W9-CGV-370

HBJ ADVANCED MATHEMATICS
A Preparation for Calculus

Arthur F. Coxford

Joseph N. Payne

Harcourt Brace Jovanovich, Publishers

Orlando   New York   Chicago   Atlanta   Dallas

ABOUT THE AUTHORS

ARTHUR F. COXFORD
Professor of Mathematics Education
University of Michigan
Ann Arbor, Michigan

JOSEPH N. PAYNE
Professor of Mathematics Education
University of Michigan
Ann Arbor, Michigan

EDITORIAL ADVISORS

Mrs. Patricia R. Connelly
Mathematics Teacher
Indian Hill High School
Cincinnati, Ohio

Brother Neal Golden, S.C.
Chairman, Department of Mathematics
  and Computer Science
Brother Martin High School
New Orleans, Louisiana

Hector Hirigoyen
Mathematics Teacher
Miami Sunset Senior High
Miami, Florida

Roger Hull
Chairman, Mathematics Department
Rowland High School
Rowland Heights, California

The contributions of Brother **Neal Golden, S.C.,** who assisted in the preparation of the Computer Applications, are gratefully acknowledged.

Contents

vi

CHAPTER **1** # Numbers, Relations, and Functions

Features

Applying Mathematical Models: Medicine

Computer Application: Multiplying Complex Numbers

Review and Testing

Mid-Chapter Review

Chapter Summary

Chapter Objectives and Review

Chapter Test

1–1 The Real Numbers

The diagram below shows the set of real numbers, R, and various subsets of R.

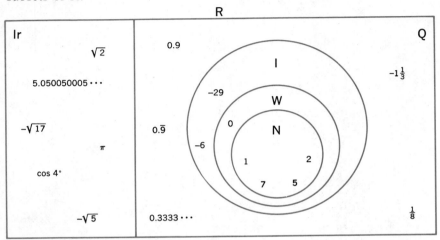

Definition The set of real numbers, R, is the set of numbers that can be named with decimals.

The real numbers can be subclassified into two subsets according to whether the decimals repeat or not. The union (∪) of these two subsets, Ir and Q, is R, that is, Ir ∪ Q = R.

Subset	Symbol	Description
Irrational Numbers	Ir	Nonterminating, nonrepeating decimals
Rational Numbers	Q	Terminating or nonterminating, repeating decimals

As an example, $\frac{5}{7}$ is a rational number and $\sqrt{2}$ is an irrational number.

The decimal for $\frac{5}{7}$ repeats in blocks of six digits.

$$\frac{5}{7} = 0.714285714285714285\ldots \longleftarrow \textbf{714285 repeats}$$

$$\frac{5}{7} = 0.\overline{714285} \longleftarrow \textbf{The bar shows the digits that repeat.}$$

$$\sqrt{2} = 1.4142135\ldots \longleftarrow \textbf{No block of repeating digits}$$

Three important subsets of Q, the rational numbers, can be described by listing their elements.

Subset	Symbol	Description
Integers	I	$\{\cdots, -2, -1, 0, 1, 2, \cdots\}$
Whole Numbers	W	$\{0, 1, 2, 3, 4, 5, \cdots\}$
Natural Numbers	N	$\{1, 2, 3, 4, 5, \cdots\}$

These are some true statements about the subsets of the real numbers.

Ir $\subseteq$ R, W $\subseteq$ I, W $\nsubseteq$ N ◄—— $\subseteq$ **means "is a subset of"**

$\sqrt{2} \in$ Ir, $0.\overline{9} \in$ Q, $\sqrt{5} \notin$ Q ◄—— $\in$ **means "is an element of"**

An alternate definition of rational numbers is often useful.

> **Definition** The set of rational numbers is the set, Q, such that
>
> $$Q = \left\{\frac{r}{s}: r \in \text{I and } s \in \text{N}\right\}$$

EXAMPLE. Show that $-5.\overline{14}$ can be expressed as $\frac{r}{s}$, $r \in$ I, $s \in$ N.

Solution: Let $x = -5.\overline{14}$

$100x = -514.\overline{14}$ ◄—— **Multiply by 10^n, where n is the number of repeating digits.**

$99x = -509$ ◄—— **Subtract the first from the second.**

$x = \dfrac{-509}{99}$ ◄—— $\frac{r}{s}, r \in$ **I**, $s \in$ **N**

CLASSROOM EXERCISES

▬ Check yourself on the symbolism of sets. Match each symbol in the column on the left with a phrase in the column on the right.

1. $\{\ \}$
2. $\cup$
3. $\in$
4. $\notin$
5. $\{x:\ \}$
6. $\cap$
7. $\subseteq$

    a. is an element of
    b. intersection
    c. the set of all x such that
    d. union
    e. is not an element of
    f. the set
    g. is a subset of

▬ Classify each number as a member of N, W, I, Q, Ir, or R. Some numbers may belong to more than one set.

8. 3   9. -3 10. $\sqrt{5}$ 11. $\frac{7}{3}$

12. $6.2\overline{3}$ 13. $1.02002002\ldots$ 14. $-0.146146146\ldots$

15. Express the numbers in Exercises 12 and 14 as $\frac{r}{s}$, $r \in$ I, $s \in$ N.

WRITTEN EXERCISES

A ━━ Classify each number as a member of N, W, I, Q, Ir or R. Some numbers may belong to more than one set.

1. $\frac{7}{2}$ **2.** $\sqrt{2}$ **3.** 0 **4.** -17

5. 8 **6.** $0.101001\cdots$ **7.** $0.\overline{101}$ **8.** $-\sqrt{7}$

9. 1.31 **10.** 1235.78901 **11.** $1.0\overline{9}$ **12.** $8.999\cdots$

━━ Write whether each statement is *True* or *False*.

13. $-5 \in W$ **14.** $0 \in W$ **15.** $R \subseteq Ir$

16. $N \subseteq I$ **17.** $I \subseteq Ir$ **18.** $W \subseteq Q$

19. $W \cup N \subseteq W$ **20.** $W \cap N \subseteq N$ **21.** $I \in Q$

22. $Ir \cap Q \subseteq R$ **23.** $0 \in Ir$ **24.** $Q \cup N = N$

━━ Write each rational number as $\frac{r}{s}$, $r \in I$, $s \in N$.

25. 1.25 **26.** 21.478 **27.** 0.1043

Example. $5.\overline{14}$, or $5.141414\cdots$

$5.\overline{14} = 5 + 0.\overline{14}$ Let $S = 0.\overline{14}$. Then, $100S = 14.\overline{14}$, and $100S - S = 14$. Thus, $99S = 14$, or $S = \frac{14}{99}$. $5.\overline{14} = 5 + \frac{14}{99}$, or $\frac{509}{99}$.

B **28.** $2.\overline{45}$ **29.** $0.00\overline{9}$ **30.** $1.30\overline{9}$

31. $37.37\overline{141}$ **32.** $0.0\overline{9}$ **33.** $0.5\overline{0}$

━━ Show that the two expressions name the same number.

34. 0.001 and $0.000\overline{9}$ **35.** 1.14 and $1.13\overline{9}$ **36.** $2.\overline{0}$ and $1.\overline{9}$

C **37.** Write an argument you would use with a classmate to convince him of the validity of the statement: *Every rational number expressed as a fraction $\frac{r}{s}$, $r \in I$, $s \in N$ can be expressed as a terminating decimal or as a repeating infinite decimal.* Hint: Consider the number of possible remainders when r is divided by s.

38. Examine each fraction. Which are usually associated with terminating decimal expressions? with infinite decimal expressions?

a. $\frac{1}{5}$ b. $\frac{1}{3}$ c. $\frac{1}{4}$ d. $\frac{1}{15}$

e. $\frac{1}{14}$ f. $\frac{1}{200}$ g. $\frac{1}{8}$ h. $\frac{1}{625}$

39. Factor each denominator of the fractions in Exercise 38. What do you notice about the factors of the denominators of the fractions expressible as terminating decimals? the others?

40. Generalize your observations of Exercise 39. Test the generalization several times. Argue that your generalization is valid.

1–2 Postulates, Definitions, and Proof

There are two basic operations defined on the set of real numbers, addition and multiplication. Each of these is a **binary operation,** that is to say, an operation that connects exactly *two* elements. The mathematical system consisting of R and the binary operations "+" and "×" has eleven properties called the **Field Postulates.**

The symbol "∀" means "for all" or "for any."

Closure Postulates (Cl P)

1. $a + b$ is unique and $a + b \in R$

6. $a \cdot b$ is unique and $a \cdot b \in R$

Commutative Postulates (Cm P)

2. $a + b = b + a$

7. $a \cdot b = b \cdot a$

Associative Postulates

3. $a + (b + c) = (a + b) + c$

8. $a \cdot (b \cdot c) = (a \cdot b) \cdot c$

Identity Postulates (Id P)

4. There exists a real number, 0, so that $a + 0 = a$.

9. There exists a real number, 1, so that $a \cdot 1 = a$.

Inverse Postulates (In P)

5. There is a real number, $-a$, so that $a + (-a) = 0$.

10. There exists a real number, $\frac{1}{a}$, so that $a \cdot \frac{1}{a} = 1, a \neq 0$.

Distributive Postulate (Di P)

11. $a(b + c) = ab + ac$

Postulate 11 states that multiplication is **distributive** over addition. Subtraction and division are defined below.

Definitions   To **subtract** b from a, add the opposite of b to a.

$$\forall a, b \in R \qquad a - b = a + (-b)$$

To **divide** a by b, multiply by the reciprocal of b. ⟵ $\frac{1}{b}$

$$\forall a, b \in R, b \neq 0 \qquad a \div b = a \cdot \frac{1}{b}$$

Recall that "$a = b$" means that a and b name the same number or that a may be substituted for b in any expression involving b. "Equality" satisfies the following properties:

IV **Equality:** $\forall a, b, c \in R$

Postulate 12 $a = a$

Postulate 13   "$a = b$" implies "$b = a$."

Postulate 14   "$a = b$ and $b = c$" implies "$a = c$."

Postulate 15   If $a = b$, then $a + c = b + c$.

The *Field Postulates* and the *Equality Postulates* together can be used to prove many relationships that are familiar to you.

The proof of Theorem 1–1, which follows, is an example of a **direct proof.** This is the type you have used most often in the past. Recall that a **theorem** is any statement proved from postulates and definitions. Furthermore, once a theorem has been proved, it can be used in the proof of other theorems.

Theorem 1–1   (Addition Cancellation Law) $\forall a, b, c \in R$
If $a + b = a + c$, then $b = c$.

Proof:
$a + b = a + c$	⟵ Given
$(a + b) + (-a) = (a + c) + (-a)$	⟵ Postulate 14
$(-a) + (a + b) = (-a) + (a + c)$	⟵ Cl Cm P+
$[a + (-a)] + b = [a + (-a)] + c$	⟵ As; Cm P+
$0 + b = 0 + c$	⟵ In P+
$b + 0 = c + 0$	⟵ Cm P+
$b = c$	⟵ Id P+

Sometimes a proof can be done in two or more parts. An important instance of this occurs when a theorem uses the phrase "if and only if." Such theorems can always be interpreted as two theorems, one the converse of the other. The following Example illustrates a two part proof that results from a theorem in which the phrase "if and only if" is used.

EXAMPLE.   Prove that $a - b = c$ if and only if (*iff*) $a = c + b$.

Solution:

Part 1:   If $a - b = c$ then $a = c + b$.

Proof:

$a - b = c$	← Given
$a + (-b) = c$	← Def. of Subtraction
$[a + (-b)] + b = c + b$.	← Add b to both sides.
Then, $a + [-b + b] = c + b$	← As P+
$a + 0 = c + b$	← In P+
$a = c + b$	← Id P+

Part 2:   If $a = c + b$ then $a - b = c$.

Proof:

$a = c + b$	← Given
$a + (-b) = [c + b] + (-b)$	← Subtract b from both sides.
$a - b = c + [b + (-b)]$	← As P+
$a - b = c + 0$	← In P+
$a - b = c$.	← Id P+

Therefore $a - b = c$ iff $a = c + b$.

As you can see, in a direct proof you reason directly toward your goal. Another type of proof that occurs frequently in more advanced mathematics is the **indirect proof.** For an indirect proof, it is sufficient to show that the opposite of your goal *is not true.* If there are only two possibilities, and the opposite of a statement is not true, then the statement is true.

The proof of Theorem 1–2, which follows, is an example of an indirect proof. You are trying to prove the uniqueness of zero. You assume zero is not unique and try to show that a contradiction results.

Theorem 1–2   (Uniqueness of zero)   There is only one real number n such that $a + n = a$ for all real numbers a.

Proof: From Postulate 4 you know that there is one number, 0, that has the property of Theorem 1–2. Now suppose that there is some other real number n, $n \neq 0$, that also has that property. Then both "$a + 0 = a$" and "$a + n = a$" are true. Now since $n \in R$, Postulate 4 may be used. Thus,

$$n + 0 = n. \qquad \mathbf{1}$$

Now use the assumption that for all real numbers a, $a + n = a$. Since 0 is a real number it follows that $0 + n = 0$.

From the Commutative Postulate,

$$n + 0 = 0 + n,$$

so $$n + 0 = 0. \qquad\qquad \textbf{2}$$

Combining equations **1** and **2** gives

$$n = n + 0 = 0, \qquad \text{or} \qquad n = 0.$$

This contradicts the assumption that $n \neq 0$ is true. Thus, 0 is unique.

CLASSROOM EXERCISES

━━ Prove the following.

1. $(-a) + a = 0$

2. $(a \cdot b) \div b = a, b \neq 0$

3. If $a = b$, then $a - c = b - c$

WRITTEN EXERCISES

A ━━ For each subset of R state which, if any, of the Field Postulates do not hold.

1. N   **2.** W   **3.** I   **4.** Q   **5.** Ir

6. Prove: The opposite of a number is unique.

7. Prove: $-0 = 0$. (*Hint:* By Postulate 4, $0 + 0 = 0$ and by Postulate 5 $0 + (-0) = 0$. Use the cancellation property.)

8. Prove: $-(-a) = a$. (*Hint:* By Postulate 5, $-a + -(-a) = 0$ and $a + (-a) = 0$. Use the cancellation property.)

9. Prove: $0 - a = -a$. (*Hint:* Use the definition of subtraction.)

10. Prove: $-(a + b) = -a + (-b)$. (*Hint:* Prove that $(a + b) + [(-a) + (-b)] = 0$ and use the result of Exercise 6.)

B **11.** Prove: $-(a - b) = b + (-a)$.

12. Prove: There is only one number having the property of Postulate 9. This is the **Uniqueness of One**.

13. Prove the Cancellation Property for Multiplication:

If $a \cdot b = a \cdot c$ and $a \neq 0$, then $b = c$

14. Prove: The reciprocal of a ($\neq 0$) is unique. (See Exercise 6.)

C **15.** Prove: $a \cdot 0 = 0$. (*Hint:* $a \cdot 0 + 0 = a \cdot 0 = a(0 + 0) = a \cdot 0 + a \cdot 0$. Use the Cancellation Property for Addition on the first and last members.)

16. Prove: If $xy = 0$, then $x = 0$ *or* $y = 0$. (The compound sentence $x = 0$ *or* $y = 0$ is true if $x = 0$ is true, $y = 0$ is true, or both are true.)

17. Prove: $a \div b = c$ if and only if $a = c \cdot b, b \neq 0$.

1–3   Order Relations

The real numbers can be placed in a one-to-one correspondence with the points on a line. The number line below shows that the real numbers can be partitioned into three disjoint sets: zero, positive numbers, and negative numbers.

The following assumptions are made about the real numbers and the idea of positiveness.

Order Postulates

Postulate 16   Some numbers are positive.

Postulate 17   For any real number a, exactly one of the following three statements is true.

$$a = 0, a \text{ is positive, or } -a \text{ is positive.}$$

Postulate 18   The sum of two positive numbers is positive.

Postulate 19   The product of two positive numbers is positive.

From Postulate 17 it follows that the number a is negative if and only if $-a$ is positive.

Why these postulates and not some other ones? Experience has shown that these postulates, when combined with appropriate definitions, give a secure basis for understanding order relationships. Check to see that you find the Order Postulates reasonable.

Order among the real numbers is indicated by signs such as $<$, $>$, $\leq$, $\geq$, and $=$. Intuitively you know that $a < b$ is true whenever a is shown to the left of b on the real line. For example, $-2 < 5$ is true. The formal definition of "is less than" is based on the Order Postulates.

Definition The symbol $<$ is defined by either of the two statements below.

  i. $a < b$ if and only if $b - a$ is positive

  ii. $a < b$ if and only if there is a positive real number x such that $a + x = b$.

EXAMPLE 1. Prove that $-2 < 5$ is a true statement.

Solution: Find $x > 0$ such that:

$$-2 + x = 5.$$
$$-2 + 7 = 5 \quad \longleftarrow \quad \textbf{Addition fact}$$
$$7 > 0 \quad \longleftarrow \quad \textbf{7 is positive.}$$
$$-2 < 5. \quad \longleftarrow \quad \textbf{By the definition of } <$$

EXAMPLE 2. Prove: $0 < a$ if and only if a is positive.

  i. If a is positive, then $0 + a = a$, and by the definition of $<$, the sentence $0 < a$ is true.

  ii. If $0 < a$, then there is a positive x such that $0 + x = a$. But $0 + x = x$, so $x = a$. Since x is positive, so is a.

The familiar relations denoted by "$>$" (is greater than) "$\leq$" (is less than or equal to) and "$\geq$" (is greater than or equal to) are defined in terms of $<$ as follows:

Definitions
  i. $a > b$ if and only if $b < a$.
  ii. $a \leq b$ if and only if $a < b$ or $a = b$.
  iii. $a \geq b$ if and only if $a > b$ or $a = b$.

Several familiar properties of inequality follow from the definition of $<$ and the Order Postulates.

Theorem 1–3 (The Trichotomy Property) $\forall a, b \in \text{R}$
Exactly one of the following is true: $a < b$, $a = b$, or $b < a$.

Proof: $a < b$ if and only if $b - a$ is positive.

$a = b$ if and only if $b - a = 0$.

$b < a$ if and only if $a - b = -(b - a)$ is positive.

By Postulate 16, exactly one of the statements below is true.

i. $b - a$ is positive.   **ii.** $b - a = 0$.   **iii.** $-(b - a)$ is positive.

Therefore, exactly one of $a < b$, $a = b$, $b < a$ is true.

Theorem 1–4 (The Transitive Property) $\forall a, b, c \in R$
If $a < b$ and $b < c$ then $a < c$.

Outline of Proof: $b - a$ and $c - b$ are positive. Thus $(b - a) + (c - b)$ is positive. Show that this means that $(c - a)$ is positive.

Theorem 1–5 (The Addition Property) $\forall a, b, c \in R$
If $a < b$ then $a + c < b + c$.

The proof is left for you, as is the proof of the following theorem.

Theorem 1–6 (The Multiplication Property) $\forall a, b \in R$
i. For all positive numbers c, if $a < b$, then $ac < bc$.
ii. For all negative numbers c, if $a < b$, then $ac > bc$.

CLASSROOM EXERCISES

━━ Complete each statement with $<$, $\leq$, $\geq$, or $>$.

1. $-2 \underline{\ ?\ } 5$ **2.** $-2 \underline{\ ?\ } 0$ **3.** $-2 \underline{\ ?\ } -3$ **4.** $-2 \underline{\ ?\ } -2$

━━ Complete each statement.

5. $5 < 7$ because $5 + \underline{\ ?\ }$ **6.** $-2 > -5$ because $-5 + \underline{\ ?\ }$

7. $3 = 3$ because $3 + \underline{\ ?\ }$ **8.** $a < a + 1$ because $a + \underline{\ ?\ }$

WRITTEN EXERCISES

A ━━ Determine whether each statement 1–8 is true or false. If a statement is false, explain why it is false.

1. $2 < 5$ **2.** $-5 < 0$ **3.** $7 < 6$ **4.** $-2 \leq -1$

5. $-5 \leq -3$ **6.** $2 \geq 2$ **7.** $-3 \leq -5$ **8.** $-2 \geq 1$

9. If $2 < 5$, why does it follow that $6 < 15$?

10. If $-4 < 2$, why does it follow that $-1 < 5$?

11. Given $x < 2$ and $2 < z$, what can you conclude about the order of x and z?

12. Given $x, y \in R$, what can you conclude about x and y?

B **13.** Prove Theorem 1–4.   **14.** Prove Theorem 1–5.

15. Prove the converse of Theorem 1–5.

16. Prove Theorem 1–6, part *i*.

17. Prove the converse of Theorem 1–6, part *i*.

18. Is it true that if $a \leq b$ and $b \leq c$, then $a \leq c$? If not, produce a counterexample. If true, prove it.

C **19.** Prove: $a < 0$ if and only if a is negative. (*Hint:* Show that $a < 0$ implies $-a$ is positive.)

20. Assume that the product of two negative numbers is a positive number. Use this assumption to prove Theorem 1–6, part *ii*.

21. Prove: If $x \leq y$ and $y \leq x$, then $x = y$.

1–4   Graphs of Real Numbers

A **graph** of a set of real numbers is the set of points on a line that correspond to the numbers. The graph of an equation or inequality is the set of points whose coordinates satisfy the equation or inequality.

The solution set of compound sentences with "or" is the **union** of the solution sets of the simple sentences. For "and" compound sentences, the solution set is the **intersection** of the sets.

EXAMPLE 1. Graph the sets of real numbers. Describe each set of points geometrically.

a. $\{r : r = -2 \ or \ r = 3\}$

b. $\{x : -1 \leq x\}$

c. $\{t : t < 5\}$

d. $\{y : -1 \leq y \leq 4\}$

e. $\{k : 3 < k \ or \ k < -2\}$

Solution:

a.

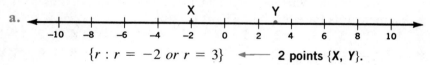

$\{r : r = -2 \ or \ r = 3\}$ ◀—— **2 points $\{X, Y\}$.**

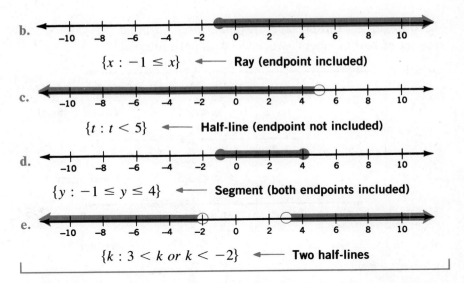

b. $\{x : -1 \le x\}$ ⟵ **Ray (endpoint included)**

c. $\{t : t < 5\}$ ⟵ **Half-line (endpoint not included)**

d. $\{y : -1 \le y \le 4\}$ ⟵ **Segment (both endpoints included)**

e. $\{k : 3 < k \text{ or } k < -2\}$ ⟵ **Two half-lines**

Example **d** is a *closed interval* because the endpoints are included. The graph of $-1 < y < 4$ is an *open interval* because the endpoints are not included.

> **Definition** The symbol $[a, b]$, where a and b are real numbers and $a < b$, denotes the set of real numbers x such that $a \le x \le b$ or the points of the segment whose endpoints have coordinates a and b. $[a, b]$ is a **closed interval**.
>
> $$[a, b] = \{x : a \le x \le b, a, b, x \in \mathbf{R}\} \text{ or its graph.}$$

Similarly, you can define an *open interval*.

> **Definition** The symbol $\langle a, b \rangle$, where $a, b \in \mathbf{R}$ and $a < b$, denotes the set $\{x : a < x < b, a, b, x \in \mathbf{R}\}$ or the graph of this set. $\langle a, b \rangle$ is an **open interval**.

An open interval is a segment without its endpoints. If one endpoint is included, an interval that is neither closed nor open is the result.

> **Definitions** $[a, b\rangle = \langle a, b \rangle \cup \{a\}$; $\langle a, b] = \langle a, b \rangle \cup \{b\}$

EXAMPLE 2. Graph [2, 3.5], ⟨2, 3.5⟩, ⟨2, 3.5], and [2, 3.5⟩. What is the set of real numbers associated with each interval?

Solution:

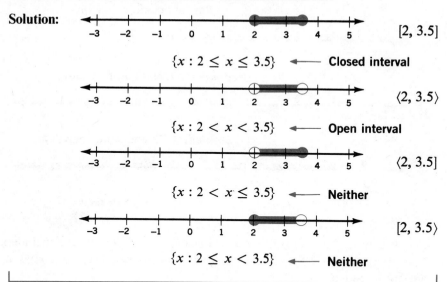

[2, 3.5]

$\{x : 2 \leq x \leq 3.5\}$ ⟵ **Closed interval**

⟨2, 3.5⟩

$\{x : 2 < x < 3.5\}$ ⟵ **Open interval**

⟨2, 3.5]

$\{x : 2 < x \leq 3.5\}$ ⟵ **Neither**

[2, 3.5⟩

$\{x : 2 \leq x < 3.5\}$ ⟵ **Neither**

Graphs of sets of real numbers are also useful in depicting the solution set of an inequality.

EXAMPLE 3. Solve $5y - 2 > 2y - 8$ where the replacement set is **R**. Graph the solution set.

Solution:

The field and order postulates of the real numbers imply that the following inequalities are equivalent to each other.

① $5y - 2 > 2y - 8$ ⟵ **(Given)**
② $5y > 2y - 6$ ⟵ **(Addition of +2) By Theorem 1–5**
③ $3y > -6$ ⟵ **(Addition of −2y) By Theorem 1–5**
④ $y > -2$ ⟵ **(Multiplication by $\frac{1}{3}$) By Theorem 1–6**

Thus the solution set is

$$\{y : y > -2, y \in \mathbf{R}\}$$

The graph is shown below.

CLASSROOM EXERCISES

━━ Describe and graph each set of real numbers.

1. $[-6, -2]$ **2.** $[-6, -2\rangle$ **3.** $\langle-6, -2]$ **4.** $\langle-6, -2\rangle$

━━ Use interval notation, $\langle$ and $]$, to express each of the following.

5. $\{x : 5 < x \leq 12\}$ **6.** $\{x : -2 \leq x < 0\}$ **7.** $\{x : -20 \leq x \leq 5\}$

WRITTEN EXERCISES

A ━━ Graph each set of real numbers.

1. $\{a : a < -1\}$ **2.** $\{b : b \geq 2.5\}$

3. $\{c : c = -2 \text{ or } c = 0\}$ **4.** $\langle0, 3\rangle$

5. $\langle0, 3]$ **6.** $[0, 3]$

7. $[\frac{2}{3}, \frac{7}{4}\rangle$ **8.** $\{d : \frac{2}{3} < d \leq 7\}$

9. $\{k : k \leq 5\}$ **10.** $\langle-2, 3\rangle \cup [3, 4]$

11. $\langle-2, 3\rangle \cap [1, 4]$ **12.** $[-2, 3] \cap [-4, 0]$

13. $[-2, 3] \cup [-4, 1]$

14. $\{v : v \in [1, 4] \text{ or } v \in [-4, -1]\}$

15. $\{r : r > -2\} \cap \{r : r < 3\}$ **16.** $\{u : u \leq 5 \text{ and } u \geq 5\}$

17. $\{p : p \geq 0, p \leq 5, p \in W\}$ **18.** $\{q : q \leq -1 \text{ and } q \geq 4\}$

19. $\{x : x \in [1, 3\rangle \text{ or } x < -2\}$ **20.** $\{y : -3 < y \text{ and } y < 3\}$

━━ Find the solution set of each inequality if the replacement set is R. Graph each nonempty solution set.

21. $2y + 3 \leq 3y - 2$ **22.** $3y + 7 \geq 5y - 7$

23. $2t - 3 + t < -t + 5$ **24.** $4n > -n$

25. $-\frac{2}{3}n < n - 6$ **26.** $-2t + 5 < -2t - 5$

27. $-t + 5 < t - 5$ **28.** $-2(t + 4) > -t - 6$

29. $-39p < 0$ **30.** $p^2 > -2$

B ━━ Graph as many points of each of the following sets as you find convenient to do (that is, you should stop when points become too close together to show).

31. $\left\{\frac{1}{2}, \frac{1}{4}, \frac{1}{8}, \frac{1}{16}, \ldots, \frac{1}{2^n}, n \in N\right\}$

32. $\left\{1, \frac{1}{2}, \frac{1}{3}, \frac{1}{4}, \frac{1}{5}, \ldots, \frac{1}{n}, n \in N\right\}$

C   **33.** $\left\{\frac{1}{2}, \frac{1}{2} + \frac{1}{4}, \frac{1}{2} + \frac{1}{4} + \frac{1}{8}, \ldots, \frac{1}{2} + \frac{1}{4} + \frac{1}{8} + \cdots + \frac{1}{2^n}, n \in N\right\}$

      34. $\left\{1, 1 + \frac{1}{2}, 1 + \frac{1}{2} + \frac{1}{3}, \ldots, 1 + \frac{1}{2} + \frac{1}{3} + \cdots + \frac{1}{n}, n \in N\right\}$

1-5   Solving and Graphing Inequalities

The compound inequality $a < x < b$ means that $a < x$ *and* $x < b$. The solution set is the intersection of the solution set of $a < x$ and the solution set of $x < b$.

$$\{x: a < x < b\} = \{x: a < x\} \cap \{x: x < b\}$$

EXAMPLE 1.   Solve and graph: $-3 < 2x + 1 < 5$

Solution:

$-3 < 2x + 1$	*and*	$2x + 1 < 5$
$-4 < 2x$		$2x < 4$
$-2 < x$		$x < 2$

Solution set: $\{x: -2 < x\} \cap \{x: x < 2\}$ ◄——— **Intersection of solution sets**

$\{x: -2 < x \text{ and } x < 2\}$

$\{x: -2 < x < 2\}$ ◄——— **Compound inequality**

Graph: $\langle -2, 2 \rangle$

To solve a **quadratic inequality**, (one involving a second-degree term), use your knowledge about the product of positive and negative numbers. The product of two real numbers is negative, if and only if one factor is positive and one is negative.

EXAMPLE 2.   Solve and graph: $x^2 + x - 6 < 0$

Solution:
$$x^2 + x - 6 < 0$$
$$(x + 3)(x - 2) < 0 \quad \text{◄——— } \textbf{In factored form}$$
$x + 3 < 0 \text{ and } x - 2 > 0 \quad or \quad x + 3 > 0 \text{ and } x - 2 < 0$
$x < -3 \text{ and } x > 2 \quad or \quad x > -3 \text{ and } x < 2$

Solution Set: $\phi \cup \{x: -3 < x < 2\}$ ◄——— **Union of ϕ and another set is the other set.**

Graph: $\langle -3, 2 \rangle$

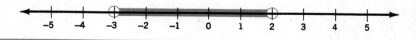

The product of two real numbers is positive if and only if both of the numbers are positive or both are negative.

EXAMPLE 3. Solve and graph: $(x + 3)(x - 2) > 0$

Solution: $(x + 3)(x - 2) > 0$ is true if and only if:

$(x + 3) > 0$ *and* $x - 2 > 0$ *or* $x + 3 < 0$ *and* $x - 2 < 0$

$x > -3$ *and* $x > 2$ *or* $x < -3$ *and* $x < 2$

Solution set: $\{x: x > 2\} \cup \{x: x < -3\}$

Graph:

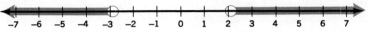

CLASSROOM EXERCISES

━━━ Write without "and."

1. $2 < x$ *and* $x < 10$ **2.** $4 < x$ *and* $x \le 8$
3. $-3.6 \le y$ *and* $y < -1$ **4.** $-8 \le m$ *and* $m \le 0$
5. $\{x: x < 5$ *and* $x < 10\}$ **6.** $\{x: x < -3$ *and* $x < 7\}$

WRITTEN EXERCISES

A ━━━Find the solution set of each inequality. Graph each nonempty solution set.

1. $4 < 3x - 2 < 5$ **2.** $0 < 5x + 4 < 6$
3. $-7 < 2x - 3 < -1$ **4.** $4 > x + 4 > 2$
5. $4 - 2x < 3x + 1 < 7$ **6.** $5 < -x + 2 < 7$
7. $3x > 4$ *and* $x > 3x - 2$ **8.** $(x + 1)(x - 2) < 0$
9. $2 > \frac{2}{3}x - 1 > -1$ **10.** $\frac{1}{6} < \frac{2}{5}x < \frac{1}{3}$
11. $(x - \frac{1}{2})(x + 2) > 0$ **12.** $x(x - 7) < 0$
13. $x^2 - 5x > 0$ **14.** $(x - \frac{1}{3})(2x - 4) < 0$
15. $(x - 1)(x - 1) < 0$ **16.** $(x - 2)(x - 2) > 0$
17. $(x - 1)(x - 1) \le 0$ **18.** $(x - 2)(x - 2) \ge 0$

B **19.** $x^2 - 4x < 5$ **20.** $x^2 + 3x \ge -2$
21. $\frac{-x^2}{10} + \frac{7x}{10} < 1$ **22.** $(2x - 1)(3x + 2) \le 0$
23. $16x^2 \le 1$ **24.** $x^2 + x + 1 < 0$
25. $2x + 1 < 5$ *or* $2x - 1 > 9$
26. $5x - 2 < 3$ *or* $-2 < 2x - 6 < 4$
27. $3x - 5 \le 4$ *and* $-2x + 2 \le -4$
28. $x^2 - 1 \ge 0$ *and* $5 < 2x + 5 < 7$

C **29.** $(x - 1)(x - 2)(x - 3) < 0$

30. $(2x - 1)(x + 3)(x - 4) > 0$

31. $(3x - 1)(2x + 3)(x + 2) < 0$

32. $(4x - 6)(x)(x + 2) \geq 0$

33. For what value of k will the solution set of $3x - k < 2$ be $\{x : x < 4\}$?

34. For what value of k will the solution set of $x^2 + x + k < 0$ be $\{x : -3 < x < 2\}$?

1–6   Mathematical Induction

Suppose that the following claim is made: For all natural numbers, n, the natural number $n^3 + 2n$ is divisible by 3.   Is the claim true?   Is it false?   To find out you might begin by examining several cases.

$$n = 1: \quad 1^3 + 2 \cdot 1 = 3; \qquad \text{3 is divisible by 3.}$$
$$n = 2: \quad 2^3 + 2 \cdot 2 = 12; \qquad \text{12 is divisible by 3.}$$
$$n = 3: \quad 3^3 + 2 \cdot 3 = 33; \qquad \text{33 is divisible by 3.}$$

So far so good.   Now check the statement for $n = 4$, $n = 5$, and $n = 6$. What are your results?

One thing is clear: You cannot possibly substantiate the claim for all natural numbers n.   Only a finite number of instances could be checked.   What you need, then, is a method of proof which verifies the claim for all natural numbers at once.   The method of proof sought is **mathematical induction.**

Mathematical induction is based on simple characteristics of the natural numbers.   They are stated in the *Axiom of Induction*.

Axiom of Induction: If T is a set of natural numbers with the properties

> i. $1 \in$ T and
> ii. $k \in$ T implies $k + 1 \in$ T,

then T is the set of natural numbers N.

The pair of conditions in the Axiom of Induction uniquely determine the set of natural numbers.   Notice that both conditions must be satisfied for the Axiom of Induction to hold.   The following example will help to illustrate the point.

For example, consider the following set T.

$$T = \{1, 2, 3\}$$

Clearly $1 \in T$, but it is not true that $k + 1 \in T$ every time $k \in T$, e.g., $3 \in T$ but $4 \notin T$. Thus $T \neq N$.

$$\text{Let } T = \{10, 11, 12, \cdots\}.$$

Clearly if $k \in T$, then $k + 1 \in T$ but $1 \notin T$. Thus, again, $T \neq N$.

The Theorem of Mathematical Induction follows directly.

Theorem 1–7 For every $n \in N$ let P_n be a statement which is either true or false. If

i. P_1 is true and

ii. whenever this statement is true for k, it is true for $k + 1$

then P_n is true for all $n \in N$.

Proof: Let T be the set of natural numbers for which P_n is true.

$1 \in T$ because of i in Theorem 1–7.

$k + 1 \in T$ whenever $k \in T$ because of ii.

Thus $T = N$ and P_n is true for all $n \in N$.

To apply the Theorem of Mathematical Induction you must do *two* things: You must verify that P_1 is true. You must also verify that P_{k+1} is true whenever P_k is true.

EXAMPLE 1. For n a natural number, P_n is the statement:

$$n^3 + 2n \text{ is divisible by 3.}$$

Prove P_n true for all $n \in N$.

Proof: The proof is by mathematical induction.

i. *Verify that P_1 is true.*

$$P_1 : 1^3 + 2 \cdot 1 \text{ is divisible by 3.}$$

P_1 is clearly true since $1^3 + 2 \cdot 1 = 3$.

ii. *Verify that whenever P_n is true for a natural number, say $n = k$, then it is true for the next natural number, $n = k + 1$.*

To carry out this portion of the argument, you must assume that P_k is true for some $k \in N$. This assumption is the *induction hypothesis*.

Assume P_k is true; i.e., $k^3 + 2k$ is divisible by 3. Next show that P_k implies P_{k+1}, i.e., prove that P_{k+1} must also be true; i.e., $(k + 1)^3 + 2(k + 1)$ is divisible by 3. First notice that

$$(k + 1)^3 + 2(k + 1) = k^3 + 3k^2 + 3k + 1 + 2k + 2$$
$$= (k^3 + 2k) + 3k^2 + 3k + 3$$
$$= P(k) + 3(k^2 + k + 1)$$

The symbol $P(k)$ is used in the last line to stand for "$k^3 + 2k$". It should not be confused with the symbol P_k which stands for the sentence "$k^3 + 2k$ is divisible by 3". Similarly, $P(k + 1)$ stands for "$(k + 1)^3 + 2(k + 1)$".

Since $P(k)$ is divisible by 3 and $3(k^2 + k + 1)$ is divisible by 3, $P(k + 1)$ is also divisible by 3. Thus both conditions of the Theorem of Mathematical Induction are satisfied. You may thus conclude that $n^3 + 2n$ is divisible by 3 for *all* $n \in$ N.

EXAMPLE 2. For n a natural number, P_n is the statement:

$$1 + 2 + 3 + \cdots + n = \frac{n(n + 1)}{2}.$$

Prove P_n true for all $n \in$ N.

Proof: i. P_1 is true, since $\frac{1(1 + 1)}{2} = 1$.

ii. Induction hypothesis:

Assume P_k is true; i.e., $1 + 2 + \cdots + k = \frac{k(k + 1)}{2}$.

Prove that P_{k+1} follows from P_k.

The left hand side of P_{k+1} is $1 + 2 + 3 + \cdots + k + (k + 1)$. But this is the left side of P_k with $k + 1$ added. This suggests that a proof may be made by adding $(k + 1)$ to both sides of the true statement P_k.

Thus
$$1 + 2 + \cdots + k + (k + 1) = \frac{k(k + 1)}{2} + (k + 1)$$
$$= \frac{k(k + 1) + 2(k + 1)}{2}$$
$$= \frac{(k + 1)(k + 2)}{2}$$
$$1 + 2 + \cdots + k + (k + 1) = \frac{(k + 1)(k + 1 + 1)}{2}$$

The last statement is P_{k+1}. Thus P_{k+1} follows from P_k.

By the Theorem of Mathematical Induction P_n is true for all $n \in$ N.

EXAMPLE 3. For n a natural number, P_n is the statement:

$$(1 + p)^n \geq 1 + np, \quad p > -1.$$

Prove P_n true for all $n \in \mathbb{N}$.

Proof: i. Verify P_1. $P_1 : (1 + p)^1 \geq 1 + 1 \cdot p$

$$1 + p \geq 1 + p, \quad p > -1$$

Thus P_1 is true.

ii. Induction Hypothesis.

Assume P_k is true, i.e., $(1 + p)^k \geq 1 + kp$. Now prove that the truth of P_{k+1} follows from that of P_k. The left hand side of the statement P_{k+1} is $(1 + p)^{k+1} = (1 + p)(1 + p)^k$. The second factor in $(1 + p)(1 + p)^k$ is the left hand side of P_k. This suggests that you may be able to make the proof by beginning with P_k and multiplying by $(1 + p)$. You know that $(1 + p)^k \geq 1 + kp$.

Since, $1 + p \geq 0$ then

$$(1 + p)(1 + p)^k \geq (1 + kp)(1 + p)$$

or $(1 + p)^{k+1} \geq 1 + kp + p + kp^2 = 1 + (k + 1)p + kp^2.$

Since $kp^2 \geq 0$

$$1 + (k + 1)p + kp^2 \geq 1 + (k + 1)p$$

Thus $(1 + p)^{k+1} \geq 1 + (k + 1)p + kp^2 \geq 1 + (k + 1)p$

or $(1 + p)^{k+1} \geq 1 + (k + 1)p$

But this is P_{k+1}! Thus the statement P_n is true for all $n \in \mathbb{N}$.

It is important to realize that both parts of the Theorem of Mathematical Induction must be satisfied for P_n to be true for all natural numbers n. For example, suppose P_n is the statement

$$1 + 2 + 3 + \cdots + n = \frac{n(n + 1)}{2} + \frac{(n - 1)}{2}$$

P_1 is true since "$1 = \frac{1(1 + 1)}{2} + \frac{(1 - 1)}{2}$" is true.

In this case, however, you cannot conclude that whenever P_k is true, P_{k+1} is also true because there is no general way to produce P_{k+1} from P_k. Thus P_n is not true for all $n \in \mathbb{N}$. The way to disprove this statement is to produce a counterexample, i.e., a natural number for which P_n is not true.

P_3 is not true because

$$6 = 1 + 2 + 3 \neq \frac{3(3 + 1)}{2} + \frac{(3 - 1)}{2} = 6 + 1 = 7.$$

On the other hand suppose that P_n is the statement

$$1 + 2 + 3 + \cdots + n = \frac{n(n + 1)}{2} + 17.$$

Then you can show that *if* P_k is true, P_{k+1} must be true also. However, it is impossible to show that P_n is true for *any n* much less for $n = 1$.

CLASSROOM EXERCISES

Write the induction hypothesis for each of the following statements.

1. $1^3 + 2^3 + 3^3 + \cdots + n^3 = \frac{n^2(n + 1)^2}{4}$

2. $1 + 4 + 7 + \cdots + (3n - 2) = \frac{n(3n - 1)}{2}$

3. $1^2 + 3^2 + 5^2 + \cdots + (2n - 1)^2 = \frac{n(2n - 1)(2n + 1)}{3}$

WRITTEN EXERCISES

A ▬ In Exercises 1–12, P_n is given. Prove by Mathematical Induction that P_n is true for all $n \in N$.

1. $1 + 3 + 5 + \cdots + (2n - 1) = n^2$

2. $2 + 4 + 6 + \cdots + 2n = n(n + 1)$

3. $\frac{1}{1 \cdot 2} + \frac{1}{2 \cdot 3} + \cdots + \frac{1}{n(n + 1)} = \frac{n}{n + 1}$

4. $\frac{1}{2} + \frac{1}{2^2} + \cdots + \frac{1}{2^n} = \frac{2^n - 1}{2^n}$

5. $-\frac{1}{2} - \frac{1}{4} - \frac{1}{8} - \cdots - \frac{1}{2^n} = \frac{1 - (2)^n}{2^n}$

6. $(b_1 - b_2) + (b_2 - b_3) + \cdots + (b_n - b_{n+1}) = b_1 - b_{n+1}$

7. $5 + 5 \cdot \frac{1}{3} + 5 \cdot \frac{1}{3^2} + \cdots + 5\frac{1}{3^{n-1}} = 5\frac{1 - (\frac{1}{3})^n}{1 - \frac{1}{3}}$

8. $5 + 7 + 9 + \cdots + [5 + 2(n - 1)] = \frac{n(10 + 2n - 2)}{2}$

B **9.** $a + aq^1 + aq^2 + \cdots + aq^{n-1} = a\frac{1 - q^n}{1 - q}$ $a, q \in R, q \neq 1$

10. $a + (a + d) + (a + 2d) + \cdots + [a + (n - 1)d] = \frac{n[(2a + (n - 1)d]}{2}$ $a, d \in R$

11. $n^3 - n$ is divisible by 6

12. $1^2 + 2^2 + \cdots + n^2 = \dfrac{n(n+1)(2n+1)}{6}$

13. Prove that the sum of n positive integers is positive. (*Hint:* See Section 1–3, Postulate 18.)

14. Prove that the product of n positive integers is positive. (*Hint:* See Section 1–3, Postulate 19.)

15. Prove that if $x_0 < x_1, x_1 < x_2, x_2 < x_3, x_3 < x_4, \ldots, x_{n-1} < x_n$, then $x_0 < x_n$. (*Hint:* Use Theorem 1–4.)

16. Prove the general distributive law:

$$y(x_1 + x_2 + \cdots + x_n) = yx_1 + yx_2 + \cdots yx_n$$

(*Hint:* Use Postulate 11.)

17. Define a positive integral power for a real number x as follows:

    i. $x^1 = x$ **ii.** $x^{n+1} = x^n \cdot x$

Prove

    a. $x^n = x \cdot x \cdot \ldots \cdot x$ (n factors of x.)

    b. $(x \cdot y)^n = x^n \cdot y^n$

    c. $x^m \cdot x^n = x^{m+n}$ (*Hint:* Use induction on n, i.e., show that $x^m \cdot x^1 = x^{m+1}$ and that $x^m x^k = x^{m+k}$ implies that $x^m \times x^{k+1} = x^{m+(k+1)}$

    d. $(x^m)^n = x^{m \cdot n}$

18. If n is a positive integer, **n factorial,** written $n!$, is defined: $n! = 1 \cdot 2 \cdot 3 \cdot \ldots n$. **Zero factorial** is defined: $0! = 1$. If r is a positive integer or zero and if $0 \le r \le n$, the binomial coefficient $\binom{n}{r}$ is defined:

$$\binom{n}{r} = \frac{n!}{(n-r)!r!}$$

    a. Establish the law of Pascal's Triangle:

$$\binom{n+1}{r} = \binom{n}{r-1} + \binom{n}{r}$$

    b. Use the result of **a** to prove that $\binom{n}{r}$ is a positive integer.

19. Let $a_1 = \sqrt{2}$, $a_2 = \sqrt{2 + \sqrt{2}}$, $a_3 = \sqrt{2 + \sqrt{2 + \sqrt{2}}}$, and so on.

Prove by induction that $a_n < 2$ for every positive integer n.

1-7 The Binomial Theorem

Binomial Theorem

Theorem 1-8 For any natural number n,

$$(a + b)^n = a^n + \frac{n}{1}a^{n-1}b + \frac{n(n-1)}{1 \cdot 2}a^{n-2}b^2 +$$

$$\frac{n(n-1)(n-2)}{1 \cdot 2 \cdot 3}a^{n-3}b^3 + \cdots + b^n.$$

A major use of the Binomial Theorem is the expansion of binomials without doing the multiplications.

EXAMPLE 1. Expand $(x + 3)^4$.

Solution: Here $a = x$ and $b = 3$.

$$(x + 3)^4 = x^4 + 4x^3 \cdot 3 + \frac{4 \cdot 3}{1 \cdot 2}x^2 \cdot 3^2 + \frac{4 \cdot 3 \cdot 2}{1 \cdot 2 \cdot 3}x^1 \cdot 3^3 + 3^4$$

$$= x^4 + 12x^3 + 54x^2 + 108x + 81$$

EXAMPLE 2. Expand $(2x - 3y)^4$.

Solution: Here $a = 2x$ and $b = -3y$. First expand $(a + b)^4$.

$$(a + b)^4 = a^4 + 4a^3b + 6a^2b^2 + 4ab^3 + b^4$$

Then substitute $2x$ for a and $-3y$ for b.

$$(2x)^4 + 4(2x)^3(-3y) + 6(2x)^2(-3y)^2 + 4(2x)(-3y)^3 + (-3y)^4$$

$$= 16x^4 - 96x^3y + 216x^2y^2 - 216xy^3 + 81y^4$$

In the following theorem, the symbol $n!$, read n factorial, means $n(n-1)(n-2)(n-3) \cdots 1$. $0! = 1$

Theorem 1-9 If $(a + b)^n$ is expanded, then its rth term is

$$\frac{n!}{(n-r+1)!(r-1)!}a^{n-r+1}b^{r-1}.$$

EXAMPLE 3. Find the fourth term of $(a - b)^7$.

Solution:

$$\frac{7!}{(7 - 4 + 1)!(4 - 1)!} a^4(-b)^3 = \frac{7!}{4! \ 3!} a^4(-b)^3 \quad \longleftarrow \quad n = 7, r = 4$$

$$= \frac{7 \cdot 6 \cdot 5 \cdot 4 \cdot 3 \cdot 2 \cdot 1}{4 \cdot 3 \cdot 2 \cdot 1 \cdot 3 \cdot 2 \cdot 1} a^4(-b)^3$$

$$= -35a^4b^3$$

The Binomial Theorem can be rewritten in a more compact form using the **binomial coefficients** $\binom{n}{0}$, $\binom{n}{1}$, $\binom{n}{2}$, and so forth.

$$(a + b)^n = \binom{n}{0}a^n + \binom{n}{1}a^{n-1}b^1 + \binom{n}{2}a^{n-2}b^2 + \binom{n}{3}a^{n-3}b^3 + \cdots + \binom{n}{n}b^n$$

The definition of $\binom{n}{r}$, the rth *binomial coefficient*, is

$$\binom{n}{r} = \frac{n!}{r!(n - r)!}$$

Binomial coefficients exhibit many interesting relationships. One of these is given in the next theorem, which will be used in the proof of the Binomial Theorem.

Theorem 1–10 $\quad \binom{n}{r} + \binom{n}{r - 1} = \binom{n + 1}{r}$

Proof: $\quad \binom{n}{r} + \binom{n}{r - 1} = \frac{n!}{r!(n - r)!} + \frac{n!}{(r - 1)!(n - r + 1)!}$

$$= \frac{n!}{(n - r)!(r - 1)!} \left(\frac{1}{r} + \frac{1}{n - r + 1)} \right)$$

$$= \frac{n!}{(n - r)!(r - 1)!} \left(\frac{n + 1 - r + r}{r(n + 1 - r)} \right)$$

$$= \frac{(n + 1)!}{r!(n + 1 - r)!}$$

$$= \binom{n + 1}{r}$$

The proof of the Binomial Theorem is by mathematical induction.

Proof: Thus, there are two statements to verify.

1. $(a + b)^1 = \binom{1}{0}a + \binom{1}{1}b$ is true $(n = 1)$.

2. If $(a + b)^k = \binom{k}{0}a^k + \binom{k}{1}a^{k-1}b^1 + \binom{k}{r}a^{k-r}b^r + \cdots + \binom{k}{k}b^k$ is true $(n = k)$, then

$$(a + b)^{k+1} = \binom{k+1}{0}a^{k+1} + \binom{k+1}{1}a^k b^1 + \cdots + \binom{k+1}{k+1}b^{k+1}$$

is true $(n = k + 1)$. Statement **1** is clearly true since

$$\binom{1}{0} = \frac{1!}{0!(1 - 0)!} = \frac{1}{1 \cdot 1} = 1$$

and

$$\binom{1}{1} = \frac{1!}{1!(1 - 1)!} = \frac{1}{1 \cdot 1} = 1.$$

To prove statement **2**, assume that "$(a + b)^k = \cdots$" in the statement is true. Then,

$(a + b)^{k+1} = (a + b)^k(a + b)$

$$= \binom{k}{0}a^{k+1} + \binom{k}{1}a^k b^1 + \binom{k}{2}a^{k-1}b^2 + \cdots + \binom{k}{r}a^{k-r+1}b^r$$

$$+ \cdots + \binom{k}{k}ab^k +$$

$$\binom{k}{0}a^k b^1 + \binom{k}{1}a^{k-1}b^2 + \cdots + \binom{k}{r-1}a^{k-r+1}b^r$$

$$+ \cdots + \binom{k}{k-1}ab^k$$

$$+ \binom{k}{k}b^{k+1}$$

$$= \binom{k}{0}a^{k+1} + \left[\binom{k}{1} + \binom{k}{0}\right]a^k b^1 + \left[\binom{k}{2} + \binom{k}{1}\right]a^{k-1}b^2 + \cdots$$

$$+ \left[\binom{k}{r} + \binom{k}{r-1}\right]a^{k-r+1}b^r + \cdots + \binom{k}{k}b^{k+1}.$$

By Theorem 1–10, this is the same as the following.

$$\binom{k+1}{0}a^{k+1} + \binom{k+1}{1}a^k b^1 + \binom{k+1}{2}a^{k-1}b^2 + \cdots$$

$$+ \binom{k+1}{r}a^{k+1-r}b^r + \cdots + \binom{k+1}{k+1}b^{k+1}$$

This is the statement of the theorem for $n = k + 1$. By mathematical induction, the theorem is true for all natural numbers.

It can be shown that if $|b| < |a|$ then $(a + b)^n$ may be expanded using exponents that are fractions or negative integers. In this case, the Binomial Theorem must be used in the form first presented, namely,

$$(a + b)^n = a^n + \frac{n}{1}a^{n-1}b + \frac{n(n-1)}{1 \cdot 2}a^{n-2}b^2 + \cdots + b^n$$

CLASSROOM EXERCISES

■ Give the first three terms of each expansion.

1. $(x + y)^8$ **2.** $(2x + y)^7$ **3.** $(3x - 2y)^5$ **4.** $(-x + 3y)^9$

■ Evaluate each expression.

5. $5!$ **6.** $5!4!$ **7.** $2 \cdot 3!$ **8.** $(5 - 1)!$

9. $\binom{8}{5}$ **10.** $\binom{4}{2}$ **11.** $\binom{12}{1}$ **12.** $\binom{12}{11}$

13. $\binom{5}{4} + \binom{5}{3}$ **14.** $\binom{7}{5} + \binom{7}{4}$

WRITTEN EXERCISES

A ■ Expand each binomial.

1. $(x + y)^7$ **2.** $(a + b)^5$ **3.** $(a - 2b)^4$ **4.** $(c - d)^6$

5. $(2 + b)^5$ **6.** $(x - 3y)^7$ **7.** $(3a + 2b)^5$ **8.** $\left(\frac{1}{2}b - 4c\right)^6$

9. $\left(\frac{x}{3} - 3y\right)^7$ **10.** $\left(y + \frac{1}{y}\right)^3$ **11.** $\left(\frac{1}{2} - x^2\right)^3$ **12.** $\left(\frac{y}{4} + \frac{4}{y}\right)^{10}$

■ Find the indicated term of the given binomial.

13. 6th term of $(x - 3y)^{10}$ **14.** 3rd term of $(2x - 4z)^{12}$

15. 4th term of $(7x + 3y)^5$ **16.** 7th term of $(a + 3b)^9$

17. 8th term of $(y - 2)^7$ **18.** 5th term of $(1 - y)^8$

19. 2nd term of $\left(3 - \frac{1}{9}x\right)^4$ **20.** 6th term of $(1 + .01)^8$

21. Write the middle term of $(2a - b)^6$.

22. Write the third term of $(x^2 - y^2)^5$.

23. Write the last term of $\left(x + \frac{4}{3}\right)^7$.

■ Use the Binomial Theorem to evaluate each of the following to the nearest hundredth.

24. $\sqrt{34}$ (*Hint:* $\sqrt{34} = (36 - 2)^{\frac{1}{2}}$) **25.** $\sqrt{1.2}$

26. $\sqrt[3]{26}$ **27.** $(1 + 0.1)^{-1}$

Applying Mathematical Models
Medicine

One of the reasons mathematics is so important in today's world is that it provides a means of examining real situations free of emotion, distractions, and irrelevant information. This is done by constructing a **mathematical model** of the situation. Such a model is simply a mathematical representation of the situation. It may be an equation, a table, a graph, or a diagram.

Public health officials use models as a means by which to estimate the course of an outbreak of a contagious disease. The following model is used to calculate the total number of persons infected at any time.

Variables Used

N represents the initial population

i_0 represents those initially infected

r_0 represents those initially recovered, isolated, and immune

s represents the susceptible people

Assumptions for the Model

The following assumptions were made about the relationships of the variables and the progress of the infection.

1. $\frac{1}{100}$ of susceptible people become infected each day.

2. $\frac{1}{10}$ of infected people recover each day and become immune.

3. $s = N -$ (infected people + immune people) $= N - (i + r)$

4. $\frac{si}{100}$ is the daily new infection rate

The Model

The model for this information is a table based on $N = 101$ thousand, $i_0 = 1$ thousand, and $r_0 = 0$. Numbers (other than the days) are given in thousands.

Day	i	s	r	New Infects	New Recovers	Add'l Infects	Total Infected
1	1.000	100.000	0.000	1.000	0.100	0.900	1.900
2	1.900	99.000	0.100	1.881	0.190	1.691	3.591
3	3.591	97.119	0.290	3.488	0.359	3.128	6.719
4	6.719	93.632	0.649	6.291	0.672	5.619	12.338
5	12.338	87.341	1.321	10.776	1.234	9.542	21.880

Calculation of the Model

1. Transfer the *Total Infected* from the previous day to the column headed i.

2. Add the previous day's r and *New Recovers*. Enter the sum under r.

3. Calculate $s = N - (i + r)$ and enter under s.

4. Calculate $\frac{si}{100}$ and enter under *New Infects*.

5. Calculate $\frac{i}{10}$ and enter under *New Recovers*.

6. Calculate $\frac{si}{100} - \frac{i}{10}$ and enter under *Additional Infects*.

7. Add i to *Additional Infects* and enter under *Total Infected*.

Continuation of this model would show that i would peak at about day 10 and then gradually decline. At the end of 40 days, the model would be as follows.

Day	i	s	r	New Infects	New Recovers	Add'l Infects	Total Infected
40	3.43	0	97.57	0	0.343	−0.343	3.087

The model shows that the epidemic would have run its course by the end of 40 days.

EXERCISES

1. Supply enough additional entries in the table to see i begin to decrease.

2. Sketch a graph with days along the x axis and i along the y axis.

3. Sketch a graph with days along the x axis and s along the y axis.

4. Another model for epidemics is given by the equation
$$i_j = 0.01(N - i_{j-1}) \cdot i_{j-1} + i_{j-1}$$
where i_j is the total infected for day j and N is the population. Make a table showing ten days of epidemic where N begins at 100 and $i_0 = 1$.

5. What does this model tell you, if anything, about the rate at which people recover from the illness?

6. Comment on the adequacy of the model in Exercise 4.

1–8 Absolute Value

On a certain number line, two points A and B have coordinates 6 and -6 respectively. The distance from 0 to A is 6 and the distance from 0 to B is 6. Distance is always non-negative and is represented by absolute value.

> **Definition** For all $x \in R$, the **absolute value** of x,
> $$|x| = \begin{cases} x \text{ if } x \geq 0 \\ -x \text{ if } x < 0 \end{cases}$$

From this definition it follows that $|6| = |-6| = 6$, since $-(-6) = 6$.

EXAMPLE 1. Graph $|x| < 3$, $x \in R$

Solution: $|x| < 3$ ⟵ **Distance from 0 is less than 3.**

Graph:

Another way to write the solution in Example 1 is $\{x: -3 < x < 3\}$. This notation illustrates the following theorem.

> **Theorem 1–11** For all $x, a \in R$, $a > 0$, $|x| < a$ if and only if $-a < x < a$, i.e., $|x| < a$ if and only if $x \in \langle -a, a \rangle$.

EXAMPLE 2. Express $x \in \langle -2, 2 \rangle$ as an inequality using absolute value.

Solution: $x \in \langle -2, 2 \rangle$

$-2 < x \text{ and } x < 2$ ⟵ **By the definition of open interval**

$|x| < 2$ ⟵ **By Theorem 1–11**

Theorem 1–11 can also be used to solve absolute value inequalities.

EXAMPLE 3. Solve and graph the solution set of $|x - 3| < 2, x \in R$.

Solution:
$$|x - 3| < 2 \text{ iff } -2 < x - 3 < 2$$
$$-2 < x - 3 < 2 \text{ iff } -2 < x - 3 \text{ and } x - 3 < 2$$
$$\text{iff} \quad 1 < x \quad \text{and } x < 5$$
$$\text{iff} \quad 1 < x < 5$$

The solution set is $\{x : 1 < x < 5\}$.

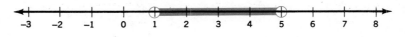

The midpoint of the interval $\langle 1, 5 \rangle$ is 3. All those real numbers that make this inequality true are less than 2 units from 3.

Theorem 1–12 The set of points whose coordinates satisfy

$$|x - a| < b, \quad \forall a, b \in R, \quad b > 0$$

are those points which are less than b units from a.

Proof:
$$|x - a| < b \text{ iff } -b < x - a < b \quad \longleftarrow \quad \textbf{By Theorem 1–11}$$
$$\text{iff } -b + a < x < b + a$$
$$\text{or } x \in \langle -b + a, b + a \rangle$$

Distance is also useful in interpreting inequalities such as $|x| > 3$ or $|x - 3| > 2$. In the first case the set of points must be more than three units from the origin. In the second the set of points must be more than 2 units from 3. The graphs are shown below.

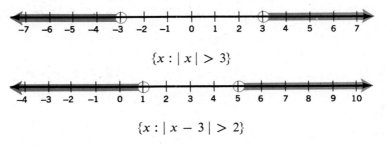

$$\{x : |x| > 3\}$$

$$\{x : |x - 3| > 2\}$$

It is clear then that $|x| > 3$ is equivalent to $x < -3 \text{ or } x > 3$, while $|x - 3| > 2$ is equivalent to $x - 3 < -2 \text{ or } x - 3 > 2$. So $x < 1 \text{ or } x > 5$.

> Theorem 1–13 $\forall x, a \in R, a > 0,$
> $|x| > a$ if and only if $x < -a \text{ or } x > a.$

EXAMPLE 4. $|2x - 1| \geq 5$

Solution:

$$2x - 1 \leq -5 \quad or \quad 2x - 1 \geq 5$$
$$2x \leq -4 \quad or \quad 2x \geq 6$$
$$x \leq -2 \quad or \quad x \geq 3$$

The solution set is $\{x : x \leq -2\} \cup \{x : x \geq 3\}.$

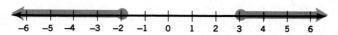

EXAMPLE 5. $|2x - 2| \leq 2 - x$

Solution:

$$|2x - 2| \leq 2 - x \text{ iff}$$
$$-(2 - x) \leq 2x - 2 \leq 2 - x \text{ iff}$$
$$x - 2 \leq 2x - 2 \text{ and } 2x - 2 \leq 2 - x \text{ iff}$$
$$x \leq 2x \text{ and } 2x \leq 4 - x \text{ iff}$$
$$0 \leq x \text{ and } 3x \leq 4 \text{ iff}$$
$$0 \leq x \text{ and } x \leq \tfrac{4}{3}$$

The solution set is $\{x : x \geq 0\} \cap \{x : x \leq \tfrac{4}{3}\}.$
Therefore, $\{x : 0 \leq x \leq \tfrac{4}{3}\} = [0, \tfrac{4}{3}].$

CLASSROOM EXERCISES

Rewrite each expression without absolute values.

1. $|4| = x$ **2.** $|x| = 4$ **3.** $|x + 2| \leq 5$
4. $|x + 2| > 5$ **5.** $|x| < 5$ **6.** $|x| > 5$
7. $|2x - 3| < 3$ **8.** $8 > |x - 5|$ **9.** $|3x + 2| \geq 5$
10. $|3x + 2| = 8$ **11.** $|2x + 3| = 5$ **12.** $-3|x + 1| = -3$

WRITTEN EXERCISES

A — Find and graph the solution set of each sentence. The replacement set for the variables is R.

1. $|x| \leq 2$ **2.** $|t| \geq 5$ **3.** $|r| < 3$
4. $|x + 1| < 3$ **5.** $|x - 1| > 2$ **6.** $|r - 3| \leq 4$

7. $|g + 4| \geq 2$ **8.** $|2 - y| < 3$ **9.** $|5 - r| < 2$

10. $|x - 5| = 4$ **11.** $|13 - (g + 2)| < 1$ **12.** $|3x - 1| < 5$

13. $|5x + 2| \leq 3$ **14.** $|2 - 4t| < 3$

B **15.** $|4 - 2(x - 1)| \leq 3$ **16.** $|3x - 2| \leq 2x - 1$

17. $|x + 5| \leq 3x - 3$ **18.** $|2x - 1| < 3x + 4$

19. $|\frac{r}{3} - 2| > r + 1$ **20.** $2|x - 1| < 4x - 2$

21. $|\frac{3y}{4} - \frac{1}{3}| > y + 1$ **22.** $|4 - x| < 2x$

23. $|x - (2x + 1)| < \frac{1}{2}x - 3$ **24.** $|y - 3| - \frac{y}{4} \geq 2$

C **25.** Prove: $|xy| = |x| \cdot |y|$ $x, y \in R$

26. Prove: $\left|\frac{x}{y}\right| = \frac{|x|}{|y|}$ $(y \neq 0)$ $x, y \in R$

27. Prove: $|x - y| = |y - x|$ $x, y \in R$

28. Prove: $xy \leq |xy|$ $x, y \in R$

29. Prove: $|x|^2 = x^2$ $x \in R$

30. Prove: $|x + y| \leq |x| + |y|$ $x, y \in R$ (*Hint:* This proof may be done by considering the following cases.

    a. $x \geq 0$ and $y \geq 0$ **b.** $x < 0$ and $y < 0$

    c. $x \geq 0$ and $y < 0$ **d.** $x < 0$ and $y \geq 0$)

31. Prove: $|x| - |y| \leq |x + y|$ $x, y \in R$ (*Hint:* You know $|(x + y) + (-y)| \leq |x + y| + |-y|$ by Exercise 30.)

32. Prove: $|x_1 \cdot x_2 \cdot \ldots x_n| = |x_1| \cdot |x_2| \ldots |x_n|$ for all $n \in N$

33. Prove the general triangle inequality: $|x_1 + x_2 + \cdots + x_n| \leq |x_1| + |x_2| + \cdots + |x_n|$ (*Hint:* Use Exercise 30 and Mathematical Induction.)

34. Prove Theorem 1–11. (*Hint:* Show that $|x| < a$ is equivalent to $(x \geq 0$ and $x < a)$ or $(x < 0$ and $-x < a).$)

MID-CHAPTER REVIEW ▭▭▭▭

▬▬ Write whether each statement is *True* or *False* (Section 1-1)

    1. $0 \in N$ **2.** $W \subseteq I$ **3.** $I \cap Q = I$

    4. Give a fractional name for 61.038.

▬▬ Name the property that gives the reason for each exercise below $a, b, c \in R$. (Section 1-2)

    5. $a + (-a) = 0$ **6.** $a \cdot (b \cdot c) = (a \cdot b) \cdot c$ **7.** $b \cdot c \in R$

Write whether each statement 8–10 is *True* or *False*. If a statement is false, explain why it is false. (Section 1-3)

8. $-3 \leq -6$ **9.** $2 \geq 2$ **10.** $10 > -13$

Find the solution set of each inequality if the replacement set is R. Graph each non-empty solution set. (Sections 1-4, 1-5)

11. $b + 2 > -3$ **12.** $3x + 4 \leq 5x - 2$

13. $-3(a + 3) < -a - 1$ **14.** $-1 < 2x + 1 < 7$

15. $(x + 4)(x - 3) < 0$ **16.** $\frac{1}{2} < \frac{5}{8}x < \frac{3}{4}$

Prove by Mathematical Induction that P_n is true for all $n \in N$. (Section 1-6)

17. P_n is the statement: $3 + 6 + 9 + \cdots + 3n = \frac{3n(n + 1)}{2}$

18. P_n is the statement: $1^2 + 2^2 + 3^2 + \cdots + n^2 = \frac{n(n + 1)(2n + 1)}{6}$

Expand each binomial. (Section 1-7)

19. $(x - y)^4$ **20.** $(a + 3b)^7$ **21.** $\left(\frac{a}{3} - \frac{1}{a}\right)^{11}$

Find the indicated term of the given binomial. (Section 1-7)

22. 4th term of $(3a - 2b)^9$ **23.** 9th term of $(4 - \frac{1}{5}y)^{12}$

Find and graph the solution set of each sentence. The replacement set for the variables is R. (Section 1-8)

24. $|x| < 4$ **25.** $|a| \geq 2$ **26.** $|6 - y| \leq 7$

1–9   Relations

How many lines, ℓ, can be drawn using p non-collinear points? You can show the solution to this problem in several ways:

Drawings:

Figure 1

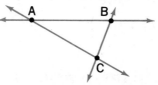

Figure 2

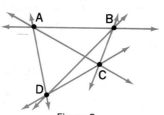

Figure 3

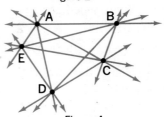

Figure 4

Table:

p	2	3	4	5
l	1	3	6	10

Formula: $l = \dfrac{p(p-1)}{2}$

Each whole number replacement for p leads to a specific number of lines l. The set of ordered pairs (p, l) thus obtained is one way to describe the relation between the number of points, no three of which are collinear, and the number of lines determined by them. Such a pairing is a *relation*.

Definition   A **relation** is a set of ordered pairs.

In set notation the relation described above is

$$\left\{ (p, l) : l = p\,\frac{(p-1)}{2} \right\}.$$

The set of replacements for p is called the *domain* of the relation. Since there can only be a whole number of points and since you need at least two points to determine a line the domain of the relation is $U = \{p : p \geq 2, p \in W\}$

If U is the set of replacement for p, you find the set of values of l to be $V = \{1, 3, 6, 10, 15, 21, 28, \ldots\}$. The set V is the *range* of the relation.

Definitions   The **domain** of a relation is the set of all its first elements, and the **range** of a relation is the set of all its second elements.

A variable associated with the domain is the **independent variable,** while a variable associated with the range is the **dependent variable.**

Commonly the domain of a relation is arbitrarily specified. In other instances it is determined by the practical example. Whenever it is not otherwise specified, the domain is taken to be the set R of real numbers for which the relation is defined.

The range of a relation is the set of all elements corresponding to elements in the domain. The **range set** is the set of elements from which the range is chosen. If the range equals the range set, then the relation is an **onto** relation. When the range does not equal the range set, then the relation is an **into** relation.

EXAMPLE 1. Let the relations T_1 and T_2 have domain = $\{1, 2, 3, 4\}$. Let the range set be $P = \{2, 5, 7\}$.

a. Let $T_1 = \{(1, 2), (2, 5), (3, 7), (4, 2)\}$.

   Then the range of T_1 is $V_1 = P$. T_1 is an **onto** relation.

b. Let $T_2 = \{(1, 2), (2, 2), (3, 2), (4, 2)\}$.

   The range of T_2 is $V_2 = \{2\} \neq P$. T_2 is an **into** relation.

You have seen that a relation may be described by a set of ordered pairs. By specifying the domain you may describe a relation by a mathematical sentence in which the independent variable may be replaced by any member of the domain. In this book if a relation is described by a sentence in x and y, x is the independent variable unless otherwise stated. A third way in which a relation may be described is by a graph.

EXAMPLE 2. Graph $y \leq x$ with domain $\{-1, 0, 1, 2\}$.

Solution:

Although the domain contains only four numbers, the range is considered to be all those $y \in R$ such that $y \leq x$ for some $x \in \{-1, 0, 1, 2\}$. Thus for each x there is an infinite subset of real numbers that satisfy the inequality $y < x$. For $x = 2$, some of the ordered pairs in the relation are $(2, 2)$, $(2, 1.9)$, $(2, 0)$, $(2, -\sqrt{.2})$, $(2, -1000)$. The set of all points corresponding to ordered pairs

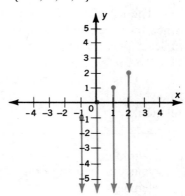

with the first coordinate 2, are those points of the ray with endpoint $(2, 2)$ and perpendicular to the horizontal, or x axis. The complete graph is shown above. It is the union of four rays.

CLASSROOM EXERCISES

━━━ Write whether each relation is an *Onto* relation, an *Into* relation or Neither.

1. $y = x$: $D = \{-2, 1, 3\}$; $R = \{-2, 1, 3, 5\}$

2. $y = x$: $D = \{1, 2, 3\}$; $R = \{3, 1, 2\}$

3. $y = x$: $D = \{0, 1\}$; $R = \{1, 1\}$

4. $\{(2, 3) (3, 2) (-2, 3)\}$: $D = \{2, 3, -2\}$; $R = \{3, 2\}$

WRITTEN EXERCISES

A ━━━Find the range of each relation given the domain.

1. $y = 2x - 3$ $x \in \{-1, -2, -3, 0, 1, 2\}$

2. $y = \frac{1}{3}x + 1$ $x \in \{-1, -\frac{1}{2}, 0, \frac{1}{2}, 1, \frac{3}{2}, 2\}$.

3. $y = x^2 - 2x + 1$ $x \in \{-1, 0, 1, 2, 3\}$

4. $r = 4(s + 2)$ $s \in \{-1, -\frac{3}{4}, -\frac{1}{2}, -\frac{1}{4}, 0, \frac{1}{4}, \frac{1}{2}, \frac{3}{4}, 1\}$

5. $z = \frac{2}{3}t - \frac{5}{3}t$ $t \in \{-3, -2, -1, 0, 1, 2, 3\}$

6. $q = \frac{1}{3}p$ $p \in \{-1, -\frac{2}{3}, -\frac{1}{3}, 0, \frac{1}{3}, \frac{2}{3}, 1\}$

7. $y = x^2$ $x \in \{0, 1, 2, 4, 8, 12\}$

8. $y = 2x - 1$ $x \in \{-5, -3, -1, 1, 3, 5\}$

9. $t > 2r$ $r \in \{-2, -1, 0, 1, 2\}$

10. $y < 2x - 3$ $x \in \{-1, 0, 2\}$

11. $y \leq 3x - 1$ $x \in \{-\frac{1}{3}, 0, \frac{1}{3}\}$

12. $y \geq \frac{5}{2}x$ $x \in \{0, 2, 4, 6\}$

13. $y = x$ $x \in \{-2, -1, 0, 1, 2\}$

━━━Given are a relation, its domain, and range set P. Is the relation onto or into?

14. $y = 2x - 3, x \in \{-1, -2, -3, 0, 1, 2\}$,
P = $\{-9, -7, -5, -3, -1, 1\}$

15. $y = \frac{1}{3}x + 1, x \in \{1, 2, 3, 4\}$, P = $\{1, 3, 4\}$

16. $y = |x|, x \in \{-4, -2, 0, 2, 4\}$, P = $\{0, 2, 4\}$

17. $y = x^2, x \in \{-4, -2, 1, 3\}$, P = $\{0, 1, 4, 9, 16\}$

18. $y = 2x, x \in N, P = N$

19. $y = 2x, x \in N, P = \{2, 4, 6, 8, \ldots\}$

20. $y = 2x + 1, x \in N, P = \{1, 3, 5, 7, \ldots\}$

21. $y = x^3, x \in \{0, 1, 2\}, P = \{-8, -1, 0, 1, 8\}$

22. $y = -x, x \in \{-1, 0, 1, 2\}, P = \{-2, -1, 0, 1\}$

23. $y = x, x \in Ir \cup Q, P = R$

24. Graph the relations described in
     a. Exercise 9.   **b.** Exercise 10.

B   **25.** Find the range and make a graph of the following relation:

$$y = |x| \qquad x \in \{-3, -2, -1, 0, 1, 2, 3\}$$

26. Find the range and make a graph of the following relation:

$$y = |x| \qquad x \in [-3, 3]$$

27. Repeat Exercises 25 and 26 for the relation $y = -|x|$.

NUMBERS, RELATIONS, AND FUNCTIONS   37

28. Graph each relation where $x \in \{-4, -3, -2, -1, 0, 1, 2, 3, 4\}$.

    a. $y = |x - 1|$ **b.** $y = |x| - 1$ **c.** $y = x - 1$

Graph the relation described by $y < |x| - 1$ over the domain $\{x : -2 \le x \le 2, x \in I\}$.

C   **29.** Suppose that postage is 8 cents for the first ounce and 8 cents for each additional ounce.

    a. What is the domain of this postage relation? the range?
    b. Describe the relation geometrically.

30. Pick five classmates. Find the ordered pairs in the relation "is taller than." Let the domain and range be the five people.

31. Use the five classmates chosen in Exercise 30 and find the ordered pairs in the relation "is heavier than." Are the relations "is taller than" and "is heavier than" the same? Could they be?

1–10 Functions and Mappings

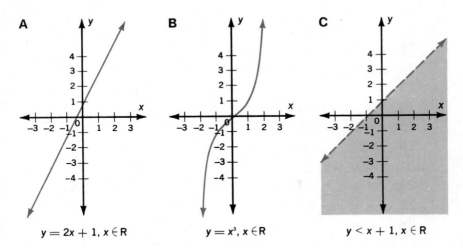

   A $y = 2x + 1, x \in R$ **B** $y = x^3, x \in R$ **C** $y < x + 1, x \in R$

Each graph above is a geometric model of a relation. A and B, however, differ from C in one important respect. For each value of x in A and B there is exactly one element y in the respective ranges. An easy way to see this is to picture a line perpendicular to the x axis at its left-hand side; by sliding the line to the right, you can observe that for each x there is only one point in the graph of the relation. This is called the **vertical-line test** for a *function*.

> **Definition**   A **function** is a relation such that for every element of the domain there is one and only one element of the range.

For each domain element in C, $y < x + 1$, $x \in$ R, there are infinitely many range elements. For example let $x = 3$.

Then
$$y < x + 1$$

So
$$y < 3 + 1$$
$$y < 4$$

So y assumes all real values less than 4. Verify that this is true for all values of x by the vertical-line test. Relation C is not a function.

When x is a domain element of a function f, then $f(x)$, read "f at x," is the corresponding range element. The function f is the set of ordered pairs of the form $(x, f(x))$. For example, if

$$f = \{(2, 3), (-4, 7)\},$$

then
$$f(2) = 3$$

and
$$f(-4) = 7.$$

When a set of ordered pairs (x, y) is a function, $f(x)$ is another name for y, an element in the range of the function. A function whose range is equal to its range set is an **onto** function. Similarly, a function whose range is a proper subset of its range set is an **into** function.

EXAMPLE.   Let a function f be defined by the following equation.
$$y = 2x - 1 \qquad x \in \text{R}$$
Find $f(x)$ for $x = -2, 1, \frac{1}{2}, p$.

Solution:

The value of $f(x)$ may be determined by substituting the corresponding value of x into the equation defining f.

$f(x) = y = 2x - 1$ ⟵ **Defining equation**

$f(-2) = 2(-2) - 1 = -4 - 1 = -5$ ⟵ **Substitute −2.**

$f(1) = 2(1) - 1 = 2 - 1 = 1$

$f(\frac{1}{2}) = 2(\frac{1}{2}) - 1 = 1 - 1 = 0$

$f(p) = 2p - 1$ ⟵ **Substitute p.**

Consider a function f with domain $U = \{0, 2, 4\}$ and range $V = \{1, 3, 5\}$. There are several ways you could associate $x \in U$ with $f(x) \in V$. Here is one which lists x and its corresponding value of $f(x)$ in table form.

x	$f(x)$
0	1
2	3
4	5

Or

$$f = \{(0, 1), (2, 3), (4, 5)\}.$$

The same function may be shown as follows.

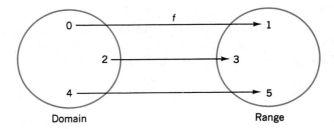

The drawing suggests a rule or procedure by which the elements of U are associated with those in V. Rather than emphasizing the ordered pairs, the drawing focuses your attention on the rule. In the instance shown here, the rule is *Add 1 to each element of U, or*

$$f(x) = x + 1.$$

Such a rule is called a **mapping** of the elements of U onto the elements of V.

A mapping is commonly denoted

$$f : x \rightarrow f(x),$$

which is read "f maps x onto $f(x)$."

In this particular example, you would write

$$f : x \rightarrow x + 1,$$

or "f maps x onto $x + 1$."

In this book there will be no distinction made between mappings and relations. The function f may be thought of as either the set of ordered pairs $\{(x, y) : y = f(x)\}$ or as the rule that associates x with $f(x)$. Sometimes one interpretation may be more useful than the other, however.

CLASSROOM EXERCISES

━━ Determine which mappings are functions.

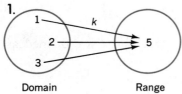

1.

Domain   Range

2.

Domain   Range

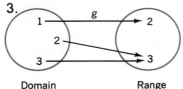

3.

Domain   Range

4.

Domain   Range

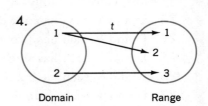

WRITTEN EXERCISES

A ━━ Let a mapping be defined by $f : x \rightarrow \frac{1}{2}x,\ x \in W$.

1. What is the range of f?

2. Find $f(4)$.   **3.** Find $3f(2)$.

4. Find $f(2x)$.   **5.** Find $2f(x)$.

6. Does $f(3) + f(5) = f(3 + 5)$?

━━ Represent each relation as a mapping. Which are functions?

7. $y = x - 1$ $U = \{x : -3 \le x < 3,\ x \in I\}$

8. $\{(1, 2), (2, 2), (3, 4), (4, 4)\}$

9. $\{(1, 2), (2, 2), (3, 4), (3, 5)\}$

10. $y = x^2$ $x \in \{-1, 0, 1\}$

11. $y = \sqrt{x}$ $x \in \{9, 4, 1, 0\}$

12. $y = \sqrt[3]{x}$ $x \in \{-8, 1, -1, 27\}$

13. $r = |t|$ $t \in \{1, \frac{1}{2}, -\frac{1}{2}, -\frac{1}{3}\} = U$

14. $r = |t|$ $r \in \{0, 1, 2\} = V$

15. $y < x + 1$ $U = \{x : 0 < x < 4,\ x \in I\},\ y \in W$

16. $y > x + 1$ $U = \{x : -3 < x < 3,\ x \in I\},$
                   $y \in \{-5, -4, \ldots, 4, 5\}$

17. $f : x \rightarrow \frac{1}{2}x + 1$ $x \in \{2, 4, 6, 8\}$

18. $f : x \rightarrow -|x|$ $x \in \{\pm 4, \pm 2, 0\}$

B **19.** In Exercises 7–18 graph each relation that is a function.

20. Let $f: x \rightarrow x^2 - 3$, $x \in \{\pm 4, \pm 3, \pm 2, \pm 10\}$.   What is the range of f?

21. Let $g: y \rightarrow y + 1$, $y \in \{13, 6, 1, -2, -3\}$.   What is the range of g?

22. Find the range of $g[f(x)]$ where g and f are defined as in Exercises 20 and 21.

C —— How many functions are there that map $x \in$ U onto $y \in$ V when

23. U and V each has one element?

24. U and V each has two elements?

25. U and V each has three elements?

26. U and V each has four elements?

27. U and V each has n elements ($n \in$ W)?

28. A **linear function** is a function described by the equation $y = mx + b$, $m \neq 0$, U $= \{x : x \in$ R$\}$.

    a. What geometric figure is the graph of a linear function?

    b. What is the significance of m?

    c. What is the significance of b?

29. The **absolute value function** is the function that maps each real number onto its absolute value. It is symbolized $f: x \rightarrow |x|$. Graph f for $x \in$ R and $-5 \leq x \leq 5$.

—— Graph.

30. $f: x \rightarrow |x + 1|$, U $= \{x : -5 \leq x \leq 5, x \in$ R$\}$

31. $g: x \rightarrow |x| + 1$, U $= \{x : -5 \leq x \leq 5, x \in$ R$\}$

32. Does $f = g$ in Exercises 30 and 31?

—— The **greatest integer function** is the function that maps each real number onto the greatest integer not greater than the given real number. It is symbolized $f: x \rightarrow [x]$.

33. Graph $f: x \rightarrow [x]$ U $= \{x : -5 \leq x \leq 5, x \in$ R$\}$.

34. Graph $g: x \rightarrow [x + 1]$ U $= \{x : -5 \leq x \leq 5, x \in$ R$\}$.

35. Graph $h: x \rightarrow [x] + 1$ U $= \{x : -5 \leq x \leq 5, x \in$ R$\}$.

36. Does $g = h$ in Exercises 34 and 35?

37. The **identity function** is the function that maps each real number onto itself. It is symbolized $I: x \rightarrow x$. Graph $I: x \rightarrow x$, U $= \{x : -5 \leq x \leq 5, x \in$ R$\}$

1—11 · Composition of Functions

Let f be a function mapping the elements of A onto those in B.
Let g be a function mapping the elements of B onto those in C.

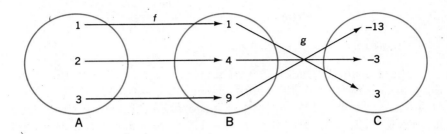

Notice that 1 maps onto 1, which in turn maps onto 3. Similarly, 2 maps onto 4, which maps onto −3, and 3 maps onto 9, which maps onto −13.

Thus, by applying f to the elements of A and then applying g to the elements in the range of f—that is, set B—the result is a mapping from A to C. This mapping is clearly a function. It is the **composition** of g with f and is denoted gf, which is read "g composition f." The function gf is the **composite function.** The mapping gf is pictured below.

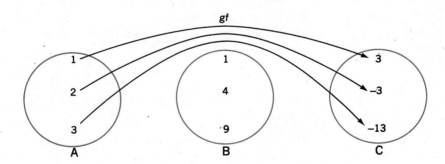

It may seem that the set B is of little consequence to the final mapping gf. This is far from the truth. In the example B was the range of f *and* the domain of g. Thus gf had domain A and range C because for each $x \in$ A there was an $f(x) \in$ B and finally a $g[f(x)]$ in C.

If the set B does not contain all the elements of the range of f nor all the elements of the domain of g, the domain of gf is lessened and so is its range. The figure at the top of page **44** illustrates this situation.

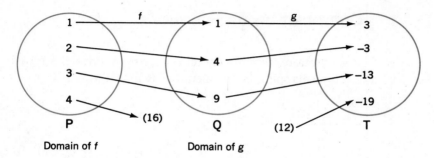

Domain of f   Domain of g

The domain of f is $\{1, 2, 3, 4\}$ and its range is $\{1, 4, 9, 16\}$. The domain of g is $\{1, 4, 9, 12\}$ and its range is $\{3, -3, -13, -19\}$. Since $f(4) = 16 \notin \{1, 4, 9, 12\}$, $g[f(4)]$ is not defined. Likewise since there is no $x \in \{1, 2, 3, 4\}$ such that $f(x) = 12$, there is no x in the domain of gf such that $g[f(x)] = -19$. Thus the domain of gf is $\{1, 2, 3\}$ and the range is $\{3, -3, -13\}$. The domain of gf is a subset of the domain of f and the range of gf is a subset of the range of g.

The following definition summarizes this discussion and gives the fundamental notation for gf.

Definition   Given two functions f and g, the function

$$gf : x \to g[f(x)]$$

is the **composite function**. The domain of gf is the set of all elements x in the domain of f for which $f(x)$ is in the domain of g. The operation of forming a composite of two functions is **composition**.

You may have noted that the functions f and g used in the discussion above could be described as follows:

$$f(x) = x^2 \qquad x \in \{1, 2, 3\}$$
$$g(x) = -2x + 5 \qquad x \in \{1, 4, 9\}$$

The composite function gf may easily be determined from the equations of f and g.

$$gf : x \to g[f(x)]$$

Thus $g[f(x)] = g[x^2]$ since $f(x) = x^2$

$$= -2(x^2) + 5 \text{ since } g(x) = -2(x) + 5.$$

So $g[f(x)] = -2x^2 + 5 \qquad x \in \{1, 2, 3\}$.

The range of $gf(x) = -2x^2 + 5$ is $\{3, -3, -13\}$. This is the set C of the example on the previous page.

CLASSROOM EXERCISES

— Given $f(x) = 3x - 1$ and $g(x) = x + 3$ for all $x \in \mathbf{R}$, find

1. $g[f(x)]$. **2.** $f[g(x)]$. **3.** $f[f(x)]$. **4.** $g[g(x)]$.

— Given $f(x) = x^2 + 1$, $g(x) = x - 2$, $h(x) = 2x + 1$, find

5. gh. **6.** fg. **7.** $f(gh)$. **8.** $(fg)h$.

WRITTEN EXERCISES

A **1.** Which exercises above prove that composition of functions is not commutative?

— Draw a mapping diagram that pictures each composite function. Specify the domain and range of the composite function.

2. $f = \{(1, 2), (3, 4), (5, 6)\}$
$g = \{(4, 5), (2, 3), (6, 7)\}$
$gf = \underline{\ ?\ }$

3. $g = \{(-5, 1), (-2, 4), (0, 2)\}$
$h = \{(2, -1), (4, -3), (1, 5)\}$
$hg = \underline{\ ?\ }$

4. $h = \{(1, 2), (3, 5), (4, 7)\}$
$f = \{(2, 3), (5, 4), (7, 6)\}$
$fh = \underline{\ ?\ }$

5. $\_ = \{(a, b), (b, c), (c, d)\}$
$H = \{(d, c), (c, b), (b, a)\}$
$H\_ = \underline{\ ?\ }$

— Given $f(x) = 3x - 4$, $h(x) = x^2 + 3$, $g(x) = -2x + 1$, $x \in \mathbf{R}$, find the following.

6. fh **7.** hf **8.** fg **9.** gf
10. $h(fg)$ **11.** $g(fh)$ **12.** $fg(2)$ **13.** $f(gh(3))$
14. $hg(-5)$ **15.** hh **16.** $f(hh)$ **17.** $f(hh(2))$

B — In Exercises 18–20, let $f : x \rightarrow ax + b$, $h : x \rightarrow cx + d$, $x \in \mathbf{R}$.

18. What is the slope of the graph of f? of the graph of h?

19. Find fh and hf.

20. What is the slope of the graph of fh? the graph of hf? Compare them with the slopes found in Exercise 18. State the generalization.

— In Exercises 21–24, let $f(x) = \frac{1}{x}$, $x \in \mathbf{R}$, $x \neq 0$.

21. Find $ff(2)$ **22.** Find $ff(-3)$ **23.** Find $ff(100)$

24. What function is ff?

— In Exercises 25–28, let $I : x \rightarrow x$ and $g : x \rightarrow x - 3$, $x \in \mathbf{R}$.

25. Find $g[I]$ and $I[g]$.

26. Find a function f such that $gf = I$, $x \in \mathbf{R}$.

27. Find a function h such that $hg = I$, $x \in \mathbf{R}$.

28. Compare h and f of Exercises 26 and 27.

C **29.** Let $f(x) = 2x + 1$ and $g(x) = 3$. Find expressions for $f[g(x)]$ and $g[f(x)]$.

30. Let $f(x) = x^3$ and $g(x) = x^2$. Find expressions for $f[g(x)]$ and $g[f(x)]$.

31. Let $f(x) = x'''$ and $g(x) = x''$. Find expressions for $f[g(x)]$ and $g[f(x)]$.

32. Let $f(x) = x^3$ and $g(x) = x^2$. Find expressions for $f \cdot g(x)$ and $g \cdot f(x)$ where $f \cdot g$ and $g \cdot f$ are products of f and g. (*i.e.*, $f \cdot g(x) = f(x) \cdot g(x)$) Compare with Exercise 30.

33. Let $f(x) = x^m$ and $g(x) = x^n$. Find an expression for the product $f \cdot g(x)$. Compare with Exercise 31.

━━━ In Exercises 34–38, let $f(x) = x + 2$, $g(x) = x - 3$, and $h(x) = x^2$. Find expressions for each of these.

34. $g \cdot f(x)$ **35.** $(g \cdot f)[h(x)]$

36. $g[h(x)]$ **37.** $f[h(x)]$

38. $[gh \cdot fh](x)$ **39.** Compare Exercises 35 and 38.

40. Does $h[g \cdot f(x)] = [hg \cdot hf](x)$ for f, g, and h in Exercises 34–38?

1–12   Inverses of Functions

Suppose f is the function

$$f : x \to x - 5$$

and g is the function

$$g : x \to x + 5.$$

The effect of f is to decrease each number by 5. The effect of g is to increase each number by 5. Then f and g are inversely related in the sense that each undoes the effect of the other. If you apply f to a real number r, you map r onto $r - 5$. If you then apply g to $r - 5$, you map $r - 5$ onto $(r - 5) + 5$, or r. The effect of the composite function gf is to map r onto r, or

$$gf : r \to r.$$

A function that maps each domain element onto itself is an **identity function** I (see Section 1–10, Exercise 37). Thus, $gf = I$. Two identity functions with unequal domains are different functions. I will be referred to as the identity function, irrespective of the domain.

In symbols, you can see that gf evaluated at r is

$$g[f(r)] = g[r - 5] = (r - 5) + 5 = r. \qquad \text{(Domain of } f = R\text{)}$$

Similary,

$$f[g(r)] = f[r + 5] = (r + 5) - 5 = r. \qquad \text{(Domain of } g = R\text{)}$$

Thus,

$$gf = I = fg. \qquad \text{(Domain of } f = \text{Domain of } g\text{)}$$

If the domain of f does not equal the domain of g then $gf \neq fg$. Consider now the function h described by

$$h(x) = \frac{3x - 1}{2}.$$

Here h tells you to take a number x, triple it, subtract 1, and divide the result by 2. To construct the inversely related mapping you would take a number x, multiply it by 2, add 1, and divide the result by 3. The resulting mapping would be

$$g(x) = \frac{2x + 1}{3}.$$

To see that h and g are inversely related, find the composite functions hg and gh.

$$h[g(x)] = \frac{3\left(\dfrac{2x + 1}{3}\right) - 1}{2} = \frac{(2x + 1) - 1}{2} = x$$

and

$$g[h(x)] = \frac{2\left(\dfrac{3x - 1}{2}\right) + 1}{3} = \frac{(3x - 1) + 1}{3} = x.$$

In both cases the result is the identity I.

$$hg = I = gh$$

This discussion is summarized by the definition of *inverse* functions.

Definition If f and g are functions so related that $fg : x \rightarrow x$ for every element x in the domain of g and $gf : y \rightarrow y$ for every element y in the domain of f, then f and g are **inverses** of each other.

In the above definition, if f and g have the same domain, then $fg = I = gf$.

Depicting a function as a mapping clearly brings out the inverse relationship between two inverse functions. If f maps x onto y, that is $y = f(x)$, then g, the inverse of f, maps y onto x; that is $g(y) = x$. This is depicted by reversing the arrows.

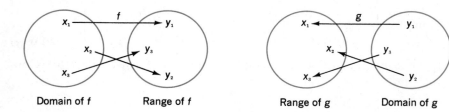

Domain of f Range of f Range of g Domain of g

For *any* mapping you can reverse the arrows and obtain another mapping. If the original mapping was a function, it does not follow, however, that the inverse mapping is also a function. Consider the diagram below.

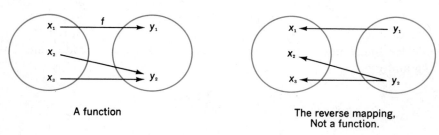

A function   The reverse mapping,
Not a function.

Any function f that associates two different elements in its domain with *one* element in the range has an inverse mapping that is not a function. In the diagram above f maps x_2 and x_3 onto y_2. Thus, the inverse mapping associates y_2 with x_2 and x_3. This inverse mapping is not a function. You can conclude that not all inverses of functions are themselves functions.

By comparing the two diagrams you can see exactly what kinds of functions have inverses that are functions. The mapping must be *one-to-one*; that is for the inverse of f to be a function $x_1 \neq x_2$ if and only if $f(x_1) \neq f(x_2)$. Frequently the inverse of f is denoted by f^{-1}.

EXAMPLE. Given $f = \{(0, 1), (2, -1)\}$ find f^{-1}.

Solution: $\qquad\qquad f : 0 \to 1 \qquad$ so $\qquad f^{-1} : 1 \to 0$
$\qquad\qquad\qquad\qquad f : 2 \to -1 \qquad$ so $\qquad f^{-1} : -1 \to 2$

Therefore $\qquad\qquad\qquad f^{-1} = \{(1, 0), (-1, 2)\}$.

CLASSROOM EXERCISES

━━ Write the inverse of each function.

1. {(2, 3) (3, 2) (4, 5)}

2. {(2, 3) (3, 3) (4, 3)}

3. {(0, 1) (2, 9) (−1, −3)}

4. {(1, 1) (−1, 1) (3, 3)}

━━ Write the equation of the inverse of each function.

5. $f(x) = 2x$

6. $f(x) = x + 3$

7. $f(x) = x - 6$

8. $f(x) = 2x + 3$

WRITTEN EXERCISES

A ━━ In Exercises 1–5, suppose $f = \{(1, 2), (3, 4), (5, 6), (7, 8)\}$ and g is the inverse of f.

1. Construct a mapping diagram for f, for g.

2. What ordered pairs are in g?

3. How can the ordered pairs of g be obtained from those of f?

4. Repeat Exercises 1–3 for $f = \{(2, -\frac{1}{2}), (3, -\frac{1}{3}), (4, -\frac{1}{4})\}$.

5. Let f be a function with an inverse that is also a function. If $f = \{(x, y) : y = f(x), x \in R\}$ find f^{-1}, the inverse of f (see Exercises 1–4).

━━ For each function find the inverse. If the inverse is not a function, explain why this is so.

6. $f : x \rightarrow 2x + 5$

7. $g : x \rightarrow \frac{1}{3}x$

8. $h : x \rightarrow \frac{1}{3}x - 1$

9. $G : r \rightarrow 2r + 1$

10. $F : t \rightarrow \frac{2}{3}t + \frac{1}{3}$

11. $H : x \rightarrow x^3$

12. $h : x \rightarrow x^3 - 8$

13. $f : x \rightarrow x^2 - 4$

14. $T : r \rightarrow \frac{4r + 5}{3}$

15. $H : y \rightarrow \frac{2}{5}y - 5$

16. In Exercises 6–15 show that the composite of the function and its inverse is the identity.

━━ Find an inverse of each of the following functions.

17. $x \rightarrow x + 3$

18. $x \rightarrow 5x - 7$

19. $x \rightarrow \frac{1}{x}, x \neq 0$

20. $x \rightarrow -x$

━━ Solve each of the following equations for x in terms of y and compare your answers with those obtained in Exercises 17–20.

21. $y = x + 3$

22. $y = 5x - 7$

23. $y = \frac{1}{x}, x \neq 0$

24. $y = -x$

25. On the basis of Exercises 17–24, describe a method that can be used to find the inverse of a function.

━━ Find the inverses of the following using Exercise 25.

26. $f(x) = \frac{7}{2}x - 1$

27. $g(x) = x^3 + 27$

28. $h(x) = x^2 - 4$

B ━━ Consider $f = \{(0, 2), (1, 0), (2, -2), (3, -4)\}$.

29. Graph f.   **30.** Graph f^{-1}.

31. Graph $I : x \rightarrow x,\ x \in$ R.

32. How are the graphs of f and f^{-1} related to that of I?

33. Repeat Exercises 29–32 for $f : x \rightarrow 3x - 4$ where

$$U = \{x : -4 \leq x \leq 4, x \in R\}.$$

34. Generalize the results of Exercises 29–33.

35. Use your generalization of Exercise 34 to graph

    a. two points of the inverse of $f(x) = \frac{1}{3}x + 1,\ x \in$ R.

    b. the complete inverse of f.

C   **36.** What function is its own inverse?

     37. Prove that every linear function has an inverse.

1–13   Complex Numbers

The set of *complex numbers* includes and is defined in terms of real numbers. You are familiar with the **imaginary unit** i with the property $i^2 = -1$. You can also identify i as $\sqrt{-1}$.

Definitions   For all, $a,\ b \in$ R, $a + bi$, $i = \sqrt{-1}$, is a **complex number.** a is the **real part** of the complex number, and bi is the **imaginary part.** The set of complex numbers is denoted C.

If in a complex number $a + bi$ the real part is zero, then $a + bi$, or bi, is a **pure imaginary** number. Likewise if in $a + bi$, $b = 0$, then $a + bi$, or a is a real number. Thus C contains pure imaginaries and real numbers as subsets.

Equality of complex numbers is defined as follows in terms of the equality of real numbers.

Definition $\forall a + bi, c + di \in C$

$a + bi = c + di$ if and only if $a = c$ and $b = d$.

The fundamental operations of addition and multiplication of complex numbers are defined so that the familiar properties of these operations for real numbers continue to apply for the complex numbers.

Definitions **Addition:** $\forall a, b, c, d \in R$

$$(a + bi) + (c + di) = (a + c) + (b + d)i$$

Multiplication: $\forall a, b, c, d \in R$

$$(a + bi)(c + di) = ac - bd + (bc + ad)i$$

With these definitions, C is *closed* with respect to addition and multiplication. Moreover it can be shown that the operations of addition and multiplication of complex numbers are *commutative* and *associative*, that *multiplication distributes over addition*, and that the *identity* elements are $0 + 0i$ and $1 + 0i$ respectively. Finally for $a + bi$, $-a + (-bi)$ and $\frac{1}{a + bi}$ $(a + bi \neq 0)$ are the *additive* and *multiplicative inverses*. You are asked to verify these statements in the exercises.

Subtraction and division are defined in terms of addition and multiplication.

Definitions **Subtraction:** $\forall z_1, z_2, z_3 \in C$,

$$z_1 - z_2 = z_3 \text{ if and only if } z_1 = z_3 + z_2.$$

Division: $\forall z_1, z_2, z_3 \in C, z_2 \neq 0,$

$$z_1 \div z_2 = z_3 \text{ if and only if } z_1 = z_3 \cdot z_2.$$

These definitions can be used to show that

$$z_1 - z_2 = z_1 + (-z_2)$$

and that

$$z_1 \div z_2 = z_1 \cdot \frac{1}{z_2}.$$

The methods are illustrated in the following two examples.

EXAMPLE 1. Given that $z_1 = a + bi$, $z_2 = c + di$ and $-z_2 = -c + (-di)$, show that $z_1 - z_2 = z_1 + (-z_2)$.

Solution: $z_1 - z_2 = z_3$ iff $z_1 = z_3 + z_2$ ◄——— **Def. of Sub.**

thus, $(a + bi) - (c + di) = x + yi$ iff

$\qquad a + bi = x + yi + c + di$ ◄——— **Def. of Sub.**

$\qquad\qquad = x + c + (y + d)i$ ◄——— **Def. of Add.**

$\qquad a = x + c,\ b = y + d$ ◄——— **Def. of Equal.**

$\qquad \left. \begin{array}{l} x = a - c = a + (-c) \\ y = b - d = b + (-d) \end{array} \right\}$ ◄——— **Def. of Sub. of real numbers**

So, $\quad z_1 - z_2 = x + yi = [a + (-c)] + [b + (-d)]i$

$\qquad\qquad\qquad = a + bi + [-c + (-di)]$

$\qquad\qquad\qquad = (a + bi) + [-(c + di)]$

$\qquad\qquad\qquad = z_1 + (-z_2)$

EXAMPLE 2. Given that $z_1 = a + bi$ and $z_2 = c + di \neq 0$, show that $z_1 \div z_2 = z_1 \cdot \dfrac{1}{z_2}$.

Solution: It is useful to keep all results in the form $A + Bi$ where A and B are real numbers. Initially show that

$$\frac{1}{z_2} = \frac{1}{c + di} = \frac{c}{c^2 + d^2} + \frac{-di}{c^2 + d^2}.$$

This is shown as follows.

$$\frac{1}{c + di} = \frac{1(c - di)}{(c + di)(c - di)} = \frac{c - di}{c^2 - d^2 i^2} \quad \text{◄——— } \textbf{Def. of Mult.}$$

$$= \frac{c - di}{c^2 + d^2} \quad \text{◄——— } i^2 = -1$$

$$= \frac{c}{c^2 + d^2} + \frac{-di}{c^2 + d^2}$$

The number $c - di$ is the **conjugate** of $c + di$. Thus,

$$z_1 \cdot \frac{1}{z_2} = (a + bi)\frac{1}{c + di}$$

$$= (a + bi)\frac{c - di}{c^2 + d^2}$$

$$= \frac{(a + bi)(c - di)}{c^2 + d^2}$$

$$= \frac{(ac + bd)}{c^2 + d^2} + \frac{(bc - ad)i}{c^2 + d^2}$$

Turning to $z_1 \div z_2$, you know that the following holds.

$$z_1 \div z_2 = z_3 \text{ iff } z_1 = z_3 \cdot z_2$$

Thus, $(a + bi) \div (c + di) = x + yi$ iff
$$a + bi = (x + yi)(c + di)$$
$$= (xc - yd) + (cy + dx)i$$

So $a = xc - yd$ and $b = xd + yc$ by the definition of equality.

Solving these equations for x and y, you find

$$x = \frac{ac + bd}{c^2 + d^2} \text{ and } y = \frac{bc - ad}{c^2 + d^2}.$$

Thus, $x + yi = \frac{(ac + bd)}{c^2 + d^2} + \frac{(bc - ad)i}{c^2 + d^2}$

$$= z_1 \cdot \frac{1}{z_2}.$$

Thus, to divide $a + bi$ by $c + di$ you can multiply $a + bi$ by $\frac{c - di}{c^2 + d^2}$, the multiplicative inverse of $c + di$.

CLASSROOM EXERCISES

━━ Perform the indicated operation. Express the number in the form $a + bi$.

1. $i + i$ **2.** $i - 2i$ **3.** $i \cdot i$ **4.** $i \div 2i$

5. i^4 **6.** $i + (i \cdot i)$ **7.** $3i - (2i)^2$ **8.** $(i + 3) - 3i$

WRITTEN EXERCISES

A ━━ Perform the indicated operation. Express the number in the form $a + bi$.

1. $(3 + 2i) - (4 - i)$ **2.** $(5 - 2i) + (3 + 7i)$

3. $(7 - i) - (7 + i)$ **4.** $(-2 + 3i) + (4 - 3i)$

5. $(2 - 3i) \cdot (-2 + i)$ **6.** $i(2 - 7i)$

7. $(1 + 5i)(5 - i)$ **8.** $(1 - i)^2$

9. $\dfrac{1 + i}{2 - i}$ **10.** $\dfrac{2 - i}{1 - i}$

11. $\dfrac{2(1 + i)}{i}$ **12.** $\dfrac{8 + 12i}{(2 + 2i)(2 - 2i)}$

B   **13.** $(3 + i)(3 - i)\left(\dfrac{2 + i}{10}\right)$ **14.** $\dfrac{1 + 2i}{3 - 4i} + \dfrac{2 - i}{5i}$

15. $\dfrac{2i}{(i - 1)(i - 2)(i - 3)}$ **16.** $\dfrac{3i}{1 + 2i} - \dfrac{4}{1 - 2i}$

17. Show that $1 + i$ and $1 - i$ satisfy $z^2 - 2z + 2 = 0$.

18. Show that the numbers $z = \dfrac{-1 \pm i\sqrt{2}}{3}$ satisfy the equation $3z^2 + 2z + 1 = 0$.

19. Prove that if $z_1 z_2 = 0$, then $z_1 = 0$ or $z_2 = 0$, $z_1, z_2 \in C$.

C **20.** Prove that if $z_1 z_2 \ldots z_n = 0$, then at least one of the complex numbers $z_1, z_2, \ldots, z_n$ is zero for all $n \in N$.

21. Establish the associative law of addition for complex numbers. Do the same for multiplication.

22. Establish the commutative law of addition for complex numbers. Do the same for multiplication.

23. Prove that multiplication distributes over addition for complex numbers.

1–14   Complex Numbers As Vectors

A complex number z written in the form $c + di$ is said to be in **standard form.** The standard form of $\dfrac{1}{a + bi}$ is $\dfrac{a}{a^2 + b^2} + \left(\dfrac{-b}{a^2 + b^2}\right) i$. An efficient way to compute the standard form of $\dfrac{1}{a + bi}$ is to multiply it by $\dfrac{a - bi}{a - bi}$. This is true because

$$
\begin{aligned}
\frac{1}{a + bi} &= \frac{1}{a + bi} \cdot \frac{a - bi}{a - bi} \\[2mm]
&= \frac{a - bi}{(a^2 + b^2) + (ab - ab)i} \\[2mm]
&= \frac{a - bi}{a^2 + b^2} \\[2mm]
&= \frac{a}{a^2 + b^2} + \frac{-b}{a^2 + b^2} \, i.
\end{aligned}
$$

For the complex number $a + bi$, $a - bi$ is the **conjugate.** The conjugate of z_1 is denoted $\bar{z}_1$ (read "z_1 conjugate"). The standard form of $\dfrac{1}{z_1}$ is $\dfrac{\bar{z}_1}{z_1 \bar{z}_1}$. This provides a simple algorithm for dividing z_2 by z_1; namely

$$
z_2 \div z_1 = z_2 \cdot \frac{1}{z_1} = \frac{z_2}{z_1} \cdot \frac{\bar{z}_1}{\bar{z}_1}.
$$

That is, multiply numerator and denominator by the conjugate of the denominator.

EXAMPLE 1. Write $\dfrac{2-3i}{1-2i}$ in standard form.

Solution: The conjugate of $1 - 2i$ is $1 + 2i$. Thus

$$\frac{2-3i}{1-2i} = \frac{2-3i}{1-2i} \cdot \frac{1+2i}{1+2i} \quad \longleftarrow \text{ Multiply by } \frac{\bar{z}}{\bar{z}}.$$

$$= \frac{(2+6)+(4-3)i}{1+4}$$

$$= \frac{8+i}{5} = \frac{8}{5} + \frac{i}{5} \quad \longleftarrow \begin{array}{l}\textbf{Standard}\\ \textbf{form}\end{array}$$

For each ordered pair (a, b) of real numbers there is a unique complex number $a + bi$. Conversely, for each complex number $a + bi$, there is a unique ordered pair (a, b) of real numbers. Thus there is a one-to-one correspondence between the ordered pairs of real numbers and the complex numbers.

Furthermore, there is a one-to-one correspondence between the ordered pairs of real numbers and the points in a rectangular coordinate system. Finally, the complex numbers and the points in the plane are associated in a one-to-one fashion.

It is natural to use this association between complex numbers and points in the plane to represent complex numbers geometrically. Usually a complex number $z = a + bi$ is represented by the directed line segment or **vector** from the origin to the point (a, b). See the figure at the right. The

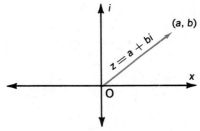

horizontal axis is the real axis and the vertical axis is the imaginary axis or the i axis. All real numbers are represented by points on the real axis; pure imaginaries by points on the i axis; and other complex numbers by points not on either axis. $z = 0 + 0i$ is the origin.

EXAMPLE 2. Show the geometric representation of z and $\bar{z}$ when

$$z = a + bi.$$

$z = a + bi$ is shown in the figure at the right. Then $\bar{z} = a - bi$, so it is a vector from 0 to $(a, -b)$. It is the reflection of the vector z in the real axis.

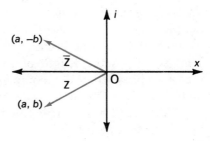

Given two complex numbers $z_1 = a + bi$ and $z_2 = c + di$; the sum $z_1 + z_2 = (a + c) + (b + d)i$. $z_1 + z_2$ is represented geometrically by the vector from the origin to $(a + c, b + d)$. The sum can be found geometrically by thinking of z_1 and z_2 as two sides of a parallelogram whose fourth vertex is $(a + c, b + d)$. Thus $z_1 + z_2$ is the diagonal from the origin to the fourth vertex. See Figure 1.

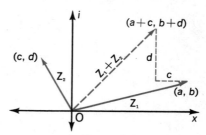

Figure 1

The same construction works for subtraction. $z_1 - z_2 = z_1 + (-z_2)$. Thus you construct the diagonal of the parallelogram with sides z_1 and $-z_2$. This is illustrated in Figure 2.

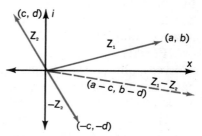

Figure 2

EXAMPLE 3. If $z_1 = 1 - 2i$, $z_2 = 2 + 3i$, exhibit $z_1 + z_2$ and $z_1 - z_2$ geometrically.

$z_1 + z_2$ is the diagonal of the parellelogram with sides z_1 and z_2. $z_1 + z_2 = 3 + i$, $z_1 - z_2 = z_1 + (-z_2)$, so $z_1 - z_2$ is the diagonal of the parallelogram with sides z_1 and $-z_2$. See Figure 3.

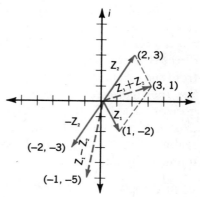

Figure 3

Recall that the absolute value of a real number x, $|x|$, is the distance from the origin to the point x. In a similar manner, the absolute value of a complex number $z = a + bi$, $|z|$, is the distance from the origin to the point (a, b). That is, $|z|$ is the length of the vector representing the complex number z. See Figure 4.

The length of z is easily found by application of the Pythagorean Theorem: if $z = a + bi$

$$|z| = \sqrt{a^2 + b^2}.$$

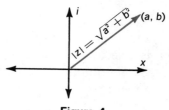

Figure 4

The following definition summarizes the discussion on page 56.

> **Definition**   Let $z = a + bi$. The **absolute value** of z, $|z|$, is defined
> $$|z| = \sqrt{a^2 + b^2}.$$

EXAMPLE 4. If $z = 5 + 12i$, find $|z|$.

Solution:
$$
\begin{aligned}
|z| &= \sqrt{5^2 + 12^2} \\
&= \sqrt{25 + 144} \\
&= \sqrt{169} \\
&= 13
\end{aligned}
$$

EXAMPLE 5. Prove: $|z| = |\bar{z}|$

Proof: Let $z = a + bi$. Then $\bar{z} = a - bi$.

$$|z| = \sqrt{a^2 + b^2} \qquad \begin{aligned} |\bar{z}| &= \sqrt{a^2 + (-b)^2} \\ &= \sqrt{a^2 + b^2} \end{aligned}$$

Thus $|z| = |\bar{z}|$.

CLASSROOM EXERCISES

━━ Find the length of each vector.

1. $3 + 2i$ **2.** $3 - 2i$ **3.** $5 + 6i$ **4.** $\frac{1}{4} - \frac{1}{2}i$

━━ Sketch the vector representation of each complex number.

5. $3 - 7i$ **6.** $-2 + 5i$ **7.** $-2 - 8i$ **8.** $4 + i$

━━ Write the conjugate of each complex number.

9. $3 - 7i$ **10.** $-2 + 5i$ **11.** $3i$ **12.** 4

WRITTEN EXERCISES

A ━━ In Exercises 1–3 find the sum and difference of z_1 and z_2. Exhibit all numbers as vectors.

1. $z_1 = -3 + i$ $z_2 = 1 + 3i$

2. $z_1 = 4 + 2i$ $z_2 = 4 - 2i$

3. $z_1 = 3 - 4i$ $z_2 = -3 - 4i$

In Exercises 4–7 find the sum and difference of z_1 and z_2. Exhibit all numbers as vectors.

4. $z_1 = -2 + 3i$ $\qquad z_2 = -2 + 3i$

5. $z_1 = 2$ $\qquad z_2 = 4i$

6. $z_1 = -3$ $\qquad z_2 = 2$

7. $z_1 = 3i$ $\qquad z_2 = 2i$

8. Find the absolute value of z_1 in each Exercise 1–7.

9. Find the conjugate of each number z_2 in Exercises 1–7.

10. Prove: $z_1 + \bar{z}_1$ is twice the real part of z_1.

Compute each quotient in Exercises 11–14.

11. $\dfrac{2 + 3i}{1 - 2i}$ $\qquad\qquad$ **12.** $\dfrac{2 - 3i}{2 + 3i}$

13. $\dfrac{5 - i}{-3 - 4i}$ $\qquad\qquad$ **14.** $\dfrac{1 + i}{-2 + 6i}$

15. Prove: $\bar{\bar{z}} = z$ if and only if z is a real number.

16. Prove: $\bar{\bar{z}} = z$.

17. Prove: $|z| = |\bar{z}|$.

B **18.** Prove: $|z| = \sqrt{z \cdot \bar{z}}$ or $|z|^2 = z \cdot \bar{z}$.

19. Prove: $\overline{z_1 + z_2} = \bar{z}_1 + \bar{z}_2$. (In words: the conjugate of the sum is the sum of the conjugates.)

20. Prove: $\overline{z_1 - z_2} = \bar{z}_1 - \bar{z}_2$.

21. Prove: $\overline{z_1 z_2} = \bar{z}_1 \cdot \bar{z}_2$.

22. Prove that $z_1 - \bar{z}_1$ is twice the imaginary part of z_1.

C **23.** Prove: $|z_1 \cdot z_2| = |z_1| \cdot |z_2|$. (*Hint:* $|z_1 \cdot z_2|^2 = z_1 z_2 \cdot \overline{z_1 z_2}$. Simplify this by using Exercise 21 and the commutativity and associativity of multiplication of complex numbers.)

24. Prove: $|z_1 \cdot z_2 \cdots z_n| = |z_1| \cdot |z_2| \cdots |z_n|$ for $n \in N$. (*Hint:* Use Exercise 23 and mathematical induction.)

25. Prove: **a.** $|z| \geq$ the absolute value of the real part of z.
$\qquad\qquad$ **b.** $|z| \geq$ the absolute value of the imaginary part of z.

26. Prove: $|z_1 + z_2| \leq |z_1| + |z_2|$. (*Hint:* $|z_1 + z_2|^2 = (z_1 + z_2)(\bar{z}_1 + \bar{z}_2)$.) Expand this. Then use Exercise 10. Use 25a and Example 5.

27. Prove: $\overline{z_1 \cdot z_2 \cdots z_n} = \bar{z}_1 \cdot \bar{z}_2 \cdots \bar{z}_n$ for all $n \in N$. (*Hint:* Use mathematical induction and Exercise 21.)

BASIC: MULTIPLYING COMPLEX NUMBERS

Computers work only with real numbers. The imaginary part of complex numbers must be handled separately from the real part.

Problem:

Given two complex numbers, write a program which computes and prints the product in $a + bi$ form.

```
100 PRINT
110 PRINT "THIS PROGRAM MULTIPLIES COMPLEX"
120 PRINT "NUMBERS A + BI AND C + DI."
130 PRINT
140 PRINT "WHAT ARE A AND B";
150 INPUT A, B
160 PRINT "WHAT ARE C AND D";
170 INPUT C, D
180 LET X = A * C - B * D
190 LET Y = B * C + A * D
200 PRINT "THE PRODUCT IS ";X;" + ";Y;"I"
210 PRINT
220 PRINT "DO ANOTHER (1=YES, 0=NO)";
230 INPUT Z
240 IF Z = 1 THEN 130
250 END
```

Output:

```
THIS PROGRAM MULTIPLIES COMPLEX
NUMBERS A + BI AND C + DI.

WHAT ARE A AND B? 5,7
WHAT ARE C AND D? 6,4
THE PRODUCT IS  2   +  62 I

DO ANOTHER (1=YES, 0=NO)? 1

WHAT ARE A AND B? 2,6
WHAT ARE C AND D? 4,-9
THE PRODUCT IS  62  +   6 I

DO ANOTHER (1=YES, 0=NO)? 0
READY
```

Analysis:

Statements 140–170: These statements accept the values of a, b, c, and d for the complex numbers $a + bi$ and $c + di$.

Statements 180–190: The formulas in these statements are based on the following algebra.

$$(a + bi)(c + di) = ac + adi + bci + bdi^2$$
$$= (ac - bd) + (ad + bc)i$$

Statement 200: The imaginary unit, i, appears in the program only in this PRINT statement. The statement prints the real and imaginary parts with a "+" sign between them and an "I" printed after the coefficient of the imaginary part (designated as "Y" in the program). (Refer to the sample output on page 59.)

EXERCISES

A   Use the program on page 59 to find each product.

1. $(2 - i)(3 + 2i)$ 2. $(\frac{1}{2} - 2i)(5 + 3i)$ 3. $(-1 + i)(-1 - i)$
4. $(i + 5)(2i + 3)$ 5. $(0 + 3i)(0 - 7i)$ 6. $(-4 + 3i)(i - 2)$

B   In Exercises 7–8, revise the program on page 59 in the manner indicated.

7. Print the result of the multiplication in the form "$(a + bi)(c + di) = x + yi$." For example, print $(2 + 3\,\text{I})(-4 + 2\,\text{I}) = -14 + -8\,\text{I}$.

8. Print the product $x + yi$ "neatly," the way it would appear in a mathematics book. For example, print $3 - 4\,\text{I}$ and not $3 + -4\,\text{I}$; print $7\,\text{I}$ and not $0 + 7\,\text{I}$; print $3 + \text{I}$ and not $3 + 1\,\text{I}$, etc.

C   Write a BASIC program for each problem.

9. Given the real and imaginary parts of the complex number $a + bi$, print its conjugate. As in Exercise 8, print the conjugate as neatly as possible.

10. Given two complex numbers, compute and print their sum.

11. Given two complex numbers, compute and print their difference.

12. Given two complex numbers, compute and print the quotient of the first divided by the second (provided the second does not equal 0).

13. Given the real and imaginary parts of three complex numbers, print their product.

CHAPTER SUMMARY

Important Terms

Absolute value (p. 30)
Associative property (p. 5)
Binary operation (p. 5)
Closed interval (p. 13)
Closure (p. 5)
Commutative property (p. 5)
Complex numbers (p. 50)
Composite function (p. 44)
Composition (p. 44)
Compound inequality (p. 16)
Conjugate (p. 52)
Dependent variable (p. 35)
Direct proof (p. 6)
Distributive property (p. 5)
Domain (p. 35)
Field Postulates (p. 5)
Function (p. 39)
Graph (p. 12)
Half line (p. 13)
Identity (p. 5)
Identity function (p. 46)
Imaginary part (p. 50)
Imaginary unit (p. 50)
Independent variable (p. 35)
Indirect proof (p. 7)
Integers (p. 3)
Into function (p. 39)

Into relation (p. 35)
Inverse (p. 5)
Inverse functions (p. 47)
Irrational numbers (p. 2)
Mapping (p. 40)
Mathematical induction (p. 18)
n factorial (p. 23)
Natural numbers (p. 3)
Onto function (p. 39)
Onto relation (p. 35)
Open interval (p. 13)
Pure imaginary number (p. 50)
Quadratic inequality (p. 16)
Range (p. 35)
Range set (p. 35)
Rational numbers (p. 3)
Ray (p. 13)
Real numbers (p. 2)
Real part (p. 50)
Reciprocal (p. 5)
Relation (p. 35)
Segment (p. 13)
Theorem (p. 6)
Vector (p. 55)
Vertical-line test (p. 38)
Whole numbers (p. 3)
Zero factorial (p. 23)

Important Ideas

1 For all a, b in R, $a < b$, $a > b$, or $a = b$.

2. For all a, b, in R, $a < b$ if and only if there is a positive real number c such that $a + c = b$.

3. $a < x < b$ means $a < x$ and $x < b$.

4. The rth term of $(x + y)^n$ is $\dfrac{n!}{(n - r + 1)!(r - 1)!} x^{(n-r+1)} y^{(r-1)}$.

5. $\left(\dfrac{n}{r}\right) = \dfrac{n!}{r!(n - r)!}$.

6. The equation of the inverse of a function can be obtained by interchanging the independent and dependent variables.

CHAPTER OBJECTIVES AND REVIEW

Objective: *To identify numbers as natural, whole, integer, rational, irrational, or real.* (Section 1-1)

━━━ Place each number in as many categories as appropriate.

1. 3   **2.** $14\frac{2}{7}$ **3.** 0   **4.** $2 + \sqrt{6}$

Objective: *To translate repeating and terminating decimal expansions into fractions and vice-versa.* (Section 1-1)

━━━ In Exercises 5–8 translate the fraction into a decimal expansion or vice-versa.

5. $\frac{2}{7}$ **6.** $0.\overline{127}$ **7.** 0.195 **8.** $\frac{11}{40}$

Objective: *To cite the field postulate, postulate of equality or order, theorem, or definition which justifies an algebraic manipulation or statement of relation.* (Section 1-2)

━━━ Cite an appropriate definition, postulate, or theorem in each of Exercises 9–14.

9. $2x + 4x = 6x$ **10.** $-5 < -3$

11. $2 - 7 = 2 + (-7)$ **12.** $0.\overline{9} = 1$ so $1 = 0.\overline{9}$

13. $2 + (3 + 5) = (3 + 5) + 2$ **14.** $3(x + 4) = 3x + 12$

Objective: *To use the Order Postulates and the definitions of the inequality symbols* $<$, $>$, $\leq$, *and* $\geq$. (Section 1-3)

━━━ Determine whether each statement in Exercises 15–18 is true or false. If a statement is false explain why it is false.

15. $3 < 7$ **16.** $9 < 8$ **17.** $5 > 0$ **18.** $-4 \leq -2$

Objective: *To graph sets of real numbers and the solution sets of simple inequalities.* (Section 1-4)

━━━ Graph each set of real numbers.

19. $\{x : x > 2\}$ **20.** $[0, 5\rangle$

21. $\langle -1, 2] \cap \langle -2, 5 \rangle$ **22.** $[-2, 0] \cup [1, 2]$

━━━ Graph the solution set of each inequality.

23. $5y \leq 6y - 2$ **24.** $6y + 1 > y + 4$

Objective: *To find and graph the solution sets of compound inequalities.* (Section 1-5)

━━━ Find and graph the solution sets of each inequality.

25. $5 < 2x + 3 \leq 9$ **26.** $(x - 3)(x + 2) \geq 0$

Objective: *To use mathematical induction.* (Section 1-6)

▬ Use mathematical induction to prove that each statement P_n is true for all $n \in$ N.

27. P_n is "$4 + 8 + 12 + \cdots + 4n = 2n(n + 1)$."

28. P_n is "$1 + 5 + 9 + \cdots + (4n - 3) = n(2n - 1)$."

Objective: *To use the binomial theorem.* (Section 1-7)

▬ Expand each binomial.

29. $(a + b)^6$ **30.** $(g - 3h)^5$

▬ Find the indicated term.

31. 4th term of $(2x - 3y)^7$ **32.** 9th term of $(a - 5b)^{10}$

Objective: *To find and graph the solution sets of inequalities that involve absolute value.* (Section 1-8)

▬ Find and graph the solution set of each inequality.

33. $|x| > 10$ **34.** $|x + 1| < 4$

Objective: *To find the range of a relation, given its domain, and to graph the relation.* (Section 1-9)

▬ Find the range of each relation. Then graph the relation.

35. $y + x = 5$ $x \in \{-3, 0, 1, 3, 4, 5\}$

36. $q \geq 3p$ $p \in \{-2, -1, 0, \frac{1}{3}, 2, 4\frac{1}{3}\}$

Objective: *To identify a relation that is a function and to graph the function.* (Section 1–10)

▬ In Exercises 37–38 state which relations are functions. Graph the relation if it is a function.

37. $f : x \rightarrow x^2$ $x \in \{-2, 0, 2\}$

38. $y = 2x$ $U = \{x : -1 < x \leq 4, x \in I\}$

Objective: *To find a composite mapping for two mappings.* (Section 1-11)

▬ Find fg and gf for the given mappings.

39. $f : x \rightarrow x - 5$ **40.** $f : x \rightarrow x^2$
     $g : x \rightarrow 2x + 1$ $g : x \rightarrow 3 - x$

Objective: *To find the inverse of a function.* (Section 1-12)

▬ Find the inverse for each function.

41. $f : x \rightarrow -3x + 5$ **42.** $g : x \rightarrow x^2 + 5$

43. Which of the inverses of Exercises 41 and 42 are functions?

Objective: *To perform the fundamental operations on complex numbers.* (Section 1-13)

▬▬ Perform the indicated operation. Express the number in the form $a + bi$.

44. $(2 - 3i) + (4i - 1)$ **45.** $(2 - 3i) \div (4i - 1)$

46. $(2 - 3i) - (4i - 1)$ **47.** $(2 - 3i) \cdot (4i - 1)$

Objective: *To represent complex numbers as vectors and to find their absolute value.* (Section 1-14)

▬▬ Find the sum and difference of z_1 and z_2. Exhibit all numbers as vectors.

48. $z_1 = -4 - i, z_2 = 5$ **49.** $z_1 = 3 - i, z_2 = 5 + i$

50. Find the absolute value of $z_1 + z_2$ in Exercises 48 and 49.

CHAPTER TEST

1. Express the number $0.\overline{2}$ as a fraction.

2. Prove $(a + b) - c = a + (b - c)$ for real numbers a, b, and c.

3. Use mathematical induction to prove that the sum of the first n even numbers is $n(n + 1)$, $n \in$ N.

4. If x is a real number and $-x$ is negative, what can you conclude about x and why?

5. What is a simpler way of describing each of the following sets?

     a. $[a, b\rangle \cup \langle a, b]$ **b.** $[a, b\rangle \cap \langle a, b]$

6. Solve for x: $-2 > |x + 2|$ **7.** Define "absolute value."

▬▬ Draw an example of each of the following on the real line.

8. segment   **9.** half line   **10.** ray   **11.** open interval

12. Expand $(2x - 7y)^5$.

▬▬ If $f : x \rightarrow x + \frac{1}{2}$ and $h : x \rightarrow 2x - 3$ find

13. fh **14.** hf **15.** f^{-1} **16.** h^{-1}

17. Produce an example of an infinite decimal which names an irrational number.

18. Find the multiplicative inverse of $\frac{1}{i}$. Write it in $a + bi$ form with a, $b \in$ R.

CHAPTER **2** **Circular Functions**

Sections

Features

Review and Testing

2–1 Distance and Circles

The **distance** on a line from A to B, represented as AB, is always a non-negative number.

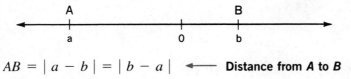

$$AB = |a - b| = |b - a| \quad \longleftarrow \quad \textbf{Distance from } A \textbf{ to } B$$

Distance between two points in a plane is also non-negative, as shown in Example 1.

EXAMPLE 1. Find the distance PQ for $P(-3, 5)$ and $Q(2, -6)$.

Solution:

Since x is -3 on PR and y is -6 on QR, $(-3, -6)$ are the coordinates of R.

$PR = |5 - (-6)| = 11$

$QR = |-3 - 2| = 5$

By the Pythagorean Theorem,
$(PQ)^2 = (PR)^2 + (QR)^2$

$(PQ)^2 = (11)^2 + (5)^2$

$\begin{aligned} PQ &= \sqrt{(11)^2 + (5)^2} \\ &= \sqrt{121 + 25} \\ &= \sqrt{146} \end{aligned}$

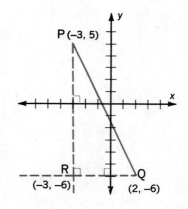

The same procedure as shown in Example 1 may be applied to any segment in the plane. Assign P and Q the coordinates $P(x_1, y_1)$ and $Q(x_2, y_2)$.

$$PQ = \sqrt{(|x_1 - x_2|)^2 + (|y_1 - y_2|)^2} \quad \longleftarrow \quad |x|^2 = x^2 \textbf{ for all real } x$$
$$PQ = \sqrt{(x_1 - x_2)^2 + (y_1 - y_2)^2} \quad \longleftarrow \quad \textbf{Distance formula}$$

The equation of a circle can be found using the distance formula. In the circle at the top of page 67, $P(x, y)$ is a point on the circle, $C(h, k)$ is the point at the center of the circle, and r represents the length of the radius of the circle.

From the distance formula,

$$r = CP = \sqrt{(x - h)^2 + (y - k)^2}$$

$$r^2 = (x - h)^2 + (y - k)^2$$

It is a simple matter to show that any point satis- fying the second equation above is on the circle with center $C(h, k)$ and radius r.

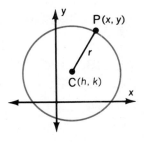

Theorem 2–1 The equation of a circle with radius r and center at (h, k) is $(x - h)^2 + (y - k)^2 = r^2$.

EXAMPLE 2. Find the equation of the circle with center $C(5, -2)$ and radius $r = 2$.

Solution:

$$(x - h)^2 + (y - k)^2 = r^2$$
$$(x - 5)^2 + (y - (-2))^2 = 2^2 \quad \longleftarrow \quad h = 5, k = -2, r = 2$$
$$(x - 5)^2 + (y + 2)^2 = 4$$

CLASSROOM EXERCISES

1. Show that $PQ = \sqrt{113}$ for $P(2, -7)$ and $Q(-5, 1)$.

2. Show that $PQ = PR$, $P(3, -4)$, $Q(8, 5)$, and $R(-6, 1)$.

3. Find the equation of the circle with center at the origin and radius 1.

4. What is the center and radius of $(x - 3)^2 + (y + 1)^2 = 10$?

WRITTEN EXERCISES

A ━━ Calculate the distance determined by each pair of points.

1. $P(0, 1)$; $Q(0, -5)$

2. $A(-3, 0)$; $B(-7, 0)$

3. $D(2, -3)$; $E(2, 5)$

4. $C(-2, 5)$; $D(-8, 5)$

5. $T(5, 1)$; $R(2, -3)$

6. $P(-1, 3)$; $Q(5, -8)$

7. $A(-5, 2)$; $D(7, -3)$

8. $Q(4, 3)$; $R(2, 1)$

9. $M(\frac{1}{2}, \frac{2}{3})$; $N(-\frac{1}{2}, -\frac{7}{3})$

10. $U(0, 0)$; $V(-4, 3)$

11. $P(1, -7)$; $Q(3, 1)$

12. $A(1003, 104)$; $B(1000, 108)$

13. $H(x + 2, y - 3)$; $J(x - 2, y)$

14. $P(a + b, a - b)$; $Q(a - b, a + b) \, b > 0$

15. $K(2a, a)$; $L(0, 0)$

16. $A(x, y)$; $B(-x, -y)$

Find the equation of each circle with center C and radius r.

17. $C(2, -5)$; $r = 3$

18. $C(1, 3)$; $r = 4$

19. $C(-5, -1)$; $r = 7$

20. $C(-2, 1)$; $r = 2$

21. $C(\frac{2}{3}, -\frac{1}{3})$; $r = \frac{1}{2}$

22. $C(-\frac{1}{4}, \frac{1}{5})$; $r = 1$

B 23. Find the equation of the circle with center $(1, 2)$ which passes through the point $(-3, 7)$.

24. For what values of k is $(-3, -5)$ ten units from $(5, k)$?

25. For what values of h is $(1, 3)$ thirteen units from $(h, -2)$?

26. Demonstrate that if R is a circle with center $C(h, k)$ and radius r, and if $P(x, y)$ satisfies $(x - h)^2 + (y - k)^2 = r^2$, then P is on circle R.

27. Find the length of the sides of the triangle PQR for the points $P(2, 1)$, $Q(3, -4)$, and $R(3, 0)$.

C 28. Find the equation of the circle for which $P(-3, 4)$ and Q $(-3, -2)$ are ends of a diameter.

29. Find the equation of the set of points that are the same distance from $P(4, 1)$ and $Q(-1, -4)$.

30. Show that $(x - h)^2 + (y - k)^2 = r^2$ can be written in the form $x^2 + y^2 + Ax + By + C = 0$. Express A, B, and C in terms of h, k, and r.

31. Given that $x^2 + y^2 - 6x - 4y - 3 = 0$ is the equation of a circle, find the center and radius.

32. What is the graph of each of the following equations?

$$(x - h)^2 + (y - k)^2 = 0, \quad (x - h)^2 + (y - k)^2 = -1$$

2-2 The Wrapping Function

You can associate points of the real number line with points of a circle by using geometric concepts.

Begin with a **unit circle**, a circle with radius 1. If a point $A(a, b)$ is on the circle, then the points $B(-a, b)$, $E(-a, -b)$, and $D(a, -b)$ are also on the circle because of the circle's symmetry. A and B are symmetric with respect to the vertical axis; A and D with respect to the horizontal axis; A and E with respect to the origin.

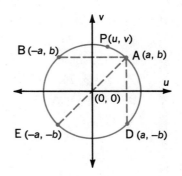

To associate points on a real number line with points on the circle, think of the line as flexible and being wrapped around the circle. The circumference of the circle is 2π because $C = 2\pi r$ or $2\pi \cdot 1$. The origin of the line is at $A(1, 0)$ of the circle.

Point $\frac{\pi}{2}$ of the line is at $B(0, 1)$ because

$$\overparen{AB} = \tfrac{1}{4}C = \tfrac{1}{4} \cdot 2\pi = \frac{\pi}{2}.$$

Thus, the following matchings are true:

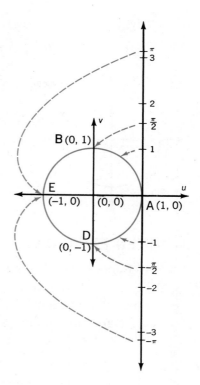

$$\pi \leftrightarrow E(-1, 0)$$

$$\frac{3\pi}{2} \leftrightarrow D(0, -1)$$

$$2\pi \leftrightarrow A(1, 0)$$

By continuing to wrap the line, any non-negative real number is matched with a point on the circle. If $P(u, v)$ is a point on the circle and x maps onto $P(u, v)$, then

$$P(u, v) \leftrightarrow x + 2\pi, \ x + 4\pi, \ \cdots, \ x + 2n\pi, \ n \in W.$$

By wrapping the negative ray clockwise,

$$D(0, -1) \leftrightarrow -\frac{\pi}{2} \qquad B(0, 1) \leftrightarrow -\frac{3\pi}{2}$$

$$E(-1, 0) \leftrightarrow -\pi \qquad A(1, 0) \leftrightarrow -2\pi$$

In general, if $P(u, v) \leftrightarrow x \in R$, $x < 0$ then $P(u, v) \leftrightarrow x - 2\pi$, $x - 4\pi, \cdots x - 2n\pi$, $n \in W$.

The wrapping procedure defines a function, the **wrapping function** W. W maps the real numbers onto the points of the unit circle.

Suppose $W: x \rightarrow (a, b)$, as shown in the figure at the right. It then follows from the symmetry of the circle that $W: -x \rightarrow (a, -b)$.

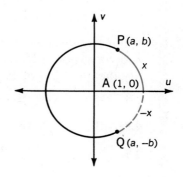

Similarly, (see figures below)

$$W : x + \pi \rightarrow (-a, -b) \qquad \text{and} \qquad W : -x + \pi \rightarrow (-a, b).$$

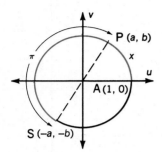
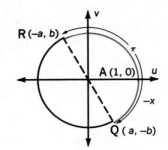

WRITTEN EXERCISES

A ▬ Suppose $W : 2 \rightarrow (u, v)$.

1. Name five positive real numbers besides 2 that map onto this same point under the wrapping function.

2. Name five negative real numbers that map onto the same point under W.

▬ Suppose $W : -3 \rightarrow (a, b)$.

3. Name four negative numbers besides -3 that W maps onto (a, b).

4. Name four positive numbers that W maps onto (a, b).

▬ Let $W : \frac{2\pi}{3} \rightarrow (r, s)$.

5. Write an expression that names all the other positive real numbers that map onto (r, s).

6. Write an expression that names all the negative real numbers that map onto (r, s).

7. Combine the results of Exercises 5 and 6 into one expression that names all the real numbers that map onto (r, s).

▬ In Exercises 8–19 let P be the point that lies on the unit circle and corresponds to the x value below for the function W. Identify the quadrant of P. Let $\pi \approx 3.142$ if necessary.

8. 1   **9.** -1 **10.** $6\pi - \frac{4\pi}{3}$ **11.** 6

12. -3 **13.** -5 **14.** $\frac{1004\pi}{3}$ **15.** $-\frac{7\pi}{6}$

16. $\frac{7\pi}{6} + \pi$ **17.** $\frac{\pi}{3} + 13\pi$ **18.** $-\frac{4\pi}{3} + \frac{\pi}{2}$ **19.** $\frac{15\pi}{2}$

20. Let $W : x \rightarrow (\frac{12}{13}, \frac{5}{13})$. What is

    a. $W(-x)$?
                    b. $W(x + \pi)$?

    c. $W(x + 2\pi)$?
               d. $W(-x + \pi)$?

21. Let $W : x \rightarrow (-\frac{3}{5}, \frac{4}{5})$. What is

    a. $W(x + \pi)$?
                b. $W(-x)$?

    c. $W(\pi - x)$?
               d. $W(2\pi + x)$?

22. Let $W : x \rightarrow \left(\frac{\sqrt{3}}{2}, -\frac{1}{2}\right)$. What is

    a. $W(2\pi + x)$?
           b. $W(x + \pi)$?

    c. $W(\pi - x)$?
               d. $W(-x)$?

23. Let $W : x \rightarrow \left(-\frac{\sqrt{13}}{14}, -\frac{1}{14}\right)$. What is

    a. $W(\pi - x)$?
          b. $W(x + 2\pi)$?

    c. $W(x + \pi)$?
             d. $W(-x)$?

24. Let $W : \frac{3\pi}{4} \rightarrow \left(-\frac{\sqrt{2}}{2}, \frac{\sqrt{2}}{2}\right)$. What is

    a. $W\left(\frac{\pi}{4}\right)$?
            b. $W\left(-\frac{3\pi}{4}\right)$?

    c. $W\left(\frac{7\pi}{4}\right)$?
           d. $W\left(\frac{5\pi}{4}\right)$?

25. Let $W : \frac{\pi}{3} \rightarrow \left(\frac{1}{2}, \frac{\sqrt{3}}{2}\right)$. What is

    a. $W\left(\frac{4\pi}{3}\right)$?
           b. $W\left(-\frac{\pi}{3}\right)$?

    c. $W\left(-\frac{4\pi}{3}\right)$?
         d. $W\left(\frac{2\pi}{3}\right)$?

C **26.** Place the square $ABCD$ as shown in the figure. Imagine a number line with its origin at $O(1, 0)$ which is wrapped counterclockwise around the square. Each point of the number line maps onto a single point on the square. This wrapping defines a function mapping non-negative real numbers onto points of the square. Call it T. For example $T : 2 \rightarrow (0, 1)$. Find the image under T of each of the following.

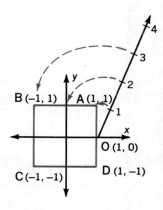

  a. 3   **b.** 4   **c.** 5   **d.** $2\frac{1}{2}$ **e.** 100   **f.** 2000

2–3 The Sine and Cosine Functions

The pairing of real numbers with points on the unit circle by the wrapping function W allows you to define two new functions. The first of these functions maps each real number x onto the *first coordinate* of $W(x) = (u, v)$ and is called the *cosine function* (abbreviated cos). The second function maps each real number x onto the *second coordinate* of $W(x) = (u, v)$ and is called the *sine function* (abbreviated sin). These functions are called **circular functions**.

Definition Let W be the wrapping function that maps $x \in R$ onto the point $P(u, v)$ that is x units from $(1, 0)$ along the circle $u^2 + v^2 = 1$. Then the **cosine** and **sine functions** are

$$\cos = \{(x, u) : u = \cos x\} \quad \text{and} \quad \sin = \{(x, v) : v = \sin x\}.$$

The definition is illustrated at the right. If x is the positive or negative length of an arc along the circle from $A(1, 0)$, then the coordinates of the corresponding point P are $(\cos x, \sin x)$.

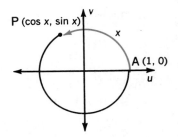

A fundamental property of the sine and cosine functions follows immediately from the definition.

Theorem 2–2 $\forall x \in R \quad \sin^2 x + \cos^2 x = 1$

Notice that $\sin^2 x$ is commonly used to represent $(\sin x)^2$. Similarly $\cos^2 x$ means $(\cos x)^2$. The proof of Theorem 2–2 is left to you.

You saw that the symmetry of the circle led to the fact that

$$\text{if } W : x \rightarrow (u, v), \text{ then } W : -x \rightarrow (u, -v).$$

Restating this in terms of $\cos x$ and $\sin x$ you have Theorem 2–3.

Theorem 2–3 $\forall x \in R$

$$\cos(-x) = \cos x \qquad \sin(-x) = -\sin x$$

By further appealing to the symmetry of the circle, you can also express cos $(\pi - x)$ and cos $(\pi + x)$ in terms of cos x. Similarly, sin $(\pi - x)$ and sin $(\pi + x)$ can be expressed in terms of sin x.

Theorem 2–4 $\forall x \in \mathrm{R}$

$$\cos (\pi - x) = -\cos x \qquad\qquad \sin (\pi - x) = \sin x$$
$$\cos (\pi + x) = -\cos x \qquad\qquad \sin (\pi + x) = -\sin x$$

The figure at the right below can be used to evaluate sin x and cos x for $x = \frac{n\pi}{2}$, $n \in \mathrm{W}$. Take, for example, $n = 0$. Then $x = 0$ also.

Note that cos$(0) = 1$ and sin $(0) = 0$ because $\mathrm{W} : 0 \rightarrow (1,\ 0)$. Now let $0 < x < \frac{\pi}{2}$. Here

$$W : x \rightarrow (\cos x,\ \sin x),$$

and $(\cos x,\ \sin x)$ is a point in Quadrant I.

Thus cos $x > 0$ and sin $x > 0$ when $0 < x < \frac{\pi}{2}$, because any point in Quadrant I has positive coordinates.

By similar reasoning you can show that the figure below is an accurate representation of the signs of cos x and sin x for all $x \in \mathrm{R}$ such that $0 \leq x < 2\pi$. When $x \in \mathrm{R}$ is associated with a point $P(\cos x,\ \sin x)$ that is in a certain quadrant, it is conventional to say that *x is in that quadrant.*

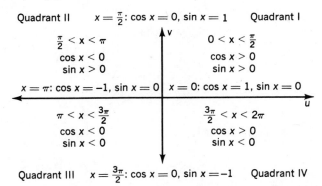

Theorem 2–5 at the top of page 74 covers the case in which $x \geq 2\pi$ or $x < 0$.

> **Theorem 2–5** $\forall x \in R$ and $\forall n \in W$
> $$\cos (x \pm 2n\pi) = \cos x$$
> $$\sin (x \pm 2n\pi) = \sin x$$

This theorem follows from the fact that the wrapping function W pairs x and $x \pm 2n\pi$ with the same point on the unit circle.

EXAMPLE 1. Determine the quadrant in which x lies and the signs of $\cos x$ and $\sin x$ if $x = \frac{21\pi}{4}$.

Solution: $\qquad\qquad x = \frac{21\pi}{4} = 5\pi + \frac{\pi}{4} = 4\pi + \frac{5\pi}{4}$

Since $\frac{5\pi}{4}$ is in Quadrant III, so is $\frac{21\pi}{4}$. Applying Theorem 2–5

$$\cos (\tfrac{5}{4}\pi + 4\pi) = \cos \frac{5\pi}{4} \quad \text{and} \quad \sin (\tfrac{5}{4}\pi + 4\pi) = \sin \frac{5\pi}{4}.$$

Thus, since $\frac{5\pi}{4}$ is in Quadrant III,

$$\cos \frac{5\pi}{4} < 0 \quad \text{and} \quad \sin \frac{5\pi}{4} < 0.$$

Consequently, $\cos \frac{21\pi}{4} < 0$ and $\sin \frac{21\pi}{4} < 0$.

EXAMPLE 2. Determine the quadrant in which x lies and the signs of $\cos x$ and $\sin x$ if $x = -\frac{16\pi}{3}$.

Solution: $\qquad\qquad x = -\frac{16\pi}{3} = -5\pi - \frac{\pi}{3}$

$$= -4\pi - \frac{4\pi}{3}$$

$$= -4\pi - \left(2\pi - \frac{2\pi}{3}\right)$$

$$= -6\pi + \frac{2\pi}{3}$$

Since $\frac{2\pi}{3}$ is in Quadrant II, so is $-\frac{16\pi}{3}$. Thus,

$$\cos \left(-\frac{16\pi}{3}\right) = \cos \left(-6\pi + \frac{2\pi}{3}\right) = \cos \frac{2\pi}{3} < 0.$$

Similarly, $\sin \left(-\frac{16\pi}{3}\right) = \sin \frac{2\pi}{3}$. so $\sin \left(-\frac{16\pi}{3}\right) > 0$.

CLASSROOM EXERCISES

━━ Express each real number as the sum of a real number and a multiple of π or 2π.

1. $\frac{23\pi}{3}$ **2.** $\frac{8\pi}{3}$ **3.** $\frac{16\pi}{6}$ **4.** $-\frac{8\pi}{3}$

5. $-\frac{15\pi}{2}$ **6.** $\frac{23\pi}{4}$ **7.** $-\frac{18\pi}{4}$ **8.** $\frac{81\pi}{4}$

━━ State the quadrant in which each real number lies.

9. $\frac{23\pi}{3}$ **10.** $\frac{8\pi}{3}$ **11.** $-\frac{18\pi}{4}$ **12.** $-\frac{8\pi}{3}$

WRITTEN EXERCISES

A ━━ In Exercises 1–15 determine the quadrant in which x lies. Then determine the signs of $\cos x$ and $\sin x$. Use the approximation $\pi \approx 3.142$ if necessary.

1. $x = 3$ **2.** $x = 4$ **3.** $x = 5$

4. $x = \frac{9\pi}{4}$ **5.** $x = -\frac{9\pi}{4}$ **6.** $x = \frac{100\pi}{3}$

7. $x = -\frac{19\pi}{4}$ **8.** $x = \frac{35\pi}{6}$ **9.** $x = -\frac{19\pi}{6}$

10. $x = -\frac{99\pi}{4}$ **11.** $x = -3$ **12.** $x = -5$

13. $x = -\frac{14\pi}{3}$ **14.** $x = -\frac{11\pi}{3}$ **15.** $x = \frac{22\pi}{5}$

━━ In Exercises 16–23 determine the other circular function, given one circular function and the quadrant in which x lies.

16. $\sin x = \frac{12}{13}$, x in Quadrant II

17. $\cos x = \frac{12}{13}$, x in Quadrant IV

18. $\sin x = -\frac{4}{5}$, x in Quadrant III

19. $\cos x = \frac{3}{5}$, x in Quadrant I

20. $\cos x = -\frac{2\sqrt{2}}{3}$, x in Quadrant II

21. $\sin x = -\frac{1}{\sqrt{5}}$, x in Quadrant IV

22. $\cos x = \frac{\sqrt{15}}{4}$, x in Quadrant IV

B   **23.** Prove that for each $x \in R$, $|\sin x| \leq 1$.

24. Prove that for each $x \in R$, $|\cos x| \leq 1$.

25. A function f is **odd** if and only if $f(-x) = -f(x)$. What theorem of this section insures that sin is odd?

26. A function f is **even** if and only if $f(-x) = f(x)$. What theorem of this section insures that cos is even?

2-4 Sines and Cosines of Special Numbers

By using the figure on page 73, sin x and cos x were evaluated when x equals 0, $\frac{\pi}{2}$, π, and $\frac{3\pi}{2}$. By applying the theorems of Section 2-3, sin x and cos x can be evaluated for any integral multiples of these numbers.

EXAMPLE 1. Evaluate:

a. sin $(-\pi)$ and cos $(-\pi)$ b. sin $\frac{5\pi}{2}$ and cos $\frac{5\pi}{2}$

a. **By Theorem 2-3:**   **By Theorem 2-3:**

$\quad$ $\sin(-\pi) = -\sin \pi$ $\cos(-\pi) = \cos \pi$

$\quad$ $\sin \pi = 0$ $\cos \pi = -1$

$\quad$ Thus, $\sin(-\pi) = 0$.   Thus, $\cos(-\pi) = -1$.

b. $\sin \frac{5\pi}{2} = \sin\left(\frac{\pi}{2} + 2\pi\right)$ $\cos \frac{5\pi}{2} = \cos\left(\frac{\pi}{2} + 2\pi\right)$

$\quad$ **By Theorem 2-5:**   **By Theorem 2-5:**

$\quad$ $\sin\left(\frac{\pi}{2} + 2\pi\right) = \sin \frac{\pi}{2}$ $\cos\left(\frac{\pi}{2} + 2\pi\right) = \cos \frac{\pi}{2}$

$\quad$ $\sin \frac{\pi}{2} = 1$ $\cos \frac{\pi}{2} = 0$

$\quad$ Thus, $\sin \frac{5\pi}{2} = 1$.   Thus, $\cos \frac{5\pi}{2} = 0$.

By using the wrapping function and the unit circle, you can evaluate the sines and cosines of any integral multiple of $\frac{\pi}{6}$ and $\frac{\pi}{4}$.

EXAMPLE 2. Evaluate sin $\frac{\pi}{4}$ and cos $\frac{\pi}{4}$.

Solution: $\qquad$ Since 2π is the distance around the circle, $\frac{\pi}{4}$ is one-
eighth the distance around. Thus,
$P(u, v)$ is the midpoint of arc AB.

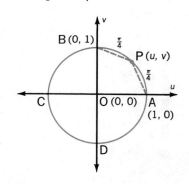

$\qquad$ It follows that $\overgroup{AP} = \overgroup{BP} = \frac{\pi}{4}$.
From geometry, the corresponding
chords are equal in length. Thus,
$AP = PB$.

$\qquad$ Now by the distance formula, $\sqrt{(x_2 - x_1)^2 + (y_2 - y_1)^2}$,

$\qquad\qquad PB = \sqrt{u^2 + (v-1)^2}$ $\qquad$ and $\qquad$ $AP = \sqrt{(u-1)^2 + v^2}$.

Therefore, $\qquad\qquad \sqrt{u^2 + (v-1)^2} = \sqrt{(u-1)^2 + v^2}$.

When you simplify this you obtain $u = v$.

Next, use the fact that $u^2 + v^2 = 1$ and the fact that u and v must be positive numbers since P is in the first quadrant.

$$u^2 + u^2 = 1$$
$$u^2 = \frac{1}{2}$$
$$u = \frac{1}{\sqrt{2}} = \frac{\sqrt{2}}{2} = v$$

It follows that $W: \frac{\pi}{4} \rightarrow \left(\frac{\sqrt{2}}{2}, \frac{\sqrt{2}}{2} \right)$. Thus,

$$\sin \frac{\pi}{4} = \frac{\sqrt{2}}{2} \text{ and } \cos \frac{\pi}{4} = \frac{\sqrt{2}}{2}.$$

EXAMPLE 3. Evaluate $\sin \frac{\pi}{6}$ and $\cos \frac{\pi}{6}$.

Solution: In the figure, let $P(u, v)$ be the point that corresponds to $\frac{\pi}{6}$.

Then $Q(u, -v)$ corresponds to $-\frac{\pi}{6}$. From the diagram you see that

$$\overset{\frown}{PB} = \overset{\frown}{AB} - \overset{\frown}{AP} \quad \text{and} \quad \overset{\frown}{QP} = \overset{\frown}{QA} + \overset{\frown}{AP}$$
$$= \frac{\pi}{2} - \frac{\pi}{6} = \frac{\pi}{3} \qquad \qquad = \frac{\pi}{6} + \frac{\pi}{6} = \frac{\pi}{3}.$$

Therefore, $\overset{\frown}{PB} = \overset{\frown}{QP}$ and $PB = QP$.

Next, use this result and the distance formula.

$$\sqrt{u^2 + (1 - v)^2} = 2v$$

Simplify this equation and use the fact that $u^2 + v^2 = 1$ to obtain:

$$2v^2 + v - 1 = 0$$

Solve the quadratic equation and discard the incorrect value, -1. The result is $v = \frac{1}{2}$. Thus,

$$\sin \frac{\pi}{6} = \frac{1}{2}.$$

Applying Theorem 2–2 and the fact that $\frac{\pi}{6}$ is in the first quadrant, you obtain

$$\cos \frac{\pi}{6} = \frac{\sqrt{3}}{2}.$$

Applying Theorem 2–4 to the results of Example 2 you can evaluate the sines and cosines for other numbers directly.

EXAMPLE 4. Evaluate $\sin \frac{5\pi}{4}$ and $\cos \frac{5\pi}{4}$.

Solution:
$$\sin \frac{5\pi}{4} = \sin \left(\pi + \frac{\pi}{4} \right) \quad \longleftarrow \quad \textbf{By Theorem 2–4}$$
$$= -\sin \frac{\pi}{4}$$

and
$$\cos \frac{5\pi}{4} = \cos \left(\pi + \frac{\pi}{4} \right)$$
$$= -\cos \frac{\pi}{4}$$

Thus,
$$\sin \frac{5\pi}{4} = -\frac{\sqrt{2}}{2} \text{ and } \cos \frac{5\pi}{4} = -\frac{\sqrt{2}}{2}.$$

CLASSROOM EXERCISES

▬ Write each real number as the sum or difference of π or 2π and a real number between 0 and $\frac{\pi}{2}$.

1. $\frac{3\pi}{2}$ **2.** $\frac{3\pi}{4}$ **3.** $\frac{5\pi}{6}$ **4.** $\frac{7\pi}{4}$

5. $\frac{11\pi}{6}$ **6.** $\frac{13\pi}{6}$ **7.** $-\frac{5\pi}{4}$ **8.** $-\frac{\pi}{4}$

WRITTEN EXERCISES

A ▬ Evaluate each of the following.

1. $\sin \left(-\frac{\pi}{2} \right)$ and $\cos \left(-\frac{\pi}{2} \right)$ **2.** $\sin \frac{3\pi}{2}$ and $\cos \frac{3\pi}{2}$

3. $\sin \left(-\frac{\pi}{4} \right)$ and $\cos \left(-\frac{\pi}{4} \right)$ **4.** $\sin \frac{3\pi}{4}$ and $\cos \frac{3\pi}{4}$

5. $\sin \frac{5\pi}{6}$ and $\cos \frac{5\pi}{6}$ **6.** $\sin \frac{7\pi}{4}$ and $\cos \frac{7\pi}{4}$

7. $\sin \frac{7\pi}{6}$ and $\cos \frac{7\pi}{6}$ **8.** $\sin \frac{11\pi}{6}$ and $\cos \frac{11\pi}{6}$

9. $\sin \frac{13\pi}{6}$ and $\cos \frac{13\pi}{6}$ **10.** $\sin \left(-\frac{17\pi}{6} \right)$ and $\cos \left(-\frac{17\pi}{6} \right)$

C ▬ In Exercises 11–14, x_1, x_2, and x are real numbers. Show that each given statement is true for all such real numbers.

11. $| \sin x_2 - \sin x_1 | \leq | x_2 - x_1 |$.
(*Hint:* An arc is longer than its chord. The hypotenuse is the longest side of a right triangle.)

12. $| \cos x_2 - \cos x_1 | \leq | x_2 - x_1 |$
13. $| \sin x | \leq | x |$
14. $| 1 - \cos x | \leq | x |$

2–5 Values of sin *x* and cos *x*

In the table below are values you have found in the examples, exercises, and discussions of Sections 2–2 and 2–3.

x	cos *x*	sin *x*
0	1	0
$\dfrac{\pi}{6}$	$\dfrac{\sqrt{3}}{2}$	$\dfrac{1}{2}$
$\dfrac{\pi}{4}$	$\dfrac{\sqrt{2}}{2}$	$\dfrac{\sqrt{2}}{2}$
$\dfrac{\pi}{3}$		
$\dfrac{\pi}{2}$	0	1
$\dfrac{2\pi}{3}$		
$\dfrac{3\pi}{4}$	$-\dfrac{\sqrt{2}}{2}$	$\dfrac{\sqrt{2}}{2}$
$\dfrac{5\pi}{6}$	$-\dfrac{\sqrt{3}}{2}$	$\dfrac{1}{2}$
π	-1	0
$\dfrac{7\pi}{6}$	$-\dfrac{\sqrt{3}}{2}$	$-\dfrac{1}{2}$
$\dfrac{5\pi}{4}$	$-\dfrac{\sqrt{2}}{2}$	$-\dfrac{\sqrt{2}}{2}$
$\dfrac{4\pi}{3}$		
$\dfrac{3\pi}{2}$	0	-1
$\dfrac{5\pi}{3}$		
$\dfrac{7\pi}{4}$	$\dfrac{\sqrt{2}}{2}$	$-\dfrac{\sqrt{2}}{2}$
$\dfrac{11\pi}{6}$	$\dfrac{\sqrt{3}}{2}$	$-\dfrac{1}{2}$
2π	1	0

The values of cos *x* and sin *x* for $x \in \left\{ \dfrac{\pi}{3}, \dfrac{2\pi}{3}, \dfrac{4\pi}{3}, \dfrac{5\pi}{3} \right\}$ are obtained in this section. For that reason you will find the next theorem useful.

$$\cos\left(\frac{\pi}{2} + x\right) = -\sin x \qquad\qquad \sin\left(\frac{\pi}{2} + x\right) = \cos x$$

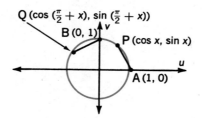

Proof: Refer to the figure above. The arc AP has length x, and the arc AQ has length $\frac{\pi}{2} + x$. Since

$$\overset{\frown}{AQ} = \overset{\frown}{AB} + \overset{\frown}{BQ}$$

and $\overset{\frown}{AB}$ is $\frac{\pi}{2}$ units, arc BQ is x units long, thus $\overline{BQ} = \overline{AP}$. (Why?)

$$
\begin{aligned}
(BQ)^2 &= \cos^2\left(\frac{\pi}{2} + x\right) + \left(\sin\left(\frac{\pi}{2} + x\right) - 1\right)^2 \\
&= \cos^2\left(\frac{\pi}{2} + x\right) + \sin^2\left(\frac{\pi}{2} + x\right) - 2\sin\left(\frac{\pi}{2} + x\right) + 1 \\
&= \qquad\qquad 1 \qquad\qquad - 2\sin\left(\frac{\pi}{2} + x\right) + 1 \\
&= 2 - 2\sin\left(\frac{\pi}{2} + x\right) \\
(AP)^2 &= (\cos x - 1)^2 + \sin^2 x \\
&= \cos^2 x - 2\cos x + 1 + \sin^2 x \\
&= (\cos^2 x + \sin^2 x) - 2\cos x + 1 \\
&= \qquad 1 \qquad\quad - 2\cos x + 1 \\
&= 2 - 2\cos x
\end{aligned}
$$

Since $BQ = AP$, $(BQ)^2 = (PA)^2$, so

$$2 - 2\sin\left(\frac{\pi}{2} + x\right) = 2 - 2\cos x$$

or

$$\sin\left(\frac{\pi}{2} + x\right) = \cos x.$$

You can now use $\cos^2 x + \sin^2 x = 1$.

$$\sin^2\left(\frac{\pi}{2} + x\right) + \cos^2\left(\frac{\pi}{2} + x\right) = 1$$

$$\cos^2\left(\frac{\pi}{2} + x\right) = 1 - \sin^2\left(\frac{\pi}{2} + x\right)$$

$$= 1 - \cos^2 x. \quad \text{(Why?)}$$

$$= \sin^2 x \quad \text{(Why?)}$$

$$\cos\left(\frac{\pi}{2} + x\right) = \sin x \text{ or } -\sin x \quad \text{(Why?)}$$

Thus, if x is in Quadrant I, then $\frac{\pi}{2} + x$ is in Quadrant II, and

$$\cos\left(\frac{\pi}{2} + x\right) = -\sin x.$$

Similarly, whatever quadrant x is in, $\frac{\pi}{2} + x$ is in the next quadrant. In each case the signs of $\sin x$ and $\cos\left(\frac{\pi}{2} + x\right)$ are opposites. Thus,

$$\forall x \in \mathbf{R} \qquad \cos\left(\frac{\pi}{2} + x\right) = -\sin x.$$

Since $\frac{2\pi}{3} = \frac{\pi}{2} + \frac{\pi}{6}$, by Theorem 2–6,

$$\sin\frac{2\pi}{3} = \cos\frac{\pi}{6} = \frac{\sqrt{3}}{2}$$

and

$$\cos\frac{2\pi}{3} = -\sin\frac{\pi}{6} = -\tfrac{1}{2}.$$

The table below summarizes many facts on $\sin x$ and $\cos x$.

1. $\forall x \in \mathbf{R}$ $\sin^2 x + \cos^2 x = 1$} **Theorem 2–2**

2. $\forall x \in \mathbf{R}$ $\sin(-x) = -\sin x$
   $\cos(-x) = \cos x$ } **Theorem 2–3**

3. $\forall x \in \mathbf{R}$ $\cos(\pi + x) = -\cos x$
   $\cos(\pi - x) = -\cos x$} **Theorem 2–4**

4. $\forall x \in \mathbf{R}$ $\sin(\pi + x) = -\sin x$
   $\sin(\pi - x) = \sin x$ } **Theorem 2–4**

5. $\forall x \in \mathbf{R}$ $n \in \mathbf{W}$ $\cos(x \pm 2n\pi) = \cos x$
   $\sin(x \pm 2n\pi) = \sin x$ } **Theorem 2–5**

6. $\forall x \in \mathbf{R}$ $\sin\left(\frac{\pi}{2} + x\right) = \cos x$
   $\cos\left(\frac{\pi}{2} + x\right) = -\sin x$ } **Theorem 2–6**

EXAMPLE. Find a real number x, $0 \leq x \leq \frac{\pi}{2}$, for which $\pm \sin x$ or $\pm \cos x$ is equal to $\cos \frac{4\pi}{5}$.

Solution: Since $\frac{4\pi}{5} = \pi - \frac{\pi}{5}$,

$$\cos \frac{4\pi}{5} = \cos\left(\pi - \frac{\pi}{5}\right)$$
$$= -\cos \frac{\pi}{5}$$

Since $\frac{4\pi}{5} = \frac{\pi}{2} + \frac{3\pi}{10}$,

$$\cos \frac{4\pi}{5} = \cos\left(\frac{\pi}{2} + \frac{3\pi}{10}\right)$$
$$= -\sin \frac{3\pi}{10}$$

CLASSROOM EXERCISES

1. Show that $\sin \frac{\pi}{3} = \frac{\sqrt{3}}{2}$ and $\cos \frac{\pi}{3} = \frac{1}{2}$. (*Hint:* Write $\frac{\pi}{3} = \frac{\pi}{2} - \frac{\pi}{6}$. Then use Theorem 2–6 and Theorem 2–3.)

2. Show that $\sin \frac{4\pi}{3} = -\frac{\sqrt{3}}{2}$ and $\cos \frac{4\pi}{3} = -\frac{1}{2}$.

3. Show that $\sin \frac{5\pi}{3} = -\frac{\sqrt{3}}{2}$ and $\cos \frac{5\pi}{3} = \frac{1}{2}$.

4. Now complete the table on page 79. Make a copy and keep it for further reference. You should memorize the entries.

WRITTEN EXERCISES

A ▬ Use the table on page 79 to determine whether each of the following is true or false.

1. $2 \sin \frac{\pi}{6} \cos \frac{\pi}{6} = \sin \frac{\pi}{3}$

2. $\sin \frac{2\pi}{3} \cos \frac{2\pi}{3} = \sin \frac{4\pi}{3}$

3. $\sin \frac{\pi}{4} \cos \frac{\pi}{4} + \cos \frac{\pi}{4} \sin \frac{\pi}{4} = 1$

4. $2 \sin \frac{3\pi}{4} \cos \frac{3\pi}{4} = -1$

5. $\sin \frac{\pi}{6} \cos \frac{\pi}{3} + \cos \frac{\pi}{6} \sin \frac{\pi}{3} = 1$

6. $\cos^2 \frac{5\pi}{6} - \sin^2 \frac{5\pi}{6} = \cos \frac{5\pi}{6}$

7. $\cos^2 \frac{5\pi}{4} - \sin^2 \frac{5\pi}{4} = 1$

8. $\cos \frac{4\pi}{3} \cos \frac{2\pi}{3} - \sin \frac{4\pi}{3} \sin \frac{2\pi}{3} = 1$

▬ In Exercises 9–20, find a real number x, $0 \leq x \leq \frac{\pi}{2}$, for which $\pm\sin x$ or $\pm\cos x$ is equal to the given number. Often there is more than one correct answer.

9. $\cos\left(-\frac{\pi}{7}\right)$ **10.** $\sin\left(-\frac{\pi}{8}\right)$ **11.** $\cos\left(\frac{11\pi}{10}\right)$ **12.** $\sin\left(\frac{10\pi}{9}\right)$

13. $\cos\left(\frac{7\pi}{8}\right)$

14. $\sin\left(\frac{7\pi}{8}\right)$

15. $\cos\left(\frac{\pi}{5} + 7\pi\right)$

16. $\sin\left(\frac{\pi}{7} + 8\pi\right)$

17. $\sin\left(\frac{4\pi}{7}\right)$

18. $\cos\left(\frac{19\pi}{3}\right)$

19. $\sin\left(-\frac{19\pi}{3}\right)$

20. $\sin\left(\frac{4n+1}{2}\pi\right),\ n \in W$

B **21.** Find an expression for $\sin\left(\frac{\pi}{2} - x\right)$ in terms of $\cos x$.

22. Find an expression for $\sin\left(x - \frac{\pi}{2}\right)$ in terms of $\cos x$.

23. Find an expression for $\cos\left(\frac{\pi}{2} - x\right)$ in terms of $\sin x$.

24. Find an expression for $\cos\left(x - \frac{\pi}{2}\right)$ in terms of $\sin x$.

25. Find an expression for $\sin(x - \pi)$ in terms of $\sin x$.

26. Find an expression for $\cos(x - \pi)$ in terms of $\cos x$.

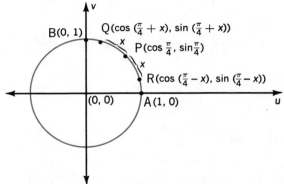

C ▬▬ Refer to the figure above. Let $x \in R$ and $0 < x < \frac{\pi}{4}$. Let A, B, P, Q and R have coordinates as indicated.

27. Show that $BQ = AR$.

28. Use Exercise 27, the distance formula, and the relation

$$\sin^2 x + \cos^2 x = 1$$

to show that

a. $\sin\left(\frac{\pi}{4} - x\right) = \cos\left(\frac{\pi}{4} + x\right)$.

b. $\cos\left(\frac{\pi}{4} - x\right) = \sin\left(\frac{\pi}{4} + x\right)$.

29. Does the result of Exercise 28 hold when $x > \frac{\pi}{4}$? $x < 0$? $x = \frac{\pi}{4}$? Explain in detail.

━━━ Find the distance between each pair of points.   (Section 2-1)

1. $A(-5, 3)$, $B(3, -5)$ **2.** $P(7, 5)$, $Q(-3, -5)$

3. Find the equation of the circle that passes through $Q(-2, 5)$ and has center $C(1, 9)$.   (Section 2-1)

4. W is the wrapping function. Name two positive and two negative numbers that map onto (u, v) if W maps 3.5 onto (u, v).   (Section 2-2)

5. If $W(x) = \left(-\frac{24}{25}, \frac{7}{25}\right)$ find:

    a. $W(-x)$ **b.** $W(x - \pi)$ (Section 2-2)

6. What are the signs of $\cos x$ and $\sin x$, if $x = \frac{31\pi}{6}$?   (Section 2-3)

7. Find $\cos x$ if $\sin x = \frac{15}{17}$ and x is in Quadrant II.   (Section 2-3)

8. Find $\sin\left(-\frac{5\pi}{6}\right)$ and $\cos\left(\frac{15\pi}{4}\right)$.   (Section 2-4)

9. Express $\sin\left(\frac{7\pi}{10}\right)$ in terms of x where $0 \le x \le \frac{\pi}{2}$.   (Section 2-5)

10. Express $\cos\left(-\frac{3\pi}{5}\right)$ in terms of x where $0 \le x \le \frac{\pi}{2}$.   (Section 2-5)

2-6   Graphs of the Sine and Cosine Functions

You know by Theorem 2–5 that for all $x \in$ R and $n \in$ W

$$\cos(x \pm 2n\pi) = \cos x \qquad \text{and} \qquad \sin(x \pm 2n\pi) = \sin x.$$

You can use Theorem 2–5 to find $\cos r$ and $\sin r$ for every real number r.

Suppose you divide the real number r by 2π. The result is a quotient $n \in$ I and a remainder x such that $0 \le x < 2\pi$. That is,

$$r \div 2\pi = n + \frac{x}{2\pi}, \quad n \in \text{I}. \qquad\qquad 1$$

Multiplying both sides of 1 by 2π, you obtain

$$r = 2\pi n + x, \qquad 0 \le x < 2\pi. \qquad\qquad 2$$

Equation 2 holds for any real number r. It says in essence that any real number is an integral multiple of 2π plus a remainder x, $0 \le x < 2\pi$. Since I = $\{-n\} \cup \{n\}$, $n \in$ W, 2 can be written

$$r = \pm 2n\pi + x, \qquad 0 \le x < 2\pi, \qquad n \in \text{W}.$$

Since every real number can be expressed $r = \pm 2n\pi + x$, the graphs of $y = \sin x$ and $y = \cos x$ for $x \in \mathbf{R}$ are determined by the graphs of $y = \sin x$ and $y = \cos x$ for $x \in [0, 2\pi)$. On each other interval that is 2π units long and has a left endpoint of $\pm 2n\pi$, the graphs of $y = \sin x$ and $y = \cos x$ are carbon copies of the graphs on $[0, 2\pi)$. Thus it suffices to graph $y = \sin x$, $x \in [0, 2\pi)$ and $y = \cos x$, $x \in [0, 2\pi)$ and to repeat these graphs on each interval $[\pm 2n\pi, \pm 2(n + 1)\pi)$ to obtain the complete graph.

A function whose graph repeats itself again and again is a *periodic function*.

Definition If f is a function with domain $\mathbf{R}$ and if there is a number $p > 0$ such that

$$\forall x \in \mathbf{R} \qquad f(x + p) = f(x)$$

then f is a **periodic function**. If p is the smallest positive number with this property, then p is the **period** of f.

The number 2π is the smallest positive p such that

$$\sin (x + p) = \sin x \qquad \text{and} \qquad \cos (x + p) = \cos x.$$

Thus the sine and cosine functions have the *period* 2π.

The figure below shows a graph of $y = \sin x$. The dots correspond to values from the table that you completed in Section 2–5.

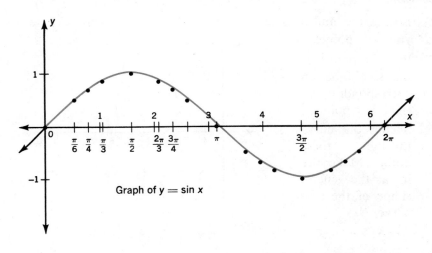

Graph of $y = \sin x$

The red portion of the graph is the graph on the interval $[0, 2\pi)$. Any interval of length 2π could be used in a repetitive fashion to construct the entire curve. Such an interval is called a **cycle** of the curve. Any interval $[x, x + 2\pi)$, $x \in R$, will determine a cycle.

The cosine function is graphed below. The red portion corresponds to the interval $[0, 2\pi)$. Again a cycle is the graph over an interval $[x, x + 2\pi)$, $x \in R$.

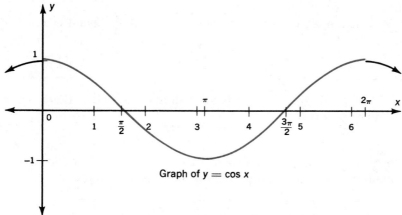

Graph of $y = \cos x$

Compare the graph of the cosine on $\left[-\frac{\pi}{2}, \frac{3\pi}{2}\right)$ with that of the sine on $[0, 2\pi)$. These two cycles are identical. It appears that the graph of $y = \cos x$ is the graph of $y = \sin x$ shifted $\frac{\pi}{2}$ units to the left.

EXAMPLE. Sketch the graph of $\sin x$ for $x \in \left[\frac{\pi}{2}, 3\pi\right]$.

Solution:

① Locate the multiples of $\frac{\pi}{2}$ and of π on the x axis. These are your key points.

② Plot the points of the sine function corresponding to these key points.

③ Sketch the curve through these points. Make sure it has the general shape of the sine curve.

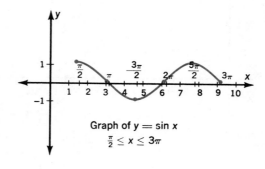

Graph of $y = \sin x$
$\frac{\pi}{2} \le x \le 3\pi$

CLASSROOM EXERCISES

▬ Express each number as a multiple of 2π and a remainder x, $0 \le x < 2\pi$.

1. $\frac{3\pi}{2}$ **2.** 7π **3.** $\frac{29\pi}{2}$

▬ If the sine or cosine is graphed on the given interval, determine the number of complete cycles represented.

4. $\left[-\frac{\pi}{2}, \frac{7\pi}{2}\right]$ **5.** $[-\pi, 0]$ **6.** $\left[\frac{\pi}{2}, \frac{13\pi}{2}\right]$

WRITTEN EXERCISES

A ▬ In Exercises 1–6 sketch the graphs of the sine and cosine functions for the interval given. First locate the key points. Then graph both functions on the same coordinate system.

1. $\left[-\frac{3\pi}{2}, \frac{3\pi}{2}\right]$ **2.** $[3\pi, 6\pi]$ **3.** $[-5\pi, -\pi]$

4. $\left[-\frac{3\pi}{4}, 3\pi\right]$ **5.** $\left[\frac{8\pi}{3}, 5\pi\right]$ **6.** $\left[-\frac{17\pi}{6}, -\frac{\pi}{6}\right]$

7. Use the following procedure to construct an accurate graph of $y = \sin x$, $x \in [0, 2\pi]$.

    a. On a piece of $8\frac{1}{2}$ by 11 graph paper construct a circle with radius $1''$ or 3 cm as depicted below. Complete the figure on your paper as depicted in the diagram. The unit is $1''$ or 3 cm.

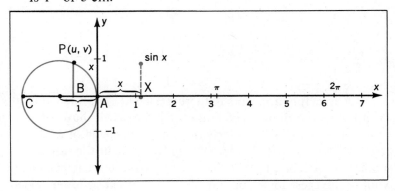

    b. Sin x is the second coordinate of $P(u, v)$ where $P(u, v)$ is x units along the circle from A. Thus $\sin x$ is the perpendicular distance from $\overline{AC}$ to $P(u, v)$. Find the point on the x axis at x, which is the fourth vertex of the rectangle PBX_-. This point is the graph of $(x, \sin x)$.

  c. Repeat this process for as many values of x as necessary to construct an accurate graph. You should plot at least 30 points.

 8. Construct an accurate graph of $y = \cos x,\ 0 \le x \le 2\pi$ by using the graph you constructed in Exercise 7. Do this by copying $y = \sin x$ for $x \in \left[\dfrac{\pi}{2}, \dfrac{5\pi}{2} \right]$ on the interval $[0, 2\pi]$.

B ━━ In Exercises 9–18 use the accurate graphs you constructed in Exercises 7 and 8 to give a reasonable estimate to the value of $x \in [0, 2\pi]$ that satisfies each of the following statements. Some statements may be satisfied by no x.

 9. $\cos x = \sin x$ **10.** $\cos x = -\sin x$

 11. $\sin x < \cos x$ **12.** $\sin x - \cos x = 0$

 13. $\sin x + \cos x = 0$ **14.** $\sin x + \cos x = 1$

 15. $\sin x - \cos x = -1$ **16.** $|\sin x + \cos x| = 1$

 17. $\sin x \cdot \cos x > 1$ **18.** $\sin x \cdot \cos x < 0$

C **19.** Sketch the graph of $y = |\sin x|,\ x \in [0, 2\pi]$.

 20. Sketch the graph of $y = 1 + \cos x,\ x \in [0, 2\pi]$.

 21. Sketch the graph of $y = 1 + |\cos x|,\ x \in [0, 2\pi]$.

 22. Sketch the graph of $y = 2\sin x,\ x \in [0, 2\pi]$.

 23. Sketch the graph of $y = \sin x + \cos x,\ x \in [0, 2\pi]$.

 24. Sketch the graph of $y = x + \sin x,\ x \in [0, 2\pi]$.

 25. Sketch the graph of $y = x + \cos x,\ x \in [0, 2\pi]$.

2-7 Amplitude and Period

  If f is a function and if there exists $M \in \mathbf{R}$ such that $f(x) \le M$ for all x in the domain of f, then f is **bounded above** by M, or M is an **upper bound** of f. Similarly, m is a **lower bound** of f, or f is **bounded below** by m, if and only if $f(x) \ge m$ for all x in the domain of f. The smallest upper bound of a function f is the **least upper bound** (l.u.b.) while the largest lower bound of f is the **greatest lower bound** (g.l.b.).

  Since 1 is the maximum value of $\sin x$ and $\cos x,\ x \in \mathbf{R}$, 1 is the least upper bound for the sine and cosine functions. Likewise, -1 is the greatest lower bound of the sine and cosine functions.

  If M and m are the least upper and greatest lower bounds of a periodic function f, then $\frac{1}{2}(M - m)$ is the **amplitude** of the function f.

EXAMPLE 1. Find the amplitude of $y = \sin x$ and $y = \cos x$, $x \in R$.

The amplitude is $\frac{1}{2}(M - m)$. Thus, the amplitude of $\cos x$ is $\frac{1}{2}[1 - (-1)] = 1$, and the amplitude of $\sin x$ is $\frac{1}{2}[1 - (-1)] = 1$.

Graphed below are

$$y = \sin x \qquad x \in [0, 2\pi] \qquad\qquad 1$$
$$y = 2 \sin x \qquad x \in [0, 2\pi]. \qquad\qquad 2$$

The functional values of **2** are each twice those of **1.** The amplitude of $y = 2 \sin x$ is $\frac{1}{2}[2 - (-2)] = 2$. The period of $y = 2 \sin x$ is 2π.

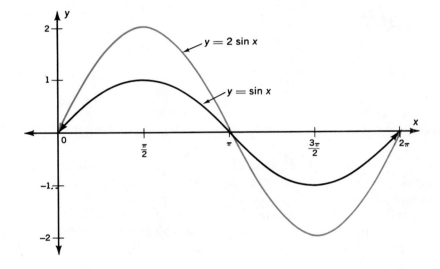

In general, the graph of $y = A \sin x$ is a sine curve with amplitude $|A|$ and period 2π.

The same situation occurs for the cosine function. In summary:

1. The graph of $y = A \sin x$ is a sine curve with amplitude $|A|$ and period 2π.
2. The graph of $y = A \cos x$ is a cosine curve with amplitude $|A|$ and period 2π.

Now consider the functions described by

$$y = \cos x$$

and

$$y = \cos (2x)$$

x	$2x$	$\cos 2x$		x	$2x$	$\cos 2x$
0	0	1		$\dfrac{7\pi}{6}$	$\dfrac{7\pi}{3}$	$\dfrac{1}{2}$
$\dfrac{\pi}{6}$	$\dfrac{\pi}{3}$	$\dfrac{1}{2}$		$\dfrac{5\pi}{4}$	$\dfrac{5\pi}{2}$	0
$\dfrac{\pi}{4}$	$\dfrac{\pi}{2}$	0		$\dfrac{4\pi}{3}$	$\dfrac{8\pi}{3}$	$-\dfrac{1}{2}$
$\dfrac{\pi}{3}$	$\dfrac{2\pi}{3}$	$-\dfrac{1}{2}$		$\dfrac{3\pi}{2}$	3π	-1
$\dfrac{\pi}{2}$	π	-1		$\dfrac{5\pi}{3}$	$\dfrac{10\pi}{3}$	$-\dfrac{1}{2}$
$\dfrac{2\pi}{3}$	$\dfrac{4\pi}{3}$	$-\dfrac{1}{2}$		$\dfrac{7\pi}{4}$	$\dfrac{7\pi}{2}$	0
$\dfrac{3\pi}{4}$	$\dfrac{3\pi}{2}$	0		$\dfrac{11\pi}{6}$	$\dfrac{11\pi}{3}$	$\dfrac{1}{2}$
$\dfrac{5\pi}{6}$	$\dfrac{5\pi}{3}$	$\dfrac{1}{2}$		2π	4π	1
π	2π	1				

Notice that when x is π, then $2x$ is 2π. Thus, $y = \cos(2x)$ forms a complete cycle on the interval $[0, \pi]$ and on $[\pi, 2\pi]$. There are 2 periods of $y = \cos(2x)$ for every one of $y = \cos x$. Consequently each period is one-half as long. The period of $y = \cos(2x)$ is $\frac{1}{2}(2\pi) = \pi$.

The graphs of $y = \cos x$ and $y = \cos(2x)$ are shown below. Notice that the amplitude of $y = \cos x$ and the amplitude of $y = \cos(2x)$ are each 1.

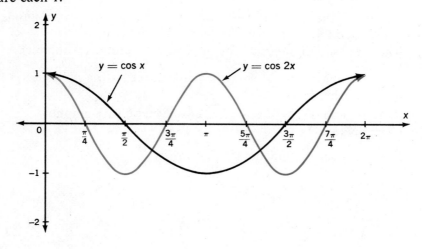

The cycle of $y = \cos(Bx)$ beginning at $x = 0$ will be complete when $|B|x = 2\pi$, or when $x = \frac{2\pi}{|B|}$. In general, then the graph of $y = \cos(Bx)$ will have period $\frac{2\pi}{|B|}$.

The same generalization applies to $y = \sin Bx$. To summarize:

3. The period of $y = \cos Bx$ is $\frac{2\pi}{|B|}$.

4. The period of $y = \sin Bx$ is $\frac{2\pi}{|B|}$.

In combination the Generalizations 1–4 tell you that $\forall x, y, A, B \in R, A, B \neq 0$

$y = A \sin Bx$ has amplitude $|A|$ and period $\frac{2\pi}{|B|}$ and

$y = A \cos Bx$ has amplitude $|A|$ and period $\frac{2\pi}{|B|}$.

The above facts on amplitude and period will help you to sketch curves of the form $y = A \sin Bx$ and $y = A \cos Bx$ using the basic curves $y = \sin x$ and $y = \cos x$.

EXAMPLE 2. Sketch the graph of one cycle of $y = -2 \cos \frac{1}{2}x$.

Solution:

The amplitude is $|-2| = 2$ and the period is $\frac{2\pi}{\frac{1}{2}} = 4\pi$. The maximum value occurs at 2π. The minimum values occur at the endpoints of $[0, 4\pi]$.

The curve crosses the x axis at the quarter and three-quarter points of $[0, 4\pi]$, or at π and 3π.

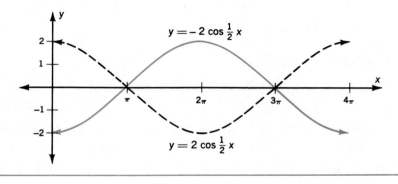

EXAMPLE 3. Sketch the graph of

$$y = 3 \sin 4x, \; x \in [0, 2\pi].$$

The amplitude is $|\,3\,| = 3$, and the period is $\frac{2\pi}{4} = \frac{\pi}{2}$. Thus there will be four complete cycles in $[0, 2\pi]$; the maximum value of $3 \sin 4x$ is 3; the minimum is -3. The maximum values occur one quarter of the way through each cycle; the minima occur three quarters of the way through each cycle; the curve crosses the x axis halfway through each cycle. Thus for $\left[0, \frac{\pi}{2}\right]$, the maximum is $\left(\frac{\pi}{8}, 3\right)$, the minimum $\left(\frac{3\pi}{8}, -3\right)$, and $y = 3 \sin 4x$ intersects the x axis at $\left(\frac{\pi}{2}, 0\right)$.

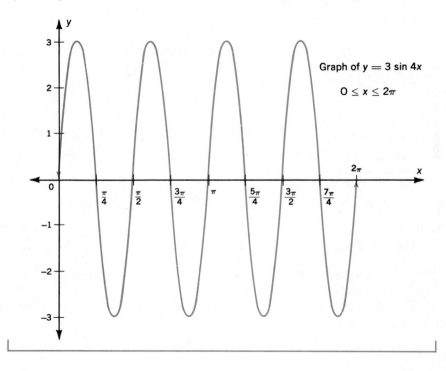

Graph of $y = 3 \sin 4x$

$0 \le x \le 2\pi$

CLASSROOM EXERCISES

━━━ Identify the amplitude and period of each function.

1. $y = 8 \cos x$ **2.** $y = -8 \cos 3x$ **3.** $y = \frac{1}{2} \sin \frac{1}{10} x$

━━━ Given the beginning point of the graph of the given function, determine at what point the second cycle begins.

4. $\frac{\pi}{4}$, $8 \cos x$ **5.** $-\frac{\pi}{4}$, $\sin \frac{1}{100} x$ **6.** 2π, $\sin 1.5x$

WRITTEN EXERCISES

A ━━Identify the amplitude and period of each function in Exercises 1–8.

1. $f(x) = 3 \sin (1 \cdot x)$

2. $g : x \rightarrow \sin (3x)$

3. $h(x) = 2 \cos (-2x)$

4. $y = -\frac{1}{2} \cos x$

5. $f : x \rightarrow -\frac{2}{3} \sin (\frac{4}{3}x)$

6. $y = -17 \cos (-8x)$

7. $h : x \rightarrow \frac{1}{18} \cos (\frac{1}{18}x)$

8. $g(x) = \frac{7}{4} \sin (\frac{3}{2}x)$

━━Find the coordinates of the

    a. maxima   **b.** minima

    c. points with y coordinates equal to zero

for each function on its period beginning with $x = 0$.

9. $g : x \rightarrow 2 \sin x$

10. $h : x \rightarrow -2 \sin x$

11. $f(x) = \frac{4}{5} \cos (2x)$

12. $y = \frac{4}{5} \cos (-2x)$

13. $h(x) = 5 \sin (\frac{2}{3}x)$

14. $g : x \rightarrow -5 \sin (-\frac{2}{3}x)$

15. $y = \cos (\frac{4}{5}x)$

16. $f : x \rightarrow -8 \cos (4x)$

━━Sketch the graph of one period of the function in each of the following exercises.

17. Exercise 9.

18. Exercise 10.

19. Exercise 11.

20. Exercise 12.

21. Exercise 13.

22. Exercise 14.

23. Exercise 15.

24. Exercise 16.

━━Write an equation describing a sine function with the given characteristics.

25. Amplitude 3 and period π

26. Amplitude $\frac{1}{2}$ and period 3π

27. Amplitude 12 and period 2

28. Amplitude $\frac{2}{3}$ and period $\frac{1}{2}$

B **29.** Amplitude 4, minimum $\left(\frac{\pi}{4}, -4\right)$

30. Amplitude $\frac{2}{5}$, maximum $\left(\frac{3\pi}{4}, \frac{2}{5}\right)$

31. Amplitude 7, contains $\left(\frac{2\pi}{3}, 0\right)$

32. Maximum $(\pi, 4)$, period 4π

33. Maximum $\left(\frac{15\pi}{4}, 2\right)$, minimum $\left(\frac{5\pi}{4}, -2\right)$

34. Maximum $\left(\frac{7\pi}{4}, 5\right)$, contains $\left(\frac{7\pi}{2}, 0\right)$

C **35.** Show that $\qquad$ $y = A \sin x, \qquad A > 0$

and $\qquad\qquad\qquad y = -A \sin x, \qquad A > 0$

have the same amplitude.

36. a. Graph $y = 2 \sin x$ and $y = 3 \cos x$ on the interval $[-2\pi, 2\pi]$. Use the same coordinate system to graph both curves.

b. Graph $y = 2 \sin x + 3 \cos x$, $x \in [-2\pi, 2\pi]$ by adding the coordinates in **a.**

c. What is the maximum and minimum value of $y = 2 \sin x + 3 \cos x$?

d. What is the amplitude of $y = 2 \sin x + 3 \cos x$?

━━━ The reciprocal of the period of a periodic function is the **frequency** of the function. The *frequency* represents the number of cycles completed by a function over an interval one unit long. What is the frequency of each of the following?

37. $y = \sin 2\pi x$ $\qquad\qquad$ **38.** $y = \sin (\frac{1}{2}x)$

39. $y = \cos 120\pi x$ $\qquad\qquad$ **40.** $y = -4 \cos 80x$

41. $y = 30 \sin 40\pi x$ $\qquad\qquad$ **42.** $y = -20 \cos (-20\pi x)$

43. $y = \cos x + \sin x$ $\qquad\qquad$ **44.** $y = 3 \cos 2x + 3 \sin 2x$

2–8   Phase Shift

Suppose you wished to graph $y = 3 \sin \left(2x - \frac{\pi}{2}\right)$. From the equation it follows that

1. the amplitude is 3, $\qquad\qquad$ 2. the period is $\frac{2\pi}{2} = \pi$, and

3. the graph is a sine curve like the graph of $y = 3 \sin (2x)$.

Suppose further that you wanted to graph $y = 3 \sin \left(2x - \frac{\pi}{2}\right)$ over an interval π units long (the period) such that y is 0 when x is either endpoint of the interval.

To find an x so that y is 0, you must find an x such that $3 \sin \left(2x - \frac{\pi}{2}\right)$ is 0. The expression $3 \sin \left(2x - \frac{\pi}{2}\right)$ is 0 when $\sin \left(2x - \frac{\pi}{2}\right)$ is 0, and the sine function is 0 when its domain value is 0. Thus, $\sin \left(2x - \frac{\pi}{2}\right) = 0$ when $2x - \frac{\pi}{2} = 0$.

Solving, you find $x = \frac{\pi}{4}$.

The left-hand endpoint of the interval is $\frac{\pi}{4}$. If x is the left-hand endpoint, then certainly $x + \pi$ is the right-hand endpoint, so the right-hand endpoint is $\frac{\pi}{4} + \pi = \frac{5\pi}{4}$.

How is the graph of $y = 3 \sin \left(2x - \frac{\pi}{2}\right)$ related to the graph of $y = 3 \sin (2x)$? The graph of $y = 3 \sin (2x)$ has amplitude 3, period π and completes a cycle on $[0, \pi]$ such that $y = 0$ at both endpoints. Likewise, the graph of $y = 3 \sin \left(2x - \frac{\pi}{2}\right)$ has amplitude 3, period π and completes a similar cycle on the interval $\left[\frac{\pi}{4}, \frac{5\pi}{4}\right]$. Thus the graph of $y = 3 \sin \left(2x - \frac{\pi}{2}\right)$ is similar to that of $y = 3 \sin (2x)$ in all respects except for the endpoints of a fundamental interval. If the graph of $y = 3 \sin 2x$ is moved $\frac{\pi}{4}$ units to the right along the x axis, then it coincides with the graph of $y = 3 \sin \left(2x - \frac{\pi}{2}\right)$. The number $\frac{\pi}{4}$ is the *phase shift* of the curve $y = 3 \sin \left(2x - \frac{\pi}{2}\right)$.

The graph of each function is shown below. Notice that the graph of $y = 3 \sin \left(2x - \frac{\pi}{2}\right)$ is always $\frac{\pi}{4}$ units ahead of the graph of $y = 3 \sin (2x)$. This is the effect of the phase shift.

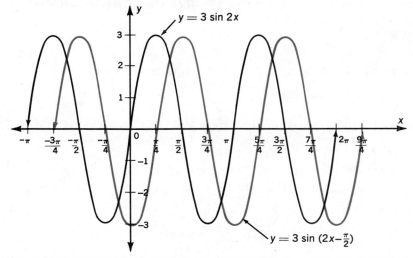

Definition The **phase shift** of a function $y = A \sin (Bx + C)$ is the number of units that the graph of $y = A \sin Bx$ must be shifted along the x axis so that it coincides with the graph of $y = A \sin (Bx + C)$.

Consider the general equation $y = A \sin (Bx + C)$ $A, B \neq 0$. To find the phase shift, find the value of x such that

$$0 = y = A \sin (Bx + C).$$

That value of x is found by solving $Bx + C = 0$. (Why?). But $Bx + C = 0$ when $x = -\frac{C}{B}$. Thus, $-\frac{C}{B}$ is the phase shift of $y = A \sin (Bx + C)$. When $-\frac{C}{B} > 0$, the shift is $\left| -\frac{C}{B} \right|$ units to the right; and the graph can be sketched by shifting the graph of $y = A \sin Bx$ $\left| -\frac{C}{B} \right|$ units to the *right*. Similarly when $-\frac{C}{B} < 0$, the graph of $y = A \sin (Bx + C)$ is similar to the graph of $y = A \sin Bx$, but is shifted $\left| -\frac{C}{B} \right|$ units to the *left*.

A similar analysis is valid for the cosine curve

$$y = A \cos (Bx + C) \qquad A, B \neq 0.$$

$-\frac{C}{B}$ is the phase shift. To obtain the graph of $y = A \cos (Bx + C)$, you first graph $y = A \cos Bx$, then shift this graph $\left| -\frac{C}{B} \right|$ units to the right when $-\frac{C}{B} > 0$ and $\left| -\frac{C}{B} \right|$ units to the left when $-\frac{C}{B} < 0$. In this case, however, the cycle graphed does not start with $y = 0$. Instead, it starts with a maximum point of the graph, where $y = A$ is true. Can you explain why?

EXAMPLE 1. Write an equation of a sine curve that has amplitude 2, period π, and phase shift $\frac{\pi}{4}$.

Solution: A sine curve defined by $y = A \sin (Bx + C)$ has amplitude $|A|$, $\frac{2\pi}{|B|}$, and phase shift $-\frac{C}{B}$.

The conditions tell you that the amplitude must be 2, so $A = 2$ or $A = -2$. Since the period is to be π, $B = 2$ or $B = -2$. If the phase shift is to be $\frac{\pi}{4}$, then $-\frac{C}{2} = \frac{\pi}{4}$ or $\frac{-C}{-2} = \frac{\pi}{4}$, so $C = -\frac{\pi}{2}$ or $C = \frac{\pi}{2}$.

The possible equations for the sine curve are as follows.

1. $y = 2 \sin \left(2x - \frac{\pi}{2} \right)$ 2. $y = -2 \sin \left(2x - \frac{\pi}{2} \right)$

3. $y = 2 \sin \left(-2x + \frac{\pi}{2} \right)$ 4. $y = -2 \sin \left(-2x + \frac{\pi}{2} \right)$

Equations 3 and 4 are equivalent to equations 2 and 1, respectively. (Why?) Thus, there are two sine curves satisfying the given characteristics.

EXAMPLE 2. Identify the amplitude, period, and phase shift in $y = 2 \cos (3x + \pi)$. Sketch the graph.

Solution:

The amplitude is $|2| = 2$. The period is $\frac{2\pi}{3}$. The phase shift is $-\frac{\pi}{3}$. The graph of $y = 2 \cos (3x + \pi)$ is shifted $\frac{\pi}{3}$ units to left of the graph of $y = 2 \cos 3x$.

To construct the graph, it is useful to begin by sketching the graph of $y = 2 \cos 3x$. This graph can be used to approximate the required graph.

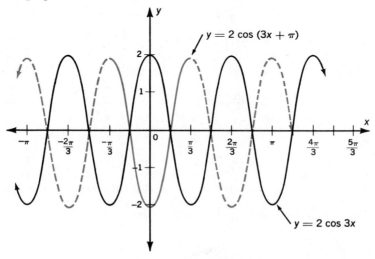

CLASSROOM EXERCISES

━━ Give the phase shift of each function.

1. $y = 3 \sin (5x + 2)$ **2.** $y = -4 \cos (2x - 1)$

3. $y = -\frac{1}{2} \sin (x + 3)$ **4.** $y = \frac{2}{3} \cos (3x)$

WRITTEN EXERCISES

A ━━ For Exercises 1–6 write an equation of a sine curve with the given characteristics.

1. Amplitude: 5; period: 2π; phase shift: $\frac{\pi}{3}$

2. Amplitude: 3; period: $\frac{2\pi}{3}$; phase shift: $\frac{\pi}{3}$

3. Amplitude: $\frac{2}{3}$; period: $\frac{\pi}{4}$; phase shift: $-\frac{\pi}{8}$

4. Amplitude: 17; period: 4π; phase shift: $\frac{\pi}{4}$

5. Amplitude: 7; period: $\frac{3\pi}{2}$; phase shift: $-\frac{\pi}{4}$

6. Amplitude: $\frac{1}{2}$; period: $\frac{5\pi}{4}$; phase shift: $-\frac{5}{8}$

For Exercises 7–12 write an equation of a cosine curve with the given characteristics.

7. Amplitude: 3; period: π; phase shift: $\frac{2\pi}{3}$

8. Amplitude: 6; period: $\frac{2\pi}{3}$; phase shift: $-\frac{5}{8}$

9. Amplitude: 100; period: 3π; phase shift: $-\pi$

10. Amplitude: $\frac{1}{5}$; period: $\frac{\pi}{5}$; phase shift: 2

11. Amplitude: $\frac{7}{3}$; period: $\frac{5\pi}{6}$; phase shift: -1

12. Amplitude: 1; period: $\frac{3\pi}{4}$; phase shift: $\frac{3\pi}{2}$

Identify the amplitude, period, and phase shift of each function in Exercises 13–28. Sketch the graph of each.

13. $y = -3 \sin \left(x - \frac{\pi}{4}\right)$ **14.** $y = \cos (3x + \pi)$

15. $y = \frac{2}{3} \sin \left(\frac{1}{2}x + \frac{\pi}{5}\right)$ **16.** $y = \cos \left(2x - \frac{\pi}{3}\right)$

17. $y = -\sin \left(\frac{2}{3}x - \pi\right)$ **18.** $y = 4 \cos \left(\frac{1}{3}x + \pi\right)$

19. $y = 2 \sin \left(-2x + \frac{\pi}{2}\right)$ **20.** $y = -\frac{1}{2} \cos (-4\pi x - 2\pi)$

B **21.** $y = 3 \sin (2\pi x + \pi)$ **22.** $y = 4 \cos \left(\frac{\pi}{2} x - \pi\right)$

23. $y = 2 \sin \left(\pi x - \frac{\pi}{2}\right)$ **24.** $y = \cos (4\pi x + \pi)$

25. $y = -3 \sin (4x + 2)$ **26.** $y = -2 \cos (6x - 4)$

27. $y = 5 \sin (x - 3)$ **28.** $y = -5 \cos (x + 4)$

C **29.** Verify that the equations $y = 2 \sin \left(3x - \frac{\pi}{2}\right)$ and

$y = -2 \sin \left(-3x + \frac{\pi}{2}\right)$ have the same graphs.

30. Verify that the equations $y = -3 \sin (-5x + \pi)$ and $y = 3 \sin (5x - \pi)$ have the same graphs.

31. You are given the following equations.

    i. $y = 3 \cos (2x - \pi)$ **iii.** $y = 3 \cos (-2x + \pi)$

    ii. $y = -3 \cos (2x - \pi)$ **iv.** $y = -3 \cos (-2x + \pi)$

Find pairs of equations with the same graphs. Explain your choices.

Applying Sine Curves

Meteorology

Meteorologists are often interested in the daily average temperature in a given region. This can be calculated by averaging the daily high and low temperatures. The monthly average temperature of a location can be found by averaging the daily average temperatures over a month. The graph below is a model of the monthly averages for a particular location.

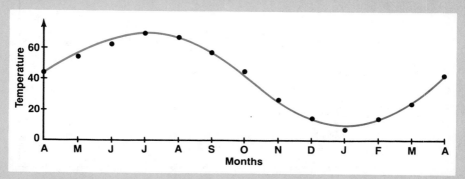

The model is a sine curve with equation

$$T(x) = A + B \sin\left(\frac{2\pi x}{12} + C\right).$$

A is the yearly mean average temperature in a location. B is the difference between the summer high or winter low and A. It is the amplitude of the graph. C is the mean number of days beyond March 21 when the average daily temperature rises above the yearly mean.

EXAMPLE. In Seattle, Washington, the yearly mean temperature is 50°F, the high average temperature is 62°F, and the temperature reaches 50°F on April 27, on the average. What is the equation for this city?

Solution: $A = 50$ $B = 62 - 50 = 12$ $C = \text{April } 27 - \text{March } 21 = 37 \text{ days}$

$$T(x) = 50 + 12 \sin\left(\frac{2\pi x}{12} + 37\right) = 50 + 12 \sin\left(\frac{\pi x}{6} + 37\right)$$

EXERCISES

For each city the yearly mean temperature, the average high temperature, and the date the temperature reaches the yearly mean are given. Write the modelling equation.

1. Detroit: 47, 71, April 23
2. Miami: 75, 84, April 25
3. Honolulu: 75, 78, May 15
4. Boston: 50, 72. April 25
5. Los Angeles: 63, 71, May 9
6. St. Louis: 55, 23, April 20

2–9 Tangent and Co-Functions

The sine and cosine functions are the fundamental circular functions. Given these functions four other circular functions can be defined. They are the *tangent* (tan), *cotangent* (cot), *secant* (sec), and *cosecant* (csc).

Definitions $\forall x \in \mathbf{R}$.

$$\tan x = \left\{(x, y) : y = \frac{\sin x}{\cos x}, \ \cos x \neq 0\right\}$$

$$\cot x = \left\{(x, y) : y = \frac{\cos x}{\sin x}, \ \sin x \neq 0\right\}$$

$$\sec x = \left\{(x, y) : y = \frac{1}{\cos x}, \ \cos x \neq 0\right\}$$

$$\csc x = \left\{(x, y) : y = \frac{1}{\sin x}, \ \sin x \neq 0\right\}$$

Notice that the tangent and cotangent functions are *reciprocals* of each other.

$$\frac{1}{\tan x} = \frac{1}{\dfrac{\sin x}{\cos x}}$$

$$= \frac{\cos x}{\sin x}$$

$$= \cot x$$

Thus, tan x and cot x are called **reciprocal functions.**

By definition sec x and cos x are also reciprocal functions as are sin x and csc x. The reciprocal relation between these pairs of functions provides a way of determining the domain, range and graph of each function.

First consider the secant function, $\sec x = \dfrac{1}{\cos x}, \ \cos x \neq 0$. The value of cos x is 0 for $x \in \left\{(2n + 1)\dfrac{\pi}{2}, \ n \in \mathbf{I}\right\}$, so sec x is *not defined* for $x \in \left\{\cdots -\dfrac{5\pi}{2}, -\dfrac{3\pi}{2}, -\dfrac{\pi}{2}, \dfrac{\pi}{2}, \dfrac{3\pi}{2}, \dfrac{5\pi}{2}, \cdots\right\}$. Sec x is defined for all other real numbers x. Thus the domain of sec x is $\mathbf{R}$ with the set $\left\{(2n + 1)\dfrac{\pi}{2}, \ n \in \mathbf{I}\right\}$ deleted.

The range of sec x can also be defined by considering the range of cos x as follows.

For all $x \in R$ such that $\cos x \neq 0$, $-1 \leq \cos x < 0$ is true or $0 < \cos x \leq 1$ is true. Dividing each term of the first expression by $\cos x < 0$, you obtain

$$-\frac{1}{\cos x} \geq 1.$$

Similarly, by dividing each term of $0 < \cos x \leq 1$ by $\cos x > 0$,

$$1 \leq \frac{1}{\cos x}.$$

Thus, since $\sec x = \frac{1}{\cos x}$, you have

$$\sec x \leq -1 \quad \longleftarrow \quad \textbf{For negative } \cos x$$

or

$$\sec x \geq 1 \quad \longleftarrow \quad \textbf{For positive } \cos x$$

It follows that the range of $\sec x$ is

$$\textbf{V} = \{y : y \leq -1 \ or \ y \geq 1, y \in \textbf{R}\}.$$

The graph of the secant function can be sketched by first sketching the graph of $y = \cos x$ and then estimating the reciprocals of $\cos x$. The dotted vertical lines have equations $x = (2n + 1)\frac{\pi}{2}$, $n \in$ I, and correspond to the values of x for which $y = \sec x$ is not defined.

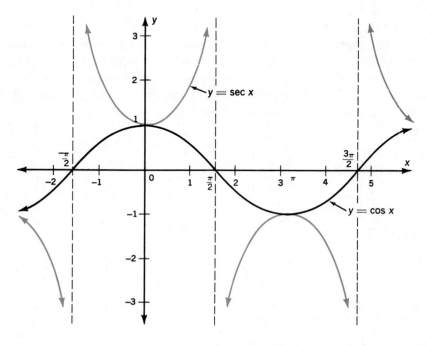

Similarly, you can verify that the domain of the cosecant functions is R with the set $\{n\pi, n \in I\}$ deleted. The range is

$$V = \{y : y \le -1 \ or \ y \ge 1, y \in R\}.$$

The graph is shown below.

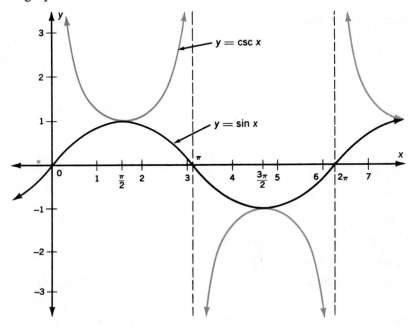

The graphs of the tangent and cotangent functions are most easily constructed from a table of values. On page 79 a partial table of values for sin x and cos x was given. It is reproduced here and on the next page with two additional rows, one for tan x and one for cot x. Notice that both tan x and cot x are undefined for certain values.

x	0	$\dfrac{\pi}{6}$	$\dfrac{\pi}{4}$	$\dfrac{\pi}{3}$	$\dfrac{\pi}{2}$	$\dfrac{2\pi}{3}$	$\dfrac{3\pi}{4}$	$\dfrac{5\pi}{6}$	π
cos x	1	$\dfrac{\sqrt{3}}{2}$	$\dfrac{\sqrt{2}}{2}$	$\dfrac{1}{2}$	0	$-\dfrac{1}{2}$	$-\dfrac{\sqrt{2}}{2}$	$-\dfrac{\sqrt{3}}{2}$	-1
sin x	0	$\dfrac{1}{2}$	$\dfrac{\sqrt{2}}{2}$	$\dfrac{\sqrt{3}}{2}$	1	$\dfrac{\sqrt{3}}{2}$	$\dfrac{\sqrt{2}}{2}$	$\dfrac{1}{2}$	0
tan x	0	$\dfrac{1}{\sqrt{3}}$	1	$\sqrt{3}$	$+\infty$	$-\sqrt{3}$	-1	$-\dfrac{1}{\sqrt{3}}$	0
cot x	$+\infty$	$\sqrt{3}$	1	$\dfrac{1}{\sqrt{3}}$	0	$\dfrac{1}{\sqrt{3}}$	-1	$-\sqrt{3}$	$-\infty$

x	$\dfrac{7\pi}{6}$	$\dfrac{5\pi}{4}$	$\dfrac{4\pi}{3}$	$\dfrac{3\pi}{2}$	$\dfrac{5\pi}{3}$	$\dfrac{7\pi}{4}$	$\dfrac{11\pi}{6}$	2π
$\cos x$	$-\dfrac{\sqrt{3}}{2}$	$-\dfrac{\sqrt{2}}{2}$	$-\dfrac{1}{2}$	0	$\dfrac{1}{2}$	$\dfrac{\sqrt{2}}{2}$	$\dfrac{\sqrt{3}}{2}$	1
$\sin x$	$-\dfrac{1}{2}$	$-\dfrac{\sqrt{2}}{2}$	$-\dfrac{\sqrt{3}}{2}$	-1	$-\dfrac{\sqrt{3}}{2}$	$-\dfrac{\sqrt{2}}{2}$	$-\dfrac{1}{2}$	0
$\tan x$	$\dfrac{1}{\sqrt{3}}$	1	$\sqrt{3}$	$-\infty$	$-\sqrt{3}$	-1	$-\dfrac{1}{\sqrt{3}}$	0
$\cot x$	$\sqrt{3}$	1	$\dfrac{1}{\sqrt{3}}$	0	$-\dfrac{1}{\sqrt{3}}$	-1	$-\sqrt{3}$	$+\infty$

The tangent is undefined for values of x for which $\cos x = 0$, i. e. for $x \in \left\{ \dfrac{\pi}{2}, \dfrac{3\pi}{2}, \ldots \dfrac{(2n-1)\pi}{2}, n \in N \right\}$. Similarly, $\cot x$ is undefined when $\sin x = 0$, i. e. for $x \in \{\pi, 2\pi, \ldots n\pi, n \in N\}$. The repetition of the values assumed by the tangent and cotangent functions suggests that the period of the function is π. You can demonstrate this by showing

$$\frac{\sin x}{\cos x} = \frac{\sin (x + \pi)}{\cos (x + \pi)}$$

and by noting that $\cot x = \dfrac{1}{\tan x}$.

The graphs are sketched below. Note that when $\tan x = 0$, $\cot x$ is undefined and vice versa.

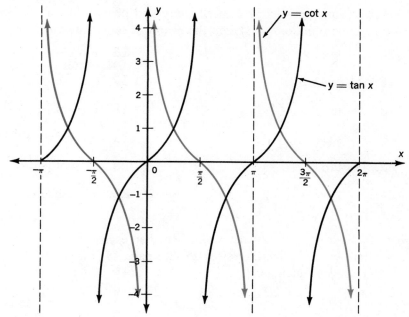

CLASSROOM EXERCISES

1. Complete the table given on pages 102-103 for the secant and cosecant functions.

2. Demonstrate that the period of tan x is π. (*Hint:* See the summary in Section 2–5.)

3. What is the period of cot x? Explain.

4. Demonstrate that the period of csc x is 2π.

5. What is the period of sec x? Explain.

WRITTEN EXERCISES

A ▬ In what quadrants does x lie if the functions have the given characteristics?

1. $\sec x \geq 1$ **2.** $\csc x \geq 1$ **3.** $\tan x > 0$

4. $\cot x > 0$ **5.** $\sec x \leq -1$ **6.** $\csc x \leq -1$

7. $\tan x < 0$ **8.** $\cot x < 0$ **9.** $\sin x < 0$

▬ State the values of x $(-2\pi \leq x \leq 2\pi)$ for which each function is undefined.

10. $\tan x$ **11.** $\cot x$ **12.** $\sec x$ **13.** $\csc x$

B ▬ Use your knowledge of periodicity and phase shift of the sine and cosine functions to sketch the graph of each function.

14. $y = \tan 2x$ **15.** $y = \cot \frac{1}{2}x$

16. $y = \sec 3x$ **17.** $y = \csc \frac{1}{3}x$

18. $y = \tan \left(x + \frac{\pi}{2}\right)$ **19.** $y = \cot \left(x - \frac{\pi}{2}\right)$

20. $y = \sec \left(x - \frac{\pi}{4}\right)$ **21.** $y = \csc \left(x + \frac{\pi}{3}\right)$

22. $y = \tan \left(2x - \frac{\pi}{2}\right)$ **23.** $y = \cot \left(\frac{1}{3}x - \frac{\pi}{2}\right)$

24. $y = \sec \left(\frac{1}{2}x + \frac{\pi}{4}\right)$ **25.** $y = \csc (3x + \pi)$

C ▬ In Exercises 26–29 determine whether each function is odd, even or neither. (See Exercises 25–26, page 75, for definitions of *odd* and *even* functions.)

26. tan   **27.** sec   **28.** cot   **29.** csc

30. How is the graph of $y = -\tan x$ related to the graph of $y = \cot\left(x + \frac{\pi}{2}\right)$? Explain your answer. (See summary, Section 2–5.)

31. How is the graph of $y = -\cot x$ related to the graph of $y = \tan\left(x + \frac{\pi}{2}\right)$? Explain.

32. Prove $|\tan x| \geq |\sin x|$, $\forall x \in R$ for which $\tan x$ is defined.

33. Prove $|\cot x| \geq |\cos x|$, $\forall x \in R$ for which $\cot x$ is defined.

34. Prove $|\sec x| \geq |\tan x|$, $\forall x \in R$ for which $\sec x$ and $\tan x$ are defined.

35. Prove $|\cot x| \leq |\csc x|$, $\forall x \in R$ for which $\cot x$ and $\csc x$ are defined.

2–10 Identities

The equation $x^2 + 3x + 2 = (x + 2)(x + 1)$ is true for *all* allowable real or complex replacements of x. An equation of this kind is called an **identity.** To emphasize that such a statement is true for all members of a given replacement set, we have used the symbol $\forall$ or the words "for all." However, $\forall$ or "for all" will not be used hereafter, as it will be assumed that statements with variables are true for all real numbers, unless otherwise stated.

Some of the identities that involve circular functions are given below.

Identities:
$$\sin^2 x + \cos^2 x = 1, \ x \in R.$$

$$\tan x = \frac{\sin x}{\cos x}, \ x \in R, \ \cos x \neq 0$$

$$\cot x = \frac{1}{\tan x}, \ x \in R, \ \tan x \neq 0$$

$$\sec x = \frac{1}{\cos x}, \ x \in R, \ \cos x \neq 0$$

$$\csc x = \frac{1}{\sin x}, \ x \in R, \ \sin x \neq 0$$

Several other identities were listed in the summary of Section 2–5.

To prove that an equation is an identity, you can manipulate *either* side of the equation until it is identical to the other side.

EXAMPLE 1. Prove $\sin^4 x - \cos^4 x = \sin^2 x - \cos^2 x$ is an identity.

Proof: Notice first that $\sin^4 x - \cos^4 x$ is the difference of two squares and consequently may be factored.

$$\sin^4 x - \cos^4 x = (\sin^2 x + \cos^2 x)(\sin^2 x - \cos^2 x)$$

Now you can use the identity $\sin^2 x + \cos^2 x = 1$.

$$\sin^4 x - \cos^4 x = (\sin^2 x + \cos^2 x)(\sin^2 x - \cos^2 x)$$
$$= 1\,(\sin^2 x - \cos^2 x)$$
$$= \sin^2 x - \cos^2 x$$

Consequently the identity is proved.

You could attack the same equation somewhat differently.

$$\sin^2 x - \cos^2 x = 1 \cdot (\sin^2 x - \cos^2 x)$$
$$= (\sin^2 x + \cos^2 x)(\sin^2 x - \cos^2 x)$$
$$= \sin^4 x - \cos^4 x.$$

EXAMPLE 2. Prove the identity $\sin x = \tan x \cdot \cos x$.

Proof:
$$\tan x \cdot \cos x = \frac{\sin x}{\cos x} \cdot \cos x$$
$$= \sin x \cdot \frac{\cos x}{\cos x}$$
$$= \sin x$$

Notice that the substitution $\frac{\cos x}{\cos x} = 1$ was made in the next-to-last step. This is permitted because you assume that the replacements for x in the original equation are exactly those for which each expression is defined. Since the original equation contains $\tan x$, you assume that $\cos x \neq 0$. In that case, $\frac{\cos x}{\cos x}$ is equal to 1.

EXAMPLE 3. Prove the identity $1 + \cot^2 x = \csc^2 x$.

Proof:
$$1 + \cot^2 x = 1 + \frac{\cos^2 x}{\sin^2 x}$$
$$= \frac{\sin^2 x}{\sin^2 x} + \frac{\cos^2 x}{\sin^2 x}$$
$$= \frac{\sin^2 x + \cos^2 x}{\sin^2 x}$$
$$= \frac{1}{\sin^2 x}$$
$$= \csc^2 x.$$

EXAMPLE 4. Express $\cos x$ in terms of $\sin x$.

Solution: Start with $\sin^2 x + \cos^2 x = 1$, and rewrite it as $\cos^2 x = 1 - \sin^2 x$. Since $\cos x > 0$ for x in Quadrants I and IV, and $\cos x < 0$ for x in Quadrants II and III,

$$\cos x = \sqrt{1 - \sin^2 x}, \qquad x \text{ in Quadrants I and IV}$$

and

$$\cos x = -\sqrt{1 - \sin^2 x}, \quad x \text{ in Quadrants II and III.}$$

EXAMPLE 5. Prove the identity $\dfrac{\csc x}{1 - \csc x} = \dfrac{\sec x}{\tan x - \sec x}$.

Solution: The procedure used to prove this identity is somewhat different from that illustrated previously. The tactic is to change both the left side and the right side to the same expression.

Left side	**Right side**
$\dfrac{\csc x}{1 - \csc x} = \dfrac{\dfrac{1}{\sin x}}{1 - \dfrac{1}{\sin x}}$	$\dfrac{\sec x}{\tan x - \sec x} = \dfrac{\dfrac{1}{\cos x}}{\dfrac{\sin x}{\cos x} - \dfrac{1}{\cos x}}$
$= \dfrac{\dfrac{1}{\sin x}}{\dfrac{\sin x - 1}{\sin x}}$	$= \dfrac{1}{\sin x - 1}$
$= \dfrac{1}{\sin x - 1}$	

Consequently, $\dfrac{\csc x}{1 - \csc x} = \dfrac{\sec x}{\tan x - \sec x}$

CLASSROOM EXERCISES

▬ Write an equivalent expression in terms of $\sin x$, $\cos x$, or both.

1. $\sec x$ **2.** $\csc x$ **3.** $\cot x$ **4.** $\dfrac{\tan x}{\csc x}$

▬ Write an equivalent expression in terms of $\sec x$, $\csc x$, or both.

5. $\dfrac{1}{\cos x}$ **6.** $\dfrac{1}{\sin x}$ **7.** $1 + \tan^2 x$ **8.** $\dfrac{1 + \cot^2 x}{\cos^2 x}$

WRITTEN EXERCISES

A ▬ Prove that each of the following equations is an identity.

1. $\tan x = \sin x \cdot \sec x$ **2.** $\cot x = \cos x \cdot \csc x$

3. $\cot^2 x = \csc^2 x - 1$ **4.** $1 + \tan^2 x = \sec^2 x$

5. $\tan^2 x = \dfrac{1 - \cos^2 x}{\cos^2 x}$ **6.** $\sec^2 x = \dfrac{\sin^2 x + \cos^2 x}{\cos^2 x}$

Prove that each of the following equations is an identity.

7. $\csc^4 x - \cot^4 x = \csc^2 x + \cot^2 x$

8. $\sec^4 x - \tan^4 x = \tan^2 x + \sec^2 x$

9. $(1 - \tan x)^2 = \sec^2 x - 2 \tan x$

10. $(1 - \sin^2 x)(1 + \tan^2 x) = 1$

11. $\dfrac{\cos^2 x}{\sin x} + \sin x = \csc x$

12. $\tan x + \cot x = \sec x \cdot \csc x$

13. $\dfrac{\tan x}{1 - \cos^2 x} = \sec x \cdot \csc x$

14. $\dfrac{\cot x}{\cos x} + \dfrac{\sec x}{\cot x} = \sec^2 x \cdot \csc x$

15. $2 \sin^2 x - 1 = 1 - 2 \cos^2 x$

16. $\csc x = \dfrac{\cot x}{\cos x}$

B **17.** Express $\tan x$ in terms of

    a. $\sin x$ **b.** $\cos x$ **c.** $\sec x$

18. Express $\cos x$ in terms of

    a. $\sin x$ **b.** $\tan x$ **c.** $\sec x$

19. Express $\cot x$ in terms of

    a. $\cos x$ **b.** $\tan x$

20. Express $\sin x$ in terms of

    a. $\cos x$ **b.** $\sec x$

In Exercises 21–32 change the first expression into the second.

21. $\dfrac{\cos x - \sin x}{\cos x}$, $1 - \tan x$

22. $\dfrac{1 + \sin x - \sin^2 x}{\cos x}$, $\cos x + \tan x$

23. $\tan x (\tan x + \cot x)$, $\sec^2 x$

24. $(\sec x - \tan x)(\sec x + \tan x)$, $\sin^2 x + \cos^2 x$

C **25.** $\dfrac{\cos x + 1}{\sin^3 x}$, $\dfrac{\csc x}{1 - \cos x}$

26. $\dfrac{\sin x}{1 - \cos x}$, $\csc x + \cot x$

27. $\dfrac{\tan x}{\sec x} + \dfrac{\cot x}{\csc x}$, $\sin x + \cos x$

28. $\dfrac{\sin x}{\csc x - 1} + \dfrac{\sin x}{\csc x + 1}$, $2 \tan^2 x$

29. $\dfrac{\sin^3 x + \cos^3 x}{1 - 2 \cos^2 x}$, $\dfrac{\sec x - \sin x}{\tan x - 1}$

30. $\dfrac{1 - 2 \sin x - 3 \sin^2 x}{\cos^2 x}$, $\dfrac{1 - 3 \sin x}{1 - \sin x}$

BASIC: TRIGONOMETRIC GRAPHS

Each microcomputer displays graphics in different ways, and uses different programming. The sample program below is for an Apple II microcomputer.

Problem:

Write a program that displays a pair of coordinate axes and the graph of $\sin x$ for $x \in [-2\pi, 2\pi]$.

```
100 REM    THIS PROGRAM GRAPHS CIRCULAR FUNCTIONS.
110 REM    TO CHANGE THE FUNCTION, RETYPE LINE 160.
120 REM
150 HOME
160 DEF FN T(X) = SIN(X)
170 HGR
180 HCOLOR = 3
190 HPLOT 0,80 TO 279,80
200 HPLOT 140,0 TO 140,159
210 FOR I = 20 TO 279 STEP 20
220 HPLOT I,78 TO I,82
230 NEXT I
240 FOR I = 0 TO 159 STEP 20
250 HPLOT 138,I TO 142,I
260 NEXT I
270 LET S = 7
280 FOR X = -140 TO 139
290 IF X = 0 THEN 340
300 LET Z = X * S / 140
310 LET Y = FN T(Z) * 140 / S
320 IF Y > 80 OR Y < -81 THEN 340
330 HPLOT X + 140, 80 - Y
340 NEXT X
350 END
```

Output:

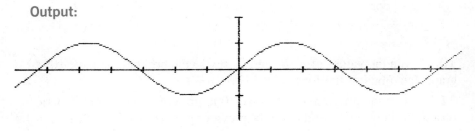

Change statement 160 to: 160 DEF FN T(X) = TAN(X)

Output:

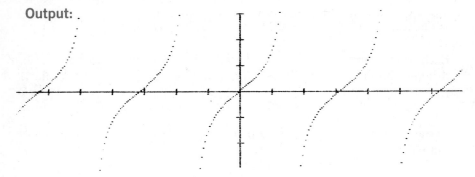

Analysis:

Statements 190–260: These statements draw the coordinate axes.

Statement 270: S is a scale factor for converting from the x–y scale to the number of dots in high–resolution graphics on the screen. Twenty screen dots represent one unit on each axis.

Statements 280–340: This loop graphs the function. Statement 290 permits inverse functions to be graphed. Statement 300 changes x into an appropriate radian measure between -7 and 7. Statement 320 causes the machine to skip y values that would be out of the range of values that fit on the screen. Finally, statement 330 plots the point on axes that are centered at $(140, 80)$ on the built–in high–resolution coordinate system. NOTE: When the program ends, the graph remains on the screen. To regain the cursor and change the function, press the RESET key.

EXERCISES

A   Use the program on page 109 to graph each function on the interval $[-2\pi, 2\pi]$.   (NOTE: The only trigonometric functions available in BASIC are sine (SIN), cosine (COS), and tangent (TAN).)

1. $y = 3 \sin x$ 2. $y = \csc x$ 3. $y = \cot x$
4. $y = \frac{1}{2} \cos x$ 5. $y = \frac{1}{5} \tan x$ 6. $y = \sin x + 2$
7. $y = -2 \sin x + 1$ 8. $y = -5 \sin x$ 9. $y = 3 \cos (x + 1) - 1$

B

10. Given the values of A, B, and C, revise the program on page 109 to graph functions of the form $y = A \sin (Bx + C)$.

11. Revise the program in Exercise 10 to graph more than one function on a single coordinate system. (The previous graph remains on the screen.)

CHAPTER SUMMARY

Important Terms

Amplitude (p. 88)
Circular function (p. 72)
Cosecant (p. 100)
Cosine function (p. 72)
Cotangent (p. 100)
Distance formula (p. 66)
Frequency (p. 94)
Greatest lower bound (p. 88)
Identity (p. 105)
Least upper bound (p. 88)

Lower bound (p. 88)
Periodic function (p. 85)
Phase shift (p. 95)
Reciprocal functions (p. 100)
Secant (p. 100)
Sine function (p. 72)
Tangent (p. 100)
Unit circle (p. 68)
Upper bound (p. 88)
Wrapping function (p. 69)

Important Ideas

1. For sine and cosine functions of the form $y = A$ trig $(Bx + C)$ the amplitude is $|A|$, the period is $\left|\frac{2\pi}{B}\right|$, and the phase shift is $-\frac{C}{B}$.

2. Trigonometric Identities: See Section 2–5 (pages 79–83) and Section 2–10 (pages 105–108).

3. To solve a trigonometric identity, transform one or the other sides of the equality so that both sides are identical.

CHAPTER OBJECTIVES AND REVIEW

Objective: *To state the distance formula and to use it to find the distance between two points.* (Section 2-1)

1. If $A(5, 3)$ and $B(-2, 7)$, find AB.

2. If $P(s, t)$ and $Q(u, v)$ are two points, what is PQ?

▬ Find the distance between the given points.

3. $A(-2, -5)$, $B(1, -7)$

4. $R(-3, \frac{1}{2})$, $S(\frac{1}{2}, -3)$

5. $M(-7, 5)$, $N(-7, -10)$

6. $U(\frac{1}{2}\sqrt{2}, \frac{1}{2}\sqrt{2})$, $V(0, 1)$

7. $A(1, 3)$, $B(6, 2)$, $C(8, 5)$, $D(3, 6)$ are the vertices of a quadrilateral. What kind of a quadrilateral is it? Explain.

Objective: *To apply the wrapping function.* (Section 2-2)

 In Exercises 8–11, suppose that W is the wrapping function that maps the given real number onto a point P of the unit circle. In which of the four quadrants does P lie? ($\pi \approx 3.142$)

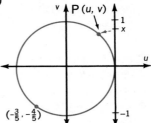

8. 2   **9.** -2

10. $\frac{2\pi}{3}$ **11.** -6

Let $W: x \rightarrow (-\frac{3}{5}, -\frac{4}{5})$. Find each of the following.

12. $W(x + 2\pi)$ **13.** $W(x + \pi)$

14. $W(-x)$ **15.** $W(-x + \pi)$

Objective: *To use the unit circle and the wrapping function to determine the sine or cosine of a number.* (Section 2-3)

Use the given circular function (sine or cosine) and the given quadrant to find the other circular function.

16. $\sin x = \frac{5}{13}$, x in Quadrant II

17. $\cos x = -\frac{4}{5}$, x in Quadrant III

Use the unit circle to find the following.

18. $\cos 3\pi$ **19.** $\sin \left(-\frac{3\pi}{2}\right)$

20. $\sin (-\pi)$ **21.** $\cos \frac{\pi}{2}$

Objective: *To use the theorems on the sine and cosine functions.* (Section 2-4 and Section 2-5)

22. If $\cos (-x) = 0.6$ and $0 < x < \pi$, find $\cos x$ and $\sin x$.

23. If $\sin (\pi + x) = -\frac{5}{13}$ and $-\frac{\pi}{2} < x < \frac{\pi}{2}$, find $\sin x$ and $\cos x$.

Objective: *To sketch the graphs of the sine and cosine functions.* (Section 2-6)

Sketch the graph of each function for the given interval.

24. $y = \sin x$, $[0, 2\pi]$ **25.** $y = \cos x$, $[-\pi, \pi]$

26. $y = \sin x$, $\left[-\frac{3\pi}{2}, \frac{\pi}{2}\right]$ **27.** $y = \cos x$, $\left[-\frac{7\pi}{2}, 0\right]$

Objective: *Given an equation $y = A \sin (Bx + C)$ or $y = A \cos (Bx + C)$, to determine* **a.** *the amplitude,* **b.** *the period, and* **c.** *the phase shift and be able to sketch the graph.* (Section 2-7 and Section 2-8)

▬▬▬ Find the amplitude, period and phase shift of each function. Sketch the graph.

28. $y = -3 \sin x$ **29.** $y = \frac{1}{2} \cos x$

30. $y = 2 \sin (4x)$ **31.** $y = -4 \cos (-2x)$

32. $y = \frac{1}{2} \sin \left(x - \frac{\pi}{2}\right)$ **33.** $y = 3 \cos (x + \pi)$

34. $y = \frac{5}{2} \sin \left(2x - \frac{\pi}{2}\right)$ **35.** $y = -2 \cos (4x + \pi)$

36. Given $y = A \sin (Bx + C)$, identify the following.
  a. amplitude
  b. period
  c. phase shift

Objective: *To sketch the tangent, cotangent, secant, and cosecant functions and to use these functions.* (Section 2-9)

▬▬▬ Sketch the graph of each function.

37. $y = \tan x$ **38.** $y = \cot x$

39. $y = \csc x$ **40.** $y = \sec x$

▬▬▬ Use the given information to find $\tan x$ and $\sec x$.

41. $\cos x = \frac{3}{5}$ $\left(0 < x < \frac{\pi}{2}\right)$

42. $\cot x = \frac{5}{12}$ $(\pi < x < 2\pi)$

Objective: *To prove trigonometric identities.* (Section 2-10)

▬▬▬ Prove that each equation is an identity.

43. $\sin^2 x = \dfrac{\sec^2 x - 1}{\sec^2 x}$

44. $\tan x = \cos x \cdot \sin x \cdot (1 + \tan^2 x)$

45. $\sec x + \tan x = (1 + \sin x)\sec x$

46. $(1 - \cot x)^2 = \csc^2 x - 2 \cot x$

47. $\tan (-x) = - \tan x$

48. $\sec (-x) = \sec x$

CHAPTER TEST

1. Find the lengths of the sides of $\triangle ABC$ where $A(2, 5)$, $B(-3, -2)$, $C(-1, 6)$.

2. $\sin 0.48 \approx 0.4617$. Find

    a. $\sin(-0.48)$ **b.** $\cos\left(\frac{\pi}{2} + 0.48\right)$ **c.** $\cos(0.48)$

3. Compute $\sin\frac{\pi}{3} \cdot \cos\frac{\pi}{6}$.

4. Sketch a graph of

    a. $y = \sin x$ $0 \le x \le 4\pi$

    b. $y = \cos x$ $0 \le x \le 4\pi$

5. In your own words define a periodic function and the period of a periodic function.

6. What is the period of $y = \sin Bx$? of $y = \cos Bx$?

7. a. What is the amplitude of a function?

    b. What is the amplitude of $y = A \sin x$? of $y = A \cos x$?

8. Sketch a graph of $y = 2 \sin 4x$.

9. Sketch the graph of $y = -2 \cos\left(2x - \frac{\pi}{2}\right)$.

10. Sketch the graph of $y = \tan x$, $0 \le x \le 2\pi$.

11. For $0 \le x \le 2\pi$ what is the range of

    a. $y = \sec x$?   **b.** $y = \csc x$?   **c.** $y = \cot x$?

12. Using $\sin^2 x + \cos^2 x = 1$ and the definitions of $\tan x$, $\cot x$, $\sec x$ and $\csc x$ find expressions for the following.

    a. $\tan^2 x$ in terms of $\sec x$.

    b. $\cot^2 x$ in terms of $\csc x$.

    c. $\sec^2 x$ in terms of $\sin x$ and $\cos x$.

    d. $\csc^2 x$ in terms of $\sin x$ and $\cos x$.

CHAPTER **3** Trigonometry

Sections

Features

Review and Testing

3–1   Angles and Rotation

In geometry an angle was defined as the union of two rays with a common endpoint. This definition met the needs of geometry. Now, however, a more general definition is needed.

Think of a ray in a plane and imagine that this ray is rotated about its endpoint to some position in the same plane. The result is an **angle**. The point is the **vertex** of the angle, the initial position of the rotating ray is the **initial side** of the angle, and the final position of the ray is the **terminal side** of the angle. See Figure 1.

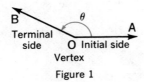

Figure 1

The curved arrow, shown in color, indicates the magnitude and direction of rotation in moving counterclockwise from $\overrightarrow{OA}$ to $\overrightarrow{OB}$. The Greek letter θ (theta) represents the magnitude and direction of rotation and is the measure of the angle.

If the ray does not rotate at all, as in Figure 2, the initial side and terminal side of the angle coincide, and the measure of the angle is 0°. If the ray makes one complete rotation in the counterclockwise direction, as in Figure 3, again the initial and terminal sides coincide, but the measure of the angle is 360°.

Figure 2   Figure 3

If the ray completes more than one complete counterclockwise rotation, the measure of the angle is greater than 360°.

A ray can be rotated in either a counterclockwise or clockwise direction to form an angle with any real number measure.

> **The measure of an angle formed by a counterclockwise rotation is indicated by a positive number.**
> **The measure of an angle formed by a clockwise rotation is indicated by a negative number.**

Thus $m\angle AOB$ is 45° while $m\angle CDE$ is −45° in the figure below.

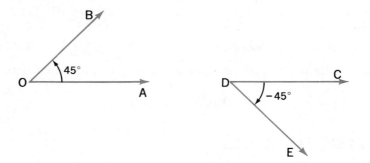

When the vertex of an angle is at the origin of a coordinate system and its initial side coincides with the positive x axis, the angle is in **standard position.** Angle AOB in the figure at the right is in standard position.

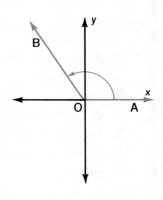

For such an angle, there are eight possible ways for the terminal side to lie. The terminal side may coincide with either the positive or negative x or y axis. This accounts for four of the possibilities. In these cases the angle is called a **quadrantal angle.** The other four possibilities are for the terminal side to lie in one of the four quadrants. An angle in standard position is said to be *in* the quadrant in which its terminal side lies. Angle AOB above is in quadrant II.

Suppose $P(x, y)$ is a point in one of the four quadrants. Then the positive x axis and the ray $\overrightarrow{OP}$ determine an angle with positive measure. If θ is the measure of $\angle AOP$ such that $0 \le \theta < 360°$, then $\theta + n \cdot 360°$, $n \in W$, is the measure of an angle in standard position with terminal side $\overrightarrow{OP}$ for each n. Angles with the same terminal side are said to be **coterminal angles.** Notice that there are also infinitely many coterminal angles with terminal side $\overrightarrow{OP}$ and having negative measures. What is an expression for the measure of these angles?

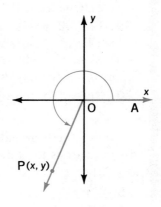

CLASSROOM EXERCISES

━━ Find the smallest positive angle that is coterminal with each angle.

1. 860°   **2.** 980°   **3.** 715°   **4.** 2453°

━━ Name the largest negative angle that is coterminal with each angle.

5. 225°   **6.** −860°   **7.** 12°   **8.** −715°

WRITTEN EXERCISES

A ━━ Sketch an angle AOB in standard position, with $\overrightarrow{OB}$ horizontal, that results from the following rotations. Determine the measure of each. ("$\frac{1}{3}$ clockwise" denotes $\frac{1}{3}$ of a complete revolution.)

1. $\frac{1}{4}$ counterclockwise   **2.** $\frac{1}{2}$ counterclockwise
3. $\frac{3}{4}$ counterclockwise   **4.** 1 counterclockwise
5. $\frac{1}{4}$ clockwise   **6.** $\frac{1}{2}$ clockwise
7. $\frac{1}{6}$ clockwise   **8.** $\frac{1}{8}$ counterclockwise
9. $\frac{5}{12}$ counterclockwise   **10.** $\frac{3}{10}$ clockwise
11. $\frac{4}{5}$ counterclockwise   **12.** $\frac{3}{2}$ clockwise
13. $\frac{17}{12}$ counterclockwise   **14.** $\frac{7}{6}$ clockwise
15. $\frac{2}{3}$ clockwise   **16.** $\frac{4}{3}$ counterclockwise

17. Let θ, $0° < \theta < 360°$, be the measure of $\angle AOB$ in standard position. What is the measure of one negative coterminal angle?

18. Let θ, $0° < \theta < 360°$, be the measure of $\angle AOB$ in standard position. What are the limits on θ if the terminal side lies in

a. Quadrant I   **b.** Quadrant II
c. Quadrant III   **d.** Quadrant IV

19. For all angles in standard position with measure $\theta > 0°$ which lie in Quadrant I, θ is between $n \cdot 360°$ and $90° + n \cdot 360°$, $n \in W$ or $n \cdot 360° < \theta < 90° + n \cdot 360°$, $n \in W$. Find similar expressions for angles in Quadrants II, III, and IV.

20. Repeat Exercise 19 for $\theta < 0°$.

━━ Use your results for Exercises 19 and 20 to find the quadrant in which the terminal side of an angle in standard position lies if its measure is the following.

21. 41°   **22.** −420°   **23.** 1000°   **24.** −290°
25. 451°   **26.** −539°   **27.** −2000°   **28.** 181°
29. 359°   **30.** −719°   **31.** 495°   **32.** 380°

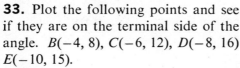

■ The angle at the right is in standard position. Its terminal side contains the point $A(-2, 4)$.

33. Plot the following points and see if they are on the terminal side of the angle. $B(-4, 8)$, $C(-6, 12)$, $D(-8, 16)$ $E(-10, 15)$.

34. Use the distance formula to find the measure of $\overline{AO}$, $\overline{BO}$, $\overline{CO}$ and $\overline{DO}$.

35. Let r represent in turn the distance from each of A, B, C, and D to O. Find $\frac{x}{r}$, $\frac{y}{r}$, and $\frac{y}{x}$ for each point.

36. For any point $P(x, y)$ on the terminal side of the angle, what is the value of $\frac{x}{r}$, $\frac{y}{r}$, $\frac{y}{x}$?

3–2 Angles Measured in Radians

It is often convenient in mathematics to use a unit of angular measure called a **radian**. An angle of one radian, that is the unit angle for radian measure, is an angle with its vertex at the center of a circle that subtends an arc of the circle the same length as the radius of the circle. In the figure at right, the radius of the circle is r, $(OA = OB = r)$, and the length of arc AB, shown in color, is r. Thus the radian measure of $\angle AOB$ is 1 radian.

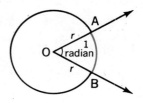

EXAMPLE 1. Suppose $\overset{\frown}{AB}$ measures 7 units and the radius r of circle O is 3 units. What is the radian measure of $\angle AOB$?

Solution:

The radius of the circle is 3. For every 3 units of arc length, an angle of one radian is determined. Since $\overset{\frown}{AB}$ has length 7, the angle AOB has measure $\frac{7}{3}$ or $2\frac{1}{3}$ radians.

Definition   A **radian** is the measure of an angle that intercepts an arc equal in length to the radius of a circle whose center is the vertex of the angle.

EXAMPLE 2. How many radians are there in one complete revolution of a ray?

Solution:

Let the ray be $\overrightarrow{OA}$ and consider a circle of radius r with center O. Since $\overrightarrow{OA}$ has made one complete revolution about O, the arc intercepted by the angle is the circle. The measure of the distance around the circle is $C = 2\pi r$. To find the number of radians in $2\pi r$ units of arc, you divide by r. Why? Consequently there are 2π radians in one revolution of a ray.

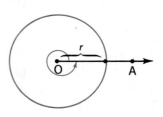

In Example 2 you found there were 2π radians in one counterclockwise revolution of a ray. In degrees, the same angle measures 360°. Thus

$$2\pi \text{ radians} = 360° \qquad \qquad 1$$

or

$$\pi \text{ radians} = 180° \qquad \qquad 2$$

Equation 2 is used to find the number of radians in one degree and the number of degrees in one radian. Dividing each member of 2 by 180, you find

$$1° = \frac{\pi}{180}. \qquad \qquad 3$$

Similarly

$$1 \text{ radian} = \frac{180°}{\pi} \qquad \qquad 4$$

Consequently

$$1° \approx 0.0174533 \text{ radians}$$

and

$$1 \text{ radian} \approx 57° \; 17' \; 44.8''$$

In indicating the measure of an angle you should feel free to use either degrees or radians. In writing 25 degrees you should use the degree symbol, °; for example, 25°. When writing the measure of an angle in radians, no additional symbol is required. For example, if $m\angle A = 1.5$, then the 1.5 is interpreted to be 1.5 radians.

Notice that the rotation of a ray needed to produce an angle measuring 3° is significantly less than that needed to produce an angle of 3 (radians).

EXAMPLE 3. Find the approximate number of

a. radians in 3° b. degrees in 3 radians

Solutions:

a. From Example 2

$$1° = \frac{\pi}{180}$$

$$3° = \frac{3\pi}{180} = \frac{\pi}{60}$$

b. From Example 2

$$1 \text{ radian} = \frac{180°}{\pi}$$

$$3 \text{ radians} = \frac{3 \cdot 180°}{\pi} = \frac{540°}{\pi}$$

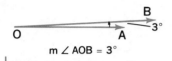
m ∠ AOB = 3°

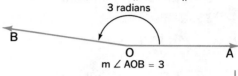
3 radians
m ∠ AOB = 3

CLASSROOM EXERCISES

━━━ Change the following degree measures to radian measures. (Leave results in terms of π.)

1. 45° **2.** 30° **3.** 105° **4.** 120°

5. −60° **6.** −120° **7.** −45° **8.** −270°

━━━ Change the following radian measures to degree measures.

9. 3π **10.** $\frac{5\pi}{6}$ **11.** 2 **12.** 6

13. -4π **14.** $-\frac{3\pi}{4}$ **15.** $-\frac{5\pi}{3}$ **16.** $-\frac{7\pi}{4}$

WRITTEN EXERCISES

A ━━━ Change each degree measure to radian measure. (Leave results in terms of π.)

1. 60° **2.** 90° **3.** −180° **4.** 270°

5. −30° **6.** −72° **7.** 135° **8.** −75°

9. 330° **10.** 495° **11.** −210° **12.** −690°

━━━ Change each radian measure to a degree measure.

13. $\frac{\pi}{6}$ **14.** $\frac{\pi}{3}$ **15.** $\frac{\pi}{2}$ **16.** $-\frac{3\pi}{2}$

17. $-\frac{4\pi}{3}$ **18.** $\frac{11\pi}{6}$ **19.** $-\frac{4\pi}{5}$ **20.** $\frac{5\pi}{12}$

21. -3π **22.** $\frac{4\pi}{3}$ **23.** $\frac{17\pi}{5}$ **24.** −4

25. −1 **26.** −7 **27.** $\frac{13\pi}{2}$ **28.** 6

B **29.** What part of a revolution does the minute hand of a clock make in 6 minutes?

30. Through how many degrees does the minute hand of a clock rotate in 6 minutes?

31. Through how many radians does the minute hand of a clock rotate in 6 minutes?

32. If the minute hand of a clock is 4 centimeters long, how far does the tip travel in 6 minutes?

33. Repeat Exercises 29–32 for the following.

a. 15 minutes   **b.** 32 minutes
c. 45 minutes   **d.** 50 minutes

34. Assume the hour hand of a clock is two centimeters long. What part of a revolution does it make in 6 minutes?

35. Through how many degrees does the hour hand of the clock in Exercise 34 rotate in 6 minutes?

36. Through how many radians does the hour hand of the clock in Exercise 34 rotate in 6 minutes?

37. How far does the tip of the hour hand in Exercise 34 travel in 6 minutes?

38. How far will a fly sitting on the outer rim of a wheel travel in one minute if the wheel has a radius of 1 foot and is turning at 10 revolutions per second?

39. The radius of a wheel of a car is 12 inches. Find the number of revolutions the wheel makes in 1 second if the car is traveling 60 mph (60 mph = 88 ft/sec).

40. Repeat Exercise 39 when the radius of the wheel of the car is 10 inches.

C **41.** Let O be the center of a circle of radius r. If $\angle AOB$ intercepts an arc s units long, what is the radian measure of $\angle AOB$?

42. A plane region bounded by an arc of a circle and the sides of a central angle is a *circular sector*. Given a circle with radius r intercepting an arc of measure s, derive a formula for the area K of a circular sector in terms of r and s.

43. Write a definition of "degree" similar to that given for radian.

44. David said to his classmate Brian that a radian and a degree were each measures of angles. Is David right? Explain your position.

3-3 The Trigonometric Functions

Let $P(x, y)$ be r units, $r \neq 0$, from the origin on the terminal side of an angle in standard position. Let θ indicate the measure of the angle. By the distance formula, $r = \sqrt{x^2 + y^2}$. For a given angle of measure θ the ratios $\frac{x}{r}$, $\frac{y}{r}$, and $\frac{y}{x}$ are independent of the point $P(x, y)$. These ratios are three basic relationships of **trigonometry.** The distance $r = \sqrt{x^2 + y^2}$ is the measure of the **radius vector** of the point P. The triangle formed by drawing a perpendicular from P to the x axis is called a **reference triangle.**

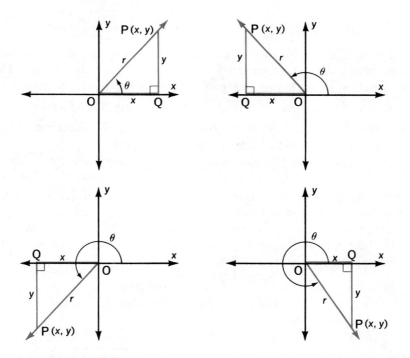

For any angle with measure θ and point $P(x, y)$ on its terminal side you have the following definitions.

sine θ (abbreviated sin θ) $= \dfrac{y}{r}$, $r = \sqrt{x^2 + y^2}$

cosine θ (abbreviated cos θ) $= \dfrac{x}{r}$, $r = \sqrt{x^2 + y^2}$

tangent θ (abbreviated tan θ) $= \dfrac{y}{x}$, $x \neq 0$

You can easily demonstrate that the sine, cosine and tangent ratios are constant for a given angle of measure θ.

In the figure $m\angle POQ = \theta$ and $P_1(x_1, y_1)$, $P_2(x_2, y_2)$, and $P_3(x_3, y_3)$ are points on the terminal side of $\angle POQ$. The triangles P_1OQ_1, P_2OQ_2, and P_3OQ_3 are similar. (Why?) Since the corresponding sides of similar triangles are proportional, you can state the following.

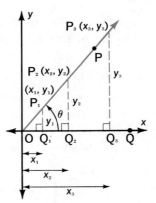

$$\sin \theta = \frac{y_1}{r_1} = \frac{y_2}{r_2} = \frac{y_3}{r_3}$$

$$\cos \theta = \frac{x_1}{r_1} = \frac{x_2}{r_2} = \frac{x_3}{r_3}$$

$$\tan \theta = \frac{y_1}{x_1} = \frac{y_2}{x_2} = \frac{y_3}{x_3}$$

For a given angle with measure θ, $\sin \theta$ has one and only one value; hence the set of ordered pairs $(\theta, \sin \theta)$ is a function. The first member of each ordered pair is the measure of an angle, the second member is the ratio $\frac{y}{r}$. Similar reasoning allows you to conclude that the cosine and tangent relations are also functions. Each of these functions is called a **trigonometric function.**

The domains of the sine and cosine functions are measures of angles, and these measures may be any real number. Therefore the domain of the sine and cosine functions is the set of real numbers. The domain of the tangent function is a subset of the real numbers, for certain members must be excluded. These excluded real numbers are the measures of angles whose terminal sides coincide with the positive or negative y axis. Explain why.

EXAMPLE 1. Sketch the angle whose terminal side contains the point $P(-5, -12)$. In which quadrant is the angle? Use the reference triangle to find the sine, cosine, and tangent of θ where θ is the measure of the angle.

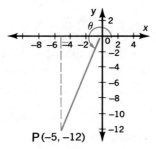

Solution: See the figure.
θ lies in Quadrant III.

$$r = \sqrt{(-5)^2 + (-12)^2}$$
$$= \sqrt{25 + 144}$$
$$= \sqrt{169} = 13.$$

$\sin \theta = \frac{y}{r} = -\frac{12}{13}$; $\quad \cos \theta = \frac{x}{r} = -\frac{5}{13}$; $\quad \tan \theta = \frac{y}{x} = \frac{12}{5}$

EXAMPLE 2. Given $\sin \theta = \frac{1}{2}$, θ in Quadrant I. Find $\cos \theta$, $\tan \theta$.

Solution: $\sin \theta = \frac{y}{r}$ and $r = \sqrt{x^2 + y^2}$ ⟵ **Definitions**

$2 = \sqrt{x^2 + 1}$ ⟵ **$r = 2, y = 1$**

$4 = x^2 + 1$ ⟵ **Square both sides.**

$3 = x^2$

Thus $x = \pm \sqrt{3}$. But since θ is in Quadrant I, $x > 0$. Thus $x = \sqrt{3}$.

$\text{Cos } \theta = \frac{\sqrt{3}}{2}$, $\tan \theta = \frac{1}{\sqrt{3}} = \frac{\sqrt{3}}{3}$.

Since the ratios $\frac{y}{r}$, $\frac{x}{r}$, $\frac{y}{x}$, $x \neq 0$ are constant for each angle in standard position, so are their reciprocals when they are defined. The reciprocals of these ratios are three other trigonometric functions for any angle with measure θ and point $P(x, y)$ in its terminal side.

---

cosecant θ (abbreviated csc θ) $= \frac{r}{y}$, $y \neq 0$

secant θ (abbreviated sec θ) $= \frac{r}{x}$, $x \neq 0$

cotangent θ (abbreviated cot θ) $= \frac{x}{y}$, $y \neq 0$

EXAMPLE 3. Let $P(2, -3)$ be a point on the terminal side of an angle in standard position which has measure θ. Find the values of the six trigonometric functions. In what quadrant does θ lie?

Solution: $x = 2$ and $y = -3$

$r = \sqrt{2^2 + (-3)^2} = \sqrt{4 + 9} = \sqrt{13}$ ⟵ **By the distance formula**

Thus $\sin \theta = -\frac{3}{\sqrt{13}}$, $\cos \theta = \frac{2}{\sqrt{13}}$, $\tan \theta = -\frac{3}{2}$

$\csc \theta = -\frac{\sqrt{13}}{3}$, $\sec \theta = \frac{\sqrt{13}}{2}$, $\cot \theta = -\frac{2}{3}$

$P(2, -3)$ is in Quadrant IV.
Thus, the angle is in Quadrant IV.
The angle is graphed at the right.
      What quadrant would $P(2, 3)$ be in?
What quadrant would $P(-2, 3)$ be in?
$P(-2, -3)$?

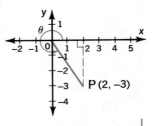

CLASSROOM EXERCISES

━━ Find the values of the six trigonometric functions for the given points.

1. $P(2, 5)$ 2. $P(-3, 5)$ 3. $P(-1, -2)$ 4. $P(1, -5)$
5. $P(1, -\frac{1}{2})$ 6. $P(0, 1)$ 7. $P(-3, 0)$ 8. $P(2, -1)$

WRITTEN EXERCISES

A ━━ Find the six trigonometric functions of θ when θ is the measure of an angle in standard position whose terminal side contains the given point. Leave answers in radical form when radicals occur.

1. $(5, 3)$ 2. $(-5, 3)$
3. $(-5, -3)$ 4. $(5, -3)$
5. $(1, -8)$ 6. $(3, 4)$
7. $(-6, 8)$ 8. $(-1, -2)$
9. $(0, 4)$ 10. $(-3, 0)$
11. $(2, 0)$ 12. $(0, -1)$
13. $(12, 5)$ 14. $(1, -3)$
15. $(-\sqrt{2}, \sqrt{2})$ 16. $(-\sqrt{3}, -1)$

B ━━ Find the five other trigonometric functions of θ when the terminal side of the angle is in the indicated quadrant.

17. $\tan \theta = \frac{2}{5}$ θ is in Quadrant I.
18. $\sin \theta = \frac{2}{3}$ θ is in Quadrant II.
19. $\cos \theta = \frac{\sqrt{3}}{2}$ θ is in Quadrant IV.
20. $\tan \theta = 1$ θ is in Quadrant III.
21. $\sin \theta = -\frac{5}{13}$ θ is in Quadrant IV.
22. $\cos \theta = -\frac{5}{13}$ θ is in Quadrant III.
23. $\cos \theta = -\frac{2}{5}$ θ is in Quadrant II.
24. $\sin \theta = \frac{1}{5}$ θ is in Quadrant I.

25. Make a table showing the sign of the trigonometric functions sine, cosine, and tangent when θ is in Quadrant I, II, III, or IV.

26. $\sin \theta = \frac{u}{v}$, θ is in Quadrant II. Find the trigonometric functions $\tan \theta$ and $\cos \theta$ in terms of u and v.

27. $\tan \theta = \frac{u}{v}$, θ is in Quadrant III. Find the trigonometric functions $\sin \theta$ and $\cos \theta$ in terms of u and v.

28. $\cos \theta = \frac{u}{v}$, θ is in Quadrant IV. Find the trigonometric functions $\sin \theta$ and $\tan \theta$ in terms of u and v.

Applying Trigonometry
Electrical Engineering

In the figure at the right, copper wire coiled around an armature is rotating through a magnetic field. When it is rotating at a constant rate, or angular velocity, ω, an **electromotive force**, or **emf**, is created. The amount, E, of this force is often of interest to **electrical engineers**, and can be expressed as a function of time t (in seconds) by the formula,

$$E = E_m \sin \omega t, \ t \geq 0,$$

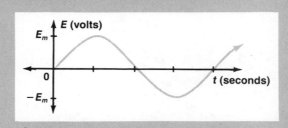

where E_m is the maximum emf. The unit of measure for E is the **volt**. This formula is an example of the formula $y = A \sin B(t - C)$, with E_m and ω used, respectively instead of A and B. E_m and ω are positive numbers and the phase shift, C, is taken to be 0.

The number of rotations, or cycles, that the coil completes in one second is the **frequency** of the alternating emf. The frequency is given by

$$f = \frac{\omega}{2\pi} \text{ cycles per second.}$$

A graph of emf as a function of time is shown below.

EXAMPLE 1. A wire cord rotates counterclockwise through a magnetic field and is described by the equation

$$E = 100 \sin 250 \pi t.$$

a. Find the frequency of rotation

b. Find E when $t = 0.001$ sec

Solutions:

a. $f = \frac{\omega}{2\pi}$

$= \frac{250\pi}{2\pi}$

$= 125$ cycles per second

b. $E = 100 \sin 250 \pi (0.001)$

$= 100 \sin 0.25 \pi$

$= 100 \frac{\sqrt{2}}{2}$

$= 50\sqrt{2} \approx 70.7$ volts

EXAMPLE 2. A wire coil rotates through a magnetic field 60 times each second. The maximum value (E_m) of the alternating emf is 110 volts. Write an equation of the form $E = E_m \sin \omega t$.

Solution: Since the frequency is 60 cycles per second,

$$f = \frac{\omega}{2\pi}$$

$$60 = \frac{\omega}{2\pi}$$

$$120\pi = \omega, \text{ or } \omega = 120\pi \text{ radians per second}$$

Since $E_m = 110$, $E = 110 \sin 120\pi t$.

Example 3 illustrates that emf can change rapidly in a small interval of time.

EXAMPLE 3. Use $E = 110 \sin 120\pi t$ to find E at the times given.
  a. $\frac{1}{2}$ sec   **b.** $\frac{181}{360}$ sec

Solutions:

a. $E = 110 \sin(120\pi \cdot \frac{1}{2})$ **b.** $E = 110 \sin(120\pi \cdot \frac{181}{360})$ ◄——— $\frac{1}{360}$ **sec later**

$\quad = 110 \sin 60\pi$

$\quad = 110 \sin(0 + 2\pi \cdot 30)$

$\quad = 110 \sin 0$

$\quad = 110(0)$, or 0 volts

$\qquad\qquad = 110 \sin \frac{181\pi}{3}$

$\qquad\qquad = 110 \sin\left(\frac{\pi}{3} + 60\pi\right)$

$\qquad\qquad = 110 \sin \frac{\pi}{3}$

$\qquad\qquad = 110 \cdot \frac{\sqrt{3}}{2} = 55\sqrt{3} \approx 95$ volts

EXERCISES

In Exercises 1 and 2, find the frequency of rotation.

1. $E = 120 \sin 90\pi t$ **2.** $E = 100 \sin 150\pi t$

3. Find E in Exercise 1 when $t = 0.1$ seconds.

4. Find E in Exercise 2 when $t = 0.01$ seconds.

In Exercises 5–8, write an equation for an alternating emf of the form $E = E_m \sin \omega t$.

5. $E_m = 220$; f $= 60$ **6.** $E_m = 110$; f $= 50$

7. $E_m = 100$; f $= 62$ **8.** $E_m = 120$; f $= 58$

In Exercises 9–12, use $E = 220 \sin 120\pi t$ to find E.

9. $t = \frac{1}{60}$ sec   **10.** $t = \frac{1}{360}$ sec   **11.** $t = 1$ sec   **12.** $t = \frac{361}{720}$ sec

3–4 Trigonometric and Circular Functions

How trigonometric functions (Section 3–3) and circular functions (Chapter 2) are related is explained below through the example of the sine function.

Recall that the circular function sine was defined to be the second coordinate of a point on the unit circle with center at the origin. If $P(x, y)$ was t units from the point $A(1, 0)$ along the circle, then $y = \sin t$. (See the figure at the right.)

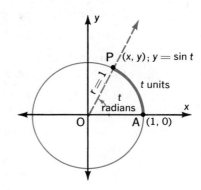

Now consider the ray OP and the measure of the angle POA *in radians*. Since the radius of the unit circle is 1, the measure of $\angle POA$ is t radians. (Why?) Consequently the value of the *trigonometric function* sin t is by definition $\frac{y}{1}$ or y.

Thus the value of the circular function sin t, $t \in$ R, is the same as the value of the trigonometric function sin t when t *is the radian measure* of the angle POA and the radius vector r is 1. But, for a given angle of measure t, the ratio $\frac{y}{r}$ is constant for all points $P(x, y)$ on the terminal side of the angle. Consequently the trigonometric function "sine" is identical to the circular function sine when the independent variable is interpreted as the radian measure of an angle in standard position. That is, if $(t, \sin t)$ is in either function, then it is in the other also.

Using similar reasoning you can conclude that each trigonometric function is equal to the circular function of the same name.

If the independent variable of a trigonometric function happens to be the degree measure of angle, then the relationship

$$1° = \frac{\pi}{180} \text{ radians}$$

allows you to convert degrees to radians. Thus even when degree measure is used to measure angles, you can equate the ordered pairs of trigonometric and circular functions. For example, the ordered pair $(30°, \sin 30°)$ corresponds to the ordered pair $\left(\frac{\pi}{6}, \sin \frac{\pi}{6}\right)$, where the last pair is an element of the sine function whether it be considered circular or trigonometric.

EXAMPLE 1. Show that the identity $\sin(-\theta) = -\sin\theta$ is valid when θ is the measure of an angle. Draw the reference triangles and show that they are similar.

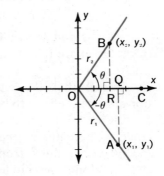

Let $-\theta$ be the measure of $\angle AOC$ in Quadrant IV. Let $\angle BOC$ be an angle in standard position with measure θ ($\theta > 0°$ and θ in Quadrant I). The reference triangles are similar, and thus $\left|\dfrac{y_2}{r_2}\right| = \left|\dfrac{y_1}{r_1}\right|$.
Since y_2 is in Quadrant I and y_1 is in Quadrant IV, y_2 and y_1 are opposite in sign. r_1 and r_2 are positive by definition of the radius vector. Thus $-\dfrac{y_2}{r_2} = \dfrac{y_1}{r_1}$ or $-\sin\theta = \sin(-\theta)$. A similar argument shows that if θ is in Quadrant I, II, or III, the relationship remains true. Thus, for all $\theta \in \mathbf{R}$

$$\sin(-\theta) = -\sin\theta.$$

Notice that the argument is independent of the unit used to measure the angle. It may be radians or degrees. Thus the identity is valid for the sine function whether it is thought of as a trigonometric or as a circular function, and whether θ is in degrees or radians.

The properties of the circular functions may be used to specify the domain and range of the trigonometric functions. This is illustrated for the tangent function in the next example.

EXAMPLE 2. Specify the range and domain of the trigonometric function tangent. For what real numbers is tangent undefined when θ is in radians? in degrees?

Solution: The range of the circular-function tangent is R. Thus the same is true of the trigonometric-function tangent.

If θ is in radians, $\tan\theta$ is undefined for $\pm\dfrac{\pi}{2}$, $\pm\dfrac{3\pi}{2}$, $\pm\dfrac{5\pi}{2}$, $\cdots$ or

$$\left\{\theta : \theta = \frac{\pi}{2} \pm n\pi, n \in \mathbf{W}\right\}.$$

In terms of degree measure, $\tan\theta$ is undefined for $\pm90°$, $\pm270°$, $\pm450° \cdots$ or $\{\theta : \theta = 90° \pm n \cdot 180°, n \in \mathbf{W}\}$.

The domain in each case is the rest of the real numbers, as follows.

$$\mathbf{R} - \left\{\frac{\pi}{2} \pm n\pi, n \in \mathbf{W}\right\} \quad \text{or} \quad \mathbf{R} - \{90° \pm n \cdot 180°, n \in \mathbf{W}\}$$

In summary, you could say that the trigonometric functions defined in this section are the circular functions of Chapter 2 with the independent variable interpreted as the radian measure of an angle in standard position. The advantage of this interpretation is that the trigonometric functions find valuable applications in triangles. Also a trigonometric function is defined for any point on the terminal side of an angle and not only for points on the unit circle. A final advantage arises from the fact that the properties you found for circular functions are also properties of trigonometric functions.

CLASSROOM EXERCISES

Specify the domain and range of each trigonometric function. Express the domain in terms of real numbers interpreted both as degree measure and as radian measure of angles.

1. sine **2.** cosine **3.** cotangent

4. cosecant **5.** secant **6.** tangent

WRITTEN EXERCISES

A ▬ Each of the following identities is valid for trigonometric as well as circular functions. Each is expressed in radians. Translate each to a statement in degrees and draw a figure showing the angles and the reference triangles. Assume for convenience that θ is an angle in Quadrant I.

1. $\cos(-\theta) = \cos\theta$

2. $\cos(\pi - \theta) = -\cos\theta$

3. $\cos(\pi + \theta) = -\cos\theta$

4. $\sin(\pi + \theta) = -\sin\theta$

5. $\sin(\pi - \theta) = \sin\theta$

6. $\sin\left(\frac{\pi}{2} + \theta\right) = \cos\theta$

7. $\cos\left(\frac{\pi}{2} + \theta\right) = -\sin\theta$

8. $\cos(\theta \pm 2n\pi) = \cos\theta,\ n \in W$

9. $\sin(\theta \pm 2n\pi) = \sin\theta,\ n \in W$

10. $\sin\left(\theta + \frac{\pi}{4}\right) = \cos\left(\theta - \frac{\pi}{4}\right)$

11. $\sin\left(\theta - \frac{\pi}{4}\right) = -\cos\left(\theta + \frac{\pi}{4}\right)$

B **12.** Use the table on page 79 to help you complete the table below. Assume x in that table is a radian measure of an angle. Leave a cell blank when the function is undefined. Keep your copy for use later. Leave entries in radical form.

	sin θ	cos θ	tan θ	csc θ	sec θ	cot θ
0°						
30°						
45°						
60°						
90°						
120°						
135°						
150°						
180°						
210°						
225°						
240°						
270°						
300°						
315°						
330°						
360°						

Use the result of Example 1 and Exercise 1 to express each of the following.

13. tan $(-\theta)$ in terms of tan θ.

14. sec $(-\theta)$ in terms of sec θ.

15. csc $(-\theta)$ in terms of csc θ.

16. cot $(-\theta)$ in terms of cot θ.

17. Use Exercises 3 and 4 to write an equivalent expression for tan $(\pi + \theta)$.

18. Use Exercises 2 and 5 to write an expression equivalent to tan $(\pi - \theta)$.

3–5 Trigonometric Functions and Triangles

The trigonometric functions may also be defined for the acute angles of a right triangle. Consider the right triangle ABC and the acute angle A with measure θ in the figure at the left below. Place a coordinate system with origin at A and positive x axis coinciding with side $\overrightarrow{AC}$ of $\angle BAC$ as in the figure at the right below. Let B have coordinates (x, y).

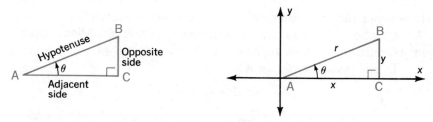

Now it is clear by comparing the two figures above that the definitions for right triangles are as follows.

Definitions	$\sin \theta = \dfrac{y}{r} = \dfrac{\text{side opposite } \theta}{\text{hypotenuse}}$
	$\cos \theta = \dfrac{x}{r} = \dfrac{\text{side adjacent } \theta}{\text{hypotenuse}}$
	$\tan \theta = \dfrac{y}{x} = \dfrac{\text{side opposite } \theta}{\text{side adjacent } \theta}$

Often when working with right triangles, the letter denoting the vertex of the angle replaces the customary symbol θ. Thus to denote the sine of the acute angle at A, you would write $\sin A$.

The table on pages 769–773 gives the sine, cosine, and tangent function values of $0°$ to $90°$ to the nearest ten-thousandth. The table can be used to solve right triangles.

The following example will illustrate the use of trigonometric functions in solving triangles.

EXAMPLE 1. If c, the length of the hypotenuse, is 100 units and A (the measure of $\angle A$) is $29°\,50'$ ($50'$ is read "50 minutes") find the length of the side opposite angle A.

Make a sketch of the right triangle and note the given information.

Solution:

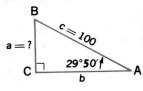

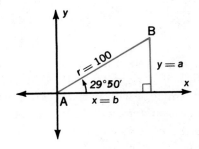

If you use the *right triangle definitions* make a sketch like the one at the left above. If you use the *coordinate-system definitions* place $\angle A$ in standard position as at the right above.

In either case by definition

$$\sin A = \frac{a}{c} = \frac{a}{100}.$$

$$\sin 29° \, 50' \approx 0.4975. \quad \longleftarrow \quad \textbf{From the table or calculator}$$

$$\frac{a}{100} \approx 0.4975$$

$$a \approx 49.75$$

EXAMPLE 2. Given the figure at the right with the lengths of sides as indicated. Find, to the nearest whole number, the length of $\overline{AC}$. Then find, to the nearest 10 minutes, the measure of angle A.

Solution:

$$18^2 = 6^2 + b^2 \quad \longleftarrow \quad \textbf{By the Pythagorean Theorem}$$

$$324 - 36 = b^2$$

$$288 = b^2.$$

$$b \approx 17 \quad \longleftarrow \quad \textbf{17}^2 = \textbf{289}$$

$$\sin A = \tfrac{6}{18} = \tfrac{1}{3} \approx 0.3333. \quad \longleftarrow \quad \textbf{By the definition}$$

$$\sin 19° \, 20' = 0.3311 \quad \longleftarrow \quad \textbf{From the table or calculator}$$

$$\sin 19° \, 30' = 0.3338.$$

Thus $\quad\quad\quad \sin A \, (\approx 0.3333)$ is nearly $\sin 19° \, 30'$.

Consequently

$$A \approx 19° \, 30' \text{ (to the nearest 10 minutes).}$$

A better approximation to the measure of angle A could be obtained by **linear interpolation**. Linear interpolation is based upon the assumption that the function being considered is linear (that its graph is a straight line) between successive entries in the table. But for a trigonometric function the range does not have a constant increase for a given constant increase in the domain. However, for a sufficiently small portion of the curve, a straight line is in fact a close approximation. (See diagram at the right below.)

To avoid errors, you may arrange your work as is demonstrated below.

$$y\left\{\begin{matrix}19°\ 20'\\ \underline{\quad ?\quad}\\ 19°\ 30'\end{matrix}\right\}10 \qquad\qquad .0022\left\{\begin{matrix}0.3311\\ 0.3333\\ 0.3338\end{matrix}\right\}.0027$$

You then write the following proportion and solve for y.

$\dfrac{y}{10} \approx \dfrac{.0022}{.0027}$

$y \approx 8'.$

Then,

$A \approx 19°\ 20' + 8'$

$\approx 19°\ 28'$

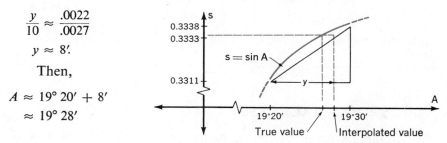

The trigonometric functions are useful in calculating lengths which are not amenable to direct measurement. Very often these applications depend on an *angle of elevation* or an *angle of depression*. An example of each of these angles is represented by Figure 1 and Figure 2 below.

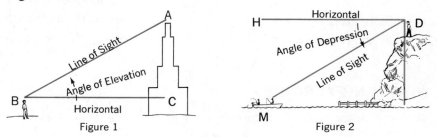

Figure 1

Figure 2

In each case the angle in question is determined by the horizontal and the line of sight.

It is important to remember that the height of the individual doing the sighting is a factor in determining the sides of the triangle used for calculation. The next example illustrates this point.

EXAMPLE 3. A man 6 feet tall stands 15 feet from a building. If the angle of elevation to the top of the building is 75°, how far is the top of the building from the ground?

Solution: Refer to Figure 1 on the previous page.

$$BC = 15', \quad \angle B \text{ is } 75°$$

The height of the building is $AC + 6$ feet.

$$\tan 75° = \frac{AC}{15} \quad \longleftarrow \quad \text{By the definition of tangent}$$

$$\tan 75° \approx 3.7321 \quad \longleftarrow \quad \text{From the table}$$

Consequently,

$$3.7321 \approx \frac{AC}{15} \quad \longleftarrow \quad \text{By substitution}$$

$$15(3.7321) \approx AC$$
$$55.98 \approx AC$$

$$AC = 56. \quad \longleftarrow \quad \text{To the nearest foot}$$

$AC + 6 = 62$ feet is the approximate height of the building.

CLASSROOM EXERCISES

▬ In the Exercises below, a, b, and c respectively represent the lengths of the sides opposite angles A, B, and C, where C is a right angle. What trigonometric function, or other means, would you use to find:

1. b, given a and A
2. b, given a and B
3. a, given c and A
4. a, given c and B
5. c, given b and B
6. c, given a and b
7. c, given b and A
8. a, given c and b

WRITTEN EXERCISES

A ▬ Use the table on pages 769–773 to find each of the following.

1. $\sin 67°$
2. $\cos 41°$
3. $\tan 14°$
4. $\sin 23° 40'$
5. $\cos 71° 30'$
6. $\tan 88° 50'$

▬ Use the table to find θ for each of the following.

7. $\sin \theta = .9730$
8. $\cos \theta = .9730$
9. $\tan \theta = 2.0353$
10. $\sin \theta = .0523$
11. $\cos \theta = .5299$
12. $\tan \theta = .2065$

Use the table and linear interpolation to find θ to the nearest minute for each of the following.

13. $\sin \theta = .2520$ **14.** $\cos \theta = .2520$ **15.** $\tan \theta = 2.0000$
16. $\sin \theta = .9080$ **17.** $\cos \theta = .7780$ **18.** $\tan \theta = 1.0029$

19. A regular pentagon is inscribed in a circle whose diameter is 24 centimeters. Find the length of its side.

20. From a point 100 meters from the base of a tower, the angle of elevation to its top is 38°. Find its height.

21. If the diameter of a planet is taken as 7912 kilometers, what is the distance of the furthest point of the surface visible from the summit of a mountain one kilometer in height? (Assume the planet is a perfect sphere.)

22. From the top of a lighthouse 44 meters above the sea, the angle of depression of a buoy is 18° 30'. Find the horizontal distance from the buoy.

23. Use the data in Exercise 22 to find the line-of-sight distance from the top of the house to the buoy.

24. The furthest point of the earth's surface visible from a mountain top is 80 miles distant. Find the height of the mountain if the earth's diameter is 7912 miles.

25. How far from the foot of a pole 26 meters high must a 2-meter person stand so that the angle of elevation of the top of the pole is 10°?

26. From the top of a tower, the angle of depression to a point 1000 meters from the base is 21°. Find the height of the tower.

27. Find the length of the side of a regular hexagon inscribed in a circle whose radius is 10 centimeters.

C **28.** In the table on pages 769–773 $\sin 36° = \cos 54°$, $\sin 19° = \cos 71°$ and $\sin 84° = \cos 6°$. Explain this phenomenon in terms of an identity given in Exercises 1–11 of Section 3–4.

MID-CHAPTER REVIEW

Sketch an angle AOB in standard position resulting from each rotation. (Section 3-1)

1. $\frac{2}{3}$ counterclockwise
2. $\frac{2}{3}$ clockwise
3. $\frac{5}{2}$ clockwise
4. $\frac{3}{5}$ counterclockwise

━━━ Convert degrees to radians. (Section 3-2)

5. 60°   **6.** 150°   **7.** 200°   **8.** −540°

━━━ Convert radians to degrees. (Section 3-2)

9. $\frac{\pi}{2}$ **10.** $-\frac{\pi}{6}$ **11.** −9   **12.** 4

━━━ Find the six trigonometric functions for θ if the terminal side of θ contains the given point. (Section 3-3)

13. $A(60, 11)$ **14.** $X(15, -8)$

━━━ Rewrite each expression using degree measure. (Section 3-4)

15. $\cos\left(\frac{\pi}{2} - x\right) = \sin x$ **16.** $\sin\left(\frac{\pi}{2} - x\right) = \cos x$

━━━ Using the standard notation for right triangle ABC, find the required parts. (Section 3-5)

17. $A = 50°$, $c = 40$; find a and b.

18. $a = 35$, $b = 17$; find A and C.

19. From the top of a lighthouse 71 meters above the sea, the angle of depression to a ship is 8°31′. Find the horizontal distance to the ship to the nearest metance to the ship to the nearest meter.

3–6   Reduction Formulas

The Table of values for the trigonometric functions includes only the measures of angles for $0° \leq \theta \leq 90°$. Suppose you were faced with finding the sine of θ where θ is greater than 90°, what would you do? Clearly you would like to express $\sin \theta$ in terms of an angle between 0° and 90° so you could use the table.

The identities given in Section 2–5 and again in the Exercises of Section 3–4 provide the necessary tools to solve this problem. They are restated here for your convenience.

	In degrees	**In radians**
1.	a. $\sin(-\theta) = -\sin\theta$	$\sin(-\theta) = -\sin\theta$
	b. $\cos(-\theta) = \cos\theta$	$\cos(-\theta) = \cos\theta$
	c. $\tan(-\theta) = -\tan\theta$	$\tan(-\theta) = -\tan\theta$
2.	a. $\sin(180° - \theta) = \sin\theta$	$\sin(\pi - \theta) = \sin\theta$
	b. $\cos(180° - \theta) = -\cos\theta$	$\cos(\pi - \theta) = -\cos\theta$
	c. $\tan(180° - \theta) = -\tan\theta$	$\tan(\pi - \theta) = -\tan\theta$
3.	a. $\sin(180° + \theta) = -\sin\theta$	$\sin(\pi + \theta) = -\sin\theta$
	b. $\cos(180° + \theta) = -\cos\theta$	$\cos(\pi + \theta) = -\cos\theta$
	c. $\tan(180° + \theta) = \tan\theta$	$\tan(\pi + \theta) = \tan\theta$

4. a. $\sin (90° + \theta) = \cos \theta$ $\qquad$ $\sin \left(\dfrac{\pi}{2} + \theta\right) = \cos \theta$

 b. $\cos (90° + \theta) = -\sin \theta$ $\qquad$ $\cos \left(\dfrac{\pi}{2} + \theta\right) = -\sin \theta$

 c. $\tan (90° + \theta) = -\cot \theta$ $\qquad$ $\tan \left(\dfrac{\pi}{2} + \theta\right) = -\cot \theta$

There are two other sets of three identities needed to complete the relationships most often used. They can be derived by using the Sets 1–4 given above.

5. a. $\sin (360° - \theta) = -\sin \theta$ $\qquad$ $\sin (2\pi - \theta) = -\sin \theta$
 b. $\cos (360° - \theta) = \cos \theta$ $\qquad$ $\cos (2\pi - \theta) = \cos \theta$
 c. $\tan (360° - \theta) = -\tan \theta$ $\qquad$ $\tan (2\pi - \theta) = -\tan \theta$

Proof of 5a:

$$\begin{aligned}
\sin (360° - \theta) &= \sin \{180° + (180° - \theta)\} \\
&= -\sin (180° - \theta) \quad \longleftarrow \quad \textbf{By 3a} \\
&= -\sin \theta \quad \longleftarrow \quad \textbf{By 2a}
\end{aligned}$$

The proofs of 5b and 5c are left for you to do.

6. a. $\sin (90° - \theta) = \cos \theta$ $\qquad$ $\sin \left(\dfrac{\pi}{2} - \theta\right) = \cos \theta$

 b. $\cos (90° - \theta) = \sin \theta$ $\qquad$ $\cos \left(\dfrac{\pi}{2} - \theta\right) = \sin \theta$

 c. $\tan (90° - \theta) = \cot \theta$ $\qquad$ $\tan \left(\dfrac{\pi}{2} - \theta\right) = \cot \theta$

Proof of 6b: $\begin{aligned}[t]
\cos (90° - \theta) &= \cos \{180° - (90 + \theta)\} \\
&= -\cos (90° + \theta) \quad \longleftarrow \quad \textbf{By 2b} \\
&= -[-\sin \theta] \quad \longleftarrow \quad \textbf{By 4b} \\
&= \sin \theta
\end{aligned}$

The proofs of 6a and 6c are left for you to do.

EXAMPLE 1. Find the value of $\cos 205° \, 10'$.

Solution: $\qquad$ $205° \, 10'$ is not in the table but
$$205° \, 10' = 180° + 25° \, 10'$$
$$\begin{aligned}
\text{So } \cos 205° \, 10' &= \cos (180° + 25° \, 10') \\
&= -\cos 25° \, 10' \quad \longleftarrow \quad \textbf{By 3b} \\
&= -0.9051 \quad \longleftarrow \quad \textbf{By the table}
\end{aligned}$$

EXAMPLE 2. Find the value of tan 123° 50′.

Solutions: **a.**   123° 50′ = 180° − 56° 10′
So tan 123° 50′ = tan (180° − 56° 10′)
= −tan 56° 10′ ⟵ **By 2c**
= −1.4919 ⟵ **By the table**

b.   123° 50′ = 90° + 33° 50′
So tan 123° 50′ = tan (90° + 33° 50′)
= −cot 33° 50′ ⟵ **By 4c**
= −1.4919 ⟵ **By the table**

CLASSROOM EXERCISES

— Find the value of each of the following.

1. tan 225° **2.** cos 220° **3.** sin 233°
4. Express cos 310° as the sine of an acute angle.
5. Express tan 150° as the tangent of an acute angle.
6. Express cos 122° as the sine of an acute angle.
7. Express tan 321° as the tangent of an acute angle.
8. Express sin 142° as the cosine of an acute angle.

WRITTEN EXERCISES

A — Express each of the following in the form (180° − θ).
1. 101° 10′ **2.** 179° 50′ **3.** 141° 30′
4. 120° 20′ **5.** 161° 40′ **6.** 97° 25′

— Express each of the following in the form (180° + θ).
7. 183° 20′ **8.** 265° 50′ **9.** 224° 50′

— Express each of the following in the form (360° − θ).
10. 285° 40′ **11.** 331° 10′ **12.** 359° 30′
13. 270° 10′ **14.** 300° 50′ **15.** 345° 20′

— Express each of the following in the form (90° + θ).
16. 142° 10′ **17.** 96° 5′ **18.** 179° 30′

— Express each of the following in the form (90° − θ).
19. 38° 20′ **20.** 97° 30′ **21.** 1° 10′

— Find the value of each of the following.
22. sin 165° **23.** $\cos \dfrac{7\pi}{6}$ **24.** tan 92°

25. $\sin 281°$ **26.** $\cos\left(-\dfrac{\pi}{4}\right)$ **27.** $\tan 265°$

28. $\sin\dfrac{4\pi}{3}$ **29.** $\cos 335°$ **30.** $\tan 271°$

B   **31.** Find reduction formulas for $\sin(270° - \theta)$, $\cos(270° - \theta)$ and $\tan(270° - \theta)$ by using the relation $270° - \theta = [360 - (90° + \theta)]$ and the formulas of this section.

    32. Repeat Exercise 31 for $\sin(270° + \theta)$, $\cos(270° + \theta)$ and $\tan(270° + \theta)$.

3–7   Sum and Difference Identities for Cosine

In Section 3–4 you saw that circular functions and trigonometric functions were related by means of the radian measure of angles. Moreover every fact that can be proved for circular functions is also true for trigonometric functions whether the independent variable represents degree or radian measure of an angle. In this Section two identities are derived using the definition of circular functions. In light of the previous comments, these identities are valid for trigonometric functions also.

The first identity relates the cosine of the sum of two numbers (or the sum of the measure of two angles) to the sine and cosine of the numbers individually. For example:

$$\cos\left(\frac{\pi}{3}\right) = \frac{1}{2}; \quad \cos\left(\frac{\pi}{6}\right) = \frac{\sqrt{3}}{2}$$

and

$$\cos\left(\frac{\pi}{3} + \frac{\pi}{6}\right) = \cos\frac{\pi}{2} = 0.$$

Clearly

$$\frac{1}{2} + \frac{\sqrt{3}}{2} \neq 0$$

and so,

$$\cos\left(\frac{\pi}{3} + \frac{\pi}{6}\right) \neq \cos\frac{\pi}{3} + \cos\frac{\pi}{6}.$$

But

$$\cos\frac{\pi}{3} \cdot \cos\frac{\pi}{6} = \frac{1}{2} \cdot \frac{\sqrt{3}}{2}$$

and

$$\sin\frac{\pi}{3} \cdot \sin\frac{\pi}{6} = \frac{\sqrt{3}}{2} \cdot \frac{1}{2}.$$

Thus

$$\cos\left(\frac{\pi}{3} + \frac{\pi}{6}\right) = \cos\frac{\pi}{3} \cdot \cos\frac{\pi}{6} - \sin\frac{\pi}{3} \cdot \sin\frac{\pi}{6}$$

$$= \frac{1}{2} \cdot \frac{\sqrt{3}}{2} - \frac{\sqrt{3}}{2} \cdot \frac{1}{2} = 0.$$

Letting the Greek letters α (alpha) and β (beta) represent real numbers (or measures of angles), the last statement can be written as follows.

$$\cos(\alpha + \beta) = \cos\alpha \cdot \cos\beta - \sin\alpha \cdot \sin\beta$$

Theorem 3-1 (The Addition Identity for the Cosine Function)
If α and β are any real numbers (measures of angles)

$$\cos(\alpha + \beta) = \cos\alpha\cos\beta - \sin\alpha\sin\beta$$

Proof: Consider the unit circle at the right. The points P, Q and R have coordinates as indicated in the figure at the right.

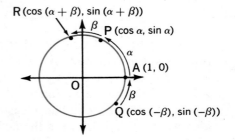

The measure of $\overset{\frown}{QA}$ and $\overset{\frown}{PR}$ is β. The measure of $\overset{\frown}{AP} = \alpha$. Thus the measure of $\overset{\frown}{QAP} = \alpha + \beta = \overset{\frown}{APR}$. Consequently the chords $\overline{PQ}$ and $\overline{RA}$ have the same measure: $PQ = RA$.

The distance formula is now used to express PQ and RA in terms of the coordinates of P, Q, and R.

$$PQ = RA$$

$$\sqrt{[\cos\alpha - \cos(-\beta)]^2 + [\sin\alpha - \sin(-\beta)]^2} = \sqrt{[\cos(\alpha+\beta) - 1]^2 + [\sin(\alpha+\beta) - 0]^2}$$

$$\cos^2\alpha - 2\cos\alpha\cos(-\beta) + \cos^2(-\beta) + \sin^2\alpha - 2\sin\alpha\sin(-\beta) + \sin^2(-\beta)$$
$$= \cos^2(\alpha+\beta) - 2\cos(\alpha+\beta) + 1 + \sin^2(\alpha+\beta) \qquad \textbf{1}$$

The fundamental identity $\sin^2 x + \cos^2 x = 1$ is used to simplify the left and right members of Equation **1**.

$$\cos^2\alpha + \sin^2\alpha = 1$$
$$\cos^2(-\beta) + \sin^2(-\beta) = 1$$
$$\cos^2(\alpha+\beta) + \sin^2(\alpha+\beta) = 1$$

Thus

$$-2\cos\alpha\cos(-\beta) - 2\sin\alpha\sin(-\beta) + 2 = -2\cos(\alpha+\beta) + 2 \qquad \textbf{2}$$

Subtracting 2 from both members of **2** and dividing by -2, you obtain

$$\cos\alpha\cos(-\beta) + \sin\alpha\sin(-\beta) = \cos(\alpha+\beta). \qquad \textbf{3}$$

You can now use the identities

$$\cos(-x) = \cos x$$

and

$$\sin(-x) = -\sin x$$

to simplify 3. The result is

$$\cos(\alpha + \beta) = \cos \alpha \cos \beta - \sin \alpha \sin \beta.$$

EXAMPLE 1.   Find the exact value of cos 75°.

Solution: $75° = 30° + 45°$,

thus, $\cos 75° = \cos(30° + 45°) = \cos 30° \cos 45° - \sin 30° \sin 45°$

$$\cos 30° = \frac{\sqrt{3}}{2}, \quad \cos 45° = \frac{\sqrt{2}}{2}, \quad \sin 30° = \frac{1}{2} \quad \text{and} \quad \sin 45° = \frac{\sqrt{2}}{2}$$

Consequently $\cos 75° = \frac{\sqrt{3}}{2} \cdot \frac{\sqrt{2}}{2} - \frac{1}{2} \cdot \frac{\sqrt{2}}{2}$

$$= \frac{\sqrt{2}}{2}\left(\frac{\sqrt{3} - 1}{2}\right)$$

$$= \frac{\sqrt{2}}{4}(\sqrt{3} - 1)$$

An identity for the cos $(\alpha - \beta)$ follows easily from Theorem 3–1.

Theorem 3–2 (The Subtraction Identity for the Cosine Function)   If α and β are any real numbers (measures of angles)

$$\cos(\alpha - \beta) = \cos \alpha \cos \beta + \sin \alpha \sin \beta.$$

Proof: $\cos(\alpha + \beta) = \cos \alpha \cos \beta - \sin \alpha \sin \beta.$ ◄——— **From Th. 3-1**

Notice that $(\alpha - \beta) = [\alpha + (-\beta)].$

Consequently

$$\cos(\alpha - \beta) = \cos[\alpha + (-\beta)]$$
$$= \cos \alpha \cos(-\beta) - \sin \alpha \sin(-\beta).$$

by Theorem 3–1.

Then $\cos(\alpha - \beta) = \cos \alpha \cos \beta + \sin \alpha \sin \beta.$

The last step follows because $\cos(-x) = \cos x$ and $\sin(-x) = -\sin x.$

EXAMPLE 2. Prove the following reduction formula.

$$\cos\left(\frac{\pi}{2} - x\right) = \sin x$$

Proof:

$$\cos\left(\frac{\pi}{2} - x\right) = \cos\frac{\pi}{2}\cos x + \sin\frac{\pi}{2}\cdot\sin x$$
$$= 0\cdot\cos x + 1\cdot\sin x$$
$$= \sin x.$$

The remainder of the reduction formulas for the cosine function given in Section 3–6 can be verified in a similar manner.

CLASSROOM EXERCISES

━━ Use Theorems 3–1 or 3–2 to verify each identity.

1. $\cos(180° - x) = -\cos x$ **2.** $\cos(180° + x) = \cos x$

3. $\cos(90° + x) = -\sin x$ **4.** $\cos(90° - x) = \sin x$

5. $\cos(2\pi - x) = \cos x$ **6.** $\cos(2\pi + x) = \cos x$

7. Find $\cos 15°$. Does your result agree with the entry in the Table of Values of Trigonometric Functions?

WRITTEN EXERCISES

A ━━ Use either Theorem 3–1 or 3–2 to find the value of the following.

1. $\cos 105°$ **2.** $\cos\frac{5\pi}{12}$ **3.** $\cos 195°$ **4.** $\cos\frac{19\pi}{12}$

5. $\cos 15°$ **6.** $\cos\frac{11\pi}{12}$ **7.** $\cos 255°$ **8.** $\cos\left(-\frac{\pi}{12}\right)$

Use either Theorem 3–1 or 3–2 to verify each identity.

9. $\cos\left(\frac{\pi}{2} + \theta\right) = -\sin\theta$ **10.** $\cos(360° - \theta) = \cos\theta$

11. $\cos(180° - \theta) = -\cos\theta$ **12.** $\cos\left(\frac{3\pi}{2} - \theta\right) = -\sin\theta$

13. $\cos(\pi + \theta) = -\cos\theta$ **14.** $\cos\left(\frac{3\pi}{2} + \theta\right) = \sin\theta$

B ━━ Let α and β be the measure of two first quadrant angles. Find $\cos(\alpha + \beta)$ given the following information.

15. $\cos\alpha = \frac{3}{5}$, $\sin\beta = \frac{3}{5}$ **16.** $\cos\alpha = \frac{5}{13}$, $\cos\beta = \frac{35}{37}$

17. $\sin\alpha = \frac{8}{17}$, $\tan\beta = \frac{7}{24}$ **18.** $\tan\alpha = \frac{4}{3}$, $\cot\beta = \frac{5}{12}$

19. $\sec\alpha = \frac{29}{21}$, $\sec\beta = \frac{5}{3}$ **20.** $\cot\alpha = \frac{12}{5}$, $\tan\beta = \frac{60}{11}$

Find $\cos(\alpha - \beta)$ for each situation.

21. $\sin \alpha = \frac{4}{5}$, $\cos \beta = \frac{4}{5}$ **22.** $\cos \alpha = \frac{12}{13}$, $\sin \beta = \frac{35}{37}$

23. $\cos \alpha = \frac{8}{17}$, $\tan \beta = \frac{24}{7}$ **24.** $\tan \alpha = \frac{3}{4}$, $\cot \beta = \frac{13}{12}$

25. $\sec \alpha = \frac{17}{8}$, $\cos \beta = \frac{3}{5}$ **26.** $\tan \alpha = \frac{5}{12}$, $\cos \beta = \frac{11}{60}$

C   **27.** Prove:

$$\cos 3x \cos 5x - \sin 3x \sin 5x = \cos 8x.$$

28. Prove:

$$\cos 3x \cos 5x + \sin 3x \sin 5x = \cos 2x.$$

29. Prove:

$$\cos(\alpha + \beta) + \cos(\alpha - \beta) = 2 \cos \alpha \cos \beta.$$

30. Prove:

$$\cos(\alpha - \beta) - \cos(\alpha + \beta) = 2 \sin \alpha \sin \beta.$$

31. Prove:

$$\cos\left(\frac{\pi}{2} + \alpha - \beta\right) = \cos \alpha \sin \beta - \sin \alpha \cos \beta.$$

32. Derive an identity for $\cos(\alpha + \beta + \theta)$ in terms of sines and cosines of α, β, and θ.

33. Assume the angles whose measures are α, β, and $\alpha + \beta$ are positive acute angles as shown at the right. Use this figure to prove $\cos(\alpha + \beta) = \cos \alpha \cos \beta - \sin \alpha \sin \beta$.

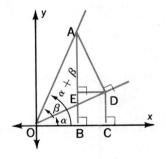

(*Hint:* $\cos(\alpha + \beta) = \dfrac{OB}{OA}$

$ = \dfrac{OC - BC}{OA}$

$ = \dfrac{OC}{OA} - \dfrac{BC}{OA}.$

What is $\cos \alpha$ in $\triangle ODC$?   What is $\sin \alpha$ in $\triangle AED$?)

34. Is the proof for Exercise 33 as general as the previous one? (Theorem 3–1) Why or why not?

35. Use the Subtraction Identity for Cosine to prove that $\sin(-\alpha) = -\sin \alpha$. (*Hint*: In the Subtraction Identity for Cosine, replace β with $90°$; in the identity in Example 2, replace x with $-\alpha$.)

3-8 Sum and Difference Identities for Sine and Tangent

The difference identity for the cosine function can be used to derive an identity for $\sin(\alpha + \beta)$. One additional fact must be recalled first, namely:

$$\sin\left(\frac{\pi}{2} - \theta\right) = \cos\theta. \qquad \qquad 1$$

The identity stated in **1** can be verified as follows:

Recall (Example 2, Section 3-7) that

$$\cos\left(\frac{\pi}{2} - x\right) = \sin x. \qquad \qquad 2$$

Replace x in **2** by $\left(\frac{\pi}{2} - \theta\right)$.

Thus
$$\cos\left[\frac{\pi}{2} - \left(\frac{\pi}{2} - \theta\right)\right] = \sin\left(\frac{\pi}{2} - \theta\right)$$

or
$$\cos\theta = \sin\left(\frac{\pi}{2} - \theta\right)$$

which is the identity stated in **1**.

Now you can prove the following theorem.

Theorem 3-3 (The Addition Identity for the Sine Function)
If α and β are any real numbers (measures of angles)

$$\sin(\alpha + \beta) = \sin\alpha\cos\beta + \cos\alpha\sin\beta.$$

Proof: In the identity, $r, s \in \mathrm{R}$,

$$\cos(r - s) = \cos r \cos s + \sin r \sin s.$$

Replace r by $\frac{\pi}{2}$ and s by $(\alpha + \beta)$. Thus

$$\cos\left[\frac{\pi}{2} - (\alpha + \beta)\right] = \cos\left[\left(\frac{\pi}{2} - \alpha\right) - \beta\right]$$
$$= \cos\left(\frac{\pi}{2} - \alpha\right)\cos\beta + \sin\left(\frac{\pi}{2} - \alpha\right)\sin\beta$$
$$= \sin\alpha\cos\beta + \cos\alpha\sin\beta.$$

But $\cos\left[\frac{\pi}{2} - (\alpha + \beta)\right] = \sin(\alpha + \beta)$ (Why?)

Thus
$$\sin(\alpha + \beta) = \sin\alpha\cos\beta + \cos\alpha\sin\beta. \qquad \qquad 3$$

Replacing β in 3 by $-\beta$ and using the identities

$$\sin(-x) = -\sin x$$
$$\cos(-x) = \cos x$$

you have

$$\sin(\alpha - \beta) = \sin \alpha \cos \beta - \cos \alpha \sin \beta$$

thus proving the next theorem.

Theorem 3–4 (The Subtraction Identity for the Sine Function)
If α and β are any real numbers (measures of angles)

$$\sin(\alpha - \beta) = \sin \alpha \cos \beta - \cos \alpha \sin \beta.$$

Theorems 3–3 and 3–4 have the same type of applications as their counterparts for the cosine function.

EXAMPLE 1. Find the value of $\sin 75°$.

Solution: $75° = 45° + 30°$ and $\sin 45° = \dfrac{\sqrt{2}}{2}$, $\cos 45° = \dfrac{\sqrt{2}}{2}$, $\sin 30° = \frac{1}{2}$, and $\cos 30° = \dfrac{\sqrt{3}}{2}$.

Thus
$$\begin{aligned}
\sin 75° &= \sin(45° + 30°) \\
&= \sin 45° \cdot \cos 30° + \cos 45° \cdot \sin 30° \\
&= \frac{\sqrt{2}}{2} \cdot \frac{\sqrt{3}}{2} + \frac{\sqrt{2}}{2} \cdot \frac{1}{2} \\
&= \frac{\sqrt{2}}{4}(\sqrt{3} + 1).
\end{aligned}$$

By definition $\tan \theta = \dfrac{\sin \theta}{\cos \theta}$, for all $\theta \in R$, $\cos \theta \neq 0$. Consequently

$$\begin{aligned}
\tan(\alpha + \beta) &= \frac{\sin(\alpha + \beta)}{\cos(\alpha + \beta)}, \quad \cos(\alpha + \beta) \neq 0 \\
&= \frac{\sin \alpha \cos \beta + \cos \alpha \sin \beta}{\cos \alpha \cos \beta - \sin \alpha \sin \beta} \\
&= \frac{\dfrac{\sin \alpha \cos \beta}{\cos \alpha \cos \beta} + \dfrac{\cos \alpha \sin \beta}{\cos \alpha \cos \beta}}{\dfrac{\cos \alpha \cos \beta}{\cos \alpha \cos \beta} - \dfrac{\sin \alpha \sin \beta}{\cos \alpha \cos \beta}} \\
&= \frac{\tan \alpha + \tan \beta}{1 - \tan \alpha \tan \beta}.
\end{aligned}$$

This argument proves the following theorem.

> **Theorem 3–5** (The Addition Identity for the Tangent Function)
> If $\alpha, \beta \in \mathbf{R}$ and $\cos \alpha$, $\cos \beta$, $\cos (\alpha + \beta) \neq 0$, then
>
> $$\tan (\alpha + \beta) = \frac{\tan \alpha + \tan \beta}{1 - \tan \alpha \tan \beta}.$$

Using $\tan (-x) = -\tan x$, you can prove the following theorem.

> **Theorem 3–6** (The Subtraction Identity for the Tangent Function) If $\alpha, \beta \in \mathbf{R}$ and $\cos \alpha$, $\cos (-\beta)$, $\cos (\alpha - \beta) \neq 0$, then
>
> $$\tan (\alpha - \beta) = \frac{\tan \alpha - \tan \beta}{1 + \tan \alpha \tan \beta}.$$

EXAMPLE 2. Find the value of $\tan 75°$.

Solution:
$$75° = 45° + 30°$$
$$\tan 45° = 1$$
$$\tan 30° = \frac{\sqrt{3}}{3}$$
$$\tan 75° = \tan (45° + 30°) \quad \longleftarrow \quad \textbf{From Th. 3–5}$$
$$= \frac{\tan 45° + \tan 30°}{1 - \tan 45° \tan 30°}$$
$$= \frac{1 + \dfrac{\sqrt{3}}{3}}{1 - 1 \cdot \dfrac{\sqrt{3}}{3}} = \frac{3 + \sqrt{3}}{3 - \sqrt{3}}$$

CLASSROOM EXERCISES

━━ Verify each identity using Theorems 3–3, 3–4, 3–5, or 3–6.

1. $\tan (180° - x) = -\tan x$
2. $\sin (180° - x) = \sin x$
3. $\tan (90° - x) = \cot x$
4. $\sin (\pi + x) = -\sin x$
5. $\sin (90° + x) = \cos x$
6. $\tan (\pi + x) = \tan x$

7. Using functions of $45°$ and $30°$ and theorems of this section, find $\sin 15°$.

8. Use the tables to find $\sin (\alpha - \beta)$ and $\cos (\alpha - \beta)$ if $\alpha = 45°$ and $\beta = 30°$.

WRITTEN EXERCISES

A ■■ Use the theorems of this section to find the following.

1. $\sin 105°$ **2.** $\sin \frac{5\pi}{12}$ **3.** $\sin(-30°)$ **4.** $\sin \frac{11\pi}{12}$

5. $\tan 105°$ **6.** $\tan \frac{5\pi}{12}$ **7.** $\tan(-30°)$ **8.** $\tan \frac{11\pi}{12}$

9. $\sin 195°$ **10.** $\sin \frac{19\pi}{12}$ **11.** $\sin 255°$ **12.** $\sin\left(-\frac{\pi}{12}\right)$

13. $\tan 195°$ **14.** $\tan \frac{19\pi}{12}$ **15.** $\tan 255°$ **16.** $\tan\left(-\frac{\pi}{12}\right)$

■■ Verify the following identities.

17. $\sin\left(\frac{\pi}{2} + x\right) = \cos x$ **18.** $\tan(90° + \theta) = -\cot\theta$

19. $\sin(180° + \theta) = -\sin\theta$ **20.** $\tan\left(\frac{\pi}{2} - x\right) = \cot x$

21. $\sin(\pi - \theta) = \sin\theta$ **22.** $\sin(270° + x) = -\cos x$

23. $\tan(180° + \theta) = \tan\theta$ **24.** $\sin\left(\frac{3\pi}{2} - \theta\right) = -\cos\theta$

25. $\tan\left(\frac{3\pi}{2} + \theta\right) = -\cot\theta$ **26.** $\tan(270° - x) = \cot x$

27. $\tan(\pi - \theta) = -\tan\theta$ (Is Theorem 3–6 applicable?)

B ■■ Verify that each of the following statements is true.

28. $2\sin^2 150° = 1 - \cos 300°$ **29.** $\tan \frac{\pi}{3} = \sqrt{\dfrac{1 - \cos \frac{2\pi}{3}}{1 + \cos \frac{2\pi}{3}}}$

30. $\cos 330° = \sqrt{\dfrac{1 + \cos 660°}{2}}$ **31.** $\tan \frac{3\pi}{4} = \dfrac{\sin \frac{3\pi}{2}}{1 + \cos \frac{3\pi}{2}}$

32. $\tan 240° = \dfrac{2\tan 120°}{1 - \tan^2 120°}$ **33.** $\cos \frac{2\pi}{3} = \cos^2 \frac{\pi}{3} - \sin^2 \frac{\pi}{3}$

■■ Prove the following statements are identities

34. $\sin(\alpha + \beta) - \sin(\alpha - \beta) = 2\cos\alpha \sin\beta$.

35. $\sin(\alpha + \beta) + \sin(\alpha - \beta) = 2\sin\alpha \cos\beta$.

36. $\cot(\alpha + \beta) = \dfrac{\cot\alpha \cot\beta - 1}{\cot\alpha + \cot\beta}$.

■■ For what values of α and β is each statement true?

37. $\cot(-\alpha) = -\cot\alpha$ **38.** $\cot(\alpha - \beta) = \dfrac{\cot\alpha \cot\beta + 1}{\cot\beta - \cot\alpha}$

39. $\sin(\alpha + \beta) \cdot \sin(\alpha - \beta) = \sin^2\alpha - \sin^2\beta$

40. $\cos(\alpha + \beta) \cdot \cos(\alpha - \beta) = \cos^2\alpha - \sin^2\beta$

41. $\sin(\alpha + \beta) \cdot \sin(\alpha - \beta) = \cos^2\beta - \cos^2\alpha$

42. $\cos(\alpha + \beta) \cdot \cos(\alpha - \beta) = \cos^2\beta - \sin^2\alpha$

BASIC: SOLVING RIGHT TRIANGLES

Problem:

Given the length of a leg of a right triangle and the degree
measure of the acute angle opposite the given leg, write a
program which solves the triangle.

```
100  PRINT
110  PRINT "THIS PROGRAM SOLVES RIGHT TRIANGLES,"
120  PRINT "GIVEN THE LENGTH OF A LEG AND THE"
130  PRINT "MEASURE OF THE ACUTE ANGLE OPPOSITE"
140  PRINT "THAT LEG."
150  LET R = .0174532925
160  PRINT
170  PRINT "WHAT IS THE DEGREE MEASURE OF THE"
180  PRINT "ACUTE ANGLE";
190  INPUT A
200  IF A <= 0 THEN 220
210  IF A < 90 THEN 240
220  PRINT "ILLEGAL ANGLE.   TRY AGAIN."
230  GOTO 190
240  LET X = A * R
250  PRINT
260  PRINT "WHAT IS THE LENGTH OF THE LEG";
270  INPUT A1
280  IF A1 > 0 THEN 310
290  PRINT "ILLEGAL LENGTH.   TRY AGAIN."
300  GOTO 270
310  LET B = 90 - A
320  LET B1 = A1/TAN(X)
330  LET C1 = SQR(A1*A1 + B1*B1)
340  PRINT
350  PRINT "THE SIDES HAVE LENGTHS"
360  PRINT A1,INT(B1*1000)/1000,INT(C1*1000)/1000
370  PRINT
380  PRINT "THE ANGLES HAVE MEASURES"
390  PRINT A,INT(B*1000)/1000," 90"
400  PRINT
410  PRINT "ANOTHER TRIANGLE (1=YES, 0=NO)";
420  INPUT Z
430  IF Z = 1 THEN 160
440  END
```

Analysis:

Statement 150: The value of R is the approximate number of radians in one degree. This value is used in statement 240 to convert the degree measure of A to the corresponding radian measure (designated as X). This is done because BASIC's TAN function (statement 320) assumes that X is in radians.

Statements 310–330: The remaining parts of the triangle are computed. B, the other acute angle, is the complement of A. The formula for the length of the other leg, B1, is based on the following.

$$\tan A = \frac{A1}{B1}$$

$$B1 \tan A = A1$$

$$B1 = \frac{A1}{\tan A}$$

Note that X is used in line 320 instead of A, since X is in radians.

Statement 330 uses the Pythagorean Theorem to compute C1, the length of the hypotenuse. SQR is the square root function of BASIC.

Statements 360 and 390: The measures of sides B1 and C1 and angle B are printed to the nearest thousandth.

EXERCISES

A Use the program on page 150 to solve each right triangle.

1. $\angle A = 50°$, $a = 5$ 2. $\angle A = 40°$, $a = 5$
3. $\angle A = 35°$, $a = 10$ 4. $\angle A = 70°$, $a = 5$
5. $\angle A = 65°$, $a = 15$ 6. $\angle A = 30°$, $a = 20$
7. $\angle A = 89°$, $a = 10$ 8. $\angle A = 0.5°$, $a = 10$
9. $\angle A = 89.8°$, $a = 20$ 10. $\angle A = 0.01°$, $a = 20$

C Write a BASIC program for each problem.

11. Given the lengths of two legs of a right triangle, solve the triangle.

12. Given the lengths of one leg and the hypotenuse of a right triangle, solve the triangle.

13. Given the length of the hypotenuse and the degree measure of an acute angle of a right triangle, solve the triangle.

14. Expand the program on page 150 so that, after solving the triangle, the computer draws a rough approximation of the solved triangle.

3–9   Double- and Half-Angle Identities

Here is a set of identities which relate the trigonometric functions of an angle to those of twice or half of the angle. Reasonably enough these are called the **double-** and **half-angle** formulas. In general their derivations are accomplished by appropriate substitutions in the angle sum identities.

Theorem 3–7   (The Double-Angle Identity for Sine)   If θ is a real number (measure of an angle), then

$$\sin 2\theta = 2 \sin \theta \cos \theta.$$

Proof: $\sin (\alpha + \beta) = \sin \alpha \cos \beta + \cos \alpha \sin \beta.$
Letting $\alpha = \beta = \theta$, you have

$$\begin{aligned} \sin (\theta + \theta) &= \sin (2\theta) \\ &= \sin \theta \cos \theta + \sin \theta \cos \theta \\ &= 2 \sin \theta \cos \theta. \end{aligned}$$

Theorem 3–8   (The Double-Angle Identity for Cosine)   If θ is a real number (measure of an angle), then

$$\begin{aligned} \cos 2\theta &= \cos^2 \theta - \sin^2 \theta \\ &= 2 \cos^2 \theta - 1 \\ &= 1 - 2 \sin^2 \theta. \end{aligned}$$

Proof: $\cos (\alpha + \beta) = \cos \alpha \cos \beta - \sin \alpha \sin \beta.$
Let $\alpha = \beta = \theta$. Then $\cos (\theta + \theta) = \cos (2\theta) = \cos^2 \theta - \sin^2 \theta$. Since $\sin^2 \theta + \cos^2 \theta = 1$ for all $\theta \in R$,

$$\begin{aligned} \cos 2\theta &= \cos^2 \theta - \sin^2 \theta \\ &= \cos^2 \theta - (1 - \cos^2 \theta) \\ &= 2 \cos^2 \theta - 1 \end{aligned}$$

and

$$\begin{aligned} \cos 2\theta &= (1 - \sin^2 \theta) - \sin^2 \theta \\ &= 1 - 2 \sin^2 \theta. \end{aligned}$$

In a similar fashion you can prove the following theorem.

> **Theorem 3-9** (The Double-Angle Identity for Tangent) If $\theta \in R$, $\cos \theta \neq 0$, $\cos 2\theta \neq 0$, then
>
> $$\tan 2\theta = \frac{2 \tan \theta}{1 - \tan^2 \theta}.$$

EXAMPLE 1. Given $\sin \theta = \frac{2}{\sqrt{5}}$, $0 < \theta < \frac{\pi}{2}$. Find the following.

a. $\cos 2\theta$,   b. $\sin 2\theta$,   c. $\tan 2\theta$.

Solutions: Since $\sin^2 \theta + \cos^2 \theta = 1$, then $\frac{4}{5} + \cos^2 \theta = 1$ and $\cos \theta = \frac{1}{\sqrt{5}}$ $\left(\text{because } 0 < \theta < \frac{\pi}{2} \right)$. It follows that $\tan \theta = \frac{2}{1}$. (Why?)

a. $\cos 2\theta = \cos^2 \theta - \sin^2 \theta$ b. $\sin 2\theta = 2 \sin \theta \cos \theta$

$ = \frac{1}{5} - \frac{4}{5} = -\frac{3}{5}$ $= 2 \cdot \frac{2}{\sqrt{5}} \cdot \frac{1}{\sqrt{5}} = \frac{4}{5}$

c. $\tan 2\theta = \dfrac{2 \tan \theta}{1 - \tan^2 \theta} = \dfrac{4}{1 - 4} = -\dfrac{4}{3}$

The half-angle identities are derived from

1
$$\cos 2\theta = 1 - 2 \sin^2 \theta$$

and

$$\cos 2\theta = 2 \cos^2 \theta - 1$$
2

Substitute $\frac{\alpha}{2}$ for θ.

$$\cos \alpha = 1 - 2 \sin^2 \frac{\alpha}{2}$$

or $\dfrac{\cos \alpha - 1}{-2} = \sin^2 \dfrac{\alpha}{2}$

or $\sin^2 \dfrac{\alpha}{2} = \dfrac{1 - \cos \alpha}{2}$

and $\sin \dfrac{\alpha}{2} = \pm \sqrt{\dfrac{1 - \cos \alpha}{2}}$

Substitute $\frac{\alpha}{2}$ for θ.

$$\cos \alpha = 2 \cos^2 \frac{\alpha}{2} - 1$$

or $\dfrac{\cos \alpha + 1}{2} = \cos^2 \dfrac{\alpha}{2}$

or $\cos \dfrac{\alpha}{2} = \pm \sqrt{\dfrac{1 + \cos \alpha}{2}}$

The "+" is used when $\frac{\alpha}{2}$ is in Quadrant I or II, otherwise the "−" is used.

The "+" is used when $\frac{\alpha}{2}$ is in Quadrant I or IV, otherwise the "−" is used.

By definition $\tan \theta = \dfrac{\sin \theta}{\cos \theta}$.

Thus

$$\tan \frac{\alpha}{2} = \pm \sqrt{\frac{1 - \cos \alpha}{1 + \cos \alpha}} \quad (\cos \alpha \neq -1)$$

the "+" being used when $\frac{\alpha}{2}$ is in Quadrant I or III, otherwise the "−" is used. In summary, you have the following theorem.

Theorem 3-10 (The Half-Angle Identities) If α is a real number (measure of an angle). Then

$$\text{i. } \sin \frac{\alpha}{2} = \pm \sqrt{\frac{1 - \cos \alpha}{2}}.$$

$$\text{ii. } \cos \frac{\alpha}{2} = \pm \sqrt{\frac{\cos \alpha + 1}{2}}.$$

$$\text{iii. } \tan \frac{\alpha}{2} = \pm \sqrt{\frac{1 - \cos \alpha}{1 + \cos \alpha}}.$$

EXAMPLE 2. Given $\cos \frac{\pi}{4} = \frac{\sqrt{2}}{2}$, find the following.

a. $\sin \frac{\pi}{8}$ **b.** $\cos \frac{\pi}{8}$ **c.** $\tan \frac{\pi}{8}$

Solutions: $\frac{\pi}{8}$ is the measure of an angle in Quadrant I. Consequently "+" is used in each identity of Theorem 3-10.

$$\text{a. } \sin \frac{\pi}{8} = \sqrt{\frac{1 - \frac{\sqrt{2}}{2}}{2}} = \sqrt{\frac{2 - \sqrt{2}}{4}} = \frac{\sqrt{2 - \sqrt{2}}}{2}$$

$$\text{b. } \cos \frac{\pi}{8} = \sqrt{\frac{1 + \frac{\sqrt{2}}{2}}{2}} = \sqrt{\frac{2 + \sqrt{2}}{4}} = \frac{\sqrt{2 + \sqrt{2}}}{2}$$

$$\text{c. } \tan \frac{\pi}{8} = \sqrt{\frac{1 - \frac{\sqrt{2}}{2}}{1 + \frac{\sqrt{2}}{2}}} = \sqrt{\frac{2 - \sqrt{2}}{2 + \sqrt{2}}}$$

CLASSROOM EXERCISES

━━ Use the half or double angle identities to find each of the following.

1. $\sin \frac{\pi}{8}$ **2.** $\cos \frac{\pi}{8}$ **3.** $\tan \frac{\pi}{8}$

━━ If $0 < \theta < \frac{\pi}{2}$, in what quadrant is

4. $\frac{1}{2}\theta$?   **5.** 2θ?

6. Explain the method for deriving double and half-angle formulas.

WRITTEN EXERCISES

A ▬ Use the half- or double-angle identities to find each of the following.

1. $\sin \frac{\pi}{12}$

2. $\cos \frac{\pi}{12}$

3. $\tan \frac{\pi}{12}$

4. $\sin \frac{7\pi}{12}$

5. $\cos \frac{7\pi}{12}$

6. $\tan \frac{7\pi}{12}$

7. $\sin \frac{3\pi}{8}$

8. $\cos \frac{3\pi}{8}$

9. $\tan \frac{3\pi}{8}$

10. $\sin \frac{11\pi}{12}$

11. $\cos \frac{11\pi}{12}$

12. $\tan \frac{11\pi}{12}$

13. $\sin \frac{5\pi}{24}$

14. $\cos \frac{3\pi}{16}$

15. $\tan \frac{\pi}{16}$

16. If $\frac{\pi}{2} < \theta < \pi$, in what quadrant is each of the following?
    a. $\frac{1}{2}\theta$
    b. 2θ

17. If $\pi < \theta < \frac{3\pi}{2}$, in what quadrant is each of the following?
    a. $\frac{1}{2}\theta$
    b. 2θ

18. If $\frac{3\pi}{2} < \theta < 2\pi$, in what quadrant is each of the following?
    a. $\frac{1}{2}\theta$
    b. 2θ

▬ Let $P(-5, -12)$ be on the terminal side of an angle in standard position with measure θ. Find each of the following.

19. $\sin \theta$

20. $\cos \theta$

21. $\tan \theta$

22. $\sin \frac{1}{2}\theta$

23. $\cos \frac{1}{2}\theta$

24. $\sin 2\theta$

25. $\cos 2\theta$

26. $\tan 2\theta$

▬ Let $P(3, -4)$ be on the terminal side of an angle in standard position with measure α. Find each of the following.

27. $\sin \frac{1}{2}\alpha$

28. $\cos \frac{1}{2}\alpha$

29. $\tan \frac{1}{2}\alpha$

30. $\sin 2\alpha$

31. $\cos 2\alpha$

32. $\tan 2\alpha$

B ▬ Prove each of the following identities.

33. $\csc 2\theta = \frac{\sec \theta \csc \theta}{2}$

34. $\sec 2\theta = \frac{\sec^2 \theta}{2 - \sec^2 \theta}$

35. $\sec 2\theta = \frac{\csc^2 \theta}{\csc^2 \theta - 2}$

36. $\sec 2\theta = \frac{\sec^2 \theta \cdot \csc^2 \theta}{\csc^2 \theta - \sec^2 \theta}$

37. $\cot 2\theta = \frac{1 + \cos 4\theta}{\sin 4\theta}$

38. $\sec \frac{1}{2}\theta = \pm \frac{\sqrt{2 + 2\cos \theta}}{1 + \cos \theta}$

39. $\csc \frac{1}{2}\theta = \pm \frac{\sqrt{2 - 2\cos \theta}}{1 - \cos \theta}$

40. $\csc \frac{1}{2}\theta = \pm \frac{\sqrt{2 + 2\cos \theta}}{\sin \theta}$

C 41. $\cos 3\alpha = 4 \cos^3 \alpha - 3 \cos \alpha$

42. $\sin 3\alpha = 3 \sin \alpha - 4 \sin^3 \alpha$

43. $\cos 4\alpha = 8 \cos^4 \alpha - 8 \cos^2 \alpha + 1$

44. $\sin 4\alpha = 4 \sin \alpha \cdot \cos \alpha \, (2 \cos^2 \alpha - 1)$

3–10   Sum and Product Identities

The final set of identities discussed in this chapter provides a means to convert products of certain trigonometric functions into sums and conversely. As was true in the derivation of the half and double angle identities, the major tools are the sum and difference identities for the sine and cosine functions.

Theorem 3–11 (The Sum-Product Identities for Sine and Cosine)   If α, β are real numbers (measures of angles), then

i. $\sin(\alpha + \beta) + \sin(\alpha - \beta) = 2\sin\alpha\cos\beta.$
ii. $\sin(\alpha + \beta) - \sin(\alpha - \beta) = 2\cos\alpha\sin\beta.$
iii. $\cos(\alpha + \beta) + \cos(\alpha - \beta) = 2\cos\alpha\cos\beta.$
iv. $\cos(\alpha + \beta) - \cos(\alpha - \beta) = -2\sin\alpha\sin\beta.$

To prove Theorem 3–11 begin with the sum and difference identities and add or subtract as indicated in the left members of i–iv.

EXAMPLE 1.   Convert the product $2\cos 7x \cos 2x$ to a sum.
Solution: Using Identity iii of Theorem 3–11

$$7x = \alpha \qquad \text{and} \qquad 2x = \beta$$

Consequently $2\cos 7x \cos 2x = \cos 9x + \cos 5x.$

The sum-product identities may be converted to an equivalent form by making the substitution of variables.

$$x = \alpha + \beta$$
$$y = \alpha - \beta$$

Solving these for α and β you find

$$\alpha = \frac{x + y}{2}$$
$$\beta = \frac{x - y}{2}$$

Making the appropriate substitutions in Theorem 3–11, you get alternate forms of Identities i–iv.

v. $\sin x + \sin y = 2\sin\dfrac{x + y}{2} \cdot \cos\dfrac{x - y}{2}$

vi. $\sin x - \sin y = 2\cos\dfrac{x + y}{2} \cdot \sin\dfrac{x - y}{2}$

vii. $\cos x + \cos y = 2 \cos \dfrac{x+y}{2} \cdot \cos \dfrac{x-y}{2}$

viii. $\cos x - \cos y = -2 \sin \dfrac{x+y}{2} \cdot \sin \dfrac{x-y}{2}$

EXAMPLE 2.   Express $\sin \dfrac{17\pi}{12} - \sin \dfrac{11\pi}{12}$ as a product. Use Identity **vi.**

Solution: $\sin \dfrac{17\pi}{12} - \sin \dfrac{11\pi}{12} = 2 \cos \dfrac{\dfrac{17\pi}{12} + \dfrac{11\pi}{12}}{2} \cdot \sin \dfrac{\dfrac{17\pi}{12} - \dfrac{11\pi}{12}}{2}$

$$= 2 \cos \dfrac{28\pi}{24} \cdot \sin \dfrac{6\pi}{24}$$

$$= 2 \cos \dfrac{7\pi}{6} \cdot \sin \dfrac{\pi}{4}$$

EXAMPLE 3.   Express $\cos 61° + \cos 73°$ as a product.
Use Identity **vii.**

Solution: $\cos 61° + \cos 73° = 2 \cos \dfrac{61° + 73°}{2} \cos \dfrac{61° - 73°}{2}$

$$= 2 \cos 67° \cdot \cos (-6°)$$

$$= 2 \cos 67° \cdot \cos 6° \quad \text{(Why?)}$$

EXAMPLE 4.   Prove the following identity.

$$\dfrac{\sin 5t + \sin 3t}{\cos 5t - \cos 3t} = \cot (-t)$$

Proof: $\dfrac{\sin 5t + \sin 3t}{\cos 5t - \cos 3t} = \dfrac{2 \sin 4t \cos t}{-2 \sin 4t \sin t}$

$$= \dfrac{\cos t}{-\sin t}$$

$$= -\cot t$$

$$= \cot (-t)$$

CLASSROOM EXERCISES

1. Express the product $\sin \dfrac{\pi}{3} \cos \dfrac{\pi}{4}$ as a sum of trigonometric functional values.

2. Express the difference $\cos \dfrac{\pi}{3} - \cos \dfrac{\pi}{4}$ as a product of trigonometric functional values.

WRITTEN EXERCISES

A ▬▬ Write each of the following products as a sum.

1. $2 \sin 3x \cos x$ **2.** $2 \cos 11t \sin 5t$

3. $2 \cos 5x \cos 2x$ **4.** $-2 \sin 7v \sin 5v$

5. $\sin 10x \sin 4x$ **6.** $\sin 15t \cos(-3t)$

7. $\cos 8x \sin 4x$ **8.** $\cos 3t \cos 5t$

▬▬ Write each of the following sums as a product.

9. $\cos 51° - \cos 23°$ **10.** $\sin \frac{\pi}{8} + \sin \frac{\pi}{16}$

11. $\sin 131° - \sin 43°$ **12.** $\cos \frac{5\pi}{7} + \cos \frac{3\pi}{7}$

13. $\sin \frac{\pi}{3} + \sin \frac{\pi}{4}$ **14.** $\sin \left(x - \frac{\pi}{2}\right) - \sin \left(x + \frac{\pi}{2}\right)$

15. $\cos \frac{1}{4} + \cos \frac{3}{4}$ **16.** $\cos(-3t) - \cos(5t)$

B ▬▬ Prove each of the following identities.

17. $\dfrac{\cos 7t + \cos 5t}{\sin 7t - \sin 5t} = \dfrac{\csc t}{\sec t}$ **18.** $\dfrac{\sin 3t + \sin t}{\sin 3t - \sin t} = \dfrac{2}{1 - \tan^2 t}$

19. $\dfrac{\sin 4x + \sin 2x}{\cos 4x + \cos 2x} = \dfrac{1}{\cot 3x}$ **20.** $\dfrac{\sin 3x + \sin x}{\cos 3x - \cos x} = -\dfrac{\csc x}{\sec x}$

21. $\dfrac{\sin 3x - \sin x}{\cos 3x + \cos x} = \tan x$ **22.** $\dfrac{\cos 9x + \cos 5x}{\sin 9x - \sin 5x} = \dfrac{1 - \tan^2 x}{2 \tan x}$

CHAPTER SUMMARY ▬▬▬▬▬▬▬▬

Important Terms

Angle (p. 116)   Radian (p. 119)
Coterminal angles (p. 117)   Radius vector (p. 123)
Double-angle formula (p. 152)   Reference triangle (p. 123)
Half-angle formula (p. 152)   Standard position (p. 117)
Initial side (p. 116)   Terminal side (p. 116)
Linear interpolation (p. 135)   Trigonometric function (p. 124)
Quadrantal angle (p. 117)   Vertex (p. 116)

Important Ideas

1. The measure of an angle formed by a counterclockwise rotation is positive; clockwise rotations produce angles with negative measures.

2. π radians $= 180°$; $1° = \frac{\pi}{180}$ radians

3. If $P(x, y)$ is a point on the terminal side of an angle θ in standard position and the distance from the origin to P is r, then $\sin = \frac{y}{r}$, $\cos \theta = \frac{x}{r}$, and $\tan \theta = \frac{y}{x}$, $x \neq 0$.

4. In a right triangle with angle A, $\sin A = \frac{\text{side opposite } A}{\text{hypotenuse}}$,

$\cos A = \frac{\text{side adjacent to } A}{\text{hypotenuse}}$ and $\tan A = \frac{\text{side opposite}}{\text{side adjacent}}$.

5. Reduction Formulas: See Section 3–6 (pages 138–141).

6. Addition and Subtraction Identities: See Section 3–7 (pages 141–145) and Section 3–8 (pages 146–149).

7. Double and Half-Angle Identities: See Section 3–9 (pages 152–155).

8. Sum and Product Identities: See Section 3–10 (pages 156–158).

CHAPTER OBJECTIVES AND REVIEW

Objective: *To sketch an angle in standard position.* (Section 3-1)

1. Identify the following for the angle AOB.
   a. Initial side
   b. Vertex
   c. Terminal side
   d. Direction of rotation

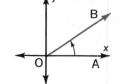

2. If $\theta = m \angle AOB$, is θ positive or negative?

━━ Sketch an angle AOB of measure θ in standard position for

3. $\theta = 120°$. **4.** $\theta = -120°$.

5. $\theta = 170°$. **6.** $\theta = -300°$.

7. $P(2, -1)$ on $\overrightarrow{OB}$. **8.** $P(-2, -3)$ on $\overrightarrow{OB}$.

9. Explain what it means for two angles to be "coterminal."

Objective: *To understand and use radian measure.* (Section 3-2)

10. If $m \angle A = 6$ radians, is $\angle A$ less than a revolution? Explain.

Objective: *Given an angle measured in radians or in degrees, to convert one to the other.* (Section 3-2)

11. What is the basic relationship relating radians and degrees?

━━ Convert each degree measure to radian measure.

12. $120°$ **13.** $-60°$ **14.** $52°$ **15.** $385°$

━━ Convert each radian measure to degree measure.

16. $\frac{\pi}{2}$ **17.** $\frac{-11\pi}{6}$ **18.** $\frac{2\pi}{9}$ **19.** $3\frac{1}{2}\pi$

Objective: *To define the trigonometric functions in terms of the radius vector r and the coordinates of P(x, y) on the terminal side of an angle of measure θ.* (Section 3-3)

━━ Define each of the following trigonometric functions. Use the radius *r* and a point *P(x, y)* on the terminal side of the angle.

20. sin θ   **21.** cos θ   **22.** tan θ

23. cot θ   **24.** sec θ   **25.** csc θ

━━ Find the six trigonometric functions of θ when θ is the measure of an angle in standard position whose terminal side contains the given point. Leave answers in radical form when radicals occur.

26. (4, 3)   **27.** (−3, 5)   **28.** (5, −12)

29. (2, 1)   **30.** (0, −3)   **31.** $(-\sqrt{3}, 1)$

Objective: *To describe the relationship between trigonometric functions and circular functions.* (Section 3-4)

32. How are trigonometric functions related to circular functions? Include in your discussion comments on the differences in definitions and in domains.

Objective: *To use the trigonometric functions to solve acute right triangles.* (Section 3-5)

━━ Find the missing measures in Exercises 33–37. Use the figure at the right.

33. $A = 60°$ $a = 3$ $b = \underline{\ ?\ }$

34. $A = 70°$ $a = 3$ $c = \underline{\ ?\ }$

35. $A = 40°$ $a = 3$ $c = \underline{\ ?\ }$

36. $a = 3$ $b = 5$ $A = \underline{\ ?\ }$

37. $a = 1$ $b = 2$ $c = \underline{\ ?\ }$

38. From an airplane two kilometers higher than the control tower of an airfield, the angle of depression to the control tower is 17°. Find the ground distance to the tower to the nearest half kilometer.

Objective: *To use the reduction formulas for the sine, cosine, and tangent functions.* (Section 3-6)

━━ Express in the form (180° − θ) or (180° + θ)

39. 98° 10′   **40.** 196° 20′   **41.** 260° 50′

━━ Find the value of each of the following.

42. $\cos 170°$ **43.** $\sin \frac{5\pi}{6}$ **44.** $\tan 190°$ **45.** $\sin 340°$

Objective: *To cite and apply the sum and difference identities for the cosine function.* (Section 3-7)

━━ Complete each identity.

46. $\cos (\alpha - \beta) = \underline{\ ?\ }$ **47.** $\cos (\alpha + \beta) = \underline{\ ?\ }$

━━ Use a sum or difference identity to find the value of each of the following.

48. $\cos \frac{\pi}{12}$ **49.** $\cos 225°$

Objective: *To cite and apply the sum and difference identities for the sine and tangent functions.* (Section 3-8)

━━ Complete each identity.

50. $\sin (\alpha - \beta) = \underline{\ ?\ }$ **51.** $\sin (\alpha + \beta) = \underline{\ ?\ }$

52. $\tan (\alpha - \beta) = \underline{\ ?\ }$ **53.** $\tan (\alpha + \beta) = \underline{\ ?\ }$

━━ Use a sum or difference identity to find the value of each of the following.

54. $\sin (-15°)$ **55.** $\sin \frac{13\pi}{12}$

56. $\tan \frac{13\pi}{12}$ **57.** $\tan 330°$

Objective: *To cite and apply the double- and half-angle formulas.* (Section 3-9)

━━ Complete each identity.

58. $\cos 2\theta = \underline{\ ?\ }$ **59.** $\sin \frac{1}{2} \alpha = \underline{\ ?\ }$

60. $\cos \frac{1}{2} \alpha = \underline{\ ?\ }$ **61.** $\tan \frac{1}{2} \alpha = \underline{\ ?\ }$

━━ Use the half- or double-angle identities to find the value of each of the following.

62. $\sin \frac{5\pi}{12}$ **63.** $\cos \frac{5\pi}{12}$

64. $\tan \frac{5\pi}{12}$ **65.** $\cos 2\theta$; $\cos \theta = \frac{3}{4}$

Objective: *To apply the sum and product identities.* (Section 3-10)

━━ Write each product or sum in the form indicated.

66. As a sum: $2 \sin \alpha \cos \beta$ **67.** As a product: $\sin \frac{1}{4} - \sin \frac{3}{4}$

CHAPTER TEST

1. Make a sketch of an angle of measure $-50°$ in standard position.
   a. What is the direction of rotation?
   b. In what quadrant is the angle?
   c. Label the initial and terminal sides.

2. Angle AOB has measure $-145°$ and is in standard position. List the measures of three angles coterminal to $\angle AOB$. Include at least one positive measure and one negative measure.

3. Change the following degree measures to radian measures.
   a. $72°$ b. $-480°$ c. $10°$

4. Change the following radian measures to degree measures.
   a. $\frac{5\pi}{18}$ b. $\frac{-15\pi}{4}$ c. 2

5. Given $P(x, y)$ with $r = OP$. Define each of the following trigonometric functions in terms of x, y and r. See the figure.
   a. $\sin\theta$ b. $\cos\theta$
   c. $\tan\theta$ d. $\cot\theta$
   e. $\sec\theta$ f. $\csc\theta$

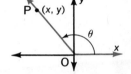

6. Complete each of the following identities.
   a. $\sin^2\theta + \cos^2\theta = $ _____.
   b. $\sin(\alpha + \beta) = $ _____.
   c. $\sin(\alpha - \beta) = $ _____.
   d. $\cos(\alpha + \beta) = $ _____.   e. $\cos(\alpha - \beta) = $ _____.

7. Prove that $\sin(\pi - \theta) = \sin\theta$.

8. Find the exact value of $\cos(15°)$ without tables.

9. Find the exact value of $\sin\frac{\pi}{8}$ without tables.

10. Find the exact value of $\tan 75°$ without tables.

11. A forest ranger spots a fire while on lookout in his 50-meter tower. The angle of depression is $4°$. How far from the base of the tower is the fire?

12. Convert the product $2\cos 9x \sin 3x$ to a sum or difference.

13. Use the tables to find approximate values for the following.
   a. $\sin(139°)$ b. $\tan(193°)$
   c. $\cos(-21°)$ d. $\tan(311°)$

14. A hunter spies a mountain goat on a cliff 250 meters higher than his position. If the angle of elevation is $20°$, what is the distance from the man to the goat?

4 Applying Trigonometry

Sections

Features

Review and Testing

4–1 Law of Sines

In Section 3–5 you learned to use trigonometric functions to solve right triangles. Trigonometry is also useful in solving triangles which contain no right angle. A major relation used in such cases is the **Law of Sines.** The following example illustrates the Law of Sines.

EXAMPLE 1. John wishes to determine the width of Perch Lake from point A to point B. The measures of sides and angles of $\triangle ABC$ are as given in the figure. To the nearest unit, how far is it from A to B?

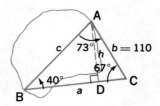

Solution: John's first thought is to construct a perpendicular from A to $\overline{BC}$. He does this, but notes that he cannot measure it directly. He notices that

$$\sin B = \frac{h}{c} \quad \longleftarrow \quad \triangle ADB$$

$$\sin C = \frac{h}{b} \quad \longleftarrow \quad \triangle ADC$$

Thus

$$h = c \sin B = b \sin C$$

or

$$\frac{b}{\sin B} = \frac{c}{\sin C}. \qquad \qquad 1$$

Since the measures of $\angle B$, $\angle C$, and b are known to John, he uses **1** to calculate the distance c from A to B as follows.

$$\frac{110}{\sin 40°} = \frac{c}{\sin 67°} \quad \text{and} \quad \frac{110 \cdot \sin 67°}{\sin 40°} = c$$

Thus

$$c = \frac{110(0.9205)}{0.6428} \quad \longleftarrow \quad \textbf{From the table}$$

Consequently $\qquad c \approx 158$

In Example 1 you saw part of the Law of Sines used to determine the distance from A to B. The complete Law of Sines follows.

Theorem 4–1 (The Law of Sines) In any triangle, the measures of the sides are proportional to the sines of the measures of the angles opposite them. In $\triangle ABC$,

$$\frac{a}{\sin A} = \frac{b}{\sin B} = \frac{c}{\sin C}.$$

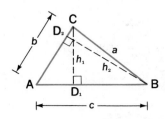
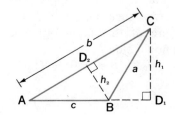

Proof: Consider two cases.

Case 1

Each angle of $\triangle ABC$ is an acute angle. h_1 and h_2 are the measures of the altitudes from C and B respectively.

In right triangles ACD_1 and BCD_1, $\frac{h_1}{b} = \sin A$ and $\frac{h_1}{a} = \sin B$.

Thus $\qquad \dfrac{b}{\sin B} = \dfrac{a}{\sin A} \qquad$ **i.**

In right triangles ABD_2 and CBD_2, $\frac{h_2}{c} = \sin A$ and $\frac{h_2}{a} = \sin C$.

Thus $\qquad \dfrac{a}{\sin A} = \dfrac{c}{\sin C} \qquad$ **ii.**

Case 2

$\angle B$ in $\triangle ABC$ is obtuse. h_1 and h_2 are the measures of the altitudes from C and B respectively.

In right triangles ACD_1 and BCD_1, $\frac{h_1}{b} = \sin A$ and $\frac{h_1}{a} = \sin (180 - B)$. Since you know $\sin (180 - B) = \sin B$, it follows that $\qquad \dfrac{b}{\sin B} = \dfrac{a}{\sin A} \qquad$ **iii.**

In right triangles ABD_2 and CBD_2, $\frac{h_2}{c} = \sin A$ and $\frac{h_2}{a} = \sin C$.

Thus $\qquad \dfrac{a}{\sin A} = \dfrac{c}{\sin C} \qquad$ **iv.**

Consequently

$$\frac{a}{\sin A} = \frac{b}{\sin B} = \frac{c}{\sin C}$$

for acute angled triangles.

Consequently

$$\frac{a}{\sin A} = \frac{b}{\sin B} = \frac{c}{\sin C}$$

for triangles with an obtuse angle.

The two arguments establish the Law of Sines for acute and obtuse triangles. Demonstrate that it is also valid for right triangles.

EXAMPLE 2. If, in $\triangle ABC$, $A = 34°$, $C = 120°$ and $b = 200$ meters, how long are sides BC and AB?

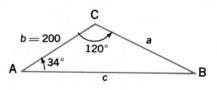

Solution: To apply the Law of Sines here, find the measure of the angle opposite the known side b.

$$B = 180° - (120° + 34) = 180° - 154° = 26°$$

$$\frac{200}{\sin 26°} = \frac{c}{\sin 120°}. \quad \longleftarrow \quad \textbf{By the Law of Sines}$$

$$c = \frac{200 \sin 120°}{\sin 26°} \quad \longleftarrow \quad \textbf{Solve for } c.$$

$$= \frac{200 \sin 60°}{\sin 26°} \quad \longleftarrow \quad \textbf{Sin 120° = sin 60°.}$$

$$\approx \frac{200(.8660)}{.4384}$$

$$\approx 395 \quad \longleftarrow \quad \textbf{Nearest integer}$$

CLASSROOM EXERCISES

━━ Use the law of sines to express the unknown side or angle in terms of known sides and angles.

1. $B = 110°$, $a = 50$, $b = 90$
$A =$ _?_

2. $A = 60°, B = 80°, a = 43$
$b =$ _?_

3. $A = 53°$, $C = 29°$, $a = 71$
$b =$ _?_

4. $B = 90°, C = 25°, c = 21$
$b =$ _?_

5. If in $\triangle ABC$, $\angle C = 90°$, is the Law of Sines valid?

6. Solve $\triangle ABC$, given $\angle B = 40°$, $\angle C = 45°$ and $BC = 10$.

WRITTEN EXERCISES

A ━━ Solve each triangle. As is customary, a, b, and c refer to the measures of the sides opposite angles A, B, and C, respectively.

1. $A = 71°$, $B = 42°$, $c = 15$

2. $A = 71°$, $a = 20$, $C = 62°$

3. $B = 41°$, $C = 130°$, $a = 10$

4. $A = 65°$, $a = 30$, $b = 20$

5. $C = 50° \, 20'$, $B = 39° \, 40'$, $c = 25$

6. $A = 90°$, $B = 40°$, $b = 12$

7. $a = 15$, $b = 20$, $B = 100°$

8. $a = 12$, $B = 110°$, $C = 35°$

Prove that each identity is true for any triangle *ABC*.

9. $\dfrac{a}{b} = \dfrac{\sin A}{\sin B}$

10. $\dfrac{a - b}{b} = \dfrac{\sin A - \sin B}{\sin B}$

B

11. Two light houses at points *A* and *B* on the coast of Maine are 40 km apart. Each has visual contact with a freighter at point *C*. If ∠*CAB* measures 20° 30′ and ∠*CBA* measures 115°, how far is the freighter from *A*? from *B*?

12. Two ranger stations located 10 km apart receive a distress call from a camper. Electronic equipment allows them to determine that the camper is at an angle of 71° from the first station and 100° from the second, each angle having as one side the line of the stations. Which station is closer to the camper? How far away is it?

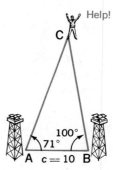

13. To find the height of a tree standing at point *C* across the Huron River from point *A*, a base line 200 meters long is established on one side of the river. The measure of ∠*BAC* was found to be 53° and that of ∠*CBA* was 74° 10′. The angle of elevation of the top of the tree from *A* measures 12°. What is the height of the tree? See the figure at the left below.

14. What is the length of a side of a regular octagon if a diagonal is 15 meters long? See the figure at the right below.

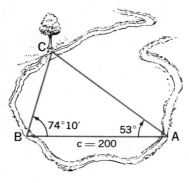

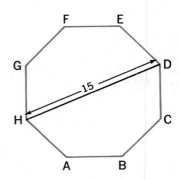

15. A tower 80 meters high stands on a cliff. From the top and bottom of the tower, the angles of depression to a ship are 18° and 14° respectively.

    a. What is the distance of the ship from the foot of the tower?

    b. What is the distance of the ship from the foot of the cliff?

    c. How high is the cliff?

C ▬▬ Prove that each identity is true for any triangle *ABC*.

16. $\dfrac{a-b}{a+b} = \dfrac{\sin A - \sin B}{\sin A + \sin B}$

17. $\dfrac{a+b}{a-b} = \dfrac{\tan \frac{1}{2}(A+B)}{\tan \frac{1}{2}(A-B)}$

(*Hint:* For Exercise 17, use Exercise 16 and the Sum-Product Identities.)

18. Area of $\triangle ABC = \frac{1}{2}a \cdot b \sin C$.

4–2   Law of Cosines

The Law of Sines may be used to solve any triangle for which you are given

    1. two angles and any one side.

The Law of Sines is of no use when you are given

    2. three sides, or

    3. two sides and their included angle.

For data as given in 2 and 3 the **Law of Cosines** is required.

Theorem 4–2 (The Law of Cosines) In any triangle, the square of a side is equal to the sum of the squares of the other sides minus twice the product of these sides times the cosine of the measure of their included angle. In $\triangle ABC$

$$a^2 = b^2 + c^2 - 2\,bc\,\cos A$$

$$b^2 = a^2 + c^2 - 2\,ac\,\cos B$$

$$c^2 = a^2 + b^2 - 2\,ab\,\cos C.$$

Proof: There are two cases to consider: 1. $\triangle ABC$ is acute, and 2. $\triangle ABC$ is obtuse. Only the proof of 2 is given.

Suppose $\triangle ABC$ is obtuse and $\overline{CD} \perp \overline{AD}$.
In $\triangle CDB$,

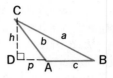

$$a^2 = h^2 + (c + p)^2$$
$$= h^2 + c^2 + 2cp + p^2. \qquad \textbf{1}$$

In $\triangle CAD$

$$h^2 = b^2 - p^2. \qquad\qquad \textbf{2}$$

Substituting for h^2 in **1**

$$a^2 = b^2 + c^2 + 2cp. \qquad\qquad \textbf{3}$$

The measure of $\angle CAD$ is θ, and $\cos \theta = \frac{p}{b}$ from which $p = b \cos \theta$. Notice that $\angle CAD$ is a supplement to $\angle A$; hence

$$\cos \theta = \cos (180° - A) = -\cos A,$$

from which

$$p = -b \cos A.$$

Substituting for p in **3**,

$$a^2 = b^2 + c^2 - 2bc \cos A.$$

EXAMPLE 1. Given $\triangle ABC$ with $A = 40°$, $b = 10$, $c = 20$. Solve the triangle.

Solution: From the Law of Cosines

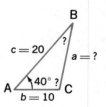

$$a^2 = b^2 + c^2 - 2b \cdot c \cos A$$
$$= (10)^2 + (20)^2 - 2 \cdot 10 \cdot 20 \cdot (0.7660)$$
$$= 100 + 400 - 400(0.7660)$$
$$= 500 - 306.4$$
$$= 193.6$$
$$a = \sqrt{193.6} \approx 13.9$$

B may be found by using the Law of Sines:

$$\sin B = \frac{b \sin A}{a}$$

and

$$C = 180° - (A + B).$$

Carry out the details and compare your results with $B \approx 27° 30'$, $C \approx 112° 30'$.

Notice that in applying either the Law of Cosines or the Law of Sines the data must include three parts of the triangle. Three types of data sets were indicated at the beginning of this section. A fourth data set, two sides and an angle opposite either side, is called the **ambiguous set** because there may be two, one, or no triangle satisfying it. (Recall that there is no SSA congruence theorem. The situation is similar here.)

Suppose the data set includes A, b and a. The situations pictured below may result for $A < 90°$ and for $A \geq 90°$.

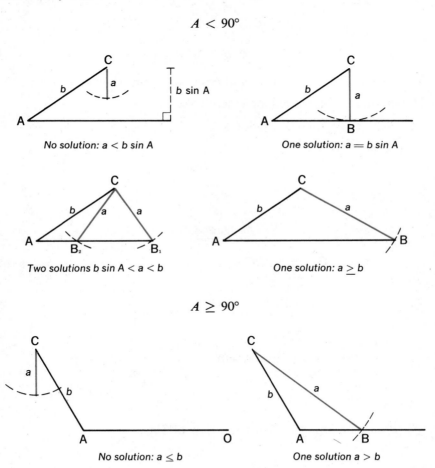

$A < 90°$

No solution: $a < b \sin A$

One solution: $a = b \sin A$

Two solutions $b \sin A < a < b$

One solution: $a \geq b$

$A \geq 90°$

No solution: $a \leq b$

One solution $a > b$

The Law of Sines may be used to solve the triangle for which the data set is ambiguous, but first you must determine whether a solution exists. The following example will illustrate the case where there are two solutions.

EXAMPLE 2. Given $\triangle ABC$ with $A = 30°$, $a = 15$, $b = 20$, find B and c.

$$\sin 30° = \tfrac{1}{2} \quad \text{and} \quad b \sin 30° = 10$$

Hence

$$b \sin 30° < a < b \qquad (10 < 15 < 20)$$

and there are two solutions.

Solution 1

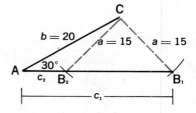

$$\frac{a}{\sin 30°} = \frac{b}{\sin B_1} \quad \text{or} \quad \frac{15}{\tfrac{1}{2}} = \frac{20}{\sin B_1}$$

Thus, $\sin B_1 = \tfrac{10}{15} = \tfrac{2}{3}$,
and $B_1 \approx 41° 50'$.
The measure of $\angle ACB_1 \approx 108° 10'$
and

$$\begin{aligned}
c &\approx \frac{\sin(108° 10') \cdot 15}{\sin 30°} \\
&\approx \sin(71° 50') \cdot 30 \\
&\approx (0.9502) \cdot 30 \\
&\approx 28.5.
\end{aligned}$$

Solution 2

Since $\angle AB_2C$ and $\angle CB_2B_1$ are supplementary and $\angle CB_2B_1 = \angle CB_1B_2$, the measure of $\angle AB_2C$ is $138° 10'$. The measure of $\angle ACB_2 = 180° - (30° + 138° 10') = 11° 50'$.

Consequently

$$\frac{c}{\sin C} = \frac{a}{\sin A}$$

or

$$c = \frac{\sin(11° 50') \cdot 15}{\sin 30°}$$

$$c \approx (0.2051)(30) \approx 6.2$$

CLASSROOM EXERCISES

1. In $\angle ABC$ it is given that $a = 6$, $b = 4$, and $c = 5$. Find the approximate measure of the angles.

2. The lengths of the sides of a triangle are 8, 9, and 13. Without using tables, determine whether the largest angle is acute or obtuse.

3. State the information that must be given to solve a triangle by the Law of Cosines.

4. The various possibilities of three given parts in a triangle are

    a. *AAA*   **b.** *ASA*

    c. *SSA*   **d.** *AAS*

    e. *SAS*   **f.** *SSS.*

Which of these do not give unique solutions? Why?

5. Using the information given in the drawings below, indicate whether the Law of Cosines can be used to solve the triangles.

a.
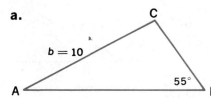

b.
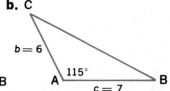

WRITTEN EXERCISES

A ▬ Use the Law of Cosines to solve each of the following.

  1. In $\triangle ABC$, $a = 5$, $b = 8$, $C = 40°$. Find c.

  2. In $\triangle ABC$, $b = 7$, $c = 10$, $A = 51°$. Find a.

  3. In $\triangle ABC$, $a = 10$, $c = 15$, $B = 171°$. Find b.

  4. In $\triangle ABC$, $a = 3$, $b = 7$, $c = 5$. Find A, B, and C.

  5. In $\triangle ABC$, $b = 9$, $c = 11$, $A = 123°$. Find a.

  6. In $\triangle ABC$, $a = 8$, $b = 6$, $C = 60°$. Find c.

  7. In $\triangle ABC$, $a = 9$, $c = 5$, $B = 120°$. Find b.

  8. In $\triangle ABC$, $a = 1$, $b = 2$, $c = 2$. Find A, B, and C.

▬ Indicate whether a solution exists and if so the number of solutions for each set of data. <u>Do not solve.</u>

  9. $a = 2$, $b = 3$, $c = 6$

10. $C = 17°$, $a = 10$, $c = 11$

11. $B = 71°$, $a = 5$, $c = 275$

12. $A = 20°$, $a = 7$, $b = 20$

13. $A = 41°$, $B = 160°$, $a = 10$

14. $C = 30°$, $b = 10$, $c = 4$

15. $A = 60°$, $b = 2$, $a = \sqrt{3}$

16. $A = 90°$, $a = 20$, $b = 19$

17. $B = 140°$, $a = 3$, $b = 2$

18. $C = 120°$, $b = 14$, $c = 13$

B **19.** Two steamships leave the same port simultaneously, one traveling 10 knots and the other 8 knots. At the end of two hours they are 15 nautical miles apart. What was the measure of the angle between their courses? (Express the measure of angle to the nearest 10'. 1 knot = 1 nautical mile per hour.) See the figure below.

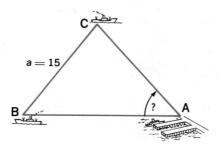

20. Two jet aircraft leave an airport at the same time. The course of the first is 160° east of north while the course of the second is 70° west of north. If the first travels 500 mph and the second 600 mph, what is the distance between them at the end of 3 hours? See the figure below.

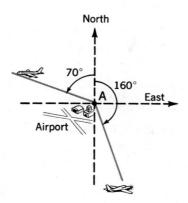

21. A woman hikes 6 km due north, then turns to the right and hikes 9 km. If the angle determined by her initial course and her final position measures 40°, through how many degrees did she turn when she turned to the right? If the angle determined by her initial course and her final position is 60°, through how many degrees did she turn when she turned to the right?

22. The radius of a circle is 20 units, and two radii OX and OY form an angle which measures 115°. How long is the chord XY?

23. Two sides and a diagonal of a parallelogram measure 7, 9, and 15 respectively. Find the measures of the angles of the parallelogram.

24. Show that if

$$t = \frac{a^2 + b^2 - c^2}{2ab}$$

then $\quad 1 + t = \dfrac{(a + b + c)(a + b - c)}{2ab}$

25. Show that if

$$t = \frac{a^2 + b^2 - c^2}{2ab}$$

then $\quad 1 - t = \dfrac{(-a + b + c)(a - b + c)}{2ab}$

26. Show that in $\triangle ABC$

$$1 + \cos C = \frac{(a + b + c)(a + b - c)}{2ab}$$

27. Show that in $\triangle ABC$

$$1 - \cos C = \frac{(-a + b + c)(a - b + c)}{2ab}$$

28. Show that in $\triangle ABC$

$$\tan \frac{C}{2} = \sqrt{\frac{(-a + b + c)(a - b + c)}{(a + b + c)(a + b - c)}}$$

C **29.** The *semiperimeter* s of a triangle with sides measuring a, b, and c is defined by $s = \dfrac{a + b + c}{2}$. Let $p = \sqrt{\dfrac{(s - a)(s - b)(s - c)}{s}}$ and use Exercises 26–28 to show that

i. $\sin\left(\dfrac{C}{2}\right) = \sqrt{\dfrac{(s - a)(s - b)}{ab}}\,.$ ii. $\cos\left(\dfrac{C}{2}\right) = \sqrt{\dfrac{s(s - c)}{ab}}\,.$

iii. $\tan\left(\dfrac{C}{2}\right) = \sqrt{\dfrac{(s - a)(s - b)}{s(s - c)}}\,.$ iv. $\tan\left(\dfrac{C}{2}\right) = \dfrac{p}{s - c}\,.$

30. Prove that the sum of the squares of the diagonals of a parallelogram is equal to the sum of the squares of the lengths of the four sides.

31. Show that in $\triangle ABC$

$$\sin C = \frac{2}{ab} \sqrt{s(s - a)(s - b)(s - c)}.$$

$\left(\textit{Hint:}\quad \sin C = 2 \sin\left(\dfrac{C}{2}\right) \cdot \cos\left(\dfrac{C}{2}\right).\right)$

4–3 Area

You will recall that if K represents the area of a triangle, then the area formula is

$$K = \tfrac{1}{2}b \cdot h \qquad\qquad 1$$

where b and h are measures of one side and the altitude to that side. Formula **1** may be used to obtain other expressions for the area when given specific sets of data.

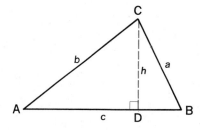 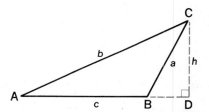

Data Set I: Given the measures of two sides and the included angle. Suppose you are given A, b and c. There are two cases to consider: $\triangle ABC$ is acute or $\triangle ABC$ is obtuse. In either case the area K is

$$K = \tfrac{1}{2}ch. \qquad\qquad 2$$

But $h = b \sin A$ in either case; hence

$$K = \tfrac{1}{2}cb \sin A. \qquad\qquad 3$$

Similarly

$$K = \tfrac{1}{2}ab \sin C \qquad\qquad 4$$

and

$$K = \tfrac{1}{2}ac \sin B. \qquad\qquad 5$$

Formulas **3–5** may be used to calculate the area of any triangle given two sides and their included angle.

EXAMPLE 1. Find the area of $\triangle ABC$ given that $B = 40°$, $a = 5$, $c = 10$. From formula 5

Solution:
$$K = \tfrac{1}{2}ac \sin B.$$
$$K = \tfrac{1}{2} \cdot 5 \cdot 10 \sin 40° \quad \longleftarrow \textbf{ By substitution}$$
$$= \tfrac{1}{2} \cdot 5 \cdot 10 \cdot (0.6428)$$
$$= \tfrac{1}{2} \cdot 5 \cdot 6.428$$
$$= 5 \cdot 3.214$$
$$= 16.070 \approx 16$$

Data Set II: Given the measures of one side and the angles. Suppose you know A, B and c. Then from formula 3

$$K = \tfrac{1}{2}bc \sin A. \qquad\qquad 6$$

But by the Law of Sines $\dfrac{b}{\sin B} = \dfrac{c}{\sin C}$ or $b = \dfrac{c \sin B}{\sin C}$.

Substituting in 6 you find

$$K = \frac{1}{2} \frac{c^2 \sin A \sin B}{\sin C}. \qquad\qquad 7$$

Similarly

$$K = \frac{1}{2} \frac{a^2 \sin B \sin C}{\sin A} \qquad\qquad 8$$

and

$$K = \frac{1}{2} \frac{b^2 \sin A \sin C}{\sin B}. \qquad\qquad 9$$

EXAMPLE 2. Find the area of $\triangle ABC$ given that $a = 10$, $A = 85°$, $B = 60°$, $C = 35°$.

Solution:

$$K = \frac{1}{2} \frac{a^2 \sin B \sin C}{\sin A} \qquad \longleftarrow \text{ Formula 8}$$

$$= \frac{1}{2} \frac{10^2(.8660)(.5736)}{(.9962)} \qquad \longleftarrow \text{ By substitution}$$

$$= 24.93$$

$$\approx 25$$

Data Set III: Given the measures of the three sides. Suppose you are given a, b, and c. Let the **semiperimeter s** be defined by

$$s = \frac{a + b + c}{2}.$$

By formula 4

$$K = \tfrac{1}{2}ab \sin C \qquad\qquad 10$$

and by Exercise 31, Section 4–2

$$\sin C = \frac{2}{ab} \sqrt{s(s - a)(s - b)(s - c)}. \qquad\qquad 11$$

Substituting 11 in 10, you find

$$K = \tfrac{1}{2}ab \left(\frac{2}{ab}\right) \sqrt{s(s - a)(s - b)(s - c)}$$

$$= \sqrt{s(s - a)(s - b)(s - c)}. \qquad\qquad 12$$

Formula 12 is known as **Heron's Formula.** (Also known as Hero's Formula.)

EXAMPLE 3. Find the area of $\triangle ABC$ if $a = 7$, $b = 8$, $c = 9$.

Solution: $\qquad s = \dfrac{7 + 8 + 9}{2}$

$\qquad\qquad\qquad = 12$

From **12**

$$K = \sqrt{12(12 - 7)(12 - 8)(12 - 9)}$$
$$= \sqrt{12(5)(4)(3)}$$
$$= 12\sqrt{5}.$$

CLASSROOM EXERCISES

Identify the formula to use to find the area of $\triangle ABC$.

1. $a = 1$, $b = 2$, $c = 1.5$ $\qquad$ **2.** $a = 1$, $b = 2$, $C = 50°$

3. $c = 5$, $a = 4$, $B = 25°$ $\qquad$ **4.** $a = 5$, $B = 30$, $C = 70°$

5. $c = 5$, $a = 4$, $b = 3$ $\qquad$ **6.** $b = 18$, $A = 70°$, $C = 80°$

7. In $\triangle ABC$, $b = 281$, $c = 358$, and $A = 32°\ 20'$. Find K.

8. In $\triangle ABC$, $a = 496$, $b = 564$, and $c = 632$. Find K.

9. In $\triangle ABC$, $A = 29°\ 40'$, $B = 78°\ 50'$, $a = 69.7$. Find K.

WRITTEN EXERCISES

A **1–12.** Find the area of the triangle or triangles (if any) satisfying the data sets in Exercises 7–18, Section 4–2.

13. Given: $K = 100$, $A = 36°$, $B = 74°$. Find b.

14. Given: $K = 50$, $A = 30°$, $b = 10$. Find c.

15. Given: $K = 50$, $a = 20$, $b = 10$, $C > 90°$. Find C.

16. The adjacent sides of a parallelogram measure 12 and 18 meters. If one angle measures 45°, find its area.

17. The sides of a rhombus measure 10 meters and one diagonal is 12 meters. Find the area.

18. The diagonals of a parallelogram have measures 60 and 40, and form an angle which measures 60°. Find the area.

B **19.** Find a formula for the area of an isosceles triangle with base b and base angles measuring θ. (Use formula **9**, page 176.)

20. In $\triangle ABC$ express the length h of the altitude to $\overline{AB}$ in terms of the lengths of the sides of the triangle. (Use formula **12**.)

21. Find an expression for the radius r of a circle inscribed in a triangle in terms of the area K and the semiperimeter s.

22. Given: $\triangle ABC$, circle O an escribed circle to $\triangle ABC$. Find an expression for the radius r of circle O in terms of K, s and the lengths of the sides of $\triangle ABC$. See figure below. (*Hint:* Area $\triangle ABC$ = Area $\triangle OCA$ + Area $\triangle OAB$ − Area $\triangle OBC$)

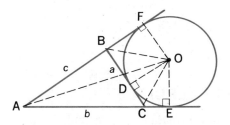

23. Show that the radius R of a circle circumscribed about a triangle ABC is given by

$$R = \frac{a}{2 \sin A} = \frac{b}{2 \sin B} = \frac{c}{2 \sin C}.$$

24. Use the results from Exercise 23 and

$$K = \frac{bc \sin A}{2}$$

to show that

$$R = \frac{abc}{4K}.$$

━━ Prove that in any $\triangle ABC$ each of the following is true.

25. $a \cos B + b \cos A = c$.

26. $a \cos B - b \cos A = \dfrac{a^2 - b^2}{c}$. (The equation for Exercise 25 is useful.)

27. $2Rr = \dfrac{abc}{a + b + c}$. r is the radius of a circle inscribed in a triangle. (See Exercise 21.) R is the radius of a circle circumscribed about a triangle. (See Exercise 24.)

28. $K = \frac{1}{2}a^2 \dfrac{\sin B \sin C}{\sin (B + C)}$.

29. $K = ab \sin \left(\dfrac{C}{2}\right) \cos \left(\dfrac{C}{2}\right)$. (See Exercises 29 and 31, Section 4–2.)

4–4   Finding Angles

If you were asked to find the values of x for which $\cos x = 2$, you would respond that the solution set is the empty set because the range of $\cos x$ is $\{-1 \leq y \leq 1\}$. However if asked to find the values of x for which $\cos x = \frac{\sqrt{2}}{2}$ you should respond that the solution set has infinitely many members. Why is this so?

You know $\cos \frac{\pi}{4} = \frac{\sqrt{2}}{2}$ and $\cos \left(-\frac{\pi}{4}\right) = \frac{\sqrt{2}}{2}$. Thus $\frac{\pi}{4}$ and $-\frac{\pi}{4}$ are elements of the solution set of $\cos x = \frac{\sqrt{2}}{2}$. You also know that $\cos(\theta \pm 2n\pi) = \cos \theta$, $n \in W$, $\theta \in R$.

Thus $\cos \left(\frac{\pi}{4} \pm 2n\pi\right) = \cos \frac{\pi}{4} = \frac{\sqrt{2}}{2}$ and $\cos \left(-\frac{\pi}{4} \pm 2n\pi\right) = \cos \left(-\frac{\pi}{4}\right) = \frac{\sqrt{2}}{2}$. It follows that the solution set of $\cos x = \frac{\sqrt{2}}{2}$ is the following.

$$\left\{x : x = \frac{\pi}{4} \pm 2n\pi \quad \text{or} \quad x = -\frac{\pi}{4} \pm 2n\pi, \, n \in W\right\}$$

This infinite set is denoted **arc cos** $\left(\frac{\sqrt{2}}{2}\right)$ or $\mathbf{cos^{-1}} \left(\frac{\sqrt{2}}{2}\right)$. Either expression may be read "the set of real numbers whose cosine is $\frac{\sqrt{2}}{2}$," or "arc cosine $\frac{\sqrt{2}}{2}$." If you think of x as representing the measure of an angle, then arc cos $\frac{\sqrt{2}}{2}$ is thought of as "the set of angle measures whose cosine is $\frac{\sqrt{2}}{2}$."

It should be noted that $\cos^{-1} \frac{\sqrt{2}}{2} \neq \left(\cos \frac{\sqrt{2}}{2}\right)^{-1}$. In the former expression the "-1" is part of the symbol for "arc cos." In the latter, the "-1" is an exponent and $\left(\cos \frac{\sqrt{2}}{2}\right)^{-1} = \dfrac{1}{\cos \frac{\sqrt{2}}{2}}$.

In general, **arc cos x** is the set of real numbers y such that **$\cos y = x$.** In other words $y \in$ arc cos x if and only if $\cos y = x$.

The sets **arc sin x, arc tan x, arc cot x, arc sec x,** and **arc csc x** are defined in a similar manner.

EXAMPLE 1. Identify the members of the set arc tan $\frac{\sqrt{3}}{3}$.

Solution:

y is an element of arc tan $\frac{\sqrt{3}}{3}$ if and only if tan $y = \frac{\sqrt{3}}{3}$. Since tan $\frac{\pi}{6} = \frac{\sqrt{3}}{3}$ and tan $\frac{7\pi}{6} = \frac{\sqrt{3}}{3}$, $\frac{\pi}{6}$ and $\frac{7\pi}{6}$ are elements of arc tan $\frac{\sqrt{3}}{3}$.

$$\tan\left(\frac{\pi}{6} \pm n\pi\right) = \frac{\sqrt{3}}{3}, \; n \in W. \quad \longleftarrow \quad \textbf{Tan } x \textbf{ has period } \pi.$$

When $n = 1$, $\frac{\pi}{6} + 1 \cdot \pi = \frac{7\pi}{6}$. Thus

$$\text{arc tan } \frac{\sqrt{3}}{3} = \left\{y : y = \frac{\pi}{6} \pm n\pi, \; n \in W\right\}$$

or

$$\text{arc tan } \frac{\sqrt{3}}{3} = \{y : y = 30° \pm n \cdot 180°, \; n \in W\} \quad \longleftarrow \quad \tfrac{\pi}{6} = \textbf{30}°$$

The key to identifying all the members of a set like arc sin x or arc cot x is to find the real numbers y such that $0 \leq y < 2\pi$ (or $0° \leq y < 360°$) and then use the period of the function to determine the remaining members.

An expression like "sin $\left(\text{arc cos } \frac{\sqrt{2}}{2}\right)$", read "sine arc cosine $\frac{\sqrt{2}}{2}$", or read as "the sine of a number whose cosine is $\frac{\sqrt{2}}{2}$" may sometimes be misinterpreted. Sin $\left(\text{arc cos } \frac{\sqrt{2}}{2}\right)$ is used to denote the values of the sines of all numbers x for which $\cos x = \frac{\sqrt{2}}{2}$ is true. Even though there are infinitely many such x, usually there are only one or two values of an expression such as sin $\left(\text{arc cos } \frac{\sqrt{2}}{2}\right)$.

EXAMPLE 2. Evaluate sin $\left(\text{arc cos } \frac{\sqrt{2}}{2}\right)$.

Solution: arc cos $\frac{\sqrt{2}}{2} = \left\{x : x = \frac{\pi}{4} \pm 2n\pi \;\; \text{or} \;\; x = \frac{-\pi}{4} \pm 2n\pi, \; n \in W\right\}$.

$$\sin\left(\text{arc cos } \frac{\sqrt{2}}{2}\right) = \sin\left(\frac{\pi}{4} \pm 2n\pi\right) \;\; \text{or} \;\; \sin\left(\frac{-\pi}{4} \pm 2n\pi\right), \; n \in W$$

$$= \sin \frac{\pi}{4} \;\; \text{or} \;\; \sin\left(\frac{-\pi}{4}\right) \quad \longleftarrow \quad \begin{array}{l} \sin \frac{\pi}{4} = \\ \sin\left(\frac{\pi}{4} \pm 2n\pi\right) \end{array}$$

$$= \frac{\sqrt{2}}{2} \;\; \text{or} \;\; \frac{-\sqrt{2}}{2}.$$

You may find it convenient to think of expressions such as arc tan 1 as sets of measures of angles. Then arc tan 1 is the set of measures of angles whose tangent is 1. Thinking this way can help you to evaluate expressions such as sec (arc tan 1) by drawing a figure.

EXAMPLE 3. Evaluate sec (arc tan 1)

Solution:

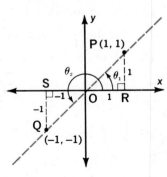

Arc tan 1 is the set of measures of angles whose tangent is 1. Thus $\tan \theta = 1$ and θ is the measure of an angle in Quadrant I or III. Also the points $P(1, 1)$ and $Q(-1, -1)$ are on the terminal sides of these angles. Complete the right triangles POR and QOS as shown in the figure.

$$\sec \theta = \frac{r}{x}, \qquad \sec \theta_1 = \frac{\sqrt{2}}{1}, \qquad \text{and} \qquad \sec \theta_2 = \frac{\sqrt{2}}{-1}.$$

Hence
$$\sec \text{ (arc tan 1)} = \frac{\sqrt{2}}{1} \quad \text{or} \quad \frac{-\sqrt{2}}{1}.$$

EXAMPLE 4. Find sin (arc cos $\frac{5}{13}$).

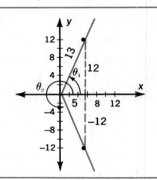

If $\cos \theta = \frac{5}{13}$, then θ is the measure of an angle in Quadrant I or IV. Also $r = 13$ and $x = 5$, and applying the Pythagorean Theorem $y = 12$.

Thus, for the drawing,

$$\sin \left(\text{arc cos } \frac{5}{13} \right) = \frac{12}{13} \quad \text{or} \quad \frac{-12}{13}.$$

CLASSROOM EXERCISES

State the quadrants in which the solutions lie.

1. $y = \text{arc tan } (-1)$
2. $y = \text{arc sin } \frac{1}{2}$
3. $y = \text{arc cos } \frac{1}{2}$
4. $y = \text{arc tan } \sqrt{3}$
5. $y = \text{arc cos } \left(-\frac{\sqrt{3}}{2} \right)$
6. $y = - \text{arc sin } \left(-\frac{\sqrt{3}}{2} \right)$

WRITTEN EXERCISES

A — Find the members of each of the following sets.

1. arc tan (-1)
2. arc sin (-1)
3. arc cos (-1)
4. arc sin 0
5. arc cos $\frac{1}{2}$
6. arc tan $\sqrt{3}$

7. arc cot $\sqrt{3}$ **8.** arc sec (-2) **9.** arc csc $\frac{2\sqrt{3}}{3}$

10. arc sin $(-\frac{1}{2})$ **11.** arc csc 1   **12.** arc cot 0

13. arc sin (0.6428)

14. arc sin $\frac{\sqrt{3}}{2} \cap$ arc cos $\left(\frac{-1}{2}\right)$

15. arc tan $(-1) \cup$ arc csc (-2)

━━ Evaluate each expression.

16. tan $\left(\text{arc sin } \frac{-3}{5}\right)$ **17.** sin (arc sin $\frac{4}{5}$)   **18.** cos (arc sec 4)

19. sec $\left(\text{arc sin } \frac{-7}{25}\right)$ **20.** csc (arc tan $\frac{1}{3}$)

21. cot (arc csc $\frac{25}{24}$)   **22.** sin (arc cos $\frac{1}{3}$)

23. csc (arc tan $[-4]$)   **24.** cos (arc cot $[-4]$)

25. tan (arc sin u) $0 \leq u < 1$ **26.** cos (arc tan u) $u > 0$

27. sin (arc cos u) $0 \leq u < 1$ **28.** cot (arc cos u) $0 \leq u < 1$

29. sec (arc tan u) $u \geq 0$ **30.** csc (arc cos u) $0 \leq u < 1$

B   Evaluate each expression.

31. cos (arc sin $\frac{3}{5}$ + arc tan $\frac{12}{13}$)   [*Hint:* What is cos $(\alpha + \beta)$?]

32. sin (arc cos $\frac{3}{5}$ + arc sec 3)

33. sin (2 arc sin $\frac{4}{5}$)   [*Hint:* What is sin 2θ?]

34. cos (2 arc cot $\frac{5}{13}$)

35. tan (2 arc sin $\frac{7}{25}$)

36. tan ($\frac{1}{2}$ arc cos $\frac{1}{2}$)   [*Hint:* What is tan $(\frac{1}{2}\theta)$?]

C   **37.** -2 sin (arc tan 1) $\cdot$ sin (arc tan $\sqrt{3}$)

    38. 2 cos (arc sec 2) $\cdot$ cos (arc csc 2)

4–5   Inverse Circular Functions

Recall that if f is a function which maps the elements of U onto the elements of V, then the inverse of f is a relation g which may or may not be a function.

Consider the sine function: $\{(x, y) : y = \sin x\}$.
The sine function maps each real number onto a unique real number y such that $-1 \leq y \leq 1$. The mapping which is the inverse of the sine function is

$$\{(x, y) : x = \sin y\}$$

or

$$\{(x, y) : y \in \text{arc sin } x\}.$$

Since arc sin x for each x such that $-1 \leq x \leq 1$ is an infinite set, the inverse of the sine function is not a function; it is a relation. By restricting the range of this relation to the set $\left\{\frac{-\pi}{2} \leq y \leq \frac{\pi}{2}\right\}$, you can pair each number x, $-1 \leq x \leq 1$, with a unique number y. The resulting mapping is a function.

The unique number y such that

$$y \in \text{arc sin } x, \frac{-\pi}{2} \leq y \leq \frac{\pi}{2},$$

is called the **principal value of arc sin x** and is denoted as follows.

$$y = \textbf{Arc sin } x$$

The capital "A" on Arc denotes the principal value. The Arc sin function is

$$\{(x, y) : y = \text{Arc sin } x, \ |x| \leq 1, \ x \in \mathbf{R}\}.$$

The graphs of $y = \sin x$, $y = \text{arc sin } x$ and $y = \text{Arc sin } x$ are shown in the next figure, Arc sin x being shown in color.

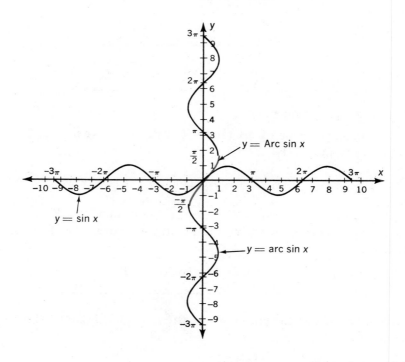

The **principal value of arc cos x,** $-1 \leq x \leq 1$, is the unique number $y \in$ arc cos x such that $0 \leq y \leq \pi$. The principal value is denoted **Arc cos x.** The Arc cos function is

$$\{(x, y) : y = \text{Arc cos } x, \ |x| \leq 1, \ x \in R\}.$$

The graph of the function described by $y = $ Arc cos x is shown below in Figure 1.

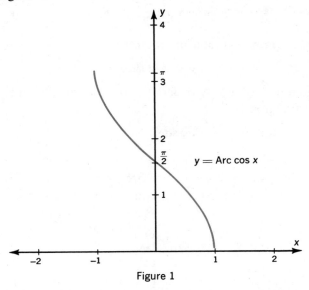

Figure 1

The unique member y, $\dfrac{-\pi}{2} < y < \dfrac{\pi}{2}$, $y \in$ arc tan x, $x \in R$, is the **principal value of arc tan x;** it is denoted **Arc tan x.** The Arc tan function is

$$\{(x, y) : y = \text{Arc tan } x, \ x \in R\}.$$

The unique member y, $0 < y < \pi$, $y \in$ arc cot x, $x \in R$, is the **principal value of arc cot x;** it is denoted **Arc cot x.** The Arc cot function is

$$\{(x, y) : y = \text{Arc cot } x, \ x \in R\}.$$

Figure 2 shows the graph of $y = $ Arc tan x and Figure 3 shows the graph of $y = $ Arc cot x.

The graph of $y = $ Arc tan x is shown below.

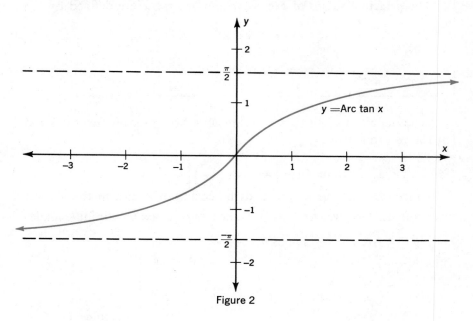

Figure 2

The graph of $y = $ Arc cot x is shown below.

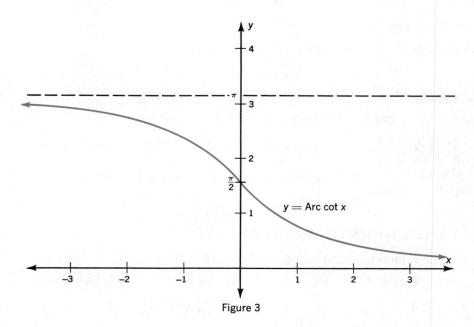

Figure 3

The **principal values of arc sec x** and **arc csc x** are defined by

$$\text{Arc sec } x = \text{Arc cos } \frac{1}{x}, \quad |x| \geq 1$$

$$\text{Arc csc } x = \text{Arc sin } \frac{1}{x}, \quad |x| \geq 1$$

The definitions of the Arc secant and Arc cosecant functions are left for you to state.

EXAMPLE 1. Evaluate $\sin\left[\text{Arc cos}\left(\frac{-7}{25}\right)\right]$.

Since $0 \leq \text{Arc cos } x \leq \pi$ and the cosine of angles in the second quadrant are negative, Arc cos $\frac{-7}{25}$ is the measure of a Quadrant II angle.

Letting $\theta = \text{Arc cos}\left(\frac{-7}{25}\right)$, $\cos \theta = \frac{-7}{25}$.

Thus $x = -7$, $r = 25$, and

$$y = \sqrt{25^2 - 7^2}$$
$$= \sqrt{576}$$
$$= 24.$$

Thus $\sin \theta = \frac{24}{25}$, and

$$\sin\left[\text{Arc cos}\left(\frac{-7}{25}\right)\right] = \frac{24}{25}.$$

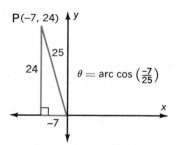

$P(-7, 24)$

$\theta = \text{arc cos}\left(\frac{-7}{25}\right)$

EXAMPLE 2. Show that

$$\sin[\text{Arc cos } x + \text{Arc sin } y] = \sqrt{1 - x^2} \cdot \sqrt{1 - y^2} + xy.$$

Solution: Let $\alpha = \text{Arc cos } x$. Then $\cos \alpha = x$ and $\sin \alpha = \sqrt{1 - x^2}$.

Let $\beta = \text{Arc sin } y$. Then $\sin \beta = y$ and $\cos \beta = \sqrt{1 - y^2}$.

Now $\sin(\alpha + \beta) = \sin \alpha \cos \beta + \cos \alpha \sin \beta$, where $\alpha = \text{Arc cos } x$ and $\beta = \text{Arc sin } y$.

Therefore, $\sin[\text{Arc cos } x + \text{Arc sin } y] = \sqrt{1 - x^2} \cdot \sqrt{1 - y^2} + xy$.

CLASSROOM EXERCISES

━━ Find the measure of each of the following angles.

1. Arc cos (-1) **2.** Arc sin 0 **3.** Arc sin $\frac{\sqrt{3}}{2}$

4. Arc tan (-1) **5.** Arc tan $\sqrt{3}$ **6.** Arc cot 0

WRITTEN EXERCISES

A ▬ Find the measure of each of the following angles.

1. Arc sin $\left(\frac{-\sqrt{2}}{2}\right)$ **2.** Arc cos $\frac{-4}{5}$ **3.** Arc tan (0.6009)

4. Arc cot (-1) **5.** Arc csc $\frac{2\sqrt{3}}{3}$ **6.** Arc sec (-2)

7. Arc sin $(\frac{1}{2})$ **8.** Arc tan $\left(\frac{-\sqrt{3}}{3}\right)$ **9.** Arc cos 0.9272

▬ Evaluate each expression.

10. sin (Arc cos $\frac{1}{3}$)   **11.** tan (Arc tan 4)

12. sin [Arc tan (-3)]   **13.** sec (Arc sin $\frac{1}{2}$)

14. csc [Arc tan (-4)]   **15.** cot (Arc cos $\frac{2}{3}$)

16. tan (Arc sin $\frac{4}{7}$)   **17.** sin $\left[\text{Arc cot}\left(\frac{-3}{4}\right)\right]$

18. cos [Arc sin $(-\frac{1}{5})$]   **19.** cot $\left[\text{Arc cos}\left(\frac{-11}{61}\right)\right]$

20. cos $\left[\text{Arc tan}\left(\frac{-12}{5}\right)\right]$ **21.** sec (Arc csc 4)

B **22.** Sketch the graph of $y =$ Arc sec x.

23. Sketch the graph of $y =$ Arc csc x.

24. Show that Arc cot $x = \frac{\pi}{2} -$ Arc tan x.

25. Show that cos (Arc sin u) = $\sqrt{1 - u^2}$, $|u| \le 1$.

26. Show that Arc tan $\frac{1}{2} +$ Arc tan $\frac{1}{3} = \frac{\pi}{4}$.

▬ Evaluate each of the following.

27. sin $\left[\text{Arc cos } \frac{4}{5} + \frac{\pi}{2}\right]$

28. cos [Arc cos $(-\frac{1}{2})$ − Arc sin $(\frac{3}{5})$]

29. sin [Arc cos $(\frac{1}{2})$ − Arc sin $\frac{5}{13}$]

30. tan $\left[\text{Arc sin } \frac{1}{\sqrt{10}} + \text{Arc cos}\left(\frac{-4}{5}\right)\right]$

31. cos $\left[\text{Arc tan}\left(\frac{-4}{3}\right) - \text{Arc sin}\left(\frac{11}{61}\right)\right]$

32. cot [Arc cot $(\frac{2}{3})$ + Arc cot $(\frac{1}{3})$]

33. sin $\left[2 \text{ Arc tan}\left(\frac{-8}{15}\right)\right]$ **34.** cos $\left[2 \text{ Arc sin}\left(\frac{-4}{5}\right)\right]$

35. tan [2 Arc cot $(\frac{24}{7})$]   **36.** sin [$\frac{1}{2}$ Arc tan $(\frac{3}{5})$]

37. cos $\left[\frac{1}{2} \text{ Arc sin}\left(\frac{-15}{17}\right)\right]$ **38.** tan $\left[\frac{1}{2} \text{ Arc sec}\left(\frac{-13}{5}\right)\right]$

C Prove the statement in the exercise below.

39. tan [Arc tan a + Arc tan 1] = $\frac{1 + a}{1 - a}$

■ Prove each statement in the exercises below.

40. $\tan [\text{Arc} \tan b - \text{Arc} \tan a] = \dfrac{b - a}{1 + ab}$

41. $\tan [\text{Arc} \cos a + \text{Arc} \sin b] = \dfrac{\sqrt{1 - a^2} \cdot \sqrt{1 - b^2} + ab}{a\sqrt{1 - b^2} - b\sqrt{1 - a^2}}$

42. $\sin [\text{Arc} \sin x + \text{Arc} \sin y] = x\sqrt{1 - y^2} + y\sqrt{1 - x^2}$

43. $\text{Arc} \sin \frac{3}{5} + \text{Arc} \cos \frac{5}{13} = \text{Arc} \sin \frac{63}{65}$

44. $\text{Arc} \tan \left(\dfrac{-3}{4}\right) + \text{Arc} \sin \left(\dfrac{-7}{25}\right) = \text{Arc} \cos \frac{3}{5}$

45. $2 \text{ Arc} \tan \frac{1}{3} + \text{Arc} \tan \frac{1}{7} = \dfrac{\pi}{4}$

46. $\text{Arc} \tan \frac{1}{5} - \text{Arc} \tan (-5) = \dfrac{\pi}{2}$

4–6 Equations Involving Trigonometric Functions

Recall that an equation which is true for all replacements of the independent variable for which the statement is defined is an identity. An equation which is not an identity is a **conditional equation.** For example, $\sin \theta = \frac{1}{2}$ is a conditional equation. The solution set is

$$\left\{\theta : \theta = \frac{\pi}{6} \pm 2n\pi \quad or \quad \theta = \frac{5\pi}{6} \pm 2n\pi, \ n \in W\right\}.$$

Notice that the solution set is infinite.

A variety of techniques may be used to find the solution set of a conditional equation involving trigonometric (or circular) functions. You may need to use algebraic techniques such as factoring, or you may need a trigonometric identity. The symbol "$\vee$" will be used to represent *or*, "$\wedge$" to represent *and*.

EXAMPLE 1. Solve $\sin 2x = 0$.

Solution: $\sin 2x = 2 \sin x \cos x.$ ⟵ **Identity**

$2 \sin x \cos x = 0.$ ⟵ **By substitution**

$\sin x = 0 \vee \cos x = 0.$ ⟵ $a \cdot b = 0$ **iff** $a = 0$ **or** $b = 0$

$\sin x = 0, \ x \in \{0 \pm n\pi\} = \text{arc} \sin 0.$

$\cos x = 0, \ x \in \left\{\dfrac{\pi}{2} \pm n\pi\right\} = \text{arc} \cos 0.$

Thus the solution set of $\sin 2x = 0$ is

$$\left\{x : x = \pm n\pi \ \vee \ x = \frac{\pi}{2} \pm n\pi, \ n \in W\right\}.$$

In this section $n \in W$ will be omitted in specifying solution sets, for you know that n represents a whole number.

EXAMPLE 2. Solve $\sin 2x = 4 \sin x$.

Solution:
$$\sin 2x = 4 \sin x$$
$$\sin 2x - 4 \sin x = 0$$
$$2 \sin x \cos x - 4 \sin x = 0$$
$$2 \sin x(\cos x - 2) = 0$$
$$2 \sin x = 0 \qquad \vee \qquad \cos x - 2 = 0$$

Since $\sin 0 = \sin \pi = 0$, the solution set of $2 \sin x = 0$ is

$$\{x : x = \pm n\pi\} = \text{arc sin } 0.$$

The solution set of $\cos x - 2 = 0$ is ϕ, because the range of $\cos x$ is $\{y : |y| \leq 1\}$. The solution set of $\sin 2x = 4 \sin x$ is

$$\{x : x = \pm n\pi\} \cup \phi = \{x : x = \pm n\pi\}.$$

EXAMPLE 3. Solve $\sin^2 x - \cos^2 x = 0$.

Solution:
$$\sin^2 x - \cos^2 x = 0$$
$$\sin^2 x - (1 - \sin^2 x) = 0 \quad \longleftarrow \quad \cos^2 x = 1 - \sin^2 x$$
$$2 \sin^2 x - 1 = 0$$
$$\sin^2 x = \tfrac{1}{2}$$
$$\sin x = \frac{1}{\sqrt{2}} \quad \vee \quad \sin x = -\frac{1}{\sqrt{2}}.$$

First, each part of the *or* statement will be solved and then the two solutions will be combined and simplified to form the final solution. The solution set of $\sin x = \dfrac{1}{\sqrt{2}}$ is

$$\left\{x : x = \frac{\pi}{4} \pm 2n\pi \ \vee \ x = \frac{3\pi}{4} \pm 2n\pi\right\} = \text{arc sin } \frac{1}{\sqrt{2}}.$$

The solution set of $\sin x = \dfrac{-1}{\sqrt{2}}$ is

$$\left\{x : x = \frac{5\pi}{4} \pm 2n\pi \ \vee \ x = \frac{7\pi}{4} \pm 2n\pi\right\} = \text{arc sin } \frac{-1}{\sqrt{2}}.$$

The solution set of $\sin^2 x - \cos^2 x = 0$ is

$$\left\{ x : x = \frac{\pi}{4} \pm 2n\pi \ \lor \ x = \frac{3\pi}{4} + 2n\pi \right\}$$

$$\cup \left\{ x : x = \frac{5\pi}{4} \pm 2n\pi \ \lor \ x = \frac{7\pi}{4} \pm 2n\pi \right\}.$$

This can be written more compactly as $\left\{ x : x = \frac{\pi}{4} \pm \frac{n\pi}{2} \right\}.$

EXAMPLE 4. Solve $2 \sin^2 x - \cos x - 1 = 0.$

Solution:

$$2 \sin^2 x - \cos x - 1 = 0$$
$$2(1 - \cos^2 x) - \cos x - 1 = 0$$
$$-2 \cos^2 x - \cos x + 1 = 0$$
$$2 \cos^2 x + \cos x - 1 = 0$$
$$(2 \cos x - 1)(\cos x + 1) = 0$$
$$(2 \cos x - 1 = 0) \ \lor \ (\cos x + 1 = 0)$$
$$(\cos x = \tfrac{1}{2}) \ \lor \ (\cos x = -1)$$

The solution sets are

a. $\cos x = \tfrac{1}{2}$ $\left\{ x : x = \frac{\pi}{3} \pm 2n\pi \ \lor \ x = \frac{5\pi}{3} \pm 2n\pi \right\}$ = arc cos $\tfrac{1}{2}$.

b. $\cos x = -1$ $\{ x : x = \pi \pm 2n\pi \}$ = arc cos (-1).

The solution set of $2 \sin^2 x - \cos x - 1 = 0$ is

$$\left\{ x : x = \frac{\pi}{3} \pm 2n\pi \ \lor \ x = \frac{5\pi}{3} \pm 2n\pi \ \lor \ x = \pi \pm 2n\pi \right\}.$$

Sometimes, the *arc-trigonometric* notation is used.

EXAMPLE 5. Solve $\tan^2 x = 5.$

Solution:

$$\tan^2 x = 5$$
$$\tan x = \sqrt{5} \ \lor \ \tan x = -\sqrt{5}$$
$$\tan x \approx 2.2361 \ \lor \ \tan x = -2.2361$$

The solution set of $\tan x \approx 2.2361$ is $\{ x : x \in \text{arc tan } 2.2361 \}.$

The solution set of $\tan x \approx -2.2361$ is $\{ x : x \in \text{arc tan } (-2.2361) \}.$

The solution set of $\tan^2 x = 5$ is most easily denoted as:

$$\{ x : x \in \text{arc tan } 2.2361 \ \lor \ x \in \text{arc tan } (-2.2361) \}$$

WRITTEN EXERCISES

A ━━ Solve each of the following equations.

1. $2 \sin x + \sqrt{3} = 0$

2. $\sqrt{3} \cot x + 1 = 0$

3. $\sqrt{2} \cos x - 1 = 0$

4. $2 \tan x - 4 = 0$

5. $\sqrt{3} \sec x + 2 = 0$

6. $3 \cos x - 1 = 0$

7. $4 \sin^2 x = 1$

8. $6 \cos^2 x + 5 \cos x + 1 = 0$

9. $3 \sin^2 x - \cos^2 x = 0$

10. $2 \tan^2 x - 3 \sec x + 3 = 0$

11. $2 \tan x - 2 \cot x = -3$

12. $\sqrt{3} \csc^2 x + 2 \csc x = 0$

13. $\cos 2x + \sin x = 1$

14. $\sin 2x + \cos x = 0$

15. $4 \tan x + \sin 2x = 0$

16. $\sin 2x = 2 \sin x$

B
17. $\tan 2x \cot x - 3 = 0$

18. $\cos^2 x + \cos 2x = \frac{5}{4}$

19. $\cos^2 x - \cos 2x = \frac{-3}{4}$

20. $\tan x + \tan 2x = 0$

21. $\sin 2x \sin x + \cos 2x \cos x = 1$

22. $\cos x = \cos 2x$

23. $\sin \left(\frac{\pi}{4} + x \right) - \sin \left(\frac{\pi}{4} - x \right) = \frac{\sqrt{2}}{2}$

24. $\cos \left(\frac{\pi}{4} + x \right) + \cos \left(\frac{\pi}{4} - x \right) = 1$

25. $\sin 2x \cos x - \cos 2x \sin x = \frac{-\sqrt{3}}{2}$

26. $|\sin x| = \frac{1}{2}$

27. $\cos 2x + 3 \cos x - 1 = 0$

28. $\cos 2x + \cos x = 0$

29. $\cos 3x + \cos x = 0$

30. $\sin 3x + \sin x = 0$

31. $\sin 2x + \cos 3x = 0$

32. $\sin^2 x - \cos^2 x - \cos x - 1 = 0$

C
33. $\sin x + \sin 2x + \sin 3x = 0$
(Use the Sum-Product Identities.)

34. $\cos x - \cos 3x - \cos 5x = 0$

35. $\sin x + \sin 2x - \sin 4x = 0$

MID-CHAPTER REVIEW

━━ Solve each triangle. (Section 4-1)

1. $a = 10, b = 15, A = 33°$

2. $C = 43°, B = 59°, b = 25$

━━ Solve each triangle. (Section 4-2)

3. $a = 6, b = 8, C = 70°$

4. $a = 5, b = 6, c = 10$

━━ Find the area of each triangle. (Section 4-3)

5. $C = 40°, B = 62°, b = 25$

6. $a = 4, b = 7, c = 10$

■ Evaluate each expression. (Sections 4-4 and 4-5)

7. arc sin (-0.5) **8.** tan (arc cos u) $0 \le u \le 1$

9. cot (Arc sin 0.3)   **10.** sin $\left(\text{Arc tan}\left(\frac{5}{12}\right)\right)$

■ Solve each equation. (Section 4-6)

11. $4 \sin^2 x = 3$ **12.** $\sin 2x + \sin x = 0$

4–7   Trigonometric Inequalities

Just as there are equations involving the trigonometric functions, inequalities may contain trigonometric functions. The methods of solution are the same as used in solving any inequality. Likewise the solution set usually is the union of intervals of real numbers.

EXAMPLE 1.   Solve $\sin x > \frac{1}{2}$, $0 \le x \le 2\pi$.

Solution: A graph of $y = \sin x$ is useful in visualizing the solution set. The portion of the graph in color represents the ordered pairs $(x, \sin x)$ for which $\sin x > \frac{1}{2}$. Since $\sin \frac{\pi}{6} = \frac{1}{2}$ and $\sin \frac{5\pi}{6} = \frac{1}{2}$, the set

$$\left\{ x : \frac{\pi}{6} < x < \frac{5\pi}{6}, \ x \in \mathbf{R} \right\}$$

is the solution set of the inequality $\sin x > \frac{1}{2}$, $0 \le x \le 2\pi$.

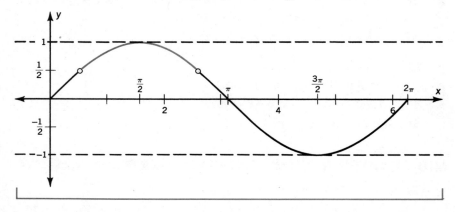

If you wanted the solution of $\sin x > \frac{1}{2}$, $x \in \mathbf{R}$ it could be obtained by adding $\pm 2n\pi$ to $\frac{\pi}{6}$ and $\frac{5\pi}{6}$. (Explain why.) Thus, in this case the solution set is

$$\left\{ x : \frac{\pi}{6} \pm 2n\pi < x < \frac{5\pi}{6} \pm 2n\pi, \ x \in \mathbf{R} \right\}.$$

EXAMPLE 2. Solve $\sin 2x > 0$, $0 \leq x \leq 2\pi$.

Solution:
$$\sin 2x > 0 \qquad \text{iff}$$
$$2 \sin x \cos x > 0 \qquad \text{iff}$$
$$\sin x > 0 \wedge \cos x > 0 \quad \text{or} \quad \sin x < 0 \wedge \cos x < 0$$

The solution set is the union of the following sets.

$$\{x : 0 < x < \pi\} \cap \left\{x : 0 < x < \frac{\pi}{2} \vee \frac{3\pi}{2} < x < 2\pi\right\}$$

and

$$\{x : \pi < x < 2\pi\} \cap \left\{x : \frac{\pi}{2} < x < \frac{3\pi}{2}\right\}$$

That union is

$$\left\{x : 0 < x < \frac{\pi}{2}\right\} \cup \left\{x : \pi < x < \frac{3\pi}{2}\right\}$$

$$= \left\{x : 0 < x < \frac{\pi}{2} \quad \text{or} \quad \pi < x < \frac{3\pi}{2}\right\}.$$

EXAMPLE 3. Solve $2 \sin^2 x - \cos x - 1 \geq 0$.

Solution: Use $\sin^2 x = 1 - \cos^2 x$.
$$2 \sin^2 x - \cos x - 1 \geq 0 \qquad \text{iff}$$
$$2(1 - \cos^2 x) - \cos x - 1 \geq 0 \qquad \text{iff}$$
$$-2 \cos^2 x - \cos x + 1 \geq 0 \qquad \text{iff}$$
$$2 \cos^2 x + \cos x - 1 \leq 0 \qquad \text{iff}$$
$$(2 \cos x - 1)(\cos x + 1) \leq 0 \qquad \text{iff}$$

$$[2 \cos x - 1 \geq 0] \wedge [\cos x + 1 \leq 0] \vee [2 \cos x - 1 \leq 0]$$
$$\wedge [\cos x + 1 \geq 0] \qquad \text{iff}$$

$$[\cos x \geq \tfrac{1}{2}] \wedge [\cos x \leq -1] \vee [\cos x \leq \tfrac{1}{2}] \wedge [\cos x \geq -1] \qquad \text{iff}$$

$$\left\{x : 0 \leq x \leq \frac{\pi}{3} \quad \text{or} \quad \frac{5\pi}{3} \leq x \leq 2\pi\right\} \cap \{x : x = \pi\}$$

$$\cup \left\{x : \frac{\pi}{3} \leq x \leq \frac{5\pi}{3}\right\} \cap \{x : 0 \leq x \leq 2\pi\}$$

$$= \phi \cup \left\{x : \frac{\pi}{3} \leq x \leq \frac{5\pi}{3}\right\} = \left\{x : \frac{\pi}{3} \leq x \leq \frac{5\pi}{3}\right\}.$$

Consequently the solution set of $2 \sin^2 x - \cos x - 1 \geq 0$ is

$$\left\{x : \frac{\pi}{3} \leq x \leq \frac{5\pi}{3}\right\} \quad \text{or} \quad \left[\frac{\pi}{3}, \frac{5\pi}{3}\right].$$

WRITTEN EXERCISES

A ▬ Find the solution set of each inequality over $0 \leq x \leq 2\pi$.

1. $2 \sin x + \sqrt{3} \leq 0$ **2.** $\sqrt{2} \cos x - 1 > 0$

3. $\tan x - 2 \leq 0$ **4.** $\sqrt{3} \cot x - 1 \leq 0$

5. $\tan x - 2 > -1$ **6.** $\sqrt{3} \sec x + 2 \geq 0$

7. $|\sin x| \leq \frac{1}{2}$ **8.** $|\cos x| \geq \frac{3}{2}$

9. $\sin^2 x - \cos^2 x \geq 0$ **10.** $\cos 2x + \sin x \leq 1$

B   **11.** $\sin 2x \geq 2 \sin x$ **12.** $\frac{\tan x}{\tan 2x} + 1 > 0$

13. $2 \cos^2 x > 1$ **14.** $2 \sin^2 x + 3 \sin x - 2 \geq 0$

15. $2 \sin^2 x + \cos x \geq 1$ **16.** $\tan^2 x + \sec x + 1 \geq 0$

17. $\cot^2 x - \csc x + 1 > 0$ **18.** $\cos x + \cos 2x > 0$

C   **19.** $\cos x \leq \sin x$ **20.** $\cos 3x + \cos x < 0$

21. $\sin 2x < \frac{2 \sin x}{\sec x}$ **22.** $\sin x \cos x \tan x < 0$

4–8   Complex Numbers in Polar Form

In Figure 1 below, the horizontal axis is the **real axis** and the vertical axis is the **imaginary axis.** The complex number $a + bi$ is represented by the point (a, b) or by the vector from the origin to (a, b). The *absolute value* of $a + bi$, or r, denoted $|a + bi|$ or r, is the length of the vector determined by (a, b).

$$r = |a + bi| = \sqrt{a^2 + b^2}$$

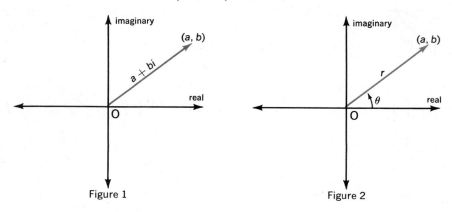

Figure 1   Figure 2

Each complex number can be represented graphically by a vector as shown in Figure 2. This vector along with the positive real axis, determines an angle in standard position. The measure of this angle is the **argument** of the complex number; it is usually denoted by the Greek letter "θ":

$$\text{argument } a + bi = \theta.$$

θ can be found by using any of the trigonometric functions, but since a and b are known, and $\tan \theta = \frac{b}{a}$, θ is defined by

$$\theta = \text{Arc} \tan \frac{b}{a}, \; a > 0 \qquad \theta = \pi + \text{Arc} \tan \frac{b}{a}, \; a < 0$$

$\left(\text{Recall } \frac{-\pi}{2} < \text{Arc} \tan x < \frac{\pi}{2}, \text{ thus } \frac{\pi}{2} < \pi + \text{Arc} \tan x < \frac{3\pi}{2}, \text{ and } \right.$
$\left. \text{thus } \frac{-\pi}{2} < \theta < \frac{3\pi}{2}. \right)$

EXAMPLE 1. Let $z = -2\sqrt{3} + 2i$. Find $r = |z|$ and θ. Graph $-2\sqrt{3} + 2i$.

Solution:
$$|z| = \sqrt{(-2\sqrt{3})^2 + 2^2}$$
$$= \sqrt{16}$$
$$= 4$$

Since $-2\sqrt{3} = a < 0$,

$$\theta = \pi + \text{Arc} \tan \frac{2}{-2\sqrt{3}}$$

$$= \pi + \left(\frac{-\pi}{6} \right)$$

$$= \frac{5\pi}{6} = 150°. \quad \text{The graph is shown above.}$$

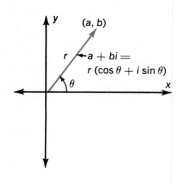

Let $a + bi$ be a complex number with absolute value r and argument θ. Notice that

$$\sin \theta = \frac{b}{r}$$
$$\cos \theta = \frac{a}{r}.$$

Thus $b = r \sin \theta$, $a = r \cos \theta$.

Hence $a + bi = r \cos \theta + ir \sin \theta$
$$= r(\cos \theta + i \sin \theta).$$

This is called the **polar form** of the complex number $a + bi$.

EXAMPLE 2. Express $3 - i\sqrt{3}$ in polar form.

Solution:
$$\theta = \text{Arc tan} \frac{-\sqrt{3}}{3} = -30°$$

$$r = \sqrt{3^2 + (\sqrt{3})^2} = \sqrt{12} = 2\sqrt{3}$$

$$3 - i\sqrt{3} = 2\sqrt{3} \left(\cos(-30°) + i\sin(-30°)\right).$$

Since $360° - 30° = 330°$, you could write

$$3 - i\sqrt{3} = 2\sqrt{3} \left(\cos 330° + i\sin 330°\right).$$

Theorem 4–3 If z_1 and z_2 are complex numbers and

$$z_1 = r_1(\cos\theta_1 + i\sin\theta_1), \qquad z_2 = r_2(\cos\theta_2 + i\sin\theta_2)$$

then

$$z_1 \cdot z_2 = r_1 r_2 \big(\cos(\theta_1 + \theta_2) + i\sin(\theta_1 + \theta_2)\big).$$

Proof:
$$z_1 \cdot z_2 = r_1(\cos\theta_1 + i\sin\theta_1) \cdot r_2(\cos\theta_2 + i\sin\theta_2)$$
$$= r_1 r_2 \cos\theta_1 \cos\theta_2 + r_1 r_2 i \cos\theta_1 \sin\theta_2 +$$
$$r_1 r_2 i \sin\theta_1 \cos\theta_2 + r_1 r_2 \cdot i^2 \sin\theta_1 \sin\theta_2$$
$$= r_1 r_2 [\cos\theta_1 \cos\theta_2 + i^2 \sin\theta_1 \sin\theta_2] +$$
$$r_1 r_2 i [\sin\theta_1 \cos\theta_2 + \cos\theta_1 \sin\theta_2]$$
$$= r_1 r_2 [\cos\theta_1 \cos\theta_2 - \sin\theta_1 \sin\theta_2] +$$
$$i r_1 r_2 \sin(\theta_1 + \theta_2)$$
$$= r_1 r_2 [\cos(\theta_1 + \theta_2) + i\sin(\theta_1 + \theta_2)]$$

EXAMPLE 3. Find $z_1 \cdot z_2$ when $z_1 = 2(\cos 40° + i\sin 40°)$ and $z_2 = 4(\cos 60° + i\sin 60°)$. Write the product in $a + bi$ form.

Solution:
$$z_1 \cdot z_2 = 2(\cos 40° + i\sin 40°) \cdot 4(\cos 60° + i\sin 60°)$$
$$= 2 \cdot 4(\cos(40° + 60°) + i\sin(40° + 60°))$$
$$= 8(\cos 100° + i\sin 100°)$$
$$= 8(-\cos 80° + i\sin 80°)$$
$$= 8(-0.1736 + 0.9848i)$$
$$= -1.3888 + 7.8784i = a + bi$$

EXAMPLE 4. If $z = r(\cos \theta + i \sin \theta)$, then show that the conjugate of z, denoted $\bar{z}$, is $\bar{z} = r(\cos(-\theta) + i \sin(-\theta))$.

Solution: The conjugate, $\bar{z}$, of $a + bi$ is $a - bi$, thus

$$\bar{z} = r(\cos \theta - i \sin \theta)$$
$$= r(\cos(-\theta) - i \sin \theta) \quad \text{(Why?)}$$
$$= r(\cos(-\theta) + i \sin(-\theta)). \quad \text{(Why?)}$$

Theorem 4–4   If $z_1 = r_1(\cos \theta_1 + i \sin \theta_1)$

and $z_2 = r_2(\cos \theta_2 + i \sin \theta_2) \neq 0 + 0i,$

then $\dfrac{z_1}{z_2} = \dfrac{r_1}{r_2}\left(\cos(\theta_1 - \theta_2) + i \sin(\theta_1 - \theta_2)\right).$

You know that $\dfrac{z_1}{z_2} = \dfrac{z_1 \cdot \bar{z}_2}{z_2 \cdot \bar{z}_2}$. Express z_1, z_2, and $\bar{z}_2$ in polar form and use Theorem 4–3. The results are immediate.

CLASSROOM EXERCISES

1. Express each of the following in polar form.

    a. $2 + 2i$ **b.** -31 **c.** $1 - \sqrt{3}i$

2. What is the absolute value of a complex number expressed in polar form?

3. Suppose you are given a complex number in the following polar form, $r(\cos \theta + i \sin \theta)$. Express x and y in terms of r and θ.

WRITTEN EXERCISES

A ━━ Graph each number on the complex plane. Find the polar form of each number.

    1. $4 + 4i$ **2.** $-1 + \sqrt{3}\,i$ **3.** $\frac{1}{2} - \frac{\sqrt{3}}{2}i$

    4. $-1 - 2i$ **5.** $-1 + 0i$ **6.** $0 + i$

    7. $0 - i$ **8.** $1 + 0i$ **9.** $0.9945 + 0.1045i$

    10. $-0.9336 + 0.3584i$

    11. $0.6428 - 0.7660i$

    12. $-2 - 3i$

Express each number in the form $a + bi$.

13. $\frac{1}{2}\left(\cos\frac{\pi}{3} + i\sin\frac{\pi}{3}\right)$

14. $2\left(\cos\frac{\pi}{2} + i\sin\frac{\pi}{2}\right)$

15. $4\left(\cos\frac{11\pi}{6} + i\sin\frac{11\pi}{6}\right)$

16. $3\left(\cos\frac{5\pi}{4} + i\sin\frac{5\pi}{4}\right)$

17. $\cos\left(\frac{-\pi}{2}\right) + i\sin\left(\frac{-\pi}{2}\right)$

18. $17(\cos\pi + i\sin\pi)$

19. $8\left(\cos\frac{\pi}{12} + i\sin\frac{\pi}{12}\right)$

20. $r(\cos\theta + i\sin\theta)$

B **21.** What is the polar form of any complex numbers whose graph is on the real axis?

22. What is the polar form of any complex numbers whose graph is on the imaginary axis?

23. Write out the details of the proof of Theorem 4–4.

24. Prove, using polar form, that $\frac{z}{z} = 1$ whenever $z \neq 0 + 0i$.

Find $z_1 \cdot z_2$ and $\frac{z_1}{z_2}$ in Exercises 25–30.

25. $z_1 = 3(\cos 80° + i\sin 80°)$, $z_2 = \frac{1}{2}(\cos 40° + i\sin 40°)$

26. $z_1 = 5\left(\cos\frac{2\pi}{3} + i\sin\frac{2\pi}{3}\right)$, $z_2 = 4\left(\cos\frac{3\pi}{4} + i\sin\frac{3\pi}{4}\right)$

27. $z_1 = 2(\cos 135° + i\sin 135°)$, $z_2 = \frac{2}{3}(\cos 150° + i\sin 150°)$

28. $z_1 = 3\left(\cos\frac{\pi}{2} + i\sin\frac{\pi}{2}\right)$, $z_2 = \left(\cos\frac{\pi}{2} + i\sin\left(\frac{-\pi}{2}\right)\right)$

29. $z_1 = 1 - i$, $z_2 = -i$

30. $z_1 = 5i$, $z_2 = 2 - 3i$

31. Draw a graph of $r_1(\cos\theta_1 + i\sin\theta_1)$ and of $r_2(\cos\theta_2 + i\sin\theta_2)$. Draw a graph of their product. Of their quotient.

32. How are the graphs of z and $\bar{z}$ related?

C **33.** Show that for $z \neq 0$,

$$\frac{1}{z} = \frac{1}{r}(\cos\theta - i\sin\theta) = \frac{1}{r^2} \cdot \bar{z}.$$

34. Show that $z^2 = [r(\cos\theta + i\sin\theta)]^2 = r^2(\cos 2\theta + i\sin 2\theta)$.

35. Show that $\frac{z}{\bar{z}} = \cos 2\theta + i\sin 2\theta$, $z \neq 0 + 0i$.

36. What is $\frac{\bar{z}}{z}$, if $z \neq 0 + 0i$?

37. Prove that the quotient of two complex numbers with the same argument is real.

38. Addition of complex numbers in polar form is more difficult than addition in rectangular form. Is this statement true for multiplication? Why or why not?

Applying Inverse Functions
Navigation

A **navigator** of a ship or an aircraft can use trigonometry to find the shortest path between any two points on the earth's surface. Since the earth may be regarded as a sphere when you are considering large distances, the shortest path between two points is the length of an arc of a great circle.

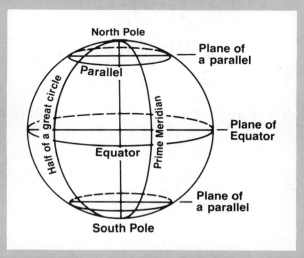

A **great circle** of a sphere is the circle formed by the intersection of the sphere and a plane passing through its center. The **equator** is the great circle formed by the plane passing through the center of the earth and perpendicular to the earth's North–South axis. A circle formed by a plane parallel to the equator is called a parallel of latitude, or simply a **parallel**. Half of a great circle passing through the North and South poles is called a **meridian of longitude,** or a **meridian.** The **prime meridian** is the meridian that passes through the city of Greenwich, England.

To find the shortest path between two points on the earth's surface, a navigator must know these data.

1. The **latitude** or angular measure of each point's parallel of latitude north or south of the equator.

2. The **longitude** or angular measure of each point's meridian east or west of the prime meridian.

In the figure at the top of page 200, α_1 represents the latitude of P_1 and β_1 represents its longitude. Thus, for $\alpha_1 = 60.5°$ and $\beta_1 = 48.2°$, the location of P_1 is represented as follows:

Latitude: 60.5° N ◄—— **60.5° north of the equator**

Longitude: 48.2° W ◄—— **48.2° west of the prime meridian**

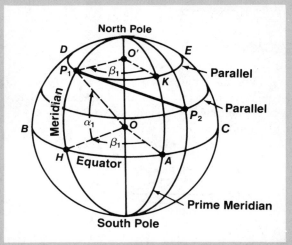

It can be shown that for any two points P_1 and P_2 in the Northern Hemisphere, the arc measure θ (in radians) of P_1P_2 can be found by the formula

$$\theta = \text{Arc cos}(\sin \alpha_1 \sin \alpha_2 + \cos \alpha_1 \cos \alpha_2 \cos \phi)$$

where α_1 and α_2 are the latitudes of points P_1 and P_2 respectively and ϕ is the change in longitude from P_1 to P_2. The distance along the arc, s, equals the radius of the arc times θ, $s = R\theta$. The length of the path from P_1 to P_2 along a great-circle route can be given by

$$s = R\theta = R \text{ Arc cos}(\sin \alpha_1 \sin \alpha_2 + \cos \alpha_1 \cos \alpha_2 \cos \phi)$$

where R is the radius of the earth. Although θ must be given in radians, α_1, α_2, and ϕ may be expressed in degree measure.

EXERCISES

1. Find the shortest flight path for a plane flying from Seattle (latitude: 47.5° N; longitude: 122.5° W) to New York (latitude: 40.5° N; longitude: 74.0° W). The radius of the earth is approximately 3959 miles. Round your answer to the nearest ten miles. (*Hint*: Since Seattle and New York are both west of the prime meridian, $\phi = 122.5° - 74°$).

2. Find the shortest flight path for a plane flying from Boston (latitude: 42.5° N; longitude: 71.0° W) to Paris (latitude: 49.0° N; longitude: 2.5° E). Round your answer to the nearest ten miles. (*Hint*: Since Boston and Paris are on opposite sides of the prime meridian, $\phi = 71.0° + 2.5°$).

3. Find the shortest flight path for a plane flying from Miami (latitude: 25.5° N; longitude: 80.3° W) to Madrid (latitude: 40.5° N; longitude: 3.8° W).

4. Find the shortest flight path for a plane flying from New Orleans (latitude: 30° N; longitude: 90° W) to Amsterdam (latitude: 52.5° N; longitude: 5° E).

4–9   De Moivre's Theorem, Roots and Powers

Suppose $\quad z = r(\cos \theta + i \sin \theta)$.

Then
$$z^2 = [r(\cos \theta + i \sin \theta)]^2$$
$$= r^2[\cos^2 \theta + 2i \sin \theta \cos \theta - \sin^2 \theta]$$
$$= r^2[\cos^2 \theta - \sin^2 \theta + i2 \sin \theta \cos \theta]$$
$$= r^2(\cos 2\theta + i \sin 2\theta)$$

Notice that the square of z is the product of the square of $r = |z|$ and the cosine of twice θ plus i times the sine of twice θ. This example illustrates a most remarkable theorem called **De Moivre's Theorem.**

Theorem 4–5 (De Moivre's Theorem). If $z = r(\cos \theta + i \sin \theta)$ and n is an integer, then

$$z^n = r^n(\cos n\theta + i \sin n\theta).$$

Proof: The proof is in two parts. (If $n = 0$, the proof is trivial.)

Part 1: n is a natural number. The proof is by *Mathematical Induction.*

Let P_n be the statement $z^n = r^n(\cos n\theta + i \sin n\theta)$.

a. P_1 is $z^1 = r^1(\cos (1 \cdot \theta) + i \sin (1 \cdot \theta))$.
   P_1 is true because
   $$z = r(\cos \theta + i \sin \theta)$$
   $$= r^1\big(\cos (1 \cdot \theta) + i \sin (1 \cdot \theta)\big).$$

b. Assume P_n is true for $k \in \mathbb{N}$:
   $$z^k = r^k\big(\cos (k\theta) + i \sin (k\theta)\big).$$

You must show that P_{k+1} is true.

$$z^{k+1} = z^k \cdot z^1$$
$$= r^k(\cos k\theta + i \sin k\theta) \cdot r(\cos \theta + i \sin \theta)$$
$$= r^k \cdot r\big(\cos (k\theta + \theta) + i \sin (k\theta + \theta)\big) \quad\longleftarrow \text{By Theorem 4–3}$$
$$z^{k+1} = r^{k+1}\big(\cos [(k + 1)\theta] + i \sin [(k + 1)\theta]\big).$$

Thus P_{k+1} is true whenever P_k is true and, by the Principle of Mathematical Induction,

$$P_n \text{ is true for all natural numbers.}$$

Part 2: $-n$ is a negative integer.

$$z^{-n} = \frac{1}{z^n}$$

$$= \frac{1}{r^n(\cos(n\theta) + i\sin(n\theta))} \quad \longleftarrow \quad \textbf{by Part 1}$$

$$= \frac{1}{r^n(\cos n\theta + i\sin n\theta)} \cdot \frac{\cos(-n\theta) + i\sin(-n\theta)}{\cos(-n\theta) + i\sin(-n\theta)}$$

$$= \frac{r^{-n}(\cos(-n\theta) + i\sin(-n\theta))}{\cos(n\theta - n\theta) + i\sin(n\theta - n\theta)}$$

$$= r^{-n}(\cos(-n\theta) + i\sin(-n\theta))$$

Combining the results of Parts 1 and 2, you have proved De Moivre's Theorem.

The formula in De Moivre's Theorem is one of the most remarkable and useful relations in elementary mathematics.

EXAMPLE 1. Derive identities for $\cos 3\theta$ and $\sin 3\theta$.

Solution: Let $(\cos\theta + i\sin\theta) = u + vi$; $u = \cos\theta$, $v = \sin\theta$.

Then $(\cos\theta + i\sin\theta)^3 = \cos 3\theta + i\sin 3\theta,$

and $(u + vi)^3 = u^3 + 3iu^2v + 3uv^2i^2 + v^3i^3 \quad \longleftarrow \quad$ **By the Binomial Theorem**

$\qquad\qquad\qquad = u^3 - 3uv^2 + i(3u^2v - v^3)$

Thus, substituting $u = \cos\theta$ and $v = \sin\theta$

$\cos 3\theta + i\sin 3\theta = \cos^3\theta - 3\cos\theta\sin^2\theta + i(3\cos^2\theta\sin\theta - \sin^3\theta)$

Two complex numbers are equal if and only if their real parts and imaginary parts are equal. Hence,

$$\cos 3\theta = \cos^3\theta - 3\cos\theta\sin^2\theta$$
$$= \cos^3\theta - 3\cos\theta(1 - \cos^2\theta)$$
$$= 4\cos^3\theta - 3\cos\theta$$

and

$$\sin 3\theta = 3\cos^2\theta\sin\theta - \sin^3\theta$$
$$= 3[1 - \sin^2\theta]\sin\theta - \sin^3\theta$$
$$= 3\sin\theta - 4\sin^3\theta.$$

The key idea in the solution of Example 1 is that a single equation with two complex numbers is equivalent to a pair of equations with real numbers. A similar procedure may be used to derive identities for $\sin n\theta$ and $\cos n\theta$, $n \in I$.

De Moivre's Theorem can be used to find roots of complex numbers. The following example is an illustration of this.

EXAMPLE 2. Find the cube roots of $-6i$.

Solution:

If $r(\cos\theta + i\sin\theta)$ is a cube root of $-6i = 6\left(\cos\frac{3\pi}{2} + i\sin\frac{3\pi}{2}\right)$,

then
$$[r(\cos\theta + i\sin\theta)]^3 = 6\left(\cos\frac{3\pi}{2} + i\sin\frac{3\pi}{2}\right)$$

or
$$r^3(\cos 3\theta + i\sin 3\theta) = 6\left(\cos\frac{3\pi}{2} + i\sin\frac{3\pi}{2}\right) \qquad \mathbf{1}$$

Complex numbers are equal if and only if their absolute values are equal and their arguments differ by $\pm 2k\pi$, $k \in W$. Thus **1** is equivalent to
$$r^3 = 6 \qquad \mathbf{2}$$

and
$$3\theta = \frac{3\pi}{2} \pm 2k\pi,\ k \in W. \qquad \mathbf{3}$$

From **2** and **3** you find,
$$r = \sqrt[3]{6} \quad \longleftarrow \quad \textbf{From Equation 2} \qquad \mathbf{4}$$

and
$$\theta = \frac{\pi}{2} \pm \frac{2k\pi}{3},\ k \in W. \quad \longleftarrow \quad \begin{array}{l}\textbf{From}\\ \textbf{Equation 3}\end{array} \qquad \mathbf{5}$$

Therefore the cube roots of $-6i$ are
$$\sqrt[3]{6}\left[\cos\left(\frac{\pi}{2} \pm \frac{2k\pi}{3}\right) + i\sin\left(\frac{\pi}{2} \pm \frac{2k\pi}{3}\right)\right]. \qquad \mathbf{6}$$

Substituting $k = 0, 1, 2, 3$, etc. in **6**, you find the cube roots to be

$$\sqrt[3]{6}\left(\cos\frac{\pi}{2} + i\sin\frac{\pi}{2}\right) = \sqrt[3]{6}\,(0 + i) \qquad \mathbf{7}$$

$$\sqrt[3]{6}\left(\cos\frac{7\pi}{6} + i\sin\frac{7\pi}{6}\right) = \sqrt[3]{6}\left(-\frac{\sqrt{3}}{2} - i\frac{1}{2}\right) \qquad \mathbf{8}$$

$$\sqrt[3]{6}\left(\cos\frac{11\pi}{6} + i\sin\frac{11\pi}{6}\right) = \sqrt[3]{6}\left(\frac{\sqrt{3}}{2} - i\frac{1}{2}\right) \qquad \mathbf{9}$$

$$\sqrt[3]{6}\left(\cos\frac{5\pi}{2} + i\sin\frac{5\pi}{2}\right) = \sqrt[3]{6}\,(0 + i) \qquad \mathbf{10}$$

Notice that roots **7** and **10** are identical. All others found by substituting $k \geq 4$ in **6** will be identical to one of **7–9** There are n roots of any complex number, one corresponding to each of the whole numbers $0, 1, 2, 3, \ldots, n - 1$.

Theorem 4–6 If $n \in \mathbb{N}$, then the n roots of $z = r(\cos \theta + i \sin \theta)$ are given by

$$\sqrt[n]{r}\left[\cos\left(\frac{\theta}{n} + \frac{2k\pi}{n}\right) + i \sin\left(\frac{\theta}{n} + \frac{2k\pi}{n}\right)\right]$$

$$k = 0, 1, 2, 3, \ldots, n - 1.$$

CLASSROOM EXERCISES

1. Use De Moivre's Theorem to evaluate each of the following expressions of complex numbers.

a. $(-2 - 2i)^5$
b. $-i^7$
c. $(3 - 5i)^{-3}$
d. $[2(\cos 30° + i \sin 30°)]^2$

2. Using De Moivre's Theorem, find the three cube roots of 8.

3. Using De Moivre's Theorem, find the three cube roots of -27.

4. Using De Moivre's Theorem, what does $(\cos \theta + i \sin \theta)^n$ equal?

WRITTEN EXERCISES

A ▬▬Use De Moivre's Theorem to evaluate each expression. Write your result in polar form and in $a + bi$ form.

1. $(1 - i)^3$
2. $(1 + i)^{-4}$
3. $(i)^4$
4. $(1 - 3i)^5$
5. $(-1 + \sqrt{3}i)^{-5}$
6. $(-\sqrt{3} - i)^3$
7. $(-i)^{-5}$
8. $(2 - 2\sqrt{3}i)^2$

▬▬Express each root in polar form. Plot the roots required in each exercise in the complex plane.

9. The fourth roots of 1
10. The cube roots of i
11. The cube roots of -1
12. The sixth roots of -1
13. The cube roots of $-1 + \sqrt{3}i$
14. The twelfth roots of 1
15. The square roots of i
16. The fifth roots of $1 - \sqrt{3}i$

B **17.** Use the procedure of Example 1 to derive identities for $\cos 4\theta$ and $\sin 4\theta$ in terms of $\sin \theta$ and $\cos \theta$.

18. Solve $z^3 = i^2$. **19.** Solve $z^3 = (1 + i)^2$.

20. Solve $z^3 = (1 + \sqrt{3}i)^2$. (Leave answers in polar form.)

21. Show that the three cube roots of 1 are 1, ω, and ω^2 where $\omega = \cos \dfrac{2\pi}{3} + i \sin \dfrac{2\pi}{3}$.

22. Show that the four fourth roots of 1 are 1, ω, ω^2, and ω^3 where $\omega = \cos \dfrac{\pi}{2} + i \sin \dfrac{\pi}{2}$.

23. Show that $[r(\cos \theta + i \sin \theta)]^{-n}$, $n \in W$ is

$$r^{-n}(\cos n\theta - i \sin n\theta)$$

C **24.** Show that $z^{\frac{p}{q}} = [r(\cos \theta + i \sin \theta)]^{\frac{p}{q}}$, $q \in N$, $p \in I$ is

$$r^{\frac{p}{q}} \left(\cos \frac{p}{q} (\theta \pm 2n\pi) + i \sin \frac{p}{q} (\theta \pm 2n\pi) \right) \qquad n = 0, 1, 2, 3, \ldots, q - 1.$$

—— Use the results of Exercise 24 to find each of the following.

25. The 3 values of $(1)^{\frac{2}{3}}$ **26.** The 3 values of $i^{\frac{2}{3}}$

27. The 4 values of $1^{\frac{3}{4}}$ **28.** The 3 values of $(-1)^{\frac{2}{3}}$

29. The 4 values of $i^{\frac{3}{4}}$ **30.** The 3 values of $(-i)^{\frac{2}{3}}$

4–10 Polar Coordinates

Each point P in the plane is on the terminal side of an angle in standard position, and it is a unique distance from the origin. The terminal side of the angle is determined by the measure θ of the angle. The distance of the point P from the origin is denoted by r. The ordered pair of numbers (r, θ) is called the **polar coordinates** of P. See Figure 1 below.

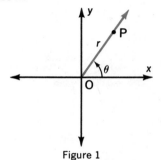

Figure 1   Figure 2

EXAMPLE 1. Plot the point P with polar coordinates $(2, 210°)$.

Draw the terminal side of the angle in standard position which measures 210°. Find the point on this ray 2 units from 0. See Figure 2.

You should observe that the polar coordinates of P given in Example 1 are not unique. The same point has polar coordinates $(2, 570°)$, $(2, 930°)$, $(2, -150°)$ and in general, $(2, 210° \pm n \cdot 360°)$, $n \in W$. Using radian measure P is $\left(2, \dfrac{7\pi}{6} \pm 2n\pi\right)$, $n \in W$.

There is still another way to identify the same point. This way makes use of $-r$ and the *convention* associated with it. When the first coordinate of a polar pair is negative, it is interpreted to mean the point $|r|$ units from the origin on the ray opposite to the terminal side of the angle with measure θ. Thus $(-2, 30°)$ is the same point as $(2, 210°)$. See Figure 3.

The polar coordinates of $P(2, 210°)$ may be given as any member of

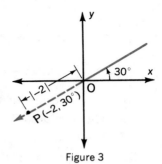

Figure 3

$\{(r, \theta) : r = 2 \text{ and } \theta = 210 \pm 2n\pi \text{ or } r = -2 \text{ and } \theta = 30° \pm 2n\pi, n \in W\}.$

In general, if r is a real number and $\overrightarrow{OQ}$ is the terminal side of an angle in standard position with measure θ, then (r, θ) are the polar coordinates of a point P $|r|$ units from O and on

a. $\overrightarrow{OQ}$ if $r > 0$

b. the ray opposite to $\overrightarrow{OQ}$ if $r < 0$

c. 0 if $r = 0$.

The vertex 0 of the angle in standard position is the pole. The initial side of the angle is the polar axis. Notice that it is not necessary to have a rectangular coordinate system on the plane in order to have polar coordinates. All that is necessary is the **pole,** the **polar axis,** the direction of rotation which will give positive θ, and the conventions **a, b,** and c above. See Figure 4.

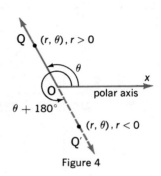

Figure 4

However, there are useful relations between polar and rectangular coordinates of a point. These are illustrated in the figure at the right.

$$(x, y) = (r \cos \theta, r \sin \theta)$$

or

$$x = r \cos \theta, \quad y = r \sin \theta \qquad \mathbf{1}$$

The equations in **1** allow you to convert from polar coordinates to rectangular coordinates.

Similarly, the following equations permit you to convert from rectangular coordinates.

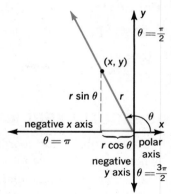

Figure 5

$$r = \sqrt{x^2 + y^2} \qquad \mathbf{2}$$

$$\theta = \text{Arc tan } \frac{y}{x} \quad x > 0 \qquad \mathbf{3}$$

$$\theta = \pi + \text{Arc tan } \frac{y}{x}, \quad x < 0 \qquad \mathbf{4}$$

EXAMPLE 2.   **a.** Find the rectangular coordinates of (3, 150°).

             b. Find polar coordinates of $(-2, -2)$ for $r > 0$ and for $r < 0$.

Solution: **a.** By Equation **1**

$$x = r \cos \theta \qquad\qquad y = r \sin \theta$$
$$= 3 \cos 150° \qquad\qquad = 3 \sin 150°$$
$$= 3\left(-\frac{\sqrt{3}}{2}\right) \qquad\qquad = 3\left(\frac{1}{2}\right)$$
$$= \frac{-3\sqrt{3}}{2}. \qquad\qquad = \frac{3}{2}.$$

        b. From **2**, you have

$$|r| = \sqrt{(-2)^2 + (-2)^2}$$
$$= \sqrt{8}$$
$$= 2\sqrt{2}.$$

Since $x < 0$, from **4** you have

$$\theta = \pi + \text{Arc tan } \frac{-2}{-2}$$
$$= \pi + \frac{\pi}{4}$$
$$= \frac{5\pi}{4}.$$

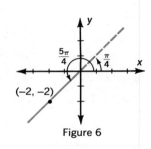

Figure 6

Consequently, for $r > 0$, polar coordinates are $\left(2\sqrt{2}, \frac{5\pi}{4}\right)$ or $(2\sqrt{2}, 225°)$. For $r < 0$, polar coordinates are $\left(-2\sqrt{2}, \frac{\pi}{4}\right)$ or $(-2\sqrt{2}, 45°)$. (See Figure 6.)

CLASSROOM EXERCISES

1. Find the polar coordinates for $r > 0$ and $r < 0$ for the point whose rectangular coordinates are $(5, -5\sqrt{3})$.

2. Find the rectangular coordinates for the point whose polar coordinates are $(-10, 60°)$.

3. Plot the point P with polar coordinates $(3, -120°)$.

WRITTEN EXERCISES

A ▬▬ Find polar coordinates a for $r > 0$ and b for $r < 0$ for each point given in rectangular coordinates.

1. $(1, 1)$ **2.** $(0, 4)$ **3.** $(-9, 0)$ **4.** $(-1, 1)$

5. $(1, -\sqrt{3})$ **6.** $(-1, -\sqrt{3})$ **7.** $(-4, 8)$ **8.** $(0, -1)$

▬▬ Find rectangular coordinates for each point given in polar coordinates.

9. $(-2, 90°)$ **10.** $\left(4, \frac{3\pi}{4}\right)$ **11.** $\left(-1, \frac{7\pi}{6}\right)$ **12.** $\left(1, \frac{7\pi}{6}\right)$

13. $\left(3, \frac{-2\pi}{3}\right)$ **14.** $\left(-\frac{3}{2}, \frac{-\pi}{4}\right)$ **15.** $\left(5, \frac{3\pi}{2}\right)$ **16.** $\left(-9, \frac{13\pi}{3}\right)$

▬▬ Use the relations $x = r \cos \theta$ and $y = r \sin \theta$ to transform each equation into an equation in polar coordinates.

17. $x = 3$ **18.** $y = -4$ **19.** $2x - y = 3$

20. $y = x$ **21.** $x^2 + y^2 = 16$ **22.** $xy = a^2$

23. $x^2 + y^2 + 4x = 0$ **24.** $x^2 + y^2 + 2y = 0$ **25.** $y^2 = 4x$

B   Use the relations 1–4 on page 207 to transform each equation into an equation in rectangular coordinates.

26. $r = 4$ **27.** $\theta = 0°$ **28.** $\theta = \frac{\pi}{4}$

29. $r = -4$ **30.** $r = 2 \sin \theta + 2 \cos \theta$ **31.** $r \sin \theta = 6$

C   **32.** $r = 4 \sec \theta$ **33.** $r = 5 \csc \theta$ **34.** $r^2 - 3r + 2 = 0$

35. Prove that if a point (x_1, y_1) has polar coordinates (r, θ) and if (x_2, y_2) has polar coordinates $(r, -\theta)$, then $x_1 = x_2$ and $y_1 = -y_2$.

4–11 Graphs of Polar Equations

Equations in polar coordinates are **polar equations**. In a plane, the set of points (r, θ) which satisfy a polar equation is a **polar graph**. Some of the polar graphs are quite beautiful as you will see.

EXAMPLE 1. Graph $r = 5$.

The polar graph of $r = 5$ is the set of all points with polar co-ordinates $(5, \theta)$. Thus, the graph is the set of all points 5 units from the pole. The graph is clearly a circle. See Figure 1. What is the equation of the same circle in rectangular coordinates? What is the polar graph of $r = -5$?

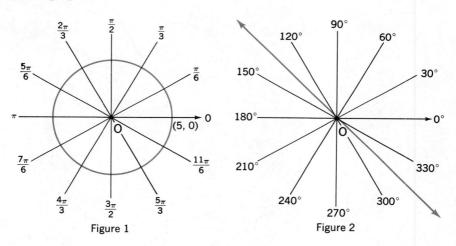

Figure 1   Figure 2

EXAMPLE 2. Sketch the polar graph of $\theta = 140°$.

The graph is all those points $(r, 140°)$ with second coordinate of $140°$ and first coordinate $r \in R$. The graph is a line through the pole. See Figure 2. What is the equation of the same line in rectangular coordinates?

EXAMPLE 3. Sketch the graph of $r = 3 \cos \theta$.

The best procedure here is to make a table of values (r, θ). For convenience the values of θ which are multiples of $\frac{\pi}{6}$ (30°) are used. These points are plotted in color on the coordinate system. Recall that a point $\left(\frac{-3}{2}, \frac{2\pi}{3}\right)$ is $\frac{3}{2}$ unit on the ray opposite to the terminal side of the angle measuring $\frac{2\pi}{3}$; i.e., $\left(\frac{3}{2}, \frac{5\pi}{3}\right)$.

Do you see that the points in the graph corresponding to (r, θ), $\pi \leq \theta \leq 2\pi$ are exactly the same points as those corresponding to $(r, \theta), 0 \leq \theta < \pi$? Thus the entire graph could be sketched by plotting only the points in the set $\{(r, \theta) : 0 \leq \theta < \pi, r = 3 \cos \theta\}$.

θ	r
0	3
$\dfrac{\pi}{6}$	$\dfrac{3\sqrt{3}}{2}$
$\dfrac{\pi}{3}$	$\dfrac{3}{2}$
$\dfrac{\pi}{2}$	0
$\dfrac{2\pi}{3}$	$\dfrac{-3}{2}$
$\dfrac{5\pi}{6}$	$\dfrac{-3\sqrt{3}}{2}$
π	-3
$\dfrac{7\pi}{6}$	$\dfrac{-3\sqrt{3}}{2}$
$\dfrac{4\pi}{3}$	$\dfrac{-3}{2}$
$\dfrac{3\pi}{2}$	0
$\dfrac{5\pi}{3}$	$\dfrac{3}{2}$
$\dfrac{11\pi}{6}$	$\dfrac{3\sqrt{3}}{2}$
2π	3

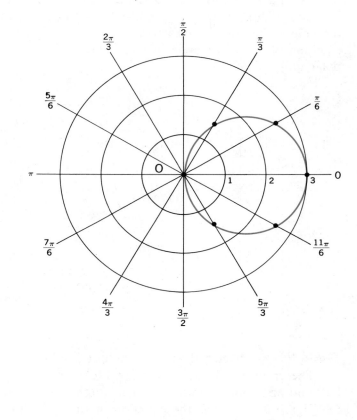

The graph is a circle. What is the equation of the same circle in rectangular coordinates? How do the following circles differ from the circle $r = \cos \theta$?

    a. $r = 6 \cos \theta$
    b. $r = \frac{3}{2} \cos \theta$
    c. $3r = 12 \cos \theta$

EXAMPLE 4. Sketch the polar graph of $r = \sin \theta + 1$.

Again, make a table of values of (r, θ). The points corresponding to the pairs in the table are plotted below. The curve is called a cardioid. (Can you guess why?)

θ	r
0	1
30°	1.5
60°	1.866
90°	2
120°	1.866
150°	1.5
180°	1
210°	0.5
240°	0.134
270°	0
300°	0.134
330°	0.5
360°	1

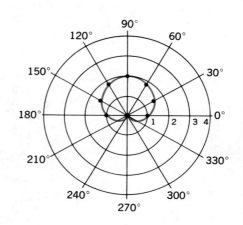

EXAMPLE 5. Sketch the polar graph of $r = \sin 2\theta$.

A table of values is valuable again. Because the equation involves 2θ, it is useful to consider values of θ at intervals of $15°$ $\left(\text{or } \frac{\pi}{12}\right)$.

θ	2θ	r
0	0	0
15°	30°	0.5
30°	60°	0.866
45°	90°	1
60°	120°	0.866
75°	150°	0.5
90°	180°	0

θ	2θ	r
105°	210°	−0.5
120°	240°	−0.866
135°	270°	−1
150°	300°	−0.866
165°	330°	−0.5
180°	360°	0
195°	390°	0.5
210°	420°	0.866
225°	450°	1
240°	480°	0.866
255°	510°	0.5
270°	540°	0
285°	570°	−0.5
300°	600°	−0.866
315°	630°	−1
330°	660°	−0.866
345°	690°	−0.5
360°	720°	0

The graph is shown in the figure. It is called a **four-leaved rose.** Each branch (petal) is identified with a number. The values in the table which produce that branch are similarly designated. The arrowheads on the graph indicate the path a point A would follow with θ increasing from 0° to 360°.

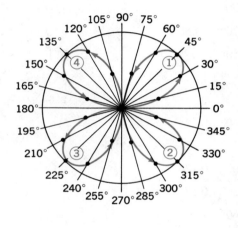

CLASSROOM EXERCISES

▬ Sketch the polar graph of each equation.

1. $r = 2$ **2.** $r = -4$ **3.** $\theta = 50°$ **4.** $\theta = -\dfrac{\pi}{4}$

WRITTEN EXERCISES

A ▬Sketch the polar graph of each equation.

1. $r = -3$ **2.** $r = 1$ **3.** $\theta = 75°$

4. $\theta = \dfrac{-\pi}{3}$ **5.** $r = \cos \theta$ **6.** $r = 2 \sin \theta$

7. $r = -3 \cos \theta$ **8.** $r = -4 \sin \theta$ **9.** $r \cos \theta = 2$

10. $r = 1 + \cos \theta$ (cardioid) **11.** $r = \sin \theta - 1$ (cardioid)

12. $r = \cos\theta - 1$ (cardioid) **13.** $r = 2\sin 3\theta$ (3-leaved rose)

14. $r = 3\cos 3\theta$ (3-leaved rose) **15.** $r = \cos 2\theta$ (4-leaved rose)

16. $r = \sin 5\theta$ (5-leaved rose) **17.** $r = \cos 4\theta$ (8-leaved rose)

B **18.** $r = 2 + \cos\theta$ (limaçon) **19.** $r = 2 + \sin\theta$ (limaçon)

20. $r = 2 + 3\cos\theta$ (limaçon) **21.** $r = 1 - 2\sin\theta$ (limaçon)

22. $r^2 = 4\sin 2\theta$ (lemniscate) **23.** $r^2 = 4\cos 2\theta$ (lemniscate)

C **24.** $r = 2\theta$ (spiral of Archimedes) **25.** $r\theta = 3$ (hyperbolic spiral)

26. $r = \dfrac{4}{1 - \cos\theta}$ (parabola) **27.** $r = \dfrac{2}{1 - \frac{1}{2}\cos\theta}$ (ellipse)

28. $r = \dfrac{16}{1 - 4\cos\theta}$ (hyperbola)

COMPUTER APPLICATION

BASIC: POLAR GRAPHS

The sample program below is for the Apple II microcomputer.

Problem:
Write a program that displays the graph of $r = 2\cos 3\theta$.

```
100 REM   THIS PROGRAM GRAPHS POLAR
110 REM   EQUATIONS R = F(T)
120 HOME
130 DEF FN R(T) = 2 * COS(3*T)
140 PRINT
150 PRINT "DOTS PER UNIT";
160 INPUT S
170 HGR
180 HCOLOR = 3
190 HPLOT 140,80 TO 279,80
200 FOR I = 140 TO 279 STEP S
210 HPLOT I,78 TO I,82
220 NEXT I
230 FOR J = 0 TO 6.3 STEP .05
240 LET X = S * FN R(J) * COS(J) + 140
250 LET Y = 80 - S * FN R(J) * SIN(J)
260 IF X < 0 OR X > 279 OR Y < 0 OR Y > 159 THEN 280
270 HPLOT X,Y                    310 GET A$
280 NEXT J                       320 TEXT
290 VTAB 21                      330 HOME
300 PRINT "PRESS A KEY TO END."  340 END
```

Output: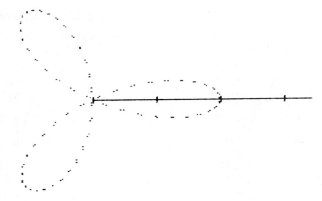

Analysis:

Statements 150–160: The user is asked for the number of dots per unit on the polar axis. The program sets the origin at position (140, 80) of the high–resolution coordinate system of the computer. Thus, S = 10 would give you 14 units to the right and left and 8 units up and down.

Statements 190–220: These statements draw the polar axis and the unit marks.

Statements 230–280: These statements graph the polar equation. Statements 240 and 250 change polar to rectangular coordinates and modify them in order to center the graph at $x = 140$, $y = 80$. In statement 260, the values of x and y are tested to see if the coordinates are off the screen. If they are, the program does not plot that point.

EXERCISES

A   Use the program on page 213 to graph each polar equation.

1. $r = \cos \theta + 1$ **2.** $r = 2 \cos 2\theta$ **3.** $r = -2 \sin \theta$

4. $r = 2\theta$ **5.** $r = 2 + \sin \theta$ **6.** $r = 3 - 2 \cos \theta$

B   In Exercises 7–8, revise the program on page 213 in the manner indicated.

7. Accept polar equations with trigonometric functions in the denominator. Do this by defining the denominator as a separate function d. Then add a statement 235 to test whether the denominator is 0.

8. Given the values of A, B, C, D, E, and F, graph polar equations of the form $r = A \sin B\theta + C \cos D\theta + E\theta + F$.

CHAPTER SUMMARY

Important Terms

Ambiguous case (p. 170)
Argument (p. 195)
Conditional equation (p. 188)
De Moivre's Theorem (p. 201)
Hero(n)'s Formula (p. 176)
Imaginary Axis (p. 194)
Inverse circular function (p. 182)
Law of Cosines (p. 168)
Law of Sines (p. 165)

Polar axis (p. 206)
Polar coordinates (p. 205)
Polar equations (p. 209)
Polar form (p. 195)
Polar graph (p. 209)
Pole (p. 206)
Principal value of an inverse
    trigonometric function (p. 183)
Real axis (p. 194)

Important Ideas

1. The area, K, of a triangle is given by

   a. $\frac{1}{2}cb \sin A = \frac{1}{2}ab \sin C = \frac{1}{2}ac \sin B$

   b. $\frac{1}{2}\frac{c^2 \sin A \sin B}{\sin C} = \frac{1}{2}\frac{a^2 \sin B \sin C}{\sin A} = \frac{1}{2}\frac{b^2 \sin A \sin C}{\sin B}$

   c. $\sqrt{s(s-a)(s-b)(s-c)}$, where $s = \frac{1}{2}(a+b+c)$

2. If $z_1 = r_1(\cos \theta + i \sin \theta_1)$ and $z_2 = r_2(\cos \theta_2 + i \sin \theta_2)$, then

   a. $z_1 z_2 = r_1 r_2(\cos(\theta_1 + \theta_2) + i \sin(\theta_1 + \theta_2))$

   b. $\frac{z_1}{z_2} = \frac{r_1}{r_2}(\cos(\theta_1 - \theta_2) + i \sin(\theta_1 - \theta_2))$

   c. $z_1{}^n = r_1{}^n(\cos(n\theta) + i \sin(n\theta_1))$

   d. $z_1^{\frac{1}{n}} = r_1^{\frac{1}{n}}\left(\cos\left(\frac{\theta_1}{n} + \frac{2k\pi}{n}\right) + i \sin\left(\frac{\theta_1}{n} + \frac{2k\pi}{n}\right)\right)$, $k = 1, 2, 3 \ldots$
   $n - 1$

CHAPTER OBJECTIVES AND REVIEW

Objective: *To cite the Law of Sines and use it to solve triangles that are not necessarily right triangles.* (Section 4-1)

1. State the Law of Sines in your own words.

■■■ Where appropriate use the Law of Sines to find the measure of the required angle or side of $\triangle ABC$. Express results to nearest unit.

2. $A = 15°$, $a = 4$, $B = 42°$. Find b.
3. $A = 15°$, $a = 4$, $C = 37°$. Find c.

4. $A = 15°$, $a = 4$, $C = 37°$. Find b.

5. $A = 15°$, $a = 4$, $b = 8$. Find B.

6. $A = 15°$, $a = 4$, $b = 8$. Find C.

Objective: *To cite the Law of Cosines and use it to solve triangles that are not necessarily right triangles.* (Section 4-2)

7. State the Law of Cosines in your own words.

━━ Find the measure of the required angle or side of $\triangle ABC$.

8. $A = 20°$, $b = 5$, $c = 3$. Find a.

9. $a = 3$, $b = 4$, $c = 6$. Find B.

10. $C = 115°$, $a = 5$, $b = 7$. Find c.

Objective: *To use trigonometric relations to calculate the area of triangles given data other than the base and altitude.* (Section 4-3)

━━ Find the area of $\triangle ABC$.

11. $A = 25°$, $b = 6$, $c = 8$.   **12.** $A = 25°$, $B = 73°$, $c = 15$.

13. $a = 6$, $b = 7$, $c = 8$.   **14.** $a = 9$, $b = 10$, $c = 8$

Objective: *To explain the meaning of the symbols arc tan x, arc cos x, etc. and evaluate expressions involving such symbols.* (Section 4-4)

15. Explain what the symbol arc sin x means. How do you think about it when working a problem?

━━ Find the members of each set.

16. arc tan $(\frac{1}{2})$ **17.** arc cos $\left(\frac{-\sqrt{3}}{2}\right)$

18. arc sin (-1) **19.** arc sin $(0) \cup$ arc cos (0)

20. arc tan $\left(\frac{-\sqrt{3}}{1}\right)$ **21.** arc cos $(\frac{1}{2})$

━━ Evaluate each expression.

22. tan (arc cos $\frac{4}{5}$)   **23.** sin (arc sin $\frac{1}{3}$)

24. cos (arc tan $\frac{5}{12}$)   **25.** sin (arc cos u) $0 \leq u < 1$

Objective: *To evaluate expressions such as Arc cos x, Arc sin x, and Arc tan x.* (Section 4-5)

━━ Find the measure of each of the following angles.

26. Arc sin $\frac{\sqrt{2}}{2}$ **27.** Arc cos $\frac{-1}{2}$

28. Arc tan $\frac{-\sqrt{3}}{1}$ **29.** Arc sin 0

■ Evaluate each expression.

30. $\sin\left(\text{Arc cos } \frac{2}{3}\right)$

31. $\tan\left(\text{Arc sin } \frac{1}{5}\right)$

32. $\cos\left(\text{Arc tan } 4\right)$

33. $\tan\left(\text{Arc cos } \frac{2}{3}\right)$

Objective: *To graph the inverse circular functions Arc sin x, Arc cos x, and Arc tan x.* (Section 4-5)

■ Graph each function. Identify the domain.

34. $y = \text{Arc sin } x$

35. $y = \text{Arc tan } x$

Objective: *To solve equations that involve circular functions.* (Section 4-6)

■ Solve each of the following equations.

36. $2 \sin x - \sqrt{3} = 0$

37. $\tan 2x = -\frac{1}{2}$

38. $2 \sin x \cos x = \frac{1}{2}$

39. $\cos^2 x - \sin^2 x = \frac{\sqrt{2}}{2}$

Objective: *To solve inequalities that involve circular functions.* (Section 4-7)

■ Find the solution set of each inequality over $0 \le x \le 2\pi$.

40. $2 \sin x - \sqrt{3} < 0$

41. $2 \sin x \cos x \le \frac{\sqrt{2}}{2}$

Objective: *To express a complex number a + bi in polar form and to multiply and divide using the polar form.* (Section 4-8)

■ Express each complex number in polar form.

42. $2 + 1i$

43. $-2 + i$

44. $-3 - \sqrt{3}i$

45. $0 - 2i$

■ Find $z_1 \cdot z_2$ and $z_1 \div z_2$ in Exercises 46–47.

46. $z_1 = 2(\cos 50° + i \sin 50°), \quad z_2 = 4(\cos 5° + i \sin 5°)$

47. $z_1 = 3\left(\cos \frac{2\pi}{3} + i \sin \frac{2\pi}{3}\right), \quad z_2 = \frac{1}{2}\left(\cos \frac{\pi}{3} + i \sin \frac{\pi}{3}\right)$

Objective: *To use DeMoivre's Theorem to find the powers and roots of complex numbers.* (Section 4-9)

■ Use DeMoivre's Theorem to evaluate each expression.

48. $[3(\cos 60° + i \sin 60°)]^5$

49. $(1 + i)^6$

■ Express the indicated roots in polar form.

50. The three cube roots of 1

51. The four fourth roots of $1 + \sqrt{3}i$

Objective: *To convert from rectangular to polar coordinates and vice-versa.* (Section 4-10)

Find the polar coordinates of the following.

52. $(-6, 6)$ **53.** $(3, 0)$ **54.** $(2, -1)$ **55.** $(1, \sqrt{3})$

Find the rectangular coordinates of the following.

56. $(-3, 270°)$ **57.** $\left(5, \frac{2\pi}{3}\right)$

58. $(-1, 60°)$ **59.** $\left(2, \frac{-\pi}{4}\right)$

Objective: *To graph equations in polar coordinates.* (Section 4-11)

Sketch the graph of each curve on a polar coordinate system.

60. $r = 5$ **61.** $\theta = -21°$

62. $r = 3 + \sin \theta$ **63.** $r = -\frac{1}{2} + \cos \theta$

CHAPTER TEST

1. Find b if $A = 43°$, $B = 17°$, and $a = 100$.

2. Find A if $a = 40$, $b = 64$, and $c = 36$.

3. Find the area of the triangle in Exercise 1.

4. Find the area of the triangle in Exercise 2.

5. Two towns are 38,500 feet apart. Fay, in one town, hears a thunder clap 8 seconds after the flash of lightening. If the angle of elevation of the flash was 75° and sound travels at 1100 feet per second, how long will it take Sue, in the other town, to hear the thunder?

Evaluate each of the following expressions.

6. $\sin \left(\arctan \frac{-2}{3} \right)$ **7.** $\tan \left(\arccos \frac{1}{-5} \right)$

8. $\cos \left(\text{Arc sin } \frac{5}{8} \right)$ **9.** Arc sin $\frac{\sqrt{2}}{2}$

Solve each of the following.

10. $\tan x = 1$

11. $2 \cos^2 x - 1 = 0$

12. $1 - 2 \sin^2 x < 0$

13. Find the four fourth roots of $-1 + i\sqrt{3}$.

14. Graph $r = \sin \theta - 2$.

━━ Choose the best answer. Choose **a, b, c,** or **d.**

1. $A = \{-3, 1.0\overline{5}, 0\}$. Which of the following is false?

    a. $A \subseteq R$ **b.** $A \subseteq Q$ **c.** $A \subseteq Ir$ **d.** $0 \in W$

2. Solve: $2x^2 - x - 6 < 0$

    a. $x < 2 \text{ and } x < -\frac{3}{2}$ **b.** $x < 2 \text{ and } x > -\frac{3}{2}$

    c. $x > 2 \text{ and } x > -\frac{3}{2}$ **d.** $x > 2 \text{ and } x < -\frac{3}{2}$

3. Find the numerical coefficient of the term with x^4 in the expansion of $(x - 2)^6$.

    a. -500 **b.** 120 **c.** 60 **d.** 480

4. Find the solution set of $|2x - 1| \geq 5$.

    a. $\{x : x \leq 2\}$ **b.** $\{x : x \geq 3\}$

    c. $\{x : x \leq 2\} \cap \{x : x \geq 3\}$ **d.** $\{x : x \leq -2\} \cup \{x : x \geq 3\}$

5. If $h(x) = 2x + 1$ and $n(x) = 3x - 2$, find $n(h(x))$.

    a. $6x + 1$ **b.** $6x - 3$ **c.** $5x - 1$ **d.** $x - 3$

6. If $z = 3 + 2i$, which of the following is true?

    a. z is a pure imaginary   **b.** $z^2 = 9 - 4i$

    c. $z = -3 + 2i$ **d.** z is complex

7. Find the length of $z = 3 - 2i$.

    a. $\sqrt{5}$ **b.** 1 **c.** $\sqrt{13}$ **d.** $-\sqrt{5}$

8. For the wrapping function W, which statement is false?

    a. $W : \pi \rightarrow (-1, 0)$

    b. If $W(r) = (x, y)$ then $y = \sin r$

    c. If $W(r) = (t, u)$ then $t = \sin r$

    d. $W : \frac{3\pi}{2} \rightarrow (0, -1)$

9. Which statement is false?

    a. Whenever $\cos x = \frac{\sqrt{3}}{2}$, $\sin x = \frac{1}{2}$.

    b. Both $\cos x$ and $\sin x$ are negative in Quadrant 3.

    c. When $\sin x = \frac{\sqrt{2}}{2}$, $\cos x$ may be $-\frac{\sqrt{2}}{2}$.

    d. $\cos^2 x + \sin^2 x = 1$ for all x.

10. If $y = -3 \sin(-2x + 1)$ then which statement is true?

    a. The amplitude is -3.   **b.** The period is 2π.

    c. The phase shift is $\frac{1}{2}$.   **d.** The period is $-\pi$.

11. $\tan x \cdot \cos^2 x =$

a. $\sin x$ **b.** $\sin x \cos x$ **c.** $\frac{\tan x}{\csc^2 x}$ **d.** $\cos x$

12. In radians, $120°$ equals

a. $\frac{2\pi}{3}$ **b.** $\frac{\pi}{3}$ **c.** $\frac{5\pi}{6}$ **d.** $\frac{2}{3}$

13. If $\sin x = -\frac{5}{13}$ and $\tan x > 0$, which statement is true?

a. $\cos x = \frac{5}{13}$ **b.** $\cos x = -\frac{12}{13}$ **c.** $\cos x = \frac{12}{13}$ **d.** $\cos x = -\frac{5}{13}$

14. In a right triangle, $\triangle ABC$, where C is the right angle, which statement is true?

a. $\sin B = \frac{BC}{AB}$ **b.** $\tan A = \frac{AC}{BC}$ **c.** $\cos A = \frac{AC}{AB}$ **d.** $\sin A = \frac{AC}{BC}$

15. Find $\sin (15°)$.

a. $\sqrt{6} - \sqrt{2}$ **b.** $\frac{\sqrt{6}}{2} - \frac{\sqrt{2}}{2}$ **c.** $\frac{\sqrt{6} - \sqrt{2}}{4}$ **d.** $\frac{1}{2} - \frac{\sqrt{3}}{4}$

16. Which of the following does not equal $\cos 2x$?

a. $\cos^2 x + \sin^2 x$ **b.** $\cos^2 x - \sin^2 x$

c. $1 - 2 \sin^2 x$ **d.** $2 \cos^2 x - 1$

17. Given $\triangle ABC$ with $A = 35°$, and $B = 81°$. Which statement is true?

a. $c = \frac{a \sin 81°}{\sin 35°}$ **b.** $a = \frac{c \sin 35°}{\sin 64°}$

c. $C = 74°$ **d.** $a = \frac{b \sin 64°}{\sin 81°}$

18. The area of $\triangle ABC$ where $B = 40°$, and $a = 10$ and $c = 15$ is

a. about 75.   **b.** about 50.   **c.** about 30.   **d.** about 60.

19. If $0 < r < 1$, then $\tan (\arcsin r) =$

a. $\frac{r}{\sqrt{1 - r^2}}$ **b.** $\frac{\sqrt{1 - r^2}}{r}$ **c.** $\frac{r}{\sqrt{1 + r^2}}$ **d.** $\frac{\sqrt{1 + r^2}}{r}$

20. Solve: $\cos 2x = \sin x$, $0 \le x \le 2\pi$

a. $x = \frac{3\pi}{2}$ **b.** $x \in \left\{ \frac{\pi}{6}, \frac{5\pi}{6} \right\}$

c. $x \in \left\{ \frac{\pi}{6}, \frac{3\pi}{2} \right\}$ **d.** $x \in \left\{ \frac{\pi}{6}, \frac{5\pi}{6}, \frac{3\pi}{2} \right\}$

21. The $a + bi$ form of $\frac{2}{3}\left(\cos \frac{5\pi}{6} + i \sin \frac{5\pi}{6} \right)$ is

a. $\frac{\sqrt{3}}{3} - \frac{i}{3}$ **b.** $\frac{\sqrt{3}}{3} + \frac{i}{3}$ **c.** $\frac{\sqrt{3}}{2} + \frac{i}{2}$ **d.** $\frac{\sqrt{3}}{2} - \frac{i}{2}$

22. The polar coordinates of $(2, -2)$ are

a. $\left(\sqrt{2}, \frac{7\pi}{4} \right)$ **b.** $\left(2\sqrt{2}, -\frac{7\pi}{4} \right)$ **c.** $\left(\sqrt{2}, -\frac{\pi}{4} \right)$ **d.** $\left(2\sqrt{2}, -\frac{\pi}{4} \right)$

CHAPTER 5 Sequences, Series, and Limits

5–1 Sequences

The concept of *limit* is fundamental in mathematics. Without it many areas of knowledge, such as physics and engineering, would not exist except in rudimentary form. The use of limits is virtually unavoidable when studying those aspects of nature that are continuous (such as temperatures and velocities). Limits are needed even in some areas of knowledge, such as statistics, that deal mainly with non-continuous (discrete) phenomena. To provide you with the background that will best illuminate the concept of limit, an important and related concept is developed first, *sequences*.

During a nine-hole golf match between two millionaires, the first millionaire suggested the following wager:

The first hole shall be worth one dollar to the winner, and each succeeding hole shall be worth twice as much as the hole immediately preceding it.

What was each of the nine holes worth?

To solve this problem set up a one-to-one correspondence between the holes and their dollar values, one dollar to the first with the value of each succeeding hole double the prior one. The following correspondence results.

Hole number	1	2	3	4	5	6	7	8	9
	↕	↕	↕	↕	↕	↕	↕	↕	↕
Dollar value	1	2	4	8	16	32	64	128	256

Consequently, the dollar value of each hole is given by one member of the ordered set of numbers: 1, 2, 4, 8, 16, 32, 64, 128, 256. The set of numbers 1, 2, 4, 8, $\cdots$, 256, in the order given is a **finite sequence** because its members are in a one-to-one correspondence with the subset $\{1, 2, 3, 4, \cdots, 9\}$ of the positive integers.

Suppose that there were a golf hole for every positive integer and that the wager remained the same. The wager then would consist of the ordered set of numbers

$$1, 2, 4, 8, 16, 32, \cdots .$$

Such a set is an **infinite sequence** since it can be put in a one-to-one correspondence with the set of positive integers

$$\{1, 2, 3, \cdots\}.$$

The three dots indicate that the numbers continue in the same pattern indefinitely. Following are the basic definitions you will need.

Definitions A **sequence** is an ordered set of numbers which is the range of a function whose domain is the positive integers or a subset thereof. If the domain is the positive integers, the sequence is an **infinite sequence.** If the domain is a subset, $1, 2, 3, \cdots, k$, of the positive integers, then it is a **finite sequence.**

  The members of the sequence are **terms** of the sequence. The term corresponding to the positive integer n is the nth term of the sequence and is denoted by a symbol such as b_n. The sequence whose nth term is b_n is denoted $\{b_n\}$.

  Each term of the sequence for the millionaire golf game can be expressed as a power of 2:

Hole number	1	2	3	4	5	6	7	8	$\cdots$	n
Dollar value	2^0	2^1	2^2	2^3	2^4	2^5	2^6	2^7	$\cdots$	2^{n-1}

If b_n denotes the nth term of this sequence, then b_n, $n \in \{1, 2, 3, \cdots\}$, is given by the formula

$$b_n = 2^{n-1}.$$

The sequence is $\{2^{n-1}\}$.

  A general expression for the nth term of a sequence permits the calculation of any specific term of the sequence.

EXAMPLE 1. Calculate the fourth and the eleventh terms of the sequence 2^{n-1}.

Solution:
$$b_n = 2^{n-1}. \quad \longleftarrow \text{ } n\text{th term}$$
$$b_4 = 2^{4-1} \quad \longleftarrow \text{ 4th term}$$
$$= 2^3$$
$$= 8.$$
$$b_{11} = 2^{11-1} \quad \longleftarrow \text{ 11th term}$$
$$= 2^{10}$$
$$= 1024.$$

  Not all sequences possess a pattern expressible in terms of a formula. The sequence

$$3, 3.1, 3.14, 3.141, 3.1415, 3.14159, 3.141592, \cdots$$

of rational approximations to π is such a sequence.

Examination of the sequence $\frac{1}{1}, \frac{1}{3}, \frac{1}{6}, \cdots$ suggests that the fourth term might be $\frac{1}{10}$ since the denominators appear to increase by 2, by 3, etc. Replacing n in the expression

$$\frac{1}{-n^3 + \frac{13}{2}n^2 - \frac{21}{2}n + 6}$$

by 1, 2, and 3, respectively, you obtain the first three terms of the sequence above. Moreover, replacing n by 4 gives $\frac{1}{4}$, not $\frac{1}{10}$ as was suggested by the apparent pattern. This example illustrates that a sequence is not necessarily determined by specifying some of its terms. (Incidentally, a general term which gives a fourth term of $\frac{1}{10}$ is $\frac{1}{\frac{1}{2}n^2 + \frac{1}{2}n}$. Check this!)

Although not every sequence can be described by a formula, the sequences in this course will usually be described by a formula.

There are two common ways used to describe a sequence:

1. Stating the general term. For example:

$$b_n = 2^n - 3 \qquad n \in \{1, 2, 3, \cdots\}.$$

2. Giving the first term, b_1, and stating the relationship between each term and its successor. For example:

$$b_1 = -1,$$
$$b_{n+1} = b_n + 2^n \qquad n \in \{1, 2, 3, \cdots\}.$$

When the second procedure is used to define a sequence, the sequence is said to be defined **recursively** or by means of a **recursion formula**.

The use of a recursive definition to find the terms of a sequence is demonstrated in the following example.

EXAMPLE 2. Let b_n be defined as follows:

$$b_1 = -1$$
$$b_{n+1} = b_n + 2^n \qquad n \in \{1, 2, 3, \cdots\}$$

a. Find the first seven terms of $\{b_n\}$.
b. Find an expression for the nth term of $\{b_n\}$.

Solutions: a. $b_1 = -1$
$b_2 = b_1 + 2^1 = -1 + 2 = 1$
$b_3 = b_2 + 2^2 = 1 + 4 = 5$
$b_4 = b_3 + 2^3 = 5 + 8 = 13$
$b_5 = b_4 + 2^4 = 13 + 16 = 29$
$b_6 = b_5 + 2^5 = 29 + 32 = 61$
$b_7 = b_6 + 2^6 = 61 + 64 = 125$

b. $b_n = b_{n-1} + 2^{n-1}$
$$= b_{n-2} + 2^{n-2} + 2^{n-1}$$
$$= b_{n-3} + 2^{n-3} + 2^{n-2} + 2^{n-1}$$
$$\vdots$$
$$= b_1 + 2^1 + 2^2 + \cdots + 2^{n-2} + 2^{n-1}$$
$$b_n = -1 + 2^1 + 2^2 + \cdots + 2^{n-2} + 2^{n-1}$$

To find a simple expression for b_n, do the following:

$$2(b_n + 1) = 2^2 + 2^3 + \cdots + 2^{n-1} + 2^n \qquad \textbf{1}$$
$$(b_n + 1) = 2^1 + 2^2 + 2^3 + \cdots + 2^{n-1} \qquad \textbf{2}$$

Subtracting **2** from **1**

$$2b_n + 2 - b_n - 1 = -2^1 + 2^n$$
or
$$b_n = 2^n - 3.$$

CLASSROOM EXERCISES

━━ Write the first three terms of the sequence with the given general term.

1. $a_n = 3n$ **2.** $a_n = n^3$ **3.** $a_n = 3^n$ **4.** $a_n = \sin\left(\frac{\pi n}{2}\right)$

━━ Write the first four terms of the sequence defined recursively.

5. $a_1 = 2$, $a_{n+1} = \frac{2}{3} a_n$ **6.** $b_1 = -3$, $b_{n+1} = 5 + b_n$

7. $c_1 = -1$, $c_{n+1} = 3 + \frac{1}{2} c_n$ **8.** $d_1 = 2$, $d_{n+1} = \frac{2}{3} - 2d_n$

9. $e_1 = 1$, $e_{n+1} = -\frac{1}{2} e_n$ **10.** $f_1 = 2$, $f_{n+1} = f_n + 3$

11. If the range of a function is to be a sequence, what restrictions must be imposed on the domain of the function?

12. Name three ways in which a sequence may be described. What are the advantages and disadvantages of each way?

WRITTEN EXERCISES

A ━━ Each sequence below is defined recursively. Write the first six terms of each.

1. $b_1 = 5$, $b_{n+1} = b_n - 2$ **2.** $b_1 = 1$, $b_{n+1} = b_n + 2^{n-1}$

3. $b_1 = 3$, $b_{n+1} = 2b_n$ **4.** $b_1 = 4$, $b_{n+1} = (-3)b_n$

5. $a_1 = 4$, $a_{n+1} = (-1)^n a_n$ **6.** $a_1 = \frac{1}{2}$, $a_{n+1} = (-1)^{n-1} a_n$

7. $c_1 = 1$, $c_{n+1} = (2c_n)^{n-1}$ **8.** $c_1 = 2$, $c_{n+1} = (c_n - 2)^2$

9. $d_1 = 5$, $d_{n+1} = \frac{1}{n} d_n$ **10.** $d_1 = 1$, $d_2 = 1$, $d_{n+1} = d_n + d_{n-1}$

The general term of a sequence is given. Write the first five terms of the sequence.

11. $a_n = \frac{4}{n}$ **12.** $b_n = 2n - 1$ **13.** $c_k = 3k^2$

14. $d_k = k(k - 1)$ **15.** $a_t = 2t - 1$ **16.** $b_t = |2t| - 3$

17. $c_t = |2t - 3|$ **18.** $d_n = \frac{n}{2n - 1}$ **19.** $a_k = \frac{k + 2}{2k + 3}$

20. $b_k = \cos \frac{k\pi}{2}$ **21.** $c_t = \cos^2 \frac{t\pi}{2}$ **22.** $d_t = (i)^t (i = \sqrt{-1})$

Give **a.** the general term and **b.** the recursive definition of each sequence.

23. $1, 2, 3, 4, \cdots$ **24.** $1, 3, 5, 7, 9, \cdots$

25. $\frac{3}{1}, \frac{3}{1 \cdot 2}, \frac{3}{1 \cdot 2 \cdot 3}, \frac{3}{1 \cdot 2 \cdot 3 \cdot 4}, \cdots$ **26.** $1, \frac{1}{2}, \frac{1}{4}, \frac{1}{8}, \cdots$

27. $1, -1, 1, -1, \cdots$ **28.** $-3, 2, 7, 12, \cdots$

B Use the following definition in Exercises 29–33.

> **Definition** An **arithmetic sequence** is a sequence with general term: $a_n = a_1 + d(n - 1)$ where a_1 is the first term and d is a constant.

29. Let $a_1 = 2$, $d = 3$. Find a_2, a_3, a_4 and a_5.

30. Let $a_1 = 5$, $d = -2$. Find a_2, a_3, a_4 and a_5.

31. If $a_n = 1 - 3(n - 1)$, find the 6th term of the sequence.

32. Prove: If $a_n = a_1 + d(n - 1)$ then $a_{k+1} - a_k = d$.

33. Write a recursive definition of the arithmetic sequence with $a_n = a_1 + d(n - 1)$.

Use the following definition in Exercises 34–38.

> **Definition** A **geometric sequence** is a sequence with general term: $a_n = a_1 \cdot r^{n-1}$ where a_1 is the first term and r is a constant.

34. Let $a_1 = 2$, $r = 3$. Find a_2, a_3, a_4, and a_5.

35. Let $a_1 = 5$, $r = \frac{1}{3}$. Find a_2, a_3, a_4, and a_5.

36. Let $a_1 = 3$, $r = \frac{1}{2}$. Find a_2, a_3, a_4, and a_5.

37. If $a_n = \frac{2}{3}(\frac{1}{2})^{n-1}$, find the 6th term of the sequence.

38. Prove: If $a_n = a_1 r^{n-1}$, then $\frac{a_{k+1}}{a_k} = r$.

C **39.** Three sequences are defined below. Show that the first three terms of each are identical, but that the fourth terms are different.

a. $a_n = \dfrac{1}{n}$ $\qquad\qquad$ **b.** $b_n = \dfrac{1}{n^3 - 6n^2 + 12n - 6}$

c. $c_n = \begin{cases} -\dfrac{1}{n} \text{ for } n \text{ a multiple of 4} \\ \dfrac{1}{n} \text{ otherwise} \end{cases}$

━━Given $a_n = 3n$. Since $(n - 1)(n - 2)(n - 3) \cdots (n - k)$ equals 0 for $n \in \{1, 2, 3, \cdots k\}$, a second sequence identical to the first for k terms can be written by adding $(n - 1)(n - 2)(n - 3) \cdots (n - k)$ to the general term $3n$. That is, $a_n = 3n$ defines the sequence 3, 6, 9, 12, 15, $\cdots$, while $b_n = 3n + (n - 1)(n - 2)(n - 3)$ gives the sequence 3, 6, 9, 18, 39, $\cdots$. $\{a_n\}$ and $\{b_n\}$ are identical for three terms, but differ for all terms thereafter.

40. Write a general term for a sequence whose first four terms are 2, 4, 8, 16, but whose fifth term is not 32.

41. Write the general term of a sequence whose first three terms are $\frac{1}{2}, \frac{2}{3}, \frac{3}{4}$, and whose fourth term is the following.

$\qquad$ **a.** $\frac{4}{5}$ $\qquad\qquad$ **b.** $\frac{4}{11}$ $\qquad\qquad$ **c.** $\frac{1}{2}$

5–2 Graphing Sequences

Finite sequences are not as useful in mathematics as are infinite sequences. There are many interesting theorems dealing with infinite sequences, and much of advanced analysis is based on these theorems. For reasons such as these, finite sequences will not be studied further. From this point forward "sequence" will mean "infinite sequence." So that you no longer have to concern yourself with finite sequences, the following convention is adopted for associating a finite sequence with an infinite sequence.

With the finite sequence

$$a_n, n \in \{1, 2, 3, \cdots, k\}$$

associate the infinite sequence

$$b_n = \begin{cases} a_n, n \in \{1, 2, 3, \cdots, k\} \\ 0, n > k. \end{cases}$$

For example, the finite sequence $\left\{1, \frac{1}{2}, \frac{1}{3}, \cdots, \frac{1}{k}\right\}$ is associated with the sequence $\left\{1, \frac{1}{2}, \frac{1}{3}, \cdots, \frac{1}{k}, 0, 0, 0, \cdots\right\}$.

A sequence $\{a_n\}$ is the range of a function that maps the positive integers into a set (possibly the same set) of numbers such as C or R. A sequence may be represented geometrically by plotting the points $(1, a_1)$, $(2, a_2)$, $(3, a_3)$, $\cdots$ in a coordinate plane. However, the usual procedure is to associate each term of the sequence with a point on a number line. The following graph shows the first seven terms of the sequence $\{a_n\} = \left\{\dfrac{n}{n+1}\right\}$. The rest of the terms lie between $\frac{7}{8}$ and 1. a_{11}, a_{23} and a_{47} are shown.

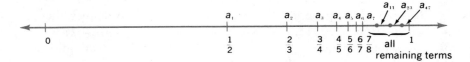

It is not possible to graph all of the terms of an infinite sequence. An adequate graph must depict accurately enough points corresponding to terms of the sequence to enable you to visualize easily the location of the remaining points.

EXAMPLE 1. Graph $\{b_n\} = \left\{(-1)^n \cdot \dfrac{1}{n}\right\}$.

Solution:

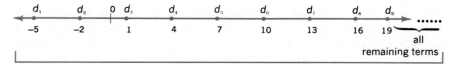

EXAMPLE 2. Graph $\{d_n\} = \{3n - 8\}$.

Solution:

EXAMPLE 3. Graph $\{a_n\} = \{(-1)^n 3\}$.

Solution:

EXAMPLE 4. Graph $\{c_n\} = \{9(\frac{2}{3})^{n-1}\}$.
Solution:

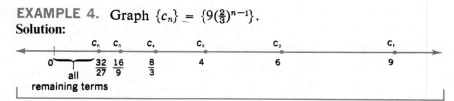

The notion of interval, first introduced in Chapter 1, is useful in describing the graph of a sequence. For example, in the graph of $\{a_n\} = \left\{\dfrac{n}{n+1}\right\}$ the points corresponding to 1, 2, $\cdots$, 7 were located. The remaining points were shown to lie between $\frac{7}{8}$ and 1. That is to say for $n > 7$

$$a_n \in \langle \tfrac{7}{8}, 1\rangle.$$

Similarly, in Example 1, for $n > 10$

$$b_n \in \langle -\tfrac{1}{9}, \tfrac{1}{8}\rangle.$$

In Example 4, for $n > 6$

$$c_n \in \langle 0, \tfrac{32}{27}\rangle.$$

The remaining points of $\{d_n\} = \{3n - 8\}$ of Example 2 can be located in an open interval also, if the notion of open interval is extended slightly. The extension needed is to include *half-lines* as open intervals, that is, the half-line $\{x : x > a, \quad a, x \in \mathbf{R}\}$.

Definition

$$\{x : x > a, \quad a, x \in \mathbf{R}\} = \langle a, \infty \rangle$$

is an **open interval with no right end.**

Also,

$$\{x : x < a, \quad a, x \in \mathbf{R}\} = \langle -\infty, a \rangle$$

is an **open interval with no left end.**

Now the remaining points in the graph of $\{d_n\} = \{3n - 8\}$ in Example 2 lie in an open interval, namely for $n > 9$,

$$d_n \in \langle 19, \infty \rangle.$$

Open intervals are useful in designating a set of points that lie within a given distance from one point. Suppose the point is 3 and the distance is 2. The interval $\langle 1, 5\rangle$ is the set of all points within two units of 3. The open interval $\langle 1, 5\rangle$ is the **neighborhood of 3 with radius 2.** Notice that 3 is the midpoint of $\langle 1, 5\rangle$.

> **Definition** Given a point M on a line; any open interval with
> M as midpoint is a **neighborhood of M**. If $\langle a, b \rangle$ is a neighbor-
> hood of M, then the **radius** of $\langle a, b \rangle$ is $\frac{b-a}{2}$ $(a < b)$.

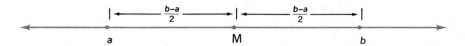

CLASSROOM EXERCISES

━━━ Find an open interval that includes all the terms of the indicated
sequence.

1. $\{a_n\} = \left\{\dfrac{1}{n+1}\right\}$ **2.** $\{a_n\} = \{n+1\}$ **3.** $\{a_n\} = \left\{\cos\dfrac{\pi n}{2}\right\}$

4. $\{a_n\} = \left\{\dfrac{n}{n+1}\right\}$ **5.** $\{a_n\} = \{2 + 3(n-1)\}$ **6.** $\{a_n\} = \left\{\sin\dfrac{\pi n}{4}\right\}$

━━━ Find the missing parts of the neighborhood: center, radius, or
endpoints.

7. $\langle -1, 5 \rangle$ **8.** center 5, radius 3

9. center 2, left endpoint -3 **10.** left endpoint -2, radius 5

11. $\langle -8, -3 \rangle$ **12.** radius 1.5, center -4.5

13. How do graphs of sequences differ from graphs of other
functions?

14. What is meant by a neighborhood of a point on a line? Explain your answer.

WRITTEN EXERCISES

A ━━━ In Exercises 1–9 graph between five and ten terms of each
sequence on a number line. When possible produce an open interval in which the remaining points lie.

1. $\{a_n\} = \{2n - 5\}$ **2.** $\{a_n\} = \left\{\dfrac{n+1}{n}\right\}$ **3.** $\{a_n\} = \left\{\dfrac{1}{2n-1}\right\}$

4. $\{b_n\} = \{(\tfrac{3}{4})^{n-1}\}$ **5.** $\{b_n\} = \{(-1)^{n-1}\}$ **6.** $\{b_n\} = \left\{6 - \dfrac{2}{n}\right\}$

7. $\{c_n\} = \{(\tfrac{3}{2})^n\}$ **8.** $\{c_n\} = \left\{\dfrac{(-1)^n}{n}\right\}$ **9.** $\{c_n\} = \left\{-3 + \dfrac{3}{n^2}\right\}$

10. For each Exercise 1–9 determine, if possible, an open interval which includes all the terms of the sequence for $n > 100$, but
excludes those terms for $n \leq 100$. For $n > 1000$, but excludes
those terms for $n \leq 1000$.

In Exercises 11–16 show graphically and express algebraically using inequalities the neighborhood of M with radius r.

11. $M = 5, r = 3$ **12.** $M = \frac{3}{2}, r = 1$ **13.** $M = 0, r = \frac{5}{2}$

14. $M = -2, r = 3$ **15.** $M = -\frac{3}{4}, r = \frac{3}{2}$ **16.** $M = t, r = p$

B   **17.** Find a neighborhood about $M = 1$ such that all the terms of $\left\{\frac{n+1}{n}\right\}$ for $n \geq 10$ lie in that neighborhood, but the preceding terms lie outside the neighborhood.

18. Repeat Exercise 17 for the sequence $\{1 + (\frac{1}{2})^n\}$.

19. Repeat Exercise 17 for the sequence $\{(-1)^n\}$. What happens here?

5–3 "Is Close To"

Examine the graph of the sequence $\{a_n\} = \left\{\frac{1}{2n}\right\}$.

Notice first that each term of $\{a_n\}$ appears to be smaller than its predecessor, that is, the sequence is decreasing. This can be verified by proving that $a_m < a_n \ (m > n)$. In particular, prove that

$$\frac{1}{2m} < \frac{1}{2n} \quad \text{whenever } m > n.$$

The proof follows. $m > n$ $m, n \in N$

Thus $\dfrac{1}{2mn} \cdot m > \dfrac{1}{2mn} \cdot n \quad \left(\dfrac{1}{2mn} > 0\right)$

or $\dfrac{1}{2n} > \dfrac{1}{2m}.$

So the terms of $\{a_n\}$ are decreasing.

Look again at the graph. It appears that if n is large enough, then a_n "is close to" zero. For example, if $n = 500$, then $a_{500} = \frac{1}{1000}$ is close to zero. In fact, it is within one one thousandth of a unit of zero. Moreover, since each succeeding term of $\{a_n\}$ is smaller than the preceding terms, all the terms of $\{a_n\}$ for $n > 500$ are closer than one one thousandth of a unit to zero.

How large would n have to be in order for all the terms of $\{a_n\}$ from n on to be as close as one millionth of a unit to zero?

If a_n is to be as close as one one millionth of a unit from zero, then a_n must be less than $\frac{1}{1,000,000}$ for some $n \in N$. This can be expressed in the inequality

$$\frac{1}{2n} < \frac{1}{1,000,000} \, .$$

1

How large must n be? Multiply both sides of **1** by $n \cdot 1,000,000$ getting

$$500,000 < n.$$

2

Thus it *appears* that n larger than $500,000$ will make a_n as close as $\frac{1}{1,000,000}$ to zero. To verify this, reverse the steps **1** and **2**, that is, let

$$n > 500,000.$$

Then
$$\frac{1}{1,000,000} > \frac{1}{2n} \, ,$$

or
$$\frac{1}{1,000,000} > a_n.$$

Consequently for $n > 500,000$, a_n is as close as $\frac{1}{1,000,000}$ to zero.

EXAMPLE. Let $\{b_n\} = \left\{\frac{n-1}{n+1}\right\}$.

a. Show that $b_n < b_{n+1}$ for $n \in N$.
b. Find $M \in N$ so that b_n is as close to 1 as $\frac{1}{50}$ for all $n \geq M$.

Solutions:

a.
$$b_n = \frac{n-1}{n+1} \qquad b_{n+1} = \frac{n}{n+2}$$

As is often the case when trying to prove an inequality, you begin with the inequality you are trying to prove and see if you can reduce it by reversible operations to an inequality known to be true. The sequence in reverse order constitutes a proof:

$$b_n < b_{n+1}$$

iff
$$\frac{n-1}{n+1} < \frac{n}{n+2}$$

iff
$$(n-1)(n+2) < n(n+1) \qquad \longleftarrow \quad \begin{array}{l}\mathbf{n+1 \text{ and}} \\ \mathbf{n+2 > 0}\end{array}$$

iff
$$n^2 + n - 2 < n^2 + n$$
iff
$$-2 < 0$$

Thus $b_n < b_{n+1}$ for $n \in N$.

b. You want to find an $M \in N$ (M is a fixed number) so that b_n is within $\frac{1}{50}$ of a unit of 1. Since each $b_n < 1$ this means

$$1 - b_n < \tfrac{1}{50} \quad \text{or} \quad 1 - \tfrac{1}{50} < b_n$$

So solve for n as follows. $\quad b_n > \frac{49}{50}$

$$\frac{n-1}{n+1} > \frac{49}{50}$$
$$50(n-1) > 49(n+1) \quad \longleftarrow \quad \boldsymbol{n+1 > 0}$$
$$50n - 50 > 49n + 49$$
$$n > 99$$

Working backwards in this derivation from $n > 99$ to $b_n > \frac{49}{50}$ constitutes a proof of the statement: *For $n \geq 100$, b_n is as close as $\frac{1}{50}$ to 1.* Thus M can be chosen to be 100 (or any larger number). A quick computation will show you that $b_{100} = \frac{99}{101}$ which is within $\frac{1}{50}$ of 1.

Recall that the direction of the inequality symbol *reverses* whenever you multiply or divide both sides of the inequality by a *negative* number. (See Theorem 1–6ii on page 11.) Thus, in part **b** of the example, the last four steps could also be done as follows.

$$49n + 49 < 50n - 50$$
$$-n < -99$$
$$(-1)(-n) > (-1)(-99) \quad \longleftarrow \quad \textbf{By Theorem 1-6ii}$$
$$n > 99$$

CLASSROOM EXERCISES

▬ Determine M such that for all $n > M$ the following is true.

1. $\dfrac{1}{2n} < \dfrac{1}{600}$ **2.** $\dfrac{1}{n-1} < \dfrac{1}{1000}$ **3.** $\dfrac{n}{n+1} > \dfrac{1}{100}$

4. $\dfrac{1}{5n} < \dfrac{1}{10^4}$ **5.** $\dfrac{1}{2^n} < \dfrac{1}{1000}$ **6.** $\dfrac{n}{4n+1} > \dfrac{1}{2000}$

WRITTEN EXERCISES

A   **1.** Let $\{a_n\} = \left\{\dfrac{1}{n}\right\}$.

     a. Show that $a_n > a_{n+1}$ for $n \in N$.

     b. Find $M \in N$ so that a_n is as close to 0 as $\frac{1}{200}$ for all $n \geq M$.

   2. Let $\{b_n\} = \left\{\dfrac{n}{n+1}\right\}$.

     a. Show that $b_n < b_{n+1}$ for $n \in N$.

     b. Find $M \in N$ so that b_n is as close to 1 as $\frac{1}{500}$ for all $n \geq M$.

3. Let $\{c_n\} = \left\{\frac{1}{2^n}\right\}$.

    a. Show that $c_n > c_{n+1}$ for $n \in \mathbb{N}$.

    b. Find $M \in \mathbb{N}$ so that c_n is as close to 0 as $\frac{1}{1000}$ for all $n \geq M$. As close to 0 as $\frac{1}{1,000,000}$.

4. Let $\{a_n\} = \left\{\frac{2n}{4n+1}\right\}$.

    a. Show that $a_n < a_{n+1}$ for $n \in \mathbb{N}$.

    b. Find $M \in \mathbb{N}$ so that a_n is as close to $\frac{1}{2}$ as $\frac{1}{100}$ for all $n \geq M$.

    c. Find $M \in \mathbb{N}$ so that a_n is as close to $\frac{1}{2}$ as $\frac{1}{500}$ for all $n \geq M$.

    d. Does the M found in **c** suffice to solve **b**? Explain.

5. Let $\{a_n\} = \left\{-\frac{1}{n}\right\}$.

    a. Show that $a_n < a_{n+1}$ for $n \in \mathbb{N}$.

    b. Find an $M \in \mathbb{N}$ so that a_n is as close to 0 as $\frac{1}{100}$ for all $n \geq M$.

B **6.** Let $\{d_n\} = \left\{-\frac{(n-1)}{n}\right\}$.

    a. Show that $d_n > d_{n+1}$ for $n \in \mathbb{N}$.

    b. Find an $M \in \mathbb{N}$ so that d_n is as close to -1 as $\frac{1}{500}$ for all $n \geq M$.

7. Let $\{c_n\} = \left\{\frac{n}{3n+1}\right\}$.

    a. Show that $c_n < c_{n+1}$ for $n \in \mathbb{N}$.

    b. Find an $M \in \mathbb{N}$ so that c_n is as close to $\frac{1}{3}$ as $\frac{1}{50}$ for all $n \geq M$.

C **8.** Let $\{a_n\} = \left\{\frac{1}{5n}\right\}$.

    a. Show that $a_n > a_{n+1}$ for $n \in \mathbb{N}$.

    b. Find an $M \in \mathbb{N}$ so that a_n is as close to 0 as $k > 0$ for all $n \geq M$.

5–4 Neighborhoods and Sequences

In the previous section you learned how to find an $M \in \mathbb{N}$ so that the terms of a sequence $\{a_n\}$ for $n \geq M$ were within a specified distance of some given number. The sequences with which you worked had all positive or all negative terms—never a mixture of positive and negative terms. The methods you learned in the last section will now be extended to a more general method which can always be used. The idea of neighborhood is central to this method. An example will clarify the idea.

EXAMPLE 1. Consider the sequence $\{a_n\} = \left\{\dfrac{n+2}{n+3}\right\}$ and the neighborhood of 1 with radius $\tfrac{1}{10}$; that is, $\langle 0.9, 1.1 \rangle$.

Which terms of $\left\{\dfrac{n+2}{n+3}\right\}$ lie in $\langle 0.9, 1.1 \rangle$? That is, how large must n be so that a_n is within $\tfrac{1}{10}$ of 1? For a term a_n to be in $\langle 0.9, 1.1 \rangle$, a_n must be between 0.9 and 1.1. That is, the compound inequality

$$0.9 < \frac{n+2}{n+3} < 1.1$$

must be true. Consequently the question can be answered by solving the compound inequality

$$0.9 < \frac{n+2}{n+3} \quad and \quad \frac{n+2}{n+3} < 1.1.$$

The solutions to these two simple inequalities follow.

$0.9 < \dfrac{n+2}{n+3}$	$\dfrac{n+2}{n+3} < 1.1$
iff $9 < \dfrac{10n+20}{n+3}$	iff $\dfrac{10n+20}{n+3} < 11$
iff $9n + 27 < 10n + 20$	iff $10n + 20 < 11n + 33$
iff $7 < n$	iff $-13 < n$

The solution set of $7 < n$ is $\{n : n > 7, n \in \mathbf{N}\}$.
The solution set of $-13 < n$ is $\{n : n > -13, n \in \mathbf{N}\}$.
Consequently the solution set of $7 < n$ *and* $-13 < n$ is

$$\{n : n > 7, n \in \mathbf{N}\} \cap \{n : n > -13, n \in \mathbf{N}\}$$
or
$$\{n : n > 7, n \in \mathbf{N}\}.$$

Hence, for all $n > 7$, a_n is in $\langle 0.9, 1.1 \rangle$. That is, if you choose M to be 8, then $a_n \in \langle 0.9, 1.1 \rangle$ for all $n \geq M = 8$. This situation is shown in the graph below.

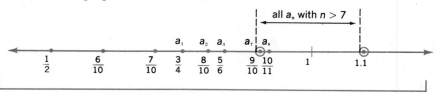

Table 1 contains similar information for other neighborhoods of 1 and the sequence $\left\{\dfrac{n+2}{n+3}\right\}$. The entries in the last column name the first term of the sequence that lies in the given neighborhood. For example, the last entry in the last row shows that a_{99998} and all succeeding terms of $\left\{\dfrac{n+2}{n+3}\right\}$ lie in the neighborhood $\langle 0.99999, 1.00001 \rangle$ of 1. In this case M could be 99998.

Neighborhood of One	Radius of Neighborhood	First Term of $\{a_n\}$ in the Neighborhood
$\langle 0.9, 1.1 \rangle$	$\dfrac{1}{10}$	a_8
$\langle 0.99, 1.01 \rangle$	$\dfrac{1}{100}$	a_{98}
$\langle 0.999, 1.001 \rangle$	$\dfrac{1}{1000}$	a_{998}
$\langle 0.9999, 1.0001 \rangle$	$\dfrac{1}{10,000}$	a_{9998}
$\langle 0.99999, 1.00001 \rangle$	$\dfrac{1}{100,000}$	a_{99998}

Table 1

The next example illustrates how using neighborhoods facilitates finding M when the sequence has both positive and negative terms. In this instance notice that both parts of the compound inequality play a vital role.

EXAMPLE 2.   Find an $M \in \mathbb{N}$ so that for $n \geq M$ the terms of $\{b_n\} = \left\{\dfrac{(-1)^n}{n}\right\}$ are in the neighborhood of 0 with radius $\dfrac{1}{1000}$, i.e., within $\dfrac{1}{1000}$ of 0.

Solution: $M \in \mathbb{N}$ is obtained by solving the compound inequality

$$-0.001 < \frac{(-1)^n}{n} < .001. \qquad \text{That is,}$$

$$-.001 < \frac{(-1)^n}{n} \qquad \qquad and \qquad \qquad \frac{(-1)^n}{n} < .001.$$

$-.001 < \dfrac{(-1)^n}{n}$ iff

$-1 < \dfrac{(-1)^n}{n} 1000$ iff

$-n < (-1)^n 1000$ iff

$n > (-1)^{n+1} 1000$

If n is even, $(-1)^{n+1} = -1$, and $n > -1 \cdot 1000$ for all n. If n is odd, $(-1)^{n+1} = 1$, and $n > 1 \cdot 1000$ when $n \geq 1001$.

$\dfrac{(-1)^n}{n} < .001$ iff

$\dfrac{(-1)^n}{n} 1000 < 1$ iff

$(-1)^n 1000 < n$

If n is odd, $(-1)^n = -1$, and $-1 \cdot 1000 < n$ for all n. If n is even, $(-1)^n = 1$, and $1 \cdot 1000 < n$ when $n > 1001$.

If $n \geq 1001$, then the conditions $n > 1001$ (n even) and $n \geq 1001$ (n odd) are both satisfied. Consequently b_{1001} and all succeeding terms are in $\langle -0.001, 0.001 \rangle$.

In the same manner it can be shown that the entries in Table 2 are accurate. Again it is clear that *most* (all but a finite number) of the terms of $\frac{(-1)^n}{n}$ are close to 0. Considering the neighborhood $\langle -0.000001, 0.000001 \rangle$, all but 1,000,000 of the terms are in the interval. In fact, no matter how small you make the radius of the neighborhood about 0, you could still prove that only a finite number of the terms of $\frac{(-1)^n}{n}$ lie outside the neighborhood.

However, there are neighborhoods of points which contain only a finite number of terms of a sequence.

Neighborhood of Zero	Radius of Neighborhood	First Term in Neighborhood
$\langle -0.01, 0.01 \rangle$	$\frac{1}{100}$	b_{101}
$\langle -0.0001, 0.0001 \rangle$	$\frac{1}{10,000}$	b_{10001}
$\langle -0.00001, 0.00001 \rangle$	$\frac{1}{100,000}$	$b_{100,001}$
$\langle -0.000001, 0.000001 \rangle$	$\frac{1}{1,000,000}$	$b_{1,000,001}$

Table 2

EXAMPLE 3. How many terms of the sequence $\{c_n\} = \left\{\frac{24}{n}\right\}$ lie in the neighborhood $\langle \frac{1}{2}, \frac{3}{2} \rangle$?

Solution:
$$\frac{1}{2} < \frac{24}{n} < \frac{3}{2}$$

$$\frac{1}{2} < \frac{24}{n} \qquad and \qquad \frac{24}{n} < \frac{3}{2}$$

$\frac{1}{2} < \frac{24}{n}$ iff $\qquad\qquad$ $\frac{24}{n} < \frac{3}{2}$ iff

$n < 48$ $\qquad\qquad\qquad$ $48 < 3n$ iff

$\qquad\qquad\qquad\qquad\qquad$ $16 < n$

The solution of the compound inequality is $16 < n < 48$. Hence for $n \in \{17, 18, \cdots, 46, 47\}$ c_n lies in $\langle \frac{1}{2}, \frac{3}{2} \rangle$. There are 31 terms of $\{c_n\}$ in this neighborhood.

There are neighborhoods of points which contain an infinite subset of the terms of a sequence, but another infinite subset of the sequence lies outside the neighborhood. For example, the neighborhood $\langle \frac{1}{2}, \frac{3}{2} \rangle$ contains an infinite number of the terms of $(-1)^n$. An infinite number also lie outside $\langle \frac{1}{2}, \frac{3}{2} \rangle$, namely all those terms for odd n.

WRITTEN EXERCISES

A ■ In Exercises 1–10 find the terms for each sequence which are in the neighborhood of radius r about m.

1. $\{a_n\} = \left\{ \frac{n}{n+1} \right\}$, $r = \frac{1}{2}$, $m = 1$

2. $\{a_n\} = \left\{ \frac{n}{n+1} \right\}$, $r = \frac{1}{1000}$, $m = 1$

3. $\{b_n\} = \{6(\frac{2}{3})^{n-1}\}$, $r = \frac{1}{2}$, $m = 1$

4. $\{b_n\} = \{6(\frac{2}{3})^{n-1}\}$, $r = \frac{1}{100}$, $m = \frac{2}{100}$

5. $\{c_n\} = \{2n - 3\}$, $r = 5$, $m = 2$

6. $\{c_n\} = \{2n - 3\}$, $r = 2$, $m = \frac{9}{10}$

7. $\{d_n\} = \left\{ (-1)^n \frac{n}{n+1} \right\}$, $r = \frac{3}{4}$, $m = 0$

8. $\{d_n\} = \left\{ (-1)^n \frac{n}{n+1} \right\}$, $r = \frac{1}{10}$, $m = 1$

9. $\{e_n\} = \left\{ \frac{2n}{n+5} \right\}$, $r = \frac{1}{4}$, $m = 1\frac{1}{4}$

10. $\{e_n\} = \left\{ \frac{2n}{n+5} \right\}$, $r = \frac{1}{100}$, $m = 2$

11. Given $\frac{n-1}{2n} < \frac{1}{10}$. Justify each step in the following argument. What statement does the argument prove?

a. $\frac{10n - 10}{2n} < 1$ iff

b. $10n - 10 < 2n$ iff

c. $-10 < -8n$ iff

d. $5 > 4n$ iff

e. $\frac{5}{4} > n$

In Exercises 12–17 you are given $\{a_n\} = \left\{ \frac{1}{2n-1} \right\}$. In each exercise for the given neighborhood of 0, what is the first term within the neighborhood? How many terms lie outside it?

12. $\langle -1, 1 \rangle$ **13.** $\langle -\frac{1}{2}, \frac{1}{2} \rangle$ **14.** $\langle -\frac{1}{10}, \frac{1}{10} \rangle$ **15.** $\langle -\frac{1}{1000}, \frac{1}{1000} \rangle$

16. $\left\langle -\frac{1}{1,000,000}, \frac{1}{1,000,000} \right\rangle$ **17.** $\langle -R, R \rangle$ where $R > 0$

B **18.** Given $\{a_n\} = \left\{ \frac{7n + 13}{3n} \right\}$. Which terms of $\{a_n\}$ are

a. greater than 2?   **b.** less than $\frac{8}{3}$?

c. in $\langle 2, 2\frac{2}{3} \rangle$?   **d.** in $\langle \frac{13}{6}, \frac{15}{6} \rangle$?

5-5   The Limit of a Sequence

What does it mean to say that "a sequence has a limit"? Here are some examples that will help you build an intuitive basis for the definition.

Examples of Sequences

1. $\{a_n\} = \left\{\frac{1}{n}\right\}$ or $1, \frac{1}{2}, \frac{1}{3}, \frac{1}{4}, \frac{1}{5}, \frac{1}{6}, \frac{1}{7}, \cdots, \frac{1}{n}, \cdots$.

2. $\{b_n\} = \{3n - 5\}$ or $-2, 1, 4, 7, 10, 13, \cdots, 3n - 5, \cdots$

3. $\{c_n\} = \left\{\frac{(-1)^n}{n}\right\}$ or $-1, \frac{1}{2}, -\frac{1}{3}, \frac{1}{4}, -\frac{1}{5}, \frac{1}{6}, \cdots, \frac{(-1)^n}{n}, \cdots$

4. $\{d_n\} = \left\{\frac{3n + 1}{n}\right\}$ or $4, \frac{7}{2}, \frac{10}{3}, \frac{13}{4}, \frac{16}{5}, \frac{19}{6}, \cdots, \frac{3n + 1}{n}, \cdots$

5. $\{e_n\} = \left\{(-1)^n \frac{2n + 1}{n}\right\}$ or $-3, \ 2\frac{1}{2}, \ -2\frac{1}{3}, \ 2\frac{1}{4}, \ -2\frac{1}{5}, \ 2\frac{1}{6}, \cdots,$
$(-1)^n \frac{2n + 1}{n}, \cdots$

EXAMPLE 1.   The terms of sequence **1** are very small for large values of n. The terms are clustered very close to zero for large n, but zero is not a term of the sequence. Zero is the limit of the sequence. The sequence is said to converge to zero.

EXAMPLE 2.   Each term in sequence **2** is three greater than its predecessor. For large values of n, the terms are large. There is no number about which the terms of the sequence cluster. This sequence has no limit; it is said to diverge.

EXAMPLE 3.   Sequence **3** is similar to sequence **1**. The terms are close to zero for large values of n, but unlike sequence **1**, there are terms to the right and to the left of zero. This sequence converges to zero.

EXAMPLE 4.   The terms of sequence **4** are very close to 3 for large values of n. To see this rewrite each term: $4, 3\frac{1}{2}, 3\frac{1}{3}, 3\frac{1}{4}, 3\frac{1}{5}, 3\frac{1}{6}, 3\frac{1}{7},$ $\cdots, 3 + \frac{1}{n}, \cdots$. Since the terms are close to 3, the sequence has a limit of 3.

EXAMPLE 5.   The terms of sequence **5** which correspond to even numbers are close to 2. The terms corresponding to odd numbers are close to -2. Consequently there is *not* a unique single number about which the terms cluster. The sequence has no limit. Therefore it is said to diverge.

The discussion of the examples suggests the following ideas:

a. Some sequences have limits; some do not.

b. If a sequence has a limit, then the limit is a unique number.

c. If a sequence has a limit, then most of the terms are close to the limit.

It is sometimes difficult to determine the limit of a sequence. You can make a guess as to the identity of the limit based upon an examination of the given sequence and then try to confirm (or refute) your guess. To confirm or refute your guess you need to know the mathematical meaning of the phrase "most of the terms are very close to the limit". The definition follows.

Definition A **sequence** $\{a_n\}$ **has a limit** A (or **a sequence** $\{a_n\}$ **converges to** A) if for every neighborhood of A a positive integer M can be found such that a_n is in the neighborhood for all $n \geq M$. If a sequence has a limit, it is a **convergent** sequence. If a sequence has no limit, it is a **divergent sequence.**

The notation $\{a_n\} \longrightarrow A$ is read: "The sequence $\{a_n\}$ converges to A" or "The limit of $\{a_n\}$ is A." Notice that one refers to *the* limit of a sequence, although there is nothing concerning uniqueness in the definition. (Definitions generally do not concern themselves with the number of objects being defined, nor even with the matter of whether the object defined exists.) It can be shown that it is indeed correct to refer to *the* limit of a sequence, that is, that the limit of a sequence *is* unique if it exists at all.

The definition of a convergent sequence is the basis of a challenge to any person who claims that a certain number is a limit of a given sequence. It says that if you claim that A is the limit, then, when challenged with a neighborhood of A, you can always find a number M such that all the terms of the sequence that correspond to positive integers greater than or equal to M will lie in that neighborhood. The following example illustrates this idea.

EXAMPLE 6.

Given: $\{a_n\} = \left\{\frac{1}{n}\right\}$.

Claim: The limit of this sequence is 0, that is $\{a_n\} \longrightarrow 0$.

Challenge: Given the neighborhood $\langle -.01, .01 \rangle$, find M such that for all $n \geq M \quad a_n \in \langle -0.01, 0.01 \rangle$.

Solution: Accepting the challenge you have the following.

$$-\frac{1}{100} < \frac{1}{n} < \frac{1}{100} \qquad \text{if and only if}$$

$$-\frac{1}{100} < \frac{1}{n} \quad and \quad \frac{1}{n} < \frac{1}{100}.$$

$$-\frac{1}{100} < \frac{1}{n} \qquad\qquad \frac{1}{n} < \frac{1}{100} \quad \text{iff}$$

is always true $100 < n$

because $n > 0$.

Hence if M is chosen to be 101, then all terms from a_{101} on are in the neighborhood

$$\langle -0.01, 0.01 \rangle.$$

The challenge is successfully met.

But the challenger may not stop. He may say; "I'm going to choose a smaller neighborhood such as $\langle -0.000001, 0.000001 \rangle$ or $\langle -10^{-17}, 10^{-17} \rangle$". These challenges can be successfully met by using the procedure above. $M = 1,000,001$ and $M = 10^{17} + 1$ will suffice.

However, no matter how many such challenges you meet, you will not have proved that 0 is the limit of $\left\{\frac{1}{n}\right\}$ because the definition requires you to show that an M can be found for *every* neighborhood. How can this be done? The answer lies in the use of a *general neighborhood*.

Definition The **general neighborhood** of A is $\langle A - \epsilon, A + \epsilon \rangle$ where ϵ is a variable whose replacement set is the set of positive real numbers.

Both ϵ and $\in$ are forms of the Greek letter *epsilon*. $\in$ will continue to be used in the sense of "is a member of" while ϵ will be used to stand for any positive number.

The general neighborhood of 0 is $\langle 0 - \epsilon, 0 + \epsilon \rangle = \langle -\epsilon, \epsilon \rangle$. You can *prove* that $\left\{\frac{1}{n}\right\} \longrightarrow 0$ by showing that you can find an M when the challenge neighborhood is the general neighborhood. This means that "most of the terms are close to 0" no matter who defines "is close to" because the real number ϵ in the definition of a general neighborhood can be as small as or smaller than any positive real number. The proof is given in Example 7.

EXAMPLE 7.

Given: $\{a_n\} = \left\{\frac{1}{n}\right\}$.

Claim: The limit of this sequence is 0.

Challenge: Find M, given the neighborhood $\langle -\epsilon, \epsilon \rangle$, $\epsilon > 0$.

Solution: Accepting the challenge:

$$-\epsilon < \frac{1}{n} < \epsilon \quad \text{iff}$$

$$-\epsilon < \frac{1}{n} \qquad and \qquad \frac{1}{n} < \epsilon.$$

$$-\epsilon < \frac{1}{n} \qquad\qquad \frac{1}{n} < \epsilon \quad \text{iff}$$

is always true $\qquad\qquad$ $\frac{1}{\epsilon} < n.$

because $n > 0.$

So choose M to be any integer greater than $\frac{1}{\epsilon}$. Therefore, the terms a_n for which $n \geq M > \frac{1}{\epsilon}$ are in the neighborhood $\langle -\epsilon, \epsilon \rangle$ because $n \geq M > \frac{1}{\epsilon}$ implies $\epsilon > \frac{1}{n}$. Also $-\epsilon < \frac{1}{n}$ for all $n \geq M$.

What has been done in this example is to show that for all values of ϵ there exists an M, namely, any number greater than $\frac{1}{\epsilon}$, such that all terms a_n with $n \geq M$ lie in the neighborhood $\langle -\epsilon, \epsilon \rangle$. Hence it has been *proved* that $\{a_n\} \longrightarrow 0$. For any neighborhood selected by a challenger, you can now find an appropriate M.

The following table lists some challenge neighborhoods, the corresponding values of $\frac{1}{\epsilon}$ and a value of M that would satisfy the condition that all the terms of the sequence corresponding to positive integers greater than or equal to M will lie in the neighborhood

$$\langle -\epsilon, \epsilon \rangle.$$

Challenge neighborhood	$\langle -10^{-6}, 10^{-6} \rangle$	$\langle -\frac{3}{4}, \frac{3}{4} \rangle$	$\langle -10^{-10}, 10^{-10} \rangle$	$\langle -\frac{1}{450}, \frac{1}{450} \rangle$
$\frac{1}{\epsilon}$	10^6	$\frac{4}{3}$	10^{10}	450
$M > \frac{1}{\epsilon}$	$10^6 + 1$	2	$10^{10} + 1$	451

The following examples prove that the suggested limits of the sequences in Examples 3 and 4 are actually the limits.

EXAMPLE 8. Prove: $\{c_n\} = \left\{\dfrac{(-1)^n}{n}\right\} \longrightarrow 0$

Challenge: Given $\langle -\epsilon, \epsilon \rangle$, find an M such that for $n \geq M$ $c_n \in \langle -\epsilon, \epsilon \rangle$.

This requires the solution of the following compound inequality.

$$-\epsilon < \frac{(-1)^n}{n} < \epsilon$$

or $\qquad -\epsilon < \dfrac{(-1)^n}{n} \qquad$ *and* $\qquad \dfrac{(-1)^n}{n} < \epsilon.$

$$-\epsilon < \frac{(-1)^n}{n} \quad \text{iff} \qquad\qquad\qquad \frac{(-1)^n}{n} < \epsilon \quad \text{iff}$$

$$-n < \frac{(-1)^n}{\epsilon} \quad \text{iff} \qquad\qquad\qquad \frac{(-1)^n}{\epsilon} < n$$

$$n > \frac{(-1)^{n+1}}{\epsilon}$$

If n is even, $(-1)^{n+1} = -1$ $\qquad$ If n is odd, $(-1)^n = -1$
and $n > -\frac{1}{\epsilon}$. $\qquad\qquad\qquad\qquad$ and $-\frac{1}{\epsilon} < n.$
If n is odd, $(-1)^{n+1} = 1$ $\qquad\quad$ If n is even, $(-1)^n = 1$
and $n > \frac{1}{\epsilon}$. $\qquad\qquad\qquad\qquad\;$ and $\frac{1}{\epsilon} < n.$

So, whether n is even or odd, choose $M > \frac{1}{\epsilon}$. Thus, for all $n \geq M$, a_n is in $\langle -\epsilon, \epsilon \rangle$ and 0 is the limit.

EXAMPLE 9. Prove: $\{d_n\} = \left\{\dfrac{3n + 1}{n}\right\} \longrightarrow 3$

Challenge: Given $\langle 3 - \epsilon, 3 + \epsilon \rangle$, find an M such that for $n \geq M$, $d_n \in \langle 3 - \epsilon, 3 + \epsilon \rangle$. This requires solving this compound inequality.

$$3 - \epsilon < \frac{3n + 1}{n} < 3 + \epsilon$$

or $\qquad 3 - \epsilon < \dfrac{3n + 1}{n} \qquad$ *and* $\qquad \dfrac{3n + 1}{n} < 3 + \epsilon.$

$$3 - \epsilon < \frac{3n + 1}{n} \quad \text{iff} \qquad\qquad \frac{3n + 1}{n} < 3 + \epsilon \quad \text{iff}$$

$$3n - \epsilon n < 3n + 1 \quad \text{iff} \qquad\qquad 3n + 1 < 3n + \epsilon n \quad \text{iff}$$

$$-\epsilon n < 1 \qquad \text{iff} \qquad\qquad\qquad 1 < \epsilon n \qquad \text{iff}$$

$$-n < \frac{1}{\epsilon} \qquad\qquad\qquad\qquad\qquad \frac{1}{\epsilon} < n$$

which is true for all positive integers n.

So choose $M > \frac{1}{\epsilon}$. Consequently for all $n \geq M > \frac{1}{\epsilon}$, d_n is in $\langle 3 - \epsilon, 3 + \epsilon \rangle$ and 3 is the limit of the sequence.

WRITTEN EXERCISES

A   **1.** Why in the proof that $\left\{ \frac{3n + 1}{n} \right\} \longrightarrow 3$ was the general neighborhood $\langle 3 - \epsilon, 3 + \epsilon \rangle$ used rather than $\langle -\epsilon, \epsilon \rangle$?

In Exercises 2–9 the claim is made that A is the limit of $\{a_n\}$. What is the general neighborhood of A for the given value of A?

   2. $A = 2$ **3.** $A = -1$ **4.** $A = 0$ **5.** $A = -\frac{2}{3}$ **6.** $A = \frac{1}{4}$

   7. $A = 100$ **8.** $A = -50$ **9.** $A = p$ (p a real number)

In Exercises 10–15, what appears to be the limit of each sequence?

   10. $a_n = \dfrac{2n + 5}{3n}$ **11.** $a_n = \dfrac{2n - 11}{n}$

   12. $a_n = \dfrac{4 - n}{n}$ **13.** $a_n = \dfrac{n^2 + 4}{3n^2}$

   14. $a_n = \dfrac{3n^2}{n^2 + 1}$ **15.** $a_n = \left(\frac{2}{3} \right)^n$

16. The limit of $\{a_n\} = \left\{ \frac{2n + 1}{3n - 2} \right\}$ appears to be $\frac{2}{3}$. Find an M such that for all $n \geq M$, a_n is in the given neighborhood.

     a. $\langle \frac{2}{3} - \frac{1}{3}, \frac{2}{3} + \frac{1}{3} \rangle$ **b.** $\langle \frac{2}{3} - 0.01, \frac{2}{3} + 0.01 \rangle$

     c. $\langle \frac{2}{3} - 10^{-6}, \frac{2}{3} + 10^{-6} \rangle$ **d.** $\langle \frac{2}{3} - \epsilon, \frac{2}{3} + \epsilon \rangle$

B   **17.** Prove: $\{a_n\} = \left\{ \frac{\frac{1}{2}n + 1}{n} \right\} \longrightarrow \frac{1}{2}$

   18. Prove: $\{b_n\} = \left\{ \frac{6n - 2}{4n} \right\} \longrightarrow \frac{3}{2}$

   19. Prove: $\{c_n\} = \left\{ \frac{-2n}{5n + 2} \right\} \longrightarrow \frac{-2}{5}$

C   **20.** Prove: $\{d_n\} = \left\{ \frac{3n^2}{n^2 + 1} \right\} \longrightarrow 3$

   21. Prove that 1 is not the limit of $\{a_n\} = \left\{ \frac{n - 1}{2n + 1} \right\}$ by finding a neighborhood of 1 which does *not* contain all terms of $\{a_n\}$ for $n \geq M$.

MID-CHAPTER REVIEW

—— Write five terms of each sequence. (Section 5-1)

   1. $a_n = \dfrac{2n}{1 + n^2}$ **2.** $b_n = (-1)\dfrac{2n}{n + 3}$

   3. $a_1 = 4, a_n = 2a_{n-1} - 3$ **4.** $b_1 = \frac{2}{3}, b_n = -b_{n-1} + 5$

—— Graph ten terms of each sequence. If possible, find an open interval which contains all the terms of the sequence. (Section 5-2)

   5. $\{a_n\} = \left\{ \frac{n}{n + 1} \right\}$ **6.** $\{b_n\} = \left\{ (-1)^n \frac{2n}{n^2} \right\}$ **7.** $\{d_n\} = \left\{ \left(\frac{5}{4} \right)^n \right\}$

8. Let $\{b_n\} = \left\{\dfrac{n}{n^2 + 1}\right\}$

   a. Show that $b_n > b_{n+1}$ for $n \in \mathsf{N}$.

   b. Find $M \in \mathsf{N}$ so that b_n is as close to 0 as $\frac{1}{100}$ for all $n \geq M$. (Section 5-3)

9. Given $\{a_n\} = \left\{\dfrac{n+1}{n}\right\}$. Which terms of $\{a_n\}$ are in a neighborhood about 1, if the radius of the neighborhood is $\frac{1}{100}$? (Section 5-4)

━━━ In Exercises 10–12, what appears to be the limit of each sequence? (Section 5-5)

10. $\{a_n\} = \left\{\dfrac{3n + 5}{2n}\right\}$ **11.** $\{b_n\} = \left\{\dfrac{5n^2}{n^2 + 1}\right\}$ **12.** $\{c_n\} = \left\{\dfrac{5n}{3n + 5}\right\}$

5–6 Convergent Sequences: Examples

Most of the sequences considered in the previous section had general terms involving only linear expressions. Here you consider sequences with general terms involving quadratic expressions and others which involve powers of real numbers. The purpose is to illustrate how such expressions are handled in the solution of the inequalities arising in limit proofs.

EXAMPLE 1.   Given: $\{a_n\} = \left\{\dfrac{2n^2 + 1}{n^2 + 1}\right\}$.   Prove: $\left\{\dfrac{2n^2 + 1}{n^2 + 1}\right\} \longrightarrow 2$.

Proof: The general neighborhood of 2 is $\langle 2 - \epsilon, 2 + \epsilon \rangle$. For 2 to be the limit, an M must be found such that $2 - \epsilon < a_n < 2 + \epsilon$ when $n \geq M$. This requires the solution of the compound inequality

$$2 - \epsilon < \frac{2n^2 + 1}{n^2 + 1} < 2 + \epsilon$$

or

$$2 - \epsilon < \frac{2n^2 + 1}{n^2 + 1} \quad and \quad \frac{2n^2 + 1}{n^2 + 1} < 2 + \epsilon.$$

The first step in solving either inequality is to divide $2n^2 + 1$ by $n^2 + 1$. You get the following

$$\frac{2n^2 + 1}{n^2 + 1} = 2 - \frac{1}{n^2 + 1}.$$

The inequalities now proceed as follows.

$$2 - \epsilon < 2 + \frac{-1}{n^2 + 1} \quad and \quad 2 + \frac{-1}{n^2 + 1} < 2 + \epsilon$$

$$-\epsilon < \frac{-1}{n^2 + 1}$$

$$n^2 + 1 > \frac{-1}{-\epsilon}$$

$$n^2 > \frac{1}{\epsilon} - 1$$

$$n > \sqrt{\frac{1}{\epsilon} - 1}$$

Since $\dfrac{-1}{n^2 + 1} < \epsilon$

$\dfrac{-1}{n^2 + 1} < 0$ and $0 < \epsilon$,

$$\frac{-1}{n^2 + 1} < \epsilon$$

is true for all $n \in \mathbf{N}$.

Thus choose $M > \sqrt{\frac{1}{\epsilon} - 1}$. Then for all $n \geq M$, a_n is in

$$\langle 2 - \epsilon, 2 + \epsilon \rangle.$$

The following table shows possible choices of M for particular values of ϵ.

ϵ	$\dfrac{1}{10}$	$\dfrac{1}{100}$	$\dfrac{1}{500}$	$\dfrac{1}{10,000}$
$\sqrt{\dfrac{1}{\epsilon} - 1}$	$\sqrt{9}$	$\sqrt{99}$	$\sqrt{499}$	$\sqrt{9,999}$
M	4	11	25	200

Notice that the choices of M given in the table are not the smallest choices possible. In fact, when $\epsilon = \dfrac{1}{10,000}$, the smallest possible choice of M is 100. Choosing an M larger than necessary is perfectly legal because the definition does *not* specify that M should be as small as possible. All that is required is that there be some M which works. Consequently, any $M > \sqrt{\frac{1}{\epsilon} - 1}$ is satisfactory.

EXAMPLE 2. Given: $\{a_n\} = \{(\frac{2}{3})^n\}$ Prove: $\{(\frac{2}{3})^n\} \longrightarrow 0$

Proof:

$$-\epsilon < (\tfrac{2}{3})^n < \epsilon \quad \text{iff}$$

$-\epsilon < (\tfrac{2}{3})^n$

Since $(\frac{2}{3})^n > 0$ and $-\epsilon$ is negative, $-\epsilon < (\frac{2}{3})^n$ for all positive integers n.

and

$(\tfrac{2}{3})^n < \epsilon.$

(Taking logarithms of both sides),

$$n \log (\tfrac{2}{3}) < \log \epsilon \qquad \text{iff}$$

(since $\log (\tfrac{2}{3}) < 0$)

$$n > \frac{\log \epsilon}{\log (\tfrac{2}{3})}.$$

Consequently, M should be chosen greater than $\dfrac{\log \epsilon}{\log (\frac{2}{3})}$. Then for all $n \geq M$, a_n will lie in $\langle -\epsilon, \epsilon \rangle$.

Possible values of M for selected replacements of ϵ are shown in the following table. As above, the value of M chosen is not necessarily the least one possible. For the table below the approximation $\log\left(\frac{2}{3}\right) \approx -0.176$ is used.

ϵ	$\dfrac{1}{100}$	$\dfrac{1}{10,000}$	10^{-8}	10^{-16}
$\dfrac{\log \epsilon}{\log \left(\frac{2}{3}\right)}$	$\dfrac{-2}{-.176}$	$\dfrac{-4}{-.176}$	$\dfrac{-8}{-.176}$	$\dfrac{-16}{-.176}$
M	12	25	50	92

EXAMPLE 3. Given: $\{a_n\} = \left\{\dfrac{\sqrt{n+1}}{n}\right\}$. Prove: $\left\{\dfrac{\sqrt{n+1}}{n}\right\} \longrightarrow 0$

Proof:
$$-\epsilon < \frac{\sqrt{n+1}}{n} < \epsilon \quad \text{iff}$$

$$-\epsilon < \frac{\sqrt{n+1}}{n} \qquad \text{and} \qquad \frac{\sqrt{n+1}}{n} < \epsilon$$

Since $\dfrac{\sqrt{n+1}}{n}$ is positive for all n and $-\epsilon$ is negative, $-\epsilon < \dfrac{\sqrt{n+1}}{n}$ is true for all n.

(Since $\dfrac{\sqrt{n+1}}{n}$ and ϵ are positive, the inequality remains valid when both terms are squared.)

So, $\dfrac{n+1}{n^2} < \epsilon^2$ iff

$$\frac{1}{\epsilon^2} < \frac{n^2}{n+1}.$$

Now $\dfrac{n^2}{n+1} \geq \dfrac{n}{2}$ for all n as you can easily show.

Thus, if $\dfrac{1}{\epsilon^2} < \dfrac{n}{2}$ it is also true that $\dfrac{1}{\epsilon^2} < \dfrac{n^2}{n+1}$.

Therefore it is sufficient to solve:

$$\frac{1}{\epsilon^2} < \frac{n}{2} \quad \text{iff}$$

$$\frac{2}{\epsilon^2} < n.$$

Consequently, choosing $M > \dfrac{2}{\epsilon^2}$ will suffice to insure that a_n is in $\langle -\epsilon, \epsilon \rangle$ for all $n \geq M$.

To prove that the M determined is satisfactory, note that the steps in the derivation are reversible.

For all $n \geq M$ $\qquad\qquad n > \dfrac{2}{\epsilon^2}$ $\qquad\qquad$ because $M > \dfrac{2}{\epsilon^2}$.

So
$$\frac{n}{2} > \frac{1}{\epsilon^2}$$

But, for all n
$$\frac{n^2}{n+1} \geq \frac{n}{2}. \quad \longleftarrow \quad \textbf{This is the key step.}$$

So
$$\frac{n^2}{n+1} > \frac{1}{\epsilon^2} \quad \longleftarrow \quad \begin{array}{l}\textbf{By transitivity of}\\ \textbf{inequality}\end{array}$$

and
$$\frac{n+1}{n^2} < \epsilon^2.$$

Thus
$$\frac{\sqrt{n+1}}{n} < \epsilon \quad \longleftarrow \quad \textbf{All terms are positive.}$$

Finally, $-\epsilon < \frac{\sqrt{n+1}}{n}$. Therefore $-\epsilon < \frac{\sqrt{n+1}}{n} < \epsilon$ for all $n \geq M$.

The key idea in the strategy is to find an expression involving n $\left(\text{in this case } \frac{n}{2}\right)$ which is less than or equal to the complex expression $\left(\frac{n^2}{n+1}\right)$ and to solve the new inequality $\left(\frac{n}{2} > \frac{1}{\epsilon^2}\right)$ to determine M.

You may wonder why, in finding an M which implies $\frac{\sqrt{n+1}}{n} < \epsilon$ for all $n \geq M$, you did not solve the inequality $\frac{1}{\epsilon^2} < \frac{n^2}{n+1}$. You could have $\left(\text{the solution is } n > \frac{1}{2\epsilon} + \frac{\sqrt{1+4\epsilon}}{2\epsilon}\right)$, but the preference was to simplify the situation by solving an inequality, $\frac{n}{2} > \frac{1}{\epsilon^2}$, whose solution would also provide a satisfactory M.

The strategies illustrated in Examples 1, 2, and 3 are typical. General terms involving quadratic expressions usually lead to a solution involving a square root of an expression in ϵ. Similarly, when $a_n = (r)^n$, the solution usually involves logarithms.

CLASSROOM EXERCISES

1. Find an M which proves that $\{a_n\} = \left\{\frac{3n^2+2}{4n^2}\right\} \longrightarrow \frac{3}{4}$.

2. Find an M which proves that $\{c_n\} = \{(\frac{4}{5})^n\} \longrightarrow 0$.

WRITTEN EXERCISES

A

1. Prove: $\{a_n\} = \left\{\frac{2n^2+1}{3n^2}\right\} \longrightarrow \frac{2}{3}$

2. Prove: $\{b_n\} = \left\{\frac{1-3n^2}{n^2}\right\} \longrightarrow -3$

3. Prove: $\{c_n\} = \{(\frac{3}{4})^n\} \longrightarrow 0$

4. Prove: $\{d_n\} = \{1 - (\frac{1}{2})^n\} \longrightarrow 1$

5. Prove: $\{e_n\} = \left\{\frac{3}{\sqrt{n+2}}\right\} \longrightarrow 0$

6. Prove: $\{f_n\} = \left\{\frac{4}{(\sqrt{n+3})^2}\right\} \longrightarrow 0$

B 7. Prove: $\{g_n\} = \left\{\dfrac{\sqrt{n+2}}{n}\right\} \longrightarrow 0$

8. Prove: $\{h_n\} = \left\{\sqrt{\dfrac{n+2}{n}}\right\} \longrightarrow 1$

9. Prove: $\{k_n\} = \left\{\dfrac{2}{n^3+5}\right\} \longrightarrow 0$

10. Prove: $\{l_n\} = \left\{\dfrac{2n}{n+1} - \dfrac{n+1}{2n}\right\} \longrightarrow \dfrac{3}{2}$

11. Prove: $\{m_n\} = \left\{\dfrac{1}{\sqrt{n^2+1}}\right\} \longrightarrow 0$

12. Prove: $\{p_n\} = \left\{\dfrac{(-1)^n}{n^2}\right\} \longrightarrow 0$

13. Prove: $\{d_n\} = \left\{\dfrac{(n-1)^2}{2n^2}\right\} \longrightarrow \dfrac{1}{2}$

14. Prove: $\{a_n\} = \left\{5 + \dfrac{n^2-3}{n^2+2}\right\} \longrightarrow 6$

Applying Recursive Definitions

Biology

Many states have resource management plans in order to effectively manage deer herds, salmon, bear, elk, etc. These resources need to be managed in order to prevent starvation from overpopulation, or extinction by overharvesting. This management is accomplished by the regulation of harvesting and the protection of the young during their growing period. (In the case of animals, harvesting is regulated by the establishment of a hunting season during which the animals may be killed.) **Biologists** do field studies to determine the pertinent natural characteristic of the resource in order to develop a management model.

The American Buffalo is a good example to use for the development of such a model. In 1830, there were approximately 40 million buffalo. In 1887, there were a mere 200 buffalo left in the United States. That means that within 57 years, 0.999995% of the buffalo died or were destroyed.

The following characteristics of buffalo can be used to construct a model.

Characteristics

    a. Two year-old buffalo are mature.

    b. 90% of the mature females bear a calf.

    c. The ratio of male to female calves is 53% to 47%.

    d. Only 30% of calves live to maturity—two years.

    e. 10% of mature buffalo die each year.

The Model

This information leads to the following model for the mature female buffalo population in year n in terms of the female population in the previous two years. This is an example of a **recursive definition** of a model.

$$F_n = 0.9F_{n-1} + 0.1269F_{n-2}$$

The term $0.1269F_{n-2}$ comes from characteristics **a, b,** and **c,** and refers to the number of female calves born in the year $n - 2$ that live until the year n. The term $0.9F_{n-1}$ arises because of characteristic e, deaths due to natural causes. If you add a harvested portion of k, the model becomes

$$F_n = (0.9 - k)F_{n-1} + 0.1269F_{n-2} \, .$$

The fraction k can be manipulated and controlled. Thus, the herd can be managed.

EXAMPLE. If the mature female buffalo population was 16 million in 1845 and 17 million in 1846, what should the harvest factor have been to ensure 16 million in 1847?

Solution: $\quad F_n = (0.9 - k)F_{n-1} + 0.1269F_{n-2}$

$$16 = (0.9 - k)17 + 0.1269 \cdot 16$$

$$16 = 15.3 - 17k + 2.0304$$

$$17k = 1.3304$$

$$k = 0.0783$$

Thus, 7.83% of the mature female population could have been harvested and still have maintained 16 million mature females.

A similar management formula can be developed for the mature male population. You are asked to develop it in the Exercises.

EXERCISES

1. Compute the term in the model for mature male buffalo in year n that comes from the number of male calves that survive from the year $n - 2$.

2. Use the term computed in Exercise 1 and a harvesting factor of c to develop a management model for mature male buffalo in the year n.

3. For females, what should the harvest constant be in order to maintain the same population each year?

4. What portion of the female herd could be harvested annually if the male herd were to decrease by 2% yearly?

5. What is the management formula for the total herd of buffalo?

5–7 Completeness and Monotone Sequences

Let $A \subseteq R$. A can be represented geometrically by a set of points on a number line.

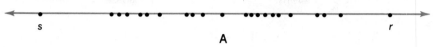

If there is a number $r \in R$ such that for each $x \in A$, x is less than or equal to r, then the subset A of R is said to be **bounded above** by r. Similarly, if there is a number $s \in R$ such that for each $x \in A$, x is greater than or equal to s, then A is **bounded below** by s. Possible positions for r and s are shown in the diagram above. (You may at this point wish to compare the above concepts with the upper and lower bounds of a function discussed in Section 2–6.)

If a set $A \subseteq R$ is bounded above and bounded below it is said to be **bounded**. Geometrically a bounded set is one that is entirely contained in a closed interval. For example, $A \subseteq [s, r]$ above.

Given a set $A \subseteq R$ with an upper bound r, it is clear that r is not unique. Any real number p such that $r < p$ is also an upper bound. Now it may happen that there is no upper bound of A that is smaller than r.

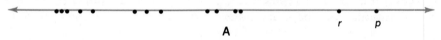

If so, then r is the **least upper bound.**

> **Definition** Let $A \subseteq R$ be bounded above. If the number r_0 is an upper bound of A and no number smaller than r_0 is an upper bound, then r_0 is the **least upper bound** of A, that is, $r_0 = $ l.u.b.A (least upper bound A).

Greatest lower bound is defined in a similar manner.

> **Definition** Let $A \subseteq R$ be bounded below. If the number s_0 is a lower bound of A and no number greater than s_0 is a lower bound, then s_0 is the **greatest lower bound** of A, that is, $s_0 = $ g.l.b.A (greatest lower bound A).

EXAMPLE. Let A = [3, 7], let B = ⟨3, 7⟩. Find a. l.u.b.A, b. g.l.b.A, c. l.u.b.B, and d. g.l.b.B.

a. l.u.b.A = 7 because for all $x \in$ A, $x \leq 7$. Moreover if $p < 7$, then p is not an upper bound of A. (Why?) Notice that l.u.b.A = 7 is an element of A.

b. g.l.b.A = 3.

c. l.u.b.B = 7 because for all $x \in$ B, $x \leq 7$. Moreover if $p < 7$, then p is not an upper bound of B because there exists a number $p_1 = \dfrac{p + 7}{2}$ which is in B and which is greater than p. Notice that l.u.b.B = 7 is not an element of B.

d. g.l.b.B = 3.

The reason for studying least upper bounds and greatest lower bounds, etc., is found in the next axiom.

Least Upper Bound Axiom: If A is any nonempty subset of R that is bounded above, then A has a least upper bound in R.

This axiom says, roughly, that the set of real numbers, R, has no "holes" in it. If R is replaced by Q, the axiom is no longer true — the set of rational numbers has holes in it. For example consider A = {1, 1.4, 1.41, 1.414, 1.4141, · · ·} of rational approximations to $\sqrt{2}$. A, as a subset of Q, has no least upper bound *in Q*, ($\sqrt{2}$ is irrational). But A, as a subset of R, has a least upper bound *in R*. Thus the significance of the axiom is that *all* sets in R which are bounded above have least upper bounds *in R*. In this sense the reals are *complete*. The axiom is one way of stating the **completeness property** of the reals.

You should be able to prove the next theorem.

Theorem 5–1 If A is any nonempty subset of R that is bounded below, then A has a greatest lower bound in R.

Proof Hint: Let B be the set of $-x$ where $x \in$ A. Apply the Axiom to B.

The completeness property stated in the Axiom is applicable to sequences which are made up of real numbers. One especially useful result is true about bounded **monotone** sequences. The definition of a monotone sequence follows.

252   CHAPTER 5

Definition Let $\{a_n\}$ be a sequence of real numbers. If $a_1 \leq a_2 \leq a_3 \leq \cdots \leq a_n \leq \cdots$, then $\{a_n\}$ is **nondecreasing.** If $a_1 \geq a_2 \geq a_3 \geq \cdots \geq a_n \geq \cdots$, then $\{a_n\}$ is **nonincreasing.** A **monotone** sequence is one which is either nondecreasing or nonincreasing (or both).

The major result about sequences follows.

Theorem 5–2 A nondecreasing sequence which is bounded above has a limit.

Proof: Let $\{a_n\}$ be the sequence. Then $A = \{a_n\}$ is a nonempty set of real numbers which is bounded above. Thus by the axiom A has a l.u.b.;
$$\text{l.u.b.}A = r_0.$$
The task now is to prove $\{a_n\} \longrightarrow r_0$. Consider the neighborhood $\langle r_0 - \epsilon, r_0 + \epsilon \rangle$, $\epsilon > 0$. Since $\epsilon > 0$ and l.u.b.$A = r_0$, $r_0 - \epsilon$ is *not* an upper bound of A. Thus for some $M \in \mathrm{N}$, $a_m > r_0 - \epsilon$. But since $a_m \leq a_n$ for all $n \geq M$, $a_n > r_0 - \epsilon$ for all $n \geq M$. Since $a_n \leq r_0$ for all $n \in \mathrm{N}$ (why?) it follows that
$$a_n \in \langle r_0 - \epsilon, r_0 + \epsilon \rangle \quad \text{for all } n \geq M.$$
Thus $\{a_n\} \longrightarrow r_0$.

Theorem 5–2 is useful because it provides a way to determine if a nondecreasing sequence has a limit, even when you do not know what the value of the limit is. For example,
$$\left\{2 - \frac{1}{2^{n-1}}\right\}$$
has a limit because it is nondecreasing and bounded above. The limit is 2.

The theorem for nonincreasing sequences similar to Theorem 5–2 is left for you to prove.

Theorem 5–3 A nonincreasing sequence which is bounded below has a limit.

CLASSROOM EXERCISES

1. Let A = [5, 8⟩.
   a. Find l. u. b. A   **b.** Find g. l. b. A
   c. Is l. u. b. A an element of A?
   d. Is g. l. b. A an element of A?

2. Suppose B = {n}. **a.** Does B have a greatest lower bound? If so what is it? **b.** Does B have a least upper bound? If so what is it?

3. Suppose C = {x : x² < 2}. Does C have a least upper bound? If so what is it?

4. Would Theorem 5–2 be true if the adjective "nondecreasing" were omitted? Why or why not?

5. Would Theorem 5–2 be true if the phrase "which is bounded above" were omitted? Why or why not?

WRITTEN EXERCISES

A **1.** When is a sequence both nonincreasing and nondecreasing?

2. Make a drawing which may be used to show geometrically the reasoning used to prove Theorem 5–2.

3. Is a nondecreasing sequence $\{a_n\}$ which is bounded above by r bounded? If so, what is its g.l.b.?

4. Prove: A bounded monotone sequence has a limit.

Determine whether or not each sequence is monotone.

5. $\{\sin n\pi\}$ **6.** $\{\cos n\pi\}$

7. $\left\{\dfrac{1}{1 + n^2}\right\}$ **8.** $\{2n + (-1)^n\}$

9. $\{\tan n\}$ **10.** $\left\{\dfrac{3n + 1}{n}\right\}$

11. $\left\{\sin \dfrac{n\pi}{2}\right\}$ **12.** $a_1 = 1$
                                $a_2 = 1$
                                $a_{n+1} = a_n + a_{n-1}, n = 3, 4, \cdots$

13. Which of the sequences in Exercises 5–12 are bounded? Explain your answer.

14. Which of the sequences in Exercises 5–12 have a limit?

15. Construct an example of a sequence which is bounded but has no limit.

16. Construct an example of a monotone sequence which has no limit.

B **17.** Prove Theorem 5–1.

18. Prove Theorem 5–3.

C ▬▬ Use the following definition in Exercises 19–21.

> **Definition** A sequence $\{a_n\}$ **diverges to infinity** if for any real number $p > 0$ there is an $M \in \mathrm{N}$ such that $a_n \geq p$ for all $n \geq M$.

19. Give three examples of sequences which diverge to infinity.

20. Give an example of a sequence which is not monotone and diverges to infinity.

21. Prove: A nondecreasing sequence which is not bounded above diverges to infinity.

5–8 Series and Their Sums

In the millionaire golf match mentioned in Section 5–1, the finite sequence of dollar values of the bet was

$$1, 2, 4, 8, 16, 32, 64, 128, 256.$$

If the millionaire who proposed the bet lost each hole, his loss in dollars would be

$$1 + 2 + 4 + 8 + 16 + 32 + 64 + 128 + 256.$$

This indicated sum is called a **series.**

> **Definition** A **series** is an indicated sum of the terms of a sequence.

EXAMPLE 1. For the arithmetic sequence

$$a, a + d, a + 2d, \ldots, a + (n - 1)d$$

write the arithmetic series.

Solution: $a + (a + d) + (a + 2d) + \cdots + [a + (n - 1)d]$

$$= na + (1 + 2 + 3 + \cdots + n - 1)d.$$

EXAMPLE 2. For the geometric sequence

$$a, ar, ar^2, \ldots, ar^{n-1}$$

write the geometric series.

Solution: $a + ar + ar^2 + \cdots + ar^{n-1}$

$$= a(1 + r + r^2 + \cdots + r^{n-1})$$

The following definition can now be stated.

Definition A **harmonic sequence** is a sequence whose terms are reciprocals of the terms of an arithmetic sequence.

EXAMPLE 3. For the harmonic sequence

$$\frac{1}{a}, \frac{1}{a+d}, \frac{1}{a+2d}, \cdots, \frac{1}{a+(n-1)d}$$

write the harmonic series.

Solution: $\dfrac{1}{a} + \dfrac{1}{a+d} + \dfrac{1}{a+2d} + \cdots + \dfrac{1}{a+(n-1)d}$

If a series has a finite number of terms it has a sum and it is easy to determine the standard name for the sum. For example,

$$3 + 5 + 7 = 15.$$

If there are infinitely many terms in a series, the task is not so simple. *Not all infinite series have sums.* For those that do, the "sum" is not always easily identified. For example, given the infinite series

$$\frac{1}{2} + \frac{1}{4} + \frac{1}{8} + \frac{1}{16} + \cdots + \frac{1}{2^n} + \cdots$$

it is not at all clear that

$$\frac{1}{2} + \frac{1}{4} + \frac{1}{8} + \frac{1}{16} + \cdots + \frac{1}{2^n} + \cdots = 1.$$

The next example illustrates the ideas used in defining the "sum of an infinite series." A key idea used in that definition is partial sum.

> **Definition** Given a series $a_1 + a_2 + \cdots + a_n + \cdots$. The **nth partial sum, S_n,** is defined by the equation
>
> $$S_n = a_1 + a_2 + \cdots + a_n.$$

EXAMPLE 4. For the infinite series $\frac{1}{2} + \frac{1}{4} + \frac{1}{8} + \cdots + \frac{1}{2^n} + \cdots$, write the partial sums.

Solution:

$$S_1 = \frac{1}{2} \qquad\qquad\qquad\qquad = \frac{1}{2}$$

$$S_2 = \frac{1}{2} + \frac{1}{4} \qquad\qquad\qquad = \frac{3}{4}$$

$$S_3 = \frac{1}{2} + \frac{1}{4} + \frac{1}{8} \qquad\qquad = \frac{7}{8}$$

$$S_4 = \frac{1}{2} + \frac{1}{4} + \frac{1}{8} + \frac{1}{16} \qquad = \frac{15}{16}$$

.
.
.

$$S_n = \frac{1}{2} + \frac{1}{4} + \frac{1}{8} + \quad\cdots\quad + \frac{1}{2^n} = \frac{2^n - 1}{2^n}$$

.
.
.

The sequence of partial sums is

$$\frac{1}{2}, \frac{3}{4}, \frac{7}{8}, \frac{15}{16}, \frac{31}{32}, \ldots, \frac{2^n - 1}{2^n}, \ldots,$$

where the general term is $\frac{2^n - 1}{2^n}$. The sequence of partial sums $\left\{\frac{2^n - 1}{2^n}\right\}$ can be shown to converge to 1. And 1 is the number that was indicated to be the sum of $\frac{1}{2} + \frac{1}{4} + \frac{1}{8} + \cdots$. The relationship between the sum of an infinite series and the limit of the sequence of partial sums is not a casual one. It is taken to be the definition of the **sum of an infinite series.**

> **Definition** Given an infinite series $a_1 + a_2 + a_3 + \cdots + a_n + \cdots$. The **sum of the infinite series** is defined to be the limit of the sequence of partial sums $\{S_n\}$ where $S_i = a_1 + a_2 + a_3 + \cdots + a_i$ for all i in the set of natural numbers. If $\{S_n\}$ has a limit, the series is a **convergent series.** If $\{S_n\}$ has no limit, the series is a **divergent series.**

Finite and infinite series are often indicated by using the Greek letter $\sum$ (sigma). For example, the sum

$$a_1 + a_2 + a_3 + \cdots + a_n$$

can be written

$$\sum_{i=1}^{n} a_i$$

which is read "the sum of a_i from $i = 1$ to $i = n$." The infinite series

$$a_1 + a_2 + a_3 + \cdots$$

can be written

$$\sum_{i=1}^{\infty} a_i$$

which is read "the sum of a_i beginning with $i = 1$ and increasing without bound." Note that i denotes natural numbers only.

EXAMPLE 5. Express the series $\sum_{i=1}^{5} (2i - 3)$ as an *indicated* sum.

Solution: $\sum_{i=1}^{5} (2i - 3) = [2(1) - 3] + [2(2) - 3] + [2(3) - 3]$

$$+ [2(4) - 3] + [2(5) - 3]$$

$$= -1 + 1 + 3 + 5 + 7$$

EXAMPLE 6. Find the sum of the series $\sum_{i=1}^{4} i$.

Solution: $$\sum_{i=1}^{4} = 1 + 2 + 3 + 4 = 10$$

EXAMPLE 7. Determine whether the geometric series $\sum_{i=1}^{\infty} \frac{2}{3}(\frac{2}{3})^{i-1}$ has a sum, and if it does, specify it.

Solution: $\sum_{i=1}^{\infty} \frac{2}{3}(\frac{2}{3})^{i-1} = \frac{2}{3} + \frac{4}{9} + \frac{8}{27} + \cdots + (\frac{2}{3})^n + \cdots$

The nth partial sum is $S_n = \frac{2}{3} + \frac{2}{3}(\frac{2}{3}) + \frac{2}{3}(\frac{2}{3})^2 + \cdots + \frac{2}{3}(\frac{2}{3})^{n-1}$. In order to find the limit of the sequence of partial sums, a simpler expression is needed for S_n. This can be found as follows.

$$S_n = \frac{2}{3} + \frac{2}{3}(\frac{2}{3}) + \frac{2}{3}(\frac{2}{3})^2 + \cdots + \frac{2}{3}(\frac{2}{3})^{n-1}$$
$$\frac{2}{3}S_n = \frac{2}{3}(\frac{2}{3}) + \frac{2}{3}(\frac{2}{3})^2 + \cdots + \frac{2}{3}(\frac{2}{3})^{n-1} + \frac{2}{3}(\frac{2}{3})^n$$

Thus $$S_n - \frac{2}{3}S_n = \frac{2}{3} - \frac{2}{3}(\frac{2}{3})^n = \frac{2}{3}(1 - (\frac{2}{3})^n)$$

So $$S_n = \frac{\frac{2}{3}(1 - (\frac{2}{3})^n)}{1 - (\frac{2}{3})} = \frac{\frac{2}{3}(1 - (\frac{2}{3})^n)}{\frac{1}{3}} = 2(1 - (\frac{2}{3})^n)$$

Thus the sequence of partial sums is $\{S_n\} = \{2[1 - (\frac{2}{3})^n]\}$. If $\sum\limits_{i=1}^{\infty} \frac{2}{3} \cdot (\frac{2}{3})^{i-1}$ is to have a sum, $\{S_n\}$ must have a limit. You can prove easily that $\{2[1 - (\frac{2}{3})^n]\}$ has a limit of 2. By the definition

$$\sum_{i=1}^{\infty} \frac{2}{3}(\frac{2}{3})^{i-1} = 2.$$

Two major ideas for determining whether an infinite series has a sum are illustrated in Example 7.

1. An expression for the partial sum S_n must be found.
2. The sequence $\{S_n\}$ must be shown either to converge or diverge. Very often **1** is more difficult than **2**.

In the case of a geometric series,

$$\sum_{i=1}^{\infty} ar^{i-1} = a + ar^1 + ar^2 + \cdots,$$

the expression for the partial sum S_n may be found in a manner similar to that used in Example 7 when $r \neq 1$.

$$S_n = a + ar + ar^2 + \cdots + ar^{n-1}$$
$$rS_n = \quad\quad ar + ar^2 + \cdots + ar^{n-1} + ar^n$$
$$S_n - rS_n = a + 0 + 0 + \cdots + \quad 0 \quad - ar^n$$
$$S_n = \frac{a - ar^n}{1 - r}, \quad r \neq 1$$
$$S_n = a \cdot n \text{ when } r = 1$$

In other cases, an expression for S_n may not be easy to determine. For example, given $\sum\limits_{i=1}^{\infty} 2i = 2 + 4 + 6 + \cdots$, the partial sums are as follows:

$$
\begin{array}{ll}
S_1 = 2 & = 2 \\
S_2 = 2 + 4 & = 6 \\
S_3 = 2 + 4 + 6 & = 12
\end{array}
$$

$$S_n = 2 + 4 + 6 + 8 + \cdots + 2n = ?$$

In such cases look for a pattern such as $S_1 = 1 \cdot 2$, $S_2 = 2 \cdot 3$, $S_3 = 3 \cdot 4$, $S_4 = 4 \cdot 5$, $\cdots$, $S_n = n \cdot (n + 1)$. When you are quite sure the pattern is right, prove it correct by using mathematical induction. Then you may use the expression for S_n to decide whether the sequence $\{S_n\}$ converges or diverges. For $\{S_n\} = n(n + 1)$ it is clear that there is no limit because the sequence is monotone and unbounded. Check this.

CLASSROOM EXERCISES

▬ Use the summation sign ($\sum$) to write each series.

1. $|x_3| + |x_4| + |x_5| + |x_6|$ **2.** $e^1 - e^2 + e^3 - e^4 + e^5$

3. $-x_1 + x_2 - x_3 + x_4$ **4.** $2 + 4 + 6 + \cdots + 2n$

5. $x_1{}^2 + x_2{}^2 + x_3{}^2 + x_4{}^2$ **6.** $\frac{1}{2} - \frac{1}{3} + \frac{1}{4} - \frac{1}{5} + \cdots$

7. How does a series differ from a sequence?

8. How is the concept of *partial sum* used to define the sum of an infinite series?

9. Define *convergent series. divergent series.*

10. State the two steps necessary for determining whether an infinite series has a sum.

WRITTEN EXERCISES

A ▬ In Exercises 1–4 classify each series as harmonic, geometric, or arithmetic.

1. $\sum\limits_{i=1}^{\infty} 4 - 2i$ **2.** $\sum\limits_{i=1}^{\infty} \frac{1}{i}$ **3.** $\sum\limits_{i=1}^{\infty} \frac{1}{2}i$ **4.** $\sum\limits_{i=1}^{\infty} \frac{1}{1 + (i - 1)}$

5. Prove by mathematical induction that

$$S_n = \frac{1}{2} + \frac{1}{4} + \frac{1}{8} + \cdots + \frac{1}{2^n} = \frac{2^n - 1}{2^n}.$$

6. Prove that the sum of the infinite series for which the nth partial sum is given in Exercise 5 is 1, i.e., $\left\{\frac{2^n - 1}{2^n}\right\} \longrightarrow 1$.

7. Prove: $S_n = \frac{2}{3} + \frac{2}{3}(\frac{2}{3})^1 + \frac{2}{3}(\frac{2}{3})^2 + \cdots + \frac{2}{3}(\frac{2}{3})^{n-1} = 2[1 - (\frac{2}{3})^n]$.

8. Prove: $\{2 - 2(\frac{2}{3})^n\} \longrightarrow 2$.

9. Prove by mathematical induction that

$$S_n = a + ar + \cdots + ar^{n-1} = a\frac{(1 - r^n)}{1 - r}, r \neq 1, \quad \text{for all } M \in \mathbf{N}.$$

10. Given the arithmetic series $\sum\limits_{i=1}^{\infty} a + d(i - 1)$. Write an expression for S_n by adding

$$S_n = a + (a + d) + (a + 2d) + \cdots + a + d(n - 2) + a + d(n - 1)$$

and

$$S_n = a + d(n - 1) + a + d(n - 2) + a + d(n - 3) + \cdots + a + d + a$$

term-by-term and solving the resulting equation for S_n.

In Exercises 11–16 write each series in expanded form.

11. $\sum_{n=1}^{5} |2 - n|$ **12.** $\sum_{i=1}^{4} (-1)^i i^2$ **13.** $\sum_{n=1}^{3} (-1)^n (n^2 - n)$

14. $\sum_{i=3}^{5} (2i - 9)$ **15.** $\sum_{i=0}^{4} \left(\frac{1}{i+1}\right)$ **16.** $\sum_{n=3}^{7} a_n$

In Exercises 17–20 use the summation sign to write each series.

17. $3 + 8 + 13 + 18$ **18.** $8 - 2 + \frac{1}{2} - \frac{1}{8}$

19. $a_1^2 + a_2^2 + a_3^2 + a_4^2$ **20.** $a_1 b_1 + a_2 b_2 + a_3 b_3$

B   In Exercises 21–23 do the two expressions name the same series?

21. $\sum_{n=1}^{4} \frac{n+3}{n+1}$ and $\sum_{n=3}^{6} \frac{n+1}{n-1}$

22. $\sum_{k=5}^{8} \frac{k-3}{k-1}$ and $\sum_{k=1}^{4} \frac{k+1}{k+8}$

23. $\sum_{i=1}^{5} \frac{i}{i+1}$ and $\sum_{i=4}^{8} \frac{i-3}{i-1}$

In Exercises 24–26 find the sum of each geometric series. Prove that your result is correct.

24. $\sum_{i=1}^{\infty} 3(\frac{4}{5})^{i-1}$ **25.** $\sum_{i=1}^{\infty} 5(-\frac{1}{3})^{i-1}$ **26.** $\sum_{i=1}^{\infty} (\frac{9}{10})^{i-1}$

C ▬▬ Here is a recursive definition of the summation sign.

$$\sum_{i=1}^{1} a_i = a_1$$

$$\sum_{i=1}^{n+1} a_i = \left(\sum_{i=1}^{n} a_i\right) + a_{n+1}$$

Use this definition to prove each statement. (Use mathematical induction.)

27. $\sum_{i=1}^{n} c \cdot a_i = c \sum_{i=1}^{n} a_i$

28. $\sum_{i=1}^{n} c = cn$

29. $\sum_{i=1}^{n} (a_i + b_i) = \sum_{i=1}^{n} a_i + \sum_{i=1}^{n} b_i$

30. $\sum_{i=1}^{n} (a_i + b_i)^2 = \sum_{i=1}^{n} a_i^2 + 2\sum_{i=1}^{n} a_i b_i + \sum_{i=1}^{n} b_i^2$

31. $\sum_{i=1}^{n} (a_i + c) = \sum_{i=1}^{n} a_i + cn$

32. $\sum_{i=1}^{n} c(a_i + b_i^2) = c \sum_{i=1}^{n} a_i + c \sum_{i=1}^{n} b_i^2$

5-9   Limits of Special Sequences

In this section you will examine some special convergent sequences. The limits of these special sequences will be quite useful in the next section.

EXAMPLE 1.   Prove: $\left\{\frac{1}{n^a}\right\} \longrightarrow 0$ where a is any positive real number.

Proof: Given the general neighborhood $\langle -\epsilon, \epsilon \rangle$ of 0, $\epsilon > 0$, you must show that there exists an M such that

$$\frac{1}{n^a} \in \langle -\epsilon, \epsilon \rangle \quad \text{for all } n \geq M.$$

Now,

$$-\epsilon < \frac{1}{n^a} < \epsilon \quad \text{iff}$$

$$-\epsilon < \frac{1}{n^a} \qquad \qquad and \qquad \qquad \frac{1}{n^a} < \epsilon.$$

Since $-\epsilon$ is negative

and $\frac{1}{n^a}$ is always

positive, $-\epsilon < \frac{1}{n^a}$ is

true for all n.

$$\frac{1}{n^a} < \epsilon \quad \text{iff}$$

$$\frac{1}{\epsilon} < n^a \quad \text{iff}$$

$$\left(\frac{1}{\epsilon}\right)^{\frac{1}{a}} < n.$$

Since $-\epsilon < \frac{1}{n^a}$ is true for all n and thus for $n \geq M > \left(\frac{1}{\epsilon}\right)^{\frac{1}{a}}$, and $\frac{1}{n^a} < \epsilon$ is true for all $n \geq M > \left(\frac{1}{\epsilon}\right)^{\frac{1}{a}}$, $\frac{1}{n^a}$ is in $\langle -\epsilon, \epsilon \rangle$ for all $n > M$. Therefore $\left\{\frac{1}{n^a}\right\} \longrightarrow 0$ for all positive real a.

Often in books on mathematics, an alternate procedure is used to indicate that the terms of a sequence are in an open interval. The method uses absolute values.

For the sequence $\left\{\frac{1}{n^a}\right\}$ in Example 1, the general neighborhood is $\langle -\epsilon, \epsilon \rangle$ about 0, the proposed limit. For $\frac{1}{n^a}$ to be in $\langle -\epsilon, \epsilon \rangle$, the distance from $\frac{1}{n^a}$ to 0 must be less than ϵ units. The distance between two points a and b on a number line is given by the absolute value of the difference in their coordinates. Thus

$$|a - b|$$

is the distance between a and b.

In particular, then, the distance $\frac{1}{n^a}$ and 0 can be written

$$\left| \frac{1}{n^a} - 0 \right|.$$

If you want $\frac{1}{n^a}$ to be in the neighborhood $\langle -\epsilon, \epsilon \rangle$, the distance between $\frac{1}{n^a}$ and 0 must be less than ϵ. Thus

$$\left| \frac{1}{n^a} - 0 \right| < \epsilon, \epsilon > 0$$

expresses the fact that the distance between $\frac{1}{n^a}$ and 0 is less than ϵ, or that $\frac{1}{n^a}$ is in $\langle -\epsilon, \epsilon \rangle$.

In general, for $\{a_n\}$ to converge to A, it must be the case that

$$| a_n - A | < \epsilon$$

for all $n \geq M$, where ϵ is the radius of the general neighborhood about A.

In summary the following statements are equivalent:

1. $| a_n - A | < \epsilon, \epsilon > 0$
2. $A - \epsilon < a_n < A + \epsilon, \epsilon > 0$
3. $a_n \in \langle A - \epsilon, A + \epsilon \rangle, \epsilon > 0$

Any one of these three equivalent statements may be used in constructing limit proofs.

EXAMPLE 2. Let $\{a_n\} = \{c\}$. That is each term of the sequence is the same: $\{c\} = c, c, c, \cdots, c, \cdots$.
Prove $\{c\} \longrightarrow c$.

The proof is especially simple if you use the absolute value notation for a neighborhood. You must show that for every $\epsilon > 0$ there is an M such that

$$| a_n - c | < \epsilon \quad \text{for all } n \geq M.$$

Proof: Since $a_n = c$ for all n,

$$| a_n - c | = | c - c |$$
$$= 0$$

which is less than ϵ by the definition of ϵ. Thus you may choose $M = 1$ or any other positive integer.

EXAMPLE 3. Prove $\{r^n\} \longrightarrow 0$ when $|r| < 1$.

Using the absolute value notation for neighborhoods, you must show that for every $\epsilon > 0$ there is an $M \in \mathbf{N}$ such that for all $n \geq M$

$$|r^n - 0| < \epsilon.$$

Proof: Recall that

$$(1 + p)^n \geq 1 + np \quad (p \geq 0, n \in \mathbf{N}).$$

Since $|r| < 1$, then $p > 0$ can be found such that $|r| = \dfrac{1}{1 + p}$. Thus

$$\frac{1}{|r|^n} = (1 + p)^n \geq 1 + np > np.$$

So

$$|r|^n < \frac{1}{np}.$$

Since you wish $|r|^n$ to be less than ϵ, it will suffice if ϵ is greater than $\dfrac{1}{np}$. Therefore choose $M > \dfrac{1}{\epsilon p}$.

Thus $n \geq M > \dfrac{1}{\epsilon p}$ implies $\epsilon > \dfrac{1}{np} > |r|^n$ for all $n \geq M$. But $|r^n - 0| = |r|^n$ and so $|r^n - 0| < \epsilon$ for all $n \geq M > \dfrac{1}{\epsilon p}$.

Why in Example 3 was the restriction $|r| < 1$ necessary? In the proof the condition was used in the second step. That is, since $|r| < 1$, $|r| = \dfrac{1}{1 + p}$ with $p > 0$. It is essential that p be positive since otherwise $|r|^n$ would not be smaller than $\dfrac{1}{np}$ for any $n \in \mathbf{N}$. If $|r|$ were greater than one, the resulting sequence has no limit (see Exercise 19, Section 5–7).

If $|r| = 1$, the proof given is not valid. (Why?) However, if $|r| = 1$, then $r = 1$ or -1. If $r = 1$, then $r^n = 1$ for all n and $\{r^n\} \longrightarrow 1$ by Example 2.

If $r = -1$, the sequence $\{r^n\}$ is

$$-1, 1, -1, 1, \cdots.$$

It is easily seen that this sequence does not converge by applying an alternate definition of convergence which can be shown to be equivalent to the definition given in Section 5–5.

Alternate Definition of Convergence of a Sequence A sequence $\{a_n\}$ **converges to** A if for any neighborhood $\langle A - \epsilon, A + \epsilon \rangle$ of A at most a finite number of terms of $\{a_n\}$ lie outside $\langle A - \epsilon, A + \epsilon \rangle$.

The usefulness of this equivalent definition is that you need find only *one* neighborhood about the proposed limit outside of which an infinite number of terms lie in order to conclude that the sequence does not have that number as its limit. The obvious possibilities for the limit of

$$-1, 1, -1, 1, -1, \cdots$$

are -1 and 1. For any other number a neighborhood can always be chosen which contains *no* terms of the sequence. Suppose 1 is chosen as the prospective limit. Then choose a neighborhood, say $\langle 1 - \frac{1}{2}, 1 + \frac{1}{2} \rangle$ or $\langle \frac{1}{2}, \frac{3}{2} \rangle$. Obviously all $a_n = (-1)^n$ for *n even* lie in $\langle \frac{1}{2}, \frac{3}{2} \rangle$. But all $a_n = (-1)^n$ for *n odd* lie outside $\langle \frac{1}{2}, \frac{3}{2} \rangle$. Consequently $\{(-1)^n\}$ does not converge to 1. Similarly $\{(-1)^n\}$ does not converge to -1. Therefore it is a divergent sequence.

The major results of this section are summarized as theorems.

Theorem 5–4 Any sequence $\{b_n\} = \frac{1}{n^a}$ with $a > 0$ and $a \in \mathbf{R}$ converges to zero.

For example: $\left\{\frac{1}{n^{\frac{1}{2}}}\right\} \longrightarrow 0$

Theorem 5–5 Any sequence $\{c\}$ of constants c converges to c.

For example: $\{5\} \longrightarrow 5$

Theorem 5–6 If $|r| < 1$, then $\{r^n\}$ converges to 0.

For example: $\{(-\frac{9}{10})^n\} \longrightarrow 0$

CLASSROOM EXERCISES

1. Translate into an inequality involving absolute value:
- **a.** a_n is in $\langle -3, 3 \rangle$.
- **b.** a_n is in $\langle 2.1, 3.5 \rangle$.
- **c.** a_n is in $\langle -\frac{1}{2}, \frac{3}{2} \rangle$
- **d.** a_n is in $\langle \frac{4}{5}, \frac{13}{5} \rangle$

2. Translate each inequality into the corresponding neighborhood statement.
- **a.** $|a_n - 1| < .2$
- **b.** $|a_n - 2| < .01$

WRITTEN EXERCISES

A ━━ In Exercises 1–8 translate each neighborhood statement into an inequality involving absolute value. a_n is in

1. $\langle -2, 2 \rangle$.
2. $\langle -.001, .001 \rangle$.
3. $\langle 1.5, 2.5 \rangle$.
4. $\langle -2.5, -1.5 \rangle$.
5. $\langle .99, 1.01 \rangle$.
6. $\langle 2, 3 \rangle$.
7. $\langle 1 - \epsilon, 1 + \epsilon \rangle$.
8. $\langle -\frac{2}{3} - \epsilon, -\frac{2}{3} + \epsilon \rangle$.

━━ In Exercises 9–16, translate each inequality involving absolute values into the corresponding neighborhood statement.

9. $|a_n - 0| < .5$
10. $|a_n - 2| < .001$
11. $|a_n + 1| < .1$
12. $|a_n - \frac{1}{3}| < \frac{1}{3}$
13. $|a_n| < \epsilon$
14. $|a_n + \frac{2}{3}| < \epsilon$
15. $|a_n - .9| < \epsilon$
16. $|a_n - .01| < .0001$

In Exercises 17–21, let a_n be the general term of a sequence. Find an M such that for all $n \geq M$ the inequality is true.

17. $a_n = \frac{2}{n}$; $|a_n - 0| < \frac{1}{2}$
18. $a_n = \frac{(-1^n)2}{n}$; $|a_n - 0| < \frac{1}{100}$
19. $a_n = 3$; $|a_n - 3| < 10^{-6}$
20. $a_n = \frac{1}{n^3}$; $|a_n - 0| < \frac{1}{100}$
21. $a_n = (\frac{9}{10})^n$; $|a_n - 0| < \frac{1}{10}$

━━ Specify the limit and the theorem which justifies it.

22. $\{100\}$
23. $\left\{\frac{1}{n^{.99}}\right\}$
24. $\{(.99)^n\}$
25. $\{-5\}$
26. $\{(-\frac{1}{3})^n\}$
27. $\left\{\frac{1}{n^{\frac{1}{3}}}\right\}$

B **28.** In your own words, explain why the two definitions of convergence for sequences are equivalent.

29. Prove: If $\{a_n\} = \left\{\frac{n}{n+1}\right\}$ then $\{a_n\} \longrightarrow 1$.

5–10   Operations with Sequences

When you add, subtract, multiply, or divide two numbers, you associate the pair of numbers with a sum, difference, product or quotient. You can perform the same operations on sequences. To do this you need to specify exactly what you mean by the sum, difference. product or quotient of two sequences:

Definitions   Given any two sequences $\{a_n\}$ and $\{b_n\}$, then

a. the sum of $\{a_n\}$ and $\{b_n\}$ is the sequence with nth term $a_n + b_n$; that is $\{a_n\} + \{b_n\} = \{a_n + b_n\}$.

b. the difference of $\{a_n\}$ and $\{b_n\}$ is the sequence with nth term $a_n - b_n$; that is $\{a_n\} - \{b_n\} = \{a_n - b_n\}$.

c. the product of $\{a_n\}$ and $\{b_n\}$ is the sequence with nth term $a_n b_n$; that is $\{a_n\} \times \{b_n\} = \{a_n \times b_n\}$.

   Given any two sequences $\{a_n\}$ and $\{b_n\}$ with $b_n = 0$ for no n, then

d. the quotient of $\{a_n\}$ and $\{b_n\}$ is the sequence with nth term $\frac{a_n}{b_n}$; that is $\{a_n\} \div \{b_n\} = \left\{\frac{a_n}{b_n}\right\}$.

Suppose $\{a_n\}$ and $\{b_n\}$ are defined as follows.

Sequence	First seven terms
$\{a_n\} = \left\{\dfrac{n+1}{n}\right\}$	$\dfrac{2}{1}, \dfrac{3}{2}, \dfrac{4}{3}, \dfrac{5}{4}, \dfrac{6}{5}, \dfrac{7}{6}, \dfrac{8}{7}$
$\{b_n\} = \left\{\dfrac{3n+2}{2n}\right\}$	$\dfrac{5}{2}, \dfrac{8}{4}, \dfrac{11}{6}, \dfrac{14}{8}, \dfrac{17}{10}, \dfrac{20}{12}, \dfrac{23}{14}$

Using the definition above gives these results.

Sequence	First seven terms
$\{a_n + b_n\} = \left\{\dfrac{5n+4}{2n}\right\}$	$\dfrac{9}{2}, \dfrac{14}{4}, \dfrac{19}{6}, \dfrac{24}{8}, \dfrac{29}{10}, \dfrac{34}{12}, \dfrac{39}{14}$
$\{a_n - b_n\} = \left\{-\dfrac{n}{2n}\right\}$	$-\dfrac{1}{2}, -\dfrac{1}{2}, -\dfrac{1}{2}, -\dfrac{1}{2}, -\dfrac{1}{2}, -\dfrac{1}{2}, -\dfrac{1}{2}$
$\{a_n \cdot b_n\} = \left\{\dfrac{3n^2 + 5n + 2}{2n^2}\right\}$	$5, 3, \dfrac{44}{18}, \dfrac{35}{16}, \dfrac{51}{25}, \dfrac{70}{36}, \dfrac{92}{49}$
$\left\{\dfrac{a_n}{b_n}\right\} = \left\{\dfrac{2n+2}{3n+2}\right\}$	$\dfrac{4}{5}, \dfrac{6}{8}, \dfrac{8}{11}, \dfrac{10}{14}, \dfrac{12}{17}, \dfrac{14}{20}, \dfrac{16}{23}$

Careful inspection suggests (and it can be proved) that:

$$\left\{\frac{n+1}{n}\right\} \longrightarrow 1 \quad \text{and} \quad \left\{\frac{3n+2}{2n}\right\} \longrightarrow \frac{3}{2}.$$

Also, $\quad \{a_n + b_n\} = \left\{\frac{5n+4}{2n}\right\} \longrightarrow \frac{5}{2} = 1 + \frac{3}{2},$

$$\{a_n - b_n\} = \left\{\frac{-n}{2n}\right\} \longrightarrow -\frac{1}{2} = 1 - \frac{3}{2},$$

$$\{a_n \cdot b_n\} = \frac{3n^2 + 5n + 2}{2n^2} \longrightarrow \frac{3}{2} = 1 \times \frac{3}{2}, \quad \text{and}$$

$$\left\{\frac{a_n}{b_n}\right\} = \left\{\frac{2n+2}{3n+2}\right\} \longrightarrow \frac{2}{3} = 1 \div \frac{3}{2}$$

Notice that the expression at the right in each statement is the sum, the difference, the product, or the quotient of the limits of $\{a_n\}$ and $\{b_n\}$. The generalization is true and is stated in the theorems following:

Theorem 5–7 **If** $\{a_n\} \longrightarrow A$ **and** $\{b_n\} \longrightarrow B$, **then**

a. $\{a_n + b_n\} \longrightarrow A + B.$

b. $\{a_n - b_n\} \longrightarrow A - B.$

c. $\{a_n \cdot b_n\} \longrightarrow A \cdot B.$

As is generally the case for division you have to be more careful.

Theorem 5–8 **If** $\{a_n\} \longrightarrow A$ **and** $\{b_n\} \longrightarrow B$ **(**$B \neq 0$**) and no** b_n **is 0, then** $\left\{\dfrac{a_n}{b_n}\right\} \longrightarrow \dfrac{A}{B}$.

The proofs of these theorems are omitted. Applications of the theorems make use of the theorems of Section 5–9.

EXAMPLE 1. Find the limit, if it exists, of $\left\{\frac{7n+5}{5n}\right\}$.

Solution:
$$\frac{7n+5}{5n} = \frac{7n}{5n} + \frac{5}{5n}$$

$$= \frac{7}{5} + \frac{1}{n}$$

Thus
$$\left\{\frac{7n+5}{5n}\right\} = \left\{\frac{7}{5}\right\} + \left\{\frac{1}{n}\right\}$$

Since $\left\{\dfrac{7}{5}\right\} \longrightarrow \dfrac{7}{5}$ (Theorem 5–5) and $\left\{\dfrac{1}{n}\right\} \longrightarrow 0$ (Theorem 5–4),

then

$$\left\{\frac{7n + 5}{5n}\right\} \longrightarrow \frac{7}{5} + 0 = \frac{7}{5} \qquad \longleftarrow \quad \textbf{By Th. 5-7a}$$

A notation which is often used in place of $\left\{\dfrac{7n + 5}{5n}\right\} \longrightarrow \dfrac{7}{5}$ is the following

$$\lim_{n \to \infty} \frac{7n + 5}{5n} = \frac{7}{5}$$

which is read: "the limit of $\dfrac{7n + 5}{5n}$ as n increases without bound is $\tfrac{7}{5}$."

Using this notation, Theorem 5–7a would read:

If $\lim\limits_{n \to \infty} a_n = \mathbf{A}$ and $\lim\limits_{n \to \infty} b_n = \mathbf{B}$, then $\lim\limits_{n \to \infty} (a_n + b_n) = \mathbf{A} + \mathbf{B}$.

EXAMPLE 2.   Find the limit of $\left\{\dfrac{6n^2 - 3n + 8}{2n^2}\right\}$ if it exists.

METHOD I $\dfrac{6n^2 - 3n + 8}{2n^2} = \dfrac{3n^2}{n^2} - \dfrac{3n}{2n^2} + \dfrac{4}{n^2}$

$$= 3 - \frac{3}{2} \cdot \frac{1}{n} + 4 \cdot \frac{1}{n^2}$$

Thus $\lim\limits_{n \to \infty} \dfrac{6n^2 - 3n + 8}{2n^2} = \lim\limits_{n \to \infty} 3 - \lim\limits_{n \to \infty} \dfrac{3}{2} \cdot \dfrac{1}{n} + \lim\limits_{n \to \infty} 4 \cdot \dfrac{1}{n^2}$

$$= 3 - \tfrac{3}{2} \cdot 0 + 4 \cdot 0$$

$$= 3.$$

METHOD II   Multiply by $\dfrac{n^{-2}}{n^{-2}}$:

$$\frac{n^{-2}}{n^{-2}} \cdot \frac{6n^2 - 3n + 8}{2n^2} = \frac{6 - \dfrac{3}{n} + \dfrac{8}{n^2}}{2}$$

Then $\lim\limits_{n \to \infty} \dfrac{6n^2 - 3n + 8}{2n^2} = \dfrac{\lim\limits_{n \to \infty} \left(6 - \dfrac{3}{n} + \dfrac{8}{n^2}\right)}{\lim\limits_{n \to \infty} 2}$

$$= \frac{6 - 0 + 0}{2} = 3.$$

The second method uses Theorem 5–8 in combination with Theorem 5–7.

EXAMPLE 3. Find $\lim\limits_{n \to \infty} \dfrac{n^3 + n}{n^2}$, if it exists.

Solution:
$$\frac{n^3 + n}{n^2} = \frac{n^3}{n^2} + \frac{n}{n^2} = n + \frac{1}{n}$$

It is clear that $\{n\}$ does not converge, that is, $\{n\}$ is a divergent sequence. Since every term of $\left\{\dfrac{n^3 + n}{n^2}\right\}$ is greater than the corresponding term of $\{n\}$, it also follows that $\left\{\dfrac{n^3 + n}{n^2}\right\}$ does not converge.

The reasoning in Example 3 can be used as a test for divergence.

Comparison Test for Divergence: If $\{a_n\}$ and $\{b_n\}$ are two sequences such that $a_n \leq b_n$ for all n or for all n greater than a fixed natural number n_0 and $\{a_n\}$ diverges, then $\{b_n\}$ diverges.

Some examples of divergent sequences are:
1. $\{n + c\}$ and $\{-n + c\}$ where c is a real number
2. $\left\{\dfrac{n}{c}\right\}$ and $\left\{\dfrac{-n}{c}\right\}$ where c is a nonzero real number
3. $\{r^n\}$ where r is a real and $|r| > 1$
4. $\{n^p\}$ where p is real and positive.

EXAMPLE 4. Use the comparison test to show that $\{2n - 3\}$ diverges.

METHOD I
$$2n - 3 \geq n \quad \text{iff} \quad 2n \geq n + 3$$
$$\text{iff} \quad n \geq 3$$

Thus for all $n \geq 3$, $2n - 3 \geq n$. Since $\{n\}$ diverges, $\{2n - 3\}$ diverges by the comparison test.

METHOD II
$$2n - 3 \geq n - 3 \quad \text{iff} \quad 2n \geq n$$
$$\text{iff} \quad n \geq 0$$

Thus for all $n > 0$, $2n - 3 > n - 3$ and $\{2n - 3\}$ diverges by comparison with $\{n - 3\}$.

CLASSROOM EXERCISES

For $\{a_n\} = \left\{\dfrac{3n + 1}{2n - 5}\right\}$ and $\{b_n\} = \left\{\dfrac{n - 2}{2n + 5}\right\}$, find the following.

1. $\{a_n + b_n\}$ 2. $\{a_n - b_n\}$ 3. $\{a_n \cdot b_n\}$

WRITTEN EXERCISES

A ▬▬ Use the theorems of this section to determine whether the sequence converges or diverges. If it converges, specify the limit.

1. $\left\{\dfrac{5n + 21}{21n}\right\}$ 　　　　　　**2.** $\left\{\dfrac{3 + 2n}{6n}\right\}$

3. $\left\{\dfrac{6 - 2n}{4n}\right\}$ 　　　　　　**4.** $\left\{\dfrac{n + 1}{n} + \dfrac{n}{2}\right\}$

5. $\left\{\dfrac{7n^2 - 2n}{5n^2}\right\}$ 　　　　　　**6.** $\left\{\dfrac{7n^2 + 2n}{5n}\right\}$

7. $\left\{\left(\dfrac{2n + 1}{n}\right)\left(5 + \dfrac{7}{n}\right)\right\}$ 　　**8.** $\left\{\dfrac{n^3}{n^2 + 10}\right\}$

9. $\left\{\left[2 + \dfrac{1}{n}\right]^4\right\}$ 　　　　　**10.** $\left\{\dfrac{n + 1}{n}\right\}$

11. $\left\{\dfrac{3n^2 + 2n + 1}{6n^2 + 3n + 2}\right\}$

12. $\left\{\dfrac{n^2 + n}{n^2 - 2}\right\}$

13. $\left\{\dfrac{(n + 1)(n + 2)(n + 3)}{3n^3}\right\}$

14. $\left\{\left(\dfrac{2n}{n}\right)\left(\dfrac{7}{10}\right)^n\right\}$

15. $\left\{5\left(\dfrac{n + 1}{n}\right)\left(\dfrac{n}{n + 1}\right)\right\}$

B **16.** Suppose $\{a_n\}$ and $\{b_n\}$ are two divergent sequences.

    a. Is $\{a_n + b_n\}$ always, sometimes, or never convergent (cite examples).

    b. Is $\{a_n \cdot b_n\}$ always, sometimes, or never convergent (cite examples).

    c. Is $\left\{\dfrac{a_n}{b_n}\right\}$ always, sometimes, or never convergent (cite examples).

17. Suppose $\{a_n\}$ is convergent and $\{b_n\}$ is divergent.

    a. Is $\{a_n + b_n\}$ always, sometimes, or never convergent (cite examples).

    b. Is $\{a_n \cdot b_n\}$ always, sometimes, or never convergent (cite examples).

    c. Is $\left\{\dfrac{a_n}{b_n}\right\}$ always, sometimes, or never convergent (cite examples).

18. a. Suppose $\{a_n\}$ and $\{b_n\}$ converge to the same number. What can you conclude, if anything, about the convergence of $\{a_n - b_n\}$?

    b. Suppose $\{a_n - b_n\}$ converges to zero. Does this mean that $\{a_n\}$ and $\{b_n\}$ converge to the same number? Explain.

BASIC: TESTING FOR CONVERGENT SEQUENCES

Problem:

Given the sequence $\{a_n\} = \left\{\dfrac{2n^2 + 1}{3n^2}\right\}$, a proposed limit L, and the radius of a neighborhood of L, write a program that computes the first term of the sequence that is in the neighborhood.

```
100 PRINT
110 PRINT "THIS PROGRAM TESTS A SEQUENCE FOR"
120 PRINT "CONVERGENCE.  TYPE THE FORMULA FOR"
130 PRINT "THE GENERAL TERM OF THE SEQUENCE"
140 PRINT "AS STATEMENT 170.  THEN TYPE"
150 PRINT "'RUN 170'."
160 STOP
170 DEF FN A(N) = (2*N*N + 1)/(3*N*N)
180 PRINT
190 PRINT "WHAT IS THE PROPOSED LIMIT";
200 INPUT L
210 PRINT "WHAT RADIUS ABOUT ";L;" DO YOU"
220 PRINT "WANT FOR A NEIGHBORHOOD";
230 INPUT R
240 PRINT
250 FOR N = 1 TO 1000
260    IF ABS(L - FN A(N)) < R THEN 310
270 NEXT N
280 PRINT "NONE OF THE FIRST 1000 TERMS OF THE"
290 PRINT "SEQUENCE ENTERS THAT NEIGHBORHOOD OF";L
300 GOTO 330
310 PRINT "THE FIRST TERM OF THE SEQUENCE THAT"
320 PRINT "IS IN THE NEIGHBORHOOD IS TERM";N
330 PRINT
340 END
```

Output:

```
RUN 170

WHAT IS THE PROPOSED LIMIT? .666667
WHAT RADIUS ABOUT  .666667  DO YOU
WANT FOR A NEIGHBORHOOD? .001

THE FIRST TERM OF THE SEQUENCE THAT
IS IN THE NEIGHBORHOOD IS TERM 19
```

Analysis:

Statements 250–270: This loop generates up to 1000 terms of the sequence. For each term statement 260 tests the inequality $|L - a_n| < R$. When this inequality checks, the computer jumps to statement 310 and prints the current value of N.

Statements 280–290: If N reaches 1000 and no term is in the neighborhood, the computer drops out of the loop to statement 280 and prints the message that none of the first 1000 terms falls within the neighborhood.

EXERCISES

A Run the program on page 272 to find the first term for each sequence which is in the neighborhood of radius *r* about *m*.

1. $\{a_n\} = \left\{\frac{1 - 3n^2}{3n^2}\right\}$, $r = 0.01$, $m = -3$

2. $\{a_n\} = \{(\frac{3}{4})^n\}$, $r = 0.005$, $m = 0$

3. $\{a_n\} = \{1 - (0.5)^n\}$, $r = 0.0001$, $m = 1$

4. $\{a_n\} = \left\{\frac{2 + 3n^2}{4n^2}\right\}$, $r = 0.0005$, $m = 0.75$

B In Exercises 5–7, revise the program on page 272 in the manner indicated.

5. Generate up to 10,000 terms.

6. Ask the user if he or she wishes to see the terms of the sequence as they are being generated. If so, print them until a term enters the neighborhood or until *n* reaches 1000.

7. Calculate the sum of the *n* terms of the sequence. When a term of the sequence enters the neighborhood, or when *n* reaches 1000, print the sum.

C Write a BASIC program for each problem.

8. Given the first term, the common difference, and a value for *n*, print the first *n* terms of an arithmetic sequence.

9. Revise the program in Exercise 8 so that it prints only the sum of the first *n* terms of the arithmetic sequence.

10. Expand the program in Exercise 8 so that it prints the first *n* terms of the arithmetic sequence and the first *n* terms of the corresponding harmonic sequence. Print the sequences in two labeled columns.

11. Given the first term, the common ratio, and a value for *n*, print the first *n* terms of a geometric sequence.

CHAPTER SUMMARY

Important Terms

Completeness property (p. 252)

Convergent sequence (p. 240)

Divergent sequence (p. 240)

Finite sequence (p. 222)

General neighborhood (p. 241)

Infinite sequence (p. 222)

Monotone sequence (p. 252)

Neighborhood (p. 230)

Series (p. 255)

Sum of an infinite series (p. 257)

Important Ideas

1. A recursive formula for a sequence expresses each term in terms of one or more of the preceding terms.

2. A sequence is said to have a limit, L, if for every neighborhood of L there exists an $M > 0$ such that for all $n > M$, a_n lies in the neighborhood.

3. Every bounded monotone sequence has a limit.

4. The following sequences converge:

   a. $\left(\frac{1}{n}\right)^a$, $a > 0$ and $a \in \mathrm{R}$, converges to 0.

   b. c, where c is a constant, converges to c.

   c. r^n, $|r| < 1$, converges to 0.

5. The sum, difference, product and quotient of two convergent sequences is convergent to the sum, difference, product, or quotient of the limits of the original sequences. (The divisor sequence in the quotient must have a nonzero limit.)

CHAPTER OBJECTIVES AND REVIEW

Objective: *To define a sequence and find any term or terms of the sequence given an expression or rule for the nth term.* (Section 5-1)

1. The first seven terms of a sequence are shown below.

$$0, 1, 8, 15, 24, 35, 48, \cdots$$

Find the general term. (*Hint:* Add 1 to each term.)

━━━ Find the first five terms of each sequence and one additional term as specified.

2. $a_n = 3n + 1$; 5th term.

3. $a_n = \frac{2}{3} + n$; 15th term.

4. $b_n = \dfrac{2}{n + 3}$; 25th term.

5. $a_1 = b$, $a_n = \frac{1}{10} a_{n-1}$; 10th term.

6. $b_n = (\frac{1}{2})^n + 10$; 10th term.

7. $c_1 = -2$, $c_n = -1c_{n-1}$; 20th term.

8. Write an expression for the nth term of the sequence.

    a. In Exercise 5.   **b.** In Exercise 7.

    c. $a_1 = 2$, $a_n = 2a_{n-1}$ **d.** $b_1 = -\frac{1}{2}$, $b_n = -1b_{n-1}$

Objective: *To graph several terms of a sequence and identify an open interval in which the remaining terms lie.* (Section 5-2)

━━ Graph five terms of each sequence. Find an open interval containing the remaining terms but not containing the first five terms.

9. $\{a_n\} = \{-3 + 2n\}$

10. $\{b_n\} = \left\{\frac{9n-1}{10}\right\}$

11. $\{c_n\} = \{(0.9)^{n-1}\}$

12. $\{d_n\} = \{(-0.5)^n\}$

Objective: *To determine whether a sequence is increasing or decreasing, and to find $M \in N$ such that for all $n \geq M$, a_n is as close as you please to some number L.* (Section 5-3)

13. Let $\{a_n\} = \left\{\frac{1}{3n}\right\}$.

    a. Show that $a_n > a_{n+1}$ for $n \in N$.

    b. Find $M \in N$ such that a_n is as close to 0 as $\frac{1}{100}$ for all $n \geq M$.

14. Let $\{b_n\} = \left\{\frac{n}{n+2}\right\}$.

    a. Show that $b_n < b_{n+1}$ for $n \in N$.

    b. Find $M \in N$ such that b_n is as close to 1 as $\frac{1}{200}$ for all $n \geq M$.

Objective: *To find all terms of a sequence which lie in a given neighborhood.* (Section 5-4)

━━ For the given sequence and neighborhood identify all the terms of the sequence lying in the neighborhood.

15. $\{a_n\} = \{-3 + 2n\}$; $\langle 23, 47 \rangle$ **16.** $\{b_n\} = \left\{\frac{4^n}{10}\right\}$; $\langle 0, 23 \rangle$

17. $\{c_n\} = \left\{\frac{2n-1}{n}\right\}$; $\langle 1.8, 2.2 \rangle$ **18.** $\{c_n\} = \left\{\frac{1}{3n}\right\}$; $\langle -\epsilon, \epsilon \rangle$, $\epsilon > 0$

19. $\{d_n\} = \left\{\left(\frac{-2}{3}\right)^n\right\}$; $\langle -0.001, 0.001 \rangle$

Objective: *To apply the definition of the limit of a sequence to prove or disprove the claim that L is the limit of* $\{a_n\}$. (Sections 5-5 and 5-6)

▬ In Exercises 20–23, what appears to be the limit of each sequence?

20. $a_n = \dfrac{3n + 1}{5n}$

21. $a_n = \dfrac{2n - 5}{n}$

22. $a_n = \dfrac{5 - n}{n}$

23. $a_n = \dfrac{n^2 - 1}{2n^2}$

▬ In each Exercise 24–26 the number L is claimed to be the limit of the sequence $\{a_n\}$. If you agree, prove you are correct. If you disagree produce a neighborhood of L which does not contain an infinite subset of $\{a_n\}$.

24. $\left\{\dfrac{2n}{n + 1}\right\}$; $L = 2$

25. $\left\{\dfrac{73}{n}\right\}$; $L = 0$

26. $\{2n - 49\}$; $L = 63$

27. Prove: $\{a_n\} = \left\{\dfrac{n^2 + 1}{2n^2}\right\} \to \dfrac{1}{2}$

Objective: *To find the least upper and greatest lower bounds of a sequence, and use these concepts to explain the completeness property of the real numbers.* (Section 5-7)

28. a. Which of the sequences in Exercise 24–26 are bounded?

   b. Find the l.u.b. and the g.l.b. for the bounded sequences.

29. a. State in your own words the least upper bound axiom.

   b. Explain what is meant by saying that the real numbers are complete.

30. Given $\{a_n\} = \left\{-1 + \dfrac{1}{n}\right\}$.

   a. Is $\{a_n\}$ bounded? Illustrate.

   b. Is $\{a_n\}$ monotone? Explain.

   c. Does $\{a_n\}$ have a limit? Explain.

Objective: *To express a series in sigma notation and to write the addends of a series that is in sigma notation.* (Section 5-8)

▬ Express each series in sigma notation.

31. $a_1^3 + a_2^3 + a_3^3 + a_4^3 + a_5^3$

32. $x_1 y - x_2 y + x_3 y - x_4 y$

▬ Write the first five addends in each series.

33. $\displaystyle\sum_{i=1}^{\infty} (4 + 2i)$

34. $\sum_{i=1}^{\infty} -3\left(\frac{i}{5}\right)$

35. $\sum_{i=1}^{\infty} |-4 + \frac{1}{2}i|$

36. $\sum_{i=1}^{\infty} \left(\frac{3}{4}\right)^{i-1}$

Objective: *To define the sum of an infinite series and to find such sums.* (Section 5-8)

37. State the definition of the sum of an infinite series in your own words. Compare your definition with the one on page 257.

━━ Find the sum of each series.

38. $\sum_{i=1}^{\infty} 2\left(\frac{3}{4}\right)^{i-1}$

39. $\sum_{i=1}^{\infty} 2\left(\frac{-3}{4}\right)^{i-1}$

Objective: *To use the limit theorems for sequences (Theorems 5–4 through 5–8 inclusive) to find limits of sequences.* (Section 5-9 and Section 5-10)

━━ Specify each limit and the theorem that justifies it.

40. $\{639\}$

41. $\left\{\frac{1}{n^2}\right\}$

42. $\{(-0.4675)^n\}$

━━ Find the limit (when possible) of each sequence.

43. $\{a_n\} = \left\{\dfrac{6n^2 + n - 1}{3n + 1}\right\}$

44. $\{b_n\} = \left\{\dfrac{n^3 + 17n^2 - 3n + 1}{43n^3 + 1}\right\}$

45. $\lim_{n \to \infty} \left[\left(\frac{2}{3}\right)^n \cdot \frac{n+1}{4n-3}\right]$

46. $\lim_{n \to \infty} \dfrac{(n-1)(n-2)(n-3)}{3n^3}$

CHAPTER TEST

1. Find the first seven terms of the sequence with nth term:

$$b_n = (-1)^n \frac{1}{2n}$$

What is b_{100}? b_{101}?

2. Find the first seven terms of the sequence defined as follows:

$$a_1 = 3, \; a_n = 2a_{n-1} - 1.$$

3. Let $c_n = 2^n + 1$. What are the first seven terms? Compare $\{c_n\}$ with $\{a_n\}$ of Exercise 2.

4. Graph $\{b_n\} = \left\{\frac{(-1)^n}{2n}\right\}$ on the number line. What is the apparent limit?

5. Graph $\{c_n\} = \{2^n + 1\}$ on the number line. Does there appear to be a limit?

6. Find an M so that all the terms of $\{a_n\} = \left\{\frac{(-1)^n}{2n}\right\}$ for $n \geq M$ lie inside the neighborhood $\langle -0.001, 0.001 \rangle$, $\langle -\epsilon, \epsilon \rangle$, $\epsilon > 0$.

7. What appears to be the limit of $\{b_n\} = \left\{\frac{2n+1}{n-2}\right\}$? Prove that your guess is correct by using the definition of limit of a sequence.

8. Construct a proof demonstrating that $\lim\limits_{n \to \infty} \frac{3}{n^2} = 0$.

9. Produce an example of a monotone sequence that is bounded; that is unbounded. Which of these sequences has a limit? Explain.

━━━━ Use the limit theorems to find the limit of each sequence.

10. $\{a_n\} = \left\{\frac{n-3}{(n+3)(n)}\right\}$

11. $\{b_n\} = \left\{\frac{2 \cdot (n-5)}{3n}\right\}$

12. $\{c_n\} = \left\{(\tfrac{4}{5})^n \cdot \left(23 - \tfrac{1}{n}\right)\right\}$

━━━━ Write out at least five addends in each series.

13. $\sum\limits_{i=1}^{\infty} \frac{(-1)^i}{3i}$

14. $\sum\limits_{i=1}^{\infty} (2i - 3)$

15. Find the sum of the geometric series.

$$\sum\limits_{i=1}^{\infty} (\tfrac{4}{5})^{i-1}$$

CHAPTER **6** **Functions and Limits**

6–1   Sequences and Functions

In Chapter 5 a *sequence* was defined as the range of a function whose domain is the positive integers. Thus, if $\{a_n\} = \left\{\dfrac{n+1}{n}\right\}$ then $\{a_n\} = \{2, \frac{3}{2}, \frac{4}{3}, \frac{5}{4}, \cdots\}$. In order to develop an understanding of the *limit of a function* it is helpful to change this point of view slightly. For the purpose of this chapter, a sequence $\{a_n\}$ will be regarded as a *function* (not simply the range of a function). The set $\{1, 2, 3, \cdots\}$ of replacements for n is the *domain* of the function; the set $\{a_1, a_2, a_3, \cdots\}$ is its *range*.

In the previous chapter you graphed many sequences on a co-ordinatized line. In Figure 1 the sequence with general term

$$a_n = \frac{n+1}{n}$$

is graphed on a coordinatized line.

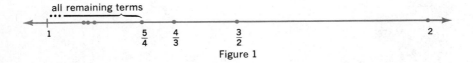

Figure 1

A sequence can just as easily be graphed in a coordinatized plane, if the sequence is defined as a function. In fact this is the standard practice for functions. Figure 2 shows the two dimensional graph of the first five terms of the sequence with general term $a_n = \dfrac{n+1}{n}$. As you know, $\lim\limits_{n\to\infty} \dfrac{n+1}{n} = 1$. In the graph you can see that the points (n, a_n) are very close to the line $y = 1$ for large n.

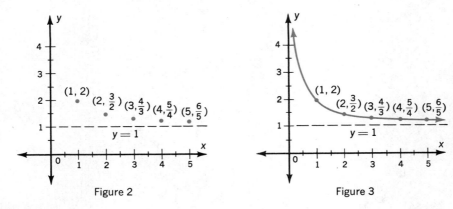

Figure 2   Figure 3

Suppose the domain of the function $a_n : n \longrightarrow \dfrac{n+1}{n}$ is extended to include all real numbers greater than 0. Then the graph of the function will resemble the one shown in Figure 3.

When the domain of a function is the set of real numbers or an interval of reals, the function is called a **function of a real variable.** These functions and their limits are the major concern of this chapter.

Recall that a sequence $\{a_n\}$ has a limit A if and only if for every $\epsilon > 0$, there is a natural number M such that for all $n \geq M$, $a_n \in \langle A - \epsilon, A + \epsilon \rangle$. The statement $n \geq M$ can be equivalently represented by the statement $n \in [M, +\infty) \quad n, M \in \{1, 2, 3, \cdots\}$, where $[M, +\infty)$ is the set of all real numbers greater than or equal to M. (See Figure 4.)

Definition $\lim\limits_{n \to \infty} a_n = A$ iff for every $\epsilon > 0$, there is an M such that for all $n \in [M, +\infty)$ $a_n \in \langle A - \epsilon, A + \epsilon \rangle$.

The sequence graphed happens to alternate on either side of A. Since the graph is given in two dimensions, the neighborhood of A, $\langle A - \epsilon, A + \epsilon \rangle$ is located on the y axis rather than on the x axis as in Chapter 5. The dotted horizontal lines $y = A + \epsilon$ and $y = A - \epsilon$ are determined by the end points of the neighborhood. Notice that for a_n to be in $\langle A - \epsilon, A + \epsilon \rangle$, a_n must be in the region between $y = A + \epsilon$ and $y = A - \epsilon$.

The interval $[M, +\infty)$ is located on the x axis. All of the terms of $\{a_n\}$ are between $y = A + \epsilon$ and $y = A - \epsilon$ for $n \geq 7$. Thus $M = 7$ (or any larger natural number). The region for which $a_n \in \langle A - \epsilon, A + \epsilon \rangle$ when $n \in [M, +\infty)$ is shaded. If there is such a region for *every* $\epsilon > 0$, then the limit of $\{a_n\}$ is A.

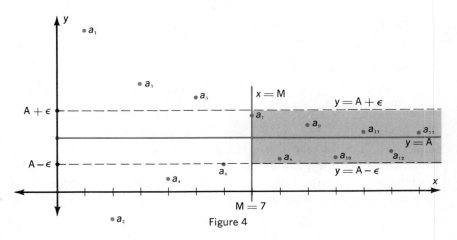

Figure 4

The situation for functions of a real variable is analogous. For the limit of $f(x)$ to be L, to each $\epsilon > 0$, there must be an x_0 (like M) such that $f(x) \in \langle L - \epsilon, L + \epsilon \rangle$ whenever $x \in \langle x_0, +\infty \rangle$. The major differences here are that x may be replaced by any real number in the interval $\langle x_0, +\infty \rangle$ and that x must assume a value greater than x_0 *but not equal to* x_0.

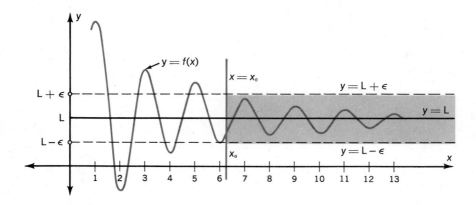

In the figure above each $f(x)$ for $x \geqslant x_0$ is in the shaded region bounded by $y = L + \epsilon$, $x = x_0$ and $y = L - \epsilon$. If such a shaded region can be found for each $\epsilon > 0$ chosen, then the limit of $f(x)$ as x increases without bound exists, and is L. This is symbolized in the following way.

$$\lim_{x \to +\infty} f(x) = L$$

or

$$f(x) \longrightarrow L \text{ as } x \longrightarrow +\infty.$$

The formal definition is much like the one for sequences.

Definition $\lim_{x \to +\infty} f(x) = L$ if and only if for each $\epsilon > 0$ there is an x_0 such that $f(x) \in \langle L - \epsilon, L + \epsilon \rangle$ whenever $x \in \langle x_0, +\infty \rangle$.

Proofs that $f(x) \longrightarrow L$ as $x \longrightarrow +\infty$ are similar to proofs involving sequences. You will recall from Chapter 5 that in doing limit proofs it is often easier to use absolute values than to use open intervals directly. Recall that a is in the open interval $\langle b - c, b + c \rangle$ if and only if a is within c units of the interval's midpoint, b. Thus

$$a \in \langle b - c, b + c \rangle \quad \text{iff} \quad |a - b| < c.$$

EXAMPLE 1. Prove: $\lim\limits_{x \to \infty} f(x) = 1$ where $f(x) = \dfrac{x+1}{x}$ and $x > 0$.

Proof: Using absolute values, an x_0 must be found such that $\left|\dfrac{x+1}{x} - 1\right| < \epsilon$ whenever $x > x_0$.

But

$$\left|\frac{x+1}{x} - 1\right| < \epsilon \quad \text{iff}$$

$$\left|\frac{x+1}{x} - \frac{x}{x}\right| < \epsilon \quad \text{iff}$$

$$\left|\frac{1}{x}\right| < \epsilon \quad \text{iff}$$

$$\frac{1}{|x|} < \epsilon \quad \text{iff}$$

$$\frac{1}{\epsilon} < |x| \quad \text{iff}$$

$$\frac{1}{\epsilon} < x \quad \longleftarrow \quad \textbf{Since } x > 0$$

Consequently, choose

$$x_0 = \frac{1}{\epsilon}.$$

It follows that if

$$x > x_0 = \frac{1}{\epsilon},$$

then

$$\left|\frac{x+1}{x} - 1\right| < \epsilon$$

and

$$\lim_{x \to \infty} \frac{x+1}{x} = 1.$$

Unlike sequences, a function of a real variable may have the set of negative real numbers for its domain. In such a case you may be asked to find the limit of the function as $|x|$ increases without bound. Since x is negative, $|x| \longrightarrow +\infty$ is equivalent to $x \longrightarrow -\infty$. This possibility may be handled by applying the next definition.

Definition $\lim\limits_{x \to -\infty} f(x) = L$ if and only if for each $\epsilon > 0$ there is an x_0 such that $f(x) \in \langle L - \epsilon, L + \epsilon \rangle$ whenever $x \in \langle -\infty, x_0 \rangle$.

EXAMPLE 2. Prove: $\lim\limits_{x \to -\infty} f(x) = 1$ where $f(x) = \dfrac{x+1}{x}$, $x < 0$

Proof:

$$\left| \frac{x+1}{x} - 1 \right| < \epsilon \quad \text{iff}$$

$$\left| \frac{x+1-x}{x} \right| < \epsilon \quad \text{iff}$$

$$\left| \frac{1}{x} \right| < \epsilon \quad \text{iff}$$

$$\frac{1}{|x|} < \epsilon \quad \text{iff}$$

$$\frac{1}{\epsilon} < |x| \quad \text{iff}$$

$$\frac{1}{\epsilon} < -x \quad \text{iff} \quad \longleftarrow \quad \textbf{Since } x < 0$$

$$-\frac{1}{\epsilon} > x \quad \longleftarrow \quad \textbf{Multiplying both sides by } -1$$

Consequently choose $x_0 = -\dfrac{1}{\epsilon}$. It follows that if $x < x_0 = -\dfrac{1}{\epsilon}$, then $\left| \dfrac{x+1}{x} - 1 \right| < \epsilon$ and $\lim\limits_{x \to -\infty} \dfrac{x+1}{x} = 1$.

CLASSROOM EXERCISES

▬ For each function indicate whether a limit exists as $x \longrightarrow +\infty$ and as $x \longrightarrow -\infty$. If so, name the limit.

1. $f(x) = \dfrac{x}{x-1}$ **2.** $f(x) = \dfrac{84x}{x-1}$ **3.** $f(x) = x$

WRITTEN EXERCISES

A ▬ Graph each sequence and the associated function of a real variable. What appears to be the limit of each as $n \longrightarrow +\infty$ or as $x \longrightarrow +\infty$?

1. $a_n = \dfrac{n-1}{n}$, $f(x) = \dfrac{x-1}{x}$ **2.** $a_n = \dfrac{1}{n}$, $f(x) = \dfrac{1}{x}$

3. $a_n = \dfrac{2n^2 + 2n + 1}{n^2}$, $f(x) = \dfrac{2x^2 + 2x + 1}{x^2}$

4. $a_n = \dfrac{1-n}{n}$, $f(x) = \dfrac{1-x}{x}$

5. $a_n = 3$, $f(x) = 3$

6. $a_n = (\tfrac{1}{2})^{n-1}$, $f(x) = (\tfrac{1}{2})^{x-1}$

7. For Exercises 1–5 what does $\lim\limits_{x \to -\infty} f(x)$ appear to be?

B ━━ For each function in Exercises 8–11 find an x_0 so that all values of the function for $x \in \langle x_0, +\infty \rangle$ will be in the neighborhood of radius $\frac{1}{10}$ about the given limit L. Construct a graph for each.

8. $f(x) = \frac{1}{x}$, $L = 0$ **9.** $f(x) = \frac{3x + 2}{x}$, $L = 3$

10. $f(x) = \frac{3 - 2x}{3x}$, $L = -\frac{2}{3}$ **11.** $f(x) = \frac{3x}{5x + 1}$, $L = \frac{3}{5}$

12. Repeat Exercises 8–11 for a radius of $\frac{1}{100}$.

C   **13.** Explain in your own words why the definitions of $\lim\limits_{x \to +\infty} f(x)$ and $\lim\limits_{x \to -\infty} f(x)$ are special cases of the following definition:

> **Definition** $\lim\limits_{x \to \infty} f(x) = L$ if and only if for each $\epsilon > 0$ there is an x_0 such that $f(x) \in \langle L - \epsilon, L + \epsilon \rangle$ whenever $|x| > |x_0|$.

━━ Prove each of the following statements.

14. $\lim\limits_{x \to +\infty} \frac{1}{x} = 0$ **15.** $\lim\limits_{x \to -\infty} \frac{1}{x} = 0$

16. $\lim\limits_{x \to +\infty} \frac{-2x + 1}{x} = -2$ **17.** $\lim\limits_{x \to +\infty} \frac{3x}{5x + 1} = \frac{3}{5}$

18. $\lim\limits_{x \to -\infty} 2 = 2$ **19.** $\lim\limits_{x \to +\infty} \frac{-x^2 + 2x}{2x^2} = -\frac{1}{2}$

20. $\lim\limits_{x \to \infty} \frac{x + 3}{x + 2} = 1$ **21.** $\lim\limits_{x \to \infty} \frac{2(x^2 - 1)}{(x - 1)(x + 1)} = 2$

22. $\lim\limits_{x \to \infty} \frac{x + 1}{x^2 - 1} = 0$ **23.** $\lim\limits_{x \to \infty} \frac{-3x + 4}{-5x} = \frac{3}{5}$

24. $\lim\limits_{x \to \infty} \frac{1}{x} = 0$ **25.** $\lim\limits_{x \to \infty} \frac{1}{x^2} = 0$

6–2   Limit of a Function at a Point $x = a$

In the previous section you studied the limit of a function $f(x)$ as $x \longrightarrow +\infty$ and as $x \longrightarrow -\infty$. In this section the meaning of "the limit of $f(x)$ as x approaches a" is discussed.

The symbolism is the same as used previously. Thus "$\lim\limits_{x \to a} f(x) = L$" means "$L$ is the limit of the function $f(x)$ as x approaches a." The intuitive idea is similar: $\lim\limits_{x \to a} f(x) = L$ means that $f(x)$ is quite close to L when x is close to but not equal to a.

Let $y = f(x)$ have a graph as shown in the diagram below. Notice that a neighborhood of L and the horizontal lines determined by its endpoints have been indicated. Also a neighborhood of a, $\langle a - \delta, a + \delta \rangle$, and the vertical lines determined by its endpoints are indicated. (δ is the Greek letter delta.) The shaded region is the intersection of the points between $y = L + \epsilon$ and $y = L - \epsilon$ and those between $x = a + \delta$ and $x = a - \delta$.

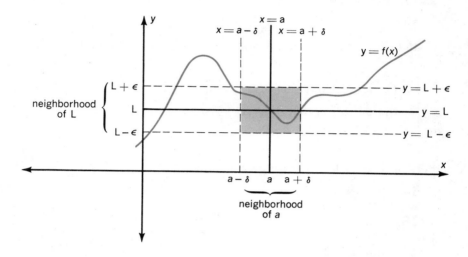

The function is said to **have a limit L as x approaches a** if and only if for every neighborhood of L a neighborhood of a can be found so that every value of the function corresponding to an $x(x \neq a)$ in the neighborhood of a lies in the neighborhood of the limit L. In graphical terms, every point of the curve between $x = a - \delta$ and $x = a + \delta$ ($x \neq a$) must also be between $y = L + \epsilon$ and $y = L - \epsilon$, that is, in the shaded region. To visualize the effect of making ϵ smaller, think of the lines $y = L + \epsilon$ and $y = L - \epsilon$ each moving close to $y = L$. If the lines $x = a - \delta$ and $x = a + \delta$ can each be moved close to $x = a$ so that the points of the graph remain in the shaded rectangular region, then L is the limit of $f(x)$ as x approaches a. These ideas are formalized in the next definition.

Definition $\lim\limits_{x \to a} f(x) = L$ if and only if for each $\epsilon > 0$ there is a $\delta > 0$ such that $f(x) \in \langle L - \epsilon, L + \epsilon \rangle$ whenever $x \in \langle a - \delta, a + \delta \rangle$ and $x \neq a$. If $\lim\limits_{x \to a} f(x) = L$, then $f(x)$ is said to **have a limit at $x = a$.**

Notice that $f(x)$ need not be defined at $x = a$ for $\lim\limits_{x \to a} f(x)$ to exist. All that need be true is for all the x in $\langle a - \delta, a + \delta \rangle$ *other than* $x = a$ to correspond to values of the function which are in $\langle L - \epsilon, L + \epsilon \rangle$. Reasoning in the same manner, if $f(x)$ is defined at $x = a$, $f(a)$ does not necessarily have to equal the limit L.

There are many examples of functions which do not have a limit at $x = a$. One of these follows.

EXAMPLE 1. Consider the function $f(x)$ defined as follows:

$$f(x) = \begin{cases} x + 2 & \text{for } x < 1 \\ 4 & \text{for } x = 1 \\ x + 4 & \text{for } x > 1 \end{cases}$$

neighborhood of 3 $\left\{ \begin{array}{l} 3+1 \\ 3 \\ 3-1 \end{array} \right.$

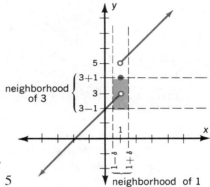

Show that $f(x)$ does not have a limit at $x = 1$.

Solution: The possible values for L are: $L = 5$, $L = 3$, or $3 < L < 5$

neighborhood of 1

a. If $L = 3$, choose $\epsilon = 1$. ◄—— ϵ is fixed first.
For all δ, if $x \in \langle 1, 1 + \delta \rangle$
$f(x) \notin \langle 2, 4 \rangle$ ◄—— See the graph.

b. If $L = 5$, choose $\epsilon = 1$.
For all δ, if $x \in \langle 1 - \delta, 1 \rangle$, $f(x) \notin \langle 4, 6 \rangle$.

c. If $3 < L < 5$, choose ϵ as the smaller of $|2 - L|$ and $|L - 5|$
For all δ, $x \in \langle 1 - \delta, 1 + \delta \rangle$
$f(x) \notin \langle L - \epsilon, L + \epsilon \rangle$

Thus, $\lim\limits_{x \to 1} f(x)$ does not exist.

Even though $\lim\limits_{x \to 1} f(x)$ does not exist for the function of Example 1, two *one-sided limits* do exist. Considering only those values of x which are less than 1, then the limit of $f(x)$ as x approaches 1 exists, and is equal to 3. This is true because the values of $f(x)$ for $x \in \langle 1 - \delta, 1 \rangle$ lie in the shaded region. Analytically this means that for a given $\epsilon > 0$, there is a $\delta > 0$ such that $f(x) \in \langle 3 - \epsilon, 3 + \epsilon \rangle$ whenever $x \in \langle 1 - \delta, 1 \rangle$ *and* $x < 1$. Since all values of x are less than 1, $f(x)$ is said to have a limit 3 *as x approaches* 1 *from the left*. In symbols: $\lim\limits_{x \to 1^-} f(x) = 3$.

It is clear that the function of Example 1 also has a *one-sided* limit at $x = 1$ when x is restricted to values greater than 1. In this case, however, the limit is 5. The limit is denoted

$$\lim_{x \to 1^+} f(x) = 5.$$

Definition   a. $f(x)$ has the **limit L as x approaches a from the right,** written

$$\lim_{x \to a^+} f(x) = L,$$

if and only if to each $\epsilon > 0$ there is a $\delta > 0$ such that $f(x) \in \langle L - \epsilon, L + \epsilon \rangle$ whenever $x \in \langle a, a + \delta \rangle$.

b. $f(x)$ has the **limit L as x approaches a from the left,** written

$$\lim_{x \to a^-} f(x) = L$$

if and only if to each $\epsilon > 0$ there is a $\delta > 0$ such that $f(x) \in \langle L - \epsilon, L + \epsilon \rangle$ whenever $x \in \langle a - \delta, a \rangle$.

EXAMPLE 2.   Graph the following.

$$f(x) = \begin{cases} \dfrac{x^2 + x}{x} & \text{for } x \neq 0 \\ 5 & \text{for } x = 0 \end{cases}$$

By inspection determine $\lim_{x \to 0} f(x)$, $\lim_{x \to 0^+} f(x)$ and $\lim_{x \to 0^-} f(x)$.

The graph is shown at the right.
By inspection

$$\lim_{x \to 0} f(x) = 1,$$

$$\lim_{x \to 0^+} f(x) = 1,$$

$$\lim_{x \to 0^-} f(x) = 1$$

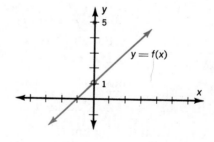

Notice that $f(0) = 5$ and is not equal to $\lim_{x \to 0} f(x)$. Also note that the limit from the left and the limit from the right equal $\lim_{x \to 0} f(x)$. Whenever a limit at a point exists, it is equal to the right and left hand limits. Also, whenever the right and left hand limits at a point both exist and are equal, the limit exists and is equal to the common value of the right and left hand limits.

WRITTEN EXERCISES

A ━━ In Exercises 1–9 use the given L and ϵ to find a neighborhood of a (if possible) so that $f(x) \in \langle L - \epsilon, L + \epsilon \rangle$ when $x \in \langle a - \delta, a + \delta \rangle$.

1. $f(x) = x + 3 \qquad L = 5, a = 2, \epsilon = \frac{1}{10}$

2. $f(x) = 2x - 3 \qquad L = -3, a = 0, \epsilon = \frac{1}{100}$

3. $f(x) = 3x + 2 \qquad L = 8, a = 2, \epsilon = \frac{1}{100}$

4. $f(x) = \frac{2}{3}x - 1 \qquad L = 0, a = 3, \epsilon = \frac{1}{100}$

5. $f(x) = \begin{cases} x - 2 & \text{for } x < 2 \\ -1 & \text{for } x = 2 \\ x - 4 & \text{for } x > 2 \end{cases} \qquad L = 0, a = 2, \epsilon = \frac{1}{2}$

6. $f(x) = \begin{cases} x - 2 & \text{for } x < 2 \\ -1 & \text{for } x = 2 \\ x - 4 & \text{for } x > 2 \end{cases} \qquad L = -2, a = 2, \epsilon = \frac{1}{2}$

7. $f(x) = \begin{cases} x - 2 & \text{for } x < 2 \\ -1 & \text{for } x = 2 \\ x - 4 & \text{for } x > 2 \end{cases} \qquad L = -1, a = 2, \epsilon = \frac{1}{2}$

8. $f(x) = \begin{cases} x + 2 & \text{for } x < 2 \\ 2x & \text{for } x \geq 2 \end{cases} \qquad L = 4, a = 2, \epsilon = \frac{1}{100}$

B **9.** $f(x) = x^2, L = 1, a = 1, \epsilon = \frac{1}{100}$ (*Hint:* Restrict δ to values less than 1. Then $|x + 1| < 3$.)

━━ In Exercises 10–13 find $\lim\limits_{x \to a} f(x)$, $\lim\limits_{x \to a^+} f(x)$ and $\lim\limits_{x \to a^-} f(x)$ (if possible) for the given function at the given point a. A graph will be of assistance.

10. $f(x) = \begin{cases} 1 & \text{for } x > 0 \\ 0 & \text{for } x = 0 \\ -1 & \text{for } x < 0 \end{cases} \qquad a = 0$

11. $f(x) = \begin{cases} |x| & \text{for } x \neq 0 \\ 5 & \text{for } x = 0 \end{cases} \qquad a = 0$

12. $f(x) = \begin{cases} \dfrac{2x^2 + x}{x} & \text{for } x \neq 0 \\ \text{undefined} & \text{for } x = 0 \end{cases} \qquad a = 0$

13. $f(x) = \begin{cases} x - 2 & \text{for } x < 2 \\ -1 & \text{for } x = 2 \\ x - 4 & \text{for } x > 2 \end{cases} \qquad a = 2$

14. Consider the following definition of the limit of a function at a point a.

> **Definition** $\lim\limits_{x \to a} f(x) = L$ if and only if $f(x)$ can be found as close as you please to L provided x is sufficiently close to a.

Compare this definition with the definition as given in the text. What are the strengths and weaknesses of each?

C **15.** Explain in your own words why "$\lim\limits_{x \to a} f(x) = L$" is equivalent to "$\lim\limits_{x \to a^-} f(x) = L$ and $\lim\limits_{x \to a^+} f(x) = L$."

6-3 Limit Theorems and Polynomials

Constructing a proof of $\lim\limits_{x \to a} f(x) = L$ in accordance with the definition given in Section 6-2 can be quite complicated even for the simplest functions.

EXAMPLE 1. Prove $\lim\limits_{x \to 2} x^2 = 4$.

Solution: Let $\epsilon > 0$ be given. Thus a δ must be found so that
$$x \in \langle 2 - \delta, 2 + \delta \rangle$$
and $x \neq 2$ implies $x^2 \in \langle 4 - \epsilon, 4 + \epsilon \rangle$. Restating these conditions using absolute values, you have
$$0 < |x - 2| < \delta \text{ implies } |x^2 - 4| < \epsilon. \qquad \text{1}$$
That is, it must be shown that
$$|x^2 - 4| = |(x + 2)(x - 2)| = |x + 2| \cdot |x - 2|$$
is as small as you please when x is sufficiently near 2. The second factor, $|x - 2|$, is certainly small if x is near 2; and the first factor, $|x + 2|$, is near 4 when x is near 2. To make this precise, first require $\delta \leq 1$. (There is nothing special about 1. Another positive number could be used and not change the nature of the argument. The details would be different, however.) If x is within a distance less than δ of 2, then certainly $|x - 2| < \delta \leq 1$.

Thus you have the following.

$$|x - 2| < 1 \qquad \text{iff}$$
$$-1 < x - 2 < 1 \qquad \text{iff}$$
$$3 < x + 2 < 5$$

Thus certainly

$$|x + 2| < 5.$$

Hence $|x^2 - 4|$ will be less than ϵ if simultaneously

$$|x + 2| < 5 \qquad\qquad\qquad 2$$

and

$$|x - 2| < \frac{\epsilon}{5} \qquad\qquad\qquad 3$$

because you want $|x^2 - 4| = |x + 2| \cdot |x - 2| < 5 \cdot \frac{\epsilon}{5} = \epsilon.$

Since $\delta \leq 1$, choose δ to be the smaller of 1 and $\frac{\epsilon}{5}$. That is, choose $\delta = \frac{\epsilon}{5}$ for $\epsilon \leq 5$ and choose $\delta = 1$ otherwise. This will force both inequalities 2 and 3 to be true. The proof is complete.

It would be tedious to prove each limit that you encountered in this manner, using only the definition. Several theorems follow which simplify matters considerably, but their proofs will not be given.

Theorem 6–1 If $f(x)$ is equal to a constant k, then $\lim_{x \to a} f(x)$ exists and $\lim_{x \to a} f(x) = k$.

Theorem 6–2 If $f(x) = x^m$ where m is a positive real number, $\lim_{x \to a} x^m = a^m$.

EXAMPLE 2. Evaluate the following two limits.

a. $\lim_{x \to 2} 3$
b. $\lim_{x \to 2} x^4$

Solutions:

a. $\lim_{x \to 2} 3 = 3$ by Theorem 6–1

b. $\lim_{x \to 2} x^4 = 2^4 = 16$ by Theorem 6–2

The next two theorems indicate how the limit of the sum, difference, product, and quotient of two functions may be found.

Theorem 6–3 If $\lim_{x \to a} f(x) = L$ and $\lim_{x \to a} g(x) = M$, then

  i. $\lim_{x \to a} [f(x) + g(x)] = L + M$,

  ii. $\lim_{x \to a} [f(x) - g(x)] = L - M$, and

  iii. $\lim_{x \to a} [f(x) \cdot g(x)] = L \cdot M$.

Parts **i** and **iii** extend to the sum and product of any finite number of functions.

Theorem 6–4 If $\lim_{x \to a} f(x) = L$ and $\lim_{x \to a} g(x) = M$, $M \neq 0$ $g(x) \neq 0$, then

$$\lim_{x \to a} \frac{f(x)}{g(x)} = \frac{L}{M} .$$

These theorems are particularly useful in finding limits of polynomial functions. An expression of the form

$$a_0 x^n + a_1 x^{n-1} + a_2 x^{n-2} + \cdots + a_{n-1} x + a_n,$$

where n denotes a nonnegative integer, is a **polynomial in x.** If x is a variable with domain D, then any polynomial in x defines a **polynomial function** whose domain is D. The value of the polynomial function is found by replacing x by a member of the domain D.

The following example shows how $\lim_{x \to a} P(x)$ relates to $P(a)$, the value of the polynomial function at a.

EXAMPLE 3. Let $P(x) = 3x^2 + 2x + 1$. Find $\lim_{x \to 2} P(x)$ and $P(2)$.

Solution: $P(2) = 3(2)^2 + 2(2) + 1 = 3 \cdot 4 + 4 + 1 = 17$.

$\lim_{x \to 2} P(x) = \lim_{x \to 2} (3x^2 + 2x + 1)$

$\qquad = \lim_{x \to 2} 3x^2 + \lim_{x \to 2} 2x + \lim_{x \to 2} 1$ ⟵   **By Theorem 6-3i**

$\qquad = 3 \cdot \lim_{x \to 2} x^2 + 2 \cdot \lim_{x \to 2} x + \lim_{x \to 2} 1$ ⟵   **By Theorems 6-1, 6-3iii**

$\qquad = 3 \cdot 2^2 + 2 \cdot 2 + 1$ ⟵   **By Theorem 6-2**

$\qquad = 17.$ Thus $\lim_{x \to 2} P(x) = P(2)$

The following theorem states this result more formally.

> **Theorem 6–5** If $P(x)$ is a polynomial.
> $$\lim_{x \to a} P(x) = P(a)$$

One of the reasons for studying polynomial functions is that they are an excellent example of a function that is *continuous*. An intuitive way to describe *continuity on an interval* is to say that if you can trace the graph of a function with your pencil without the pencil tip leaving the paper, then the function is continuous on that interval. (Polynomial functions are noteworthy for being continuous on *any* interval.) Before considering a precise definition of continuity on an interval, it is necessary to define continuity *at a point*.

> **Definition** A function $f(x)$ is **continuous at** $x = a$ if and only if the three conditions following are satisfied:
>
> i. $f(x)$ is defined at $x = a$,
>
> ii. $\lim_{x \to a} f(x)$ exists, and
>
> iii. $\lim_{x \to a} f(x) = f(a)$.
>
> A function which fails to satisfy one or more of conditions i., ii., or iii., at $x = a$ is said to be **discontinuous** at $x = a$. A function is said to be **continuous on an interval** if and only if it is continuous at each point of the interval.

It is important to realize that although it is natural to think of continuity in connection with intervals, continuity is fundamentally a property that a function has or does not have at a particular *point*.

EXAMPLE 4. Let $f(x) = 4$ for all real x. Show that $f(x)$ is continuous at $x = 7$.

Solution: Check each criterion in the definition.

  i. $f(7)$ is defined.   ←——— **7 is a real number.**

  ii. $\lim_{x \to 7} 4$ exists.   ←——— **By Theorem 6-1**

  iii. $\lim_{x \to 7} 4 = f(7) = 4$ ←——— **By Theorem 6-1**

CLASSROOM EXERCISES

▬ Evaluate each limit.

1. $\lim_{x \to 4} x^2 - 5$

2. $\lim_{x \to 3} \frac{x-3}{x-2}$

3. $\lim_{x \to -1} x^3 - 3x$

4. $\lim_{x \to 2} (x+1)(x-1)$

5. $\lim_{x \to 10} 3$

6. $\lim_{x \to -2} 3x^2 + (x+1)^2$

WRITTEN EXERCISES

A ▬ In Exercises 1–14 find the indicated limit (if possible).

1. $\lim_{x \to 3} (2x^2 - 5x + 1)$

2. $\lim_{x \to 2} (-3x^2 + 1)$

3. $\lim_{x \to -2} (x^2 + 2x - 3)$

4. $\lim_{x \to -3} (-\frac{1}{3}x^2 - 2x + 8)$

5. $\lim_{x \to -2} \left(\frac{3x^2 - 5}{2x + 17} \right)$

6. $\lim_{x \to -1} \left(\frac{x^2 - 1}{x} \right)$

7. $\lim_{x \to -1} \left(\frac{x}{x^2 - 1} \right)$

8. $\lim_{x \to 1} \left[\frac{(x-2)(x+1)}{x^2 - x - 2} \right]$

9. $\lim_{x \to 3} (x^5 - 240)$

10. $\lim_{x \to 3} [x(x+1)(x+2)]$

11. $\lim_{x \to 4} (3x^2 - 5x)$

12. $\lim_{x \to -5} \left(\frac{1}{x} \right)$

13. $\lim_{x \to 1} \left(\frac{4x^2 - 1}{5x + 2} \right)$

14. $\lim_{x \to 2} \frac{3x}{4x - 7}$

B Each function is discontinuous at the point $x = a$. Determine which of the conditions which define continuity are not satisfied. Graph each function over the given interval.

15. $f(x) = \begin{cases} \frac{2x^2 + x}{x} & \text{for } x \neq 0 \\ 0 & \text{for } x = 0 \end{cases}$ $a = 0, [-2, 2]$

16. $f(x) = \begin{cases} \frac{1}{x} & \text{for } x \neq 0 \\ \text{undefined} & \text{for } x = 0 \end{cases}$ $a = 0, [-2, 2]$

17. $f(x) = \begin{cases} x^2 + 2 & \text{for } x < 0 \\ 4 & \text{for } x = 0 \\ x + 2 & \text{for } x > 0 \end{cases}$ $a = 0, [-2, 2]$

18. $f(x) = \begin{cases} 2x - 3 & \text{for } x < 2 \\ 1 & \text{for } x = 2 \\ -x & \text{for } x > 2 \end{cases}$ $a = 2, [0, 4]$

Use the pattern of proof in Example 1 to find the required limit and to prove that it is the limit by direct use of the definition.

19. $\lim\limits_{x \to 2} 3x$

20. $\lim\limits_{x \to 2} \dfrac{1}{x}$

21. $\lim\limits_{x \to 1} x^2 + 2$

22. $\lim\limits_{x \to 2} \dfrac{3x+1}{2x}$

23. Prove: $\lim\limits_{x \to a} k = k$ (Theorem 6–1).

24. Prove: $\lim\limits_{x \to a} x^m = a^m$, m a positive integer (Theorem 6–2).

C **25.** Prove Theorem 6–5.

■ **26.** Prove that every polynomial $P(x)$ is continuous at $x = a$.

6–4   Rational Functions and Discontinuities

An expression of the form

$$\frac{P(x)}{Q(x)}$$

where $P(x)$ and $Q(x)$ are polynomials is a rational expression in x. If x is a variable with domain D then a rational expression in x defines a rational function with domain D. A value of a rational function $R(x)$ at $x = a$ can be found by substituting a for x in $R(x)$.

EXAMPLE 1.   Let $P(x) = 2x^2 + 3x$, $Q(x) = x + 5$.   What is the rational function

$$R(x) = \frac{P(x)}{Q(x)} \, ?$$

Solution: $\qquad\qquad R(x) = \dfrac{2x^2 + 3x}{x + 5}$

Find the value of $R(x)$ at $x = -2$.

$$R(-2) = \frac{2(-2)^2 + 3(-2)}{(-2) + 5}$$

$$= \frac{2 \cdot 4 - 6}{3}$$

$$= \tfrac{2}{3}$$

Whereas polynomial functions are always continuous at every finite point, a rational function may be *discontinuous* at one or more points. There are essentially two types of discontinuities for rational functions: (1) removable discontinuities and (2) discontinuities associated with the nonexistence of at least one one-sided limit.

EXAMPLE 2.   (A removable discontinuity.)

Consider the function defined by the following equation.   (See Figure 5 below.)

$$f(x) = \frac{x^2 - x}{x - 1}, \quad x \in R$$

Since

$$x - 1 = 0 \quad \text{when } x = 1,$$

$f(x)$ is not defined for $x = 1$.   Thus $f(x)$ is not continuous at $x = 1$.

On the other hand,

$$\lim_{x \to 1} \frac{x^2 - x}{x - 1} = 1.$$

To see this, factor the numerator of $\frac{x^2 - x}{x - 1}$.

Since

$$x^2 - x = x(x - 1)$$

then

$$\frac{x^2 - x}{x - 1} = \frac{x(x - 1)}{x - 1}.$$

In determining the value of $\lim\limits_{x \to 1} \frac{x(x - 1)}{x - 1}$, *x can never be equal to one.*
Thus $x - 1$ is never equal to zero.   Moreover under these restrictions
$\frac{x - 1}{x - 1}$ *always* equals 1. ($x \neq 1$)

Thus

$$\lim_{x \to 1} \frac{x(x - 1)}{x - 1} = \lim_{x \to 1} x = 1.$$

Consequently, $f(x) = \frac{x^2 - x}{x - 1}$ has a removable discontinuity at
$x = 1$.   The discontinuity can be removed by *defining* $f(x) = 1$, for
$x = 1$.   In the graph, the discontinuity can be thought of as a hole!
By defining $f(x) = 1$ when $x = 1$, the hole is filled and the resulting function is continuous at every finite point.   (The reason that this approach works, of course, is that

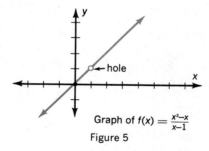

Graph of $f(x) = \frac{x^2 - x}{x - 1}$

Figure 5

it is permissible to define $f(1)$ any way you please since there exists no prior definition of $f(1)$ with which to be in conflict.)

There is a general procedure implicit in Example 2.   If both the numerator and denominator of a rational function $R(x) = \frac{P(x)}{Q(x)}$ approach 0 as $x \longrightarrow a$, then you may be able to factor out the common terms and find the limit of the new function.

EXAMPLE 3. (At least one one-sided limit fails to exist.)

Consider the function

$$f(x) = \frac{1}{x - 1} \qquad x \in \mathbf{R}.$$

$f(x)$ is not defined at $x = 1$ because division by zero is not defined. Hence, $f(x)$ is discontinuous at $x = 1$. Notice that $x - 1$ cannot be factored out. So the discontinuity is not removable.

However, the question remains: What happens to $f(x) = \frac{1}{x-1}$ as $x \longrightarrow 1$, but is not equal to 1? Considering first values of $x > 1$, it is clear that $x - 1$ is very small and positive for values of x very close to 1. Since $x - 1$ is *small* and *positive*, $f(x) = \frac{1}{x-1}$ is *large* and *positive* when x is close to 1. In fact $\frac{1}{x-1}$ can be made larger than any predetermined large real number by taking x close enough to 1. This is illustrated below.

x	$\dfrac{1}{x-1}$
1.2	5
1.1	10
1.05	20
1.01	100
1.001	1000

Thus the one-sided limit

$$\lim_{x \to 1+} \frac{1}{x - 1}$$

does not exist; it equals no *finite real number*.

Since $f(x) = \frac{1}{x-1}$ increases without bound as $x \longrightarrow 1^+$, it is convenient to have a simple manner to indicate such a state of affairs. The statement " $\lim\limits_{x \to 1+} \frac{1}{x-1} = +\infty$ " is used to indicate this. In general, the statement

$$\lim_{x \to a^+} f(x) = +\infty \quad (\text{or} -\infty)$$

means that as $x \longrightarrow a^+$, the function assumes values larger (smaller) than a preassigned real number M.

In a similar manner, $\lim\limits_{x \to 1-} \frac{1}{x-1} = -\infty$, for when x is less than 1 and close to 1, $\frac{1}{x-1}$ is negative and large in absolute value. Consequently, $\frac{1}{x-1}$ decreases without bound as $x \longrightarrow 1^-$.

The line $x = 1$ is an *asymptote* for the function $f(x) = \frac{1}{x-1}$. An **asymptote** is a line that the graph of a function approaches as the variable x nears a fixed point a or tends to $+\infty$ or $-\infty$. A rational function $R(x) = \frac{P(x)}{Q(x)}$ has a *vertical asymptote* at a point a where $P(a) \neq 0$ and $Q(a) = 0$. For $f(x) = \frac{1}{x-1}$, the line $x = 1$ is a vertical asymptote.

$R(x) = \frac{P(x)}{Q(x)}$ has a *horizontal asymptote* $y = b$ whenever $\lim\limits_{x \to +\infty} R(x) = b$ or $\lim\limits_{x \to -\infty} R(x) = b$. For $f(x) = \frac{1}{x-1}$, $\lim\limits_{x \to +\infty} \frac{1}{x-1} = 0$. Thus $y = 0$ is an horizontal asymptote for $f(x)$.

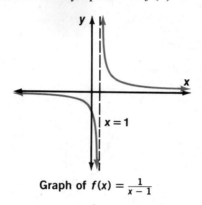

$x = 1$

Graph of $f(x) = \frac{1}{x-1}$

CLASSROOM EXERCISES

━━ Identify the discontinuities of each function and their nature.

1. $f(x) = \frac{x^2 - 4}{x + 2}$

2. $f(x) = \frac{x - 2}{x^2 - 4}$

3. $f(x) = \frac{1}{x^2 - 4}$

4. $f(x) = \begin{cases} \dfrac{1}{x - 2} & \text{for } x < 2 \\ x + 2 & \text{for } x \geq 2 \end{cases}$

WRITTEN EXERCISES

A ━━ In Exercises 1–4 evaluate each rational function at the point specified.

1. $f(x) = \frac{x^2 - 2x}{x^2 + 2}$ $x = 3$

2. $f(x) = \frac{-2x^3 + 3x}{x - 4}$ $x = -2$

3. $f(x) = \frac{1}{x^3 + 2x^2 + 1}$ $x = -2$

4. $f(x) = \frac{-(x + 2)(x - 1)}{(-x + 1)(x - 3)}$ $x = \frac{1}{2}$

In Exercises 5–14 determine the real number(s) if any for which each function is undefined.

5. $f(x) = \dfrac{x}{x^2 - x - 2}$

6. $f(x) = \dfrac{1}{x^2 + 2x - 2}$

7. $f(x) = \dfrac{x^2 + 2x - 1}{x}$

8. $f(x) = \dfrac{(x - 2)(x - 1)(x - 3)}{x(x + 2)(x + 1)}$

9. $f(x) = \dfrac{x^3 - 1}{(x - 1)(x^2 + x + 1)}$

10. $f(x) = \dfrac{x - 2}{x^2 + 2}$

11. $f(x) = \dfrac{x^2 + 2}{x - 2}$

12. $f(x) = \dfrac{(x + 1)}{x^3 + 1}$

13. $f(x) = \dfrac{1}{x^4 + 1}$

14. $f(x) = \dfrac{x(x - 1)}{x(x - 1)}$

In Exercises 15–26 find the indicated limit. When an indicated limit does not exist, find the two one-sided limits. Use the notation $\lim\limits_{x \to a^+} f(x) = +\infty(-\infty)$ and $\lim\limits_{x \to a^-} f(x) = +\infty(-\infty)$.

15. $\lim\limits_{x \to 2} \dfrac{(2x - x^2)}{2 - x}$

16. $\lim\limits_{x \to -1} \left(\dfrac{x^2 + 4x + 3}{x^2 - x - 2} \right)$

17. $\lim\limits_{x \to 5} \dfrac{x^2 - 25}{x^2 - 4x - 5}$

18. $\lim\limits_{x \to -1} \dfrac{x}{x + 1}$

19. $\lim\limits_{x \to 2} \dfrac{x^2 - 4x + 4}{x - 2}$

20. $\lim\limits_{x \to 2} -\dfrac{x - 2}{x^2 - 4x + 4}$

21. $\lim\limits_{x \to -4} \dfrac{x}{x^2 + 16}$

22. $\lim\limits_{x \to -3} \dfrac{x + 3}{(x + 3)(x^2 + 6x + 9)}$

23. $\lim\limits_{x \to 3} \dfrac{x + 3}{(x - 3)^2}$

24. $\lim\limits_{x \to 0} \dfrac{2}{x^2 - 2x}$

25. $\lim\limits_{x \to 2} \dfrac{2}{x^2 - 2x}$

26. $\lim\limits_{x \to 1} \dfrac{2}{x^2 - 2x}$

In Exercises 27–30 find the horizontal asymptotes using the limits: $\lim\limits_{x \to +\infty} f(x)$ and $\lim\limits_{x \to -\infty} f(x)$.

27. $f(x) = \dfrac{2x + 3}{x}$

28. $f(x) = \dfrac{2x + 3}{x^2 - 4}$

29. $f(x) = \dfrac{3x^2 - 2x}{x^2}$

30. $f(x) = \dfrac{3x^2 - 2x}{4x^2 + 4x + 1}$

31. Find all vertical asymptotes for the functions given in Exercises 27–30.

B In Exercises 32–42 you are given that $f(x) = \dfrac{x + 1}{x(x + 1)(x - 2)}$.

32. What type of discontinuity does $f(x)$ have at $x = -1$, at $x = 0$, at $x = 2$?

33. Does $f(x)$ have any vertical asymptotes? If so identify them.

━━ Find the following limits.

34. $\lim\limits_{x \to -\infty} f(x)$

35. $\lim\limits_{x \to -1^-} f(x)$

36. $\lim\limits_{x \to -1^+} f(x)$

37. $\lim_{x \to 0^-} f(x)$ **38.** $\lim_{x \to 0^+} f(x)$ **39.** $\lim_{x \to 2^-} f(x)$

40. $\lim_{x \to 2^+} f(x)$ **41.** $\lim_{x \to +\infty} f(x)$

42. Sketch the graph of $f(x)$.

C ▬▬ A rational function $R(x) = \dfrac{P(x)}{Q(x)}$ for which $\lim_{x \to a} P(x) = 0$ and $\lim_{x \to a} Q(x) = 0$ is said to be **indeterminate at** $x = a$ because $\lim_{x \to a} R(x) = \lim_{x \to a} \dfrac{P(x)}{Q(x)} = \dfrac{0}{0}$. The symbol "$\dfrac{0}{0}$" has no meaning and does not in itself imply anything about the limit of $R(x)$. It happens that the true limit may be any finite real number or $P(x)$ may increase or decrease without bound. Find the limit (if possible) of each indeterminate form.

43. $\lim_{x \to 1} \dfrac{x-1}{x-1}$ **44.** $\lim_{x \to 0} \dfrac{x}{x^2}$ **45.** $\lim_{x \to 2} \dfrac{(x-2)^2}{x-2}$

46. $\lim_{x \to 0} \dfrac{17x}{x}$ **47.** $\lim_{x \to 1} \dfrac{x-1}{1-x}$

▬▬ Find a rational function $R(x)$ whose numerator and denominator tend to zero as x approaches a but such that $\lim_{x \to a} R(x)$ equals each of the following.

48. -4 **49.** 1000 **50.** 0 **51.** $-\infty$ **52.** a

▬▬ Very often $\lim_{x \to +\infty} \dfrac{P(x)}{Q(x)}$ appears to have the form $\dfrac{\infty}{\infty}$ because $\lim_{x \to +\infty} P(x) = \infty$ and $\lim_{x \to +\infty} Q(x) = \infty$. For example, if

$$P(x) = 3x$$

and

$$Q(x) = x^2,$$

then

$$\lim_{x \to +\infty} \dfrac{P(x)}{Q(x)}$$

has the form

$$\dfrac{\infty}{\infty}.$$

This is an indeterminate form similar to the form $\dfrac{0}{0}$. Again the function $\dfrac{P(x)}{Q(x)}$ may have any finite number as its limit as $x \longrightarrow +\infty$ or it may increase or decrease without bound. Find the true limits of each indeterminate form.

53. $\lim_{x \to +\infty} \dfrac{3x}{x^2}$ **54.** $\lim_{x \to +\infty} \dfrac{3x^2}{x^2}$ **55.** $\lim_{x \to +\infty} \dfrac{3x^3}{x^2}$

56. $\lim_{x \to +\infty} \dfrac{-3x^3}{x^2}$ **57.** $\lim_{x \to +\infty} \dfrac{2x^2 + 2x^1}{5x^2}$

━━━ Graph each sequence and the associated function of a real variable. What appears to be the limit of each as $n \to +\infty$ or as $x \to +\infty$? (Section 6-1)

1. $a_n = \frac{n+1}{n}$, $f(x) = \frac{x+1}{x}$

2. $a_n = \frac{1}{n_2}$, $f(x) = \frac{1}{x_2}$

━━━ Find a neighborhood of a so that $f(x) \in \langle L - \epsilon, L + \epsilon \rangle$ when $x \in \langle a - \delta, a + \delta \rangle$. (Section 6-2)

3. $f(x) = x + 6$ $L = 8$, $a = 2$, $\epsilon = \frac{1}{10}$

4. $f(x) = 2x - 1$ $L = 5$, $a = 3$, $\epsilon = \frac{1}{100}$

━━━ Find the indicated limits. (Section 6-3)

5. $\lim\limits_{x \to 5} (-2x^2 + 10x - 1)$

6. $\lim\limits_{x \to 3} \frac{x-5}{x+3}$

━━━ Determine the real number(s) if any for which each function is undefined. (Section 6-4)

7. $f(x) = \frac{3x^2 - 3}{x + 2}$

8. $f(x) = \frac{x^2 + 4x + 4}{x^2 - 4}$

━━━ Find the two one-sided limits at each point of discontinuity. (Section 6-4).

9. $f(x) = \frac{3x^3 - 3}{x + 2}$

10. $f(x) = \frac{(x+2)^2}{x^2 - 4}$

6–5   The Derived Function: An Application of Limits

Previous sections were devoted to limits of functions as $x \to a$, $x \to +\infty$, or $x \to -\infty$. Here a new function $f'(x)$ is derived from a function $f(x)$ by using limits. The discussion will be restricted to real-valued functions of a real variable x which are defined in a neighborhood of the particular value of x under consideration.

Definition   Given a function $y = f(x)$, $f(x)$ is said to have a derived function at x if and only if the following limit exists and is finite; the function $f'(x)$ defined by the limit is called the **derived function of $f(x)$**:

$$f'(x) = \lim\limits_{h \to 0} \frac{f(x+h) - f(x)}{h}$$

The expression $\dfrac{f(x+h) - f(x)}{h}$ can be interpreted as the *slope* of a line passing through two points on the graph of the function $f(x)$. The geometric interpretation of the *limit* of this expression as $h \longrightarrow 0$ is important and will be considered in the next section.

For any particular value of x, the limit in the definition of $f'(x)$ will be a number; that is, the value of the derived function at that value of x.

EXAMPLE 1. Find the derived function of $f(x) = x^2 + 1$ at $x = 2$.

Solution:
$$f(2 + h) - f(2) = (2 + h)^2 + 1 - (2^2 + 1)$$
$$= 4 + 4h + h^2 + 1 - 4 - 1$$
$$= 4h + h^2$$

$$\dfrac{f(2 + h) - f(2)}{h} = \dfrac{4h + h^2}{h} \quad \longleftarrow \quad \boldsymbol{h \neq 0}$$

$$= 4 + h$$

$$\lim_{h \to 0} \dfrac{f(2) + h) - f(2)}{h} = \lim_{h \to 0} (4 + h)$$

$$= 4$$

The derived function of $f(x) = x^2 + 1$ at $x = 2$ is equal to 4: $f'(2) = 4$.

EXAMPLE 2. Find the derived function of $f(x) = \dfrac{1}{x}$ at $x = 3$.

Solution:
$$f'(3) = \lim_{h \to 0} \dfrac{f(3 + h) - f(3)}{h} \quad \longleftarrow \quad \textbf{By definition}$$

$$f(3 + h) = \dfrac{1}{3 + h}$$

$$f(3) = \tfrac{1}{3}$$

$$f(3 + h) - f(3) = \dfrac{1}{3 + h} - \dfrac{1}{3}$$

$$= \dfrac{3 - (3 + h)}{(3 + h) \cdot 3}, \quad \longleftarrow \quad \substack{\textbf{Combined} \\ \textbf{fractions}}$$

$$\dfrac{f(3 + h) - f(3)}{h} = \dfrac{-h}{h \cdot (3 + h) \cdot 3}$$

$$= \dfrac{-1}{3(3 + h)},$$

$$f'(3) = \lim_{h \to 0} \frac{-1}{3(3 + h)}$$

$$= \frac{-1}{3^2} = -\frac{1}{9}$$

so

$$f'(3) = -\tfrac{1}{9}.$$

A general expression for $f'(x)$ can be derived in a similar manner. All that need be done is substitute a symbol like x_0 for the particular value of x. Evaluation of the resulting expression at $x = a$ gives the value of the derived function at $x = a$ (when it exists).

EXAMPLE 3. Find the derived function of $f(x) = x^2 + 1$ at a general point $x = x_0$.

Solution:
$$f(x_0) = x_0^2 + 1$$
$$f(x_0 + h) = (x_0 + h)^2 + 1$$
$$= x_0^2 + 2hx_0 + h^2 + 1$$

So
$$f(x_0 + h) - f(x_0) = x_0^2 + 2hx_0 + h^2 + 1 - x_0^2 - 1$$
$$= 2hx_0 + h^2.$$

Then
$$\frac{f(x_0 + h) - f(x_0)}{h} = \frac{2hx_0 + h^2}{h}$$
$$= 2x_0 + h$$
$$f'(x_0) = \lim_{h \to 0} (2x_0 + h) = 2x_0.$$

Thus $f'(x_0) = 2x_0$ when $f(x) = x^2 + 1$.

Since $2x_0$ is defined for all x_0 which are finite, the subscript is dropped and the derived function $f'(x)$ for $f(x) = x^2 + 1$ is $f'(x) = 2x$ for any real number x.

For example, $f'(2) = 2 \cdot 2 = 4$, which is the same as the result in Example 1.

EXAMPLE 4. Find the derived function of $f(x) = \frac{1}{x}$, $x \ne 0$.

Solution:
$$f(x_0 + h) = \frac{1}{x_0 + h}, \quad f(x_0) = \frac{1}{x_0} \quad \text{and}$$

$$f(x_0 + h) - f(x_0) = \frac{1}{x_0 + h} - \frac{1}{x_0}$$

$$= \frac{x_0 - x_0 - h}{(x_0 + h)x_0}$$

so $\quad \dfrac{f(x_0 + h) - f(x_0)}{h} = \dfrac{-h}{h \cdot (x_0 + h) \cdot x_0}$ and

$$f'(x_0) = \lim_{h \to 0} \frac{-1}{(x_0 + h)x_0} = -\frac{1}{x_0{}^2}.$$

Thus

$$f'(x) = -\frac{1}{x^2}, \quad x \neq 0.$$

If $x = 3$, $f'(x) = -\frac{1}{3^2} = -\frac{1}{9}$ which corresponds to the result of Example 2.

CLASSROOM EXERCISES

For each function, find $\dfrac{f(x + h) - f(x)}{h}$ in simplest form.

1. $f(x) = 3x^2$ **2.** $f(x) = x^2 + 2x$ **3.** $f(x) = 3x - 5$

4. $f(x) = \frac{1}{3x}$ **5.** $f(x) = \frac{5}{x}$ **6.** $f(x) = \frac{1}{x^2}$

For each function, find $f'(x)$.

7. $f(x) = 3x^2$ **8.** $f(x) = x^2 + 2x$ **9.** $f(x) = 3x - 5$

10. $f(x) = \frac{1}{3x}$ **11.** $f(x) = \frac{5}{x}$ **12.** $f(x) = \frac{1}{x^2}$

WRITTEN EXERCISES

A Use the definition of derived function at $x = a$ to find the indicated values.

1. $f'(3)$ where $f(x) = 2x + 5$

2. $f'(2)$ where $f(x) = x^2 + x$

3. $f'(0)$ where $f(x) = x^2 - 2$

4. $f'(7)$ where $f(x) = 4x - 17$

5. $f'(-1)$ where $f(x) = \dfrac{1}{x - 1}$

6. $f'(2)$ where $f(x) = -x^2$

7. $f'(-3)$ where $f(x) = -5x + 6$

8. $f'(2)$ where $f(x) = -\dfrac{1}{x} \ (x \neq 0)$

9. $f'(-2)$ where $f(x) = -x^2 + x$

10. $f'(a)$ where $f(x) = x + 2x^2$

B ___ Find the derived function of $f(x)$ at a general point.

11. $f(x) = 3x^2 - 1$ **12.** $f(x) = \dfrac{1}{x+1}$ $(x \neq -1)$

13. $f(x) = x^2 - 3x$ **14.** $f(x) = \dfrac{-1}{x^2}$

15. $f(x) = x^3$ **16.** $f(x) = \dfrac{x}{x+1}$ $(x \neq -1)$

17. $f(x) = x^2 - x$ **18.** $f(x) = \dfrac{1}{x^3}$

19. $f(x) = \sqrt{x}$ **20.** $f(x) = x^{\frac{1}{3}}$

C   The *one-sided* derived function at a point is defined in a manner similar to the one-sided limit at a point. That is, the right (left) derived function of $f(x)$ at $x = a$ is the one-sided limit

$$\lim_{h \to 0^+} \frac{f(a+h) - f(a)}{h} \quad \left(\lim_{h \to 0^-} \frac{f(a+h) - f(a)}{h} \right).$$

21. Find the right and left derived functions at $x = 2$ of the following function.

$$f(x) = \begin{cases} x + 2 & \text{for } x < 2 \\ 2x & \text{for } x \geq 2 \end{cases}$$

22. Find the right and left derived functions at $x = 0$ of the following function.

$$f(x) = \begin{cases} -x & \text{for } x \leq 0 \\ x & \text{for } x > 0 \end{cases}$$

23. Find the right and left derived functions at $x = 1$ of the following function.

$$f(x) = \begin{cases} x^2 & \text{for } x < 1 \\ 3x - 2 & \text{for } x \geq 1 \end{cases}$$

24. Find the right and left derived functions at $x = 2$ of the following function.

$$f(x) = \begin{cases} x + 4 & \text{for } x < 2 \\ x^2 & \text{for } x \geq 2 \end{cases}$$

25. Explain in your own words why a function has a derived function at a point if and only if the right and left derived functions are equal at the point.

26. Explain why a function is continuous at a point $x = x_0$ whenever the derived function at $x = x_0$ exists. (*Hint:* consider $f(x_0 + h) - f(x_0) = h \cdot \dfrac{f(x_0 + h) - f(x_0)}{h}$ and take limits of both sides.)

Applying Limits
Audio Technology

Feedback, the ability of a mechanical system to adjust to changes in input, is an important concept for **audio technicians.** They must design systems with built-in feedback, so that the system output is not greatly disturbed by random disturbances in the input.

Suppose the output of a system is described by the equation

$$y = 10x$$

where x is the value of the input. This is an example of direct variation and, thus, changes in the output are directly proportional to changes in input of the system. The constant, 10, describes the **gain** of the system, the ratio of the output to the input.

An automatically adjusting system is described by the equation

$$y = A\left(x - \frac{y}{10}\right)$$

where A is a constant and $\frac{y}{10}$ is the "correcting feedback term."

EXAMPLE 1. Find a value of A so that $y = A\left(x - \frac{y}{10}\right)$ closely approximates $y = 10x$.

Solution:
$$y = Ax - \frac{Ay}{10}$$

$$y + \frac{Ay}{10} = Ax$$

$$\frac{10y + Ay}{10} = Ax$$

$$y\frac{(10 + A)}{10} = Ax$$

$$y = Ax\left(\frac{10}{10 + A}\right)$$

$$y = \frac{10A}{10 + A}x$$

Thus, $\frac{10A}{10 + A}$ must approximate 10. But $\lim\limits_{A \to \infty} \frac{10A}{10 + A} = 10$, so the approximation improves as A increases. Choose $A = 10,000$. Then $\frac{10A}{10 + A} = 9.99$. Thus

$$y = 10,000\left(x - \frac{y}{10}\right)$$

describes an amplifier system whose output is approximately 10 times the input.

How do these two systems react to a 10% decrease in amplifier gain? The non-feedback model becomes $y = 9x$. Output decreases by 10% also.

However, the feedback system with $A = 9000(10,000 - 0.1 \cdot 10,000)$ behaves differently.

$$y = 9000\left(x - \frac{y}{10}\right)$$

$$y = 9000x - 900y$$

$$901y = 9000x$$

$$y = \frac{9000}{901}x = 9.989x$$

The feedback system effectively nullifies the apparent 10% decrease in amplified output.

EXAMPLE 2. For what value of R would $y = R\left(x - \frac{y}{10}\right)$ produce an amplifier gain of 90%, i.e., ($9x$ rather than $10x$)?

Solution:

$$y = R\left(x - \frac{y}{10}\right)$$

$$9x = R\left(x - \frac{9x}{10}\right) \quad \longleftarrow \text{ Substitute } 9x \text{ for } y.$$

$$9x = R\left(\frac{x}{10}\right)$$

$$90 = R$$

Thus, the amplifier gain must drop to 90 before the feedback system loses 10%.

You can see from the above examples that systems with built-in feedback lead to more uniform output under varying input conditions.

EXERCISES

1. If the output drops to 80%, how much will the amplifier gain drop in the feedback system?

2. An output system is given by $y = 40x + 10d$, where the output is 40 times input plus 10 times disturbances. The corresponding feedback system is given by $y = 40(A(x - By)) + 10d$. If you wish the feedback system to reduce the effects of the disturbances by a factor of 50, how should A and B be chosen? (*Hint*: Reducing by a factor of *50* is equivalent to dividing by *50*—solve the feedback system for y and set the values of A and B accordingly.)

3. Repeat Exercise 2 if $y = 15x + 5d$ and you wish a reduction in the effect of disturbances by 20.

6-6 Geometric Interpretation of the Derived Function

Let $y = f(x)$ have a graph as seen at right. Let $x = a$ be a point for which $f(a)$ exists and let $f'(a)$ exist. The y coordinate of point B is $f(a)$.

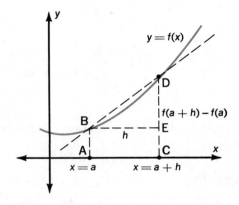

Let h be a real number, either positive or negative. Then $a + h$ is a point on the x axis and $f(a + h)$ is the y coordinate of point D. Consequently, $f(a + h) - f(a)$ is the difference in the y coordinates of points D and B and may be positive or negative. Its absolute value is depicted in the diagram as DE, the difference in the lengths of $\overline{CD}$ and $\overline{AB}$. Notice that the length of the segment BE is $|h|$.

The ratio

$$\frac{f(a + h) - f(a)}{h}$$

is the *slope* of the line determined by B and D. Such a line is a *secant* line. Now think of h taking on values close to 0. For each h the ratio $\frac{f(a + h) - f(a)}{h}$ is the slope of the corresponding secant line. When h is very close to 0, the points B and D are each on the graph of $y = f(x)$ and are very close together. Consequently, for small h, the secant line through B and D is very close to the line *tangent* to $f(x)$ at $x = a$.

Since the secant lines through B approach the line tangent to $f(x)$ at $x = a$, the slopes of the secant lines approach the slope of the tangent line. Since the slope of each secant line is given by

$$\frac{f(a + h) - f(a)}{h},$$

the slope of the tangent is given by

$$\lim_{h \to 0} \frac{f(a + h) - f(a)}{h}.$$

That is by the derived function of $f(x)$ evaluated at $x = a$.

The following is a statement of the geometric interpretation of $f'(a)$ and summarizes the above discussion.

> Geometric Interpretation of $f'(a)$: $f'(a)$ is the slope of the line tangent to $y = f(x)$ at $x = a$.

EXAMPLE 1. A line with equation $f(x) = 3x - 5$ has slope 3 at $x = 6$ because the slope is the coefficient of x when the equation is in the form $f(x) = mx + b$. Verify that $f'(6) = 3$ also.

$$\frac{f(6 + h) - f(6)}{h} = \frac{3(6 + h) - 5 - (3 \cdot 6 - 5)}{h}$$

$$= \frac{18 + 3h - 5 - 18 + 5}{h}$$

$$= \frac{3h}{h} \quad \longleftarrow \quad h \neq 0$$

$$= 3.$$

$$f'(6) = \lim_{h \to 0} 3 = 3$$

Notice that in this example $f'(x)$ does not depend on x, that is, $f'(x) = 3$ for all x. Hence, the slope of $f(x) = 3x - 5$ is 3 for all x. This is as it should be because the slope of a line is constant.

EXAMPLE 2. Find the slope of the tangent to $f(x) = x^2$ at $x = 1$.

$$f'(1) = \lim_{h \to 0} \frac{(1 + h)^2 - 1^2}{h} \quad \longleftarrow \quad \textbf{By the definition}$$

$$= \lim_{h \to 0} \frac{2h + h^2}{h} \quad \longleftarrow \quad \textbf{h} \neq \textbf{0}$$

$$= \lim_{h \to 0} (2 + h)$$

$$= 2 \quad \longleftarrow \quad \textbf{The slope of the tangent}$$

CLASSROOM EXERCISES

▬ For $f(x) = 3x^2 - 2x$, find the slope of the secant between the points with the given x coordinates.

1. $x = 0$ and $x = 1$ **2.** $x = 0$ and $x = 0.5$

3. $x = 0$ and $x = 0.1$ **4.** $x = 0$ and $x = h$

▬ For $f(x) = 3x^2 - 2x$, find the slope of the line tangent to $f(x)$ at the given value of x.

5. $x = 0$ **6.** $x = 1$ **7.** $x = 0.5$ **8.** $x = -1$

WRITTEN EXERCISES

A ▬▬Find the slope of the tangent to the graph of the function at the given point.

1. $f(x) = \frac{2}{3}x - 1$ at $x = 5$ **2.** $f(x) = \frac{1}{x}$ at $x = 2$

3. $f(x) = -x^2$ at $x = 4$ **4.** $f(x) = \frac{1}{x-1}$ at $x = 0$

5. $f(x) = 2x^2 + 3x$ at $x = 1$ **6.** $f(x) = 5$ at $x = 100$

7. $f(x) = 3x - x^2$ at $x = 0$

8. $f(x) = -x^2 + 4x - 1$ at $x = 1$

B ▬▬For Exercises 9–12 sketch a graph of the function. Estimate the slope of the line tangent at $x = a$. Find that slope and compare with your estimate.

9. $f(x) = x^2$ at $x = 3$ **10.** $f(x) = \frac{1}{x}$ at $x = -2$

11. $f(x) = x^2 - 2x$ at $x = 1$ **12.** $f(x) = 4x + 2$ at $x = -1$

13. What is the slope of a line that passes through points B and D if their coordinates are:

   a. $B(x_1, y_1)$, $D(x_2, y_2)$?
   b. $B(x, y_1)$, $D(x + h, y_2)$?
   c. $B(x, f(x))$, $D(x + h, f(x + h))$?
   d. $B(x + h, f(x + h))$, $D(x, f(x))$?

14. The expression $\lim\limits_{h \to 0} \dfrac{f(a + h) - f(a)}{h}$

may or may not exist at a. What is the geometric interpretation if it does not exist?

C ▬▬For a quadratic function

$$f(x) = ax^2 + bx + c \quad (a \neq 0),$$

the value of $f(x)$ at $x = -\dfrac{b}{2a}$ is the maximum or minimum value of the function. For each function find $f'(x)$ at $x = -\dfrac{b}{2a}$.

15. $f(x) = x^2$ **16.** $f(x) = -x^2 + 2x$

17. $f(x) = 2x^2 + x - 1$ **18.** $f(x) = -3x^2 + x - 5$

19. $f(x) = ax^2 + bx + c$

20. Generalize the results of Exercises 15–19.

21. Even though $f(x) = \dfrac{1}{x}$ is not defined at $x = 0$, for all $x \neq 0$ the function is defined. Find $f'(x)$ and discuss what happens to $f'(x)$ for x close to 0. What does this mean geometrically?

6-7   Rules for Finding $f'(x)$

The derived function for most functions can be written down by application of simple rules. Several of these rules are given in this section. Their use will allow you to determine the slope of a line tangent to a given curve quickly — a skill which will be useful in later chapters. The rules are stated as theorems, not all of which will be proved.

Theorem 6-6   If $f(x) = k$, k a constant, then $f'(x) = 0$.

Theorem 6-7   The derived function of the product of a constant k and a function $f(x)$ is the product of k and $f'(x)$.

EXAMPLE 1.   Find $f'(x)$ when

a. $f(x) = 17$ **b.** $f(x) = 4(x^2 + 1)$

Solutions:

a. If $f(x) = 17$, $f'(x) = 0$ by Theorem 6-6. This agrees with intuition because the line $f(x) = 17$ is horizontal and its slope is therefore 0.
b. Think of $f(x)$ as the product of 4 and $(x^2 + 1)$. The derived function for $x^2 + 1$ is $2x$ (Example 3 Section 6-5). Thus by Theorem 6-7,

$$f'(x) = 4 \cdot 2x$$
$$= 8x.$$

The proof of the next theorem is based upon the Binomial Theorem. (For a review of this important theorem, see pages 24–27.)

Theorem 6-8   If $f(x) = x^m$ where m is a positive integer, then $f'(x) = mx^{m-1}$.

Proof: For Theorem 6-8 to be true, $\lim\limits_{h \to 0} \dfrac{(x+h)^m - x^m}{h}$ must be mx^{m-1}. This can be shown by using the binomial formula to expand $(x+h)^m$. $(x + h)^m = x^m + mx^{m-1}h + $ (terms with powers of h greater than 1 such as h^2, h^3, h^4, $\cdots$). Thus $\dfrac{(x+h)^m - x^m}{h} = mx^{m-1} + $ (terms with powers of h greater than 0 such as h, h^2, h^3, $\cdots$). Each of the terms other than mx^{m-1} tends to zero as $h \longrightarrow 0$. Consequently: $f'(x) = mx^{m-1}$.

EXAMPLE 2.   Find $f'(x)$ if $f(x) = x^5$.

Solution: $\qquad f'(x) = 5x^4.$ ◄——— **By Theorem 6-8**

The derived function of a function with a negative exponent is found similarly.

> **Theorem 6–9**   If $f(x) = \dfrac{1}{x^m}$, m a positive integer, $x \neq 0$, then
>
> $$f'(x) = \frac{-m}{x^{m+1}}, \text{ or } f'(x) = -mx^{-m-1}$$

Proof: $\qquad f(x + h) - f(x) = \dfrac{1}{(x + h)^m} - \dfrac{1}{x^m}$

$$= \frac{x^m - (x + h)^m}{(x + h)^m \cdot x^m}$$

$$= \frac{x^m - \left(x^m + mx^{m-1}h + \dfrac{m(m - 1)}{2} x^{m-2}h^2 + \cdots + h^m\right)}{(x + h)^m \cdot x^m}$$

$$= \frac{-mx^{m-1}h - \dfrac{m(m - 1)}{2} x^{m-2}h^2 - \cdots - h^m}{(x + h)^m \cdot x^m}$$

The quotient $\dfrac{f(x + h) - f(x)}{h}$ is

$$\frac{-mx^{m-1}h - \dfrac{m(m - 1)}{2} x^{m-2}h^2 - \cdots - h^m}{h \cdot (x + h)^m \cdot x^m}$$

$$= \frac{-mx^{m-1} - \dfrac{m(m - 1)}{2} x^{m-2}h - \cdots - h^{m-1}}{(x + h)^m \cdot x^m}$$

Now as $h \longrightarrow 0$, the numerator approaches $-mx^{m-1}$ because all other addends approach zero. The denominator $(x + h)^m \cdot x^m \longrightarrow x^m \cdot x^m$ as $h \longrightarrow 0$. Thus

$$\lim_{h \to 0} \frac{f(x + h) - f(x)}{h} = \frac{-mx^{m-1}}{x^m \cdot x^m}$$

$$= \frac{-m}{x^m \cdot x^m \cdot x^{-m} \cdot x^1}$$

$$= \frac{-m}{x^{m+1}}$$

Even when the exponent is not integral, the same procedure is used.

> **Theorem 6-10**   If $f(x) = x^r$, r a rational number, $x > 0$, then
> $$f'(x) = r \cdot x^{r-1}.$$

EXAMPLE 3.   Find $f'(x)$ when **a.** $f(x) = 3x^{-4}$ and **b.** $f(x) = 3x^{\frac{2}{3}}$

Solution: **a.** $f'(x) = 3(-4x^{-4-1})$ ⟵ **By Theorem 6-9**

$\qquad\qquad\quad = -12x^{-5}$

b. $f'(x) = 3(\frac{2}{3}x^{\frac{2}{3}-1})$ ⟵ **By Theorem 6-10**

$\qquad\qquad = 2x^{-\frac{1}{3}}$

> **Theorem 6-11**   If $f(x) = f_1(x) + f_2(x) + \cdots + f_n(x)$,
> and $f_n'(x)$ exists for all n
> then $\qquad f'(x) = f_1'(x) + f_2'(x) + \cdots + f_n'(x)$.

Theorems 6–6, 6–8 and 6–11 combine to provide a means of determining the derived function of any polynomial function.

EXAMPLE 4.   Find $f'(x)$ when $f(x) = 2x^4 + 3x^2 + 7x + 2$.

Solution: $f(x) = 2x^4 + 3x^2 + 7x + 2$
$\qquad\qquad = f_1(x) + f_2(x) + f_3(x) + f_4(x)$
$f'(x) = f_1'(x) + f_2'(x) + f_3'(x) + f_4'(x)$ ⟵ **By Theorem 6-11**
$\qquad = 2 \cdot 4x^3 + 3 \cdot 2x^1 + 7 \cdot 1 + 0$ ⟵ **By Theorems 6-6, 6-7, 6-8**
$\qquad = 8x^3 + 6x + 7$

EXAMPLE 5.   Find $f'(x)$ when $f(x) = 2x^5 + 3x - 1$.

Solution: $f'(x) = 2 \cdot 5x^4 + 3$
$\qquad\qquad = 10x^4 + 3$

EXAMPLE 6.   What is the slope of the tangent to the graph of $f(x) = 4x^3 + 2x$ at $x = 2$?

$$f'(x) = 12x^2 + 2$$
$$f'(2) = 12 \cdot 4 + 2 = 50$$

CLASSROOM EXERCISES

Find $f'(x)$ for each $f(x)$.

1. $f(x) = x^2$ **2.** $f(x) = 6x^2$ **3.** $f(x) = 46x^{\frac{3}{2}}$

WRITTEN EXERCISES

A   Find $f'(x)$ for each $f(x)$.

1. $f(x) = x^7$ **2.** $f(x) = 13x^4$ **3.** $f(x) = 4$

4. $f(x) = 3x^2 + 2$ **5.** $f(x) = \frac{1}{x^{100}}$ **6.** $f(x) = \frac{7}{x^5}$

7. $f(x) = 5x^{10} + x^5 - 2x^2 + 1$ **8.** $f(x) = x^5 - x^4 + x^2 - x + 1$

9. $f(x) = 12x^{-3}$ **10.** $f(x) = \frac{1}{x^4} - \frac{2}{x^2} + x$

Find the slope of the line tangent to each function at $x = 2$.

11. $f(x) = x^7$ **12.** $f(x) = x^{-2}$

13. $f(x) = x^2 + 2x - 3$ **14.** $f(x) = x^{\frac{1}{2}}$

B   Use the point-slope form of the equation of a line to determine the equation of the line tangent to $f(x)$ at $x = a$. (Point-Slope form: $y - y_1 = m(x - x_1)$, m is the slope, point (x_1, y_1) is on the line.)

15. $f(x) = \frac{1}{2}x^2 + 2x$, $x = 3$ **16.** $f(x) = -\frac{1}{2}x^2 + 2x$, $x = 1$

17. $f(x) = 2x + 3$, $x = 1$ **18.** $f(x) = x^3 - x$, $x = -1$

19. $f(x) = \frac{1}{x^2}$, $x = 3$ **20.** $f(x) = \frac{20}{x^2}$, $x = -2$

21. $f(x) = x^{\frac{4}{3}}$, $x = 8$ **22.** $f(x) = x^{\frac{1}{2}}$, $x = 4$

C   **23.** Prove Theorem 6–6.   **24.** Prove Theorem 6–7.

25. Suppose $f(x)$ and $g(x)$ have derived functions $f'(x)$ and $g'(x)$.

Let $p(x) = f(x) \cdot g(x)$. Show that $p'(x) = f(x) \cdot g'(x) + g(x)f'(x)$

Hint: $\dfrac{p(x + h) - p(x)}{h} = \dfrac{f(x + h) \cdot g(x + h) - f(x)g(x)}{h}$

$= \dfrac{f(x + h)g(x + h) - f(x + h)g(x) + f(x + h)g(x) - f(x)g(x)}{h}$

Simplify the last statement and consider $\lim\limits_{h \to 0} \dfrac{p(x + h) - p(x)}{h}$.

Use the above rule to find the derived function of

26. $x^2 x^4$.   **27.** $x^2 \cdot \frac{1}{x^4}$.   **28.** $(x^2 + 1)(x^3 - 2)$.

BASIC: SLOPE OF A POLYNOMIAL FUNCTION

Problem:

Given the coefficients of a polynomical function, write a program which computes the slope of the tangent to the function for any *x* value.

```
100 PRINT
110 PRINT "THIS PROGRAM COMPUTES THE SLOPE OF A"
120 PRINT "POLYNOMIAL P(X) FOR ANY X."
130 PRINT
140 PRINT "WHAT IS THE DEGREE OF THE POLYNOMIAL";
150 INPUT N
160 PRINT "ENTER THE COEFFICIENTS."
170 FOR I = N TO 0 STEP -1
180    PRINT "X↑";I;
190    INPUT A(I)
200 NEXT I
210 PRINT
220 PRINT "AT WHAT X VALUE DO YOU WANT THE SLOPE";
230 INPUT X
240 LET D = 0
250 FOR I = N TO 1 STEP -1
260    LET D = D + I * A(I) * X↑(I-1)
270 NEXT I
280 PRINT
290 PRINT "SLOPE AT X = ";X;" IS ";D
300 PRINT
310 PRINT "ANOTHER X VALUE FOR SAME FUNCTION"
320 PRINT "(1=YES,0=NO)";
330 INPUT Q
340 IF Q = 1 THEN 210
350 PRINT "ANOTHER FUNCTION (1=YES, 0=NO)";
360 INPUT Q
370 IF Q = 1 THEN 130
380 PRINT
390 END
```

Output:

```
THIS PROGRAM COMPUTES THE SLOPE OF A
POLYNOMIAL P(X) FOR ANY X.
```

```
WHAT IS THE DEGREE OF THE POLYNOMIAL? 3
ENTER THE COEFFICIENTS.
X↑ 3 ? 1
X↑ 2 ? -1
X↑ 1 ? 2
X↑ 0 ? 5

AT WHAT X VALUE DO YOU WANT THE SLOPE? 1

SLOPE AT X = 1 IS 3

ANOTHER X VALUE FOR SAME FUNCTION
(1=YES,0=NO)? 0
ANOTHER FUNCTION (1=YES,0=NO)? 0
```

Analysis:

Statements 140–230: This section accepts the coefficients of the polynomial, where the user first enters the degree N of the polynomial. Then the x value is accepted.

Statements 240–270: The derived function of $P(x)$ is evaluated term by term. The key line is statement 260. The formula is based on the fact that the derived function of $a_i x^i$ is $ia_i x^{i-1}$.

EXERCISES

A　　Run the program on page 315 to calculate the slopes of the tangents to the graphs of each function at the given points.

1. $f(x) = x^2 - 3x + 4$ at $x = -1, 2, 5$

2. $f(x) = 3x^3 + x - 7$ at $x = 0, 3, -2$

3. $f(x) = -x^4 + x^2 - 1$ at $x = -2, 2, 3$

4. $f(x) = 2x^5 + 3x - 1$ at $x = -1\frac{1}{2}, \frac{1}{2}, 4\frac{1}{2}$

B　　In Exercises 5–7, revise the program on page 315 in the manner indicated.

5. The degree of a polynominal function must be a nonnegative integer. Add a "bad data test" to catch an invalid value for n (statement 150).

6. When accepting the coefficients of the polynomial, print X ? instead of X↑1 ?, and print CONSTANT? instead of X↑0 ?

7. Have the user enter the x value before entering the coefficients. Then combine the input and calculation loops (statements 170–200 and 240–270) into one loop.

316　COMPUTER APPLICATION

CHAPTER SUMMARY

Important Terms

Asymptote (p. 298)
Continuous function (p. 293)
Derived function (p. 301)
Discontinuous function (p. 295)

Function of a real variable (p. 281)
Indeterminate function (p. 300)
Polynomial function (p. 292)
Polynomial in x (p. 292)

Important Ideas

1. The limit of $f(x)$ at $x = a$ equals L if and only if for every neighborhood about L, there exists a neighborhood about a such that $f(x)$ is in the neighborhood about L whenever x is in the neighborhood about a.

2. If the limit of a function $f(x)$ at $x = a$ is $f(a)$, then the function is continuous at the point $x = a$.

3. The limit of a polynomial $P(x)$ at $x = a$ is $P(a)$.

4. If the limit of a rational function does not exist at a point $x = a$, then the function is discontinuous at $x = a$.

5. The derived function of a function $f(x)$ is $f'(x)$ where

$$f'(x) = \lim_{h \to 0} \frac{f(x + h) - f(x)}{h}$$

6. The derived function of a function evaluated at a point $x = a$ gives the slope of the line tangent to the function at the point $(a, f(a))$.

7. Rules for finding $f'(x)$

    a. If $f(x) = k$, then $f'(x) = 0$.

    b. If $f(x) = kg(x)$, then $f'(x) = kg'(x)$

    c. If $f(x) = x^m$, m a rational number, then $f'(x) = mx^{m-1}$

CHAPTER OBJECTIVES AND REVIEW

Objective: *To illustrate geometrically functions for which $|x|$ increases without bound and to find the limit, if one exists.* (Section 6-1)

━━━ Graph each function. What appears to be the limit, if any, as $x \longrightarrow \infty$ or $x \longrightarrow -\infty$?

1. $f(x) = \dfrac{x + 2}{x}$

2. $f(x) = -\dfrac{1}{x}$

3. $f(x) = \dfrac{3x^2 - 4x + 2}{x^2}$

4. $f(x) = \left(\dfrac{1}{2}\right)^x$

Objective: *For any neighborhood of a number L, to find, when possible, a neighborhood of a point x = a such that f(x) is in the neighborhood of L whenever x is in the neighborhood of a.* (Section 6-2)

▬▬ Use the given L and ϵ to find a neighborhood of a such that $f(x) \in \langle L - \epsilon, L + \epsilon \rangle$ when $x \in \langle a - \delta, a + \delta \rangle$.

5. $f(x) = 2x$, $L = 6$, $a = 3$, $\epsilon = \frac{1}{5}$

6. $f(x) = x - 2$, $L = 4$, $a = 6$, $\epsilon = \frac{1}{10}$

7. $f(x) = 3x - 2$, $L = 7$, $a = 3$, $\epsilon = \frac{1}{100}$

8. $f(x) = 4$, $L = 4$, $a = 1$, $\epsilon = \frac{1}{100}$

Objective: *To cite and use theorems about limits to calculate limits of functions.* (Section 6-3)

▬▬ In Exercises 9–13 complete the statement of each limit theorem. $\lim\limits_{x \to a} f(x) = M$, $\lim\limits_{x \to a} g(x) = N$.

9. $\lim\limits_{x \to a} c = $ _____

10. $\lim\limits_{x \to a} x^n = $ _____

11. $\lim\limits_{x \to a} [f(x) \pm g(x)] = $ _____

12. $\lim\limits_{x \to a} [f(x) \cdot g(x)] = $ _____

13. $\lim\limits_{x \to a} \dfrac{f(x)}{g(x)} = $ _____

▬▬ Use the limit theorems in Exercises 9–13 to demonstrate the truth of each statement.

14. $\lim\limits_{x \to 1} (2 \cdot x^2) = 2$

15. $\lim\limits_{x \to -3} (x^2 - 2x) = 15$

16. $\lim\limits_{x \to 1} \dfrac{x + 1}{x + 2} = \dfrac{2}{3}$

17. $\lim\limits_{x \to +\infty} \dfrac{x + 1}{x} = 1$

Objective: *To find the limit, if it exists, of a rational function f(x) at a point of discontinuity.* (Section 6-4)

▬▬ In Exercises 18–19 find the indicated limit.

18. $\lim\limits_{x \to 3} \dfrac{3x - x^2}{3 - x}$

19. $\lim\limits_{x \to 4} \dfrac{x^2 - 16}{x - 4}$

Objective: *To use the definition of the derived function f'(x) to find its value for a given value of x.* (Section 6-5)

▬▬ Use the definition of derived function to find the indicated values.

20. $f'(2)$ where $f(x) = 4x - 3$

21. $f'(3)$ where $f(x) = x^2 + 1$

22. $f'(2)$ where $f(x) = -\dfrac{1}{x}$

23. $f'(1)$ where $f(x) = x^2 - x$

Objective: *To use the derived function to find the slope of a tangent to a graph of a function at a given point.* (Section 6-6)

━━ Find the slope of the tangent to the graph of the given function at the given point.

24. $f(x) = \frac{1}{2}x + 1$ at $x = 2$ **25.** $f(x) = x^2$ at $x = -3$

26. $f(x) = \dfrac{1}{x+1}$ at $x = 0$ **27.** $f(x) = 3$ at $x = 12$

Objective: *To use Theorems 6–6 through 6–11 to find $f'(x)$.* (Section 6-7)

━━ Find $f'(x)$ for each $f(x)$.

28. $f(x) = x^3$ **29.** $f(x) = 6x^5$

30. $f(x) = -2$ **31.** $f(x) = 2x^2 - 7$

32. $f(x) = \dfrac{1}{x^7}$ **33.** $f(x) = \dfrac{1}{x^3} - \dfrac{3}{x^4}$

34. $f(x) = x^{-\frac{2}{3}}$ **35.** $f(x) = x^{\frac{4}{3}}$

CHAPTER TEST

━━Given $f(x) = x^2 - 2$. In Exercises 1–4 answer each question about $f(x)$.

1. What is $\lim_{x \to 2} f(x)$?

2. What are $\lim_{x \to 2^-} f(x)$ and $\lim_{x \to 2^+} f(x)$?

3. Is $f(x)$ continuous at $x = 2$? Explain.

4. Draw a diagram illustrating geometrically the fact that the limit of $f(x)$ as x nears 2 is 2.

━━Evaluate each limit in Exercises 5–10.

5. $\lim_{x \to 1} x^5 - 2x^3 + x$

6. $\lim_{x \to -3} \frac{x - 3}{2x^2}$

7. $\lim_{x \to 0} \frac{x^2 + x}{x}$

8. $\lim_{x \to \infty} \frac{2x}{x^2}$

9. $\lim_{x \to 2^+} \frac{4}{x - 2}$

10. $\lim_{x \to 2^-} \frac{4}{x - 2}$

11. If $f(x) = 3x^2 - x + 1$, then use the definition of $f'(x)$ to calculate $f'(x)$.

12. Draw a diagram illustrating and explain the geometric significance of $f'(a)$.

━━Find $f'(x)$ for each function of Exercises 13–17.

13. $f(x) = 4x^4 + 3x^2 - 2x + 1$

14. $f(x) = 3$

15. $f(x) = 4x - 5$

16. $f(x) = x^{-5}$

17. $f(x) = 8x^{\frac{4}{3}}$

CHAPTER 7 Algebraic Functions

Sections

Features

Review and Testing

7–1   Polynomial Functions

Suppose that you are given a symbol x and a set of numbers A. Many different expressions in x can be generated by a finite number of arithmetic operations upon x and the members of A. For example, $3 \cdot \pi \cdot x \cdot x + \sqrt{2}$. If the only operations permitted are multiplication, addition, and subtraction, the resulting expressions in x are polynomials in x *over the set* A, where A is either the set of integers, the set of rational numbers, the set of real numbers, or the set of complex numbers. Since each of these sets is closed with respect to the operations of multiplication, addition, and subtraction, the coefficients of the polynomials are in set A also.

EXAMPLE 1.   Name the smallest set to which the coefficients of each polynomial belong.

   a. $16x^3 + 4x - 2$ **b.** $2x^3 + \frac{15}{2}$

   c. $\sqrt{2}x^{100} + 50x - \pi$ **d.** $(2i)x^5 + 1$

Solution: **a.** Integers   **b.** Rational numbers
   c. Real numbers   **d.** Complex numbers

If you are also permitted to use the operation of division to generate expressions in x, the resulting expressions are **rational expressions** in x *over the set* A.

EXAMPLE 2.   Name the smallest set to which the coefficients of each rational expression belong.

   a. $\dfrac{x^2 + 2}{x + 1}$ **b.** $\dfrac{\frac{x^3}{3} + 2x}{\frac{14}{5}x^4}$

   c. $\dfrac{x^5 + x^4 + x^3}{\sqrt{2}\,x^3}$ **d.** $\dfrac{\frac{3}{2}x + 2i}{\frac{9}{4}x^3 - 3i^3}$

Solution: **a.** Integers   **b.** Rational numbers
   c. Real numbers   **d.** Complex numbers

Notice that all polynomial expressions are also rational expressions. Why?

If you may also use extraction of roots as an operation in generating expressions, the result is an **algebraic expression.** The following example illustrates the idea.

EXAMPLE 3. Name the smallest set to which the coefficients of each algebraic expression belong.

a. $\dfrac{5^3\sqrt{x}}{\sqrt{x}+1} - 2^3\sqrt{x}$ b. $\frac{1}{3}\sqrt{x} + 2^4\sqrt{x}$

c. $\sqrt{3^3}\sqrt{x^2} + \pi$ d. $3 + 2i^3\sqrt{x}$

Solution:
a. Integers   b. Rational numbers
c. Real numbers   d. Complex numbers

The set of algebraic expressions includes rational and polynomial expressions.

A **polynomial** in the symbol x over the real numbers R is an algebraic expression that can be written

$$a_n x^n + a_{n-1} x^{n-1} + a_{n-2} x^{n-2} + \cdots + a_1 x + a_0$$

where n is a nonnegative integer, the **coefficients** a_i are in R, and $a_n \neq 0$. The number n is said to be the degree of the polynomial, and a_n is called the **leading coefficient.**

If x is a variable whose domain is the set of real numbers R, then the association denoted by

$$f : x \rightarrow a_n x^n + a_{n-1} x^{n-1} + \cdots + a_1 x + a_0$$

or

$$f(x) = a_n x^n + a_{n-1} x^{n-1} + \cdots + a_1 x + a_0$$

is called a **polynomial function.** The range of a polynomial function is $\{y : y = f(x), x \in \text{R}\}$.

The range may be all of R or a subset of R. The degree of a polynomial function is the same as that of its defining polynomial.

EXAMPLE 4. Name the degree of each polynomial over the reals.

a. $f : x \rightarrow x^5 + 2x^3 + x$ b. $g(x) = 2x^3 + 1$
c. $h(x) = \sqrt{x} + x^3$ d. $r(x) = \frac{3}{2} i x^2 + 2$

Solution:
a. Degree 5   b. Degree 3
c. Not a polynomial ($x^{\frac{1}{2}}$ not permissible)
d. Not a polynomial ($\frac{3}{2} i \notin \text{R}$)

You are already familiar with the properties of the *constant, linear,* and *quadratic* functions.

Properties of the Constant Function

The **constant function** associates with every element x of its domain the number c. The range of the function is the single number c, and hence the graph of the function is either a line parallel to the x axis when $c \neq 0$ or the x axis itself when $c = 0$. The point at which the graph of a function intersects the y axis is called the **y intercept** of the function. The y intercept is the point $(0, f(0))$. The y intercept for the constant function is $(0, c)$. The slope of the graph of $f(x) = c$ is 0 at every point.

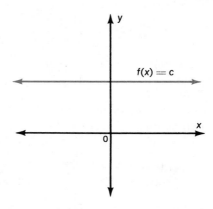

Of course, the constant function $f(x) = c$, $c \neq 0$, is just the polynomial function $f(x) = a_0 = c$ and hence the degree is 0. If, however, $c = 0$, then $f(x) = 0$ is *not* a polynomial function (Why?) and has no degree associated with it. Nevertheless, it is common practice to call $f(x) = 0$ the **zero polynomial.** You can conclude that every line with zero slope is associated with a polynomial function of degree 0 or with the zero polynomial.

Properties of the Linear Function

The graph of the **linear function** $f(x) = mx + b$, $m \neq 0$, is a line with slope m and y intercept $(0, b)$. The graph intersects the x axis at the point with x coordinate $-\dfrac{b}{m}$.

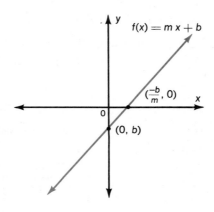

If the graph of a function and the x axis have any points in common, these points are called the **real zeros** of the function. Otherwise the zeros are imaginary. Stated more formally, the set of *zeros* of a function f is the set of all x in the domain of f for which $f(x) = 0$. The zeros of a function are found by setting $f(x)$ equal to 0 and solving the resulting equation for x.

For example, the zeros of the linear function

$$f(x) = 4x - 3$$

are found by solving

$$0 = 4x - 3$$
$$3 = 4x$$
$$\tfrac{3}{4} = x.$$

Hence the set of zeros of $f(x) = 4x - 3$ is

$$\{\tfrac{3}{4}\}.$$

In other words the line, $4x - 3$, crosses the x axis at $x = \tfrac{3}{4}$.

Properties of the Quadratic Function

The graph of the **quadratic function**

$$f(x) = ax^2 + bx + c, \qquad a \neq 0,$$

is a *parabola*. The y intercept is $(0, c)$.

The following two cases will be considered, the first when a is greater than zero, the second when a is less than zero. If $a > 0$, the parabola is *concave upward* (opens upward).

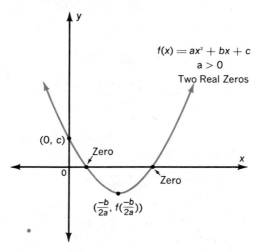

If $a < 0$, the parabola is *concave downward* (opens downward).

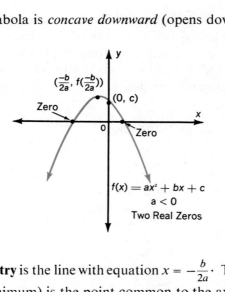

The **axis of symmetry** is the line with equation $x = -\dfrac{b}{2a}$. The **turning point** (maximum or minimum) is the point common to the axis of symmetry and the parabola. The y coordinate of this point is $f\left(-\dfrac{b}{2a}\right)$. (See Exercises 15–21, page 310.) The zeros (if any) are found by applying the **quadratic formula.**

$$x = \frac{-b \pm \sqrt{b^2 - 4ac}}{2a}$$

The nature of the zeros of a quadratic function can be determined by examining the **discriminant,**

$$b^2 - 4ac.$$

① If $b^2 > 4ac$, then $b^2 - 4ac > 0$. Thus $\sqrt{b^2 - 4ac}$ is a positive real number and there are *two real zeros.*

$$\frac{-b + \sqrt{b^2 - 4ac}}{2a} \quad \text{and} \quad \frac{-b - \sqrt{b^2 - 4ac}}{2a}$$

② If $b^2 = 4ac$, then $b^2 - 4ac = 0$. Thus $\sqrt{b^2 - 4ac}$ is zero and there is *one real zero*: $-\dfrac{b}{2a}$

③ If $b^2 < 4ac$, then $b^2 - 4ac < 0$. Thus $\sqrt{b^2 - 4ac}$ is a pure imaginary number and there are *two complex zeros.*

$$\frac{-b + i\sqrt{4ac - b^2}}{2a} \quad \text{and} \quad \frac{-b - i\sqrt{4ac - b^2}}{2a}$$

The slope of the line tangent to the graph at a point $(x_0, f(x_0))$ is found by evaluating the derived function $f'(x) = 2ax + b$ at $x = x_0$.

CLASSROOM EXERCISES

▬ For each expression in Exercises 1–6, identify the type of expression and the smallest set that includes all its coefficients.

1. $\dfrac{x - \frac{2}{3}}{x^2 + \sqrt{5}}$

2. $50x^2 - \sqrt{4}x + 3$

3. $\sqrt{3x + 1}$

4. $\dfrac{x^2 + 3x - 5}{x + 1}$

5. $\dfrac{1}{x} + x^4 - \frac{3}{2}$

6. $\dfrac{i\sqrt{2}x^2 - 1}{x^4 + 1}$

WRITTEN EXERCISES

A ▬ Identify the degree and leading coefficient of each polynomial.

1. $3x^4 - 2x + 1$

2. $\dfrac{7x^2 - 2x}{5}$

3. $x(4x + 2)$

4. $x^2 - 3x^4 + 2x$

5. $-x^9 - 2x^3 + x$

6. $1 - 3x$

▬ For each linear and quadratic function determine the y intercept, the real zeros (if any), and the slope at $x = 3$. For the quadratic functions determine also the axis of symmetry, the coordinates of the turning point, and whether the graph opens upward or downward.

7. $f(x) = -2x - 3$

8. $f(x) = \frac{1}{2}x + 5$

9. $f(x) = 2x$

10. $f(x) = x^2$

11. $f(x) = x^2 - 4$

12. $f(x) = x^2 + 2x + 1$

13. $f(x) = -x^2$

14. $f(x) = 3x^2 + x + 1$

15. $f(x) = -2x^2 + 4x$

16. $f(x) = x^2 - 5x - 50$

B **17.** What is the slope of the line tangent to $f(x) = ax^2 + bx + c$ at $x = -\dfrac{b}{2a}$?

18. Find the equation of the line tangent to $f(x) = 3x^2$ at

a. $x = 0.$

b. $x = 2.$

c. $x = -3.$

d. $x = x_0.$

19. Find the y intercept of the line tangent to $f(x) = 3x^2$ at

a. $x = 2.$

b. $x = x_0.$

20. In Exercise 19, is there any relationship between the y intercepts found in **a** and **b** and $f(2)$ and $f(x_0)$? Explain.

C **21.** Show that the sum of two polynomials over a set A is also a polynomial over A. Is this true also for the product of two polynomials?

7–2 Synthetic Substitution

Suppose that you were asked to graph the polynomial function

$$f(x) = a_n x^n + a_{n-1} x^{n-1} + \cdots + a_1 x + a_0.$$

One of the first things you would have to do is to calculate values of the function corresponding to particular values of x. This can always be done by substitution. For $x = c$,

$$f(c) = a_n c^n + a_{n-1} c^{n-1} + \cdots + a_1 c + a_0.$$

EXAMPLE 1. Find the value of $f(x) = 4x^4 - 2x^3 - 3x^2 - x$ evaluated at $x = 3$.

Solution:
$$\begin{aligned}
f(3) &= 4(3)^4 - 2(3)^3 - 3(3)^2 - 3 \\
&= 4(81) - 2(27) - 3(9) - 3 \\
&= 324 - 54 - 27 - 3 \\
&= 240
\end{aligned}$$

Certainly for polynomial functions of large degree or for large values of x, substitution leads to many tedious calculations. There is a simpler method to calculate values called **synthetic substitution.**

EXAMPLE 2. Find the value of $f(x) = 2x^3 - 3x^2 - 5x + 4$ at $x = 3$.
Solution: Write $2x^3 - 3x^2 - 5x + 4$ in the alternate form

$$[(2x - 3)x - 5]x + 4.$$

When $x = 3$, this becomes $[(2(3) - 3)3 - 5]3 + 4$.

The evaluation in stages is as follows.

① Multiply 2 (the coefficient of x^3) by 3 and add the product to -3 (the coefficient of x^2): $6 - 3 = 3$.
② Multiply the result of ①, 3, by 3 and add the product to -5 (the coefficient of x): $9 - 5 = 4$.
③ Multiply the result of ②, 4, by 3 and add the product to 4 (the constant term): $12 + 4 = 16$.

Consequently $f(3) = 16$ when $f(x) = 2x^3 - 3x^2 - 5x + 4$. The evaluation of $f(x)$ at $x = c$ in Example 2 follows a definite pattern.

Multiply the leading coefficient by c, add the result to the next coefficient, multiply the sum by c, add, multiply, etc. in the same manner.

EXAMPLE 3. Evaluate $f(x) = \frac{1}{2}x^3 + 2x^2 + 5x - 5$ at $x = 2$.

Solution:

Write the coefficients of successive terms (arranged in descending order of powers of x), and write 2 at the far right as shown.

$$\frac{1}{2} \quad 2 \quad 5 \quad -5 \quad \underline{|2}$$

To begin the process, bring down the leading coefficient, $\frac{1}{2}$. Multiply $\frac{1}{2}$ by 2 and add the product to the next coefficient, 2.

$$
\begin{array}{ccccc}
\frac{1}{2} & 2 & 5 & -5 & \underline{|2} \\
 & (\frac{1}{2} \times 2) = 1 & (3 \times 2) = 6 & (11 \times 2) = 22 & \\
\hline
\frac{1}{2} & 3 & 11 & 17 = f(2) &
\end{array}
$$

The sum is 3. The process is repeated as shown above. By synthetic substitution, $f(2) = 17$. You can verify this by direct substitution.

Synthetic substitution works for a polynomial function of any degree and for any replacement for x. This is not proved here, but the general case for a third degree polynomial function is worked out in the next example.

EXAMPLE 4. The polynomial function of degree 3 may be written as follows:

$$f(x) = a_3x^3 + a_2x^2 + a_1x + a_0, \quad a_3 \neq 0$$

or

$$f(x) = [(a_3x + a_2)x + a_1]x + a_0$$

Verify that the result of synthetic substitution of c is $f(c)$.

Solution: By direct replacement,

$$f(c) = a_3c^3 + a_2c^2 + a_1c + a_0.$$

Synthetic substitution gives the following result:

$$
\begin{array}{ccccc}
a_3 & a_2 & a_1 & a_0 & \underline{|c} \\
 & a_3c & (a_3c + a_2)c & [(a_3c + a_2)c + a_1]c & \\
\hline
a_3 & (a_3c + a_2) & [(a_3c + a_2)c + a_1] & [(a_3c + a_2)c + a_1]c + a_0 &
\end{array}
$$

The last entry in the third row is $f(c)$ and is the same as the result obtained by direct substitution.

EXAMPLE 5. Given $f(x) = x^4 - 3x^2 - 2x - 5$, determine $f(2)$.

Solution: $x^4 - 3x^2 - 2x - 5 = x^4 + 0x^3 - 3x^2 - 2x - 5$

The complete set of coefficients must be used in the synthetic substitution as shown.

$$
\begin{array}{rrrrr|r}
1 & 0 & -3 & -2 & -5 & \underline{2} \\
  & 2 & 4 & 2 & 0 & \\
\hline
1 & 2 & 1 & 0 & -5 \\
\end{array}
$$

Thus $f(2) = -5$. Check this by direct substitution.

CLASSROOM EXERCISES

▬ Evaluate each polynomial by direct substitution and synthetic substitution.

1. $f(x) = x^3 - 2x^2 + x - 1$ $x = -1, 0, 2$

2. $f(x) = -2x^2 + 3x + 1$ $x = 2, 3, -1$

WRITTEN EXERCISES

A ▬ Use synthetic substitution to evaluate each function at the designated values of x.

1. $f(x) = x^4 - 2x^3 + 3x^2 - x + 5$ $x = -2, 1, 3$

2. $g(x) = x^4 + x - 3$ $x = -2, 1, 3$

3. $f(x) = -3x^3 + x^2 + x - 2$ $x = -1, -3, 0, 2, 4$

4. $h(x) = 2x^3 - 3x^2 + 1$ $x = \frac{1}{2}, \frac{1}{3}, 1$

5. $g(x) = x^4 - x^3 + 2x + 3$ $x = \frac{2}{3}, \frac{1}{4}, -2$

6. $s(x) = 3x^2 + x - x^4 + 2$ $x = -\frac{1}{2}, \frac{1}{3}, -2, 2$

B   **7.** If $r(x) = 2x^3 + 3x^2 - 3x + k$, find k so that $r(2) = 8$.

      8. If $s(x) = x^3 - 7x + 3k$, find k so that $s(-1) = 6$.

      9. If $f(x) = 3x^3 - kx^2 + 2x$, find k so that $f(1) = -5$.

   10. If $f(x) = 2x^3 - kx^2 + 3x - 2k$, find k so that $f(2) = 4$.

C   **11.** If $f(x) = 2x^4 - 3x^2 + cx + k$, find c and k so that $f(-2) = 20$ and $f(2) = 24$.

   12. If $f(x) = x^4 + 2x^3 - x^2 + cx + k$, find c and k so that $f(1) = 0$ and $f(-1) = 0$.

   13. Let $f(x) = x^3 + 3x^2 + 6x - 20$. By synthetic substitution evaluate $f(x)$ for $x \in \{\pm 4, \pm 3.5, \pm 3, \pm 2.5, \pm 2, \pm 1.5, \pm 1, \pm 0.5, 0\}$. Plot three points on a coordinate plane and connect them with a smooth curve to obtain an approximate graph of $f(x)$.

7-3 The Remainder and Factor Theorems

The first theorem in this chapter is motivated by examining the evaluation of

$$f(x) = x^3 - 4x^2 + x + 6$$

at $x = 4$ using synthetic substitution.

$$
\begin{array}{rrrr|r}
1 & -4 & 1 & 6 & \underline{4} \\
  & 4 & 0 & 4 & \\
\hline
1 & 0 & 1 & 10 &
\end{array}
$$

Now rewrite the first row in the pattern so that it appears as the original polynomial. Then attach the same power of x to each number in a given column.

$$
\begin{array}{rrrr|r}
1x^3 & -4x^2 & +1x & +6 & \underline{4} \\
     & +4x^2 & +0x & +4 & \\
\hline
1x^3 & 0x^2 & +1x & +10 &
\end{array}
$$

The polynomial in the third row is the sum of the polynomials in the first two rows.
Since

$$f(x) = x^3 - 4x^2 + x + 6 \qquad \text{and} \qquad f(4) = 10,$$

the addition can be rewritten as follows.

$$f(x) + (4x^2 + 0x + 4) = x^3 + 0x^2 + x + f(4).$$

Factoring gives

$$f(x) + 4(x^2 + 0x + 1) = x(x^2 + 0x + 1) + f(4).$$

Notice that $x^2 + 0x + 1$ appears on both sides of this equation. Now solve the equation for $f(x)$ by combining terms and factoring.

$$f(x) = x(x^2 + 0x + 1) - 4(x^2 + 0x + 1) + f(4)$$
$$f(x) = (x - 4)(x^2 + 0x + 1) + f(4)$$

This last expression has the same form as the well-known relationship,

$$\text{Dividend} = (\text{Divisor})(\text{Quotient}) + \text{Remainder}.$$

Thus, if $f(x) = x^3 - 4x^2 + x + 6$ is divided by $x - 4$, the quotient will be $x^2 + 1$, the remainder will be $f(4) = 10$, and both the quotient and remainder can be found by synthetically substituting $x = 4$ in $f(x)$. The generalization of this result is called the *Remainder Theorem*.

> **Theorem 7–1** **Remainder Theorem** If $f(x)$ is a polynomial function of degree n, $n > 0$, and if c is a number, then the remainder in the division of $f(x)$ by $x - c$ is $f(c)$. In symbols,
>
> $$f(x) = (x - c)Q(x) + f(c)$$
>
> where the quotient $Q(x)$ is a polynomial of degree $n - 1$.

Proof: Dividing $f(x)$ by $x - c$, you obtain a quotient $Q(x)$ and a remainder r (a real number). Then

$$f(x) = (x - c)Q(x) + r$$

for all values of x. If the degree of $f(x)$ is n, the degree of $Q(x)$ is $n - 1$. Since the equation is true for all x, it must be true for $x = c$. Then,

$$f(c) = (c - c)Q(c) + r, \quad \text{or } f(c) = r.$$

It is important to note that the theorem is stated in terms of $x - c$, the *difference* between x and the number c.

EXAMPLE 1. Divide $f(x) = 2x^3 + x - 2$ by $x - 1$. Find the quotient $Q(x)$ and the remainder.
Solution: Use synthetic substitution.

$$
\begin{array}{rrrr|l}
2 & 0 & 1 & -2 & \underline{1} \\
  & 2 & 2 & 3 & \\
\hline
2 & 2 & 3 & 1 &
\end{array}
$$

The numbers in the third row, other than the last one at the right which is the remainder, are the coefficients of the quotient $Q(x)$. Thus

$$Q(x) = 2x^2 + 2x + 3 \quad \text{and} \quad f(1) = 1.$$

Consequently $\quad f(x) = (x - 1)(2x^2 + 2x + 3) + 1.$

Since the synthetic substitution of $x = c$ in $f(x)$ can also be used to divide $f(x)$ by $x - c$, the process is alternately called **synthetic division** of $f(x)$ by $x - c$. The polynomial $Q(x)$ is called the **depressed polynomial.**

EXAMPLE 2. Use synthetic division to divide $f(x) = x^3 - 4x^2 + x + 6$ by $x + 1$. Identify the quotient and remainder.
Solution: To divide by $x - c$, c is substituted synthetically. Since $x + 1 = x - (-1)$, -1 is substituted synthetically in $f(x)$.

$$
\begin{array}{rrrr|r}
1 & -4 & 1 & 6 & \underline{-1} \\
& -1 & 5 & -6 & \\
\hline
1 & -5 & 6 & \;0
\end{array}
$$

The remainder is 0, and the depressed polynomial is $Q(x) = x^2 - 5x + 6$, hence:

$$f(x) = (x + 1)(x^2 - 5x + 6) + 0.$$

In Example 2, the remainder $f(-1)$ is 0 and therefore -1 is a zero of $f(x)$. Consequently $x + 1$ and $Q(x)$ are factors of $f(x)$. Stated formally, this result is the *Factor Theorem*.

Theorem 7–2 **Factor Theorem** A number c is a zero of a polynomial function f of degree n, $n > 0$, if and only if $x - c$ is a factor of $f(x)$.

Proof Part I (only if):

The Remainder Theorem implies that there exists a polynomial $Q(x)$ of degree $n - 1$ such that

$$f(x) = (x - c)Q(x) + f(c).$$

If c is a zero, then $f(c) = 0$ and

$$f(x) = (x - c)Q(x).$$

Consequently $x - c$ is a factor of $f(x)$.

Part 2 (if):

If $x - c$ is a factor of $f(x)$ then there is a polynomial $Q(x)$ such that you have the following.

$$f(x) = (x - c)Q(x)$$

When x is replaced by c,

$$
\begin{aligned}
f(c) &= (c - c)Q(c) \\
&= 0.
\end{aligned}
$$

Consequently c is a zero of f.

There are two reasons for the importance of the Factor Theorem. First, it provides a test as to whether or not a number is a zero of a polynomial function. This test is simplified by using synthetic substitution. The second reason is that linear factors of $f(x)$ may be found by identification of the zeros of f. Synthetic substitution simplifies this task.

To test whether or not a linear polynomial $mx + b$, $m \neq 0$, is a factor of $f(x)$, you write

$$mx + b = m\left(x + \frac{b}{m}\right)$$

$$= m\left[x - \left(-\frac{b}{m}\right)\right]$$

and see whether $f\left(-\frac{b}{m}\right) = 0$. (By the Factor Theorem, $mx + b$ is a factor of $f(x)$ if and only if $f\left(-\frac{b}{m}\right) = 0$.)

WRITTEN EXERCISES

A ━━━ Find $Q(x)$ and $f(c)$ so that $f(x) = (x - c)Q(x) + f(c)$.

1. $f(x) = 3x^3 + 4x^2 - 10x - 15$ $c = 2$

2. $f(x) = x^3 + 3x^2 + 2x + 12$ $c = -3$

3. $f(x) = -2x^4 + 3x^3 + 6x - 10$ $c = 1$

4. $f(x) = 2x^4 + 3x^3 - x^2 + 1$ $c = -\frac{1}{2}$

5. $f(x) = 9x^3 - x + 1$ $c = \frac{2}{3}$

━━━ Find the quotient and remainder when $f(x)$ is divided by the linear factor at the right.

6. $f(x) = 2x^3 - 3x^2 + 2x - 4$ $x - 2$

7. $f(x) = 2x^3 - 3x^2 + 2x - 8$ $x - 2$

8. $f(x) = x^4 - x^3 + x - 5$ $x + 1$

9. $f(x) = 3x^3 + x^2 - 6x + 3$ $x + \frac{1}{3}$

10. $f(x) = x^7 - 31x^2$ $x - 2$

B   **11.** If $f(x)$ of degree n, $n > 0$, is divided by $g(x)$ of degree m, $m > 0$, so that a quotient $Q(x)$ and a remainder $r(x)$ are obtained, what is the degree of $Q(x)$? of $r(x)$?

12. Find the value of $f(x) = x^3 - x^2 - 4x + 4$ at $x = -3, -2, -1$, 0, 1, 2, 3. What are the factors of $f(x)$?

13. Find the value of $f(x) = 6x^3 + 35x^2 - 7x - 6$ at $x = -6, -2$, $-\frac{1}{3}, \frac{1}{2}, 3$. Name three linear factors of $f(x)$.

14. Find the value of k so that $f(x) = x^4 + kx^3 - 2kx^2 + 3x - 5$ has a factor $x - 1$.

15. Find the values of k so that $f(x) = x^3 - x^2 + kx - 12$ has a factor $x - 3$.

16. Determine k so that $x - k$ will divide $f(x) = x^2 + 4x + 2$ with a remainder of -1.

C **17.** If $f(x) = x^2 + px + q$ is exactly divisible by $x - a$ and $x - b$, show that $p = -a - b$ and $q = ab$.

18. Show that $x - a$ is a factor of $x^n - a^n$ when n is even.

19. Show that $x + a$ is a factor of $x^n + a^n$ when n is odd. What is $Q(x)$?

20. Show that $3x - 6$ is a factor of $3x^3 - 15x + 6$.

21. Prove Theorem 7–1 for the case

$$f(x) = a_3x^3 + a_2x^2 + a_1x + a_0.$$

(*Hint:* Follow the pattern used in the text for $f(x) = x^3 - 4x^2 + x + 6$.)

━━ Use the quadratic formula to find the zeros of each quadratic function in Exercises 22–25. Express the quadratic function as the product of two linear functions with complex coefficients (real or imaginary).

22. $f(x) = 2x^2 + 7x - 15$

23. $f(x) = x^2 - x - 1$

24. $f(x) = 2x^2 - 3x + 2$

25. $f(x) = x^2 + 4$

7–4 Locating Real Zeros

The Factor Theorem enables you to answer the question: Given a polynomial function f and a real number c, is c a zero of f? This theorem does not, however, tell you *how* to find c.

For polynomial functions of degree one and two, linear and quadratic functions, you already know how to find the zeros. There are also methods that can be used to determine the zeros of third and fourth degree polynomial functions. Surprising as it may seem, the best way to determine the zeros of a polynomial function of degree greater than two is to *guess*. The following theorem is an aid to making intelligent guesses.

● **Theorem 7–3** **Locater Theorem** If f is a polynomial function and a and b are real numbers such that $f(a)$ and $f(b)$ have opposite signs, then there is at least one zero of f between a and b.

Geometrically the Locater Theorem says that if the point $(a, f(a))$ is below the x axis and the point $(b, f(b))$ is above the x axis, then there must be *at least one* point between $x = a$ and $x = b$ on the x axis where the graph intersects the axis.

Although this Theorem is not proved here, the basic reason for its validity lies in the fact that every polynomial function is continuous on each interval $[a, b]$. Consequently there are no "gaps" in the graph, and it must intersect the x axis at least once.

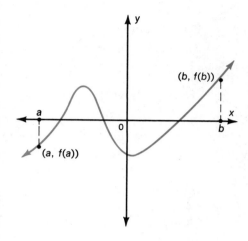

The figure at the right illustrates the Locater Theorem. Since $f(a) < 0$ and $f(b) > 0$, $f(a)$ and $f(b)$ have opposite signs. Thus, the graph of f must intersect the x axis at least once between $x = a$ and $x = b$. In fact, in the figure, f intersects the x axis three times and thus at least once.

EXAMPLE 1. Locate between successive tenths a real zero of the following function.

$$f(x) = x^4 - 2x^3 + 4x - 4$$

Solution: Use synthetic substitution to find two integers a and b, for which $f(a)$ and $f(b)$ have opposite signs. The work is tabulated below, using selected values for c.

		Coefficients			
	1	−2	0	4	−4
−2 **zero**	1	−4	8	−12	20
−1	1	−3	3	1	−5
0	1	−2	0	4	−4
1 **zero**	1	−1	−1	3	−1
2	1	0	0	4	4
3	1	1	3	13	35
c				$f(c)$	

Hence there is at least one zero between -2 and -1 and at least one zero between 1 and 2.

Choose one of the pairs of numbers, say 1 and 2, and "close in" on the zero by finding $f(c)$ for $1 < c < 2$. Since $-1(f(1))$ is closer to 0 than is 4 $(f(2))$, pick a number that is closer to 1, such as 1.3.

1	-2	0	4	-4	$\lfloor 1.3$
	1.3	-0.91	-1.183	3.6621	
1	-0.7	-0.91	2.817	-0.3379	

Because $f(1.3) = -0.3379$ and $f(2) = 4$ there is a zero of the polynomial function between 1.3 and 2.

1	-2	0	4	-4	$\lfloor 1.4$
	1.4	-0.84	-1.176	3.9536	
1	-0.6	-0.84	2.824	-0.0464	

Hence $f(1.4) = -0.0464$, and there is a zero between 1.4 and 2.

1	-2	0	4	-4	$\lfloor 1.5$
	1.5	-0.75	-1.125	4.3125	
1	-0.5	-0.75	2.875	0.3125	

Since $f(1.4)$ and $f(1.5)$ have opposite signs, there is at least one zero between 1.4 and 1.5.

In Example 1 at least two real zeros of a polynomial function f were located, but no mention was made of the possibility of there being other real zeros. In fact, the table in Example 1 allows you to conclude that all of the real zeros of f are between $x = -2$ and $x = 3$.

Theorem 7–4 Let f be a polynomial function. Let c be a positive real number substituted synthetically in $f(x)$. If
(1) all the coefficients of the depressed polynomial $Q(x)$ are nonnegative, and
(2) $f(c)$ is positive, then all the real zeros of f are less than c, and thus c is an **upper bound** for the zeros of f.

Proof: By the Remainder Theorem, $f(x) = (x - c)Q(x) + f(c)$. For $x = c, f(x) = f(c) > 0$. Thus, $x = c$ is not a zero.
For $x > c, (x - c) > 0, Q(x) > 0$ and $f(c) > 0$. Thus,

$$(x - c)Q(x) + f(c) > 0.$$

Consequently, any x equal to or greater than c is not a zero of f, and all real zeros must be less than c.

You may ask how a real number that is less than all the real zeros of a polynomial function can be determined. If such a number exists, it is called a **lower bound** for the zeros of a function f. One way to determine a lower bound for the zeros of f is to examine $f(-x)$ and apply Theorem 7–4.

Suppose c is a zero of $f(x)$, $c < 0$.
Then
$$f(x) = (x - c)Q(x)$$
and
$$\begin{aligned} f(-x) &= (-x - c)Q(-x) \\ &= -(x + c)Q(-x) \\ &= -(x - [-c])Q(-x). \end{aligned}$$

Thus, $-c > 0$ is a zero of $f(-x)$. That is, the negative zeros of $f(x)$ are positive zeros of $f(-x)$. Consequently, an upper bound for the positive zeros of $f(-x)$ is a lower bound for the negative zeros of $f(x)$.

EXAMPLE 2. Find an upper bound and a lower bound for the roots of the polynomial function of Example 1.
$$f(x) = x^4 - 2x^3 + 4x - 4$$

Solution: Find $f(3)$ by synthetic substitution and observe the signs of the coefficients of the depressed polynomial.

1	−2	0	4	−4	$\underline{3}$
	3	3	9	39	
1	1	3	13	35	

The coefficients 1, 1, 3, and 13 are positive, and hence by Theorem 7–4 the number 3 is an *upper bound* for the zeros of f. A lower bound for the zeros of f may be found by finding an upper bound for the zeros of $f(-x)$.
$$f(-x) = x^4 + 2x^3 - 4x - 4$$

1	2	0	−4	−4	$\underline{2}$
	2	8	16	24	
1	4	8	12	20	

Hence −2 is a lower bound for the zeros of f.

There is a simpler test for a lower bound of the zeros of f that is frequently substituted for the one described above. Substitute synthetically a negative number c in a polynomial. If the coefficients of the depressed polynomial of $f(x)$ and the number $f(c)$ alternate in sign, then c is a lower bound for the zeros of f.

Use the test just stated to find a lower bound for the zeros of the function

$$f(x) = x^4 - 2x^3 + 4x - 4.$$

Solution: By synthetic substitution,

1	-2	0	4	-4	$\lfloor -2$
	-2	8	-16	24	
1	-4	8	-12	20	← **The signs alternate.**

Thus, -2 is a lower bound.

CLASSROOM EXERCISES

—— Find the smallest integral upper bound and the largest integral lower bound for the zeros of each polynomial.

1. $f(x) = x^3 + 3x^2 - 3$ **2.** $f(x) = 2x^4 + 2x + 3$

3. $f(x) = x^4 - 3x^2 + 6x - 2$ **4.** $f(x) = 2x^3 - 5x^2 + 4$

5. $f(x) = 4x^2 - 3x + 2$ **6.** $f(x) = 5x^4 - 2x^2 + 7$

WRITTEN EXERCISES

A —— Find the intervals between consecutive integers that contain real zeros of f.

1. $f(x) = x^3 - 3x^2 + 3$

2. $f(x) = 2x^4 - 2x - 3$

3. $f(x) = x^4 - 3x^2 - 6x - 2$

4. $f(x) = x^3 - 6x^2 + 11x - 5$

5. $f(x) = x^4 + 3x - 13$

6. $f(x) = x^3 - 12x + 3$

7. $f(x) = 3x^3 - 3x + 1$ (*Hint:* Try $f(\frac{1}{2})$.)

8. Determine the upper and lower bounds for the zeros of the functions in Exercises 1–7.

B —— Locate between successive tenths one real zero of each polynomial function.

9. $f(x) = x^3 + 3x - 2$ **10.** $f(x) = x^4 + x - 1$

11. $f(x) = x^3 - x + 7$ **12.** $f(x) = -x^3 + 2x - 1$

13. Determine the range of values of k for which $f(x) = x^3 - 2x^2 + 4x - k$ has at least one real zero between

a. 0 and 1.   **b.** 1 and 2.

7–5   Rational Zeros

In this section you will be concerned only with polynomials over the integers, that is, polynomials with integral coefficients. The following theorem is of major importance. It is extremely useful in helping you to find possible rational zeros for polynomial functions over the integers.

Theorem 7–5   Let f be a polynomial function over the integers.

$$f(x) = a_n x^n + a_{n-1} x^{n-1} + \cdots + a_1 x + a_0, \quad a_i \in I$$

If f has a rational zero $\frac{r}{s}$, $\frac{r}{s} \neq 0$, $s > 0$, and $\frac{r}{s}$ is expressed in lowest terms, then r is a divisor of a_0 and s is a divisor of a_n.

Proof:

By assumption, $\frac{r}{s}$ is a zero of f. Thus $f\left(\frac{r}{s}\right) = 0$ and

$$a_n \frac{r^n}{s^n} + a_{n-1} \frac{r^{n-1}}{s^{n-1}} + a_{n-2} \frac{r^{n-2}}{s^{n-2}} + \cdots + a_1 \frac{r}{s} + a_0 = 0. \qquad 1$$

Multiplying 1 by s^n ($s \neq 0$) gives

$$a_n r^n + a_{n-1} r^{n-1} s + a_{n-2} r^{n-2} s^2 + \cdots + a_1 r s^{n-1} + a_0 s^n = 0. \qquad 2$$

Equation 2 can be written in two convenient forms. The first is obtained by solving 2 for $a_0 s^n$ and dividing by r; the second by solving 2 for $a_n r^n$ and dividing by s.

$$\frac{a_0 s^n}{r} = -[a_n r^{n-1} + a_{n-1} r^{n-2} s + a_{n-2} r^{n-3} s^2 + \cdots + a_1 s^{n-1}] \qquad 3$$

$$\frac{a_n r^n}{s} = -[a_{n-1} r^{n-1} + a_{n-2} r^{n-2} s + \cdots + a_1 r s^{n-2} + a_0 s^{n-1}] \qquad 4$$

The coefficients $a_0, a_1, \cdots, a_n$ and n and s are integers and so the expressions on the right side of equations 3 and 4 are also integers. Thus the left side must also be integers. Since $\frac{r}{s}$ is in lowest terms, s does not divide r, and r does not divide s. Thus r does not divide s^n (Why?), and s does not divide r^n. Consequently, $\frac{a_0 s^n}{r}$ being an integer and r not dividing s^n implies r divides a_0. In a similar manner it follows from 4 that s divides a_n. Thus the theorem is proved.

Theorem 7–6 is a special case of Theorem 7–5.

Theorem 7–6 If

$$f(x) = x^n + a_{n-1}x^{n-1} + a_{n-2}x^{n-2} + \cdots + a_1 x + a_0$$

is a polynomial with integral coefficients, $a_0 \neq 0$, and the coefficient of the highest power of x is one, then the only rational numbers that may be zeros of f are the integral divisors of a_0.

EXAMPLE 1. Find the only rational numbers that may be zeros of

$$f(x) = 3x^3 - 8x^2 + 3x + 2.$$

Solution: For $f(x) = 3x^3 - 8x^2 + 3x + 2$, $a_n = 3$ and $a_0 = 2$.

$r \in \{1, 2, -1, -2\}$ ◄——— **Factors of a_0**

$s \in \{1, 3\}$ ◄——— **Factors of a_n**

$\frac{r}{s} \in \{\pm 1, \pm 2, \pm \frac{1}{3}, \pm \frac{2}{3}\}$ ◄——— **By Theorem 7-5**

EXAMPLE 2. Find the only rational numbers that may be zeros of

$$f(x) = x^4 - 2x^3 + 3x^2 - 2x + 2.$$

The possible rational zeros are ± 1 and ± 2 by Theorem 7–6. To find the *actual* rational zeros, the *possible* zeros must be tested.

EXAMPLE 3. Find the rational zeros of the following function.

$$f(x) = 3x^4 - 5x^3 - 5x^2 - 19x - 6$$

Solution: $\frac{r}{s} \in \{\pm 1, \pm 2, \pm 3, \pm 6, \pm \frac{1}{3}, \pm \frac{2}{3}\}$ ◄——— $\begin{array}{l} a_0 = -6 \\ a_n = 3 \end{array}$

Substituting synthetically you find that 3 is a zero of f.

3	-5	-5	-19	-6	$\underline{|3}$
	9	12	21	6	
3	4	7	2	$|\ 0$	

Thus $f(x) = (x - 3)(3x^3 + 4x^2 + 7x + 2)$. If $f(x)$ has any other rational zeros, they must be zeros of the depressed polynomial $3x^3 + 4x^2 + 7x + 2$. This is true because if $x - c$, $c \neq 3$, is to divide $f(x)$, it must divide $3x^3 + 4x^2 + 7x + 2$. Hence $3x^3 + 4x^2 + 7x + 2$ can be used to determine the remaining zeros (if any).

For the depressed polynomial, the only rational numbers that may be the zeros are: ± 1, ± 2, $\pm\frac{1}{3}$, $\pm\frac{2}{3}$. Notice that the number of possible zeros has been decreased by using the depressed polynomial. Synthetic substitution shows that $-\frac{1}{3}$ is a zero.

3	4	7	2	$\underline{\;-\frac{1}{3}}$
	-1	-1	-2	
3	3	6	0	

Thus $f(x) = (x - 3)(x + \frac{1}{3})(3x^2 + 3x + 6)$. Again, $3x^2 + 3x + 6$ is a depressed polynomial that can be written $Q(x) = 3(x^2 + x + 2)$. The only possible rational zeros of $Q(x)$ are integers, namely, ± 1 and ± 2. Synthetic substitution shows that none of these is a zero. Thus the rational zeros of $f(x)$ are 3, $-\frac{1}{3}$, and $f(x) = 3(x - 3)(x + \frac{1}{3})(x^2 + x + 2)$.

WRITTEN EXERCISES

A ▬▬ Find all rational zeros and, if possible, all other real zeros of $f(x)$.

1. $f(x) = x^3 - x^2 - 14x + 24$
2. $f(x) = x^3 - 8x^2 + 5x + 14$
3. $f(x) = x^3 - 2x^2 - 7x - 4$
4. $f(x) = x^3 + 2x^2 - x - 2$
5. $f(x) = 8x^3 - 26x^2 + 23x - 6$
6. $f(x) = 6x^3 + 5x^2 - 8x - 7$
7. $f(x) = 3x^3 - x^2 - 6x + 2$ (*Hint:* Use the quadratic formula to find the real zeros that are not rational.)
8. $f(x) = 2x^3 - 5x^2 + 1$
9. $f(x) = x^3 - x^2 - 14x + 24$
10. $f(x) = 2x^3 - x^2 + 2x - 1$
11. $f(x) = x^3 + 5x^2 + 8x + 6$
12. $f(x) = 8x^5 - 27x^2$ (Three rational and two complex zeros.)
13. $f(x) = x^4 - 4x^3 - 14x^2 + 36x + 45$
14. $f(x) = 4x^4 - 8x^3 - 5x^2 + 2x + 1$
15. $f(x) = 12x^3 + x^2 - 15$

B **16.** Show that if all the coefficients of $f(x)$ have the same sign, then $f(x)$ has no positive real zeros.

17. Find a cubic polynomial function whose zeros are -1, 2, and -3.

18. Find a cubic polynomial function whose zeros are $\frac{1}{2}$, $-\frac{2}{3}$, and 6.

C ▬ You may know that if $f(x) = ax^2 + bx + c$ has zeros r_1 and r_2, then

$$r_1 + r_2 = -\frac{b}{a} \quad \text{and} \quad r_1 \cdot r_2 = \frac{c}{a}.$$

Similar relationships exist between the zeros and the coefficients of polynomials of third degree and higher. The following exercises develop this relationship for third degree polynomials. Use the zeros of the polynomial derived in Exercise 17 in each of the following Exercises.

19. Find the sum of the zeros. Compare the sum with the coefficient of x^2.

20. Find the sum of all possible two-factor products of the zeros, for example, $(-1 \cdot 2) + (-1 \cdot -3) + (2 \cdot -3)$. Compare the result with the coefficient of x.

21. Find the product of the zeros. Compare the result with the constant term.

▬ The zeros of a third degree polynomial function are 2, $\frac{1}{2}$, and $-\frac{3}{2}$. Use this information in Exercises 22–25.

22. Find the sum of the zeros.

23. Find the sum of all possible two-factor products of the zeros.

24. Find the product of the zeros.

25. Write the equation of a polynomial function having the given zeros. Check your result by using the Factor Theorem.

26. Use the Factor Theorem to write the equation of a third-degree polynomial function with zeros r_1, r_2, and r_3.

27. Use the result of Exercise 26 and the fact that $f(x) = a_3x^3 + a_2x^2 + a_1x + a_0$ can be written

$$f(x) = a_3 \left(x^3 + \frac{a_2}{a_3}x^2 + \frac{a_1}{a_3}x + \frac{a_0}{a_3} \right)$$

to find expressions for the coefficients $\frac{a_2}{a_3}$, $\frac{a_1}{a_3}$, and $\frac{a_0}{a_3}$ in terms of r_1, r_2 and r_3.

28. Find the polynomial function f of degree three that has rational zeros 2, -1, and 3, and that satisfies the condition $f(0) = 18$.

29. Follow the procedure of Exercises 26 and 27 to find expressions for the coefficients $\frac{a_3}{a_4}$, $\frac{a_2}{a_4}$, $\frac{a_1}{a_4}$, and $\frac{a_0}{a_4}$ of the function

$$f(x) = a_4 \left(x^4 + \frac{a_3x^3}{a_4} + \frac{a_2x^2}{a_4} + \frac{a_1x}{a_4} + \frac{a_0}{a_4} \right)$$

in terms of the zeros r_1, r_2, r_3 and r_4 of f.

7–6 Number of Zeros of a Polynomial Function

Two important questions about the zeros of a polynomial function have not been answered. Does every polynomial function have a zero? How many zeros does such a polynomial function have? The first question is answered by the following theorem called the **Fundamental Theorem of Algebra.**

Theorem 7–7 Every polynomial function of degree greater than zero has at least one real or imaginary zero.

The proof of the theorem is not given, since it is beyond the scope of this book.

Notice that the Fundamental Theorem does not tell you how to find a zero, but it does assure you that a zero exists.

Before the second question can be answered, the notion of a *multiple zero* and the *multiplicity* of a zero must be discussed. The function

$$f(x) = x^2 + 8x + 16 = (x + 4)(x + 4)$$

has exactly one zero, namely $x = -4$. Since it appears in more than one factor, -4 is called a *multiple zero*. Since -4 appears in exactly two factors, it has *multiplicity* 2. More formally:

Definitions Given a polynomial function f and a zero r of f.
a. r is a **multiple zero** of f if and only if $(x - r)^k$, $k > 1$, divides $f(x)$. If $k = 1$, the zero is called a **simple zero.**
b. The **multiplicity** of a zero r is the greatest exponent k such that $(x - r)^k$ divides $f(x)$.

EXAMPLE 1. It is easy to verify that 0 and 1 are zeros of $f(x) = x^5 - 3x^4 + 3x^3 - x^2$. Find the multiplicity of each zero.

Since $x^5 - 3x^4 + 3x^3 - x^2 = x^2(x^3 - 3x^2 + 3x - 1)$, $x^2 = (x - 0)^2$ divides $f(x)$. Thus $x = 0$ is a zero of multiplicity 2. Since $(x - 1)^3 = x^3 - 3x^2 + 3x - 1$, $x = 1$ is a zero of multiplicity 3. In factored form, $f(x) = x^2(x - 1)^3$. The number of zeros can now be determined for a polynomial of degree n.

Theorem 7–8 Let f be a polynomial of degree n, $n > 0$. Then f has at least one and at most n complex zeros (including real zeros), and the sum of the multiplicities of the zeros is n.

The proof is based on Theorem 7–7 and is left for you to do.

EXAMPLE 2. Find all the complex zeros of

$$f(x) = 2x^5 - 4x^3 + 4x^2 - 6x + 4$$

and write $f(x)$ as the product of linear terms and a constant.

First note that $f(x) = 2(x^5 - 2x^3 + 2x^2 - 3x + 2)$. Using synthetic substitution you can show easily that 1 is a zero of multiplicity 2 and -2 is a simple zero. Thus

$$f(x) = 2(x - 1)(x - 1)(x + 2)(x^2 + 1).$$

Now $x^2 + 1$ has no real zero, but i and $-i$ are zeros. So $x^2 + 1 = (x - i)(x + i)$. Consequently, the complex zeros of f are 1, 1, -2, i, $-i$ and $f(x) = 2(x - 1)(x - 1)(x + 2)(x - i)(x + i)$.

Example 2 illustrates two ideas. First, some of the complex zeros may be real. (Recall that the real numbers are complex numbers of the form $a + 0i$.) Secondly, when there is a nonreal complex zero of a polynomial with *real* coefficients, there is another such zero. In fact, if $a + bi$ is a complex zero of f, then its conjugate $a - bi$ is also a zero. Since nonreal complex zeros occur in pairs, every polynomial of odd degree with real coefficients has at least one real zero.

Theorem 7–9 If f is a polynomial function with real coefficients and $f(a + bi) = 0$, $b \neq 0$, then $f(a - bi) = 0$.

Theorem 7–10 If f is a polynomial function of odd degree with real coefficients, then f has at least one *real* zero.

The proofs of these two theorems are left for you.

CLASSROOM EXERCISES

━━ Find all the complex zeros and their multiplicity.

1. $f(x) = x^4 - 8x^2 + 16$ 2. $f(x) = x^4 - 5x^2 + 4$
3. $f(x) = x^4 + 4x^2 + 3$ 4. $f(x) = x^4 + 4x^3 + 6x^2 + 4x + 1$

WRITTEN EXERCISES

A ━━ For Exercises 1–12 find the zeros of each function. Show that the sum of the multiplicities in each exercise equals the degree of the polynomial.

1. $f(x) = x^3 - 3x - 2$

2. $f(x) = x^3 - 3x + 2$

3. $f(x) = x^4 + 5x^3 + 9x^2 + 7x + 2$

4. $f(x) = x^5 + 4x^4 + x^3 - 10x^2 - 4x + 8$

5. $f(x) = x^3 - 1$

6. $f(x) = x^3 + 1$

7. $f(x) = x^4 + 5x^2 + 4$

8. $f(x) = x^4 - 2x^3 + 10x^2 - 18x + 9$

9. $f(x) = x^6 - 2x^3 + 1$

10. $f(x) = x^6 + 2x^3 + 1$

11. $f(x) = x^6 + 2x^5 + 3x^4 + 4x^3 + 3x^2 + 2x + 1$

12. $f(x) = x^6 - 2x^5 + 3x^4 - 4x^3 + 3x^2 - 2x + 1$

B ━━ Let f be a polynomial function with the given zeros. Write a polynomial with the smallest degree and integral coefficients that could define f.

13. $1, -1, 2$

14. $\frac{1}{2}, \frac{3}{2}, -1$

15. $1 + \sqrt{3}, 2$

16. $1, \dfrac{1 + \sqrt{3}i}{2}$

17. $2, 0, 1 + i$

18. $5, 2, -3i$

19. A double zero $1 + 2i$.

20. A double zero 2; $1 + 2i$.

21. A triple zero of i.

22. Given the polynomial function

$$f(x) = x^3 - 3x^2 + 9x + 13,$$

find the other zeros if one zero is $2 + 3i$.

23. Given the polynomial function

$$f(x) = 2x^4 - 9x^3 + 13x^2 - 81x - 45,$$

find the other zeros if one zero is $3i$.

24. A triple zero of

$$f(x) = 8x^5 - 12x^4 + 38x^3 - 49x^2 + 24x - 4$$

is $\frac{1}{2}$. Find the other zeros.

C **25.** Prove Theorem 7–8. (*Hint:* By Theorem 7–7, f has at least one zero, r. Thus, by the factor Theorem

$$f(x) = (x - r)Q(x),$$

where $Q(x)$ has degree $n - 1$. If $n - 1 = 0$, you are finished. If $n - 1 \neq 0$, repeat the process on $Q(x)$.)

26. Prove Theorem 7–9.

7–7 Maxima and Minima

In Section 6–6 the derived function f' evaluated at $x = c$ was given a geometric interpretation: $f'(c)$ is the slope of the line tangent to the graph of f at the point $(c, f(c))$. If $f'(c) = 0$, then the tangent at $(c, f(c))$ is a line parallel to the x axis. Two of the forms that the graph of the function may take in a small neighborhood of $(c, f(c))$ are shown below.

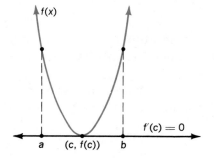

Figure 1

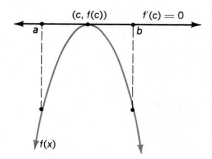

Figure 2

In Figure 1, the graph of f is above the tangent for all values of x in a small closed interval $[a, b]$ and in this case $(c, f(c))$ is called a **relative minimum** for f. It is indeed a *minimum* since $f(c) < f(x)$ for all $x \in [a, b]$. It is a *relative* minimum because there may be values of $f(x)$ that are less than $f(c)$ if x is not in $[a, b]$. If $f(c)$ is less than all other $f(x)$ for x in the domain of f, then $(c, f(c))$ is an **absolute minimum** for f.

In Figure 2, each point of the graph of f for x in a small neighborhood $[a, b]$ of c is below the tangent and $(c, f(c))$ is a **relative maximum** of the function. If $f(c)$ is greater than $f(x)$ for all x in the domain of f, then $(c, f(c))$ is an **absolute maximum** for f.

A function f is graphed in Figure 3 on the interval $[a, b]$. The points for which $f'(x) = 0$ are as follows:

a. Relative minimum — $(c_1, f(c_1))$.
b. Absolute (as well as relative) minimum — $(c_2, f(c_2))$.
c. Relative maximum — $(c_3, f(c_3))$.

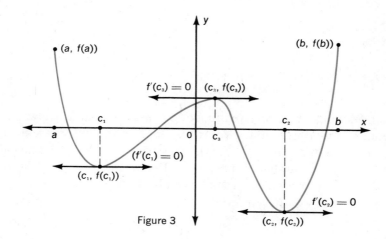

Figure 3

The graph shows clearly that $(b, f(b))$ is an absolute maximum and that an absolute maximum (or minimum) does not necessarily correspond to a point at which $f'(x)$ is zero.

The set of zeros of a derived function f' are called **critical points** of the function f. The relative maxima and minima are in the set of critical points of the function.

EXAMPLE. Find the relative maxima and minima of
$$f(x) = 2x^3 - 3x^2 - 12x - 7.$$

Solution: First find the derived function.
$$f'(x) = 6x^2 - 6x - 12$$
$$= 6(x - 2)(x + 1)$$

Find the values of x when $f'(x) = 0$.
$$f'(x) = 0 = 6(x - 2)(x + 1)$$
$$x - 2 = 0 \quad \text{or} \quad x + 1 = 0$$

You must now determine the character of f near $x = 2$ and $x = -1$.
$$f(x) = 2x^3 - 3x^2 - 12x - 7$$
$$= (2x - 7)(x + 1)(x + 1)$$

①
$$f(-1) = (-9)(0)(0) = 0$$
$$f(-\tfrac{1}{2}) = (-8)(\tfrac{1}{2})(\tfrac{1}{2}) = -2$$
$$f(-\tfrac{3}{2}) = (-10)(-\tfrac{1}{2})(-\tfrac{1}{2}) = -2.5$$

By further testing you see that $(-1, 0)$ is a relative maximum.

②
$$f(2) = (-3)(3)(3) = -27$$
$$f(\tfrac{3}{2}) = (-4)(2.5)(2.5) = -25$$
$$f(\tfrac{5}{2}) = (-2)(3.5)(3.5) = -24.50$$

By further testing you see that $(2, -27)$ is a relative minimum.

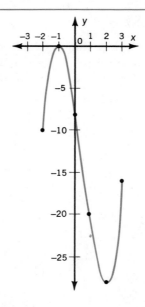

The graph of f for $x \in [-2, 3]$ is shown above. (Note that the scales on the x and y axes are in a 2 : 1 ratio.) Notice that the relative maximum and relative minimum that have been identified are also absolute for $x \in [-2, 3]$. The absolute maximum and minimum will change if the domain of f is changed. For instance, if the domain is $[-3, 4]$, then $f(-3) = -52$, $f(4) = 25$, and $(-3, -52)$ is the absolute minimum while $(4, 25)$ is the absolute maximum. For $x \in R$ there is no absolute maximum or minimum. However, the relative maximum and minimum found in the example remain unchanged. Notice also that $f'(-3) = 60$ and $f'(4) = 60$. Thus, a point may be an absolute maximum or minimum and not be associated with a tangent line with zero slope. For this reason the discussion in this section is restricted to finding relative maxima and minima that are associated with values of x for which $f'(x) = 0$.

CLASSROOM EXERCISES

▬▬ Find the derived function and the critical points of each polynomial.

1. $f(x) = x^3 + 3x^2 + 3x$

2. $f(x) = 2x^3 - 15x^2 + 12$

3. $f(x) = x^3 - 3x - 6$

4. $f(x) = x^4 - 8x^3 + 7$

5. $f(x) = 4x^5 + 2x^3 + 8$

6. $f(x) = 7x^3 - 6x^2 - 5x$

7. $f(x) = 6x^7 - 8x^6 - 5$

8. $f(x) = 3x^2 - 7x + 4$

WRITTEN EXERCISES

A ▬▬ Identify the critical points of each polynomial function f. Determine whether each critical point is a relative maximum or minimum.

1. $f(x) = 2x^3 - 3x^2 - 12x$

2. $f(x) = x^3 + 3x^2$

3. $f(x) = x^3 - 3x^2$

4. $f(x) = x^2 - 7x + 6$

5. $f(x) = -x^2 + 7x - 6$

6. $f(x) = 3 - 2x - x^2$

7. $f(x) = x^3 + 12x$

8. $f(x) = \frac{x^3}{3} + \frac{3x^2}{2} + 2x - 11$

9. $f(x) = x^3 - 2x^2 + 5$

10. $f(x) = x^4 - 16x^2 - 12$

11. $f(x) = -2x^3 - 3x^2 + 11$

12. $f(x) = x^7 - 31$

13. $f(x) = ax^2 + 6x + c, a \neq 0$

14. $f(x) = ax^3 - 2x + c, a > 0$

B ▬▬ A ball is thrown upward so that its height t seconds later is s feet above the earth. Use this information and $s = 96t - 16t^2$, where s is in feet and t is in seconds, in the following exercises.

15. What is the height of the ball after

    a. 1 second?

    b. 4 seconds?

    c. 6 seconds?

16. What is the time when the ball reaches its maximum height?

17. What is the maximum height of the ball?

■ The formula $s = 160t - 16t^2$ describes the motion (vertically upward) of a toy rocket, where s is in feet and t is in seconds. Use this information in Exercises 18–20.

18. How high is the rocket when $t = 3$? when $t = 7$?

19. Explain why the height of the rocket is the same when $t = 3$ and when $t = 7$.

20. Use the derived function to determine at what time t the rocket reached a maximum height. (*Hint:* At what time t does the derived function equal zero?)

C **21.** Find the dimensions of a rectangle with perimeter 72 meters that will enclose the maximum area.

22. Find the dimensions of a rectangular field with maximum area to be enclosed with 200 meters of fencing if one side of the field is along a straight river and needs no fence.

MID-CHAPTER REVIEW

1. Identify the degree and leading coefficient of the polynomial function $f(x) = 2x - 3x^4 + 5x^2$. (Section 7-1)

2. Determine the slope, y intercept, and real zeros of $f(x) = -8x + 5$. (Section 7-1)

3. Determine the coordinates of the turning point, the equation of the axis of symmetry, and the real zeros of $f(x) = x^2 + 7x - 8$. (Section 7-1)

4. Determine the slope of the tangent to $f(x) = x^2 + 3x - 5$ at $x = 3$. (Section 7-1)

5. Use synthetic substitution to evaluate $f(x) = x^4 - 3x^3 + 2x - 1$ at $x = -1$, 0 and 4. (Section 7-2)

6. Find $Q(x)$ and $f(5)$ so that $f(x) = x^5 - 2x^2 + 3 = Q(x)(x - 5) + f(5)$. (Section 7-3)

7. Find the quotient and remainder when $3x^5 - 2x^2 + x - 1$ is divided by $x - 2$. (Section 7-3)

8. Find the intervals between consecutive integers that contain real zeros of $P(x) = 24x^3 + 22x^2 - 97x + 40$. (Section 7-4)

9. Find all the rational zeros of $P(x) = 24x^3 + 22x^2 - 97x + 40$. (Section 7-5)

10. Write a cubic polynomial function whose zeros are $-\frac{3}{4}$, $\frac{1}{2}$, and $\frac{5}{3}$. (Section 7-5)

11. How many real zeros may $f(x) = x^6 - 16x^3 + 64$ have? Find all the zeros, real and complex and state the multiplicities of each. (Section 7-6)

12. Identify the critical points of $f(x) = x^3 - 2x^2 + x - 7$. Determine whether each is a relative maximum or minimum. (Section 7-7)

BASIC: FINDING A ZERO OF A FUNCTION

Problem:

Write a program which computes and prints a real zero of the function $g(x) = x^3 + 2x - 5$ to the nearest thousandth, given the upper and lower bounds.

```
100  DIM A(50),B(50),X(51)
110  PRINT
120  PRINT "THIS PROGRAM CALCULATES A ZERO OF A"
130  PRINT "FUNCTION, GIVEN TWO CONSECUTIVE"
140  PRINT "INTEGERS THAT THE ROOT LIES BETWEEN."
150  PRINT
160  DEF FN G(X) = X↑3 + 2*X - 5
170  PRINT "WHAT ARE THE TWO BOUNDING INTEGERS";
180  INPUT A(N), B(N)
190  LET X(N) = A(N)
200  PRINT
210  PRINT " N";TAB(4);"A(N)";TAB(12);"B(N)";
TAB(20);"X(N+1)";TAB(30);"F(X)"
220  PRINT "---------------------------------------"
230  LET X(N+1) = .5 * (A(N) + B(N))
240  LET F = FN G(X(N+1))
250  GOSUB 360
260  IF ABS(X(N) - X(N+1)) < .001 THEN 420
270  LET N = N + 1
280  IF F <= 0 THEN 320
290  LET B(N) = X(N)
300  LET A(N) = A(N-1)
310  GOTO 230
320  LET A(N) = X(N)
330  LET B(N) = B(N-1)
340  GOTO 230
350  REM   PRINT ROUTINE
360  LET A = INT((A(N)+.00005)*10000)/10000
370  LET B = INT((B(N)+.00005)*10000)/10000
380  LET X = INT((X(N+1)+.00005)*10000)/10000
390  LET F1 = INT((F+.00005)*10000)/10000
400  PRINT N;TAB(4);A;TAB(12);B;TAB(20);X;
TAB(30);F1
410  RETURN
420  END
```

Output:

```
WHAT ARE THE TWO BOUNDING INTEGERS? 1,2
```

N	A(N)	B(N)	X(N+1)	F(X)
0	1	2	1.5	1.375
1	1	1.5	1.25	-.5469
2	1.25	1.5	1.375	.3496
3	1.25	1.375	1.3125	-.114
4	1.3125	1.375	1.3437	.1139
5	1.3125	1.3437	1.3281	-1E-03
6	1.3281	1.3437	1.3359	.0562
7	1.3281	1.3359	1.332	.0275
8	1.3281	1.332	1.3301	.0132
9	1.3281	1.3301	1.3291	6.1E-03

Analysis:

Statements 230–250: The procedure for approximating the zero is to approach the zero by repeatedly halving the interval between A(N) and B(N) (statement 230). (NOTE: At the lower bound, $g(x) < 0$, and at the upper bound, $g(x) > 0$. To adapt the program for a decreasing function, replace G(X) by $-G(X)$.) In statement 240, the new x value, X(N + 1), is substituted in the formula for function G and the function value assigned to F. Statement 250 sends the computer to the subroutine beginning at statement 350, which prints the current values (as shown in the sample output above).

Statements 260–340: In line 260 the computer tests x_{n+1} to see if it is within 0.001 of the previous x_n. If it is, the run ends and a zero is approximated. In the sample run, a zero was found at approximately $x = 1.3291$. At that point, $g(x) \approx 0.0061$.

Statements 360–400: This subroutine uses the INT function to round the values to be printed to the nearest ten–thousandth.

EXERCISES

A   Use the program on page 352 to find real zeros for each function.

1. $x^3 + 2x^2 - 0.5$ (3 zeros)   2. $x^3 - 2x^2 + 3x - 1$

3. $x^4 - 2x^2 - 6$ 4. $x^4 - x^3 - 3$

B   Revise the program on page 352 as indicated.

5. Find real zeros to the nearest ten thousandth.

6. Handle increasing and decreasing functions.

7–8 Points of Inflection

In a small neighborhood of $(c, f(c))$, a point at which $f'(c) = 0$, the graph of the polynomial function f may also appear as in Figures 1 and 2 below.

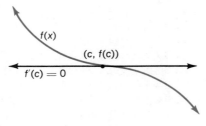

Figure 1

In Figure 1 the graph of f is above the tangent at $(c, f(c))$ for $x < c$ and below the tangent for $x > c$. The situation is reversed in Figure 2. The point $(c, f(c))$ is called a **point of inflection** of f.

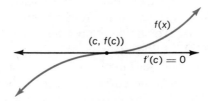

Figure 2

You have undoubtedly noticed that the horizontal line through $(c, f(c))$ in Figures 1 and 2 is not what you have been accustomed to call a tangent since it crosses the graph of f. Rather than relying on intuitive notions of the tangent (from geometry), you must now think of the tangent to the graph of a function at a point $(a, f(a))$ as the line whose slope is the limit of

$$\frac{f(a + h) - f(a)}{h}$$

as h tends to 0 (see Section 6–6). That is, the **tangent** is the limiting position of a secant through $(a, f(a))$ and $(a + h, f(a + h))$. (There are inflection points at which the slope of the tangent is not 0, but they will not be discussed until a later section.)

Since $f' = 0$ at $(c, f(c))$, a point of inflection is also a critical point. To identify such a point, you must investigate the values of $f(x)$ for $x > c$ and for $x < c$.

The results of this and the previous section can now be summarized.

Given a polynomial function f and its derived function f'. Suppose c is a critical point; that is, $f'(c) = 0$:
- i. If $f(x) > f(c)$ for all x close to c, then $(c, f(c))$ is a **relative minimum** of f.
- ii. If $f(x) < f(c)$ for all x close to c, then $(c, f(c))$ is a **relative maximum** of f.
- iii. If $f(x) < f(c)$ for $x < c$ and $f(x) > f(c)$ for $x > c$; or if $f(x) > f(c)$ for $x < c$ and $f(x) < f(c)$ for $x > c$, then $(c, f(c))$ is a **point of inflection**.

EXAMPLE 1. Find the relative maxima and minima and the points of inflection of $f(x) = 2x^3 - 3x^2 - 36x + 75$.

Solution: First find the zeros of the derived function.

$$f'(x) = 6x^2 - 6x - 36$$
$$= 6(x^2 - x - 6)$$
$$= 6(x - 3)(x + 2)$$

Hence, $f'(x) = 0$ when $x = 3$ and $x = -2$. Now compute $f(3)$, $f(3.1)$, and $f(2.9)$.

$$
\begin{array}{ccccc}
2 & -3 & -36 & +75 & \underline{|3} \\
 & 6 & 9 & -81 & \\
\hline
2 & 3 & -27 & -6 = f(3) &
\end{array}
$$

$$
\begin{array}{ccccc}
2 & -3 & -36 & 75 & \underline{|3.1} \\
 & 6.2 & 9.92 & -80.848 & \\
\hline
2 & 3.2 & -26.08 & -5.848 = f(3.1) &
\end{array}
$$

$$
\begin{array}{ccccc}
2 & -3 & -36 & 75 & \underline{|2.9} \\
 & 5.8 & 8.12 & -80.852 & \\
\hline
2 & 2.8 & -27.88 & -5.852 = f(2.9) &
\end{array}
$$

You can see that $(3, -6)$ is a relative minimum.

Similarly $\qquad\qquad f(-2) = 119$

and $\qquad\qquad f(-2.1) = 118.848$
$$f(-1.9) = 118.852.$$

You can see that $(-2, 119)$ is a relative maximum of f. No points of inflection have been found.

EXAMPLE 2. Find the relative maxima and minima, and the points of inflection of $f(x) = x^3$.

Solution:
$$f'(x) = 3x^2$$
$$f'(x) = 0 \quad \text{when } x = 0$$

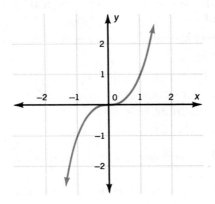

By substitution you can verify the following:
$$f(0) = 0$$
$$f(0.1) = 0.001$$
$$f(-0.1) = -0.001$$

You can see that $(0, 0)$ is a point of inflection of f. There are no relative maxima or minima.

WRITTEN EXERCISES

A ━━ Find the relative maxima, the relative minima, and the points of inflection of each function f.

1. $f(x) = 2x^3 + 3x^2 - 12x + 1$

2. $f(x) = x^3 - 12x$

3. $f(x) = x^4 - 2x^3 + 5$

4. $f(x) = (x - 2)(x + 3)^2$

5. $f(x) = \dfrac{x^4 - 6x^2 + 6}{8}$

6. $f(x) = x^2(2x + 5)$

7. $f(x) = 8x^2 - x^4$

8. $f(x) = -x^3 + 3x - 1$

9. $f(x) = x^4$

10. $f(x) = x^3 - 2x^2 + 5$

11. $f(x) = x^7 - 31$

12. $f(x) = 3x^4 - 8x^3 + 6x^2 + 1$

13. $f(x) = 12x^5 - 30x^4 + 20x^3 - 1$

14. $f(x) = x^m, m \geq 1, m \in N$

15. $f(x) = (x - a)^3$

16. $f(x) = (x - a)^4$

B ▬▬ The point $A(1, 1)$ is on the graph of each function below. For which function is A a relative minimum, a relative maximum, a point of inflection, or none of these?

17. $f(x) = 2x^3 - 6x^2 + 6x - 1$

18. $g(x) = 2x^3 - 9x^2 + 12x - 4$

19. $h(x) = 2x^3 - 3x^2 - 12x + 14$

20. $r(x) = 2x^3 - 6x + 5$

C **21.** Find two numbers whose sum is 10 such that

    a. their product is a maximum.

    b. the sum of their squares is a minimum.

22. Find two numbers whose sum is 12 such that the sum of one number and the square of the second is a minimum.

23. Find two numbers whose sum is 50 such that the product of the first and twice the second is a maximum.

7–9   Sketching Polynomials

You are now in a position to sketch an accurate graph of a polynomial function quite easily. The information that is available from the equation defining a polynomial function and that is also valuable in graphing the function follows.

    Given: $f(x) = a_n x^n + a_{n-1} x^{n-1} + \cdots + a_1 x + a_0$

① The y intercept is $(0, a_0)$.

② The value of f at $x = c$ is found by direct or synthetic substitution.

③ The real zeros of f are found (when possible) by application of the ideas in Sections 7–3 to 7–5.

④ The relative maxima and minima and inflection points are found by determining the zeros of $f'(x)$.

EXAMPLE 1. Sketch the graph of $f(x) = x^3 + 3x^2 - 4$.

Solution:

① The y intercept is $(0, -4)$ because $f(0) = -4$.

② Using synthetic substitution,

$$f(x) = x^3 + 3x^2 - 4$$
$$= (x + 2)^2(x - 1).$$

Thus the zeros of f are $x = -2$ and $x = 1$; $x = -2$ is a zero of multiplicity two.

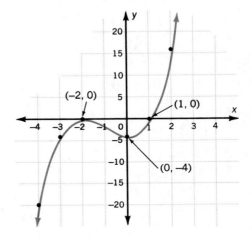

③ Compile a table of values of f for an interval that includes the zeros of f, in this case $[-4, 3]$.

x	-4	-3	-2	-1	0	1	2	3
$f(x)$	-20	-4	0	-2	-4	0	16	50

④ $f'(x) = 3x^2 + 6x = x(3x + 6)$

The zeros of f' are $x = 0$ and $x = -2$. Since $f(x) < f(-2)$ for x close to -2, $(-2, 0)$ is a *relative maximum*. Since $f(x) > f(0)$ for x close to 0, $(0, -4)$ is a *relative minimum*.

Two questions which have not been answered in the analysis of Example 1 are: What happens to the graph of f as $x \longrightarrow +\infty$? What happens to the graph of f as $x \longrightarrow -\infty$? You can answer these questions by considering the following limits.

a. $\lim\limits_{x \to +\infty} x^3 + 3x^2 - 4$ **b.** $\lim\limits_{x \to -\infty} x^3 + 3x^2 - 4$

It is clear that $x^3 + 3x^2 - 4 \longrightarrow +\infty$ as $x \longrightarrow +\infty$. That is, as x increases without bound so does $x^3 + 3x^2 - 4$. The fact is denoted as follows.

$$\lim\limits_{x \to +\infty} x^3 + 3x^2 - 4 = +\infty$$

Geometrically this means that the graph continues to rise to the right as x increases.

The situation for **b** is not quite as clear, for as $x \longrightarrow -\infty$, $x^3 \longrightarrow -\infty$ and $3x^2 \longrightarrow +\infty$. Thus it appears that the limit of $x^3 + 3x^2$ could be zero. However this is not the case, for x^3 *dominates* x^2. That is, as $x \longrightarrow -\infty$, $\frac{x^3}{3x^2} = \frac{x}{3} \longrightarrow -\infty$. Thus x^3 approaches $-\infty$ so fast that it counteracts the effect of $3x^2$ approaching $+\infty$.
Consequently

$$x^3 + 3x^2 - 4 \longrightarrow -\infty \quad \text{as} \quad x \longrightarrow -\infty,$$

or

$$\lim_{x \to -\infty} x^3 + 3x^2 - 4 = -\infty.$$

Geometrically this means that the graph continues to drop to the left as x decreases ($x \longrightarrow -\infty$).

In general, the power of x with the greatest positive exponent dominates all other sums of powers of x, and the limit of

$$a_n x^n + a_{n-1} x^{n-1} + a_{n-2} x^{n-2} + \cdots + a_0$$

approaches the same limit as $a_n x^n$ does as x approaches $+\infty$ or $-\infty$.

The nature of $\lim_{x \to +\infty} f$ and $\lim_{x \to -\infty} f$ is a fifth characteristic of f which should be determined when graphing f. This is illustrated in the next example.

EXAMPLE 2.   Sketch the graph of $f(x) = x^3 - 3x$.

Solution:

① Since $f(0) = 0$, the y intercept is $(0, 0)$.

② The zeros of $f(x) = x(x^2 - 3)$ are 0, $\sqrt{3}, -\sqrt{3}$.

③ Compile a table of values of f for

$$x \in [-3, 3].$$

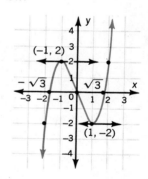

x	-3	-2	-1	0	1	2	3
$f(x)$	-18	-2	2	0	-2	2	18

④ $f'(x) = 3x^2 - 3$. The zeros of f' are $x = 1$ and $x = -1$. Consequently, $(1, -2)$ and $(-1, 2)$ are critical points. Since $f(x) > -2$ for x near 1, $(1, -2)$ is a relative minimum. Since $f(x) < 2$ for x near -1, $(-1, 2)$ is a relative maximum.

⑤ $\lim_{x \to +\infty} x^3 - 3x = +\infty$, $\lim_{x \to -\infty} x^3 - 3x = -\infty$.

WRITTEN EXERCISES

A ▬▬ Find the y intercept, functional values for $-4 < x < 4$, zeros, relative maxima and minima and inflection points, and $\lim\limits_{x \to -\infty} f$ and $\lim\limits_{x \to +\infty} f$ for each function. Graph the function.

1. $f(x) = 3x^2 - 12x + 12$

2. $f(x) = \dfrac{4x^3 + 15x^2 - 72x + 6}{6}$

3. $f(x) = x^3 - 3x^2 + 4$

4. $f(x) = 2x^3 - 9x^2 + 12x + 1$

5. $f(x) = 2x^3 + 3x^2 - 12x - 2$

6. $f(x) = x^4 - 6x^2 + 8x$

7. $f(x) = x^4 - 4x^3 + 6x^2$

8. $f(x) = 2x^3 + 3x^2 - 12x - 7$

9. $f(x) = x^4 + 5x^3 + 9x^2 + 7x + 2$

10. $f(x) = -2x^3 + 3x^2 + 12x + 7$

11. $f(x) = x^4$

12. $f(x) = x^5$

13. $f(x) = (x - 4)^3$

14. $f(x) = (x - 4)^4$

15. $f(x) = 12x^5 - 30x^4 + 20x^3 - 1$

16. $f(x) = 3x^4 - 8x^3 + 6x + 1$

17. $f(x) = -3x^4 + 8x^3 - 6x - 1$

18. $f(x) = 2x^3 - 3x^2 - 12x + 14$

19. $f(x) = x^3 + x^2 - x + 5$

20. $f(x) = x^2(x - 6)^3$

B   **21.** $f(x) = x^6 + 2x^5 + 3x^4 + 4x^3 + 3x^2 + 2x + 1$

     22. $f(x) = x^6 - 2x^5 + 3x^4 - 4x^3 + 3x^2 - 2x + 1$

     23. $f(x) = (x - 1)^3(x^2 + 1)$

     24. $f(x) = (x - 1)^3(x + 1)(x^2 + 1)$

     25. $f(x) = (x - 7)^2$

     26. $f(x) = 5x^4 + 2x^3 - 3x^2 - 4x - 5$

     27. $f(x) = (2x^2 - 3x - 2)^2$

     28. $f(x) = x(x + 2)^2(x - 2)^3$

     29. $f(x) = x^5 - 5x^4$

     30. $f(x) = 3x^5 - 20x^3$

     31. $f(x) = (2 + x)^2(1 - x)^3$

     32. $f(x) = -2x^3 - 3x^2 + 12x + 10$

7–10 Concavity and other Inflection Points

Before considering inflection points at which f' is not 0, several other concepts must be introduced.

> A function f is increasing on an interval $[a, b]$ if and only if for all $x_1, x_2 \in [a, b]$ and $x_2 > x_1, f(x_2) > f(x_1)$.
>
> A function f is decreasing on $[a, b]$ if and only if for all $x_1, x_2 \in [a, b]$ and $x_2 > x_1, f(x_2) < f(x_1)$.

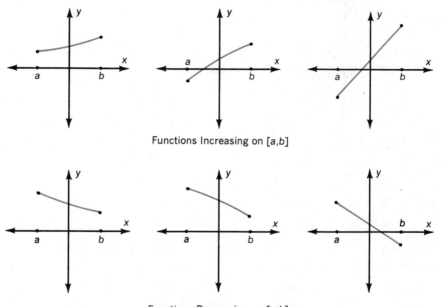

Functions Increasing on [a,b]

Functions Decreasing on [a,b]

Choose any point on a graph of one of the increasing functions depicted above. At that point place a straightedge tangent to the curve and notice that the slope of the tangent is positive. Repeat the procedure for the decreasing functions. What do you notice about the slope? In general it is true that if a function f is increasing on $[a, b]$, then $f'(x) > 0$ for all $x \in \langle a, b \rangle$. (If f is decreasing on $[a, b]$ then $f'(x) < 0$ for all $x \in \langle a, b \rangle$.) The converse statement is also true, that is, if $f'(x) > 0$ $(f'(x) < 0)$ for all $x \in \langle a, b \rangle$ then f is an increasing (decreasing) function on $[a, b]$.

A polynomial function may be increasing on one subset of an interval, yet decreasing on another subset of the same interval. In Figure 1 $f(x)$ is increasing on $[a, c]$ and decreasing on $[c, b]$. Notice that f changes from an increasing to a decreasing function at $(c, f(c))$ and that $f'(c) = 0$. Thus c is a critical point for f, and c separates the graph into an increasing part and a decreasing part. In general, the set of critical points of a polynomial function determines the end points of the intervals for which the function is increasing or decreasing.

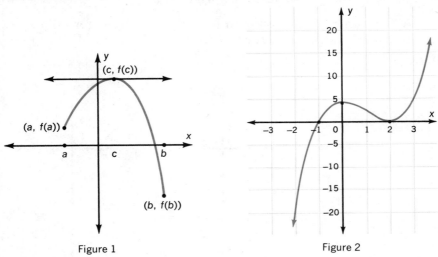

Figure 1   Figure 2

EXAMPLE 1. Given the polynomial function

$$f(x) = x^3 - 3x^2 + 4,$$

find the critical points and the intervals on which $f(x)$ is increasing and decreasing. See Figure 2.

Solution: $f'(x) = 3x^2 - 6x = 3x(x - 2)$
            $f'(x) = 0$, when $x = 0$ and   when $x = 2$

Consider now the intervals

$$\langle -\infty, 0], \qquad [0, 2], \qquad \text{and} \qquad [2, +\infty).$$

① For $x \in \langle -\infty, 0 \rangle$, $3x < 0$ and $x - 2 < 0$.   Consequently $3x(x - 2) > 0$ and $f(x)$ is increasing on $\langle -\infty, 0]$.

② For $x \in \langle 0, 2 \rangle$, $3x > 0$ and $x - 2 < 0$. Thus $3x(x - 2) < 0$ and $f(x)$ is decreasing on $[0, 2]$.

③ For $x \in \langle 2, +\infty \rangle$, $3x > 0$ and $x - 2 > 0$. Hence, $3x(x - 2) > 0$ and $f(x)$ is increasing on $[2, +\infty)$.

The function $f(x) = x^3 - 3x^2 + 4$ of Example 1 has a derived function $f'(x) = 3x^2 - 6x$. See Figure 3. Notice that $f'(x)$ is itself a polynomial and thus it has a derived function. The derived function of the derived function is called the **second derived function** of f and is denoted $f''(x)$ (read "f double prime of x"). In this case $f''(x) = 6x - 6$.

The derived function, $f'(x) = 3x^2 - 6x$, can be analyzed with the aid of its derived function, $f''(x) = 6x - 6$. The critical point of $f'(x)$ occurs where $x = 1$ because $f''(x) = 0$ at $x = 1$. Since $f''(x) < 0$ when $x \in \langle -\infty, 1 \rangle$, $f'(x)$ is decreasing on $\langle -\infty, 1]$. Similarly $f''(x) > 0$ for $x \in \langle 1, +\infty \rangle$, and $f'(x)$ is increasing on $[1, +\infty)$. See Figure 4.

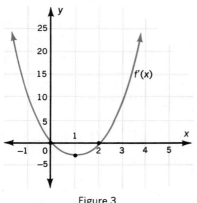

Figure 3

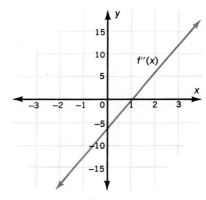

Figure 4

The question to be answered now is: What does the fact that $f'(x)$ is increasing or decreasing tell you about the shape of the graph of $f(x)$?

Consider two lines l_1 and l_2 with slopes m_1 and m_2, $m_2 < m_1$, and $l_1 \cap l_2 = \{T\}$, as in the figure at the right. It is clear that if $m_2 < m_1$, then l_1 must be rotated clockwise about T to make it coincide with l_2. That is, *decreasing* the slope of a line corresponds to turning it *clockwise*. A similar argument shows that *increasing* the slope of a line corresponds to turning it *counterclockwise*.

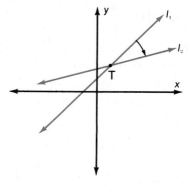

Now $f''(x) > 0$ implies $f'(x)$ is increasing for increasing x, and thus the tangents to f are turning counterclockwise. When the tangents to a curve turn counterclockwise as x increases, the curve is said to be **concave upward**. See Figure 5.

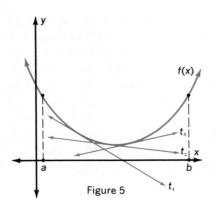

Figure 5

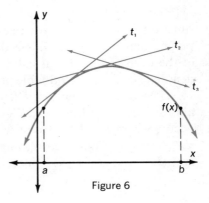

Figure 6

Similarly $f''(x) < 0$ implies $f'(x)$ is decreasing. Thus the tangents to f are turning clockwise. When the tangents to a curve turn clockwise as x increases, the curve is said to be **concave downward**. See Figure 6.

The graph of a function f is **concave downward** on an interval $[a, b]$ if and only if $f''(x) < 0$ for all $x \in \langle a, b \rangle$.

The graph of a function f is **concave upward** on an interval $[a, b]$ if and only if $f''(x) > 0$ for all $x \in \langle a, b \rangle$.

Points at which the graph changes concavity are points of inflection. Since the second derived function must change sign when the curve changes concavity, $f''(x)$ is zero at a point of inflection. However, the converse is not true; that is, $f''(c) = 0$ *does not* imply a point of inflection at $x = c$. Thus the points of inflection will be a subset of the zeros of $f''(x)$.

EXAMPLE 2. Determine the points of inflection and the intervals on which $f(x)$ is concave upward and concave downward if

$$f(x) = x^3 - 3x^2 + 4.$$
$$f'(x) = 3x^2 - 6x$$
$$f''(x) = 6x - 6$$

The set of zeros of $f''(x)$ is $\{1\}$. Thus, if there is an inflection point it must be $x = 1$. Since $f''(x) < 0$ for all $x \in I_1 = \langle -\infty, 1 \rangle$, $f(x)$ is concave downward on I_1. Since $f''(x) > 0$ for all $x \in I_2 = \langle 1, +\infty \rangle$, $f(x)$ is concave upward on I_2. Since $f(x)$ changes from concave downward to concave upward at the point where $x = 1$, $(1, 2)$ is a point of inflection. See Figure 2 on page 362.

CLASSROOM EXERCISES

— Find the second derived function for each polynomial.

1. $f(x) = x^4 + 2x^3 - x^2 + 1$ **2.** $f(x) = -x^3 + 3x^2 - 3x + 1$

3. $f(x) = x^5 - 4x^3 + x - 2$ **4.** $f(x) = -3x^6 - 7x^2 + 9x - 5$

WRITTEN EXERCISES

A — Find the intervals over which each function is concave upward and concave downward. Name the inflection points.

1. $f(x) = 3x^2 - 12x + 12$

2. $f(x) = 2x^3 - 9x^2 + 12x + 1$

3. $f(x) = 2x^3 + 3x^2 - 12x - 2$

4. $f(x) = x^4 - 4x^3 + 6x^2$

5. $f(x) = 2x^3 + 3x^2 - 12x - 7$

6. $f(x) = x^4 + 5x^3 + 9x^2 + 7x + 2$

— Find the y-intercept, zeros, maxima and minima, points of inflection, intervals where the graph is concave upward or downward, and limits as $x \longrightarrow +\infty$ and $x \longrightarrow -\infty$. Sketch the graph of each function.

7. $f(x) = 2x^2 - x^3$

8. $f(x) = x^3$

9. $f(x) = x^4$

10. $f(x) = x^3 + 2x^2 + x - 2$

11. $f(x) = x^3 - 6x^2 + 9x + 1$

12. $f(x) = x^4 - 9x^2$.

B   **13.** $f(x) = 4x^3 - 9x^2 + 5$

14. $f(x) = \frac{x^3}{3} + 4x - 4$

15. $f(x) = (x - 1)^2(x + 1)^2$

16. $f(x) = x^3 + x^2 + x + 1$

17. $f(x) = 2x^3 - 3x^2 - 36x + 25$

18. $f(x) = 24x^2 - x^4$

19. $f(x) = x(x^2 - 4)^2$

20. Given: $f'(x) = 0$ at $x = c$

a. Suppose $f''(c) > 0$. What can you conclude about the point $(c, f(c))$?

b. Suppose $f''(c) < 0$. What can you conclude about the point $(c, f(c))$?

C **21.** The following theorem is proved in more advanced mathematics.

Mean Value Theorem If f is continuous on $[a, b]$ and has a derived function on $\langle a, b \rangle$, then there is a point $x_0 \in \langle a, b \rangle$ such that

$$f'(x_0) = \frac{f(b) - f(a)}{b - a}$$

---

a. Geometrically, what is $\dfrac{f(b) - f(a)}{b - a}$?

b. Interpret $f'(x_0)$ geometrically.

c. Depict the equality of $f'(x_0)$ and $\dfrac{f(b) - f(a)}{b - a}$.

7–11 Rational Functions

Polynomial functions in x are obtained by a finite number of additions, subtractions, and multiplications of constants and x's. When division of these expressions is also permitted, the class of functions called **rational functions** results.

Recall from Section 6–4 that a rational function $R(x)$ is the quotient of two polynomials.

$$R(x) = \frac{P(x)}{Q(x)}$$

For $R(x)$ to be zero, clearly $P(x)$ must be zero. However, if $P(x)$ is zero, it may be that $R(x)$ is not defined. For example, if $R(x) = \dfrac{(x - 1)(x - 2)}{x - 1}$, then $P(2) = 0$ and $P(1) = 0$, but $R(x)$ is zero at $x = 2$. At $x = 1$, $R(x)$ is undefined. Thus every zero of a rational function $R(x)$ is also a zero of the polynomial $P(x)$.

Whenever the denominator $Q(x)$ of $R(x)$ is zero, the rational function is undefined. Thus the domain of $R(x)$ must be restricted to those real numbers for which $Q(x) \neq 0$.

The set of numbers excluded from the domain and the set of zeros of a rational function are valuable aids in sketching a graph. Additional valuable aids are the limits discussed in Section 6–4 and the idea of an asymptote. The next example illustrates how these ideas can be used to sketch a graph of a rational function.

EXAMPLE 1. Sketch a graph of the rational function

$$R(x) = \frac{(x - 1)(x - 4)}{(x - 3)(x + 1)}.$$

① Notice that $R(x)$ is not defined
for $x \in \{-1, 3\}$. Sketch the
graphs of $x = -1$ and $x = 3$.
These lines are to remind you
that $R(x)$ is not defined for
$x \in \{-1, 3\}$. Furthermore,
there may be either a "hole" in
the graph or an asymptote at
these points. See Figure 1.

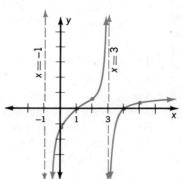

Figure 1

② Determine the zeros of $R(x)$.
They are $x = 1$ and $x = 4$. Plot
these points on the graph. Cal-
culate a few additional values of $R(x)$. Plot them.

x	0	1	2	4	5
$R(x)$	$-\frac{4}{3}$	0	$\frac{2}{3}$	0	$\frac{1}{3}$

③ Examine the nature of the graph near the lines where $R(x)$ is un-
defined (near $x = -1$ and $x = 3$). A systematic approach is best.
Determine first what the graph is on either side of $x = -1$ and of
$x = 3$. This is done by evaluating four limits.

a. $\lim\limits_{x \to -1^-} \dfrac{(x - 1)(x - 4)}{(x - 3)(x + 1)}$ b. $\lim\limits_{x \to -1^+} \dfrac{(x - 1)(x - 4)}{(x - 3)(x + 1)}$

c. $\lim\limits_{x \to 3^-} \dfrac{(x - 1)(x - 4)}{(x - 3)(x + 1)}$ d. $\lim\limits_{x \to 3^+} \dfrac{(x - 1)(x - 4)}{(x - 3)(x + 1)}$

(Recall that $x \longrightarrow -1^-$ means x
near -1 but always less than
-1.) As in Section 6–4, these
limits are as follows:

a. $\lim\limits_{x \to -1^-} R(x) = +\infty$

b. $\lim\limits_{x \to -1^+} R(x) = -\infty$

c. $\lim\limits_{x \to 3^-} R(x) = +\infty$

d. $\lim\limits_{x \to 3^+} R(x) = -\infty$

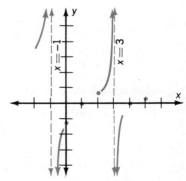

Figure 2

Thus, $x = -1$ and $x = 3$ are
vertical asymptotes to the graph
of $R(x)$. You can sketch part of the graph as in Figure 2.

④ The final step is to see what the graph is like for large and for small values of x. This is done by evaluating these two limits.

   a. $\lim\limits_{x \to -\infty} R(x)$ b. $\lim\limits_{x \to +\infty} R(x)$

These each have 1 as a limit. Thus, $y = 1$ is a horizontal asymptote. Notice that for $x \longrightarrow -\infty$, $R(x)$ is always larger than 1. Thus, the graph nears $y = 1$ from above. The opposite happens for $x \longrightarrow +\infty$. See Figure 3.

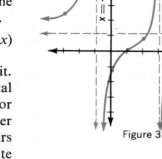

Figure 3

EXAMPLE 2. Sketch a graph of $R(x) = \frac{1}{x}$.

① Zeros: None (why?).

② Undefined points: $x = 0$ (Why?)

③ Calculate a few points:

x	-3	-2	-1	1	2	3
$R(x)$	$-\frac{1}{3}$	$-\frac{1}{2}$	-1	1	$\frac{1}{2}$	$\frac{1}{3}$

Plot them.

④ Vertical asymptotes:

Evaluate: $\lim\limits_{x \to 0^-} \frac{1}{x} = -\infty$

and

$$\lim\limits_{x \to 0^+} \frac{1}{x} = +\infty$$

The line $x = 0$ is a vertical asymptote.

⑤ Horizontal asymptotes:

Evaluate: $\lim\limits_{x \to -\infty} \frac{1}{x} = 0$ (Through values less than zero or greater than zero?)

and

$$\lim\limits_{x \to +\infty} \frac{1}{x} = 0$$ Thus, $y = 0$ is a horizontal asymptote.

⑥ Sketch the graph using steps ①–⑤, as in Figure 4.

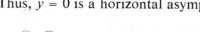

Vertical asymptote

Horizontal asymptote

Figure 4

WRITTEN EXERCISES

A ▬ For each rational function identify (a) zeros, (b) excluded points, (c) vertical asymptotes, (d) horizontal asymptotes, and (e) a few points on the graph. Sketch the graph.

1. $f(x) = \dfrac{1}{x-1}$

2. $f(x) = \dfrac{1}{x+1}$

3. $f(x) = \dfrac{-2}{x-3}$

4. $f(x) = \dfrac{-6}{2x-5}$

5. $f(x) = \dfrac{2x}{x+5}$

6. $f(x) = \dfrac{-x}{2-x}$

7. $f(x) = \dfrac{2x-3}{x+4}$

8. $f(x) = \dfrac{3x+4}{2x-5}$

9. $f(x) = \dfrac{-3x}{x^2+3x+2}$

10. $f(x) = \dfrac{4x}{(x-2)(2x+3)}$

11. $f(x) = \dfrac{x-5}{(x+1)(x-5)}$

12. $f(x) = \dfrac{3x-4}{(2x-3)(3x-2)}$

13. $f(x) = \dfrac{x(x-5)}{(x+2)(4x-1)}$

14. $f(x) = \dfrac{x}{x^2+1}$

15. $f(x) = \dfrac{x^2-5x+6}{x^2+5x+6}$

16. $f(x) = \dfrac{x(x-1)(x+4)}{(x+1)(x+2)(x+3)}$

17. $f(x) = \dfrac{2x}{x^2+x+1}$

18. $f(x) = \dfrac{-x(2-x)}{x^2-16}$

B **19.** Graph

$$f(x) = \frac{1}{x-1}$$

and

$$g(x) = \frac{x+2}{(x+2)(x-1)}.$$

20. How do the graphs of $f(x)$ and $g(x)$ in Exercise 19 differ?

21. Suppose $P(x) = t(x)s(x)$ and $Q(x) = t(x)g(x)$. Let $R_1(x) = \dfrac{P(x)}{Q(x)}$ and $R_2(x) = \dfrac{s(x)}{g(x)}$. How do the graphs of $R_1(x)$ and $R_2(x)$ differ?

▬ Sketch the graph of each rational function.

22. $f(x) = \dfrac{x^2(x-2)}{x(x-2)}$

23. $f(x) = \dfrac{x^2(x-2)}{x(x-2)^2}$

24. $f(x) = \dfrac{(x-1)(x-2)}{(x^2-1)(x)}$

25. $f(x) = \dfrac{(x-1)x}{(x-1)^2}$

C **26.** In Exercise 25 the graph of

$$f(x) = \frac{x(x-1)}{(x-1)^2}$$

did not have a "hole" in it like those in Exercises 22–24. Explain.

7-12 Real Algebraic Functions

Polynomial functions and rational functions can be obtained by a finite number of additions, subtractions, multiplications, and divisions of expressions in a variable x. If the additional operation of extraction of roots is allowed, a larger class of functions results, namely, the **algebraic functions.**

Recall that the domain of a rational function

$$R(x) = \frac{P(x)}{Q(x)}$$

must be restricted to those real numbers for which $Q(x) \neq 0$. In a similar manner, the domain of a real algebraic function $A(x)$ is restricted to those real numbers r for which $A(r)$ is a real number. Only real algebraic functions are discussed.

EXAMPLE 1. Restrict the real replacements for x so that the range of $A(x) = \sqrt{16 - x^2}$ is a subset of the real numbers.

The range of $A(x)$ is real when the expression under the radical is positive or zero. You must find the set of real numbers such that

$$16 - x^2 \geq 0.$$

This is equivalent to

$$(4 - x)(4 + x) \geq 0.$$

This last inequality is true when

1. both factors are positive or zero, or
2. both factors are negative or zero.

Condition **1** implies

$$4 - x \geq 0 \quad and \quad 4 + x \geq 0$$

or

$$4 \geq x \quad and \quad 4 \geq -x$$

which is equivalent to

$$-4 \leq x \leq 4.$$

Condition **2** implies

$$4 - x \leq 0 \quad and \quad 4 + x \leq 0$$

or

$$4 \leq x \quad and \quad 4 \leq -x$$

and there are no values of x that satisfy these inequalities simultaneously. Thus if the domain is $\{x : -4 \leq x \leq 4\}$, then the range of $A(x)$ will be a subset of **R**.

EXAMPLE 2. Is the range of $A(x) = \sqrt[3]{x}$ a subset of the real numbers or must the domain be restricted?

Solution:

Every real number has exactly one real cube root. The following illustrates the situation for positive and negative numbers and for 0.

$$\sqrt[3]{-8} = -2 \qquad \sqrt[3]{0} = 0 \qquad \sqrt[3]{27} = 3$$

Because $\sqrt[3]{x}$ is defined and is a real number for all $x \in$ R, there is no need to restrict the domain.

EXAMPLE 3. Specify the domain of

$$A(x) = 4 - \frac{1}{\sqrt{x}}$$

so that its range will be a subset of the real numbers. Then graph $A(x)$.

Solution:

Since $\sqrt{x}$ is real only for $x \geq 0$, the largest possible domain is $[0, +\infty)$. However, since $\sqrt{x}$ appears in a denominator, $x = 0$ must be excluded from the domain. Consequently the domain is

$$\langle 0, +\infty \rangle \quad \text{or} \quad x > 0, \quad \textit{and} \quad x \text{ real.}$$

Once the domain of an algebraic function has been defined, the procedures used in graphing the function follow those used in graphing rational functions.

① The zeros are found by solving $A(x) = 0$.

$$4 - \frac{1}{\sqrt{x}} = 0$$
$$4\sqrt{x} = 1$$
$$\sqrt{x} = \tfrac{1}{4}$$
$$x = \tfrac{1}{16}$$

② The line $x = 0$ is a vertical asymptote. For $x = 0$, the numerator of $A(x)$ is nonzero, but the denominator is zero.

$$\lim_{x \to 0^+}\left(4 - \frac{1}{\sqrt{x}}\right) = -\infty$$

$A(x)$ decreases without bound as x tends to zero from the right.

③ The line $y = 4$ is a horizontal asymptote because

$$\lim_{x \to \infty}\left(4 - \frac{1}{\sqrt{x}}\right) = 4.$$

④ Selected values of x and $A(x)$ and a portion of the graph are shown below. See Figure 1.

x	$\frac{1}{16}$	1	2	3	4
$A(x)$	0	3	3.293	3.423	3.500

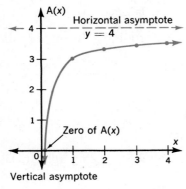

Figure 1

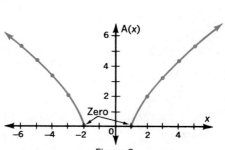

Figure 2

EXAMPLE 4. Sketch the graph of $A(x) = \sqrt{(x - 1)(x + 2)}$ on the appropriate domain.

Solution: The domain of A is found by solving

$$(x - 1)(x + 2) \geq 0.$$

This inequality is satisfied if and only if

$$(x - 1) \geq 0 \quad and \quad (x + 2) \geq 0$$
or $$(x - 1) \leq 0 \quad and \quad (x + 2) \leq 0$$

that is, if and only if

$$x \geq 1 \quad and \quad x \geq -2 \qquad 1$$
or $$x \leq 1 \quad and \quad x \leq -2. \qquad 2$$

Inequality **1** is satisfied when $x \geq 1$ and inequality **2** is satisfied when $x \leq -2$.

So $(x - 1)(x + 2) \geq 0$ when

$$x \geq 1 \quad or \quad x \leq -2.$$

Thus, the domain of $A(x)$ is $\langle -\infty, -2] \cup [1, +\infty\rangle$. The zeros of $A(x)$ are -2 and 1.

There are no vertical or horizontal asymptotes.

Selected values of x and $A(x)$ are as follows. See Figure 2.

x	1	2	3	4	5	-2	-3	-4	-5	-6
$A(x)$	0	2	3.16	4.24	5.29	0	2	3.16	4.24	5.29

372   CHAPTER 7

CLASSROOM EXERCISES

Find the largest domain of $A(x)$ such that the range is a subset of the real numbers.

1. $A(x) = \sqrt{x^2 - 5}$

2. $A(x) = \sqrt{4 - x^2}$

3. $A(x) = \sqrt[3]{x^2 - 5}$

4. $A(x) = \sqrt[3]{4 - x^2}$

WRITTEN EXERCISES

A Find the largest domain of $A(x)$ such that the range is a subset of the real numbers.

1. $A(x) = \sqrt{x^2 - 4}$

2. $A(x) = \sqrt[3]{x^2 - 4}$

3. $A(x) = \sqrt[4]{x^2 - 4}$

4. $A(x) = 1 - \dfrac{1}{\sqrt{x - 1}}$

5. $A(x) = 1 - \dfrac{1}{\sqrt{1 - x}}$

6. $A(x) = x - 2 + \dfrac{1}{\sqrt{x - 2}}$

7. $A(x) = \sqrt{(x - 1)(x - 2)}$

8. $A(x) = \sqrt{(x^2 + 1)(x + 1)}$

9. $A(x) = \sqrt{(x + 2)x(x - 2)}$

10. $A(x) = \sqrt[3]{x - 1} + \sqrt[2]{x - 1}$

11. $A(x) = x^{\frac{2}{3}}$

12. $A(x) = \dfrac{1}{(1 - x)^{\frac{2}{3}}}$

Graph each function on the appropriate domain.

13. $A(x) = \sqrt[3]{x^2 - 4}$

14. $A(x) = 1 - \dfrac{1}{\sqrt{1 - x}}$

15. $A(x) = \sqrt{(x + 2)(x - 3)}$

16. $A(x) = \sqrt{(x + 2)(3 - x)}$

17. $A(x) = \dfrac{-\sqrt{x + 1}}{\sqrt{x}}$

18. $A(x) = \dfrac{1}{\sqrt{(x + 2)(3 - x)}}$

19. $A(x) = \sqrt[3]{x^2}$

20. $A(x) = \sqrt{x^3}$

B **21.** Often algebraic functions are written in an implicit form like

$$y^2 - 2y - x^2 = 0,$$

where

$$y = A(x).$$

In a case like this, you can find an explicit representation by solving the equation for $y = A(x)$.

$$y = 1 + \sqrt{1 + x^2} \quad or \quad y = 1 - \sqrt{1 + x^2}$$

Thus, two explicit algebraic functions result from the one implicit representation. Graph each on the same coordinate system.

22. Find the two explicit algebraic functions that result from solving

$$y^2 - 2y + x^2 = 0$$

for y. Graph each on the same coordinate system.

C ▬▬ In general, if A is a continuous function and if $y = A(x)$ and x and y satisfy an algebraic equation

$$P_0(x)y^n + P_1(x)y^{n-1} + P_2(x)y^{n-2} + \cdots + P_n(x) = 0, \qquad \textbf{1}$$

where $P_0, P_1, P_2, \cdots, P_n$ are polynomials in x, then A is an **algebraic function.** For example, in the algebraic equation

$$y^2 - 2y - x^2 = 0, \; P_0(x) = 1, \; P_1(x) = -2 \quad and \quad P_2(x) = -x^2.$$

Show that $y = A(x)$ satisfies an equation of the form **1** when $A(x)$ equals each of the following.

23. $y = 1 - \sqrt{1 - x^2}$ **24.** $y = 1 + \sqrt[3]{x}$

25. $y = \sqrt{x + \sqrt{x}}$ **26.** $y = \sqrt[3]{x^2}$

27. $y = \sqrt[3]{\dfrac{x}{x^2 + 1}}$ **28.** $y = \sqrt{x} + \dfrac{1}{\sqrt{x}}$

7–13   Polynomial Curve Fitting

Suppose that a chemist has a solution that is at $-12°$ Celsius at the beginning of an experiment. He subjects the solution to a constant heat and notes that one minute later the temperature is $-6°$ Celsius. After two and three minutes the temperature is found to be 6°C and 36°C, respectively. The chemist wants to approximate

 ① the time when the solution will have a temperature of 0°C, and

 ② the temperature after 2.7 minutes.

Eliminating the physical ideas, the problem can be stated: Given $(0, -12)$, $(1, -6)$, $(2, 6)$, and $(3, 36)$, is there a continuous function f that contains these ordered pairs and that closely approximates the temperature of the solution at any time t for $0 \le t \le 3$? Such a function is a mathematical model of the physical situation.

To solve his problem the chemist uses the following theorem.

Theorem 7–11   If (x_1, y_1), (x_2, y_2), $\cdots$, (x_n, y_n) are n distinct points and if all the x_i are distinct, then there exists a polynomial function of degree less than or equal to $n - 1$ that contains the n points.

EXAMPLE. Find a polynomial function of degree less than or equal to 3 that contains $(0, -12)$, $(1, -6)$, $(2, 6)$, and $(3, 36)$.

According to Theorem 7–11, $f(x) = a_3x^3 + a_2x^2 + a_1x + a_0$ will contain the four given points. This is called *fitting the polynomial to the points*. Proceed now to determine the coefficients a_0, a_1, a_2, and a_3. Substitution of the ordered pairs yields four equations.

$$-12 = a_3(0) + a_2(0) + a_1(0) + a_0 = a_0$$
$$-6 = a_3(1) + a_2(1) + a_1(1) + a_0$$
$$6 = a_3(8) + a_2(4) + a_1(2) + a_0$$
$$36 = a_3(27) + a_2(9) + a_1(3) + a_0$$

This is a system of four linear equations in the four variables a_0, a_1, a_2, and a_3 and hence has a unique solution. A method ordinarily employed for simultaneous equations will be used to solve this system.

From the first equation it is clear that $a_0 = -12$. Substitute this value of a_0 in the remaining equations.

$$a_3 + a_2 + a_1 = 6$$
$$8a_3 + 4a_2 + 2a_1 = 18$$
$$27a_3 + 9a_2 + 3a_1 = 48$$

Eliminate a_1.

$$6a_3 + 2a_2 = 6$$
$$24a_3 + 6a_2 = 30$$

Then eliminate a_2.

$$6a_3 = 12$$
$$a_3 = 2$$

It follows that $a_2 = -3$ and $a_1 = 7$. Consequently,

$$f(x) = 2x^3 - 3x^2 + 7x - 12.$$

The chemist's problem requires that you find x when $f(x) = 0$ and $f(x)$ when $x = 2.7$. Verify by synthetic substitution that $f(1.62) = -.0301$. Consequently, $f(x) = 0$ when x is approximately 1.62. Verify by synthetic substitution that $f(2.7) = 24.396$.

For the chemist to accept this model, function values $f(x)$ other than the four used in finding the coefficients must be good approximations of his laboratory data. If the "fit" is acceptable, that is, if the temperatures computed from f are close to observed values, then $f(x) = 2x^3 - 3x^2 + 7x - 12$ will be a useful model for the variation of temperature of the solution in the time interval $0 \leq x \leq 3$. If f does not produce results consistent with observations, the scientist will construct a more accurate model by taking more laboratory data and finding another polynomial function of higher degree.

WRITTEN EXERCISES

A — Find a polynomial of smallest degree which contains the members of the set of ordered pairs.

  1. $(0, 1), (1, 2), (3, 21), (-1, 0)$
  2. $(-1, 0), (1, 8), (2, 57), (-2, -7)$
  3. $(-1, -25), (0, 0), (1, 1), (2, -16)$
  4. $(-2, -15), (-1, -8), (1, -6), (2, 1)$
  5. $(1, 0), (2, 0), (3, 0), (4, 6)$
  6. $(-2, -15), (-1, 0), (0, 9), (1, 0), (2, 15)$
  7. $(0, 3), (1, -3), (2, 3), (4, 9)$

B — The following ordered pairs represent hour of the day and temperature at that hour. Use this information in Exercises 8–10.

$$(1, 32), (2, 35), (3, 30), (4, 25)$$

  8. Find a polynomial function f which could be a model for the temperature for time t if $1 \leq t \leq 4$.
  9. Find $f(2.5)$. Interpret the result.
  10. Is there a relative maximum of f for $1 \leq t \leq 4$? If so, what is the value of t and the corresponding value of f?
  11. A mile off shore on Lake Michigan a fisherman searches for Coho Salmon. With an electronic thermometer he finds the following depth-temperature readings.

$$(5, 71°), (20, 65°), (30, 60°), (45, 50°)$$

His thermometer then failed after the reading $(45, 50°)$. If Coho Salmon stay in water near 55°F, approximately at what depth should the fisherman fish?

7–14 Maxima and Minima: Applications

Problems in the physical world often require for their solution the maximum or minimum value that a variable can assume under certain conditions. You will see in the following examples how information in such problems can be used to construct a polynomial function which may then be maximized or minimized by finding the zeros of the derived function.

EXAMPLE 1. What is the area of the largest rectangular garden that a farmer can enclose with 400 feet of fencing if one side of the garden has already been fenced?

The quantity you wish to maximize in this problem is the area A of the rectangular garden. You must express A as a function of a single variable and then find the derived function, A'. A sketch will be helpful. The garden is to be rectangular, so you can let two sides have the same measure, say x, and the third side have some other measure, say y.

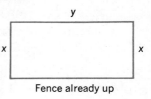
Fence already up

The area of a rectangular region is the product of its length and its width, so the formula

$$A = xy \qquad \mathbf{1}$$

expresses the relationship between the area and the linear dimensions.

In $\mathbf{1}$, the area A is expressed as a function of *two* variables. Since you do not know how to find the derived function of such an expression, you must find a way to express A as a function of *one* variable. You can do this by using the condition that only 400 feet of fencing are available. Hence

$$400 = 2x + y$$

or

$$400 - 2x = y.$$

Substitute the last expression for y in $\mathbf{1}$ to obtain

$$A = x(400 - 2x)$$
$$= 400x - 2x^2.$$

Now that the area A is expressed as a polynomial in x, the task of finding the zeros of the derived function A' is easy.

$$A' = 400 - 4x$$

The zeros of A' are found by solving

$$0 = 400 - 4x.$$
$$x = 100,$$

and

$$y = 400 - 2x$$
$$= 400 - 200$$
$$= 200.$$

It is easy to check that this is indeed a relative maximum of A. The maximum area the farmer can enclose with 400 feet of fencing is

$$A = 100 \cdot 200 = 20,000 \text{ square feet.}$$

Summarizing, the main steps in the solution of the problem are as follows:

① Find the quantity (A) that is to be maximized or minimized.
② Express that quantity as a function of the other variables ($A = xy$).
③ Express either x or y in terms of the other ($y = 400 - 2x$).
④ Calculate the derived function of the polynomial function. (If $A = 400x - 2x^2$, then $A' = 400 - 4x$.)
⑤ Find the zeros of the derived function ($x = 100$).
⑥ Determine whether or not the zero corresponds to a maximum (or minimum).
⑦ Calculate the maximum or minimum.

EXAMPLE 2. A manufacturer has 100 tons of a product that he can sell now with a profit of $5 per ton. For each week that he delays shipment, he can produce an additional 10 tons. However, for each week's delay the profit decreases 25¢ per ton. If he can sell all of the product that he has on hand at any time, when should he ship so that his profit will be a maximum?

The profit is to be a maximum.
Let x = the number of weeks delay.
Then $100 + 10x$ = number of tons shipped after x weeks delay.
$5.00 - 0.25x$ = number of dollars profit per ton after delay.

Since the profit equals the number of tons times the profit per ton,

$$P = (100 + 10x)(5.00 - 0.25x).$$
$$P = 500 + 25x - 2.5x^2$$
$$P' = 25 - 5x$$

1

Next find the zeros of the derived function P'.

$$0 = 25 - 5x$$
$$x = 5$$

The maximum occurs when $x = 5$. Substitute 5 in **1**.

$$P = 500 + 25x - 2.5x^2$$
$$P = 500 + 25(5) - 2.5(5)^2$$
$$P = \$562.50$$

In order to make the maximum profit of $562.50, the manufacturer should ship the product at the end of five weeks.

EXAMPLE 3. Given a 20-unit square of sheet metal, find the dimensions of the open box of greatest volume that can be made from the metal by cutting congruent squares from the corners.

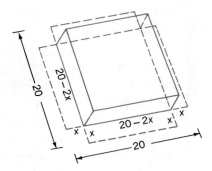

If the squares to be cut from the corners measure x units by x units, then the dimensions of the completed box will be x units, $20 - 2x$ units, and $20 - 2x$ units. The volume V is to be a maximum. V is the product of three linear measures. Hence

$$V = x(20 - 2x)^2$$
$$= 400x - 80x^2 + 4x^3.$$

The maximum will be found at a zero of V'.

$$V' = 400 - 160x + 12x^2$$
$$= 4(100 - 40x + 3x^2)$$
$$= 4(10 - 3x)(10 - x)$$

Thus the zeros of V' are $x = 10$ and $x = \frac{10}{3}$. When $x = 10$, the volume of the box is certainly a minimum — there is no box! It is easy to show that $x = \frac{10}{3}$ gives the maximum volume, namely,

$$\frac{10}{3}\left(20 - \frac{20}{3}\right)^2 = \frac{16{,}000}{27}.$$

WRITTEN EXERCISES

A **1.** A rectangular garden is to be enclosed on three sides by fencing; the fourth side is the side of a barn. What is the largest garden that can be enclosed by 50 meters of fencing? What are the dimensions of the garden?

2. Find a number such that the sum of the number and its square will be as small as possible.

3. Show that the largest rectangle with a perimeter of 20 meters is a square.

4. A trough with a rectangular cross section is to be made from a long sheet of metal 24 meters wide by turning up strips along each side. Find the amount that must be turned up to give the greatest cross section.

5. A rectangle has two of its vertices as the x axis. The other two vertices are on the parabola whose equation is $y = 18 - x^2$. What are the dimensions of the rectangle if its area is to be a maximum?

6. A body moves such that its distance, s, in kilometers from a point, A, is expressed by the formula $s = 5t^2 - 3t + 6$. For what value of t is the body closest to point A? At that time, how far will it be from A?

B **7.** Find three numbers such that the first is the sum of the second and third, the second is the square of the third, and the sum of the three numbers is a minimum.

8. There are 900 units of fencing available to enclose a rectangular plot of ground with a fence down the middle and parallel to two ends. What is the maximum area which can be enclosed?

9. A bus line carries 2000 passengers per day at a rate of 20¢ per passenger. In contemplating a rate change, the management estimates that they would lose 200 passengers for every 5¢ they increased the rates. What rate should they charge to maximize their revenue?

10. A wire 14 cm in length is cut into two pieces. One part is used to make a square. The other part is bent into a rectangle such that $l = 3w$. How should the wire be cut if the sum of the areas is to be a minimum?

11. Find the dimensions of the right circular cylinder of greatest volume that can be inscribed in a right circular cone with a height of 9 units and a base with a radius of 6 units.

C **12.** The sum of two positive numbers is 5. Find the numbers such that:

  a. Their product is a maximum.

  b. The sum of their squares is a minimum.

  c. The product of one number and the square of the other will be a maximum.

13. Find the dimensions of the right circular cylinder of greatest volume that can be inscribed in a right circular cone with radius of base r and height P.

14. Find the least amount of material needed to make a square-based open box that has a volume of 4000 cubic meters.

15. Find the least amount of material needed to make a square-based box with a top that has a volume of N cubic units. What are the dimensions when $N = 81$?

Applying Functions

Economics

Economists seek efficient ways to describe manufacturing cost, sales revenue, and business profit. For simplification, it is assumed here that cost, revenue, and profit are functions of the number of items produced.

A variety of **cost functions** $C(x)$ are possible, depending on the industry and market conditions. The following three could be used.

$$C_1(x) = 10x + 5,\ x \geq 0 \quad \longleftarrow \quad \textbf{\$5 fixed costs—taxes, etc.}$$
$$\textbf{\$10 per item}$$

$$C_2(x) = -0.001x^2 + 10x + 5,\ x \geq 0 \quad \longleftarrow \quad \textbf{Cost reduction from large lots of raw materials}$$

$$C_3(x) = 0.001x^2 + 10x + 5,\ x \geq 0 \quad \longleftarrow \quad \textbf{Cost increase from competition for labor}$$

Revenues (income) can also be represented by functions. Since no revenues are realized if nothing is sold, revenue functions contain the origin. The following two functions are examples of **revenue functions.**

$$R_1(x) = 20x,\ x \geq 0 \quad \longleftarrow \quad \textbf{\$20 per item}$$

$$R_2(x) = 20x - 0.01x^2,\ x \geq 0 \quad \longleftarrow \quad \textbf{Price reduction from decreased popularity}$$

The **profit function** for an item is the difference between the revenue function and the cost function.

$$P(x) = R(x) - C(x)$$

EXAMPLE. Write the profit function for $C(x) = 10x + 2000$ and $R(x) = 20x$. Is a profit made when **a.** $x = 10$? **b.** $x = 100$? **c.** $x = 1000$? **d.** How many items should be produced to "break even?"

Solution: $P(x) = R(x) - C(x) = 20x - (10x + 2000) = 10x - 2000$

     a. $P(10) = 100 - 2000 = -1900$ $\longleftarrow$ **A loss, since $P(x) < 0$.**

     b. $P(100) = 1000 - 2000 = -1000$ $\longleftarrow$ **A loss, since $P(x) < 0$.**

     c. $P(1000) = 10,000 - 2000 = 8000$ $\longleftarrow$ **A profit, since $P(x) > 0$.**

     d. $P(x) = 0$ for the "break-even" point.

          $10x - 2000 = 0$ Thus, $x = 200$ items.

EXERCISES

1. Graph $C_1(x)$, $C_2(x)$, and $C_3(x)$ on the same coordinate system.

2. Graph $R_1(x)$ and $R_2(x)$ on the same coordinate system.

3. Answer the questions in the Example for $C(x) = 0.01x^2 + 10x + 100$ and $R(x) = 20x - 0.01x^2$.

CHAPTER SUMMARY

Important Terms

Absolute minimum or
  maximum (p. 347)
Algebraic expression (p. 322)
Algebraic function (p. 370)
Axis of symmetry (p. 326)
Concave upward or
  downward (p. 364)
Constant function (p. 324)
Critical points (p. 348)
Depressed polynomial (p. 332)
Discriminant (p. 326)
Factor Theorem (p. 333)
Fundamental Theorem of
  Algebra (p. 344)
Linear function (p. 324)

Point of inflection (p. 354)
Quadratic formula (p. 326)
Quadratic function (p. 325)
Rational expression (p. 322)
Rational function (p. 366)
Relative minimum or
  maximum (p. 347)
Remainder Theorem (p. 332)
Second derived function (p. 363)
Synthetic division (p. 332)
Synthetic substitution (p. 328)
Turning point (p. 326)
y intercept (p. 324)
Zero of a function (p. 325)
Zero polynomial (p. 324)

Important Ideas

1. If the remainder, $P(c)$, is zero when $P(x)$ is divided by $x - c$, then $x - c$ is a factor of $P(x)$.

2. If f is a polynomial function and a and b are real numbers such that $f(a)$ and $f(b)$ have opposite signs, then there is at least one zero of f between a and b.

3. Let f be a polynomial of degree n, $n > 0$. Then f has at least one and at most n complex zeros.

4. Let f be a polynomial with real coefficients. If one zero of f is $a + bi$, then $a - bi$, is another zero of f.

5. The relative minimum and maximum points of a polynomial function f can be found among the set of values for which the derived function for f has a value of 0.

6. The second derived function is used to determine the concavity of the graph of a function $f(x)$. If $f''(x) > 0$, then the graph is concave downward. If $f''(x) < 0$, then the graph is concave upward.

7. For any set of n distinct points with distinct x coordinates in the plane, a polynomial of maximum degree $n - 1$ can be found containing all the points.

CHAPTER OBJECTIVES AND REVIEW

Objective: *To recognize polynomial functions.* (Section 7-1)

━━Write "polynomial" or "not polynomial" for each of the following functions. If the function is a polynomial write the degree and the leading coefficient.

1. $2x^3 - 7$

2. $\dfrac{8x^2 - 4}{5}$

3. $3x^4 - x^{-2}$

4. $\dfrac{1}{3x^2 + x - 9}$

Objective: *To apply the properties of linear functions and quadratic functions.* (Section 7-1)

━━For each linear and quadratic function determine (a) the y intercept, (b) the real zeros, if any, and (c) the slope at $x = 3$. For the quadratic functions determine also (d) the axis of symmetry, (e) the coordinates of the turning point, and (f) whether the graph opens upward or downward.

5. $f(x) = 3x + 7$

6. $f(x) = 3x^2 + 7$

7. $f(x) = x^2 - 2x + 1$

8. $f(x) = x(x - 1)$

Objective: *To use synthetic substitution to evaluate polynomial functions.* (Section 7-2)

━━Evaluate each polynomial for the given values of x. Use synthetic substitution.

9. $f(x) = x^3 + 3x^2 - 2$ $x = 1, 4, -3, 0$

10. $f(x) = x^4 - 2x^3 + 2x^2 - 5$ $x = 2, \frac{1}{2}, 3, 0$

11. $g(x) = -5x^3 - 2x + 7$ $x = -1, 0, 1, 2$

12. $h(x) = x^4 - 16$ $x = -3, -2, -1, 0, 1, 2, 3$

Objective: *To apply the Remainder Theorem and Factor Theorem.* (Section 7-3)

━━Find the quotient and remainder when $f(x)$ is divided by the given linear factor.

13. $f(x) = 2x^3 + x^2 - 3x - 5; \quad x - 3$

14. $f(x) = x^4 + x^2 - x + 7; \quad x + 1$

━━Which, if any, of the linear expressions shown at the right are factors of the given polynomial?

15. $f(x) = x^4 - 2x^3 + 2x^2 - 5$ $(x - 1); (x + 1); (x - 2)$

16. $g(x) = -5x^3 - 2x + 7$ $\qquad\qquad (x-1); (x+1); (x+2)$

17. $h(x) = x^4 - 16$ $\qquad\qquad (x-1); (x+1); (x+2); (x-2)$

Objective: *To use synthetic substitution to locate real zeros of a polynomial and to identify upper and lower bounds on the real zeros.* (Section 7-4)

━━ Find the intervals that contain real zeros of each polynomial function.

18. $f(x) = x^3 + 3x^2 - 3$

19. $f(x) = x^4 - 2x^3 + 2x^2 - 5$

20. Identify upper and lower bounds for the real zeros of Exercises 18 and 19.

Objective: *To identify the possible rational zeros of a polynomial over the integers.* (Section 7-5)

━━ Find the set of possible rational zeros for each polynomial function. Determine which, if any, of these are actually zeros of the polynomial.

21. $f(x) = 2x^4 + 15x^3 + 28x^2 + 15x$

22. $g(x) = -5x^3 - 2x + 7$

23. $h(x) = 9x^3 + 6x^2 - 5x - 2$

Objective: *To express a polynomial as a product of linear factors with complex coefficients.* (Section 7-6)

24. Write each polynomial of Exercises 21–23 as a product of linear factors with complex coefficients.

25. Find all the zeros of the polynomial $f(x) = x^6 - 4x^5 + 8x^4 - 16x^3 + 16x^2$. Identify all multiple zeros and their multiplicity.

Objective: *To identify critical points of a polynomial function and to determine whether a critical point is a relative maximum, a relative minimum, or a point of inflection.* (Section 7-7 and Section 7-8)

━━ Find the relative maxima, relative minima, and points of inflection of each function.

26. $f(x) = x^3$

27. $f(x) = x^3 - 9x$

28. $f(x) = x^5 - 1$

29. $f(x) = 3x^4 - 20x^3 + 36x^2 + 60$

Objective: *To sketch the graphs of polynomials using y intercepts, zeros, relative maxima and minima, inflection points, and limits.* (Section 7-9)

━━━ For each function find (a) the y intercept, (b) functional values over the interval $-3 \leq x \leq 3$, (c) zeros, and (d) relative maxima, relative minima, and inflection points. Also (e) note the behavior of the function as $x \to +\infty$ and $x \to -\infty$. Then graph the function.

30. $f(x) = x^4 - 4x^3 + 8x^2 - 16x + 16$

31. $f(x) = x^3 - 1$

32. $f(x) = x^3 - 3x^2 - 6x + 8$

33. $f(x) = 9x^3 + 81x^2 - 45x - 36$

Objective: *To use the second derived function to identify intervals over which a function is concave upward or concave downward.* (Section 7-10)

34. Find the intervals over which the functions of Exercises 30–33 are concave upward and concave downward. Use the second derived function.

Objective: *To identify restricted domain values and asymptotes of rational functions and to graph such functions.* (Section 7-11)

━━━ For each rational function find the (a) zeros, (b) excluded points, (c) vertical asymptotes, (d) horizontal asymptotes, and (e) a few points on the graph. Then (f) sketch the graph.

35. $f(x) = \dfrac{x(x - 4)}{(x + 2)(x - 2)}$
　　　　　36. $f(x) = \dfrac{3x(x + 3)}{(x - 1)(x - 5)}$

Objective: *To graph algebraic functions.* (Section 7-12)

━━━ Graph each function on the appropriate domain.

37. $f(x) = \sqrt{x^2 - 25}$
　　　　　38. $f(x) = x + \sqrt{x}$

Objective: *To fit a polynomial to a given set of noncollinear points.* (Section 7-13)

━━━ Find a polynomial function that contains the given points.

39. $(3, 2), (2, 3), (-3, -2)$
　　　　　40. $(1, 0), (0, 1), (-1, 0), (-4, 0)$

Objective: *To apply the concepts of maximum and minimum of polynomial functions to verbal problems.* (Section 7-14)

41. A lot has the shape of a right triangle with legs of 240 feet and 300 feet. Find the ground dimensions of the largest 20-story rectangular building that can be constructed on the lot so that the sides of the building are parallel to the legs of the triangle.

CHAPTER TEST

▬▬ Given $P(x)$, find $P(a)$ for each value of a by synthetic substitution.

1. $P(x) = -3x^4 + 2x^2 + 5$ $\qquad\qquad a = -2, \frac{5}{3}, 1, 0$

2. $P(x) = 3x^4 - 2x^3 - 27x^2 + 18x$ $\qquad a = 3, 1, 0, -1, -3$

3. Determine all rational zeros for $P(x)$ in Exercise 1. Determine all zeros, irrational and complex, in Exercise 1.

4. Repeat Exercise 3 for: $P(x) = 3x^4 - 2x^3 - 27x^2 + 18x$.

5. Express in your own words the meaning of the Factor Theorem and the Remainder Theorem.

6. What is the maximum number of complex zeros of a degree 7 polynomial with real coefficients? Explain your answer.

7. Locate one real zero of $P(x) = 2x^3 + x - 1$ between successive tenths.

▬▬ Identify the critical points of each polynomial function. Determine whether each critical point is a relative maximum or minimum or a point of inflection.

8. $P(x) = x^4 - 4x^2$

9. $P(x) = (x - 1)^3$

10. $P(x) = 3x^4 + 24x^3 + 30x^2 - 168x - 1$

▬▬ Identify the y intercepts, the real zeros, the critical points of each polynomial. Sketch the graph using this information.

11. $P(x) = x^4 - 4x^2$

12. $P(x) = x^3 - 3x^2$

13. $P(x) = x^3 - 6x^2 + 12x - 8$

14. For each polynomial in Exercises 11–13 find the intervals for which the graph is concave upward or concave downward.

▬▬ Sketch the graph of each function. Restrict the domain where necessary.

15. $f(x) = 1 + \sqrt{25 - x^2}$

16. $f(x) = \dfrac{x^4 - 4x^2}{x^2 - 4}$

17. $f(x) = \dfrac{1}{(x + 1)(x - 3)}$

18. Find a polynomial of degree 3 which contains the four points $A(1, 2)$, $B(2, 3)$, $C(0, 0)$ and $D(-1, 1)$.

19. The sum of two positive numbers is 12. Find the numbers so that the product of one and the square of the other is a maximum.

CHAPTER

8 Exponential and Logarithmic Functions

Sections

Features

Review and Testing

8–1   Rational Exponents

In your earlier study of mathematics, integral exponents were defined by the following equations.

1 $\qquad\qquad\qquad a^0 = 1$ if $a \neq 0$ $\quad\longleftarrow$ **0^0 is not defined.**

2 $\qquad\qquad\qquad a^1 = a$

3 $\qquad\qquad\qquad a^n = a \cdot a \cdot \;\cdots\; \cdot a \qquad$ to n factors when n is an integer greater than 1.

4 $\qquad\qquad\qquad a^{-n} = \dfrac{1}{a^n}, \qquad$ when n is a positive integer.

You are familiar with the properties of integral exponents from these theorems.

5 $\qquad\qquad\quad a^n \cdot a^m = a^{n+m}$

6 $\qquad\qquad\quad \dfrac{a^n}{a^m} = a^{n-m} \quad \text{or} \quad \dfrac{1}{a^{m-n}}, \, a \neq 0$

7 $\qquad\qquad\quad (a^m)^n = a^{m \cdot n}$

The next step is to assign meaning to a symbol such as $3^{\frac{2}{3}}$. This step is not hard to take because there is a natural relationship between $\sqrt[p]{a}$ and $a^{\frac{1}{p}}$ when p is a positive integer. First,

$$y = \sqrt[p]{a} \qquad \text{iff} \qquad y^p = a.$$

In words, y is the pth root of a if and only if the pth power of y is a. Now you want to define $a^{\frac{1}{p}}$ in such a way that properties 5, 6, and 7 hold. In particular, you want property 7 to be valid for rational exponents. Thus, you want

$$y = a^{\frac{1}{p}}$$

to imply

$$y^p = (a^{\frac{1}{p}})^p$$

and 7 to imply

$$(a^{\frac{1}{p}})^p = a^{\frac{p}{p}} = a.$$

Thus, since

$$y = \sqrt[p]{a} \qquad \text{iff} \qquad y^p = a$$

and you want $y = a^{\frac{1}{p}}$ to imply $y^p = a$ by property 7, you make the following definition.

8 $$a^{\frac{1}{p}} = \sqrt[p]{a} \qquad p \in \mathbf{N}$$

To extend **8** to the case where the numerator of the exponent is not 1, you make the following definition.

9 $$a^{\frac{q}{p}} = (a^{\frac{1}{p}})^q \qquad a \neq 0, q \text{ an integer, } p \text{ a natural}$$
$$\text{number, and } \frac{q}{p} \text{ in lowest terms.}$$

From **8** and **9**, properties **5**, **6**, and **7** are easily shown to be valid for rational exponents.

So that there is no ambiguity about the meaning of $\sqrt[p]{a}$ and $a^{\frac{1}{p}}$, both symbols are taken to indicate the *principal root*. The **principal root**, $\sqrt[p]{a}$ or $a^{\frac{1}{p}}$, is the positive root when there is more than one real root and the real root when there is only one real root. Thus, $\sqrt[3]{8} = 2$ and $\sqrt{9} = 3$, not -3.

The symbol $\sqrt[p]{a}$ names a real number except when $a < 0$ and p is even. In this case, $\sqrt[p]{a}$ is imaginary. For example, $\sqrt[2]{-4} = 2i$.

Another irregularity occurs when a is a negative real number. There are cases for which $[a^{r_1}]^{r_2}$ may not equal $[a^{r_2}]^{r_1}$ for $a < 0$. The following example illustrates what occurs if a is not restricted to nonnegative real numbers when p is an even number in Definition **9**.

EXAMPLE 1. Evaluate $[(-4)^2]^{\frac{1}{2}}$ and $[(-4^{\frac{1}{2}})]^2$ by performing the operations in order left to right. This will show that $[(-4)^2]^{\frac{1}{2}} \neq [(-4)^{\frac{1}{2}}]^2$.

Solution:
$$[(-4)^2]^{\frac{1}{2}} = [16]^{\frac{1}{2}}$$
$$= 4 \quad \longleftarrow \textbf{ Principal root}$$
$$[(-4)^{\frac{1}{2}}]^2 = [2i]^2$$
$$= -4 \quad \longleftarrow \quad i^2 = -1$$

Since $4 \neq -4$, the result is *not* independent of the order of operations when the base is a *negative* real number and the root is even. The solution to this dilemma is to restrict the base to only nonnegative real numbers for even roots. When this is done, the order of exponentiation does not affect the result.

A property of a number raised to a rational exponent is given in the next theorem. Notice that it is an obvious extension of a similar result for integral exponents.

> **Theorem 8–1** If r and s are rational numbers and $r < s$ and $a > 1$, then $a^r < a^s$.

Proof: Suppose that n is a whole number. Now recall that if

    a. $a > 1$, then $a^n > 1$.
    b. $a = 1$, then $a^n = 1$.
    c. $0 < a < 1$, then $a^n < 1$.

You can now prove that for $a > 1$,

$$a^{\frac{m}{n}} > 1 \text{ for } m, n \in \text{W.}$$

The proof is indirect.

① Suppose $a^{\frac{m}{n}} = 1$.
    Then $a^m = 1^n = 1$. (Why?)

But this contradicts **a** above.

② Suppose $a^{\frac{m}{n}} < 1$.
    Then $a^m < 1^n = 1$. (Why?)

But this contradicts **a** above.

③ Since $a^{\frac{m}{n}}$ is not equal to 1 nor less than 1, it must be greater than 1 by the Trichotomy Principle. Now the rest of the proof is easy. Let r and s be any rational numbers such that $r < s$. Then $s - r$ is some positive rational number, say $\frac{m}{n}$. Since

$$a^{s-r} = a^{\frac{m}{n}} > 1$$

it follows that $a^r(a^{s-r}) > a^r$ (because $a^r > 0$) or

$$a^s > a^r.$$

EXAMPLE 2.   Simplify $[(x^{-2})(x^3y^{-4})(5y^{-3})]^{-\frac{1}{2}}$

Solution:

$$[(x^{-2})(x^3y^{-4})(5y^{-3})]^{-\frac{1}{2}} = (5xy^{-7})^{-\frac{1}{2}}$$

$$= \left(\frac{5x}{y^7}\right)^{-\frac{1}{2}} = \sqrt{\frac{y^7}{5x}} = y^3\sqrt{\frac{y}{5x}}$$

CLASSROOM EXERCISES

━━ Evaluate each of the following.

1. $(8^{-\frac{2}{3}})^3$ **2.** $(-45)^{\frac{1}{2}}$ **3.** $(.0016)^{\frac{1}{4}} \cdot (27)^{\frac{2}{3}}$

━━ Perform the indicated operations.

4. $(x^{\frac{2}{3}} \cdot x^{-\frac{3}{4}})^{-1}$ **5.** $2y^{-2} \cdot 3y^{-3}$ **6.** $[(2x^2)(y^{-3})]^{\frac{1}{2}}$

7. What is the formal definition of $a^{\frac{p}{q}}$? In your own words, state the definition.

8. What restriction must be placed on a in $a^{\frac{p}{q}}$ when q is even? Explain.

WRITTEN EXERCISES

A ━━ Evaluate each of the following.

1. $4^{-2} \cdot 4^{\frac{1}{2}}$ **2.** $5^{-1} \cdot 8^{\frac{1}{3}}$

3. $7^6 \cdot 7^{-3}$ **4.** $5^{-2} \cdot 5^2$

5. $(4^{\frac{3}{2}})^{-1}$ **6.** $(\sqrt[3]{-8})^2$

━━ Simplify each of the following. The replacement set for each variable is the set of positive real numbers.

7. $(x^3)(2y^{-1})(x^2 \cdot y^{-2})^{-1}$ **8.** $[(x^2)(2^{-2} \cdot y^4]^{-\frac{1}{2}}$

9. $[(a^4)(a^{-\frac{2}{3}})]^{\frac{3}{2}}$ **10.** $(x^{\frac{3}{4}})(x^{-\frac{2}{3}})(x^{\frac{1}{5}})$

11. $\left(\frac{x^{-2}}{x^{-3}}\right)^2\left(\frac{x^{-2}}{x^{-1}}\right)^2$ **12.** $(a^{\frac{1}{2}} - b^{\frac{1}{2}})(a^{\frac{1}{2}} + b^{\frac{1}{2}})$

━━ Evaluate each of the following.

13. $800(8^{-\frac{2}{3}})$ **14.** $[(-8)^3]^{\frac{1}{3}}$

15. $64(\frac{16}{9})^{-\frac{3}{2}}$ **16.** $[(-8)^{\frac{1}{3}}]^3$

17. What do the results to Exercises 14 and 16 illustrate with regard to $(a^q)^{\frac{1}{p}}$ and $(a^{\frac{1}{p}})^q$?

18. Arrange the following numbers in increasing order of magnitude.

$$2, (4^{\frac{7}{2}})(16^{-1}), (\tfrac{1}{2})^{-\frac{4}{3}}, 2^{-3}, (2^{-\frac{2}{5}})^5$$

B ━━ Find the value of p in each of the following.

19. $8^p = (2^3)^3$ **20.** $8^p = 2^{(3^3)}$

21. $(3^2)^3 = 9^p$ **22.** $3^{(2^3)} = 9^p$

23. $16^p = 2^{(4^5)}$ **24.** $16^p = (2^4)^5$

■■■ Solve for x.

25. $x^{\frac{2}{3}} = 16$ **26.** $2x^{\frac{3}{2}} = 8$

27. $2x^{\frac{1}{2}} = 4$ **28.** $x^{-\frac{3}{2}} = 8$

29. Prove: If $a > 0$ and r_1 and r_2 are rational numbers, then the following are true.

     a. $a^{r_1} \cdot a^{r_2} = a^{r_1 + r_2}$ **b.** $\dfrac{a^{r_1}}{a^{r_2}} = a^{r_1 - r_2}$

     c. $(a^{\frac{1}{p}})^{\frac{1}{q}} = a^{\frac{1}{pq}}$ $(p, q \in W)$

30. Prove: If r and s are rational numbers, $r < s$, and $0 < a < 1$, then $a^r > a^s$.

8–2   Real Exponents

At the moment the symbol a^x $(a > 0)$ has been defined for all rational replacements of x. If you were to graph the function

$$f(x) = a^x \quad (a > 0),$$

the domain of f would have to be restricted to rational x, because a^x has not been defined for irrational numbers.

For example, choose $a = 2$ and consider 2^x where x is a real number. You know how 2^x is defined for rational numbers, but no meaning has been attached to, say, $2^{\sqrt{3}}$ or to 2^{π} since $\sqrt{3}$ and π are irrational numbers. The method of defining 2^x for irrational x is illustrated in the following example.

EXAMPLE 1.   Define $2^{\sqrt{3}}$.

By Theorem 8–1, $2^r < 2^s$ when r and s are rational and $r < s$. It seems reasonable to require that this same property hold when r and s are irrational numbers. Thus, for $x = \sqrt{3}$ and for all rational numbers r and s such that

$$r < \sqrt{3} < s \hspace{4cm} 1$$

you would like to have

$$2^r < 2^{\sqrt{3}} < 2^s. \hspace{3.5cm} 2$$

Clearly, **1** and **2** place severe restriction on the choice of the value of $2^{\sqrt{3}}$. In fact, **1** and **2** uniquely determine the value of $2^{\sqrt{3}}$. To see why this is true consider two sets of rational approximations to $\sqrt{3}$ given in the table.

r		$<$	$\sqrt{3}$	$<$	s
1.7		$<$	$\sqrt{3}$	$<$	1.8
1.73		$<$	$\sqrt{3}$	$<$	1.74
1.732		$<$	$\sqrt{3}$	$<$	1.733
1.7320		$<$	$\sqrt{3}$	$<$	1.7321

By 1 and 2 you have the following table.

2^r	$<$	$2^{\sqrt{3}}$	$<$	2^s
$2^{1.7}$	$<$	$2^{\sqrt{3}}$	$<$	$2^{1.8}$
$2^{1.73}$	$<$	$2^{\sqrt{3}}$	$<$	$2^{1.74}$
$2^{1.732}$	$<$	$2^{\sqrt{3}}$	$<$	$2^{1.733}$
$2^{1.7320}$	$<$	$2^{\sqrt{3}}$	$<$	$2^{1.7321}$

Converting the left and right hand columns to approximations to their real number equivalents, you have the following. (The method for conversion will be considered later.)

2^r	$<$	$2^{\sqrt{3}}$	$<$	2^s
3.25	$<$	$2^{\sqrt{3}}$	$<$	3.48
3.317	$<$	$2^{\sqrt{3}}$	$<$	3.340
3.3219	$<$	$2^{\sqrt{3}}$	$<$	3.3242
3.32188	$<$	$2^{\sqrt{3}}$	$<$	3.32211

Thus, if 2 is to hold, you have a three decimal place approximation to $2^{\sqrt{3}}$.
$$2^{\sqrt{3}} \approx 3.322$$

The procedure is one of "pinching down" on the value of $2^{\sqrt{3}}$ by using rational approximations of $\sqrt{3}$ and $2^{\sqrt{3}}$.

The pinching down process is illustrated graphically as follows.

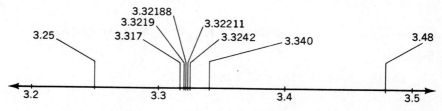

It is proved in advanced mathematics texts that there is one unique number y in each of the intervals of the following sequence of intervals.

$$[2^{1.7}, 2^{1.8}][2^{1.73}, 2^{1.74}][2^{1.732}, 2^{1.733}], \cdots$$

That number y is defined to be $2^{\sqrt{3}}$.

The process illustrated for $2^{\sqrt{3}}$ can be applied to any real number x and positive real number a to define a^x, $a > 0$, $x \in R$. Explicitly, this is done as follows:

① Let $r_1, r_2, r_3, \ldots, r_n, \ldots$ be an increasing sequence of rational numbers all less than x and such that $\lim\limits_{n \to \infty} r_n = x$. Let $s_1, s_2, s_3, \ldots,$ $s_n, \ldots$ be a decreasing sequence of rational numbers all greater than x and such that $\lim\limits_{n \to \infty} s_n = x$.

② Let $a > 1$, and consider the sequences $\{a^{r_n}\}$ and $\{a^{s_n}\}$. For each $n \in N$,
$$a^{r_n} \leq y \leq a^{s_n}.$$

③ There is a number y in each of the intervals in the following sequence of intervals.
$$[a^{r_1}, a^{s_1}], [a^{r_2}, a^{s_2}], [a^{r_3}, a^{s_3}], \cdots, [a^{r_n}, a^{s_n}], \cdots$$

The number y in each interval $[a^{r_n}, a^{s_n}]$ is defined to be a^x. A similar procedure is used to define a^x when x is real and $0 < a < 1$.

It is no longer necessary to restrict the domain of the function
$$f : x \longrightarrow a^x, a > 0$$
to the rational numbers only. The function f is now defined for all $x \in R$. In fact, $f(x) = a^x$, $a > 0$ is a *continuous* function, for the definition of a^x for x irrational "fills in" all the holes in the graph of $f(r) = a^r$, $a > 0$ and $r \in Q$. Functions of this type in which the exponent is a variable are called **exponential functions.** (Functions such as $f(x) = x^2$ in which the *base* is a variable are called **power functions.**)

An accurate graph of $f(x) = 2^x$ (for $-2 \leq x \leq 2.75$) is shown at the right. It can be used to obtain a good approximation to 2^x for $-2 \leq x \leq 2.75$, as the next example illustrates.

EXAMPLE 2. Use the graph of $f(x) = 2^x$ to approximate $2^{1.5}$.

Solution: METHOD I

On the graph of $f(x) = 2^x$ when $x = 1.5$
$$f(x) \approx 2.83$$
Thus $2^{1.5} \approx 2.83$

METHOD II

Notice that $2^{1.5} = 2^1 \cdot 2^{0.5}$
$$= 2 \cdot 2^{0.5} \quad \text{(Why?)}$$

Hence you can read $2^{0.5}$ on the graph and multiply the result by 2.

From the graph $\qquad 2^{0.5} \approx 1.41$

Thus $\qquad 2^{1.5} \approx 2(1.41) = 2.82.$

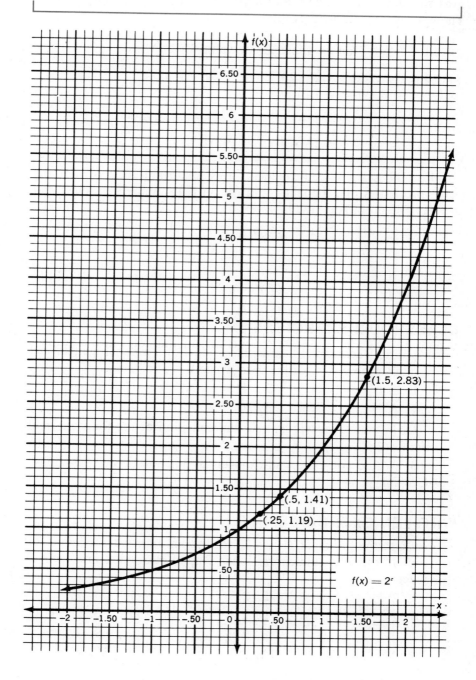

Method II illustrates a procedure whereby 2^x can be approximated using only the graph of $f(x) = 2^x$ for $0 \leq x \leq 1$. The idea is to write x as the sum of an integer and a rational number between 0 and 1. The next example illustrates this.

EXAMPLE 3. Find an approximate value for $2^{4.25}$.

Solution:

$2^{4.25} = 2^4 \cdot 2^{0.25}$, $\longleftarrow$ $a^{m+n} = a^m \cdot a^n$

$2^{4.25} = 16 \cdot 2^{0.25}$

$2^{0.25} \approx 1.19$ $\longleftarrow$ **From the graph**

$2^{4.25} \approx 16 \times 1.19 \approx 19.04.$

For the sake of completeness, it is important to note that the usual properties of exponents hold for all real numbers x and y and $a > 0$. The proof is omitted.

$$a^x \cdot a^y = a^{x+y}$$

$$\frac{a^x}{a^y} = a^{x-y}$$

$$(a^x)^y = a^{x \cdot y}$$

CLASSROOM EXERCISES

Write each expression as the product of a rational number and a rational power, p, of the base where $0 < p < 1$.

1. $2^{3.8}$ **2.** $2^{2.4}$ **3.** $5^{1.632}$

4. $6^{6.32}$ **5.** $2^{-1.51}$ **6.** $3^{-3.98}$

7. In your own words, give the definition of a^x, for x any real number.

8. Would you expect all exponential functions to be continuous? Explain.

WRITTEN EXERCISES

A Use the graph of $f(x) = 2^x$ to find an approximate value for each of the following expressions. Round answers to one decimal place.

1. $2^{0.25}$ **2.** $2^{0.50}$ **3.** $2^{0.75}$

4. $2^{-0.25}$ **5.** $2^{-0.50}$ **6.** $2^{-0.75}$

7. $2^{2.6}$ **8.** 2^{π} **9.** $2^{-0.40}$

10. $2^{-4.5}$ **11.** $2^{3.5}$ **12.** $4^{0.75}$

From the graph of $f(x) = 2^x$, $2^{1.59} \approx 3$. This fact may be used to approximate 3^x for $x \in \mathbf{R}$.

Example.

$$3^{0.5} \approx (2^{1.59})^{0.5}$$
$$\approx 2^{0.795}$$
$$\approx 2^{0.8}$$

From the graph of $f(x) = 2^x$,

$$2^{0.8} \approx 1.7.$$

Thus

$$3^{0.5} \approx 1.7.$$

Use the procedure in the above example to approximate each power of 3.

13. $3^{0.25}$ **14.** $3^{1.2}$ **15.** $3^{-0.5}$

16. $3^{0.75}$ **17.** $3^{2.4}$ **18.** $3^{-1.5}$

Use the graph of $f(x) = 2^x$ to estimate the value of x in Exercises 19–24.

19. $2^x = 5$ **20.** $2^x = 0.4$ **21.** $2^x = 1.62$

22. $2^x = 3$ **23.** $2^x = 0.27$ **24.** $2^x = 6$

B Given a positive real number x, you can express x as an integral power of 2 multiplied by a number r such that $1 \le r \le 2$.

Example. Let $x = 5$.

The greatest power of 2 in 5 is 4.
By division you find

$$5 = 2^2(1.25).$$

Thus 5 can be expressed as a power of 2 by expressing 1.25 as a power of 2.

From the graph of $f(x) = 2^x$,

$$1.25 \approx 2^{0.31}.$$

Thus

$$5 \approx 2^2(2^{0.31}) = 2^{2.31}.$$

Use the procedure in the above example to express each of the following numbers as a power of 2.

25. 10   **26.** 3.5   **27.** 18   **28.** 0.25

29. 24   **30.** 6   **31.** 0.75   **32.** 0.10

C **33.** Construct an accurate graph of the function $f : x \longrightarrow (\frac{1}{2})^x$ for $-3 \le x \le 2$.

34. Construct an accurate graph of the function $f : x \longrightarrow 3^x$ for $0 \le x \le 1$.

35. Construct an accurate graph of the function $f : x \longrightarrow 5^x$ for $0 \le x \le 1$.

(*Hint:* Is the fact that $5 \approx 2^{2.31}$ helpful?)

36. How is the graph of $f(x) = a^x$, $a > 0$, related to the graph of $f(x) = \left(\frac{1}{a}\right)^x$, $a > 0$?

8–3   The Number *e*

There are two quite famous irrational numbers in mathematics. The first, π, is familiar to you through your work in geometry. To twenty decimal places,

$$\pi \approx 3.14159265358979323846.$$

Using electronic computers, π has been computed to more than 100,000 places.

The second famous number

$$e \approx 2.7182818,$$

is probably less familiar to you.

The numbers π and e are defined as sums of infinite series.

$$\pi = 4\left(\sum_{n=0}^{\infty} (-1)^n \frac{1}{2n + 1}\right)$$

That is, $\pi = 4(1 - \frac{1}{3} + \frac{1}{5} - \frac{1}{7} + \frac{1}{9} - \frac{1}{11} + \cdots)$

$$e = \sum_{n=0}^{\infty} \frac{1}{n!} \qquad (n! = 1 \cdot 2 \cdot 3 \cdot \ \cdots \ \cdot n \text{ and } 0! = 1)$$

That is, $e = 1 + \frac{1}{1!} + \frac{1}{2!} + \frac{1}{3!} + \frac{1}{4!} + \frac{1}{5!} + \cdots$

From the definition of *e* as an infinite series, it is clear that $2 < e$. If you let S_n be the partial sum corresponding to the whole number n then you have the following.

$$S_1 = 1 + \frac{1}{1!} = 2$$

Also, if $n > 1$, then S_n is greater than 2 because the addends are all positive. Thus, $2 < e$.

It is also true that $e < 3$. This follows because

$$a_n = \frac{1}{n!} = \frac{1}{1 \cdot 2 \cdot 3 \cdot \ \cdots \ \cdot n} < \frac{1}{2} \cdot \frac{1}{2} \cdot \ \cdots \ \cdot \frac{1}{2} = \frac{1}{2^{n-1}}$$

and thus

$$S_n < 1 + 1 + \frac{1}{2} + \frac{1}{2^2} + \frac{1}{2^3} + \cdots + \frac{1}{2^{n-1}} = 1 + 2 - \frac{1}{2^{n-1}} < 3.$$

It follows that $2 < e < 3$.

The sequence $\{S_n\}$ of partial sums is an increasing sequence because $S_{n+1} = S_n + \frac{1}{(n+1)!}$. Since $\{S_n\}$ is increasing and each term is less than 3, it follows that $\{S_n\}$ has a limit. (See Theorem 5-2 of Section 5-7.) This limit is by definition the irrational number e.

$$e = \lim_{n \to \infty} S_n$$

where
$$S_n = 1 + \frac{1}{1!} + \frac{1}{2!} + \cdots + \frac{1}{n!} \quad (n \in \{0, 1, 2, \cdots\})$$

The series $\sum_{n=0}^{\infty} \frac{1}{n!}$ can be used to calculate decimal approximations for e. You are asked to do this in the exercises.

There are other equivalent ways of expressing e as a limit. One of the most common is

$$e = \lim_{n \to \infty} \left(1 + \frac{1}{n}\right)^n. \tag{1}$$

If e is raised to the real power x then

$$e^x = \lim_{n \to \infty} \left(1 + \frac{x}{n}\right)^n. \tag{2}$$

If $x = -1$, then from 2 it follows that

$$e^{-1} = \frac{1}{e} = \lim_{n \to \infty} \left(1 - \frac{1}{n}\right)^n. \tag{3}$$

Since $n \longrightarrow \infty$ is equivalent to $h \longrightarrow 0$ when $h = \frac{1}{n}$, the following limits may also be used to obtain e or e^x.

$$e = \lim_{h \to 0} (1 + h)^{\frac{1}{h}} \tag{4}$$

and

$$e^x = \lim_{h \to 0} (1 + xh)^{\frac{1}{h}} \tag{5}$$

The following expression

$$\lim_{n \to \infty} \left(1 + \frac{1}{n}\right)^n$$

is equivalent to

$$e = \sum_{n=0}^{\infty} \frac{1}{n!}$$

as can be seen by expanding $\left(1 + \frac{1}{n}\right)^n$, using the binomial theorem, and simplifying. (For a review of the binomial theorem, see page 24.)

$$\left(1 + \frac{1}{n}\right)^n = 1 + n \cdot \frac{1}{n} + \frac{(n)(n-1)}{2!} \cdot \frac{1^2}{n^2} + \frac{n(n-1)(n-2)}{3!} \cdot \frac{1^3}{n^3} + \cdots + \frac{1^n}{n^n}$$

or

$$\left(1 + \frac{1}{n}\right)^n = 1 + \frac{1}{1!} + \frac{1^2}{2!}\left(1 - \frac{1}{n}\right) + \frac{1^3}{3!} \cdot \left(1 - \frac{1}{n}\right)\left(1 - \frac{2}{n}\right) + \cdots$$
$$+ \frac{1^n}{n!}\left(1 - \frac{1}{n}\right)\left(1 - \frac{2}{n}\right) \cdots \left(1 - \frac{n-2}{n}\right)\left(1 - \frac{n-1}{n}\right)$$

Passage to the limit as $n \longrightarrow \infty$ can be accomplished by replacing $\frac{1}{n}$ by 0 in each term as follows.

$$e = 1 + \frac{1}{1!} + \frac{1}{2!} + \frac{1}{3!} + \cdots + \frac{1}{n!} + \cdots$$

If e^x is desired, the same procedure applied to $\left(1 + \frac{x}{n}\right)^n$ yields

$$e^x = 1 + \frac{x}{1!} + \frac{x^2}{2!} + \frac{x^3}{3!} + \cdots + \frac{x^n}{n!} + \cdots. \qquad 6$$

CLASSROOM EXERCISES

━━ Use 6 to approximate e^x to 3 decimal places.

1. $x = 2$ **2.** $x = -2$ **3.** $x = 1.5$

WRITTEN EXERCISES

A   **1.** Use

$$e = 1 + \frac{1}{1!} + \frac{1}{2!} + \cdots + \frac{1}{n!} + \cdots$$

to approximate e correct to 3 decimal places. How many terms of the series are needed to obtain the desired degree of accuracy?

2. Repeat Exercise 1 for 6 decimal places.

3. Use

$$e^x = 1 + \frac{x}{1!} + \frac{x^2}{2!} + \frac{x^3}{3!} + \cdots + \frac{x^n}{n!} + \cdots$$

to approximate $e^{0.01}$ correct to four decimal places. How many terms of the series are needed to obtain the desired degree of accuracy?

4. Repeat Exercise 3 for 8 decimal places.

5. Use

$$e^x = 1 + \frac{x}{1!} + \frac{x^2}{2!} + \cdots + \frac{x^n}{n!} + \cdots$$

to write an expression for e^{-1}.

6. Approximate e^{-1} correct to 3 decimal places.

B **7.** Use the graph of $f(x) = 2^x$ to estimate x in the equation

$$2^x = e.$$

8. In Exercise 7 you found that $2^{1.44} \approx e$. Use this result to construct a graph of

$$f(x) = e^x \quad \text{for} \quad -1 \le x \le 2.$$

C **9.** Prove that the sum of the first 13 terms of the infinite series for e provides an estimate for e which is accurate to 8 decimal places.

(*Hint:*

$$e = 1 + \frac{1}{1!} + \cdots + \frac{1}{12!} + \frac{1}{13!} + \cdots$$

Thus to show that the "error" of estimation is less than 0.000000005 you must show that

$$\frac{1}{13!} + \frac{1}{14!} + \cdots < 0.000000005.$$

To do this use the fact that

$$\frac{1}{13!} + \frac{1}{14!} + \frac{1}{15!} + \cdots < \frac{1}{13!}\left(1 + \frac{1}{13} + \frac{1}{13^2} + \cdots\right).)$$

10. Use the procedure of Exercise 9 to show that your answer to Exercise 1 is correct.

11. Use the procedure of Exercise 9 to show that your answer to Exercise 2 is correct.

12. Use $e^x = 1 + \frac{x}{1!} + \frac{x^2}{2!} + \frac{x^3}{3!} + \cdots + \frac{x^n}{n!}$ to approximate $x^2 e^x$ where x is the following.

    a. $x = 2$
    b. $x = -2$

8–4   The Function $f : x \longrightarrow e^x$

As stated in Section 8–2, $f(x) = a^x$, $a > 0$, is a continuous function. In particular, for $x \in R$,

$$f(x) = e^x$$

is a continuous function with domain equal to R.

Values of e^x and e^{-x}

x	e^x	e^{-x}
0.00	1.0000	1.00000
0.01	1.0101	0.99005
0.02	1.0202	0.98020
0.03	1.0305	0.97045
0.04	1.0408	0.96079
0.05	1.0513	0.95123
0.10	1.1052	0.90484
0.15	1.1618	0.86071
0.20	1.2214	0.81873
0.25	1.2840	0.77880
0.30	1.3499	0.74082
0.35	1.4191	0.70469
0.40	1.4918	0.67032
0.45	1.5683	0.63763
0.50	1.6487	0.60653
0.55	1.7333	0.57695
0.60	1.8221	0.54881
0.65	1.9155	0.52205
0.70	2.0138	0.49659
0.75	2.1170	0.47237
0.80	2.2255	0.44933
0.85	2.3396	0.42741
0.90	2.4596	0.40657
0.95	2.5857	0.38674
1.00	2.7183	0.36788
1.50	4.4817	0.22313
2.00	7.3891	0.13534
3.00	20.086	0.04979
4.00	54.598	0.01832
5.00	148.41	0.00674

The graph of $f(x) = e^x$ is shown below.

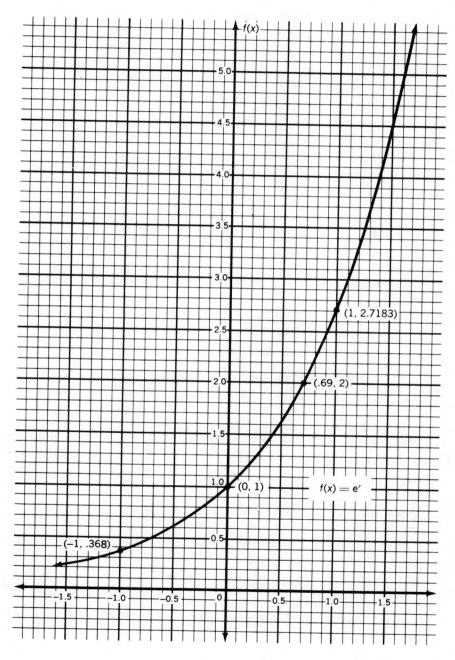

EXAMPLE. Use the graph of $f(x) = e^x$ to estimate x when $e^x = 2$.

Solution: Reading from the graph,

$$x \approx 0.69 \text{ corresponds to } f(x) = 2.$$

Checking this estimate in the table, you find $e^{0.70} \approx 2.0138$ and $e^{0.65} \approx$ 1.9155. Thus the estimate of $x = 0.69$ seems fairly good.

A second check on the accuracy of the estimate can be made as follows:

$$e^{0.69} = e^{0.65} \times e^{0.04} \quad \longleftarrow \quad a^{x+y} = a^x \cdot a^y$$
$$\approx 1.9155 \times 1.0408$$
$$\approx 1.9936$$

Thus, when $x = 0.69$, $e^x \approx 2$.

The graph of $f(x) = e^x$ has a strange property—a property no other elementary function possesses. If you place a ruler tangent to $f(x) = e^x$ at:

1. $(0, 1)$, you find the slope of the line is 1.
2. $(1, 2.7183)$, you find the slope of the line is 2.7183.
3. $(-1.0, 0.36788)$, you find the slope of the line is 0.36788.

In general, if you place a ruler tangent to $f(x) = e^x$ at (x, e^x) you find the slope of the line is e^x.

Since the slope of a tangent line at a point $(x, f(x))$ is given by the derived function f' evaluated at x, you have the following theorem.

Theorem 8–2 If $f(x) = e^x$, then $f'(x) = e^x$.

The proof of Theorem 8–2 is given in Section 8–11. However, you should convince yourself of its validity by using the graph given on page 403. Copy the curve and draw tangents to the curve at randomly chosen points (x_1, e^{x_1}) and see if the slope of each line is not nearly equal to e^{x_1}.

Applying Theorem 8–2, you can prove that the graph of $f(x) = e^x$ is everywhere concave upward.

First note that $e^x > 0$ for all $x \in R$. Thus, if $f(x) = e^x$ then $f'(x) = e^x$. Since $f'(x) = f(x) = e^x$, $f''(x) = e^x$. Thus $f''(x) > 0$ for all $x \in R$ and $f(x)$ is concave upward.

Note that $\lim_{x \to -\infty} e^x = 0$. Thus the x axis is an asymptote for $f(x) = e^x$. Also, $\lim_{x \to +\infty} e^x = +\infty$ and $f(x) = e^x$ increases without bound as $x \longrightarrow +\infty$.

CLASSROOM EXERCISES

▬ Use the table on page 402 to find an approximation of the value of x.

1. $e^x = 90.02$ **2.** $e^x = 0.0111$ **3.** $x = 1.5^{2.3}$

▬ Determine e^x for each of these values of x.

4. $x = 5$ **5.** $x = 1.6$ **6.** $x = 0.222$
7. $x = 2.4$ **8.** $x = 0.45$ **9.** $x = 1.32$

WRITTEN EXERCISES

A ▬ Use the table on page 402 to estimate the value of the variable.

1. $e^x = 2.65$ **2.** $e^{1.10} = y$ **3.** $e^x = 3$
4. $e^{-1.10} = y$ **5.** $e^x = 0.50$ **6.** $e^{2.5} = y$

▬ Use the table on page 402 to estimate the slope of the tangent to $f(x) = e^x$ at the given point.

7. $(-1, e^{-1})$ **8.** $(0.3, e^{0.3})$
9. $(1.5, e^{1.5})$ **10.** $(-1.5, e^{-1.5})$

11. Use the graph of $f(x) = e^x$ to estimate the slope of the tangent at the points given in Exercises 7–10. Compare your results.

12. Write an equation of the tangent to the graph of f at each point given in Exercises 7–10.

B **13. a.** Through the point $(4, 5)$, draw a line t_1 with slope $m = \frac{2}{3}$.

b. Draw a line t_2 which is the mirror image of t_1 with respect to the y axis.

c. To which point on t_2 does $(4, 5)$ correspond?

d. What is the slope of t_2?

e. Let (r, s) be on the line t_1 with slope m. Let t_2 be the mirror image of t_1 with respect to the y axis. What point on t_2 corresponds to (r, s)? What is the slope of t_2?

14. a. Plot the point (x, e^x) for which x has the following values.

$$-1.5, -1, -0.5, 0, 0.5, 1.0, 1.5$$

b. What is the slope of each tangent to $f(x) = e^x$ for the points in **a**? Draw these tangents.

15. Locate the points that are mirror images of the points in Exercise 14a with respect to the y axis.

16. Draw the lines which are mirror images of the lines in Exercise 14**b** with respect to the y axis.

17. Show that each point of Exercise 15 is on the graph of

$$g(x) = e^{-x}.$$

8–5 Applications – Compound Interest

Several applications of exponential functions will now be considered. The first, *compound interest* is particularly interesting because the number e occurs naturally in the analysis of the problem.

Suppose a sum of money P dollars is invested at an interest rate of r per cent, or $\frac{r}{100}$ per year. Thus at the end of one year you will have

$$P + P\left(\frac{r}{100}\right)$$

or

$$P\left(1 + \frac{r}{100}\right).$$

If no money is withdrawn and the rate remains $\frac{r}{100}$ per year, at the end of a second year you will have

$$P\left(1 + \frac{r}{100}\right) + P\left(1 + \frac{r}{100}\right)\frac{r}{100}$$

or

$$P\left(1 + \frac{r}{100}\right)^2.$$

The process of adding the interest to the principal P is called **compounding.**

In general, if you invest P dollars at an interest rate of $\frac{r}{100}$ per year and compound the interest annually, the total amount A_t you have at the end of t years is given by the following formula.

$$A_t = P\left(1 + \frac{r}{100}\right)^t$$

For some investments the interest is compounded semiannually, quarterly, or, in general, n times per year. In a situation in which the interest is compounded n times a year, the interest rate is $\frac{r}{100n}$ per period, and the number of periods in t years is nt. It follows that the amount A_{nt} after nt periods is

$$A_{nt} = P\left(1 + \frac{r}{100n}\right)^{nt}.$$

EXAMPLE 1. At the end of two years how much money do you have if you invest \$100 at an annual interest rate of 4% and the interest is compounded semiannually (every 6 months)?

Solution: $\qquad P = 100 \qquad n = 2 \qquad \dfrac{r}{100} = \dfrac{4}{100} \qquad t = 2$

$$A_4 = 100 \left(1 + \frac{4}{2 \cdot 100} \right)^{2 \cdot 2}$$

$$= 100(1.02)^4$$

$$\approx 100(1.0824)$$

$$\approx 108.24$$

Hence, you have \$108.24 at the end of two years.

The more often you compound the interest the more complex the calculation of A_{nt} becomes. In Example 1, if $n = 10$, you would have to calculate $100(1.004)^{20}$, which is clearly not simple. Thus, you need a way of approximating A_{nt}. This is obtained by letting the number of periods, n, increase without bound. Theoretically, this is equivalent to letting the interest be compounded *continuously*.

Compounding interest continuously is equivalent to evaluating the following limit.

$$\lim_{n \to \infty} P \left(1 + \frac{r}{100n} \right)^{nt} \qquad\qquad\qquad \textbf{1}$$

The limit **1** can be simplified as follows.

$$\lim_{n \to \infty} P \left(1 + \frac{r}{100n} \right)^{nt} = P \lim_{n \to \infty} \left(1 + \frac{r}{100n} \right)^{nt} \qquad \longleftarrow \textbf{\textit{P} is constant.}$$

$$= P \lim_{n \to \infty} \left[\left(1 + \frac{\frac{r}{100}}{n} \right)^n \right]^t \qquad\qquad\qquad \textbf{2}$$

The limit **2** is equal to $Pe^{\frac{rt}{100}}$ because

$$\lim_{n \to \infty} \left(1 + \frac{x}{n} \right)^n = e^x \qquad \longleftarrow \textbf{See Section 8-3.}$$

Thus if interest is **compounded continuously**

$$A_t = Pe^{\frac{rt}{100}} \qquad (t \text{ in years}).$$

The surprising thing here is the occurrence of e.

That $A_t = Pe^{\frac{rt}{100}}$ is a fair approximation to A_{nt} is illustrated in the next example.

EXAMPLE 2. If $P = 100$, $\dfrac{r}{100} = \dfrac{4}{100}$ and $t = 2$, what is the amount of money when interest is compounded continuously for two years?

Solution: $\qquad A_t = Pe^{\frac{4 \cdot 2}{100}} \quad \text{or} \quad A_t = 100(e^{0.08})$

The table in Section 8–4 can be used to show the following.

$$e^{0.08} = e^{0.05} \cdot e^{0.03}$$
$$= (1.0513)(1.0305)$$
$$\approx 1.0834$$

Thus $\qquad\qquad\qquad A_t = 100(1.0834) = 108.34$

Comparing this result with Example 1, you find earnings of 10 cents more by continuous compounding.

CLASSROOM EXERCISES

1. Find the compound interest on $100 at 3% semiannually for 2 years.

2. Find the compound amount on $200 at 4% semiannually, for 10 years.

3. Compute the interest in Exercise 2 when it is compounded continuously.

WRITTEN EXERCISES

A **1.** Find the amount of money A_t if $1000 is compounded continuously for 15 years at a rate of 2 per cent.

In Exercises 2 and 3 find the amount of money $\mathbf{A}_t$ if $1000 is invested as stated.

2. Compounded continuously for 3 years at 2 per cent.

3. Compounded quarterly for 3 years at 2 per cent.

4. Compare the results of Exercises 2 and 3.

Calculate the number of years it would take to double P dollars under the given conditions. Use the approximation $2 \approx e^{0.693}$.

5. 4 per cent compounded continuously.

6. 8 per cent compounded continuously.

7. n per cent compounded continuously.

In Exercises 8–10, find the annual interest rate compounded continuously in order to double P dollars for the given time period.

8. 1 year **9.** 3 years **10.** 23 years

BASIC: COMPOUND INTEREST

Problem:

Given the principal, rate, number of compounding periods per year, and number of years, write a program which prints the value of an investment.

```
100 PRINT
110 PRINT "THIS PROGRAM COMPUTES COMPOUND INTEREST"
120 PRINT "GIVEN THE PRINCIPAL (P), RATE (R),"
130 PRINT "COMPOUNDING PERIODS PER YEAR (N) AND"
140 PRINT "NUMBER OF YEARS (T)."
150 PRINT
160 PRINT "ENTER P, R, N, AND T, IN THAT ORDER,"
170 PRINT "SEPARATED BY COMMAS."
180 INPUT P, R, N, T
190 LET A = P * (1 + R/(100*N)) ↑ (N * T)
200 LET A = INT(100 * (A + .005))/100
210 PRINT
220 PRINT "PRINCIPAL";TAB(11);"RATE";TAB(16);"PERIODS";
230 PRINT TAB(24);"YEARS";TAB(32);"AMOUNT"
240 FOR I = 1 TO 39
250    PRINT "-";
260 NEXT I
270 PRINT
280 PRINT P;TAB(11);R;TAB(18);N;TAB(25);T;TAB(31);A
290 PRINT
300 PRINT "ANY MORE PROBLEMS (1=YES, 0=NO)";
310 INPUT Z
320 IF Z = 1 THEN 150
330 END
```

Output:

```
ENTER P, R, N, AND T, IN THAT ORDER,
SEPARATED BY COMMAS.
? 10000,8.5,12,3

PRINCIPAL  RATE PERIODS YEARS   AMOUNT
---------------------------------------
  10000     8.5    12     3     12893
```

```
ANY MORE PROBLEMS (1=YES, 0=NO)? 1

ENTER P, R, N, AND T, IN THAT ORDER,
SEPARATED BY COMMAS.
? 15000,12.25,4,15

PRINCIPAL  RATE PERIODS YEARS    AMOUNT
--------------------------------------------
 15000         12.25   4         15      91648.9

ANY MORE PROBLEMS (1=YES, 0=NO)? 0
READY
```

Analysis:

Statement 190: This line contains the following formula, which computes the amount (A) that an investment will be worth in t years (see page 406).

$$A_{nt} = P\left(1 + \frac{r}{100n}\right)^{nt}$$

Statement 200: This line rounds A to the nearest hundredth.

EXERCISES

A   Use the program on page 409 to find the amount, A.

1. $P = \$1000$, $r = 15$, $n = 6$, $t = 10$

2. $P = \$15\,000$, $r = 12$, $n = 4$, $t = 5$

3. $P = \$200\,000$, $r = 10$, $n = 12$, $t = 1$

4. $P = \$1$, $r = 10$, $n = 24$, $t = 1$

5. $P = \$4500$, $r = 8.5$, $n = 12$, $t = 2.5$

6. $P = \$8750$, $r = 11.25$, $n = 52$, $t = 0.5$

B   In Exercises 7–9, revise the program on page 409 in the manner indicated.

7. The program "assumes" that the numbers entered are valid. Insert statements to test whether the values entered are legitimate. For example, the principal (P) must be a positive number.

8. Compute the amount accumulated on a period-by-period basis, instead of at the end of the investment period only.

9. Compute and print the amount accumulated as n increases from 1 to 365, while P, r, and t remain fixed ($t = 1$).

8–6 Applications – Population Growth

Consider the phenomenon of population growth. It is natural to expect the number of births (and deaths) in equal time intervals for a population to be proportional to the number of members in the population at the beginning of each interval. That is if N_0, N_1 and N_2 represent the number of members in a population at the beginning of equal time intervals, then

$$N_1 = kN_0$$
$$N_2 = kN_1$$

and

$$N_2 = k(kN_0) = k^2 N_0$$

where k is the constant of proportionality. Thus, the population N_t at the beginning of the $(t + 1)$th equal time interval is given by the following formula

$$N_t = k^t N_0 \qquad\qquad 1$$

Equation 1 defines an *exponential function*. If you agree that the variable t need not be restricted to integers, then 1 defines a *continuous exponential function* of the constant k.

Consider a population of bacteria. Suppose at time 0 ($t = 0$), there are $N_0 = 1000$ bacteria. Suppose further that the bacteria double in number every day. Thus, the number of bacteria N equals

$$N_0 \quad \text{when } t = 0$$
$$2N_0 \quad \text{when } t = 1 \text{ (day)}$$
$$2(2N_0) = 2^2 N_0 \quad \text{when } t = 2 \text{ (days)}$$

and

$$2^n N_0 \quad \text{when } t = n \text{ (days)}$$

In general, then the number N of bacteria present after t days is given by

$$N = 2^t N_0 \qquad\qquad 2$$

or when $N_0 = 1000$

$$N = 2^t(1000) \quad (t \text{ in days})$$

Surely the bacteria do not double themselves exactly at the end of each day. Rather, they reproduce continuously throughout the 24 hours in each interval. Thus it is reasonable to assume that 2 represents the number of bacteria in the colony for all real numbers t greater than or equal to 0.

EXAMPLE. Let $N = 2^t N_0$ represent the number of bacteria in a culture at time $t \geq 0$ (days). If $N_0 = 100$, is the number of bacteria initially,

a. how many bacteria are there $2\frac{1}{2}$ days later?

b. when will there be 500 bacteria?

Solutions: a. Here $t = 2\frac{1}{2}$.

$$N = 2^{\frac{5}{2}}(100)$$
$$= 4 \cdot 2^{\frac{1}{2}}(100)$$
$$= 400 \cdot \sqrt{2}$$
$$\approx 400 \cdot (1.414)$$
$$\approx 566 \text{ to the nearest whole number.}$$

There are approximately 566 bacteria when $t = \frac{5}{2}$.

b. Here $N = 500$ and t is unknown.

$$500 = 2^t \cdot (100)$$
$$5 = 2^t$$

Since
$$5 = 2^2 \cdot (1.25) \quad \text{and} \quad 1.25 \approx 2^{0.32},$$
$$5 = 2^{2.32} \quad \text{and} \quad t \approx 2.32 \text{ days.}$$

Notice that even though the discussion in the example dealt with bacteria, the equation

$$N = k^t N_0$$

may be used to estimate the number of members in any population when N_0 and k are known.

WRITTEN EXERCISES

A ▬ Let a bacteria colony double its members in 24 hours.

1. What equation gives the number of members t days after the beginning of the experiment?

2. The number of bacteria present at the end of $n + 7$ days is how many times the number present at $n + 3$ days from the first count?

3. If there are N bacteria present after 50 days, after how many days were there $\dfrac{N}{8}$ present?

▬ Suppose that there were 90,000 bacteria present at the end of 2 days and 202,500 present at the end of 4 days.

4. Find the number present at the beginning of the count.

5. Find the number present at the end of 5 days.

6. Find the number present at the end of $\frac{1}{2}$ day.

7. Find the number of days at the end of which there are 60,000 bacteria.

8. Find the approximate number of days at the end of which there are 80,000 bacteria.

▬ Suppose a city increases its population by $\frac{1}{8}$ every year. Let N_0 be the number of people at $t = 0$. Use this information in Exercises 9 and 10.

9. Write an equation giving the number N of people in the city at the end of t years.

10. Find the approximate number of years required for the population to double $(N(t) = 2N_0)$.

11. Suppose lemmings triple their population every year and that 1 acre of land supports 100 lemmings. If a herd of 100 lemmings have 100 acres of land, how many years can pass before the land will no longer support the herd? (Assume no lemming dies in the period.)

8–7 Applications – Radioactive Decay

While population growth is an instance of exponential growth, radioactive decay is an example of the opposite phenomenon. You may think of radioactive material as containing a very large number of unstable atoms. These atoms can change spontaneously into stable atoms of another substance. As a result, the number of the unchanged atoms decreases with time. The number $N(x)$ of unchanged atoms at time x, is given by

$$N(x) = N_0 a^{-x}, \qquad\qquad 1$$

where N_0 is the number $N(0)$ at $x = 0$ and a is a suitable constant greater than one.

Since, for all $a > 1$, there is a unique number α (alpha) such that $a = 2^{\alpha}$, equation 1 may be expressed as follows.

$$N(x) = N_0 2^{-\alpha x} \qquad\qquad 2$$

Moreover, since $2 \approx e^{0.693}$, equation 2 may be written as follows.

$$N(x) = N_0 e^{-\alpha(0.693)x}$$

If you let $c = -\alpha(0.693)$ this can be written as follows.

$$N(x) = N_0 e^{-cx} \qquad\qquad 3$$

Clearly, the fraction of radioactive atoms which remain after a given time t is fixed, since

$$\frac{N(x + t)}{N(x)} = \frac{N_0 a^{-(x+t)}}{N_0 a^{-x}} = a^{-t}$$

is independent of the starting time x.

As $t \longrightarrow +\infty$, $\frac{N(x + t)}{N(x)} \longrightarrow 0$. Thus, for some time T, $N(x + T)$ must be equal to one half of $N(x)$. The time T at which exactly one half of the radioactive atoms remain is called the half-life of the radioactive matter.

To find the half-life T of a radioactive substance it is convenient to use equation 2. You must solve

$$\tfrac{1}{2}N_0 = N_0 2^{-\alpha x},$$

because you want to determine the time when the number of radioactive atoms equals one half the original number N_0.

The solution follows.

$$\tfrac{1}{2}N_0 = N_0 2^{-\alpha T}$$

and
$$2^{-1} = 2^{-\alpha T}.$$

Thus
$$\alpha T = 1$$

$$T = \frac{1}{\alpha} \quad \text{or} \quad \alpha = \frac{1}{T}.$$

Consequently the equation describing radioactive decay can be written

$$N(x) = N_0 2^{-\frac{x}{T}}, \qquad\qquad 4$$

where T is the half-life of the substance.

EXAMPLE. If a substance decomposes in such a way that at the end of 400 years only one half of it remains, what fraction of the substance remains after 80 years?

Solution: The fraction which remains after 80 years is

$$\frac{N(80)}{N(0)}.$$

The data imply that the half-life is 400 years. Thus equation 4 gives you

$$N(80) = N_0 2^{-\frac{80}{400}} = N_0 2^{-\frac{1}{5}},$$

from which you have the following.

$$\frac{N(80)}{N(0)} = 2^{-\frac{1}{5}} \approx e^{-\frac{0.693}{5}} \approx e^{-0.14} \approx 0.869$$

WRITTEN EXERCISES

A   **1.** The half-life of radon is 385 days. What fraction of a sample with N_0 atoms remains at the end of 7.7 days? After 23.1 days?

2. Find the half-life of uranium if $\frac{1}{3}$ of the substance decomposes in 0.26 billion years.

3. The half-life of a radioactive substance is 25 minutes. What fraction of the sample remains after

    a. 12.5 minutes?
    b. 75 minutes?
    c. 150 minutes?

4. The half-life of Polonium (212) is 3×10^{-7} seconds. How much of a given sample remains after

    a. 1 minute?
    b. 12.2 minutes?
    c. 1 day?
    d. 3 days?

B   **5.** In living matter the proportion of carbon which is radioactive does not vary with time (supposedly), but it decays from the time of death with a half-life of 5600 years. Date a piece of wood in which the radioactive carbon is 0.78 of the radioactive carbon of a similar specimen of living wood.

6. The half-life of a radioactive substance is 1 hour. What fraction of the substance is radioactive at the end of 1 second? at the end of 3 seconds?

MID-CHAPTER REVIEW

━━ Simplify each of the following. The replacement set for each variable is the set of positive real numbers. (Section 8-1)

    1. $(8^{\frac{2}{3}})^{-2}$ **2.** $(5^{-1})^{\frac{1}{2}}$

    3. $(x^{\frac{2}{3}})^3 (x^{-4})^{\frac{1}{2}}$ **4.** $((x^4)(x^2 y^{-2}))^{\frac{1}{2}}$

━━ Use the graph of $f(x) = 2^x$ to estimate the value of each expression. (Section 8-2)

    5. $2^{0.6}$ **6.** $2^{-0.6}$ **7.** $3^{0.25}$ **8.** $4^{1.6}$

    9. Use $e^x = 1 + \frac{x}{1!} + \frac{x^2}{2!} + \cdots + \frac{x^n}{n!} + \cdots$ to approximate e^3 to two decimal places. (Section 8-3)

━━━ Use the graph of $f(x) = e^x$ to estimate the value of x.   (Section 8-4)

10. $x = e^{0.57}$ **11.** $e^x = 2.5$

12. Find the compound interest on $1000 at 12% compounded quarterly for 3 years.   (Section 8-5)

13. How many years will it take to double $1000 if it is invested at 12% and compounded continuously?   (Section 8-5)

14. How many bacteria would exist at the end of 5 days, if there were 2000 at the end of the first day and 2500 at the end of 1.5 days? (Section 8-6)

15. The half life of a radioactive substance is 60 minutes. What fraction of the sample remains after 90 minutes?   (Section 8-7)

8–8   Inverses

In order to proceed with the major topic of this chapter, it is necessary to review and extend the idea of the inverse of a function. Recall that if f is a function and if g (which may or may not be a function) is the *inverse* of f, then

$$f : x \longrightarrow y \quad (x \in f, y \in g) \qquad g : y \longrightarrow x \quad (x \in f, y \in g).$$

Each $x \in f$ corresponds to a unique $y \in g$ in the above mappings. However, since g need not be a function, each $y \in g$ need not correspond to a unique $x \in f$. The following examples will illustrate the case where g is a function and the case where g is not a function.

EXAMPLE 1.   Identify the inverse of the function sin $= \{(x, y) : y = \sin x, x \in R\}$ and tell whether it is a function.
Solution: The inverse is

$$g = \text{arc sin} = \{(x, y) : x = \sin y, x \in [-1, 1]\}$$
$$= \{(x, y) : y = \text{arc sin } x, x \in [-1, 1]\}.$$

Thus, arc sin is not a function.

If the inverse of a function is itself a function then it is referred to as the **inverse function** of f and may be denoted by f^{-1}, which is read "f inverse."

EXAMPLE 2.   Identify the inverse and tell whether it is a function.

$$\text{Sin} = \left\{ (x, y) : y = \sin x, x \in \left[-\frac{\pi}{2}, \frac{\pi}{2} \right] \right\}$$

Solution: The inverse is

$$f^{-1} = \text{Arc sin} = \{(x, y) : x = \text{Sin } y, x \in [-1, 1]\}$$
$$= \{(x, y) : y = \text{Arc sin } x, x \in [-1, 1]\}$$

Because of the restricted domain of Sin, Arc sin *is* a function.

A good way to picture a function f and its inverse function, f^{-1}, is to think of a diagram such as the following.

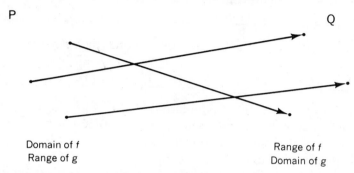

P

Q

Domain of f
Range of g

Range of f
Domain of g

If f associates each member of P with one and only one member of Q, then the inverse function of f associates each number of Q with one and only one member of P. The function f would be represented by arrows going from P to Q while for f^{-1} the same arrows would point in the opposite direction. Clearly turning the arrows around can be done in only one way. Thus it is intuitively evident that the inverse of a function is unique. By definition it follows that

$$f^{-1}((f(x)) = x \quad \text{and} \quad f(f^{-1}(y)) = y.$$

Theorem 8–3 If f has an inverse function, f^{-1}, and $x_1 \neq x_2$ are points in the domain of f, then $f(x_1) \neq f(x_2)$.

Proof: The proof is indirect. Suppose $f(x_1) = f(x_2)$, f has an inverse function and $x_1 \neq x_2$, then

$$f^{-1}(f(x_1)) = f^{-1}(f(x_2))$$

and $$x_1 = x_2$$

by the definition of inverse function. But

$$x_1 \neq x_2 \qquad \text{by assumption.}$$

Thus you have a contradiction, and the theorem is proved.

A function for which $f(x_1) \neq f(x_2)$ whenever $x_1 \neq x_2$ is a **one-to-one function.** Theorem 8–3 may be restated as:

> If a function f has an inverse function then it is one-to-one.

The converse of Theorem 8–3 is also true. You shall find it and a related theorem valuable in the next section.

> **Theorem 8–4** If a function f is one-to-one, then f has an inverse function.

Proof: The hypothesis that f is one-to-one allows you to construct a function g which will turn out to be the inverse function of f.

Let y be an element in the range of f. Then, since f is one-to-one, there is one and only one element x in the domain of f such that $y = f(x)$. Let g be the function that associates each y with the unique x, that is $g(y) = x$ when $y = f(x)$. Clearly the domain of g is the range of f. Also, since $y = f(x)$,

$$g(y) = g(f(x)) = x$$

and since

$$x = g(y)$$

$$f(x) = f(g(y)) = y.$$

Thus g is the inverse of f and $g = f^{-1}$.

> **Definition** A function f is **strictly increasing** if and only if for any two elements x_1 and x_2 in the domain of f, $x_1 < x_2$ implies $f(x_1) < f(x_2)$.

Intuitively, a strictly increasing function has a graph which is everywhere rising to the right.

> **Theorem 8–5** If f is a strictly increasing function, then f has an inverse function.

Proof: Let x_1 and x_2 be any two distinct members of the domain of f. There are two possible relations between x_1 and x_2. They are the following.

$$x_1 < x_2 \quad \text{or} \quad x_2 < x_1$$

If $x_1 < x_2$, then by hypothesis $f(x_1) < f(x_2)$.
If $x_2 < x_1$, then $f(x_2) < f(x_1)$.
   In either case, $f(x_1) \neq f(x_2)$, and f is one-to-one. Hence, f has an inverse function by Theorem 8–4.

The simple relation between the graph of a function f and its inverse function f^{-1} is familiar to you. If t and u are real numbers so that $t = f(u)$, then $P(u, t)$ is a point of the graph of f. But if $t = f(u)$, then $u = f^{-1}(t)$ and $Q(t, u)$ is a point of the graph of f^{-1}. Thus the graph f^{-1} can be obtained from the graph of f by plotting the points obtained by interchanging the coordinates of the points of f. This relation is illustrated in the figure below.

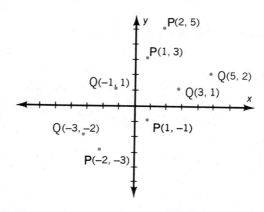

It can be shown that each point $Q(t, u)$ of the graph of f^{-1} is the mirror image of the point $P(u, t)$ of f with respect to the line $y = x$. This is done by showing that $y = x$ is the perpendicular bisector of the segment PQ. It is left for you to do in the exercises.

WRITTEN EXERCISES

A —— In Exercises 1–4, find the inverse of each function.

1. $f : x \longrightarrow 3x - 2$

2. $f : x \longrightarrow -\frac{1}{2}x + 1$

3. $f : x \longrightarrow \frac{2}{x} + 1$

4. $f : x \longrightarrow x^3 - 2$

In Exercises 5–8, solve each equation for x in terms of y. Compare your results with those you obtained in Exercises 1–4.

5. $y = 3x - 2$

6. $y = -\frac{1}{2}x + 1$

7. $y = \frac{2}{x} + 1$

8. $y = x^3 - 2$

9. Sketch the graph of $f(x) = x^2$, $x \in R$.

    a. Show that f does not have an inverse function.

    b. Sketch the graphs of $f_1(x) = x^2$, $x \geq 0$ and $f_2(x) = x^2$, $x < 0$, and identify the inverse functions.

    c. What relationship exists among the domains of f, f_1 and f_2? (f_1 is said to be the **restriction** of f to the domain $\{x : x \geq 0\}$ and f_2 is the restriction of f to the domain $\{x : x < 0\}$.)

10. Sketch the graph of $f(x) = \sqrt{9 - x^2}$. Does f have an inverse function? If not, how could the domain be restricted so that the resulting functions have inverses?

B   **11.** Define a strictly decreasing function.

12. Prove: Every strictly decreasing function has an inverse function.

13. Prove: The line $y = x$ is the perpendicular bisector of the segment $\overline{PQ}$, where the coordinates of P are (t, u) and for Q are (u, t), thus showing that the graphs of a function and its inverse are mirror images.

14. Sketch the graph of f and its inverse. (Use Exercise 13.)

    a. $f(x) = 3x - 2$

    b. $f(x) = x^3 - 2$

C   **15.** For $f(x) = \frac{2}{3}x - 4$ sketch the graphs and find the slopes of f and f^{-1}.

16. Repeat Exercise 15 for $g(x) = \frac{1}{2}x + 1$ and $h(x) = mx + b$, $m \neq 0$.

17. State a relation between the slope of a linear function and the slope of its inverse.

Use the function $f(x) = x^2$, $x \geq 0$ in Exercises 18–20.

18. What is the slope of the tangent to f at $x = 4$?

19. Find f^{-1} and the slope of the tangent to f^{-1} at $x = 16$.

20. State a relation suggested by Exercises 18 and 19.

21. Prove: The inverse of a strictly increasing function is a strictly increasing function.

8–9 Logarithmic Functions

Does an exponential function have an inverse function? Clearly the answer is yes, for when $a > 1$, $a^{x_1} < a^{x_2}$ whenever $x_1 < x_2$. Thus applying Theorem 8–5 (or Exercise 12, Section 8–8 when $0 < a < 1$) the exponential function $f : x \longrightarrow a^x$, $a > 0$ has an inverse function. For the remainder of this section let a be restricted to real numbers greater than 1.

If $f(x) = a^x$, then the graph of $f^{-1}(x)$ is the mirror image of the graph of f with respect to the line $y = x$ since (u, t) is in f^{-1} if and only if (t, u) is in f. Since the domain of f is R and the range is the set of positive real numbers, the domain of f^{-1} is the set of positive real numbers, and the range is R. The graphs of f and f^{-1} are shown.

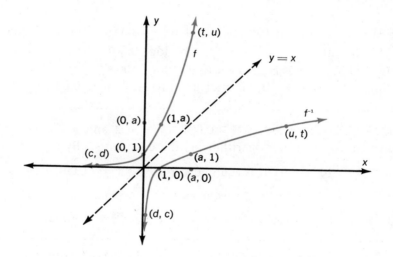

The function f^{-1} is called the **logarithm to the base a** and is denoted by the symbol $\log_a$. Thus

$$f^{-1} : x \longrightarrow \log_a x.$$

Now

$$f : x \longrightarrow a^x$$

and

$$f^{-1} : x \longrightarrow \log_a x$$

are inverse functions. Thus

$$f(f^{-1}(x)) = x$$

and

$$f^{-1}(f(x)) = x.$$

From this it follows that

$$f(\log_a x) = x \qquad\qquad 1$$

and

$$f^{-1}(a^x) = x \qquad\qquad 2$$

or using exponential and logarithmic notation exclusively

$$a^{\log_a x} = x \qquad\qquad 1'$$

and

$$\log_a a^x = x. \qquad\qquad 2'$$

From **1'** you can see that $\log_a x$ is an exponent. Call it y. Then y is the inverse of x; that is, y is the only number for which $x = a^y$. Thus,

$$y = \log_a x \quad \text{if and only if} \quad x = a^y. \qquad\qquad 3$$

Because of this fact, logarithms are often *defined* as exponents.

EXAMPLE 1.   Given $10^2 = 100$ and $10^{-3} = 0.001$, find the following.

    a. $\log_{10} 100$ **b.** $\log_{10} 0.001$

a. By **3**, $100 = 10^2$ is equivalent to $2 = \log_{10} 100$.

b. Similarly, $0.001 = 10^{-3}$ is equivalent to $-3 = \log_{10} 0.001$.

EXAMPLE 2.   Express $10^{-3} = 0.001$, $e^{0.693} \approx 2$ and $e^{-1} \approx 0.3679$ in equivalent forms using logarithms as the exponents. By **1**, $a^{\log_a x} = x$.

Thus $10^{-3} = 0.001$ is equivalent to $10^{\log_{10} 0.001} \approx 0.001$.

$$e^{0.693} \approx 2 \text{ is equivalent to } e^{\log_e 2} \approx 2.$$

and $e^{-1} \approx 0.3679$ is equivalent to $e^{\log_e 0.3679} \approx 0.3679$.

The familiar properties of logarithms follow easily from the definition of a logarithmic function as the inverse of an exponential function.

Theorem 8–6 $\log_a 1 = 0.$

Proof: If $f : x \longrightarrow a^x$, then $f(x) = a^x$ and $f(0) = a^0 = 1$. Thus $f^{-1}(1) = 0$ or $\log_a 1 = 0$.

Theorem 8–7 $\log_a y_1 \cdot y_2 = \log_a y_1 + \log_a y_2.$

Proof: If $f : x \longrightarrow a^x$, then $f(x) = a^x$ and

$$f(x_1 + x_2) = a^{x_1 + x_2} = a^{x_1} \cdot a^{x_2} = f(x_1) \cdot f(x_2).$$

Thus $$f^{-1}(f(x_1 + x_2)) = f^{-1}(f(x_1) \cdot f(x_2)). \qquad 4$$

By definition: $$f^{-1}(f(x_1 + x_2)) = x_1 + x_2.$$

Let $y_1 = f(x_1)$ and $y_2 = f(x_2)$. Thus $f^{-1}(y_1) = x_1$ and $f^{-1}(y_2) = x_2$. Substitution in **4** gives

$$x_1 + x_2 = f^{-1}(y_1 \cdot y_2).$$

But $$x_1 + x_2 = f^{-1}(y_1) + f^{-1}(y_2).$$

Thus $$f^{-1}(y_1 \cdot y_2) = f^{-1}(y_1) + f^{-1}(y_2).$$

Changing to logarithmic notation you have

$$\log_a y_1 \cdot y_2 = \log_a y_1 + \log_a y_2$$

for all positive real numbers y_1 and y_2.

Theorem 8–8 $\log_a y^p = p \log_a y.$

Proof: If $$f : x \longrightarrow a^x,$$
then

$$f(x) = a^x.$$

Therefore

$$\begin{aligned} f(xp) &= a^{xp} \\ &= [a^x]^p \\ &= [f(x)]^p. \end{aligned}$$

Using the inverse relation

$$\begin{aligned} f^{-1}([f(x)]^p) &= f^{-1}[f(xp)] \\ &= xp. \end{aligned} \qquad 5$$

Let $y = f(x)$ and $x = f^{-1}(y)$.

Substitute in **5**.

$$f^{-1}(y^p) = [f^{-1}(y)]p$$

Changing to logarithmic notation you have the following.

$$\log_a y^p = p \log_a y$$

The following theorems are easy consequences of Theorems 8–7 and 8–8. They are left for you to prove in the exercises.

Theorem 8–9 $\log_a \frac{y_1}{y_2} = \log_a y_1 - \log_a y_2$.

Theorem 8–10 $\log_a \sqrt[c]{y} = \frac{1}{c} \log_a y,\ c \in W$.

The table of values for e^x in Section 8–4 can be used to find the logarithms to the base e of certain numbers. Since

$$e^{0.65} \approx 1.9155,$$
$$\log_e 1.9155 \approx 0.65.$$

But what is $\log_e 2$? That is, if $e^x = 2$, what is x? A method of finding $\log_e 2$ is illustrated in Example 3.

EXAMPLE 3. Find $\log_e 2$.

Solution:

The procedure is to express 2 as a product of factors which are in the table of Section 8–4. In this way, using Theorem 8–7 you can find $\log_e 2$.

The largest number not greater than 2 in column 2 of the table is 1.9155.

$$2 \div 1.9155 \approx 1.0441$$

and so

$$2 \approx 1.9155 \cdot 1.0441$$

1.0441 is not in the second column of the table, so choose the greatest entry not greater than 1.0441 and divide.

$$1.0441 \div 1.0408 \approx 1.003$$

Thus

$$1.0441 \approx 1.0408 \cdot 1.003$$

and

$$2 \approx 1.9155 \cdot 1.0408 \cdot 1.003$$

Hence, $\log_e 2 \approx \log_e 1.9155 + \log_e 1.0408 + \log_e 1.003$
$$\approx .65 + .04 + .003 = .693$$

Finally,

$$\log_e 2 \approx .693 \quad \text{or} \quad e^{0.693} \approx 2.$$

In a manner similar to that illustrated in Example 3 you can show that $\log_e 3 \approx 1.099$.

EXAMPLE 4. Find

      a. $\log_e 6.$ **b.** $\log_e 4.$

Solutions:

a.
$$\log_e 6 = \log_e 2 + \log_e 3 \quad \longleftarrow \text{ By Theorem 8-7}$$

From Example 3,
$$\log_e 2 \approx 0.693$$

From the comment above,
$$\log_e 3 \approx 1.099$$

Thus
$$\log_e 6 \approx 0.693 + 1.099$$
$$= 1.792$$

b. Since $4 = 2^2$, by Theorem 8–8

$$\log_e 4 = \log_e 2^2$$
$$= 2 \log_e 2$$
$$\approx 2(0.693)$$
$$= 1.386$$

An accurate graph of $f : x \longrightarrow \log_e x$ is shown on page 427. You will be asked to use it in the exercises.

CLASSROOM EXERCISES

  1. Given the expression $y = 2^x$, find
    a. its inverse.
    b. an equivalent logarithmic form.
  2. Find the inverse of $y = e^x$.

  ━━ Express each of the following in exponential form.
  3. $\log_2 8 = 3$ **4.** $\log_6 6 = 1$ **5.** $\log_{16} 2 = \frac{1}{4}$

WRITTEN EXERCISES

A ━━ Use the results of Examples 3 and 4 to find the following.
  1. $\log_e 8$ **2.** $\log_e 12$ **3.** $\log_e 18$
  4. $\log_e 9$ **5.** $\log_e \frac{3}{2}$ **6.** $\log_e \frac{9}{4}$

  7. Find $\log_e 5$ given that $5 \approx (4.4817)(1.1052)(1.009)$. Use the table in Section 8–4.

  8. Use the results of Example 3 and Exercise 7 to find $\log_e 10$ and $\log_e 100$.

In Exercises 9–14, use the results of Examples 3 and 4 and Exercise 7 to find the following.

9. $\log_e 0.25$ **10.** $\log_e 0.20$ **11.** $\log_e \frac{5}{3}$

12. $\log_e \frac{3}{5}$ **13.** $\log_e \frac{2}{3}$ **14.** $\log_e \frac{2}{5}$

In Exercises 15–20, use the graph of $f(x) = \log_e x$ to estimate

15. $\log_e 0.25$ **16.** $\log_e 0.20$ **17.** $\log_e \frac{5}{3}$

18. $\log_e \frac{3}{5}$ **19.** $\log_e \frac{2}{3}$ **20.** $\log_e \frac{2}{5}$

21. Compare the results you obtained in Exercises 9–14 and Exercises 15–20.

22. By measuring the appropriate segments on the graph of $f(x) = e^x$, verify the following.

    a. $\log_e 2 + \log_e 3 = \log_e 6$ **b.** $\log_e 1.5 + \log_e 2 = \log_e 3$

B In Exercises 23–28, express each in the exponential form.

23. $\log_{10} x = 5$ **24.** $\log_{10} 19 = y$

25. $\log_3 25 = y$ **26.** $\log_n m = p$

27. $2 \log_3 5 = y$ **28.** $\log_e 5 + \log_e 7 = x$

29. Prove Theorem 8–9.

30. Prove Theorem 8–10.

31. Prove: $\log_a a = 1$.

In Exercises 32–37, write each statement in logarithmic form.

32. $81 = 3^4$ **33.** $\sqrt[3]{125} = 5$

34. $10^{-2} = 0.01$ **35.** $\frac{1}{6} = (36)^{-\frac{1}{2}}$

36. $0.04^{\frac{3}{2}} = 0.008$ **37.** $\sqrt{\sqrt{16}} = 2$

Given $\log_{10} 5 = 0.6990$, find the following.

38. $\log_{10} 2$ **39.** $\log_{10} \frac{1}{5}$

40. $\log_{10} \frac{25}{4}$ **41.** $\log_{10} \frac{64}{25}$

C **42.** Find x if

    a. $\log_4 x + \log_4 (x + 6) = 2$

    b. $2 \log_2 x = -2$

Given that $a^x = a^y$ if and only if $x = y$, that $a^{\log_a b} = b$, and the laws of exponents prove the following.

43. $\log_a b \cdot c = \log_a b + \log_a c$ (*Hint:* Let $b = a^{\log_a b}$, $c = a^{\log_a c}$ and $bc = a^{\log_a bc}$. Substitute the exponential expressions for b and c in $a^{\log_a bc} = bc$ and simplify.)

44. $\log_a \frac{b}{c} = \log_a b - \log_a c$

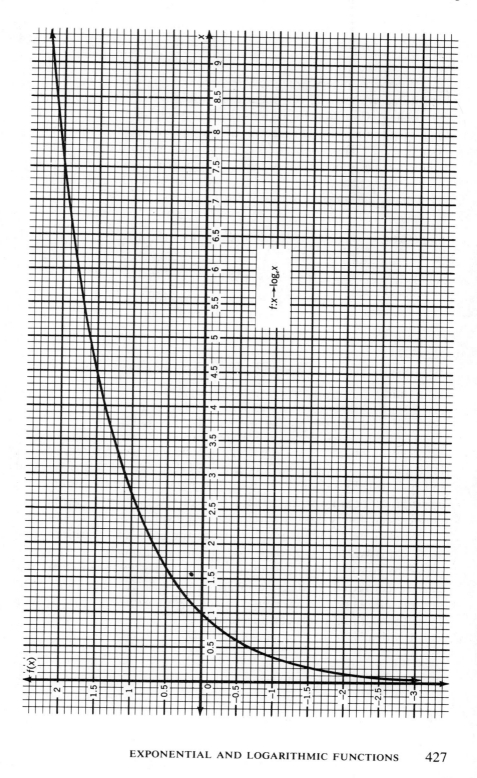

$f : x \rightarrow \log_e x$

8–10   Logarithms with Special Bases

The two numbers which are most commonly used as the bases of logarithms are ten and *e*. Logarithms with the base ten are **common logarithms.** Common logarithms are extremely useful in performing long calculations involving repeated multiplication, division, and exponentiation. This application is directly related to the facts that the Hindu-Arabic numeration system uses ten as its base and that every number may be expressed as the product of a number between one and ten and an integral power of ten.

EXAMPLE 1.   Given $\log_{10} 2 \approx 0.3010$ find the following.

   a. $\log_{10} 200$ b. $\log_{10} 0.0002$

Solutions: a.   Since $200 = 2 \times 10^2$,

$$\begin{aligned} \log_{10} 200 &= \log_{10} 2 + \log_{10} 10^2 \\ &\approx 0.3010 + 2 \log_{10} 10 \\ &= 0.3010 + 2 \\ &= 2.3010. \end{aligned}$$

b. Similarly, $0.0002 = 2 \times 10^{-4}$.

   Thus $\begin{aligned} \log_{10} 0.0002 &= \log_{10} 2 + \log_{10} 10^{-4} \\ &\approx 0.3010 + -4 \\ &= -4 + .3010, \text{ or } -3.6990 \end{aligned}$

The number $e \approx 2.7183$ is the second commonly used base of logarithms. Logarithms with base *e* are called **natural logarithms** and $\log_e x$ is usually denoted "ln *x*." The name "natural logarithm" is appropriate because when *e* is the base of a logarithmic function the derived function is especially simple as you will see in Section 8–11.

Since *e* and ten are usually used as the bases of logarithms, and since extensive tables of these logarithms are available, it is appropriate to consider the question of how a logarithm to another base may be converted to a base *e* logarithm or base ten logarithm. The general problem of converting the logarithm with any base *a* to a logarithm with base *b* is considered first.

By identity **1'** of Section 8–9, page 422,

$$x = b^{\log_b x}. \tag{1}$$

Taking the logarithm to base *a* of *x* you find

$$\log_a x = \log_a (b^{\log_b x})$$

or $\log_a x = \log_b x \cdot \log_a b$ 2

You can use equation 2 to change from logarithms with base a to those with base b, as Example 2 illustrates.

EXAMPLE 2. Express $\log_4 16$ as a base 2 logarithm.
Solution: By 2, you have

$$\log_4 16 = \log_2 16 \cdot \log_4 2$$

or

$$\log_2 16 = \frac{\log_4 16}{\log_4 2}$$

Since $\log_4 16 = 2$ and $\log_4 2 = \frac{1}{2}$, $\log_2 16 = \frac{2}{\frac{1}{2}} = 4$.

Common logarithms can be expressed in terms of natural logarithms in the manner illustrated in Example 2.

$$\ln x = (\log_{10} x) \ln 10$$
$$\log_{10} x = \frac{\ln x}{\ln 10}$$

From Exercise 8, Section 8–9 you know that

$$\ln 10 \approx 2.303.$$

Thus

$$\log_{10} x \approx \frac{\ln x}{2.303} \qquad\qquad 3$$
$$\log_{10} x \approx 0.434(\ln x) \qquad\qquad 4$$
$$\ln x \approx 2.303(\log_{10} x) \qquad\qquad 5$$

EXAMPLE 3. Find $\log_{10} e$ and $\ln 10$.
Solution: Equation 4 for $x = e$ implies

$$\log_{10} e \approx 0.434(\ln e) = 0.434.$$

Equation 5 for $x = 10$ implies $\ln 10 = 2.303(\log_{10} 10) = 2.303.$

The solution of Example 3 has an interesting sidelight.   Since $\frac{1}{2.303} \approx 0.434$, it appears that

$$\frac{1}{\ln 10} = \log_{10} e. \qquad\qquad 6$$

This relation is valid and can be proved by setting $x = 10$, $a = 10$, and $b = e$ in equation 2. More generally:

Theorem 8–11 $\log_a b = \dfrac{1}{\log_b a}$

WRITTEN EXERCISES

A ━━ Given $\log_{10} 2 = 0.3010$, $\log_{10} 3 = 0.4771$, $\log_{10} 5 = 0.6990$, and $\log_{10} 7 = 0.8451$, find each logarithm.

1. $\log_{10} 12$

2. $\log_{10} 15$

3. $\log_{10} 6$

4. $\log_{10} 1.2$

5. $\log_{10} 0.15$

6. $\log_{10} 0.006$

7. $\log_{10} 48$

8. $\log_{10} 60$

9. $\log_{10} 128$

10. Convert the common logarithms found in Exercises 1–6 to natural logarithms.

━━ Express each logarithm in simplified form.

11. $\log_{0.01} 0.001$

12. $\log_3 \sqrt{81}$

13. $\log_5 \frac{1}{125}$

14. $\log_4 128$

15. $\log_{\frac{1}{2}} 8$

16. $\ln e^3$

17. $\ln \sqrt[3]{e}$

18. $\log_3 \frac{1}{27}$

19. $\log_2 \sqrt[3]{32}$

B ━━ Find the value of x in Exercises 20–31.

20. $3^{\log_3 2} + 5^{\log_5 7} = 6^{\log_6 x}$

21. $\ln (x^2 - 1) - 2 \ln (x - 1) = \ln 5 \quad (x > 0)$

22. $\ln 4 + 2 \ln x - \ln (x^2 + x) = \ln 2 \quad (x > 0)$

23. $11^{\log_x 7} = 7$

24. $7^{\log_7 x} = 3$

25. $\ln x = 0$

26. $\ln x + 1 = 0$

27. $\ln x = 1$

28. $\ln (x - 2) = 3$

29. $\ln x - 2 = -4$

30. $\ln x^2 - 1 = 3$

31. $\ln (2x - 1) + 2 = 0$

C **32.** For what values of x does $(\ln x)^2 = \ln x^2$?

33. For what values of x does $(\log_{10} x)^2 = \log_{10} x^2$?

34. For what values of x does $(\log_b x)^2 = \log_b x^2$?

35. Prove Theorem 8–11.

36. Find x if $\log_{10} x - 2 + \log_x 10 = 0$.

37. Prove: $(\log_a b)(\log_b c)(\log_c d) = \log_a d$

38. Sketch the graph of $f(x) = |\ln x|$.

39. Solve for x. $2^{2x+2} - 8^{x+2} = 0$.

40. Solve for x. $4^{3x} - 8^{4x+1} = 0$.

41. Solve for x. $3^{3x} - 9^{x+1} = 0$.

42. Solve for x. $7^{2x} - 49^{3x+1} = 0$.

8–11   Derived Function of e^x

In Exercises 15–20 of Section 8–8 you found that there was a simple relationship between the derived function of an increasing (or decreasing) function f and the derived function of f^{-1}. The theorem summarizing these results is stated here without proof.

Theorem 8–12 If $y = f(x)$ is increasing (or decreasing) and has a derived function at every point of this interval and $f'(x) \neq 0$ in this interval, then the inverse function $x = g(y)$ has a derived function in the corresponding interval and

$$g'(y) = \frac{1}{f'(x)}.$$

EXAMPLE 1. Verify Theorem 8–12 when $f(x) = mx + b$, $m \neq 0$.

Since $f(x) = mx + b$, $f'(x) = m$. By Theorem 8–12, $g'(y)$ should be $\frac{1}{m}$. You can verify that $g'(y) = \frac{1}{m}$ by finding the inverse of $f(x) = y$. Since $y = mx + b$, it follows that

$$x = \frac{y}{m} - \frac{b}{m},$$

or

$$g(y) = \frac{y}{m} - \frac{b}{m}.$$

Then $g'(y) = \frac{1}{m}$ is obtained by finding the derived function of the polynomial function $g(y)$. Hence, the theorem is verified.

EXAMPLE 2. Verify Theorem 8–12 for

$$f(x) = 3x^2 \qquad x > 0.$$

Solution: The function $f(x) = 3x^2$ implies

$$f'(x) = 2 \cdot (3x)$$
$$= 6x.$$

Thus by the theorem,

$$g'(y) = \frac{1}{6x}.$$

But since

$$y = 3x^2$$
$$x = \sqrt{\frac{y}{3}}$$

and

$$g'(y) = \frac{1}{6\sqrt{\frac{y}{3}}}$$
$$= \frac{1}{2\sqrt{3y}}.$$

Solving $y = 3x^2$ for x yields

$$g(y) = x = \tfrac{1}{3}\sqrt{3y}.$$

By definition, you have the following.

$$g'(y) = \lim_{h \to 0} \left[\frac{1}{3} \frac{\sqrt{3(y + h)} - \sqrt{3y}}{h} \right]$$

(You treat y just as you would x.)

$$= \frac{1}{3} \lim_{h \to 0} \left[\frac{3(y + h) - 3y}{h(\sqrt{3(y + h)} + \sqrt{3y})} \right]$$

(Multiply numerator and denominator by $\sqrt{3(y + h)} + \sqrt{3y}$.)

$$= \frac{1}{3} \lim_{h \to 0} \frac{3}{\sqrt{3(y + h)} + \sqrt{3y}}$$

$$= \frac{1}{2\sqrt{3y}}$$

The two results above are the same and Theorem 8–12 is verified.

Theorem 8–12 will be useful to you in proving that if $f(x) = e^x$ then $f'(x) = e^x$. But to use it, you must first find $f'(x)$ when $f(x) = \ln x$. This is done next.

Let $f(x) = \ln x$. Then by definition,

$$f'(x) = \lim_{h \to 0} \left(\frac{\ln (x + h) - \ln x}{h} \right)$$

$$= \lim_{h \to 0} \frac{\ln \left(\dfrac{x + h}{x} \right)}{h}$$

$$= \lim_{h \to 0} \left[\frac{1}{h} \ln \left(1 + \frac{h}{x} \right) \right]$$

$$= \lim_{h \to 0} \ln \left(1 + \frac{h}{x} \right)^{\frac{1}{h}}$$

$$= \ln \left[\lim_{h \to 0} \left(1 + \frac{h}{x} \right)^{\frac{1}{h}} \right]$$

$$= \ln (e^{\frac{1}{x}}) \quad \longleftarrow \quad \textbf{By equation 5, Section 8-3}$$

$$= \frac{1}{x} \ln e \quad \longleftarrow \quad \textbf{By Theorem 8-8}$$

$$= \frac{1}{x}.$$

Thus the derived function of $f(x) = \ln x$ is $f'(x) = \frac{1}{x}$. This is a remarkably simple expression for $f'(x)$. Notice how naturally e arose in the derivation. This is one reason logarithms with base e are called *natural logarithms*.

These results are summarized by the following theorem.

Theorem 8–13   If $f(x) = \ln x$, then $f'(x) = \frac{1}{x}$.

You can now prove Theorem 8–2 (page 404).

$$\text{If } f(y) = e^y, \text{ then } f'(y) = e^y.$$

Proof: Let $y = \ln x$, then $y' = \frac{1}{x}$.

But $f(y) = e^y$ is the inverse of $y = \ln x$.

Thus
$$f'(y) = \frac{1}{y'} \quad \longleftarrow \quad \textbf{By Theorem 8-12}$$

$$= \frac{1}{\dfrac{1}{x}} \quad \longleftarrow \quad \textbf{By Theorem 8-13}$$

$$= x.$$

But $x = e^y$ since $y = \ln x$. Thus $f'(y) = e^y$, and the theorem is proved.

EXAMPLE 3. Find the derived function $f'(x)$ if $f(x) = \log_a x$.

Since you know that $g(x) = \ln x$ has a derived function $g'(x) = \frac{1}{x}$, it is desirable to change $f(x)$ to a natural logarithm. By equation **2** of Section 8–10,

$$f(x) = \log_a x = (\log_a e)(\ln x).$$

Thus, since $\log_a e$ is constant.

$$f'(x) = (\log_a e) \cdot \frac{1}{x}$$

$$= \frac{\log_a e}{x}$$

WRITTEN EXERCISES

A — Find the derived function for each function f. Evaluate at the given value of the variable.

1. $f(x) = e^x$; $x = \frac{1}{2}$

2. $f(x) = \ln x$; $x = 1$

3. $f(x) = \log_2 x$; $x = 4$

4. $f(x) = \log_{10} x$; $x = 2$

5. $f(x) = \log_{\frac{1}{2}} x$; $x = 2$

6. $f(x) = \log_{\frac{1}{e}} x$; $x = e$

7. $f(x) = \log_b x$; $x = \frac{1}{b}$

8. $f(x) = \log_{(e^2)} x$; $x = e^3$

9. $f(x) = e^x + \ln x$, $x > 0$; $x = 1$

10. $f(x) = \ln x + \ln x$; $x = 2$

B **11.** In Exercises 1–5, write the equation of the line tangent to the curve at the point with the given x coordinate.

12. Prove: $\log_{\frac{1}{b}} a = (-1)(\log_b a)$

13. Use Exercise 12 to prove:

$$\text{If } f(x) = \log_{\frac{1}{b}} x, \text{ then } f'(x) = \frac{-\log_b e}{x} .$$

14. Show that if $f(x) = \log_{\frac{1}{e}} x$, then $f'(x) = -\frac{1}{x} .$

C **15.** Use the definition of the derived function to prove:

$$\text{If } f(x) = \ln (ax), \text{ then } f'(x) = \frac{1}{x} .$$

16. Use the definition of the derived function to prove:

$$\text{If } f(x) = a \ln x, \text{ then } f'(x) = \frac{a}{x} .$$

17. Use the inverse relation between $f(x) = \log_a x$ and $g(y) = a^y$ and Theorem 8–12 to prove:

$$\text{If } g(y) = a^y, \text{ then } g'(y) = (\ln a)a^y.$$

Applying Logarithms
Industrial Engineering

Psychologists are often concerned with the **learning curve.** This is the graph that results when the time needed to complete a given task is plotted against the number of times the task is done. The more times a task is performed, the less time it takes to do it, up to a minimum value of time.

Industrial engineers have also noted that a group learning curve can describe the process involved in manufacturing an item. In this context, the curve is called a manufacturing progress curve. The figure on the right is the graph of a general learning curve.

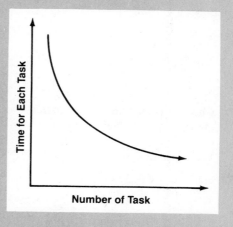

It has been demonstrated in the aircraft industry that the number of hours to complete aircraft number 2 was 80% of the time needed for aircraft number 1; number 4 was completed in 80% of the time needed for number 2; number 8 needed 80% of the time to complete number 4; in general, number 2^n took 80% of the time needed for number 2^{n-1}.

The table below shows this relationship.

Aircraft Number	Hours Used
1	32,000
2	$32,000 \cdot 0.8$
4	$32,000 \cdot 0.8^2$
8	$32,000 \cdot 0.8^3$
$\vdots$	$\vdots$
2^n	$32,000 \cdot 0.8^n$

A general equation can be derived as a model for this relationship.

$$x = 2^n \text{ and } y = 32{,}000(0.8)^n$$

$$\log_2 x = \log_2 2^n$$

$$= n$$

Thus $y = 32{,}000(0.8)^{\log_2 x}$

1

Taking the base 2 logarithm of both sides of **1** yields

$$\log_2 y = \log_2(32{,}000) + \log_2 x \cdot \log_2(0.8)$$
$$= \log_2(32{,}000) + \log_2 x^{\log_2(0.8)}$$
$$= \log_2(32{,}000 \cdot x^{\log_2(0.8)})$$

Thus $y = 32{,}000 \cdot x^{\log_2(0.8)}$.

Since $\log_2(0.8) = -0.322$

$$y = 32{,}000 \cdot x^{-0.322}. \qquad\qquad \textbf{2}$$

The general equation is

$$y = M \cdot x^{\log_2 r} \qquad\qquad \textbf{3}$$

where M is the number of manhours necessary to build the first item, r is the learning rate, x is the item number, and y is the number of hours for completion.

EXAMPLE. How many hours of labor were needed to build aircraft number 40?

Solution: $y = 32{,}000 \cdot x^{-0.322}$

$y = 32{,}000 \cdot 40^{-0.322}$ ◀——— **Use a calculator.**

$= 32{,}000(0.3049)$

$= 9757$ ◀——— **To the nearest hour**

The manufacturing progress curve discussed above is used by industry to forecast output, to set pricing, and to determine costs and borrowing needs when a new item is produced.

EXERCISES

In Exercises 1–6, determine the number of hours needed to build each aircraft.

1. Number 5

2. Number 100

3. Number 300

4. Number 500

5. Number 10,000

6. Number 100,000

7. Do you think the model $y = 32{,}000 \cdot x^{-0.322}$ is accurate for large numbers such as that in Exercise 6? Discuss.

8. In the petroleum industry $r = 0.9$. Write the equation for this industry.

9. Find the time needed to make the first 8 aircraft.

(Note: If $T_n = y_1 + y_2 + \cdots + y_n$, then T_n is approximated by $M \cdot \dfrac{n^{a+1}}{a+1}$, where $a = \log_2 r$. Calculate the time exactly, using **2** and using the approximation.)

CHAPTER SUMMARY

Important Terms

Common logarithms (p. 428)   Natural logarithms (p. 428)
Exponential function (p. 394)   One-to-one function (p. 418)
Inverse function (p. 416)   Principal nth root of a
Logarithmic function (p. 421)   number (p. 389)
Logarithms to the base a (p. 421) Strictly increasing function (p. 418)

Important Ideas

1. The exponential function $f(x) = a^x$, $a > 0$, is a continuous function on the real numbers.

2. The number e can be expressed as the sum of the following infinite series: $1 + \frac{1}{1!} + \frac{1}{2!} + \frac{1}{3!} + \cdots + \frac{1}{n!} + \cdots$, and equals approximately 2.7182818.

3. $e^x = 1 + \frac{x}{1!} + \frac{x^2}{2!} + \frac{x^3}{3!} + \cdots + \frac{x^n}{n!} + \cdots$

4. The derived function of e^x is e^x.

5. $y = \log_a x$ if and only if $x = a^y$

6. **General properties of logarithms:** See pages 422–424.

7. $\log_a b = \dfrac{1}{\log_b a}$

8. If $f(x) = \ln x$, then $f'(x) = \dfrac{1}{x}$

CHAPTER OBJECTIVES AND REVIEW

Objective: *To evaluate expressions involving rational exponents easily and accurately.* (Section 8-1)

■■■■ Simplify each expression. The set of positive real numbers is the replacement set for all variables.

1. $x^{\frac{3}{4}} \cdot x^{-\frac{2}{3}}$

2. $[a^{\frac{4}{5}} \cdot b^{\frac{2}{3}}]^{-\frac{1}{2}}$

3. $\left(\frac{y^{-2}}{x^3}\right)^{\frac{1}{6}} \cdot \left(\frac{x^3}{y^{-2}}\right)^{\frac{1}{3}}$

4. $200 \cdot (16^{-\frac{3}{4}})$

5. $[(-32)^{\frac{1}{5}}]^5$

6. $\left(\frac{9}{16}\right)^{-\frac{5}{2}}$

■■■■ Find x in each equation.

7. $4^x = 2^{\frac{6}{5}}$

8. $x^{\frac{2}{3}} = 4$

9. $16^x = 32^{\frac{2}{3}}$

10. $x^{\frac{3}{5}} = 8$

11. $8^x = 16^{\frac{1}{2}}$

12. $x^{\frac{3}{4}} = 125$

Objective: *To use the graph of f : x ⟶ 2ˣ to find values of 2ˣ and x.* (Section 8-2)

━━ Use the graph of 2^x on page 395 to find an approximate value of t for each of the following.

13. $2^{0.30} = t$ **14.** $2^{2.30} = t$

15. $2^t = 0.5$ **16.** $2^{-1} = t$

Objective: *To express the number e and the expression eˣ each as an infinite series.* (Section 8-3)

17. Use $e = 1 + \dfrac{1}{1!} + \dfrac{1}{2!} + \cdots + \dfrac{1}{n!} + \cdots$ to approximate e correct to four decimal places.

18. Use $e^x = 1 + \dfrac{x}{1!} + \dfrac{x^2}{2!} + \dfrac{x^3}{3!} + \cdots + \dfrac{x^n}{n!} + \cdots$ to approximate $e^{0.1}$ correct to four decimal places.

Objective: *To describe and sketch the graph of the exponential function.* (Section 8-4)

19. Describe the characteristics of the graph of $f : x \longrightarrow e^x$. Include domain, range, zeros, y intercepts, concavity, and asymptotes. Make a sketch.

Objective: *To use the graph of f : x ⟶ eˣ to find values of eˣ and x.* (Section 8-4)

━━ Use the graph of e^x on page 403 to find an approximate value of t for each of the following.

20. $e^{0.30} = t$ **21.** $e^{2.30} = t$

22. $e^t = 0.5$ **23.** $e^t = 2$

Objective: *To use exponential functions to solve problems involving compound interest, population growth, and radioactive decay.* (Sections 8-5 through 8-7)

24. Two thousand dollars is compounded continuously for ten years at an annual rate of five per cent. Find the amount of money A_t at the end of the ten years.

438 CHAPTER 8

■ The city of Adrian doubled its population in the ten years from 1970 to 1980. In 1970 there were 3000 residents.

25. How many people will reside in Adrian in 1995 if the population continues to grow at the same rate?

26. In what year will the population be 9000?

27. The half-life of a substance is 80 days. A sample of the substance has N_0 atoms. What fraction of the sample remains at the end of 20 days?

Objective: *To find the inverse of a function and to determine whether or not the inverse is a function.* (Section 8-8)

■ Find the inverse of each function. Then indicate whether the inverse is also a function.

28. $f : x \longrightarrow 2x - 1$ **29.** $f : x \longrightarrow 2 - x^2$

Objective: *To describe the graph of the logarithmic function.* (Section 8-9)

30. Describe the characteristics of the graph of $f : x \longrightarrow \log_e x$ (i.e. $x \longrightarrow \ln x$). Describe domain, range, zeros, y intercepts, concavity, and asymptotes.

Objective: *To use the relationship between logarithms and exponents.* (Section 8-9 and Section 8-10)

■ Write each statement in logarithmic form.

31. $27 = 3^3$ **32.** $125^{-\frac{1}{3}} = \frac{1}{5}$

33. $8^{\frac{2}{3}} = 4$ **34.** $5^0 = 1$

35. $\log_{10} 2 = 0.3010$ and $\log_{10} 3 = 0.4771$. Find the value of $\log_{10} 18$.

Objective: *To find the derived function of e^x and $\ln x$.* (Section 8-11)

■ Find the derived function and its value at $x = 3$.

36. $f(x) = e^x$ **37.** $f(x) = \ln x$

CHAPTER TEST

1. Calculate $(4^{\frac{5}{2}})^{-1}$
2. Simplify $(x^{\frac{4}{3}}) \cdot (x^{-\frac{2}{5}}) \cdot (x^{\frac{2}{3}})^{-2}$
3. Find x : $(\frac{2}{3})^{\frac{x}{3}} = \frac{4}{9}$
4. Approximate $2^{0.45}$ using the graph on page 395.
5. Approximate x if $2^x = 2.35$. Use the graph on page 395.
6. What is the base of the natural logarithms?
7. Write $8^{\frac{2}{3}} = 4$ in logarithmic form.
8. Write $\log_2 \frac{1}{4} = -2$ in exponential form.
9. Express $\log_5 10$ as a logarithm with base ten.
10. Express $\log_{10} 5$ as a natural logarithm.
11. Find the amount of money A_t if \$100 is compounded continuously at a rate of 3 per cent for 20 years.
12. How are sequences and limits used to define a^r for real exponents?
13. Explain why the logarithmic function is the inverse of the exponential function with the same base. Sketch the graphs of each on the same set of coordinate axes.
14. If $f(x) = \ln x$ and $g(x) = e^x$ what are
    a. $f'(x)$ and
    b. $g'(x)$?
15. What happens to the slope of a line tangent to $y = \ln x$ as $x \longrightarrow +\infty$? as $x \longrightarrow 0$?

Choose the best answer. Choose **a**, **b**, **c**, or **d**.

1. For $\left\{1 - \frac{(-1)^n}{n}\right\}$, which statement is true?

  a. There is no open interval with radius 0.001 that contains all but a finite number of the terms.

  b. $\left\langle \frac{1}{2}, \frac{3}{2} \right\rangle$ contains all but 5 terms of $\left\{1 - \frac{(-1)^n}{n}\right\}$.

  c. All intervals centered at 1 contain all but a finite number of the terms.

  d. All intervals centered at 0 contain all but a finite number of the terms.

2. For $\frac{1}{3n}$ to be as close to zero as $\frac{1}{1000}$, n must be greater than

  a. 200   **b.** 300   **c.** 330   **d.** 400

3. Find the limit of $\left\{\frac{\sqrt{2n+1}}{n}\right\}$ as n increases without bound.

  a. 0   **b.** $\sqrt{2}$ **c.** $\sqrt{3}$ **d.** undefined

4. Suppose $a_n > 0$ for all n and $a_n < 5$ for all n, and $a_n \le a_{n+1}$ for all n, then which statement is true?

  a. $\{a_n\} \to 5$.   **b.** $\{a_n\}$ has a limit.

  c. $\{a_n\}$ has no limit.   **d.** Nothing can be determined.

5. For $\sum\limits_{n=1}^{\infty} ar^n$, which statement is true?

  a. It always has a finite sum.   **b.** It has a sum of $r < 1$.

  c. It has a sum when $|r| < 1$.   **d.** It never has a sum.

6. $\{a_n\} = \left\{\frac{3n-1}{n}\right\}$, $\{b_n\} = \left\{\frac{n+1}{n}\right\}$. Which statement is true?

  a. $\{a_n \cdot b_n\} \to 3$ **b.** $\{a_n + b_n\} \to 3$

  c. $\{a_n - b_n\} \to 0$ **d.** $\left\{\frac{a_n}{b_n}\right\} \to 2$

7. What value of δ will ensure that $f(x) \in \langle 3 - \epsilon, \ 3 + \epsilon \rangle$ when $f(x) = 3x - 3$, $\epsilon = \frac{1}{2}$ and $x = 2$ whenever $x \in \langle 2 - \delta, 2 + \delta \rangle$?

  a. $\frac{1}{2}$ **b.** $\frac{1}{3}$ **c.** $\frac{1}{5}$ **d.** $\frac{1}{6}$

8. Find $\lim\limits_{x \to -2} (x)(x-1)(x+3)$.

  a. 6   **b.** 0   **c.** -30 **d.** does not exist

9. Find the slope of the function $f(x) = 3x^2 + 2x - 1$ at $x = 3$.

  a. 20   **b.** 11   **c.** 24   **d.** not defined

10. Which function has a removable discontinuity at $x = -2$?

    a. $f(x) = \frac{x-2}{x+2}$ **b.** $f(x) = \frac{2(x+2)}{x-2}$

    c. $f(x) = \frac{x^2-4}{x+2}$ **d.** $f(x) = \frac{x-2}{x^2-4}$

11. Find the depressed polynomial when $x^4 + 2x^3 - 8x - 16$ is divided by $x - 2$.

    a. $x^3 + 4x^2 + 8x + 8$ **b.** $x^2 + 4x$

    c. $x^2 - 8$ **d.** $x^3 - 8$

12. If a polynomial, $P(x)$, of degree N is divided evenly by $x - a$, then which statement is true?

    a. $P(a) = 0$ **b.** $P(x) = Q(x) \cdot (x - a)$

    c. The degree at $Q(x)$ is $N - 1$.   **d.** All are true.

13. Every polynomial of degree $n > 0$ has which of the following?

    a. one real zero   **b.** one complex zero

    c. n distinct zeros   **d.** n zeros

14. If $a + bi$ is a zero of $f(x) = 2x^3 - 3x^2 + 5x - 2$, which is true?

    a. $f(x)$ has two real zeros.   **b.** All the zeros are complex.

    c. $f(x)$ has one real zero.   **d.** $-a + bi$ is also a zero.

15. For the function $f(x) = 2x^3 - 15x^2 + 36x - 48$, which statement is true?

    a. There is a point of inflection at $x = 2.5$.

    b. There is a relative maximum at $x = 3$.

    c. There is a relative minimum at $x = 2$.

    d. **a, b,** and **c** are true.

16. Identify the false statement.

    a. $[(-9)^2]^{\frac{1}{3}} = [(-9)^{\frac{1}{3}}]^2$ **b.** $[(-2)^3]^{\frac{1}{3}} = [(-2)^{\frac{1}{3}}]^3$

    c. $[(-9)^{\frac{1}{2}}]^2 = [(-9)^2]^{\frac{1}{2}}$ **d.** $[(-16)^{-2}]^{\frac{1}{3}} = [(-16)^{\frac{1}{3}}]^{-2}$

17. The number e is

    a. larger than π **b.** equal to 2.71828

    c. irrational   **d.** $\approx 4(1 - \frac{1}{3} + \frac{1}{5} - \frac{1}{7} + \cdots)$

18. Which statement is true for logarithmic functions?

    a. $\log_a xy = \log_a x + \log_a y$ **b.** $\log_a x^y = y \log_a x$

    c. $\log_a b = \frac{1}{\log_b a}$ **d.** **a, b,** and **c** are true.

19. Find the slope of the line tangent to $y = e^x$ at $x = 4$.

    a. 4   **b.** $\frac{1}{4}$ **c.** e^4 **d.** $\frac{1}{e^2}$

CHAPTER 9 Vectors, Lines, and Planes

Sections

Features

Applying Optimal Paths: Business Administration

Computer Application: The Angle Between Two Vectors

Review and Testing

Mid-Chapter Review

Chapter Summary

Chapter Objectives and Review

Chapter Test

9–1 Vectors and Operations

Analytic geometry is a wedding of algebra and geometry. In analytic geometry the geometric concepts such as lines, planes, circles, angles, etc., are examined from an algebraic point of view. For example, the equation

$$y - 2x + 4 = 0, \quad x \in \mathbf{R}$$

is an algebraic model of a line, since each point $A(x, y)$ whose coordinates satisfy $y - 2x + 4 = 0$ is on a line, and each point on that line has coordinates which satisfy $y - 2x + 4 = 0$.

Central to the study of analytic geometry is the derivation of algebraic expressions which describe geometric ideas. In this regard, **vectors** play an important role.

Definition A **vector** is a directed line segment.

A vector is usually denoted by a letter with an arrow over it such as $\vec{A}$ or $\vec{r}$. Since a vector is a segment, it has a *length* or *magnitude*. The length of a vector v is symbolized as $|\vec{v}|$. The length of a vector is often called the *absolute value* of the vector. Thus, $|\vec{v}|$ is the *absolute value*, the *length*, or the *magnitude* of $\vec{v}$.

A vector has two endpoints. The direction of the vector is specified by naming the endpoints in *order*. The first named point is the *initial point* or *foot* of the vector; the second named point is the *terminal point* or *tip* of the vector. Thus a vector from A to B can be represented as $\overrightarrow{AB}$; A is the foot, B is the tip.

Vectors are generally represented geometrically by *arrows*. The end with the arrow head is the tip of the vector. Three vectors are illustrated below.

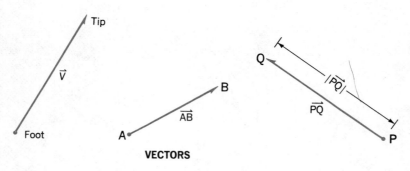

VECTORS

> **Definition** Two vectors, say $\overrightarrow{PQ}$ and $\overrightarrow{RS}$, are said to be **equal** if
> **a.** *PQSR* is a parallelogram or
> **b.** $\overrightarrow{PQ}$ and $\overrightarrow{RS}$ are collinear and have the same direction and length.

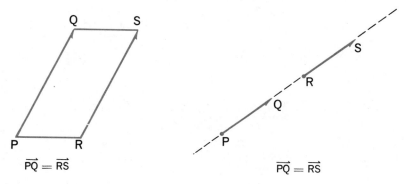

$\overrightarrow{PQ} = \overrightarrow{RS}$ $\overrightarrow{PQ} = \overrightarrow{RS}$

In the definition of equal vectors it is important to notice that the order of the vertices of the parallelogram is important. It is the parallelogram formed by joining in order foot to tip, to tip, to foot, to foot of the given vectors. If a parallelogram is not obtained in this way, the vectors are *not equal.*

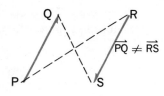

$\overrightarrow{PQ} \neq \overrightarrow{RS}$

Using the definition of equal vectors, you can move a vector to any position in space you may wish. The following example illustrates how this may be done.

EXAMPLE. Find the vector equal to $\vec{v}$ that has its foot at *C*. See the figure at the right.

Let *D* be the tip of the vector with foot *C* and equal to $\vec{v}$. Then *D* is the fourth vertex of parallelogram *ABDC*. The required vector is $\overrightarrow{CD}$ as shown in the figure at the right in red. If *C* were on the line containing $\overleftrightarrow{AB}$, how would you proceed to find the vector equal to $\vec{v}$ with foot at *C*?

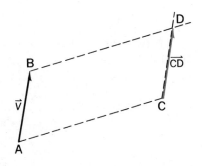

Two or more vectors may be added by the **polygon rule:** from the tip of the first vector, the second vector is drawn; from the tip of the second, the third is drawn, and so on. The sum of the vectors is the vector with the same foot as the first vector and the same tip as the last vector. The diagram below illustrates how to add four vectors by the polygon rule.

$$\vec{v} = \vec{v}_1 + \vec{v}_2 + \vec{v}_3 + \vec{v}_4$$

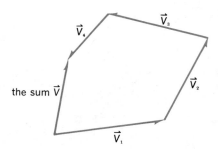

Definition   Two vectors $\vec{v}_1$ and $\vec{v}_2$ are **parallel** whenever the lines containing them are parallel or are the same line.

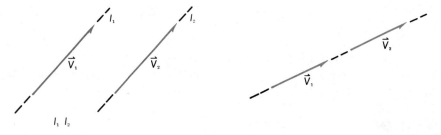

If two nonparallel vectors $\vec{v}_1$ and $\vec{v}_2$ are added, the sum $\vec{v}$ is the third side of a triangle:

$$\vec{v} = \vec{v}_1 + \vec{v}_2.$$

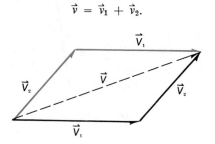

If a vector is added to itself, the result is a vector in the same direction and twice as long:

$$\vec{v} + \vec{v} = 2\vec{v}.$$

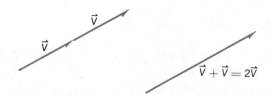

In general if k is any real number, $k \cdot \vec{v}$ is a vector $|\,k\,|$ times as long as $\vec{v}$. If $k > 0$, then $k \cdot \vec{v}$ and $\vec{v}$ have the same direction. If $k < 0$, then $k \cdot \vec{v}$ and $\vec{v}$ have opposite directions. If $k = 0$, then $k \cdot \vec{v}$ is the **zero vector,** denoted $\vec{0}$. No direction is given to the zero vector. These ideas are illustrated in the diagram below.

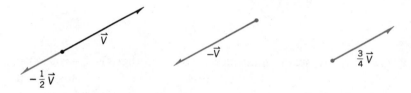

In $k \cdot \vec{v}$ the real number k is called a **scalar.** Thus, $k \cdot \vec{v}$ is a *scalar multiple* of $\vec{v}$. If one vector is a scalar multiple of another, the two vectors are parallel. Conversely if $\vec{v}_1 \parallel \vec{v}_2$, then

$$m \cdot \vec{v}_1 = n \cdot \vec{v}_2,$$

for some $m, n \neq 0$ as pictured below. That is, two vectors are parallel if and only if one is equal to a nonzero scalar multiple of the other.

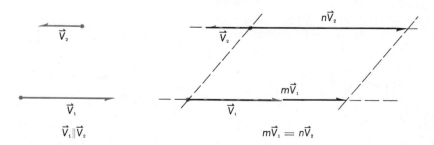

Subtraction of vectors is defined in terms of addition. $\vec{v}_1 - \vec{v}_2$ is the vector which when added to $\vec{v}_2$ gives $\vec{v}_1$.

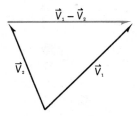

$\vec{v}_1 - \vec{v}_2$, then, is the vector from the tip of $\vec{v}_2$ to the tip of $\vec{v}_1$. $\vec{v}_1 - \vec{v}_2$ can also be obtained by adding $-\vec{v}_2$ to $\vec{v}_1$. That is, $\vec{v}_1 - \vec{v}_2 = \vec{v}_1 + (-\vec{v}_2)$. This is easily seen by referring to the following diagram.

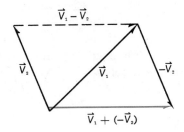

Since $\vec{v}_2$ and $-\vec{v}_2$ are scalar multiples of one another, $\vec{v}_2 \parallel -\vec{v}_2$. Also $|\vec{v}_2| = |-\vec{v}_2|$. Since, from plane geometry, you know a quadrilateral is a parallelogram if two sides are parallel and equal, the figure is a parallelogram and

$$\vec{v}_1 - \vec{v}_2 = \vec{v}_1 + (-\vec{v}_2).$$

Suppose you are given $\vec{A}$ and $\vec{B}$ as below.

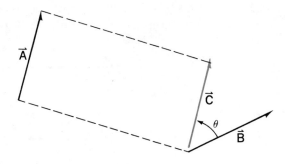

By the definition of equality $\vec{A} = \vec{C}$. Thus the angle determined by $\vec{A}$ and $\vec{B}$ is the angle determined by $\vec{C}$ and $\vec{B}$. Its measure is θ, where $0° \leq \theta \leq 180°$.

WRITTEN EXERCISES

A ━━━ In Exercises 1–2 use the procedure illustrated in the discussion to find the vector equal to $\vec{A}$ with foot at C.

1.

2.

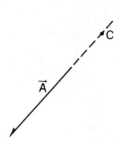

━━━ In Exercises 3–4, find the measure of the angle between the vectors $\vec{A}$ and $\vec{B}$ by first moving each to C and then measuring with a protractor.

3.

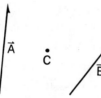

4.

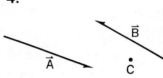

━━━ In Exercises 5–9, copy the diagram and find the following.

$$\vec{V} = \vec{A} + \vec{B} \quad \text{and} \quad \vec{T} = \vec{A} - \vec{B}$$

5.

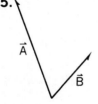

6.

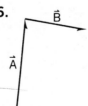

7.

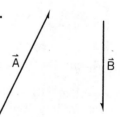

8.

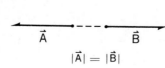

$$|\vec{A}| = |\vec{B}|$$

9.

$$\vec{A} = \vec{B}$$

━━ Draw a vector and call it $\vec{A}$. Draw $m\vec{A}$ when m is as follows.

10. 3   **11.** $\frac{5}{3}$ **12.** $\frac{1}{3}$ **13.** -2

14. $-\frac{2}{3}$ **15.** $-\frac{7}{2}$ **16.** 0   **17.** $\frac{1}{4}$

18. Let $\vec{A} \parallel \vec{B}$, $|\vec{A}| = 3$, $|\vec{B}| = 2$, and $m\vec{A} = n\vec{B}$. Find m or n as indicated for each of the following.

    a. m if $n = 3$.

    b. n if $m = \frac{2}{3}$.

    c. n if $m = -\frac{2}{3}$ and $\vec{A}$ and $\vec{B}$ have the same direction.

    d. n if $m = -\frac{2}{3}$ and $\vec{A}$ and $\vec{B}$ are opposite in direction.

    e. m if $n = \frac{3}{4}$ and $\vec{A}$ and $\vec{B}$ are opposite in direction.

    f. n if $m = \frac{7}{2}$ and $\vec{A}$ and $\vec{B}$ are in the same direction.

    g. n if $m = -\frac{7}{2}$ and $\vec{A}$ and $\vec{B}$ are in the same direction.

    h. n if $m = -\frac{7}{2}$ and $\vec{A}$ and $\vec{B}$ are opposite in direction.

    i. m if $n = \frac{8}{3}$ and $\vec{A}$ and $\vec{B}$ are opposite in direction.

    j. m if $n = -\frac{8}{3}$ and $\vec{A}$ and $\vec{B}$ are in the same direction.

    k. m if $n = 1$ and $\vec{A}$ and $\vec{B}$ are in the same direction.

    l. m if $n = 1$ and $\vec{A}$ and $\vec{B}$ are opposite in direction.

    m. n if $m = -1$ and $\vec{A}$ and $\vec{B}$ are in the same direction.

    n. n if $m = -1$ and $\vec{A}$ and $\vec{B}$ are opposite in direction.

    o. m if $n = k$ and $\vec{A}$ and $\vec{B}$ are in the same direction.

    p. m if $n = k$ and $\vec{A}$ and $\vec{B}$ are opposite in direction.

━━ Draw a diagram showing each of the following.

19. $\vec{A} + (-\vec{A}) = \vec{0}$.

20. $\vec{0} + \vec{B} = \vec{B} + \vec{0} = \vec{B}$.

21. $\vec{A} + (\vec{B} + \vec{C}) = (\vec{A} + \vec{B}) + \vec{C}$ (Associative property).

22. $m(n\vec{A}) = (m \cdot n)\vec{A}$; m, n are scalars.

23. $(m + n)\vec{A} = m\vec{A} + n\vec{A}$, m, n are scalars.

24. $m(\vec{A} + \vec{B}) = m\vec{A} + m\vec{B}$, m a scalar.

B   **25.** Prove that $m(n\vec{A}) = (m \cdot n)\vec{A}$. (*Hint:* You must show that both vectors have the same direction and the same length.)

    26. Prove that the length of $(m + n)\vec{A}$ is the same as the length of $m\vec{A} + n\vec{A}$ by showing that

        a. $|m + n|\,|\vec{A}| = |m|\,|\vec{A}| + |n|\,|\vec{A}|$ when m and n are of the same sign and

        b. $|m + n|\,|\vec{A}| = |(|m| - |n|)|\,|\vec{A}|$ when m and n are of opposite signs.

27. Prove $m(\vec{A} + \vec{B}) = m\vec{A} + m\vec{B}$, $m > 0$ by showing that

    a. $m\vec{A} + m\vec{B}$ is in the same direction as $\vec{A} + \vec{B}$ and therefore of $m(\vec{A} + \vec{B})$, and

    b. $|m\vec{A} + m\vec{B}|$ is m times as long as $|\vec{A} + \vec{B}|$.

    (*Hint:* Draw a figure and show that the triangles formed by $\vec{A}$, $\vec{B}$ and $\vec{A} + \vec{B}$ and by $m\vec{A}$, $m\vec{B}$ and $m\vec{A} + m\vec{B}$ are similar.)

28. Given two nonparallel vectors $\vec{A}$ and $\vec{B}$ and that θ is the measure of the angle determined by $\vec{A}$ and $\vec{B}$,

    a. Express $|\vec{A} - \vec{B}|$ in terms of $|\vec{A}|$, $|\vec{B}|$, and θ. (*Hint:* Use the Law of Cosines.)

    b. Express $|\vec{A} + \vec{B}|$ in terms of $|\vec{A}|$, $|\vec{B}|$, and θ. (*Hint:* Use the Law of Cosines.)

9–2 Basis Vectors

The properties of vectors studied so far are valid whether the vectors all lie in space or are restricted to a single plane in space. Now it is advantageous to discuss vectors lying in a single plane separately from those lying in space.

Consider two nonparallel vectors $\vec{A}$ and $\vec{B}$ lying in the same plane. The vector sum $2\vec{A} + 5\vec{B}$ is a vector in the same plane as shown in Figure 2. In fact for any scalars m and n, $m\vec{A} + n\vec{B}$ is a vector in the same plane.

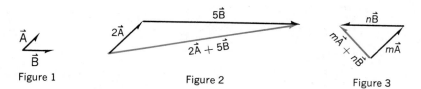

Figure 1   Figure 2   Figure 3

Suppose you have two nonparallel vectors, say $\vec{A}$, $\vec{B}$, in a plane and a vector, call it $\vec{C}$, in the same plane. Are there scalars m and n such that $\vec{C} = m\vec{A} + n\vec{B}$? This leads to a definition and Theorem 9–1.

Definition   Given scalars m and n and vectors $\vec{A}$ and $\vec{B}$, the vector $\vec{C} = m\vec{A} + n\vec{B}$ is a **linear combination** of $\vec{A}$ and $\vec{B}$.

Theorem 9–1 Any given vector $\vec{C}$ can be written as a unique linear combination of two given nonparallel, nonzero vectors $\vec{A}$ and $\vec{B}$ in the same plane. Thus $\vec{C} = m\vec{A} + n\vec{B}$, where m and n are unique scalars.

Proof: Let $\vec{A}$, $\vec{B}$, and $\vec{C}$ have the same foot O. Let P be the tip of $\vec{C}$. Construct the line through P parallel to $\vec{B}$. It intersects the line of $\vec{A}$ in Q. Let $\overrightarrow{OQ} = m\vec{A}$. Since $\overrightarrow{QP}$ is parallel to $\vec{B}$, $\overrightarrow{QP}$ is a scalar multiple of $\vec{B}$. That is $\overrightarrow{QP} = n\vec{B}$. By the construction and the definition of vector addition

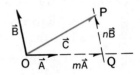

$$\vec{C} = m\vec{A} + n\vec{B}.$$

To show uniqueness, suppose

$$\vec{C} = m_1\vec{A} + n_1\vec{B} = m_2\vec{A} + n_2\vec{B}.$$

Then $(m_1 - m_2)\vec{A} = (n_2 - n_1)\vec{B}$. In this case either ① $\vec{A}$ is parallel to $\vec{B}$ because one is a nonzero scalar multiple of the other ② $\vec{A} = \vec{B} = \vec{0}$ or ③ $m_1 - m_2 = n_2 - n_1 = 0$. In either ① or ② a contradiction is reached because $\vec{A}$ and $\vec{B}$ were two nonparallel nonzero vectors. Thus $m_1 = m_2$ and $n_2 = n_1$ and it follows that $m_1\vec{A} + n_1\vec{B} = m_2\vec{A} + n_2\vec{B} = m\vec{A} + n\vec{B}$.

EXAMPLE. Find m and n such that $\vec{C} = m\vec{A} + n\vec{B}$ where $\vec{A}$, $\vec{B}$, and $\vec{C}$ are given as in the figure below.

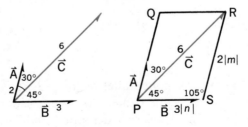

Solution: Complete the parallelogram with $\vec{C}$ as diagonal.

$$\overrightarrow{SR} = m\vec{A}, \quad \overrightarrow{PS} = n\vec{B}$$
$$|\overrightarrow{SR}| = |m||\vec{A}| = |m|2$$
$$|\overrightarrow{PS}| = |n||\vec{B}| = |n|3$$

By the Law of Sines you can find the values of m and n.

i. $\dfrac{6}{\sin 105°} = \dfrac{2|\,m\,|}{\sin 45°}$ ii. $\dfrac{6}{\sin 105°} = \dfrac{3|\,n\,|}{\sin 30°}$

From the table $\sin 105° = \sin 75° = 0.9659$; $\sin 45° = \dfrac{\sqrt{2}}{2}$; $\sin 30° = \frac{1}{2}$.
Thus:

i. $\dfrac{6}{0.9659} = \dfrac{2|\,m\,|}{\dfrac{\sqrt{2}}{2}}$ or $2|\,m\,| = \dfrac{3\sqrt{2}}{0.9659}$ and $|\,m\,| = \dfrac{3\sqrt{2}}{1.9318}$

ii. $\dfrac{6}{0.9659} = \dfrac{3|\,n\,|}{\frac{1}{2}}$ or $3|\,n\,| = \dfrac{3}{0.9659}$ and $|\,n\,| = \dfrac{1}{0.9659}$

From the figure it is clear that $m > 0$, $n > 0$,

so $\qquad\qquad\qquad \vec{C} = \dfrac{3\sqrt{2}}{1.9318}\,\vec{A} + \dfrac{1}{0.9659}\,\vec{B}.$

For vectors in space there is a theorem similar to Theorem 9–1.

Theorem 9–2 In three dimensional space let $\vec{A}$, $\vec{B}$, and $\vec{C}$ be any three nonzero vectors not all three parallel to the same plane, with no two of them parallel to each other. Then any given vector $\vec{D}$ is a unique linear combination of $\vec{A}$, $\vec{B}$, and $\vec{C}$. Thus $\vec{D} = l\vec{A} + m\vec{B} + n\vec{C}$, where l, m, and n are unique scalars.

The proof is similar to that of Theorem 9–1. An outline follows.

Outline of Proof:

The three vectors have the same foot O. Let the line through P, the tip of $\vec{D}$, parallel to $\vec{C}$ intersect the plane of $\vec{A}$ and $\vec{B}$ in Q. Then $\overrightarrow{OQ} = l\vec{A} + m\vec{B}$. (Why?), $\overrightarrow{QP} = n\vec{C}$ and $\vec{D} = \overrightarrow{OQ} + \overrightarrow{QP} = l\vec{A} + m\vec{B} + n\vec{C}$.

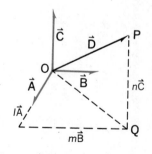

The vectors $\vec{A}$, $\vec{B}$ of Theorem 9–1 and $\vec{A}$, $\vec{B}$ and $\vec{C}$ of Theorem 9–2 form a **base** or **basis** for all the vectors in the plane or space. From the theorems it is clear that there are two basis vectors for a plane (2-dimensional space), and three for space (3-dimensional space). The scalars l, m, and n are the **components** of the vector $\vec{D} = l\vec{A} + m\vec{B} + n\vec{C}$. A similar statement is true for $\vec{C} = m\vec{A} + n\vec{B}$ in a plane.

CLASSROOM EXERCISES

1. Give a geometric interpretation of the concept of basis vectors in a plane.

2. Give a geometric interpretation of the concept of basis vectors in space.

3. State in your own words what is meant by a linear combination of vectors.

4. What are the components of a vector?

WRITTEN EXERCISES

A ▬ Use a ruler to approximate the values of the scalars m and n when

$$\vec{C} = m\vec{A} + n\vec{B}.$$

1.

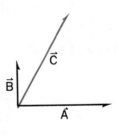

2.

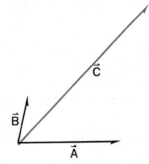

3.

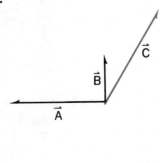

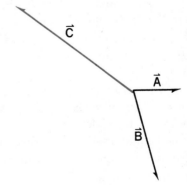

In Exercises 5–12 use the basis vectors $\vec{A}$, $\vec{B}$, and $\vec{C}$ as given in Figure 1 to draw each vector $\vec{D}$. The three vectors are perpendicular to each other. Trace the basis vectors on your paper first.

5. $\vec{D} = \vec{A} + \vec{B} + \vec{C}$

6. $\vec{D} = 2\vec{A} + \vec{B} + \frac{1}{2}\vec{C}$

7. $\vec{D} = \vec{A} + 2\vec{B} - 2\vec{C}$

8. $\vec{D} = -2\vec{A} - \frac{1}{2}\vec{B} + 3\vec{C}$

9. $\vec{D}$ has components $(-\frac{1}{2}, 3, -1)$

10. $\vec{D}$ has components $(-1, -1, -1)$

11. $\vec{D}$ has components $(0, 1, 0)$

12. $\vec{D}$ has components $(2, 0, -3)$

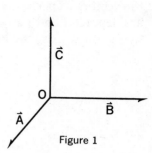

Figure 1

B **13.** Find $\vec{C}$ as a linear combination of $\vec{A}$ and $\vec{B}$ when

$$|\vec{A}| = 2, \quad |\vec{B}| = 2, \quad |\vec{C}| = 1$$

and the angles are as indicated in Figure 2. ($\vec{A}$, $\vec{B}$, and $\vec{C}$ are in the same plane.)

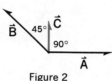

Figure 2

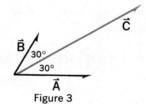

Figure 3

14. Repeat Exercise 13 when

$$|\vec{A}| = 3, \quad |\vec{B}| = 2, \quad |\vec{C}| = 6$$

and angles are as shown in Figure 3.

15. Repeat Exercise 13 when

$$|\vec{A}| = 2, \quad |\vec{B}| = 3, \quad |\vec{C}| = 4,$$

and angles are as shown in the figure below.

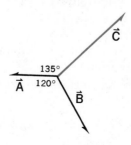

9-3 Perpendicular Basis

In **two-space** (a plane) it is advantageous to choose the basis for the vectors as perpendicular vectors each of unit length. These vectors are denoted **i** and **j** and their common foot by O. The line determined by **i** is the x axis; the line determined by **j** is the y axis.

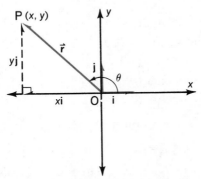

Any vector $\vec{r}$ in the plane with foot at O can be expressed as a linear combination of the basis vectors **i** and **j**.

$$\vec{r} = x\mathbf{i} + y\mathbf{j}$$

The components of $\vec{r} = x\mathbf{i} + y\mathbf{j}$ are the coordinates of the tip P of $\vec{r}$.

$$P = (x, y)$$

The vector $\vec{r} = \overrightarrow{OP}$ is a **position vector** because its foot is at the origin and its components are the coordinates of its tip P. A position vector $\vec{r}$ may be designated by the rectangular coordinates of its tip. That is, the coordinates (x, y) of a point P may be thought of as the position vector $\overrightarrow{OP}$:

$$\overrightarrow{OP} = (x, y)$$

Notice that you now have two systems of notation for position vectors.

1. Unit basis vector notation: $x\mathbf{i} + y\mathbf{j}$
2. Ordered pair notation: (x, y)

The first (unit basis) notation will be used more often here than the second (ordered pair) notation.

The angle from **i** to $\vec{r}$ has measure θ. θ ranges in value from $0°$ to $360°$ (2π radians).

$$\theta = \arctan \frac{y}{x} \qquad 0 \leq \arctan \frac{y}{x} \leq 360° \ (2\pi)$$

Moreover, using your knowledge of polar coordinates (see page 207) and letting $|\vec{r}| = r$, you can see that the following is true.

$$x = r \cos \theta$$
$$y = r \sin \theta$$
$$|\vec{r}| = r = \sqrt{x^2 + y^2}$$

EXAMPLE 1. Let the position vector $\vec{r} = -2\mathbf{i} + 2\mathbf{j}$.
        a. Find $|\vec{r}| = r$.   **b.** Find θ.

Solutions: **a.** $\vec{r} = -2\mathbf{i} + 2\mathbf{j}$.   ⟵ $|\vec{r}| = \sqrt{x^2 + y^2}$

Thus

$$r = \sqrt{(-2)^2 + (2)^2}$$
$$= \sqrt{8}$$
$$= 2\sqrt{2}$$

Since the x component of $\vec{r}$ is negative and the y component is positive,

$$\textbf{b. } \theta = \arctan \frac{2}{-2} \quad \longleftarrow \quad x = -2, y = 2$$

$\theta = 135°$ since $\tan 135° = \dfrac{2}{-2}$ and $(-2, 2)$ is in Quadrant II.

Consider now three-dimensional space. Choosing a set of mutually perpendicular vectors of unit length one for the basis is advantageous here also. The basis vectors are denoted as $\mathbf{i}$, $\mathbf{j}$, and $\mathbf{k}$. Their common foot is O.

The position vector

$$\vec{r} = x\mathbf{i} + y\mathbf{j} + z\mathbf{k}$$

has for its components the rectangular coordinates of the point at its tip:

$$P = (x, y, z).$$

(See Figure 1 on page 458.)

As in the two dimensional case, the ordered triple of coordinates of the tip of the position vector $\vec{r} = \overrightarrow{OP}$ is identified with the following vector.

$$\overrightarrow{OP} = (x, y, z)$$

The length of a position vector $\vec{r}$ is given by

$$|\vec{r}| = r = \sqrt{x^2 + y^2 + z^2}. \quad \longleftarrow \quad \textbf{See Figure 2, page 458.}$$

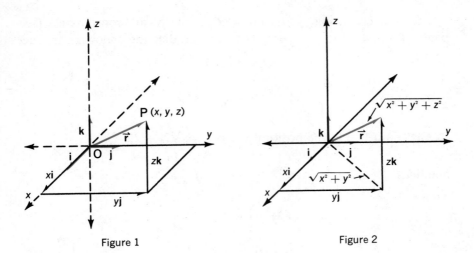

Figure 1   Figure 2

EXAMPLE 2. Show that any vector $\overrightarrow{PQ}$ in space can be expressed as a linear combination of **i**, **j**, and **k**. That is, any vector $\overrightarrow{PQ}$ can be expressed as follows.

$$\overrightarrow{PQ} = l\mathbf{i} + m\mathbf{j} + n\mathbf{k}$$

Solution:

Choose a point O for origin and let $P = (x_1, y_1, z_1)$ and $Q = (x_2, y_2, z_2)$. Then $\overrightarrow{OP}$ and $\overrightarrow{OQ}$ are position vectors.

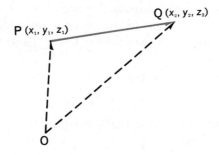

Furthermore,

$$\begin{aligned}
\overrightarrow{PQ} &= \overrightarrow{OQ} - \overrightarrow{OP} \\
&= (x_2\mathbf{i} + y_2\mathbf{j} + z_2\mathbf{k}) - (x_1\mathbf{i} + y_1\mathbf{j} + z_1\mathbf{k}) \\
&= (x_2 - x_1)\mathbf{i} + (y_2 - y_1)\mathbf{j} + (z_2 - z_1)\mathbf{k}
\end{aligned}$$

Let

$$(x_2 - x_1) = l, \quad (y_2 - y_1) = m, \quad \text{and} \quad (z_2 - z_1) = n.$$

Thus

$$\overrightarrow{PQ} = l\mathbf{i} + m\mathbf{j} + n\mathbf{k}.$$

The same result is valid in two-space. (See Exercise 14.)

The result of Example 2 can be carried further. The length of $\overrightarrow{PQ}$ is

$$|\overrightarrow{PQ}| = \sqrt{l^2 + m^2 + n^2}.$$

But

$$l = (x_2 - x_1), \quad m = (y_2 - y_1), \quad \text{and} \quad n = (z_2 - z_1).$$

Thus

$$|\overrightarrow{PQ}| = \sqrt{(x_2 - x_1)^2 + (y_2 - y_1)^2 + (z_2 - z_1)^2}$$

where

$$P = (x_1, y_1, z_1) \quad \text{and} \quad Q = (x_2, y_2, z_2).$$

This can be stated as follows.

> **The length of a vector is the square root of the sum of the squares of the differences of the coordinates of the tip and foot of a vector.**

Any vector, by Example 2, may be expressed as $\vec{A} = l\mathbf{i} + m\mathbf{j} + n\mathbf{k}$. The components l, m, and n are called **direction numbers** of $\vec{A}$. When each is divided by $|\vec{A}| = \sqrt{l^2 + m^2 + n^2}$ the ratios are **direction cosines** of $\vec{A}$.

In particular

$$\cos \alpha = \frac{l}{|\vec{A}|}$$

$$\cos \beta = \frac{m}{|\vec{A}|}$$

$$\cos \gamma = \frac{n}{|\vec{A}|}$$

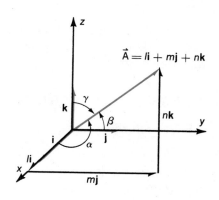

where α, β, and γ are the measures of the angles $\vec{A}$ makes with $\mathbf{i}$, $\mathbf{j}$, and $\mathbf{k}$ respectively. (See the figure at the right.) α, β, and γ are called **direction angles**.

> **Theorem 9–3** If $\alpha, \beta,$ and γ are direction angles then
> $$\cos^2 \alpha + \cos^2 \beta + \cos^2 \gamma = 1.$$

Proof: By definition

$$\cos \alpha = \frac{l}{|\vec{A}|}, \quad \cos \beta = \frac{m}{|\vec{A}|}, \quad \text{and} \quad \cos \gamma = \frac{n}{|\vec{A}|}.$$

Therefore,

$$\cos^2 \alpha + \cos^2 \beta + \cos^2 \gamma = \frac{l^2 + m^2 + n^2}{|\vec{A}|^2}$$

$$= \frac{l^2 + m^2 + n^2}{l^2 + m^2 + n^2}$$

$$= 1.$$

EXAMPLE 3.   Suppose $\vec{A}$ has direction angles of $\alpha = 45°$ and $\beta = 45°$. What is γ? Draw the vector.

By Theorem 9–3, $\cos^2 \alpha + \cos^2 \beta + \cos^2 \gamma = 1$. Consequently, since $\cos \alpha = \cos 45 = \frac{\sqrt{2}}{2} = \cos \beta$,

$$\left(\frac{\sqrt{2}}{2}\right)^2 + \left(\frac{\sqrt{2}}{2}\right)^2 + \cos^2 \gamma = 1$$

$$\cos^2 \gamma = 0$$

Thus $\gamma = 90°$. The diagram is at the right. $\vec{A}$ is in the xy plane.

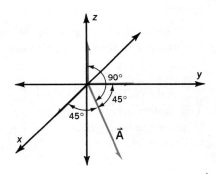

Since its length was unspecified it may have any nonzero length. When only the direction of a vector is required, the vector is called a **direction vector.**

CLASSROOM EXERCISES

1. A vector has $\cos \alpha = \cos \beta = \frac{-1}{\sqrt{2}}$. Find γ.

2. What are the direction cosines of
  a. the x axis?
  b. the y axis?
  c. the z axis?

3. Suppose that the direction numbers of a line are l, m, and n. What are the direction cosines?

4. Explain the geometric difference between direction numbers, direction cosines and direction angles.

WRITTEN EXERCISES

A ▬▬ Given the position vector $\vec{r}$, find its length and the measure θ of the angle it makes with **i**. (Express θ to nearest 10′.)

1. $\vec{r} = 2\mathbf{i} + 3\mathbf{j}$

2. $\vec{r} = -2\mathbf{i} + 3\mathbf{j}$

3. $\vec{r} = -2\mathbf{i} - 3\mathbf{j}$

4. $\vec{r} = 2\mathbf{i} - 3\mathbf{j}$

5. $\vec{r} = 2\mathbf{i} - \sqrt{3}\mathbf{j}$

6. $\vec{r} = 1\mathbf{i} - 1\mathbf{j}$

7. $\overrightarrow{OP} = (-\sqrt{3}, 1)$

8. $\vec{r} = (-1, 0)$

9. $\vec{r} = (-1, 0)$

10. $\overrightarrow{OP} = (1, -1)$

11. $\overrightarrow{OP} = (0, -5)$

12. $\vec{r} = (3, 4)$

13. Sketch each vector in Exercises 1–6.

14. Let $P = (x_1, y_1)$, $Q = (x_2, y_2)$. Prove: If $\overrightarrow{PQ}$ is any vector in two-space then

$$\overrightarrow{PQ} = m\mathbf{i} + n\mathbf{j}.$$

15. Prove: If $P = (x_1, y_1)$ and $Q = (x_2, y_2)$ then

$$|\overrightarrow{PQ}| = \sqrt{(x_2 - x_1)^2 + (y_2 - y_1)^2} \qquad \text{(See Exercise 14).}$$

▬▬ In Exercises 16–23 find $|\overrightarrow{PQ}|$.

16. $P = (1, 5)$, $Q = (-3, 2)$

17. $P = (-1, 1)$, $Q = (4, 13)$

18. $P = (a, b)$, $Q = (a - 1, b - 3)$

19. $P = (x, y)$, $Q = (x + 2, y + 2)$

20. $P = (1, 1, 1)$, $Q = (2, -1, 3)$

21. $P = (0, 1, 2)$, $Q = (-\sqrt{10}, -4, 1)$

22. $P = (x, y, z)$, $Q = (x + 1, y - 1, z + \sqrt{2})$

23. $P = (a, 2a, -a)$, $Q = (4a, 6a, 4a)$

24. What are the direction cosines of the vector from $(2, -1, 4)$ to $(-1, 3, -8)$?

B **25.** A vector has direction angles $\alpha = 30°$, $\beta = 60°$. Find the third angle γ. Make a sketch of the vector.

26. Repeat Exercise 25 when $\alpha = 45°$ and $\beta = 120°$. How many answers are there?

27. A *unit vector* is a vector with length 1. What is the unit vector in the same direction as

$$\vec{A} = 12\mathbf{i} - 4\mathbf{j} + 3\mathbf{k}?$$

28. What is the unit vector in the same direction as $\vec{A}$, if

$$\vec{A} = l\mathbf{i} + m\mathbf{j} + n\mathbf{k}?$$

Applying Optimal Paths
Business Administration

One of the important functions of those in **business administration** is to minimize costs related to the transportation of goods or services from one place to another. **Optimal path analysis,** which deals with the problem of finding the best (least costly) path from one place to another, addresses this situation. We shall use a **grid** as the mathematical model.

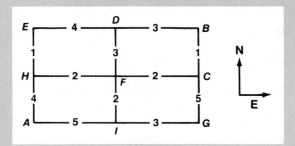

The numbers in the grid state the cost from point to point. Thus, to go north from I to F costs 2 units and to go east from E to D costs 4 units.

The Problem

Find an optimal path from corner A to corner B in the grid above.

Conditions

1. You must always go north or east at any junction (no doubling back).

2. The optimal path is the one for which the sum of the side numbers is a minimum.

Solution to the Problem

To solve the problem, you work backwards from B. Suppose you were at C. What is the optimal path to B? North to B. What is the cost of this path? It is 1. This is shown on the diagram with an arrow and a 1.

Similarly at D the arrow points east and has a 3. Now suppose you were at F with two choices. If you go north, the cost to B is $3 + 3$, or 6. Going east, the cost is $2 + 1$, or 3. Thus, 3 indicates the choice to make.

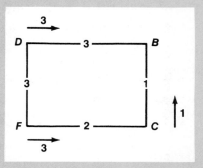

The expanded diagram at the right shows an east arrow and 7 at E, a north arrow and 6 at G. If you were at H, what path is optimal? North to B costs 8, while east to B costs 5. Thus, an east arrow and 5 go at H. Similarly, a north arrow and 5 go at I.

Finally, you are at A with two paths to choose from. North to H costs 9 to B, while east to I costs 10. A north arrow and a 9 go at A. The optimal path follows the arrows from A to B.

$$A \rightarrow H \rightarrow F \rightarrow C \rightarrow B.$$

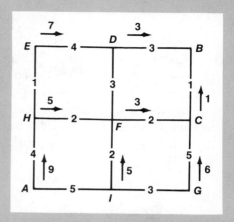

EXERCISES

In Exercises 1–3, find the optimal path and its cost from A to B.

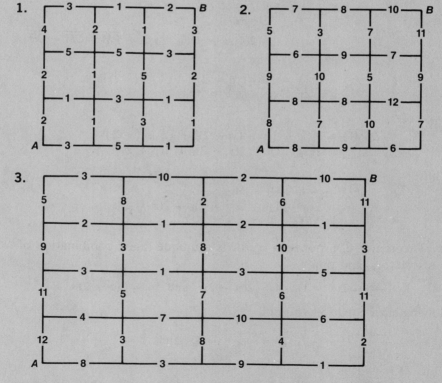

4. For the grid in Exercise 1, devise a procedure to find the **maximum** cost path from A to B going only north or east, and find this path.

9–4 Dividing a Segment

Consider a segment $\overrightarrow{PQ}$ in space. Let $P = (1, 2, -2)$ and $Q = (-3, 6, 4)$. What are the coordinates of the midpoint of $\overrightarrow{PQ}$?

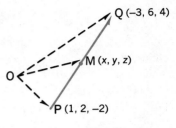

Vector methods may be used to answer this question. Let O be the origin and consider $\overrightarrow{OP}$, $\overrightarrow{OQ}$, and $\overrightarrow{PQ}$.

By the definition of subtraction,

$$\overrightarrow{PQ} = \overrightarrow{OQ} - \overrightarrow{OP} \qquad \mathbf{1}$$

Let $M(x, y, z)$ be the midpoint of $\overrightarrow{PQ}$. $\overrightarrow{PM}$ has the same direction as $\overrightarrow{PQ}$, $2\overrightarrow{PM} = \overrightarrow{PQ}$, and $\overrightarrow{PM} = \overrightarrow{OM} - \overrightarrow{OP}$.

Thus

$$\begin{aligned}
\overrightarrow{PQ} &= \overrightarrow{OQ} - \overrightarrow{OP} \\
&= 2\overrightarrow{PM} \\
&= 2(\overrightarrow{OM} - \overrightarrow{OP}). \qquad \longleftarrow \quad \overrightarrow{PM} = \overrightarrow{OM} - \overrightarrow{OP}
\end{aligned}$$

But

$$\begin{aligned}
\overrightarrow{PQ} &= (-3 - 1)\mathbf{i} + (6 - 2)\mathbf{j} + (4 - (-2))\mathbf{k} \\
&= -4\mathbf{i} + 4\mathbf{j} + 6\mathbf{k}
\end{aligned}$$

and

$$\begin{aligned}
2(\overrightarrow{PM}) &= 2[(x - 1)\mathbf{i} + (y - 2)\mathbf{j} + (z - (-2))\mathbf{k}] \\
&= 2(x - 1)\mathbf{i} + 2(y - 2)\mathbf{j} + 2(z + 2)\mathbf{k}.
\end{aligned}$$

Thus

$$\begin{aligned}
\overrightarrow{PQ} &= -4\mathbf{i} + 4\mathbf{j} + 6\mathbf{k} \\
&= 2(x - 1)\mathbf{i} + 2(y - 2)\mathbf{j} + 2(z + 2)\mathbf{k} \\
&= 2\overrightarrow{PM}.
\end{aligned}$$

By Theorem 9–2, a nonzero vector is a unique linear combination of basis vectors, and thus

$$-4 = 2(x - 1), \quad 4 = 2(y - 2), \quad \text{and} \quad 6 = 2(z + 2).$$

Solving each equation you find

$$x = \frac{-4 + 2}{2} = -1, \quad y = \frac{4 + 4}{2} = 4, \quad \text{and} \quad z = \frac{6 - 4}{2} = 1.$$

Thus $M = (-1, 4, 1)$.

The procedure used above can be applied in the general case to get a formula for the coordinates of the midpoint.

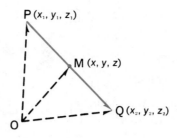

Let $P = (x_1, y_1, z_1)$ and $Q = (x_2, y_2, z_2)$. Let $M = (x, y, z)$ be the midpoint of $\overrightarrow{PQ}$. See the figure above.

$$\overrightarrow{PQ} = (x_2 - x_1)\mathbf{i} + (y_2 - y_1)\mathbf{j} + (z_2 - z_1)\mathbf{k}$$
$$\overrightarrow{PM} = (x - x_1)\mathbf{i} + (y - y_1)\mathbf{j} + (z - z_1)\mathbf{k}$$

and

$$\overrightarrow{PQ} = 2\overrightarrow{PM}.$$

It follows that

$$(x_2 - x_1)\mathbf{i} + (y_2 - y_1)\mathbf{j} + (z_2 - z_1)\mathbf{k}$$
$$= 2(x - x_1)\mathbf{i} + 2(y - y_1)\mathbf{j} + 2(z - z_1)\mathbf{k}.$$

By Theorem 9–2,

$$x_2 - x_1 = 2(x - x_1),\ y_2 - y_1 = 2(y - y_1),\ (z_2 - z_1) = 2(z - z_1).$$

Solving for x, y, and z you find the following.

$$x = \frac{x_2 + x_1}{2}, \quad y = \frac{y_2 + y_1}{2}, \quad z = \frac{z_2 + z_1}{2}$$

The midpoint M of $\overrightarrow{PQ}$ is

$$\left(\frac{\text{sum of } x\text{'s}}{2}, \frac{\text{sum of } y\text{'s}}{2}, \frac{\text{sum of } z\text{'s}}{2}\right).$$

The following theorem summarizes the above discussion and gives a general formula for finding the midpoint.

Theorem 9–4 If $P = (x_1, y_1, z_1)$ and $Q = (x_2, y_2, z_2)$ then the midpoint of $\overrightarrow{PQ}$ is

$$M = \left(\frac{x_1 + x_2}{2}, \frac{y_1 + y_2}{2}, \frac{z_1 + z_2}{2}\right)$$

See if you can modify this theorem so it is valid for a segment in the xy plane.

Similar methods can be used to find the point of a segment which divides it into any fractional part.

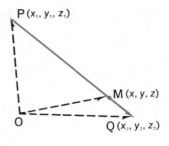

EXAMPLE. Given points $P(x_1, y_1, z_1)$ and $Q(x_2, y_2, z_2)$, find the point M which is $\frac{4}{5}$ the way from P to Q. Stating this in terms of vectors, find the vector $\overrightarrow{PM}$ which is $\frac{4}{5}\overrightarrow{PQ}$, or $4\overrightarrow{PQ} = 5\overrightarrow{PM}$.

Solution:

Writing $\overrightarrow{PQ}$ and $\overrightarrow{PM}$ in terms of the basis vector $\mathbf{i}$, $\mathbf{j}$, and $\mathbf{k}$, you find

$$4(x_2 - x_1)\mathbf{i} + 4(y_2 - y_1)\mathbf{j} + 4(z_2 - z_1)\mathbf{k}$$
$$= 5(x - x_1)\mathbf{i} + 5(y - y_1)\mathbf{j} + 5(z - z_1)\mathbf{k}$$

and since the components are equal,

$$4(x_2 - x_1) = 5(x - x_1), \; 4(y_2 - y_1) = 5(y - y_1), \; 4(z_2 - z_1) = 5(z - z_1).$$

Solving for x, y, and z, you find

$$x = \frac{4x_2 + x_1}{5}, \quad y = \frac{4y_2 + y_1}{5}, \quad z = \frac{4z_2 + z_1}{5}.$$

The point $M = \left(\frac{4x_2 + x_1}{5}, \frac{4y_2 + y_1}{5}, \frac{4z_2 + z_1}{5}\right)$ is the point $\frac{4}{5}$ of the way from P to Q. It is also the point which divides $\overrightarrow{PQ}$ in the ratio 4 to 1.

$$\frac{|\overrightarrow{PM}|}{|\overrightarrow{MQ}|} = \frac{4}{1}$$

CLASSROOM EXERCISES

1. What is the z component of any vector in the xy plane?

2. What are the coordinates of the midpoint of a vector in the xy plane if its endpoints are (x_1, y_1) and (x_2, y_2)?

▬▬ Find the midpoint of $\overrightarrow{PQ}$ with endpoints as follows.

3. $P(2, -1, 1)$, $Q(-4, 0, 3)$

4. $P(3, 1)$, $Q(-5, 5)$

5. $P(1, 2, 3)$, $Q(-6, -5, -4)$

6. $P(x_1, y_1, z_1)$, $Q(x_2, y_2, z_2)$

7. $P(a, b)$, $Q(c, 0)$

8. $P(3, 2, -4)$, $Q(9, 0, 6)$

WRITTEN EXERCISES

A **1.** State the result for Exercise 2 of *Classroom Exercises* as a theorem and prove it.

▬ Find the midpoint of $\overrightarrow{PQ}$ with endpoints as follows.

2. $P(2, -3), Q(4, 1)$ **3.** $P(1, 2, 3), Q(3, 2, 1)$

4. $P(-5, -3), Q(-2, -1)$ **5.** $P(1, 0, -5), Q(2, 1, 5)$

6. $P(-2, 1), Q(4, 5)$ **7.** $P(-2, -4, -3), Q(1, -3, 2)$

8. $P(4, 2), Q(-1, -3)$ **9.** $P(a, b, c), Q(a+1, b+2, c+3)$

10. $P(a, b), Q(3-a, 5-b)$ **11.** $P(a, b, c), Q(-a, -b, -c)$

12. If M is the midpoint of $\overrightarrow{PQ}$, show that $|\overrightarrow{PM}| = |\overrightarrow{QM}|$ for
     a. $\overrightarrow{PQ}$ in the xy plane
     b. $\overrightarrow{PQ}$ in space

13. In the derivation of the coordinates of the midpoint M of $\overrightarrow{PQ}$ in Theorem 9–4, does it make any difference if you consider $\overrightarrow{QP}$ rather than $\overrightarrow{PQ}$? Explain.

B ▬ In Exercises 14–20, M is a point between P and Q where $P(4, 5, 8)$ and $Q(2, -3, 4)$. Find M for each exercise.

14. M is $\frac{2}{3}$ the way from P to Q.

15. M is $\frac{2}{3}$ the way from Q to P.

16. M is $\frac{3}{4}$ the way from P to Q.

17. $\dfrac{|\overrightarrow{PM}|}{|\overrightarrow{MQ}|} = \dfrac{5}{1}$ **18.** $\dfrac{|\overrightarrow{QM}|}{|\overrightarrow{MP}|} = \dfrac{3}{2}$

19. $\dfrac{|\overrightarrow{PM}|}{|\overrightarrow{PQ}|} = \dfrac{1}{6}$ **20.** $\dfrac{|\overrightarrow{QM}|}{|\overrightarrow{QP}|} = \dfrac{2}{5}$

C ▬ A point M is said to *divide* $\overrightarrow{PQ}$ *externally* in the ratio $\frac{a}{b}$ if M is not between P and Q and $\dfrac{|\overrightarrow{PM}|}{|\overrightarrow{QM}|} = \dfrac{a}{b}$.

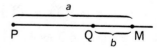

▬ If $P = (4, 5, 8)$ and $Q = (2, -3, 4)$, find M such that M divides $\overrightarrow{PQ}$ externally in the ratio as indicated in Exercises 21–24.

21. $\frac{4}{3}$ **22.** $\frac{7}{4}$ **23.** $\frac{1}{3}$ **24.** $\frac{2}{5}$

25. Given $P(x_1, y_1, z_1)$ and $Q(x_2, y_2, z_2)$. Let M be the point between P and Q which is $\frac{p}{q}$ $(0 < \frac{p}{q} < 1)$ of the way from P to Q. Find the coordinates of the point M.

9–5   Lines

Two points P and Q in space determine a unique line. Those same two points taken in a prescribed order also determine a unique vector: $\overrightarrow{PQ}$. If R is any other point on the line through P and Q, $\overrightarrow{QR}$ is a scalar multiple of $\overrightarrow{PQ}$.

$$\overrightarrow{QR} = t \cdot \overrightarrow{PQ}$$

This is true because the vectors $\overrightarrow{QR}$ and $\overrightarrow{PQ}$ are collinear. These facts are used to derive several different equations of a line.

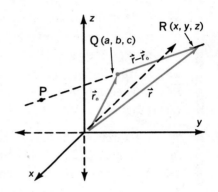

Suppose, as in the figure at the right, P and Q are two fixed points on the line. By Example 2 Section 9–3, $\overrightarrow{PQ}$ is a unique linear combination of $\mathbf{i}$, $\mathbf{j}$, and $\mathbf{k}$:

$$\overrightarrow{PQ} = l\mathbf{i} + m\mathbf{j} + n\mathbf{k} \qquad \mathbf{1}$$

Let $R(x, y, z)$ be any point on the line. (You may think of R as a variable point if you wish.) Then $\overrightarrow{QR} = \vec{r} - \vec{r}_0$ is a scalar multiple of $\overrightarrow{PQ}$:

Thus

$$\overrightarrow{QR} = \vec{r} - \vec{r}_0 = t \cdot \overrightarrow{PQ}, \; t \text{ a scalar} \qquad \mathbf{2}$$

But

$$\vec{r} - \vec{r}_0 = (x - a)\mathbf{i} + (y - b)\mathbf{j} + (z - c)\mathbf{k} \qquad \mathbf{3}$$

Substituting 1 and 3 in 2 you find

$$\vec{r} - \vec{r}_0 = (x - a)\mathbf{i} + (y - b)\mathbf{j} + (z - c)\mathbf{k} = t(l\mathbf{i} + m\mathbf{j} + n\mathbf{k}) \qquad \mathbf{4}$$

By the uniqueness of the linear combination of $\mathbf{i}$, $\mathbf{j}$, and $\mathbf{k}$, you find

$$x - a = t \cdot l, \; y - b = t \cdot m, \text{ and } z - c = t \cdot n. \qquad \mathbf{5}$$

Thus

$$\frac{x - a}{l} = t, \quad \frac{y - b}{m} = t, \quad \text{and} \quad \frac{z - c}{n} = t, \quad l, m, n \neq 0$$

and

$$\frac{x - a}{l} = \frac{y - b}{m} = \frac{z - c}{n} \quad l, m, n \neq 0. \qquad \mathbf{6}$$

The equations in 6 are the **standard equations** of a line.

Solving for x, y, and z in **5**, gives the **parametric equations** of a line:

$$x = a + t \cdot l$$
$$y = b + t \cdot m \qquad\qquad 7$$
$$z = c + t \cdot n$$

Notice that in the parametric equations of line the first column contains the coordinates of the variable point on the line; the second column, the coordinates (a, b, c) of a fixed point; and the third column, the products of the scalar t (a parameter) and the direction numbers of the fixed vector. These direction numbers are also called **the direction numbers of the line.**

Given the parametric equations of a line, a point $R(x, y, z)$ on the line can be found by assigning a specific real number to t and evaluating each equation. (a, b, c, l, m, n are assumed to be known.) Not all of l, m, and n can be zero because $\overrightarrow{PQ}$ was assumed to be a nonzero vector.

Equation **2** can be written in the shorthand form

$$\vec{r} = \vec{r}_0 + t\overrightarrow{PQ} \qquad\qquad 8$$

where $\vec{r}$ is the position vector of the variable point, $\vec{r}_0$ is the position vector of the fixed point, and $\overrightarrow{PQ}$ is the fixed vector. Equation **8** is the vector equation of a line.

EXAMPLE 1. A line has parametric equations

$$x = 2 + t \cdot 5, \quad y = -1 + t \cdot (-1), \quad z = 0 + t \cdot 3.$$

a. Find the point on the line corresponding to $t = -2$.

b. What are the direction numbers of this line?

c. Write the standard equations of the line.

Solutions:

a. Substituting $t = -2$ in the parametric equations, you find
$$x = -8, y = 1, z = -6.$$
The point is $(-8, 1, -6)$.

b. The direction numbers of the line and the fixed vector are identical: l, m, and n. In this case they are 5, -1, and 3.

c. Solve each equation for t:

$$t = \frac{x-2}{5}, \; t = \frac{y+1}{-1}, \; t = \frac{z}{3}$$

The standard equations are thus $\frac{x-2}{5} = \frac{y+1}{-1} = \frac{z}{3}$.

EXAMPLE 2. Find the parametric equations of the line through $P(1, 2, 3)$ and $Q(-2, 3, -4)$.

Solution: Let the fixed vector be $\overrightarrow{PQ}$.

$$\begin{aligned} \overrightarrow{PQ} &= (-2 - 1)\mathbf{i} + (3 - 2)\mathbf{j} + (-4 - 3)\mathbf{k} \\ &= -3\mathbf{i} + 1\mathbf{j} - 7\mathbf{k} \end{aligned}$$

Let the fixed point be $P(1, 2, 3)$, and let the variable point be $R(x, y, z)$. The position vector to R is

$$\vec{r} = x\mathbf{i} + y\mathbf{j} + z\mathbf{k}$$

while the position vector to P is

$$\vec{r}_0 = 1\mathbf{i} + 2\mathbf{j} + 3\mathbf{k}.$$

By equation 8

$$\begin{aligned} x\mathbf{i} + y\mathbf{j} + z\mathbf{k} &= 1\mathbf{i} + 2\mathbf{j} + 3\mathbf{k} + t(-3\mathbf{i} + 1\mathbf{j} - 7\mathbf{k}) \\ &= (1 - 3t)\mathbf{i} + (2 + 1t)\mathbf{j} + (3 - 7t)\mathbf{k}. \end{aligned}$$

Thus by uniqueness, the parametric equations are

$$\begin{aligned} x &= 1 - 3t \\ y &= 2 + t \\ z &= 3 - 7t. \end{aligned}$$

Find the parametric equations if $Q(-2, 3, -4)$ is chosen to be the fixed point.

Since $\vec{r}_2 = -2\mathbf{i} + 3\mathbf{j} - 4\mathbf{k}$, the parametric equations are

$$\begin{aligned} x &= -2 - 3t \\ y &= 3 + 1t \\ z &= -4 - 7t \end{aligned}$$

The equations 6, 7, and 8, can be modified to include lines in the xy plane (that is in two-space). Notice that the direction number, n, equals 0. This is true because the angle from any line in the xy plane to the z axis is $90°$ ($\cos 90° = 0$). Furthermore the fixed point has co-ordinates $(a, b, 0)$ because every point in the xy plane has a z coordinate equal to 0.

Thus the standard equations of a line in the xy plane are

$$\frac{x - a}{l} = \frac{y - b}{m}, \quad z = 0, \quad l, m \neq 0. \qquad 9$$

The parametric equations of the same line are

$$\begin{aligned} x &= a + t \cdot l \\ y &= b + t \cdot m \qquad\qquad 10 \\ z &= 0. \end{aligned}$$

The vector equation is identical to equation 8 when it is understood that $\vec{r}$, $\vec{r}_0$, and $\overrightarrow{PQ}$ are vectors in one plane. (See the figure.)

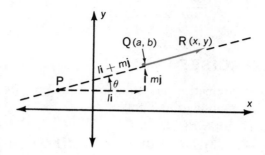

EXAMPLE 3. Find parametric, standard, and vector equations of the line containing $P(1, 4)$ and $Q(2, 7)$.

The fixed vector is $\overrightarrow{PQ} = 1\mathbf{i} + 3\mathbf{j}$. Let $Q(2, 7)$ be the fixed point and $R(x, y)$ be the variable point.

$$\vec{r} = x\mathbf{i} + y\mathbf{j}, \quad \vec{r}_0 = 2\mathbf{i} + 7\mathbf{j}$$

The vector equation is

$$\vec{r} = \vec{r}_0 + t\overrightarrow{PQ}$$

or
$$\begin{aligned} x\mathbf{i} + y\mathbf{j} &= 2\mathbf{i} + 7\mathbf{j} + t(1\mathbf{i} + 3\mathbf{j}) \\ &= (2 + t)\mathbf{i} + (7 + 3t)\mathbf{j}. \end{aligned}$$

By uniqueness of the linear combination of $\mathbf{i}$ and $\mathbf{j}$

$$\begin{aligned} x &= 2 + t \\ y &= 7 + 3t \\ z &= 0 \end{aligned}$$

are the parametric equations. The standard equations are

$$\frac{x - 2}{1} = \frac{y - 7}{3}, \quad z = 0.$$

CLASSROOM EXERCISES

━━ Find the parametric equation of $\overrightarrow{AB}$ if A and B are as follows.

1. $A(1, 2, -3)$, $B(-1, -4, 7)$ **2.** $A(x_1, y_1, z_1)$, $B(x_2, y_2, z_2)$
3. $A(2, -1, 4)$, $B(-3, 1, 5)$ **4.** $A(2, 1, 0)$, $B(5, 3, 0)$
5. $A(0, 2, 5)$, $B(1, 3, 4)$ **6.** $A(3, -2, 1)$, $B(1, 4, 3)$

━━ Find the direction numbers of each line.

7. $x = 2 - 3t$, $y = 5 + 7t$, $z = 8 - t$

8. $\dfrac{x+1}{-2} = \dfrac{y+4}{-6} = \dfrac{z-7}{10}$

9. $\dfrac{1-x}{2} = \dfrac{2-y}{6} = \dfrac{z+3}{10}$

WRITTEN EXERCISES

A ▬ Find the parametric and standard equations (when possible) of each line containing the points A and B.

1. $A(-2, 1, 3)$ $B(1, 0, -3)$ **2.** $A(1, 2, 3)$ $B(5, 5, 5)$

3. $A(-1, -2, -3)$ $B(0, 0, 0)$ **4.** $A(1, 5, -3)$ $B(2, -1, -2)$

5. $A(1, 2, 5)$ $B(2, 1, 5)$ **6.** $A(1, 3, 5)$ $B(2, 3, 5)$

7. $A(1, 2, 0)$ $B(3, 3, 0)$ **8.** $A(1, 2)$ $B(3, 3)$

9. $A(2, -3)$ $B(-4, 5)$ **10.** $A(-2, 1)$ $B(2, 1)$

11. $A(5, -3)$ $B(5, -2)$ **12.** $A(-2, -5)$ $B(5, -2)$

▬ Use the figure at the right for Exercises 13–15.   Let $\overrightarrow{OB} = l\mathbf{i} + m\mathbf{j} + n\mathbf{k}$.

13. If $\overrightarrow{OB}$ is in the xy plane, then $n = \underline{\ ?\ }$

14. If $\overrightarrow{OB}$ is in the yz plane, then $l = \underline{\ ?\ }$

15. If $\overrightarrow{OB}$ is in the xz plane, then $m = \underline{\ ?\ }$

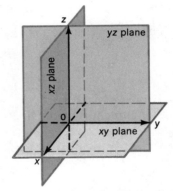

16. What are the standard equations of a line in the xz plane?

17. What are the parametric equations of a line in the yz plane?

18. What are the parametric equations of a line in the

   a. plane parallel to the xy plane and 5 units above it?

   b. plane parallel to xz plane and 3 units to the left?

   c. plane parallel to yz plane and $\frac{1}{2}$ unit in front of it?

B   **19.** Find the parametric equations of the line with standard equations $2x - 1 = 4y + 8 = 3z - 5$.

20. What are the direction numbers of the line in Exercise 19?

21. Let $A = (1, -2, 3)$ and $B = (2, 1, 5)$.   Find the parametric equations of the line through A and B.

   a. when $\overrightarrow{AB}$ is the fixed vector and B is the fixed point.

   b. when $\overrightarrow{AB}$ is the fixed vector and A is the fixed point.

   c. when $\overrightarrow{BA}$ is the fixed vector and A is the fixed point.

22. Below are given two sets of parametric equations of lines.

$$\begin{array}{lll} x = 2 + t & x = 1 - s \\ y = 3 + t & \text{and} \quad y = 2 - s \quad & t \text{ and } s \text{ parameters.} \\ z = 1 - 2t & z = 3 + 2s \end{array}$$

a. What are the direction numbers of the lines?
b. What is the fixed vector for each line?
c. How are the direction vectors related?
d. Are the equations equations of the same line? Explain.

23. How many sets of parametric equations of a line are there? Explain.

C **24.** Find the equation of the line containing the midpoint of $\overline{AB}$ and C when $A = (2, 5)$, $B = (3, 1)$, and $C = (-2, 3)$.

25. Find the parametric equations of the medians of the triangle with vertices $(a, 0)$, $(0, b)$, $(0, c)$.

26. Find the points on each median in Exercise 25 which is $\frac{2}{3}$ the distance from the vertex to the midpoint of the opposite side. What do you notice about these points?

9–6 Lines in two-space

The standard equations of a line in the xy plane are

$$\frac{x - a}{l} = \frac{y - b}{m}, \quad z = 0, \quad l, m \neq 0.$$

It is customary to omit the second equation; $z = 0$.
    A direction vector of this line is

$$\vec{A} = l\mathbf{i} + m\mathbf{j}.$$

The slope of the vector $\vec{A}$ is defined to be

$$slope\ \vec{A} = \frac{m}{l} \quad l \neq 0. \qquad \mathbf{1}$$

In words, the slope of a vector $\vec{A} = l\mathbf{i} + m\mathbf{j}$ is the length of the vertical vector $|m\mathbf{j}|$ divided by the length of the horizontal vector $|l\mathbf{i}|$ (recall $|\mathbf{i}| = |\mathbf{j}| = 1$) or the **j**-component divided by the **i**-component of the vector.

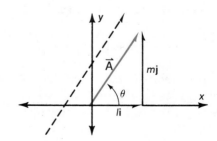

The **slope of a line in two-space** is defined to be the slope of any of its direction vectors. The slope of a line is a unique number because any two direction vectors are parallel and thus have proportional components. That is, if $\vec{A}$ and $\vec{B}$ are direction vectors for the same line,

$$\vec{A} = t\vec{B} \text{ where } t \text{ is a scalar.}$$

Then if slope $\vec{B} = \dfrac{m}{l}$,

$$\text{slope } \vec{A} = \frac{tm}{tl} = \frac{m}{l} = \text{slope } \vec{B}.$$

If a direction vector $\vec{A}$ of a line makes an angle of measure θ with the positive x axis,

$$\frac{m}{l} = \tan \theta, \quad l \neq 0.$$

Thus

$$\text{slope } \vec{A} = \tan \theta = \frac{m}{l} = \lambda. \quad (\lambda \text{ is the Greek letter } \textit{lambda}.) \qquad 2$$

If $\vec{A} = l\mathbf{i} + m\mathbf{j}$ is a direction vector for a line, then $\vec{A} = l(\mathbf{i} + \lambda\mathbf{j})$ and $\mathbf{i} + \lambda\mathbf{j}$ is a direction vector for the same line. The standard equations of the line containing (x, y) and fixed point (a, b) are

$$\frac{x - a}{1} = \frac{y - b}{\lambda}$$

or

$$y - b = \lambda(x - a). \qquad 3$$

Clearly every point on the line through (a, b) and of slope λ satisfies equation 3. Conversely, any point (x, y) different from (a, b), that satisfies equation 3 must lie on the line; for

$$y - b = \lambda \, (x - a) \quad \text{implies} \quad \frac{y - b}{x - a} = \lambda.$$

Thus the vector from (a, b) to (x, y),

$$(x - a)\mathbf{i} + (y - b)\mathbf{j} = (x - a)\left[\mathbf{i} + \frac{y - b}{x - a}\mathbf{j}\right] = (x - a)[\mathbf{i} + \lambda\mathbf{j}],$$

is a nonzero scalar multiple of the direction vector $\mathbf{i} + \lambda\mathbf{j}$. Therefore, (x, y) is on the line.

Finally (a, b) satisfies equation 3, and any point satisfying 3 lies on the line. Equation 3 is the **point-slope equation of a line**.

EXAMPLE 1. Let a line have a direction vector $3\mathbf{i} + 2\mathbf{j}$ and contain the point $(5, 2)$. Find the equation of the line.

Solution: Since $3\mathbf{i} + 2\mathbf{j}$ is a direction vector, then the slope of the line is $\frac{2}{3}$ and, by the point slope equation, the line has equation $(y - 2) = \frac{2}{3}(x - 5)$.

The parametric equations of a line in two-space through (a, b) are

$$x = a + tl$$
$$y = b + tm$$

If $l = 0$, then a direction vector of the line is $\vec{A} = 0\mathbf{i} + m\mathbf{j} = m\mathbf{j}$. Thus the line is parallel to the y axis. It has parametric equations

$$x = a$$
$$y = b + tm$$

Since y takes on all real values and x is always a, only the first equation is used to denote the line. In other words

$$x = a, \qquad\qquad\qquad 4$$

is the equation of a line parallel to the y axis. Similarly, when $m = 0$,

$$y = b \qquad\qquad\qquad 5$$

is the equation of a line parallel to the x axis.

The equations **3**, **4**, and **5** are first degree equations. The derivations of these equations prove the following theorem.

Theorem 9–5 Any line in the xy plane is described by an equation of the first degree.

The converse of Theorem 9–5 which follows is also true.

Theorem 9–6 Any equation of the first degree in x and y describes a line in the xy plane.

Proof: Let such an equation be $Ax + By + C = 0$, where A, B, and C are constants with A and B not both zero. The strategy is to find a line which has this equation.

Case 1

Let $B \neq 0$. Consider the line containing $\left(0, \frac{-C}{B}\right)$ with slope $\frac{-A}{B}$. By the *point slope* equation, this line is described by

$$y - \left(\frac{-C}{B}\right) = -\frac{A}{B}\ (x - 0)$$

or

$$Ax + By + C = 0.$$

Since there is a unique line with y intercept $\left(0, \frac{-C}{B}\right)$ and slope $\frac{-A}{B}$, the original equation describes that line.

Case 2

Let $B = 0$. Consider the line containing $\left(\frac{-C}{A}, 0\right)$ and parallel to the y axis. The equation of this line is

$$x = \frac{-C}{A}$$

or

$$Ax + 0y + C = 0.$$

Case 3

Let $A = 0$. Consider the line through $\left(0, \frac{-C}{B}\right)$ and parallel to the x axis. Its equation is

$$y = \frac{-C}{B}$$

which reduces to

$$0x + By + C = 0.$$

Thus the linear equation $Ax + By + C = 0$ is always the equation of a line in the xy plane.

EXAMPLE 2. The equation of a line in two-space is $2x + 3y - 4 = 0$.
a. Find the slope, λ, of the line.
b. Find a direction vector for the line.

Solutions: a. $2x + 3y - 4 = 0$ is equivalent to $\frac{2}{3}x + y - \frac{4}{3} = 0$

This is equivalent to $y = -\frac{2}{3}x + \frac{4}{3}$ ⟵ **Slope-intercept form**

Thus $\lambda = -\frac{2}{3}$

b. Since $\lambda = -\frac{2}{3}$, a direction vector is the following.

$$\vec{A} = \mathbf{i} - \frac{2}{3}\mathbf{j}$$

Find the x and y intercepts.

The x and y intercepts are found by alternately setting y and x equal to zero and solving for x and y.

When $y = 0$,

$$2x + 3 \cdot 0 - 4 = 0 \text{ implies } x = 2.$$

When $x = 0$,

$$2 \cdot 0 + 3y - 4 = 0 \text{ implies } y = \tfrac{4}{3}.$$

Sketch the graph of the line.

From the steps above, we see that $(0, \tfrac{4}{3})$ and $(2, 0)$ are on the line. These two points, or any others, uniquely determine the line. Plot the two points and the line determined by them. (See the figure below.)

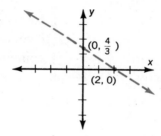

CLASSROOM EXERCISES

▬▬ Find the equation of the line satisfying the given conditions.

1. The line through $(4, 2)$ with slope $\tfrac{3}{2}$.

2. The line through $(-3, 2)$ with slope $\tfrac{3}{4}$.

3. The line having direction vector $5\mathbf{i} + 4\mathbf{j}$ and containing the point $(7, 4)$.

▬▬ Given the following equation of a line in two-space,

$$4x + 3y - 8 = 0$$

find each of the following:

4. the slope λ of the line.

5. the x and y intercepts.

6. a direction vector for the line.

7. Repeat Exercises 4–6 for the line in two-space with the following equation.

$$6x - 2y - 9 = 0$$

WRITTEN EXERCISES

A — Find the equation of the line satisfying the given conditions.

1. Slope is $\frac{1}{5}$, contains $(2, -3)$.

2. Slope is $-\frac{5}{3}$, contains $(0, 3)$.

3. Parallel to y axis, contains $(-2, 3)$.

4. Parallel to x axis, contains $(1, 5)$.

5. Slope is 0, contains $(2, -3)$.

6. Slope is undefined, contains $(1, -17)$.

7. A direction vector is $\vec{A} = 3\mathbf{i} - 2\mathbf{j}$, contains $(1, 1)$.

8. A direction vector is $\vec{A} = -5\mathbf{i} + 2\mathbf{j}$, contains $(-3, -1)$.

9. Slope is $\frac{5}{8}$, contains $(7, 1)$.

10. Slope is -8, contains $(0, 0)$.

11. A direction vector is $\vec{A} = \mathbf{i} - 3\mathbf{j}$, contains $(-5, 1)$.

12. A direction vector is $\vec{A} = -\mathbf{i} + 3\mathbf{j}$, contains $(-5, 1)$.

13. A direction vector is $\vec{A} = \mathbf{i} + \frac{2}{7}\mathbf{j}$, contains $(0, 0)$.

14. A direction vector is $\vec{A} = \mathbf{i} + a\mathbf{j}$, contains (b, c).

— Find a direction vector for each line whose equation is given.

15. $y - 2 = 3(x - 1)$

16. $y + 5 = -2(x + 3)$

17. $y + \frac{2}{3} = x - 1$

18. $3x + 2y + 4 = 0$

19. $y + 2x - 3 = 0$

20. $x + 2y - 3 = 0$

21. $4x - 3y - 7 = 0$

22. $\frac{1}{2}x - \frac{2}{3}y - \frac{4}{5} = 0$

23. $x = 3 + t5$, $y = 4 + t3$

24. $x = -1 - 4t$, $y = 2 - 3t$

25. Graph each line given in Exercises 15–22.

B **26.** Show that two vectors $\overrightarrow{P_1P_2}$, $\overrightarrow{P_3P_4}$, where $P_1(x_1, y_1)$, $P_2(x_2, y_2)$, $P_3(x_3, y_3)$, $P_4(x_4, y_4)$ are equal if and only if $x_2 - x_1 = x_4 - x_3$, and $y_2 - y_1 = y_4 - y_3$.

27. Using the vectors given in Exercise 26, show that two vectors are parallel if and only if $x_2 - x_1 = t(x_4 - x_3)$ and $y_2 - y_1 = t(y_4 - y_2)$, where t is a real nonzero number.

28. Show that if $P_1(x_1, y_1)$ and $P_2(x_2, y_2)$ are two points on a line, then $\lambda = \dfrac{y_2 - y_1}{x_2 - x_1}$.

29. Make a geometric argument demonstrating that the slope of a line may be determined by dividing the difference of the y coordinates by the difference (nonzero) of the x coordinates of any two points on the line. (*Hint:* Choose two different pairs of points and consider similar triangles.)

Use the result of Exercises 28 and 29 to write the equation of the line that contains each of the following.

30. $(2, 1)$ and $(5, 4)$

31. $(17, 84)$ and $(19, 82)$

32. $(-5, 2)$ and $(2, -4)$

33. $(3, -2)$ and $(-1, -3)$

34. (x_1, y_1) and (x_2, y_2), $x_1 \neq x_2$ (Note: Your result is the two point equation of a line.)

C **35. a.** Show that $Ax + By + C = 0$ may be written in the following form

$$\frac{x}{a} + \frac{y}{b} = 1$$

when $A, B, C \neq 0$.

b. Interpret a and b in terms of the graph of the equation $Ax + By + C = 0$.

36. a. Show that $Ax + By + C = 0$, $B \neq 0$, can be written in the form

$$y = mx + b.$$

b. What interpretation can be given to m and to b?

37. You are given $Ax + By + 5 = 0$, $B \neq 0$.

a. Express the slope of this line in terms of the constants A, B, and 5.

b. What is a direction vector for this line?

c. What is a direction vector for a vector parallel to the vector in Exercise **b?**

d. Using your vector in Exercise **c,** write a linear equation of the line with that direction vector which contains $(2, 3)$.

e. How are the given line and the line you found in Exercise **d** related?

f. How are the equations related?

g. What generalization does the results found in Exercises **a, b, c, d, e,** and **f** suggest?

MID-CHAPTER REVIEW

■■ Draw a vector $\overrightarrow{AB}$ on your paper. Use $\overrightarrow{AB}$ for Exercises 1–4.
(Section 9-1)

1. Draw $2\overrightarrow{AB}$

2. Draw $-\overrightarrow{AB}$

3. Draw $\overrightarrow{CD} = \overrightarrow{AB}$ through a point C not on $\overrightarrow{AB}$.

4. Draw $\overrightarrow{CD} \neq \overrightarrow{AB}$. Then draw $\overrightarrow{AB} + \overrightarrow{CD}$.

■■ Let $\vec{A} \parallel \vec{B}$, $|\vec{A}| = 4$, $|\vec{B}| = 5$, and $m\vec{A} = n\vec{B}$. Find m or n as indicated for each of the following. (Section 9-1)

5. m if $n = 2$

6. n if $m = -\frac{3}{4}$ and $\vec{A}$ and $\vec{B}$ have the same direction.

7. m if $n = \frac{2}{5}$ and $\vec{A}$ and $\vec{B}$ are opposite in direction.

8. n if $m = \frac{1}{8}$ and $\vec{A}$ and $\vec{B}$ are opposite in direction.

9. Find m and n such that $\vec{C} = m\vec{A} + n\vec{B}$ where $|\vec{A}| = 2$, $|\vec{B}| = 3$, $|\vec{C}| = 10$, the angle between $\vec{A}$ and $\vec{B}$ is $45°$, and the angle between $\vec{A}$ and $\vec{C}$ is $15°$. (Section 9-2)

■■ Given the position vector $\vec{r}$, find its length and the measure θ of the angle it makes with **i**. (Section 9-3)

10. $\vec{r} = -3\mathbf{i} + 2\mathbf{j}$ **11.** $\vec{r} = 3\mathbf{i} - 2\mathbf{j}$ **12.** $\vec{r} = -3\mathbf{i} - 2\mathbf{j}$

■■ Find $|\overrightarrow{PQ}|$. (Section 9-3)

13. $P = (1, 2, 3)$, $Q = (4, -2, 1)$

14. $P = (0, 4, 6)$, $Q = (-2, 1, 0)$

15. Given $P(1, 2)$ and $Q(5, 7)$, find the two points that divide $\overrightarrow{PQ}$ into thirds. (Section 9-4)

■■ Find the parametric and standard equations of each line containing A and B. (Section 9-5)

16. $A(1, 2, 1)$, $B(3, 5, 2)$ **17.** $A(-1, 0, 4)$, $B(3, 2, 1)$

18. $A(3, 6)$, $B(4, 7)$ **19.** $A(6, 2)$, $B(-1, 3)$

20. A line containing $(2, -3)$ has a direction vector $2\mathbf{i} - 3\mathbf{j}$. Find the equation of the line. (Section 9-6)

■■ Find a direction vector for each line whose equation is given.
(Section 9-6)

21. $y - 3 = 2(x + 4)$ **22.** $y + 7 = -3(x + 2)$

23. $y + 7 = x - 9$ **24.** $y - 81. = -4x + 7$

25. $6x + 3y - 2 = 19$ **26.** $-4x - 5y - 17 = 0$

9-7 The Angle Between Two Vectors

Two nonzero vectors, $\vec{A}$ and $\vec{B}$, in space may or may not intersect. However, the angle between the vectors may be determined uniquely because each vector is equal to some unique position vector. (See Example 2, Section 9–3.)

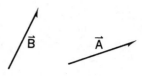

Let $\vec{V}_1 = a_1\mathbf{i} + a_2\mathbf{j} + a_3\mathbf{k}$ and $\vec{V}_2 = b_1\mathbf{i} + b_2\mathbf{j} + b_3\mathbf{k}$

be the two position vectors that correspond to $\vec{A}$ and $\vec{B}$. The measure of the angle between the vector $\vec{V}_1$ and $\vec{V}_2$ is θ. Clearly $0° \leq \theta \leq 180°$. $\theta = 0$ when $\vec{V}_2 = t\vec{V}_1$, $t > 0$ and $\theta = 180°$ when $\vec{V}_2 = t\vec{V}_1$, $t < 0$.

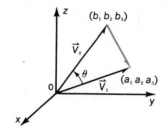

Notice that the vector $\vec{V}_1 - \vec{V}_2$ is the third side of the triangle formed by $\vec{V}_1$ and $\vec{V}_2$. The Law of Cosines (page 168) can be used to find $\cos \theta$.

$$|\vec{V}_1 - \vec{V}_2|^2 = |\vec{V}_1|^2 + |\vec{V}_2|^2 - 2|\vec{V}_1||\vec{V}_2| \cos \theta$$

or

$$\cos \theta = \frac{-|\vec{V}_1 - \vec{V}_2|^2 + |\vec{V}_1|^2 + |\vec{V}_2|^2}{+2|\vec{V}_1| \cdot |\vec{V}_2|}. \qquad \mathbf{1}$$

But

$$-|\vec{V}_1 - \vec{V}_2|^2 = -[(a_1 - b_1)^2 + (a_2 - b_2)^2 + (a_3 - b_3)^2]$$
$$= -[a_1^2 - 2a_1b_1 + b_1^2 + a_2^2 - 2a_2b_2 + b_2^2 + a_3^2 - 2a_3b_3 + b_3^2]$$

$$|\vec{V}_1|^2 = a_1^2 + a_2^2 + a_3^2$$

and

$$|\vec{V}_2|^2 = b_1^2 + b_2^2 + b_3^2.$$

Substituting the expressions in $\mathbf{1}$, you find

$$\cos \theta = \frac{2(a_1b_1 + a_2b_2 + a_3b_3)}{2|\vec{V}_1| \cdot |\vec{V}_2|}$$

or

$$\cos \theta = \frac{a_1b_1 + a_2b_2 + a_3b_3}{\sqrt{a_1^2 + a_2^2 + a_3^2} \cdot \sqrt{b_1^2 + b_2^2 + b_3^2}}. \qquad \mathbf{2}$$

EXAMPLE 1. Find the measure of the angle between the vectors $\vec{A} = \mathbf{i} + \mathbf{j} + \mathbf{k}$ and $\vec{B} = 2\mathbf{i} + 3\mathbf{j} + 5\mathbf{k}$. Express your answer to the nearest degree.

Solution:

$$\cos \theta = \frac{a_1b_1 + a_2b_2 + a_3b_3}{|\vec{A}| \cdot |\vec{B}|}. \qquad \longleftarrow \text{ By equation 2}$$

so

$$\cos \theta = \frac{1 \cdot 2 + 1 \cdot 3 + 1 \cdot 5}{\sqrt{3} \cdot \sqrt{38}}$$

$$= \frac{10}{\sqrt{114}}$$

$$\approx \frac{10}{10.68} \approx .94$$

Thus $\theta \approx 20°$.

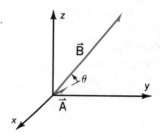

Equation **2** for the cosine of the angle between two vectors in space needs little modification for vectors in the xy plane. The z component for such vectors is 0.

Thus

$$\cos \theta = \frac{a_1b_1 + a_2b_2}{\sqrt{a_1^2 + a_2^2} \cdot \sqrt{b_1^2 + b_2^2}}. \qquad 3$$

Therefore,

$$\vec{V}_1 = a_1\mathbf{i} + a_2\mathbf{j} \quad \text{and} \quad \vec{V}_2 = b_1\mathbf{i} + b_2\mathbf{j}.$$

Notice that the numerator of equation **2** is the sum of the products of the corresponding components of $\vec{V}_1$ and $\vec{V}_2$. This sum is called the **inner product** or **dot product**.

Definition The **inner product (dot product)** of two vectors $\vec{V}_1 = a_1\mathbf{i} + a_2\mathbf{j} + a_3\mathbf{k}$ and $\vec{V}_2 = b_1\mathbf{i} + b_2\mathbf{j} + b_3\mathbf{k}$ is:

$$\vec{V}_1 \cdot \vec{V}_2 = a_1b_1 + a_2b_2 + a_3b_3 \qquad 4$$

If $\vec{V}_1$ and $\vec{V}_2$ are in the xy plane, then

$$\vec{V}_1 \cdot \vec{V}_2 = a_1 b_1 + a_2 b_2. \qquad \qquad 5$$

This leads to Theorem 9–7 which you will be asked to prove in the exercises.

Theorem 9–7   **a.** $\vec{V}_1 \cdot \vec{V}_2 = \vec{V}_2 \cdot \vec{V}_1$ (Commutative Property)

            b. $\vec{V}_1 \cdot (\vec{V}_2 + \vec{V}_3) = \vec{V}_1 \cdot \vec{V}_2 + \vec{V}_1 \cdot \vec{V}_3$

                                  (Distributive Property)

In terms of inner products,

$$\cos \theta = \frac{\vec{V}_1 \cdot \vec{V}_2}{|\vec{V}_1| \cdot |\vec{V}_2|}$$

for all nonzero vectors $\vec{V}_1$ and $\vec{V}_2$. Notice that the multiplication shown in the denominator is an ordinary product of two numbers, not a dot product.

EXAMPLE 2.   Find the angle between the vectors

$$\vec{A} = 2\mathbf{i} + 4\mathbf{j} + 2\mathbf{k} \quad \text{and} \quad \vec{B} = 3\mathbf{i} - 5\mathbf{j} + 7\mathbf{k}.$$

Interpret the results.

Solution: $\cos \theta = \dfrac{2 \cdot 3 + 4(-5) + 2 \cdot 7}{\sqrt{24} \cdot \sqrt{83}}$

$$= \frac{6 - 20 + 14}{\sqrt{24} \cdot \sqrt{83}} = 0$$

Since $\cos \theta = 0$, $\theta = 90°$. Thus the vectors $\vec{A}$ and $\vec{B}$ are perpendicular.

Example 2 suggests the next theorem.

Theorem 9–8   Two vectors $\vec{A}$ and $\vec{B}$ are perpendicular if and only if $\vec{A} \cdot \vec{B} = 0$.

The proof follows from the fact that $\vec{A}$ and $\vec{B}$ are perpendicular if and only if $\theta = 90° \pm 180k$.   ($k = 0, 1, 2, 3, \cdots$) and that will happen if and only if $\cos \theta$ is zero. But $\cos \theta = 0$ if and only if $\vec{A} \cdot \vec{B} = 0$. The zero vector is considered to be perpendicular to all vectors.

EXAMPLE 3. Find a nonzero vector $\vec{B}$ perpendicular to $\vec{A} = 2\mathbf{i} - 3\mathbf{j}$.

Solution: Let $\vec{B} = b_1\mathbf{i} + b_2\mathbf{j}$
$$\vec{A} \cdot \vec{B} = 2b_1 - 3b_2 = 0 \quad \longleftarrow \quad \vec{A} \perp \vec{B} \text{ implies } \vec{A} \cdot \vec{B} = 0.$$

Therefore $\dfrac{b_1}{b_2} = \dfrac{3}{2}$.

Thus b_1 and b_2 may be any numbers whose ratio is $\frac{3}{2}$.
Suppose $b_1 = 12$. Then $b_2 = 8$ and $\vec{B} = 12\mathbf{i} + 8\mathbf{j}$.

If you wished $\vec{B}$ to have length one, then it is easiest to choose $b_2 = \dfrac{2}{\sqrt{13}}$ and $b_1 = \dfrac{3}{\sqrt{13}}$. In this case

$$\vec{B} = \frac{3}{\sqrt{13}}\mathbf{i} + \frac{2}{\sqrt{13}}\mathbf{j}.$$

The vectors found in Example 3 have special names. A vector which is perpendicular to a given vector is said to be a **normal vector** or a **normal** to the given vector. If the normal has length one, it is called a **unit normal.**

The idea of the angle between two vectors is used to define the **angle between two lines.**

> **Definition**   The **angle between two lines** l_1 and l_2 is the nonobtuse angle between any two of the direction vectors for the lines.

A **normal to a line** is a vector perpendicular to a direction vector of the line.

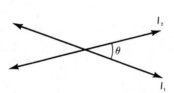

Angle between two lines.

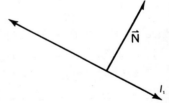

$\vec{N}$ is a normal to l_1.

EXAMPLE 4. Let line l_1 have equations $\dfrac{x-1}{1} = \dfrac{y-3}{1} = \dfrac{z-7}{1}$ and line l_2 have equations $\dfrac{x-5}{2} = \dfrac{y+1}{3} = \dfrac{z}{5}$.

a. Find the angle between l_1 and l_2.

b. Find a normal to l_1, and a normal to l_2.

484   CHAPTER 9

Solutions: **a.** Direction vectors for l_1 and l_2 are

$$\vec{r}_1 = 1\mathbf{i} + 1\mathbf{j} + 1\mathbf{k}$$

and
$$\vec{r}_2 = 2\mathbf{i} + 3\mathbf{j} + 5\mathbf{k}$$

Thus
$$\cos \theta = \frac{1 \cdot 2 + 1 \cdot 3 + 1 \cdot 5}{\sqrt{3} \cdot \sqrt{38}} = \frac{10}{\sqrt{114}}$$

By Example 1, $\theta \approx 20°$.

b. Let $\vec{N}_1 = n_1\mathbf{i} + n_2\mathbf{j} + n_3\mathbf{k}$ be normal to l_1.

Then
$$\vec{N}_1 \cdot \vec{r}_1 = n_1 \cdot 1 + n_2 \cdot 1 + n_3 \cdot 1$$
$$= n_1 + n_2 + n_3 = 0$$

One choice for a solution to this equation is

$$n_1 = 2, \ n_2 = -1, \text{ and } n_3 = -1.$$

Thus $\vec{N}_1$ could equal $2\mathbf{i} - \mathbf{j} - \mathbf{k}$. Any other triple that satisfies the equation will also do.

One normal to l_2 is $\vec{N}_2 = \mathbf{i} + \mathbf{j} - \mathbf{k}$. Find another.

WRITTEN EXERCISES

A ▬▬ Find the cosine of the angle between each pair of vectors.

1. $\vec{A} = \mathbf{i} + \mathbf{j}$
$\vec{B} = \mathbf{i}$

2. $\vec{A} = \mathbf{i} + \mathbf{j}$
$\vec{B} = \mathbf{j}$

3. $\vec{A} = \mathbf{i} + \mathbf{j} + \mathbf{k}$
$\vec{B} = \mathbf{i} + \mathbf{j}$

4. $\vec{A} = \mathbf{i} + \mathbf{j} + \mathbf{k}$
$\vec{B} = \mathbf{j}$

5. $\vec{A} = \mathbf{i}$
$\vec{B} = \mathbf{j}$

6. $\vec{A} = \mathbf{k}$
$\vec{B} = 5\mathbf{k}$

7. $\vec{A} = 2\mathbf{i} + 3\mathbf{j} + 7\mathbf{k}$
$\vec{B} = -3\mathbf{i} + 5\mathbf{k}$

8. $\vec{A} = 2\mathbf{j} - 3\mathbf{k}$
$\vec{B} = \mathbf{i} + 4\mathbf{j} + 2\mathbf{k}$

9. $\vec{A} = 7\mathbf{i} + 1\mathbf{j}$
$\vec{B} = -3\mathbf{i} + 2\mathbf{j}$

10. $\vec{A} = \mathbf{i} - 2\mathbf{k}, \vec{B} = 3\mathbf{j}$

11. $\vec{A} = 3\mathbf{j} - 2\mathbf{k}, \vec{B} = 2\mathbf{i} - \mathbf{j} - \mathbf{k}$

12. $\vec{P}$ is the vector from $(-4, 2)$ to $(2, 1)$.
$\vec{Q}$ is the vector from $(5, 8)$ to $(6, 2)$.

13. $\vec{r}$ is the vector from $(-2, 1, -3)$ to $(0, 1, 3)$.
$\vec{v}$ is the vector from $(1, 0, 3)$ to $(5, -2, 1)$.

14. $\vec{A}$ is the vector from $(1, 8, 5)$ to $(8, 5, 11)$.
$\vec{B}$ is the vector from $(-2, -3, -4)$ to $(1, 0, -6)$.

15. Find a normal to each vector in Exercises 7–9.

16. Find a unit normal to each vector in Exercises 11 and 13.

B ━━ Find the measure θ of the acute angle between each pair of lines. Find θ to the nearest degree.

17. $\dfrac{x-3}{2} = \dfrac{y-3}{5}, z = 0$

$\dfrac{x+1}{3} = \dfrac{y+2}{1}, z = 0$

18. $\dfrac{x+1}{2} = \dfrac{y-2}{2} = \dfrac{z-1}{2}$

$\dfrac{x-1}{3} = \dfrac{y-2}{5} = \dfrac{z+3}{1}$

19. $y = -3(x - 1)$

$y = \tfrac{1}{2}(x + 2)$

20. $\dfrac{x+1}{1} = \dfrac{y-2}{3}, z = 0$

$\dfrac{x-3}{1} = \dfrac{y+5}{2}, z = 0$

21. $x = 2 - 4t, x = 1 + 5t$

$y = 1 - 2t, y = -2 - t$

$z = 1 + 2t, z = 1 - 2t$

22. $x = 5, y = 2x + 4$

23. Find a unit normal to each line in Exercises 17–22.

24. **a.** Let $\vec{A} = a\mathbf{i} + b\mathbf{j} + c\mathbf{k}$. Find the cosine of the angles formed by $\vec{A}$ and $\mathbf{i}, \mathbf{j}, \mathbf{k}$.

b. What do your answers in part **a** represent?

C **25.** **a.** The standard equations of a line in the xy plane can be written $\dfrac{x-a}{1} = \dfrac{y-b}{\lambda}$, where λ is the slope of the line. If the lines

$$\dfrac{x-a}{1} = \dfrac{y-b}{\lambda_1}$$

and

$$\dfrac{x-c}{1} = \dfrac{y-d}{\lambda_2}$$

are perpendicular, how must λ_1 and λ_2 be related?

b. Is the converse statement true? Prove or disprove.

26. Prove that the vectors

$$\vec{V}_1 = 7\mathbf{i} - 3\mathbf{j} + 6\mathbf{k}$$
$$\vec{V}_2 = 3\mathbf{i} + 3\mathbf{j} - 2\mathbf{k}$$
$$\vec{V}_3 = 6\mathbf{i} - 16\mathbf{j} - 15\mathbf{k}$$

are mutually perpendicular.

27. Find the equation of a line perpendicular to the line with standard equations $\frac{x-1}{2} = \frac{y+3}{1} = \frac{z-1}{5}$.

(*Hint:* What is a direction vector for the desired line?)

28. Prove Theorem 9–7.

9–8 Parallel and Perpendicular Lines: Distance

Clearly, all vertical lines are parallel. Suppose, however, you have two nonvertical lines with equations

$$Ax + By + C_1 = 0 \quad \text{and} \quad Ax + By + C_2 = 0 \qquad B \neq 0. \quad \mathbf{1}$$

Then

$$\mathbf{i} + \frac{-A}{B}\mathbf{j}$$

is a direction vector for each line because $\frac{-A}{B}$ is the slope of each line. Since the lines have the same direction vector, the lines are parallel.

Conversely if two lines are parallel, they have parallel direction vectors. Then one vector is a scalar multiple of the other. If the vectors are $l_1\mathbf{i} + m_1\mathbf{j}$ and $l_2\mathbf{i} + m_2\mathbf{j}$ then

$$l_1\mathbf{i} + m_1\mathbf{j} = tl_2\mathbf{i} + tm_1\mathbf{j}, \quad t \neq 0.$$

Thus the slopes are equal since

$$\lambda_1 = \frac{m_1}{l_1} = \frac{tm_2}{tl_2} = \frac{m_2}{l_2} = \lambda_2.$$

Letting $\lambda_1 = \lambda_2 = \frac{-A}{B}$, the lines have equations **1** where C_1 and C_2 are constants. The following theorem can now be stated.

Theorem 9–9 Two nonvertical lines are parallel if and only if they have the same slope.

With regard to Theorem 9–9, two lines $A_1x + B_1y + C_1 = 0$ and $A_2x + B_2y + C_2 = 0$ are parallel if and only if $A_1 = KA_2$ and $B_1 = KB_2$.

Clearly, a vertical line and a horizontal line are perpendicular. The following theorem excludes this case.

> **Theorem 9–10** Two lines with nonzero slopes are perpendicular if and only if the product of the slopes is -1.

Proof: The direction vector of $Ax + By + C = 0$ is $\vec{V_1} = \mathbf{i} + \frac{-A}{B}\mathbf{j}$. Another line is perpendicular to $Ax + By + C = 0$ if and only if the inner product of its direction vector $\vec{V_2} = \mathbf{i} + \lambda\mathbf{j}$ and $\mathbf{i} + \frac{-A}{B}\mathbf{j}$ is zero. (Note: A and B are nonzero. Why?) Thus,

$$V_1 \cdot V_2 = 1 + \lambda\left(\frac{-A}{B}\right) = 0$$

But
$$1 + \lambda\left(\frac{-A}{B}\right) = 0 \quad \text{iff}$$

$$\lambda\left(\frac{-A}{B}\right) = -1 \qquad\qquad 2$$

From equation 2 it follows that $\lambda = \frac{B}{A}$. Thus the equation of a line perpendicular to

$$Ax + By + C = 0 \qquad\qquad 3$$

is
$$Bx - Ay + C_1 = 0. \qquad\qquad 4$$

Notice that in Equation 4 the coefficient of the x and y terms are the reverse of those in 3. Furthermore the sign of one coefficient has been reversed. This fact can help you quickly write the equation of a line perpendicular to a given line. The constant C_1 can be found when a point on the perpendicular line is known.

EXAMPLE 1. Given line $2x + 3y + 5 = 0$. Find
a. the parallel line through $(-2, 1)$.
b. the perpendicular line through $(-2, 1)$.

Solutions: a. The equation to use is $2x + 3y + C_1 = 0$.
$$2(-2) + 3(1) + C_1 = 0 \quad \longleftarrow \quad \text{Substitute } (-2, 1).$$
$$C_1 = 1$$
Thus $2x + 3y + 1 = 0$ is the equation of the parallel line.

   b. The equation to use is $-3x + 2y + C_2 = 0$.
$$-3(-2) + 2(1) + C_2 = 0 \quad \longleftarrow \quad \text{Substitute } (-2, 1)$$
$$C_2 = -8$$
Thus $-3x + 2y - 8$ is the equation of the perpendicular line.

The equation of a line perpendicular to a given line, the distance formula, and elementary algebra are useful in deriving a formula for the distance from a point to a line.

Theorem 9-11 The distance d from $P(a, b)$ to line $Ax + By + C = 0$ is given by the formula

$$d = \frac{|Aa + Bb + C|}{\sqrt{A^2 + B^2}}.$$

Proof: If $B = 0$, then the line is parallel to the y axis, and d is the absolute value of the difference of a and $x = \frac{-C}{A}$. (Why?) Thus such lines can be excluded from further discussion.

Consider the line $Ax + By + C = 0$ as shown in the figure. The line through $P(a, b)$ parallel to $Ax + By + C = 0$ has equation

$$Ax + By + C_1 = 0 \qquad\qquad 5$$

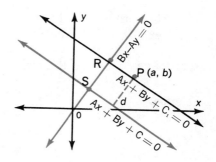

where C_1 can be determined by substituting $x = a$ and $y = b$ in 5. This substitution will be performed later in the proof since it complicates the manipulations if done now.

The line through the origin which is perpendicular to the parallel lines is defined by the following equation.

$$Bx - Ay + C_2 = 0$$

Since $(0, 0)$ is on this line, $C_2 = 0$ and the equation is

$$Bx - Ay = 0.$$

Let the intersection of $Bx - Ay = 0$ with the parallel lines be R and S. Then $|\overrightarrow{SR}| = d$. (Why?)

The coordinates of R and S can be found by solving these systems.

$$\begin{array}{ll} Bx - Ay = 0 & \\ Ax + By + C_1 = 0 & \end{array} \quad\text{and}\quad \begin{array}{ll} Bx - Ay = 0 \\ Ax + By + C = 0 \end{array}$$

The solutions are

$$R\left(\frac{-C_1 A}{A^2 + B^2}, \frac{-C_1 B}{A^2 + B^2}\right) \quad\text{and}\quad S\left(\frac{-CA}{A^2 + B^2}, \frac{-CB}{A^2 + B^2}\right)$$

Now
$$d^2 = |\overrightarrow{RS}|^2 = \left(\frac{-C_1 A + CA}{A^2 + B^2}\right)^2 + \left(\frac{-C_1 B + CB}{A^2 + B^2}\right)^2$$
$$= \frac{A^2(-C_1 + C)^2 + B^2(-C_1 + C)^2}{(A^2 + B^2)^2}$$
$$= \frac{(A^2 + B^2)(-C_1 + C)^2}{(A^2 + B^2)^2}$$
$$= \frac{(-C_1 + C)^2}{A^2 + B^2}$$

But
$$C_1 = -Aa - Bb, \quad \text{so}$$
$$d = \sqrt{\frac{(Aa + Bb + C)^2}{A^2 + B^2}}$$
$$= \frac{|Aa + Bb + C|}{\sqrt{A^2 + B^2}}$$

The formula for the distance from a point to a line is easier to apply than it is to derive.

EXAMPLE 2. Find the distance from $(2, -5)$ to $3x + 4y - 3 = 0$.

Solution:
$$d = \frac{|Aa + Bb + C|}{\sqrt{A^2 + B^2}}$$

Thus
$$d = \frac{|3 \cdot 2 + 4(-5) - 3|}{\sqrt{9 + 16}}$$
$$= \frac{|6 - 20 - 3|}{5}$$
$$= \frac{17}{5} = 3\frac{2}{5}$$

CLASSROOM EXERCISES

State whether the vectors in each pair are parallel or perpendicular.

1. $(1, 2); (-2, 1)$ **2.** $(1, 2); (2, 4)$ **3.** $(1, 2, 3); (2, -1, 0)$

Find the distance from the origin to the lines whose equations are given below. Leave answers in radical form when radicals occur.

4. $x + y + 8 = 0$ **5.** $5x + 12y - 30 = 0$ **6.** $3x + 5y - 8 = 0$

Find the distance from $(-3, 5)$ to each line.

7. $x + y + 8 = 0$ **8.** $2x - y + 3 = 0$ **9.** $2x - y + 11 = 0$

10. How do you determine whether two lines are parallel?

11. How do you determine whether two lines are perpendicular?

WRITTEN EXERCISES

A ▬ Find equations of two lines containing A; one line parallel to the given line and one line perpendicular to the given line.

1. $A(4, 1)$, $2x - 3y + 5 = 0$ **2.** $A(2, -1)$, $2x - y + 1 = 0$

3. $A(2, -1)$, $2x - y = 0$ **4.** $A(3, 4)$, $7x + 5y + 4 = 0$

5. $A(0, 0)$, $x - y + 3 = 0$ **6.** $A(2, -3)$, $8x - y = 0$

7. $A(6, 0)$, $3x + 3y - 1 = 0$ **8.** $A(2, 5)$, $x = 4$

9. $A(7, 9)$, $y = -3$ **10.** $A(-2, -5)$, $y = 2x - 1$

11. $A(0, 7)$, $9y + x + 3 = 0$ **12.** $A(-5, 1)$, $\frac{x}{2} + \frac{y}{3} = 1$

13. Find the distance from the line to the point in Exercises 1–12 above. Leave answers in radical form when radicals occur.

B **14.** For the line $Ax + By + C = 0$, find an expression for the distance from the origin to the line.

▬ Use your results in Exercise 14 to find the distance from the origin to

15. $2x - 3y + 7 = 0$ **16.** $4x + 5y - 15 = 0$

17. $x = 4$ **18.** $y = 3$

19. $5x - 12y = 0$ **20.** $\frac{x}{a} + \frac{y}{b} - 1 = 0$

21. $y = mx + b$

▬ Let $A(1, 0)$, $B(9, 2)$, $C(3, 6)$ be the vertices of a triangle. Find each of the following.

22. The equations of the lines containing the sides.

23. The equations of the lines containing the medians.

24. The equations of the lines containing the altitudes.

25. The equations of the lines containing the perpendicular bisectors of the sides.

26. The point common to the lines in Exercises 23, 24, and 25.

27. Show that the three points found in Exercise 26 are collinear.

28. Repeat Exercises 22–27, for the vertices $A(0, 0)$, $B(9, 2)$, and $C(2, 7)$.

C **29. a.** Given the line $3x + 2y + 4 = 0$, find a vector $\vec{N}$ normal to this line.

b. How are the components of the normal $\vec{N}$ related to the coefficients of the line?

c. Verify that $P(2, -5)$ is on the line.

d. Let $Q(x, y)$ be a point on the line. Find the components of $\vec{PQ}$.

e. What is the value of the inner product $\vec{N} \cdot \vec{PQ}$?

f. Find $\vec{N} \cdot \vec{PQ}$ and simplify. What is the result?

30. Repeat Exercise 29 for $Ax + By + C = 0$.

31. Generalize your results in Exercises 29 and 30, that is, if $\vec{N}$ is a normal to a line and $\vec{PQ}$ is a direction vector, the equation of the line is found by what means?

9-9   The Cross Product of Two Vectors

In two-space, if you were asked to find a vector perpendicular to each of two nonparallel, nonzero vectors, you would respond that there was no satisfactory nonzero vector. If one existed, a triangle could have two right angles as shown in Figure 1. Since the zero vector is thought of as perpendicular to any vector, it is the only vector in two-space perpendicular to two nonparallel, nonzero vectors.

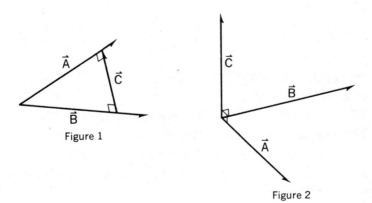

Figure 1

Figure 2

For two (nonzero) nonparallel vectors in three-space, there are many nonzero vectors perpendicular to each. For example, **i** is perpendicular to **j** and to **k**. Another example is shown in Figure 2. It

492   CHAPTER 9

happens that there is a simple relationship between the components of $\vec{A}$ and $\vec{B}$ and a vector $\vec{C}$ in three-space which is perpendicular to $\vec{A}$ and $\vec{B}$. Let $\vec{A} = a_1\mathbf{i} + a_2\mathbf{j} + a_3\mathbf{k}$, $\vec{B} = b_1\mathbf{i} + b_2\mathbf{j} + b_3\mathbf{k}$, and the required vector be $\vec{C} = l\mathbf{i} + m\mathbf{j} + n\mathbf{k}$. Then $\vec{C} \perp \vec{A}$ and $\vec{C} \perp \vec{B}$ if and only if

$$\vec{C} \cdot \vec{A} = 0 \quad \text{and} \quad \vec{C} \cdot \vec{B} = 0.$$

Or $\qquad a_1l + a_2m + a_3n = 0 \quad \text{and} \quad b_1l + b_2m + b_3n = 0.$ **1**

Since the components of $\vec{A}$ and $\vec{B}$ are known, equations **1** can be solved simultaneously for l and m in terms of n.

Thus:
$\qquad$ i. $\qquad a_1l + a_2m = -a_3n$

and
$$b_1l + b_2m = -b_3n$$

$\qquad$ ii. $a_1b_2l + a_2b_2m = -a_3b_2n$ $\qquad\longleftarrow$ **Eliminate m.**
$\qquad\quad a_2b_1l + a_2b_2m = -a_2b_3n$

$\qquad$ iii. $(a_1b_2 - a_2b_1)l = (a_2b_3 - a_3b_2)n$ $\qquad\longleftarrow$ **Solve for l.**

$\qquad$ iv. $l = \dfrac{(a_2b_3 - a_3b_2)n}{a_1b_2 - a_2b_1}$, $a_1b_2 - a_2b_1 \neq 0$

Similarly $m = \dfrac{(a_1b_3 - a_3b_1)n}{a_2b_1 - a_1b_2} = \dfrac{a_3b_1 - a_1b_3}{a_1b_2 - a_2b_1}\, n$ where $a_1b_2 - a_2b_1 \neq 0$.

The value of n is arbitrary, so choose it to be

$$n = a_1b_2 - a_2b_1.$$
Then
$$l = a_2b_3 - a_3b_2$$
$$m = a_3b_1 - a_1b_3.$$

Thus $\qquad \vec{C} = (a_2b_3 - a_3b_2)\mathbf{i} + (a_3b_1 - a_1b_3)\mathbf{j} + (a_1b_2 - a_2b_1)\mathbf{k}.$ **2**

The vector $\vec{C}$ in **2** is determined by the components of $\vec{A}$ and $\vec{B}$. To help you remember how the components of $\vec{A}$ and $\vec{B}$ combine to give you the components of $\vec{C}$ define the symbol

$$\begin{vmatrix} a_2 & a_3 \\ b_2 & b_3 \end{vmatrix} = a_2b_3 - a_3b_2.$$ **3**

Then using **3**, **2** becomes

$$\vec{C} = \begin{vmatrix} a_2 & a_3 \\ b_2 & b_3 \end{vmatrix}\mathbf{i} + \begin{vmatrix} a_3 & a_1 \\ b_3 & b_1 \end{vmatrix}\mathbf{j} + \begin{vmatrix} a_1 & a_2 \\ b_1 & b_2 \end{vmatrix}\mathbf{k}.$$ **4**

Definition Given $\vec{A} = a_1\mathbf{i} + a_2\mathbf{j} + a_3\mathbf{k}$ and $\vec{B} = b_1\mathbf{i} + b_2\mathbf{j} + b_3\mathbf{k}$, the vector $\vec{C}$ is the *cross product* of $\vec{A}$ and $\vec{B}$, $\vec{A} \times \vec{B}$, and defined by equation **4**.

EXAMPLE. Find $\vec{C} \times \vec{D}$ in each of the following.

a. When $\vec{C} = 2i - 3j + 4k$ and $\vec{D} = 5i + 2j - 3k$.

$$\vec{C} \times \vec{D} = \begin{vmatrix} -3 & 4 \\ 2 & -3 \end{vmatrix} i + \begin{vmatrix} 4 & 2 \\ -3 & 5 \end{vmatrix} j + \begin{vmatrix} 2 & -3 \\ 5 & 2 \end{vmatrix} k$$

$$= (9 - 8)i + (20 + 6)j + (4 + 15)k$$

$$= 1i + 26j + 19k$$

b. When $\vec{C} = i$ and $\vec{D} = j$.

$$i \times j = \begin{vmatrix} 0 & 0 \\ 1 & 0 \end{vmatrix} i + \begin{vmatrix} 0 & 1 \\ 0 & 0 \end{vmatrix} j + \begin{vmatrix} 1 & 0 \\ 0 & 1 \end{vmatrix} k$$

$$= 0i + 0j + 1k = k$$

c. When $\vec{C} = j$ and $\vec{D} = i$.

$$j \times i = \begin{vmatrix} 1 & 0 \\ 0 & 0 \end{vmatrix} i + \begin{vmatrix} 0 & 0 \\ 0 & 1 \end{vmatrix} j + \begin{vmatrix} 0 & 1 \\ 1 & 0 \end{vmatrix} k$$

$$= 0i + 0j - 1k = -k$$

Parts b and c suggest that $\vec{A} \times \vec{B} \neq \vec{B} \times \vec{A}$, that is, that the operation "cross product" is not commutative. This is, in fact, true. The proofs of the following theorems are left for you.

Theorem 9–12 $\vec{A} \times \vec{B} = -\vec{B} \times \vec{A}$.

Theorem 9–13 (Distributive Property)

$$\vec{A} \times (\vec{B} + \vec{C}) = \vec{A} \times \vec{B} + \vec{A} \times \vec{C}$$

Theorem 9–14 (An Associative Property)

$$m(\vec{A}) \times \vec{B} = m(\vec{A} \times \vec{B}).$$

Remaining unanswered is the question of the length of the vector $\vec{A} \times \vec{B}$. From 2

$$|\vec{A} \times \vec{B}| = \sqrt{(a_2b_3 - a_3b_2)^2 + (a_3b_1 - a_1b_3)^2 + (a_1b_2 - a_2b_1)^2} \qquad 5$$

There is a more compact form of 5 as indicated in the next theorem.

Theorem 9–15 If $\vec{A} = a_1i + a_2j + a_3k$, $\vec{B} = b_1i + b_2j + b_3k$ and the angle between $\vec{A}$ and $\vec{B}$ has measure θ, $0 \leq \theta \leq 180°$, then

$$|\vec{A} \times \vec{B}| = |\vec{A}| \cdot |\vec{B}| \sin \theta.$$

Proof:

$$|\vec{A} \times \vec{B}| = \sqrt{(a_2b_3 - a_3b_2)^2 + (a_3b_1 - a_1b_3)^2 + (a_1b_2 - a_2b_1)^2}$$

$$= \sqrt{a_2b_3^2 - 2a_2a_3b_2b_3 + a_3^2b_2^2 + a_3^2b_1^2 - 2a_1a_3b_1b_3}$$
$$\overline{+ a_1^2b_3^2 + a_1^2b_2^2 - 2a_1a_2b_1b_2 + a_2^2b_1^2}$$

$$= \sqrt{(a_1^2 + a_2^2 + a_3^2)(b_1^2 + b_2^2 + b_3^2)}$$
$$\overline{- [a_1^2b_1^2 + a_2^2b_2^2 + a_3^2b_3^2 + 2a_1a_2b_1b_2 + 2a_1a_3b_1b_3 + 2a_2a_3b_2b_3]}$$

$$= \sqrt{|\vec{A}|^2 \cdot |\vec{B}|^2 - (\vec{A} \cdot \vec{B})^2} \quad (\text{since } \vec{A} \cdot \vec{B} = a_1b_1 + a_2b_2 + a_3b_3).$$

$$= |\vec{A}| \cdot |\vec{B}| \cdot \sqrt{1 - \left(\frac{\vec{A} \cdot \vec{B}}{|\vec{A}| \cdot |\vec{B}|}\right)^2}$$

Now since $\cos\theta = \dfrac{\vec{A} \cdot \vec{B}}{|\vec{A}||\vec{B}|}$, $\left(\dfrac{\vec{A} \cdot \vec{B}}{|\vec{A}||\vec{B}|}\right)^2 = \cos^2\theta$,

so $$|\vec{A} \times \vec{B}| = |\vec{A}| \cdot |\vec{B}| \sqrt{1 - \cos^2\theta}$$

or since $\sin\theta = \sqrt{1 - \cos^2\theta}$, $|\vec{A} \times \vec{B}| = |\vec{A}| \cdot |\vec{B}| \sin\theta$.

The geometric interpretation of Theorem 9–15 is interesting. Consider $\vec{A}$ and $\vec{B}$ as shown in the figure.

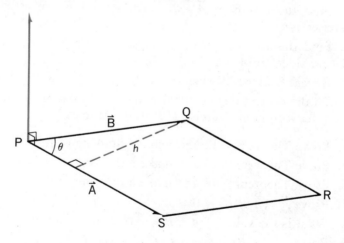

Let h be the length of the perpendicular from the tip of $\vec{B}$ to $\vec{A}$. Then $h = |\vec{B}| \cdot \sin\theta$ (Why?), and h is the altitude of the parallelogram $PQRS$. The length of the base of $PQRS$ is $|\vec{A}|$. Thus the area of $PQRS$ is

$$|\vec{A}| \cdot |\vec{B}| \sin\theta.$$

Consequently, the *length of the cross product* of $\vec{A}$ and $\vec{B}$ is the *area* of the parallelogram determined by $\vec{A}$ and $\vec{B}$.

WRITTEN EXERCISES

A ━━ Find each cross product $\vec{A} \times \vec{B}$.

1. $\vec{A} = 2\mathbf{i} + 3\mathbf{j} - 4\mathbf{k}, \vec{B} = \mathbf{i} - 2\mathbf{j} + \mathbf{k}$
2. $\vec{A} = \mathbf{i} - 2\mathbf{j} - 2\mathbf{k}, \vec{B} = 3\mathbf{i} - 4\mathbf{j} - 2\mathbf{k}$
3. $\vec{A} = \mathbf{i} + \mathbf{j} + \mathbf{k}, \vec{B} = \mathbf{i} - \mathbf{j} + \mathbf{k}$
4. $\vec{A} = 6\mathbf{i} - 3\mathbf{j} - 14\mathbf{k}, \vec{B} = 3\mathbf{i} + 2\mathbf{j} - 3\mathbf{k}$
5. $\vec{A} = 4\mathbf{i} + 5\mathbf{j} - 6\mathbf{k}, \vec{B} = \mathbf{i} - 2\mathbf{j} + 3\mathbf{k}$
6. $\vec{A} = 4\mathbf{i} - 2\mathbf{j}, \vec{B} = 3\mathbf{i} + 2\mathbf{k}$
7. $\vec{A} = \mathbf{i} - 3\mathbf{k}, \vec{B} = \mathbf{j}$
8. $\vec{A} = 2\mathbf{i} + 3\mathbf{j}, \vec{B} = 4\mathbf{i} - \mathbf{j}$
9. $\vec{A} = \mathbf{k}, \vec{B} = 3\mathbf{i} + 2\mathbf{j} - 7\mathbf{k}$
10. $\vec{A} = \frac{1}{3}\mathbf{i} - \frac{2}{3}\mathbf{k}, \vec{B} = \mathbf{j} + 4\mathbf{k}$

━━ Find the cross product of each ordered pair of vectors.

11. (i, i)   **12.** (i, j)   **13.** (i, k)
14. (j, i)   **15.** (j, j)   **16.** (j, k)
17. (k, i)   **18.** (k, j)   **19.** (k, k)

20. Find the length of $\vec{A} \times \vec{B}$ when $\vec{A}$ and $\vec{B}$ are as given in Exercises 1–6.

21. Find the area of the parallelogram in three-space when the adjacent sides are $\vec{A} = 2\mathbf{i} + 4\mathbf{j} - 3\mathbf{k}$ and $\vec{B} = \mathbf{i} - 2\mathbf{k}$.

22. Repeat Exercise 21 when $\vec{A} = -4\mathbf{i} + 2\mathbf{j} - 3\mathbf{k}$ and $\vec{B} = \mathbf{i} + \mathbf{j} + \mathbf{k}$.

23. To the nearest degree, what is the measure θ of the angle between the vectors in Exercise 21? in Exercise 22?

B **24.** Prove Theorem 9–12 and make a drawing of it.
25. Prove Theorem 9–13 and make a drawing of it.
26. Prove Theorem 9–14 and make a drawing of it.
27. Prove $\vec{A} \cdot (\vec{A} \times \vec{B}) = 0$.
28. What is the value of $\vec{A} \cdot (\vec{B} \times \vec{A})$? Prove your answer.
29. Prove: $(\vec{A} \times \vec{B}) \times \vec{C} = (\vec{A} \cdot \vec{C})\vec{B} - (\vec{B} \cdot \vec{C})\vec{A}$.
(This is called the *triple cross product*.)
30. Find the vector perpendicular to the plane of the points $(3, -1, 2)$, $(4, 5, 3)$ and $(-2, 4, 6)$.
31. Find the area of the triangle having the vertices given in Exercise 30.
32. What is the formula for the area of a triangle with vectors $\vec{A}$ and $\vec{B}$ for two sides?

C **33. a.** Show that $\vec{A} \times (\vec{B} \times \vec{C}) \neq (\vec{A} \times \vec{B}) \times \vec{C}$.

b. Find a formula for $\vec{A} \times (\vec{B} \times \vec{C})$. (See Exercises 24 and 29.)

34. $\begin{vmatrix} a_1 & a_2 \\ b_1 & b_2 \end{vmatrix} = a_1 b_2 - a_2 b_1$ is the *determinant* of the **matrix**

$$\begin{bmatrix} a_1 & a_2 \\ b_1 & b_2 \end{bmatrix}.$$

(A **matrix** is a rectangular array of numbers.)

a. Show that

$$\begin{vmatrix} ma_1 & ma_2 \\ b_1 & b_2 \end{vmatrix} = m \begin{vmatrix} a_1 & a_2 \\ b_1 & b_2 \end{vmatrix}.$$

b. Show that

$$\begin{vmatrix} a_1 & a_2 \\ b_1 & b_2 \end{vmatrix} = - \begin{vmatrix} a_2 & a_1 \\ b_2 & b_1 \end{vmatrix}.$$

35. The determinant of a matrix $\begin{bmatrix} a_1 & a_2 & a_3 \\ b_1 & b_2 & b_3 \\ c_1 & c_2 & c_3 \end{bmatrix}$ is

$$a_1 \begin{vmatrix} b_2 & b_3 \\ c_2 & c_3 \end{vmatrix} - a_2 \begin{vmatrix} b_1 & b_3 \\ c_1 & c_3 \end{vmatrix} + a_3 \begin{vmatrix} b_1 & b_2 \\ c_1 & c_2 \end{vmatrix} = \begin{vmatrix} a_1 & a_2 & a_3 \\ b_1 & b_2 & b_3 \\ c_1 & c_2 & c_3 \end{vmatrix}.$$

Show that $\vec{A} \times \vec{B} = \begin{vmatrix} \mathbf{i} & \mathbf{j} & \mathbf{k} \\ a_1 & a_2 & a_3 \\ b_1 & b_2 & b_3 \end{vmatrix}.$

9–10 The Equation of a Plane

A plane is to three-space as a line is to two-space. In each case the dimension of the subset is one less than the dimension of the space: 2 to 3 and 1 to 2. The analogy goes further: In two-space the equation of a line is

$$Ax + By + C = 0. \qquad \qquad \mathbf{1}$$

In three-space, as you shall see, the equation of a plane is also a linear equation,

$$Ax + By + Cz + D = 0. \qquad \qquad \mathbf{2}$$

The major task of this section is to show that equation **2** is the equation of a plane.

Let Ω (Greek letter *omega*) be a plane, $P(a, b, c)$ a fixed point in Ω, $Q(x, y, z)$ any other point in Ω, and $\vec{N} = A\mathbf{i} + B\mathbf{j} + C\mathbf{k}$ the normal to Ω.

$\vec{N}$, being perpendicular to Ω is perpendicular to every vector in Ω. In particular $\vec{N} \perp \vec{PQ}$.

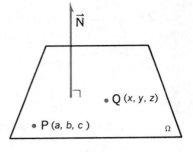

Consequently,

$$\vec{N} \cdot \vec{PQ} = 0$$

or $\quad (A\mathbf{i} + B\mathbf{j} + C\mathbf{k}) \cdot ((x - a)\mathbf{i} + (y - b)\mathbf{j} + (z - c)\mathbf{k}) = 0$

and $\qquad\qquad A(x - a) + B(y - b) + C(z - c) = 0$

or $\qquad\qquad Ax + By + Cz + (-Aa - Bb - Cc) = 0.$

Let $D = -Aa - Bb - Cc$, substitute, and you find

$$Ax + By + Cz + D = 0$$

is the equation of the plane Ω.

Conversely, any equation like **2** is the equation of a plane. Let $P(a, b, c)$ be a point satisfying **2**. Then

$$Aa + Bb + Cc + D = 0 \qquad\qquad\qquad 3$$

Subtracting **3** from **2** you find the following.

$$A(x - a) + B(y - b) + C(z - c) = 0. \qquad\qquad 4$$

Equation **4** is the inner product of

$$\vec{N} = A\mathbf{i} + B\mathbf{j} + C\mathbf{k}$$

and $\qquad\qquad \vec{PQ} = (x - a)\mathbf{i} + (y - b)\mathbf{j} + (z - c)\mathbf{k},$

where $Q(x, y, z)$ is any point satisfying **2**, and $P(a, b, c)$ is a fixed point. The set of all $Q(x, y, z)$ such that $\vec{PQ}$ is perpendicular to $\vec{N}$ is a plane. This leads to the following theorem.

Theorem 9–16   A figure Ω in three-space is a plane if and only if each point (x, y, z) in Ω satisfies $Ax + By + Cz + D = 0$ (A, B, and C not all zero).

The coefficients of x, y, and z are the components of the normal to the plane. (Compare with Exercises 29 and 30, Section 9–8.)

EXAMPLE 1. Find the equation of the plane containing $(1, 3, 4)$ whose normal is $\vec{N} = 2\mathbf{i} - 3\mathbf{j} - 4\mathbf{k}$.

Solution:

Since the normal is $\vec{N} = 2\mathbf{i} - 3\mathbf{j} - 4\mathbf{k}$, the equation of the plane is

$$2x - 3y - 4z + D = 0.$$

Consequently,

$$2 \cdot 1 - 3 \cdot 3 - 4 \cdot 4 + D = 0 \quad \longleftarrow \quad \textbf{(1, 3, 4) is on the plane.}$$

and

$$D = 23.$$

The equation is

$$2x - 3y - 4z + 23 = 0.$$

EXAMPLE 2. Find the equation of the plane determined by $A(1, 1, 1)$, $B(2, -3, 4)$, and $C(-1, 3, 2)$.

Solution:

Since A, B, and C are in the plane, $\overrightarrow{AB}$ and $\overrightarrow{AC}$ are also. The cross product $\overrightarrow{AB} \times \overrightarrow{AC}$ is a vector perpendicular to $\overrightarrow{AB}$ and $\overrightarrow{AC}$ and is a normal to the plane. Consequently

$$\overrightarrow{AB} \times \overrightarrow{AC} = (\mathbf{i} - 4\mathbf{j} + 3\mathbf{k}) \times (-2\mathbf{i} + 2\mathbf{j} + \mathbf{k})$$

$$= \begin{vmatrix} -4 & 3 \\ 2 & 1 \end{vmatrix} \mathbf{i} + \begin{vmatrix} 3 & 1 \\ 1 & -2 \end{vmatrix} \mathbf{j} + \begin{vmatrix} 1 & -4 \\ -2 & 2 \end{vmatrix} \mathbf{k}$$

$$= -10\mathbf{i} - 7\mathbf{j} - 6\mathbf{k} = \vec{N}$$

The plane has equation

$$-10x - 7y - 6z + D = 0.$$

$$-10x - 7y - 6z + 23 = 0. \quad \longleftarrow \quad D = 23$$

You may find it difficult to sketch planes in space. The **traces** of the plane are helpful in making such a sketch.

Definition The *xy-trace* is the intersection of the given plane with the *xy* plane.

The *yz-trace* is the intersection of the given plane with the *yz* plane.

The *xz-trace* is the intersection of the given plane with the *xz* plane.

Each trace is a line. They are found by respectively setting z, x, and y equal to zero in $Ax + By + Cz + D = 0$ and graphing the resulting lines. This is shown in the figure below.

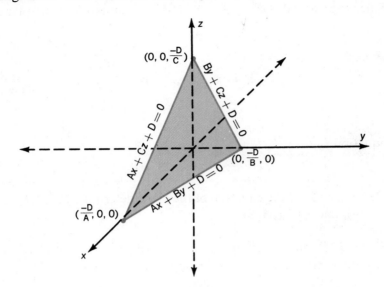

For the plane $Ax + By + Cz + D = 0$. $Ax + By + D = 0$ is the xy-trace. $By + Cz + D = 0$ is the yz-trace. $Ax + Cz + D = 0$ is the xz-trace. Shading helps you to visualize the plane. Only the portion in one octant is usually shown.

EXAMPLE 3. Given

$$2x - 3y - 6z + 12 = 0.$$

Find the three traces and sketch the graph.

The traces are

$$2x - 3y + 12 = 0$$
$$-3y - 6z + 12 = 0$$
$$2x - 6z + 12 = 0.$$

The points common to the axis and the plane are

$(-6, 0, 0)$, $(0, 4, 0)$, $(0, 0, 2)$.

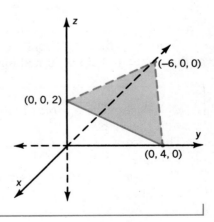

The graph is shown at the right. Notice that the portion shown is behind the yz plane. The dotted traces indicate this fact.

CLASSROOM EXERCISES

1. Find a vector normal to $3x + 2y - 3z + 5 = 0$

2. Write the equations of three planes with normal $\vec{N} = -2\mathbf{i} + 3\mathbf{j} + \mathbf{k}$.

3. Find the equation of the plane containing $(2, 6, -1)$ whose normal is $\vec{N} = -\mathbf{i} + \frac{2}{3}\mathbf{j} - \mathbf{k}$.

WRITTEN EXERCISES

A ▬▬ Find the equation of the plane satisfying the conditions. $\vec{N}$ is the normal to the plane.

1. $\vec{N} = 3\mathbf{i} + 2\mathbf{j} - 5\mathbf{k}$, contains $(1, 1, 2)$

2. $\vec{N} = 3\mathbf{i} - 2\mathbf{j} - 5\mathbf{k}$, contains $(2, -1, -1)$

3. $\vec{N} = 4\mathbf{i} - \mathbf{j} - \mathbf{k}$, contains $(0, 2, 3)$

4. $\vec{N} = 7\mathbf{i} - 3\mathbf{j} - 2\mathbf{k}$, contains $(1, 1, 2)$

5. $\vec{N} = \frac{1}{2}\mathbf{i} - \frac{2}{3}\mathbf{j} + \frac{3}{4}\mathbf{k}$, contains $(-2, -3, -4)$

6. Parallel to the plane $5x - 2y + 7z + 1 = 0$, contains $(2, 1, 0)$

7. Parallel to the plane $-2x + 3y - 4z - 5 = 0$, contains $(1, -3, -2)$

8. Parallel to the plane $7x - 3y - 2z + 1 = 0$, contains $(1, 0, 2)$

9. Contains $(1, 4, 3)$, $(2, 1, 5)$, $(3, 2, 1)$

10. Contains $(-2, -5, 1)$, $(4, 8, -2)$, $(7, 1, 5)$

11. Contains $(0, 1, 2)$, $(2, 0, 4)$, $(4, 3, 0)$

12. Contains $(2, -2, -1)$, $(-3, 4, 1)$, $(4, 2, 3)$

B **13.** Perpendicular to $5x - 2y + 7z + 1 = 0$, contains $(0, 1, 2)$

14. Perpendicular to $3x - 2y + z - 5 = 0$, contains $(2, 2, 3)$

15. Perpendicular to $x - y - z + 10 = 0$, contains $(0, 0, 0)$

16. Perpendicular to the segment with endpoints $(2, 0, 4)$ and $(0, -8, 4)$ and contains its midpoint.

17. Repeat Exercise 16 where the points are $(1, 1, 2)$ and $(-5, 7, 2)$.

18. Graph each plane in Exercises 1–17. Identify the traces.

19. What is the equation of the xy plane? xz plane? yz plane?

C **20.** Present a convincing argument demonstrating that the measure of the angle between two planes is the same as that of the angles between their normals.

21. What is the measure, to the nearest degree, of the angle between the planes

$$2x + 3y + z = 0 \quad \text{and} \quad -x + 2y + 5z - 8 = 0?$$

BASIC: THE ANGLE BETWEEN TWO VECTORS

To a computer, a three-dimensional vector is simply three numbers. A program must allow the machine to handle these numbers.

Problem:
Given the components of two three-dimensional vectors, write a program which prints the degree measure of the angle between the vectors. If the angle is 90°, print that the vectors are perpendicular.

```
110  PRINT "THIS PROGRAM COMPUTES THE ANGLE"
120  PRINT "BETWEEN TWO 3-DIMENSIONAL VECTORS"
130  PRINT "AND DECIDES WHETHER THE VECTORS ARE"
140  PRINT "PERPENDICULAR."
150  PRINT
160  PRINT "FOR THE VECTOR AI + BJ + CK, WHAT"
170  PRINT "ARE A, B, AND C";
180  INPUT A, B, C
190  PRINT "FOR THE VECTOR DI + EJ + FK, WHAT"
200  PRINT "ARE D, E, AND F";
210  INPUT D, E, F
220  LET P = A*D + B*E + C*F
230  IF P = 0 THEN 360
240  LET V1 = SQR(A*A + B*B + C*C)
250  LET V2 = SQR(D*D + E*E + F*F)
260  IF V1 * V2 <> 0 THEN 290
270  PRINT "ONE OF THE VECTORS WAS 0."
280  GOTO 370
290  LET C1 = P/(V1*V2)
300  LET S = SQR(1 - C1*C1)
310  LET T = S/C1
320  LET X = ATN(T)
330  LET X = 180 * X / 3.14159
340  PRINT "ANGLE BETWEEN VECTORS = ";X;" DEGREES"
350  GOTO 370
360  PRINT "VECTORS ARE PERPENDICULAR."
370  PRINT
380  PRINT "ANY MORE PROBLEMS (1=YES,0=NO)";
390  INPUT Z
400  IF Z = 1 THEN 150
410  PRINT
420  END
```

Analysis:

The central logic of the program is based on the following equation (see page 483).

$$\cos \theta = \frac{\vec{V}_1 \cdot \vec{V}_2}{|\vec{V}_1| \cdot |\vec{V}_2|}.$$

Statements 220–230: P is the inner product of the vectors, the numerator of the fraction in the formula above. If P = 0, the vectors are perpendicular.

Statements 240–280: The product of the magnitudes of the vectors is computed. If the product (the denominator of the formula above) equals 0, then one of the vectors is 0, and the computer prints statement 270.

Statements 290–340: At statement 290, the computer calculates the cosine (CI) of the angle between the vectors. Statement 300 computes S, the sine of the angle, using the identity $\sin^2 \theta + \cos^2 \theta = 1$. In statement 310, T is the tangent of θ. Statement 320 computes the arctangent (ATN in BASIC) of T, producing the radian measure, X, of the angle between the vectors. Finally, statement 330 converts the radian measure of X to the degree measure before printing the result (statement 340). (This approach is necessary because most versions of BASIC have no arccosine or arcsine functions.)

EXERCISES

A Use the program on page 502 to compute the degree measure of the angle between each pair of vectors.

1. $\vec{A} = i + j + k, \vec{B} = i + j$
2. $\vec{A} = 2i + 3j + 7k, \vec{B} = -3i + 5k$
3. $\vec{A} = 2j - 3k, \vec{B} = i + 4j + 2k$
4. $\vec{A} = 7i + j, \vec{B} = -3i + 2j$

B In Exercises 5–7, revise the program on page 502 in the manner indicated.

5. Combine statements 300–320 into one LET statement.
6. Print both the radian and the degree measures of the angle.
7. Change the given information to the endpoints of the two vectors.

C Write a BASIC program.

8. Given coordinates of two three-dimensional points, print the parametric equations of the line through the points.

9-11 Intersecting Planes and Distance

As you know, the intersection of two planes is either the empty set or a line. Two planes Ω_1 and Ω_2 are parallel if and only if their normals $\vec{N_1}$ and $\vec{N_2}$ are parallel. Since vectors are parallel if and only if

$$\vec{N_1} = t \cdot \vec{N_2}, \; t \text{ a scalar}, \; t \neq 0,$$

and the components of the normals are the coefficients of x, y, and z, two planes

$$Ax + By + Cz + D = 0 \quad \text{and} \quad A_1x + B_1y + C_1z + D_1 = 0$$

are parallel if and only if

$$A_1x + B_1y + C_1z = tAx + tBy + tCz. \tag{1}$$

Further, if $D_1 = tD$, then the planes are identical; otherwise they are distinct.

Two nonparallel planes intersect in a line. If the two planes Ω_1 and Ω_2 have normals $\vec{N_1}$ and $\vec{N_2}$, then $\vec{N_1}$ and $\vec{N_2}$ are each perpendicular to the line of intersection. Since the cross product (a vector) $\vec{N_1} \times \vec{N_2}$ is perpendicular to both $\vec{N_1}$ and $\vec{N_2}$, the direction of the line is given by $\vec{N_1} \times \vec{N_2} = \vec{L_1}$.

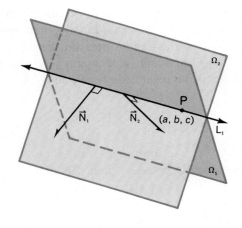

Let $P(a, b, c)$ be a fixed point on the line. Then if $Q(x, y, z)$ is any other point on the line,

$$\vec{PQ} = (x - a)\mathbf{i} + (y - b)\mathbf{j} + (z - c)\mathbf{k} = t(\vec{N_1} \times \vec{N_2}). \tag{2}$$

Equation 2 is the vector equation of the line. Simplifying, you get the parametric equations of the line:

$$x - a = t \begin{vmatrix} B_1 & C_1 \\ B_2 & C_2 \end{vmatrix} \qquad \vec{N_1} = A_1\mathbf{i} + B_1\mathbf{j} + C_1\mathbf{k}$$

$$y - b = t \begin{vmatrix} C_1 & A_1 \\ C_2 & A_2 \end{vmatrix} \qquad \vec{N_2} = A_2\mathbf{i} + B_2\mathbf{j} + C_2\mathbf{k}$$

$$z - c = t \begin{vmatrix} A_1 & B_1 \\ A_2 & B_2 \end{vmatrix}$$

EXAMPLE 1. Find the parametric equations of the line which is the intersection of

$$x + 2y + 3z - 8 = 0$$

and

$$3x - 3y + z + 3 = 0$$

Solution: First find the direction vector for the line.

$$\vec{L} = \vec{N_1} \times \vec{N_2} = \begin{vmatrix} 2 & 3 \\ -3 & 1 \end{vmatrix} \mathbf{i} + \begin{vmatrix} 3 & 1 \\ 1 & 3 \end{vmatrix} \mathbf{j} + \begin{vmatrix} 1 & 2 \\ 3 & -3 \end{vmatrix} \mathbf{k}$$

$$= 11\mathbf{i} + 8\mathbf{j} - 9\mathbf{k}$$

Now you must find a point on the line. Since the line must intersect at least one of the xy, the xz, or the yz planes, you can find one point by setting x, y, or z equal to zero and solving the resulting equations for the other two variables.

Here let $z = 0$, then

$$x + 2y = 8$$
$$3x - 3y = -3$$

so

$$-3x - 6y = -24$$
$$3x - 3y = -3$$

or

$$-9y = -27$$
$$y = 3$$

so

$$x = 2.$$

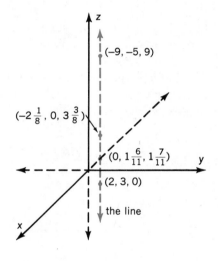

Thus the point $(2, 3, 0)$ is on the line. The parametric equations are the following.

$$x - 2 = 11t$$
$$y - 3 = 8t$$
$$z = -9t$$

Plot two points on the line such as $(2, 3, 0)$ and $(-9, -5, 9)$ (when $t = -1$) and draw the line in question. See the figure. The point $(-2\frac{1}{8}, 0, 3\frac{3}{8})$ is the intersection of the line and the xz plane. The point $(0, 1\frac{6}{11}, 1\frac{7}{11})$ is the intersection of the line and the yz plane.

Vector techniques let you derive an equation for the distance from a point to a plane. It is similar to the equation for the distance from a point to a line.

> **Theorem 9–17** Let $Ax + By + Cz + D = 0$ be a plane and $P(a, b, c)$ a point. The distance d from the point to the plane is given by
>
> $$d = \frac{|\, Aa + Bb + Cc + D\, |}{\sqrt{A^2 + B^2 + C^2}}$$
>
> 3

Proof: If $A \neq 0$, then the point $R\left(\frac{-D}{A}, 0, 0\right)$ is on the plane. $\Bigl($If $A = 0$, choose the point $\left(0, \frac{-D}{B}, 0\right)$ or $\left(0, 0, \frac{-D}{C}\right)$ instead.$\Bigr)$ Let Q be the point in the plane such that $\overrightarrow{QP}$ is perpendicular to the plane. Notice that $d = |\, \overrightarrow{QP}\, |$.

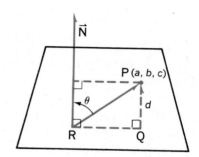

Let θ be the measure of the acute angle between the normal $\vec{N}$ to the plane and the vector $\overrightarrow{RP}$.

Then

$$d = |\, \overrightarrow{QP}\, | = |\, \overrightarrow{RP}\, | \cos \theta \quad \text{(Why?)}$$

But

$$\cos \theta = \frac{\vec{N} \cdot \overrightarrow{RP}}{|\, \vec{N}\, | \cdot |\, \overrightarrow{RP}\, |} \quad \text{(inner product)}$$

or

$$|\, \overrightarrow{RP}\, | \cos \theta = \frac{\vec{N} \cdot \overrightarrow{RP}}{|\, \vec{N}\, |}. \qquad 4$$

Now

$$\vec{N} = A\mathbf{i} + B\mathbf{j} + C\mathbf{k}$$

and

$$\overrightarrow{RP} = \left(a + \frac{D}{A}\right)\mathbf{i} + b\mathbf{j} + c\mathbf{k}.$$

Substituting these in equation 4, you find

$$d = |\, \overrightarrow{RP}\, | \cos \theta = \frac{(A\mathbf{i} + B\mathbf{j} + C\mathbf{k}) \cdot \left[\left(a + \frac{D}{A}\right)\mathbf{i} + b\mathbf{j} + c\mathbf{k}\right]}{\sqrt{A^2 + B^2 + C^2}}$$

$$= \frac{A\left(a + \frac{D}{A}\right) + Bb + Cc}{\sqrt{A^2 + B^2 + C^2}}$$

$$= \frac{Aa + Bb + Cc + D}{\sqrt{A^2 + B^2 + C^2}}$$

Since $Aa + Bb + Cc + D$ could be negative, the absolute value is used to ensure that d is positive.

Thus
$$d = \frac{|Aa + Bb + Cc + D|}{\sqrt{A^2 + B^2 + C^2}}$$

EXAMPLE 2. Find the distance from $(1, 3, -2)$ to the plane $x - 2y + 3z + 7 = 0$.

Solution:
$$d = \frac{|Aa + Bb + Cc + D|}{\sqrt{A^2 + B^2 + C^2}}$$

Thus

$$d = \frac{|1 \cdot 1 - 2 \cdot 3 + 3(-2) + 7|}{\sqrt{1 + 4 + 9}}$$

$$= \frac{|-4|}{\sqrt{14}} = \frac{4}{\sqrt{14}}$$

WRITTEN EXERCISES

A ━━ Find the parametric equations of the line that is the intersection of the given planes (if such a line exists). Graph each line.

1. $2x - 3y + 4z + 1 = 0$
   $x + y - z - 2 = 0$

2. $-3x + 2y + 4z - 5 = 0$
   $5x - y + 3z + 6 = 0$

3. $5x + 7y - 2z - 3 = 0$
   $x - y - z = 0$

4. $3x + y + 4z + 2 = 0$
   $x + 3y - z + 3 = 0$

5. $4x + 2y - z - 4 = 0$
   $x - y + 2z - 1 = 0$

6. $x - 2y - 3z - 4 = 0$
   $3x + y + z + 1 = 0$

7. $4x - 2y + z - 3 = 0$
   $-8x + 4y - 2z + 6 = 0$

8. $-x - 3y + z - 4 = 0$
   $2x + 6y - 2y - 4 = 0$

9. $4x - 3y + z + 2 = 0$
   $4x - 3y + 2z + 1 = 0$

10. $x + y + z - 7 = 0$
    $x + 2y + z - 9 = 0$

━━ Find the distance from the given point to the given plane.

11. $2x - y + 2z + 3 = 0$, $(1, 1, 3)$

12. $6x + 2y - 3z + 5 = 0$, $(4, -2, 1)$

13. $4x - 2y + 2z - 3 = 0$, $(-1, 2, 1)$

14. $4x - 5y - 3z - 1 = 0$, $(3, 2, -1)$

15. $3x - y - z + 6 = 0$, $(1, 3, -4)$

16. $4x - 2y + 7z - 16 = 0$, $(0, 0, 0)$

17. What formula gives the distance from the origin to the plane $Ax + By + Cz + D = 0$?

B **18.** Find the distance between the parallel planes $4x - 2y + 3z - 4 = 0$ and $4x - 2y + 3z + 16 = 0$. How do you know the planes are parallel?

C **19. a.** Let $\vec{K}$ be the direction vector of a line l. Let $P(a, b, c)$ be a point in space not on l. Let d be the distance from P to l. If R is a point on l, show that $d = |\overrightarrow{RP}| \sin \theta$.

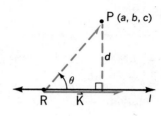

b. What is $|\overrightarrow{RP} \times \vec{K}|$ in terms of $|\overrightarrow{RP}|$, $|\vec{K}|$, and $\sin \theta$?

c. Use your results of **a** and **b** to find a vector formula for d.

20. Use the results of Exercise 19 to find the distance from $P(1, 3, 2)$ and the line of

a. Exercise 1. **b.** Exercise 2. **c.** Exercise 3. **d.** Exercise 4.

CHAPTER SUMMARY

Important Terms

Angle between two lines (p. 484)
Base (basis) (p. 453)
Components (p. 453)
Cross product (p. 493)
Direction angles (p. 459)
Direction cosines (p. 459)
Direction numbers (p. 459)
Direction numbers of the
  line (p. 469)
Direction vector (p. 460)
Inner (dot) product (p. 482)
Normal to a line (p. 484)
Normal vector (p. 484)

Parametric equations (p. 469)
Point-slope equation (p. 474)
Polygon rule (p. 446)
Position vector (p. 456)
Scalar (p. 447)
Slope of a line (two-space)
  (p. 474)
Standard equations (p. 468)
Trace (p. 499)
Two-space (p. 456)
Unit normal (p. 484)
Vectors (p. 444)
Zero vector (p. 447)

Important Ideas

1. Every vector is a linear combination of basis vectors.

2. If $l\mathbf{i} + m\mathbf{j} + n\mathbf{k}$ is a direction vector for a line, the standard equations are

$$\frac{x - a}{l} = \frac{y - b}{m} = \frac{z - c}{n} \text{ where } l, m, n \neq 0$$

3. Any line in the *xy* plane is described by an equation of the first degree. The converse of this is also true.

4. If $\vec{A} = (a_1, a_2, a_3)$ and $\vec{B} = (b_1, b_2, b_3)$ and θ is the angle between $\vec{A}$ and $\vec{B}$, then

$$\cos \theta = \frac{\vec{A} \cdot \vec{B}}{|\vec{A}| \, |\vec{B}|}$$

5. Two vectors are perpendicular if and only if the dot product is zero.

6. The distance, *d*, from $P(a, b)$ to $Ax + By + C = 0$ is

$$d = \frac{|Aa + Bb + C|}{\sqrt{A^2 + B^2}}$$

7. If $a\mathbf{i} + b\mathbf{j} + c\mathbf{k}$ is normal to a plane, the equation of the plane is $ax + by + cz + D = 0$.

CHAPTER OBJECTIVES AND REVIEW

Objective: *To explain and illustrate the concept of vector and the definition of equality of vectors.* (Section 9-1)

1. What are the essential characteristics of a vector? Illustrate these characteristics geometrically.

2. How do you determine whether or not two vectors $\vec{A}$ and $\vec{B}$ are equal? Illustrate geometrically.

━━ In each diagram below which vectors appear equal? Explain.

3.

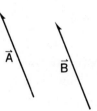

4.

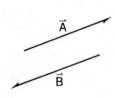

5.

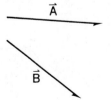

6.

Objective: *To illustrate scalar multiplication of a vector, addition of vectors, and subtraction of vectors.* (Section 9-1)

7. Copy $\vec{A}$ and $\vec{B}$ on your paper.
Make a diagram showing

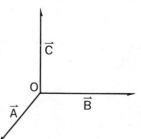

    a. $3\vec{A}$ **b.** $-2\vec{B}$
    c. $\vec{A} + \vec{B}$ **d.** $2\vec{B} + \vec{A}$
    e. $\vec{B} - \vec{A}$ **f.** $\vec{A} - \vec{B}$
    g. $2\vec{A} - \vec{B}$ **h.** $\frac{2}{3}\vec{A} + \frac{4}{3}\vec{B}$
    i. $\frac{4}{5}\vec{A} + \frac{2}{5}\vec{B}$ **j.** $\frac{4}{5}\vec{A} - \frac{2}{5}\vec{B}$

■■■ Draw a diagram showing each of the following relationships.

8. $\vec{A} + \vec{B} = \vec{B} + \vec{A}$ (Commutative property)
9. $\vec{A} + (-\vec{B}) = \vec{A} - \vec{B}$

Objective: *To write a vector as a linear combination of basis vectors.* (Section 9-2)

■■■ Use a ruler to approximate the values of the scalars m and n when $\vec{C} = m\vec{A} + n\vec{B}$

10.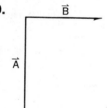

11.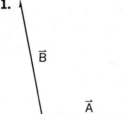

■■■ In Exercises 12–17, copy the mutually perpendicular basis vectors $\vec{A}$, $\vec{B}$, and $\vec{C}$. Then use these basis vectors to draw each vector $\vec{D}$.

12. $\vec{D} = 0\vec{A} + \vec{B} + \vec{C}$
13. $\vec{D} = \vec{A} + \vec{B} + 0\vec{C}$
14. $\vec{D} = \vec{A} + 2\vec{B} + \vec{C}$
15. $\vec{D} = -\vec{A} + \frac{1}{2}\vec{B} + 2\vec{C}$
16. $\vec{D}$ has components $(\frac{1}{2}, 2, 1)$.
17. $\vec{D}$ has components $(0, 2, -1)$.

Objective: *To use unit perpendicular basis vectors to represent the position of a vector and to find the magnitude of a vector.* (Section 9-3)

━━ In Exercises 18–23, find the length of the given position vector $\vec{r}$, and the measure θ of the angle that it makes with the unit vector **i**. (Express θ to the nearest ten minutes.)

18. $\vec{r} = \mathbf{i} + \mathbf{j}$

19. $\vec{r} = \mathbf{i} - \mathbf{j}$

20. $\vec{r} = 3\mathbf{i} + 2\mathbf{j}$

21. $\vec{r} = 3\mathbf{i} - 2\mathbf{j}$

22. $\vec{r} = (5, 12)$

23. $\overrightarrow{OP} = (1, \sqrt{3})$

━━ In Exercises 24–25, find each vector $\overrightarrow{PQ}$ and its length $|\overrightarrow{PQ}|$. Leave answers in radical form.

24. $P = (0, 3); \quad Q = (-2, 1)$

25. $P = (1, 0, 1); \quad Q = (4, -2, 0)$

26. Find the direction cosines of the vectors of Exercises 24 and 25.

Objective: *To find the midpoint of a vector.* (Section 9-4)

━━ In Exercises 27–30, find the coordinates of the midpoint of $\overrightarrow{PQ}$.

27. $P(0, 0); Q(6, -8)$

28. $P(1, 0, 4); Q(-3, 4, 2)$

29. $P(3, 1); Q(-1, 5)$

30. $P(3, -1, 2); Q(2, -2, 3)$

Objective: *To find the equations of a line in two-space or three-space.* (Section 9-5 and Section 9-6)

━━ Find the parametric equations and standard equations of each line that contains the given points, has the given slope, or has the given direction vector.

31. $A(2, 3, 1); B(0, 4, 1)$

32. $A(-1, 0);$ Slope: 5.

33. $A(4, 4, 4); B(3, -1, 2)$

34. $A(-3, 1);$ Direction vector: $2\mathbf{i} + \mathbf{j}$.

35. $A(3, -2);$ Slope: $-\frac{1}{2}$.

36. $A(0, 0);$ Direction vector: $\mathbf{i} - 2\mathbf{j}$.

Objective: *To define the inner product of two vectors and to use it to find the nonobtuse angle between two lines.* (Section 9-7)

━━ Suppose that

$$\vec{A} = a_1\mathbf{i} + b_1\mathbf{j} + c_1\mathbf{k} \text{ and } \vec{B} = a_2\mathbf{i} + b_2\mathbf{j} + c_2\mathbf{k}$$

are two vectors.

37. What is $\vec{A} \cdot \vec{B}$?

38. Suppose that θ is the measure of the nonobtuse angle between $\overrightarrow{A}$ and $\overrightarrow{B}$. Find $\cos \theta$.

━━━ Find the cosine of the nonobtuse angle between each pair of vectors.

39. $\overrightarrow{A} = \mathbf{i} - \mathbf{j}$
$\quad\; \overrightarrow{B} = \mathbf{i}$

40. $\overrightarrow{A} = 3\mathbf{j} + 2\mathbf{k}$
$\quad\;\; \overrightarrow{B} = \mathbf{j} - \mathbf{k}$

41. $\overrightarrow{A} = \mathbf{i} - \mathbf{j} + \mathbf{k}$
$\quad\; \overrightarrow{B} = \mathbf{i} + 2\mathbf{j} - \mathbf{k}$

42. $\overrightarrow{A} = 2\mathbf{i} + \mathbf{j} - \mathbf{k}$
$\quad\;\; \overrightarrow{B} = \mathbf{i} + \mathbf{j} - 2\mathbf{k}$

43. Find a vector that is normal to each vector in Exercises 39–42.

44. Find a unit normal vector for each vector in Exercises 39–40.

Objective: *To find equations of lines that are parallel to or perpendicular to a given line.* (Section 9-8)

━━━ In each exercise an equation of a line is given. Find an equation of a line that is parallel to the given line and an equation of a line that is perpendicular to the given line. Choose the parallel or perpendicular line so that it includes the given point A.

45. $2x - 3y + 5 = 0; \quad A(2, 1)$

46. $\dfrac{x - 4}{2} = \dfrac{y + 3}{1}; \quad A(5, -2)$

Objective: *To find the distance between a given point and a given line.* (Section 9-8)

━━━ Find the distance between the given point and the given line in Exercises 47–48.

47. $2x - 3y + 5 = 0; \quad A(2, 1)$

48. $\dfrac{x - 4}{2} = \dfrac{y + 3}{1}; \quad A(5, -2)$

Objective: *To find the cross product of two vectors and the length of the vector that is the cross product.* (Section 9-9)

━━━ Find each cross product $\overrightarrow{A} \times \overrightarrow{B}$.

49. $\overrightarrow{A} = 3\mathbf{i} + 2\mathbf{j} - \mathbf{k}; \quad \overrightarrow{B} = -\mathbf{i} + \mathbf{j} + \mathbf{k}$

50. $\overrightarrow{A} = \mathbf{i} + \mathbf{j} + \mathbf{k}; \quad \overrightarrow{B} = 2\mathbf{j} - \mathbf{k}$

51. $\overrightarrow{A} = -2\mathbf{i} - 3\mathbf{j} + \mathbf{k}; \quad \overrightarrow{B} = \mathbf{i} + \mathbf{j} - 4\mathbf{k}$

52. Find the length of the vector $\overrightarrow{A} \times \overrightarrow{B}$ in Exercise 49.

53. Let θ be the measure of the angle between $\overrightarrow{A}$ and $\overrightarrow{B}$ in Exercise 49. Find $\sin \theta$.

Objective: *To find the equation of a plane.* (Section 9-10)

■ In Exercises 54–56, write the equation of the plane that satisfies the given conditions.

54. $\vec{N} = 2\mathbf{i} - 3\mathbf{j} - 2\mathbf{k}$ is a normal to the plane. The plane contains the point (0, 2, 3).

55. The plane is parallel to the plane with equation $7x - 2y + 3z + 4 = 0$ and contains the point (1, 1, 1).

56. The plane contains the points (1, 1, 1), (2, −3, 1) and (−4, 3, 0).

57. $\vec{N}$ is a vector that is normal to the plane $Ax + By + Cz + D = 0$. Find the components of $\vec{N}$.

58. Sketch the graph of the plane in Exercise 54 using its traces.

Objective: *To find the equation of the line of intersection of two planes and to find the distance from a point to a plane.* (Section 9-11)

■ Find the parametric equations of the line that is the intersection of the given planes.

59. $3x - 2y - 4z + 2 = 0$
 $x + y + z - 3 = 0$

60. $x - y - z + 4 = 0$
 $x + y + z - 2 = 0$

■ Find the distance from the given point to the given plane.

61. $x - 2y + z - 1 = 0$; $(2, -1, 4)$

CHAPTER TEST

■ Use the vectors $\vec{A}, \vec{B}, \vec{C}, \vec{D}$, and $\vec{E}$ for Exercises 1–7. Copy these vectors on your paper.

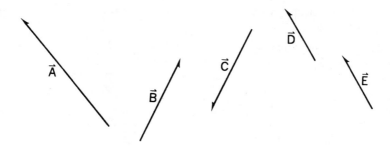

1. Which pair(s) of vectors are equal? What test would you use to prove their equality?

2. Which pair(s) of vectors have the same magnitude?

3. Which pair(s) of vectors are parallel?

4. Find $\vec{A} + \vec{B}$ and $\vec{B} - \vec{E}$.

5. With a protractor measure the angle between $\vec{D}$ and $\vec{C}$.

6. Draw the vector $3\vec{D}$.

7. Estimate the values of m and n such that $\vec{A} = m\vec{C} + n\vec{D}$.

8. Sketch the usual basis vectors for a two-space and those for three-space. Describe each set.

9. Find $\vec{PQ}$ in terms of i, j, and k.
   a. $P(2, -5)$, $Q(-1, 3)$
   b. $P(1, 5, -2)$, $Q(0, -3, 1)$

10. Calculate the length of the vector
$$\vec{A} = 2i - 2j - k.$$

11. Find the standard equations and the parametric equations of the line containing
   a. $A(2, 1)$, $B(-3, 7)$.
   b. $A(1, -3, 5)$, $B(2, 5, -3)$.

12. Given
$$\vec{A} = 2i - 6j + 1k \quad \text{and} \quad \vec{B} = -3i - j + 5k,$$
calculate $\vec{A} \cdot \vec{B}$.

13. What is the angle between $\vec{A}$ and $\vec{B}$ in Exercise 12?

14. a. Find a vector $\vec{N}$ which is normal to
$$\vec{A} = 2i - 6j + 1k \quad \text{and} \quad \vec{B} = -3i - j + 5k.$$

   b. What is another name for $\vec{N}$?

15. Let $\vec{N} = 5i + 7j - k$ be a normal to a plane which contains $P(2, -3, 1)$. What is the equation of the plane?

16. Find the equation of the plane which contains $P(1, 2, -3)$ and is parallel to $\vec{A} = 2i - k$.

17. Find the parametric equations of the line that is the intersection of the planes whose equations appear below.

$$x + y - z = 0$$
$$4x - 2y + z = 0$$

CHAPTER **10** # Matrices, Vectors, and Linear Transformations

Sections

Features

Applying Network Theory: Civil Engineering

Computer Application: Solving Linear Systems

Review and Testing

Mid-Chapter Review

Chapter Summary

Chapter Objectives and Review

Chapter Test

Cumulative Review: Chapters 9–10

10-1 Matrices and Addition

Each of the four arrays of numbers shown below is a **matrix.** Notice that each is a set of numbers arranged in rows and columns and enclosed by a pair of brackets.

$$\begin{bmatrix} 1 & \sqrt{2} \\ 5 & 1 \end{bmatrix} \quad \begin{bmatrix} 3 \\ 0.4 \end{bmatrix} \quad [1 \quad 2i \quad 3] \quad \begin{bmatrix} -2 & -1 & -4 & \sqrt[3]{5} \\ \pi & 3i & 2 & 4-2i \\ 0 & \sqrt{2} & e & 0 \end{bmatrix}$$

> **Definition**   A **matrix** is a rectangular array of numbers arranged into rows and columns. A matrix is written as follows:
>
> $$\begin{bmatrix} a_{11} & a_{12} & \cdots & a_{1n} \\ a_{21} & a_{22} & \cdots & a_{2n} \\ \vdots & \vdots & \vdots & \vdots \\ a_{m1} & a_{m2} & \cdots & a_{mn} \end{bmatrix}$$

This matrix has *m rows* and *n columns.* The numbers *m* and *n* are the *dimensions* of the matrix; it is an *m by n* or $m \times n$ matrix. The numbers a_{ij} $(i = 1, \cdots, m; j = 1, \cdots, n)$ are *entries* of the matrix. The entry a_{ij} is in the *i*th row and *j*th column of the matrix.

EXAMPLE 1.

$$\text{Let } C = \begin{bmatrix} 17 & -2 & 3 \\ 0 & -1 & \sqrt{5} \\ 6 & 1 & -7i \\ 5 & -4 & 2 \end{bmatrix}$$

a. Find the dimensions of *C*.   **b.** Identify the entries c_{32}, c_{21} and c_{13}.

Solutions: **a.**   *C* is a 4 by 3 matrix ⟵ **4 rows**
                                                          3 columns

   b. $C_{32} = 1, C_{21} = 0, C_{13} = 3$

> **Definition**   Matrices *A* and *B* are **equal** if and only if
> **a.** the dimensions of *A* equal the dimensions of *B*
> **b.** for all *i* and *j*, $a_{ij} = b_{ij}$.

$$\text{If } A = \begin{bmatrix} 1 & -3 \\ -2 & 5 \end{bmatrix} \text{ and } B = \begin{bmatrix} \frac{2}{2} & (5-8) \\ \frac{4}{-2} & (1+4) \end{bmatrix}, \text{ then } A = B.$$

Matrices with the same dimensions may be added.

Definition   The **sum** C of a matrix A with dimensions $m \times n$ and a matrix B with the same dimensions is an $m \times n$ matrix whose entries are given by the following.

$$c_{ij} = a_{ij} + b_{ij} \qquad i \in \{1, 2, \cdots, m\} \quad j \in \{1, 2, \cdots, n\}$$

EXAMPLE 2.   Let $A = \begin{bmatrix} 1 & 2 & 4 \\ -2 & -5 & 0 \end{bmatrix}$ and $B = \begin{bmatrix} -2 & 1 & -3 \\ 1 & 4 & -5 \end{bmatrix}$

Find $A + B$.

Solution:
$$A + B = \begin{bmatrix} 1 & 2 & 4 \\ -2 & -5 & 0 \end{bmatrix} + \begin{bmatrix} -2 & 1 & -3 \\ 1 & 4 & -5 \end{bmatrix}$$

$$= \begin{bmatrix} (1 + (-2)) & (2 + 1) & (4 + (-3)) \\ (-2 + 1) & (-5 + 4) & (0 + (-5)) \end{bmatrix}$$

$$= \begin{bmatrix} -1 & 3 & 1 \\ -1 & -1 & -5 \end{bmatrix}$$

Definition   If A is an $m \times n$ matrix and k is a real number, the **scalar product** of k and A (kA) is the $m \times n$ matrix with entries ka_{ij} for all i and j.

EXAMPLE 3.   Let $A = \begin{bmatrix} 1 & 2 \\ 3 & 4 \end{bmatrix}$. Find $3A$, $-\frac{1}{2}A$ and kA.

Solution:
$$3A = \begin{bmatrix} 3 \cdot 1 & 3 \cdot 2 \\ 3 \cdot 3 & 3 \cdot 4 \end{bmatrix} = \begin{bmatrix} 3 & 6 \\ 9 & 12 \end{bmatrix}$$

$$-\tfrac{1}{2}A = \begin{bmatrix} -\frac{1}{2} \cdot 1 & -\frac{1}{2} \cdot 2 \\ -\frac{1}{2} \cdot 3 & -\frac{1}{2} \cdot 4 \end{bmatrix} = \begin{bmatrix} -\frac{1}{2} & -1 \\ -\frac{3}{2} & -2 \end{bmatrix}$$

$$kA = \begin{bmatrix} k \cdot 1 & k \cdot 2 \\ k \cdot 3 & k \cdot 4 \end{bmatrix} = \begin{bmatrix} k & 2k \\ 3k & 4k \end{bmatrix}$$

Square matrices have the same number of rows and columns. This number is the **order** of the matrix.

Let M_2 be the set of all two-by-two matrices (matrices of order 2).

Then $A = \begin{bmatrix} 1 & 3 \\ 2 & 1 \end{bmatrix}$, $B = \begin{bmatrix} 0 & 1 \\ 0 & 1 \end{bmatrix}$ and $C = \begin{bmatrix} 5 & 0 \\ 1 & 5 \end{bmatrix}$ are members of M_2.

The system of M_2 with the operation $+$ has many familiar properties. These are summarized in the following theorems.

Theorem 10–1 (Addition is Commutative and Associative)
If A, B, C are in M_2, then

    i. $A + B = B + A$

    ii. $A + (B + C) = (A + B) + C$.

You can see that $O = \begin{bmatrix} 0 & 0 \\ 0 & 0 \end{bmatrix}$ has the property that for all matrices A in M_2, $A + O = O + A = A$. O is the only member of M_2 with this property. It is the *additive identity* in the set M_2. Theorem 10–2 follows.

Theorem 10–2 There is a unique member O of M_2, called the **zero matrix,** with the property that for all A in M_2,

$$O + A = A + O = A.$$

If you add $A = \begin{bmatrix} -2 & 1 \\ -5 & -3 \end{bmatrix}$ to $B = \begin{bmatrix} 2 & -1 \\ 5 & 3 \end{bmatrix}$, the sum is the zero matrix. Thus B is an *additive inverse* (or **opposite**) of A.

Definition The matrix $-A$ is the **opposite** of A. That is, $-A$ has the property that $A + (-A) = (-A) + A = O$.

In a system in which the associative property holds, if there is an opposite for an element, then that opposite is unique. It is also easy to show that $(-1)A$ is an opposite of A.

Theorem 10–3 For each A in M_2 there is a unique member $-A$ of M_2 with the property that $A + (-A) = (-A) + A = O$. Furthermore, $-A = (-1)A$. Thus $(-1)A$ is the unique opposite of A.

You can now define subtraction of matrices in M_2. A similar definition can be stated for other sets of matrices on which addition is defined.

> **Definition** For A and B in M_2, the **difference** $A - B$ is defined by $A - B = A + (-B)$.

Clearly
$$A - B = \begin{bmatrix} a_{11} - b_{11} & a_{12} - b_{12} \\ a_{21} - b_{21} & a_{22} - b_{22} \end{bmatrix}$$

The next theorem is an easy consequence of the definitions given in Section 10–1 and the properties of real numbers.

> **Theorem 10–4** For any A, B in M_2 and p, q in R,
>
> i. $1A = A$
>
> ii. $p(qA) = pq(A)$
>
> iii. $(p + q)A = pA + qA$
>
> iv. $p(A + B) = pA + pB$

The theorems and definitions given for 2×2 matrices are true for any set of matrices with specified dimensions. Thus, Theorems 10–1 through 10–4 are true for A_{mn} where A_{mn} is the set of all $m \times n$ matrices with real entries.

CLASSROOM EXERCISES

Assume that A, B, C are $m \times n$ matrices and that a_{ij}, b_{ij}, c_{ij} are respectively the elements in row i and column j, for each i and each j. Answer the following:

1. What element is in the ith row and jth column of $A + B$?

2. What element is in the ith row and jth column of $B + A$?

3. What element is in the ith row and jth column of the sum $(A + B) + C$?

WRITTEN EXERCISES

A Use the following matrices in Exercises 1–8.

$$A = \begin{bmatrix} 2 & -5 & 1 \\ 3 & 1 & -7 \end{bmatrix} \quad B = \begin{bmatrix} -12 & 4 & 6 \\ 8 & -2 & -4 \end{bmatrix} \quad C = \begin{bmatrix} 6 & -2 & -3 \\ -4 & 1 & 2 \end{bmatrix}$$

Find each of the following.

1. $A + B$

2. $A + C$

3. $B + C$

4. $(A + B) + C$

5. $A + -2B$

6. $A + \frac{1}{2}B$

7. $B + 2C$

8. $(2A + -3B) + -6C$

9. How would you define subtraction of matrices?

A — Let $A = \begin{bmatrix} a_{11} & a_{12} \\ a_{21} & a_{22} \end{bmatrix}$, $B = \begin{bmatrix} b_{11} & b_{12} \\ b_{21} & b_{22} \end{bmatrix}$ and $C = \begin{bmatrix} c_{11} & c_{12} \\ c_{21} & c_{22} \end{bmatrix}$

Prove:

10. Theorem 10–1, part **ii.**   **11.** Theorem 10–3.

12. Theorem 10–4, part **i.**   **13.** Theorem 10–4, part **ii.**

14. Theorem 10–4, part **iii.**   **15.** Theorem 10–4, part **iv.**

Let $A = \begin{bmatrix} 1 & -3 \\ -2 & 1 \end{bmatrix}$ $B = \begin{bmatrix} 0 & 1 \\ -4 & 2 \end{bmatrix}$ $C = \begin{bmatrix} -3 & 2 \\ 2 & 1 \end{bmatrix}$. Find each of the following:

16. $-A$ **17.** $-B + 2C$

18. $(4 + 3)A$ **19.** $-3(2B)$

20. $5(B + C)$ **21.** $(4 + 2)(A - B)$

22. $-4(A + B - C)$ **23.** $2(3A - 4C)$

24. X if $A + 2X = C$ **25.** Y if $B - 3Y = A + 2C$

B **26.** Solve the matrix equation

$$\begin{bmatrix} 2 & 1 & 5 \\ 3 & 4 & 1 \end{bmatrix} = C + \begin{bmatrix} 1 & 2 & -3 \\ 2 & 1 & 4 \end{bmatrix}$$

for the 2×3 matrix C.

27. Given

$$\vec{A} = 2\mathbf{i} + 3\mathbf{j} - 2\mathbf{k},$$

how might you represent $\vec{A}$ as a matrix? (There are two ways.)

Definition   A **mathematical system,** denoted $\langle S; \circ \rangle$, is a set S and one or more operations $\circ$, defined on the set S. For example if W is the set of whole numbers, then $\langle W; + \rangle$ is a mathematical system.

Tell for which of the following systems **a.** the associative property holds, **b.** the commutative property holds, **c.** there is an identity element, **d.** there is an inverse element for each element a.

28. $\langle R; + \rangle$ **29.** $\langle Q; + \rangle$

30. $\langle N; + \rangle$ **31.** $\langle W; + \rangle$

32. $\langle M_2; + \rangle$ **33.** $\langle D; \times \rangle$ D $= \{i, -i, 1, -1\}$

C 34. Prove that if h is an identity element of S under the operation $\circ$ in a mathematical system $\langle S; \circ \rangle$, then h is unique. (*Hint:* Suppose h_1 and h_2 were identity elements. Show that $h_1 = h_2$.)

35. Use the results of Exercise 34 to show that $O = \begin{bmatrix} 0 & 0 \\ 0 & 0 \end{bmatrix}$ is unique in $\langle M_2; + \rangle$.

10–2 Multiplication of Two Matrices

There are many ways to define the product of two matrices in M_2. Experience has shown that the way which is most useful is what is often called *row-by-column* multiplication.

Definition (Multiplication of Matrices) Let $A = \begin{bmatrix} a_{11} & a_{12} \\ a_{21} & a_{22} \end{bmatrix}$ and $B = \begin{bmatrix} b_{11} & b_{12} \\ b_{21} & b_{22} \end{bmatrix}$ be two matrices in M_2. The product C of A and B is the matrix defined by

$$C = AB = \begin{bmatrix} a_{11} & a_{12} \\ a_{21} & a_{22} \end{bmatrix} \begin{bmatrix} b_{11} & b_{12} \\ b_{21} & b_{22} \end{bmatrix} = \begin{bmatrix} (a_{11}b_{11} + a_{12}b_{21}) & (a_{11}b_{12} + a_{12}b_{22}) \\ (a_{21}b_{11} + a_{22}b_{21}) & (a_{21}b_{12} + a_{22}b_{22}) \end{bmatrix}.$$

Notice that if the *rows* of A are thought of as components of vectors and the *columns* of B are also thought of as components of vectors, then the entries in the product matrix can be thought of as *inner products* of vectors.

EXAMPLE 1. Find the product of $A = \begin{bmatrix} 1 & -2 \\ -3 & 1 \end{bmatrix}$ and $B = \begin{bmatrix} 2 & -3 \\ 1 & 4 \end{bmatrix}$.

Solution:
$$AB = \begin{bmatrix} 1 & -2 \\ -3 & 1 \end{bmatrix} \begin{bmatrix} 2 & -3 \\ 1 & 4 \end{bmatrix}$$

row 1 $\times$ column 1 $= (1)(2) + (-2)(1) = 2 + -2 = 0 = c_{11}$
row 1 $\times$ column 2 $= (1)(-3) + (-2)(4) = -3 - 8 = -11 = c_{12}$
row 2 $\times$ column 1 $= (-3)(2) + (1)(1) = -6 + 1 = -5 = c_{21}$
row 2 $\times$ column 2 $= (-3)(-3) + (1)(4) = 9 + 4 = 13 = c_{22}$

Thus

$$AB = \begin{bmatrix} 0 & -11 \\ -5 & 13 \end{bmatrix}.$$

Example 1 illustrates the fact that the entry in the ith row and jth column of the product matrix is the *inner product* of the ith row and jth column of the factor matrices. The product of two matrices in M_2 is thus always a matrix in M_2.

EXAMPLE 2. Find AB and BA when $A = \begin{bmatrix} 2 & 1 \\ 4 & 3 \end{bmatrix}$ and $B = \begin{bmatrix} 5 & 1 \\ -3 & 2 \end{bmatrix}$.

Solution:
$$AB = \begin{bmatrix} 2 & 1 \\ 4 & 3 \end{bmatrix}\begin{bmatrix} 5 & 1 \\ -3 & 2 \end{bmatrix} = \begin{bmatrix} 7 & 4 \\ 11 & 10 \end{bmatrix}$$

$$BA = \begin{bmatrix} 5 & 1 \\ -3 & 2 \end{bmatrix}\begin{bmatrix} 2 & 1 \\ 4 & 3 \end{bmatrix} = \begin{bmatrix} 14 & 8 \\ 2 & 3 \end{bmatrix}$$

Notice that $\quad\quad\quad\quad A \cdot B \neq B \cdot A.$

Thus multiplication of matrices in M_2 is *not commutative*.

Even though multiplication of matrices in M_2 is not commutative several other properties which hold for matrices under addition hold for multiplication of matrices.

The next theorem is a direct consequence of the definition of multiplication. The proof is straightforward but somewhat intricate. It is left for you to do in the exercises.

Theorem 10–5 (Associativity of Multiplication) If A, B and C are matrices in M_2, then

$$A(BC) = (AB)C.$$

An important matrix is the **unit matrix** I defined as follows.

$$I = \begin{bmatrix} 1 & 0 \\ 0 & 1 \end{bmatrix}$$

If

$$A = \begin{bmatrix} a_{11} & a_{12} \\ a_{21} & a_{22} \end{bmatrix}$$

then,

$$AI = \begin{bmatrix} a_{11} & a_{12} \\ a_{21} & a_{22} \end{bmatrix}\begin{bmatrix} 1 & 0 \\ 0 & 1 \end{bmatrix} = \begin{bmatrix} a_{11} & a_{12} \\ a_{21} & a_{22} \end{bmatrix} = A \quad \text{and}$$

$$IA = \begin{bmatrix} 1 & 0 \\ 0 & 1 \end{bmatrix}\begin{bmatrix} a_{11} & a_{12} \\ a_{21} & a_{22} \end{bmatrix} = \begin{bmatrix} a_{11} & a_{12} \\ a_{21} & a_{22} \end{bmatrix} = A.$$

Thus I is a unit matrix or a *multiplicative identity* for the set of matrices M_2. From Exercise 34 Section 10–1, it follows that I is unique. Thus you have proved the following theorem.

Theorem 10-6   There is a unique element $I = \begin{bmatrix} 1 & 0 \\ 0 & 1 \end{bmatrix}$ of M_2 with the property that for any A in M_2

$$IA = AI = A.$$

Using the definition of the product of a real number and a matrix, you can easily prove the next theorem. The proof is left for you.

Theorem 10-7   If k is in R and A and B are in M_2, then

$$A(kB) = (kA)B = k(AB).$$

EXAMPLE 3.   Compute $\begin{bmatrix} 2 & 8 \\ 4 & 2 \end{bmatrix} \left(\frac{1}{2} \begin{bmatrix} 3 & 1 \\ -2 & 1 \end{bmatrix} \right)$.

Solution: Theorem 10-7 allows you to compute as follows.

$$\frac{1}{2} \left(\begin{bmatrix} 2 & 8 \\ 4 & 2 \end{bmatrix} \begin{bmatrix} 3 & 1 \\ -2 & 1 \end{bmatrix} \right) = \frac{1}{2} \begin{bmatrix} -10 & 10 \\ 8 & 6 \end{bmatrix} = \begin{bmatrix} -5 & 5 \\ 4 & 3 \end{bmatrix}$$

CLASSROOM EXERCISES

▬ Multiply.

1. $\begin{bmatrix} 2 & 1 \\ -3 & 4 \end{bmatrix} \begin{bmatrix} 0 & 5 \\ 2 & 4 \end{bmatrix}$

2. $\begin{bmatrix} 0 & 1 \\ 1 & 0 \end{bmatrix} \begin{bmatrix} 5 & 1 \\ -9 & 7 \end{bmatrix}$

3. $\begin{bmatrix} 5 & -2 \\ 1 & -3 \end{bmatrix} \begin{bmatrix} 1 & 0 \\ 0 & 1 \end{bmatrix}$

4. $\left(\begin{bmatrix} 2 & -3 \\ 1 & 5 \end{bmatrix} \begin{bmatrix} 1 & 1 \\ 2 & 1 \end{bmatrix} \right) \begin{bmatrix} 2 & -3 \\ 3 & -2 \end{bmatrix}$

WRITTEN EXERCISES

A ▬ In each exercise find AB, BA, $A(2B)$, and $(2A)(3B)$.

1. $A = \begin{bmatrix} 1 & -1 \\ 0 & 1 \end{bmatrix}$ $B = \begin{bmatrix} 2 & 1 \\ 1 & 2 \end{bmatrix}$

2. $A = \begin{bmatrix} 0 & -1 \\ 1 & 0 \end{bmatrix}$ $B = \begin{bmatrix} 1 & 1 \\ -1 & -1 \end{bmatrix}$

3. $A = \begin{bmatrix} 0 & 1 \\ 1 & 1 \end{bmatrix}$ $B = \begin{bmatrix} -1 & -1 \\ 1 & 1 \end{bmatrix}$

4. $A = \begin{bmatrix} 4 & 1 \\ 3 & 2 \end{bmatrix}$ $B = \begin{bmatrix} 2 & -1 \\ -3 & 4 \end{bmatrix}$

5. Let A^2 denote AA, A^3 denote AAA, etc.

    a. Compute A^2 if $A = \begin{bmatrix} 2 & 1 \\ 1 & 3 \end{bmatrix}$

    b. Compute A^3 if $A = \begin{bmatrix} 1 & 2 \\ 0 & 1 \end{bmatrix}$

6. For $A = \begin{bmatrix} 7 & 1 \\ 5 & -2 \end{bmatrix}$, prove or disprove that $A^2A = AA^2$.

7. For $A = \begin{bmatrix} 1 & 0 \\ 0 & -1 \end{bmatrix}$ compute A^2, A^3, A^4, and A^5. Do you see any pattern?

8. For $A = \begin{bmatrix} 0 & -1 \\ 1 & 0 \end{bmatrix}$ compute A^2, A^3, A^4, A^5, and A^6. Do you see any pattern?

9. Let A, B be in $\mathbf{M}_2$.

    a. Find $(A - B)(A + B)$

    b. Does $(A - B)(A + B)$ equal $A^2 - B^2$? Explain.

10. Let A, B be in $\mathbf{M}_2$.

    a. Find $(A + B)^2$.

    b. Find $A^2 + 2AB + B^2$.

    c. Compare the results of **a** and **b**.

11. For $A = \begin{bmatrix} 1 & 2 \\ 3 & 1 \end{bmatrix}$, verify that $A^2 - 2A - 5I = O$

$$\left(I = \begin{bmatrix} 1 & 0 \\ 0 & 1 \end{bmatrix}, \quad O = \begin{bmatrix} 0 & 0 \\ 0 & 0 \end{bmatrix} \right)$$

12. Prove Theorem 10–5.

13. Prove Theorem 10–7.

14. Let $L_1 = l_1I$ and $L_2 = l_2I$, $l_1, l_2 \in \mathbf{R}$. Prove or disprove:

    a. $L_1 + L_2 = (l_1 + l_2)I$.   **b.** $L_1L_2 = (l_1l_2)I$.

15. Prove or disprove: If l_1 and l_2 are real numbers and $A \in \mathbf{M}_2$, then $A^2 - (l_1 + l_2)A + l_1l_2I = (A - l_1I)(A - l_2I)$.

Definition   If A is an $m \times n$ matrix and B is an $n \times p$ matrix, then the **product** of A and B, $AB = C$, is an $m \times p$ matrix defined by

$$c_{ij} = a_{i1}b_{1j} + a_{i2}b_{2j} + a_{i3}b_{3j} + \cdots + a_{in}b_{nj}$$
$$i = 1, 2, \cdots, m \qquad j = 1, 2, \cdots, p.$$

Perform the indicated computations when possible.

16. $\begin{bmatrix} 2 & 1 & 3 & 7 \end{bmatrix} \begin{bmatrix} 5 & 1 \\ -2 & 7 \\ -3 & -4 \\ 1 & 0 \end{bmatrix}$

17. $\begin{bmatrix} 1 & 3 & 5 \\ 7 & 2 & -3 \\ -1 & 0 & -5 \end{bmatrix} \begin{bmatrix} 5 & 1 \\ -2 & 7 \\ -3 & -4 \end{bmatrix}$

18. $\begin{bmatrix} 5 & 1 \\ -2 & 7 \\ -3 & -4 \end{bmatrix} \begin{bmatrix} 1 & 3 & 5 \\ 7 & 2 & -3 \\ -1 & 0 & -5 \end{bmatrix}$

19. $\begin{bmatrix} 1 \\ 2 \\ 3 \\ 4 \end{bmatrix} \begin{bmatrix} 4 & -3 & -2 & 1 \end{bmatrix}$

20. Let A be an $m \times n$ matrix, B be an $n \times p$ matrix, C be an $n \times p$ matrix, and k be any real number. Prove the following:

a. $A(B - C) = AB - AC$ **b.** $A(kB) = k(AB)$

> **Definition** If A is an $m \times n$ matrix, then the **transpose of A, A^T,** is an $n \times m$ matrix defined by $a_{ij}^T = a_{ji}$.

Find A^T for each matrix

21. $\begin{bmatrix} 2 & 1 & 3 \\ -3 & 2 & 0 \end{bmatrix}$

22. $\begin{bmatrix} 0 & 1 \\ -3 & 5 \end{bmatrix}$

23. $\begin{bmatrix} 1 & -1 & 2 & -2 \\ -3 & 3 & -1 & 1 \\ 0 & 2 & -3 & 1 \end{bmatrix}$

24. $\begin{bmatrix} 0 & 2 & -1 \\ -2 & 0 & -3 \\ 1 & 3 & 0 \end{bmatrix}$

10–3   Vectors and Matrices

Recall that any vector in two-space can be identified by the coordinates of its tip (a, b). Since each ordered pair, (a, b), represents a unique vector and each vector $\vec{v}$ is equal to a unique position vector with tip at (a, b), the following theorem is true.

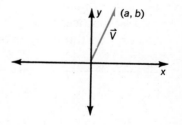

> **Theorem 10–8** There is a one-to-one correspondence between the vectors in the plane and the ordered pairs of real numbers.

Since ordered pairs uniquely determine vectors, you may think of an ordered pair of real numbers as a vector. When you read "the vector (4, 2)," you should think of the position vector whose tip has coordinates (4, 2).

Identifying vectors with ordered pairs of real numbers lets you use matrix notation to denote vectors.

Definition The vector (a, b) is denoted by the 2×1 matrix $\begin{bmatrix} a \\ b \end{bmatrix}$, where a is the first or **i** component of the vector and b is the second or **j** component. $\begin{bmatrix} a \\ b \end{bmatrix}$ is a **column vector**.

EXAMPLE 1. Name the vector $\overrightarrow{PQ}$, where $P = (2, 5)$ and $Q = (1, 7)$, as a column vector. Sketch the vector.

Solution: $\overrightarrow{PQ} = (1 - 2)\mathbf{i} + (7 - 5)\mathbf{j} = -\mathbf{i} + 2\mathbf{j}$

Thus

$$\overrightarrow{PQ} = \begin{bmatrix} -1 \\ 2 \end{bmatrix}. \quad \longleftarrow \text{ \textbf{Column vector}}$$

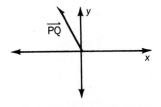

Column vectors and matrices in M_2 can be multiplied. *The product is another column vector.* The procedure used is like that used to multiply two matrices in M_2, except that there is only one column in a column vector, and thus only two inner products are found.

Definition The product of a matrix, $A = \begin{bmatrix} a_{11} & a_{12} \\ a_{21} & a_{22} \end{bmatrix}$ and a vector, $\vec{v} = \begin{bmatrix} x \\ y \end{bmatrix}$, is the column vector, $A\vec{v}$, defined by the following system.

$$\begin{bmatrix} a_{11} & a_{12} \\ a_{21} & a_{22} \end{bmatrix} \begin{bmatrix} x \\ y \end{bmatrix} = \begin{bmatrix} a_{11}x + a_{12}y \\ a_{21}x + a_{22}y \end{bmatrix}$$

EXAMPLE 2. Compute $\begin{bmatrix} 1 & -3 \\ 2 & -1 \end{bmatrix}\begin{bmatrix} 1 \\ 3 \end{bmatrix}$. Sketch the original vector and the product vector.

Solution: 1st row by column

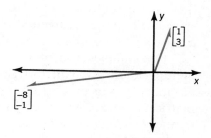

$$(1)(1) + (-3)(3) = -8$$

2nd row by column

$$(2)(1) + (-1)(3) = -1$$

Thus $\begin{bmatrix} 1 & -3 \\ 2 & -1 \end{bmatrix}\begin{bmatrix} 1 \\ 3 \end{bmatrix} = \begin{bmatrix} -8 \\ -1 \end{bmatrix}$.

Both vectors are shown at the right.

A theorem like Theorem 10–7 is true for products of matrices and column vectors. It is stated below as Theorem 10–9.

Theorem 10–9 For any vector $\vec{v}$ in two-space, for any matrix A in M_2, and for any real number k,
$$A(k\vec{v}) = (kA)\vec{v} = k(A\vec{v}).$$

Multiplying a matrix A and vector $\vec{v}$ gives a vector $\vec{r}$, that is

$$A\vec{v} = \vec{r}. \qquad \qquad \textbf{1}$$

The equation is reminiscent of a linear equation

$$ax = b \qquad \qquad \textbf{2}$$

where a and b are real numbers and x is a variable. Equation 2 can be solved when $a \neq 0$. Equation 1 can often be solved also.

EXAMPLE 3. Find $\vec{v} = \begin{bmatrix} x \\ y \end{bmatrix}$ when $\begin{bmatrix} 2 & 1 \\ 4 & 3 \end{bmatrix}\begin{bmatrix} x \\ y \end{bmatrix} = \begin{bmatrix} 1 \\ 0 \end{bmatrix}$.

Solution: $A\vec{v} = \vec{r}$ where $A = \begin{bmatrix} 2 & 1 \\ 4 & 3 \end{bmatrix}$ and $\vec{r} = \begin{bmatrix} 1 \\ 0 \end{bmatrix}$.

$$\begin{bmatrix} 2 & 1 \\ 4 & 3 \end{bmatrix}\begin{bmatrix} x \\ y \end{bmatrix} = \begin{bmatrix} 2x + y \\ 4x + 3y \end{bmatrix} = \begin{bmatrix} 1 \\ 0 \end{bmatrix} \quad \longleftarrow \quad \begin{array}{l}\textbf{By multiplication} \\ \textbf{of matrices}\end{array}$$

Thus
$$\begin{aligned} 2x + y &= 1 \\ 4x + 3y &= 0 \end{aligned} \quad \longleftarrow \quad \begin{array}{l}\textbf{By equality} \\ \textbf{of matrices}\end{array}$$

Solving this system by the addition method yields

$y = -2$ and $x = \frac{3}{2}$. Thus, $\vec{v} = \begin{bmatrix} -2 \\ \frac{3}{2} \end{bmatrix}$.

Notice that the *solution vector* is found by finding the coordinates of the point common to the two lines $2x + y = 1$ and $4x + 3y = 0$. If these lines are parallel there is no solution. If they are the same line, there are many solutions. How can you identify parallel lines? The same line? In the next section you will learn an easier method of solving a matrix and vector equation like $A\vec{v} = \vec{r}$.

For completeness, it must be mentioned that the definitions of multiplication given in this section and in Section 10–2 are special instances of a general definition of matrix multiplication. Any two matrices A and B with dimensions $m \times n$ and $n \times p$ may be multiplied by the row-column procedure. The *ij*th entry in $C = A \cdot B$ is the inner product of the *i*th row of A and the *j*th column of B. The dimensions of C are $m \times p$. See Exercises 16–19, Section 10–2.

EXAMPLE 5. Compute $\begin{bmatrix} 2 & 1 & 4 \\ 3 & 1 & 7 \end{bmatrix} \begin{bmatrix} 1 & 4 & 1 & 5 \\ 2 & 6 & 3 & 2 \\ 3 & 1 & 5 & 7 \end{bmatrix} = AB$.

Solution:

$$AB = \begin{bmatrix} 2 & 1 & 4 \\ 3 & 1 & 7 \end{bmatrix} \begin{bmatrix} 1 & 4 & 1 & 5 \\ 2 & 6 & 3 & 2 \\ 3 & 1 & 5 & 7 \end{bmatrix} = \begin{bmatrix} 16 & 18 & 25 & 40 \\ 26 & 25 & 41 & 66 \end{bmatrix} = C$$

Dimensions of Matrix: $\qquad 2 \times 3 \qquad 3 \times 4 \longrightarrow 2 \times 4$

WRITTEN EXERCISES

A ━━ Find the column vector, $\vec{v} = \begin{bmatrix} x \\ y \end{bmatrix}$, for $\overrightarrow{PQ}$ in each of the following.

1. $P(2, 1)$ and $Q = (3, 4)$

2. $P(3, 4)$ and $Q = (2, 1)$

3. $P(-3, 1)$ and $Q = (2, -5)$

4. $P = (\frac{1}{2}, -3)$ and $Q = (4, 2)$

5. $P = (-4, 2)$ and $Q = (2, -1)$

6. $P = (-1, -3)$ and $Q = (1, 2)$

7. $P = (103, 47)$ and $Q = (100, 49)$

8. $P = (1, 3)$ and $Q = (-\frac{2}{3}, -\frac{4}{5})$

━━ Let $A = \begin{bmatrix} 1 & 2 \\ 4 & 1 \end{bmatrix}$, $B = \begin{bmatrix} -2 & 1 \\ 3 & -1 \end{bmatrix}$, $C = \begin{bmatrix} 0 & 1 \\ 2 & 1 \end{bmatrix}$, $\vec{r} = \begin{bmatrix} 2 \\ -2 \end{bmatrix}$, $\vec{t} = \begin{bmatrix} -1 \\ 4 \end{bmatrix}$.

Find the column vector. Make a sketch of each vector.

9. $A\vec{r}$ **10.** $B\vec{r}$ **11.** $C\vec{r}$ **12.** At

13. $B\vec{t}$ **14.** $C\vec{t}$ **15.** $A(2\vec{r})$ **16.** $B(\frac{1}{2}\vec{r})$

17. $C(\vec{r}+\vec{t})$ **18.** $C\vec{r}+C\vec{t}$ **19.** $(AB)\vec{r}$ **20.** $A(B\vec{r})$

21. $(AC)\vec{t}$ **22.** $A(C\vec{t})$ **23.** $(A+B)\vec{r}$ **24.** $A\vec{r}+B\vec{r}$

25. Compare the results of Exercises
     a. 17 and 18.   **b.** 19 and 20.   **c.** 23 and 24.

B   Solve for the vector $\begin{bmatrix} x \\ y \end{bmatrix}$ when possible.

26. $\begin{bmatrix} 4 & 1 \\ 3 & 1 \end{bmatrix}\begin{bmatrix} x \\ y \end{bmatrix} = \begin{bmatrix} 2 \\ 1 \end{bmatrix}$ **27.** $\begin{bmatrix} -3 & 4 \\ -6 & 1 \end{bmatrix}\begin{bmatrix} x \\ y \end{bmatrix} = \begin{bmatrix} -2 \\ 3 \end{bmatrix}$

28. $\begin{bmatrix} 2 & -3 \\ -4 & 6 \end{bmatrix}\begin{bmatrix} x \\ y \end{bmatrix} = \begin{bmatrix} 1 \\ 0 \end{bmatrix}$ **29.** $\begin{bmatrix} 1 & 0 \\ 0 & 1 \end{bmatrix}\begin{bmatrix} x \\ y \end{bmatrix} = \begin{bmatrix} 4 \\ 5 \end{bmatrix}$

30. $\begin{bmatrix} 0 & 5 \\ 1 & 0 \end{bmatrix}\begin{bmatrix} x \\ y \end{bmatrix} = \begin{bmatrix} 2 \\ -1 \end{bmatrix}$ **31.** $\begin{bmatrix} 1 & -2 \\ -2 & 4 \end{bmatrix}\begin{bmatrix} x \\ y \end{bmatrix} = \begin{bmatrix} 2 \\ -4 \end{bmatrix}$

32. $\begin{bmatrix} 1 & 5 \\ 0 & 1 \end{bmatrix}\begin{bmatrix} x \\ y \end{bmatrix} = \begin{bmatrix} 7 \\ 2 \end{bmatrix}$ **33.** $\begin{bmatrix} 4 & 1 \\ 1 & 0 \end{bmatrix}\begin{bmatrix} x \\ y \end{bmatrix} = \begin{bmatrix} 2 \\ 8 \end{bmatrix}$

C ▬▬ Complete the products.

34. $\begin{bmatrix} 1 \\ 4 \end{bmatrix}\begin{bmatrix} 2 & 3 \end{bmatrix}$

35. $\begin{bmatrix} 1 & 1 & 1 \\ 4 & 3 & 2 \end{bmatrix}\begin{bmatrix} 1 & 2 \\ 0 & 1 \\ 1 & 4 \end{bmatrix}$

36. $\begin{bmatrix} 1 & 2 & 4 & 1 \\ 5 & 1 & 0 & 3 \end{bmatrix}\begin{bmatrix} 1 & 4 & 3 \\ -2 & 1 & 2 \\ 1 & -5 & 0 \\ 0 & 1 & 0 \end{bmatrix}$

37. $\begin{bmatrix} 1 & 1 & 3 \\ 1 & 3 & 1 \\ 3 & 1 & 1 \end{bmatrix}\begin{bmatrix} 2 & 1 & 1 \\ 1 & 2 & 1 \\ 1 & 1 & 2 \end{bmatrix}$

▬▬ Let $A = \begin{bmatrix} a_{11} & a_{12} \\ a_{21} & a_{22} \end{bmatrix}$ $B = \begin{bmatrix} b_{11} & b_{12} \\ b_{21} & b_{22} \end{bmatrix}$ $\vec{r} = \begin{bmatrix} x \\ y \end{bmatrix}$ $\vec{t} = \begin{bmatrix} u \\ v \end{bmatrix}$ and k a real number. Prove each of the following.

38. $A(\vec{r}+\vec{t}) = A\vec{r}+A\vec{t}$

39. $A(B\vec{r}) = (AB)\vec{r}$

40. $(A+B)\vec{r} = A\vec{r}+B\vec{r}$

41. $A(k\vec{r}) = (kA)\vec{r} = k(A\vec{r})$ (Theorem 10–9).

> **Definition** If A is an $n \times n$ matrix, then the trace of A, $\mathrm{Tr}(A)$, is defined to be the sum
> $$a_{11} + a_{22} + a_{33} + \cdots + a_{nn}.$$

42. a. Prove: $\mathrm{Tr}(cA) = c(\mathrm{Tr}A)$, $c \in \mathrm{R}$, A is $n \times n$.
  b. Prove: $\mathrm{Tr}(A + B) = \mathrm{Tr}(A) + \mathrm{Tr}(B)$, A and B are both $n \times n$ matrices.

43. Compute the trace of each matrix if it exists.

  a. $\begin{bmatrix} 1 & 2 \\ 3 & 4 \end{bmatrix}$

  b. $\begin{bmatrix} 2 & -1 & 3 \\ 2 & -5 & 1 \\ 7 & 9 & 2 \end{bmatrix}$

  c. $\begin{bmatrix} 1 & 0 & 0 & 0 \\ 0 & -1 & 0 & 0 \\ 0 & 0 & 0 & -1 \end{bmatrix}$

44. When is the trace of an $n \times n$ matrix zero?

10–4 Inverses and Determinants

In Section 10–3 you learned how to solve a matrix vector equation

$$A\vec{v} = \vec{r}$$

by solving a pair of linear equations. The major objective of this section is to develop matrix methods which can be employed in finding the solution.

The means sought are motivated by the solution procedures used in determining x in the real number equation

$$ax = b.$$

Here, when $a \neq 0$, multiplication of left and right members by $\frac{1}{a}$, the multiplicative inverse of a, provides the solution easily.

If $\qquad\qquad ax = b,$

then $\qquad\qquad \dfrac{1}{a}(ax) = \dfrac{1}{a} \cdot b$

or $\qquad\qquad x = \dfrac{b}{a}$

Similarly, if there is a matrix A^{-1} (read "A inverse") such that $A^{-1}A = I = AA^{-1}$, then $\vec{v}$ will equal $A^{-1}\vec{r}$ because $I\vec{v} = \vec{v}$ and $A^{-1}\vec{r}$ is a column matrix. The procedure would be as follows.

$$A\vec{v} = \vec{r},$$

so

$$A^{-1}(A\vec{v}) = A^{-1}\vec{r}$$

Thus

$$I\vec{v} = A^{-1}\vec{r}$$

or

$$\vec{v} = A^{-1}\vec{r}.$$

There are three questions to be answered: **1.** Are there any matrices that have inverses? **2.** If there are, which ones are they? **3.** What is the inverse of a matrix A?

The first question is easy to answer: Some matrices have inverses. For example, let $A = \begin{bmatrix} 0 & -1 \\ 1 & 0 \end{bmatrix}$. Then if $B = \begin{bmatrix} 0 & 1 \\ -1 & 0 \end{bmatrix}$, B is the inverse of A, because

$$AB = \begin{bmatrix} 0 & -1 \\ 1 & 0 \end{bmatrix}\begin{bmatrix} 0 & 1 \\ -1 & 0 \end{bmatrix} = \begin{bmatrix} 1 & 0 \\ 0 & 1 \end{bmatrix} = I.$$

$$BA = \begin{bmatrix} 0 & 1 \\ -1 & 0 \end{bmatrix}\begin{bmatrix} 0 & -1 \\ 1 & 0 \end{bmatrix} = \begin{bmatrix} 1 & 0 \\ 0 & 1 \end{bmatrix} = I.$$

Thus $AB = BA = I$ and $B = A^{-1}$ (or $A = B^{-1}$).

Theorem 10–10 If A is a matrix in M_2 and if A^{-1} is a matrix with the property that

$$AA^{-1} = A^{-1}A = I,$$

then A^{-1} is unique.

This theorem is a consequence of Exercise 34, Section 10–1 and Theorem 10–5.

It is also true that not all matrices have inverses. For example $O = \begin{bmatrix} 0 & 0 \\ 0 & 0 \end{bmatrix}$ has no inverse for $\begin{bmatrix} 0 & 0 \\ 0 & 0 \end{bmatrix}\begin{bmatrix} a_{11} & a_{12} \\ a_{21} & a_{22} \end{bmatrix} = \begin{bmatrix} 0 & 0 \\ 0 & 0 \end{bmatrix}$ for all matrices A. Thus OA is never equal to $I = \begin{bmatrix} 1 & 0 \\ 0 & 1 \end{bmatrix}$. There are many other square matrices that do not have inverses, also. For example: $\begin{bmatrix} 1 & 0 \\ 0 & 0 \end{bmatrix}$.

The next two examples illustrate the method used to find the inverse of a matrix. The first is a particular case, the second is the general case which constitutes a proof of necessary and sufficient conditions for a matrix A to have an inverse A^{-1}.

EXAMPLE 1. Let $A = \begin{bmatrix} 0 & 2 \\ -1 & 3 \end{bmatrix}$. Find the matrix B, if it exists, such that $AB = BA = I$.

Solution: Let $B = \begin{bmatrix} a & b \\ c & d \end{bmatrix}$,

Then

$$AB = \begin{bmatrix} 0 & 2 \\ -1 & 3 \end{bmatrix}\begin{bmatrix} a & b \\ c & d \end{bmatrix}$$

$$= \begin{bmatrix} 2c & 2d \\ -a + 3c & -b + 3d \end{bmatrix} = \begin{bmatrix} 1 & 0 \\ 0 & 1 \end{bmatrix}$$

Thus

$$2c = 1 \qquad 2d = 0$$
$$-a + 3c = 0 \qquad -b + 3d = 1$$

Solving these equations you find $c = \frac{1}{2}$, $d = 0$, $a = \frac{3}{2}$, and $b = -1$.

Thus

$$B = \begin{bmatrix} \frac{3}{2} & -1 \\ \frac{1}{2} & 0 \end{bmatrix} = A^{-1} \quad \longleftarrow \quad \boldsymbol{BA = AB = I}$$

EXAMPLE 2. Let $A = \begin{bmatrix} p & q \\ r & s \end{bmatrix}$. Find the matrix $B = \begin{bmatrix} a & b \\ c & d \end{bmatrix}$ such that $AB = BA = I$ and the conditions on A such that B exists.

Solution: For B to satisfy the conditions,

$$AB = \begin{bmatrix} p & q \\ r & s \end{bmatrix}\begin{bmatrix} a & b \\ c & d \end{bmatrix} = \begin{bmatrix} 1 & 0 \\ 0 & 1 \end{bmatrix} = I.$$

Then by multiplication

$$\begin{bmatrix} pa + qc & pb + qd \\ ra + sc & rb + sd \end{bmatrix} = \begin{bmatrix} 1 & 0 \\ 0 & 1 \end{bmatrix}.$$

This matrix equation is equivalent to the four equations:

i. $pa + qc = 1$ iii. $pb + qd = 0$
ii. $ra + sc = 0$ iv. $rb + sd = 1$

Now you must solve these equations for the real numbers a, b, c, and d in terms of the real numbers p, q, r, and s. Solving i and ii for a, (multiply i by s and ii by $-q$ and add the resulting equations) you find

$$psa - qra = s \text{ or } (ps - qr)a = s. \qquad\qquad 1$$

Similarly you find

$$(ps - qr)c = -r \qquad\qquad 2$$
$$(ps - qr)b = -q \qquad\qquad 3$$
$$(ps - qr)d = p. \qquad\qquad 4$$

Equations 1, 2, 3, and 4 have a unique solution if and only if the number $ps - qr$ is *not* 0. Thus a matrix $A = \begin{bmatrix} p & q \\ r & s \end{bmatrix}$ has no inverse when $ps - qr = 0$.

If, on the other hand, $ps - qr \neq 0$, then $A = \begin{bmatrix} p & q \\ r & s \end{bmatrix}$ has an inverse $\begin{bmatrix} a & b \\ c & d \end{bmatrix}$ whose entries are the following.

$$a = \frac{s}{ps - qr} \qquad b = \frac{-q}{ps - qr}$$

$$c = \frac{-r}{ps - qr} \qquad d = \frac{p}{ps - qr}$$

Thus

$$B = \begin{bmatrix} \dfrac{s}{ps - qr} & \dfrac{-q}{ps - qr} \\ \dfrac{-r}{ps - qr} & \dfrac{p}{ps - qr} \end{bmatrix} = \frac{1}{ps - qr} \begin{bmatrix} s & -q \\ -r & p \end{bmatrix}. \qquad 5$$

Direct multiplication verifies that B satisfies $BA = I$. Thus $B = A^{-1}$.

In Example 2 the number $ps - qr$ plays a key role in determining whether a matrix $\begin{bmatrix} p & q \\ r & s \end{bmatrix}$ has an inverse. This number is the **determinant** of the matrix A. It is denoted *det A*.

Following is a formal definition of the determinant of a matrix A in M_2.

Definition For a matrix $A = \begin{bmatrix} a_{11} & a_{12} \\ a_{21} & a_{22} \end{bmatrix}$ the **determinant of** A, written "det A", is the number defined by,

$$\det A = a_{11}a_{22} - a_{12}a_{21}.$$

Now the necessary and sufficient conditions for the existence of an inverse of a matrix A in M_2 can be stated.

Theorem 10-11 If A is a matrix in M_2, then A has an inverse A^{-1} if and only if det $A \neq 0$. If det $A \neq 0$ and $A = \begin{bmatrix} a_{11} & a_{12} \\ a_{21} & a_{22} \end{bmatrix}$, then

$$A^{-1} = \begin{bmatrix} \dfrac{a_{22}}{\det A} & \dfrac{-a_{12}}{\det A} \\ \dfrac{-a_{21}}{\det A} & \dfrac{a_{11}}{\det A} \end{bmatrix} = \frac{1}{\det A} \begin{bmatrix} a_{22} & -a_{12} \\ -a_{21} & a_{11} \end{bmatrix}.$$

> **Definition**   A matrix A which has an inverse A^{-1} is an **invertible matrix.**

EXAMPLE 3.   Find the inverse, if it exists, of $A = \begin{bmatrix} 2 & 1 \\ 1 & 2 \end{bmatrix}$.

Solution: $\det A = 2 \cdot 2 - 1 \cdot 1 = 4 - 1 = 3$

Since $\det A \neq 0$, A has an inverse.

$$A^{-1} = \tfrac{1}{3}\begin{bmatrix} 2 & -1 \\ -1 & 2 \end{bmatrix} = \begin{bmatrix} \frac{2}{3} & -\frac{1}{3} \\ -\frac{1}{3} & \frac{2}{3} \end{bmatrix}$$

EXAMPLE 4.   Find the inverse, if it exists, of $B = \begin{bmatrix} 4 & 3 \\ -8 & -6 \end{bmatrix}$.

Solution: $\det B = 4(-6) - 3(-8) = -24 - (-24) = 0$

There is no inverse for B.

EXAMPLE 5.   Find the inverse, if it exists, of $C = \begin{bmatrix} -1 & 0 \\ 0 & 1 \end{bmatrix}$.

Solution: $\det C = (-1)1 - (0)(0) = -1$

$$C^{-1} = \frac{1}{-1}\begin{bmatrix} 1 & 0 \\ 0 & -1 \end{bmatrix} = \begin{bmatrix} -1 & 0 \\ 0 & 1 \end{bmatrix}$$

Thus C is its own inverse.

EXAMPLE 6.   Solve the matrix vector equation $\begin{bmatrix} 2 & 2 \\ 1 & 2 \end{bmatrix}\begin{bmatrix} x \\ y \end{bmatrix} = \begin{bmatrix} 4 \\ 5 \end{bmatrix}$.

Solution:

If $\begin{bmatrix} 2 & 2 \\ 1 & 2 \end{bmatrix}$ has an inverse, the system can be solved by multiplying both sides of the equation above by that inverse.   Since

$$\det A = 2 \times 2 - 2 \times 1 = 4 - 2 = 2$$

the inverse of $\begin{bmatrix} 2 & 2 \\ 1 & 2 \end{bmatrix}$ is $\tfrac{1}{2}\begin{bmatrix} 2 & -2 \\ -1 & 2 \end{bmatrix} = \begin{bmatrix} 1 & -1 \\ -\frac{1}{2} & 1 \end{bmatrix}$

Thus $\begin{bmatrix} 1 & -1 \\ -\frac{1}{2} & 1 \end{bmatrix}\begin{bmatrix} 2 & 2 \\ 1 & 2 \end{bmatrix}\begin{bmatrix} x \\ y \end{bmatrix} = \begin{bmatrix} 1 & -1 \\ -\frac{1}{2} & 1 \end{bmatrix}\begin{bmatrix} 4 \\ 5 \end{bmatrix}$

and $I\begin{bmatrix} x \\ y \end{bmatrix} = \begin{bmatrix} -1 \\ 3 \end{bmatrix}$

or $\begin{bmatrix} x \\ y \end{bmatrix} = \begin{bmatrix} -1 \\ 3 \end{bmatrix}$

WRITTEN EXERCISES

A ━━ Find the determinant of each matrix.

1. $\begin{bmatrix} -4 & -1 \\ 6 & 2 \end{bmatrix}$ **2.** $\begin{bmatrix} 0 & -1 \\ 1 & 0 \end{bmatrix}$ **3.** $\begin{bmatrix} -1 & 0 \\ 0 & -1 \end{bmatrix}$

4. $\begin{bmatrix} 1 & 0 \\ 0 & -1 \end{bmatrix}$ **5.** $\begin{bmatrix} 1 & 7 \\ 1 & 5 \end{bmatrix}$ **6.** $\begin{bmatrix} 10 & 4 \\ 5 & 2 \end{bmatrix}$

7. $\begin{bmatrix} 0 & 1 \\ 0 & 5 \end{bmatrix}$ **8.** $\begin{bmatrix} 3 & 8 \\ 2 & 5 \end{bmatrix}$ **9.** $\begin{bmatrix} a & b \\ 0 & 0 \end{bmatrix}$

10. $\begin{bmatrix} 17 & 3 \\ 5 & 1 \end{bmatrix}$ **11.** $\begin{bmatrix} 84 & 55 \\ 3 & 2 \end{bmatrix}$ **12.** $\begin{bmatrix} p & q \\ 2 & 3 \end{bmatrix}$

13. For each matrix in Exercises 1–11 find the inverse, if it exists.

14. For the inverse of the matrix in Exercise 12 to exist, what conditions must be placed on p and q?

━━ Solve each matrix vector equation for the vector $\begin{bmatrix} x \\ y \end{bmatrix}$ when possible. Use the method of Example 6.

15. $\begin{bmatrix} 4 & 1 \\ 3 & 1 \end{bmatrix}\begin{bmatrix} x \\ y \end{bmatrix} = \begin{bmatrix} 2 \\ 1 \end{bmatrix}$ **16.** $\begin{bmatrix} -3 & 4 \\ -6 & 1 \end{bmatrix}\begin{bmatrix} x \\ y \end{bmatrix} = \begin{bmatrix} -2 \\ 3 \end{bmatrix}$

17. $\begin{bmatrix} 2 & -3 \\ -4 & 6 \end{bmatrix}\begin{bmatrix} x \\ y \end{bmatrix} = \begin{bmatrix} 1 \\ 0 \end{bmatrix}$ **18.** $\begin{bmatrix} 1 & 0 \\ 0 & 1 \end{bmatrix}\begin{bmatrix} x \\ y \end{bmatrix} = \begin{bmatrix} 4 \\ 5 \end{bmatrix}$

19. $\begin{bmatrix} 0 & 1 \\ 1 & 0 \end{bmatrix}\begin{bmatrix} x \\ y \end{bmatrix} = \begin{bmatrix} 2 \\ -1 \end{bmatrix}$ **20.** $\begin{bmatrix} 1 & -2 \\ -2 & 4 \end{bmatrix}\begin{bmatrix} x \\ y \end{bmatrix} = \begin{bmatrix} 2 \\ -4 \end{bmatrix}$

21. $\begin{bmatrix} 1 & 5 \\ 0 & 1 \end{bmatrix}\begin{bmatrix} x \\ y \end{bmatrix} = \begin{bmatrix} 7 \\ 2 \end{bmatrix}$ **22.** $\begin{bmatrix} 4 & 1 \\ 1 & 0 \end{bmatrix}\begin{bmatrix} x \\ y \end{bmatrix} = \begin{bmatrix} 2 \\ 8 \end{bmatrix}$

B   **23.** For $a, b \in R$ and $a \neq 0 \neq b$, find the inverse of $A = \begin{bmatrix} a & 0 \\ 0 & b \end{bmatrix}$.

24. For $a \in R$, $a \neq 0$, find the inverse of $A = \begin{bmatrix} a & 0 \\ 0 & a \end{bmatrix}$.

25. Find the inverse of $\begin{bmatrix} 1 & k \\ 0 & 1 \end{bmatrix}$ for $k \in R$.

26. Find the inverse of $\begin{bmatrix} k & 1 \\ 1 & 0 \end{bmatrix}$ for $k \in R$.

27. Find the inverse of $\begin{bmatrix} 1 & a \\ a & 1 \end{bmatrix}$ for $a \in R$, $a \neq \pm 1$.

28. A pair of linear equations

     i. $ax + by = r$
     ii. $cx + dy = s$ r and s not both zero

has a unique solution if and only if the lines are not parallel or identical. State this condition in terms of the slopes of **i** and **ii**.

Applying Network Theory

Civil Engineering

A **network** is a set of nodes and the arcs connecting them as shown at the right. **Civil engineers** often use networks as models for electrical systems, road systems, railway systems, etc.

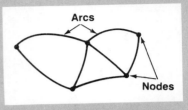

Arcs

Nodes

Matrices are used to describe networks. These descriptions can be classified as **incidence matrices** or **route matrices**.

EXAMPLE 1. For the network shown below, construct the following.

a. The incidence matrix **b.** The route matrix

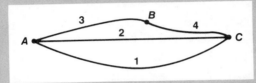

Solutions:

a. The incidence matrix at the right has a 1 in row A, column 1 because route 1 contains A. Thus, row A has 1's in columns 1, 2, and 3 and a 0 in column 4. The rest of the matrix is filled in the same manner.

$$\text{Nodes} \begin{array}{c} A \\ B \\ C \end{array} \begin{bmatrix} 1 & 1 & 1 & 0 \\ 0 & 0 & 1 & 1 \\ 1 & 1 & 0 & 1 \end{bmatrix}$$

Arcs: 1 2 3 4

Incidence Matrix

b. The route matrix at the right is constructed by placing the number of arcs connecting two nodes in the row and column identified by the nodes. Thus, a 0 goes in A, A, since there is no route from A to A; a 1 goes in A, B and a 2 in A, C because there are, respectively, 1 and 2 routes connecting these nodes.

$$\text{Nodes} \begin{array}{c} A \\ B \\ C \end{array} \begin{bmatrix} 0 & 1 & 2 \\ 1 & 0 & 1 \\ 2 & 1 & 0 \end{bmatrix}$$

Nodes: A B C

Route Matrix

Two networks having identical incidence or route matrices are equivalent. That is, the networks are the same even though they may appear to be different.

EXAMPLE 2. Produce two networks described by the route matrix $\begin{bmatrix} 1 & 1 \\ 1 & 1 \end{bmatrix}$.

Solution: **a.** 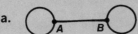 **b.**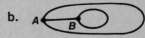

The arcs beginning and ending at A or B produce the 1's on the diagonal of the matrix. These networks are topologically equivalent.

Shown at the right is a network representing a small part of a water system. The arrowheads on the arcs indicate the direction of flow. Water enters A and flows toward D. From B to C it can flow in either direction. The usual route for the water is along the single arc AD; but in the case of an emergency some two-arc routes can be found by multiplying the route matrix by itself and reading the resulting route matrix.

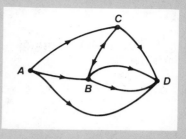

$$
\begin{array}{c}
\begin{array}{cccc} A & B & C & D \end{array} \\
\begin{array}{c} A \\ B \\ C \\ D \end{array}
\begin{bmatrix}
0 & 1 & 1 & 1 \\
0 & 0 & 1 & 2 \\
0 & 1 & 0 & 1 \\
0 & 0 & 0 & 0
\end{bmatrix}
\end{array}
\times
\begin{array}{c}
\begin{array}{cccc} A & B & C & D \end{array} \\
\begin{array}{c} A \\ B \\ C \\ D \end{array}
\begin{bmatrix}
0 & 1 & 1 & 1 \\
0 & 0 & 1 & 2 \\
0 & 1 & 0 & 1 \\
0 & 0 & 0 & 0
\end{bmatrix}
\end{array}
=
\begin{array}{c}
\begin{array}{cccc} A & B & C & D \end{array} \\
\begin{array}{c} A \\ B \\ C \\ D \end{array}
\begin{bmatrix}
0 & 1 & 1 & 3 \\
0 & 1 & 0 & 1 \\
0 & 0 & 1 & 2 \\
0 & 0 & 0 & 0
\end{bmatrix}
\end{array}
$$

Directed Route Matrix   ×   Directed Route Matrix   =   Tow-arc Directed Route Matrix

The "two-arc directed route matrix" above shows that from A to D there are three two-arc routes: $A - C - D$ and $A - B - D$ twice. In general, if A is a route matrix, then A^n, $n \in W$, is the n-arc route matrix for the network.

EXERCISES

Construct the route and incidence matrices for each network.

1.
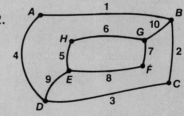

2.

3. For the water system shown above, find the three-arc route matrix. Check your results by tracing each route.

4. How many two-arc routes connect each node in the network at the right?

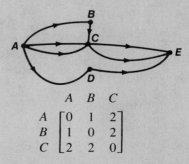

5. Draw a network described by the route matrix at the right.

$$
\begin{array}{c}
\begin{array}{ccc} A & B & C \end{array} \\
\begin{array}{c} A \\ B \\ C \end{array}
\begin{bmatrix}
0 & 1 & 2 \\
1 & 0 & 2 \\
2 & 2 & 0
\end{bmatrix}
\end{array}
$$

10–5   Systems of Linear Equations

The system of linear equations below has m equations and n variables.

$$a_{11}x_1 + a_{12}x_2 + \cdots + a_{1n}x_n = b_1$$
$$a_{21}x_1 + a_{22}x_2 + \cdots + a_{2n}x_n = b_2$$

1

$$a_{m1}x_1 + a_{m2}x_2 + \cdots + a_{mn}x_n = b_m$$

Letting
$$A = \begin{bmatrix} a_{11} & a_{12} \cdots a_{1n} \\ a_{21} & a_{22} \cdots a_{2n} \\ & \\ & \\ & \\ a_{m1} & a_{m2} \cdots a_{mn} \end{bmatrix}, \quad X = \begin{bmatrix} x_1 \\ x_2 \\ \\ \\ x_n \end{bmatrix} \text{ and } B = \begin{bmatrix} b_1 \\ b_2 \\ \\ \\ b_m \end{bmatrix}$$

system 1 can be written $AX = B$.   **2**

A solution to 2 is an X satisfying 2. The system is **homogeneous** if all the b_i in B are zero. Otherwise, the system is **nonhomogeneous.**

You are familiar with basic methods for solving simple systems. The main idea behind any method of solving a system of equations is to construct a new system that is equivalent to the original one. To construct such a system it is necessary to use one or more of the following three manipulations.

I. Interchange the ith and the jth equations.

II. Multiply an equation by a nonzero real number, c.

III. Replace the ith equation by the sum of the ith equation and c times the jth equation, $i \neq j$. That is, replace

$$a_{i1}x_1 + a_{i2}x_2 + \cdots + a_{in}x_n = b_i$$

by

$$(a_{i1} + ca_{j1})x_1 + (a_{i2} + ca_{j2})x_2 + \cdots + (a_{in} + ca_{jn})x_n = b_i + cb_j$$

EXAMPLE 1. Solve $\begin{cases} 2x_1 - 2x_2 = 6 \\ x_1 + 2x_2 = 0 \end{cases}$ by using operations I, II, III.

Solution:
$$\begin{cases} 2x_1 - 2x_2 = 6 \\ x_1 + 2x_2 = 0 \end{cases}$$

is equivalent to

$$\begin{cases} x_1 + 2x_2 = 0 \\ 2x_1 - 2x_2 = 6 \end{cases} \longleftarrow \textbf{By I}$$

which is equivalent to

$$\begin{cases} x_1 + \ \ 2x_2 = 0 \\ 0x_1 + -6x_2 = 6 \end{cases}$$ ⟵ **By** III

which is equivalent to

$$\begin{cases} x_1 + 2x_2 = 0 \\ \qquad x_2 = -1 \end{cases}$$ ⟵ **By** II

which is equivalent to

$$\begin{cases} x_1 = 2 \\ x_2 = -1 \end{cases}$$ ⟵ **By** III

Thus $x_1 = 2$, $x_2 = -1$ is the solution to the original system.

Look back over the solution to Example 1. The essential feature of this solution procedure is that by employing operations I, II and III the original system is replaced by an equivalent system in which the coefficients are either zero or one. The variables $x_1, x_2, \cdots, x_n$ play little part in this process. In fact the same manipulations could be carried out on the coefficients and constants of the given system. One way to organize the coefficients conveniently is into a matrix. A matrix of coefficients is the *coefficient* matrix. Here the coefficient matrix is

$$\begin{bmatrix} 2 & -2 \\ 1 & 2 \end{bmatrix}.$$

The elementary manipulations do not leave the constants b_i unchanged. Thus they are included along with the coefficients in the *augmented matrix*.

$$\begin{bmatrix} 2 & -2 & \vdots & 6 \\ 1 & 2 & \vdots & 0 \end{bmatrix}$$

A set of vertical dots is used to separate the coefficients from the constants b_i. For the system **1** the augmented matrix is

$$\begin{bmatrix} a_{11} & a_{12} & \cdots & a_{1n} & \vdots & b_1 \\ a_{21} & a_{22} & \cdots & a_{2n} & \vdots & b_2 \\ \cdot & & & & \vdots & \\ \cdot & & & & \vdots & \\ \cdot & & & & \vdots & \\ a_{n1} & a_{n2} & \cdots & a_{mn} & \vdots & b_m \end{bmatrix}$$

3

You can now perform manipulations on the rows of the augmented matrix identical to those that you performed on the equations. In this way you can produce an augmented matrix which corresponds to a system equivalent to the original and in which the solution is evident. When performed on a matrix, these manipulations are called **elementary row operations**.

EXAMPLE 2. Use elementary row operations on the augmented matrix to solve

$$\begin{bmatrix} 2 & 1 & -1 \\ -2 & 1 & 2 \\ 1 & 1 & 1 \end{bmatrix} \begin{bmatrix} x_1 \\ x_2 \\ x_3 \end{bmatrix} = \begin{bmatrix} -1 \\ 1 \\ 2 \end{bmatrix}$$

Solution: First write the augmented matrix.

$$\left[\begin{array}{ccc:c} 2 & 1 & -1 & -1 \\ -2 & 1 & 2 & 1 \\ 1 & 1 & 1 & 2 \end{array} \right]$$

Replace *row 2* by the sum of *row 1* and *row 2*.

$$\left[\begin{array}{ccc:c} 2 & 1 & -1 & -1 \\ 0 & 2 & 1 & 0 \\ 1 & 1 & 1 & 2 \end{array} \right]$$

Replace *row 3* by the sum of *row 3* and $-\frac{1}{2}$ times *row 1*.

$$\left[\begin{array}{ccc:c} 2 & 1 & -1 & -1 \\ 0 & 2 & 1 & 0 \\ 0 & \frac{1}{2} & \frac{3}{2} & \frac{5}{2} \end{array} \right]$$

Replace *row 1* by the sum of *row 1* and $-\frac{1}{2}$ times *row 2*.

$$\left[\begin{array}{ccc:c} 2 & 0 & -\frac{3}{2} & -1 \\ 0 & 2 & 1 & 0 \\ 0 & \frac{1}{2} & \frac{3}{2} & \frac{5}{2} \end{array} \right]$$

Replace *row 3* by the sum of *row 3* and $-\frac{1}{4}$ times *row 2*.

$$\left[\begin{array}{ccc:c} 2 & 0 & -\frac{3}{2} & -1 \\ 0 & 2 & 1 & 0 \\ 0 & 0 & \frac{5}{4} & \frac{5}{2} \end{array} \right]$$

Multiply *row 3* by $\frac{4}{5}$.

$$\left[\begin{array}{ccc:c} 2 & 0 & -\frac{3}{2} & -1 \\ 0 & 2 & 1 & 0 \\ 0 & 0 & 1 & 2 \end{array} \right]$$

Replace *row 2* by the sum of *row 2* and -1 times *row 3*.

$$\left[\begin{array}{ccc:c} 2 & 0 & -\frac{3}{2} & -1 \\ 0 & 2 & 0 & -2 \\ 0 & 0 & 1 & 2 \end{array} \right]$$

Replace *row 1* by the sum of *row 1* and $\frac{3}{2}$ times *row 3*.

$$\left[\begin{array}{ccc:c} 2 & 0 & 0 & 2 \\ 0 & 2 & 0 & -2 \\ 0 & 0 & 1 & 2 \end{array} \right]$$

Multiply *row 2* by $\frac{1}{2}$.

$$\left[\begin{array}{ccc:c} 2 & 0 & 0 & 2 \\ 0 & 1 & 0 & -1 \\ 0 & 0 & 1 & 2 \end{array} \right]$$

Multiply *row 1* by $\frac{1}{2}$.

$$\left[\begin{array}{ccc:c} 1 & 0 & 0 & 1 \\ 0 & 1 & 0 & -1 \\ 0 & 0 & 1 & 2 \end{array} \right]$$

Clearly you do not have to obtain the last equivalent system to calculate the values of x_1, x_2, and x_3 easily. Any of the 5 systems preceding the last could be used for this purpose. Of course the last one represents the solution most obviously.

CLASSROOM EXERCISES

▬ Use the augmented matrix and elementary row manipulation method to solve each of the following systems.

1.
$$\begin{cases} x + 2y - z = 4 \\ 2x - y + 3z = 3 \\ 7x - 2y + 4z = 7 \end{cases}$$

2.
$$\begin{cases} x + y + z = 4 \\ 2x - 3y - z = 1 \\ x + 2y + 2z = 5 \end{cases}$$

WRITTEN EXERCISES

A ━━ Use the augmented matrix and elementary row manipulation method to solve each system of equations.

1. $\begin{cases} -3x + 2y = -1 \\ x + y = 2 \end{cases}$ **2.** $\begin{cases} 3x - 2y = 1 \\ 6x + 6y = 7 \end{cases}$

3. $\begin{cases} x - 2y = -5 \\ 2x + 3y = 4 \end{cases}$ **4.** $\begin{cases} x - 7y = 3 \\ -2x + 7y = 1 \end{cases}$

5. $\begin{cases} x - 3y = 5 \\ -2x + 6y = 5 \end{cases}$ **6.** $\begin{cases} 2x + y = 5 \\ -4x - 2y = -10 \end{cases}$

7. $\begin{cases} x + y + z = 6 \\ -2x - 3y + 3x = 1 \\ x - 4y + 2z = -1 \end{cases}$ **8.** $\begin{cases} x + y + z = 0 \\ 2x - 2y - z = 9 \\ 3x + 2y + z = 1 \end{cases}$

9. $\begin{cases} x - 2y + z = -2 \\ 2x + 2y - 4z = -1 \\ 4x + y + 2z = 7 \end{cases}$ **10.** $\begin{cases} x + y + 2z = 2 \\ 2x - y + 3z = 5 \\ x - y - z = -2 \end{cases}$

11. $\begin{cases} x + 5y - 3z = 0 \\ x + y + z = 0 \\ 2x - 3y + z = 0 \end{cases}$

12. $\begin{cases} w - x + y - z = 0 \\ w + x + y + z = 6 \\ 2w - x + y - z = 1 \\ -4w + x - 2y + 4z = 1 \end{cases}$

B **13.** $\begin{cases} x_1 + x_2 + x_3 + x_4 + x_5 = 3 \\ x_1 + x_5 = 0 \\ 2x_1 + x_2 + x_3 = 2 \\ x_2 + x_3 + x_4 = 3 \\ x_3 + x_4 + x_5 = 0 \end{cases}$

14. $\begin{cases} 2x_1 + x_2 + 3x_3 = 1 \\ x_1 + 2x_3 = 1 \end{cases}$

15. Write the matrix form, $AX = B$, of each of the systems in Exercises 10–14.

C ━━ Elementary row operations can be used to find the inverse of a square matrix of any order. Write $A : I$ as one matrix. Use elementary row operations to change A to I and I will change to A^{-1}. Find A^{-1} for each A.

16. $A = \begin{bmatrix} 1 & -2 & 1 \\ 2 & 2 & -4 \\ 4 & 1 & 2 \end{bmatrix}$ **17.** $A = \begin{bmatrix} 1 & 1 & 1 \\ -2 & -3 & 3 \\ 1 & -4 & 2 \end{bmatrix}$

10–6   Homogeneous Systems of Equations

A non-square system is a system with more or fewer equations than variables. These systems may be either homogeneous or non-homogeneous.

EXAMPLE 1. Solve the following homogeneous system.

$$\begin{bmatrix} 1 & 3 & 0 & 0 & -2 \\ 0 & 0 & 1 & 0 & 1 \\ 0 & 0 & 0 & 1 & 2 \\ 0 & 0 & 0 & 0 & 0 \end{bmatrix} \begin{bmatrix} x_1 \\ x_2 \\ x_3 \\ x_4 \\ x_5 \end{bmatrix} = \begin{bmatrix} 0 \\ 0 \\ 0 \\ 0 \end{bmatrix}$$

Solution:

The coefficient matrix is simplified as far as possible because in each row with a non-zero element, the first non-zero element is 1. Also, the first non-zero elements are further to the right as the row numbers increase. The matrix is said to be in **reduced row echelon form.**

Multiplying you find

$$x_1 + 3x_2 \qquad\qquad - 2x_5 = 0$$
$$x_3 \qquad + x_5 = 0$$
$$x_4 + 2x_5 = 0$$

The variables x_1, x_3, and x_4, may be expressed in terms of x_2 and x_5. The solution is:

$$x_1 = -3x_2 + 2x_5$$
$$x_2 = x_2$$
$$x_3 = -x_5$$
$$x_4 = -2x_5$$
$$x_5 = x_5$$

where x_2 and x_5 may be any real numbers. Thus, the solution to this homogeneous system of linear equations is an infinite set of solutions. In matrix notation this solution can be written either as one matrix or as the sum of matrices.

$$\begin{bmatrix} x_1 \\ x_2 \\ x_3 \\ x_4 \\ x_5 \end{bmatrix} = \begin{bmatrix} -3x_2 + 2x_5 \\ x_2 \\ - x_5 \\ - 2x_5 \\ x_5 \end{bmatrix}$$

$$= x_2 \begin{bmatrix} -3 \\ 1 \\ 0 \\ 0 \\ 0 \end{bmatrix} + x_5 \begin{bmatrix} 2 \\ 0 \\ -1 \\ -2 \\ 1 \end{bmatrix}, \quad x_2, x_5 \in R$$

This is called the *general solution* of the system.

Any row in the augmented matrix which consists entirely of zeros may be ignored since it will place no restrictions on the variables.

EXAMPLE 2. Find all solutions for the following homogeneous system.

$$\begin{bmatrix} 1 & 2 & 1 & 1 \\ 2 & 4 & -1 & 0 \end{bmatrix} \begin{bmatrix} x_1 \\ x_2 \\ x_3 \\ x_4 \end{bmatrix} = \begin{bmatrix} 0 \\ 0 \end{bmatrix}$$

Solution:

The augmented matrix is $\begin{bmatrix} 1 & 2 & 1 & 1 & \vdots & 0 \\ 2 & 4 & -1 & 0 & \vdots & 0 \end{bmatrix}$.

This reduces to $\begin{bmatrix} 1 & 2 & 1 & 1 & \vdots & 0 \\ 0 & 0 & -3 & -2 & \vdots & 0 \end{bmatrix} \longrightarrow \begin{bmatrix} 1 & 2 & 1 & 1 & \vdots & 0 \\ 0 & 0 & 1 & \frac{2}{3} & \vdots & 0 \end{bmatrix}$

or to the reduced row echelon form

$$\begin{bmatrix} 1 & 2 & 0 & \frac{1}{3} & \vdots & 0 \\ 0 & 0 & 1 & \frac{2}{3} & \vdots & 0 \end{bmatrix}.$$

Thus,
$$x_1 + 2x_2 \qquad + \tfrac{1}{3}x_4 = 0$$
$$x_3 + \tfrac{2}{3}x_4 = 0 \qquad \longleftarrow \text{ Homogeneous equations}$$

Solving for x_1 and x_3 in terms of x_2 and x_4, you get

$$x_1 = -2x_2 - \tfrac{1}{3}x_4$$
$$x_3 = 0x_2 - \tfrac{2}{3}x_4$$

Thus the general solution is:
$$\begin{bmatrix} x_1 \\ x_2 \\ x_3 \\ x_4 \end{bmatrix} = \begin{bmatrix} -2x_2 - \tfrac{1}{3}x_4 \\ x_2 + 0x_4 \\ 0x_2 - \tfrac{2}{3}x_4 \\ 0x_2 + x_4 \end{bmatrix} = x_2 \begin{bmatrix} -2 \\ 1 \\ 0 \\ 0 \end{bmatrix} + x_4 \begin{bmatrix} -\tfrac{1}{3} \\ 0 \\ -\tfrac{2}{3} \\ 1 \end{bmatrix}$$

where x_2 and x_4 can be replaced by any real numbers.

EXAMPLE 3. Find all solutions of

$$\begin{bmatrix} 1 & 1 & 1 \\ 1 & 0 & 0 \\ 1 & 2 & 1 \end{bmatrix} \begin{bmatrix} x_1 \\ x_2 \\ x_3 \end{bmatrix} = {}_3O_1.$$

Solution:

$$\begin{bmatrix} 1 & 1 & 1 & \vdots & 0 \\ 1 & 0 & 0 & \vdots & 0 \\ 1 & 2 & 1 & \vdots & 0 \end{bmatrix} \to \begin{bmatrix} 1 & 0 & 0 & \vdots & 0 \\ 1 & 1 & 1 & \vdots & 0 \\ 1 & 2 & 1 & \vdots & 0 \end{bmatrix} \to \begin{bmatrix} 1 & 0 & 0 & \vdots & 0 \\ 0 & 1 & 1 & \vdots & 0 \\ 1 & 2 & 1 & \vdots & 0 \end{bmatrix}$$

$$\begin{bmatrix} 1 & 0 & 0 & \vdots & 0 \\ 0 & 1 & 1 & \vdots & 0 \\ 0 & 2 & 1 & \vdots & 0 \end{bmatrix} \to \begin{bmatrix} 1 & 0 & 0 & \vdots & 0 \\ 0 & 1 & 1 & \vdots & 0 \\ 0 & 0 & -1 & \vdots & 0 \end{bmatrix} \to \begin{bmatrix} 1 & 0 & 0 & \vdots & 0 \\ 0 & 1 & 0 & \vdots & 0 \\ 0 & 0 & -1 & \vdots & 0 \end{bmatrix}$$

$$\to \begin{bmatrix} 1 & 0 & 0 & \vdots & 0 \\ 0 & 1 & 0 & \vdots & 0 \\ 0 & 0 & 1 & \vdots & 0 \end{bmatrix}$$

Thus the only solution is the trivial solution: $x_1 = 0$, $x_2 = 0$, $x_3 = 0$.

Notice that in Example 3 each row of the reduced row echelon form is nonzero and that there are exactly as many nonzero rows as variables; namely 3. This illustrates a useful theorem.

> **Theorem 10–12** A system of homogeneous equations in n variables $x_1, x_2, \ldots x_n$ has a unique solution if the reduced row echelon matrix has exactly n rows with nonzero entries. That solution is the trivial solution.

CLASSROOM EXERCISES

Find the general solution for each homogeneous system in Exercises 1 and 2.

1. $\begin{aligned} x_1 + + x_3 &= 0 \\ x_1 + 2x_2 - 3x_3 &= 0 \end{aligned}$

2. $\begin{aligned} x_1 + x_2 &= 0 \\ x_1 + + 2x_3 + x_4 &= 0 \\ x_2 + x_3 + x_4 &= 0 \end{aligned}$

WRITTEN EXERCISES

A In Exercises 1–14 find the general solution for each homogeneous system.

1. $\begin{aligned} 3x_1 + 2x_2 - x_3 &= 0 \\ 2x_1 - x_2 + 2x_3 &= 0 \end{aligned}$

2. $\begin{aligned} 2x_1 - x_2 &= 0 \\ x_1 + 4x_2 &= 0 \\ 0x_1 + 0x_2 &= 0 \\ 3x_1 - 3x_2 &= 0 \end{aligned}$

3. $\begin{aligned} x_1 - 3x_2 &= 0 \\ 2x_1 + x_2 &= 0 \end{aligned}$

4. $\begin{bmatrix} 2 & -\frac{1}{2} \\ 4 & -1 \end{bmatrix} \begin{bmatrix} x_1 \\ x_2 \end{bmatrix} = \begin{bmatrix} 0 \\ 0 \end{bmatrix}$

5.
$$\begin{bmatrix} 3 & -2 & 7 \\ 3 & 2 & -7 \end{bmatrix} \begin{bmatrix} x_1 \\ x_2 \\ x_3 \end{bmatrix} = {}_2O_1$$

6.
$$\begin{bmatrix} 2 & -1 \\ 1 & 2 \\ 3 & -2 \end{bmatrix} \begin{bmatrix} x_1 \\ x_2 \end{bmatrix} = \begin{bmatrix} 0 \\ 0 \\ 0 \end{bmatrix}$$

7.
$$\begin{aligned} 6x_1 - x_2 + 2x_3 &= 0 \\ -x_1 + 3x_2 - x_3 &= 0 \\ 2x_1 + 7x_2 &= 0 \end{aligned}$$

8.
$$\begin{bmatrix} 10 & 12 & -1 \\ 3 & -7 & 6 \end{bmatrix} \begin{bmatrix} x_1 \\ x_2 \\ x_3 \end{bmatrix} = \begin{bmatrix} 0 \\ 0 \end{bmatrix}$$

9.
$$\begin{bmatrix} 3 & -2 & 1 \end{bmatrix} \begin{bmatrix} x_1 \\ x_2 \\ x_3 \end{bmatrix} = \begin{bmatrix} 0 \end{bmatrix}$$

10.
$$\begin{bmatrix} 1 & 1 & 1 & 1 \\ 1 & -1 & 1 & 1 \\ 1 & -1 & -1 & 1 \\ 1 & -1 & -1 & -1 \end{bmatrix} \begin{bmatrix} x_1 \\ x_2 \\ x_3 \\ x_4 \end{bmatrix} = {}_4O_1$$

B

11.
$$\begin{bmatrix} 2 & 1 & 3 & 0 & 1 & 0 \\ 2 & -2 & 0 & -6 & 0 & 1 \\ 1 & -1 & 0 & -3 & -1 & 0 \\ -2 & 4 & -3 & 6 & 1 & 1 \end{bmatrix} \begin{bmatrix} x_1 \\ x_2 \\ x_3 \\ x_4 \\ x_5 \\ x_6 \end{bmatrix} = {}_4O_1$$

12.
$$\begin{aligned} 3x_1 + 2x_2 - 7x_3 + 2x_4 + x_5 &= 0 \\ -x_1 + x_2 \qquad\quad - 7x_4 + x_5 + 3x_6 &= 0 \end{aligned}$$

C

13.
$$\begin{aligned} ix_1 + (1 + i)x_2 + 2x_3 &= 0 \\ 2x_1 - (1 - i)x_2 + ix_3 &= 0 \end{aligned} \qquad i = \sqrt{-1}$$

14.
$$\begin{aligned} (1 + i)x_1 - ix_2 + 2ix_3 &= 0 \\ (1 - 2i)x_1 + x_2 \qquad\quad &= 0 \end{aligned} \qquad i = \sqrt{-1}$$

15. Show that if for all x, $c_3x^3 + c_2x^2 + c_1x + c_0 = 0$

then $$c_0 = c_1 = c_2 = c_3 = 0.$$

(*Hint:* Make four substitutions for x yielding 4 linear equations in c_0, c_1, c_2, and c_3.)

16. Find all values of k such that the system

$$\begin{bmatrix} 2 & 1 \\ 3 & k \end{bmatrix} \begin{bmatrix} x_1 \\ x_2 \end{bmatrix} = \begin{bmatrix} 0 \\ 0 \end{bmatrix}$$

has only the trivial solution. For what values of k does the system have an infinite number of solutions?

17. Repeat Exercise 16 for the following system.

$$\begin{bmatrix} 1 & 3 \\ 3 & k^2 \end{bmatrix} \begin{bmatrix} x_1 \\ x_2 \end{bmatrix} = \begin{bmatrix} 0 \\ 0 \end{bmatrix}$$

10–7 Nonhomogeneous Systems of Equations

A nonhomogeneous system of m linear equations in n variables

$$AX = B$$

can be reduced to the reduced row echelon form as follows.

$$x_1 + c_{12}x_2 + 0x_3 + c_{14}x_4 + \cdots = d_1$$
$$x_3 + c_{24}x_4 + \cdots = d_2$$

$$\cdot \quad \cdot \quad \cdot \quad \cdot \quad \cdot \quad \cdot \quad \cdot \quad \cdot$$

$$x_{n-1} = d_{k-1}$$
$$x_n = d_k$$
$$0x_1 + 0x_2 + \cdots + 0x_k + \cdots + 0x_n = d_{k+1}$$
$$0x_1 + 0x_2 + \cdots + 0x_k + \cdots + 0x_n = d_m$$

In this system there are k ($k \leq m$) equations with at least one non-zero coefficient. There are $m - k$ equations with all zero coefficients. Denote this system

$$[C : D].$$

Note that if $d_{k+1} = 1$, then $[C : D]$ has no solution because there is at least one equation which can be satisfied by no replacements for x_i, $i = 1, \ldots n$. If $d_{k+1} = 0$, then $d_{k+2} = d_{k+3} = \cdots = d_m = 0$ because the augmented matrix is in reduced row echelon form. In this case there is at least one solution found by setting $x_n = d_k$, $x_{n-1} = d_{k-1}$, and so on, working backwards to find the remaining variables.

If some variables are expressed in terms of others that can take on a real number value, then the system $[C : D]$ has infinitely many solutions. However, if every variable is determined the solution is unique.

EXAMPLE 1. Let $[C : D] = \begin{bmatrix} 1 & 0 & 0 & 0 & : & 4 \\ 0 & 1 & 0 & 0 & : & 2 \\ 0 & 0 & 1 & 0 & : & 1 \\ 0 & 0 & 0 & 1 & : & 2 \end{bmatrix}$.

The solution is unique: $\begin{bmatrix} x_1 \\ x_2 \\ x_3 \\ x_4 \end{bmatrix} = \begin{bmatrix} 4 \\ 2 \\ 1 \\ 2 \end{bmatrix}$

In this case every unknown is determined.

The following example will illustrate the case where there is an infinite set of solutions for the variables.

EXAMPLE 2.   Let $[C : D] = \begin{bmatrix} 1 & 0 & 3 & 0 & \vdots & 3 \\ 0 & 1 & 1 & 0 & \vdots & 2 \\ 0 & 0 & 0 & 1 & \vdots & 6 \\ 0 & 0 & 0 & 0 & \vdots & 0 \end{bmatrix}$.

This system has an infinite set of solutions because x_1 and x_2 can be expressed in terms of x_3:

$$\begin{aligned} x_1 &= 3 - 3x_3 \\ x_2 &= 2 - x_3 \\ x_3 &= x_3 \\ x_4 &= 6 \end{aligned}$$

Thus the general solution is:

$$\begin{bmatrix} x_1 \\ x_2 \\ x_3 \\ x_4 \end{bmatrix} = \begin{bmatrix} 3 - 3x_3 \\ 2 - x_3 \\ 0 + x_3 \\ 6 + 0x_3 \end{bmatrix} = \begin{bmatrix} 3 \\ 2 \\ 0 \\ 6 \end{bmatrix} + x_3 \begin{bmatrix} -3 \\ -1 \\ 1 \\ 0 \end{bmatrix}, \quad x_3 \in \mathbf{R}$$

The general solution to this system illustrates an interesting theorem. Before this theorem is stated consider the next example.

EXAMPLE 3.   Find the general solution to the homogeneous system:

$$[C : O] = \begin{bmatrix} 1 & 0 & 3 & 0 & \vdots & 0 \\ 0 & 1 & 1 & 0 & \vdots & 0 \\ 0 & 0 & 0 & 1 & \vdots & 0 \\ 0 & 0 & 0 & 0 & \vdots & 0 \end{bmatrix}$$

Solution:

$$\begin{aligned} x_1 &= -3x_3 \\ x_2 &= -x_3 \\ x_3 &= x_3 \\ x_4 &= 0 \end{aligned}$$

The general solution then is $\begin{bmatrix} x_1 \\ x_2 \\ x_3 \\ x_4 \end{bmatrix} = x_3 \begin{bmatrix} -3 \\ -1 \\ 1 \\ 0 \end{bmatrix}$.

Now compare the results of Examples 2 and 3. You see that the general solution to the homogeneous system $[C : O]$ is part of the general solution to the nonhomogeneous system $[C : D]$. The other part of the general solution of $[C : D]$ is one particular solution. Thus the solution of the nonhomogeneous system is a linear combination of a particular solution to $[C : D]$ and the general solution to the homogeneous system $[C : O]$. This result is stated in the next theorem.

Theorem 10–13 Y is a solution of $AX = B$ iff $Y = Z + c_1Z_1 + c_2Z_2 + \cdots + c_kZ_k$ where Z is a particular solution to $AX = B$ and $c_1Z_1 + c_2Z_2 + \cdots + c_kZ_k$ is the general solution to $AX = O$.

Proof: Suppose $AY = B$.

Then, $A(Y - Z) = AY - AZ = B - B = 0$ ◄——— See Exercise 20, page 525.

It follows that $Y - Z$ is a solution to $AX = O$.

Thus

$$Y - Z = c_1Z_1 + c_2Z_2 + \cdots + c_kZ_k$$

or

$$Y = Z + c_1Z_1 + c_2Z_2 + \cdots + c_kZ_k.$$

Conversely if

$$Y = Z + c_1Z_1 + c_2Z_2 + \cdots + c_kZ_k$$

then

$$AY = A(Z + c_1Z_1 + c_2Z_2 + \cdots + c_kZ_k).$$

It follows that:

$$AY = AZ + c_1AZ_1 + c_2AZ_2 + \cdots + c_kAZ_k$$ ◄——— See Exercise 20, page 525.
$$= B + O + O + \cdots + O$$
$$= B$$

Thus Y is a solution to $AX = B$.

Theorem 10–14 If $AX = O$ has only one solution (the trivial solution) then $AX = B$ has no more than one solution.

Proof: Suppose X_1 and X_2 are solutions to $AX = B$ and $X_1 \neq X_2$. Then

$$X_1 - X_2 \neq 0$$

and

$$A(X_1 - X_2) = AX_1 - AX_2$$
$$= B - B$$
$$= O$$

Thus $X_1 - X_2 \neq O$ is a second solution to $AX = O$. This contradicts the assumption that $AX = O$ has only the trivial solution.

EXAMPLE 4. For $A = \begin{bmatrix} 1 & -2 & 3 & 2 \\ -2 & -1 & 4 & 1 \end{bmatrix}$, $X = \begin{bmatrix} 1 \\ 0 \\ 2 \\ -1 \end{bmatrix}$, $B = \begin{bmatrix} 5 \\ 5 \end{bmatrix}$

$AX = B$. Find the general solution and 3 other particular solutions.

Solution:

Since $X = \begin{bmatrix} 1 \\ 0 \\ 2 \\ -1 \end{bmatrix}$ is a particular solution, you need only find the general solution to $AX = O$.

$\begin{bmatrix} 1 & -2 & 3 & 2 \\ -2 & -1 & 4 & 1 \end{bmatrix}$ is row equivalent to $\begin{bmatrix} 1 & 0 & -1 & 0 \\ 0 & 1 & -2 & -1 \end{bmatrix}$.

The general solution to $AX = O$ is therefore

$$\begin{bmatrix} x_1 \\ x_2 \\ x_3 \\ x_4 \end{bmatrix} = \begin{bmatrix} x_3 \\ 2x_3 + x_4 \\ x_3 \\ 0x_3 + x_4 \end{bmatrix} = x_3 \begin{bmatrix} 1 \\ 2 \\ 1 \\ 0 \end{bmatrix} + x_4 \begin{bmatrix} 0 \\ 1 \\ 0 \\ 1 \end{bmatrix}, \quad x_3, x_4 \in R$$

The general solution to $AX = B$ is a linear combination of a particular solution to $AX = B$ and the general solution to $AX = O$.

$$\begin{bmatrix} x_1 \\ x_2 \\ x_3 \\ x_4 \end{bmatrix} = \begin{bmatrix} 1 \\ 0 \\ 2 \\ -1 \end{bmatrix} + c_1 \begin{bmatrix} 1 \\ 2 \\ 1 \\ 0 \end{bmatrix} + c_2 \begin{bmatrix} 0 \\ 1 \\ 0 \\ 1 \end{bmatrix}, \quad c_1, c_2 \in R$$

Three particular solutions are as follows.

$c_1 = 1, c_2 = 0$	$c_1 = 0, c_2 = 1$	$c_1 = 1, c_2 = 10$
$\begin{bmatrix} 2 \\ 2 \\ 3 \\ -1 \end{bmatrix}$	$\begin{bmatrix} 1 \\ 1 \\ 2 \\ 0 \end{bmatrix}$	$\begin{bmatrix} 2 \\ 12 \\ 3 \\ 9 \end{bmatrix}$

CLASSROOM EXERCISES

▬ Write the general and 3 particular solutions if they exist.

1. $x_1 - x_2 = -1$
$x_1 + x_2 = 6$
$x_1 + x_2 = 7$

2. $x_1 - x_2 - x_3 = 3$
$3x_1 + 6x_2 - 7x_3 = -13$

WRITTEN EXERCISES

A — Which of the ordered triples in Exercises 1–6 are solutions to

$$\begin{bmatrix} 1 & 1 & 1 \\ 1 & -1 & 1 \end{bmatrix} \begin{bmatrix} x_1 \\ x_2 \\ x_3 \end{bmatrix} = \begin{bmatrix} 0 \\ 0 \end{bmatrix}?$$

1. $\begin{bmatrix} -2 \\ 0 \\ 2 \end{bmatrix}$
2. $\begin{bmatrix} 2 \\ 1 \\ -3 \end{bmatrix}$
3. $\begin{bmatrix} -1 \\ 0 \\ 1 \end{bmatrix}$

4. $\begin{bmatrix} 1 \\ 1 \\ -2 \end{bmatrix} + \begin{bmatrix} -1 \\ 0 \\ 1 \end{bmatrix}$
5. $\begin{bmatrix} 0 \\ 0 \\ 0 \end{bmatrix}$
6. $\begin{bmatrix} -c \\ 0 \\ c \end{bmatrix} c \in R$

— Which of the ordered triples in Exercise 7–12 are solutions to

$$\begin{bmatrix} 1 & 1 & 1 \\ 1 & -1 & 1 \end{bmatrix} \begin{bmatrix} x_1 \\ x_2 \\ x_3 \end{bmatrix} = \begin{bmatrix} 0 \\ -2 \end{bmatrix}?$$

7. $\begin{bmatrix} -2 \\ 0 \\ 2 \end{bmatrix}$
8. $\begin{bmatrix} 2 \\ 1 \\ -3 \end{bmatrix}$
9. $\begin{bmatrix} -1 \\ 0 \\ 1 \end{bmatrix}$

10. $\begin{bmatrix} -1 \\ 1 \\ 0 \end{bmatrix} + \begin{bmatrix} -1 \\ 0 \\ 1 \end{bmatrix}$
11. $\begin{bmatrix} -6 \\ 1 \\ 5 \end{bmatrix}$
12. $\begin{bmatrix} 1 \\ 1 \\ -2 \end{bmatrix} + \begin{bmatrix} -c \\ 0 \\ c \end{bmatrix} c \in R$

— Write the general and 3 particular solutions if they exist.

13. $\begin{aligned} x_1 - 3x_2 &= 1 \\ 2x_1 - x_2 &= 4 \end{aligned}$

14. $\begin{aligned} x_1 - 5x_2 &= 2 \\ -3x_1 + 15x_2 &= -6 \end{aligned}$

15. $\begin{aligned} 2x_1 + x_2 + 4x_3 &= 3 \\ x_1 + x_2 + 2x_3 &= 2 \\ 3x_1 + x_2 + 6x_3 &= 6 \end{aligned}$

16. $\begin{aligned} 2x_1 + x_2 + x_3 &= 1 \\ -2x_1 - x_2 + x_3 &= 2 \\ 4x_1 + 2x_2 + 3x_3 &= 1 \end{aligned}$

17.
$$\begin{bmatrix} 2 & 1 & 0 & 1 \\ 3 & 3 & 3 & 5 \\ 3 & 0 & -3 & -2 \end{bmatrix} \begin{bmatrix} x_1 \\ x_2 \\ x_3 \\ x_4 \end{bmatrix} = \begin{bmatrix} 2 \\ 4 \\ 3 \end{bmatrix}$$

18. $\begin{aligned} 2x_1 + x_2 \quad\quad + x_4 &= 2 \\ 3x_1 \quad\quad - 3x_3 - 2x_4 &= 3 \\ 3x_1 + 3x_2 + 3x_3 + 5x_4 &= 3 \end{aligned}$

19. $\begin{aligned} x_1 \quad\quad + x_3 + x_4 \quad\quad - x_6 &= -4 \\ x_1 + x_2 + x_3 \quad\quad\quad\quad &= 1 \\ - x_2 + x_3 \quad\quad + x_5 + x_6 &= 0 \\ x_1 - x_2 + x_3 + x_4 + x_5 + x_6 &= 1 \\ -x_1 \quad\quad - x_3 \quad\quad - x_5 + x_6 &= 3 \\ x_4 + x_5 + x_6 &= 4 \end{aligned}$

20.
$$\begin{bmatrix} 2 & 1 & 2 & 3 & 1 & 1 \\ 0 & 1 & 1 & 2 & 2 & 0 \\ 2 & 1 & 3 & 1 & 0 & 5 \\ 4 & 3 & 6 & 6 & 3 & 10 \\ 0 & 0 & 0 & 3 & 1 & 1 \\ 0 & 1 & 1 & 2 & 4 & 0 \end{bmatrix} \begin{bmatrix} x_1 \\ x_2 \\ x_3 \\ x_4 \\ x_5 \\ x_6 \end{bmatrix} = \begin{bmatrix} 7 \\ -1 \\ 1 \\ -1 \\ 1 \\ 0 \end{bmatrix}$$

21.
$$\begin{aligned} 2x_1 + x_2 + 2x_3 + 3x_4 + x_5 &= 1 \\ x_2 + x_3 + 2x_4 + x_5 &= -1 \\ 2x_1 + x_2 + 3x_3 + x_4 &= 3 \end{aligned}$$

In Exercises 22–25 determine all values of k, if possible, for which the resulting system has

   a. no solution.

   b. a unique solution.

   c. infinitely many solutions.

22.
$$\begin{aligned} x_1 + x_2 - x_3 &= 2 \\ x_1 + 2x_2 + x_3 &= 3 \\ x_1 + x_2 + (k^2 - 5)x_3 &= k \end{aligned}$$

23.
$$\begin{aligned} x_1 + x_2 + x_3 &= 2 \\ 2x_1 + 3x_2 + 2x_3 &= 5 \\ 2x_1 + 3x_2 + (k^2 - 1)x_3 &= k + 1 \end{aligned}$$

24.
$$\begin{aligned} x_1 + x_2 + x_3 &= 2 \\ x_1 + 2x_2 + x_3 &= 3 \\ x_1 + x_2 + (k^2 - 5)x_3 &= k \end{aligned}$$

25.
$$\begin{aligned} x_1 + x_2 + x_3 &= 2 \\ x_1 + 2x_2 - x_3 &= -3 \\ x_1 + 2x_2 + (k^2 - 10)x_3 &= k \end{aligned}$$

26. A trucking company owns three types of trucks, numbered I, II, III. The trucks are equipped to haul three different types of machines per load according to the following chart.

	Trucks		
	I	II	III
Machine X	1	1	1
Machine Y	0	1	2
Machine Z	2	1	1

How many trucks of each type should be sent to haul exactly 15 type X machines, 17 type Y machines, and 20 type Z machines? Assume each truck is fully loaded.

27. A company produces products A, B, and C. Each unit of each product requires work to be done by a technician and by an unskilled laborer.

Product A requires a day's work from each of 5 technicians and 5 laborers for each unit produced.

Product B requires 10 technicians and 10 laborers.

Product C requires 2 technicians and 4 laborers for each unit produced.

a. How many units of each product A, B, and C should be produced each day to keep all 100 technicians and 150 laborers employed?

b. Is there a unique answer?

c. If product B is in greater demand than product A, what is the solution?

MID-CHAPTER REVIEW

Let $A = \begin{bmatrix} 1 & -3 \\ 2 & -5 \end{bmatrix}$ and $B = \begin{bmatrix} -2 & 1 \\ 3 & 4 \end{bmatrix}$. Find each of the following.

(Sections 10–1 and 10–2)

1. $-A$ **2.** $A - B$ **3.** $5B$ **4.** $B - 3A$

5. AB **6.** BA **7.** $3BA$ **8.** $-\frac{1}{2}AB$

9. Represent $3i + 2j$ with a column matrix. (Section 10–3)

10. Solve: $\begin{bmatrix} 2 & 1 \\ 3 & 4 \end{bmatrix} \begin{bmatrix} x \\ y \end{bmatrix} = \begin{bmatrix} 4 \\ 5 \end{bmatrix}$ (Section 10–3)

11. If $A = \begin{bmatrix} 2 & -3 \\ 1 & 5 \end{bmatrix}$, find A^{-1}. (Section 10–4)

12. If $A = \begin{bmatrix} 2 & -3 \\ 1 & 5 \end{bmatrix}$, find det A. (Section 10–4)

13. Use the augmented matrix and elementary row manipulations to solve the following system. (Section 10–5)

$$\begin{cases} 3x + 2y - z = 0 \\ x + y + z = 2 \\ -x + y + z = 0 \end{cases}$$

14. Find the general solution and two particular solutions to

$$\begin{bmatrix} 1 & 2 & 0 & 0 & 3 \\ 0 & 0 & 1 & 0 & 4 \\ 0 & 0 & 0 & 1 & 2 \end{bmatrix} \begin{bmatrix} x_1 \\ x_2 \\ x_3 \\ x_4 \\ x_5 \end{bmatrix} = \begin{bmatrix} 0 \\ 0 \\ 0 \end{bmatrix}$$

(Section 10–6)

15. Find the general solution and 3 particular solutions to

$$\begin{bmatrix} 1 & 2 & 3 & 1 \\ 2 & 1 & 3 & 2 \end{bmatrix} \begin{bmatrix} x_1 \\ x_2 \\ x_3 \\ x_4 \end{bmatrix} = \begin{bmatrix} 1 \\ 2 \end{bmatrix}$$

(Section 10–7)

10–8 Matrices and Linear Transformations of Vectors

A **transformation** is a rule by which one object is paired with another. If the objects happen to be vectors, then a transformation of a vector pairs the vector with another vector.

Transformations of vectors can be described in various ways: by words, by equations, and by matrices (to name just three). Below are four examples of transformations of vectors. In each case the transformation is applied to the vector $\vec{v} = \begin{bmatrix} 1 \\ 2 \end{bmatrix}$, and the graphical representation of $\vec{v}$ and the transformed vector are shown.

EXAMPLE 1. Let T be the transformation defined by the rule: T pairs each vector $\vec{v}$ with itself. The graph in Figure 1 shows $\vec{v} = \begin{bmatrix} 1 \\ 2 \end{bmatrix}$ and "T of $\vec{v}$" which is written $T(\vec{v})$. Here $T(\vec{v}) = \vec{v}$. T is the **identity transformation.**

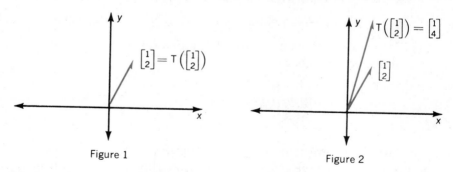

Figure 1   Figure 2

EXAMPLE 2. Let T be the transformation defined by the rule: T pairs each vector $\vec{v} = \begin{bmatrix} x \\ y \end{bmatrix}$ with the vector $T(\vec{v}) = \begin{bmatrix} x \\ y^2 \end{bmatrix}$ when $\vec{v} = \begin{bmatrix} 1 \\ 2 \end{bmatrix}$, $T(\vec{v}) = \begin{bmatrix} 1 \\ 4 \end{bmatrix}$. (See Figure 2 above.) The original vector, $\vec{v}$, is the **pre-image** and the transformed vector $T(\vec{v})$ is the **image** of $\vec{v}$ under the transformation T.

EXAMPLE 3. Let a transformation T be defined by the following statement.

For all $\vec{v}$, $T(\vec{v}) = \vec{v} + \begin{bmatrix} 2 \\ 3 \end{bmatrix}$. For the vector $\begin{bmatrix} 1 \\ 2 \end{bmatrix}$, $T(\vec{v}) = \begin{bmatrix} 1 \\ 2 \end{bmatrix} + \begin{bmatrix} 2 \\ 3 \end{bmatrix} = \begin{bmatrix} 3 \\ 5 \end{bmatrix}$.
The vector $\vec{v}$ and its image are shown in Figure 3 below.

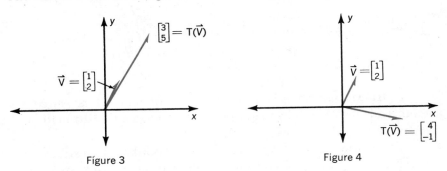

Figure 3   Figure 4

EXAMPLE 4. Define a transformation as follows: For all $\vec{v}$, $T(\vec{v}) = A\vec{v}$ where $A = \begin{bmatrix} 2 & 1 \\ -5 & 2 \end{bmatrix}$. For $\vec{v} = \begin{bmatrix} 1 \\ 2 \end{bmatrix}$, $T(\vec{v}) = \begin{bmatrix} 2 & 1 \\ -5 & 2 \end{bmatrix}\begin{bmatrix} 1 \\ 2 \end{bmatrix} = \begin{bmatrix} 4 \\ -1 \end{bmatrix}$.

This transformation (see Figure 4 above) is an example of a special kind of transformation called a *linear transformation*. It is defined by two properties.

Definition   A **linear transformation** on the set of vectors in two-space is a rule which pairs each vector $\vec{v} = \begin{bmatrix} x \\ y \end{bmatrix}$ with a vector $T(\vec{v})$ of two-space such that for all vectors, $\vec{v}_1$ and $\vec{v}_2$ in two-space and any real number k

       i. $T(\vec{v}_1 + \vec{v}_2) = T(\vec{v}_1) + T(\vec{v}_2)$
       ii. $T(k\vec{v}_1) = k \cdot T(\vec{v}_1)$.

It can also be shown that every linear transformation of the vectors in the plane into themselves can be represented by a two-by-two matrix and conversely. (The proof is omitted.) Thus the set M_2 of two-by-two matrices with real number entries can be thought of as the set of linear transformations of the vectors of the plane into themselves. The transformation is carried out by multiplying the vector v_1 by the matrix A in M_2. You can partially convince yourself of the validity of the statements made above by referring to Theorem 10–9 and to Exercise 38 in Section 10–3.

EXAMPLE 5. Verify for the transformation defined by matrix $A = \begin{bmatrix} 1 & 2 \\ 0 & 1 \end{bmatrix}$ that

$$\text{i. } A(\vec{v}_1 + \vec{v}_2) = A\vec{v}_1 + A\vec{v}_2$$
$$\text{ii. } A(k\vec{v}_1) = k(A\vec{v}_1)$$

Solutions: Let $\vec{v}_1 = \begin{bmatrix} x_1 \\ y_1 \end{bmatrix}$, $\vec{v}_2 = \begin{bmatrix} x_2 \\ y_2 \end{bmatrix}$. Then

i. $A(\vec{v}_1 + \vec{v}_2) = \begin{bmatrix} 1 & 2 \\ 0 & 1 \end{bmatrix} \left(\begin{bmatrix} x_1 \\ y_2 \end{bmatrix} + \begin{bmatrix} x_2 \\ y_2 \end{bmatrix} \right) = \begin{bmatrix} 1 & 2 \\ 0 & 1 \end{bmatrix} \begin{bmatrix} x_1 + x_2 \\ y_1 + y_2 \end{bmatrix}$

$\qquad = \begin{bmatrix} x_1 + x_2 + 2y_1 + 2y_2 \\ y_1 + y_2 \end{bmatrix}$

$A\vec{v}_1 = \begin{bmatrix} 1 & 2 \\ 0 & 1 \end{bmatrix} \begin{bmatrix} x_1 \\ y_1 \end{bmatrix} = \begin{bmatrix} x_1 + 2y_1 \\ y_1 \end{bmatrix}$, $\quad A\vec{v}_2 = \begin{bmatrix} 1 & 2 \\ 0 & 1 \end{bmatrix} \begin{bmatrix} x_2 \\ y_2 \end{bmatrix} = \begin{bmatrix} x_2 + 2y_2 \\ y_2 \end{bmatrix}$

So $A\vec{v}_1 + A\vec{v}_2 = \begin{bmatrix} x_1 + 2y_1 + x_2 + 2y_2 \\ y_1 + y_2 \end{bmatrix} = \begin{bmatrix} x_1 + x_2 + 2y_1 + 2y_2 \\ y_1 + y_2 \end{bmatrix}$

$\qquad = A(\vec{v}_1 + \vec{v}_2)$

ii. $A(k\vec{v}_1) = \begin{bmatrix} 1 & 2 \\ 0 & 1 \end{bmatrix} \begin{bmatrix} kx_1 \\ ky_1 \end{bmatrix} = \begin{bmatrix} kx_1 + 2ky_1 \\ ky_1 \end{bmatrix} = k \begin{bmatrix} x_1 + 2y_1 \\ y_1 \end{bmatrix} = k(A\vec{v}_1)$

Often it is interesting to determine the effects of a linear transformation on a set of vectors. See Example 6 below.

EXAMPLE 6. Consider the set of vectors V such that $\vec{v} \in V$ if and only if $\vec{v} = \begin{bmatrix} x \\ y \end{bmatrix} = \begin{bmatrix} 1 + 2t \\ 2 + 3t \end{bmatrix}$, $t \in R$. Let $T = \begin{bmatrix} 1 & 2 \\ 0 & 1 \end{bmatrix}$ define a transformation of V. Find the image of V.

Notice first that the vectors in V are exactly those vectors whose tips are on the line

$$\begin{cases} x = 1 + 2t \\ y = 2 + 3t. \quad t \in R \end{cases}$$

This is the line containing $(1, 2)$ with slope $\frac{3}{2}$. This line is graphed at right. Now apply the transformation $T = \begin{bmatrix} 1 & 2 \\ 0 & 1 \end{bmatrix}$ to the vectors in V.

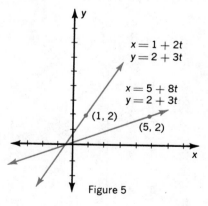

$x = 1 + 2t$
$y = 2 + 3t$

$x = 5 + 8t$
$y = 2 + 3t$

$(1, 2)$

$(5, 2)$

Figure 5

$T(\vec{v}) = \begin{bmatrix} 1 & 2 \\ 0 & 1 \end{bmatrix} \begin{bmatrix} 1 + 2t \\ 2 + 3t \end{bmatrix} = \begin{bmatrix} 1 & 2 \\ 0 & 1 \end{bmatrix} \left(\begin{bmatrix} 1 \\ 2 \end{bmatrix} + \begin{bmatrix} 2t \\ 3t \end{bmatrix} \right) = \begin{bmatrix} 5 \\ 2 \end{bmatrix} + \begin{bmatrix} 8t \\ 3t \end{bmatrix} = \begin{bmatrix} 5 + 8t \\ 2 + 3t \end{bmatrix}$

The image of the set of vectors V is the set of vectors $\vec{u} = \begin{bmatrix} 5 + 8t \\ 2 + 3t \end{bmatrix}$, $t \in \mathbf{R}$.

This is the set of vectors with their tips on the line

$$\begin{cases} x = 5 + 8t \\ y = 2 + 3t \end{cases}$$

that is, the line containing $(5, 2)$ with slope $\frac{3}{8}$. This line is shown in color in Figure 5.

This example demonstrates that the image of the given line is again a line under the transformation $\begin{bmatrix} 1 & 2 \\ 0 & 1 \end{bmatrix}$. Example 6 illustrates why these transformations are called linear transformations; they map lines into lines.

CLASSROOM EXERCISES

— Let $A = \begin{bmatrix} 1 & 2 \\ 4 & 3 \end{bmatrix}$ and $\vec{v} = \begin{bmatrix} 3 \\ 1 \end{bmatrix}$. Find the following.

1. Determine the vector onto which A maps $\vec{v}$.

2. Determine the line onto which A maps the line containing $\vec{v}$. (Recall that $\vec{v}$ is a position vector.)

3. Let $\vec{v} = \begin{bmatrix} 3 \\ 0 \end{bmatrix}$. T maps $\begin{bmatrix} x \\ y \end{bmatrix}$ onto $\begin{bmatrix} x \\ y \end{bmatrix} + \begin{bmatrix} -2 \\ -3 \end{bmatrix}$.
Find $T(\vec{v})$.

WRITTEN EXERCISES

A — For each of Exercises 1–10 you are given a transformation matrix and three vectors. Find the image of each vector and sketch the pre-image vectors and the image vectors on a coordinate plane.

1. $A = \begin{bmatrix} 1 & 1 \\ 1 & 0 \end{bmatrix}$ $\qquad \vec{v}_1 = \begin{bmatrix} 2 \\ 1 \end{bmatrix}$ $\qquad \vec{v}_2 = \begin{bmatrix} -4 \\ 5 \end{bmatrix}$ $\qquad \vec{v}_3 = \begin{bmatrix} 3 \\ -7 \end{bmatrix}$

2. $A = \begin{bmatrix} 2 & 3 \\ -1 & 2 \end{bmatrix}$ $\qquad \vec{v}_1 = \begin{bmatrix} 1 \\ 1 \end{bmatrix}$ $\qquad \vec{v}_2 = \begin{bmatrix} 5 \\ -2 \end{bmatrix}$ $\qquad \vec{v}_3 = \begin{bmatrix} -2 \\ -3 \end{bmatrix}$

3. $A = \begin{bmatrix} 2 & 3 \\ 0 & 0 \end{bmatrix}$ $\qquad \vec{v}_1 = \begin{bmatrix} 0 \\ 1 \end{bmatrix}$ $\qquad \vec{v}_2 = \begin{bmatrix} -2 \\ 4 \end{bmatrix}$ $\qquad \vec{v}_3 = \begin{bmatrix} 4 \\ -1 \end{bmatrix}$

4. $A = \begin{bmatrix} 1 & 0 \\ 0 & 1 \end{bmatrix}$ $\qquad \vec{v}_1 = \begin{bmatrix} 4 \\ 7 \end{bmatrix}$ $\qquad \vec{v}_2 = \begin{bmatrix} -3 \\ -6 \end{bmatrix}$ $\qquad \vec{v}_3 = \begin{bmatrix} 1 \\ 0 \end{bmatrix}$

5. $A = \begin{bmatrix} -1 & 0 \\ 0 & 1 \end{bmatrix}$ $\qquad \vec{v}_1 = \begin{bmatrix} 1 \\ 2 \end{bmatrix}$ $\qquad \vec{v}_2 = \begin{bmatrix} 2 \\ 4 \end{bmatrix}$ $\qquad \vec{v}_3 = \begin{bmatrix} -3 \\ -6 \end{bmatrix}$

6. $A = \begin{bmatrix} -1 & 0 \\ 0 & -1 \end{bmatrix}$ $\quad \vec{v}_1 = \begin{bmatrix} 5 \\ 2 \end{bmatrix}$ $\quad \vec{v}_2 = \begin{bmatrix} -3 \\ 1 \end{bmatrix}$ $\quad \vec{v}_3 = \begin{bmatrix} 0 \\ -8 \end{bmatrix}$

7. $A = \begin{bmatrix} 0 & 0 \\ 0 & 0 \end{bmatrix}$ $\quad \vec{v}_1 = \begin{bmatrix} 1 \\ 1 \end{bmatrix}$ $\quad \vec{v}_2 = \begin{bmatrix} 100 \\ 2 \end{bmatrix}$ $\quad \vec{v}_3 = \begin{bmatrix} x \\ y \end{bmatrix}$

8. $A = \begin{bmatrix} 0 & -1 \\ -1 & 0 \end{bmatrix}$ $\quad \vec{v}_1 = \begin{bmatrix} -3 \\ 1 \end{bmatrix}$ $\quad \vec{v}_2 = \begin{bmatrix} 1 \\ -5 \end{bmatrix}$ $\quad \vec{v}_3 = \begin{bmatrix} 3 \\ 4 \end{bmatrix}$

9. $A = \begin{bmatrix} 4 & -2 \\ -2 & 1 \end{bmatrix}$ $\quad \vec{v}_1 = \begin{bmatrix} 4 \\ 7 \end{bmatrix}$ $\quad \vec{v}_2 = \begin{bmatrix} 2 \\ -3 \end{bmatrix}$ $\quad \vec{v}_3 = \begin{bmatrix} -1 \\ -3 \end{bmatrix}$

10. $A = \begin{bmatrix} 0 & 1 \\ 0 & 3 \end{bmatrix}$ $\quad \vec{v}_1 = \begin{bmatrix} 4 \\ 2 \end{bmatrix}$ $\quad \vec{v}_2 = \begin{bmatrix} -1 \\ 5 \end{bmatrix}$ $\quad \vec{v}_3 = \begin{bmatrix} 6 \\ -8 \end{bmatrix}$

11. Prove that under any linear transformation the image of $\begin{bmatrix} 0 \\ 0 \end{bmatrix}$ is itself.

12. Show that under a linear transformation with matrix $\begin{bmatrix} a & b \\ 0 & 0 \end{bmatrix}$, a or $b \neq 0$, every vector in two-space maps onto a vector on the x axis.

13. Show that under a linear transformation with matrix $\begin{bmatrix} 0 & 0 \\ a & b \end{bmatrix}$, a or $b \neq 0$, every vector in two-space maps onto a vector on the y axis.

14. Show that every vector in the plane maps onto a vector on the line through the origin with slope $-\frac{1}{2}$ when the transformation is

$$\begin{bmatrix} 4 & -2 \\ -2 & 1 \end{bmatrix}.$$

B **15.** Find the image of the line $\begin{cases} x = 2 - 3t \\ y = 1 + 2t \end{cases}$

under the transformation $\begin{bmatrix} 2 & 3 \\ 1 & 1 \end{bmatrix}$. Graph the pre-image and image.

16. Repeat Exercise 15 for line $\begin{cases} x = -3 + t \\ y = 0 + 3t \end{cases}$

and transformation $\begin{bmatrix} 0 & -1 \\ 1 & 0 \end{bmatrix}$.

17. Repeat Exercise 15 for line $\begin{cases} x = 7t \\ y = 3t \end{cases}$

and transformation $\begin{bmatrix} 0 & 1 \\ -1 & 0 \end{bmatrix}$.

18. Repeat Exercise 15 for line $\begin{cases} x = 1 - 2t \\ y = 2 + t \end{cases}$

and transformation $\begin{bmatrix} 1 & 0 \\ 0 & -1 \end{bmatrix}$.

19. Find the image of the triangle with vertices $A = \begin{bmatrix} 2 \\ 4 \end{bmatrix}$, $B = \begin{bmatrix} 2 \\ 1 \end{bmatrix}$
$C = \begin{bmatrix} -1 \\ 1 \end{bmatrix}$ under

    a. $\begin{bmatrix} 1 & 0 \\ 0 & -1 \end{bmatrix}$ **b.** $\begin{bmatrix} -1 & 0 \\ 0 & 1 \end{bmatrix}$

    c. $\begin{bmatrix} 4 & 2 \\ -3 & 1 \end{bmatrix}$ **d.** $\begin{bmatrix} 1 & 5 \\ 0 & 1 \end{bmatrix}$

Graph each pre-image and image.

C   **20.** Prove: If A is an invertible matrix in M_2 and V is the set of all vectors in two-space, then

      i. the image of V is V.

      ii. the transformation A is one-to-one.

21. Prove: If A is an invertible matrix and L is a line:

$$\begin{cases} x = a + lt \\ y = b + mt \end{cases}$$

Then the image of L under the linear transformation represented by A is a line.

22. Prove that the transformation which maps each vector $\begin{bmatrix} x \\ y \end{bmatrix}$ into the vector $\begin{bmatrix} x + 2 \\ y + 3 \end{bmatrix}$ is not a linear transformation. (*Hint:* Show that at least one of the conditions **i** or **ii** of the definition is not satisfied.)

10–9   Special Linear Transformations

    There are several linear transformations of a set of vectors which are of particular importance. They also happen to be examples of linear transformations which have easy and useful geometric interpretations.

    Consider the linear transformation whose matrix is

$$\begin{bmatrix} 1 & 0 \\ 0 & -1 \end{bmatrix} = A.$$

Notice that det $A = -1$. Thus A is an invertible matrix and maps the set of all vectors in the plane onto themselves in a one-to-one manner. (See Exercise 20, Section 10–8.)

Think now of a vector $\vec{v} = \begin{bmatrix} x \\ y \end{bmatrix}$ and find its image under A; that is, find $A\vec{v}$.

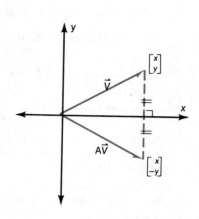

$$A\vec{v} = \begin{bmatrix} 1 & 0 \\ 0 & -1 \end{bmatrix} \begin{bmatrix} x \\ y \end{bmatrix} = \begin{bmatrix} x \\ -y \end{bmatrix}$$

$\vec{v}$ and $A\vec{v}$ are shown at the right. Notice that the line determined by the tips of $\vec{v}$ and $A\vec{v}$ is perpendicular to the x axis. Also each point is the same distance from the x axis. Thus $\vec{v}$ and $A\vec{v}$ are *mirror images* or *reflections* of each other with respect to the x axis. Since $\vec{v}$ is an arbitrary vector each vector has the same property except those of the form $\begin{bmatrix} x \\ 0 \end{bmatrix}$. These latter vectors are their own images. (Why?)

Summarizing this discussion you find the following.

a. Under the linear transformation $\begin{bmatrix} 1 & 0 \\ 0 & -1 \end{bmatrix}$ each image vector $\begin{bmatrix} x \\ -y \end{bmatrix}$, $y \neq 0$ is the reflection with respect to the x axis of its pre-image.

b. Vectors $\vec{v} = \begin{bmatrix} x \\ 0 \end{bmatrix}$ are their own images.

The linear transformation $\begin{bmatrix} 1 & 0 \\ 0 & -1 \end{bmatrix}$ is denoted $r_{x\,\text{axis}}$ and is called the *reflection with respect to the x axis.*

By a similar argument you can show that $\begin{bmatrix} x \\ y \end{bmatrix}$, $x \neq 0$ is mapped onto $\begin{bmatrix} -x \\ y \end{bmatrix}$ by $\begin{bmatrix} -1 & 0 \\ 0 & 1 \end{bmatrix}$ and $\begin{bmatrix} 0 \\ y \end{bmatrix}$ is mapped by $\begin{bmatrix} -1 & 0 \\ 0 & 1 \end{bmatrix}$ onto itself for all y. $\begin{bmatrix} -1 & 0 \\ 0 & 1 \end{bmatrix}$ is denoted

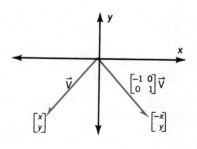

$r_{y\,\text{axis}}$ and is called the *reflection with respect to the y axis.* An example is shown at the right.

The linear transformations $r_{x\,\text{axis}}$ and $r_{y\,\text{axis}}$ provide a natural way to define symmetry with respect to the x axis and the y axis. The formal definition follows.

EXAMPLE 1. $V = \left\{ \begin{bmatrix} x \\ y \end{bmatrix} : \begin{bmatrix} x \\ y \end{bmatrix} = \begin{bmatrix} t \\ t^2 \end{bmatrix}, t \in R \right\}$.   Show that V is symmetric to the y axis.

Several members of V are shown in Figure 1.   Notice that each vector, $\vec{v}$ in V, has its tip on the graph with equation $x = t$, $y = t^2$.   This is a parabola.

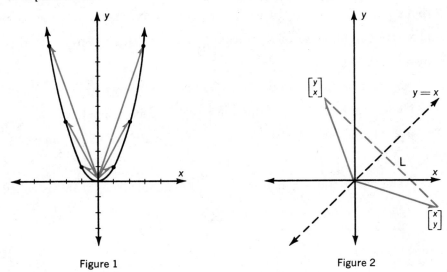

Figure 1   Figure 2

To prove that V is symmetric with respect to the y axis, compute the following.

$$r_{y\,axis} \cdot \vec{v} = \begin{bmatrix} -1 & 0 \\ 0 & 1 \end{bmatrix} \begin{bmatrix} t \\ t^2 \end{bmatrix}$$

$$= \begin{bmatrix} -t \\ t^2 \end{bmatrix}$$

$$= \begin{bmatrix} -t \\ (-t)^2 \end{bmatrix} \quad \text{since } t^2 = (-t)^2$$

Thus the image of each $\vec{v} \in V$ is in V and V is symmetric with respect to the y axis.

The matrix $\begin{bmatrix} 0 & 1 \\ 1 & 0 \end{bmatrix}$ is another important linear transformation. If $\begin{bmatrix} x \\ y \end{bmatrix}$ is any vector, then

$$\begin{bmatrix} 0 & 1 \\ 1 & 0 \end{bmatrix}\begin{bmatrix} x \\ y \end{bmatrix} = \begin{bmatrix} y \\ x \end{bmatrix}.$$

(See Figure 2.) Considering the line L determined by the tips of the vectors $\begin{bmatrix} x \\ y \end{bmatrix}$ and $\begin{bmatrix} y \\ x \end{bmatrix}$ you see that the slope is $\dfrac{x-y}{y-x} = -1$. Thus L is perpendicular to the line $y = x$. Moreover the midpoint of the vector from $\begin{bmatrix} x \\ y \end{bmatrix}$ to $\begin{bmatrix} y \\ x \end{bmatrix}$ is $\left(\dfrac{x+y}{2}, \dfrac{y+x}{2}\right)$. Thus the midpoint of L is on the line $y = x$ and the line $y = x$ is the perpendicular bisector of the segment determined by $\begin{bmatrix} x \\ y \end{bmatrix}$ and its image $\begin{bmatrix} y \\ x \end{bmatrix}$. The vectors are mirror images of each other with respect to the line $y = x$.

The linear transformation $\begin{bmatrix} 0 & 1 \\ 1 & 0 \end{bmatrix}$ is denoted $r_{y=x}$ and is called the *reflection with respect to $y = x$*.

Using a similar argument you can show that the *reflection with respect to $y = -x$* is given by the matrix

$$\begin{bmatrix} 0 & -1 \\ -1 & 0 \end{bmatrix}.$$

This transformation is denoted

$$r_{y=-x}.$$

The image of $\begin{bmatrix} x \\ y \end{bmatrix}$ under $r_{y=-x}$ is $\begin{bmatrix} -y \\ -x \end{bmatrix}$. This is shown in Figure 3 below.

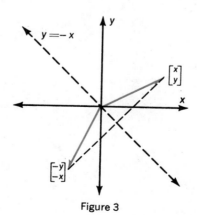

Figure 3

EXAMPLE 2.   Show that the set of vectors

$$V = \left\{ \begin{bmatrix} x \\ y \end{bmatrix} : \begin{bmatrix} x \\ y \end{bmatrix} = \begin{bmatrix} t \\ 1 \\ \frac{1}{t} \end{bmatrix}, \; t \in R, \quad t \neq 0 \right\}$$

is symmetric with respect to $y = x$.

Several of the vectors in V are shown in Figure 4. For this set to be symmetric with respect to the line $y = x$, the image vector must be in V. Let

$$\vec{v} = \begin{bmatrix} t \\ 1 \\ \frac{1}{t} \end{bmatrix}.$$

Then,

$$r_{y=x}\vec{v} = \begin{bmatrix} 0 & 1 \\ 1 & 0 \end{bmatrix} \begin{bmatrix} t \\ \frac{1}{t} \end{bmatrix} = \begin{bmatrix} \frac{1}{t} \\ t \end{bmatrix}$$

Since $t \neq 0$, $\frac{1}{t}$ is a real number and $t = \dfrac{1}{\frac{1}{t}}$.

Thus

$$\begin{bmatrix} \frac{1}{t} \\ t \end{bmatrix} = \begin{bmatrix} \frac{1}{t} \\ \frac{1}{\frac{1}{t}} \end{bmatrix}$$

and therefore is in V. Thus V is symmetric with respect to the line $y = x$. Is V symmetric with respect to the line $y = -x$?

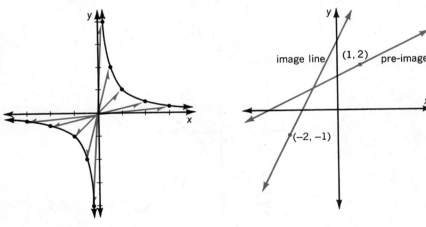

Figure 4   Figure 5

EXAMPLE 3. Find the image of the set of vectors

$$V = \left\{ \begin{bmatrix} x \\ y \end{bmatrix} : \begin{bmatrix} x \\ y \end{bmatrix} = \begin{bmatrix} 1 + 2t \\ 2 + t \end{bmatrix}, \ t \in \mathbf{R} \right\}$$

under $r_{y=-x}$. Graph the pre-image and image.

Solution: V is the set of vectors with tips on the line

$$x = 1 + 2t$$
$$y = 2 + t \quad t \in \mathbf{R}.$$

This is the line which contains $(1, 2)$ and has slope $\frac{1}{2}$. (Why?) (See Figure 5.)

The image set is

$$\begin{bmatrix} 0 & -1 \\ -1 & 0 \end{bmatrix} \begin{bmatrix} 1 + 2t \\ 2 + t \end{bmatrix} = \begin{bmatrix} -2 - t \\ -1 - 2t \end{bmatrix}.$$

The image vectors thus have their tips on

$$\begin{cases} x = -2 - t \\ y = -1 - 2t \end{cases}$$

or the line containing $(-2, -1)$ with slope 2. The lines are shown in Figure 5. Show that their intersection is the point $(-1, 1)$.

CLASSROOM EXERCISES

━━ Find the image of each vector under $r_{x\text{-axis}}$, $r_{y\text{-axis}}$, $r_{y=x}$, and $r_{y=-x}$.

1. $\begin{bmatrix} 2 \\ -3 \end{bmatrix}$ **2.** $\begin{bmatrix} 5 \\ 0 \end{bmatrix}$ **3.** $\begin{bmatrix} 0 \\ 5 \end{bmatrix}$ **4.** $\begin{bmatrix} 2 \\ 2 \end{bmatrix}$ **5.** $\begin{bmatrix} 2 \\ -2 \end{bmatrix}$

WRITTEN EXERCISES

A ━━ Match each transformation with the appropriate matrix.

1. $r_{x\,\text{axis}}$ **2.** $r_{y=x}$

3. $r_{y\,\text{axis}}$ **4.** $r_{y=-x}$

a. $\begin{bmatrix} 1 & 0 \\ 0 & -1 \end{bmatrix}$ **b.** $\begin{bmatrix} 1 & 0 \\ 0 & 1 \end{bmatrix}$

c. $\begin{bmatrix} 0 & -1 \\ -1 & 0 \end{bmatrix}$ **d.** $\begin{bmatrix} -1 & 0 \\ 0 & -1 \end{bmatrix}$

e. $\begin{bmatrix} -1 & 0 \\ 0 & 1 \end{bmatrix}$ **f.** $\begin{bmatrix} 0 & 1 \\ 1 & 0 \end{bmatrix}$

Match each transformation with the appropriate image of $\begin{bmatrix} r \\ s \end{bmatrix}$.

5. $r_{x\,\text{axis}}$　　　　　　　　　　　**6.** $r_{y\,\text{axis}}$

7. $r_{y=x}$　　　　　　　　　　　　**8.** $r_{y=-x}$

a. $\begin{bmatrix} r \\ -s \end{bmatrix}$　　　　　　　　b. $\begin{bmatrix} r \\ s \end{bmatrix}$

c. $\begin{bmatrix} -s \\ -r \end{bmatrix}$　　　　　　　　d. $\begin{bmatrix} -r \\ -s \end{bmatrix}$

e. $\begin{bmatrix} -r \\ s \end{bmatrix}$　　　　　　　　f. $\begin{bmatrix} s \\ r \end{bmatrix}$

Given the vectors $\begin{bmatrix} 3 \\ 1 \end{bmatrix}$, $\begin{bmatrix} -4 \\ 2 \end{bmatrix}$, $\begin{bmatrix} -1 \\ -3 \end{bmatrix}$, and $\begin{bmatrix} 3 \\ -4 \end{bmatrix}$. Make a graph of these vectors and their images under each of the following.

9. $r_{x\,\text{axis}}$　　　　　　　　　　**10.** $r_{y\,\text{axis}}$

11. $r_{y=-x}$　　　　　　　　　　**12.** $r_{y=x}$

Given a triangle with vertices at $(2, 1)$, $(3, 5)$, $(7, 3)$. Make a graph of the triangle and its image under each of the following.

13. $r_{x\,\text{axis}}$　　　　　　　　　　**14.** $r_{y\,\text{axis}}$

15. $r_{y=x}$　　　　　　　　　　**16.** $r_{y=-x}$

17. Find the inverse of $r_{x\,\text{axis}}$, $r_{y\,\text{axis}}$, $r_{y=x}$, and $r_{y=-x}$. What do you notice?

In Exercises 18–21, determine the line with respect to which the set V is symmetric.

18. $V = \left\{ \begin{bmatrix} 2 \\ 1 \end{bmatrix}, \begin{bmatrix} -3 \\ 2 \end{bmatrix}, \begin{bmatrix} 2 \\ -1 \end{bmatrix}, \begin{bmatrix} 4 \\ 0 \end{bmatrix}, \begin{bmatrix} -3 \\ -2 \end{bmatrix} \right\}$

19. $V = \left\{ \begin{bmatrix} 2 \\ 1 \end{bmatrix}, \begin{bmatrix} 2 \\ 2 \end{bmatrix}, \begin{bmatrix} -3 \\ 2 \end{bmatrix}, \begin{bmatrix} 2 \\ -3 \end{bmatrix}, \begin{bmatrix} 1 \\ 2 \end{bmatrix} \right\}$

20. $V = \left\{ \begin{bmatrix} 2 \\ 1 \end{bmatrix}, \begin{bmatrix} 0 \\ 3 \end{bmatrix}, \begin{bmatrix} -3 \\ -2 \end{bmatrix}, \begin{bmatrix} -2 \\ 1 \end{bmatrix}, \begin{bmatrix} 3 \\ -2 \end{bmatrix} \right\}$

21. $V = \left\{ \begin{bmatrix} 2 \\ 1 \end{bmatrix}, \begin{bmatrix} 3 \\ -3 \end{bmatrix}, \begin{bmatrix} -5 \\ 5 \end{bmatrix}, \begin{bmatrix} -1 \\ -2 \end{bmatrix} \right\}$

B　In Exercises 22–34, determine the line(s) with respect to which each set is symmetric.

22. $V = \left\{ \begin{bmatrix} x \\ y \end{bmatrix} : \begin{bmatrix} x \\ y \end{bmatrix} = \begin{bmatrix} t \\ |t| \end{bmatrix}, t \in R \right\}$

23. $V = \left\{ \begin{bmatrix} x \\ y \end{bmatrix} : \begin{bmatrix} x \\ y \end{bmatrix} = \begin{bmatrix} t \\ |t| - 3 \end{bmatrix}, t \in R \right\}$

24. $V = \left\{ \begin{bmatrix} x \\ y \end{bmatrix} : \begin{bmatrix} x \\ y \end{bmatrix} = \begin{bmatrix} t \\ -\frac{1}{t} \end{bmatrix}, t \in R, t \neq 0 \right\}$

25. $V = \left\{ \begin{bmatrix} x \\ y \end{bmatrix} : \begin{bmatrix} x \\ y \end{bmatrix} = \begin{bmatrix} t^2 \\ t \end{bmatrix}, t \in R \right\}$

26. $V = \left\{ \begin{bmatrix} x \\ y \end{bmatrix} : \begin{bmatrix} x \\ y \end{bmatrix} = \begin{bmatrix} t \\ t^2 + t^4 \end{bmatrix}, t \in R \right\}$

27. $V = \left\{ \begin{bmatrix} x \\ y \end{bmatrix} : \begin{bmatrix} x \\ y \end{bmatrix} = \begin{bmatrix} t \\ \pm\sqrt{4 - t^2} \end{bmatrix}, t \in R, -2 \le t \le 2 \right\}$

28. $V = \left\{ \begin{bmatrix} x \\ y \end{bmatrix} : \begin{bmatrix} x \\ y \end{bmatrix} = \begin{bmatrix} |t| \\ t \end{bmatrix}, t \in R \right\}$

29. $V = \left\{ \begin{bmatrix} x \\ y \end{bmatrix} : \begin{bmatrix} x \\ y \end{bmatrix} = \begin{bmatrix} t \\ \pm 2\sqrt{1 - t^2} \end{bmatrix}, -1 \le t \le 1, t \in R \right\}$

30. $V = \left\{ \begin{bmatrix} x \\ y \end{bmatrix} : \begin{bmatrix} x \\ y \end{bmatrix} = \begin{bmatrix} t \\ t \end{bmatrix}, t \in R \right\}$

31. $V = \left\{ \begin{bmatrix} x \\ y \end{bmatrix} : \begin{bmatrix} x \\ y \end{bmatrix} = \begin{bmatrix} t \\ t^2 + 1 \end{bmatrix}, t \in R \right\}$

32. $V = \left\{ \begin{bmatrix} x \\ y \end{bmatrix} : \begin{bmatrix} x \\ y \end{bmatrix} = \begin{bmatrix} t^2 + 2 \\ t \end{bmatrix}, t \in R \right\}$

33. $V = \left\{ \begin{bmatrix} x \\ y \end{bmatrix} : \begin{bmatrix} x \\ y \end{bmatrix} = \begin{bmatrix} t\sqrt{25 - t^2} \\ t \end{bmatrix}, t \in R \right\}$

34. $V = \left\{ \begin{bmatrix} x \\ y \end{bmatrix} : \begin{bmatrix} x \\ y \end{bmatrix} = \begin{bmatrix} t\sqrt{16 - 2t^2} \\ t \end{bmatrix}, t \in R \right\}$

C **35.** Prove that the four reflections

$$r_{x \text{ axis}}, \qquad r_{y \text{ axis}}, \qquad r_{y=x}, \quad \text{and} \quad r_{y=-x}$$

preserve distance between points.

36. Prove that the four reflections

$$r_{x \text{ axis}}, \qquad r_{y \text{ axis}}, \qquad r_{y=x}, \quad \text{and} \quad r_{y=-x}$$

preserve the measure of angles between vectors.

37. Under each of the following find the image of the line

$$\begin{cases} x = 1 - 3t \\ y = 2 + t \, . \end{cases}$$

a. $r_{x=y}$
c. $r_{y \text{ axis}}$

b. $r_{x \text{ axis}}$
d. $r_{y=-x}$

Graph each image and pre-image. Find the point of intersection.

38. What line(s) is its own image under

a. $r_{y \text{ axis}}$
c. $r_{y=x}$

b. $r_{x \text{ axis}}$
d. $r_{y=-x}$

10–10   Rotations about the Origin

In Figure 1, vector $\vec{v}$ has been rotated 75° counterclockwise about the origin. The image vector is in color. The purpose of this section is to find a matrix representation of a rotation about the origin.

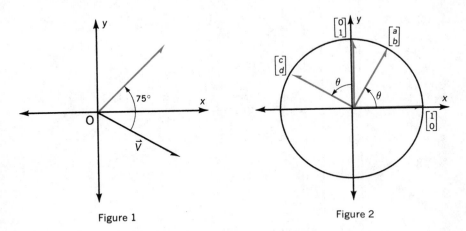

Figure 1   Figure 2

Every vector may be expressed as

$$\vec{v} = a\mathbf{i} + b\mathbf{j},$$

where $\mathbf{i} = \begin{bmatrix} 1 \\ 0 \end{bmatrix}$ and $\mathbf{j} = \begin{bmatrix} 0 \\ 1 \end{bmatrix}$. If a vector is transformed, its image is determined by the images of $\mathbf{i}$ and $\mathbf{j}$. Suppose that $\begin{bmatrix} 1 \\ 0 \end{bmatrix} \rightarrow \begin{bmatrix} a \\ b \end{bmatrix}$ and $\begin{bmatrix} 0 \\ 1 \end{bmatrix} \rightarrow \begin{bmatrix} c \\ d \end{bmatrix}$ and that A is the matrix of this transformation. Then $A\begin{bmatrix} 1 \\ 0 \end{bmatrix} = \begin{bmatrix} a \\ b \end{bmatrix}$ and $A\begin{bmatrix} 0 \\ 1 \end{bmatrix} = \begin{bmatrix} c \\ d \end{bmatrix}$. This can be written in the following form.

$$A\begin{bmatrix} 1 & 0 \\ 0 & 1 \end{bmatrix} = \begin{bmatrix} a & c \\ b & d \end{bmatrix}$$

But $\begin{bmatrix} 1 & 0 \\ 0 & 1 \end{bmatrix}$ is the identity matrix. Thus, the following statement must be true.

$$A = \begin{bmatrix} a & c \\ b & d \end{bmatrix}$$

This result is formalized in Theorem 10–15 which is stated at the top of the next page.

> **Theorem 10–15**   If A is the matrix for the transformation such that $\begin{bmatrix} 1 \\ 0 \end{bmatrix} \rightarrow \begin{bmatrix} a \\ b \end{bmatrix}$ and $\begin{bmatrix} 0 \\ 1 \end{bmatrix} \rightarrow \begin{bmatrix} c \\ d \end{bmatrix}$, then $A = \begin{bmatrix} a & c \\ b & d \end{bmatrix}$.

Now consider the rotation of θ degrees about the origin. The image of $\begin{bmatrix} 1 \\ 0 \end{bmatrix}$ is $\begin{bmatrix} a \\ b \end{bmatrix}$. But a and b can be written in terms of θ and trigonometric functions as follows (see Section 2–3):

$$a = \cos \theta$$
$$b = \sin \theta$$

If $A \begin{bmatrix} 0 \\ 1 \end{bmatrix} = \begin{bmatrix} c \\ d \end{bmatrix}$, then from Theorem 2–6 on page 80,

$$c = \cos (90 + \theta) = -\sin \theta$$
$$d = \sin (90 + \theta) = \cos \theta.$$

Applying Theorem 10–15,

$$A = \begin{bmatrix} \cos \theta & -\sin \theta \\ \sin \theta & \cos \theta \end{bmatrix}.$$

This is the matrix for a rotation about the origin. Since the rotation has measure θ this particular linear transformation is called the **rotation of θ about the origin** and is denoted R_θ.

EXAMPLE 1. Find the image of $\begin{bmatrix} 2 \\ 3 \end{bmatrix}$ under R_{135}. Make a sketch showing the two vectors.

$$R_{135} = \begin{bmatrix} \cos 135 & -\sin 135 \\ \sin 135 & \cos 135 \end{bmatrix}$$

$$= \begin{bmatrix} \dfrac{-\sqrt{2}}{2} & \dfrac{-\sqrt{2}}{2} \\ \dfrac{\sqrt{2}}{2} & \dfrac{-\sqrt{2}}{2} \end{bmatrix}$$

$$= \frac{\sqrt{2}}{2} \begin{bmatrix} -1 & -1 \\ 1 & -1 \end{bmatrix}.$$

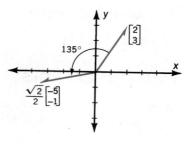

Thus,

$$R_{135} \cdot \begin{bmatrix} 2 \\ 3 \end{bmatrix} = \frac{\sqrt{2}}{2} \begin{bmatrix} -1 & -1 \\ 1 & -1 \end{bmatrix} \begin{bmatrix} 2 \\ 3 \end{bmatrix}$$

$$= \frac{\sqrt{2}}{2} \begin{bmatrix} -5 \\ -1 \end{bmatrix}$$

EXAMPLE 2. Find the image of the line $\begin{cases} x = 1 + 2t \\ y = 2 + t, \end{cases} t \in R$

under R_{270}. Graph the pre-image and image.

Solution: The given line contains $(1, 2)$ and has slope $\frac{1}{2}$. The image is found by multiplying R_{270} by $\begin{bmatrix} 1 + 2t \\ 2 + t \end{bmatrix}$:

$R_{270} \cdot \begin{bmatrix} 1 + 2t \\ 2 + t \end{bmatrix}$

$= \begin{bmatrix} \cos 270 & -\sin 270 \\ \sin 270 & \cos 270 \end{bmatrix} \begin{bmatrix} 1 + 2t \\ 2 + t \end{bmatrix}$

$= \begin{bmatrix} 0 & 1 \\ -1 & 0 \end{bmatrix} \begin{bmatrix} 1 + 2t \\ 2 + t \end{bmatrix}$

$= \begin{bmatrix} 2 + t \\ -1 - 2t \end{bmatrix}$

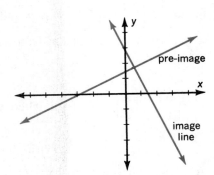

The image line is $\begin{cases} x = 2 + t \\ y = -1 - 2t \end{cases}$.

This line contains $(2, -1)$ and has slope -2. Where do the lines intersect?

CLASSROOM EXERCISES

— Find the image of $\begin{bmatrix} 3 \\ -2 \end{bmatrix}$ under the following.

1. R_{120} **2.** R_{45} **3.** R_{270} **4.** R_{90} **5.** R_{180}

6. Find the image of $\begin{cases} x = t \\ y = 3t. \end{cases} t \in R$

under R_{180} and R_{90}.

WRITTEN EXERCISES

A — For Exercises 1–8, if $R_\theta = \begin{bmatrix} \cos\theta & -\sin\theta \\ \sin\theta & \cos\theta \end{bmatrix}$ find the explicit expression for R_θ when θ equals

1. $0°$ **2.** $45°$

3. $90°$ **4.** $180°$

5. $270°$ **6.** $30°$

7. $60°$ **8.** $54°$

9. Show that $R_{90°} = R_{-270°}$.

10. Show that $R_\theta = R_{\theta - 360°}$.

In Exercises 11–18, find the image of each vector under **a.** $R_{90°}$, **b.** $R_{180°}$, **c.** $R_{270°}$, **d.** $R_{45°}$. (Use the results of Exercises 2, 3, 4, 5.)

11. $\begin{bmatrix} 2 \\ -3 \end{bmatrix}$ **12.** $\begin{bmatrix} \sqrt{2} \\ -\sqrt{2} \end{bmatrix}$ **13.** $\begin{bmatrix} -3 \\ -4 \end{bmatrix}$ **14.** $\begin{bmatrix} 4 \\ 5 \end{bmatrix}$

15. $\begin{bmatrix} 0 \\ 4 \end{bmatrix}$ **16.** $\begin{bmatrix} -2 \\ 1 \end{bmatrix}$ **17.** $\begin{bmatrix} 4 \\ 1 \end{bmatrix}$ **18.** $\begin{bmatrix} 5 \\ 0 \end{bmatrix}$

Find the image of the triangle with vertices $(2, 7)$, $(4, 1)$, $(6, 3)$ under each rotation. Graph the pre-image and image.

19. $R_{90°}$ **20.** $R_{45°}$

21. $R_{180°}$ **22.** $R_{270°}$ **23.** $R_{30°}$

In Exercises 24–27, find the image of each line under the rotations in Exercises 19–23. Make a graph of each.

24. $\begin{cases} x = -3 + 2t \\ y = 0 - t \end{cases}$ **25.** $\begin{cases} x = 1 - 3t \\ y = 2 + 3t \end{cases}$

26. $\begin{cases} x = 1 + \frac{1}{2}t \\ y = -2 - 2t \end{cases}$ **27.** $\begin{cases} x = -3 - 2t \\ y = -2 + 5t \end{cases}$

B   **28.** Show that the length of the vector $\begin{bmatrix} x \\ y \end{bmatrix}$ is identical to that of $R_\theta \begin{bmatrix} x \\ y \end{bmatrix}$. (*Hint:* $\sin^2 \theta + \cos^2 \theta = 1$)

29. Show that the angle between the vectors $\begin{bmatrix} a \\ b \end{bmatrix}$ and $\begin{bmatrix} c \\ d \end{bmatrix}$ is the same as the angle between $R_\theta \cdot \begin{bmatrix} a \\ b \end{bmatrix}$ and $R_\theta \cdot \begin{bmatrix} c \\ d \end{bmatrix}$. (*Hint:* Use the results of Exercise 28 and the hint given there.)

30. Show that every vector on the line $\begin{cases} x = t \\ y = nt \end{cases}$ $t \in R$ has an image on the same line under $R_{180°}$.

C   **31.** The rotation R_{180} is a *half turn*. A set of vectors is called symmetric to the origin if and only if the image of every vector under R_{180} is in the original set. For example $\left\{ \begin{bmatrix} 1 \\ 2 \end{bmatrix}, \begin{bmatrix} -1 \\ -2 \end{bmatrix} \right\}$ is symmetric to the origin because $R_{180} \cdot \begin{bmatrix} 1 \\ 2 \end{bmatrix} = \begin{bmatrix} -1 \\ -2 \end{bmatrix}$ and $R_{180} \cdot \begin{bmatrix} -1 \\ -2 \end{bmatrix} = \begin{bmatrix} 1 \\ 2 \end{bmatrix}$. Show that each set below is symmetric to the origin.

a. $V = \left\{ \begin{bmatrix} x \\ y \end{bmatrix} : \begin{bmatrix} x \\ y \end{bmatrix} = \begin{bmatrix} t \\ t^3 \end{bmatrix}, t \in R \right\}$

b. $V = \left\{ \begin{bmatrix} x \\ y \end{bmatrix} : \begin{bmatrix} x \\ y \end{bmatrix} = \begin{bmatrix} t \\ \frac{1}{t} \end{bmatrix}, t \neq 0, t \in R \right\}$

c. $V = \left\{ \begin{bmatrix} x \\ y \end{bmatrix} : \begin{bmatrix} x \\ y \end{bmatrix} = \begin{bmatrix} t \\ \pm\sqrt{4 - t^2} \end{bmatrix}, -2 \leq t \leq 2, t \in R \right\}$

BASIC: SOLVING LINEAR SYSTEMS

Problem:

Given an $n \times n$ system of linear equations, write a program which uses elementary row operations on the augmented coefficient matrix to solve the system. This method is called **Gauss–Jordan reduction.**

```
100  DIM A(10,20)
120  PRINT "THIS PROGRAM SOLVES N X N SYSTEMS"
130  PRINT "OF LINEAR EQUATIONS BY GAUSS-JORDAN"
140  PRINT "ROW REDUCTIONS."
150  PRINT
160  PRINT "WHAT IS THE VALUE OF N";
170  INPUT N
180  PRINT
190  PRINT "ENTER THE COEFFICIENTS OF EACH"
200  PRINT "EQUATION,INCLUDING THE CONSTANT."
210  FOR I = 1 TO N
220     PRINT "EQUATION";I;":"
230     FOR J = 1 TO N+1
240        INPUT A(I,J)
250     NEXT J
260  NEXT I
270  PRINT
280  FOR I = 1 TO N
290     IF A(I,I) <> 0 THEN 390
300     FOR K = I+1 TO N
310        IF A(K,I) <> 0 THEN 340
320     NEXT K
330     GOTO 580
340     FOR J = 1 TO N+1
350        LET Z = A(I,J)
360        LET A(I,J) = A(K,J)
370        LET A(K,J) = Z
380     NEXT J
390     IF A(I,I) = 1 THEN 440
400     LET M = A(I,I)
410     FOR J = 1 TO N+1
420        LET A(I,J) = A(I,J)/M
430     NEXT J
440     FOR L = 1 TO N
450        IF L = I THEN 510
```

```
460     IF A(L,I) = 0 THEN 510
470     LET M = A(L,I)
480     FOR J = 1 TO N+1
490       LET A(L,J) = A(L,J)-M*A(I,J)
500     NEXT J
510   NEXT L
520 NEXT I
530 PRINT "SOLUTION IS:"
540 FOR I = 1 TO N
550   PRINT "X(";I;") = ";A(I,N+1)
560 NEXT I
570 GOTO 590
580 PRINT "NO UNIQUE SOLUTION"
590 PRINT
600 PRINT "ANY MORE EQUATIONS (1=YES,0=NO)";
610 INPUT Q
620 IF Q = 1 THEN 150
630 PRINT
640 END
```

Analysis:

Statements 290–330: The program keys on the "pivot" element A(I,I) on the main diagonal of the coefficient matrix. If this element is zero, the loop in lines 300–320 searches for a later row that has a nonzero element in that column. If there is none, the computer ends the loop and reaches line 330, which sends it to statement 580.

Statements 340–430: The loop in lines 340–380 is executed when A(I,I) = 0, but a later row (K) has a nonzero element in column I. These steps interchange rows K and J in order to put a nonzero element in the pivot position. If A(I,I) is not 1, the loop in lines 410–430 divides each element of row I by the pivot element.

Statements 440–510: This section creates zeros in all positions in column I except for the pivot position (row I). It does this by adding the appropriate multiple of the pivot row I to row L.

EXERCISES

A   Use the program on page 570 to solve each system of equations.

1. $\begin{cases} 5x - 2y = 19 \\ 7x + 3y = 15 \end{cases}$ **2.** $\begin{cases} x - y = 5 \\ 2x + 3y = 10 \end{cases}$ **3.** $\begin{cases} 2x - 3y = 16 \\ -5x - y = 28 \end{cases}$

C

4. Given the elements of a 2×2 matrix, write a program which prints the determinant and the multiplicative inverse (if any) of the matrix.

10–11   Compositions of Linear Transformations

In the figure, vector $\begin{bmatrix} 2 \\ -1 \end{bmatrix}$ is shown. The linear transformation $\begin{bmatrix} 1 & 1 \\ 2 & 1 \end{bmatrix}$ is applied to $\begin{bmatrix} 2 \\ -1 \end{bmatrix}$ yielding

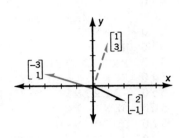

$\begin{bmatrix} 1 & 1 \\ 2 & 1 \end{bmatrix}\begin{bmatrix} 2 \\ -1 \end{bmatrix} = \begin{bmatrix} 1 \\ 3 \end{bmatrix}.$ Then   the linear transformation $\begin{bmatrix} 0 & -1 \\ 1 & 0 \end{bmatrix}$ is applied to $\begin{bmatrix} 1 \\ 3 \end{bmatrix}$ yielding

$$\begin{bmatrix} 0 & -1 \\ 1 & 0 \end{bmatrix}\begin{bmatrix} 1 \\ 3 \end{bmatrix} = \begin{bmatrix} -3 \\ 1 \end{bmatrix}.$$

The latter two vectors are shown in color in the figure.

The operation of applying one transformation to the vectors of a set, then applying a second transformation to the vectors in the image set is called **composing transformations.** If A_1 is the matrix of the first transformation and A_2 is the matrix of the second, then the composition of A_1 and A_2 applied to V is

$$A_2(A_1 \vec{v}). \qquad\qquad 1$$

Since matrix multiplication is associative, the following is true.

$$A_2(A_1 \vec{v}) = (A_2 A_1)\vec{v} \qquad\qquad 2$$

(See Exercise 39, Section 10–3.) Thus the composition of two linear transformations may be accomplished by first computing the product $A_2 A_1$ and then applying this transformation to $\vec{v}$.

A_1 and A_2 are two-by-two matrices, thus $A_2 A_1$ is a two-by-two matrix. Therefore, the composite of two linear transformations is again a linear transformation. This argument proves the following theorem.

Theorem 10–16   If A_1 and A_2 are linear transformations then the composite of A_1 and A_2 is a linear transformation A and

$$A_2(A_1 \vec{v}) = (A_2 A_1)\vec{v} = A\vec{v}$$

for all $\vec{v}$.

EXAMPLE 1. Verify Theorem 10–16 for $A_1 = \begin{bmatrix} 1 & 2 \\ -3 & 4 \end{bmatrix}$, $A_2 = \begin{bmatrix} 1 & -2 \\ 1 & 3 \end{bmatrix}$ and $\vec{v} = \begin{bmatrix} -1 \\ 2 \end{bmatrix}$.

$$A_2(A_1\vec{v}) = \begin{bmatrix} 1 & -2 \\ 1 & 3 \end{bmatrix} \left(\begin{bmatrix} 1 & 2 \\ -3 & 4 \end{bmatrix} \begin{bmatrix} -1 \\ 2 \end{bmatrix} \right)$$

$$= \begin{bmatrix} 1 & -2 \\ 1 & 3 \end{bmatrix} \begin{bmatrix} 3 \\ 11 \end{bmatrix} = \begin{bmatrix} -19 \\ 36 \end{bmatrix}$$

$$(A_2A_1)\vec{v} = \left(\begin{bmatrix} 1 & -2 \\ 1 & 3 \end{bmatrix} \begin{bmatrix} 1 & 2 \\ -3 & 4 \end{bmatrix} \right) \begin{bmatrix} -1 \\ 2 \end{bmatrix}$$

$$= \begin{bmatrix} 7 & -6 \\ -8 & 14 \end{bmatrix} \begin{bmatrix} -1 \\ 2 \end{bmatrix} = \begin{bmatrix} -19 \\ 36 \end{bmatrix}$$

Thus $A_2(A_1\vec{v}) = (A_2A_1)\vec{v}$. Since the composite is representable by a 2 by 2 matrix, it is a linear transformation.

Composites of the special linear transformations introduced in Sections 10–9 and 10–10 are particularly interesting because of the patterns which occur. Consider initially the composite of two rotations about the origin, say $R_\phi R_\theta$.

$$R_\phi R_\theta = \begin{bmatrix} \cos\phi & -\sin\phi \\ \sin\phi & \cos\phi \end{bmatrix} \begin{bmatrix} \cos\theta & -\sin\theta \\ \sin\theta & \cos\theta \end{bmatrix}$$

$$= \begin{bmatrix} \cos\phi\cos\theta - \sin\phi\sin\theta & -\cos\phi\sin\theta - \sin\phi\cos\theta \\ \sin\phi\cos\theta + \cos\phi\sin\theta & -\sin\phi\sin\theta + \cos\phi\cos\theta \end{bmatrix} \qquad 3$$

Recall the identities: $\cos(\phi + \theta) = \cos\phi\cos\theta - \sin\phi\sin\theta$ and
$$\sin(\phi + \theta) = \sin\phi\cos\theta + \cos\phi\sin\theta$$

Substituting these expressions in 3 you find:

$$R_\phi R_\theta = \begin{bmatrix} \cos(\phi + \theta) & -\sin(\phi + \theta) \\ \sin(\phi + \theta) & \cos(\phi + \theta) \end{bmatrix}$$

$$= \begin{bmatrix} \cos\alpha & -\sin\alpha \\ \sin\alpha & \cos\alpha \end{bmatrix}, \quad \text{where } \alpha = \phi + \theta. \qquad 4$$

The matrix 4 is the matrix of a rotation about the origin with the angle measuring

$$\alpha = \phi + \theta.$$

Theorem 10–17 The composite of two rotations, R_θ and R_ϕ, about the origin is a rotation $R_{\phi+\theta}$ about the origin. The angle of rotation is the sum of the angles of the original rotations. That is

$$R_\phi R_\theta = R_{\phi+\theta}.$$

EXAMPLE 2. Find the matrix for R_{75} without reference to tables.

Solution: Since $75 = 30 + 45$, $R_{75} = R_{30}R_{45}$.

Thus,
$$R_{75} = R_{30}R_{45} = \begin{bmatrix} \dfrac{\sqrt{3}}{2} & \dfrac{-1}{2} \\ \dfrac{1}{2} & \dfrac{\sqrt{3}}{2} \end{bmatrix} \begin{bmatrix} \dfrac{\sqrt{2}}{2} & \dfrac{-\sqrt{2}}{2} \\ \dfrac{\sqrt{2}}{2} & \dfrac{\sqrt{2}}{2} \end{bmatrix}$$

$$= \left(\frac{1}{2} \begin{bmatrix} \sqrt{3} & -1 \\ 1 & \sqrt{3} \end{bmatrix} \right) \left(\frac{\sqrt{2}}{2} \begin{bmatrix} 1 & -1 \\ 1 & 1 \end{bmatrix} \right)$$

$$= \frac{\sqrt{2}}{4} \begin{bmatrix} \sqrt{3} & -1 \\ 1 & \sqrt{3} \end{bmatrix} \begin{bmatrix} 1 & -1 \\ 1 & 1 \end{bmatrix}$$

$$= \frac{\sqrt{2}}{4} \begin{bmatrix} \sqrt{3} - 1 & -(\sqrt{3} + 1) \\ \sqrt{3} + 1 & \sqrt{3} - 1 \end{bmatrix}$$

Composing reflections also yields an interesting pattern. Whereas the composite of two rotations is a rotation, the composite of two reflections is *not* a reflection. To see what it may be, consider the following examples.

1. $r_{y=x}r_{x \text{ axis}} = \begin{bmatrix} 0 & 1 \\ 1 & 0 \end{bmatrix} \begin{bmatrix} 1 & 0 \\ 0 & -1 \end{bmatrix} = \begin{bmatrix} 0 & -1 \\ 1 & 0 \end{bmatrix} = R_{90}$

2. $r_{y \text{ axis}}r_{x \text{ axis}} = \begin{bmatrix} -1 & 0 \\ 0 & 1 \end{bmatrix} \begin{bmatrix} 1 & 0 \\ 0 & -1 \end{bmatrix} = \begin{bmatrix} -1 & 0 \\ 0 & -1 \end{bmatrix} = R_{180}$

3. $r_{y=-x}r_{x \text{ axis}} = \begin{bmatrix} 0 & -1 \\ -1 & 0 \end{bmatrix} \begin{bmatrix} 1 & 0 \\ 0 & -1 \end{bmatrix} = \begin{bmatrix} 0 & 1 \\ -1 & 0 \end{bmatrix} = R_{270}$

In each case above the composite of two reflections is a rotation. The generalization is the following.

The composite of two reflections with respect to intersecting lines is a rotation about the point of intersection.

The converse statement is also true, but neither statement can be proved here since your knowledge of reflections is not extensive enough.

CLASSROOM EXERCISES

━━━ Find the single matrix that is the composition of A followed by B.

1. $A = \begin{bmatrix} 2 & 1 \\ 1 & 2 \end{bmatrix}$ $B = \begin{bmatrix} -2 & 3 \\ 3 & 1 \end{bmatrix}$ **2.** $A = \begin{bmatrix} 1 & 0 \\ 1 & 1 \end{bmatrix}$ $B = \begin{bmatrix} 1 & 1 \\ 0 & 1 \end{bmatrix}$

WRITTEN EXERCISES

A ▬ Find the single matrix which is the composition of A followed by B.

1. $A = \begin{bmatrix} 1 & 2 \\ 1 & 4 \end{bmatrix}$ $B = \begin{bmatrix} 2 & 1 \\ -3 & -1 \end{bmatrix}$

2. $A = \begin{bmatrix} 2 & -1 \\ 1 & 5 \end{bmatrix}$ $B = \begin{bmatrix} 1 & 1 \\ 1 & 2 \end{bmatrix}$

3. $A = \begin{bmatrix} -1 & -2 \\ -5 & 1 \end{bmatrix}$ $B = \begin{bmatrix} -3 & 4 \\ 1 & 2 \end{bmatrix}$

4. $A = \begin{bmatrix} 3 & 4 \\ 5 & 7 \end{bmatrix}$ $B = \begin{bmatrix} 7 & -4 \\ -5 & 3 \end{bmatrix}$

5. Find the image of **a.** $\begin{bmatrix} -1 \\ +3 \end{bmatrix}$ **b.** $\begin{bmatrix} 0 \\ 2 \end{bmatrix}$ **c.** $\begin{bmatrix} 4 \\ -1 \end{bmatrix}$ **d.** $\begin{bmatrix} -3 \\ 0 \end{bmatrix}$ and **e.** $\begin{bmatrix} -2 \\ -1 \end{bmatrix}$

under the composite transformation BA using the transformations given in Exercises 1–4. Draw graphs showing each vector and its image.

▬ Find each rotation matrix without using tables.

6. $R_{105°}$ **7.** $R_{165°}$

8. $R_{15°}$ ($15° = 45° - 30°$)   **9.** $R_{195°}$

10. Find the image of the triangle with vertices at (1, 2), (2, 1) and (4, 5) under the composite transformation $B \cdot A$ where $A = \begin{bmatrix} 1 & 0 \\ -2 & 1 \end{bmatrix}$ and $B = \begin{bmatrix} 1 & 3 \\ 0 & 1 \end{bmatrix}$. Draw a graph of the triangle and its image.

11. Repeat Exercise 10 for the composite AB. Are the results the same?

12. Find the image of the line $\begin{cases} x = -3 + t \\ y = 2 + 2t \end{cases}$ under the composite transformation BA given in Exercise 10. Graph the two lines.

13. Repeat Exercise 12 for the line $\begin{cases} x = 1 + t \\ y = 3t. \end{cases}$

B **14.** Show that composition of rotations about the origin is commutative, that is,

$$R_\phi R_\theta = R_\theta R_\phi.$$

15. Prove that the determinant of a composite transformation AB is the product of the determinants of A and B, that is, $\det(AB) = (\det A)(\det B)$.

16. Prove: If A and B are inverse matrices; then $\det B = \dfrac{1}{\det A}$.

17. Describe the effect on a vector of the composite transformation of the following.

    a. $A^{-1}A$ **b.** AA^{-1}

18. If A transforms $\vec{v}$ into $\vec{r}$ and A has nonzero determinant, what transformation will transform $\vec{r}$ into $\vec{v}$?

C **19.** Find the area of the triangle with vertices at $(0, 0)$, (a, b) and $(c, 0)$ using the cross product of vectors $a\mathbf{i} + b\mathbf{j} + 0\mathbf{k}$ and $c\mathbf{i} + 0\mathbf{j} + 0\mathbf{k}$. (See Section 9–9).

20. Let $A = \begin{bmatrix} p & q \\ r & s \end{bmatrix}$ be a linear transformation with nonzero determinant. Let $|\det A| = k$.

    a. Find the image of the triangle given in Exercise 19 under the linear transformation A.

    b. Find the cross product of the images of the vectors $a\mathbf{i} + b\mathbf{j} + 0\mathbf{k}$ and $c\mathbf{i} + 0\mathbf{j} + 0\mathbf{k}$.

    c. Find the length of this cross product.

    d. What is the area of the image triangle?

    e. How are the areas of the pre-image and image triangles related?

    f. State a generalization.

    g. Is the generalization valid for a triangle which has no vertex at the origin? Explain.

21. What does a rotation about the origin do to the area of a triangle? Explain.

22. Answer Exercise 21 for the reflections of Section 10–9.

23. It can be shown that the reflection with respect to $y = mx$ is

$$r_{y=mx} = \begin{bmatrix} \cos 2\theta & \sin 2\theta \\ \sin 2\theta & -\cos 2\theta \end{bmatrix}$$

where θ is the measure of the angle between the positive x axis and the line through the origin $y = mx$. Verify this statement for each of the following.

    a. x axis   **b.** y axis

    c. the line $y = x$ **d.** the line $y = -x$

24. Use Exercise 23 to find the reflection matrix for

    a. $r_{y=\frac{1}{2}x}$ **b.** $r_{y=2x}$

    c. $r_{y=-2x}$ **d.** $r_{y=-\frac{1}{2}x}$

    e. $r_{y=3x}$ **f.** $r_{y=\frac{1}{3}x}$

10–12   Translations

The transformations considered so far have been ones which left the origin fixed. Thus they were identified with 2×2 matrices. The transformation discussed in this section pairs each point in the plane with a new point. This transformation is called a **translation**.

Let (x, y) be any point in the plane. Then the position vector $\begin{bmatrix} x \\ y \end{bmatrix}$ has its tip at the point (x, y). Suppose you are given a constant vector $\begin{bmatrix} a \\ b \end{bmatrix}$. The vector $\begin{bmatrix} x \\ y \end{bmatrix} + \begin{bmatrix} a \\ b \end{bmatrix} = \begin{bmatrix} x + a \\ y + b \end{bmatrix}$ is a position vector which has its tip at $(x + a, y + b)$. The point (x, y) has been translated to the new position $(x + a, y + b)$. See the figure below.

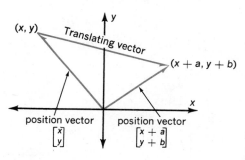

Definition   A **translation** is a transformation which pairs each point (x, y) with a point $(x + a, y + b)$. The translation is performed by adding the **translating vector** $\begin{bmatrix} a \\ b \end{bmatrix}$ to the position vector $\begin{bmatrix} x \\ y \end{bmatrix}$.

EXAMPLE 1. Let $\begin{bmatrix} 2 \\ -3 \end{bmatrix}$ be a translating vector. Find the images of $(1, 1)$, $(-1, -2)$ and $(-4, 3)$. Graph the points and their images.

$$\begin{bmatrix} 1 \\ 1 \end{bmatrix} + \begin{bmatrix} 2 \\ -3 \end{bmatrix} = \begin{bmatrix} 3 \\ -2 \end{bmatrix}$$

$$\begin{bmatrix} -1 \\ -2 \end{bmatrix} + \begin{bmatrix} 2 \\ -3 \end{bmatrix} = \begin{bmatrix} 1 \\ -5 \end{bmatrix}$$

$$\begin{bmatrix} -4 \\ 3 \end{bmatrix} + \begin{bmatrix} 2 \\ -3 \end{bmatrix} = \begin{bmatrix} -2 \\ 0 \end{bmatrix}$$

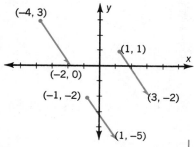

Each point in the figure is connected to its image by the translating vector $\begin{bmatrix} 2 \\ -3 \end{bmatrix}$.

It is clear from the definition of translation that each point has unique image and each point is the image of a unique point. It is also true, but perhaps not quite so obvious, that under a translation the

    a. image of a line is a line.

    b. distance between pre-image points and image points is equal.

    c. measure of the angles between two vectors and the image vectors is the same.

These results are left for you to prove in the exercises.

Knowing that the image of a line is a line allows you to find the equation of the image of a line. This is illustrated in the next example.

EXAMPLE 2. Given $y - x = 3$. Find the image of this line under the translation $\begin{bmatrix} 1 \\ -2 \end{bmatrix}$. Write the equation of the image and graph both lines.

Each point on $y - x = 3$ has the form $(t,\ t + 3)$. Thus, the image of $(t,\ t + 3)$ is

$$\begin{bmatrix} t \\ t+3 \end{bmatrix} + \begin{bmatrix} 1 \\ -2 \end{bmatrix} = \begin{bmatrix} t+1 \\ t+1 \end{bmatrix}.$$

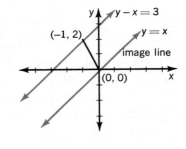

The image vector $\begin{bmatrix} t+1 \\ t+1 \end{bmatrix}$ shows that the x and y coordinates of the points in the image line are equal. Thus, the equation of the image line is $y = x$.

There is a more efficient method of finding the equation of the image line of Example 2. It is described at the top of the next page.

Let $(x',\ y')$ be the coordinates of the image of $(x,\ y)$. Then:

$$\begin{bmatrix} x \\ y \end{bmatrix} + \begin{bmatrix} 1 \\ -2 \end{bmatrix} = \begin{bmatrix} x+1 \\ y-2 \end{bmatrix} = \begin{bmatrix} x' \\ y' \end{bmatrix}$$

$$x' = x + 1$$
$$y' = y - 2 \qquad\qquad\qquad \mathbf{1}$$

Equations 1 can be solved for x and y

$$\begin{cases} x = x' - 1 \\ y = y' + 2 \end{cases}. \qquad\qquad\qquad \mathbf{2}$$

Substituting these values in the equation of the line $y - x = 3$, you find

$$(y' + 2) - (x' - 1) = 3$$

or

$$y' - x' + 3 = 3$$

or

$$y' = x'.$$

Dropping the primes, you find the equation of the image

$$y = x.$$

Theorem 10–18 The equation of the image of a curve under a translation with vector $\begin{bmatrix} h \\ k \end{bmatrix}$ is obtained by substituting

$$x = x' - h$$
$$y = y' - k$$

in the equation of the preimage.

EXAMPLE 3. Find the equation of the line which is the image of $y = 2x - 3$ under a translation with vector $\begin{bmatrix} -3 \\ 2 \end{bmatrix}$. Graph each line.

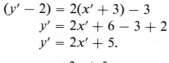

Solution: By Theorem 10–18,

$$\begin{cases} x = x' + 3. \\ y = y' - 2 \end{cases}$$

Thus, the equation is

$$(y' - 2) = 2(x' + 3) - 3$$
$$y' = 2x' + 6 - 3 + 2$$
$$y' = 2x' + 5.$$

or

$$y = 2x + 5.$$

The equations

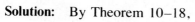

$$\begin{cases} x = x' - h \\ y = y' - k \end{cases} \qquad\qquad 3$$

are called the translation equations.

Theorem 10–18 can be generalized to include three-space. The equations obtained are $\begin{cases} x = x' - h \\ y = y' - k \\ z = z' - l \end{cases}$ where $\begin{bmatrix} h \\ k \\ l \end{bmatrix}$ is the translating vector.

CLASSROOM EXERCISES

1. Translate the line $3x + 2y = 6$ so that the y-intercept maps onto the origin. Find the equation of the new line.

2. Given the set of points $\{(1, 2), (3, 4), (6, 8), (3, 5), (1, 7)\}$, list their translations, where $\begin{bmatrix} 3 \\ 0 \end{bmatrix}$ is the translating vector.

WRITTEN EXERCISES

A ━━ Give the coordinates of the new point if the translating vector is $\begin{bmatrix} -3 \\ 5 \end{bmatrix}$.

1. (0, 0)	**2.** (1, 4)	**3.** (3, 5)
4. (−2, −3)	**5.** (−4, 7)	**6.** (0, 5)
7. (8, 0) **8.** (−5, −5)	**9.** (7, −4)	**10.** (−1, 0)

━━ Translate each line so that the y-intercept maps onto the origin. Graph each line. Find the equation.

11. $y = 2x - 1$ **12.** $y - 3x + 2 = 0$

13. $2y + 4x = 6$ **14.** $3y - 2x - 5 = 0$

15. $y + 5x = 0$ **16.** $7y - 2x = 14$

17. Translate each line in Exercises 11–16 so that the x-intercept maps onto the origin. Graph the lines and find the equation.

B   **18.** Prove: The image of a line under a translation is a line.

19. Prove: Distance between points is preserved by a translation.

20. Prove: The measure of an angle is preserved by a translation.

21. Find the image of the triangle with vertices at (1, 3), (4, 5), and (6, 1) under the translation with vector $\begin{bmatrix} -7 \\ 4 \end{bmatrix}$. Graph each.

22. Find the areas of the triangle and its image in Exercise 21.

C ━━ Find the image of the plane under the translation with vector $\begin{bmatrix} -2 \\ 1 \\ 3 \end{bmatrix}$.

23. $x + y + 2 = 0$ **24.** $2x - 3y + 4z = 5$

25. $\frac{1}{2}x - 2y + 3z = 7$ **26.** $x - 7y - 4z = -16$

27. Construct an argument which you could use to convince a classmate that the intersection of two lines maps onto the intersection of the image lines under a translation.

CHAPTER SUMMARY ▬▬▬▬▬

Important Terms

Composing transformations (p. 572)
Determinant (p. 533)
Elementary row operations (p. 539)
Homogeneous system of linear
  equations (p. 538)
Identity transformation (p. 553)
Image (p. 553)
Invertible matrix (p. 534)
Linear transformation (p. 554)
Matrix (p. 516)
Nonhomogeneous system of
  linear equations (p. 538)

Opposite (p. 518)
Order of a matrix (p. 517)
Pre-image (p. 553)
Reduced row echeleon
  form (p. 542)
Rotation through an
  angle of θ (p. 567)
Scalar product (p. 517)
Transformation (p. 553)
Translation (p. 577)
Unit matrix (p. 522)
Zero matrix (p. 518)

Important Ideas

1. Square matrices of order n satisfy properties such as associativity, closure, and the existence of an identity and zero matrix under multiplication and addition.

2. For $A = \begin{bmatrix} a_{11} & a_{12} \\ a_{21} & a_{22} \end{bmatrix}$, det $A = a_{11}a_{22} - a_{12}a_{21}$ and

$$A^{-1} = \frac{1}{\det A} \begin{bmatrix} a_{22} & -a_{12} \\ -a_{21} & a_{11} \end{bmatrix}, \text{ det } A \neq 0.$$

3. Homogeneous systems of linear equations with more variables than equations generally have an infinite number of solutions.

4. The solution to a nonhomogeneous system of linear equations is made up of a particular solution and the general solution of the corresponding homogeneous system.

5. Compositions of two reflections in intersecting lines give rotations about the point common to the lines.

CHAPTER OBJECTIVES AND REVIEW ▬▬▬▬▬

Objective: *To explain and illustrate the concepts of matrix and equality of matrices.* (Section 10-1)

1. Describe what is meant by the dimensions of a matrix.

2. Illustrate your description using a 5 by 3 matrix.

3. Explain under what conditions two matrices A and B are equal.

4. Which pair of the matrices below are equal?

a. $\begin{bmatrix} 2 & -3 \\ 7 & 1 \end{bmatrix}$

b. $\begin{bmatrix} 2 & -3 & 4 \\ 7 & 1 & 0 \end{bmatrix}$

c. $\begin{bmatrix} \frac{4}{2} & (5-8) \\ 7 & -i^2 \end{bmatrix}$

d. $\begin{bmatrix} 2 & 7 \\ -3 & 1 \\ 4 & 0 \end{bmatrix}$

Objective: *To find the sum of two matrices when the sum exists and to recognize when the sum of two matrices does not exist.* (Section 10-1)

▬▬ Use the following matrices for Exercises 5–8. In each case find the sum if it exists. If the sum does not exist explain why.

$$A = \begin{bmatrix} 2 & -3 \\ 4 & 5 \end{bmatrix} \qquad B = \begin{bmatrix} 6 & -3 & 1 \\ 2 & 0 & 5 \end{bmatrix} \qquad C = \begin{bmatrix} 0 & 1 \\ -1 & 0 \end{bmatrix}$$

5. $A + C$ **6.** $B + C$

7. $A + A$ **8.** $A + (C + C)$

Objective: *To multiply a vector by a scalar.* (Section 10-1)

▬▬ Use the following matrices to find the sums and products of Exercises 9–12.

$$A = \begin{bmatrix} 4 & 2 & 1 \\ 0 & 1 & -3 \end{bmatrix} \qquad B = \begin{bmatrix} 10 & -2 & 0 \\ 8 & 2 & -6 \end{bmatrix} \qquad C = \begin{bmatrix} 5 & 1 & 1 \\ -1 & 2 & 3 \end{bmatrix}$$

9. $A + \frac{1}{2}B$ **10.** $B + (-2C)$

11. $5(A + B)$ **12.** $3A + (-1C)$

Objective: *To add and subtract two-by-two square matrices.* (Section 10-1)

▬▬ Use the following matrices to find the sums, products, and inverses of Exercises 13–16.

$$A = \begin{bmatrix} 3 & 1 \\ -1 & 6 \end{bmatrix} \qquad B = \begin{bmatrix} -2 & 0 \\ 1 & 4 \end{bmatrix} \qquad C = \begin{bmatrix} -3 & -1 \\ 1 & -6 \end{bmatrix}$$

13. $-B$ **14.** $A + C$

15. $2A - B$ **16.** $-2(-3B + C)$

Objective: *To find the product of two square matrices.* (Section 10-2)

▬▬ Use the following matrices for Exercises 17–20.

$$A = \begin{bmatrix} 2 & -3 \\ 1 & 2 \end{bmatrix} \qquad B = \begin{bmatrix} 1 & 1 \\ -3 & 5 \end{bmatrix} \qquad C = \begin{bmatrix} 6 & -3 \\ 2 & 0 \end{bmatrix} \qquad D = \begin{bmatrix} 1 & 0 \\ 0 & 1 \end{bmatrix}$$

■■ Find the given product. Express as a two-by-two matrix.
17. AB **18.** BA
19. $A(2C)$ **20.** DB

Objective: *To represent a vector in matrix form as a column vector and to multiply a square matrix by a column vector.* (Section 10-3)

■■ Use the following matrices for Exercises 21–24.

$$A = \begin{bmatrix} 2 & 3 \\ 5 & 1 \end{bmatrix} \qquad B = \begin{bmatrix} 0 & 2 \\ 1 & 1 \end{bmatrix} \qquad \vec{r} = \begin{bmatrix} 1 \\ -1 \end{bmatrix} \qquad \vec{t} = \begin{bmatrix} 1 \\ 0 \end{bmatrix}$$

■■ Find each column vector. Make a sketch of each vector.
21. $A\vec{r}$ **22.** $B\vec{r}$
23. $A\vec{t}$ **24.** $(A + B)\vec{t}$

Objective: *To calculate the inverse of a matrix when the inverse exists.*
(Section 10-4)

■■ Find the inverse, if it exists.

25. $\begin{bmatrix} 2 & -1 \\ 4 & -3 \end{bmatrix}$ **26.** $\begin{bmatrix} 8 & 4 \\ 4 & 2 \end{bmatrix}$

27. $\begin{bmatrix} 1 & 5 \\ 0 & 1 \end{bmatrix}$ **28.** $\begin{bmatrix} 0 & 2 \\ -2 & 0 \end{bmatrix}$

Objective: *To use the augmented matrix and elementary row manipulation method to solve systems of equations.* (Section 10-5)

■■ Use the augmented matrix and elementary row manipulation method to solve each system of equations.
29. $\begin{cases} -5x + 4y = -39 \\ x + y = 6 \end{cases}$ **30.** $\begin{cases} w + x + y + z = 0 \\ w - x - y - z = 2 \\ 3w + x + 2y - z = 9 \\ w + x - 4y + z = -15 \end{cases}$

Objective: *To solve homogeneous and nonhomogeneous systems of linear equations.* (Section 10-6 and Section 10-7)

■■ Write the general solution for each system in Exercises 31–32.

31. $\begin{bmatrix} 3 & -1 & 1 \\ 1 & 1 & 1 \end{bmatrix} \begin{bmatrix} x_1 \\ x_2 \\ x_3 \end{bmatrix} = \begin{bmatrix} 0 \\ 2 \end{bmatrix}$ **32.** $3x_1 - x_2 + x_3 = 0$
$x_1 + x_2 + x_3 = 0$

Write the general solution for each system in Exercises 33–34.

33. $\begin{bmatrix} 1 & 1 & 1 \\ 3 & -1 & 1 \\ 4 & 0 & 2 \end{bmatrix} \begin{bmatrix} x_1 \\ x_2 \\ x_3 \end{bmatrix} = \begin{bmatrix} 2 \\ 0 \\ 2 \end{bmatrix}$

34. $\begin{bmatrix} 1 & 1 & 1 \\ 3 & -1 & 1 \\ 4 & 0 & 2 \end{bmatrix} \begin{bmatrix} x_1 \\ x_2 \\ x_3 \end{bmatrix} = \begin{bmatrix} 0 \\ 0 \\ 0 \end{bmatrix}$

Objective: *To illustrate linear transformations using two-by-two matrices.*
(Section 10-8)

For Exercises 35 and 36 a transformation matrix and three vectors are given. Find the image of each vector. Sketch the pre-image vector and the image vector on a coordinate plane.

35. $A = \begin{bmatrix} 1 & -1 \\ -1 & 0 \end{bmatrix}$ $\quad \vec{v}_1 = \begin{bmatrix} 2 \\ 0 \end{bmatrix}$ $\quad \vec{v}_2 = \begin{bmatrix} -3 \\ 2 \end{bmatrix}$ $\quad \vec{v}_3 = \begin{bmatrix} 6 \\ 1 \end{bmatrix}$

36. $A = \begin{bmatrix} -2 & 0 \\ 0 & 1 \end{bmatrix}$ $\quad \vec{v}_1 = \begin{bmatrix} 0 \\ -1 \end{bmatrix}$ $\quad \vec{v}_2 = \begin{bmatrix} 5 \\ 3 \end{bmatrix}$ $\quad \vec{v}_3 = \begin{bmatrix} 0 \\ 0 \end{bmatrix}$

Objective: *To illustrate reflections about the x axis, the y axis, the line* $y = x$, *and the line* $y = -x$. (Section 10-9)

Make a graph of $\begin{bmatrix} -3 \\ 2 \end{bmatrix}$ and its image under each of the following reflections.

37. $r_{x \text{ axis}}$ 　　　 38. $r_{y \text{ axis}}$ 　　　 39. $r_{y = x}$ 　　　 40. $r_{y = -x}$

Objective: *To find the image of a vector or line under a rotation.*
(Section 10-10)

Find the image under $R_{45°}$.

41. $\begin{bmatrix} 0 \\ 1 \end{bmatrix}$ 　　　 42. $\begin{bmatrix} 2 \\ -1 \end{bmatrix}$ 　　　 43. $\begin{bmatrix} -\sqrt{2} \\ \sqrt{2} \end{bmatrix}$ 　　　 44. $\begin{bmatrix} 3 \\ 0 \end{bmatrix}$

Find the image of each line under $R_{90°}$.

45. $\begin{cases} x = 2 - t \\ y = 0 + t \end{cases}$ 　　　　 46. $\begin{cases} x = 1 + t \\ y = 1 - t \end{cases}$

Objective: *To find a composition of two linear transformations.*
(Section 10-11)

Find the composition of A followed by B.

47. $A = \begin{bmatrix} -1 & 2 \\ 2 & 3 \end{bmatrix}$ $\quad B = \begin{bmatrix} 0 & 1 \\ 5 & 7 \end{bmatrix}$

48. $A = R_{90°}$ $\quad B = R_{45°}$

Objective: *To find the image of a vector or line under a translation.*
(Section 10-12)

▬▬ Each of the following points is translated by the vector $\begin{bmatrix} -2 \\ 4 \end{bmatrix}$. Find the coordinates of the new point.

49. $A(0, 0)$ **50.** $B(2, 3)$ **51.** $C(-2, 5)$ **52.** $D(-4, -7)$

53. Find the equation of the image of the line $y = 2x + 1$ after a translation with vector $\begin{bmatrix} -2 \\ -1 \end{bmatrix}$. Graph the line and its image.

CHAPTER TEST

1. $A = \begin{bmatrix} -5 & 3 \\ 0 & 1 \end{bmatrix}$ and $B = \begin{bmatrix} -5 & (2+1) \\ 0 & -1 \end{bmatrix}$. Does $A = B$? Explain.

2. $C = \begin{bmatrix} 2 & -1 & 3 & 1 \\ 4 & 1 & -5 & 7 \\ 0 & -2 & 3 & -6 \end{bmatrix}$

    a. What are the dimensions of C?

    b. Name the entries of C represented by c_{13}, c_{24}, c_{31}.

3. Find the sum of the following matrices if it exists.

$$\begin{bmatrix} 2 & -3 & 1 \\ 4 & -8 & -5 \end{bmatrix} + \begin{bmatrix} 0 & 2 & -1 \\ -3 & 1 & 2 \end{bmatrix}$$

4. Find the product of the following matrices if it exists.

$$\begin{bmatrix} 2 & 5 \\ 0 & 1 \end{bmatrix} \begin{bmatrix} -2 & -5 & 1 \\ 0 & -1 & 3 \end{bmatrix}$$

5. A and B are two matrices for which $A + B$ is defined and AB is defined. What can you conclude about the dimensions of A and B?

6. For matrices in M_2 and k real is it true that

    a. $(A + B) + C = A + (B + C)$?

    b. $(AB)C = A(BC)$?

    c. $(kA)B = k(AB)$?

    d. $AB = BA$?

7. $A = \begin{bmatrix} u & v \\ w & x \end{bmatrix}$. Find det A.

8. If $A = \begin{bmatrix} p & q \\ r & s \end{bmatrix}$ is to have an inverse, what is true about det A?

9. Find the inverse of $\begin{bmatrix} 2 & -3 \\ 1 & -5 \end{bmatrix}$, if it exists.

10. Find the inverse of $\begin{bmatrix} k & -1 \\ -1 & 0 \end{bmatrix}$, if it exists.

▬▬ In Exercises 11–14 use matrix methods to find the general solution to each system.

11. $\begin{bmatrix} 1 & 3 \\ -2 & 5 \end{bmatrix} \begin{bmatrix} x_1 \\ x_2 \end{bmatrix} = \begin{bmatrix} 7 \\ 5 \end{bmatrix}$

12. $\begin{bmatrix} 1 & 3 \\ -2 & -6 \end{bmatrix} \begin{bmatrix} x_1 \\ x_2 \end{bmatrix} = \begin{bmatrix} 1 \\ -2 \end{bmatrix}$

13. $\begin{bmatrix} 1 & 2 & -3 \\ 2 & 1 & -5 \end{bmatrix} \begin{bmatrix} x_1 \\ x_2 \\ x_3 \end{bmatrix} = \begin{bmatrix} 0 \\ 0 \end{bmatrix}$

14. $\begin{bmatrix} 2 & 4 & -2 \\ 2 & 3 & -1 \\ 1 & 1 & 1 \end{bmatrix} \begin{bmatrix} x_1 \\ x_2 \\ x_3 \end{bmatrix} = \begin{bmatrix} 0 \\ 0 \\ 1 \end{bmatrix}$

15. Let $A = \begin{bmatrix} 2 & 1 \\ 3 & 2 \end{bmatrix}$ represent a transformation.

    a. Find the image of the vectors $\begin{bmatrix} 2 \\ -2 \end{bmatrix}$, $\begin{bmatrix} 1 \\ 0 \end{bmatrix}$, and $\begin{bmatrix} 0 \\ 2 \end{bmatrix}$.

    b. The tips of the vectors in **a** are collinear. Are the tips of the image vectors collinear? Explain.

16. Let $A = \begin{bmatrix} 2 & 1 \\ 3 & 2 \end{bmatrix}$ and $B = \begin{bmatrix} 2 & -1 \\ -3 & 1 \end{bmatrix}$.

    a. What is the composite transformation AB?

    b. What is the composite transformation BA?

17. Find the composite of $r_{y \text{ axis}}$ with itself.

18. Find the composite of $r_{y \text{ axis}}$ with $r_{y=-x}$.

19. Find the image of the line

$$x = 3t + 1$$
$$y = -t - 1$$

under the transformation with matrix $\begin{bmatrix} 2 & -1 \\ 3 & -1 \end{bmatrix}$.

20. Find the image of the line

$$x = t + 1$$
$$y = -t + 1$$

under the translation with vector $\begin{bmatrix} -2 \\ 3 \end{bmatrix}$.

CUMULATIVE REVIEW: CHAPTERS 9–10

━━ Choose the best answer. Choose **a**, **b**, **c**, or **d**.

1. Two vectors are always equal if
   a. They have the same magnitude.
   b. They lie on the same line.
   c. They have the same direction.
   d. They have magnitudes and directions equal.

2. If $\overrightarrow{OP}$ is a vector in three-space with its tip at $P(2, -3, 5)$ then
   a. The position vector is $2\mathbf{i} - 3\mathbf{j} + 5\mathbf{k}$.
   b. The length is $\sqrt{38}$.
   c. $\overrightarrow{OP} = \overrightarrow{QR}$ where $Q(1, 3, 5)$ and $R(3, 0, 10)$.
   d. All of **a, b, c**

3. For $\vec{v} = 2\mathbf{i} + \mathbf{j} - 2\mathbf{k}$ the unit direction vector is
   a. $\vec{u} = \mathbf{i} + \mathbf{j} + \mathbf{k}$
   b. $\vec{u} = \frac{2}{3}\mathbf{i} + \frac{1}{3}\mathbf{j} - \frac{2}{3}\mathbf{k}$
   c. $\vec{u} = -\frac{1}{3}\mathbf{i} + \frac{2}{3}\mathbf{j} + \frac{2}{3}\mathbf{k}$
   d. $\vec{u} = -\mathbf{i} - \mathbf{j} + \mathbf{k}$

4. Find the midpoint of $\overrightarrow{PQ}$ where $P(-2, 3, -1)$ and $Q(5, -3, 1)$.
   a. $M(\frac{7}{2}, -3, 1)$
   b. $M(-\frac{7}{2}, 3, -1)$
   c. $M(\frac{3}{2}, 0, 0)$
   d. $M(-\frac{3}{2}, 0, 1)$

5. Find the equations for the line containing $Q(2, -3, 1)$ with direction $\vec{r} = 5\mathbf{i} + 3\mathbf{j} - 2\mathbf{k}$.
   a. $\frac{x + 2}{5} = \frac{y - 3}{3} = \frac{z + 1}{-2}$
   b. $\frac{x - 2}{2} = \frac{y + 3}{3} = \frac{z + 1}{2}$
   c. $\frac{x - 2}{5} = \frac{y + 3}{3} = \frac{z - 1}{-2}$
   d. None of the above

6. Find the slope of the line that has $\vec{r} = -3\mathbf{i} + 5\mathbf{j}$ as a direction vector.
   a. $-\frac{5}{3}$
   b. $\frac{5}{3}$
   c. $\frac{3}{5}$
   d. $-\frac{3}{5}$

7. Find the equation of the line through $(-5, 2)$ with the direction vector $\vec{r} = 2\mathbf{i} - \mathbf{j}$.
   a. $y - 2x - 12 = 0$
   b. $y + 2x + 8 = 0$
   c. $2y + x + 1 = 0$
   d. $2y - x - 9 = 0$

8. Find the cosine of the angle between $\vec{r} = 2\mathbf{i} - 3\mathbf{j} + 4\mathbf{k}$ and $\vec{v} = -\frac{1}{2}\mathbf{i} + \mathbf{j} - 5\mathbf{k}$.
   a. $-\frac{96}{\sqrt{29 \cdot 105}}$
   b. $-\frac{48}{\sqrt{105 \cdot 29}}$
   c. $-\frac{24}{105 \cdot 29}$
   d. $-\frac{24}{25}$

9. Find the distance from the origin to $3x - 4y = 5$.
   a. zero
   b. negative
   c. 1
   d. 20

10. The plane containing $A(1, 1, 1)$, $B(2, -3, 4)$ and $C(-1, 3, 2)$
    a. is perpendicular to $-10\mathbf{i} - 7\mathbf{j} - 6\mathbf{k}$
    b. contains $\overline{AC}$ and $\overline{BC}$
    c. has equation $10x + 7y + 6z - 23 = 0$
    d. All of the above.

11. Find the distance from $Q(1, 1, -1)$ to $5x - 3y + 2z - 5 = 0$.
    a. $\frac{-5}{\sqrt{13}}$ **b.** $\frac{15}{\sqrt{34}}$ **c.** 3 **d.** $\frac{5}{\sqrt{38}}$

12. Which of the following is an example of a 2×3 matrix?

    a. $\begin{bmatrix} 5 & 1 \\ 3 & 4 \end{bmatrix}$ **b.** $\begin{bmatrix} 2 & 3 \\ 3 & 2 \\ 1 & 5 \end{bmatrix}$ **c.** $\begin{bmatrix} 2 & 1 & 4 \\ 3 & 1 & 5 \end{bmatrix}$ **d.** $\begin{bmatrix} 2 & 1 & 5 \\ 3 & 2 & 7 \\ 4 & 9 & 1 \end{bmatrix}$

13. $\begin{bmatrix} 2 & 1 \\ -3 & 5 \end{bmatrix} \cdot \begin{bmatrix} 1 & 2 & 3 \\ 2 & 1 & 5 \end{bmatrix}$

    a. equals $\begin{bmatrix} -4 & 1 & -9 \\ 11 & 7 & 28 \end{bmatrix}$ **b.** equals $\begin{bmatrix} 4 & 5 & 11 \\ 7 & -1 & 16 \end{bmatrix}$

    c. is undefined   **d.** is a 3 by 2 matrix

14. Find $\vec{v} = \begin{bmatrix} x \\ y \end{bmatrix}$ such that $\begin{bmatrix} 2 & 1 \\ -3 & 1 \end{bmatrix} \begin{bmatrix} x \\ y \end{bmatrix} = \begin{bmatrix} 0 \\ 1 \end{bmatrix}$.

    a. $\vec{v}$ is not defined   **b.** $x = -1$, $y = 2$
    c. $x = -\frac{1}{5}$, $y = \frac{2}{5}$ **d.** $x = -5$, $y = +10$

15. Find the solution to $\begin{cases} x - 2y + z = 2 \\ -x - 3y - z = 3 \\ x + y - 3z = 3 \end{cases}$.

    a. $(1, 1, 1)$ **b.** $(1, -1, -1)$ **c.** $(1, 1, -1)$ **d.** $(-1, 1, -1)$

16. Find a particular solution to $\begin{bmatrix} 1 & 2 & 1 \\ 1 & 4 & -1 \end{bmatrix} \begin{bmatrix} x_1 \\ x_2 \\ x_3 \end{bmatrix} = \begin{bmatrix} 0 \\ 0 \end{bmatrix}$.

    a. $\begin{bmatrix} -2 \\ 1 \\ 0 \end{bmatrix}$ **b.** $\begin{bmatrix} -1 \\ 0 \\ -2 \end{bmatrix}$ **c.** $\begin{bmatrix} -3 \\ 1 \\ -2 \end{bmatrix}$ **d.** None of the above

17. What is the image of $\vec{v} = \begin{bmatrix} -3 \\ 2 \end{bmatrix}$ under a transformation with matrix $\begin{bmatrix} 3 & -2 \\ 1 & 2 \end{bmatrix}$?

    a. $\begin{bmatrix} -13 & 1 \\ 1 & -13 \end{bmatrix}$ **b.** $\frac{1}{8}\begin{bmatrix} 2 & 2 \\ -1 & 3 \end{bmatrix}$ **c.** $\begin{bmatrix} -13 \\ 1 \end{bmatrix}$ **d.** $\begin{bmatrix} 1 \\ -13 \end{bmatrix}$

18. What is the image of $Q(2, 3)$ under a $90°$ rotation about the origin?
    a. $P(-3, 2)$ **b.** $P(-2, 3)$ **c.** $P(-3, -2)$ **d.** $P(3, 2)$

CHAPTER **11** The
Conic Sections

Sections

Features

Applying Non-Linear Programming: Cost Analysis

Computer Application: Rotating a Conic

Review and Testing

Mid-Chapter Review

Chapter Summary

Chapter Objectives and Review

Chapter Test

11–1   Historical Perspective

The four plane curves circle, parabola, ellipse, and hyperbola are called the **conic sections.** They are called *conic sections* because each curve may be obtained by the intersection of a plane with a right circular conic surface. The figures below show these curves as intersections of planes and conic surfaces.

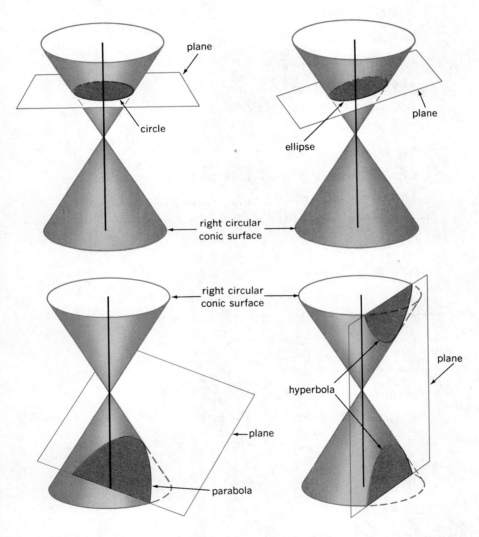

In the early history of Greek mathematics the definitions of the conic sections were stated in terms of planes and conic surfaces. Their properties were studied intensively. Apollonius (ca 220 B.C.) wrote an extensive treatise on these curves. It was called "Conic Sections" and had eight books and about 400 propositions (theorems). Apollonius is also credited with supplying the names *ellipse, parabola,* and *hyperbola.*

Even though each conic section is a subset of a three dimensional figure, each curve lies entirely in one plane. Thus the conic sections are plane curves, and they may be defined in several different ways which make no use of solid geometry. The definitions of the conic sections given in this chapter depend only on the geometry of the plane for their understanding. You should, however, remember that these curves were originally studied as a part of space geometry.

CLASSROOM EXERCISES

1. Name the four conic sections.

2. Describe how conic sections are obtained from the conic surfaces in the Figures.

WRITTEN EXERCISES

A **1.** Obtain a book on the history of mathematics from your library or teacher. Look up Apollonius (ca 220 B.C.). Describe some of his mathematical works.

2. Repeat Exercise 1 for Menaechmus (ca 350 B.C.). How is he associated with conic sections?

11–2   The Ellipse

Any plane curve can be described as a set of points which satisfy a given set of conditions. Often such a set of points is called a *locus.* For example, you know that a circle is the set of all points at a given distance from a given point called the center. From these conditions you can derive the equation of the circle by using the distance formula. (See Section 2–1.) Here are two examples.

1. The circle with center $(0, 0)$ and radius r has equation $x^2 + y^2 = r^2$.

2. The circle with center (h, k) and radius r has equation $(x - h)^2 + (y - k)^2 = r^2$.

An **ellipse** is defined in a similar manner by using a locus.

Definition   Let F and F' be two points in a plane. The set of all points P in the plane such that the sum of the distances PF and PF' is constant is an **ellipse.**

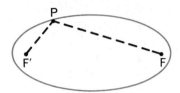

PF' + PF is a constant

The points F' and F are called the **foci** of the ellipse. The ellipse can be thought of as the curve traced by a pencil restrained by a string of constant length and tied at the ends to F' and F. If $F' = F$, then the curve so traced is a circle. A circle is a special case of an ellipse.

The line determined by the foci F' and F is the **transverse axis** of the ellipse. The perpendicular bisector of $\overline{F'F}$ is the **conjugate axis.** The intersection of the transverse and conjugate axes is the **center** of the ellipse.

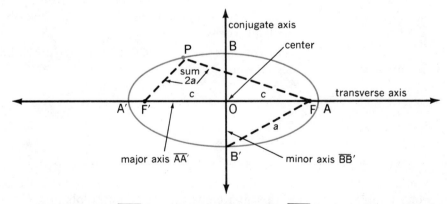

The segment $\overline{A'A}$ is the **major axis** while $\overline{BB'}$ is the **minor axis.** Letting

$$F'F = 2c \quad \text{and} \quad PF' + PF = 2a,$$

you see that

$$F'O = OF = c.$$

($2a$ and $2c$ are used to simplify the algebra that will follow.)

Moreover
$$F'A + FA = 2c + 2FA = 2a$$
and
$$F'A' + FA' = 2c + 2F'A' = 2a$$
so
$$FA = F'A'.$$
Thus

$$A'A = A'F' + F'A$$
$$= FA + F'A$$
$$A'A = 2a.$$

That is, the *major axis* is 2a units long.
   Note also that
$$F'B = FB = a. \qquad \text{(Why?)}$$
Thus
$$BO = \sqrt{a^2 - c^2}.$$
Similarly
$$F'B' = FB' = a$$
and
$$B'O = \sqrt{a^2 - c^2}.$$
Thus
$$BB' = 2\sqrt{a^2 - c^2}.$$
Let
$$\sqrt{a^2 - c^2} = b,$$
then
$$BB' = 2b.$$

That is, the *minor axis* is 2b units long.
   Clearly $a > c$, and since $b = \sqrt{a^2 - c^2}$, $a > b$ also. $\overline{OA}$ is the **semimajor axis** while $\overline{OB}$ is the **semiminor axis.** The points A' and A are the vertices of the ellipse.
   Having named some of the parts of the ellipse, the next task is to obtain an equation for the curve. For convenience the center is taken to be the origin and the transverse and conjugate axes chosen as the coordinate axes. The foci F' and F have coordinates $(-c, 0)$ and $(c, 0)$ since $FF' = 2c$.

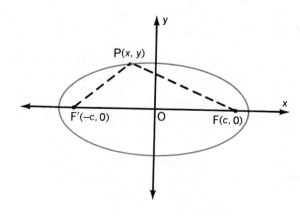

The definition of an ellipse says that $P(x, y)$ must satisfy

$$F'P + FP = 2a \qquad\qquad 1$$

Applying the distance formula you find the following.

$$\sqrt{(x + c)^2 + y^2} + \sqrt{(x - c)^2 + y^2} = 2a \qquad\qquad 2$$

Thus
$$\sqrt{(x + c)^2 + y^2} = 2a - \sqrt{(x - c)^2 + y^2}$$

$$x^2 + 2cx + c^2 + y^2 = 4a^2 - 4a\sqrt{(x - c)^2 + y^2} + x^2$$
$$- 2cx + c^2 + y^2$$

$$a\sqrt{(x - c)^2 + y^2} = a^2 - cx \qquad\qquad 3$$

$$a^2(x^2 - 2cx + c^2 + y^2) = a^4 - 2a^2cx + c^2x^2$$

$$a^2x^2 - 2ca^2x + c^2a^2 + a^2y^2 = a^4 - 2a^2cx + c^2x^2$$

$$(a^2 - c^2)x^2 + a^2y^2 = a^4 - a^2c^2 = a^2(a^2 - c^2)$$

$$b^2x^2 + a^2y^2 = a^2b^2 \quad \longleftarrow \quad \mathbf{b^2 = a^2 - c^2}$$

or
$$\frac{x^2}{a^2} + \frac{y^2}{b^2} = 1. \qquad\qquad 4$$

Before you can say equation 4 is the equation of the ellipse, you must prove that any point $P(x, y)$ which satisfies 4 also satisfies $F'P + FP = 2a$. You are asked to do this in the exercises. Equation 4 is called the *standard form* of the equation of an ellipse with center at the origin, semimajor axis of length a, semiminor axis of length b, and foci $(c, 0)$ and $(-c, 0)$.

If the transverse axis is the y axis rather than the x axis, then the standard equation of an ellipse is

$$\frac{x^2}{b^2} + \frac{y^2}{a^2} = 1, \quad a > b \qquad\qquad 5$$

with center at the origin, semimajor axis of length a, semiminor axis of length b, and foci $(0, c)$ and $(0, -c)$.

EXAMPLE. Identify the transverse axis, the length of the semimajor axis and the semiminor axis, and the coordinates of the foci for equations a and b.

a. $\frac{x^2}{9} + \frac{y^2}{25} = 1.$ b. $9x^2 + 25y^2 = 225$

a. (See Figure 1.) Since $25 > 9$, the transverse axis is the y axis. Thus $a = 5$ and $b = 3$. The length of the semimajor axis is 5, that of the semiminor axis is 3. Since $b^2 = a^2 - c^2$, $9 = 25 - c^2$ or $c^2 = 16$ and $c = 4$. Thus the foci have coordinates $(0, 4)$, $(0, -4)$.

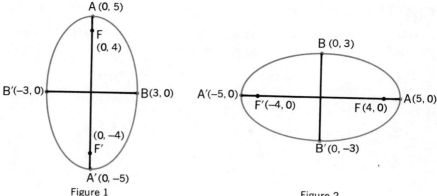

A (0, 5)
F (0, 4)
B'(-3, 0)
B(3, 0)
(0, -4) F'
A'(0, -5)

Figure 1

B (0, 3)
A'(-5, 0)
F'(-4, 0)
F (4, 0)
A(5, 0)
B'(0, -3)

Figure 2

b. (See Figure 2.) The first step is to write the equation in standard form. This is done by dividing both sides by 225.

$$\frac{9x^2}{225} + \frac{25y^2}{225} = \frac{225}{225}$$

$$\frac{x^2}{25} + \frac{y^2}{9} = 1$$

The transverse axis is the x axis because $25 > 9$ and 25 is the denominator of the term involving x^2.

The procedures used in **a** now produce semimajor axis length = 5, semiminor axis length = 3, coordinates of foci = (4, 0) and (-4, 0).

CLASSROOM EXERCISES

■■■ Find the lengths of the semimajor and semiminor axes and the coordinates of the vertices for the following.

1. $\frac{x^2}{36} + \frac{y^2}{25} = 1$

2. $\frac{x^2}{9} + \frac{y^2}{100} = 1$

3. $\frac{x^2}{64} + \frac{y^2}{81} = 1$

■■■ Put the following equations into standard form.

4. $9x^2 + 8y^2 = 72$

5. $32x^2 + 16y^2 = 64$

6. $162x^2 + 128y^2 = 10368$

7. Find the equation of the ellipse having foci at $(\pm 4, 0)$ and the length of the semimajor axis 5.

WRITTEN EXERCISES

A ━━ Find the lengths of the axes and the coordinates of the foci, and sketch the curve for Exercises 1–8.

1. $\frac{x^2}{16} + \frac{y^2}{4} = 1$

2. $x^2 + 2y^2 = 32$

3. $\frac{x^2}{4} + \frac{y^2}{36} = 1$

4. $5x^2 + 2y^2 = 20$

5. $\frac{x^2}{36} + \frac{y^2}{16} = 1$

6. $16x^2 + 25y^2 = 400$

7. $\frac{x^2}{8} + \frac{y^2}{16} = 1$

8. $16x^2 + 4y^2 = 64$

━━ Find the equation of each ellipse for Exercises 9–16.

9. Foci at $(\pm 3, 0)$, vertices at $(\pm 5, 0)$.

10. Foci at $(0, \pm 4)$, vertices at $(0, \pm 7)$.

11. Foci at $(\pm 2, 0)$, minor axis of length 3.

12. Foci at $(0, \pm 5)$, major axis of length 26.

13. Foci at $(0, \pm 3)$, vertices at $(0, \pm 6)$.

14. Vertices at $(\pm 4, 0)$, end of minor axis at $(0, 3)$.

15. Foci at $(0, \pm 2)$, one vertex at $(0, -4)$.

16. Vertices at $(\pm 8, 0)$, contains $(4, \sqrt{3})$.

B **17.** The transverse axis of an ellipse is the x axis. The lengths of the major and minor axes are in the ratio 3 : 2. The ellipse contains the point $(2, 1)$. Find its equation.

18. The foci of an ellipse are on the y axis, the major axis is twice as long as the distance FF', the center is $(0, 0)$, and $(\frac{9}{2}, 3)$ is on the ellipse. Find the equation.

19. Let ABC be a triangle with base AB and $A = (2, 0)$, $B = (-2, 0)$. Find the equation such that for all points $C(x, y)$, the product of the slopes of $\overleftrightarrow{AC}$ and $\overleftrightarrow{BC}$ is -4.

20. Using the information in Exercise 19, graph the locus of $C(x, y)$ and a representative triangle ABC. Are the points A and B on the curve? Explain.

21. Generalize the results of Exercises 19–20. Will the generalization be true when the product of the slopes is positive?

22. Show that if $P(x, y)$ satisfies $\frac{x^2}{a^2} + \frac{y^2}{b^2} = 1$, then $PF' + PF = 2a$.

23. Show that $FP = a - \frac{c}{a}x$, $(F(c, 0))$. (*Hint:* See Equation 3.)

C **24.** Suppose the foci of an ellipse are at $(0, 0)$ and $(6, 0)$. Then the center is at $(3, 0)$. Neither standard equation of the ellipse **4** nor **5** is the equation of this ellipse. Use the definition of the ellipse to find the equation of this ellipse when the major axis has length 10.

11-3 Properties of Ellipses

In the derivation of the standard equations of an ellipse in Section 11-2, equation **3** on page 594 is an intermediate result. Thus,

$$a\sqrt{(x - c)^2 + y^2} = a^2 - cx$$

or

$$\sqrt{(x - c)^2 + y^2} = a - \frac{c}{a}x \cdot \qquad \qquad 1$$

The left hand expression in equation **1** is the distance from $F(c, 0)$ to $P(x, y)$; that is $FP = \sqrt{(x - c)^2 + y^2}$.

After slight modification, the right hand side of **1** may also be interpreted geometrically.

$$FP = a - \frac{c}{a}x = \frac{c}{a}\left(\frac{a^2}{c} - x\right) \qquad \qquad 2$$

You can see that $\left(\frac{a^2}{c} - x\right)$ is the distance, k, from $P(x, y)$ to the line $x = \frac{a^2}{c}$. (See the figure.) $\frac{c}{a}$ is a constant which is less than 1. Thus

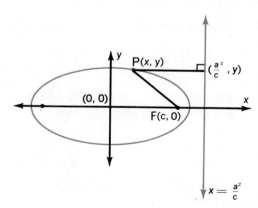

$\frac{c}{a}\left(\frac{a^2}{c} - x\right)$ is a constant times the distance from $P(x, y)$ to $x = \frac{a^2}{c}$.

You can say that the ratio of the distance FP to the distance, k, from P to $x = \frac{a^2}{c}$ is a constant for *all points P on the ellipse.*

$$\frac{FP}{k} = \frac{\frac{c}{a}\left(\frac{a^2}{c} - x\right)}{\left(\frac{a^2}{c} - x\right)} = \frac{c}{a}$$

The constant ratio $0 < \frac{c}{a} = e < 1$ is the **eccentricity** of the ellipse. The line $x = \frac{a^2}{c}$ is a *directrix* of the ellipse. Each ellipse has two *directrix* lines, (directrices), one for each focus. What is the equation of the other directrix line for the ellipse $\frac{x^2}{a^2} + \frac{y^2}{b^2} = 1$ $(a > b)$? $\left(x = -\frac{a^2}{c}\right)$

> **Theorem 11–1** An ellipse is the set of all points whose distance from a fixed point F (the focus) is equal to a constant e $(0 < e < 1)$ times the distance to a fixed line d (the directrix).

Theorem 11–1 is often taken as a definition of an ellipse.

Any segment whose endpoints are on an ellipse is called a **chord** of the ellipse. If the chord contains a focus, it is a **focal chord.** The focal chord which is perpendicular to the transverse axis is called the **latus rectum.**

The lengths of the *latera recta* (latera recta is the plural of latus rectum) of an ellipse are easily found. It is left for you to show that the following theorem is true.

> **Theorem 11–2** The latera recta of an ellipse have length $\frac{2b^2}{a}$.

EXAMPLE. Find the eccentricity, the length of the latera recta, and the equations of the directrices for the following.

a. $\frac{x^2}{9} + \frac{y^2}{25} = 1$

$a = 5, b = 3, c = 4$

The length of the latera recta is $\frac{18}{5}$. The equations of the directrices are $y = \frac{25}{4}$ and $y = -\frac{25}{4}$. The eccentricity is $\frac{4}{5}$.

b. $\frac{x^2}{25} + \frac{y^2}{9} = 1$

$a = 5, b = 3, c = 4$

The length of the latera recta is $\frac{18}{5}$. The equations of the directrices are $x = \frac{25}{4}$ and $x = -\frac{25}{4}$. The eccentricity is $\frac{4}{5}$.

CLASSROOM EXERCISES

━━ Find the eccentricity and the length of the latera recta for each ellipse.

1. $\frac{x^2}{64} + \frac{y^2}{16} = 1$ **2.** $\frac{x^2}{16} + \frac{y^2}{25} = 1$

3. $\frac{x^2}{16} + \frac{y^2}{64} = 1$ **4.** $\frac{x^2}{10} + \frac{y^2}{9} = 1$

━━ Find the equations of the directrices for each ellipse.

5. $\frac{x^2}{36} + \frac{y^2}{9} = 1$ **6.** $\frac{x^2}{9} + \frac{y^2}{36} = 1$

7. $2x^2 + 5y^2 = 100$ **8.** $4x^2 + 3y^2 = 48$

9. Define an ellipse in terms of a directrix and a focus.

10. Describe $\frac{c}{a}$ as a ratio of two distances.

11. What is meant by a latus rectum of an ellipse?

WRITTEN EXERCISES

A ━━ For the ellipses of Exercises 1–8 find the eccentricity, the length of the latera recta, and the equations of the directrices.

1. $\frac{x^2}{16} + \frac{y^2}{4} = 1$ **2.** $x^2 + 2y^2 = 32$

3. $\frac{x^2}{4} + \frac{y^2}{36} = 1$ **4.** $5x^2 + 2y^2 = 20$

5. $\frac{x^2}{36} + \frac{y^2}{16} = 1$ **6.** $16x^2 + 25y^2 = 400$

7. $\frac{x^2}{8} + \frac{y^2}{16} = 1$ **8.** $16x^2 + 4y^2 = 64$

B   **9.** The orbit of the earth around the sun is an ellipse with the sun as a focus. If the shortest and longest distances (center to center) from the sun to earth are 9.3×10^7 miles and 9.6×10^7 miles, what is the eccentricity of the earth's orbit?

10. There are two ellipses with center at the origin, eccentricity $\frac{2}{3}$, and containing the point (2, 1). Find their equations.

11. On the same coordinate axes draw the set of ellipses with vertices A at (5, 0) and A' at (−5, 0) and having eccentricity

     a. $\frac{9}{10}$.   **b.** $\frac{7}{10}$.   **c.** $\frac{5}{10}$.   **d.** $\frac{3}{10}$.   **e.** $\frac{1}{10}$.

12. a. What pattern is exhibited by the ellipses of Exercise 11?

     b. When e is close to 1 what is the shape of the ellipse?

     c. When e is close to 0 what is the shape of the ellipse?

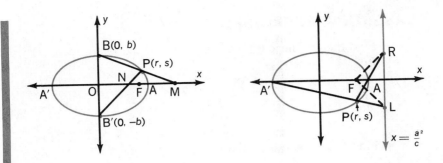

C **13.** Let $P(r, s)$ be any point on the ellipse $\frac{x^2}{a^2} + \frac{y^2}{b^2} = 1 \ (a > b)$. See the figure at the left above. Draw $\overleftrightarrow{BP}$ and $\overleftrightarrow{B'P}$ intersecting the transverse axis in M and N respectively. Prove that $ON \cdot OM = a^2$.

14. Let $P(r, s)$ be any point on the ellipse $\frac{x^2}{a^2} + \frac{y^2}{b^2} = 1 \ (a > b)$. See the figure at the right above. Draw the directrix $x = \frac{a^2}{c}$. Draw $\overleftrightarrow{A'P}$ intersecting $x = \frac{a^2}{c}$ in L, and $\overleftrightarrow{AP}$ intersecting $x = \frac{a^2}{c}$ in R. Prove that $\overleftrightarrow{FR} \perp \overleftrightarrow{FL}$. $\left(F \text{ is the focus corresponding to } x = \frac{a^2}{c} \cdot \right)$

15. Let C be a circle with center at the origin and radius r. See the figure at the left below. Let A be any point interior to C. What equation does the set of all points P satisfy if P is equidistant from A and the circle?

16. Given the x axis with points $A'(-a, 0)$ and $A(a, 0)$. See the figure at the right below. Draw the line $x = p$ and let $D(p, r)$ be any point on $x = p$. Draw $\overleftrightarrow{A'D}$, $\overleftrightarrow{AD}$ and $\overleftrightarrow{A'X}$ where $\overleftrightarrow{A'X} \perp \overleftrightarrow{A'D}$. Let the intersection of $\overleftrightarrow{A'X}$ and $\overleftrightarrow{AD}$ be $T(x, y)$. Find the equation that all points $T(x, y)$ satisfy.

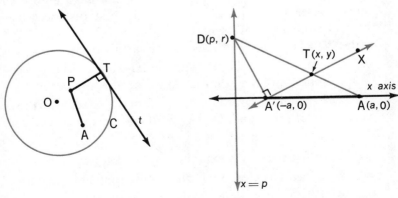

11–4   The Hyperbola

A hyperbola is defined in a manner similar to an ellipse.

> **Definition**   A **hyperbola** is the set of all points such that for any point in the set the difference of its distances from two fixed points is a constant.

The fixed points are the *foci* F' and F which are $2c$ units apart. The constant difference is denoted by $2a$. Letting the coordinates of F' and F be $(-c, 0)$ and $(c, 0)$ respectively, the point $P(x, y)$ is on the hyperbola whenever

$$F'P - FP = 2a \quad \text{or} \quad FP - F'P = 2a$$

Thus $\qquad\qquad F'P - FP = \pm 2a \qquad\qquad \left(\begin{array}{l} + \text{ for right branch} \\ - \text{ for left branch} \end{array} \right)$

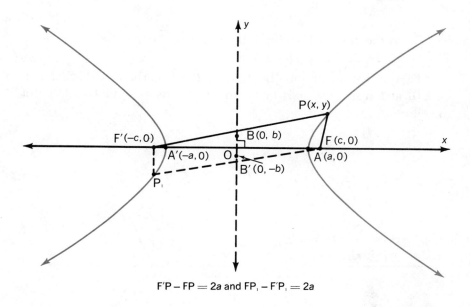

$$F'P - FP = 2a \text{ and } FP_1 - F'P_1 = 2a$$

$\overleftrightarrow{F'F}$ is the transverse axis, A' and A are the vertices, and $\overline{A'A}$ is the major axis. In triangle $F'PF$, when $P(x, y)$ is on the right branch, $a < c$ because $F'P - FP < F'F$. Thus $2a < 2c$ and $a < c$. In a similar manner you can show $a < c$ when $P(x, y)$ is on the left branch.

The conjugate axis is the perpendicular bisector of the transverse axis $\overleftrightarrow{F'F}$. The intersection, O, of the two axes is the **center of the hyperbola**. The points B and B' on the conjugate axis at a distance $b = \sqrt{c^2 - a^2}$ from the center of the hyperbola determine the minor axis $\overline{BB'}$. The length of the semiminor axis, b, may be greater than, equal to, or less than the length of the semimajor axis, a, for a hyperbola. Of course c is greater than either a or b.

The major axis is $2a$ units long, since

$$2a = F'A - FA$$
$$2a = F'A' + A'A - FA \tag{1}$$

and also

$$2a = FA' - F'A'$$
$$2a = FA + A'A - F'A' \tag{2}$$

Subtracting 2 from 1 you get

$$0 = 2(F'A' - FA)$$

or

$$F'A' = FA. \tag{3}$$

Then substituting 3 in 1, you see that

$$2a = F'A' + A'A - F'A'$$
$$= A'A.$$

As in the case of the ellipse the quotient $\dfrac{c}{a} = e$ is the *eccentricity*. Since $c > a$, the eccentricity $e > 1$.

The derivation of the equation of the hyperbola with center at $O(0, 0)$ and transverse axis equal to the x axis is similar to that for the ellipse.

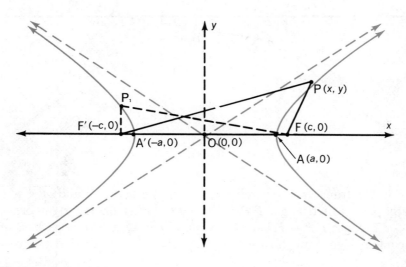

From the definition of a hyperbola, if follows that

$$F'P - FP = \sqrt{(x + c)^2 + y^2} - \sqrt{(x - c)^2 + y^2} = \pm 2a \qquad\qquad 4$$

Thus

$$\sqrt{(x + c)^2 + y^2} = \pm 2a + \sqrt{(x - c)^2 + y^2} \qquad \begin{pmatrix} + \text{ for right branch} \\ - \text{ for left branch} \end{pmatrix}$$

$$x^2 + 2cx + c^2 + y^2 = 4a^2 \pm 4a\sqrt{(x - c)^2 + y^2} + x^2 - 2cx + c^2 + y^2$$

$$cx - a^2 = \pm a\sqrt{(x - c)^2 + y^2} \qquad\qquad 5$$

$$c^2x^2 - 2ca^2x + a^4 = a^2(x^2 - 2cx + c^2 + y^2)$$

$$c^2x^2 + a^4 = a^2x^2 + c^2a^2 + a^2y^2$$

$$(c^2 - a^2)x^2 - a^2y^2 = a^2(c^2 - a^2) \qquad\qquad (c^2 - a^2 = b^2)$$

$$b^2x^2 - a^2y^2 = a^2b^2$$

or

$$\frac{x^2}{a^2} - \frac{y^2}{b^2} = 1 \qquad\qquad 6$$

Not all of the steps in the derivation are reversible, but it can be shown that 6 is the equation of a hyperbola with the center at the origin, transverse axis on the x axis, and conjugate axis on the y axis.

The standard equation of the hyperbola with the y axis for transverse axis and x axis for conjugate axis is

$$\frac{y^2}{a^2} - \frac{x^2}{b^2} = 1 \qquad\qquad 7$$

EXAMPLE. A latus rectum of a hyperbola is a focal chord perpendicular to the transverse axis. What is the length of either latus rectum of the hyperbola $\frac{x^2}{a^2} - \frac{y^2}{b^2} = 1$?

Since the transverse axis is the x axis, the line containing the latus rectum is $x = c$ or $x = -c$.

For $x = c$, $\frac{c^2}{a^2} - \frac{y^2}{b^2} = 1$

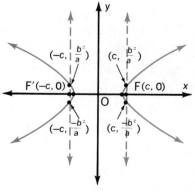

or

$$\frac{c^2}{a^2} - \frac{a^2}{a^2} = \frac{y^2}{b^2}$$

or

$$\frac{c^2 - a^2}{a^2} = \frac{y^2}{b^2}$$

or

$$\frac{b^4}{a^2} = y^2 \quad \text{and} \quad y = \pm \frac{b^2}{a}$$

Thus the length of the latus rectum is $\frac{2b^2}{a}$. This is the same formula which gives the length of the latus rectum for an ellipse.

CLASSROOM EXERCISES

▬▬ Find the length of the semimajor and semiminor axes and state whether the x or y axis is the transverse axis for Examples 1–3.

1. $\dfrac{x^2}{25} - \dfrac{y^2}{9} = 1$ **2.** $\dfrac{y^2}{9} - \dfrac{x^2}{36} = 1$ **3.** $\dfrac{x^2}{4} - \dfrac{y^2}{9} = 1$

▬▬ Sketch each hyperbola.

4. $\dfrac{y^2}{16} - \dfrac{x^2}{9} = 1$ **5.** $\dfrac{x^2}{27} - \dfrac{y^2}{9} = 1$ **6.** $\dfrac{y^2}{9} - \dfrac{x^2}{9} = 1$

WRITTEN EXERCISES

A ▬▬ For Exercises 1–12 identify each curve and find the vertices, foci, ends of latera recta, and eccentricity. Sketch each curve.

1. $\dfrac{x^2}{16} - \dfrac{y^2}{9} = 1$ **2.** $\dfrac{x^2}{36} - \dfrac{y^2}{64} = 1$

3. $4y^2 - 9x^2 = 36$ **4.** $\dfrac{y^2}{9} - \dfrac{x^2}{25} = 1$

5. $4x^2 - y^2 + 1 = 0$ **6.** $4y^2 - 25x^2 = 100$

7. $y^2 - x^2 = 36$ **8.** $x^2 - 16y^2 - 16 = 0$

9. $\dfrac{x^2}{4} - \dfrac{y^2}{21} = 1$ **10.** $\dfrac{x^2}{9} + \dfrac{y^2}{16} = 1$

11. $\dfrac{y^2}{2} - \dfrac{2x^2}{9} = 2$ **12.** $k^2x^2 - y^2 = k^2, \; k > 0$

▬▬ For Exercises 13–20 write the equation of the hyperbola whose axes are the coordinate axes and which satisfies the given conditions. Sketch the graph of each curve.

13. Vertex at $(4, 0)$, end of minor axis at $(0, 3)$.

14. Minor axis of length 8, foci at $(0, \pm5)$.

15. Latus rectum of length 5, focus $(3, 0)$.

16. Major axis of length 8, foci at $(\pm5, 0)$.

17. Minor axis of length 8, foci at $(\pm5, 0)$.

18. Passes through $(2, 1)$, $(4, 3)$, x axis is the transverse axis.

19. End of minor axis at $(3, 0)$ and contains $(4, \frac{20}{3})$.

B **20.** Latus rectum of length 6, eccentricity 3, center at $(0, 0)$, y axis is the transverse axis.

21. Prove or disprove: $\dfrac{x^2}{25} + \dfrac{y^2}{9} = 1$ and $\dfrac{x^2}{4} - \dfrac{y^2}{12} = 1$ have the same foci.

22. What is the equation of a locus of points if the distance of every point from $A(4, 0)$ is twice the distance of the point from the line $x = 1$?

11–5   Asymptotes of the Hyperbola

In Section 6–4 an asymptote to a curve was defined to be a line which the curve approached as the independent variable x neared a fixed number a or as x increased (or decreased) without bound. A hyperbola $\frac{x^2}{a^2} - \frac{y^2}{b^2} = 1$ has two asymptotes given by the equations

$$y = \frac{bx}{a} \quad \text{and} \quad y = \frac{-bx}{a} \qquad\qquad 1$$

To show that equations 1 are equations of asymptotes, you must prove that as x increases (decreases) without bound the limit of the distance between the curve and the line is zero. That is, if d is the distance from the curve to the line then $\lim\limits_{x \to \pm\infty} d = 0$.

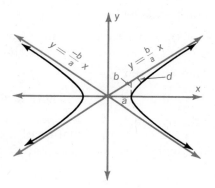

Let $P(r, s)$ be any point on the hyperbola $b^2x^2 - a^2y^2 = a^2b^2$ in the first quadrant. Then the distance d from the curve to the line $bx - ay = 0$ is equal to the following. Remember, the distance, d, from a point $P(x_1, y_1)$ to a line $kx + ly + m = 0$ is equal to

$$d = \frac{|\, kx_1 + ly_1 + m \,|}{\sqrt{k^2 + l^2}} \qquad \longleftarrow \textbf{See page 489.}$$

$$d = \frac{|\, br - as \,|}{\sqrt{b^2 + a^2}} = \frac{|\, br - as \,|}{c} \qquad\qquad 2$$

Multiply numerator and denominator of 2 by $br + as$ and noting that $b^2r^2 - a^2s^2 = a^2b^2$ (Why?) you therefore find the following.

$$d = \frac{|\, b^2r^2 - a^2s^2 \,|}{c(br + as)} = \frac{a^2b^2}{c} \cdot \frac{1}{br + as}$$

But $a^2s^2 = b^2r^2 - a^2b^2$ and therefore $as = b\sqrt{r^2 - a^2}$, so

$$d = \frac{a^2b^2}{c} \cdot \frac{1}{br + b\sqrt{r^2 - a^2}}$$

$$= \frac{a^2b}{c} \cdot \frac{1}{r + \sqrt{r^2 - a^2}}$$

Then

$$\lim_{r \to \infty} d = \lim_{r \to \infty} \frac{a^2b}{c} \cdot \frac{1}{r + \sqrt{r^2 - a^2}} = 0$$

because

$$\frac{1}{r + \sqrt{r^2 - a^2}} \longrightarrow 0 \quad \text{as} \quad r \longrightarrow \infty.$$

Thus $y = \frac{b}{a}x$ is an asymptote to the curve $\frac{x^2}{a^2} - \frac{y^2}{b^2} = 1$. Because of the symmetry of the curve and the lines, it is clear that both lines $y = \pm \frac{b}{a}x$ are asymptotes of the hyperbola.

The equations of the asymptotes for any hyperbola whose equation is in standard form may be found by replacing the constant 1 by 0 and factoring. That is, given $\frac{x^2}{a^2} - \frac{y^2}{b^2} = 1$, set $\frac{x^2}{a^2} - \frac{y^2}{b^2} = 0$ and factor. Then you have $\frac{x}{a} - \frac{y}{b} = 0$ or $\frac{x}{a} + \frac{y}{b} = 0$. These last two equations are the asymptotes for the hyperbola.

EXAMPLE 1. Find the equations of the asymptotes of $\frac{y^2}{a^2} - \frac{x^2}{b^2} = 1$.

Solution:

Let $\frac{y^2}{a^2} - \frac{x^2}{b^2} = 0$. Factor, then you have

$$\frac{y}{a} - \frac{x}{b} = 0 \quad \text{or} \quad \frac{y}{a} + \frac{x}{b} = 0.$$

$by - ax = 0$ and $by + ax = 0$ are the equations of the asymptotes.

Determining the asymptotes of a hyperbola and sketching them will help you to sketch the associated hyperbola.

EXAMPLE 2. Sketch the graph of $\frac{x^2}{9} - \frac{y^2}{16} = 1$. First find the asymptotes. If $\frac{x^2}{9} - \frac{y^2}{16} = 0$, then $\frac{x}{3} \pm \frac{y}{4} = 0$ or $y = \pm\frac{4}{3}x$. Notice that the slope of the asymptote $y = \frac{4}{3}x$ is the ratio: $\frac{\text{semiminor axis}}{\text{semimajor axis}}$. Thus the line $y = \frac{4}{3}x$ is determined by the opposite vertices of the rectangle with base $2a$ and height $2b$. (See the figure.) Similarly for $y = -\frac{4}{3}x$.

The asymptotes are $\overleftrightarrow{PR}$ and $\overleftrightarrow{QS}$. The hyperbola may now be sketched, tangent to $\overline{PS}$ at A and tangent to $\overline{QR}$ at A' and approaching the asymptotes as $x \longrightarrow \pm\infty$.

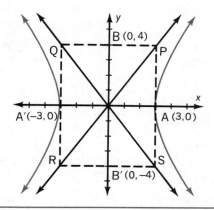

If the asymptotes of a hyperbola are perpendicular, the hyperbola is called a **rectangular hyperbola.** Clearly the asymptotes of a hyperbola are perpendicular whenever their slopes are negative reciprocals, and this occurs only when $a = b$. (This is left for you to prove in the exercises.)

A hyperbola $\frac{x^2}{a^2} - \frac{y^2}{b^2} = 1$ has major axis of length $2a$ along the x axis and minor axis of length $2b$ along the y axis. The hyperbola $\frac{y^2}{b^2} - \frac{x^2}{a^2} = 1$ has major axis of length $2b$ along the y axis and minor axis of length $2a$ along the x axis. Thus the major and minor axes of these two hyperbolas are interchanged. Such hyperbolas are called **conjugate hyperbolas.** Can you show that conjugate hyperbolas have the same asymptotes?

CLASSROOM EXERCISES

▬ Find the equations of the asymptotes for the following curves, if they exist.

1. $\frac{x^2}{25} - \frac{y^2}{36} = 1$

2. $\frac{y^2}{9} - \frac{x^2}{4} = 1$

3. $\frac{x^2}{25} + \frac{y^2}{36} = 1$

4. $\frac{x^2}{16} - \frac{y^2}{9} = 1$

━━━ Write the equation of the hyperbola conjugate to each hyperbola.

5. $\frac{x^2}{25} - \frac{y^2}{36} = 1$　　　　**6.** $\frac{y^2}{9} - \frac{x^2}{4} = 1$　　　　**7.** $6x^2 - 6y^2 = 36$

8. Given the standard equation of a hyperbola, how do you find the equations of the asymptotes?

9. What conditions must be satisfied for a hyperbola to be called a rectangular hyperbola?

10. When are two hyperbolas conjugate?

WRITTEN EXERCISES

A **1–12.** For each Exercise 1–12 in Section 11–4 find the equations of the asymptotes if the curve is a hyperbola and sketch the curve using the technique of Example 2.

13. Prove that the asymptotes of $\frac{x^2}{a^2} - \frac{y^2}{b^2} = 1$ are perpendicular if and only if $a = b$.

14. Prove that conjugate hyperbolas have identical asymptotes.

15. Are conjugate hyperbolas congruent when $a = b$?

16. Sketch, on the same axes, the hyperbola $\frac{x^2}{25} - \frac{y^2}{9} = 1$ and its conjugate.

━━━ For Exercises 17–20, find the equation of the hyperbola.

17. Vertices at $(\pm 6, 0)$, asymptotes $2x \pm y = 0$.

18. Foci at $(0, \pm 5)$, one asymptote containing $(6, 5)$.

19. Foci at $(\pm 4, 0)$, slope of asymptotes ± 3.

20. Center at the origin, slope of asymptotes $\pm\frac{1}{3}$, and length of latus rectum $\frac{4}{3}$. (two answers)

B **21.** Prove that the product of the distances of any point on the hyperbola $x^2 - 4y^2 = 4$ from its asymptotes is constant.

22. Prove the product of the distances of any point on a hyperbola from its asymptotes is constant.

23. Show that the ellipse $9x^2 + 25y^2 = 900$ and the hyperbola $7x^2 - 9y^2 = 252$ have the same foci.

━━━ For Exercises 24 and 25, find the equation of the set of points satisfying the given conditions.

24. The distance from $(5, 0)$ is $\frac{5}{4}$ the distance from $x = \frac{16}{5}$.

25. The distance from $y = \frac{25}{3}$ is $\frac{3}{5}$ the distance from $(0, 5)$.

26. Prove that for two conjugate hyperbolas the sum of the squares of the reciprocals of the eccentricities is one.

C **27.** Let $\overleftrightarrow{AP}$ and $\overleftrightarrow{A'P}$ cut d, a directrix, in points M and N respectively where $P(x, y)$ is on the hyperbola. Show that $\angle MFN$ is a right angle (F is the focus on the same side of the center as d.) (See the figure below.)

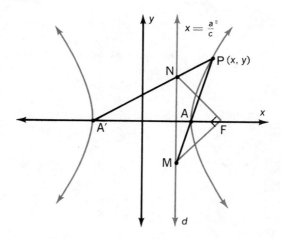

28. Let C be a circle with center at the origin and radius r. Let A be any point exterior to circle C. What equation does the set of all points P satisfy if P is equidistant from point A and the circle C? (*Hint:* See Exercise 15, Section 11–3.) (See the figure at the left below.)

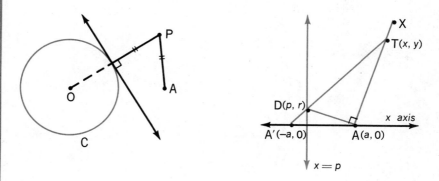

29. Given the x axis with points $A'(-a, 0)$ and $A(a, 0)$. Draw the line $x = p$ ($-a < p < a$) and let $D(p, r)$ be any point on $x = p$. Draw $\overleftrightarrow{A'D}$, $\overleftrightarrow{AD}$ and $\overleftrightarrow{AX}$ where $\overleftrightarrow{AX} \perp \overleftrightarrow{AD}$. Let $\overleftrightarrow{AX} \cap \overleftrightarrow{A'D} = T(x, y)$. Find the equation which all points $T(x, y)$ satisfy. (*Hint:* Find equations for $\overleftrightarrow{A'D}$ and $\overleftrightarrow{AX}$ and eliminate r from these two equations to get one equation.) (See the figure at the right above).

Applying Non-Linear Programming
Cost Analysis

Cost Analysts try to minimize costs and maximize profit. In such situations, there are usually a large number of conditions, or constraints, that must be satisfied simultaneously. When the graphs of these constraints are straight lines, finding values that satisfy the conditions is called **linear programming**. However, not all conditions give rise to straight lines. These situations are examples of **non-linear programming**.

EXAMPLE. Cindy has two horses to pasture. The pair requires at least 640 square meters of pasturage. She can use an existing straight fence for one side of the pasture, and she has 50 prefabricated fence panels, each 2 meters wide, to use on the other three sides of the rectangular pasture. What is the smallest number of panels she can use?

Solution: Suppose x is the number of panels for each of the two equal sides and y is the number for the other side. Then

$$2x + y \leq 50 \quad \longleftarrow \textbf{ Only 50 panels}$$

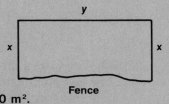

Since each panel is 2 meters wide,

$$2x \cdot 2y \geq 640 \quad \longleftarrow \textbf{ The horses need at least 640 m}^2.$$

or $xy \geq 160$.

The graph is shown below.

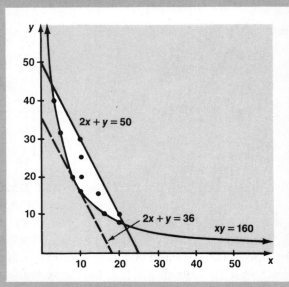

The shaded portion of the graph on page 610 is the excluded region. All solutions lie on or inside the region bounded by $xy = 160$ and $2x + y = 50$. Note that the graph of $xy = 160$ for positive x and y, is a rectangular hyperbola with the axes as its asymptotes.

Since Cindy can use only an integral number of panels, the points in the region that have integral coordinates are displayed. Possible solutions are displayed in the table below.

x	4	5	10	10	10	8	15	16	20	20
y	40	32	30	25	20	20	15	10	10	8
$2x + y$	48	42	50	45	40	36	45	42	50	48

It is clear from the table that 36 panels is the smallest number. This can be shown on the graph by thinking of lines parallel to $2x + y = 50$. The last such line intersecting the critical region at a critical point is $2x + y = 36$. Notice that the 36 indicates the number of panels needed. The line is dashed on the graph.

Linear and non-linear programming problems that arise in business and industry may have hundreds of variables and constraints. They are usually solved by computers.

EXERCISES

1. Solve the problem in the Example if the area to be enclosed is reduced to 480 square meters.

2. In making a new alloy, two materials are used. The sum of the amounts of the materials must be at least 3 units, while the sum of the weights cannot exceed 4. The weight of the first material is approximated by the amount itself. The weight of the second is approximated by the square of the amount. Find the amount of each material used so that the sum of the amounts is maximized.

3. The distance, d, that can be traveled in a motor boat at a constant rate, r, is given by

$$d \le 12r - r^2.$$

If a motor boat trip is to last at least 3 hours, find the rate for the longest time possible. $\left(\text{NOTE: Time is given by the expression } \frac{d}{r}.\right)$

4. Given the same conditions as in Exercise 3, find the rate for the shortest time possible.

11-6   The Parabola

The parabola is the final conic section to be discussed in this chapter. Its definition follows.

> **Definition**   A **parabola** is the set of all points P equidistant from a fixed point and a fixed line.

The fixed point is the **focus,** the fixed line is the **directrix.** The line perpendicular to the directrix from F is the **axis of symmetry.** The point of intersection of the curve and the axis of symmetry is the **vertex.** The focal chord which is perpendicular to the axis is the **latus rectum.** (See Figure 1.)

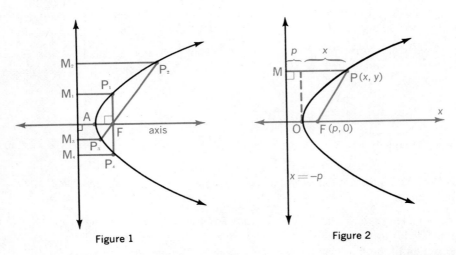

Figure 1   Figure 2

The equation of the parabola with axis of symmetry along the x axis and vertex at the origin is easily obtained. In Figure 2 let F have coordinates $(p, 0)$ and the directrix have equation $x = -p$. By the definition of a parabola $FP = PM$. (See Figure 2.) $FP = \sqrt{(x - p)^2 + y^2}$ by the distance formula, and $PM = p + x$. Thus

$$FP = \sqrt{(x - p)^2 + y^2} = p + x = PM \qquad 1$$

Squaring this expression you find

$$x^2 - 2px + p^2 + y^2 = p^2 + 2px + x^2$$

or $$y^2 = 4px \qquad 2$$

The equation $y^2 = 4px$ is the equation of the parabola with vertex at the origin and focus at the point $F(p, 0)$. If $p > 0$ then the parabola opens to the right; if $p < 0$, the parabola opens to the left.

The parabola with vertex at the origin and focus at $F(0, p)$ has equation

$$x^2 = 4py \qquad\qquad 3$$

It opens up when $p > 0$ and down when $p < 0$. You should verify these statements.

For the parabola

$$y^2 = 4px,$$

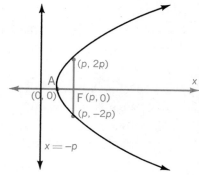

the latus rectum has equation $x = p$ and intersects the curve at $x = p$. Its length is found by substituting p for x in $y^2 = 4px$. You get $y^2 = 4p^2$ and therefore $y = \pm 2p$. (Similarly for the parabola $x^2 = 4py$.)

Thus the length of the latus rectum is $4p$. More accurately the length is $|\,4p\,|$, because if the curve opens to the left or downward, p is less than zero. This result is stated in the following theorem.

Theorem 11–3 The length of the latus rectum of a parabola $y^2 = 4px$ or $x^2 = 4py$ is $|\,4p\,|$.

EXAMPLE. Find the coordinates of the focus, the equation of the directrix, and coordinates of the endpoints of the latus rectum of the parabola $y^2 = -12x$ and sketch the curve.

Solution:

From the equation $y^2 = -12x$, it follows that $4px = -12x$ and $p = -3$. Thus the focus is $F(-3, 0)$ and $x = 3$ is the directrix. The endpoints of the latus rectum are $(-3, 6)$ and $(-3, -6)$. The curve is sketched at the right to go through $(0, 0)$, $(-3, 6)$, and $(-3, -6)$.

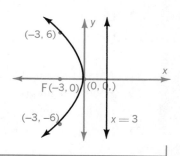

CLASSROOM EXERCISES

Find the value of p, the axis of symmetry and state in which direction the parabola opens for Exercises 1–8. (p is the nonzero coordinate of the focus of a parabola whose vertex is at the origin.)

1. $y^2 = -16x$
2. $x^2 = 16y$
3. $x^2 = -36y$
4. $y^2 = 12x$
5. $y^2 = 18x$
6. $x^2 = -18y$
7. $x^2 = -26y$
8. $y^2 = 14x$

Find the length of the latus rectum for each parabola.

9. $y^2 = -16x$
10. $x^2 = 16y$
11. $x^2 = -24y$
12. $y^2 = 24x$
13. Define a parabola as a set of points.
14. What is the axis of symmetry of a parabola?
15. How does the equation for a parabola differ from that of an ellipse and a hyperbola?

WRITTEN EXERCISES

A ━━ Find the coordinates of the focus, equation of the directrix, and coordinates of the endpoints of the latus rectum, and sketch each parabola for Exercises 1–9.

1. $y^2 = 4x$
2. $x^2 = y$
3. $y^2 = -11x$
4. $x^2 = -24y$
5. $y^2 = -6x$
6. $x^2 = 8y$
7. $y^2 = 3x$
8. $x^2 = \frac{1}{4}y$
9. $4x^2 - 9y = 0$

In Exercises 10–22 use the information given to write the equation of each parabola with vertex at the origin. Sketch each curve.

10. Focus is $(3, 0)$
11. Focus is $(-\frac{3}{2}, 0)$
12. Directrix: $x = -2$
13. Directrix: $x = 4$
14. Focus is $(0, 2)$
15. Focus is $(0, -\frac{7}{8})$
16. Directrix: $y = -1$
17. Directrix: $y = 3$
18. Axis of symmetry along x axis; $(4, -8)$ on the parabola.
19. Focus on y axis; $(-3, 2)$ on the parabola.
20. Focus on x axis; $(-4, -2)$ on the parabola.
21. Length of latus rectum is 12; parabola opens downward.
22. Parabola opens to the left; $(-1, -1)$ on the parabola.

B **23.** Show that the angle whose vertex is at the vertex of the parabola $y^2 = 4x$ and whose sides contain the points $(1, 2)$ and $(16, -8)$ is a right angle.

24. Given the line determined by the two points $(1, 2)$ and $(16, -8)$ and the parabola $y^2 = 4x$. Let M be the point of intersection of the line and the axis of symmetry of the parabola. Show that the distance from the point M to the vertex of the parabola is equal to the length of the latus rectum.

25. Suppose $x = -2$ is the directrix of a parabola with focus $F(4, 0)$, then the vertex is $A(1, 0)$. Then the standard forms for the equation of a parabola that were derived are not applicable. Use the definition of a parabola to derive an equation for the parabola described above.

26. Given a parabola with vertex at $A(-3, 0)$ and focus at $F(-1, 0)$. The standard forms for the equation of a parabola that were derived are not applicable. Use the definition of a parabola to derive an equation for this parabola.

27. Given a parabola with directrix $y = 2$ and focus at $F(0, -6)$. The standard forms for the equation of a parabola that were derived are not applicable. Use the definition of a parabola to derive an equation for this parabola.

C **28.** In the figure at the left below let $P(x_1, y_1)$ and $Q(x_2, y_2)$ be the ends of a focal chord for $y^2 = 4px$. Show that

    a. $PQ = x_1 + x_2 + 2p$. (See Equation 1.)

    b. the distance from the midpoint M of focal chord PQ to the directrix is $\frac{1}{2}PQ$.

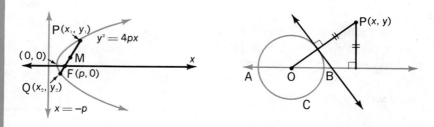

29. Let C be a circle with center at the origin and radius r. In the figure at the right above let $\overleftrightarrow{AB}$ be a line determined by a fixed diameter. Find the equation of the set of all points $P(x, y)$ satisfying the condition that P is equidistant from the line $\overleftrightarrow{AB}$ and the circle C.

MID-CHAPTER REVIEW

▬ Find the length of the axes, the coordinates of the foci, and sketch each conic. (Sections 11-2 and 11-4)

1. $\dfrac{x^2}{36} + \dfrac{y^2}{16} = 1$

2. $\dfrac{x^2}{16} + \dfrac{y^2}{36} = 1$

3. $\dfrac{x^2}{36} - \dfrac{y^2}{16} = 1$

4. $\dfrac{x^2}{16} - \dfrac{y^2}{36} = 1$

▬ Find the eccentricity, the length of the latera recta, and the equations of the directrices of each conic. (Section 11-3 and 11-4)

5. $2x^2 + 5y^2 = 20$

6. $2x^2 - 5y^2 = 20$

7. $4y^2 + 16x^2 = 64$

8. $25y^2 - 4x^2 = 100$

▬ Find the asymptotes for each hyperbola. Sketch each graph. (Section 11-5).

9. $16x^2 - 64y^2 = 64$

10. $25y^2 - x^2 = 25$

11. $\dfrac{x^2}{25} - \dfrac{y^2}{16} = 1$

12. $\dfrac{y^2}{9} - \dfrac{x^2}{25} = 1$

▬ Find the coordinates of the focus and vertex and sketch the curve. (Section 11-6)

13. $y^2 = -12x$

14. $x^2 - 8y = 0$

15. $x^2 = 36y$

16. $y^2 - 18x = 0$

11–7   Translating Conics

In Section 10–12 you learned that a point (x, y) was translated to a point (x', y') by adding the translating vector to the initial point written as a vector,

$$\begin{bmatrix} x \\ y \end{bmatrix} + \begin{bmatrix} a \\ b \end{bmatrix} = \begin{bmatrix} x' \\ y' \end{bmatrix}$$

or by adding the coordinates of the translating point to the original point.

$$(x + a, y + b) = (x', y')$$

You also saw in Section 10–12 that a set of points could be translated to a new position by employing the *translation equations*

$$x = x' - h$$
$$y = y' - k$$

where the translation vector is $\begin{bmatrix} h \\ k \end{bmatrix}$. The translation equations can be used to obtain equations of conics that do not have their centers at the origin (or vertex at the origin for a parabola). When a conic is translated to a new position in the plane the properties of the conic section are preserved. That is, the original conic and its translation image are congruent.

Standard Equations for the Parabola

Given

$$y^2 = 4px$$

and the translation equations $x = x' - h$, $y = y' - k$. By substituting, you find

$$(y' - k)^2 = 4p(x' - h) \qquad \textbf{1}$$

Since $(0, 0)$ maps onto (h, k) under the translation, the vertex of the image parabola is at (h, k). See Figure 1 below. Thus, dropping primes, the equation of the parabola with vertex at (h, k) and axis parallel to the x axis is

$$(y - k)^2 = 4p(x - h) \qquad \textbf{2}$$

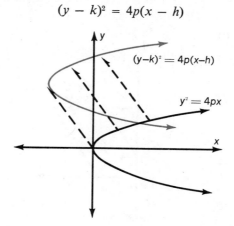

Figure 1

The corresponding equation for the parabola with its axis parallel to the y axis is

$$(x - h)^2 = 4p(y - k) \qquad \textbf{3}$$

EXAMPLE 1. Find the focus, the vertex, and the latus rectum of the parabola $(x - 2)^2 = 8(y + 3)$ and sketch the curve.

Solution:

$(x - 2)^2 = 8(y + 3)$
$ = 4 \cdot 2(y + 3)$

Thus, $A(2, -3)$ is the vertex, and $F(2, -1)$ is the focus. The endpoints of the latus rectum are $B(-2, -1)$ and $C(6, -1)$.

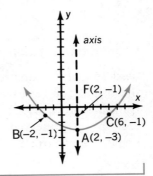

Standard Equations for the Ellipse

Translating the ellipse $\frac{x^2}{a^2} + \frac{y^2}{b^2} = 1$ by means of the translating equations

$$x = x' - h \qquad y = y' - k$$

and dropping the primes, yields the standard equation.

$$\frac{(x - h)^2}{a^2} + \frac{(y - k)^2}{b^2} = 1, a > b \qquad \qquad \mathbf{4}$$

The center of $\mathbf{4}$ is at (h, k), the vertices have coordinates $(h - a, k)$ and $(h + a, k)$, the ends of the minor axis are at $(h, k + b)$ and $(h, k - b)$, and the latus rectum is $\frac{2b^2}{a}$ in length.

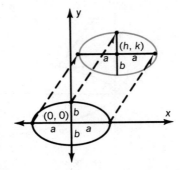

The standard equation for an ellipse with transverse axis parallel to the y axis and with center at (h, k) is

$$\frac{(y - k)^2}{a^2} + \frac{(x - h)^2}{b^2} = 1, a > b \qquad \qquad \mathbf{5}$$

EXAMPLE 2. Find the coordinates of the center, the vertices and the foci for the given ellipse.

$$\frac{(x-6)^2}{25} + \frac{(y+10)^2}{9} = 1$$

The center has coordinates $(6, -10)$. $a^2 = 25$, therefore the length of the semimajor axis is 5. The coordinates of the vertices are

$$(6-5, -10) \quad \text{and} \quad (6+5, -10)$$

or

$$(1, -10) \quad \text{and} \quad (11, -10)$$

$a^2 = 25$ and $b^2 = 9$, therefore $c^2 = \sqrt{a^2 - b^2} = \sqrt{25 - 9} = \sqrt{16} = 4$. The coordinates of the foci are therefore,

$$(6-4, -10) \quad \text{and} \quad (6+4, -10)$$

or

$$(2, -10) \quad \text{and} \quad (10, -10)$$

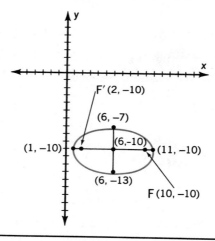

Standard Equations for the Hyperbola

By translating the hyperbolas $\frac{x^2}{a^2} - \frac{y^2}{b^2} = 1$ and $\frac{y^2}{a^2} - \frac{x^2}{b^2} = 1$ using the translating equations $x = x' - h$ and $y = y' - k$ and dropping the primes you can derive the equations

$$\frac{(x-h)^2}{a^2} - \frac{(y-k)^2}{b^2} = 1 \qquad\qquad 6$$

and

$$\frac{(y-k)^2}{a^2} - \frac{(x-h)^2}{b^2} = 1 \qquad\qquad 7$$

Each of these hyperbolas has center (h, k). 6 has a horizontal transverse axis. And 7 has a vertical transverse axis.

EXAMPLE 3. Find the equation of the hyperbola with foci at $F'(-4, 2)$ and $F(2, 2)$ and semiminor axis of length 1 unit. Sketch the curve.

The center of the hyperbola is the midpoint of $\overline{F'F}$, which is the point $(-1, 2)$. Since the transverse axis is parallel to the x axis, the equation has standard form 6. Since you know $b = 1$, at this point you can write,

$$\frac{(x + 1)^2}{a^2} - \frac{(y - 2)^2}{1} = 1.$$

c is half of $F'F = 6$, so $c = 3$ and $a^2 = c^2 - b^2 = 9 - 1 = 8.$ Thus

$$\frac{(x + 1)^2}{8} - \frac{(y - 2)^2}{1} = 1.$$

The sketch is easily drawn by finding the asymptotes of the curve. These are found by setting $\frac{(x + 1)^2}{8} - \frac{(y - 2)^2}{1}$ equal to zero. They are $\frac{x + 1}{2\sqrt{2}} \pm (y - 2) = 0$ and contain the center of the hyperbola $(-1, 2)$.

CLASSROOM EXERCISES

1. Find the coordinates of the vertex and focus and the equation of the axis of symmetry for the parabola $(y - 2)^2 = 12(x - 3)$.

2. Find the coordinates of the center, vertices, and ends of the minor axis for the ellipse $\frac{(x + 3)^2}{16} + \frac{(y - 2)^2}{9} = 1$.

3. Find the coordinates of the center, foci and the equations of the, asymptotes for the hyperbola $\frac{(x - 2)^2}{9} - \frac{(y - 4)^2}{4} = 1$.

━━━ Find the equation of each conic.

4. Parabola: Vertex $(2, 0)$ directrix, $x = 0$.

5. Parabola: Focus $(1, 0)$, vertex $(1, 3)$.

6. Ellipse: Semimajor axis $= 5$, foci at $(0, 2)$ and $(8, 2)$.

7. Ellipse: Center $(2, 2)$, focus $(5, 2)$, length of semimajor axis is 8.

8. Hyperbola: Vertices $(8, 3)$ and $(-3, 3)$, eccentricity $\frac{3}{2}$.

9. Hyperbola: Center $(2, 1)$, focus $(-2, 1)$, eccentricity $\frac{4}{3}$.

WRITTEN EXERCISES

A ▬▬ Find the equation of each conic for Exercises 1–16 and sketch each curve.

1. Hyperbola: Center $(1, 3)$, vertex $(4, 3)$, end of minor axis at $(1, 1)$.

2. Hyperbola: Vertex $(-4, 0)$, foci at $(-5, 0)$ and $(1, 0)$.

3. Hyperbola: Ends of minor axis at $(3, -1)$ and $(3, 5)$, focus at $(-1, 2)$.

4. Hyperbola: Vertices at $(-1, 3)$ and $(5, 3)$, length of minor axis is 6.

5. Hyperbola: Vertices at $(0, 0)$ and $(12, 0)$, asymptotes $4x - 3y - 24 = 0$ and $4x + 3y - 24 = 0$.

6. Ellipse: Center at $(5, 1)$, vertex at $(5, 4)$, end of minor axis at $(3, 1)$.

7. Ellipse: Vertex at $(6, 3)$, foci at $(-4, 3)$ and $(4, 3)$.

8. Ellipse: Ends of minor axis at $(-1, 2)$ and $(-1, -4)$, focus at $(1, -1)$.

9. Ellipse: Vertices at $(-1, 3)$ and $(5, 3)$, length of minor axis is 4.

10. Ellipse: One vertex at $(9, 2)$, ends of minor axis at $(4, -1)$ and $(4, 5)$.

11. Parabola: Vertex at $(2, 3)$, focus at $(6, 3)$.

12. Parabola: Vertex at $(-2, 5)$, focus at $(-2, -2)$.

13. Parabola: Vertex at $(3, -2)$, endpoints of latus rectum at $(-3, 1)$ and $(9, 1)$.

14. Parabola: Vertex at $(-1, -2)$, length of latus rectum is 12, opens downward.

15. Parabola: Focus at $(4, -1)$, latus rectum has length 8, opens to left.

B **16.** Prove that the length of the latus rectum of the parabola $(y - k)^2 = 4p(x - h)$ is $4p$.

17. Prove that the length of the latera recta of the hyperbola $\dfrac{(x - h)^2}{a^2} - \dfrac{(y - k)^2}{b^2} = 1$ and the ellipse $\dfrac{(x - h)^2}{a^2} + \dfrac{(y - k)^2}{b^2} = 1$ is $\dfrac{2b^2}{a}$.

18. Find the directrix for $\dfrac{(x - h)^2}{a^2} - \dfrac{(y - k)^2}{b^2} = 1$.

19. Find the directrix for $\dfrac{(x - h)^2}{a^2} + \dfrac{(y - k)^2}{b^2} = 1$.

11-8   Equations of the Second Degree: Translations

If A, B, C, D, E, and F are real numbers (A, B, C not all zero) the equation

$$Ax^2 + Bxy + Cy^2 + Dx + Ey + F = 0 \qquad 1$$

is an equation of the second degree. In general every equation in the form of **1** is usually a conic. However, some second-degree equations describe no points at all or describe *degenerate conics*, such as points (degenerate circles or ellipses), intersecting lines (degenerate hyperbolas), or parallel lines (degenerate parabolas). An example is $x^2 + y^2 = 0$ which is an equation of the origin. Other examples are $x^2 + y^2 = -2$ (no graph) and $x^2 - y^2 = 0$ (intersecting lines).

In order to identify the conic section represented by **1**, you would like to change the equation so that the curve is more recognizable. This can be accomplished by moving the curve to a new position.

Translation can be used to change the position in the plane of the curve represented by **1** and also to get a new equation. By choosing the correct translation you get a new equation of the conic that has at most one first degree term and possibly none at all.

For example, when $B = 0$ in equation **1**, by use of a translation you could reduce equation **1** to the form

$$A'x^2 + C'y^2 + F' = 0 \qquad 2$$

If A' and C' have the same sign, then equation **2** describes an ellipse, a circle, a point, or no graph. If A' and C' have opposite signs, the equation describes a hyperbola or two intersecting straight lines. Equation **1** can also be reduced to the following form.

$$A'x^2 + E'y + F' = 0 \qquad 3$$

Equation **3** describes a parabola or two parallel straight lines.

The procedure used to obtain these equations from Equation **1** is illustrated below. First, recall that the translation equations are

$$x = x' - h$$
$$y = y' - k.$$

If $B = 0$, then equation **1** has the form

$$Ax^2 + Cy^2 + Dx + Ey + F = 0. \qquad 1'$$

Substituting the translation equations in **1'** you have

$$A(x' - h)^2 + C(y' - k)^2 + D(x' - h) + E(y' - k) + F = 0. \qquad 2'$$

Simplifying, you have the following equation.

$$Ax'^2 + Cy'^2 + (-2Ah + D)x' + (-2Ck + E)y'$$
$$+ (Ah^2 + Ck^2 - Dh - Ek + F) = 0 \qquad 3'$$

To eliminate the x' and y' terms, you need

and
$$\begin{aligned} -2Ah + D &= 0 \\ -2Ck + E &= 0 \end{aligned} \qquad 4'$$

This system has a solution in h and k if and only if $\begin{bmatrix} -2A & 0 \\ 0 & -2C \end{bmatrix}$ has an inverse. The matrix has an inverse if and only if the determinant

or
$$\begin{aligned} 4AC - 0 &\neq 0 \\ 4AC &\neq 0. \end{aligned} \qquad 5'$$

When $4AC = 0$, one of x' and y' cannot be eliminated. Notice that when $4AC = 0$, then either A or C must be zero. (Why?) In this case, the curve is a parabola. (See Equation 3.) When $4AC < 0$, A and C are opposite in sign and the curve is a hyperbola, or a degenerate conic. (See Equation 2.) Similarly when $4AC > 0$, the curve is an ellipse or circle, or a degenerate conic. (See Equation 2.)

In general when $B \neq 0$, substitution of the translation equations in 1 gives the following

$$A(x' - h)^2 + B(x' - h)(y' - k) + C(y' - k)^2$$
$$+ D(x' - h) + E(y' - k) + F = 0. \qquad 4$$

Simplifying you find

$$Ax'^2 + Bx'y' + Cy'^2 + (-2Ah - Bk + D)x' + (-2Ck - Bh + E)y'$$
$$+ (Ah^2 + Bkh + Ck^2 - Dh - Ek + F) = 0 \qquad 5$$

To eliminate the x' and the y' terms, you need

and
$$\begin{aligned} -2Ah - Bk + D &= 0 \\ -Bh - 2Ck + E &= 0. \end{aligned} \qquad 6$$

This system has a solution if and only if the matrix $\begin{bmatrix} -2A & -B \\ -B & -2C \end{bmatrix}$ has an inverse. The matrix has an inverse if and only if the determinant
$$4AC - B^2 \neq 0. \qquad 7$$

When $4AC - B^2 = 0$, the curve must be a parabola because one of x' and y' cannot be eliminated. It is also true that when $4AC - B^2 < 0$, the curve is a hyperbola and when $4AC - B^2 > 0$ it is an ellipse.

EXAMPLE 1. Translate the curve represented by

$$4x^2 + 9y^2 + 8x - 36y + 4 = 0$$

so that the curve is in standard position and the equation is a standard form.

Solution:

The curve is an ellipse. ⟵ **4AC = 4 · 4 · 9 > 0.**

To find the correct translation, substitute $x = x' - h$, $y = y' - k$ and simplify.

$$4(x'^2 - 2hx' + h^2) + 9(y'^2 - 2ky' + k^2)$$
$$+ 8(x' - h) - 36(y' - k) + 4 = 0$$
$$4x'^2 + 9y'^2 + (-8h + 8)x' + (-18k - 36)y'$$
$$+ (4h^2 + 9k^2 - 8h + 36k + 4) = 0 \qquad \text{8}$$

For x' and y' to be eliminated, you need

$$-8h + 8 = 0$$
$$h = 1$$

$$-18k - 36 = 0$$
$$k = -2.$$

Substituting $h = 1$, $k = -2$ in equation 8 you find

$$4x'^2 + 9y'^2 + (4 + 36 - 8 - 72 + 4) = 0$$

or $\qquad 4x'^2 + 9y'^2 = 36.$ ⟵ **An ellipse**

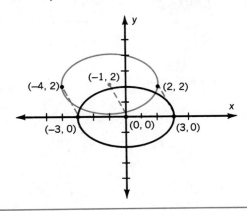

Notice that the translating vector is $\begin{bmatrix} 1 \\ -2 \end{bmatrix}$. To sketch a graph of the original curve all you need do is translate $4x^2 + 9y^2 = 36$ under the vector $\begin{bmatrix} -1 \\ 2 \end{bmatrix}$ which is the opposite of the original vector.

EXAMPLE 2. Translate the curve represented by

$$2x^2 - 4x - y + 5 = 0$$

so that the curve is in standard position and the equation is in a standard form.

Solution:

The curve is a parabola. ⟵ $4AC = 4 \cdot 2 \cdot 0 = 0$

Find the correct translation by substituting $x = x' - h$, $y = y' - k$.

$$2(x'^2 - 2x'h + h^2) - 4(x' - h) - (y' - k) + 5 = 0$$

or $\qquad 2x'^2 + (-4h - 4)x' - y' + (2h^2 + 4h + k + 5) = 0 \qquad$ 9

Clearly $-4h - 4 = 0$ when $h = -1$. For the moment leave k unspecified. Substituting $h = -1$ in 9 and dropping primes, you have

$$2x^2 - y + (2 - 4 + 5 + k) = 0$$

or $\qquad 2x^2 = y - (3 + k)$

For this to be in standard form $(3 + k)$ must be zero so $k = -3$. Then the image of $2x^2 - 4x - y + 5 = 0$ under the translation with vector $\begin{bmatrix} -1 \\ -3 \end{bmatrix}$ is $2x^2 = y$ or $x^2 = \frac{1}{2}y$.

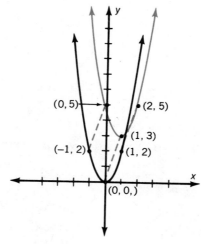

(0, 5)   (2, 5)

(1, 3)

(−1, 2)   (1, 2)

(0, 0,)

CLASSROOM EXERCISES

▬ Find the values of h and k that will eliminate the x and y terms in Exercises 1 and 2. Also use $4AC$ to identify each curve.

1. $x^2 + y^2 - 6x + 12y + 33 = 0$ **2.** $x^2 + y^2 + 6x - 12y + 33 = 0$

3. $x^2 - 2y^2 - 3x + 4y + 7 = 0$ **4.** $x^2 - y^2 + 2x - 5y + 3 = 0$

WRITTEN EXERCISES

A ━━ Translate each curve so that its center (or vertex for the parabola) is at the origin. Sketch the image curve and then the original curve.

1. $x^2 + y^2 - 2x - 4y - 20 = 0$

2. $x^2 - 4y^2 - 2x - 16y - 19 = 0$

3. $x^2 - 4y^2 + 8x + 24y - 20 = 0$

4. $2x^2 - 4x - y + 5 = 0$

5. $y^2 - 6x - 4y + 22 = 0$

6. $3x^2 + 4y^2 + 12x + 8y + 8 = 0$

7. $9x^2 + y^2 + 36x - 8y + 43 = 0$

8. $2x^2 + 2y^2 - 8x + 5 = 0$

9. $16x^2 - 4y^2 - 160x - 24y + 300 = 0$

10. $2y^2 - 6x + 12y + 33 = 0$

11. $x^2 + y^2 - 4x - 2y - 20 = 0$

12. $2y^2 - 4y - x + 5 = 0$

13. $9x^2 + 4y^2 - 36x + 8y + 4 = 0$

11–9   The General Second Degree Equation: Rotations

In the last section you learned how to remove the linear (first degree) terms from

$$Ax^2 + Bxy + Cy^2 + Dx + Ey + F = 0 \qquad\qquad 1$$

by translating the curve to a new position. When $B \neq 0$ the term Bxy can be removed from **1** by rotating the curve through an angle θ.

Before discussing how to eliminate Bxy, recall that the equations (see Section 10–10)

$$\begin{bmatrix} \cos \theta & -\sin \theta \\ \sin \theta & \cos \theta \end{bmatrix} \begin{bmatrix} x \\ y \end{bmatrix} = \begin{bmatrix} x' \\ y' \end{bmatrix} \qquad\qquad 2$$

rotate a point (x, y) through an angle of θ to (x', y'). However, the rotation desired is the inverse of **2** since you want equations for x and y in terms of x' and y'. The equations are easily found by multiplying both sides of **2** by the inverse of the rotation matrix. (See Section 10-4.)

(Note that the inverse exists for all θ. Why?) The result is:

$$\begin{bmatrix} x \\ y \end{bmatrix} = \begin{bmatrix} \cos\theta & \sin\theta \\ -\sin\theta & \cos\theta \end{bmatrix}\begin{bmatrix} x' \\ y' \end{bmatrix}$$

or
$$x = x'\cos\theta + y'\sin\theta$$
$$y = -x'\sin\theta + y'\cos\theta$$

3

Equations 3 are the *rotation equations*.

EXAMPLE 1. Rotate the curve represented by $x^2 - y^2 - 9 = 0$ through an angle of 45°. Sketch both curves.

Solution: When $\theta = 45°$, the rotation equations are:

$$x = \frac{x'}{\sqrt{2}} + \frac{y'}{\sqrt{2}} \qquad y = \frac{-x'}{\sqrt{2}} + \frac{y'}{\sqrt{2}}$$

Substitution in $x^2 - y^2 - 9 = 0$ yields

$$\left(\frac{x'+y'}{\sqrt{2}}\right)^2 - \left(\frac{-x'+y'}{\sqrt{2}}\right)^2 - 9 = 0$$

or
$$x'^2 + 2x'y' + y'^2 - x'^2 + 2x'y' - y'^2 - 18 = 0$$

or
$$2x'y' = 9.$$

Since $2x'y' = 9$ is the image of $x^2 - y^2 = 9$ under a rotation and the properties of conics are preserved under rotations, both are hyperbolas.

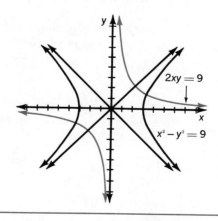

In Example 1 you found that the rotation image of $x^2 - y^2 = 9$ had an equation which involved an xy-term. Conversely, given a second degree equation with an xy-term, rotations can be used to eliminate that term. Clearly the major objective is to find the angle θ through which you should rotate.

Suppose you have a second degree equation with $B \neq 0$.

$$Ax^2 + Bxy + Cy^2 + Dx + Ey + F = 0$$

Rotate this curve through an angle θ by substituting the rotation equations below.

$$x = x' \cos \theta + y' \sin \theta \qquad y = -x' \sin \theta + y' \cos \theta$$

The results, in simplified form, are

$$A'x'^2 + B'x'y' + C'y'^2 + D'x' + E'y' + F' = 0$$

where
$$
\begin{aligned}
A' &= A \cos^2 \theta - B \sin \theta \cos \theta + C \sin^2 \theta \\
B' &= B(\cos^2 \theta - \sin^2 \theta) + (2A - 2C) \sin \theta \cos \theta \\
C' &= A \sin^2 \theta + B \sin \theta \cos \theta + C \cos^2 \theta \\
D' &= D \cos \theta - E \sin \theta \\
E' &= D \sin \theta + E \cos \theta \\
F' &= F.
\end{aligned}
$$

To eliminate $x'y'$, B' must be zero.

Let $\qquad B' = B(\cos^2 \theta - \sin^2 \theta) + (2A - 2C) \sin \theta \cos \theta = 0$

or $\qquad\qquad\qquad\qquad B \cos 2\theta + (A - C) \sin 2\theta = 0.$

(See the double-angle formulas on page 152.) Since $B \neq 0$, $\sin 2\theta \neq 0$. (Why?) Thus,

$$\frac{\cos 2\theta}{\sin 2\theta} = \frac{C - A}{B}$$

or $\qquad\qquad\qquad\qquad \cot 2\theta = \frac{C - A}{B}.$ **4**

By restricting θ to an acute angle, $\sin \theta$ and $\cos \theta$ can be computed by using the half-angle formulas (see page 154).

$$\sin \theta = \sqrt{\frac{1 - \cos 2\theta}{2}}, \quad \cos \theta = \sqrt{\frac{1 + \cos 2\theta}{2}}$$ **5**

Thus to eliminate the xy-term from **1**, find $\cot 2\theta$ by using **4**, $\sin \theta$ and $\cos \theta$ using **5** and rotate using the rotation equations **3**.

EXAMPLE 2. Rotate $2x^2 + \sqrt{3}xy + y^2 - 8 = 0$ in such a manner that the xy term is eliminated.

Solution: By **4** $\cot 2\theta = \frac{1 - 2}{\sqrt{3}} = \frac{-1}{\sqrt{3}}$. The

angle θ is acute and $\cot 2\theta = \frac{x}{y}$, and so

$x = -1, y = \sqrt{3}$. (See the diagram.) Re-

call that $\cos 2\theta = \frac{x}{r}$ where $r = \sqrt{x^2 + y^2}$.

Thus $\cos 2\theta = -\frac{1}{2}$.

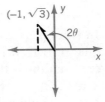

Now substituting in **5**, you see that

$$\sin \theta = \sqrt{\frac{1 - \frac{-1}{2}}{2}} \qquad \cos \theta = \sqrt{\frac{1 + \frac{-1}{2}}{2}}$$

$$= \sqrt{\frac{2 + 1}{4}} \qquad\qquad = \sqrt{\frac{1}{4}}$$

$$= \frac{\sqrt{3}}{2} \qquad\qquad = \frac{1}{2}$$

The rotating equations are

$$x = \frac{x' + \sqrt{3}y'}{2}$$

$$y = \frac{-\sqrt{3}x' + y'}{2}$$

Substituting these in the original equation, you get

$$2\left(\frac{x' + y'\sqrt{3}}{2}\right)^2 + \sqrt{3}\left(\frac{x' + y'\sqrt{3}}{2}\right)\left(\frac{-x'\sqrt{3} + y'}{2}\right)$$
$$+ \left(\frac{-x'\sqrt{3} + y'}{2}\right)^2 - 8 = 0$$

Multiplying out and collecting terms you find

$$2x'^2 + 10y'^2 = 32 \text{ or } x'^2 + 5y'^2 = 16.$$

The figure below shows the original ellipse and its image in standard position. What is the measure of the angle through which the ellipse was rotated? (*Hint:* What is $\sin \theta$? $\cos \theta$?)

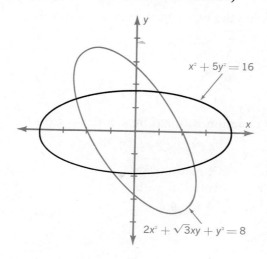

EXAMPLE 3. By a translation and a rotation move the curve $4x^2 - 4xy + 7y^2 + 12x + 6y - 9 = 0$ to the standard position. Find the equation of the curve in standard position.

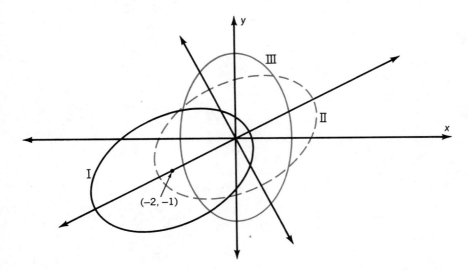

Check $4AC - B^2$. It is greater than zero, so a translation will eliminate the linear terms. Use the equations

$$x = x' - h$$
$$y = y' - k$$

Then

$$4(x'^2 - 2x'h + h^2) - 4(x'y' - x'k - y'h + hk)$$
$$+ 7(y'^2 - 2y'k + k^2) + 12(x' - h) + 6(y' - k) - 9 = 0 \qquad 6$$

Thus to eliminate the linear terms you need to solve

$$-8h + 4k + 12 = 0$$
$$4h - 14k + 6 = 0$$

or
$$h = 2$$
$$k = 1.$$

The resulting equation is found by substituting $h = 2$, $k = 1$ in 6.

$$4x'^2 - 4x'y' + 7y'^2 - 24 = 0 \qquad 7$$

The $x'y'$ term in this equation can be eliminated by a rotation with

$\cot 2\theta = \dfrac{7-4}{-4} = -\frac{3}{4}.$ $\operatorname{Sin} \theta = \dfrac{2}{\sqrt{5}}$

and $\cos \theta = \dfrac{1}{\sqrt{5}}.$

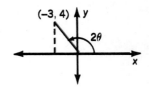

The rotating equations are therefore

$$x' = \frac{x' + 2y'}{\sqrt{5}}; \quad y' = \frac{-2x' + y'}{\sqrt{5}}.$$

Substitution in 7 yields

$$8x'^2 + 3y'^2 - 24 = 0.$$

Thus the curve is an ellipse with major axis along the y axis.

In the figure, the original ellipse is I. It was translated to position II, and finally II was rotated to position III.

CLASSROOM EXERCISES

— Find the cosine and sine of the angle of rotation that will eliminate the xy term from the following equations.

1. $2x^2 + 12xy + 7y^2 - 4x + 5y - 23 = 0$

2. $-2x^2 + 4xy + y^2 - 10x - 11y - 17 = 0$

WRITTEN EXERCISES

A — Translate and rotate each curve until it is in standard position and its equation is in standard form. Sketch each curve.

1. $2x^2 + 4xy + 5y^2 - 8x - 14y + 5 = 0$

2. $x^2 - 2xy + y^2 - 8\sqrt{2}y - 8 = 0$

3. $3x^2 + 12xy + 8y^2 - 24x - 40y + 60 = 0$

4. $73x^2 - 72xy + 52y^2 + 380x - 160y + 400 = 0$

5. $11x^2 + 6xy + 3y^2 - 12x - 12y - 12 = 0$

6. $3x^2 - 10xy + 3y^2 + 22x - 26y + 43 = 0$

7. $6x^2 + 12xy + y^2 - 36x - 6y = 0$

8. $104x^2 + 60xy + 41y^2 - 60x - 82y - 75 = 0$

9. $12x^2 - 7xy - 12y^2 - 17x + 31y - 13 = 0$

10. $25x^2 + 120xy + 144y^2 + 86x - 233y + 270 = 0$ (Rotate this curve before translating it.)

11. $x^2 - 2xy + y^2 - 5x = 0$

12. $3x^2 + 2xy - y^2 + 4y - 3 = 0$

B — The similarity transformation is defined by the equations $x = cx'$, $y = cy'$. Find the image of each conic under this transformation for $c = \frac{1}{2}, 2, 3$.

13. $x^2 + y^2 = 9$

14. $\frac{x^2}{9} + \frac{y^2}{16} = 1$

15. $x^2 - y^2$ 1

16. $y^2 = 4x$

BASIC: ROTATING A CONIC

Problem:
Given the coefficients of the second–degree equation of the form
$Ax^2 + Bxy + Cy^2 + Dx + Ey + F = 0$, write a program which determines the angle of rotation and the coefficients of the equation of the
rotated curve.

```
110 PRINT "THIS PROGRAM CALCULATES THE EQUATION"
120 PRINT "OF A CONIC SECTION AFTER IT HAS BEEN"
130 PRINT "ROTATED THROUGH AN ANGLE THETA."
140 PRINT
150 PRINT "FOR THE EQUATION"
170 PRINT "AX↑2 + BXY + CY↑2 + DX + EY + F = 0"
190 PRINT "WHAT ARE A, B, C, D, E, AND F";
200 INPUT A, B, C, D, E, F
210 IF B = 0 THEN 440
220 IF A = C THEN 280
230 LET T = .5 * ATN(B/(C-A))
240 LET S = SIN(T)
250 LET C2 = COS(T)
260 LET T = 180 * T / 3.14159
270 GOTO 310
280 LET T = 45
290 LET S = .707106
300 LET C2 = .707106
320 PRINT "USE A ROTATION ANGLE OF ";T;" DEGREES"
330 LET A1 = A*C2*C2 - B*S*C2 + C*S*S
340 LET B1 = 0
350 LET C1 = A*S*S + B*S*C2 + C*C2*C2
360 LET D1 = D*C2 - E*S
370 LET E1 = D*S + E*C2
380 LET F1 = F
390 PRINT
400 PRINT "FOR ROTATED EQUATION, USE"
410 PRINT "A' = ";A1;" B' = ";B1;" C' = ";C1
420 PRINT "D' = ";D1;" E' = ";E1;" F' = ";F1
430 GOTO 450
440 PRINT "NO ROTATION NECESSARY"
450 PRINT
460 PRINT "ANY MORE EQUATIONS (1=YES,0=NO)";
470 INPUT Z                   490 PRINT
480 IF Z = 1 THEN 140         500 END
```

Output:

```
FOR THE EQUATION
AX↑2 + BXY + CY↑2 + DX + EY + F = 0
WHAT ARE A, B, C, D, E, AND F? 4,-4,7,12,6,-9

USE A ROTATION ANGLE OF -26.5651   DEGREES

FOR ROTATED EQUATION, USE
A' =    3  B' =   0  C' =   8
D' =   13.4164  E' =  4.76837E-07  F' = -9

ANY MORE EQUATIONS (1=YES,0=NO)? 0
```

Analysis:

Statements 210–300: This part of the program determines the angle of rotation, T. Statement 230 is based on the formula given on page 628: $\cot 2\theta = \frac{C - A}{B}$. Because BASIC has no arccotangent function, the ATN (arctangent) function is used. If $A = C$, then the computer is sent to statements 280–300, which set T as 45° and S and C2 as the sine and cosine of 45°, respectively.

Statements 330–380: The equations on page 628 are used to determine the coefficients of the equation of the rotated curve.

EXERCISES

A   Use the program on page 632 to determine the angle of rotation and the coefficients of the equation of the rotated curve.

1. $2x^2 + 4xy + 4y^2 - 8x - 14y + 5 = 0$

2. $3x^2 + 12xy + 8y^2 - 24x - 40y + 60 = 0$

3. $73x^2 - 72xy + 52y^2 + 380x - 160y + 400 = 0$

4. $11x^2 + 6xy + 3y^2 - 12x - 12y - 12 = 0$

C   Write a BASIC program for each problem.

5. Given h, k, a, and b of the equation $\frac{(x - h)^2}{a^2} + \frac{(y - k)^2}{b^2} = 1$, print the coordinates of the center, foci, and vertices of the ellipse and the lengths of the major and minor axes and the latera recta.

6. Given a, b, and c of the equation $y = ax^2 + bx + c$, print the coordinates of the vertex and focus of the parabola, the equations of the directrix and axis of symmetry, and the length of the latus rectum.

CHAPTER SUMMARY

Important Terms

Axis of symmetry (p. 612)
Center of a hyperbola (p. 602)
Center of an ellipse (p. 592)
Conic sections (p. 590)
Conjugate axis (p. 592)
Conjugate hyperbola (p. 607)
Eccentricity (p. 598)
Ellipse (p. 592)
Focal chord (p. 598)

Foci (p. 592)
Hyperbola (p. 601)
Latus rectum (p. 598)
Parabola (p. 612)
Rectangular hyperbola (p. 607)
Semimajor axis (p. 593)
Semiminor axis (p. 593)
Transverse axis (p. 592)
Vertex of a parabola (p. 612)

Important Ideas

1. Standard equations for the ellipse: See page 618.

2. Standard equations for the hyperbola: See page 619.

3. Standard equations for the parabola: See page 617.

4. The asymptotes for a hyperbola are found by factoring
$b^2x^2 - a^2y^2 = 0$ or $b^2(x - h)^2 - a^2(y - k)^2 = 0$

5. The equation $Ax^2 + Bxy + Cy^2 + Dx + Ey + F = 0$ represents a conic or a degenerate conic. If $4AC - B^2 = 0$, it is a parabola. If $4AC - B^2 < 0$, it is a hyperbola; if $4AC - B^2 > 0$, it is an ellipse.

6. Applying the transformation

$$x = x' \cos \theta + y' \sin \theta$$
$$y = -x' \sin \theta + y' \cos \theta$$

rotates a graph through an angle with measure θ.

CHAPTER OBJECTIVES AND REVIEW

Objective: *To relate the circle, parabola, ellipse, and hyperbola to a right circular conic surface.* (Section 11-1)

In each case tell what figure or figures may be formed when a plane cuts a right circular conic surface in the fashion described.

1. The plane is perpendicular to the axis of the cone.

2. The plane is parallel to the axis of the cone.

3. The plane intersects the axis of the cone.

Objective: *To use the equation of an ellipse to find its vertices, foci, major axis, and minor axis.* (Section 12-2)

▬▬ Find the lengths of the axes and the coordinates of the foci of each ellipse.

4. $\dfrac{x^2}{4} + \dfrac{y^2}{16} = 1$ **5.** $x^2 + 2y^2 = 8$ **6.** $x^2 + 3y^2 = 27$

Objective: *To find the equation of an ellipse from information given about its foci, vertices, axes, or other parts of the ellipse.* (Section 11-2)

▬▬ Find an equation of each ellipse in Exercises 7 and 8.

7. Foci at $(0, \pm 3)$, vertices at $(0, \pm 5)$.

8. Foci at $(\pm 4, 0)$, minor axis of length 6.

Objective: *To sketch an ellipse.* (Section 11-2)

9–10. Sketch the ellipses of Exercises 4 and 6.

Objective: *To use the equation of an ellipse to find its eccentricity, the length of the latera recta, and the equations of the directrices.* (Section 11-3)

11–12. For the ellipses of Exercises 4 and 6 find the eccentricity, the length of the latera recta, and the equations of the directrices.

Objective: *To use the equation of a hyperbola to find its vertices, foci, latera recta, and eccentricity.* (Section 11-4)

▬▬ For the hyperbolas of Exercises 13–14 find the coordinates of the vertices, foci, and the ends of the latera recta. Also find the eccentricity.

13. $\dfrac{x^2}{9} - \dfrac{y^2}{16} = 1$ **14.** $25y^2 - 4x^2 = 100$

Objective: *To find the equation of a hyperbola from information given about its foci, vertices, axes, or other parts of the hyperbola.* (Section 11-4)

▬▬ Find an equation for each hyperbola in Exercises 15–16.

15. Vertex at $(0, -4)$, end of minor axis at $(3, 0)$.

16. Major axis of length 6, foci at $(\pm 4, 0)$.

Objective: *To sketch a hyperbola.* (Section 11-4)

17–18. Sketch the hyperbolas of Exercises 13–14.

Objective: *To find the asymptotes of a hyperbola and to write their equations.* (Section 11-5)

19–20. Find the equations of the asymptotes of the hyperbolas of Exercises 13–14. Sketch the asymptotes in the drawings that you made in Exercises 17–18.

Objective: *To use the equation of a parabola to find its focus, directrix, and latus rectum.* (Section 11-6)

━━━ Find the coordinates of the focus, the equation of the directrix, and coordinates of the endpoints of the latus rectum for the parabolas of Exercises 21–22.

21. $y^2 = -4x$ **22.** $x^2 = 12y$

Objective: *To find the equation of a parabola from information given about its focus, directrix, latus rectum, or other parts of the parabola.* (Section 11-6)

━━━ Find an equation of each parabola in Exercises 23–25.

23. Focus: $(0, -6)$

24. Directrix: $y = 4$

25. Length of latus rectum is 10; parabola opens upward.

Objective: *To sketch a parabola.* (Section 11-6)

26–27. Sketch the parabolas of Exercises 21–22.

Objective: *To find the standard equation of a conic that does not have its center at the origin when information concerning the conic is given.* (Section 11-7)

━━━ Find the equation of each conic in Exercises 28–30.

28. Ellipse: vertex at $(2, 8)$; foci at $(2, -4)$ and $(2, 4)$.

29. Parabola: vertex at $(3, 1)$; focus at $(3, 3)$.

30. Hyperbola: center at $(2, -3)$; vertex at $(7, -3)$; end of minor axis at $(2, 1)$.

Objective: *To translate a curve of the form $Ax^2 + Cy^2 + Dx + Ey + F = 0$ so that its center (or vertex for the parabola) is at the origin.* (Section 11-8)

━━━ Translate each curve so that its center (or vertex for the parabola) is at the origin.

31. $-3x^2 - 3y^2 + 2x + 2y = -25$

32. $9x^2 + 3x + 2y - 1 = 0$

33. $x^2 + 2y^2 - 4x + 3y - 8 = 0$

Objective: *To recognize the nature of a conic section from its equation.*
(Sections 11-2 through 11-8)

━━━ Identify whether each equation is the equation of a parabola, circle, ellipse, or hyperbola.

34. $\dfrac{x^2}{12} + \dfrac{y^2}{16} = 1$

35. $\dfrac{x^2}{16} - \dfrac{y^2}{9} = 1$

36. $\dfrac{(x-1)^2}{25} + \dfrac{(y+5)^2}{9} = 1$

37. $\dfrac{(y-2)^2}{64} - \dfrac{(x+3)^2}{36} = 1$

38. $(x-3)^2 = 12(y+2)$

39. $y^2 = -8x$

━━━ Use the discriminant to determine whether each equation represents a parabola, ellipse, or hyperbola. (None of the curves is a degenerate conic or circle.)

40. $3x^2 + 2xy - y^2 + 2x = 5$

41. $3x^2 + 2xy + y^2 + 2x = 5$

42. $3x^2 + 6xy + 3y^2 + 2x = 5$

43. $2x^2 + 2xy + y^2 + 2y = 5$

Objective: *To translate and rotate a conic so that it may be represented by an equation of a congruent conic in standard position.* (Section 11-9)

━━━ In Exercises 44–47 use translation, rotation or both, to move each curve so that its center (or vertex for parabolas) is at the origin and so that its axis is the x or y axis. In each case identify the translation vector and angle of rotation.

44. $x^2 + y^2 - 4x - 2y - 20 = 0$

45. $-4x^2 + y^2 - 16x - 2y - 19 = 0$

46. $x^2 - 6y - 4x + 22 = 0$

47. $16x^2 - 9y^2 + 32x + 36y + 205 = 0$

CHAPTER TEST ▬▬▬▬▬▬▬▬▬▬▬▬

1. Write the equation of the parabola with axis of symmetry parallel to the x axis and containing $(4, 2)$, $(2, -1)$, $(4, 1)$.

2. Write the equation of the ellipse with axes on, or parallel to, the coordinate axes whose

    a. foci are at $(0, \pm1)$ and vertices are at $(0, \pm3)$

    b. semiminor axis is 4 and foci are at $(\pm3, 0)$

    c. center is at $(2, -3)$, one vertex at $(2, -9)$ and eccentricity is $\frac{2}{3}$.

3. Write the equation of the hyperbola with axes on, or parallel to, the coordinate axes whose

    a. foci are at $(0, \pm 7)$ and vertices are at $(0, \pm 5)$.

    b. foci are at $(-2, -2)$ and $(6, -2)$, and the eccentricity is $\frac{4}{3}$.

    c. center is at the origin, one focus is at $(-10, 0)$ and minor axis has length 12.

4. What are the equations of the asymptotes of

$$\frac{y^2}{25} - \frac{x^2}{24} = 1?$$

5. Find the length of the latus rectum of

$$\frac{(x-1)^2}{9} + \frac{(y-3)^2}{4} = 1.$$

6. What is the equation of the directrix of

$$y^2 + 2x - 4y - 14 = 0?$$

7. What are the lengths of the semimajor and semiminor axes of

$$\frac{(y-3)^2}{36} + \frac{(x-2)^2}{20} = 1?$$

8. What are the coordinates of the center, vertices, and foci of

$$\frac{(y-3)^2}{36} + \frac{(x-2)^2}{20} = 1?$$

9. What conic is represented by

$$4x^2 + 3y^2 - 32y - 48 = 0?$$

10. What conic is represented by

$$5x^2 - 4y^2 + 12x + 16y - 124 = 0?$$

11. What conic is represented by

$$3y^2 - 4x - y + 2 = 0?$$

12. Use translation to eliminate the first degree terms in

$$5x^2 - 4y^2 + 10x + 16y - 124 = 0.$$

13. Remove the xy term in

$$9x^2 - 12xy + 4y^2 - 4 = 0$$

by rotating the conic through an angle θ.

14. Use translation and rotation to remove the x, the y, and the xy terms in

$$46x^2 + 48xy + 32y^2 + 5x + 12y - 7 = 0.$$

CHAPTER **12** # Graphs in Three-Space

Sections

Feature

Review and Testing

12–1   Cylinders

In Section 9–11 you learned that the equation

$$Ax + By + Cz + D = 0 \qquad\qquad \textbf{1}$$

is the equation of a plane in space whenever A, B, and C are not all zero and x, y, $z \in$ R. A plane is an example of a surface. A set of points in space which is the graph of a relation described by a single equation is a **surface.**

A second example of a surface is a sphere. A **sphere** is the set of all points at a fixed distance r from a fixed point O (a, b, c). By the distance formula it follows that each point on the sphere satisfies the following equation.

$$(x - a)^2 + (y - b)^2 + (z - c)^2 = r^2 \qquad\qquad \textbf{2}$$

Figure 1 below illustrates Equation **2.**

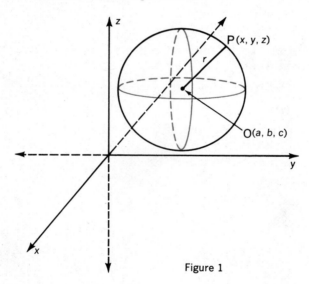

Figure 1

There are many other surfaces in space. One of the simplest classes of surfaces is the **cylinders.**

Let C be a curve in a plane π. Let L be the set of lines which are perpendicular to π and contain a point of the curve C. The set of all points on the lines in L is a cylindrical surface, or a cylinder. See Figure 2.

The curve C is the *directrix* of the cylinder, and each line in L is an *element* of the cylinder. Do you know why the elements of a cylinder are parallel to each other?

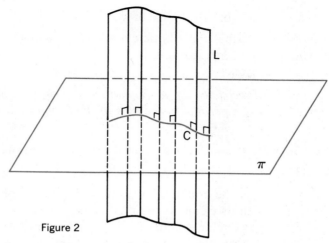

Figure 2

The intersection of a plane perpendicular to an element of a cylinder is a **normal section of the cylinder.** Each normal section of a cylinder is congruent to the directrix. Can you explain why?

A cylinder is often named after the curve which is its directrix. If the directrix is a parabola, the cylinder is a parabolic cylinder. In a similar manner a cylinder could be *hyperbolic, elliptic,* or even a plane.

As you know, you may arbitrarily choose a coordinate system for space. The equations of cylinders are quite simple if you choose the coordinate system so that one of the coordinate planes is perpendicular to the elements of the cylinder.

For example, in the figure at the right suppose that the directrix of a cylinder is an ellipse. Choose the coordinate system so that the ellipse is in standard position in the xy plane. Then that ellipse has equation

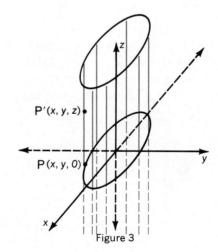

Figure 3

$$\frac{x^2}{a^2} + \frac{y^2}{b^2} = 1$$

in the xy plane. Notice that each element of the cylinder is perpendicular to the xy plane. Thus if $P(x, y, 0)$ is a point on the directrix, then $P'(x, y, z)$, for $z \in R$, is a point on the cylinder. This follows because each point on one element of the cylinder has the same x and y coordinates.

Since z is arbitrary for any choice of x and y satisfying $\frac{x^2}{a^2} + \frac{y^2}{b^2} = 1$, this equation also describes the elliptic cylinder with its elements parallel to the z axis. The generalization is:

The graph in three-space of an equation in two variables is a cylinder with its elements parallel to the axis of the unnamed variable.

EXAMPLE. Identify the surfaces described by each equation.

a. $x^2 + z^2 = 4$ **b.** $y^2 = 4(z - 2)$

a. Since $x^2 + z^2 = 4$ is the equation of a circle in the xz plane, it is a circular cylinder with its elements parallel to the y axis.

    The graph of the circular cylinder is illustrated below.

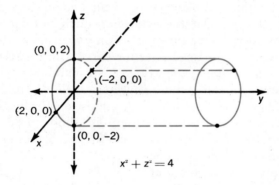

b. $y^2 = 4(z - 2)$ is a parabola in the yz plane with vertex at $(0, 0, 2)$. Thus the surface is a parabolic cylinder with its elements parallel to the x axis.

    The graph of the parabolic cylinder is illustrated below.

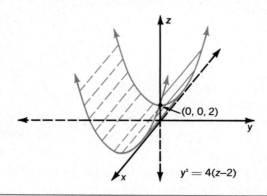

CLASSROOM EXERCISES

━━━ Given the following graphs in two-space, identify the cylindrical surface and the axis to which its elements are parallel.

1. $\frac{x^2}{16} + \frac{y^2}{8} = 1$

2. $3x^2 + 3z^2 = 9$

3. $3y^2 - 4z^2 = 12$

4. $4y^2 + 4z^2 = 16$

━━━ Write an equation of each cylindrical surface.

5. Hyperbolic cylinder with elements parallel to the x axis.

6. Elliptical cylinder with elements parallel to the z axis.

7. A plane surface with elements parallel to the y axis.

8. Define a "surface".

9. Describe in your own words what a cylindrical surface is.

10. What determines the name of the cylindrical surface (that is, elliptical, circular, etc.)?

WRITTEN EXERCISES

A ━━━ Identify each surface and construct its graph for Exercises 1–14.

1. $(x - 2)^2 + y^2 = 9$

2. $(x - 2)^2 + z^2 = 9$

3. $(y - 2)^2 + z^2 = 9$

4. $3x + 4y = 12$

5. $x^2 + y^2 + z^2 = 4$

6. $x^2 = 8z$

7. $y^2 = 4z$

8. $\frac{x^2}{16} - \frac{y^2}{9} = 1$

9. $4x^2 + 9z^2 = 36$

10. $x^2 + z^2 - 4x - 6z + 9 = 0$

11. $x^2 + 4y^2 - 4x - 32y = 64$

12. $z^2 + y^2 - 4y = 0$

13. $y = \sin x \quad 0 \le x \le \pi$

14. $y = e^x$

15. Compare the graphs of **a.** $x^2 + 4y^2 = 16$ and **b.** $x^2 + 4y^2 = 16$, $z = 2$. Sketch each graph.

━━━ Sketch a graph of each equation for Exercises 16–21.

16. $x^2 + y^2 + z^2 = 16$

17. $x^2 + y^2 + z^2 = 16, z = 3$

18. $y^2 = 8(z - 3)$

19. $y^2 = 8(z - 3), x = -2$

20. $(x - 2)^2 + 4z^2 = 4$

21. $(x - 2)^2 + 4z^2 = 4, y = 1$

B **22.** Find the equation of the surface whose points have the property that the square of the distance of each point from the x axis is equal to twice its distance from the xy plane. Construct the graph.

23. Find the equation of the set of points which are equidistant from $(1, 2, 7)$ and $(1, 5, 7)$. Construct the graph.

12-2 Surfaces of Revolution

Given a curve C and a line L in a plane π, the surface generated by revolving C about L is called a **surface of revolution.** The line L is the **axis of rotation.** The curve C is the **generating curve.**

The curve formed by the intersection of a plane and a surface is a **plane section** of the surface. When the intersecting plane is perpendicular to the axis of rotation of a surface of revolution the

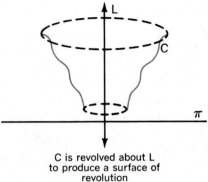

C is revolved about L to produce a surface of revolution

plane section is said to be perpendicular to the axis of rotation. It should be clear to you that each perpendicular plane section of a surface of revolution is either a circle, one point, or the empty set. The converse of the previous statement is also true. The following is a statement of the converse.

> If for a given surface there is a line L such that each plane section perpendicular to L is a circle, one point, or the empty set, then the surface is a surface of revolution.

These comments imply that whenever you are given the equation of a surface you can determine whether it is a surface of revolution by identifying the nature of the plane sections perpendicular to some line L. The catch here is that choosing L is difficult. The problem is substantially simplified by specifying initially that you are only interested in determining whether a surface is a surface of revolution with respect to one of the coordinate axes. Then, because of the simple nature of the equation of a plane perpendicular to an axis, the procedure is straightforward. That procedure is illustrated in the next example.

EXAMPLE 1. Show that $4x^2 + y^2 + 4z^2 - 6y = 0$ is a surface of revolution with the y axis as the axis of rotation.
Solution: To accomplish the task you must show that for each plane perpendicular to the y axis the plane section is a circle, a point, or the empty set.

Recall that the equation of a plane perpendicular to the y axis is $y = k$, where k is some real number. The intersection of the surface $4x^2 + y^2 + 4z^2 - 6y = 0$ and the plane $y = k$ is the set of points with y-coordinate k and therefore satisfying the following equation.

$$4x^2 + 4z^2 + k^2 - 6k = 0$$

or
$$4x^2 + 4z^2 = k(6 - k) \qquad\qquad \mathbf{1}$$

Thus, in the plane $y = k$, the plane section is described by **1**. Is the graph of **1** a circle, a point, or the empty set for every $k \in R$ and *never* anything else? Clearly such is the case because

$$x^2 + z^2 = \tfrac{1}{4}k(6 - k)$$

is a circle for $0 < k < 6$; it is a point for $k = 0$ or $k = 6$; and it is the empty set when $k < 0$ or $k > 6$. Another way to say the same thing is to say that it is a circle when $k(6 - k) > 0$; a point when $k(6 - k) = 0$ and the empty set when $k(6 - k) < 0$.

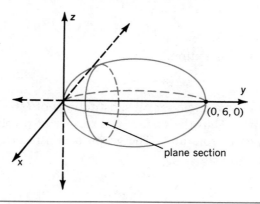

plane section

Recall that to graph a plane in three-space you made use of the traces, that is, the intersections of the plane with the coordinate planes. These were found by setting successively x, y, and z equal to zero and graphing the resulting line in the appropriate coordinate plane. The same idea applies here.

Setting $z = 0$, in $4x^2 + y^2 + 4z^2 - 6y = 0$, you have the ellipse in the xy plane with equation

$$4x^2 + y^2 - 6y = 0.$$

in the xy plane. Similarly the trace of the surface in the yz plane is an ellipse with equation

$$4z^2 + y^2 - 6y = 0.$$

These two ellipses are used to graph the surface shown above.

EXAMPLE 2. Determine the coordinate axis for which the graph of

$$x^2 + y^2 - 9z^2 = 25$$

is a surface of revolution. What are the traces of the surface in the three coordinate planes?

Solution: Check the traces first. If a trace is not a circle then the surface is not a surface of revolution with the eliminated variable as axis of rotation.

$x = 0$	$y^2 - 9z^2 = 25$	◄—— **A hyperbola**
$y = 0$	$x^2 - 9z^2 = 25$	◄—— **A hyperbola**
$z = 0$	$x^2 + y^2 = 25$	◄—— **A circle**

Thus the axis of rotation *may* be the z axis. Check further by determining the nature of all perpendicular plane sections. You see that substituting

$$z = k$$

into

$$x^2 + y^2 - 9z^2 = 25$$

yields the following equation.

$$x^2 + y^2 = 25 + 9k^2$$

The graph of this is a circle for all substitutions of k because $25 + 9k^2$ is always positive. Thus the surface is a surface of revolution with the z axis as the axis of rotation. The graph is constructed by using the traces. It is shown below.

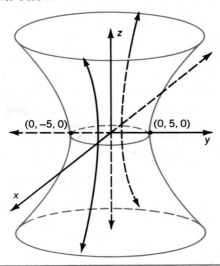

CLASSROOM EXERCISES

━━ Find the traces and identify the axis or axes of rotation.

1. $3x^2 + 3y^2 + 3z^2 = 1$

2. $7x^2 - 8y^2 - 8z^2 = -2$

3. $x^2 - 4y^2 - 4z^2 = 25$

4. $y^2 + x^2 + z^2 = 36$

WRITTEN EXERCISES

A ━━ For each equation find the traces and determine if the graph is a surface of revolution. If it is, identify the axis or axes of rotation. Sketch the graph of the surface.

1. $\frac{1}{4}(x^2 + z^2) = y$

2. $y^2 = x^2 + z^2$

3. $9z^2 + 16(x^2 + y^2) = 25$

4. $x^2 + y^2 + z^2 = 25$

5. $x^2 + 4y^2 + 9z^2 = 36$

6. $y^2 + x^2 = 4z$

7. $x^2 + y^2 + z^2 = 6y$

8. $9y^2 - 16x^2 - 16z^2 = 144$

9. $x^2 - 16y^2 + z^2 = 0$

10. $8x^2 + 8y^2 - z^2 = 0$

B **11.** The graph of the equation

$$Ax^2 + By^2 + Cz^2 + Dx + Ey + Fz + G = 0$$

is, under certain circumstances, a surface of revolution. What are the circumstances?

12. How would you determine the axis of rotation for the surface in Exercise 11 when it was a surface of revolution?

12-3 Quadric Surfaces

The graph of a second degree equation in space is a **quadric surface.** Many of the surfaces you studied earlier in this chapter are quadric surfaces. The study of general quadric surfaces is quite difficult, but, by restricting the second degree equations to those with no xy-, xz-, and yz-terms the properties of the resulting surfaces are relatively easy to study.

There are three tools valuable in describing a quadric surface. These are 1. traces, 2. the plane sections, and 3. symmetry with respect to a plane. You are familiar with the methods used to find the traces and to identify plane sections. Symmetry with respect to a plane is equally as easy.

Two points P and Q are symmetric with respect to a plane π if and only if π is the perpendicular bisector of the line segment PQ. (See Figure 1.)

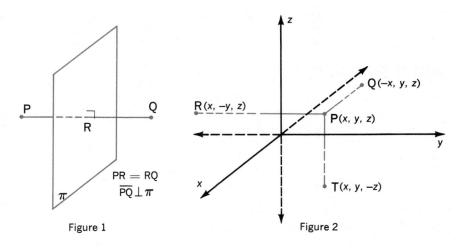

Figure 1

Figure 2

The symmetry planes of greatest interest are the coordinate planes. For example, in Figure 2 $P(x, y, z)$ and $Q(-x, y, z)$ are symmetric with respect to the yz plane. Similarly $P(x, y, z)$ and $R(x, -y, z)$ are symmetric to the xz plane and $P(x, y, z)$ and $T(x, y, -z)$ are symmetric with respect to the xy plane.

Now if a surface S is to be symmetric with respect to, say, the yz plane, then for each point P of S there is a point Q of S such that P and Q are symmetrically located with respect to the yz plane. Thus $P(x, y, z)$ being in S implies $Q(-x, y, z)$ is in S. This means that the equation of the surface is satisfied by the coordinates of each point. This can happen only when even powers of x occur in the equation because only then will $(x)^n = (-x)^n$. Therefore, a quadric surface is symmetric to the yz plane if and only if x occurs only to even powers in the equation of the surface. Corresponding statements hold for symmetry with respect to the xz and xy planes. Can you state them?

A simple and familiar quadric surface is the sphere:

$$x^2 + y^2 + z^2 = r^2. \qquad \textbf{1}$$

The properties of the sphere are easily summarized: The sphere **1**

is symmetric to each coordinate plane,

has traces that are circles, and

has plane sections that are circles, single points, or the empty set.

The next quadric surface discussed here is the *ellipsoid*. The equation of an **ellipsoid** is the following

$$\frac{x^2}{a^2} + \frac{y^2}{b^2} + \frac{z^2}{c^2} = 1.$$

2

The characteristics of an ellipsoid are not hard to derive: First, since x, y, and z occur raised to the exponent 2, the ellipsoid is symmetric with respect to each coordinate plane. The traces are formed by setting x, y, and z equal to zero one at a time. In each case you see that the trace is an ellipse. The equations of the traces are the following.

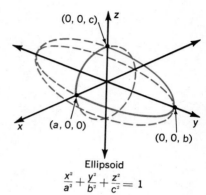

Ellipsoid
$$\frac{x^2}{a^2} + \frac{y^2}{b^2} + \frac{z^2}{c^2} = 1$$

xy plane:

$$\frac{x^2}{a^2} + \frac{y^2}{b^2} = 1, z = 0.$$

xz plane:

$$\frac{x^2}{a^2} + \frac{z^2}{c^2} = 1, y = 0.$$

yz plane:

$$\frac{y^2}{b^2} + \frac{z^2}{c^2} = 1, x = 0.$$

The plane section perpendicular to the z axis is the graph of the system:

$$\frac{x^2}{a^2} + \frac{y^2}{b^2} = 1 - \frac{k^2}{c^2}, \quad z = k.$$

For $1 - \frac{k^2}{c^2} > 0$, the plane section is an ellipse and for $1 - \frac{k^2}{c^2} = 0$, the section is a point. Similar remarks may be made for plane sections perpendicular to the x and y axes. A graph of an ellipsoid is shown above.

Notice that when $a^2 = b^2 = c^2$ the ellipsoid is a sphere. What conditions on the constants a^2, b^2, and c^2 would allow you to conclude that the ellipsoid is a surface of revolution?

There are five other quadric surfaces with which you should be familiar. These are identified on pages 650–1, along with their graphs. The determination of the characteristics of each is left for you.

Elliptic Paraboloid:

$$\frac{x^2}{a^2} + \frac{y^2}{b^2} = cz, c > 0 \qquad 3$$

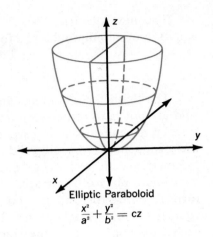

Elliptic Paraboloid
$$\frac{x^2}{a^2} + \frac{y^2}{b^2} = cz$$

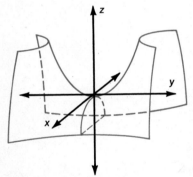

Hyperbolic Paraboloid
$$\frac{y^2}{a^2} - \frac{x^2}{b^2} = cz$$

Hyperbolic Paraboloid:

$$\frac{y^2}{a^2} - \frac{x^2}{b^2} = cz, c > 0 \qquad 4$$

Elliptic Cone:

$$\frac{x^2}{a^2} + \frac{y^2}{b^2} - \frac{z^2}{c^2} = 0 \qquad 5$$

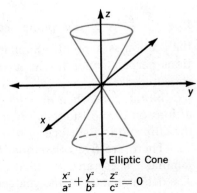

Elliptic Cone
$$\frac{x^2}{a^2} + \frac{y^2}{b^2} - \frac{z^2}{c^2} = 0$$

Hyperboloid of one Sheet:

$$\frac{x^2}{a^2} + \frac{y^2}{b^2} - \frac{z^2}{c^2} = 1 \qquad \qquad 6$$

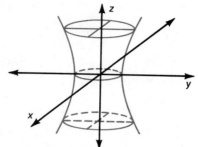

Hyperboloid of one sheet
$$\frac{x^2}{a^2} + \frac{y^2}{b^2} - \frac{z^2}{c^2} = 1$$

Hyperboloid of two Sheets:

$$\frac{y^2}{b^2} - \frac{x^2}{a^2} - \frac{z^2}{c^2} = 1 \qquad \qquad 7$$

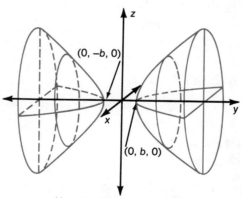

Hyperboloid of two sheets
$$\frac{y^2}{b^2} - \frac{x^2}{a^2} - \frac{z^2}{c^2} = 1$$

Since the hyperboloid and paraboloid have centers of symmetry, they are called **central quadrics.**

It should be noted that similar diagrams will result if the variables x, y, and z are interchanged in any of the quadric surfaces listed above.

In addition to the quadric surfaces described here there are *degenerate* quadric surfaces. For example the graph of the equation

$$(x - a)^2 + (y - b)^2 + (z - c)^2 = 0 \qquad \qquad 8$$

is a single point, namely (a, b, c).

The equation

$$(x - a)^2 + (y - b)^2 = 0 \qquad \qquad 9$$

is satisfied by all points $P(a, b, z)$, $z \in R$. Therefore the graph is a line through the point $(a, b, 0)$.

The equation

$$(x - a)^2 = b^2 \qquad \qquad 10$$

represents *two parallel planes*: $x - a = b$ and $x - a = -b$. The graph of the equation

$$(x - a)^2 = 0 \qquad \qquad 11$$

represents a single plane with equation $x - a = 0$.

Finally the graph of

$$\frac{x^2}{a^2} - \frac{y^2}{b^2} = 0 \qquad \qquad 12$$

represents two intersecting planes with equations $\frac{x}{a} + \frac{y}{b} = 0$ and $\frac{x}{a} - \frac{y}{b} = 0$. Their intersection is the z axis.

CLASSROOM EXERCISES

▬ For Exercises 1–3, identify symmetries of the quadric surfaces.

1. $2x^2 + y^2 + 3y + z^2 - 2z = 7$

2. $3x^2 + 4y^2 + 2z = 3$

3. $x^2 - 2x + y^2 - 2y + z^2 = 3$

▬ For Exercises 4–7, identify the quadric surface.

4. $\frac{x^2}{4} - \frac{z^2}{10} = 3y$

5. $\frac{x^2}{3} + \frac{y^2}{3} + \frac{z^2}{3} = 1$

6. $\frac{x^2}{4} - \frac{y^2}{16} + z^2 = 1$

7. $z^2 - \frac{x^2}{4} - y^2 = 1$

8. Name three characteristics used to describe a quadric surface.

9. Define symmetry with respect to a plane.

WRITTEN EXERCISES

A ▬ Determine the characteristics of each quadric surface, that is, identify symmetries, find equations of the traces, and determine the character of the plane sections which are perpendicular to the coordinate axes for Exercises 1–5.

1. Elliptic Paraboloid: $\dfrac{x^2}{a^2} + \dfrac{y^2}{b^2} = cz \quad c > 0$

2. Hyperbolic Paraboloid: $\dfrac{x^2}{a^2} - \dfrac{y^2}{b^2} = cz \quad c > 0$

3. Elliptic Cone: $\dfrac{x^2}{a^2} + \dfrac{y^2}{b^2} - \dfrac{z^2}{c^2} = 0$

4. Hyperboloid of one Sheet: $\dfrac{x^2}{a^2} + \dfrac{y^2}{b^2} - \dfrac{z^2}{c^2} = 1$

5. Hyperboloid of two Sheets: $\dfrac{x^2}{a^2} - \dfrac{y^2}{b^2} - \dfrac{z^2}{c^2} = 1$

▬ For Exercises 6–39, identify the quadric surface and use the traces to sketch the graph of the surface.

6. $\dfrac{x^2}{9} + \dfrac{y^2}{4} + \dfrac{z^2}{16} = 1$

7. $\dfrac{x^2}{4} + \dfrac{y^2}{4} + \dfrac{z^2}{9} = 1$

8. $16x^2 + 9y^2 - z^2 = 144$

9. $\dfrac{x^2}{9} + \dfrac{y^2}{16} - \dfrac{z^2}{4} = 1$

10. $16x^2 - 9y^2 - z^2 = 144$

11. $\dfrac{x^2}{9} - \dfrac{y^2}{16} - \dfrac{z^2}{4} = 1$

12. $16x^2 + 9y^2 - z^2 = 0$

13. $\dfrac{x^2}{9} + \dfrac{y^2}{16} - \dfrac{z^2}{4} = 0$

14. $4x^2 + 9y^2 = 36z$

15. $x^2 + 4z^2 = 12y$

16. $4x^2 - 9y^2 = 36z$

17. $x^2 - 4z^2 = 12y$

18. $x^2 + (y - 4)^2 + z^2 = 0$

19. $x^2 + y^2 + z^2 = 1$

20. $(x + 1)^2 + (y - 2)^2 = 0$

21. $x^2 + (y - 2)^2 = 4$

22. $\dfrac{x^2}{9} - \dfrac{y^2}{16} = 0$

23. $\dfrac{x^2}{9} - \dfrac{y^2}{4} + \dfrac{z^2}{25} = 0$

24. $x^2 + y^2 = 9$

25. $x^2 + y^2 = 9x$

26. $x^2 + y^2 = 9z$

27. $x^2 + y^2 = 0$

28. $\frac{x^2}{25} + \frac{y^2}{9} - \frac{z^2}{64} = 1$

29. $-3x^2 - 3y^2 - 3z^2 = -1$

30. $\frac{z^2}{16} - \frac{y^2}{4} = 1$

31. $2x^2 + y^2 - 3z^2 = 6$

32. $-\frac{x^2}{2} + \frac{y^2}{4} - z^2 = 1$

33. $y^2 + z^2 = 3x$

34. $\frac{x^2}{7} + \frac{z^2}{49} = 0$

35. $2y^2 + z^2 = 4$

36. $\frac{y^2}{4} - \frac{z^2}{8} = 1$

37. $-\frac{x^2}{12} + \frac{z^2}{16} = 1$

38. $-\frac{x^2}{9} + \frac{y^2}{64} - \frac{z^2}{25} = 1$

39. $\frac{(x-3)^2}{9} + \frac{(y-2)^2}{16} - z^2 = 1$

12–4   Cylindrical and Spherical Coordinates

When the directed distance from three mutually perpendicular planes is used to locate a point in space, the coordinates are called *Cartesian coordinates* or *rectangular coordinates*. You are familiar with rectangular coordinates, however there are other coordinate systems which are used to locate points in space.

One such system is called the **cylindrical coordinate system.** In this system each point in space is identified by an ordered triple (r, θ, z). If (x, y, z) and (r, θ, z) name the same point, then the first two coordinates of (r, θ, z) are the polar coordinates of the point $(x, y, 0)$ in the xy plane; that is, r is the length of the vector from $(0, 0, 0)$ to $(x, y, 0)$ and θ is the measure of the angle from $\overrightarrow{OQ}$ to $\overrightarrow{OR}$. This is shown in the figure.

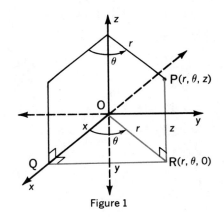

Figure 1

You should be able to derive the following relations between rectangular and cylindrical coordinates.

$$x = r \cos \theta \qquad y = r \sin \theta \qquad r^2 = x^2 + y^2$$

$$\tan \theta = \frac{y}{x} \quad \text{and} \quad z = z$$

EXAMPLE 1. Describe the surface whose equation in cylindrical coordinates is

$$r = 5.$$

There are two solutions. The first is that the set of points satisfying $r = 5$ is the set of all points 5 units from the z axis. Since θ and z are not restricted by the equation they may take on all values. The graph shown in Figure 2 below is clearly a right circular cylinder with its axis being the z axis.

A second solution uses the fact that $r^2 = x^2 + y^2$ and thus $r = 5$, becomes

$$25 = x^2 + y^2.$$

You know that in space, the latter equation has a right circular cylinder for its graph.

A second coordinate system, shown in Figure 3, is the system of **spherical coordinates.** This system uses two angles and a vector to locate each point in space. The coordinates are given by the ordered triple (ρ, θ, ϕ) (rho, theta, phi). If $P(x, y, z)$ and $P(\rho, \theta, \phi)$ name the same point, rho (ρ) is the length of the vector $\overrightarrow{OP}$

$$\rho = |\overrightarrow{OP}|.$$

Theta (θ) is the measure of the same angle as in the cylindrical coordinates for the point (x, y, z). Phi (ϕ) is the measure of the angle between the positive z axis and $\overrightarrow{OP}$.

It is customary to restrict the spherical coordinates (ρ, θ, ϕ) as follows: $\qquad \rho \geq 0, \qquad 0 \leq \theta \leq 2\pi, \qquad 0 \leq \phi \leq \pi$

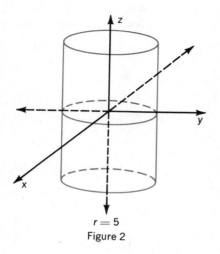

$r = 5$

Figure 2

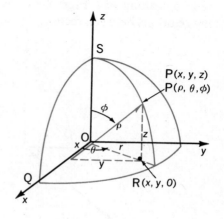

Figure 3

EXAMPLE 2. Identify the surfaces which satisfy the spherical co-ordinate equations

$$\text{a. } \rho = 3 \qquad \text{b. } \phi = \frac{\pi}{4}$$

Solution:

a. The equation $\rho = 3$ implies that each point on the surface is three units from the origin. Thus the surface is a sphere of radius 3, center at the origin. See Figure 4 below.

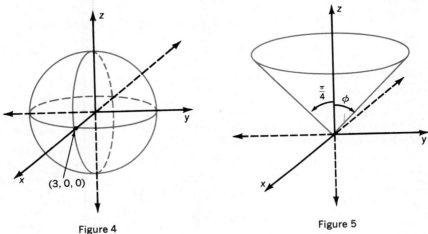

Figure 4   Figure 5

b. In Figure 5, ϕ is the measure of the angle from the z axis to a position vector $\overrightarrow{OP}$. All such points P are on the right circular cone with its axis along the z axis.

Recall that $\sin(90 - \phi) = \cos \phi$ and $\cos(90 - \phi) = \sin \phi$. These relations along with Figure 6 below will allow you to derive the following relations between rectangular, cylindrical and spherical coordinates:

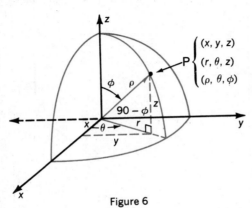

Figure 6

$$r = \rho \cos (90 - \phi) = \rho \sin \phi$$
$$z = \rho \sin (90 - \phi) = \rho \cos \phi \qquad \qquad 1$$
$$\theta = \theta.$$

$$x = r \cos \theta$$
$$y = r \sin \theta \qquad \qquad 2$$
$$z = z.$$

Therefore:

$$x = \rho \sin \phi \cos \theta$$
$$y = \rho \sin \phi \sin \theta \qquad \qquad 3$$
$$z = \rho \cos \phi.$$

The equations in 3 are obtained by appropriate substitution of those in 1 into those in 2.

EXAMPLE 3. Express the equation

$$x^2 + y^2 = 25$$

(a right circular cylinder) in spherical coordinates. Does the equation have a sensible geometric interpretation? $x = \rho \sin \phi \cos \theta$ and $y = \rho \sin \phi \sin \theta$ by 3. Thus $x^2 + y^2 = 25$ is

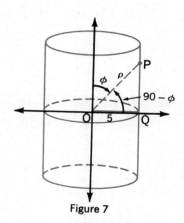

Figure 7

$$\rho^2 \sin^2 \phi \cos^2 \theta + \rho^2 \sin^2 \phi \sin^2 \theta = 25$$
$$\rho^2 \sin^2 \phi \, (\cos^2 \theta + \sin^2 \theta) = 25$$

or

$$\rho^2 \sin^2 \phi = 25.$$

But since $\rho \geq 0$ and $\sin \phi \geq 0$ for $0 \leq \phi \leq \pi$ you can write

$$\rho \sin \phi = 5$$

This equation may be interpreted geometrically by writing

$$\sin \phi = \frac{5}{\rho}$$
$$\cos (90 - \phi) = \frac{5}{\rho}$$

In the figure the base of the triangle OPQ is always 5, and angle POQ always measures $90 - \phi$ for every point on the cylinder. Thus the relation $\cos (90 - \phi) = \sin \phi = \frac{5}{\rho}$ holds for all points on the cylinder.

CLASSROOM EXERCISES

▬ For Exercises 1–4, change the cylindrical coordinates to rectangular coordinates.

1. $\left(4, \frac{\pi}{3}, 2\right)$

2. $(5, 2\pi, -7)$

3. $\left(1, \frac{\pi}{2}, 9\right)$

4. $\left(10, \frac{\pi}{4}, 0\right)$

▬ For Exercises 5–8, change the spherical coordinates to rectangular coordinates.

5. $\left(2, 2\pi, \frac{\pi}{2}\right)$

6. $\left(4, \frac{\pi}{4}, \frac{\pi}{3}\right)$

7. $\left(5, \frac{\pi}{3}, \frac{\pi}{6}\right)$

8. $\left(20, \pi, \frac{2\pi}{3}\right)$

9. Compare polar and cylindrical coordinates.

10. Compare cylindrical and spherical coordinates.

WRITTEN EXERCISES

A ▬ Change cylindrical coordinates to rectangular coordinates for Exercises 1–6.

1. $(3, 0, 2)$

2. $\left(2, \frac{\pi}{4}, -2\right)$

3. $\left(7, \frac{\pi}{2}, 4\right)$

4. $(1, \pi, -2)$

5. $\left(2, \frac{4\pi}{3}, 3\right)$

6. $\left(4, \frac{3\pi}{2}, -5\right)$

▬ Change the spherical coordinates to rectangular coordinates for Exercises 7–12.

7. $\left(7, \frac{\pi}{4}, 0\right)$

8. $\left(7, 0, \frac{\pi}{4}\right)$

9. $\left(7, \pi, \frac{\pi}{2}\right)$

10. $\left(12, \frac{2\pi}{3}, \frac{5\pi}{6}\right)$

11. $\left(8, \frac{\pi}{13}, \pi\right)$

12. $\left(2, \frac{11\pi}{6}, \frac{\pi}{3}\right)$

13. Express ρ in terms of x, y, and z.

14. Express $\cos \phi$ in terms of x, y, and z.

15. Express $\tan \theta$ in terms of x, y, and z.

16. Express $\cos \theta$ in terms of x, y and z.

17. Express r in terms of x, y and z.

18. Express $\sin \phi$ in terms of x, y and z.

For Exercises 19–25 change each equation from an equation in the given coordinates into an equation in the two remaining coordinate systems.

19. $x^2 + y^2 + z^2 = 9$

20. $x^2 + y^2 + z^2 - 2z = 0$

21. $z^2 = r^2$ (Change to rectangular coordinates first.)

22. $x^2 + y^2 - x = 0$

23. $\rho = 8 \cos \phi$ (See Exercise 13.)

24. $\frac{x^2}{4} + \frac{y^2}{16} + 2z^2 = 1$

25. $\rho = 4 \sin \theta$

12–5   Curves in Space

A curve in space is the set of points which make up the intersection of two surfaces. For example, you may think of a line as the intersection of two planes. Given the equations of Chapter 9 the planes are the following. (See Section 9–10.)

$$A_1 x + B_1 y + C_1 z + D_1 = 0$$

and

$$A_2 x + B_2 y + C_2 z + D_2 = 0$$

The line of intersection is the set of points satisfying the two equations simultaneously. Thus you may say that the system

$$A_1 x + B_1 y + C_1 z + D_1 = 0$$
$$and$$
$$A_2 x + B_2 y + C_2 z + D_2 = 0$$

is the algebraic representation of a line.

More generally if $F_1(x, y, z) = 0$ and $F_2(x, y, z) = 0$ are equations of surfaces, then the system

$$F_1(x, y, z) = 0 \quad and \quad F_2(x, y, z) = 0 \qquad \qquad 1$$

describes a curve in space. The system 1 is the *two-surface representation* of a curve.

If one of the surfaces in 1 is a plane, then the curve is a **plane curve.** You are familiar with plane sections of quadric surfaces; these are examples of plane curves.

On the other hand, when there is no plane which completely contains the space curve, that curve is then a **twisted curve.**

An example of a twisted curve is the graph of the system

$$x^2 + y^2 + z^2 = 16 \quad and \quad (x - 2)^2 + y^2 = 16$$

This curve, illustrated in Figure 1, is the intersection of a sphere and a right circular cylinder. Its graph in the first octant is shown below in color. (Three mutually perpendicular planes having a common origin divide space into eight equal regions, each of which is called an octant.)

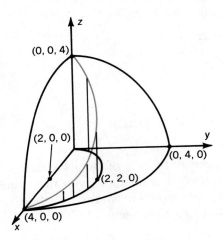

Figure 1

In addition to the two surface representation of a space curve, the curves may be represented by *parametric equations*. Recall that the parametric equations of a line were

$$x = a + t \cdot l$$
$$y = b + t \cdot m$$
$$z = c + t \cdot n$$

where $P(a, b, c)$ was a point on the line, the direction vector was $l\mathbf{i} + m\mathbf{j} + n\mathbf{k}$, and $t \in R$ was the parameter.

In a similar manner a curve can be represented parametrically by three equations

$$x = F_1(t)$$
$$y = F_2(t) \qquad\qquad 2$$
$$z = F_3(t)$$

The three equations are the *parametric representation of a curve* in space. For each replacement of the parameter t, the point with coordinates $x = F_1(t)$, $y = F_2(t)$, $z = F_3(t)$ is on the curve.

As an example the curve with parametric equations

$$x = a \cos t, \quad y = a \sin t, \quad z = bt$$

is called a *circular helix*. Notice that (see Figure 2)

$$x^2 + y^2 = a^2 (\cos^2 t + \sin^2 t) = a^2. \qquad \qquad 3$$

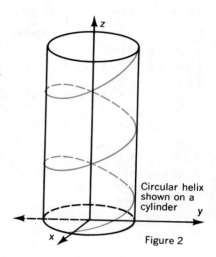

Thus each point of the helix is on a right circular cylinder. Also for each t, the point is bt units up (or down) from the xy plane. Thus the helix winds around the cylinder, moving further and further away from the xy plane for increasing values of t. A portion of the graph is shown at the right.

Circular helix shown on a cylinder

Figure 2

   In graphing a curve from its parametric equations, it is often useful to eliminate the parameter from a pair of the parametric equations as was done in equation 3 above. Doing this sometimes allows you to identify a simple surface on which the curve lies. Otherwise the procedure used is to plot points, usually in the first octant, and sketch the curve using these points.

WRITTEN EXERCISES

A ▬▬ Sketch each curve in the first octant for Exercises 1–11.

1. $x = 6 \sin t, y = 6 \cos t, z = 5t$

2. $x = 3 \sin 2t, y = 3 \cos 2t, z = 4t$

3. $x = 3t \cos t, y = 3t \sin t, z = 4t$

4. $x = t, y = 2t, z = t^2$

5. $x = t, y = t, z = \frac{2}{3}t^{\frac{2}{3}}$

6. $x^2 + y^2 = 36, y - z = 0$

7. $x^2 + y^2 = 25, z - x = 0$

8. $y^2 = 4x, z = 4x$

9. $x^2 + y^2 - 4y = 0, y = 2x$

10. $x^2 + y^2 + z^2 = 25, x^2 = 9$

11. $x = t, y = \frac{t^2}{\sqrt{2}}, z = \frac{1}{3}t^3$

BASIC: CHANGING TO RECTANGULAR COORDINATES

Problem:

Given the cylindrical or spherical coordinates of a point, write a program which computes and prints the point's rectangular coordinates.

```
110 PRINT "THIS PROGRAM CONVERTS CYLINDRICAL"
120 PRINT "AND SPHERICAL COORDINATES TO"
130 PRINT "RECTANGULAR COORDINATES."
140 PRINT
150 PRINT "WILL YOU ENTER 1. CYLINDRICAL"
160 PRINT "OR                2. SPHERICAL"
170 PRINT "COORDINATES";
180 INPUT Q
190 PRINT
200 IF Q = 2 THEN 310
210 PRINT "WHAT IS R";
220 INPUT R
230 PRINT "WHAT IS THETA (IN DEGREES)";
240 INPUT T
250 LET T = 3.14159 * T / 180
260 PRINT "WHAT IS Z";
270 INPUT Z
280 LET X = R * COS(T)
290 LET Y = R * SIN(T)
300 GOTO 420
310 PRINT "WHAT IS P (RHO)";
320 INPUT P
330 PRINT "WHAT IS THETA (IN DEGREES)";
340 INPUT T
350 LET T = 3.14159 * T / 180
360 PRINT "WHAT IS PHI (IN DEGREES)";
370 INPUT H
380 LET H = 3.14159 * H / 180
390 LET X = P * SIN(H) * COS(T)
400 LET Y = P * SIN(H) * SIN(T)
410 LET Z = P * COS(H)
420 PRINT
430 PRINT "RECTANGULAR COORDINATES ARE"
440 PRINT "(";X;",";Y;",";Z;")"
450 PRINT
460 PRINT "ANY MORE PROBLEMS (1=YES,0=NO)";
470 INPUT C
```

```
480 IF C = 1 THEN 140
490 PRINT
500 END
```

Output:

```
WILL YOU ENTER 1. CYLINDRICAL
OR              2. SPHERICAL
COORDINATES? 2

WHAT IS P (RHO)? 12
WHAT IS THETA (IN DEGREES)? 120
WHAT IS PHI (IN DEGREES)? 90

RECTANGULAR COORDINATES ARE
(-5.99998 , 10.3923 , 1.34823E-05 )

ANY MORE PROBLEMS (1=YES,0=NO)? 0
```

Analysis:

Statements 210–300: This section accepts the cylindrical coordinates of a point and changes them to rectangular coordinates. Line 250 converts the degree measure of angle T to radians, since BASIC's COS and SIN functions (lines 280–290) accept T in radians.

Statements 310–410: Here spherical coordinates are changed to rectangular coordinates. Lines 350 and 380 convert T and H from degrees to radians.

EXERCISES

A   Use the program on page 662 to change cylindrical coordinates to rectangular coordinates for Exercises 1–6. (All angles are in degrees.)

1. $(4, 0, 3)$ **2.** $(4, 90, -2)$ **3.** $(0, 135, -1)$

4. $(2, 210, 5)$ **5.** $(20, 75, 6)$ **6.** $(15, -50, -2)$

Use the program on page 662 to change spherical coordinates to rectangular coordinates for Exercises 7–12. (All angles are in degrees.)

7. $(8, 15, 80)$ **8.** $(1, 100, 35)$ **9.** $(4, 0, 165)$

10. $(22, 43, 67)$ **11.** $(6, 40, 110)$ **12.** $(2, 110, 10)$

C   Write a BASIC program for each problem.

13. Change cylindrical coordinates to spherical coordinates.

14. Change spherical coordinates to cylindrical coordinates.

CHAPTER SUMMARY

Important Terms

Axis of rotation (p. 644)
Central quadric (p. 651)
Cylinders (p. 640)
Cylindrical coordinates (p. 654)
Generating curve (p. 644)
Normal section of a
  cylinder (p. 641)
Plane curve (p. 659)

Plane section of a
  surface (p. 644)
Quadric surface (p. 647)
Sphere (p. 640)
Spherical coordinates (p. 655)
Surface (p. 640)
Surface of revolution (p. 644)
Twisted curve (p. 659)

Important Ideas

1. The equation of a cylinder with elements parallel to an axis is an equation in two variables.

2. Plane sections perpendicular to an axis of revolution are circular for surfaces of revolution.

3. Common quadric surfaces:

  a. Ellipsoid: $\dfrac{x^2}{a^2} + \dfrac{y^2}{b^2} + \dfrac{z^2}{c^2} = 1$

  b. Elliptic paraboloid: $\dfrac{x^2}{a^2} + \dfrac{y^2}{b^2} = cz,\ c > 0$

  c. Hyperbolic paraboloid: $\dfrac{y^2}{a^2} - \dfrac{x^2}{b^2} = cz,\ c > 0$

  d. Elliptic cone: $\dfrac{x^2}{a^2} + \dfrac{y^2}{b^2} - \dfrac{z^2}{c^2} = 0$

  e. Hyperboloid of one Sheet: $\dfrac{x^2}{a^2} + \dfrac{y^2}{b^2} - \dfrac{z^2}{c^2} = 1$

  f. Hyperboloid of two Sheets: $\dfrac{x^2}{a^2} - \dfrac{y^2}{b^2} - \dfrac{z^2}{c^2} = 1$

4. The equations that relate cylindrical coordinates with rectangular coordinates are $x = r \cos \theta$, $y = r \sin \theta$, $z = z$.

5. Equations that relate spherical coordinates with rectangular coordinates are $x = \rho \sin \phi \cos \theta$, $y = \rho \sin \phi \sin \theta$, $z = \rho \cos \phi$.

6. Space curves are often described by giving the equations of two surfaces that intersect in the curve, or by giving a set of parametric equations specifying the coordinates of each point on the curve.

CHAPTER OBJECTIVES AND REVIEW

Objective: *To identify and graph cylindrical surfaces.* (Section 12-1)

1. Define a directrix and an element of a cylinder.

Identify each cylindrical surface by name and sketch its graph.

2. $\frac{y^2}{16} + \frac{z^2}{9} = 1$ **3.** $x^2 - y = 0$ **4.** $x - y = 3$

5. $yz = 4$ **6.** $x^2 + z^2 = 9$ **7.** $x^2 - 4y^2 - 4 = 0$

Objective: *To identify and sketch surfaces of revolution.* (Section 12-2)

Identify each surface which is a surface of revolution. Determine the traces in each coordinate plane, indicate the axis or axes of rotation, and sketch each surface of revolution.

8. $x^2 + z^2 - 4y = 0$ **9.** $9x^2 + 4y^2 + 9z^2 - 36 = 0$

10. $9x^2 - 9y^2 + 4z^2 - 36 = 0$ **11.** $x^2 + 4y^2 + z^2 - 4 = 0$

12. $4x^2 + 4y^2 + 4z^2 = 16$ **13.** $x^2 - 16y^2 + z^2 = 0$

Objective: *To identify and graph quadric surfaces.* (Section 12-3)

Identify each quadric surface by name and sketch it.

14. $9x^2 + 4y^2 + 6z^2 = 36$ **15.** $\frac{x^2}{16} + \frac{y^2}{25} = 9z$

16. $4x^2 + 4y^2 - \frac{z^2}{16} = 0$ **17.** $x^2 + y^2 + z^2 = 25$

18. $9x^2 - 4y^2 = 72z$ **19.** $\frac{x^2}{16} - \frac{y^2}{25} - \frac{z^2}{36} = 1$

Objective: *To illustrate how a point in three-space may be located using rectangular, cylindrical and spherical coordinates and to illustrate and use the relationships between these coordinate systems.* (Section 12-4)

20. Given a point P which has coordinates

a. (x, y, z) **b.** (r, θ, z) **c.** (ρ, θ, ϕ)

Make one or more sketches illustrating the meaning of each coordinate.

21. Given $P(r, \theta, z)$. What are the rectangular coordinates of P?

22. Given $P(x, y, z)$. What are the cylindrical coordinates of P?

23. Given $P(\rho, \theta, \phi)$. What are the rectangular coordinates of P?

Change the cylindrical coordinates to rectangular coordinates.

24. $(2, 0, 4)$ **25.** $(3, \frac{\pi}{3}, -1)$

Change the spherical coordinates to rectangular coordinates.

26. $(6, 0, \frac{\pi}{3})$

27. $(4, \frac{\pi}{4}, 0)$

Objective: *To sketch the graph of a curve in space given a two surface representation or a parametric representation.* (Section 12-5)

28. Sketch the first octant graph of the curve defined by the curves $y^2 - 4x = 0$ and $z - 4x = 0$.

29. Sketch the first octant graph of the following curve.

$$x = 3 \sin t, \quad y = 3 \cos t, \quad z = \tfrac{1}{2}t.$$

CHAPTER TEST

1. Sketch the graph of the cylindrical surface whose equation is $z^2 - 4y = 0$.

2. Write the equation of the right circular cylinder whose axis is the x axis and whose directrix is a circle with radius 5.

3. Find the equations of the traces of $4x^2 + y^2 - 4z^2 = 4$. Is this a surface of revolution? Explain your answer.

4. Find the traces of $16x^2 - y^2 + 16z^2 = 9$. What is the axis of rotation? Sketch the curve.

5. What quadric surface is represented by $4x^2 + y^2 - 4z^2 = 4$? Sketch it.

6. Let P have spherical coordinates $\left(1, \frac{2\pi}{3}, \frac{3\pi}{4}\right)$. Find the rectangular coordinates for P.

7. Let Q have cylindrical coordinates $\left(2, \frac{\pi}{6}, 5\right)$. Find the rectangular coordinates for Q.

CHAPTER **13** Introduction to Calculus

Sections

Features

Review and Testing

13–1   The Derivative

In Section 6–5 the derived function $f'(x)$ of a given function $f(x)$ was defined by the following limit .

$$f'(x) = \lim_{h \to 0} \frac{f(x + h) - f(x)}{h} \qquad \qquad 1$$

The derived function $f'(x)$ is also called the **derivative** of $f(x)$ and the process of finding the derivative is called **differentiation.** A function f which has a derivative at a point $x = a$ is said to be **differentiable** at $x = a$.

EXAMPLE 1.   Use the definition above to find the derivative of $f(x) = x^2 - 2x$.

Solution: By definition you must evaluate $\lim\limits_{h \to 0} \frac{f(x + h) - f(x)}{h}$.

$$f(x + h) = (x + h)^2 - 2(x + h) = x^2 + 2xh + h^2 - 2x - 2h$$
$$f(x) \qquad\qquad\qquad = x^2 \qquad\qquad - 2x$$
$$f(x + h) - f(x) \qquad = \qquad 2xh - 2h + h^2$$
$$\frac{f(x + h) - f(x)}{h} \qquad = \qquad 2x - 2 + h$$

Thus

$$\lim_{h \to 0} \frac{f(x + h) - f(x)}{h} = \lim_{h \to 0} (2x - 2 + h) = 2x - 2.$$

So

$$f'(x) = 2x - 2.$$

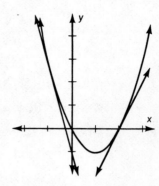

The geometric interpretation of the derivative was discussed in Section 6–6. There you found that $f'(x)$ evaluated at $x = a$ was the slope of the line tangent to the curve $f(x)$ at the point $(a, f(a))$. The graph of $f(x) = x^2 - 2x$ is shown at the right. Since $f'(x) = 2x - 2$, the tangent lines at $(2, 0)$ and $(-1, 3)$ have slopes of 2 and -4 respectively. They are shown at the right.

From your previous work you are familiar with the derivatives of several functions. They are summarized here for easy reference.

If $f(x) = c$, (c is a constant) then $f'(x) = 0$

If $f(x) = a \cdot x^m \; m \in W$, a is a constant then $f'(x) = a \cdot m \cdot x^{m-1}$

3. If $f(x) = f_1(x) + f_2(x) + \cdots + f_n(x)$ then $f'(x) =$
$$f_1'(x) + f_2'(x) + \cdots + f_n'(x)$$

4. If $f(x) = \dfrac{1}{x^m}$ $m \in W$ then $f'(x) = \dfrac{-m}{x^{m+1}}$

5. If $f(x) = \ln x$ then $f'(x) = \dfrac{1}{x}$ (See Section 8–11)

6. If $f(x) = e^x$ then $f'(x) = e^x$ (See Section 8–11)

EXAMPLE 2. Find the derivative of $f(x) = 3x^4 - 2x^2 - 3$.

Let $f_1(x) = 3x^4$, $f_2(x) = -2x^2$, $f_3(x) = -3$ then $f_1'(x) = 12x^3$, $f_2'(x) = -4x^1$, $f_3'(x) = 0$. Thus $f'(x) = 12x^3 - 4x$.

The next formula allows you to calculate the derivative of a function f which is the product of two differentiable functions.

Theorem 13–1 If $f(x) = r(x)s(x)$ where r and s are differentiable functions, then $f'(x) = r(x)s'(x) + s(x)r'(x)$.

Proof: By definition

$$f'(x) = \lim_{h \to 0} \frac{r(x+h)s(x+h) - r(x)s(x)}{h}$$

$$= \lim_{h \to 0} \frac{r(x+h)s(x+h) - r(x+h)s(x) + r(x+h)s(x) - r(x)s(x)}{h}$$

$$= \lim_{h \to 0} \frac{r(x+h)[s(x+h) - s(x)] + s(x)[r(x+h) - r(x)]}{h}$$

$$= \lim_{h \to 0} r(x+h) \lim_{h \to 0} \frac{s(x+h) - s(x)}{h} + s(x) \lim_{h \to 0} \frac{r(x+h) - r(x)}{h}$$

$$= r(x)s'(x) + s(x)r'(x)$$

EXAMPLE 3. Find the derivative of $f(x) = (x^2 - 3x)(x^4 + 2x^3)$.

Solution: Let $r(x) = x^2 - 3x$ $s(x) = x^4 + 2x^3$.

Then $r'(x) = 2x - 3$ $s'(x) = 4x^3 + 6x^2$

$f'(x) = (x^2 - 3x)(4x^3 + 6x^2) + (x^4 + 2x^3)(2x - 3)$ ⟵   **By Th. 13-1**

      $= 6x^5 - 5x^4 - 24x^3$.

If $f(x)$ had been expanded first then

$$f(x) = x^6 - x^5 - 6x^4$$

and thus $f'(x) = 6x^5 - 5x^4 - 24x^3$.

Not all products of two functions can be simplified into one function by expansion as was done in the check for Example 3. This fact is the reason for introducing Theorem 13-1. The following example illustrates such a case.

EXAMPLE 4. Find the derivative of $f(x) = xe^x$.

Solution: Let $\quad\quad r(x) = x \quad\quad s(x) = e^x.$

Then $\quad\quad\quad\quad\quad r'(x) = 1 \quad\quad s'(x) = e^x.$

Thus by Theorem 13-1 $\quad\quad f'(x) = xe^x + e^x = e^x(x+1).$

CLASSROOM EXERCISES

━━ Find the derivatives of the functions in Exercises 1–4.

1. $f(x) = x^3 + 2x^2 - x$
2. $f(x) = x^{-5} + 3$
3. $f(x) = x^2 e^x$
4. $f(x) = \ln(x^3)$

WRITTEN EXERCISES

A ━━ Find the derivative of the function described by the given equation for Exercises 1–14.

1. $f(x) = -2x^2 + 3x - 1$
2. $f(x) = 7x^{100} - 3x^{50}$
3. $f(x) = 7$
4. $f(x) = x^{-4}$
5. $f(x) = \dfrac{3}{x^7}$
6. $f: x \longrightarrow 5e^x$
7. $f(x) = \ln x + e^x - 4x^3$
8. $f: x \longrightarrow 7 \ln x + 3x^{-8}$
9. $f(x) = (x^2 + x)(x - 3)$
10. $f: x \longrightarrow (x^2 - x^4)e^x$
11. $f(x) = (e^x + 2)(x^2 - x)$
12. $f: x \longrightarrow (\ln x)(x^3 - x^2)$
13. $f(x) = e^x \left(\dfrac{1}{x} - x^2 \right)$
14. $f: x \longrightarrow \ln(x^x)$

B **15.** Let $f(x) = e^x$. Then $f'(x) = e^x$. If $f(x) = e^{2x}$ find $f'(x)$ by employing Theorem 13-1. (*Hint:* $e^x \cdot e^x = e^{2x}$)

━━ Use Exercise 15 to aid you in calculating $f'(x)$ for Exercises 16–19.

16. $f(x) = e^{3x}$
17. $f(x) = e^{4x}$
18. $f(x) = e^{5x}$
19. $f(x) = e^{nx}$

C ━━ $g(x)$, $h(x)$ and $k(x)$ are differentiable functions. Find $f'(x)$ for

20. $f(x) = g(x)h(x)k(x).$
21. $f(x) = \dfrac{h(x)}{g(x)}$, $g(x) \neq 0.$

13-2 The Derivative of a Quotient

Theorem 13–1 provides the formula for finding the derivative of products. Theorem 13–2 does the same for quotients.

Theorem 13-2 If $f(x) = \dfrac{r(x)}{s(x)}$, $s(x) \neq 0$, where r and s are differentiable functions, then

$$f'(x) = \frac{s(x)r'(x) - r(x)s'(x)}{s^2(x)}$$

Proof:

$$f'(x) = \lim_{h \to 0} \frac{\dfrac{r(x+h)}{s(x+h)} - \dfrac{r(x)}{s(x)}}{h}$$

$$= \lim_{h \to 0} \frac{s(x)r(x+h) - r(x)s(x+h)}{s(x)s(x+h)h}$$

$$= \lim_{h \to 0} \frac{s(x)r(x+h) - r(x)s(x) + r(x)s(x) - r(x)s(x+h)}{s(x)s(x+h)h}$$

$$= \lim_{h \to 0} \frac{s(x)}{s(x)s(x+h)} \left[\frac{r(x+h) - r(x)}{h} \right] - \frac{r(x)}{s(x)s(x+h)} \left[\frac{s(x+h) - s(x)}{h} \right]$$

$$= \frac{s(x)r'(x) - r(x)s'(x)}{s^2(x)}$$

EXAMPLE 1. Find the derivative of $\dfrac{x^2 - 1}{x + 1}$.

Solution: $\qquad r(x) = x^2 - 1 \qquad\qquad s(x) = x + 1$

Then $\qquad\qquad r'(x) = 2x \qquad\qquad\quad s'(x) = 1$

$$f'(x) = \frac{(x+1)(2x) - (x^2 - 1)(1)}{(x+1)^2} \quad\longleftarrow \textbf{ By Theorem 13-2}$$

$$= \frac{2x^2 + 2x - x^2 + 1}{(x+1)^2}$$

$$= \frac{x^2 + 2x + 1}{(x+1)^2}$$

$$= \frac{(x+1)(x+1)}{(x+1)^2} = 1$$

Notice that $f(x) = \dfrac{x^2 - 1}{x + 1} = x - 1$.

Then $f'(x) = 1$. This confirms Theorem 13–2 for one example.

EXAMPLE 2. Find the derivative of $f(x) = \frac{e^x}{2x}$.

Solution: $r(x) = e^x \qquad\qquad s(x) = 2x$

Then $\qquad\qquad r'(x) = e^x \qquad\qquad s'(x) = 2$

$$f'(x) = \frac{2xe^x - 2e^x}{4x^2} = \frac{(x-1)e^x}{2x^2} \quad\longleftarrow \textbf{ By Theorem 13-2}$$

CLASSROOM EXERCISES

━━ Find $r(x)$, $s(x)$, $r'(x)$, $s'(x)$ and $f'(x)$ for each quotient.

1. $f(x) = \frac{x^2 + x}{x - 1}$

2. $f(x) = \frac{e^x + x}{x}$

3. $f(x) = \frac{4x^2}{2 - x}$

4. $f(x) = \frac{3x^4 - 3x^2}{1 - x}$

WRITTEN EXERCISES

A ━━ Find the derivative of each function.

1. $f(x) = \frac{3x^3}{x + 2}$

2. $f(x) = \frac{x + 2}{3x^2}$

3. $f(x) = \frac{2x^2 + 3x + 1}{x}$

4. $f(x) = \frac{x}{x^2 + 2x + 1}$

5. $f(x) = \frac{\ln(x)}{x}$

6. $f(x) = \frac{e^x}{2x}$

7. $f(x) = \frac{ax + bx^2}{ax}$

8. $f(x) = \frac{x^2 - 2x}{e^x}$

B **9.** $f(x) = \frac{xe^x}{x + 1}$

10. $f(x) = \frac{e^x \ln x}{2 - x}$

11. $f(x) = \frac{x^2 \ln x}{2x - 1}$

12. $f(x) = \frac{x - 1}{xe^x}$

13. $f(x) = \frac{(x + 1)^2}{e^2}$

14. $f(x) = \frac{(x - 1)e^x}{x(x + 2)}$

━━ The slope of a line tangent to a curve at a point $x = a$ is given by derivative $f'(a)$. Find the slope of the line tangent to the function at the given point.

15. $f(x) = \frac{1}{x - 2}, x = 4$

16. $f(x) = \frac{e^x - e^{-x}}{x}, x = 1$

17. $f(x) = \frac{x}{4 - x}, x = 0$

18. $f(x) = \frac{\ln x}{x - 1}, x = 3$

━━ Find the coordinates of the points on the graph of $f(x)$ at which $f'(x) = 0$.

19. $f(x) = \frac{x^2}{1 + x^2}$

20. $f(x) = \frac{x}{1 + x^2}$

21. $f(x) = \frac{1 + x^2}{x}$

22. $f(x) = \frac{x - 2}{x + 2}$

13-3   The Chain Rule

In order to find the derivative of $(x^2 - x + 1)^2$, you would need to expand the expression first and then find the derivative. Thus, if

$$f(x) = (x^2 - x + 1)^2 = x^4 - 2x^3 + 3x^2 - 2x + 1.$$

then
$$f'(x) = 4x^3 - 6x^2 + 6x - 2$$
$$= 2(2x^3 - 3x^2 + 3x - 1)$$
$$= 2(x^2 - x + 1)(2x - 1) \qquad \textbf{1}$$

But, this approach will not work on $f(x) = (x^2 + 2x)^{\frac{1}{2}}$ or $f(x) = e^{x^2}$. Because of this fact, mathematicians developed the **chain rule**. The chain rule provides a way to find the derivative of composite functions.

Let
$$f(x) = (x^2 - x + 1)^2.$$

Let
$$u(x) = (x^2 - x + 1).$$

Then
$$f(x) = f(u) = u^2$$
$$f'(u) = 2u \qquad\qquad u'(x) = 2x - 1$$

Let
$$f'(x) = f'(u) \cdot u'(x)$$
$$= 2u(2x - 1) \quad\longleftarrow\quad \textbf{Replace } u \textbf{ with } x^2 - x + 1.$$
$$= 2(x^2 - x + 1)(2x - 1) \qquad \textbf{2}$$

If you compare **2** with **1** above, you will see that the results are identical. Thus the chain rule is verified in this case. Theorem 13–3 formalizes this result.

Theorem 13–3   If f and u are functions such that $u(x)$ is differentiable at x and $f(u)$ is differentiable at $u(x)$, then the chain rule

$$f'(x) = f'(u) \cdot u'(x)$$

is valid at x.

EXAMPLE 1.   Let $f(x) = (x^2 + 2x)^{\frac{1}{2}}$. Find $f'(x)$.

Solution: Use the chain rule.

Let
$$u(x) = x^2 + 2x \qquad\qquad f(u) = u^{\frac{1}{2}}$$

Then
$$u'(x) = 2x + 2 \qquad\qquad f'(u) = \tfrac{1}{2} u^{-\frac{1}{2}}$$

$$f'(x) = f'(u) \cdot u'(x) = \tfrac{1}{2} u^{-\frac{1}{2}}(2x + 2) \quad\longleftarrow\quad \textbf{By Theorem 13-3}$$
$$= \tfrac{1}{2}(x^2 + 2x)^{-\frac{1}{2}}(2x + 2)$$
$$= (x + 1)(x^2 + 2x)^{-\frac{1}{2}}$$

EXAMPLE 2. Let $f(x) = e^{x^2}$. Find $f'(x)$.

Solution: Use the chain rule.

Let	$u(x) = x^2$	$f(u) = e^u$
Then	$u'(x) = 2x$	$f'(u) = e^u$

$f'(x) = f'(u) \cdot u'(x) = e^u \cdot 2x = 2xe^{x^2}$ ◄——— **By Theorem 13-3**

CLASSROOM EXERCISES

▬ For each composite function, identify u, $u'(x)$, $f(u)$, $f'(u)$, and $f'(x)$.

1. $f(x) = (x^2 + 3x)^3$

2. $f(x) = 3(x^2 - 1)^4$

3. $f(x) = (x^3 - x)^{\frac{1}{2}}$

4. $f(x) = \left(\frac{1}{x+1}\right)^2$

WRITTEN EXERCISES

A ▬ Use the chain rule to find the derivative of each function.

1. $f(x) = (x + 1)^5$

2. $f(x) = (x^2 + 1)^5$

3. $f(x) = (x^2 + 1)^{-5}$

4. $f(x) = (3x^2 - 2)^{-3}$

5. $f(x) = (x^3 - x)^{\frac{1}{2}}$

6. $f(x) = (x^4 + 2x)^{-\frac{1}{2}}$

7. $f(x) = \left(\frac{1}{x}\right)^4$

8. $f(x) = \left(\frac{1}{x+2}\right)^3$

9. $f(x) = \left(\frac{2x}{x+2}\right)^3$

10. $f(x) = \left(\frac{x+2}{2x}\right)^4$

11. $f(x) = (e^x - e^{-x})^2$

12. $f(x) = e^{(x^2+x)}$

13. $f(x) = e^{\frac{1}{x}}$

14. $f(x) = e^{5x}$

B **15.** $f(x) = (x^2 + 1)^2(x^3 - x)^3$

16. $f(x) = (x\,e^x)^3$

17. $f(x) = e^{x^2} \cdot x^4$

18. $f(x) = (e^x + \ln x)^2$

19. $f(x) = \left(\frac{x}{1+e^{2x}}\right)^2$

20. $f(x) = \frac{1}{e^x + e^{-x}}$

C ▬ If $f(x) = \sin x$, then $f'(x) = \cos x$. Similarly, if $f(x) = \cos x$, then $f'(x) = -\sin x$. Using this information, find $f'(x)$.

21. $f(x) = \sin 2x$

22. $f(x) = \cos 3x$

23. $f(x) = (\ln(\sin 2x))^2$

24. $f(x) = \ln(\sin(2x)^2)$

▬ For each formula below calculate the derivative of each side. Then show that the results are identical.

25. $e^{(a+b)x} = e^{ax} \cdot e^{bx}$

26. $\ln ax = \ln a + \ln x$

27. $\sin(a + b)x = \sin ax \cos bx + \cos ax \sin bx$

28. $\cos(a + b)x = \cos ax \cos bx - \sin ax \sin bx.$

13–4 Velocity and Acceleration: Rates

Imagine an automobile traveling due west at the rate of 180 miles per hour on the Bonneville Salt Flats. To determine the distance S it traveled from a point O in t minutes at the rate of 180 mph (or 3 miles per minute) you would use the formula $S = 3t$.

On the other hand, if you observed the car at point O at time t_1 and at point P at t_2 and O and P were 1 mile apart, the *average rate* of the car could be determined by dividing the distance traveled by the elapsed time, $t_2 - t_1$. In this case the rate is $\frac{1}{t_2 - t_1}$. In general the **average rate** or **average velocity** of an object moving in a straight line is given by the formula

$$\text{Average velocity} = \frac{S_2 - S_1}{t_2 - t_1} \qquad \qquad 1$$

where S_2 and S_1 are distances and t_2 and t_1 are measures of time.

EXAMPLE 1. Find the average velocity of an aircraft flying due west if at 2:00 P.M. it is over O'Hare Field in Chicago and at 3:30 P.M. it is 700 kilometers west.

Solution:

Let $\qquad\qquad S_1 = 0 \quad \text{at} \quad t_1 = 2\text{:}00 \text{ P.M.}$

Then $\qquad\qquad S_2 = 700 \quad \text{when} \quad t_2 = 3\text{:}30 \text{ P.M.}$

Thus $\qquad S_2 - S_1 = 700 \text{ kilometers}$

$\qquad\qquad\quad t_2 - t_1 = 1.5 \text{ hours}$

and $\qquad \dfrac{S_2 - S_1}{t_2 - t_1} = \dfrac{700}{\frac{3}{2}}$

$$= \frac{1400}{3} \approx 467 \text{ kilometers per hour}$$

Motion in a straight line is called rectilinear motion. Often a function $S(t)$ is used to describe the distance S of an object from a fixed point at a time t. $S(t)$ is called a **position function.** In such cases no restriction is placed on the moving object other than that it is rectilinear motion. Thus the object need not move at a uniform rate as the car did on the Bonneville Salt Flats; nor does it need to move in only one direction; it may move in opposite directions.

For rectilinear motion described by a position function $S(t)$, the average velocity of the object over an interval of time $[t_1, t_2]$ is defined by

$$\text{average velocity} = \frac{S(t_2) - S(t_1)}{t_2 - t_1}. \qquad \qquad 2$$

For example, a freely falling body will travel $16t^2$ feet in t seconds, thus $S(t) = 16t^2$ for a freely falling body.

The average velocity of the body using equation **2** is

$$\frac{16t_2^2 - 16t_1^2}{t_2 - t_1} = 16(t_2 + t_1).$$

Thus, for the time interval $[1, 3]$, the average velocity is $16(1 + 3) = 64$ feet per second, while in the interval $[5, 7]$ the average velocity is $16(5 + 7) = 16(12) = 192$ feet per second.

The average velocity of a moving object is a useful concept, but it does not indicate the velocity of an object *at* a given time t. Something more must be done to get the **instantaneous velocity** of an object.

Suppose you wished to know the velocity of a freely falling body 3 seconds from the time it began to fall. The position function is $S(t) = 16t^2$. If you calculate average velocities for small time intervals $[t_1, t_2]$ with $t_1 = 3$, you can get an approximation to the *instantaneous velocity* at $t = 3$. Several of these calculations are shown in the table. Here $t_2 = t_1 + h$, $S(t_1) = 144$, $t_1 = 3$.

t_2	$S(t_2)$	$S(t_2) - S(t_1)$	$t_2 - t_1 = h$	$\dfrac{S(t_2) - S(t_1)}{t_2 - t_1}$
4	256	$256 - 144 = 112$	$4 - 3 = 1$	$\dfrac{112}{1} = 112$
3.5	196	$196 - 144 = 52$	$3.5 - 3 = .5$	$\dfrac{52}{.5} = 104$
3.1	153.76	$153.76 - 144 = 9.76$	$3.1 - 3 = .1$	$\dfrac{9.76}{.1} = 97.6$
3.01	144.9616	$144.9616 - 144 = 0.9616$	$3.01 - 3 = .01$	$\dfrac{.9616}{.01} = 96.16$
$3 + h$	$16(9 + 6h + h^2)$	$16(9 + 6h + h^2) - 16 \cdot 9 = 16(6h + h^2)$	$3 + h - 3 = h$	$\dfrac{16(6h + h^2)}{h} = 16(6 + h)$

Each entry in the last column of the table is an average velocity. Each is also an approximation to the velocity at $t = 3$. These approximations improve as the length of time interval h approaches zero. Thus the velocity of the falling body at $t = t_1$ is defined by this limit, if it exists.

$$\text{instantaneous velocity at time } t_1 = \lim_{h \to 0} \frac{S(t_1 + h) - S(t_1)}{h} \qquad 3$$

But notice that $\lim\limits_{h \to 0} \dfrac{S(t_1 + h) - S(t_1)}{h} = S'(t)$ evaluated at $t = t_1$.

> **Definition** Let $S(t)$ be the position function for a rectilinear motion. The **velocity** of the moving body at $t = t_1$ is the derivative of $S(t)$ evaluated at $t = t_1$. Let $v(t)$ represent the velocity as a function of t. Then
> $$v(t) = S'(t) \qquad \qquad 4$$

EXAMPLE 2. Let a particle have a position function

$$S(t) = t^3 - 6t^2 + 9t + 2 \quad \text{for } t \in [0, 4].$$

What is $v(t)$? Find the velocity of the particle at $t = 0, 1, 2, 3,$ and 4.

Solution: $\qquad\qquad\qquad v(t) = S'(t).$

Thus $\qquad\qquad\qquad\quad v(t) = 3t^2 - 12t + 9$

$$= 3(t^2 - 4t + 3)$$

$v(0) = 9$ — This is the initial velocity.

$v(1) = 0$ — The particle is not moving.

$v(2) = {}^-3$ — The particle is moving backwards.

$v(3) = 0$ — The particle has stopped.

$v(4) = 9$ — The particle is moving forward.

Notice that the velocity of the particle in Example 2 is not constant. In fact at $t = 2$, it is actually negative. The rate of change in the velocity of a particle is the **acceleration** of the particle. The **average acceleration** and **instantaneous acceleration** of a particle are defined by equations 5 and 6 respectively.

$$\text{average acceleration} = \frac{v(t_1 + h) - v(t_1)}{h} \qquad\qquad 5$$

$$\text{instantaneous acceleration} = \lim_{h \to 0} \frac{v(t_1 + h) - v(t_1)}{h} = v'(t_1) \qquad 6$$

Equation 6 tells you that the derivative of the velocity function $v(t)$ evaluated at $t = t_1$, is the **acceleration function** $a(t)$ for the moving particle, that is

$$a(t) = v'(t). \qquad\qquad 7$$

Since $\qquad\qquad\qquad\quad v(t) = S'(t)$

it follows that $\qquad\qquad\quad a(t) = S''(t) \qquad\qquad 8$

that is, the second derivative of the *position function* is the *acceleration function*.

EXAMPLE 3.

$$S(t) = t^3 - 6t^2 + 9t + 2, \quad t \in [0, 4]$$

What is the acceleration function $a(t)$? Find the acceleration at $t = 0, 1, 2, 3, 4$.

Solution: Since

$$a(t) = v'(t)$$
$$v(t) = 3t^2 - 12t + 9$$
$$a(t) = 6t - 12$$
$$= 6(t - 2)$$

$a(0) = -12$—The particle is slowing down.

$a(1) = -6$—The particle is slowing down.

$a(2) = 0$—There is no change in the velocity.

$a(3) = 6$—The particle is going faster.

$a(4) = 12$—The particle continues to pick up speed.

Velocity and acceleration are each a rate of change of one variable per unit change in a second variable. In general, for a function $f(x)$, the derivative $f'(x)$ may always be interpreted as the instantaneous rate of change of $f(x)$ per unit change in x.

WRITTEN EXERCISES

A ━━━ For Exercises 1–5, let the position function of a moving particle be $S(t) = t^2 - 25$. Find the average velocity from $t = 3$ to

1. $t = 5$. **2.** $t = 4$. **3.** $t = 3.1$. **4.** $t = 3.01$. **5.** $t = 3 + h$.

━━━ For Exercises 6–10, let the position function of a moving particle be $100 - 4t^2$. Find the average velocity from $t = 2$ to

6. $t = 0$. **7.** $t = 1$. **8.** $t = 1.9$. **9.** $t = 1.99$. **10.** $t = 1.999$.

━━━ For Exercises 11–13, let the position function of a moving particle be $S(t) = 3t^2 - 2t + 1$.

11. What is the average velocity of the particle on each interval $[0, 2]$, $[0, 1]$, $[0, 0.1]$, $[0, 0.01]$, $[0, h]$?

12. What is the instantaneous velocity at $t = 0$?

13. What is the instantaneous acceleration of the particle at $t = 0$?

━━━ For each position function in Exercises 14–21 find $v(t)$ and $a(t)$. Evaluate each at $t = 0, 1, 2, 3, 4$.

14. $S(t) = 2t^2 + 5t - 12$ **15.** $S(t) = 4t + 3$

16. $S(t) = 4 - 2t - t^2$ **17.** $S(t) = (2t + 3)^2$

18. $S(t) = (4 - t)^2$

19. $S(t) = 64t - 16t^2$

20. $S(t) = 2t^3 - 18t^2 + 48t - 6$

21. $S(t) = 2t^3 - 9t^2 + 12$

B ━━ Use the following information for Exercises 22–26.
If a ball is thrown vertically upward with an initial velocity of 128 feet per second, the ball's height after t seconds is given by $S(t) = 128t - 16t^2$.

22. What is the velocity function?

23. What is the velocity when $t = 2, 4, 6$?

24. At what time is the velocity 48 feet per second? 16 feet per second? -48 feet per second?

25. When is the velocity zero? What is the height of the ball at that time? Is this the maximum height?

26. When does the ball hit the ground? What is its velocity at that time?

━━ Use the following information for Exercises 27–29.
If a ball is thrown vertically upward with a velocity of 32 feet per second, the ball's height after t seconds is given by $S(t) = 32t - 16t^2$.

27. At what time t does the ball reach its maximum height?

28. What is the maximum height?

29. At what time does the ball hit the ground?

MID-CHAPTER REVIEW ▮▮▮▮▮▮▮▮▮▮▮▮▮▮

━━ Find the derivative of each function. (Sections 13-1, 13-2, 13-3)

1. $f(x) = 5x^4$

2. $f(x) = x^4 \cdot e^x$

3. $f(x) = x^{-3} - 3x^{-2}$

4. $f(x) = (x^2 - 2x)e^x$

5. $f(x) = (x - 1)(x + 1)x$

6. $f(x) = (e^x - e^{-x})(e^{-x} + e^x)$

7. $f(x) = \dfrac{x + 1}{x^2 + 1}$

8. $f(x) = \dfrac{(x - 1)(x + 1)}{x - 3}$

9. $f(x) = (x^2 + 6x - 1)^3$

10. $f(x) = (3x^2 - 7)^{-2}$

11. $f(x) = e^{(x^3 - 2x)}$

12. $f(x) = 3(x^2 - 3)^2 - 2(x^2 - 3)$

13. Find the values of x for which $f'(x) = 0$, if $f(x) = (2x^2 - 3)^4$. (Section 13-3)

14. If the position function of a moving particle is $S(t) = 3t^3 - 18t + 4$, find each of the following. (Section 13-4)

    a. $v(t)$ and $a(t)$.

    b. $v(t)$ and $a(t)$ at $t = 0, 1, \sqrt{2}, 3$.

    c. The time at which $v(t) = 18$.

INTRODUCTION TO CALCULUS   679

Applying Derivatives
Economics

Cost, revenue and profit functions are important tools for analysis by **economists.**
The derivatives of these functions, the marginal cost, $C'(x)$, the marginal revenue,
$R'(x)$, and the marginal profit, $P'(x)$, are also important tools. If $R(x)$ is the
revenue function, then

$$\frac{R(x+h) - R(x)}{h}$$

is the average revenue on the interval $\langle x, x + h \rangle$. Taking the limit

$$\lim_{h \to 0} \frac{R(x+h) - R(x)}{h} = R'(x).$$

$R'(x)$ is, therefore, the instantaneous change in the revenue at $(x, R(x))$. If
$R'(x) = 0$, then $R(x)$ may have a maximum value, a minimum value, or an inflection point at x.

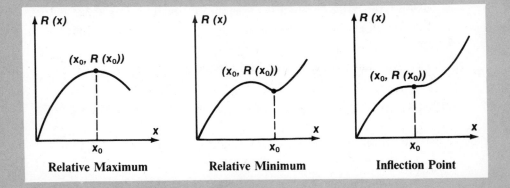

| Relative Maximum | Relative Minimum | Inflection Point |

Analysis of these factors can help economists in planning production and fore-
casting economic trends.

EXAMPLE 1. Find the marginal revenue function if $R(x) = 20x - 0.01x^2$,
$x \le 0$. Is there a production quantity that yields a maximum revenue?

Solution: $R(x) = 20x - 0.01x^2$

$R'(x) = 20 - 0.02x$ ◄——— **Marginal revenue function**

$R'(x) = 0$ when

$20 - 0.02x = 0$

or when $x = 1000$

Thus, maximum revenue occurs when production is 1000 items.

EXAMPLE 2. Find the marginal cost function if $C(x) = 0.001x^2 + 10x + 5$, $x \geq 0$. Is there a production quantity that gives a minimum cost?

Solution: $C(x) = 0.001x^2 - 10x + 5$

$C'(x) = 0.002x - 10$ ◄──── **Marginal cost function**

$C'(x) = 0$ when

$0.002x - 10 = 0$

or when $x = 5000$

Thus, when 5000 items are produced, the cost, when figured according to this cost function, is a minimum.

EXERCISES

1. Find $R'(x)$ for each revenue function. Locate the points, if any, satisfying $R'(x) = 0$. ($x \geq 0$ for each $R(x)$)

    a. $R(x) = 8x$

    b. $R(x) = 200x - 5x^2$

    c. $R(x) = 540x - \dfrac{x^2}{18}$

2. Find $C'(x)$ for each cost function. Locate the points, if any, satisfying $C'(x) = 0$. ($x \geq 0$ for each $C(x)$)

    a. $C(x) = 7x + 9$

    b. $C(x) = 5x + \dfrac{1}{x} + 2000$

    c. $C(x) = 12x + \dfrac{200}{x} + 200$

3. The profit function, $P(x)$, is given by $P(x) = R(x) - C(x)$. Form three different profit functions from the revenue and cost functions in Exercises 1 and 2. For what values, if any, does $P'(x) = 0$?

4. When $D(x)$ is a demand function (price as a function of the number of items demanded) then $R(x) = xD(x)$. Calculate $R'(x)$.

5. For each demand function, compute $D'(x)$, $R'(x)$ and the zeros, if any, of these marginal functions.

    a. $D(x) = 8 - x$

    b. $D(x) = \dfrac{24}{x + 2}$

    c. $D(x) = \dfrac{200}{x + 10}$

13-5 Area and Approximation

You know how to calculate the area of many plane regions that are enclosed by simple polygons. Likewise, you know that the area of a circular region of radius r is πr^2. But how can you calculate the area of a plane region such as the one shown at the right? The answer to this question is the subject of this section and the sections which follow. In this chapter, the only curves considered are $y = f(x)$ where $f(x)$ is continuous for all x in $[a, b]$. You may assume the above condition is true for all functions discussed in this chapter unless otherwise indicated.

Clearly you must assume that each plane region bounded by plane curves has a unique number associated with it which is its area. Otherwise further discussion would be futile.

Since you do not know the area of a region bounded by curves, it is reasonable to attempt to approximate the area using the areas of regions you can calculate. Consider a simple case first. The triangular region bounded by

$$y = \tfrac{1}{2}x, \quad \text{the } x \text{ axis}, \quad \text{and} \quad x = 8.$$

The region is shown in Figure 1.

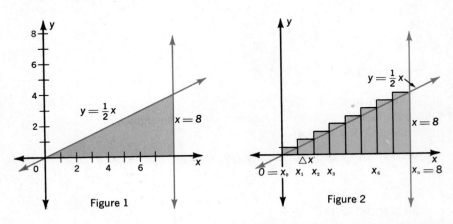

Figure 1   Figure 2

You know that the area, A, of the triangular region is 16, but that is not important here. What is important is the method of approximation used, for it is applicable to regions whose areas you do not know beforehand. The method used is to approximate the area you wish to find with the sum of the areas of rectangles.

First partition the interval $[0, 8]$ into a finite number, n, of intervals of the same length. See Figure 2. Each of these intervals will have length.

$$\frac{8 - 0}{n} = \Delta x$$

Call the endpoints of these intervals

$$0 = x_0, x_1, x_2, \cdots, x_{n-1}, x_n = 8.$$

If $n = 8$ then $\Delta x = 1$ and the intervals are

$$[0, 1], [1, 2], \cdots, [7, 8].$$

Now form the n rectangles of *width* Δx and *length equal to the ordinate of the right hand endpoint of each interval*. The ordinate is $y_i = \frac{1}{2}(0 + i \cdot \Delta x)$. These are shown in Figure 2. Therefore each rectangle has area

$$y_i \Delta x, \, i = 1, 2, \cdots, n$$

and the approximation to the area of the triangular region is the sum of the areas of the rectangles.

$$y_1 \Delta x + y_2 \Delta x + y_3 \Delta x + \cdots + y_{n-1} \Delta x + y_n \Delta x = \sum_{i=1}^{n} y_i \Delta x = A_n$$

When $n = 8$, $\Delta x = 1$, the approximation is

$$\sum_{i=1}^{8} y_i \Delta x = 1 \cdot (\tfrac{1}{2} + 1 + \tfrac{3}{2} + 2 + \tfrac{5}{2} + 3 + \tfrac{7}{2} + 4)$$
$$= 1(\tfrac{16}{2} + 10)$$
$$= 18$$

Notice that the approximation to the area is larger than the area. You could get an approximation that was smaller than the area by choosing the ordinate of the left-hand endpoint of each interval as the length of each rectangle. In that case the area would be approximated by 14. (You should verify this.)

A better approximation to the true area could be obtained by making a finer partition of the x axis. If, say, sixteen intervals were used rather than 8, the area approximation would be the following. $\left(\text{Remember from Section 1–6, that } \sum_{i=1}^{n} i = \frac{n(n + 1)}{2} .\right)$

$$\sum_{i=1}^{16} y_i \Delta x = \tfrac{1}{2}(\tfrac{1}{4} + \tfrac{2}{4} + \tfrac{3}{4} + \tfrac{4}{4} + \tfrac{5}{4} + \cdots + \tfrac{14}{4} + \tfrac{15}{4} + \tfrac{16}{4})$$
$$= \tfrac{1}{8}(1 + 2 + 3 + \cdots + 16)$$
$$= \tfrac{1}{8} \cdot 136 = 17$$

Consider now an example in which you cannot calculate the exact area, but in which the "sum of rectangles" area will give you an approximation to the true area. Let the region be bounded by the curve $y = \frac{1}{4}x^2$, the x axis, and the line $x = 4$.

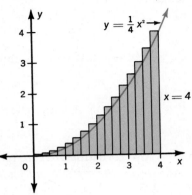

Following the procedure described above, partition $[0, 4]$ into n intervals of length $\Delta x = \dfrac{4 - 0}{n} = \dfrac{4}{n}$. Again choose the right-hand endpoint of each interval and use the ordinate of that point as the length of the rectangle. Thus the area of each rectangle is

$$y_i \, \Delta x, \ i = 1, 2, \cdots, n.$$

The approximation to the area is given by

$$A_n = \sum_{i=1}^{n} y_i \, \Delta x \qquad \qquad \textbf{1}$$

Since the right-hand endpoints of the n intervals are $x_1 = \Delta x$, $x_2 = 2 \, \Delta x$, $x_3 = 3 \, \Delta x, \ldots, x_i = i \cdot \Delta x$, the ordinates of these points are

$$y_1 = \tfrac{1}{4}(\Delta x)^2, \ y_2 = \tfrac{1}{4}(2 \, \Delta x)^2, \ y_3 = \tfrac{1}{4}(3 \, \Delta x)^2, \cdots, y_i = \tfrac{1}{4}(i \cdot \Delta x)^2$$

and therefore

$$A_n = \sum_{i=1}^{n} \tfrac{1}{4}(i \, \Delta x)^2 \cdot \Delta x$$

$$= \tfrac{1}{4} \sum_{i=1}^{n} i^2 (\Delta x)^3 \qquad \qquad \textbf{2}$$

Suppose that $n = 16$. Then $\Delta x = \frac{4}{16} = \frac{1}{4}$ and applying **2** you have the following. $\left(\text{Remember from Section 1–6, Exercise 12 that } \displaystyle\sum_{i=1}^{n} i^2 = \frac{n(n + 1)(2n + 1)}{6}.\right)$

$$A_{16} = \tfrac{1}{4} \sum_{i=1}^{16} i^2 (\tfrac{1}{4})^3$$

$$= (\tfrac{1}{4})^4 \sum_{i=1}^{16} i^2$$

$$= \tfrac{1}{256} \cdot (1 + 4 + 9 + \cdots + 256)$$

$$= \tfrac{1}{256} \cdot 1496$$

$$= \tfrac{187}{32} \approx 5.84$$

The true area of this region is 5.$\overline{3}$. The approximate value of 5.84 is too large (as expected) but relatively close to the true value.

CLASSROOM EXERCISES

▬ For Exercises 1–3 consider the triangular region bounded by the x axis and the lines $x = 0$, $x = 3$ and $y = x$.

1. Find the true area of the region.

2. Find the approximate area using rectangles whose lengths are determined by the right-hand endpoint of each interval and let the number of intervals be 6.

3. Find the approximate area using rectangles whose lengths are determined by the left-hand endpoint of each interval and let the number of intervals be 6.

WRITTEN EXERCISES

A ▬ Let a region be bounded by the following curves: $y = \frac{3}{2}x$, $x = 0$, $x = 2$ and the x axis. Find an approximation to the area using n intervals for the given values of n in Exercises 1–3.

1. $n = 2$ **2.** $n = 4$ **3.** $n = 16$

4. What is the true area of the region given above?

5. Repeat Exercises 1–4 when the region is bounded by $y = 2x + 1$, the y axis, the x axis, and $x = 2$.

6. Repeat Exercises 1–3, but use the left-hand endpoints of the intervals to determine the rectangles.

7. Repeat Exercise 5, but use the left-hand endpoints of the intervals to determine the rectangles.

▬ Let a region be bounded by $y = x^2$, $x = 0$, $x = 2$ and the x axis. Approximate the area of this region using the intervals given in Exercises 8 and 9.

8. 4 intervals   **9.** 8 intervals

▬ Let a region be bounded by $y = \sqrt{x}$, $x = 4$ and the x axis. Approximate the area of the region using the intervals given in Exercises 10 and 11.

10. 4 intervals   **11.** 16 intervals

12. Repeat Exercises 8–11 but use the left-hand endpoints of the intervals to determine the rectangles.

B ━━ Let a region be bounded by $y = x^3$, the x axis, $x = 0$ and $x = 2$. Approximate the area using the intervals given in Exercises 13 and 14.

13. 4 intervals   **14.** 8 intervals

━━ For Exercises 15–16, use the following information. Let a region be bounded by $y = \frac{1}{4}x^2$, $x = 2$, $x = 4$ and the x axis.

15. If there are 4 intervals, how long is each?

16. What is the approximate area of the region for 4 intervals?

13–6   Trapezoidal Approximation for Area

In the last section you approximated the area of a region bounded by curves with the sum of areas of rectangles. For small numbers of intervals "approximation by rectangles" does not result in a value extremely close to the true area. One method of improving the approximations is to substitute trapezoids for the rectangles.

Suppose you want the area of the region bounded by $y = f(x)$, $f(x) \geq 0$ for all x in $[a, b]$, $x = a$, $x = b$, and the x axis. $f(x)$ must be continuous in $[a, b]$. Partition the interval $[a, b]$ into n intervals, each of length $\Delta x = \dfrac{b - a}{n}$. The points which do this partitioning are $x_0 = a$, $x_1 = a + \Delta x$, $x_2 = a + 2\Delta x, \ldots, x_{n-1} = a + (n-1)\Delta x$, $x_n = b$.

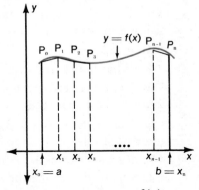

Let $P_0, P_1, \ldots, P_{n-1}, P_n$ be the points on the curve $y = f(x)$ corresponding to $x_0, x_1, \ldots, x_{n-1}, x_n$.

Consider the trapezoid $aP_0P_1x_1$. It has width Δx and the length of its bases are $y_0 = f(x_0)$ and $y_1 = f(x_1)$. Its area is

$$\text{Area } aP_0P_1x_1 = \tfrac{1}{2}(y_0 + y_1)\,\Delta x.$$

Similarly, the areas of the other trapezoids $x_1P_1P_2x_2$, $x_2P_2P_3x_3, \ldots,$ $x_{n-1}P_{n-1}P_nx_n$ are as follows.

$$\text{Area } x_1P_1P_2x_2 = \tfrac{1}{2}(y_1 + y_2)\,\Delta x$$
$$\text{Area } x_2P_2P_3x_3 = \tfrac{1}{2}(y_2 + y_3)\,\Delta x$$
$$\text{Area } x_{n-1}P_{n-1}P_nx_n = \tfrac{1}{2}(y_{n-1} + y_n)\,\Delta x$$

The sum of the areas of the trapezoids is an approximation to the area of the region. If you call that sum T, it follows that

$$T = \tfrac{1}{2}(y_0 + y_1)\,\Delta x + \tfrac{1}{2}(y_1 + y_2)\,\Delta x + \tfrac{1}{2}(y_2 + y_3)\,\Delta x$$
$$+ \cdots + \tfrac{1}{2}(y_{n-1} + y_n)\,\Delta x$$
$$= \tfrac{1}{2}(y_0 + 2y_1 + 2y_2 + 2y_3 + \cdots + 2y_{n-1} + y_n)\,\Delta x$$
$$= (\tfrac{1}{2}y_0 + y_1 + y_2 + y_3 + \cdots + y_{n-1} + \tfrac{1}{2}y_n)\,\Delta x \qquad\qquad 1$$

Equation 1 is the formula for the trapezoidal approximation to the area bounded by $y = f(x)$, $x = a$, $x = b$ and the x axis, where $y_i = f(x_i)$ and $\Delta x = \dfrac{b - a}{n}$.

EXAMPLE 1. Approximate the area of the region bounded by $y = \tfrac{1}{4}x^2$, $x = 0$, $x = 4$ and the x axis with the trapezoidal approximation for 16 intervals.

Solution: $\qquad\qquad \Delta x = \dfrac{4 - 0}{16} = \tfrac{1}{4}.$ ⟵ **a = 0, b = 4**

$y_0 = \tfrac{1}{4}(0)^2 = 0$ $\qquad y_6 = \tfrac{1}{4}(\tfrac{6}{4})^2 = \tfrac{1}{4}\cdot\tfrac{36}{16}$ $\qquad y_{12} = \tfrac{1}{4}(\tfrac{12}{4})^2 = \tfrac{1}{4}\cdot\tfrac{144}{16}$

$y_1 = \tfrac{1}{4}(\tfrac{1}{4})^2 = \tfrac{1}{4}\cdot\tfrac{1}{16}$ $\qquad y_7 = \tfrac{1}{4}(\tfrac{7}{4})^2 = \tfrac{1}{4}\cdot\tfrac{49}{16}$ $\qquad y_{13} = \tfrac{1}{4}(\tfrac{13}{4})^2 = \tfrac{1}{4}\cdot\tfrac{169}{16}$

$y_2 = \tfrac{1}{4}(\tfrac{2}{4})^2 = \tfrac{1}{4}\cdot\tfrac{4}{16}$ $\qquad y_8 = \tfrac{1}{4}(\tfrac{8}{4})^2 = \tfrac{1}{4}\cdot\tfrac{64}{16}$ $\qquad y_{14} = \tfrac{1}{4}(\tfrac{14}{4})^2 = \tfrac{1}{4}\cdot\tfrac{196}{16}$

$y_3 = \tfrac{1}{4}(\tfrac{3}{4})^2 = \tfrac{1}{4}\cdot\tfrac{9}{16}$ $\qquad y_9 = \tfrac{1}{4}(\tfrac{9}{4})^2 = \tfrac{1}{4}\cdot\tfrac{81}{16}$ $\qquad y_{15} = \tfrac{1}{4}(\tfrac{15}{4})^2 = \tfrac{1}{4}\cdot\tfrac{225}{16}$

$y_4 = \tfrac{1}{4}(\tfrac{4}{4})^2 = \tfrac{1}{4}\cdot\tfrac{16}{16}$ $\qquad y_{10} = \tfrac{1}{4}(\tfrac{10}{4})^2 = \tfrac{1}{4}\cdot\tfrac{100}{16}$ $\qquad y_{16} = \tfrac{1}{4}(\tfrac{16}{4})^2 = \tfrac{1}{4}\cdot\tfrac{256}{16}$

$y_5 = \tfrac{1}{4}(\tfrac{5}{4})^2 = \tfrac{1}{4}\cdot\tfrac{25}{16}$ $\qquad y_{11} = \tfrac{1}{4}(\tfrac{11}{4})^2 = \tfrac{1}{4}\cdot\tfrac{121}{16}$

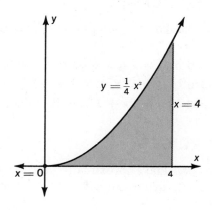

$y = \tfrac{1}{4}x^2$

$x = 4$

$x = 0$

You now add $\tfrac{1}{2}y_0$ and $\tfrac{1}{2}y_{16}$ to the remaining y_i's, $i = 2, 15$. The sum is

$\tfrac{1}{4}\cdot\tfrac{1}{16}(1 + 4 + 9 + 16 + \cdots + 196 + 225 + 128)$ or $\tfrac{1}{4}\cdot\tfrac{1}{16}\cdot 1368$

Thus $\quad T = (\tfrac{1}{4}\cdot\tfrac{1}{16}\cdot 1368)\cdot\Delta x = (\tfrac{1}{4}\cdot\tfrac{1}{16}\cdot 1368)\cdot\tfrac{1}{4} = \tfrac{171}{32} \approx 5.34$

The true area of the region is 5.3̄3̄. Thus the trapezoidal approximation for 16 intervals is less than one one-hundredth too large. This is a better approximation than the one obtained using rectangles, (page 684). The approximate value obtained then (5.84) was about five tenths too large.

EXAMPLE 2. Find the trapezoidal approximation for the area of the region bounded by $y = x^2$, $x = 1$, $x = 2$ and the x axis, using $n = 4$.

Solution: $\Delta x = \dfrac{2 - 1}{4} = \frac{1}{4}$. Thus

$$x_0 = a = 1 \qquad y_0 = 1^2 = \tfrac{16}{16}$$
$$x_1 = a + \Delta x = 1\tfrac{1}{4} \qquad y_1 = (\tfrac{5}{4})^2 = \tfrac{25}{16}$$
$$x_2 = a + 2\Delta x = 1\tfrac{2}{4} \qquad y_2 = (\tfrac{6}{4})^2 = \tfrac{36}{16}$$
$$x_3 = a + 3\Delta x = 1\tfrac{3}{4} \qquad y_3 = (\tfrac{7}{4})^2 = \tfrac{49}{16}$$
$$x_4 = b = 2 \qquad y_4 = (\tfrac{8}{4})^2 = \tfrac{64}{16}$$

Then $\frac{1}{2}y_0 = \tfrac{8}{16}$ and $\frac{1}{2}y_4 = \tfrac{32}{16}$. Thus

$$T = \tfrac{1}{4}(\tfrac{8}{16} + \tfrac{25}{16} + \tfrac{36}{16} + \tfrac{49}{16} + \tfrac{32}{16})$$
$$= \tfrac{1}{4} \cdot \tfrac{75}{8}$$
$$= \tfrac{75}{32} \approx 2.34$$

$y = x^2$

The true area of the region is 2.3̄3̄. The next section shows why.

CLASSROOM EXERCISES

Find the trapezoidal approximation for the areas of the regions in Exercises 1–3, using $n = 3$.

1. Region bounded by $y = 2x$, $x = 0$, $x = 1$ and the x axis.
2. Region bounded by $y = \sqrt{x}$, $x = 0$, $x = 9$ and the x axis.
3. Region bounded by $y = 2x + 1$, $x = 0$, $x = 6$, and the x axis.

WRITTEN EXERCISES

A Find the trapezoidal approximation for the areas of the regions in Exercises 1–12, using the given n. Round answers to two decimal places.

1. $f(x) = x$, $x = 0$, $x = 2$, x axis, $n = 4$
2. $f(x) = x^3$, $x = 0$, $x = 2$, x axis, $n = 4$
3. $f(x) = x^3$, $x = 1$, $x = 2$, x axis, $n = 4$
4. $f(x) = \sqrt{x}$, $x = 0$, $x = 4$, x axis, $n = 4$

5. $f(x) = \sqrt{x}$, $x = 2$, $x = 4$, x axis, $n = 4$

6. $f(x) = \frac{1}{x^2}$, $x = 1$, $x = 2$, x axis, $n = 2$

B **7.** $f(x) = \sqrt{x^3 - 1}$, $x = 2$, $x = 3$, x axis, $n = 6$

8. $f(x) = \sqrt{4 - x^2}$, $x = -1$, $x = 1$, x axis, $n = 5$

9. $f(x) = 3x^2$, $x = 1$, $x = 9$, x axis, $n = 8$

10. $f(x) = x\sqrt{9 + x^2}$, $x = 0$, $x = 4$, x axis, $n = 4$

11. $f(x) = x\sqrt{9 + x^2}$, $x = 0$, $x = 4$, x axis, $n = 8$

12. $f(x) = \frac{1}{\sqrt{4 + x^3}}$, $x = 0$, $x = 4$, x axis, $n = 4$

13. Let $y = mx$, $x = a$, $x = b$ (a, b, $m > 0$) and the x axis define a region. What is the trapezoidal approximation to the area of the region for $n = 4$? for $n = 8$? How do you explain the two results found?

13–7   Area as a Limit

You have seen how the area of a region can be approximated by summing areas of rectangles or areas of trapezoids. In either case, as the number of intervals increases the approximate area nears the true area of the region. The definition of the area of a region bounded by curves involves approximations by rectangles and a limit. Note that as the number of intervals increases without bound the width of each rectangle decreases and approaches zero as a limit.

Definition   Suppose that $f(x) \geq 0$ for all x in $[a, b]$. Then the **area** of the region, A, bounded by $y = f(x)$, $x = a$, $x = b$, and the x axis is given by

$$A_a^b f(x) = \lim_{n \to \infty} \left(\sum_{i=1}^{n} f(x_i) \Delta x \right)$$

where $\Delta x = \frac{b - a}{n}$ and x_i is the right-hand endpoint of the ith interval $[x_{i-1}, x_i]$.

In the above definition if $f(x) < 0$ for all x in $[a, b]$, then the area is defined as $-\lim\limits_{n \to \infty} \left(\sum\limits_{i=1}^{n} f(x_i) \Delta x \right)$.

Thus in either case

$$A_a^b f(x) = \left| \lim_{n \to \infty} \left(\sum_{i=1}^{n} f(x_i) \Delta x \right) \right|.$$

Figure 1 below depicts a typical rectangle used in calculating the area bounded by $y = f(x)$, $f(x) \geq 0$, $x = a$, $x = b$, and the x axis. The sum of the areas of all such rectangles as the width of the rectangles nears zero is very close to the exact area of the region.

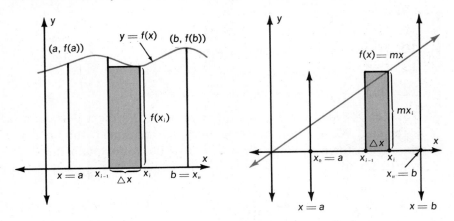

Figure 1   Figure 2

EXAMPLE 1. Find the area of the region bounded by $f(x) = mx$, $x = a$, $x = b$, and the x axis. $(a, b, m > 0, a < b)$ See Figure 2.

The first step is to find the expression for the approximate value of the area for n. As usual: $\Delta x = \dfrac{b-a}{n}$ and $x_0 = a$, $x_1 = a + \Delta x$, $x_2 = a + 2\Delta x$, $\cdots$, $x_i = a + i\Delta x$, $\cdots$, $x_n = b$. Thus $f(x_1) = m(a + \Delta x)$, $f(x_2) = m(a + 2\Delta x)$, $\cdots$, $f(x_i) = m(a + i\Delta x)$, $\cdots$, $f(x_n) = mb$. The approximate area A_n for n intervals is the following.

$$A_n = \sum_{i=1}^{n} m(a + i \cdot \Delta x)\, \Delta x$$

$$= \sum_{i=1}^{n} \left[ma\,\frac{(b-a)}{n} + mi \cdot \left(\frac{b-a}{n}\right)^2 \right]$$

$$= ma\,\frac{(b-a)}{n} \cdot n + m\left(\frac{b-a}{n}\right)^2 \sum_{i=1}^{n} i$$

$$A_n = ma(b-a) + m\left(\frac{b-a}{n}\right)^2 \cdot \sum_{i=1}^{n} i \qquad\qquad \mathbf{1}$$

You know that $\qquad \displaystyle\sum_{i=1}^{n} i = 1 + 2 + 3 + \cdots + n = \frac{n(n+1)}{2}. \qquad \mathbf{2}$

Substituting **2** in equation **1** you get

$$A_n = ma(b-a) + m\left(\frac{b-a}{n}\right)^2 \cdot \frac{n(n+1)}{2}. \qquad\qquad \mathbf{3}$$

Equation 3 will yield an approximate value for the area for any given n. For example, if $m = \frac{1}{2}$, $a = 0$, $b = 8$ and $n = 8$, $A_n = 18$. (Compare this with the results obtained in Section 13–5.)

By definition the exact area of the region is

$$A_a^b(mx) = \lim_{n \to \infty} \left(\sum_{i=1}^{n} m(a + i \cdot \Delta x) \Delta x \right) = \lim_{n \to \infty} A_n$$

$$= \lim_{n \to \infty} \left[ma(b - a) + m \left(\frac{b - a}{n} \right)^2 \cdot \frac{n(n + 1)}{2} \right]$$

$$= ma(b - a) + m(b - a)^2 \lim_{n \to \infty} \frac{n(n + 1)}{2n^2}$$

$$= ma(b - a) + \left(m(b - a)^2 \right) \tfrac{1}{2} \qquad \text{(Why?)}$$

$$= m \left[ab - a^2 + \frac{b^2}{2} - ab + \frac{a^2}{2} \right]$$

$$= m \left(\frac{b^2}{2} - \frac{a^2}{2} \right).$$

Thus $\qquad A_a^b(mx) = \dfrac{m}{2} (b^2 - a^2).$ 4

Equation 4 can be read as follows: The area between $y = mx$ and the x axis from $x = a$ to $x = b$ is $\frac{m}{2} (b^2 - a^2)$.

Equation 4 may be used to calculate the area bounded by any line through the origin, $x = a$, $x = b$ ($a < b$) and the x axis. If $m < 0$ then the area is $-\frac{m}{2} (b^2 - a^2)$.

EXAMPLE 2. Find the area bounded by the curves, $f(x) = x^2$, $x = a$, $x = b$, and the x axis. ($a < b$). $\Delta x = \dfrac{b - a}{n}$, $x_0 = a$, $x_1 = a + \Delta x$, $x_2 = a + 2 \Delta x, \cdots, x_i = a + i \cdot \Delta x, \cdots, x_n = b$.

$f(x_i) = (a + i \Delta x)^2$. Thus for n,

$$A_n = \sum_{i=1}^{n} f(x_i) \Delta x = \sum_{i=1}^{n} (a + i \Delta x)^2 \Delta x$$

$$= \sum_{i=1}^{n} [a^2 \Delta x + 2ai(\Delta x)^2 + i^2(\Delta x)^3] \qquad \longleftarrow \quad \begin{array}{l} \textbf{Expansion of} \\ \textbf{(} a + i \, \Delta \, x \textbf{)}^2 \end{array}$$

$$= \sum_{i=1}^{n} \left[a^2 \left(\frac{b - a}{n} \right) + 2ai \left(\frac{b - a}{n} \right)^2 + i^2 \left(\frac{b - a}{n} \right)^3 \right]$$

$$= na^2 \left(\frac{b - a}{n} \right) + 2a \left(\frac{b - a}{n} \right)^2 \sum_{i=1}^{n} i + \left(\frac{b - a}{n} \right)^3 \sum_{i=1}^{n} i^2$$

Recall that $\sum_{i=1}^{n} i = \dfrac{n(n+1)}{2}$ and $\sum_{i=1}^{n} i^2 = \dfrac{n(n+1)(2n+1)}{6}$. (See Section 1–6 page 20 and page 23 Exercise 12.) Thus

$$A_n = a^2(b-a) + 2a\left(\frac{b-a}{n}\right)^2 \frac{n(n+1)}{2}$$
$$+ \left(\frac{b-a}{n}\right)^3 \frac{n(n+1)(2n+1)}{6}. \qquad 5$$

The required area is therefore

$$A_a^b(x^2) = \lim_{n\to\infty} A_n$$

$$= \lim_{n\to\infty} a^2(b-a) + \lim_{n\to\infty}\left[2a\left(\frac{b-a}{n}\right)^2 \frac{n(n+1)}{2}\right]$$
$$+ \lim_{n\to\infty}\left[\left(\frac{b-a}{n}\right)^3 \frac{n(n+1)(2n+1)}{6}\right]$$

$$= a^2(b-a) + a(b-a)^2 \lim_{n\to\infty} \frac{n(n+1)}{n^2}$$
$$+ \frac{(b-a)^3}{6} \lim_{n\to\infty} \frac{n(n+1)(2n+1)}{n^3}$$

$$= a^2 b - a^3 + a(b^2 - 2ab + a^2) + \left(\frac{b^3 - 3b^2 a + 3ba^2 - a^3}{6}\right)\cdot 2$$

$$= \frac{b^3 - a^3}{3}.$$

Thus the area from $x = a$ to $x = b$ of the region between $y = x^2$ and the x axis is

$$A_a^b(x^2) = \frac{b^3 - a^3}{3}.$$

The key in calculating exact areas is to change the expression for the sum of the areas of the rectangles to a form whose limit as n increases without bound is easily determined. The following facts will help you to do this.

1. $\sum_{i=1}^{n} p = np$, p a constant

2. $\sum_{i=1}^{n} pi = p \sum_{i=1}^{n} i$

3. $\sum_{i=1}^{n} i = 1 + 2 + 3 + \cdots + n = \dfrac{n(n+1)}{2}$

4. $\sum_{i=1}^{n} i^2 = 1^2 + 2^2 + \cdots + n^2 = \dfrac{n(n+1)(2n+1)}{6}$

5. $\sum_{i=1}^{n} i^3 = 1^3 + 2^3 + \cdots + n^3 = \dfrac{n^2(n+1)^2}{4}$

CLASSROOM EXERCISES

▬ Calculate the exact area of the regions in Exercises 1–3.
1. The region bounded by $y = 2x + 1$, the x axis, $a = 0$ and $b = 2$.
2. The region bounded by $y = x^3$, $a = 0$, $b = 4$ and the x axis.
3. The region bounded by $y = x^2$, $a = 1$, $b = 4$ and the x axis.
4. The region bounded by $y = 2x^2$, $a = 2$, $b = 5$ and the x axis.

WRITTEN EXERCISES

A ▬ Use the formulas found in Example 1 and Example 2 to calculate the exact areas for Exercises 1–16.

1. $y = 2x$, $a = 2$, $b = 5$
2. $y = 5x$, $a = 2$, $b = 5$
3. $y = 3x$, $a = 2$, $b = 5$
4. $y = \frac{1}{2}x$, $a = 1$, $b = 4$
5. $y = 0.1x$, $a = 5$, $b = 20$
6. $y = \frac{1}{100}x$, $a = 0$, $b = 100$
7. $y = x^2$, $a = 0$, $b = 3$
8. $y = x^2$, $a = 1$, $b = 7$
9. $y = x^2$, $a = 5$, $b = 6$
10. $y = x^2$, $a = 7$, $b = 8$
11. $y = x^2$, $a = -2$, $b = 4$
12. $y = x^2$, $a = -3$, $b = 3$

B 13. $y = -x$, $a = 2$, $b = 4$
14. $y = -2x$, $a = 3$, $b = 7$
15. $y = x$, $a = -2$, $b = 0$ (The answer is negative. Can you explain why?)
16. $y = 4x$, $a = -2$, $b = 0$ and $a = 0$, $b = 4$. What would the area from $a = -2$ to $b = 4$ be?

▬ Use the definition of exact area to calculate the true area for Exercises 17–23. Assume $f(x) \geq 0$ for all x in $[a, b]$.
17. $f(x) = px^2$, $x = a$, $x = b$, x axis
18. $f(x) = p$, $x = a$, $x = b$, x axis
19. $f(x) = x^3$, $x = a$, $x = b$, x axis
20. $f(x) = px^3$, $x = a$, $x = b$, x axis

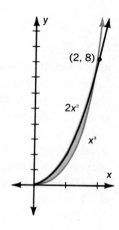

C 21. $f(x) = x^2 + 1$, $x = a$, $y = b$, x axis
22. $f(x) = x^2 + x + 1$, $x = a$, $x = b$, x axis
23. $f(x) = x^3 + 3$, $x = a$, $x = b$, x axis

24. By any means you wish find the area of the region bounded by $f(x) = x^3$ and $g(x) = 2x^2$. (*Hint:* You can use subtraction if you are clever.)

13-8   The Definite Integral

The definition of area as stated in the previous section made use of sums which had two essential characteristics:

1. The number of terms was increasing, and
2. The size of each term was decreasing.

Thus the area of a region became the limit of the sum of an increasing number of addends of decreasing absolute value.

In studying other physical quantities such as work done by a variable force, volumes, fluid pressure, and arc length, the same sort of sums and their limits occur. Mathematicians, transcending physical interpretations, have *defined* the definite integral as the limit of a sum of an increasing number of addends of decreasing absolute value.

Definition   Let $f(x)$ be a function whose domain contains the closed interval $[a, b]$. The **definite integral** of $f(x)$ from $x = a$ to $x = b$, denoted $\int_a^b f(x)\,dx$, is defined by the equation

$$\int_a^b f(x)\,dx = \lim_{n \to \infty} \left(\sum_{i=1}^{n} f(x_i)\,\Delta x \right) \qquad\qquad 1$$

where $a = x_0, x_1, \cdots, x_{n-1}, x_n = b$ effect the partitioning of $[a, b]$ into n equal intervals of length $\Delta x = \dfrac{b - a}{n}$, and $f(x_i)$ is the ordinate of an arbitrary point x_i in $[x_{j-1}, x_j]$.

The definite integral exists when the limit in 1 is a finite number. In $\int_a^b f(x)\,dx$ a is called the **lower bound of integration,** b is called the **upper bound of integration** and $f(x)$ is called the **integrand.** The terms lower bound and upper bound as used here are not to be confused with the upper and lower bounds of a function as those terms have been used in earlier chapters.

It can be shown that the partitioning points, x_j, $j = 0, 1, \ldots, n$ need not be equally spaced as long as the longest interval nears zero as n increases without bound. The definite integral defined here is called the **Riemann integral.** There are also other types of integrals such as the **Lebesgue** and the **Stieljes integrals.**

From the definition of the definite integral when the addends in the defining sum are interpreted as areas of rectangles you have

$$A_a^b(f(x)) = \int_a^b f(x)\, dx, \ f(x) \geq 0, \ x \in [a, b].$$

In a later section another application of the definite integral will be discussed. At this moment the first task is to get some means of evaluating definite integrals so that you need not evaluate the limit of the sum as you did to find the area bounded by curves. The theorems stated below will not be proved here, but reference to the definition should make them seem reasonable.

Since $\lim\limits_{n \to \infty} \sum\limits_{i=1}^{n} pf(x_i)\Delta x = p \lim\limits_{n \to \infty} \sum\limits_{i=1}^{n} f(x_i)\Delta x$, p a constant, the following theorem seems reasonable.

> **Theorem 13–4** $\quad \int_a^b pf(x)\, dx = p \int_a^b f(x)\, dx \qquad p$ a constant

In other words, the integral of a constant times a function is equal to the constant times the integral of the function.

You also know that $\lim\limits_{n \to \infty} \sum\limits_{i=1}^{n} [f_1(x_i) + f_2(x_i)]\Delta x = \lim\limits_{n \to \infty} \sum\limits_{i=1}^{n} f_1(x_i)\Delta x +$ $\lim\limits_{n \to \infty} \sum\limits_{i=1}^{n} f_2(x_i)\Delta x$. The same results are true for any finite number of addends $f_j(x_i)\Delta x$. Thus the next theorem is reasonable.

> **Theorem 13–5** $\quad \int_a^b [f_1(x) + f_2(x) + \cdots + f_n(x)]\, dx$
>
> $$= \int_a^b f_1(x)\, dx + \cdots + \int_a^b f_n(x)\, dx$$

That is, the integral of the sum of functions is the sum of the integrals of the functions.

In Section 13–7 you found

in Example 1 $\qquad\qquad A_a^b(mx) = \dfrac{m}{2}(b^2 - a^2)$

in Example 2

$$A_a^b(x^2) = \tfrac{1}{3}(b^3 - a^3),$$

and in Exercise 18

$$A_a^b(p) = \left| \frac{p}{1}(b - a) \right|$$

Each of these definite integrals interpreted as an area is a specific instance of the next theorem. Do you see the pattern?

$$\boxed{\textbf{Theorem 13–6} \quad \int_a^b x^m \, dx = \frac{1}{m+1}(b^{m+1} - a^{m+1}), \ m \in W}$$

Theorems 13–4, 13–5, and 13–6 are sufficient to find the definite integral of any polynomial function.

EXAMPLE 1. Evaluate $\int_1^3 (2x + 3) \, dx$. Cite a reason for each step.

Solution:
$$\int_1^3 (2x + 3) \, dx = \int_1^3 2x \, dx + \int_1^3 3 \, dx \qquad \longleftarrow \quad \textbf{By Th. 13–5}$$
$$= 2\int_1^3 x \, dx + 3\int_1^3 dx \qquad \longleftarrow \quad \textbf{By Th. 13–4}$$
$$= \tfrac{2}{2}(3^2 - 1^2) + 3(3 - 1) \qquad \longleftarrow \quad \textbf{By Th. 13–6}$$
$$= 8 + 6$$
$$= 14$$

EXAMPLE 2. Evaluate $\int_{-1}^1 (5x^3 + x) \, dx$.

Solution:
$$\int_{-1}^1 (5x^3 + x) \, dx = \int_{-1}^1 5x^3 \, dx + \int_{-1}^1 x \, dx$$
$$= 5\int_{-1}^1 x^3 \, dx + \int_{-1}^1 x \, dx$$
$$= \tfrac{5}{4}((1)^4 - (-1)^4) + \tfrac{1}{2}(1^2 - (-1)^2)$$
$$= \tfrac{5}{4}(0) + \tfrac{1}{2}(0) = 0$$

(Can you explain geometrically why the answer is 0?)

EXAMPLE 3. Show that $\int_{-2}^1 x^2 \, dx + \int_1^2 x^2 \, dx = \int_{-2}^2 x^2 \, dx$.

Solution:
$$\int_{-2}^1 x^2 \, dx = \tfrac{1}{3}[1^3 - (-2)^3] = \tfrac{1}{3} \cdot 9 = 3$$

$$\int_1^2 x^2 \, dx = \tfrac{1}{3}[2^3 - 1^3] = \tfrac{1}{3} \cdot 7 = 2\tfrac{1}{3}$$

$$\int_{-2}^2 x^2 \, dx = \tfrac{1}{3}[2^3 - (-2)^3] = \tfrac{1}{3} \cdot 16 = 5\tfrac{1}{3}$$

Since
$$3 + 2\tfrac{1}{3} = 5\tfrac{1}{3},$$

you have shown that
$$\int_{-2}^1 x^2 \, dx + \int_1^2 x^2 \, dx = \int_{-2}^2 x^2 \, dx.$$

CLASSROOM EXERCISES

━━━ Evaluate the definite integral for Exercises 1–4.

1. $\int_0^2 x^2\, dx$

2. $\int_1^5 (x + 3)\, dx$

3. $\int_{-1}^0 x^{101}\, dx$

4. $\int_1^3 x^3\, dx$

5. $\int_2^4 (x - 2)\, dx$

6. $\int_3^1 (x^2 - 2x)\, dx$

7. How are the definite integral and the true area of a region related?

8. If $\int_a^b f(x)\, dx = 0$, $(a < b)$, interpret this geometrically. How could integrals be used to find the true area of the region bounded by $x = a$, $x = b$, the x axis, and $f(x)$? (Ignore the case where $f(x) = 0\ \forall x$.)

WRITTEN EXERCISES

A ━━━ Evaluate the definite integral for Exercises 1–12.

1. $\int_0^3 3x^2\, dx$

2. $\int_{-1}^4 2x^3\, dx$

3. $\int_1^2 -\tfrac{1}{2}x^2\, dx$

4. $\int_{-2}^2 (x^2 - 1)\, dx$

5. $\int_{-2}^2 (x^2 - 3x + 2)\, dx$

6. $\int_0^1 25x^{49}\, dx$

7. $\int_2^4 (x - 2)^2\, dx$

8. $\int_{-3}^0 5(x^4 + x^2)\, dx$

9. $\int_4^9 5\, dx$

10. $\int_{-1}^1 (x^7 - x^3)\, dx$

11. $\int_0^1 (x^6 - x^2)\, dx$

12. $\int_{-4}^2 (x - 3)\, dx$

B ━━━ Compare the values of each pair of definite integrals, for Exercises 13–18.

13. $\int_1^2 x\, dx,\ \int_2^1 x\, dx$

14. $\int_0^3 2x^2\, dx,\ \int_3^0 2x^2\, dx$

15. $\int_{-1}^3 x^4\, dx,\ \int_3^{-1} x^4\, dx$

16. $\int_{-2}^{-3} 2x\, dx,\ \int_{-3}^{-2} 2x\, dx$

17. $\int_{-2}^0 x^3\, dx,\ \int_0^{-2} x^3\, dx$

18. $\int_a^b (x^2 + x)\, dx,\ \int_b^a (x^2 + x)\, dx$

19. What relationship did you find between the pairs of integrals in Exercises 13–18. State your generalization and test it for other examples.

Compare the sum of the first two integrals with the value of the third for Exercises 20–23.

20. $\int_{-2}^{0} x\,dx,\ \int_{0}^{3} x\,dx,\ \int_{-2}^{3} x\,dx$

21. $\int_{1}^{2} 2x^2\,dx,\ \int_{2}^{5} 2x^2\,dx,\ \int_{1}^{5} 2x^2\,dx$

22. $\int_{-3}^{-2} (x^2-1)\,dx,\ \int_{-2}^{0} (x^2-1)\,dx,\ \int_{-3}^{0} (x^2-1)\,dx$

23. $\int_{a}^{c} 3x^2\,dx,\ \int_{c}^{b} 3x^2\,dx,\ \int_{a}^{b} 3x^2\,dx\quad a < c < b$

24. What pattern did you observe in Exercises 20–23? State your generalization and test your generalization on other examples.

C ━━ Let $G(x) = 2x^3 - x + 2$, for Exercises 25–27.

25. Find $G'(x)$.

26. Find $\int_{a}^{b} G'(x)\,dx$.

27. Find $G(b) - G(a)$.

28. Compare the results of Exercises 26 and 27.

━━ The generalization implied in Exercises 28 is: If $G'(x) = f(x)$, then $\int_{a}^{b} f(x)\,dx = G(b) - G(a)$. Test this generalization for Exercises 29–34. (This generalization is true. It is called the **Fundamental Theorem of Calculus.**)

29. $G(x) = x$

30. $G(x) = x^2$

31. $G(x) = x^3$

32. $G(x) = 2x^2$

33. $G(x) = x^2 - 1$

34. $G(x) = x^m$

13–9 Areas by Integration

You have already seen that the definition of the definite integral and the definition of the area of the region bounded by $f(x) \geq 0$, $x = a$, $x = b$, $(a < b)$ and x axis are the same.

$$A_a^b f(x) = \int_{a}^{b} f(x)\,dx \qquad f(x) \geq 0 \qquad x \in [a, b]$$

Determining areas of plane regions bounded by curves was one of the initial applications of integration. (Attempts to find areas led to the definition of the integral.) In the physical sciences specification of such areas remains an important application.

The next three examples illustrate the definite integral used to determine areas of regions. Study these examples thoroughly.

EXAMPLE 1. Area between Two Curves. Find the area of the region bounded by the parabola

$$f(x) = 2 - x^2$$

and the line $g(x) = -x$

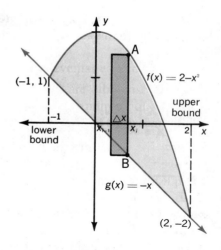

Solution:

The first step in the solution is to sketch a graph of the region. Notice that the curves intersect at the points $(-1, 1)$ and $(2, -2)$. Thus the lower bound of integration is -1, while the upper bound of integration is 2.

    The region under consideration can be approximately covered by rectangular regions like the one shown in the diagram. Each such rectangular region has *width*

$$\Delta x = \frac{2 - (-1)}{n} = \frac{3}{n}. \qquad\qquad 1$$

The height of the rectangular region is the length of the segment AB. This length is found by *subtracting the y-coordinate of B from that of A.* (Why?) But the y-coordinate of A for $x = x_i$ is $f(x_i) = 2 - x_i^2$ and the y-coordinate of B is $g(x_i) = -x_i$. Thus the length of AB is

$$f(x_i) - g(x_i) = 2 - x_i^2 - (-x_i). \qquad\qquad 2$$

    Multiplying 1 and 2 you get the area of the rectangular region

$$[f(x_i) - g(x_i)]\,\Delta x = [2 - x_i^2 + x_i]\,\Delta x. \qquad\qquad 3$$

The sum of all such terms (for x_i, $i = 1, \ldots, n$)

$$\sum_{i=1}^{n} [f(x_i) - g(x_i)]\,\Delta x = \sum_{i=1}^{n} [2 - x_i^2 + x_i]\,\Delta x \qquad\qquad 4$$

is the approximate area. The exact area is found by taking the limit of 4 as n increases without bound. But this is the definite integral

$$\int_{-1}^{2} [f(x) - g(x)]\,dx = \int_{-1}^{2} (2 - x^2 + x)\,dx. \qquad\qquad 5$$

$$\text{Area} = \int_{-1}^{2} (2 - x^2 + x)\,dx$$

$$= \left[2 \cdot 2 - \frac{(2^3)}{3} + \frac{(2)^2}{2}\right] - \left[2(-1) - \frac{(-1)^3}{3} + \frac{(-1)^2}{2}\right] = 4\tfrac{1}{2}$$

EXAMPLE 2. Area by Two Integrals. Find the area of the region bounded by the lines

$$y = 2x - 8$$
$$y = -\tfrac{2}{7}x + \tfrac{24}{7}$$
$$y = -\tfrac{6}{5}x + \tfrac{8}{5}$$

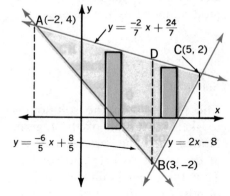

Solution:

Solving the equations in pairs you see that the vertices of the triangle they form are $(3, -2)$, $(5, 2)$ and $(-2, 4)$. The area can be found by using the procedures of Example 1, but *not in one step*. By considering the figure you can see that every rectangle with sides parallel to the y axis used to approximate the area has one vertex on the line $y = -\tfrac{2}{7}x + \tfrac{24}{7}$. However at the other end, some rectangles have a vertex on $y = -\tfrac{6}{5}x + \tfrac{8}{5}$ and others on $y = 2x - 8$. Thus the area of $\triangle ABC$ cannot be found in one step; it must be calculated using two steps. Since area of $\triangle ABD +$ area of $\triangle BCD =$ area of $\triangle ABC$, you must find 1. the area of $\triangle ABD$, 2. the area of $\triangle BCD$.

$$\text{Area of } \triangle ABD = \int_{-2}^{3}\left[\left(-\frac{2x}{7} + \frac{24}{7}\right) - \left(-\frac{6}{5}x + \frac{8}{5}\right)\right]dx$$

$$= \int_{-2}^{3} \tfrac{1}{35}(32x + 64)\,dx$$

$$= \tfrac{32}{35}\int_{-2}^{3}(x + 2)\,dx$$

$$= \tfrac{32}{35}(\tfrac{25}{2}) = \tfrac{80}{7} = 11\tfrac{3}{7}$$

$$\text{Area of } \triangle BCD = \int_{3}^{5}[(-\tfrac{2}{7}x + \tfrac{24}{7}) - (2x - 8)]\,dx$$

$$= \int_{3}^{5} \tfrac{16}{7}(-x + 5)\,dx$$

$$= \tfrac{16}{7}(2)$$

$$= 4\tfrac{4}{7}$$

Area of $\triangle ABC =$ Area $\triangle ABD +$ Area $\triangle BCD$
So Area of $\triangle ABC = 11\tfrac{3}{7} + 4\tfrac{4}{7} = 16$

EXAMPLE 3. Area of Region Below The x Axis. Find the area of the region bounded by the x axis and

$$f(x) = x^2 + x - 6.$$

The zeros of $f(x) = x^2 + x - 6$ are $(-3, 0)$ and $(2, 0)$. Thus the region is the shaded portion in the figure below. A typical rectangular region is shown. Since the x axis has equation $y = 0$, the desired area can be considered as the area of a region between the two following curves.

$$y = 0 \quad \text{and} \quad f(x) = x^2 + x - 6.$$

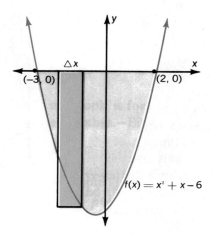

Thus the height of a typical rectangle is

$$0 - (x^2 + x - 6). \hspace{2cm} 6$$

The width of a typical rectangle is Δx and therefore the area is equal to the following integral.

$$\int_{-3}^{2} [0 - (x^2 + x - 6)]\, dx$$

or

$$\int_{-3}^{2} (-x^2 - x + 6)\, dx$$

$$= \left(-\frac{(2)^3}{3} - \frac{(2)^2}{2}\right) + 6(2) - \left[\left(-\frac{(-3)^3}{3} - \frac{(-3)^2}{2}\right) + 6(-3)\right]$$

$$= -\tfrac{8}{3} - 2 + 12 - 9 + \tfrac{9}{2} + 18$$

$$= 19 + 4\tfrac{1}{2} - 2\tfrac{2}{3} = 20\tfrac{5}{6}$$

EXAMPLE 4. Area of Region Symmetric to x axis. Find the area of the region bounded by the x axis, $f(x) = x^3$, $a = -3$ and $b = +3$.

Sketching the curve you can see that part of the region falls below the x axis and part above. A typical rectangular region is shown. The height of a typical rectangle is x^3. The width of a typical rectangle is Δx and therefore

$$A^3_{-3}(x^3) = \int_{-3}^{3} x^3\, dx = 0.$$

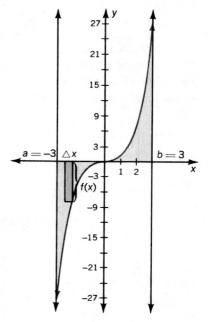

This is clearly incorrect. For this problem there are two ways of finding the true area.

Since the part of the region below the x axis gives a negative value for the area and the part of the region above the x axis gives a positive value for the area, then the area is the following.

$$A^3_{-3}(x^3) = \left| \int_{-3}^{0} x^3\, dx \right| + \int_{0}^{3} x^3\, dx$$

$$= \left| -\tfrac{81}{4} \right| + \tfrac{81}{4} = \tfrac{81}{2}$$

Another way of approaching the problem is to realize that the region below the x axis is symmetric to the region above the x axis and therefore

$$A^3_{-3}(x^3) = 2\int_{0}^{3} x^3\, dx \qquad \text{or} \qquad 2\left| \int_{-3}^{0} x^3\, dx \right|$$

$$= 2(\tfrac{81}{4}) = \tfrac{81}{2}$$

The key idea illustrated in Examples 1–3 is that the area of a region bounded by two or more curves can be found by integration. The integrand is $(g(x) - f(x))$ when $g(x) > f(x)$ for all x in the interval of integration. The bounds of integration are usually found by determining the points of intersection of the curves. In some cases it may be necessary to use more than one integral. The idea illustrated in Example 4 is that if $f(x)$ or $(g(x) - f(x))$ crosses the x axis in $[a, b]$ then more than one integral may be necessary.

CLASSROOM EXERCISES

━━ Using the definite integral, find the area of the given regions in Exercises 1–3.

1. The region bounded by $y = x^2$, $x = 0$, $x = 4$ and the x axis.

2. The region bounded by the curves $y = x^2$, and $y = x$.

3. The region bounded by the curves x^3, $x = 0$ and $x = 4$ and the x axis.

WRITTEN EXERCISES

A ━━ Find the area of the region bounded by the given curves. Sketch each region.

1. x axis and $y = 2x - x^2$

2. $y = x^2$, $y = 0$, $x = 2$, $x = 4$

3. $y = x^2 - 9$, $y = 0$, $x = 1$, $x = 4$

4. $y = 6x - x^2$, $y = 0$

5. $y = 2x - x^2$, $y = -3$

6. $y = x^2$, $y = x$

7. $y = x^4 - 2x^2$, $y = 2x^2$

8. $y = 9 - x^2$, $y = x + 7$

9. $y = x^3 - x^2 - 2x$, $y = 0$

10. $y = x^3 - 6x^2 + 9x$, $y = x$

11. $y = x^3 - x$, $y = 3x$

12. $y = x^3 - 3x$, $y = x$

B **13.** Interpret $\int_0^1 x^n \, dx$ ($n \in W$) as the area of a region.

14. How is the area of Exercise 13 related to the unit square?

15. What happens to the number $\int_0^1 x^n \, dx$ as n increases?

16. Find the area of the region bounded by $y = x^2$, $y = 0$, $x = 0$, and $x = 2$.

17. Find the area of the region bounded by $y = x^2 + x$, $y = x$, $x = 0$, and $x = 2$.

18. Are the areas in Exercises 16 and 17 the same?

19. Are the regions in Exercises 16 and 17 the same?

20. $\int_1^3 (x^2 - x) \, dx$ can be interpreted as the area of many different regions. Draw two such regions.

BASIC: AREA UNDER A CURVE

Problem:

Given the lower and upper bounds and the number of intervals, write a program which computes and prints the rectangular region approximation for the function $f(x) = x^2 - 1$.

```
100 PRINT
110 PRINT "THIS PROGRAM GIVES THE DEFINITE "
120 PRINT "INTEGRAL OF F(X) BETWEEN A AND B."
130 PRINT
140 PRINT "ENTER YOUR FUNCTION AS LINE 170 AND"
150 PRINT "TYPE 'RUN 170'."
160 STOP
170 DEF FN F(X) = X*X - 1
180 PRINT "WHAT IS THE LEFT ENDPOINT OF THE"
190 PRINT "INTERVAL";
200 INPUT A
210 PRINT "RIGHT ENDPOINT";
220 INPUT B
230 IF B > A THEN 260
240 GOSUB 450
250 GOTO 210
260 PRINT "HOW MANY SUBDIVISIONS (> 0)";
270 INPUT N
280 IF N > 0 THEN 310
290 GOSUB 450
300 GOTO 260
310 REM   AREA CALCULATION BEGINS AT LINE 320.
320 LET D = (B - A)/N
330 LET X = A
340 LET S = 0
350 FOR I = 0 TO N
360   LET Y = FN F(X) * D
370   LET S = S + Y
380   LET X = X + D
390 NEXT I
400 PRINT
410 PRINT "THE INTEGRAL FROM ";A;"TO";B;"FOR"
420 PRINT N;" SUBDIVISIONS IS ";S
430 PRINT
440 STOP
```

```
450 REM    ILLEGAL INPUT ERROR ROUTINE
460 PRINT
470 PRINT "LAST ENTRY ILLEGAL.   PLEASE  REENTER."
480 PRINT
490 RETURN
500 END
```

Output:

```
>RUN 170
WHAT IS THE LEFT ENDPOINT OF THE
INTERVAL? 3
RIGHT ENDPOINT? 5
HOW MANY SUBDIVISIONS (> 0)? 100

THE INTEGRAL FROM  3 TO 5 FOR
 100   SUBDIVISIONS IS   30.9868
```
$\longleftarrow \int_3^5 (x^2 - 1)\,dx = 30\tfrac{2}{3}$

Analysis:

Statements 320–390: This is the core of the program. In statement 320, the width of the rectangles (D) is set at $\frac{B - A}{N}$ and X is set at A. In statement 360, Y, the area of the rectangle, is calculated. The variable S stores the sum of the areas of the rectangles. In statement 380, D is added to X to produce the new value of X for the next execution of the loop.

EXERCISES

A   Use the program on page 704 to approximate the value of each integral. Use $n = 100$.

1. $\int_{-3}^{2} (x^2 - 2x + 1)\,dx$ **2.** $\int_{0}^{3} (x^3 - 1)\,dx$ **3.** $\int_{-1}^{2} (2x^2 - 3x)\,dx$

B   Revise the program on page 704 in the manner indicated.

4. Use the right endpoint of each rectangle as the value at which the function is evaluated.

5. Use the midpoint of each interval as the value at which the function is evaluated.

6. Allow the user to choose the point at which the function is evaluated in each interval: left endpoint, right endpoint, or midpoint.

C   Write a BASIC program.

7. Use the trapezoidal approximation formula to calculate the area bounded by $y = f(x)$, $x = a$, $x = b$, and the x axis.

13–10   Volumes by Integration

You have seen that the area of a plane region with curves for boundaries can be found by evaluating a definite integral. In the same manner the volume (a number) of a space region with *surfaces* for boundaries can be found by integration.

The space regions (solids) for which it is easiest to calculate volumes are those bounded by *surfaces of revolution*. These regions are the only ones discussed here.

The procedures for calculating the volume of a space region are similar to those used in area; that is, the space region is approximated by regions for which a means of calculating the volume is known. Then these volumes are added, and the limit is taken.

For solids of revolution a convenient space region which may be used to approximate the solid is the *circular cylinder*. Since a plane perpendicular to the axis of rotation intersects a solid of revolution in a *circular disc*, that solid and its volume may be approximated by a "stack of thin circular cylinders."

The procedures used are illustrated in the next examples.

EXAMPLE 1.   Consider the solid of revolution formed by rotating the line $y = \frac{1}{2}x + 1$ about the x axis. Find the volume of the portion of the solid between $x = 0$ and $x = 4$.

Solution:

The solid of revolution is shown in the figure on page 707. Now partition the interval $[0, 4]$ into n intervals, each of length

$$\Delta x = \frac{4 - 0}{n},$$

with the points $x_0 = 0$, x_1, x_2, x_3, . . . , $x_n = 4$. Imagine planes perpendicular to the x axis at each point x_i, $i = 0, 1, 2, \ldots, n$. They intersect the solid in circular discs. Then think of the stack of cylinders, each having as its base the circular disc at x_i, $i = 1, 2, \ldots, n$ respectively and having height Δx. The solid is approximated by the stack of cylinders, and the volume is approximated by the sum of the volumes of these cylinders.

The volume of a circular cylinder with height $= h$ and the radius of the base $= r$, is

$$V = \pi r^2 h.$$

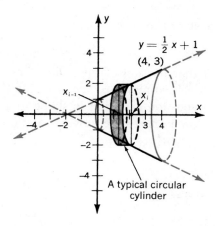

For each cylinder above, $h = \Delta x$, and the radius of the base is the distance from the x axis at $x = x_i$ to the line $y = \frac{1}{2}x + 1$, so

$$r_i = y_i = \tfrac{1}{2}x_i + 1 \text{ for each } i = 1, 2, \ldots, n.$$

Thus the volume of one circular cylinder is

$$V_i = \pi(y_i)^2 \, \Delta x = \pi(\tfrac{1}{2}x_i + 1)^2 \, \Delta x.$$

The volume of *all* the circular cylinders is

$$\sum_{i=1}^{n} V_i = \sum_{i=1}^{n} \pi(\tfrac{1}{2}x_i + 1)^2 \, \Delta x.$$

Therefore the volume of the solid is by definition

$$V = \lim_{n \to \infty} \sum_{i=1}^{n} V_i = \lim_{n \to \infty} \sum_{i=1}^{n} \pi(\tfrac{1}{2}x_i + 1)^2 \, \Delta x.$$

The last limit is the type that defines a definite integral. Thus the volume V of the solid is given by the equation

$$V = \int_0^4 \pi(\tfrac{1}{2}x + 1)^2 \, dx. \qquad\qquad 1$$

$$= 17\tfrac{1}{3}\,\pi \text{ cubic units.}$$

Equation 1 for the volume of a solid of revolution with the x axis as the axis of rotation can be easily generalized to

$$V = \pi \int_a^b y^2 \, dx = \pi \int_a^b [f(x)]^2 \, dx. \qquad\qquad 2$$

The factor "$\pi[f(x)]^2$" is the area of the base and "dx" is the height of the circular cylinder.

The same procedures may be used when a plane curve is rotated about the y axis.

EXAMPLE 2. Consider the curve

$$y = \sqrt{x}.$$

Find the volume of that portion of the solid of revolution formed by rotating the region bounded by $y = \sqrt{x}$, $y = 2$, and the y axis about the y axis. The solid in question is similar in shape to a trumpet. (See the figure at the left below.) Since the axis of rotation is the y axis, the interval $[0, 2]$ on the y axis is partitioned—each interval is $\dfrac{2 - 0}{n} = \Delta y$.

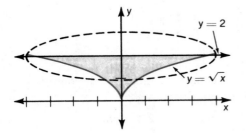
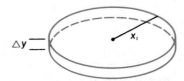

A typical circular cylinder

The radius of a typical cylinder is the distance from the y axis to the curve (see the figure at the right above)—that is, the radius is x_i. Thus, the volume of a circular cylinder is $V_i = \pi x_i^2 \Delta y$. Since $y_i = \sqrt{x_i}$, $y_i^4 = x_i^2$ and thus

$$V_i = \pi y_i^4 \, \Delta y.$$

Thus the integral

$$\pi \int_0^2 y^4 \, dy = V$$

gives the volume. Thus, $V = \frac{32}{5} \pi$ cubic units.

EXAMPLE 3. Find the volume of the solid formed by rotating the region in the first quadrant bounded by y axis, $y = 4$ and $y = x^2$ about the x axis.

The solid is shown in the diagram. Since the axis of rotation is the x axis, the interval $[0, 2]$ on the x axis is partitioned into n intervals of length

$$\frac{2 - 0}{n} = \Delta x.$$

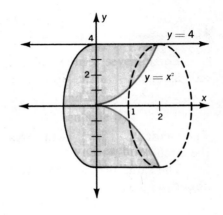

A typical "slice" of the solid is no longer a circular cylinder. It resembles more a metal washer. Such a "washer" is sketched at the right. Its thickness is Δx. The area of its base is $\pi(r_2{}^2 - r_1{}^2)$ because it is the difference of the areas of the two circular regions.

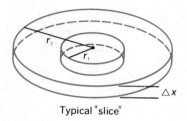

Typical "slice"

For the solid under discussion r_2 is the distance from the x axis to the line $y = 4$. Thus

$$r_2 = 4$$

r_1 is the distance from the x axis to the curve $y = x^2$. Thus

$$r_1 = y_i = x_i{}^2$$

Thus the volume of a typical slice of the solid is

$$V_i = \pi(r_2{}^2 - r_1{}^2)\,\Delta x = \pi(4^2 - (y_i)^2)\,\Delta x$$
$$= \pi(4^2 - x_i{}^4)\,\Delta x$$

The volume then is the value of the definite integral

$$V = \pi \int_0^2 (4^2 - x^4)\,dx.$$

It is easy to find V. $V = 32 \cdot \frac{4}{5}\pi = \frac{128}{5}\pi.$

CLASSROOM EXERCISES

━━ For Exercises 1–3, find the volume of the solid generated by rotating the given region about the x axis.

1. $y = x$, $x = 0$ and $x = 4$

2. $y = x^3$, $x = 0$ and $x = 2$

3. $y^2 = x - 9$, $y \geq 0$ and $x = 12$

WRITTEN EXERCISES

A ━━ For Exercises 1–10 find the volume of the solid generated by rotating the given region about the x axis.

1. $y = 2x + 1$, x axis, y axis, $x = 3$

2. $y = 2x + 1$, $y = 7$, y axis

3. $y = x^2 + 1$, x axis, y axis, $x = 2$

4. $y = x^2 + 1$, y axis, $y = 5$

5. $y = x - x^2$, x axis

6. $y = 3x - x^2$, x axis

7. $y = 5x - x^2$, $y = x$

8. $y = x^3$, x axis, $x = 2$

9. $y = x^3$, y axis, $y = 8$

10. $y = x$, $y = 2$, y axis

B **11.** Find the volume of the solid generated by rotating the region bounded by $y = x^2$, $y = 2$ and y axis about the y axis. (The height is Δy.)

12. Find the volume of the solid generated by rotating the region bounded by $y = x^2$ and $y = x$ about the x axis.

13. Repeat Exercise 12 with the y axis as the axis of rotation.

14. Find the volume of the solid generated by rotating the region bounded by $y = x^2$ and $y = x^3$ about the x axis.

C ▬▬ Find the volume of the solid generated by rotating the region bounded by the y axis, $y = 4$ and $y = x^2$ about the given axis.

15. the y axis

16. the x axis

17. the line $y = 4$

18. the line $x = 2$

19. the line $x = 4$

20. the line $y = 6$

21. Find the volume of the ellipsoid generated by rotating the region bounded by the x axis and $y = \frac{b}{a}\sqrt{a^2 - x^2}$ about the x axis.

22. Find the volume of the sphere of radius r generated by rotating the region bounded by the x axis and $y = \sqrt{r^2 - x^2}$ about the x axis.

CHAPTER SUMMARY ▬▬▬▬▬▬▬▬

Important Terms

Acceleration function $a(t)$ (p. 677)

Average acceleration (p. 677)

Average velocity (p. 675)

Derivative of $f(x)$ (p. 688)

Differentiable (p. 668)

Differentiation (p. 668)

Instantaneous acceleration (p. 677)

Instantaneous velocity (p. 676)

Integrand (p. 694)

Lower bound of integration (p. 694)

Position function (p. 675)

Riemann integral (p. 694)

Upper bound of integration (p. 694)

Important Ideas

1. If $f(x) = r(x) \cdot s(x)$, then $f'(x) = r(x)s'(x) + r'(x)s(x)$.

2. If $f(x) = \dfrac{r(x)}{s(x)}$, then $f'(x) = \dfrac{s(x)r'(x) - r(x)s'(x)}{s^2(x)}$.

3. If $f(x) = f(u(x))$, then $f'(x) = f'(u) \cdot u'(x)$.

4. $A_a^b f(x) = \lim\limits_{n \to \infty} \left(\sum\limits_{i=1}^{n} f(x_i \Delta x) \right)$ 5. $\displaystyle\int_a^b f(x)\,dx = \lim\limits_{n \to \infty} \left(\sum\limits_{i=1}^{n} f(x_i \Delta x) \right)$

6. $\displaystyle\int_a^b x^m\,dx = \dfrac{1}{m+1}(b^{m+1} - a^{m+1})$

CHAPTER OBJECTIVES AND REVIEW

Objective: *To calculate derivatives of polynomial, exponential, and logarithmic functions and their products.* (Section 13-1)

━━ In Exercises 1–6 calculate the derivative for each function.

1. $f(x) = x^3$
2. $f(x) = 5e^x$
3. $f(x) = \ln x^2$
4. $f(x) = 3x^4 - 2x^3 + 3$
5. $f(x) = 7x^{-5} \cdot e^x$
6. $f(x) = (x^2 + 1)(x^3 - 3x)$

Objective: *To calculate derivatives of quotients of differentiable functions.* (Section 13-2)

━━ Calculate each derivative.

7. $f(x) = \dfrac{x^2}{x-3}$
8. $f(x) = \dfrac{x-3}{x^4}$
9. $f(x) = \dfrac{e^x}{x}$
10. $f(x) = \dfrac{2\ln x}{x+2}$

Objective: *To calculate derivatives of composite functions by using the Chain Rule.* (Section 13-3)

━━ Calculate each derivative.

11. $f(x) = (x^2 + 1)^4$
12. $f(x) = e^{3x^2 - 1}$
13. $f(x) = (x^2 - 2)^{\frac{3}{2}}$
14. $f(x) = \ln(x^2 - 3x + 1)$

Objective: *To define and calculate average and instantaneous rates of change for position functions describing rectilinear motion.* (Section 13-4)

15. In your own words define the average velocity of a particle from t_1 to t_2 whose motion is given by $R(t)$. Define the instantaneous velocity of the particle at $t = 4$.

16. Let $R(t) = 7t^2 - 5t + 3$ be a position function describing rectilinear motion of a particle.

    a. Find the average velocity of the particle from $t = 1$ to $t = 3$.

    b. Find the instantaneous velocity of the particle at $t = 3$.

17. Let $S(t) = 12t^2 - 6t$ be a position function for a particle.

    a. Find $v(t)$.

    b. Find $a(t)$.

    c. What is the velocity at $t = 3$?

    d. What is the acceleration at $t = 3$?

    e. What is the velocity at $t = 0$?

    f. What is the acceleration at $t = 0$?

18. A bullet is shot straight upward with an initial velocity of 1280 feet per second. The bullet's height after t seconds is given by $S(t) = 1280t - 16t^2$.

    a. What is the velocity function?

    b. What is the velocity when $t = 20, 40, 60$?

    c. What is the acceleration function?

    d. At what time t does the bullet hit the ground?

    e. What is the velocity of the bullet when it hits the ground?

Objective: *To use rectangular regions to calculate an approximate value for the area of a region bounded by a plane curve, the x and y axes, and a vertical line.* (Section 13-5)

■■■ Let a region be bounded by the following curves: $y = \frac{2}{3}x$, $x = 0$, $x = 3$, and the x axis. Find an approximation to the area of the region using n rectangles for the given values of n.

19. $n = 2$ **20.** $n = 4$ **21.** $n = 16$

22. Let a region be bounded by the following curves: $y = 4x^2$, $x = 0$, $x = 3$, and the x axis. Find an approximation of the area of the region using 16 rectangles.

Objective: *To use trapezoidal regions to calculate an approximate value for the area of a region bounded by a plane curve, the x axis, and two vertical lines.* (Section 13-6)

■■■ Find the trapezoidal approximation for the areas of the regions in Exercises 23–24 using the given n. Round answers to two decimal places.

23. $f(x) = 3x^2$, $x = 0$, $x = 4$, x axis, $n = 4$

24. $f(x) = \sqrt{x}$, $x = 1$, $x = 7$, x axis, $n = 6$

Objective: *To use the formulas for calculating the exact area bounded by the curve* $y = mx$ *or* $y = x^2$, *the x axis, and the lines* $x = a$, $x = b$.
(Section 13-7)

━━ Calculate the exact areas bounded by the x axis and the indicated curves or lines.

25. $y = 4x$, $a = 1$, $b = 6$ **26.** $y = x^2$, $a = 2$, $b = 5$

Objective: *To evaluate the definite integral of a polynomial function.*
(Section 13-8)

━━ Evaluate the definite integrals.

27. $\int_1^2 5x^3 \, dx$ **28.** $\int_1^3 (x^4 - x^3) \, dx$

29. $\int_0^2 18x^{27} \, dx$ **30.** $\int_{-2}^2 (x^6 + 8x) \, dx$

31. $\int_{-2}^2 (x^5 + x) \, dx$ **32.** $\int_{-4}^3 (x + 2) \, dx$

33. $\int_6^{10} -3 \, dx$ **34.** $\int_{-3}^0 2(x^2 + x^8) \, dx$

Objective: *To use the definite integral to determine the area of a region bounded by plane curves.* (Section 13-9)

━━ In Exercises 35–39 use definite integrals to find the area of the region bounded by the given curves.

35. $f(x) = 3x^2$, $x = 3$, $x = 9$, x axis
36. $f(x) = x^4$, $g(x) = x^3$, y axis
37. $f(x) = x^4$, $g(x) = x^3$, $x = 2$, y axis
38. $y = -\frac{1}{2}x + \frac{1}{2}$, $y = \frac{2}{3}x + \frac{5}{3}$, $y = 3x - 3$
39. $y = x^2$, $y = 2$

Objective: *To use the definite integral to calculate volumes of surfaces of revolution.* (Section 13-10)

40. Find the volume of the solid generated by rotating about the x axis, the region bounded by $y = 3x + 1$, $x = 1$, $x = 3$, and the x axis.

41. Find the volume of the solid generated by rotating about the y axis, the region bounded by $y = x^2$, $y = 4$, and the y axis.

42. Find the volume of the solid generated by rotating about the x axis, the region bounded by $y = x^3$, $x = 2$, and the x axis.

CHAPTER TEST

1. Find $f'(x)$ if $f(x) = x^2 - 3x + e^x$.

2. Find $f'(x)$ if $f(x) = xe^x$.

3. Find $g'(x)$ if $g(x) = e^x \ln x$.

4. Find $f'(x)$ if $f(x) = (x^2 - 3x + 4)^4$.

5. Find $f'(x)$ if $f(x) = \dfrac{2x^3 - x}{x^2 + 1}$.

━━━ For Exercises 6–11 let $S(t) = 24t^2 - 6t^3$ be the position function for a rectilinearly moving particle, with $0 \leq t \leq 4$.

6. Find $v(t)$.

7. Find $a(t)$.

8. For what value of t is the particle not moving?

9. For what values of t is the acceleration positive?

10. How far from its starting point is the particle at $t = 1, 2, 3, 4$?

11. What is the average velocity of the particle from $t = 1$ to $t = 3$?

12. Calculate two approximations to the area of the region bounded by the curves $y = x^3$, $x = 2$ and the x axis for 16 subdivisions of $[0, 2]$. The first approximation should use rectangles; the second trapezoids.

13. Calculate the true area of the region in Exercise 12 by using a definite integral.

━━━ Evaluate each integral in Exercises 14–17.

14. $\displaystyle\int_{-1}^{2} x^3 \, dx$

15. $\displaystyle\int_{0}^{5} (3x^2 + 5x^4) \, dx$

16. $\displaystyle\int_{1}^{2} (x + 1)(2x - 3) \, dx$

17. $\displaystyle\int_{0}^{5} (mx + b) \, dx$

18. Find the volume of the surface of revolution obtained by rotating the region bounded by $y = \frac{2}{3}x^2 + 1$, y axis, x axis, and $x = 3$ about the x axis.

Choose the best answer. Choose **a, b, c,** or **d.**

1. The ellipse with major axis on the x-axis with length of 8 is

   a. $\frac{x^2}{8} + \frac{y^2}{4} = 1$ **b.** $\frac{x^2}{16} + \frac{y^2}{9} = 1$ **c.** $\frac{x^2}{16} + \frac{y^2}{25} = 1$ **d.** $\frac{x^2}{8} + \frac{y^2}{9} = 1$

2. Find the eccentricity of $25x^2 + 9y^2 = 225$.

   a. $\frac{4}{5}$ **b.** $\frac{5}{4}$ **c.** $\frac{3}{5}$ **d.** $\frac{5}{3}$

3. Find the length of the latus rectum for $4y^2 - 25x^2 = 100$.

   a. $\frac{4}{5}$ **b.** $\frac{10}{4}$ **c.** $\frac{8}{5}$ **d.** $\frac{4}{25}$

4. Find the asymptote of the hyperbola $4y^2 - 25x^2 = 100$.

   a. $4y - 25x = 0$ **b.** $5x - 2y = 0$
   c. $5y - 2x = 0$ **d.** $25y - 4x = 0$

5. For the parabola, $y^2 = 4px$, which statement is true?
   a. The focus is at $F(p, 0)$.
   b. The directrix has equation $x = -p$.
   c. The latus rectum has a length $|4p|$.
   d. All of the above are true.

6. Which of the following is the equation of the parabola with vertex at $(0, 0)$, axis of symmetry $y = 0$, and containing $P(-2, 4)$?
   a. $x^2 = -8y$ **b.** $x^2 = 4y$ **c.** $y^2 = -8x$ **d.** $y^2 = -4x$

7. Which is the equation of the parabola with vertex $V(1, 5)$ and focus $F(1, 0)$?

   a. $y^2 = 20x - 100$ **b.** $(y - 5)^2 = 4(x - 1)$
   c. $y^2 = 4x - 20$ **d.** $(y - 1)^2 = 10(x - 5)$

8. Which vector will translate $y^2 - 4y - 8x - 4 = 0$ to standard position?

   a. $\begin{bmatrix} -3 \\ 4 \end{bmatrix}$ **b.** $\begin{bmatrix} -2 \\ 1 \end{bmatrix}$ **c.** $\begin{bmatrix} -2 \\ 2 \end{bmatrix}$ **d.** $\begin{bmatrix} -3 \\ 1 \end{bmatrix}$

9. $9x^2 - 6xy + y^2 + 12x + 6y + 4 = 0$ is the equation of which conic?
   a. circle   **b.** ellipse   **c.** hyperbola   **d.** parabola

10. The graph of $y^2 + 8x^2 = 16$ in three-space is
    a. a plane   **b.** an ellipse   **c.** a sphere
    d. a cylinder with elliptic cross sections.

11. Which of the following surfaces is a surface of revolution?
    a. $x^2 - y^2 + 9z^2 = 36$ **b.** $4x^2 - 9y^2 + 4z^2 = 36$
    c. $x^2 - 9y^2 + 4z^2 = 36$ **d.** All of the above

12. What are the rectangular coordinates of the point with spherical coordinates $\left(8, \frac{3\pi}{4}, \frac{5\pi}{3}\right)$?

a. $(-2\sqrt{6}, 2\sqrt{6}, -4)$ b. $(-2\sqrt{3}, 2\sqrt{3}, 2)$

c. $(2\sqrt{6}, -2\sqrt{6}, -4)$ d. $(2\sqrt{3}, -\sqrt{3}, 4)$

13. Find the derivative of $3x^2 - 2x + 5$.

a. $3x^2 - 2x$ b. $3x^2 - 2$ c. $6x^2 - 2$ d. $6x - 2$

14. If $f(x) = (x - 2x^3) \ln x$, find $f'(x)$.

a. $\ln x - 6x^2 \ln x + 1 - 2x^2$ b. $(1 - x^2) \ln x + 1 - 2x^2$

c. $(1 - 6x^2) \ln x + (x - 2x^3) \ln x$

d. $\ln x - 6x^2 \ln x + x - 2x$

15. If $f(x) = \frac{x-3}{x^2 + 2x}$, find $f'(x)$.

a. $\frac{6-x}{x^2(x+2)}$ b. $\frac{-x^2 + 6x + 6}{x^2(x+2)^2}$

c. $\frac{x(-x+6)}{x^2(x+2)}$ d. $\frac{-x^2 + 6x + 6}{x^2(x+2)}$

16. If $f(x) = e^{x^3}$, find $f'(x)$.

a. $3xe^{x^3}$ b. $3x^2 e^{x^2}$ c. $3x^2 e^{x^3}$ d. $x^2 e^{x^3}$

17. What is the slope of the line tangent to $f(x) = 3x^2 + 2x$ at $x = -2$?

a. 8   b. -4 c. -10 d. -16

18. A particle moves according to the function $s(t) = \frac{1}{3}t^3 - 4t^2 + 3t - 2$ for $t \in [0, 8]$. What is the acceleration of the particle when $t = 4$?

a. -13 b. 0   c. 4   d. 20

19. Find the area of the region bounded by $f(x) = x^2$, $x = 1$, $x = 4$, and the x axis.

a. 20   b. 21   c. $21\frac{2}{3}$ d. $21\frac{1}{3}$

20. Evaluate: $\int_{-1}^{3} (3x^2 - 2x) \, dx$

a. 20   b. 18   c. 16   d. 11

21. Find the area enclosed by $x = -1$, $f(x) = 3 - x^2$, $x = 1$, $g(x) = \frac{1}{2}x$.

a. $4\frac{5}{6}$ b. 5   c. $5\frac{1}{3}$ d. $7\frac{1}{6}$

22. Find the area bounded by $x = -2$, $f(x) = x^3 - 8$, $x = 3$, and $y = 0$.

a. $64\frac{1}{4}$ b. $15\frac{3}{4}$ c. $23\frac{3}{4}$ d. 40

23. Find the volume of the solid made by rotating $f(x) = 2x + 1$ between $x = 1$ and $x = 3$ about the x axis.

a. $42\frac{2}{3}$ b. $52\frac{2}{3}\pi$ c. 10   d. 10π

CHAPTER **14** Introduction to Probability

Sections

Features

Review and Testing

14–1   Counting

The menu at a restaurant includes three kinds of hamburgers, two sizes of French fried potatoes, and four choices of beverage. The **tree diagram** below shows all of the different dinners of a hamburger, French fries, and a beverage that can be ordered. For each "hamburger" branch of the tree there are two "French-fries" branches. For each "French-fries" branch there are four "beverage" branches. The number of choices of meals equals the number of branches on the extremities of the tree—namely, 24 choices.

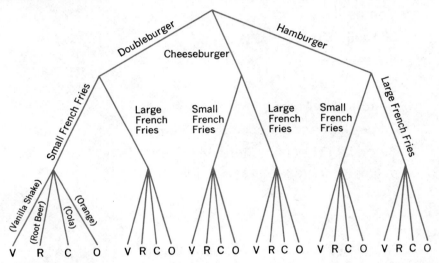

EXAMPLE 1.   A restaurant offers pie, cake, and ice cream for dessert and offers coffee, tea, milk, and soda for its beverage. How many different orders of dessert and beverage can you choose from?

Begin the tree diagram with a branch for each dessert.

To each branch add a branch for each beverage.

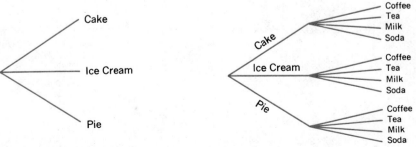

There are 12 different dessert-beverage orders.

Note that in the first situation, there are two French-fries choices for every hamburger choice. Thus there are 2×3 "French-fries and hamburger" choices. Similarly, there are four beverage choices for every "French-fries and hamburger" choice. There are $4 \times (2 \times 3)$ "French-fries, burger, beverage" choices. This illustrates the *Fundamental Counting Principle*.

Fundamental Counting Principle If one event can occur in m different ways, and if, after it occurs or at the same time, a second event can occur in n ways, then the two events can occur in $m \cdot n$ different ways.

To generalize, for acts that occur in n_1, n_2, n_3, $\cdots$, n_k ways respectively, the total act can occur in

$$n_1 \cdot n_2 \cdot n_3 \cdot \ \cdots \ \cdot n_k$$

ways.

EXAMPLE 2. A multiple-choice test has ten items with four choices each. Find the number of ways in which a student could select his answers.

Solution:

Each of the ten items is an event with four possible outcomes.

$$n_1 = n_2 = n_3 = \cdots = n_{10} = 4$$

From the Fundamental Counting Principle the number of ways is

$$4 \cdot 4 \cdot 4 \cdot 4 \cdot 4 \cdot 4 \cdot 4 \cdot 4 \cdot 4 \cdot 4.$$

There are 4^{10} or 1,048,576 ways to mark the answers.

CLASSROOM EXERCISES

1. In Example 1 suppose that you never eat pie or drink coffee. Find the number of different orders of dessert and beverage.

2. In Example 2 find the number of ways there are for a student to get every item wrong.

3. A mail questionnaire includes eight questions with five responses to each question. Find the number of ways in which a person can answer the eight questions.

WRITTEN EXERCISES

A   **1.** Make a tree diagram showing the 15 ways of choosing vanilla, chocolate, or strawberry ice cream each with a topping of marshmallow, chocolate, hot fudge, butterscotch, or crushed nuts.

—— Use a tree diagram to solve Exercises 2–4.

2. A baseball team has five pitchers and three catchers. How many different batteries (a pitcher and a catcher) are possible?

3. In how many ways can John choose a coat and a pair of trousers if he has two sport coats and three pairs of trousers?

4. How many pairs of letters are possible if each pair contains one of the vowels {a, i, u} followed by one of the consonants {b, c, d, f, g}?

—— Use the Fundamental Principle of Counting to solve Exercises 4–25.

5. A certain make of automobile is available with a choice of six different colors, of four different body styles, and of either six or eight cylinders. How many choices do you have in buying this particular make of automobile?

6. In how many ways can you form a committee consisting of one junior and one senior if there are 100 juniors and 84 seniors?

7. How many pairs of letters are possible if each pair contains one of the five vowels followed by one of the 21 consonants?

8. In a school election, there are two candidates for president, three for vice-president, four for secretary, and one for treasurer. In how many ways may the election result?

9. At a dance there are 25 boys and 22 girls. In how many ways may a boy invite a girl to dance? In how many ways may a girl invite a boy to dance?

10. From city A to city B there are eight roads, and from city B to city C there are ten roads. How many routes are possible from A to C?

11. On three shelves in the library there are 15 books, 14 books, and 20 books, respectively. In how many ways may you choose one book from each shelf?

B —— Each Sunday, a newspaper carries a list of the eight best-selling fiction books and the ten best-selling nonfiction books.

12. In how many different ways can one book from each list be chosen?

13. On a particular Sunday, three fiction and six nonfiction books were on the lists for the first time. Suppose that your selection must include one book from each of the following categories: fiction-first time on the list, fiction-not on list for the first time, nonfiction-first time on the list, and nonfiction-not on the list for the first time? In how many ways can you select the four books?

14. In how many ways can you select two fiction books that are new on the list? (Use the same Sunday as in Exercise 13.)

▬ A student takes a 20-item true-false test.

15. In how many different ways can the items be answered if the student answers every question?

16. In how many different ways can the items be answered if the student leaves one question unanswered?

17. Mary is going to college. In how many different ways can she take along at least one of her 10 favorite recordings? (*Hint: at least one* includes taking 1, 2, ⋯, or 10 records. For each record there are two possibilities: she can take it or she can leave it.)

▬ In Exercises 18–20, use only the digits 1, 2, 3, 4, 5, 7, and 8.

18. How many numbers of five digits can be formed?

19. How many numbers of five different digits can be formed?

20. How many even numbers of five digits can be formed?

21. For the digits 1, 2, 3, 4, 7, 8, 9, how many even numbers of three different digits can be formed?

22. Two cubical dice, each face containing one of 1, 2, 3, 4, 5, 6, are tossed. In how many recognizably different ways can they fall?

23. In how many ways can seven people be assigned consecutive positions in a receiving line if the first two positions must be filled from four of the people?

24. For a final examination, four science students and four history students are assigned alternate seats in a row of eight. In how many ways can this be done if the first seat may be occupied by any one of the eight students?

25. Find the number of ways in which the students of Exercise 24 can be assigned if the first seat must be occupied by a history student.

14-2 Permutations

The Fundamental Principle of Counting may be used to derive formulas for special counting situations called *permutations*.

> **Definition** A **permutation** of n objects is an arrangement of those objects.

EXAMPLE 1. How many permutations are there of four cards drawn from a deck of 52 cards?

Solution: First card: 52 ways   Second card: 51 ways
Third card: 50 ways   Fourth card: 49 ways

From the Fundamental Principle of Counting the total number of ways is

$$52 \times 51 \times 50 \times 49 = 6,497,400 \text{ permutations.}$$

The symbol "$_{52}P_4$" is used to represent "the number of permutations of 52 objects taken four at a time."

The method of Example 1 suggests Theorem 14–1.

> **Theorem 14-1** **a.** $_nP_n = n(n-1)(n-2) \cdots 1 = n!$
>
> **b.** $_nP_r = n(n-1)(n-2) \cdots (n-r+1)$
> $$= \frac{n!}{(n-r)!}$$

(Recall that n! is called "n factorial" or "factorial n.")

Proof: a. Suppose that there are n objects that are to be placed in a row. The first place can be filled in n ways. This leaves $n-1$ objects to use in the second place, $n-2$ in the third place, $\cdots$, $n-(r-1)$ in the rth place and $n-(n-1)$ in the last. By the Fundamental Principle of Counting, the number of permutations, $_nP_n$, is the product of these numbers.

The proof of b is asked for in the exercises.

EXAMPLE 2. A club has 25 members. In how many ways can it elect a president, vice-president, secretary, and treasurer? No person can hold two offices and all members are eligible.

Solution: To select four officers from 25 members requires a permutation of 25 things taken 4 at a time.

$$_{25}P_4 = \frac{25!}{(25-4)!} = 25 \cdot 24 \cdot 23 \cdot 22$$
$$= 303,600$$

EXAMPLE 3. In how many ways can five adults be seated in a row of five chairs?

Solution:
$$_5P_5 = 5! = 5 \times 4 \times 3 \times 2 \times 1$$
$$= 120$$

EXAMPLE 4. In how many ways can you arrange the letters in the word "ROOM?"

Solution:

There are $_4P_4 = 24$ ways to arrange the letters R, O, O, M. However, not all of these can be distinguished from one another. For example, you have R, O_1, O_2, M and R, O_2, O_1, M. For every arrangement with the O's in the order O_1, O_2 there is another with the O's in the opposite order. That is, there are 2! or $_2P_2$ arrangements of the O's. Thus there are

$$\frac{_4P_4}{_2P_2} = \frac{4!}{2!} = 12$$

distinguishable orders of the letters in "ROOM."

Theorem 14-2 If in a set of n objects r of them are alike, then the number of distinguishable permutations is

$$\frac{_nP_n}{_rP_r} = \frac{n!}{r!}$$

If there are r_1 of one thing, r_2 of another, and so forth then there are

$$\frac{_nP_n}{_{r_1}P_{r_1} \cdot _{r_2}P_{r_2} \cdot \ \cdots} = \frac{n!}{r_1! \cdot r_2! \cdot \ \cdots}$$

permutations of the n objects.

EXAMPLE 5. How many permutations are there of the letters in the word BALLOON?

Solution: There are two L's and two O's. Thus,

$$\frac{7!}{2!\ 2!} = 1260.$$

EXAMPLE 6. How many permutations are there of the letters in the word BALLOON if the first and last letters must be either B or N?

Solution: Use the Fundamental Principle and Theorem 14–1.

$$\begin{pmatrix} \text{Number of ways to select} \\ \text{the first and last letters} \end{pmatrix} \times \begin{pmatrix} \text{Number of permutations} \\ \text{of the remaining letters} \end{pmatrix}$$

$$2 \qquad\qquad \times \qquad\qquad \frac{5!}{2!\ 2!}$$

There are 2×30 or 60 ways.

WRITTEN EXERCISES

A ══Compute the value of each of the following.

1. $_7P_4$ **2.** $_8P_5$ **3.** $_5P_5$ **4.** $\frac{_8P_8}{_2P_2}$

5. How many arrangements are there of five playing cards drawn from a stack of five cards?

6. How many arrangements are there of five playing cards drawn from a deck of 52 cards?

7. How many nine-digit numbers can be formed using the digits 1, 2, 3, 4, 5, 6, 7, 8, 9 each only once?

8. How many three-digit numbers can be formed using the digits 1, 2, 3, 4, 5, 6, 7, 8, 9 each only once?

9. How many three-digit numbers can be formed from the digits 1, 2, 3, 4, 5, 6, 7, 8, 9? Each digit may be used either no times, once, twice, or three times in each number.

══Find the number of distinct permutations of the letters or digits taken all at a time.

10. $\{a, a, a, b, b, c, d, e, e\}$ **11.** $\{1, 2, 3, 3, 5, 5, 5, 7\}$

12. COMMOTION   **13.** MISSISSIPPI

14. How many different six-digit numbers can be formed using each of 2, 1, 1, 3, 3, 3 exactly once?

15. How many of the numbers found in Exercise 14 are even?

16. In how many ways can you distribute eight hats, all of which are alike, to eight boys?

17. In Exercise 16 suppose that five hats are green and three white. In how many distinct ways can the distribution be done?

18. Six nickels, three dimes, and a quarter are distributed among 10 children. Each child receives one coin. In how many ways can the coins be distributed?

B **19.** How many four-digit even numbers can you form from the digits 3, 4, 5, 6, 7, 9 using each no more than once in each number?

20. How many five-digit numbers can you form from the digits 1, 2, 3, 4, 5, 6, 7 using each digit no more than once in each number and with the digits 1, 2, 3 in consecutive order?

21. Find the number of batting orders for nine baseball players.

22. In how many ways can a batting order be formed when the best three batters must be in first, fourth, and fifth positions?

23. In how many ways can you seat two children and three adults in a row of five seats if the children are not to sit in consecutive seats?

━━ In Exercises 24–26 you are to schedule eight commercials for a television program. The commercials are presented in eight predetermined one-minute time slots. In how many ways can you schedule the commercials under the conditions specified?

24. Each of eight commercials is to be seen once.

25. Each of four commercials is to be seen two times.

26. There are two comic commercials and one serious one. Each comic commercial is shown twice and the serious one is shown four times.

━━ In Exercises 27–30 find in how many ways two admirals, three generals, and four diplomats can be seated in a row of nine seats under the conditions specified.

27. With an admiral at each end.

28. With an admiral at each end and all generals and all diplomats, respectively, in two consecutive groups of seats.

29. With a general at each end and the diplomats in consecutive seats.

30. With the generals and diplomats in alternating seats.

31. Prove part **b** of Theorem 14–1.

14-3 Combinations

In working with permutations, you must take into account the *order* of the objects. Thus, there are $n!$ permutations of a set with n members. On the other hand, there is only one *combination* of a set with n members.

> **Definition**   A **combination** of r objects is an unordered set of r objects.

EXAMPLE 1.   Compare the number of permutations of a set that has five members with the number of combinations of the set.

Permutations: $_5P_5 = 5! = 120$ permutations
Combinations: Since order is not significant there is just one combination of the five objects.

It is possible to have more than one combination providing the number of objects selected is fewer than the number of objects available. Each combination is simply a subset of the available objects.

EXAMPLE 2.   How many single-person committees can be formed from a group of five people: {Bob, Jim, Lisa, Stan, Sue}?
There are obviously five such committees or subsets.

{Bob}   {Jim}   {Lisa}   {Stan}   {Sue}

EXAMPLE 3.   How many four-person committees can be formed from a group of five people?

Every committee of four is a four-member subset of the five-person group. There are five four-person groups, each formed by removing a different one of the five persons. Thus, the number of four-person committees equals the number of single-person committees, five.

The symbol "$_5C_4$" is read "the number of combinations of five objects taken four at a time." Similarly, the symbol "$_nC_r$" is read "the number of combinations of n objects taken r at a time."

> **Definition** $_nC_r$ is the number of r-membered subsets of an n-membered set.

Note: Sometimes the symbol

$$\binom{n}{r}$$

is used rather than $_nC_r$. (See, for example, the proof of the Binomial Theorem on pages 25–26.)

EXAMPLE 4. List the six permutations of the letters a, b, and c taken two at a time. Then find the number of combinations of the letters taken two at a time.

Solution: The permutations are shown below.

(a, b)	(a, c)	(b, c)
(b, a)	(c, a)	(c, b)
1	**2**	**3**

Notice that each pair of permutations **1**, **2**, and **3** corresponds to a single combination:

$$\{a, b\} \qquad \{a, c\} \qquad \{b, c\}$$

Thus, there are three combinations.

Example 4 illustrates a way of finding the number of combinations of n things taken r at a time. You choose a subset consisting of r members from a set consisting of n members in $_nC_r$ ways. You arrange each subset in $r!$ ways. Using the Fundamental Principle of Counting, multiply these two numbers to find the permutations of n things taken r at a time.

$$_nP_r = {_nC_r} \cdot r!$$

Solving for $_nC_r$ you obtain the following.

$$_nC_r = \frac{_nP_r}{r!}$$

$$= \frac{n!}{(n - r)! \cdot r!}$$

This is the same as the binomial coefficient.

Theorem 14–3 $\quad _nC_r = \dfrac{n!}{(n - r)! \cdot r!}$

EXAMPLE 5. Find the number of ways in which each group can be chosen from 12 people.

a. A group of five people

b. A president, vice-president, treasurer, secretary, and membership chairman

Solutions:

a. The order is not important. Use combinations.

$$_{12}C_5 = \frac{12!}{5! \cdot 7!} = 792$$

b. The order is important. Use permutations.

$$_{12}P_5 = \frac{12!}{7!} = 95,040$$

EXAMPLE 6. How many five-card hands are there in a 52-card deck?

Solution: $$_{52}C_5 = \frac{52!}{5! \cdot 47!} = 2,598,960$$

Note: Unless there is a statement to the contrary you should assume that a "deck of cards" refers to a standard 52-card deck with four suits.

The proof of the following theorem is asked for in the exercises.

Theorem 14–4 $_nC_r = {}_nC_{n-r}$

Thus, by Theorem 14–4 $_7C_2 = {}_7C_5$, $_{14}C_3 = {}_{14}C_{11}$, and so forth. Examples 2 and 3 also illustrate this theorem, with $_5C_1$ (from Example 2) equal to $_5C_4$ (Example 3).

CLASSROOM EXERCISES

1. How many four-card hands are there in a 52-card deck?

2. How many four-card hands are there in a 52-card deck if one of them must be a five of clubs?

3. In a toss of five dice, in how many ways can exactly two sixes come up?

WRITTEN EXERCISES

A ━━━ Complete the value of each of the following.

1. $_7C_4$ **2.** $_8C_5$ **3.** $_8C_3$ **4.** $_5C_5$

5. In how many ways can a committee of three be chosen from a group of 10 members of the League of Women Voters?

6. In how many ways can a motel chain select three sites for the construction of new motels if 14 sites are available?

7. A federal accountant must audit three tax returns from 12 that are before her. In how many ways can she choose?

8. In how many ways can you form a party of six from 10 friends?

9. In how many ways may Fred select five rides from 13 at an amusement park?

10. From a penny, nickel, dime, quarter, and half-dollar, how many different sums of money can be made from three coins?

━━━ A ten-item true-false test is given. For Exercises 11–14, find in how many ways a person can get the given results.

11. One right, nine wrong   **12.** Three right, seven wrong

13. Five right, five wrong   **14.** Seven right, three wrong

━━━ In Exercises 15 and 16 leave factorials in your answer.

15. How many 13-card hands are there in a 52-card deck?

16. In Exercise 15, how many hands contain four nines?

17. Ten points lie in a plane. No three are collinear. How many triangles can be drawn using vertices chosen from these points?

18. In Exercise 17 suppose that one of the points is always a vertex of a triangle? How many triangles are there?

━━━ At a high school a four-person faculty committee is chosen from 15 teachers and a principal. For each set of given conditions find in how many ways the committee can be formed.

19. The principal must be on the committee.

20. The principal or any teacher may be on the committee.

21. The principal may not serve on the committee.

B **22.** In how many ways can Dorothy invite two girls and three boys to a party if she chooses from eight girls and six boys and if Dennis, one of the six boys, must be invited?

23. Prove Theorem 14–4.

14-4 Mutually Exclusive Events

Events, acts, or choices that cannot occur simultaneously are **mutually exclusive events.** Two such events are obtaining a head on a toss of a coin and obtaining a tail on the same toss.

The Fundamental Principle of Counting shows how to find the number of cases in compound simultaneous events. The *Addition Principle of Counting* does the same for mutually exclusive events.

Addition Principle of Counting   If a first event can occur in m ways and a second event in n ways, and if the events are mutually exclusive, then one or the other of the events can occur in $m + n$ ways.

EXAMPLE 1. A bag contains five red tokens and two green tokens. In how many ways can you select one red or one green token?

Solution: You can select one red token in $_5C_1$ ways.
You can select one green token in $_2C_1$ ways.
You can select one red token *or* one green token in

$$_5C_1 + {}_2C_1 = 5 + 2 = 7 \text{ ways.}$$

EXAMPLE 2. How many numbers greater than 3000 can you form from the digits 0, 1, 2, 4, 5 using each digit no more than once in each number?

Solution: There are two mutually exclusive events, each of which is a permutation.

i. Four-digit numbers greater than 3000.
ii. Five-digit numbers greater than 3000.

For i, there are two choices for the first digit (4, 5) and then four, three, and two choices for the remaining digits.

$$2 \cdot 4 \cdot 3 \cdot 2 = 48$$

For ii, there are four choices for the first digit (1, 2, 4, 5) and then four, three, two, and one choices for the remaining digits.

$$4 \cdot 4 \cdot 3 \cdot 2 \cdot 1 = 96$$

$48 + 96 = 144$ possible numbers greater than 3000. ◄——— By the Addition Prin. of Counting

EXAMPLE 3. A bag contains four red and three green tokens. In how many ways can a set of three tokens be drawn if the set must contain at least two red tokens?

Solution: There are two mutually exclusive events, each of which is a combination.

  i. Two red tokens and one green token. $_4C_3 \cdot {}_3C_0 = 4 \times 1 = 4$

  ii. Three red tokens and no green tokens. $_4C_2 \cdot {}_3C_1 = 6 \times 3 = 18$

The desired event can occur in $18 + 4 = 22$ ways.

In Examples 4 and 5 a standard 52-card deck of cards is used. Each of the thirteen cards of each suit will be referred to as a *value* of a card in that suit.

EXAMPLE 4. In how many ways can you deal a five-card hand that has exactly one pair (two aces, or two twos, and so forth)?

  There are 13 values from which the pair may come. ⟵ $_{13}C_1$

  Each value has four cards; choose two. ⟵ $_4C_2$

Thus, you can choose the pair in $_{13}C_1 \cdot {}_4C_2$ ways. Now you must choose the other three cards from the remaining 12 values so that no new pair is formed.

  Choose three values. ⟵ $_{12}C_3$

  Choose one card from each value. ⟵ $_4C_1 \cdot {}_4C_1 \cdot {}_4C_1$

Thus, the number of hands with exactly one pair is

$$_{13}C_1 \cdot {}_4C_2 \cdot {}_{12}C_3 \cdot ({}_4C_1)^3 = 1{,}098{,}240.$$

EXAMPLE 5. In how many ways can you deal a five-card hand with exactly one pair or a royal flush (Ace, King, Queen, Jack, Ten of the same suit)?

Solution: There are two mutually exclusive events.

 i. Exactly one pair (1,098,240 ways; see Example 4).

 ii. Royal flush.

Choose a suit. ⟵ $_4C_1 = 4$

There is only one way to choose the A, K, Q, J, 10. ⟵ $_5C_5 = 1$

The number of ways to have a royal flush: $4 \times 1 = 4$

The desired event can occur in $1{,}098{,}240 + 4 = 1{,}098{,}244$ ways.

WRITTEN EXERCISES

A ■ In Exercises 1–2 a box of candy contains five creams and six caramels. Find the number of ways in which each given event can ocur.

1. Two creams and three caramels are selected.

2. Two creams or three caramels are selected.

■ In Exercises 3–6 a sack contains five red tokens, eight blue tokens, and four green tokens. Find the number of ways in which each given event can occur.

3. Three red tokens or three blue tokens are drawn.

4. Two red tokens and two green tokens are drawn.

5. Two red tokens, two blue tokens, or two green tokens are drawn.

6. Two red tokens, two blue tokens, and two green tokens are drawn.

■ In Exercises 7–14 find the number of ways in which each given event can occur. Each digit may be used more than once unless otherwise stated.

7. A number greater than 4000 is constructed from the digits 2, 3, 4, 5, and 6.

8. A number greater than 4000 is constructed from the digits 2, 3, 4, 5, and 6 with each digit used no more than once.

9. A number greater than 500 is constructed from the digits 0, 1, 2, 3, 7.

10. A number greater than 500 is constructed from the digits 2, 3, 5, 8, 9.

11. A number smaller than 4000 is constructed from the digits 2, 3, 4, 5, 6.

12. A number smaller than 4000 is constructed from the digits 0, 2, 3, 4, 5, 6.

13. A number smaller than 200 is constructed from the digits 0, 1, 2, 3.

14. A number smaller than 200 is constructed from the digits 1, 2, 3, 4.

15. A host invites five dinner guests from 10 people. He must avoid having two of the ten, Mr. Kent and Mr. Batson, attend together. Find the number of ways in which the guests may be chosen.

In each of Exercises 16–19 a committee of six is selected from six boys and eight girls. Find the number of ways in which the given selections can occur.

16. Three girls and three boys. **17.** Six boys or six girls.

18. At least five boys. **19.** At most two girls.

In each of Exercises 20–22 seven recipes are available. Find the number of ways in which each event can occur.

20. Exactly four recipes are chosen.

21. At least four recipes are chosen.

22. At most four recipes are chosen.

23. Nine different books are distributed among Lars, Georgette, and Maria so that they receive four, three, and two books respectively. Find the number of ways in which the books can be distributed.

24. A committee of six people is formed from nine people, two of whom refuse to serve together. Find the number of committees that can be formed.

In Exercises 25–29 a five-card hand is dealt from a 52-card deck of playing cards. Find the number of ways in which each given event can occur.

25. Exactly one pair of threes.

26. Exactly one pair of threes or one pair of kings.

27. Three of a kind. (No four-of-a-kind is included.)

28. At least a pair of threes.

29. At least one pair.

30. A thirteen-card hand is dealt consisting of five hearts and eight clubs. Find the number of ways in which this can be done.

B **31.** The table shows the frequency of all five-card poker hands. Complete the table. The ace may be used as a high or low card.

Poker Hand	Description	Calculating Formula	Value
Royal Flush	A, K, Q, J, 10 of the same suit	$_?C_?$	4
Straight Flush	Any five-card sequence in the same suit except Royal Flush	?	36

Poker Hand	Description	Calculating Formula	Value
Four of a Kind	Any four cards all of the same value	?	?
Full House	Any three of a kind and any pair	?	?
Flush	Five cards in the same suit, but not a straight flush or royal flush	$_4C_1 \cdot {}_{13}C_5 - ?$	?
Straight	Five cards in a sequence, but not all in the same suit	$10(_?C_?)^5 - 40$	?
Three of a Kind	Exactly three cards all of the same kind, but not a full house	?	54,912
Two Pairs	Two cards of one kind, two cards of another kind and a fifth card of a third kind	?	?
One Pair	Exactly two cards of one kind, the other three cards of three different kinds	See Example 4.	1,098,240
"Nothing"	No pairs, straights, or anything else.	None	1,302,540

All 5-card Hands: 2,598,960

MID-CHAPTER REVIEW

1. How many ensembles of 3 hats, 5 coats and 4 pairs of gloves can be made?   (Section 14-1)

2. How many "words" can be formed using $\{a, i, o\}$ as possible first letters and $\{s, t, n, r\}$ as second letters? (Section 14-1)

Compute each permutation or combination. (Section 14-2 and 14-3)

3. $_{10}P_3$ **4.** $_5P_2$ **5.** $_{10}C_3$ **6.** $_5C_2$

7. How many committees of 8 can be chosen from a panel of 12?
(Section 14-3)

8. How many ways can you draw a 5 or a jack from a 52-card deck?
(Section 14-4)

9. How many ways can you throw an even number on a standard die and choose an ace from a 52-card deck, or throw a 5 and draw a king?
(Section 14-4)

14-5 Probability

The following four cards are face down on a table.

A heart   A spade   A club   A diamond

Two of the cards are now drawn. This can be done in six ways.

{H, S}, {H, C}, {H, D}, {S, C}, {S, D}, {C, D}

A complete listing of this kind shows all the possible outcomes of an experiment and is called a **sample space.** The above sample space is for the experiment "Draw two cards from a hand of one heart, one spade, one club, and one diamond."

Any subset of a sample space is called an **event.** Here are three events from the sample space described above.

Description of Draw	Event
A heart.	{H, S}, {H, C}, {H, D}
Two red cards.	{H, D}
Two cards of the same color.	{H, D}, {S, C}

Now it is possible to define the *probability* of an event.

Definition. The **probability** of an event E is the ratio of the number of elements in the event to the number of elements in the sample space. A probability is represented as *p* or *p*(E).

This definition assumes that each element of the sample space is *equally likely;* that is, you are just as likely to get one element as another on any trial of an experiment.

EXAMPLE 1. Find the probability of each event in the table above.

Solutions:

a. Draw a heart.

$$p(E) = \frac{\text{Number of ways of drawing a heart}}{\text{Number of ways of drawing two cards}} = \frac{3}{6} = \frac{1}{2}$$

b. Draw two red cards.

$$p(E) = \frac{1}{6}$$

c. Draw two cards of the same color.

$$p(E) = \frac{2}{6} = \frac{1}{3}$$

EXAMPLE 2. Find the probability of dealing a five-card hand that contains:

a. A, K, Q, J, 10 of spades. **b.** A, K, Q, J, 10 of the same suit.
Solutions:
a. The number of all five-card hands is $_{52}C_5$. Of these, the number of ways to obtain A, K, Q, J, 10 of spades is $_5C_5$ or 1. Thus,

$$p \text{ (A, K, Q, J, 10 of spades)} = \frac{_5C_5}{_{52}C_5}$$

$$= \frac{1}{2,598,960} \approx 3 \times 10^{-7}$$

b. There are four hands in the desired event. The sample space is the same as for part **a**. Thus,

$$p \text{ (A, K, Q, J, 10 of same suit)} = \frac{4}{2,598,960} \approx 12 \times 10^{-7}$$

EXAMPLE 3. What is the probability of drawing two red cards from a 52-card deck?

Solution: The sample space has $_{52}C_2$ elements.
The event has $_{26}C_2$ elements.

$$p = \frac{_{26}C_2}{_{52}C_2} = \frac{25}{102}$$

$$\approx 0.245$$

EXAMPLE 4. A five-digit number is built at random from the digits 1, 2, 3, 4, 5, 6, and 8. Each digit is used no more than once. Find the probability that the number will begin and end with even digits.

Solution: The sample contains $_7P_5$ elements.
The event has $4 \times 5 \times 4 \times 3 \times 3$ elements.

$$p = \frac{4 \cdot 5 \cdot 4 \cdot 3 \cdot 3}{7 \cdot 6 \cdot 5 \cdot 4 \cdot 3} = \frac{2}{7}$$

EXAMPLE 5. One die is rolled. Find the probability of getting:

a. a seven. **b.** a number less than seven.

Solutions: The sample space has six elements in each case.
a. The event is empty. **b.** The event equals the sample space.

$$p = \frac{0}{6} = 0 \qquad\qquad p = \frac{6}{6} = 1$$

The following are the basic postulates of probability.

Probability Postulates

i. For every event A of a sample space S, $0 \leq p(A) \leq 1$.

ii. If event A equals the sample space S, then $p(A) = p(S) = 1$.

iii. If events A and B are subsets of S and have no elements in common, then

$$p(A \cup B) = p(A) + p(B).$$

Postulates i and ii are illustrated by Examples 1–5. Postulate iii can be extended to three or more events. Example 6 illustrates Postulate iii for the case of three events.

EXAMPLE 6. Find the probability of getting at least one five in a roll of three fair dice.

Solution: The number of elements in the sample space is

$$6 \times 6 \times 6 = 216.$$

There are three events with no elements in common: A. rolling one five, B. rolling two fives, and C. rolling three fives. Thus,

$$p(\text{at least one five}) = p(A \cup B \cup C) = p(A) + p(B) + p(C).$$

Event A: Rolling one five

One five can be obtained in $_3C_1$ ways.

Two non-fives can be obtained in $(_5C_1)^2$ ways.

$$p(A) = p(\text{one five}) = \frac{_3C_1 \cdot (_5C_1)^2}{6 \cdot 6 \cdot 6} = \frac{75}{216}$$

Event B: Rolling two fives

Two fives can be obtained in $_3C_2$ ways.

One non-five can be obtained in $_5C_1$ ways.

$$p(B) = p(\text{two fives}) = \frac{_3C_2 \cdot {_5C_1}}{6 \cdot 6 \cdot 6} = \frac{15}{216}$$

Event C: Rolling three fives

Three fives can be obtained in $_3C_3$ ways.

$$p(C) = p(\text{three fives}) = \frac{_3C_3}{6 \cdot 6 \cdot 6} = \frac{1}{216}$$

Finally, the probability of the desired event is found by addition.

$$p(\text{at least one five}) = \frac{75}{216} + \frac{15}{216} + \frac{1}{216}$$

$$= \frac{91}{216}$$

Sometimes it is easier to find the probability of an event by finding the probability of its *complement* first. For example the complement of the event "at least one five is rolled" is the event "no five is rolled."

Definition B is called the **complement** of A with respect to a set S if

    i. $A \cup B = S$ and   ii. $A \cap B = \phi$.

The proof of the following theorem is asked for in the exercises.

Theorem 14-5 If B is the complement of an event A with respect to sample space S, then $p(B) = 1 - p(A)$.

Note: In all exercises and examples that involve dice or coins, you should assume that the dice or coins are "fair" (not loaded or unbalanced) unless you are told otherwise.

EXAMPLE 7. Find the probability of getting at least one five in a roll of three dice (see Example 6) by first finding the complement of this event.

Solution: The complement is the event that *no* five is rolled.

No fives can be obtained in $({}_5C_1)^3$ ways.

$$p(\text{no fives}) = \frac{({}_5C_1)^3}{216} = \frac{125}{216} \text{ ways}$$

Now use Theorem 14-5.

$$p(\text{at least one five}) = 1 - p(\text{no fives})$$

$$= 1 - \frac{125}{216} = \frac{91}{216}$$

CLASSROOM EXERCISES

▬▬ Four cubes are drawn, without replacement, from a box that contains five red cubes and six white cubes. Find the probability of each event below.

1. Two red and two white cubes   **2.** All cubes the same color

3. At least three white cubes   **4.** At least one white cube

▬▬ Five lettered tiles are drawn, without replacement, from a box that contains seven A tiles and nine B tiles. Find the probability of each event below.

5. Three A's and two B's   **6.** All A tiles

7. At least two B's   **8.** At least one A

WRITTEN EXERCISES

A ▬▬ A bag contains 26 tokens, five of them white, six red, and 15 black. One token is drawn. Find the probability that the color will be as described.

1. Red   **2.** Red or white

3. White or black   **4.** Red and black

▬▬ A die is rolled. Find the probability that the die will show the result described.

5. One or three   **6.** An even number

7. At least a four   **8.** A multiple of three

▬▬ One card is drawn from a shuffled deck of 52 cards. Find the probability of each event.

9. Drawing a red king

10. Drawing a jack, queen, king, or ace

11. Drawing a card that is neither an ace nor a king

12. Drawing a diamond or a spade

13. Drawing a four, five, six, seven, or nine of any suit

▬▬ Let H stand for heads and T for tails. Construct a sample space for three successive tosses of a coin. (There are $2^3 = 8$ events.) Find the probability of each event.

14. No heads   **15.** Exactly one head

16. Exactly two heads   **17.** At least one head

A hat contains 100 slips of paper labeled with the numbers 1 through 100. One slip of paper is drawn at random. Find the probability that the number will be as described.

18. Less than 40   **19.** Odd

20. Even   **21.** Divisible by seven

A six-digit number is built at random by use of the digits one through seven inclusive. No digit appears more than once in each number. Find the probability that the number will be as described.

22. Odd   **23.** Even

24. Divisible by five   **25.** Greater than 500,000

26. Four cards are drawn from a 52-card deck. Find the probability that there will be one spade, one diamond, one heart, and one club.

27. Eight books are placed on a shelf. Two of these are mathematics books. Find the probability that the two mathematics books are next to each other.

28. For the books in Exercise 27 find the probability that there is exactly one book between the two mathematics books.

Thirty tickets in a box are numbered from 1 to 30. Two tickets are selected in one draw. Find the probability of each indicated event.

29. The sum of the two numbers is even.

30. The product of the numbers is even.

B   Group A has four men and two women. Group B has five men and 10 women. One person is chosen by lot from each group. Find the probability of each arrangement.

31. Two women.   **32.** Two men.

33. One man, one woman.   **34.** At least one man.

Four men and three women are seated in a seven-chair row. Find the probability for each arrangement.

35. A man in the first seat   **36.** Men and women alternate.

37. The women side by side.   **38.** The men side by side.

Six coins are tossed. Find the probability of each event.

39. Exactly four heads   **40.** Exactly four tails

41. All tails   **42.** At most two heads

Five couples attend a party at which the hostess matches dance partners by lot. Find the probability of each event.

43. Each original couple are also dance partners.

44. Exactly three original couples are also dance partners.

45. Six dice are thrown. Find the probability that all the numbers one through six inclusive will appear.

46. In the game of bridge each player, N, E, S, and W (North, East, South, and West) is dealt thirteen cards. When one pair, (N, S) or (E, W), wins the bid, one of the two hands is laid out face up. Thus, the winning bidders know 26 of the cards. Suppose that between them the winning bidders, say N and S, have nine hearts. The event that the remaining four hearts are split so that E or W has three of the hearts is called a 3-1 split. The probability that this will occur is:

$$p = \frac{{}_4C_3 \cdot {}_{22}C_{10} + {}_4C_1 \cdot {}_{22}C_{12}}{{}_{26}C_{13}} = \frac{2({}_4C_3 \cdot {}_{22}C_{10})}{{}_{26}C_{13}} = \frac{286}{575} = 0.4974$$

Complete the table. Use logarithms or a calculator.

Total Hearts Revealed (N and S)	Splits of Remaining Hearts (E and W)	Probability (Fractional Form)	Probability (Decimal Form)
7	3-3	$\frac{286}{805}$	0.3553
	4-2	?	?
	5-1	?	?
	6-0	?	?
8	3-2	?	?
	4-1	?	?
	5-0	?	?
9	2-2	?	?
	3-1	?	0.4974
	4-0	?	?
10	2-1	?	?
	3-0	?	?
11	1-1	?	?
	2-0	?	?

47. Refer to Exercise 31 of Section 14–4. Then construct a probability table for poker hands similar to the one you constructed for heart-splits in Exercise 46.

Applying Probability
Systems Design

Many businesses deal in service. Except when service is given by appointment, the person who arrives first is served first. If no one is available to serve the customer, the customer waits. The waiting line is called the **queue.**

Systems designers for such service businesses study queuing theory to prevent long queues, which lead to dissatisfied customers. The study of **queuing theory** includes the effects of the rate of arrival, the rate of service, the number of service stations, etc. and the length of time needed to be served. Many banks have gone to a common queue for all tellers, whereas supermarkets have several independent queues.

To analyze queues, a computer is often used to **simulate** the situation by assuming customers arrive randomly at some fixed rate. For example, one customer may arrive at a supermarket every 4 minutes, on the average. The probability of a customer arriving in a short interval T is $\frac{T}{4}$.

The Problem

Analyze a queuing situation in which customers arrive at an average rate of 1 every 4 minutes and can be served in 3 minutes.

Simulation of the Problem

The following output was generated by a computer programmed to simulate the arrival times. The numbers indicate the time (in minutes) at which each customer arrived within an hour.

2	4.5	8	12.5
16	19.5	24	35.5
36	40.5	48.5	50.5
54	56.5		

There were 14 arrivals in the simulated hour.

Analysis

Question 1. Can one checkout person handle all the customers?

The answer is yes if the ratio of the average servicing time to the average time between arrivals is less than 1.

In this case, the ratio is $\frac{3}{4} = 0.75 < 1$.

Question 2. How long does the queue become in this simulation?

The answer can be shown graphically. The graph below shows the queue length for each $\frac{1}{2}$ minute. The person being served is assumed to be in the queue, and each person's service time of 3 minutes starts when the person is first in line.

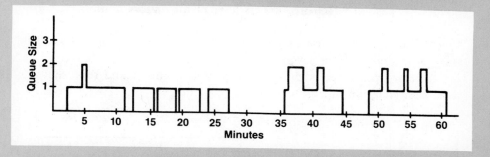

The graph can be understood as follows:

The person arriving at 2 minutes is served for 3 minutes, so that person's time extends to 5. However, a person arrives at 4.5 minutes, so for 0.5 minutes the queue is 2 persons long. At 5 minutes the first person leaves, the second person moves up and begins service time, and so on.

Question 3. What is the average queue length?

This can be calculated from the graph.

Queue of 0 for 37 half-minutes

Queue of 1 for 67 half-minutes

Queue of 2 for 16 half-minutes

$$q = \frac{37 \cdot 0 + 67 \cdot 1 + 16 \cdot 2}{120}$$

$$= \frac{67 + 32}{120} = 0.825$$

On the average, there are 0.825 customers in the store.

EXERCISES

Using the method in the analysis above, draw the queue size graph and calculate the average queue length, q, for the given data.

1.

1	2	2.5	5
10.5	13.5	20	22
22.5	23	24.5	25
28.5	29.5	32.5	35
37	40	43	45
37	40	43	45
46	52.5	53	59

24 arrivals

2.

1.5	12	16.5
20.5	33.5	36.
36.5	39.5	41
41.5	49	50.5
51	52	55
51	52	55
57.5	58.5	

17 arrivals

14-6   General Addition Rule

In this section an addition rule for probabilities is found that covers the case in which two events have elements in common.

EXAMPLE 1.   In a toss of two dice, find the probability of exactly one "two" or a sum of seven.

The sample space is shown explicitly in Figure 1 and represented as a **Venn diagram** in Figure 2.

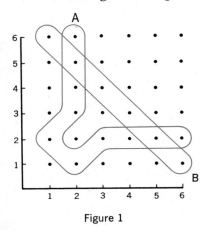

Figure 1

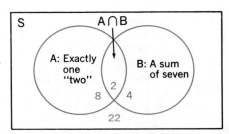

A has $8 + 2 = 10$ elements
B has $4 + 2 = 6$ elements
S has $8 + 2 + 4 + 22 = 36$ elements

Figure 2

A is the event of getting exactly one "two."
B is the event of getting a sum of seven.

By counting the elements in A, B, and $A \cup B$, the following probabilities are found.

$$p(A) = \frac{10}{36} \qquad p(B) = \frac{6}{36} \qquad p(A \cup B) = \frac{14}{36}$$

In Example 1 notice that $p(A \cup B) \neq p(A) + p(B)$.   The reason for this is that some elements are counted twice—namely, the elements of $A \cap B$.   Since $p(A \cap B) = \frac{2}{36}$, $p(A \cup B)$ can be found by subtracting $p(A \cap B)$ from $p(A) + p(B)$, that is, from $\frac{16}{36}$.   This suggests the following theorem.

Theorem 14-6   General Addition Rule   For any two events A and B

$$p(A \cup B) = p(A) + p(B) - p(A \cap B)$$

Proof: If $A \cap B = \phi$, then $p(A \cap B) = 0$ and the theorem follows from Probability Postulate **iii** in Section 14–5.

If $A \cap B \neq \phi$, then the sample space S must be partitioned into **disjoint** sets (sets with no elements in common). Let A′ be the complement of A in S. Let B′ be the complement of B in S.

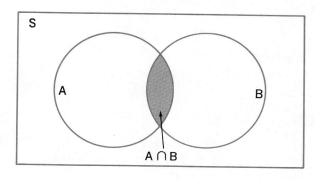

Then

$$A \cup B = A \cup (A' \cap B) \text{ and } A \cap (A' \cap B) = \phi \qquad 1$$
$$B = (A' \cap B) \cup (A \cap B) \text{ and } (A' \cap B) \cap (A \cap B) = \phi. \qquad 2$$

From **1** and Theorem 14–5 in Section 14–5,

$$p(A \cup B) = p(A) + p(A' \cap B). \qquad 3$$

Similarly, from **2** and Theorem 14–5,

$$p(B) = p(A' \cap B) + p(A \cap B) \text{ or } p(A' \cap B) = p(B) - p(A \cap B). \qquad 4$$

Combining **3** and **4**, you obtain the desired result.

$$p(A \cup B) = p(A) + p(B) - p(A \cap B)$$

EXAMPLE 2. Find the probability that a face card (J, Q, or K) or a heart will appear on a draw of one card from a deck.
Solution:

Let A be the event *Face Cards.*   A has 12 elements.

Let B be the event *Hearts.*   B has 13 elements.

Then $A \cap B$ is the event *Heart Face Cards.* $A \cap B$ has three elements.

$$p(A \cup B) = p(A) + p(B) - p(A \cap B)$$
$$= \frac{12}{52} + \frac{13}{52} - \frac{3}{52}$$
$$= \frac{11}{26} = 0.423$$

CLASSROOM EXERCISES

━━ One card is drawn from a 52-card deck. Find the probability of each indicated event.

1. An ace, king, or queen is drawn.

2. A red card is drawn.

3. A red ace, king, or queen is drawn.

4. An ace, king, queen, or red card is drawn.

5. An eight, nine, or ten is drawn.

6. An eight, nine, ten, or black card is drawn.

WRITTEN EXERCISES

A ━━ Given two mutually exclusive events A and B such that $p(A) = 0.30$ and $p(B) = 0.55$, find each of the following.

1. $p(A')$ **2.** $p(B')$

3. $p(A \cup B)$ **4.** $p(A \cap B)$

5. $p(A \cap B')$ **6.** $p(B \cap A')$

7. $p(A' \cap B')$ **8.** $p(A' \cup B')$

━━ Given two events A and B such that $p(A) = 0.67$, $p(B) = 0.23$ and $p(A \cap B) = 0.12$, find each of the following.

9. $p(A')$ **10.** $p(B')$

11. $p(A' \cap B)$ **12.** $p(A \cap B')$

13. $p(A \cup B)$ **14.** $p(A' \cap B')$

━━ A number is selected from $\{1, 2, 3, \cdots, 11, 12\}$. Find the probability of each event.

15. The number is even.

16. The number is divisible by three.

17. The number is even or divisible by three.

18. On a toss of two dice find the probability of a 10 or a double.

━━ In a class of 30 seniors, 22 like rock music, 12 like country-western music, and two like neither. Draw a Venn diagram for this situation. Then find the probability that a senior likes the kind of music indicated in each of Exercises 19–22.

19. Rock music   **20.** Country-western

21. Rock or country-western   **22.** Rock or neither

23. Find the probability of drawing a pair or two red cards when two cards are drawn at random from a 52-card deck.

The local pep club sells raffle tickets numbered from 1 through 200. Find the probability that the winning number will be divisible by one of the following.

24. Four   **25.** Five   **26.** Twenty   **27.** Four or five

28. For suburban married couples, the probabilities that the husband, wife, or both will watch a certain TV program are 0.18, 0.23, and 0.14 respectively. Find the probability that at least one of them watches the program.

29. Julia Chang feels that the probability of her striking out the first batter in a softball game is $\frac{2}{5}$, the probability of striking out the second batter is $\frac{1}{2}$, and the probability of striking out both is $\frac{1}{5}$. Assume that these probabilities are correct and find the probability that Julia will strike out at least one batter.

B   **30.** Show by Venn diagrams that $(A \cap B) \cup (A \cap B') = A$.

31. Use Exercise 30 to show that $p(A) \geq p(A \cap B)$ for any events A and B.

32. Show that $A \cup B = (A \cap B) \cup (A' \cap B) \cup (A \cap B')$. Use Venn diagrams.

33. Use Exercises 30 and 32 to show that $p(A \cup B) \geq p(B)$ and that $p(A \cup B) \geq p(A)$ for events A and B.

Mr. Wayne stops for gas. Assume that the following probabilities are true.

Event	Probability
He has the battery checked.	0.23
He has the tires checked.	0.18
He has the battery and tires checked.	0.08

What is the probability that Mr. Wayne will do each of the following?

34. Have the battery checked, but not the tires.

35. Have the battery or the tires checked.

36. Have neither the battery nor the tires checked.

37. Have the battery or tires checked, but not both.

38. Draw a Venn diagram to represent the fact that the following is true.

$$p(A \cup B \cup C) = (p(A) + p(B) + p(C)) - \\ (p(A \cap B) + p(A \cap C) + p(B \cap C)) + \\ p(A \cap B \cap C)$$

14-7   Conditional Probability

If some information about the possible outcomes of a probability experiment happens to be known, then that information affects the probability of each outcome.

EXAMPLE 1. Two dice are tossed in succession and the first die shows a three. Knowing this, find the probability that the sum shown by the dice is five, six, or seven.

Solution: Let A be the event of getting a three on the first die.
Let B be the event of getting a sum of five, six, or seven on the two dice.
Then A ∩ B is the event of getting a three on the first die while also getting a sum of five, six, or seven.
These events are all shown in the figure below.

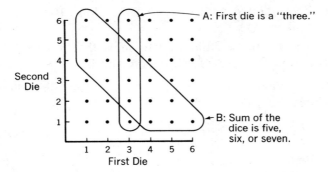

Placing a condition on the first die reduces the size of the sample space considered when using the second condition. Thus, the sample space changes to A.

The diagram shows that the event for this new sample space is the intersection of B with A, that is, A ∩ B.

$$p(5, 6, \text{ or } 7, \text{ given } 3 \text{ on die } 1) = \frac{\text{number in } A \cap B}{\text{number in } A}$$

$$= \frac{3}{6} = \frac{1}{2}$$

The same result may be obtained by using probabilities related to the original sample space. Thus, in Example 1, $p(A \cap B) = \frac{3}{36}$, $p(A) = \frac{6}{36}$, and

$$p(B \text{ given } A) = \frac{p(A \cap B)}{p(A)} = \frac{\frac{3}{36}}{\frac{6}{36}} = \frac{1}{2}.$$

The reason that this works is that the probabilities involved are proportional to the number of elements in the corresponding sets (events). This leads to the definition of *conditional probability*, $p(\text{B} \mid \text{A})$, that is, the probability of "B given A" or "B under the condition that A has occurred."

Definition   The **conditional probability** of an event B when event A has occurred is the ratio of $p(\text{A} \cap \text{B})$ to the probability of A. In symbols,

$$p(\text{B} \mid \text{A}) = \frac{p(\text{A} \cap \text{B})}{p(\text{A})}. \qquad \text{A} \neq \emptyset$$

EXAMPLE 2. Let sample space S be all families with two children. If one child in a family is a girl, find the probability that the other child is also a girl. (Assume that the probability that a child is a girl is $\frac{1}{2}$ – actually this is not quite accurate.)

Solution: Let A = the event that at least one child is a girl.
Let B = the event that the other child is a girl.
$$S = \{(G, G), (B, G), (G, B), (B, B)\}$$

$$p(\text{A}) = \frac{3}{4} \qquad p(\text{A} \cap \text{B}) = \frac{1}{4}$$

$$p(\text{B} \mid \text{A}) = \frac{\frac{1}{4}}{\frac{3}{4}} = \frac{1}{3}$$

The definition of conditional probability leads to the following.

Theorem 14–7 $p(\text{A} \cap \text{B}) = p(\text{A}) \cdot p(\text{B} \mid \text{A})$

EXAMPLE 3. Find the probability of drawing two spades in succession from a 52-card deck if the first card is not replaced.

Solution: Let A = the event that the first card is a spade.
Let B = the event that the second card is a spade.
S has 52×51 or 2652 elements.

Clearly, $p(\text{A}) = \frac{13}{52}$ and $p(\text{B} \mid \text{A}) = \frac{12}{51}$ because there are 12 spades remaining in the deck. Thus, by Theorem 14–7

$$p(\text{A} \cap \text{B}) = \frac{13}{52} \times \frac{12}{51} = \frac{1}{17} \approx 0.059.$$

CLASSROOM EXERCISES

■■■ A red die and a green die are tossed. Find the probability that the sum that shows is greater than eight if:

1. nothing else is known.   **2.** the red die shows a four.

3. the green die shows a six.   **4.** the red die shows a three.

WRITTEN EXERCISES

A   **1.** Two dice are tossed in succession and it is known that the sum is five, six, or seven. Find the probability that the first die shows a three. (*Hint:* Represent the sample space in a manner similar to that of Example 1.)

2. A red die and a green die are tossed. It is known that the red die shows a six. Find the probability that the sum that shows is at least 11.

3. A red die and a green die are tossed. It is known that the sum that shows is at least 11. Find the probability that the red die shows a six.

4. A box contains four poker chips colored blue, yellow, red, and green. Three of the chips are drawn and it is known that the green chip is among them. Find the probability that the red chip is also one of the three drawn.

5. Three coins are tossed in succession. It is known that the third coin came up tails. Find the probability that all three coins are tails.

6. A machine with two dials is constructed so that the probability of obtaining a certain reading a on both the first and second dial is 0.1. The probability of obtaining a on just the first dial is 0.5. Find the probability of obtaining a on the second dial when the first dial has already shown a.

■■■ In Exercises 7–8 two cards are drawn in succession from a 52-card deck.

7. Find the probability of drawing two aces.

8. Use the result of Exercise 7 to find the probability of drawing two aces if the first card is known to be an ace.

9. Six tokens numbered 1, 2, 3, 4, 5, and 6 are in a bag. Find the probability of drawing 1 and 2 in that order. Assume that the first token is not replaced before drawing the second.

14-8 Dependent and Independent Events

Suppose that two tokens are drawn in succession from a hat that contains five red and two blue tokens. Can you determine the probability that the first is red, the second blue? Not unless you know whether the first token is replaced before the second is drawn.

EXAMPLE 1. Find the probability for the experiment just described. Assume that before the second token is drawn, the first token:
a. is replaced. **b.** is not replaced.

Solutions: Let A = the event that the first token is red.
  Let B = the event that the second token is blue.
To solve **a** and **b** use Theorem 14–7.

a.

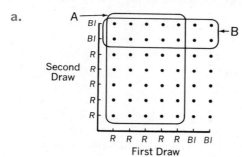

With Replacement (49 elements)

$$p(A \cap B) = p(A) \cdot p(B \mid A)$$
$$= \frac{35}{49} \cdot \frac{10}{35}$$
$$= \frac{5}{7} \cdot \frac{2}{7}$$
$$= \frac{10}{49}$$

b.

Second Draw
BI BI R R R R R
R R R R R BI BI
First Draw
Without Replacement (42 elements)

$$p(A \cap B) = p(A) \cdot p(B \mid A)$$
$$= \frac{30}{42} \cdot \frac{10}{30}$$
$$= \frac{5}{7} \cdot \frac{2}{6}$$
$$= \frac{5}{21}$$

In **a** the outcome of the first event, A, does not affect the outcome of the second event, B. Thus, these events are *independent*. In **b**, the outcome of the first event does affect the outcome of the second. These two events are *dependent*.

Note that in part **a** $p(B \mid A) = \frac{2}{7}$ and in part **b** $p(B \mid A) = \frac{2}{6}$. The first value is $p(B)$, the probability of B when B is independent of A. This suggests the following definition.

> **Definition**   Two events (or trials) A and B are **independent** if
> $$p(B) = p(B \mid A).$$
> Otherwise A and B are **dependent.**

This definition and Theorem 14–7 lead to Theorem 14–8.

> **Theorem 14–8**   The events A and B are independent if and only if $p(A \cap B) = p(A) \cdot p(B)$.

This theorem can be extended to three or more events. Thus, A, B, and C are independent if and only if

$$p(A \cap B \cap C) = p(A) \cdot p(B) \cdot p(C).$$

EXAMPLE 2.   Show that, in Example 1, the probabilities are unchanged if the blue token is drawn first.

a.   (Independent events)

$$p(B \cap A) = p(B) \cdot p(A)$$
$$= \frac{2}{7} \cdot \frac{5}{7} = \frac{10}{49}$$

b.   (Dependent events)

$$p(B \cap A) = p(B) \cdot p(A \mid B)$$
$$= \frac{2}{7} \cdot \frac{5}{6} = \frac{5}{21}$$

Examples 1 and 2 illustrate the fact that in the formulas for independent and dependent events, A and B are interchangeable.

EXAMPLE 3.   An experiment consists of a roll of one die.

Let A = the event that a 2, 3, or 4 appears.
Let B = the event that a 4, 5, or 6 appears.
Show that A and B are dependent events.

Solution: The sample space has six elements. Therefore.

$$p(A) = \frac{3}{6} = \frac{1}{2} \text{ and } p(B) = \frac{3}{6} = \frac{1}{2}.$$

Thus,

$$p(A) \cdot p(B) = \frac{1}{2} \cdot \frac{1}{2} = \frac{1}{4}.$$

Since $A \cap B = \{4\}$,

$$p(A \cap B) = \frac{1}{6}.$$

Thus, $p(A) \cdot p(B) \neq p(A \cap B)$ and A and B are dependent by Theorem 14–8.

EXAMPLE 4. Suppose the die used in Example 3 was *not* fair so that

$$p(2) = p(3) = p(5) = p(6) = \frac{1}{8}$$

and

$$p(1) = p(4) = \frac{1}{4}.$$

Show that events A and B are independent for this die.

Solution: $p(A) = \frac{1}{8} + \frac{1}{8} + \frac{1}{4} = \frac{1}{2}$ $p(B) = \frac{1}{4} + \frac{1}{8} + \frac{1}{8} = \frac{1}{2}$

$$p(A \cap B) = \frac{1}{4} = \frac{1}{2} \cdot \frac{1}{2} = p(A) \cdot p(B)$$

EXAMPLE 5. Find the probability of getting two black marbles in succession from a bag of three red and two black marbles if the first is replaced.

Solution:

The first marble is replaced. The events are independent.

$p(\text{black on first draw}) = \frac{2}{5}$ $p(\text{black on second draw}) = \frac{2}{5}$

$$p(A \cap B) = p(A) \cdot p(B) = \frac{2}{5} \times \frac{2}{5} = \frac{4}{25}$$

CLASSROOM EXERCISES

Classify events A and B as *independent* or *dependent*.

1. A. First toss of a coin: heads   B. Second toss: tails

2. From a bag of four red and five blue tokens, two tokens are drawn in succession without replacement.

A. First draw: a red token   B. Second draw: a blue token

3. Repeat Exercise 2, but assume that the first token *is* replaced.

4–6. Find the probability of event A followed by event B in each of Exercises 1–3.

WRITTEN EXERCISES

A   **1.** Find the probability of drawing two aces from a deck of cards if the first card is replaced before the second is drawn.

2. Repeat Exercise 1 but assume the first card is *not* replaced.

A pair of dice is thrown. Find the probability of each event.

3. Both are sixes.   **4.** Neither is a three.   **5.** Both show prime numbers.

■ A box contains 10 red, 8 green, and 12 blue tickets. Two successive tickets are drawn without replacement. Find the probability of drawing (without regard to order):

6. One blue and one green ticket. **7.** Two red tickets.

8. One green and one red ticket. **9.** No blue ticket.

■ The senior class has 42 girls and 48 boys; the junior class 50 girls and 40 boys. One representative each is chosen from the senior and junior classes. Find the probability that:

10. both will be girls.

11. both will be boys.

12. the junior will be a boy and the senior a girl.

13. the junior will be a girl and the senior a boy.

14. A deck of 52 cards contains four tens. Find the probability of getting two successive tens if the first card is replaced before the second is drawn.

15. Repeat Exercise 14 but assume the first card is *not* replaced.

B **16.** A die is rolled four times. Find the probability that it shows a six at least once.

17. A coin is tossed four times. Find the probability of getting the same number of heads and tails.

■ A bag has seven red and three green tokens. Two tokens are drawn in sequence. Find the probability that:

18. the second token is green.

19. the second token is green given that the first is red.

20. the second token is green given that the first is green.

■ A bag contains three black tokens and five white tokens.

21. Find the probability of drawing two white tokens if the first token is replaced before the second is drawn.

22. Repeat Exercise 21 but assume the first token is *not* replaced.

23. Find the probability of drawing three white tokens in succession if each token is replaced after selection.

24. Repeat Exercise 23 but assume the tokens are *not* replaced.

25. From a deck of 52 cards in which aces are high, two successive cards are drawn without replacement. Find the probability of getting a card whose value is less than five on both draws.

14-9   Binomial Probability Function

Suppose that an event E and its probability $p(E)$ are defined as follows.

E: Toss a coin and obtain "Heads."

$$p(E) = \frac{1}{2}$$

The toss of a coin is independent of any previous toss. Thus, if the coin is tossed n times, the probability of obtaining n heads is found by evaluating the following product

$$\underbrace{\frac{1}{2} \cdot \frac{1}{2} \cdot \frac{1}{2} \cdot \ \cdots \ \cdot \frac{1}{2}}_{n \text{ factors}} = \left(\frac{1}{2}\right)^n,$$

since Theorem 14-8 for two independent events can be extended to three or more trials.

Moreover, if E is *any* event with probability p, and if there are n independent trials, then the probability that E will occur exactly n times is p^n.

Of course, E does not occur on every trial. Call the occurrence of E a success, S, and the nonoccurrence of E a failure, F. Then the sample space is divided into two mutually exclusive events, S and F.

This leads to the definition of *binomial trials*, which are also called *Bernoulli trials*.

Definition   Binomial (Bernoulli) Trials

A sequence of **binomial trials** is a sequence of independent repeated trials under identical conditions. There are two possible outcomes on each trial: S or F.

Since a binomial trial has only two outcomes, the probability of success p and probability of failure q are related by the equation

$$p + q = 1,$$

which follows from the *Probability Postulates* on page 737.

Example 1 on the next page shows how to determine the probability of any specified combination of successes and failures.

EXAMPLE 1. The probability that Phyllis will win whenever she plays bridge is $\frac{1}{4}$. Suppose that she plays six games. Find the probability that she will win four times and lose twice.

In each set of six games a particular win-loss pattern can be represented in a diagram. For example, suppose that the middle four games are wins and that the first and last games are losses. Then the diagram is as follows.

(Loss) (Win) (Win) (Win) (Win) (Loss)

The probability of "Win" is $\frac{1}{4}$ and of "Loss" is

$$1 - \frac{1}{4} = \frac{3}{4}.$$

The probability of the pattern's occurring is the product of the probabilities for "Win" and "Loss." Thus, the probability of the win-loss pattern "LWWWL" is

$$\left(\frac{1}{4}\right)^4 \cdot \left(\frac{3}{4}\right)^2.$$

Any other pattern of four wins and two losses, for example, WLWWWL, also has probability $(\frac{1}{4})^4 \cdot (\frac{3}{4})^2$. There are $_6C_4$ such patterns. Since all of these 4–2 win-loss patterns are mutually exclusive, the total probability is the sum of the $_6C_4$ probabilities. This is found by forming the product of $_6C_4$ and $(\frac{1}{4})^4 \cdot (\frac{3}{4})^2$, namely,

$$_6C_4 \left(\frac{1}{4}\right)^4 \left(\frac{3}{4}\right)^2 = 15 \left(\frac{1}{4}\right)^4 \left(\frac{3}{4}\right)^2$$

$$= 15 \cdot \frac{3^2}{4^6}$$

$$= \frac{135}{4098} \approx 0.033.$$

Example 1 illustrates Theorem 14–9.

Theorem 14–9 The probability of exactly k successes in n binomial trials is

$$_nC_k \cdot p^k q^{n-k} \qquad\qquad (n \geq k; q = 1 - p)$$

The proof is asked for in the exercises.

> **Theorem 14–10** The probability of at least k successes in n binomial trials ($n \geq k$) is given by the following expressions.
>
> $$p^n + {_nC_{n-1}} \cdot p^{n-1}q^1 + {_nC_{n-2}} \cdot p^{n-2}q^2 + \cdots + {_nC_k} \cdot p^k q^{n-k}.$$

Proof: The term $_nC_k \cdot p^k q^{n-k}$ gives the probability of exactly k successes. Each other term to the left of $_nC_k \cdot p^k q^{n-k}$ in the expression gives the probability of more than k successes. Since all possible numbers of successes greater than k are included, the sum gives the probability of at least k successes.

EXAMPLE 2. On a True-False test, Art has to guess at the answers to each of the ten questions. However, he estimates his probability of guessing correctly at $\frac{2}{3}$. Assume that his estimate is correct and find the probability of his getting at least seven answers correct.

Solution: Use Theorem 14–10.

$$\left(\frac{2}{3}\right)^{10} + {_{10}C_9} \cdot \left(\frac{2}{3}\right)^9\left(\frac{1}{3}\right)^1 + {_{10}C_8} \cdot \left(\frac{2}{3}\right)^8\left(\frac{1}{3}\right)^2 + {_{10}C_7} \cdot \left(\frac{2}{3}\right)^7\left(\frac{1}{3}\right)^3$$

$$= \frac{2^7}{3^{10}}(8 + 40 + 90 + 120) = \frac{33{,}024}{59{,}049} \approx 0.559$$

Notice that $_nC_k p^k q^{n-k}$ is a term of the expansion by the Binomial Theorem (see page 24) of $(p + q)^k$. The most probable number of successes in n trials is the value of k for which $_nC_k p^k q^{n-k}$ is largest. An investigation of such terms would show that the most probable number of successes is approximately np. (See the last exercise of Section 14–10.) This fact and Theorem 14–9 are important in statistics.

CLASSROOM EXERCISES

━━━ At a carnival game, the probability of hitting a target with a bean bag in one throw is $\frac{1}{4}$. Margo makes five throws. Find the probability of each indicated event if she makes:

1. exactly two hits.　　　　　　**2.** at least two hits.

3. exactly three hits.　　　　　**4.** at least three hits.

5. at most two hits.　　　　　　**6.** at most three hits.

WRITTEN EXERCISES

A   **1.** In the World Series one year, Boston and Cincinnati are evenly matched with each having a probability of $\frac{1}{2}$ of winning each game. When one team wins four games, the Series is over. Find the probability that Boston wins in exactly four games.

2. For the Series game in Exercise 1 find the probability that Cincinnati wins in exactly seven games.

━━In Exercise 3–5 a die is rolled five times.

3. Find the probability of getting exactly two threes.

4. Find the probability of getting at least two threes.

5. Find the probability of getting at most two threes.

━━In Exercises 6–7 a coin is flipped eight times.

6. Find the probability of getting exactly six heads.

7. Find the probability of getting at most six heads.

8. Mrs. Cranston owns a motel. She has five T.V.'s that she supplies to guests. There are eight guests and the probability that a guest wants a T.V. set is $\frac{1}{2}$. Find the probability that there will be more requests than sets.

━━Assume that $\frac{3}{4}$ of the drivers of seat-belted cars use them on long trips and that four seat-belted cars are checked on a tollway. Find the probability that seat belts are used by:

9. none of the drivers.   **10.** all the drivers.

11. exactly one driver.   **12.** at most two drivers.

B   **13.** An airplane is to drop supplies to a stranded expedition. The probability of doing this in one drop is $\frac{1}{3}$. Find the smallest number of drops necessary in order to be at least 95 per cent sure of getting at least one batch of supplies to the expedition.

14. A batter has a batting average of 0.350. Find the probability that the batter will get two hits in five times at bat.

15. Seven coins are tossed. Find the most probable number of heads, and the corresponding probability of this number, by expanding $(\frac{1}{2} + \frac{1}{2})^7$. Compare this result with the value of np (*i.e.* of $7 \cdot \frac{1}{2} = 3.5$).

16. For a certain infection the probability that one animal will get well after one week is 0.3. Find the probability that exactly four of six animals will get well after one week.

17. Prove Theorem 14–9.

14–10 Expected Value

At a local state fair there is a game of chance with the following rules.

>   i. Eight tickets, marked 1, 1, 2, 2, 3, 3, 4, and 4 respectively, are placed in a bowl.
>   ii. The customer reaches into the bowl and draws two tickets.
> iii. The customer wins one-tenth the dollar value of the sum of the numbers on the tickets.

What is a fair price for the customer to pay for the opportunity to play the game? The answer to this question is provided by the concept of *expected value*.

> **Definition** If the probabilities of receiving the amounts $a_1, a_2, \cdots,$ or a_k, are $p_1, p_2, \cdots,$ and p_k, respectively, then the *mathematical expectation* or <u>expected</u> value E is given by
>
> $$E = a_1 p_1 + a_2 p_2 + \cdots + a_k p_k.$$

EXAMPLE 1. Apply the above definition to the game of chance described earlier.

Solution: First construct a sample space for the problem.

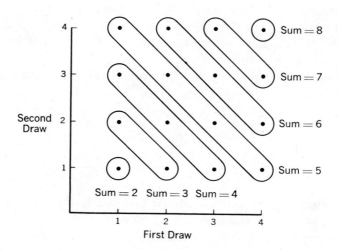

There are 16 sample points, but there are only seven possible sums.

The probabilities of these sums are as follows.

$$p(2) = \frac{1}{16} \qquad p(3) = \frac{2}{16} \qquad p(4) = \frac{3}{16} \qquad p(5) = \frac{4}{16}$$

$$p(6) = \frac{3}{16} \qquad p(7) = \frac{2}{16} \qquad p(8) = \frac{1}{16}$$

The expected value, E, is

$$\frac{2}{10} \cdot \frac{1}{16} + \frac{3}{10} \cdot \frac{2}{16} + \frac{4}{10} \cdot \frac{3}{16} + \frac{5}{10} \cdot \frac{4}{16} + \frac{6}{10} \cdot \frac{3}{16} + \frac{7}{10} \cdot \frac{2}{16} + \frac{8}{10} \cdot \frac{1}{16}.$$

This simplifies to

$$\frac{1}{160} (2 + 6 + 12 + 20 + 18 + 14 + 8)$$

or,

$$\frac{1}{160} (80) = \frac{1}{2}.$$

This value for E means that if you play long enough and if the game is fair, you will average $\frac{1}{2}$ dollar in winnings per play of the game. Thus, the mathematical expectation or expected value, E, is the average payoff for the game. Since you win $\frac{1}{2}$ dollar, on the average, for each game, a fair price for you to pay is $\frac{1}{2}$ dollar. Of course, the game operator wishes to make a profit, so the operator will charge more than $\frac{1}{2}$ dollar.

EXAMPLE 2. Roulette is sometimes played with a wheel that has 37 slots numbered 0–36. The player makes a wager on a number. If the ball falls in a slot with that number, the player will win 35 times the wager. If the ball stops on another number, the wager is lost. Find the expected value of this game.

The probability that the ball falls into a certain numbered slot is $\frac{1}{37}$. The loss of one dollar is represented by -1. Then, for a wager of one dollar,

$$E = 35 \cdot \frac{1}{37} + (-1) \frac{36}{37}$$

$$= \frac{-1}{37} \approx -0.027$$

The result means that you would lose nearly three cents for each dollar you wagered if you played long enough. Conversely, it says that your opponent would win nearly three cents for each dollar wagered. A *fair game* is one for which $E = 0$. Roulette, as described, is not a fair game.

EXAMPLE 3. In a certain board game, you move your piece as many spaces as appears on the upper face of the rolled die. Find the expected number of spaces for a move.

Solution: Each number one through six is equally likely with probability $\frac{1}{6}$.

$$E = \tfrac{1}{6}(1 + 2 + 3 + 4 + 5 + 6)$$
$$= \tfrac{1}{6} \times 21$$
$$= 3.5$$

The expected number of spaces for a move is 3.5 spaces.

CLASSROOM EXERCISES

A club sells 500 raffle tickets for a color T.V. worth $400.

1. Find the expected value of the purchase of one ticket.

2. Find the smallest purchase price for which the club will not lose money.

WRITTEN EXERCISES

A — Patricia Joyce receives $2.60 if she draws an ace from a 52-card deck.

1. Find the expected value of the game.

2. How much should Patricia be charged to play so that the game will be fair?

To introduce microwave ovens to the public, a store offers a cash prize of $1000 to anyone who comes to the store to fill out an application card. Suppose that 2500 people do this.

3. Find the expected value of filling out the card.

4. Is it worth the $1.00 for the transportation cost of getting to the store? Explain.

In a golf tournament, the winner will get $15,000 and the loser $9000. Find the expected value of the tournament for Player A in each case below.

5. The two players are equally likely to win.

6. The odds that Player A will win are 5 to 4, that is, the probability that Player A will win is $\frac{5}{5+4}$, or $\frac{5}{9}$.

7. Suppose that a person will pay you the face value of a die if it comes up 1, 2, or 3. Find what you should pay that person for a 4, 5, or 6 in order to make it a fair game ($E = 0$).

8. Alex's parents promise him $10 for an A in probability, $5.00 for a B, and nothing for a C, D or E. His probability of getting an A is 0.21 and his probability of getting a B is 0.47. Find his mathematical expectation.

B ▬ In a game called "Fish," you choose one package from a bucket that contains 20 packages worth seven cents each, 20 packages worth 12 cents each, and five worth 14 cents each. Determine whether it is worthwhile to pay the given amount in order to play the game.

9. Eight cents   **10.** Twelve cents

11. A friend offers to pay you twenty-five dollars if you draw the ace of spades and four dollars for any other spade. However, you must pay your friend two dollars for any nonspade drawn. Should you accept the offer? Explain.

▬ Suppose that on the draw of a card from a 52-card deck, the dealer will pay ten dollars for an ace, five dollars for a king or queen, three dollars for a jack or ten, and nothing for any other card.

12. Find the expected value of the game.

13. Would you pay $1.00 to play? Explain.

14. A man rolling a pair of dice will pay n dollars if the number showing is the product of n primes (not necessarily distinct), where $n = 2$ or 3. He will collect three dollars if he rolls a prime sum. Find the expected value of the game.

15. An importer is offered a shipment of radios for $5000. The probabilities that they can be sold for $6000, $5500, $5000, or $4500 are 0.25, 0.46, 0.19, and 0.10, respectively. Find the expected profit if the radios are accepted.

16. In a certain board game, you move your piece as many spaces as the sum of the values showing on two dice. Find the expected number of spaces for a move.

C **17.** Prove the following theorem:

> *In a sequence of n binomial trials, the expected value of the number of successes is np, where p is the probability of success on each trial.*

COMPUTER APPLICATION

BASIC: SIMULATIONS

Computers are useful in simulating events that are otherwise difficult to duplicate. For example, randomly generating the number of samples of people necessary to estimate the probability that two of them share a birthday would be very expensive and time-consuming.

Problem:

Write a program which simulates a given number of samples of n people in order to determine the probability that at least two were born on the same month and day (not year).

```
100 PRINT
110 PRINT "THIS PROGRAM CALCULATES THE"
120 PRINT "PROBABILITY THAT TWO PERSONS IN 'N'"
130 PRINT "HAVE THE SAME BIRTHDAY."
140 PRINT
150 PRINT "HOW MANY PERSONS";
160 INPUT N
170 PRINT "HOW MANY SAMPLES TO DRAW (> = 100)";
180 INPUT M
190 DIM P(N)
200 LET C = 0
210 FOR I = 1 TO M
220    FOR J = 1 TO N
230       LET P(J) = INT(365*RND(.5)+1)
240       IF J = 1 THEN 280
250       FOR K = 1 TO J-1
260          IF P(K) = P(J) THEN 300
270       NEXT K
280    NEXT J
290    GOTO 310
300    LET C = C + 1
310 NEXT I
320 PRINT
330 PRINT M;" SAMPLES OF";N;" PERSONS EACH"
340 PRINT "PRODUCED MATCHES";C;" TIMES."
350 PRINT
360 PRINT "THE PROBABILITY OF TWO PERSONS IN";N
370 PRINT "HAVING THE SAME BIRTHDATE IS "; C/M
380 PRINT
390 END
```

Output:

```
HOW MANY PERSONS? 10
HOW MANY SAMPLES TO DRAW (> = 100)? 100

100 SAMPLES OF 10 PERSONS EACH
PRODUCED MATCHES 11 TIMES.

THE PROBABILITY OF TWO PERSONS IN 10
HAVING THE SAME BIRTHDAY IS .11
```

NOTE: The probability that <u>no two people</u> in a group of n people share a birthday can be found using the equation

$$p(E) = \frac{365 P_n}{365^n}.$$

Analysis:

Statements 210–310: The I–loop is based on the number of samples, M, to be tested. The second loop (J–loop) generates random numbers between 1 and 365 corresponding to the days in a (non-leap) year. Statements 250–270 check to see if, upon generating a new P(J), the new number equals a previous P(J). If it does, generation of P(J)'s is stopped, one added to the count (C) of samples with a match, and a new sample is begun (NEXT I). This technique is used to reduce the time needed to run the simulation.

EXERCISES

A   Use the program on page 763 to determine each probability, using the given values for n and m.

1. $n = 24$, $m = 200$ **2.** $n = 30$, $m = 100$

3. Run the program for 100 samples for each sample size 10 through 25. Make a table of the probabilities obtained.

4. Calculate the mathematical probability that at least two people will have the same birth date in a random sample of n people, where n is 10 through 25. Compare these results with the results obtained in Exercise 3.

B   Revise the program on page 763 in the manner indicated.

5. Add statements to the program to check for bad input. For example, the number of people and the number of samples must be positive integers.

C   Write a BASIC program.

6. Find the average number of birth date matches in a sample of n people.

CHAPTER SUMMARY

Important Terms

Addition Principle of Counting (p. 730)
Binomial trials (p. 755)
Combination (p. 726)
Complement (p. 738)
Conditional Probability (p. 749)
Discount sets (p. 745)
Event (p. 735)
Expected value (p. 759)
Fundamental Counting Principle (p. 719)

General Addition Rule (p. 744)
Independent events (p. 752)
Mathematical expectation (p. 759)
Mutually exclusive events (p. 730)
Permutation (p. 722)
Probability (p. 735)
Sample space (p. 735)
Tree diagram (p. 718)
Venn diagram (p. 744)

Important Ideas

1. $_nP_r = \dfrac{n!}{(n-r)!}$ where $n! = n \cdot (n-1)(n-2). \ldots \cdot 1$

2. $_nC_r = \dbinom{n}{r} = \dfrac{n!}{r!(n-r)!}$

3. For every event A in a sample space S, $0 \le p(A) \le 1$.

4. $p(A \cup B) = p(A) + p(B) - p(A \cap B)$

5. $p(B \mid A) = \dfrac{p(A \cap B)}{p(A)}$, $p(A) \ne 0$

6. $p(A \cap B) = p(A) \cdot p(B)$, if A and B are independent.

CHAPTER OBJECTIVES AND REVIEW

Objective: *To apply the Fundamental Principle of Counting.* (Section 14-1)

1. Find the number of ways in which a blue sock and a red sock can be chosen from three blue socks and five red socks.

2. Find the number of ways in which a sandwich and drink can be chosen from five sandwiches and four drinks.

3. A true-false exam has 10 questions. Find the number of ways in which a student can mark his answers.

Objective: *To evaluate and apply permutations.* (Section 14-2)

▬▬Evaluate each expression.

4. $_{10}P_3$ **5.** $_{100}P_0$ **6.** $_5P_2$ **7.** $_nP_{n-r}$

8. Find the number of ways in which three identical T.V. sets and identical record players can be arranged side by side.

9. Find the number of permutations of nine coins: three identical pennies, four identical dimes and two identical quarters.

10. Find the number of permutations of the letters in TENNESSEE.

Objective: *To evaluate and apply combinations.* (Section 14-3)

━━━ Evaluate each expression.

11. $_{12}C_1$ **12.** $\dfrac{_nP_r}{r!}$ **13.** $_5C_2$ **14.** $_nC_n$

15. Find the number of committees of four persons that can be selected from a set of 15 people.

━━━ Find the number of committees of four persons that can be selected from eight men and ten women in each instance below.

16. Two must be men and two must be women.

17. Three must be women and one must be a man.

18. Find the number of ways in which you can select five cards from a standard deck with kings, queens, and jacks removed. How many of these selections have at least one pair?

Objective: *To apply the Addition Principle of Counting.* (Section 14-4)

19. Find the number of ways in which you can select a red token or a green token from a box with seven red and two green tokens.

━━━ Find the number of committees of four persons that can be selected from eight men and ten women in each instance below.

20. At least two members must be men.

21. At most one member must be a man.

22. Describe what is meant by *mutually exclusive events.*

Objective: *To find probabilities of simple events.* (Section 14-5)

23. Find the probability of getting exactly one pair of sevens in a five-card hand.

24. Find the probability of getting exactly three fours in seven tosses of a die.

25. Find the number of whole numbers made up of the digits 1, 3, 5, 6, and 8. (Use no digit more than once.) Then find the probability of choosing an even four-digit number from these numbers.

Objective: *To apply the General Addition Rule for probabilities.*
(Section 14-6)

26. Complete: $p(A \cup B) = p(A) + \underline{\ ?\ } - \underline{\ ?\ }$.

27. Find the probability that an ace, king, queen, jack, or a spade will appear on a single draw of one card from a 52-card deck.

28. Find the probability of drawing two black cards or a pair from a 52-card deck.

Objective: *To find conditional probabilities.* (Section 14-7)

29. Complete: $p(B \mid A) = \underline{\ ?\ }$.

30. Find the probability of getting a sum of nine on two dice if the first die already show a five.

31. Find the probability of getting a sum of eight, nine, or ten on two dice if the first die already shows a six.

Objective: *To identify independent and dependent events and to find the probability of such events.* (Section 14-8)

■■■ Two tokens are drawn from a box. In each case determine whether the events of drawing the tokens is *independent* or *dependent*.

32. The first token drawn is replaced.

33. No replacement is made.

■■■ Find the probability of getting a green token and a red token from a bag of eight red and five green tokens in each case.

34. The first token is replaced.   **35.** The first token is not replaced.

Objective: *To apply the Binomial Probability Function.* (Section 14-9)

■■■ Mary wins the game of Hearts three-fourths of the times that she plays. Suppose that she plays six games.

36. Find the probability that she will win exactly four times.

37. Find the probability that she will win at least twice.

38. Find the probability that she will win at most four times.

Objective: *To calculate and interpret expected values.* (Section 14-10)

■■■ On a roll of one die, an odd number pays 50 cents, six pays 60 cents and two pays 90 cents.

39. Find the expected value of the game.

40. Would 40 cents be too much to pay for the honor of playing? Explain.

CHAPTER TEST

━━ Find the value of each expression in Exercises 1–3.

1. $_5C_3$ **2.** $_8P_4$ **3.** $\dfrac{(n-1)!}{n!}$

━━ Find a numeral or a symbol to complete each statement in Exercises 4–8.

4. $n! = \underline{\ ?\ }$ **5.** $\underline{\ ?\ } \leq p(E) < \underline{\ ?\ }$

6. $p(E) + p(E') = \underline{\ ?\ }$ (E' is the complement of E.)

7. Given $E_1 \cap E_2 = \phi$, $p(E_1 \cup E_2) = \underline{\ ?\ } + \underline{\ ?\ }$.

8. Given $E_1 \cap E_2 \neq \phi$, $p(E_1 \cup E_2) = p(E_1) + p(E_2) - \underline{\ ?\ }$.

9. Draw a sample space for tossing three coins. (It consists of eight points.) Find the probability of each point.

10. There are five roads from city A to city B, and seven roads from city B to city C. Find the number of roads you could take from city A via city B to city C.

11. Find the number of ways you can arrange five people in a row.

12. Find the number of committees of three people each that you can form from a set of eight people.

13. Find the probability of getting four heads and three tails when seven coins are tossed.

14. From a bag containing nine red tokens and six green tokens, two tokens are drawn in succession. Find the probability of drawing two red tokens with replacement.

15. Repeat Exercise 14 but assume that the tokens are not replaced after they are drawn.

━━ In Exercises 16–19, two dice, X and Y, are rolled. Find the probability that:

16. the numbers on the two dice are the same.

17. the number on die X is less than three and the number on die Y is greater than three.

18. the number on die X is greater than or equal to four *or* the number on die Y is greater than two.

19. the sum of the numbers on the two dice is greater than eight.

20. In a board game the number of spaces that a piece may move is determined by the throw of a tetrahedral die. The "down" face counts. The four faces are marked 2, 4, 6, and 8, respectively. Find the expected number of spaces that a piece will move after a die is rolled.

Table of Values of the Trigonometric Functions

θ Deg.	θ Rad.	Sin θ	Cos θ	Tan θ	Cot θ	Sec θ	Csc θ		
0° 00'	.0000	.0000	1.0000	.0000		1.000		1.5708	90° 00'
10'	.0029	.0029	1.0000	.0029	343.77	1.000	343.8	1.5679	50'
20'	.0058	.0058	1.0000	.0058	171.89	1.000	171.9	1.5650	40'
30'	.0087	.0087	1.0000	.0087	114.59	1.000	114.6	1.5621	30'
40'	.0116	.0116	.9999	.0116	85.940	1.000	85.95	1.5592	20'
50'	.0145	.0145	.9999	.0145	68.750	1.000	68.76	1.5563	10'
1° 00'	.0175	.0175	.9998	.0175	57.290	1.000	57.30	1.5533	89° 00'
10'	.0204	.0204	.9998	.0204	49.104	1.000	49.11	1.5504	50'
20'	.0233	.0233	.9997	.0233	42.964	1.000	42.98	1.5475	40'
30'	.0262	.0262	.9997	.0262	38.188	1.000	38.20	1.5446	30'
40'	.0291	.0291	.9996	.0291	34.368	1.000	34.38	1.5417	20'
50'	.0320	.0320	.9995	.0320	31.242	1.001	31.26	1.5388	10'
2° 00'	.0349	.0349	.9994	.0349	28.636	1.001	28.65	1.5359	88° 00'
10'	.0378	.0378	.9993	.0378	26.432	1.001	26.45	1.5330	50'
20'	.0407	.0407	.9992	.0407	24.542	1.001	24.56	1.5301	40'
30'	.0436	.0436	.9990	.0437	22.904	1.001	22.93	1.5272	30'
40'	.0465	.0465	.9989	.0466	21.470	1.001	21.49	1.5243	20'
50'	.0495	.0494	.9988	.0495	20.206	1.001	20.23	1.5213	10'
3° 00'	.0524	.0523	.9986	.0524	19.081	1.001	19.11	1.5184	87° 00'
10'	.0553	.0552	.9985	.0553	18.075	1.002	18.10	1.5155	50'
20'	.0582	.0581	.9983	.0582	17.169	1.002	17.20	1.5126	40'
30'	.0611	.0610	.9981	.0612	16.350	1.002	16.38	1.5097	30'
40'	.0640	.0640	.9980	.0641	15.605	1.002	15.64	1.5068	20'
50'	.0669	.0669	.9978	.0670	14.924	1.002	14.96	1.5039	10'
4° 00'	.0698	.0698	.9976	.0699	14.301	1.002	14.34	1.5010	86° 00'
10'	.0727	.0727	.9974	.0729	13.727	1.003	13.76	1.4981	50'
20'	.0756	.0756	.9971	.0758	13.197	1.003	13.23	1.4952	40'
30'	.0785	.0785	.9969	.0787	12.706	1.003	12.75	1.4923	30'
40'	.0814	.0814	.9967	.0816	12.251	1.003	12.29	1.4893	20'
50'	.0844	.0843	.9964	.0846	11.826	1.004	11.87	1.4864	10'
5° 00'	.0873	.0872	.9962	.0875	11.430	1.004	11.47	1.4835	85° 00'
10'	.0902	.0901	.9959	.0904	11.059	1.004	11.10	1.4806	50'
20'	.0931	.0929	.9957	.0934	10.712	1.004	10.76	1.4777	40'
30'	.0960	.0958	.9954	.0963	10.385	1.005	10.43	1.4748	30'
40'	.0989	.0987	.9951	.0992	10.078	1.005	10.13	1.4719	20'
50'	.1018	.1016	.9948	.1022	9.7882	1.005	9.839	1.4690	10'
6° 00'	.1047	.1045	.9945	.1051	9.5144	1.006	9.567	1.4661	84° 00'
10'	.1076	.1074	.9942	.1080	9.2553	1.006	9.309	1.4632	50'
20'	.1105	.1103	.9939	.1110	9.0098	1.006	9.065	1.4603	40'
30'	.1134	.1132	.9936	.1139	8.7769	1.006	8.834	1.4573	30'
40'	.1164	.1161	.9932	.1169	8.5555	1.007	8.614	1.4544	20'
50'	.1193	.1190	.9929	.1198	8.3450	1.007	8.405	1.4515	10'
7° 00'	.1222	.1219	.9925	.1228	8.1443	1.008	8.206	1.4486	83° 00'
10'	.1251	.1248	.9922	.1257	7.9530	1.008	8.016	1.4457	50'
20'	.1280	.1276	.9918	.1287	7.7704	1.008	7.834	1.4428	40'
30'	.1309	.1305	.9914	.1317	7.5958	1.009	7.661	1.4399	30'
40'	.1338	.1334	.9911	.1346	7.4287	1.009	7.496	1.4370	20'
50'	.1367	.1363	.9907	.1376	7.2687	1.009	7.337	1.4341	10'
8° 00'	.1396	.1392	.9903	.1405	7.1154	1.010	7.185	1.4312	82° 00'
10'	.1425	.1421	.9899	.1435	6.9682	1.010	7.040	1.4283	50'
20'	.1454	.1449	.9894	.1465	6.8269	1.011	6.900	1.4254	40'
30'	.1484	.1478	.9890	.1495	6.6912	1.011	6.765	1.4224	30'
40'	.1513	.1507	.9886	.1524	6.5606	1.012	6.636	1.4195	20'
50'	.1542	.1536	.9881	.1554	6.4348	1.012	6.512	1.4166	10'
9° 00'	.1571	.1564	.9877	.1584	6.3138	1.012	6.392	1.4137	81° 00'
		Cos θ	Sin θ	Cot θ	Tan θ	Csc θ	Sec θ	θ Rad.	θ Deg.

Table of Values of the Trigonometric Functions

θ Deg.	θ Rad.	Sin θ	Cos θ	Tan θ	Cot θ	Sec θ	Csc θ		
9°00′	.1571	.1564	.9877	.1584	6.3138	1.012	6.392	1.4137	81°00′
10′	.1600	.1593	.9872	.1614	6.1970	1.013	6.277	1.4108	50′
20′	.1629	.1622	.9868	.1644	6.0844	1.013	6.166	1.4079	40′
30′	.1658	.1650	.9863	.1673	5.9758	1.014	6.059	1.4050	30′
40′	.1687	.1679	.9858	.1703	5.8708	1.014	5.955	1.4021	20′
50′	.1716	.1708	.9853	.1733	5.7694	1.015	5.855	1.3992	10′
10°00′	.1745	.1736	.9848	.1763	5.6713	1.015	5.759	1.3963	80°00′
10′	.1774	.1765	.9843	.1793	5.5764	1.016	5.665	1.3934	50′
20′	.1804	.1794	.9838	.1823	5.4845	1.016	5.575	1.3904	40′
30′	.1833	.1822	.9833	.1853	5.3955	1.017	5.487	1.3875	30′
40′	.1862	.1851	.9827	.1883	5.3093	1.018	5.403	1.3846	20′
50′	.1891	.1880	.9822	.1914	5.2257	1.018	5.320	1.3817	10′
11°00′	.1920	.1908	.9816	.1944	5.1446	1.019	5.241	1.3788	79°00′
10′	.1949	.1937	.9811	.1974	5.0658	1.019	5.164	1.3759	50′
20′	.1978	.1965	.9805	.2004	4.9894	1.020	5.089	1.3730	40′
30′	.2007	.1994	.9799	.2035	4.9152	1.020	5.016	1.3701	30′
40′	.2036	.2022	.9793	.2065	4.8430	1.021	4.945	1.3672	20′
50′	.2065	.2051	.9787	.2095	4.7729	1.022	4.876	1.3643	10′
12°00′	.2094	.2079	.9781	.2126	4.7046	1.022	4.810	1.3614	78°00′
10′	.2123	.2108	.9775	.2156	4.6382	1.023	4.745	1.3584	50′
20′	.2153	.2136	.9769	.2186	4.5736	1.024	4.682	1.3555	40′
30′	.2182	.2164	.9763	.2217	4.5107	1.024	4.620	1.3526	30′
40′	.2211	.2193	.9757	.2247	4.4494	1.025	4.560	1.3497	20′
50′	.2240	.2221	.9750	.2278	4.3897	1.026	4.502	1.3468	10′
13°00′	.2269	.2250	.9744	.2309	4.3315	1.026	4.445	1.3439	77°00′
10′	.2298	.2278	.9737	.2339	4.2747	1.027	4.390	1.3410	50′
20′	.2327	.2306	.9730	.2370	4.2193	1.028	4.336	1.3381	40′
30′	.2356	.2334	.9724	.2401	4.1653	1.028	4.284	1.3352	30′
40′	.2385	.2363	.9717	.2432	4.1126	1.029	4.232	1.3323	20′
50′	.2414	.2391	.9710	.2462	4.0611	1.030	4.182	1.3294	10′
14°00′	.2443	.2419	.9703	.2493	4.0108	1.031	4.134	1.3265	76°00′
10′	.2473	.2447	.9696	.2524	3.9617	1.031	4.086	1.3235	50′
20′	.2502	.2476	.9689	.2555	3.9136	1.032	4.039	1.3206	40′
30′	.2531	.2504	.9681	.2586	3.8667	1.033	3.994	1.3177	30′
40′	.2560	.2532	.9674	.2617	3.8208	1.034	3.950	1.3148	20′
50′	.2589	.2560	.9667	.2648	3.7760	1.034	3.906	1.3119	10′
15°00′	.2618	.2588	.9659	.2679	3.7321	1.035	3.864	1.3090	75°00′
10′	.2647	.2616	.9652	.2711	3.6891	1.036	3.822	1.3061	50′
20′	.2676	.2644	.9644	.2742	3.6470	1.037	3.782	1.3032	40′
30′	.2705	.2672	.9636	.2773	3.6059	1.038	3.742	1.3003	30′
40′	.2734	.2700	.9628	.2805	3.5656	1.039	3.703	1.2974	20′
50′	.2763	.2728	.9621	.2836	3.5261	1.039	3.665	1.2945	10′
16°00′	.2793	.2756	.9613	.2867	3.4874	1.040	3.628	1.2915	74°00′
10′	.2822	.2784	.9605	.2899	3.4495	1.041	3.592	1.2886	50′
20′	.2851	.2812	.9596	.2931	3.4124	1.042	3.556	1.2857	40′
30′	.2880	.2840	.9588	.2962	3.3759	1.043	3.521	1.2828	30′
40′	.2909	.2868	.9580	.2994	3.3402	1.044	3.487	1.2799	20′
50′	.2938	.2896	.9572	.3026	3.3052	1.045	3.453	1.2770	10′
17°00′	.2967	.2924	.9563	.3057	3.2709	1.046	3.420	1.2741	73°00′
10′	.2996	.2952	.9555	.3089	3.2371	1.047	3.388	1.2712	50′
20′	.3025	.2979	.9546	.3121	3.2041	1.048	3.356	1.2683	40′
30′	.3054	.3007	.9537	.3153	3.1716	1.049	3.326	1.2654	30′
40′	.3083	.3035	.9528	.3185	3.1397	1.049	3.295	1.2625	20′
50′	.3113	.3062	.9520	.3217	3.1084	1.050	3.265	1.2595	10′
18°00′	.3142	.3090	.9511	.3249	3.0777	1.051	3.236	1.2566	72°00′
		Cos θ	Sin θ	Cot θ	Tan θ	Csc θ	Sec θ	θ Rad.	θ Deg.

Table of Values of the Trigonometric Functions

θ Deg.	θ Rad.	Sin θ	Cos θ	Tan θ	Cot θ	Sec θ	Csc θ		
18° 00'	.3142	.3090	.9511	.3249	3.0777	1.051	3.236	1.2566	72° 00'
10'	.3171	.3118	.9502	.3281	3.0475	1.052	3.207	1.2537	50'
20'	.3200	.3145	.9492	.3314	3.0178	1.053	3.179	1.2508	40'
30'	.3229	.3173	.9483	.3346	2.9887	1.054	3.152	1.2479	30'
40'	.3258	.3201	.9474	.3378	2.9600	1.056	3.124	1.2450	20'
50'	.3287	.3228	.9465	.3411	2.9319	1.057	3.098	1.2421	10'
19° 00'	.3316	.3256	.9455	.3443	2.9042	1.058	3.072	1.2392	71° 00'
10'	.3345	.3283	.9446	.3476	2.8770	1.059	3.046	1.2363	50'
20'	.3374	.3311	.9436	.3508	2.8502	1.060	3.021	1.2334	40'
30'	.3403	.3338	.9426	.3541	2.8239	1.061	2.996	1.2305	30'
40'	.3432	.3365	.9417	.3574	2.7980	1.062	2.971	1.2275	20'
50'	.3462	.3393	.9407	.3607	2.7725	1.063	2.947	1.2246	10'
20° 00'	.3491	.3420	.9397	.3640	2.7475	1.064	2.924	1.2217	70° 00'
10'	.3520	.3448	.9387	.3673	2.7228	1.065	2.901	1.2188	50'
20'	.3549	.3475	.9377	.3706	2.6985	1.066	2.878	1.2159	40'
30'	.3578	.3502	.9367	.3739	2.6746	1.068	2.855	1.2130	30'
40'	.3607	.3529	.9356	.3772	2.6511	1.069	2.833	1.2101	20'
50'	.3636	.3557	.9346	.3805	2.6279	1.070	2.812	1.2072	10'
21° 00'	.3665	.3584	.9336	.3839	2.6051	1.071	2.790	1.2043	69° 00'
10'	.3694	.3611	.9325	.3872	2.5826	1.072	2.769	1.2014	50'
20'	.3723	.3638	.9315	.3906	2.5605	1.074	2.749	1.1985	40'
30'	.3752	.3665	.9304	.3939	2.5386	1.075	2.729	1.1956	30'
40'	.3782	.3692	.9293	.3973	2.5172	1.076	2.709	1.1926	20'
50'	.3811	.3719	.9283	.4006	2.4960	1.077	2.689	1.1897	10'
22° 00'	.3840	.3746	.9272	.4040	2.4751	1.079	2.669	1.1868	68° 00'
10'	.3869	.3773	.9261	.4074	2.4545	1.080	2.650	1.1839	50'
20'	.3898	.3800	.9250	.4108	2.4342	1.081	2.632	1.1810	40'
30'	.3927	.3827	.9239	.4142	2.4142	1.082	2.613	1.1781	30'
40'	.3956	.3854	.9228	.4176	2.3945	1.084	2.595	1.1752	20'
50'	.3985	.3881	.9216	.4210	2.3750	1.085	2.577	1.1723	10'
23° 00'	.4014	.3907	.9205	.4245	2.3559	1.086	2.559	1.1694	67° 00'
10'	.4043	.3934	.9194	.4279	2.3369	1.088	2.542	1.1665	50'
20'	.4072	.3961	.9182	.4314	2.3183	1.089	2.525	1.1636	40'
30'	.4102	.3987	.9171	.4348	2.2998	1.090	2.508	1.1606	30'
40'	.4131	.4014	.9159	.4383	2.2817	1.092	2.491	1.1577	20'
50'	.4160	.4041	.9147	.4417	2.2637	1.093	2.475	1.1548	10'
24° 00'	.4189	.4067	.9135	.4452	2.2460	1.095	2.459	1.1519	66° 00'
10'	.4218	.4094	.9124	.4487	2.2286	1.096	2.443	1.1490	50'
20'	.4247	.4120	.9112	.4522	2.2113	1.097	2.427	1.1461	40'
30'	.4276	.4147	.9100	.4557	2.1943	1.099	2.411	1.1432	30'
40'	.4305	.4173	.9088	.4592	2.1775	1.100	2.396	1.1403	20'
50'	.4334	.4200	.9075	.4628	2.1609	1.102	2.381	1.1374	10'
25° 00'	.4363	.4226	.9063	.4663	2.1445	1.103	2.366	1.1345	65° 00'
10'	.4392	.4253	.9051	.4699	2.1283	1.105	2.352	1.1316	50'
20'	.4422	.4279	.9038	.4734	2.1123	1.106	2.337	1.1286	40'
30'	.4451	.4305	.9026	.4770	2.0965	1.108	2.323	1.1257	30'
40'	.4480	.4331	.9013	.4806	2.0809	1.109	2.309	1.1228	20'
50'	.4509	.4358	.9001	.4841	2.0655	1.111	2.295	1.1199	10'
26° 00'	.4538	.4384	.8988	.4877	2.0503	1.113	2.281	1.1170	64° 00'
10'	.4567	.4410	.8975	.4913	2.0353	1.114	2.268	1.1141	50'
20'	.4596	.4436	.8962	.4950	2.0204	1.116	2.254	1.1112	40'
30'	.4625	.4462	.8949	.4986	2.0057	1.117	2.241	1.1083	30'
40'	.4654	.4488	.8936	.5022	1.9912	1.119	2.228	1.1054	20'
50'	.4683	.4514	.8923	.5059	1.9768	1.121	2.215	1.1025	10'
27° 00'	.4712	.4540	.8910	.5095	1.9626	1.122	2.203	1.0996	63° 00'
		Cos θ	Sin θ	Cot θ	Tan θ	Csc θ	Sec θ	θ Rad.	θ Deg.

Table of Values of the Trigonometric Functions

θ Deg.	θ Rad.	Sin θ	Cos θ	Tan θ	Cot θ	Sec θ	Csc θ		
27° 00′	.4712	.4540	.8910	.5095	1.9626	1.122	2.203	1.0996	63° 00′
10′	.4741	.4566	.8897	.5132	1.9486	1.124	2.190	1.0966	50′
20′	.4771	.4592	.8884	.5169	1.9347	1.126	2.178	1.0937	40′
30′	.4800	.4617	.8870	.5206	1.9210	1.127	2.166	1.0908	30′
40′	.4829	.4643	.8857	.5243	1.9074	1.129	2.154	1.0879	20′
50′	.4858	.4669	.8843	.5280	1.8940	1.131	2.142	1.0850	10′
28° 00′	.4887	.4695	.8829	.5317	1.8807	1.133	2.130	1.0821	62° 00′
10′	.4916	.4720	.8816	.5354	1.8676	1.134	2.118	1.0792	50′
20′	.4945	.4746	.8802	.5392	1.8546	1.136	2.107	1.0763	40′
30′	.4974	.4772	.8788	.5430	1.8418	1.138	2.096	1.0734	30′
40′	.5003	.4797	.8774	.5467	1.8291	1.140	2.085	1.0705	20′
50′	.5032	.4823	.8760	.5505	1.8165	1.142	2.074	1.0676	10′
29° 00′	.5061	.4848	.8746	.5543	1.8040	1.143	2.063	1.0647	61° 00′
10′	.5091	.4874	.8732	.5581	1.7917	1.145	2.052	1.0617	50′
20′	.5120	.4899	.8718	.5619	1.7796	1.147	2.041	1.0588	40′
30′	.5149	.4924	.8704	.5658	1.7675	1.149	2.031	1.0559	30′
40′	.5178	.4950	.8689	.5696	1.7556	1.151	2.020	1.0530	20′
50′	.5207	.4975	.8675	.5735	1.7437	1.153	2.010	1.0501	10′
30° 00′	.5236	.5000	.8660	.5774	1.7321	1.155	2.000	1.0472	60° 00′
10′	.5265	.5025	.8646	.5812	1.7205	1.157	1.990	1.0443	50′
20′	.5294	.5050	.8631	.5851	1.7090	1.159	1.980	1.0414	40′
30′	.5323	.5075	.8616	.5890	1.6977	1.161	1.970	1.0385	30′
40′	.5352	.5100	.8601	.5930	1.6864	1.163	1.961	1.0356	20′
50′	.5381	.5125	.8587	.5969	1.6753	1.165	1.951	1.0327	10′
31° 00′	.5411	.5150	.8572	.6009	1.6643	1.167	1.942	1.0297	59° 00′
10′	.5440	.5175	.8557	.6048	1.6534	1.169	1.932	1.0268	50′
20′	.5469	.5200	.8542	.6088	1.6426	1.171	1.923	1.0239	40′
30′	.5498	.5225	.8526	.6128	1.6319	1.173	1.914	1.0210	30′
40′	.5527	.5250	.8511	.6168	1.6212	1.175	1.905	1.0181	20′
50′	.5556	.5275	.8496	.6208	1.6107	1.177	1.896	1.0152	10′
32° 00′	.5585	.5299	.8480	.6249	1.6003	1.179	1.887	1.0123	58° 00′
10′	.5614	.5324	.8465	.6289	1.5900	1.181	1.878	1.0094	50′
20′	.5643	.5348	.8450	.6330	1.5798	1.184	1.870	1.0065	40′
30′	.5672	.5373	.8434	.6371	1.5697	1.186	1.861	1.0036	30′
40′	.5701	.5398	.8418	.6412	1.5597	1.188	1.853	1.0007	20′
50′	.5730	.5422	.8403	.6453	1.5497	1.190	1.844	.9977	10′
33° 00′	.5760	.5446	.8387	.6494	1.5399	1.192	1.836	.9948	57° 00′
10′	.5789	.5471	.8371	.6536	1.5301	1.195	1.828	.9919	50′
20′	.5818	.5495	.8355	.6577	1.5204	1.197	1.820	.9890	40′
30′	.5847	.5519	.8339	.6619	1.5108	1.199	1.812	.9861	30′
40′	.5876	.5544	.8323	.6661	1.5013	1.202	1.804	.9832	20′
50′	.5905	.5568	.8307	.6703	1.4919	1.204	1.796	.9803	10′
34° 00′	.5934	.5592	.8290	.6745	1.4826	1.206	1.788	.9774	56° 00′
10′	.5963	.5616	.8274	.6787	1.4733	1.209	1.781	.9745	50′
20′	.5992	.5640	.8258	.6830	1.4641	1.211	1.773	.9716	40′
30′	.6021	.5664	.8241	.6873	1.4550	1.213	1.766	.9687	30′
40′	.6050	.5688	.8225	.6916	1.4460	1.216	1.758	.9657	20′
50′	.6080	.5712	.8208	.6959	1.4370	1.218	1.751	.9628	10′
35° 00′	.6109	.5736	.8192	.7002	1.4281	1.221	1.743	.9599	55° 00′
10′	.6138	.5760	.8175	.7046	1.4193	1.223	1.736	.9570	50′
20′	.6167	.5783	.8158	.7089	1.4106	1.226	1.729	.9541	40′
30′	.6196	.5807	.8141	.7133	1.4019	1.228	1.722	.9512	30′
40′	.6225	.5831	.8124	.7177	1.3934	1.231	1.715	.9483	20′
50′	.6254	.5854	.8107	.7221	1.3848	1.233	1.708	.9454	10′
36° 00′	.6283	.5878	.8090	.7265	1.3764	1.236	1.701	.9425	54° 00′
		Cos θ	Sin θ	Cot θ	Tan θ	Csc θ	Sec θ	θ Rad.	θ Deg.

Table of Values of the Trigonometric Functions

θ Deg.	θ Rad.	Sin θ	Cos θ	Tan θ	Cot θ	Sec θ	Csc θ		
36°00′	.6283	.5878	.8090	.7265	1.3764	1.236	1.701	.9425	54°00′
10′	.6312	.5901	.8073	.7310	1.3680	1.239	1.695	.9396	50′
20′	.6341	.5925	.8056	.7355	1.3597	1.241	1.688	.9367	40′
30′	.6370	.5948	.8039	.7400	1.3514	1.244	1.681	.9338	30′
40′	.6400	.5972	.8021	.7445	1.3432	1.247	1.675	.9308	20′
50′	.6429	.5995	.8004	.7490	1.3351	1.249	1.668	.9279	10′
37°00′	.6458	.6018	.7986	.7536	1.3270	1.252	1.662	.9250	53°00′
10′	.6487	.6041	.7969	.7581	1.3190	1.255	1.655	.9221	50′
20′	.6516	.6065	.7951	.7627	1.3111	1.258	1.649	.9192	40′
30′	.6545	.6088	.7934	.7673	1.3032	1.260	1.643	.9163	30′
40′	.6574	.6111	.7916	.7720	1.2954	1.263	1.636	.9134	20′
50′	.6603	.6134	.7898	.7766	1.2876	1.266	1.630	.9105	10′
38°00′	.6632	.6157	.7880	.7813	1.2799	1.269	1.624	.9076	52°00′
10′	.6661	.6180	.7862	.7860	1.2723	1.272	1.618	.9047	50′
20′	.6690	.6202	.7844	.7907	1.2647	1.275	1.612	.9018	40′
30′	.6720	.6225	.7826	.7954	1.2572	1.278	1.606	.8988	30′
40′	.6749	.6248	.7808	.8002	1.2497	1.281	1.601	.8959	20′
50′	.6778	.6271	.7790	.8050	1.2423	1.284	1.595	.8930	10′
39°00′	.6807	.6293	.7771	.8098	1.2349	1.287	1.589	.8901	51°00′
10′	.6836	.6316	.7753	.8146	1.2276	1.290	1.583	.8872	50′
20′	.6865	.6338	.7735	.8195	1.2203	1.293	1.578	.8843	40′
30′	.6894	.6361	.7716	.8243	1.2131	1.296	1.572	.8814	30′
40′	.6923	.6383	.7698	.8292	1.2059	1.299	1.567	.8785	20′
50′	.6952	.6406	.7679	.8342	1.1988	1.302	1.561	.8756	10′
40°00′	.6981	.6428	.7660	.8391	1.1918	1.305	1.556	.8727	50°00′
10′	.7010	.6450	.7642	.8441	1.1847	1.309	1.550	.8698	50′
20′	.7039	.6472	.7623	.8491	1.1778	1.312	1.545	.8668	40′
30′	.7069	.6494	.7604	.8541	1.1708	1.315	1.540	.8639	30′
40′	.7098	.6517	.7585	.8591	1.1640	1.318	1.535	.8610	20′
50′	.7127	.6539	.7566	.8642	1.1571	1.322	1.529	.8581	10′
41°00′	.7156	.6561	.7547	.8693	1.1504	1.325	1.524	.8552	49°00′
10′	.7185	.6583	.7528	.8744	1.1436	1.328	1.519	.8523	50′
20′	.7214	.6604	.7509	.8796	1.1369	1.332	1.514	.8494	40′
30′	.7243	.6626	.7490	.8847	1.1303	1.335	1.509	.8465	30′
40′	.7272	.6648	.7470	.8899	1.1237	1.339	1.504	.8436	20′
50′	.7301	.6670	.7451	.8952	1.1171	1.342	1.499	.8407	10′
42°00′	.7330	.6691	.7431	.9004	1.1106	1.346	1.494	.8378	48°00′
10′	.7359	.6713	.7412	.9057	1.1041	1.349	1.490	.8348	50′
20′	.7389	.6734	.7392	.9110	1.0977	1.353	1.485	.8319	40′
30′	.7418	.6756	.7373	.9163	1.0913	1.356	1.480	.8290	30′
40′	.7447	.6777	.7353	.9217	1.0850	1.360	1.476	.8261	20′
50′	.7476	.6799	.7333	.9271	1.0786	1.364	1.471	.8232	10′
43°00′	.7505	.6820	.7314	.9325	1.0724	1.367	1.466	.8203	47°00′
10′	.7534	.6841	.7294	.9380	1.0661	1.371	1.462	.8174	50′
20′	.7563	.6862	.7274	.9435	1.0599	1.375	1.457	.8145	40′
30′	.7592	.6884	.7254	.9490	1.0538	1.379	1.453	.8116	30′
40′	.7621	.6905	.7234	.9545	1.0477	1.382	1.448	.8087	20′
50′	.7650	.6926	.7214	.9601	1.0416	1.386	1.444	.8058	10′
44°00′	.7679	.6947	.7193	.9657	1.0355	1.390	1.440	.8029	46°00′
10′	.7709	.6967	.7173	.9713	1.0295	1.394	1.435	.7999	50′
20′	.7738	.6988	.7153	.9770	1.0235	1.398	1.431	.7970	40′
30′	.7767	.7009	.7133	.9827	1.0176	1.402	1.427	.7941	30′
40′	.7796	.7030	.7112	.9884	1.0117	1.406	1.423	.7912	20′
50′	.7825	.7050	.7092	.9942	1.0058	1.410	1.418	.7883	10′
45°00′	.7854	.7071	.7071	1.0000	1.0000	1.414	1.414	.7854	45°00′
		Cos θ	Sin θ	Cot θ	Tan θ	Csc θ	Sec θ	θ Rad.	θ Deg.

Table of Common Logarithms

N	0	1	2	3	4	5	6	7	8	9
1.0	0000	0043	0086	0128	0170	0212	0253	0294	0334	0374
1.1	0414	0453	0492	0531	0569	0607	0645	0682	0719	0755
1.2	0792	0828	0864	0899	0934	0969	1004	1038	1072	1106
1.3	1139	1173	1206	1239	1271	1303	1335	1367	1399	1430
1.4	1461	1492	1523	1553	1584	1614	1644	1673	1703	1732
1.5	1761	1790	1818	1847	1875	1903	1931	1959	1987	2014
1.6	2041	2068	2095	2122	2148	2175	2201	2227	2253	2279
1.7	2304	2330	2355	2380	2405	2430	2455	2480	2504	2529
1.8	2553	2577	2601	2625	2648	2672	2695	2718	2742	2765
1.9	2788	2810	2833	2856	2878	2900	2923	2945	2967	2989
2.0	3010	3032	3054	3075	3096	3118	3139	3160	3181	3201
2.1	3222	3243	3263	3284	3304	3324	3345	3365	3385	3404
2.2	3424	3444	3464	3483	3502	3522	3541	3560	3579	3598
2.3	3617	3636	3655	3674	3692	3711	3729	3747	3766	3784
2.4	3802	3820	3838	3856	3874	3892	3909	3927	3945	3962
2.5	3979	3997	4014	4031	4048	4065	4082	4099	4116	4133
2.6	4150	4166	4183	4200	4216	4232	4249	4265	4281	4298
2.7	4314	4330	4346	4362	4378	4393	4409	4425	4440	4456
2.8	4472	4487	4502	4518	4533	4548	4564	4579	4594	4609
2.9	4624	4639	4654	4669	4683	4698	4713	4728	4742	4757
3.0	4771	4786	4800	4814	4829	4843	4857	4871	4886	4900
3.1	4914	4928	4942	4955	4969	4983	4997	5011	5024	5038
3.2	5051	5065	5079	5092	5105	5119	5132	5145	5159	5172
3.3	5185	5198	5211	5224	5237	5250	5263	5276	5289	5302
3.4	5315	5328	5340	5353	5366	5378	5391	5403	5416	5428
3.5	5441	5453	5465	5478	5490	5502	5514	5527	5539	5551
3.6	5563	5575	5587	5599	5611	5623	5635	5647	5658	5670
3.7	5682	5694	5705	5717	5729	5740	5752	5763	5775	5786
3.8	5798	5809	5821	5832	5843	5855	5866	5877	5888	5899
3.9	5911	5922	5933	5944	5955	5966	5977	5988	5999	6010
4.0	6021	6031	6042	6053	6064	6075	6085	6096	6107	6117
4.1	6128	6138	6149	6160	6170	6180	6191	6201	6212	6222
4.2	6232	6243	6253	6263	6274	6284	6294	6304	6314	6325
4.3	6335	6345	6355	6365	6375	6385	6395	6405	6415	6425
4.4	6435	6444	6454	6464	6474	6484	6493	6503	6513	6522
4.5	6532	6542	6551	6561	6571	6580	6590	6599	6609	6618
4.6	6628	6637	6646	6656	6665	6675	6684	6693	6702	6712
4.7	6721	6730	6739	6749	6758	6767	6776	6785	6794	6803
4.8	6812	6821	6830	6839	6848	6857	6866	6875	6884	6893
4.9	6902	6911	6920	6928	6937	6946	6955	6964	6972	6981
5.0	6990	6998	7007	7016	7024	7033	7042	7050	7059	7067
5.1	7076	7084	7093	7101	7110	7118	7126	7135	7143	7152
5.2	7160	7168	7177	7185	7193	7202	7210	7218	7226	7235
5.3	7243	7251	7259	7267	7275	7284	7292	7300	7308	7316
5.4	7324	7332	7340	7348	7356	7364	7372	7380	7388	7396

Table of Common Logarithms

N	0	1	2	3	4	5	6	7	8	9
5.5	7404	7412	7419	7427	7435	7443	7451	7459	7466	7474
5.6	7482	7490	7497	7505	7513	7520	7528	7536	7543	7551
5.7	7559	7566	7574	7582	7589	7597	7604	7612	7619	7627
5.8	7634	7642	7649	7657	7664	7672	7679	7686	7694	7701
5.9	7709	7716	7723	7731	7738	7745	7752	7760	7767	7774
6.0	7782	7789	7796	7803	7810	7818	7825	7832	7839	7846
6.1	7853	7860	7868	7875	7882	7889	7896	7903	7910	7917
6.2	7924	7931	7938	7945	7952	7959	7966	7973	7980	7987
6.3	7993	8000	8007	8014	8021	8028	8035	8041	8048	8055
6.4	8062	8069	8075	8082	8089	8096	8102	8109	8116	8122
6.5	8129	8136	8142	8149	8156	8162	8169	8176	8182	8189
6.6	8195	8202	8209	8215	8222	8228	8235	8241	8248	8254
6.7	8261	8267	8274	8280	8287	8293	8299	8306	8312	8319
6.8	8325	8331	8338	8344	8351	8357	8363	8370	8376	8382
6.9	8388	8395	8401	8407	8414	8420	8426	8432	8439	8445
7.0	8451	8457	8463	8470	8476	8482	8488	8494	8500	8506
7.1	8513	8519	8525	8531	8537	8543	8549	8555	8561	8567
7.2	8573	8579	8585	8591	8597	8603	8609	8615	8621	8627
7.3	8633	8639	8645	8651	8657	8663	8669	8675	8681	8686
7.4	8692	8698	8704	8710	8716	8722	8727	8733	8739	8745
7.5	8751	8756	8762	8768	8774	8779	8785	8791	8797	8802
7.6	8808	8814	8820	8825	8831	8837	8842	8848	8854	8859
7.7	8865	8871	8876	8882	8887	8893	8899	8904	8910	8915
7.8	8921	8927	8932	8938	8943	8949	8954	8960	8965	8971
7.9	8976	8982	8987	8993	8998	9004	9009	9015	9020	9025
8.0	9031	9036	9042	9047	9053	9058	9063	9069	9074	9079
8.1	9085	9090	9096	9101	9106	9112	9117	9122	9128	9133
8.2	9138	9143	9149	9154	9159	9165	9170	9175	9180	9186
8.3	9191	9196	9201	9206	9212	9217	9222	9227	9232	9238
8.4	9243	9248	9253	9258	9263	9269	9274	9279	9284	9289
8.5	9294	9299	9304	9309	9315	9320	9325	9330	9335	9340
8.6	9345	9350	9355	9360	9365	9370	9375	9380	9385	9390
8.7	9395	9400	9405	9410	9415	9420	9425	9430	9435	9440
8.8	9445	9450	9455	9460	9465	9469	9474	9479	9484	9489
8.9	9494	9499	9504	9509	9513	9518	9523	9528	9533	9538
9.0	9542	9547	9552	9557	9562	9566	9571	9576	9581	9586
9.1	9590	9595	9600	9605	9609	9614	9619	9624	9628	9633
9.2	9638	9643	9647	9652	9657	9661	9666	9671	9675	9680
9.3	9685	9689	9694	9699	9703	9708	9713	9717	9722	9727
9.4	9731	9736	9741	9745	9750	9754	9759	9763	9768	9773
9.5	9777	9782	9786	9791	9795	9800	9805	9809	9814	9818
9.6	9823	9827	9832	9836	9841	9845	9850	9854	9859	9863
9.7	9868	9872	9877	9881	9886	9890	9894	9899	9903	9908
9.8	9912	9917	9921	9926	9930	9934	9939	9943	9948	9952
9.9	9956	9961	9965	9969	9974	9978	9983	9987	9991	9996

Table of Natural Logarithms

N	0	1	2	3	4	5	6	7	8	9
1.0	0.0000	0.0100	0.0198	0.0296	0.0392	0.0488	0.0583	0.0677	0.0770	0.0862
1.1	0.0953	0.1044	0.1133	0.1222	0.1310	0.1398	0.1484	0.1570	0.1655	0.1740
1.2	0.1823	0.1906	0.1989	0.2070	0.2151	0.2231	0.2311	0.2390	0.2469	0.2546
1.3	0.2624	0.2700	0.2776	0.2852	0.2927	0.3001	0.3075	0.3148	0.3221	0.3293
1.4	0.3365	0.3436	0.3507	0.3577	0.3646	0.3716	0.3784	0.3853	0.3920	0.3988
1.5	0.4055	0.4121	0.4187	0.4253	0.4318	0.4383	0.4447	0.4511	0.4574	0.4637
1.6	0.4700	0.4762	0.4824	0.4886	0.4947	0.5008	0.5068	0.5128	0.5188	0.5247
1.7	0.5306	0.5365	0.5423	0.5481	0.5539	0.5596	0.5653	0.5710	0.5766	0.5822
1.8	0.5878	0.5933	0.5988	0.6043	0.6098	0.6152	0.6206	0.6259	0.6313	0.6366
1.9	0.6419	0.6471	0.6523	0.6575	0.6627	0.6678	0.6729	0.6780	0.6831	0.6881
2.0	0.6931	0.6981	0.7031	0.7080	0.7129	0.7178	0.7227	0.7275	0.7324	0.7372
2.1	0.7419	0.7467	0.7514	0.7561	0.7608	0.7655	0.7701	0.7747	0.7793	0.7839
2.2	0.7885	0.7930	0.7975	0.8020	0.8065	0.8109	0.8154	0.8198	0.8242	0.8286
2.3	0.8329	0.8372	0.8416	0.8459	0.8502	0.8544	0.8587	0.8629	0.8671	0.8713
2.4	0.8755	0.8796	0.8838	0.8879	0.8920	0.8961	0.9002	0.9042	0.9083	0.9123
2.5	0.9163	0.9203	0.9243	0.9282	0.9322	0.9361	0.9400	0.9439	0.9478	0.9517
2.6	0.9555	0.9594	0.9632	0.9670	0.9708	0.9746	0.9783	0.9821	0.9858	0.9895
2.7	0.9933	0.9969	1.0006	1.0043	1.0080	1.0116	1.0152	1.0188	1.0225	1.0260
2.8	1.0296	1.0332	1.0367	1.0403	1.0438	1.0473	1.0508	1.0543	1.0578	1.0613
2.9	1.0647	1.0682	1.0716	1.0750	1.0784	1.0818	1.0852	1.0886	1.0919	1.0953
3.0	1.0986	1.1019	1.1053	1.1086	1.1119	1.1151	1.1184	1.1217	1.1249	1.1282
3.1	1.1314	1.1346	1.1378	1.1410	1.1442	1.1474	1.1506	1.1537	1.1569	1.1600
3.2	1.1632	1.1663	1.1694	1.1725	1.1756	1.1787	1.1817	1.1848	1.1878	1.1909
3.3	1.1939	1.1969	1.2000	1.2030	1.2060	1.2090	1.2119	1.2149	1.2179	1.2208
3.4	1.2238	1.2267	1.2296	1.2326	1.2355	1.2384	1.2413	1.2442	1.2470	1.2499
3.5	1.2528	1.2556	1.2585	1.2613	1.2641	1.2669	1.2698	1.2726	1.2754	1.2782
3.6	1.2809	1.2837	1.2865	1.2892	1.2920	1.2947	1.2975	1.3002	1.3029	1.3056
3.7	1.3083	1.3110	1.3137	1.3164	1.3191	1.3318	1.3244	1.3271	1.3297	1.3324
3.8	1.3350	1.3376	1.3403	1.3429	1.3455	1.3481	1.3507	1.3533	1.3558	1.3584
3.9	1.3610	1.3635	1.3661	1.3686	1.3712	1.3737	1.3762	1.3788	1.3813	1.3838
4.0	1.3863	1.3888	1.3913	1.3938	1.3962	1.3987	1.4012	1.4036	1.4061	1.4085
4.1	1.4110	1.4134	1.4159	1.4183	1.4207	1.4231	1.4255	1.4279	1.4303	1.4327
4.2	1.4351	1.4375	1.4398	1.4422	1.4446	1.4469	1.4493	1.4516	1.4540	1.4563
4.3	1.4586	1.4609	1.4633	1.4656	1.4679	1.4702	1.4725	1.4748	1.4770	1.4793
4.4	1.4816	1.4839	1.4861	1.4884	1.4907	1.4929	1.4951	1.4974	1.4996	1.5019
4.5	1.5041	1.5063	1.5085	1.5107	1.5129	1.5151	1.5173	1.5195	1.5217	1.5239
4.6	1.5261	1.5282	1.5304	1.5326	1.5347	1.5369	1.5390	1.5412	1.5433	1.5454
4.7	1.5476	1.5497	1.5518	1.5539	1.5560	1.5581	1.5602	1.5623	1.5644	1.5665
4.8	1.5686	1.5707	1.5728	1.5748	1.5769	1.5790	1.5810	1.5831	1.5851	1.5872
4.9	1.5892	1.5913	1.5933	1.5953	1.5974	1.5994	1.6014	1.6034	1.6054	1.6074
5.0	1.6094	1.6114	1.6134	1.6154	1.6174	1.6194	1.6214	1.6233	1.6253	1.6273
5.1	1.6292	1.6312	1.6332	1.6351	1.6371	1.6390	1.6409	1.6429	1.6448	1.6467
5.2	1.6487	1.6506	1.6525	1.6544	1.6563	1.6582	1.6601	1.6620	1.6639	1.6658
5.3	1.6677	1.6696	1.6715	1.6734	1.6752	1.6771	1.6790	1.6808	1.6827	1.6845
5.4	1.6864	1.6882	1.6901	1.6919	1.6938	1.6956	1.6974	1.6993	1.7011	1.7029

Table of Natural Logarithms

N	0	1	2	3	4	5	6	7	8	9
5.5	1.7047	1.7066	1.7084	1.7102	1.7120	1.7138	1.7156	1.7174	1.7192	1.7210
5.6	1.7228	1.7246	1.7263	1.7281	1.7299	1.7317	1.7334	1.7352	1.7370	1.7387
5.7	1.7405	1.7422	1.7440	1.7457	1.7475	1.7492	1.7509	1.7527	1.7544	1.7561
5.8	1.7579	1.7596	1.7613	1.7630	1.7647	1.7664	1.7681	1.7699	1.7716	1.7733
5.9	1.7750	1.7766	1.7783	1.7800	1.7817	1.7843	1.7851	1.7867	1.7884	1.7901
6.0	1.7918	1.7934	1.7951	1.7967	1.7984	1.8001	1.8017	1.8034	1.8050	1.8066
6.1	1.8083	1.8099	1.8116	1.8132	1.8148	1.8165	1.8181	1.8197	1.8213	1.8229
6.2	1.8245	1.8262	1.8278	1.8294	1.8310	1.8326	1.8342	1.8358	1.8374	1.8390
6.3	1.8405	1.8421	1.8437	1.8453	1.8469	1.8485	1.8500	1.8516	1.8532	1.8547
6.4	1.8563	1.8579	1.8594	1.8610	1.8625	1.8641	1.8656	1.8672	1.8687	1.8703
6.5	1.8718	1.8733	1.8749	1.8764	1.8779	1.8795	1.8810	1.8825	1.8840	1.8856
6.6	1.8871	1.8886	1.8901	1.8916	1.8931	1.8946	1.8961	1.8976	1.8991	1.9006
6.7	1.9021	1.9036	1.9051	1.9066	1.9081	1.9095	1.9110	1.9125	1.9140	1.9155
6.8	1.9169	1.9184	1.9199	1.9213	1.9228	1.9242	1.9257	1.9272	1.9286	1.9301
6.9	1.9315	1.9330	1.9344	1.9359	1.9373	1.9387	1.9402	1.9416	1.9430	1.9445
7.0	1.9459	1.9473	1.9488	1.9502	1.9516	1.9530	1.9544	1.9559	1.9573	1.9587
7.1	1.9601	1.9615	1.9629	1.9643	1.9657	1.9671	1.9685	1.9699	1.9713	1.9727
7.2	1.9741	1.9755	1.9769	1.9782	1.9796	1.9810	1.9824	1.9838	1.9851	1.9865
7.3	1.9879	1.9892	1.9906	1.9920	1.9933	1.9947	1.9961	1.9974	1.9988	2.0001
7.4	2.0015	2.0028	2.0042	2.0055	2.0069	2.0082	2.0096	2.0109	2.0122	2.0136
7.5	2.0149	2.0162	2.0176	2.0189	2.0202	2.0215	2.0229	2.0242	2.0255	2.0268
7.6	2.0281	2.0295	2.0308	2.0321	2.0334	2.0347	2.0360	2.0373	2.0386	2.0399
7.7	2.0412	2.0425	2.0438	2.0451	2.0464	2.0477	2.0490	2.0503	2.0516	2.0528
7.8	2.0541	2.0554	2.0567	2.0580	2.0592	2.0605	2.0618	2.0631	2.0643	2.0656
7.9	2.0669	2.0681	2.0694	2.0707	2.0719	2.0732	2.0744	2.0757	2.0769	2.0782
8.0	2.0794	2.0807	2.0819	2.0832	2.0844	2.0857	2.0869	2.0882	2.0894	2.0906
8.1	2.0919	2.0931	2.0943	2.0956	2.0968	2.0980	2.0992	2.1005	2.1017	2.1029
8.2	2.1041	2.1054	2.1066	2.1078	2.1090	2.1102	2.1114	2.1126	2.1138	2.1150
8.3	2.1163	2.1175	2.1187	2.1199	2.1211	2.1223	2.1235	2.1247	2.1258	2.1270
8.4	2.1282	2.1294	2.1306	2.1318	2.1330	2.1342	2.1353	2.1365	2.1377	2.1389
8.5	2.1401	2.1412	2.1424	2.1436	2.1448	2.1459	2.1471	2.1483	2.1494	2.1506
8.6	2.1518	2.1529	2.1541	2.1552	2.1564	2.1576	2.1587	2.1599	2.1610	2.1622
8.7	2.1633	2.1645	2.1656	2.1668	2.1679	2.1691	2.1702	2.1713	2.1725	2.1736
8.8	2.1748	2.1759	2.1770	2.1782	2.1793	2.1804	2.1815	2.1827	2.1838	2.1849
8.9	2.1861	2.1872	2.1883	2.1894	2.1905	2.1917	2.1928	2.1939	2.1950	2.1961
9.0	2.1972	2.1983	2.1994	2.2006	2.2017	2.2028	2.2039	2.2050	2.2061	2.2072
9.1	2.2083	2.2094	2.2105	2.2116	2.2127	2.2138	2.2148	2.2159	2.2170	2.2181
9.2	2.2192	2.2203	2.2214	2.2225	2.2235	2.2246	2.2257	2.2268	2.2279	2.2289
9.3	2.2300	2.2311	2.2322	2.2332	2.2343	2.2354	2.2364	2.2375	2.2386	2.2396
9.4	2.2407	2.2418	2.2428	2.2439	2.2450	2.2460	2.2471	2.2481	2.2492	2.2502
9.5	2.2513	2.2523	2.2534	2.2544	2.2555	2.2565	2.2576	2.2586	2.2597	2.2607
9.6	2.2618	2.2628	2.2638	2.2649	2.2659	2.2670	2.2680	2.2690	2.2701	2.2711
9.7	2.2721	2.2732	2.2742	2.2752	2.2762	2.2773	2.2783	2.2793	2.2803	2.2814
9.8	2.2824	2.2834	2.2844	2.2854	2.2865	2.2875	2.2885	2.2895	2.2905	2.2915
9.9	2.2925	2.2935	2.2946	2.2956	2.2966	2.2976	2.2986	2.2996	2.3006	2.3016
10.0	2.3026	2.3036	2.3046	2.3056	2.3066	2.3076	2.3086	2.3096	2.3106	2.3116

Index

Boldfaced numerals indicate the pages that contain formal or informal definitions. Numerals in parentheses refer to exercises.

ANSWERS TO SELECTED EXERCISES

The answers are provided for all of the problems in the <u>Mid-Chapter Reviews</u> and <u>Chapter Tests</u>. The answers for the <u>Computer Applications</u> appear in the <u>Solution Key</u>. For all other types of exercises, the answers to the odd-numbered problems are provided.

CHAPTER 1   NUMBERS, RELATIONS, AND FUNCTIONS

PAGE 3   CLASSROOM EXERCISES

1. f 3. a 5. c 7. g 9. R, I, Q 11. R, Q 13. R, Q 15. $\frac{187}{30}$, $-\frac{146}{999}$

PAGE 4   WRITTEN EXERCISES

1. R, Q 3. R, Q, I, W 5. R, Q, I, W, N 7. R, Q 9. R, Q 11. R, Q 13. False. 15. False. 17. False.
19. True. 21. True. 23. False. 25. $\frac{5}{4}$ 27. $\frac{1043}{10,000}$ 29. $\frac{1}{100}$ 31. $\frac{311,117}{8325}$ 33. $\frac{1}{2}$ 35. Let x = .00$\overline{9}$. Then
1.13$\overline{9}$ = 1.13 + x. 10x = .0$\overline{9}$ = .09 + x. Therefore, 9x = .09 and x = .01. Therefore, 1.139 = 1.13 + .01 = 1.14.
37. Upon dividing r by s, the resulting decimal either terminates or does not. If it doesn't terminate, there are at most s different remainders occurring in the division process after the decimal point, and since all digits of the numerator are 0 after the decimal point, a given remainder in one place will lead to the same remainder in the next place time and again; thus we get a repeating decimal. 39. In those decimals which terminate, the denominators have, aside from the factor 1, only factors which are expressible as products of only twos and fives. The others involve different primes in their factorization.

PAGE 8   CLASSROOM EXERCISES

1. $(-a) + a = a + (-a)$ (Postulate 2)
    $a + (-a) = 0$ (Postulate 5)
    $(-a) + a = 0$ (Postulate 14)

3. a = b Given
   $a + (-c) = b + (-c)$ Post. 15
   $a - c = b - c$ Def. of Subt.

PAGES 8-9   WRITTEN EXERCISES

1. 4, 5, 10 3. 10 5. 1, 4, 6, 9 7. The result follows immediately from Theorem 1-1 with a = 0, b = −0, c = 0.

9. $0 - a = 0 + (-a)$ Def. of subt.
   $0 + (-a) = (-a) + 0$ Post. 2.
   $(-a) + 0 = -a$ Post. 4.
   Using Post. 14 completes the proof.

11. $-(a - b) = -[a + (-b)]$ Def. of subt.
    $-[a + (-b)] = -a + [-(-b)]$ Ex. 10.
    $-a + [-(-b)] = -a + b$ Ex. 8.
    $-a + b = b + (-a)$ Post. 2.

13. By Postulate 10, the reciprocal, $\frac{1}{a}$, exists.
    Then, $[a \cdot (\frac{1}{a})] \cdot b = [a \cdot (\frac{1}{a})] \cdot c$
    $1 \cdot b = 1 \cdot c$ (Postulate 10)
    $b \cdot 1 = c \cdot 1$ (Postulate 7)
    $b = c$ (Postulate 9)

    Multiplying both sides by $\frac{1}{a}$ gives $\frac{1}{a} \cdot (a \cdot b) = \frac{1}{a} \cdot (a \cdot c)$.
    (Postulates 7 and 8)

15. $a \cdot 0 + 0 = a \cdot 0$ (Postulate 4)
     $a \cdot 0 = a(0 + 0)$ (Postulate 4)
     $a \cdot (0 + 0) = a \cdot 0$ (Postulate 11)
     $a \cdot 0 + 0 = a \cdot 0 + a \cdot 0$ (Postulate 14)
     $0 = a \cdot 0$ (Theorem 1-1: Addition Cancellation Law)
     $a \cdot 0 = 0$ (Postulate 13)

17. Part 1: If $a \div b = c$, then $a = c \cdot b$ Proof: $a \div b = c$

$$a \cdot (\frac{1}{b}) = c \qquad \text{(Definition of division)}$$

Multiply both sides by b. Then $[a \cdot (\frac{1}{b})] \cdot b = c \cdot b$.

$$a \cdot (\frac{1}{b} \cdot b) = c \cdot b \qquad \text{(Postulate 8)}$$
$$a \cdot 1 = c \cdot b \qquad \text{(Postulate 10)}$$
$$a = c \cdot b \qquad \text{(Postulate 9)}$$

Part 2: If $a = c \cdot b$, then $a \div b = c$ $(b \neq 0)$.   Proof: $a = c \cdot b$; divide both sides by b, i.e. multiply by $\frac{1}{b}$.

$$\text{Then, } a \cdot (\frac{1}{b}) = (c \cdot b) \cdot (\frac{1}{b})$$
$$a \div b = c \cdot (b \cdot \frac{1}{b}) \qquad \text{(Def. of division and Post. 8)}$$
$$a \div b = c \cdot 1 \qquad \text{(Postulate 10)}$$
$$a \div b = c \qquad \text{(Postulate 9)}$$

PAGE 11 CLASSROOM EXERCISES

1. $<$ 3. $>$ 5. $5 + 2 = 7$ 7. $3 + \underline{0} = \underline{3}$

PAGES 11-12 WRITTEN EXERCISES

1. True. 3. False. 5. True. 7. False. 9. Theorem 1-6 with a = 2, b = 5, c = 3. 11. $x < z$ by Theorem 1-4.

13. Continuing from the text's outline, $(b - a) + (c - b) = (b + (-a)) + (c + (-b))$. (Definition of subtraction.)

$$(b + (-a)) + (c + (-b)) = (-a + b) + (-b + c) \qquad \text{(Postulate 2)}$$
$$(-a + b) + (-b + c) = ((-a + b) + (-b)) + c \qquad \text{(Postulate 3)}$$
$$((-a + b) + (-b)) + c = (-a + (b + (-b))) + c \qquad \text{(Postulate 3)}$$
$$(-a + (b + (-b))) + c = (-a + 0) + c \qquad \text{(Postulate 5)}$$
$$(-a + 0) + c = -a + c \qquad \text{(Postulate 4)}$$
$$-a + c = c + (-a) \qquad \text{(Postulate 2)}$$
$$c + (-a) = c - a \qquad \text{(Def. of subtraction.)}$$

Thus, $(b - a) + (c - b) = c - a$ which is therefore positive.

15. All steps in showing $(b + c) - (a + c) = b - a$ are reversible; therefore the converse of Theorem 1-5 follows easily. 17. If $ac < bc$ with c positive, then $\frac{1}{c}$ exists. It can be shown that $\frac{1}{c}$ must be positive, and therefore from Theorem 1-6i, we have $ac(\frac{1}{c}) < bc(\frac{1}{c})$ or from Postulate 8, $a \cdot (c \cdot (\frac{1}{c})) < b \cdot (c \cdot (\frac{1}{c}))$ which implies $a \cdot 1 < b \cdot 1$ or $a < b$. 19. Part 1: Assume $a < 0$. Then $0 - a$ is positive. But $0 - a = 0 + (-a) = -a + 0 = -a$. Thus $-a$ is positive; hence a is negative. Part 2: The steps in Part 1 are reversible completing the proof. 21. $x \leq y$ implies that either $x = y$ or $y - x$ is positive. $y \leq x$ implies that either $x = y$ or $x - y$ is positive. If in either of the above assertions, $x = y$ we are finished, since if $x = y$, neither $x - y$ nor $y - x$ may be positive. However, in the remaining case, if both $x - y$ and $y - x$ are assumed positive, this would imply $(x - y) + (y - x)$ is positive. However, it is easily shown that $(x - y) + (y - x) = 0$ which leads to a contradiction. Therefore, this case is impossible, and $x = y$.

PAGE 15 CLASSROOM EXERCISES

1. All real numbers between −6 and −2, including −6 and −2. 3. All real numbers between −6 and −2, including −2 but not −6. 5. $< 5, 12]$ 7. $[-20, 5]$

PAGE 15 WRITTEN EXERCISES

1. All real numbers less than −1 but not including −1. 3. The numbers −2 and 0. 5. All real numbers between 0 and 3, including 3 but not 0. 7. All real numbers between $\frac{2}{3}$ and $\frac{7}{4}$, including $\frac{2}{3}$ but not $\frac{7}{4}$. 9. All real numbers less than 5 and including 5. 11. All real numbers between 1 and 3, including 1 but not 3.

13. All real numbers between -4 and 3, including both -4 and 3. 15. All real numbers between -2 and 3, not including -2 or 3. 17. The integers, 0, 1, 2, 3, 4, 5. 19. All real numbers less than -2, not including -2, also all real numbers between 1 and 3, including 1 but not 3. 21. $\{y : y \geq 5\}$ 23. $\{t : t < 2\}$ 25. $\{n : n > \frac{18}{5}\}$ 27. $\{t : t > 5\}$ 29. $\{p : p > 0\}$

31. 33.

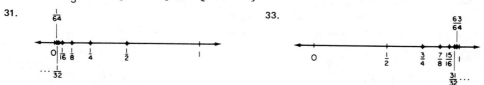

PAGE 17 CLASSROOM EXERCISES

1. $2 < x < 10$. 3. $-3.6 \leq y < -1$ 5. $x < 5$

PAGES 17-18 WRITTEN EXERCISES

1. $\{x : 2 < x < \frac{7}{3}\}$ 3. $\{x : -2 < x < 1\}$ 5. $\{x : \frac{3}{5} < x < 2\}$ 7. Empty set. 9. $\{x : 0 < x < \frac{9}{2}\}$
11. $\{x : x < -2\} \cup \{x : x > \frac{1}{2}\}$ 13. $\{x : x < 0\} \cup \{x : x > 5\}$ 15. Empty set. 17. $\{x : x = 1\}$
19. $\{x : -1 < x < 5\}$ 21. $\{x : x < 2\} \cup \{x : x > 5\}$ 23. $\{x : -\frac{1}{4} \leq x \leq \frac{1}{4}\}$
25. $\{x : x < 2\} \cup \{x : x > 5\}$ 27. $\{x : x = 3\}$ 29. $\{x : x < 1\} \cup \{x : 2 < x < 3\}$
31. $\{x : x < -2\} \cup \{x : -\frac{3}{2} < x < \frac{1}{3}\}$ 33. 10

PAGE 22 CLASSROOM EXERCISES

1. Assume P_k is true, i.e., $1^3 + 2^3 + 3^3 + \cdots + k^3 = \frac{k^2(k+1)^2}{4}$. Then show that P_k implies P_{k+1}.
3. Assume P_k is true, i.e., $1^2 + 3^2 + 5^2 + \cdots + (2k-1)^2 = \frac{k(2k-1)(2k+1)}{3}$. Then show that P_k implies P_{k+1}.

PAGES 22-23 WRITTEN EXERCISES

1. $2(1) - 1 = 1$; $1^2 = 1$; therefore P_1 is true. Assume P_k true, i.e. $1 + 3 + 5 + \cdots + (2k-1) = k^2$. Since $k^2 + 2(k+1) - 1 = k^2 + 2k + 2 - 1 = (k+1)^2$, it follows that P_{k+1} is true; hence P_n is true for all $n \in N$.

3. $\frac{1}{1(1+1)} = \frac{1}{2}$; $\frac{1}{1+1} = \frac{1}{2}$. $\frac{k}{k+1} + \frac{1}{(k+1)(k+2)} = \frac{k(k+2)+1}{(k+1)(k+2)} = \frac{k+1}{k+2}$

5. For $n = 1$; $\frac{1-2^1}{2^1} = -\frac{1}{2}$. For $k + 1$; $-\frac{1}{2} - \frac{1}{4} - \frac{1}{8} - \cdots - \frac{1}{2^k} - \frac{1}{2^{k+1}} = \frac{1-(2^k)}{2^k} - \frac{1}{2^{k+1}}$

$= \frac{2 - 2^{k+1} - 1}{2^{k+1}} = \frac{1 - 2^{k+1}}{2^{k+1}}$ 7. For $n = 1$; $\frac{5(1-(\frac{1}{3})^1)}{1-\frac{1}{3}} = \frac{5(\frac{2}{3})}{\frac{2}{3}} = 5$. For $k + 1$; $5 + 5(\frac{1}{3}) + 5(\frac{1}{3^2}) + \cdots$

$+ 5(\frac{1}{3^{k-1}}) + 5(\frac{1}{3^k}) = 5\frac{(1-(\frac{1}{3})^k)}{1-\frac{1}{3}} + 5(\frac{1}{3^k}) = 5\left[\frac{1-\frac{1}{3^k}}{1-\frac{1}{3}} + \frac{1}{3^k}\right] = 5\left[\frac{3^k - 1 + (1-\frac{1}{3})}{(1-\frac{1}{3})3^k}\right]$

$= 5\left[\frac{3^k - \frac{1}{3}}{3^k(1-\frac{1}{3})}\right] = 5\left[\frac{1-\frac{1}{3^{k+1}}}{1-\frac{1}{3}}\right] = 5\left[\frac{1-(\frac{1}{3})^{k+1}}{1-\frac{1}{3}}\right]$ 9. $aq^{1-1} = a$. $a(\frac{1-q^1}{1-q}) = a$; $a(\frac{1-q^k}{1-q})$

$+ aq^{(k+1)-1} = a((\frac{1-q^k}{1-q}) + q^k) = a((1 + q + q^2 + \cdots + q^{k-1}) + q^k) = a(\frac{1-q^{k+1}}{1-q})$ 11. $1^3 - 1 = 0$ which is divisible by 6. Assume $k^3 - k$ divisible by 6. Then $(k+1)^3 - (k+1) = k^3 + 3k^2 + 3k + 1 - k - 1 = (k^3 - k) + (3k^2 + 3k) = (k^3 - k) + 3(k^2 + k)$. $k^3 - k$ is divisible by 6 by assumption. $3(k^2 + k)$ is obviously divisible by 3 and by 2 also since $k^2 + k$ is even for any k. Therefore, $3(k^2 + k)$ and also $(k^3 - k) + 3(k^2 + k)$ is divisible by 6. **13.** The "sum" of one positive integer is clearly positive. Let s_k be the sum of k positive integers. Then s_k is a positive integer by assumption. Let a be any positive integer. Consider $s_{k+1} = s_k + a$. By Postulate 18, s_{k+1} is positive.

15. For n = 1. $x_0 < x_1$, given. For k + 1. If $x_0 < x_1 < x_2 < \cdots < x_k < x_{k+1}$, then $x_0 < x_k$ and $x_k < x_{k+1}$. By Theorem 1-4 $x_0 < x_{k+1}$. **17.** Inductive step only is given in Exercise 17.

a. $x^{k+1} = x^k \cdot x = \underbrace{(x \cdot x \cdot x \cdot \cdots \cdot x)}_{\text{k factors of x}} \cdot x = \underbrace{(x \cdot x \cdot \cdots \cdot x)}_{\text{k + 1 factors}}$

b. $(x \cdot y)^{k+1} = (x \cdot y)^k (xy) = \underbrace{(xy \cdot xy \cdot \cdots \cdot xy)}_{\text{k factors of xy}}(xy)$

$= \underbrace{(xy \cdot xy \cdot \cdots \cdot xy)}_{\text{k + 1 factors of xy}} = \underbrace{(x \cdot x \cdot \cdots \cdot x)}_{\substack{\text{k + 1 factors} \\ \text{of x}}} \underbrace{(y \cdot y \cdot \cdots \cdot y)}_{\substack{\text{k + 1 factors} \\ \text{of y}}} = x^{k+1} \cdot y^{k+1}$

c. $x^m \cdot x^1 = x^{m+1}$ by Definition II. Assume $x^m \cdot x^k = x^{m+k}$. Then $x^m \cdot x^{k+1} = x^m \cdot (x^k \cdot x^1)$

$= (x^m \cdot x^k) \cdot x^1 = x^{m+k} \cdot x^1 = \underbrace{(x \cdot x \cdot \cdots \cdot x)}_{\substack{\text{m + k factors} \\ \text{of x}}} \cdot x = \underbrace{(x \cdot x \cdot \cdots \cdot x)}_{\substack{\text{m + k + 1 factors} \\ \text{of x}}} = x^{m+(k+1)}$

19. $a_1 = \sqrt{2}$ which is less than 2, so P_1 is true.
Assume P_k is true. Thus, $a_k = \sqrt{2 + a_{k-1}} < 2$. But $a_{k+1} = \sqrt{2 + a_k}$. Since $a_k < 2$, $\sqrt{2 + a_k} < \sqrt{2 + 2}$. But $\sqrt{2 + 2} = \sqrt{4} = 2$. Thus $a_{k+1} = \sqrt{2 + a_k} < 2$. Thus, by induction, $a_n < 2$ for all n.

PAGE 27 CLASSROOM EXERCISES
1. $x^8 + 8x^7y + 28 x^6y^2$ **3.** $243x^5 - 810x^4y + 1080x^3y^2$ **5.** 120 **7.** 12 **9.** 56 **11.** 12 **13.** 15

PAGE 27 WRITTEN EXERCISES
1. $x^7 + 7x^6y + 21x^5y^2 + 35x^4y^3 + 35x^3y^4 + 21x^2y^5 + 7xy^6 + y^7$ **3.** $a^4 - 8a^3b + 24a^2b^2 - 32ab^3 + 16b^4$
5. $32 + 80b + 80b^2 + 40b^3 + 10b^4 + b^5$ **7.** $243a^5 + 810a^4b + 1080a^3b^2 + 720a^2b^3 + 240ab^4 + 32b^5$
9. $\frac{1}{2187}x^7 - \frac{7}{243}x^6y + \frac{7}{9}x^5y^2 = \frac{35}{3}x^4y^3 + 105x^3y^4 - 567x^2y^5 + 1701xy^6 - 2187y^7$
11. $\frac{1}{8} - \frac{3}{4}x^2 + \frac{3}{2}x^4 - x^6$ **13.** $-61,236x^5y^5$ **15.** $13,230x^2y^3$ **17.** -128 **19.** $-12x$ **21.** $-160a^3b^3$
23. $\frac{16,384}{2187}$ **25.** 1.10 **27.** .091

PAGE 29 EXERCISES

1.

Day	i	s	r	New Infects	New Re- covers	Add'l Infects	Total In- fected
6	21.880	76.565	2.565	16.752	2.188	14.564	36.444
7	36.444	59.813	4.743	21.798	3.644	18.154	54.598
8	54.598	38.015	8.387	20.755	5.460	15.295	69.893
9	69.893	17.26	13.847	12.064	6.989	5.075	74.968
10	74.968	5.196	20.836	3.896	7.497	-3.602	71.366
11	71.366	1.301	28.333	0.428	7.137	-6.209	65.157

3. See the Solution Key.

5. It does not tell you anything about the rate of recovery.

PAGE 32 CLASSROOM EXERCISES

1. $4 = x$ 3. $x + 2 \geq -5$ and $x + 2 \leq 5$ 5. $x > -5$ and $x < 5$ 7. $2x - 3 > -3$ and $2x - 3 < 3$
9. $3x + 2 \leq -5$ or $3x + 2 \geq 5$ 11. $2x + 3 = -5$ or $2x + 3 = 5$

PAGES 32-33 WRITTEN EXERCISES

1. $\{x : -2 \leq x \leq 2\}$ 3. $\{r : -3 < r < 3\}$ 5. $\{x : x < -1\} \cup \{x : x > 3\}$ 7. $\{g : g \leq -6\} \cup$
$\{g : g \geq -2\}$ 9. $\{r : 3 < r < 7\}$ 11. $\{g : 10 < g < 12\}$ 13. $\{x : -1 \leq x \leq \frac{1}{5}\}$ 15. $\{x : \frac{3}{2} \leq x \leq \frac{9}{2}\}$
17. $\{x : x \geq 4\}$ 19. $\{r : r < \frac{3}{4}\}$ 21. $\{y : y < -\frac{8}{21}\}$ 23. The empty set. 25. If $x \geq 0$, $y \geq 0$, then
$|x| = x$, $|y| = y$, $|xy| = xy$. If $x < 0$, $y < 0$, then $|x| = -x$, $|y| = -y$, $|xy| = xy$. If $x > 0$, $y < 0$,
$y < 0$, $|x| = x$, $|y| = -y$, $|xy| = -y$, $|xy| = -xy$. If $x < 0$, $y \geq 0$, then $|x| = -x$, $|y| = y$, $|xy| = -xy$.
In any of these cases, we therefore have $|xy| = |x| \cdot |y|$. 27. If $x - y \geq 0$, then $|x - y| = x - y$.
However, $x - y \geq 0$ implies $y - x < 0$. Thus $|y - x| = x - y$ also. Now, if $x - y < 0$, we have $|x - y| = y - x$. But $x - y < 0$ implies $y - x \geq 0$. Thus $|y - x| = y - x$ also. In either case $|x - y| = |y - x|$.
29. If $x \geq 0$, $|x| = x$, and $|x|^2 = x^2$. If $x < 0$, $|x| = -x$, and $|x|^2 = (-x)^2 = x^2$. 31. By Exercise 30, $|(x + y) + (-y)| \leq |x + y| + |-y|$. But by Ex. 27, $|-y| = |y|$. Thus, since $|(x + y) - y| = |x|$, we obtain $|x| \leq |x + y| + |y|$ which implies $|x| - |y| \leq |x + y|$. 33. By Ex. 30, $|x_1 + x_2| \leq |x_1| + |x_2|$. Assume $|x_1 + x_2 + \cdots + x_k| \leq |x_1| + |x_2| + \cdots + |x_k|$ for some $k \in N$. Then $|x_1 + x_2 + \cdots + x_{k+1}| = |(x_1 + x_2 + \cdots + x_k) + x_{k+1}| \leq |x_1 + x_2 + \cdots + x_k| + |x_{k+1}| \leq |x_1| + |x_2| + \cdots + |x_k| + |x_{k+1}|$.

PAGES 33-34 MID-CHAPTER REVIEW

1. False 2. True 3. True 4. Terminating decimal $61.038 = \frac{61038}{1000} = \frac{30519}{500}$ 5. Inverse postulate of
Addition 6. Associative Postulate of Multiplication 7. Closure Postulate of Multiplication 8. False because
$-6 + 3 = -3$ So $-6 \leq -3$ or $-3 \geq -6$ 9. True 10. True 11. $\{b : b > -5\}$ 12. $\{x : x \geq 3\}$
13. $\{a : a > -4\}$ 14. $\{x : -1 < x < 3\}$ 15. $\{x : -4 < x < 3\}$ 16. $\{x : \frac{4}{5} < x < \frac{6}{5}\}$ 17. i. Verify P_1:
$P_1 : 3 = \frac{3(2)}{2} = 3$. Thus, P_1 is true. ii. Induction Hypothesis. Assume P_k is true; i.e., $3 + 6 + 9 + \cdots + 3k = \frac{3k(k + 1)}{2}$. Prove that P_{k+1} follows from P_k. Thus $3 + 6 + 9 + \cdots + 3k + 3(k + 1) = \frac{3k(k + 1)}{2} + 3(k + 1) = \frac{3(k + 1)[k + 2]}{2} = \frac{3(k + 1)[(k + 1) + 1]}{2}$. The last statement is P_{k+1}. Thus P_{k+1} follows from P_k.
18. i. Verify $P_1 : P_1 : 1^2 = \frac{1(1 + 1)(2 + 1)}{6} = \frac{2(3)}{6} = 1$. Thus P_1 is true. ii. Induction Hypothesis: Assume P_k
is true; i.e. $1^2 + 2^2 + 3^2 + \cdots + k^2 = \frac{k(k + 1)(2k + 1)}{6}$. Prove that P_{k+1} follows from P_k. Thus
$1^2 + 2^2 + 3^2 + \cdots + k^2 + (k + 1)^2 = \frac{k(k + 1)(2k + 1)}{6} + (k + 1)^2 = \frac{(k + 1)}{6}[k(2k + 1) + 6(k + 1)] = \frac{(k + 1)}{6}[2k^2 + 7k + 6] = \frac{(k + 1)(k + 2)(2k + 3)}{6} = \frac{(k + 1)[(k + 1) + 1][2(k + 1) + 1]}{6}$. The last statement is
P_{k+1}. Thus P_{k+1} follows from P_k. 19. $x^4 - 4x^3y + 6x^2y^2 - 4xy^3 + y^4$ 20. $a^7 + 21a^6b + 189a^5b^2 + 945a^4b^3 + 2835a^3b^4 + 5103a^2b^5 + 5103ab^6 + 2187b^7$. 21. $\frac{a^{11}}{177,147} - \frac{11a^9}{59,049} + \frac{55a^7}{19,683} - \frac{55a^5}{2187} + \frac{110a^3}{729} - \frac{154a}{243} + \frac{154}{81a} - \frac{110}{27a^3} + \frac{55}{9a^5} - \frac{55}{9a^7} + \frac{11}{3a^9} - \frac{1}{a^{11}}$ 22. $-489,888\, a^6b^3$ 23. $\frac{25,344}{78,125}y^8$ 24. $<-4, 4> = \{x : -4 < x < 4\}$ 25. $\{a : a \leq -2\} \cup \{a : a \geq 2\}$ 26. $[-1, 13] = \{x : -1 \leq y \leq 13\}$

PAGE 36 CLASSROOM EXERCISES

1. Into 3. Into

PAGES 37-38 WRITTEN EXERCISES

1. $\{-5, -7, -9, -3, -1, 1\}$ 3. $\{4, 1, 0\}$ 5. $\{3, 2, 1, 0, -1, -2, -3\}$ 7. $\{0, 1, 4, 16, 64, 144\}$

9. $\{t : t > -4\}$ 11. $\{y : y \le 0\}$ 13. $\{-2, -1, 0, 1, 2\}$ 15. Into. 17. Into. 19. Onto. 21. Into. 23. Onto.

25. Range: $\{0, 1, 2, 3\}$; Graph consists of the following points: $\{(-3, 3), (-2, 2), (-1, 1), (0, 0), (1, 1),$ $(2, 2), (3, 3)\}$ 27. (25) Range = $\{0, -1, -2, -3\}$; Graph consists of the following points: $\{(-3, -3),$ $(-2, -2), (-1, -1), (0, 0), (1, -1), 2, -2), (3, -3)\}$; (26) Range = $[-3, 0]$. Graph is an inverted "V" with vertex at (0, 0) and end points at $(-3, -3)$ and $(3, -3)$.

29. a. Domain = $\{x : x > 0\}$. Range = $\{y : y = 8x, x \in N\}$. b. The graph of the relation consists of line segments, 1 unit in length, and parallel to the x axis, for $y \in \{8, 16, 24, \cdots\}$. Each segment is located between two consecutive integral values of x and includes only the right hand endpoint. For example, one segment has the domain $< 0, 1$] and is 8 units above the x axis. 31. Answers will vary. This exercise is done in the same way as Exercise 30. Replace the heights of the students by their weights and compare each of the 5 students to the other 4 by weight. The heavier student is listed first in each pair. This is not the same relation as "is taller than" in general. However, if the heaviest student is the tallest student, the next heaviest is the next tallest, and so on for all 5 students, the same set of pairs would be obtained.

PAGE 41 CLASSROOM EXERCISES   1 and 3 are functions.

PAGES 41-42 WRITTEN EXERCISES

1. $\left\{0, \frac{1}{2}, 1, \frac{3}{2}, 2, \cdots\right\}$ 3. 3 5. x 7. The relations in Exercises 7, 8, 10-14, 17, and 18 are functions.

19.

21. $\{14, 7, 2, -1, -2\}$ 29.

23. 1

25. 6

27. n!

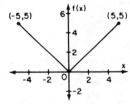

The graphs for Exercises 8, 10, 11, 12, 13, 14, 17, and 18 are done in a similar manner. 31. Two line segments with common endpoint at (0, 1). One has slope 1 and one has slope -1. 33. Line segments parallel to the x axis for $y \in \{-5, -4, \cdots, 4, 5\}$. Each segment contains all real numbers between two specific consecutive integers, but including only the left endpoint. Example: One line segment has domain $-5 \le x < -4$ and range y = -5. 35. Similar to Exercise 34. 37. A line segment passing through (0,0) having a slope of 1.

PAGE 45 CLASSROOM EXERCISES   1. 3x + 2 3. 9x − 4 5. 2x − 1 7. $4x^2 - 4x + 2$

PAGES 45-46 WRITTEN EXERCISES

1. 1, 2 3. hg = $\{(-5, 5), (-2, -3), (0, -1)\}$; Domain: $\{-5, -2, 0\}$, Range: $\{-3, -1, 5\}$. 5. The diagram is done in a similar manner to Exercise 3. Define the first function as F. Then HF = $\{(a, a), (b, b), (c, c)\}$; Domain = $\{a, b, c\}$, Range = $\{a, b, c\}$. 7. $(3x - 4)^2 + 3$ 9. $-6x + 9$ 11. $-6x^2 - 9$ 13. -73 15. $(x^2 + 3)^2 + 3$ 17. 152 19. fh(v) = acx + ad + b; hf(x) = acx + bc + d 21. 2 23. 100 25. g[l(x)] = x − 3; l[g(x)] = x − 3 27. h(x) = x + 3 29. f[g(x)] = 7; g[f(x)] = 3 31. f[g(x)] = x^{nm}; g[f(x)] = x^{mn} 33. f · g(x) = x^{m+n}. f · g(x) $\ne$ f[g(x)] = g[f(x)] = x^{mn} 35. (g · f)[h(x)] = $(x^2 - 3)(x^2 + 2)$ 37. f[h(x)] = $x^2 + 2$ 39. They are equal.

PAGE 49 CLASSROOM EXERCISES

1. $f^{-1} = \{(3, 2), (2, 3), (5, 4)\}$ 3. $f^{-1} = \{(1, 0), (9, 2), (-3, -1)\}$ 5. $f^{-1} : x \to \frac{x}{2}$ 7. $f^{-1} : x \to x + 6$

PAGES 49-50 WRITTEN EXERCISES

1.

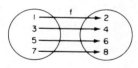 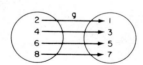

3. Interchanging first and second coordinates in each ordered pair. 5. $f^{-1} = \{(y, x) : y = f(x)\}$ 7. $3x$ 9. $\frac{r-1}{2}$

11. $\sqrt[3]{x}$ 13. $\pm\sqrt{x+4}$ Not a function, e.g., $f^{-1} : 0 \overset{2}{\underset{-2}{\diagdown}}$. 15. $\frac{5}{2}(y + 5)$ 17. $x - 3$ 19. $\frac{1}{x}$ 21. and 23. Same

answers as 17. and 19 except y and x are interchanged. 25. Solve for x in terms of y, then replace y by x in

the final answer. 27. $y = x^3 + 27$; $x = \sqrt[3]{y - 27}$; Thus, the inverse is $y = \sqrt[3]{x - 27}$. 29. The four given points.

31. Line passing through (0, 0) with slope 1. 33. f is a line segment through (0, −4) with a slope of 3. f^{-1} is

a line segment through $(0, \frac{4}{3})$ with a slope of $\frac{1}{3}$. The graphs of f, f^{-1} are reflections of each other in

$y = x(1 : x \to x)$.

35. a.

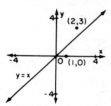

b. It is a line passing through (1, 0) and (2, 3). The line has slope of 3 and a y intercept of −3.

37. Consider $f : x \to ax + b, a \neq 0$. $x \in R$. Then

$$f^{-1} : x \to \frac{x-b}{a}, x \in R.$$

PAGE 53 CLASSROOM EXERCISES

1. $0 + 2i$ 3. $-1 + 0i$ 5. $1 + 0i$ 7. $4 + 3i$

PAGES 53-54 WRITTEN EXERCISES

1. $-1 + 3i$ 3. $0 - 2i$ 5. $-1 + 8i$ 7. $10 + 24i$ 9. $\frac{1}{5} + \frac{3}{5}i$ 11. $2 - 2i$ 13. $2 + i$ 15. $\frac{1}{5}$ 17. $(1 + i)^2 - 2(1 + i) +$

$2 = 1 + 2i - 1 - 2 - 2i + 2 = 0$. Also $(1 - i)^2 - 2(1 - i) + 2 = 1 - 2i - 1 - 2 + 2i + 2 = 0$. 19. Assume

$z_1 z_2 = 0$ and suppose $z_1 \neq 0$ and $z_2 \neq 0$. Let $z_1 = a + bi$ and $a_2 = c + di$ a, b, c, d $\in$ R. Then either a $\neq 0$ or

b $\neq 0$ or both and either c $\neq 0$ or d $\neq 0$ or both. There are nine possible cases. In the first one a $\neq 0$, b = 0,

c $\neq 0$, d = 0. Then $z_1 z_2 = (ac - bd) + (bc + ad)i$ and ac − bd $\neq 0$ since ac $\neq 0$ and bd = 0. Hence $z_1 z_2 \neq 0$.

This contradicts our assumption. Similarly, the eight other cases result in contradictions. Therefore, the

supposition must be false and $z_1 = 0$ or $z_2 = 0$ or both. 21. Let $z_1 = a_1 + b_1 i, z_2 = a_2 + b_2 i, z_3 = a_3 + b_3 i$,

$a_1, a_2, a_3, b_1, b_2, b_3 \in$ R. Then $(z_1 + z_2) + z_3 = ((a_1 + b_1 i) + (a_2 + b_2 i)) + (a_3 + b_3 i) = ((a_1 + a_2) + a_3) +$

$((b_1 + b_2) + b_3)i = (a_1 + b_1 i) + ((a_2 + b_2 i) + (a_3 + b_3 i)) = z_1 + (z_2 + z_3)$. 23. Let $z_1 = a_1 + b_1 i, z_2 = a_2 +$

$b_2 i, z_3 = a_3 + b_3 i, a_1, a_2, a_3, b_1, b_2, b_3 \in$ R. Then $z_1(z_2 + z_3) = (a_1 + b_1 i)((a_2 + a_3) + (b_2 + b_3)i) =$

$a_1(a_2 + a_3) - b_1(b_2 + b_3) + (b_1(a_2 + a_3) + a_1(b_2 + b_3))i = [(a_1 a_2 - b_1 b_2) + (a_2 b_1 + a_1 b_2)i] + [(a_1 a_3 -$

$b_1 b_3) + (a_3 b_1 + a_1 b_3)] = z_1 z_2 + z_1 z_3$.

PAGE 57 CLASSROOM EXERCISES

1. $\sqrt{13}$

3. $\sqrt{61}$

9. $3 + 7i$

11. $-3i$

5.

$3 - 7i$

$(3, -7)$

7.

$-2 - 8i$

$(-2, -8)$

1. $z_1 + z_2 = -2 + 4i$

   $z_1 - z_2 = -4 - 2i$

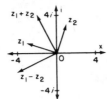

3. $z_1 + z_2 = -8i, z_1 - z_2 = 6$

5. $z_1 + z_2 = 2 + 4i, z_1 - z_2 = 2 - 4i$

7. $z_1 + z_2 = 5i, z_1 - z_2 = i$

9. Exercise 1: $1 - 3i$; Exercise 2: $4 + 2i$; Exercise 3: $-3 + 4i$; Exercise 4: $-2 - 3i$; Exercise 5: $-4i$; Exercise 6: 2; Exercise 7: $-2i$. 11. $\dfrac{-4 + 7i}{5}$ 13. $\dfrac{-11 + 23i}{25}$ 15. Let $z = a + bi$, where $a, b \in R$. $\bar{z} = z \Leftrightarrow a - bi = a + bi \Leftrightarrow 2bi = 0 \Leftrightarrow b = 0 \Leftrightarrow z$ is real. 17. Let $z = a + bi$, where $a, b \in R$. Then $|z| = \sqrt{a^2 + b^2} = \sqrt{a^2 + (-b)^2} = |\bar{z}|$

19. $\overline{z_1 + z_2} = \overline{(a_1 + a_2) + (b_1 + b_2)i} = a_1 + a_2 - (b_1 + b_2)i = (a_1 - b_1 i) + (a_2 - b_2 i) = \bar{z_1} + \bar{z_2}$

21. $\overline{z_1 z_2} = \overline{(a_1 + b_1 i)(a_2 + b_2 i)} = \overline{(a_1 a_2 - b_1 b_2) + (a_1 b_2 + a_2 b_1)i} = (a_1 a_2 - b_1 b_2) - (a_1 b_2 + a_2 b_1)i$

$= (a_1 - b_1 i) \cdot (a_2 - b_2 i) = \bar{z_1} \cdot \bar{z_2}$ 23. $|z_1 \cdot z_2|^2 = z_1 \cdot z_2 \cdot \overline{z_1 z_2} = (z_1 \bar{z_1})(z_2 \bar{z_2}) = |z_1|^2 \cdot |z_2|^2$

Therefore $|z_1 z_2| = |z_1||z_2|$ 25. Let $z = a + bi, a, b \in R$. a. $|z| = \sqrt{a^2 + b^2}$. Since $b^2 \geq 0$, we have

$a^2 + b^2 \geq a^2, \therefore \sqrt{a^2 + b^2} \geq a$. b. $|z| = \sqrt{a^2 + b^2}$. Since $a^2 \geq 0, a^2 + b^2 \geq b^2$. But $|bi|$

$= \sqrt{b^2} = |b|. \therefore a^2 + b^2 \geq |bi|^2 \therefore \sqrt{a^2 + b^2} \geq |bi|$. 27. Inductive step: $\overline{z_1 z_2 \cdots z_{k+1}}$

$= \overline{z_1 \cdot z_2 \cdot \cdots \cdot z_k} \cdot \bar{z}_{k+1}$ by Exercise 21., and this in turn is equal to $(\bar{z_1} \cdot \bar{z_2} \cdot \cdots \cdot \bar{z_k}) \cdot \bar{z}_{k+1}$ by the inductive hypothesis. The last expression is then equal to $\bar{z_1} \cdot \bar{z_2} \cdot \cdots \cdot \bar{z}_{k+1}$ by the associative property.

1. Natural, whole, integer, rational, real 3. Whole, integer, rational, real 5. $0.\overline{285714}$ 7. $\dfrac{39}{200}$ 9. Distributive Prop. 11. Definition of Subtraction 13. Commutativity of Addition 15. True 17. True 19. All real numbers greater than 2, not including 2. 21. All real numbers between -1 and 2, not including -1, including 2. 23. All real numbers greater than 2, including 2. 25. All real numbers between 1 and 3, not including 1, including 3. 27. P_1 is true since $4 = 2(1)(1 + 1) = 4$. Assume that P_k is true; we must show that P_{k+1} is also true. Then, $4 + 8 + 12 + \cdots + 4k = 2k(k + 1)$ and, $[4 + 8 + 12 + \cdots + 4k] + 4(k + 1) = 2k(k + 1) + 4(k + 1) = (k + 1)(2k + 4) = 2(k + 1)[(k + 1) + 1]$. But this is P_{k+1}. Thus the statement P_n is true for all $n \in N$. 29. $a^6 + 6a^5 b + 15a^4 b^2 + 20a^3 b^3 + 15a^2 b^4 + 6ab^5 + b^6$ 31. $-15{,}120\, x^4 y^3$ 33. All real numbers less than -10, not including -10; also all real numbers greater than 10, not including 10.

35. $R = \{0, 1, 2, 4, 5, 8\}$

37. It is a function.

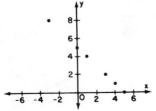

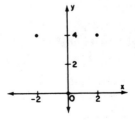

39. $fg: x \to (2x + 1) - 5 = 2x - 4$; $gf: x \to 2(x - 5) + 1 = 2x - 9$ 41. $f^{-1}: x \to \dfrac{5 - x}{3}$ 43. The inverse of Exercise 41 is a function. 45. $\dfrac{-14}{17} \dfrac{-5}{17}i$ 47. $10 + 11i$ 49. $z_1 + z_2 = 8$; $z_1 - z_2 = -2 - 2i$

PAGE 64   CHAPTER TEST

1. $\frac{2}{9}$ 2. $(a + b) - c = (a + b) + (-c)$ (Definition of subtraction)

                        $= a + (b + (-c))$ (Associative property of addition)

                        $= a + (b - c)$ (Definition of subtraction)

3. If $n = 1$, $2(1) = 1(1 + 1) = 2$, so that P_1 is true. Assume that P_k is true, that is, $2 + 4 + \cdots + 2k = k(k + 1)$. Then, $2 + 4 + \cdots + 2k + 2(k + 1) = k(k + 1) + 2(k + 1) = (k + 1)(k + 2)$. This is $P_{k + 1}$. Thus, P_k implies $P_{k + 1}$ and therefore, P_n is true for all $n \in N$. 4. x is positive, since $-x$ is the additive inverse of a positive number, $-x = -(x)$. 5. a. [a, b] b. $<a, b>$ 6. The empty set. 7. $|x| = \begin{cases} x \text{ if } x \geq 0 \\ -x \text{ if } x < 0 \end{cases}$ 8. See page 13. 9. See page 13. 10. See page 13. 11. See page 13. 12. $32x^5 - 560x^4y + 3920x^3y^2 - 13{,}720\ x^2y^3 + 24{,}010\ xy^4 - 16{,}807\ y^5$ 13. $2x - \frac{5}{2}$ 14. $2x - 2$ 15. $x - \frac{1}{2}$ 16. $\frac{x + 3}{2}$ 17. $.101001000100001 \cdots$ 18. $0 + 1i$

CHAPTER 2   CIRCULAR FUNCTIONS

PAGE 67   CLASSROOM EXERCISES

1. $PQ = \sqrt{(2 - (-5))^2 + (-7 - 1)^2} = \sqrt{(7)^2 + (-8)^2} = \sqrt{49 + 64} = \sqrt{113}$ 3. $x^2 + y^2 = 1$

PAGES 67-68   WRITTEN EXERCISES

1. 6 3. 8 5. 5 7. 13 9. $\sqrt{10}$ 11. $\sqrt{68}$ 13. 5 15. $\sqrt{5}a$ 17. $9 = (x - 2)^2 + (y + 5)^2$ 19. $49 = (x + 5)^2 + (y + 1)^2$ 21. $\frac{1}{4} = (x - \frac{2}{3})^2 + (y + \frac{1}{3})^2$ 23. $41 = (x - 1)^2 + (y - 2)^2$ 25. 13, -11 27. $PQ = \sqrt{26}$; $QR = 4$; $PR = \sqrt{2}$ 29. $y = -x$ 31. $C(3, 2)$, $r = 4$

PAGES 70-71   WRITTEN EXERCISES

1. $2 + 2\pi, 2 + 4\pi, 2 + 6\pi, 2 + 8\pi, 2 + 10\pi$ 3. $-3 - 2\pi, -3 - 4\pi, -3 - 6\pi, -3 - 8\pi$ 5. $\frac{2\pi}{3} + 2\pi n, n \in N$ 7. $\frac{2\pi}{3} \pm 2\pi n, n \in W$ 9. IV 11. IV 13. I 15. II 17. III 19. Quadrantal between quadrants III and IV.

21. a. $(\frac{3}{5}, -\frac{4}{5})$ b. $(-\frac{3}{5}, -\frac{4}{5})$ c. $(\frac{3}{5}, \frac{4}{5})$ d. $(-\frac{3}{5}, \frac{4}{5})$ 23. a. $(\frac{\sqrt{13}}{14}, -\frac{1}{14})$ b. $(-\frac{\sqrt{13}}{14}, -\frac{1}{14})$ c. $(\frac{\sqrt{13}}{14}, \frac{1}{14})$ d. $(-\frac{\sqrt{13}}{14}, \frac{1}{14})$ 25. a. $(-\frac{1}{2}, -\frac{\sqrt{3}}{2})$ b. $(\frac{1}{2}, -\frac{\sqrt{3}}{2})$ c. $(-\frac{1}{2}, \frac{\sqrt{3}}{2})$ d. $(-\frac{1}{2}, \frac{\sqrt{3}}{2})$

PAGE 75   CLASSROOM EXERCISES

1. $6\pi + \frac{5\pi}{3}$ 3. $2\pi + \frac{2\pi}{3}$ 5. $-8\pi + \frac{\pi}{2}$ 7. $-6\pi + \frac{3\pi}{2}$ 9. IV 11. on axis between quadrants III and IV.

PAGE 75   WRITTEN EXERCISES

1. II, $-$, $+$ 3. IV, $+$, $-$ 5. IV, $+$, $-$ 7. III, $-$, $-$ 9. II, $-$, $+$ 11. III, $-$, $-$ 13. III, $-$, $-$ 15. I, $+$, $+$ 17. $-\frac{5}{13}$ 19. $\frac{4}{5}$ 21. $\frac{2}{\sqrt{5}}$ 23. For each $x \in [0, 2\pi]$, $\sin x \in [-1, 1]$, since the range of y on the unit circle is $-1 \leq y \leq 1$. Thus, since all other values of $\sin x$ are obtained by repeating points on the unit circle, the result follows. 25. Theorem 2-3

1. $\pi + \dfrac{\pi}{2}$ 3. $\pi - \dfrac{\pi}{6}$ 5. $2\pi - \dfrac{\pi}{6}$ 7. $-\pi - \dfrac{\pi}{4}$

PAGE 78 WRITTEN EXERCISES

1. $-1, 0$ 3. $-\dfrac{\sqrt{2}}{2}, \dfrac{\sqrt{2}}{2}$ 5. $\dfrac{1}{2}, -\dfrac{\sqrt{3}}{2}$ 7. $-\dfrac{1}{2}, -\dfrac{\sqrt{3}}{2}$ 9. $\dfrac{1}{2}, \dfrac{\sqrt{3}}{2}$ 11. In the figure $CB \le m\overset{\frown}{CB}$. Now, $|\sin x_2 -$
$\sin x_1| = CS$ and $|x_2 - x_1| = m\overset{\frown}{CB}$. But $CS \le CB$ and $CB \le m\overset{\frown}{CB}$. Therefore, $|\sin x_2 - \sin x_1| \le |x_2 -$
$x_1|$ by substitution. 13. Let $x_2 = x$ and $x_1 = 0$ and the result follows from Exercise 11.

PAGE 82 CLASSROOM EXERCISES

1. $\dfrac{\pi}{3} = \dfrac{\pi}{2} - \dfrac{\pi}{6}$; $\sin \dfrac{\pi}{3} = \sin (\dfrac{\pi}{2} - \dfrac{\pi}{6}) = \cos (\dfrac{-\pi}{6})$ (Theorem 2-6); $= \cos \dfrac{\pi}{6}$ (Theorem 2-3) $= \dfrac{\sqrt{3}}{2}$. $\cos \dfrac{\pi}{3} =$
$\cos (\dfrac{\pi}{2} - \dfrac{\pi}{6}) = -\sin (\dfrac{-\pi}{6})$ (Theorem 2-6) $= -(-\sin \dfrac{\pi}{6})$ (Theorem 2-3) $= +\sin \dfrac{\pi}{6} = +\dfrac{1}{2}$. 3. $\dfrac{5\pi}{3} = \pi + \dfrac{2\pi}{3}$;
$\sin \dfrac{5\pi}{3} = \sin (\pi + \dfrac{2\pi}{3}) = -\sin \dfrac{2\pi}{3}$ (Theorem 2-4) $= -\dfrac{\sqrt{3}}{2}$. (See Example, page 81) $\cos \dfrac{5\pi}{3} = \cos (\pi + \dfrac{2\pi}{3}) =$
$-\cos \dfrac{2\pi}{3}$ (Theorem 2-4) $= -(-\dfrac{1}{2})$ (Example, page 81) $= \dfrac{1}{2}$.

PAGES 82-83 WRITTEN EXERCISES

1. True 3. True 5. False; $\sin \dfrac{\pi}{6} \cos \dfrac{\pi}{3} + \cos \dfrac{\pi}{2} \sin \dfrac{\pi}{3} = \dfrac{1}{2} \cdot \dfrac{1}{2} + 0 \cdot \dfrac{\sqrt{3}}{2} = \dfrac{1}{4} \ne 1$ 7. False; $\cos^2 \dfrac{5\pi}{4} -$
$\sin^2 \dfrac{5\pi}{4} = (-\dfrac{\sqrt{2}}{2})^2 - (-\dfrac{\sqrt{2}}{2})^2 = 0 \ne 1$ 9. $\cos \dfrac{\pi}{7}$ 11. $-\cos \dfrac{\pi}{10}$ 13. $\cos \dfrac{7\pi}{8} = \cos (\pi - \dfrac{\pi}{8}) = -\cos \dfrac{\pi}{8}$;
$\cos \dfrac{7\pi}{8} = \cos (\dfrac{\pi}{8} + \dfrac{3\pi}{8}) = -\sin \dfrac{3\pi}{8}$ 15. $-\cos \dfrac{\pi}{5}$ 17. $\sin \dfrac{\pi}{7}, \cos \dfrac{\pi}{14}$ 19. $-\sin \dfrac{\pi}{3}$ 21. $\sin (\dfrac{\pi}{2} - x) = \sin (\dfrac{\pi}{2} +$
$(-x)) = \cos (-x) = \cos x$ 23. $\cos (\dfrac{\pi}{2} - x) = \cos (\dfrac{\pi}{2} + (-x)) = -\sin (-x) = \sin x$ 25. $\sin (x - \pi) = \sin [-(\pi - x)] =$
$-\sin (\pi - x) = -\sin x$ 27. $\overset{\frown}{AP} = \dfrac{\pi}{4}$, $\overset{\frown}{BP} = \dfrac{\pi}{4}$; Therefore $\overset{\frown}{BP} = \overset{\frown}{AP}$. $\overset{\frown}{BP} - x = \overset{\frown}{BQ}$ and $\overset{\frown}{AP} - x = \overset{\frown}{AR}$;
Therefore $\overset{\frown}{BQ} = \overset{\frown}{AR}$ and $BQ = AR$. 29. Yes. If $x > \dfrac{\pi}{4}$, $x - \overset{\frown}{BP} = \overset{\frown}{BQ}$ and $x - \overset{\frown}{AP} = \overset{\frown}{AR}$. Therefore, $\overset{\frown}{BQ} = \overset{\frown}{AR}$
and $BQ = AR$. If $x < 0$, $|\overset{\frown}{BP} - |x|| = \overset{\frown}{BQ}$ and $|\overset{\frown}{AP} - |x|| = \overset{\frown}{AR}$. Therefore, $\overset{\frown}{BQ} = \overset{\frown}{AR}$ and $BQ = AR$. If
$x = \dfrac{\pi}{4}$, points B and Q coincide and points R and A coincide. Thus, $BQ = AR = 0$.

PAGE 84 MID-CHAPTER REVIEW

1. $8\sqrt{2}$ 2. $10\sqrt{2}$ 3. $(x - 1)^2 + (y - 9)^2 = 25$ 4. $3.5 + 2\pi, 3.5 + 4\pi, 3.5 - 2\pi, 3.5 - 4\pi$ 5. a. $(\dfrac{-24}{25}, \dfrac{-7}{25})$
b. $(\dfrac{+24}{25}, \dfrac{-7}{25})$ 6. Both negative 7. $\dfrac{-8}{17}$ 8. $-\dfrac{1}{2}, \dfrac{\sqrt{2}}{2}$ 9. $\cos \dfrac{\pi}{5}$ 10. $-\cos \dfrac{2\pi}{5}$

PAGE 87 CLASSROOM EXERCISES

1. $\dfrac{3}{4} (2\pi)$ 3. $7 (2\pi) + \dfrac{\pi}{2}$ 5. None

PAGES 87-88 WRITTEN EXERCISES

1. Only the graph for Exercise 1 is shown
as the graphs for Exercises 3 and 5
are similar.

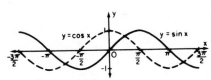

7. The graph should look like the figure at the bottom of page 85 with the graph beginning at 0 and ending at 2π.

9. $\dfrac{\pi}{4}, \dfrac{5\pi}{4}$ 11. $x \in \langle 0, \dfrac{\pi}{4} \rangle \cup \langle \dfrac{5\pi}{4}, 2\pi \rangle$ 13. $\dfrac{3\pi}{4}, \dfrac{7\pi}{4}$ 15. $0, \dfrac{3\pi}{2}, 2\pi$ 17. None.

19.

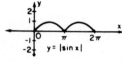

21.

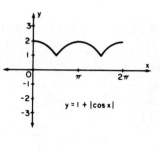

23.

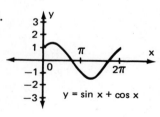

25.

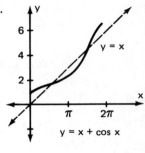

PAGE 92 CLASSROOM EXERCISES

1. 8, 2π 3. $\frac{1}{2}$, 20π 5. $\frac{799}{4}\pi$

PAGES 93-94 WRITTEN EXERCISES

1. 3, 2π 3. 2, π 5. $\frac{2}{3}$, $\frac{3\pi}{2}$ 7. $\frac{1}{18}$, 36π 9. a. $(\frac{\pi}{2}, 2)$ b. $(\frac{3\pi}{2}, -2)$ c. $(0, 0)$, $(\pi, 0)$, $(2\pi, 0)$ 11. a. $(0, \frac{4}{5})$ and $(\pi, \frac{4}{5})$ b. $(\frac{\pi}{2}, -\frac{4}{5})$ c. $(\frac{\pi}{4}, 0)$, $(\frac{3\pi}{4}, 0)$ 13. a. $(\frac{3\pi}{4}, 5)$ b. $(\frac{9\pi}{4}, -5)$ c. $(0, 0)$, $(\frac{3\pi}{2}, 0)$, $(3\pi, 0)$ 15. a. $(0, 1)$, $(\frac{5\pi}{2}, 1)$ b. $(\frac{5\pi}{4}, -1)$ c. $(\frac{5\pi}{4}, 0)$, $(\frac{15\pi}{4}, 0)$ 17. Amplitude is 2, period is 2π. 19. Amplitude is $\frac{4}{5}$, period is π. 21. Amplitude is 5, period is 3π. 23. Amplitude is 1, period is $\frac{5}{2}\pi$. 25. $y = \pm3 \sin 2x$ 27. $y = \pm12 \sin (\pi x)$ 29. $y = 4 \sin 6x$, $y = -4 \sin 2x$ 31. $y = \pm7 \sin (\frac{3}{2}x)$ or $y = \pm7 \sin 3x$ 33. $y = -2 \sin (\frac{2}{5}x)$ or $y = 2 \sin \frac{6}{5}x$ 35. Amplitude of A sin x is $|A|$. Amplitude of $-A$ sin x is $|-A|$, and $|A| = |-A|$ for all $A \in R$. 37. 1 39. 60 41. 20 43. $\frac{1}{2\pi}$

PAGE 97 CLASSROOM EXERCISES

1. $\frac{-2}{5}$ 3. -3

PAGES 97-98 WRITTEN EXERCISES

1. $y = \pm5 \sin (x - \frac{\pi}{3})$ 3. $y = \pm\frac{2}{3}\sin (8x + \pi)$ 5. $y = \pm7 \sin (\frac{4x}{3} + \frac{\pi}{3})$ 7. $y = \pm3 \cos (2x - \frac{4\pi}{3})$ 9. $y = \pm100 \cos (\frac{2x}{3} + \frac{2\pi}{3})$ 11. $y = \pm\frac{7}{3}\cos (\frac{12x}{5} + \frac{12}{5})$

	Amplitude	Period	Phase Shift
13.	3	2π	$\frac{\pi}{4}$
15.	$\frac{2}{3}$	4π	$-\frac{2\pi}{5}$
17.	1	3π	$\frac{3\pi}{2}$
19.	2	π	$\frac{\pi}{4}$
21.	3	1	$-\frac{1}{2}$
23.	2	2	$\frac{1}{2}$
25.	3	$\frac{\pi}{2}$	$-\frac{1}{2}$
27.	5	2π	3

29. Since $2 \sin (3x - \frac{\pi}{2}) = -2 \sin (-(3x - \frac{\pi}{2}))$ $= -2 \sin (-3x + \frac{\pi}{2})$, result follows.

31. i. and iii, have identical graphs. Likewise with ii. and iv. This follows from the fact that for $a \in R$, $\cos (-a) = \cos a$.

PAGE 99 EXERCISES

1. $T(x) = 47 + 24 \sin \left(\frac{\pi x}{6} + 33\right)$ 3. $T(x) = 75 + 3 \sin \left(\frac{\pi x}{6} + 55\right)$ 5. $T(x) = 63 + 8 \sin \left(\frac{\pi x}{6} + 49\right)$

PAGE 104 CLASSROOM EXERCISES

	Secant	Cosecant		Secant	Cosecant
1. 0	1	undefined	$\frac{7\pi}{6}$	$\frac{-2}{\sqrt{3}}$	-2
$\frac{\pi}{6}$	$\frac{2}{\sqrt{3}}$	2	$\frac{5\pi}{4}$	$-\sqrt{2}$	$-\sqrt{2}$
$\frac{\pi}{4}$	$\sqrt{2}$	$\sqrt{2}$	$\frac{4\pi}{3}$	-2	$\frac{-2}{\sqrt{3}}$
$\frac{\pi}{3}$	2	$\frac{2}{\sqrt{3}}$	$\frac{3\pi}{2}$	undefined	-1
$\frac{\pi}{2}$	undefined	1	$\frac{5\pi}{3}$	2	$\frac{-2}{\sqrt{3}}$
$\frac{2\pi}{3}$	-2	$\frac{2}{\sqrt{3}}$	$\frac{7\pi}{4}$	$\sqrt{2}$	$-\sqrt{2}$
$\frac{3\pi}{4}$	$-\sqrt{2}$	$\sqrt{2}$	$\frac{11\pi}{6}$	$\frac{2}{\sqrt{3}}$	-2
$\frac{5\pi}{6}$	$\frac{-2}{\sqrt{3}}$	2	2π	1	undefined
π	-1	undefined			

3. $\cot x = \frac{\cos x}{\sin x} = \frac{-\cos (x + \pi)}{-\sin (x + \pi)} = \cot (x + \pi)$; therefore, cot x also has period π

5. $\sec x = \frac{1}{\cos x} = -\frac{1}{\cos (x + 2\pi)} = \sec (x + 2\pi)$. Since the function is the same for x and x + 2π, it has a period of 2π.

PAGES 104-105 WRITTEN EXERCISES

1. I, IV 3. I, III 5. II, III 7. II, IV 9. III, IV 11. $-2\pi, -\pi, 0, \pi, 2\pi$ 13. $-2\pi, -\pi, 0, \pi, 2\pi$

15-23. Refer to the graphs of the tan, cot, sec, and csc on Pages 101-103 of the text. Only the graph for Exercise 25 is shown as the others are similar. 25. Period $\frac{2\pi}{3}$, phase shift $-\frac{\pi}{3}$ 27. Even 29. Odd

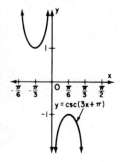

$y = \csc(3x + \pi)$

31. $-\cot x = \frac{\cos x}{-\sin x} = \frac{\sin (x + \frac{\pi}{2})}{\cos (x + \frac{\pi}{2})} = \tan (x + \frac{\pi}{2})$; therefore the graphs are the

same. 33. $|\cot x| = |\frac{\cos x}{\sin x}| = \frac{|\cos x|}{|\sin x|}$. For sin x $\neq$ 0, $|\cot x||\sin x| = |\cos x|$.

Then because $|\sin x| \leq 1$, $|\cot x| \geq |\cos x|$. 35. $|\cot x| = |\frac{\cos x}{\sin x}|$

$= |\cos x||\frac{1}{\sin x}|$, $|\csc x| = |\frac{1}{\sin x}|$. And $|\cos x||\frac{1}{\sin x}| \leq |\frac{1}{\sin x}|$ follows

from the fact that $|\cos x| \leq 1$. Thus, $|\cot x| \leq |\csc x|$.

PAGE 107 CLASSROOM EXERCISES

1. $\frac{1}{\cos x}$ 3. $\frac{\cos x}{\sin x}$ 5. sec x 7. $\sec^2 x$

796 *Answers to Selected Exercises*

1. $\tan x = \dfrac{\sin x}{\cos x} = \sin x \left(\dfrac{1}{\cos x}\right) = \sin x \sec x$ 3. $\cot^2 x = \dfrac{\cos^2 x}{\sin^2 x} = \dfrac{1 - \sin^2 x}{\sin^2 x} = \dfrac{1}{\sin^2 x} - \dfrac{\sin^2 x}{\sin^2 x} = \csc^2 x - 1$

5. $\tan^2 x = \dfrac{\sin^2 x}{\cos^2 x} = \dfrac{1 - \cos^2 x}{\cos^2 x}$ 7. $\csc^4 x - \cot^4 x = (\csc^2 x + \cot^2 x) \cdot (\csc^2 x - \cot^2 x) = (\csc^2 x + \cot^2 x) \cdot 1$

9. $(1 - \tan x)^2 = 1 - 2 \tan x + \tan^2 x = (1 + \tan^2 x) - 2 \tan x = \sec^2 x - 2 \tan x$ 11. $\dfrac{\cos^2 x}{\sin x} + \sin x =$

$\dfrac{\cos^2 x + \sin^2 x}{\sin x} = \dfrac{1}{\sin x} = \csc x$ 13. $\dfrac{\tan x}{1 - \cos^2 x} = \dfrac{\tan x}{\sin^2 x} = \dfrac{\sin x}{\cos x} \cdot \dfrac{1}{\sin^2 x} = \dfrac{1}{\sin x \cos x} = \sec x \csc x$

15. $2 \sin^2 x - 1 = 2(1 - \cos^2 x) - 1 = 1 - 2 \cos^2 x$ 17. a. $\pm \dfrac{\sin x}{\sqrt{1 - \sin^2 x}}$ b. $\pm \dfrac{\sqrt{1 - \cos^2 x}}{\cos x}$

c. $\pm \sqrt{\sec^2 x - 1}$ 19. a. $\pm \dfrac{\cos x}{\sqrt{1 - \cos^2 x}}$ b. $\dfrac{1}{\tan x}$ 21. $\dfrac{\cos x - \sin x}{\cos x} = \dfrac{\cos x}{\cos x} - \dfrac{\sin x}{\cos x} = 1 - \tan x$ 23. $\tan x$

$(\tan x + \cot x) = \tan^2 x + 1 = \sec^2 x$ 25. $\dfrac{\cos x + 1}{\sin^3 x} = \dfrac{\cos x + 1}{\sin x \, (1 - \cos^2 x)} = \dfrac{\cos x + 1}{(\cos x + 1)(1 - \cos x) \sin x} =$

$\dfrac{1}{1 - \cos x} \cdot \dfrac{1}{\sin x} = \dfrac{\csc x}{1 - \cos x}$ 27. $\dfrac{\tan x}{\sec x} + \dfrac{\cot x}{\csc x} = \dfrac{\frac{\sin x}{\cos x}}{\frac{1}{\cos x}} + \dfrac{\frac{\cos x}{\sin x}}{\frac{1}{\sin x}} = \sin x + \cos x$ 29. $\dfrac{\sin^3 x + \cos^3 x}{1 - 2 \cos^2 x} =$

$\dfrac{(\sin x + \cos x)(\sin^2 x - \sin x \cos x + \cos^2 x)}{1 - 2 \cos^2 x} = \dfrac{(\sin x + \cos x)(1 - \sin x \cos x)}{1 - 2 \cos^2 x} =$

$\dfrac{(\sin^2 x - \cos^2 x)(1 - \sin x \cos x)}{(1 - 2 \cos^2 x)(\sin x - \cos x)} = \dfrac{1 - \sin x \cos x}{\sin x - \cos x} = \dfrac{\sec x - \sin x}{\tan x - 1}$

PAGES 111-113 CHAPTER OBJECTIVES AND REVIEW

1. $\sqrt{65}$ 3. $\sqrt{13}$ 5. 15 7. ABCD is a parallelogram. 9. Third quadrant 11. First quadrant 13. $\left(\dfrac{3}{5}, \dfrac{4}{5}\right)$

15. $\left(\dfrac{3}{5}, \dfrac{-4}{5}\right)$ 17. $\sin x = \dfrac{-3}{5}$ 19. 1 21. 0 23. $\sin x = \dfrac{5}{13}$; $\cos x = \dfrac{12}{13}$ 25. See page 85.

27.

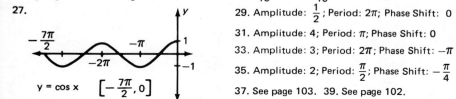

$y = \cos x \quad \left[-\dfrac{7\pi}{2}, 0\right]$

29. Amplitude: $\dfrac{1}{2}$; Period: 2π; Phase Shift: 0

31. Amplitude: 4; Period: π; Phase Shift: 0

33. Amplitude: 3; Period: 2π; Phase Shift: $-\pi$

35. Amplitude: 2; Period: $\dfrac{\pi}{2}$; Phase Shift: $-\dfrac{\pi}{4}$

37. See page 103. 39. See page 102.

41. $\tan x = \dfrac{4}{3}$, $\sec x = \dfrac{5}{3}$ 43. $\sin^2 x = 1 - \cos^2 x = 1 - \dfrac{1}{\sec^2 x} = \dfrac{\sec^2 x - 1}{\sec^2 x}$ 45. $\sec x + \tan x = \sec x$

$\left(1 + \dfrac{\tan x}{\sec x}\right) = \sec x \, (1 + \tan x \cdot \cos x) = \sec x \left(1 + \dfrac{\sin x}{\cos x} \cdot \cos x\right) = (1 + \sin x) \cdot \sec x$ 47. $\tan (-x) =$

$\dfrac{\sin (-x)}{\cos (-x)} = \dfrac{-\sin x}{\cos x} = -\tan x$

PAGE 114 CHAPTER TEST

1. $AB = \sqrt{74}$; $BC = \sqrt{68}$; $AC = \sqrt{10}$ 2. a. -0.4617 b. -0.4617 c. 0.89 3. $\dfrac{3}{4}$ 4. See answer to Ex. 1 on

page 87. 6. $\dfrac{2\pi}{|B|}$; $\dfrac{2\pi}{|B|}$ 7. a. $\dfrac{1}{2}(M - m)$ b. $|A|$; $|A|$ 8. Amplitude: 2; Period: $\dfrac{\pi}{2}$; No Phase Shift.

9. Amplitude: 2; Period: π; Phase Shift: $\dfrac{\pi}{4}$ 10. See page 103 of text. 11. a. $\{y : y \leq -1 \text{ or } y \geq 1\}$

b. $\{y : y \leq -1 \text{ or } y \geq 1\}$ c. All reals 12. a. $\sec^2 x - 1$ b. $\csc^2 x - 1$ c. $\dfrac{\sin^2 x}{\cos^2 x} + 1$ d. $\dfrac{\cos^2 x}{\sin^2 x} + 1$

CHAPTER 3 TRIGONOMETRY

PAGE 118 CLASSROOM EXERCISES
1. $140°$ 3. $355°$ 5. $-135°$ 7. $-348°$

PAGES 118-119 WRITTEN EXERCISES
1. $90°$ 3. $270°$ 5. $-90°$ 7. $-60°$ 9. $150°$ 11. $288°$ 13. $510°$ 15. $-240°$ 17. Ans. will vary. $\theta - 360°$ or $\theta - n \cdot 360°$, $n \in W$ 19. In Quadrant II, $90° + n \cdot 360° < \theta < 180° + n \cdot 360°$, $n \in W$. In Quadrant III, $180° + n \cdot 360° < \theta < 270° + n \cdot 360°$, $n \in W$. In Quadrant IV, $270° + n \cdot 360° < \theta < (n + 1) 360°$, $n \in W$. 21. I 23. IV 25. II 27. II 29. IV 31. II 33. Points B, C, and D are on the terminal side. Point E is not. 35. A: $\frac{x}{r} = \frac{-1}{\sqrt{5}}$, $\frac{y}{r} = \frac{2}{\sqrt{5}}$, $\frac{y}{x} = -2$. For B, C, and D $\frac{x}{r}$, $\frac{y}{r}$, and $\frac{y}{x}$ are the same as for A.

PAGE 121 CLASSROOM EXERCISES
1. $\frac{\pi}{4}$ 3. $\frac{7\pi}{12}$ 5. $-\frac{\pi}{3}$ 7. $-\frac{\pi}{4}$ 9. $540°$ 11. $114° \, 35' \, 29.6''$ 13. $-720°$ 15. $-300°$

PAGES 121-122 WRITTEN EXERCISES
1. $\frac{\pi}{3}$ 3. $-\pi$ 5. $-\frac{\pi}{6}$ 7. $\frac{3\pi}{4}$ 9. $\frac{11\pi}{6}$ 11. $-\frac{7\pi}{6}$ 13. $30°$ 15. $90°$ 17. $-240°$ 19. $-144°$ 21. $-540°$ 23. $612°$ 25. $-57° \, 17' \, 45''$ 27. $1170°$ 29. $\frac{1}{10}$ 31. $\frac{\pi}{5}$ 33. a. $\frac{1}{4}$, $90°$, $\frac{\pi}{2}$, 2π cm b. $\frac{8}{15}$, $192°$, $\frac{16\pi}{15}$, $\frac{64\pi}{15}$ cm c. $\frac{3}{4}$, $270°$, $\frac{3\pi}{2}$, 6π cm d. $\frac{5}{6}$, $300°$, $\frac{5\pi}{3}$, $\frac{20\pi}{3}$ cm 35. $3°$ 37. $\frac{\pi}{30}$ cm 39. $\frac{44}{\pi}$ revolutions 41. $\frac{s}{r}$ 43. A degree is the measure of an angle that intercepts an arc equal in length to $\frac{1}{360}$ the circumference of a circle whose center is the vertex of the angle.

PAGE 126 CLASSROOM EXERCISES

	$\sin \theta$	$\cos \theta$	$\tan \theta$	$\csc \theta$	$\sec \theta$	$\cot \theta$
1.	$\frac{5}{\sqrt{29}}$	$\frac{2}{\sqrt{29}}$	$\frac{5}{2}$	$\frac{\sqrt{29}}{5}$	$\frac{\sqrt{29}}{2}$	$\frac{2}{5}$
3.	$-\frac{2}{\sqrt{5}}$	$-\frac{1}{\sqrt{5}}$	2	$-\frac{\sqrt{5}}{2}$	$-\sqrt{5}$	$\frac{1}{2}$
5.	$-\frac{1}{\sqrt{5}}$	$\frac{2}{\sqrt{5}}$	$-\frac{1}{2}$	$-\sqrt{5}$	$\frac{\sqrt{5}}{2}$	-2
7.	0	-1	0	undefined	-1	undefined

PAGE 126 WRITTEN EXERCISES

	$\sin \theta$	$\cos \theta$	$\tan \theta$	$\csc \theta$	$\sec \theta$	$\cot \theta$
1.	$\frac{3}{\sqrt{34}}$	$\frac{5}{\sqrt{34}}$	$\frac{3}{5}$	$\frac{\sqrt{34}}{3}$	$\frac{\sqrt{34}}{5}$	$\frac{5}{3}$
3.	$-\frac{3}{\sqrt{34}}$	$-\frac{5}{\sqrt{34}}$	$\frac{3}{5}$	$-\frac{\sqrt{34}}{3}$	$-\frac{\sqrt{34}}{5}$	$\frac{5}{3}$
5.	$-\frac{8}{\sqrt{65}}$	$\frac{1}{\sqrt{65}}$	-8	$-\frac{\sqrt{65}}{8}$	$\sqrt{65}$	$-\frac{1}{8}$
7.	$\frac{4}{5}$	$-\frac{3}{5}$	$-\frac{4}{3}$	$\frac{5}{4}$	$-\frac{5}{3}$	$-\frac{3}{4}$

	sin θ	cos θ	tan θ	csc θ	sec θ	cot θ
9.	1	0	undefined	1	undefined	0
11.	0	1	0	undefined	1	undefined
13.	$\dfrac{5}{13}$	$\dfrac{12}{13}$	$\dfrac{5}{12}$	$\dfrac{13}{5}$	$\dfrac{13}{12}$	$\dfrac{12}{5}$
15.	$\dfrac{1}{\sqrt{2}}$	$-\dfrac{1}{\sqrt{2}}$	-1	$\sqrt{2}$	$-\sqrt{2}$	-1
17.	$\dfrac{2}{\sqrt{29}}$	$\dfrac{5}{\sqrt{29}}$	$\dfrac{2}{5}$	$\dfrac{\sqrt{29}}{2}$	$\dfrac{\sqrt{29}}{5}$	$\dfrac{5}{2}$
19.	$-\dfrac{1}{2}$	$\dfrac{\sqrt{3}}{2}$	$-\dfrac{1}{\sqrt{3}}$	-2	$\dfrac{2}{\sqrt{3}}$	$-\sqrt{3}$
21.	$-\dfrac{5}{13}$	$\dfrac{12}{13}$	$-\dfrac{5}{12}$	$-\dfrac{13}{5}$	$\dfrac{13}{12}$	$-\dfrac{12}{5}$
23.	$\dfrac{\sqrt{21}}{5}$	$-\dfrac{2}{5}$	$-\dfrac{\sqrt{21}}{2}$	$\dfrac{5}{\sqrt{21}}$	$-\dfrac{5}{2}$	$-\dfrac{2}{\sqrt{21}}$

25. sin θ $\begin{array}{c|c} + & + \\ \hline - & - \end{array}$ cos θ $\begin{array}{c|c} - & + \\ \hline - & + \end{array}$ tan θ $\begin{array}{c|c} - & + \\ \hline + & - \end{array}$ 27. sin $\theta = -\dfrac{u}{\sqrt{u^2+v^2}}$, cos $\theta = -\dfrac{v}{\sqrt{u^2+v^2}}$

PAGE 128 EXERCISES   1. 45 3. 0 5. E = 220 sin 120 πt 7. E = 100 sin 124 πt 9. 0 11. 0

PAGE 131 CLASSROOM EXERCISES

1. Domain: R; Range: [−1, 1] 3. Domain: R − $\{\pi \pm n\pi, n \in W\}$ or R − $\{180° \pm n \cdot 180°, n \in W\}$;
Range: R 5. Domain: R − $\{\dfrac{\pi}{2} \pm n\pi, n \in W\}$ or R − $\{90° \pm n \cdot 180°, n \in W\}$; Range: R

PAGES 131-132 WRITTEN EXERCISES

1. cos $(-\theta)$ = cos θ 3. cos $(180° + \theta)$ = −cos θ 5. sin$(180° - \theta)$ = sin θ 7. cos$(90° + \theta)$ = −sin θ

9. sin$(\theta \pm 360° \cdot$ n) = sin θ, n $\in$ W

11. sin$(\theta - 45°)$ = −cos$(\theta + 45°)$ 13. −tan θ

15. −csc θ 17. tan θ

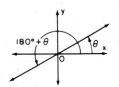

PAGE 136 CLASSROOM EXERCISES   1. tangent 3. sine 5. sine 7. cosine

PAGES 136-137 WRITTEN EXERCISES

1. .9205 3. .2493 5. .3173 7. 76° 40′ 9. 63° 50′ 11. 58° 13. 14° 36′ 15. 63° 26′ 17. 38° 55′ 19. 14.1
centimeters 21. 89.0 kilometers 23. 138.7 meters 25. 136.1 meters 27. 10 centimeters

PAGES 137-138 MID-CHAPTER REVIEW

1. 240° 2. −240° 3. −450° 4. 216° 5. $\dfrac{\pi}{3}$ 6. $\dfrac{5\pi}{6}$ 7. $\dfrac{10\pi}{9}$ 8. −3π 9. 90° 10. −30° 11. −515° 39′ 43.2″

12. 229° 10′ 59.2″ 13. sin $\theta = \dfrac{11}{61}$, cos $\theta = \dfrac{60}{61}$, tan $\theta = \dfrac{11}{60}$, csc $\theta = \dfrac{61}{11}$, sec $\theta = \dfrac{61}{60}$, cot $\theta = \dfrac{60}{11}$

14. sin $\theta = -\dfrac{8}{17}$, cos $\theta = \dfrac{15}{17}$, tan $\theta = -\dfrac{8}{15}$, csc $\theta = -\dfrac{17}{8}$, sec $\theta = \dfrac{17}{15}$, cot $\theta = -\dfrac{15}{8}$ 15. cos $(90° - x)$ = sin x

16. sin $(90° - x)$ = cos x 17. a = 30.6 b = 25.7 18. A = 64.1°, C = 90° 19. x = $\dfrac{71}{\tan 8° 31′} \cong 474.$

1. 1 3. −.7986 5. − tan 30° 7. − tan 39°

PAGES 140-141 WRITTEN EXERCISES

1. $180° − 78° 50'$ 3. $180° − 38° 30'$ 5. $180° − 18° 20'$ 7. $180° + 3° 20'$ 9. $180° + 44° 50'$ 11. $360° −$ 28° 50' 13. $360° − 89° 50'$ 15. $360° − 14° 40'$ 17. $90° + 6° 5'$ 19. $90° − 51° 40'$ 21. $90° − 88° 50'$

23. $\cos \frac{7\pi}{6} = \cos(\pi + \frac{\pi}{6}) = -\cos \frac{\pi}{6} = -\frac{\sqrt{3}}{2}$ 25. $\sin 281° = \sin(360° − 79°) = -\sin 79° = -.9816$ 27. $\tan 265° =$ $\tan(180° + 85°) = \tan 85° = 11.430$ 29. $\cos 335° = \cos(360° − 25°) = .9063$ 31. $\sin(270° − \theta) = \sin$ $[360° − (90° + \theta)] = -\sin(90° + \theta) = -\cos \theta$, $\cos(270° − \theta) = \cos(90° + \theta) = -\sin \theta$, $\tan(270° − \theta) =$ $-\tan(90° + \theta) = \cot \theta$

PAGE 144 CLASSROOM EXERCISES

1. $\cos(x − y) = \cos x \cos y + \sin x \sin y$; $\cos(180° − x) = \cos 180° \cos x + \sin 180° \sin x = −1 \cos x +$ $0 \sin x = -\cos x$ 3. $\cos(x + y) = \cos x \cos y − \sin x \sin y$; $\cos(90° + x) = \cos 90° \cos x − \sin 90° \sin x =$ $0 \cos x − 1 \sin x = -\sin x$ 5. $\cos(x − y) = \cos x \cos y + \sin x \sin y$; $\cos(2\pi − x) = \cos 2\pi \cos x +$ $\sin 2\pi \sin x = 1 \cos x + 0 \sin x = \cos x$ 7. $\cos 15° = .966$; yes

PAGES 144-145 WRITTEN EXERCISES

1. $\frac{\sqrt{2}}{4}(1 − \sqrt{3})$ 3. $-\frac{\sqrt{2}}{4}(1 + \sqrt{3})$ 5. $\frac{\sqrt{2}}{4}(\sqrt{3} + 1)$ 7. $\frac{\sqrt{2}}{4}(1 − \sqrt{3})$ 9. $\cos(\frac{\pi}{2} + \theta) = \cos \frac{\pi}{2} \cos \theta - \sin \frac{\pi}{2}$ $\sin \theta = 0 \cdot \cos \theta − 1 \cdot \sin \theta = -\sin \theta$ 11. $\cos(180° − \theta) = \cos 180° \cos \theta + \sin 180° \sin \theta = −1 \cdot \cos \theta +$ $0 \cdot \sin \theta = -\cos \theta$ 13. $\cos(\pi + \theta) = \cos \pi \cos \theta − \sin \pi \sin \theta = (−1) \cos \theta − 0 \cdot \sin \theta = -\cos \theta$ 15. 0 17. $\frac{304}{425}$ 19. $-\frac{17}{145}$ 21. $\frac{24}{25}$ 23. $\frac{416}{425}$ 25. $\frac{84}{85}$ 27. $\cos 3x \cdot \cos 5x − \sin 3x \cdot \sin 5x = \cos(3x + 5x) = \cos 8x$ 29. $\cos(\alpha + \beta) + \cos(\alpha − \beta) = \cos \alpha \cos \beta − \sin \alpha \sin \beta + \cos \alpha \cos \beta + \sin \alpha \sin \beta = 2 \cos \alpha \cos \beta$ 31. $\cos(\frac{\pi}{2} + \alpha − \beta) = \cos((\frac{\pi}{2} + \alpha) − \beta) = \cos(\frac{\pi}{2} + \alpha) \cos \beta + \sin(\frac{\pi}{2} + \alpha) \sin \beta = -\sin \alpha \cos \beta + \cos \alpha \sin \beta =$ $\cos \alpha \sin \beta − \sin \alpha \cos \beta$ 33. $\cos(\alpha + \beta) = \frac{OB}{OA} = \frac{OC − BC}{OA} = \frac{OC}{OA} − \frac{BC}{OA}$. In $\triangle ODC$, $\cos \alpha = \frac{OC}{OD}$ or $OD \cdot$ $\cos \alpha = OC$. In $\triangle AED$, $m < DAE = \alpha$, therefore $\sin \alpha = \frac{ED}{AD} = \frac{BC}{AD}$ or $AD \cdot \sin \alpha = BC$. Therefore $\cos$ $(\alpha + \beta) = \frac{OD \cdot \cos \alpha}{OA} − \frac{AD \cdot \sin \alpha}{OA}$. But $\frac{OD}{OA} = \cos \beta$ and $\frac{AD}{OA} = \sin \beta$ so $\cos(\alpha + \beta) = \cos \beta \cos \alpha − \sin \beta \sin \alpha$. 35. $\sin(-\alpha) = -\sin \alpha$; $\cos(90° − (-\alpha)) = \cos(90° + \alpha) = \cos 90° \cos \alpha − \sin 90° \sin \alpha = 0 \cdot \cos \alpha − 1 \sin \alpha =$ $-\sin \alpha$

PAGE 148 CLASSROOM EXERCISES

1. $\tan(180° − x) = \frac{\tan 180° − \tan x}{1 + \tan 180° \tan x} = \frac{0 − \tan x}{1 + 0} = -\tan x$ 3. $\tan(90° − x) = \frac{\sin(90° − x)}{\cos(90° − x)} =$ $\frac{\sin 90° \cos x − \cos 90° \sin x}{\cos 90° \cos x + \sin 90° \sin x} = \frac{\cos x − 0}{0 + \sin x} = \frac{\cos x}{\sin x} = \cot x$ 5. $\sin(90° + x) = \sin 90° \cos x + \cos 90° \sin x =$ $1 \cos x + 0 \sin x = \cos x$ 7. $\sin 15° = .2588$

PAGE 149 WRITTEN EXERCISES

1. $\frac{\sqrt{6} + \sqrt{2}}{4}$ 3. $-\frac{1}{2}$ 5. $\frac{1 + \sqrt{3}}{1 − \sqrt{3}}$ 7. $-\frac{\sqrt{3}}{3}$ 9. $\frac{\sqrt{2} − \sqrt{6}}{4}$ 11. $\frac{-\sqrt{6} − \sqrt{2}}{4}$ 13. $\frac{\sqrt{3} − 1}{\sqrt{3} + 1}$

15. $\frac{\sqrt{3} + 1}{\sqrt{3} − 1}$ 17. $\sin(\frac{\pi}{2} + x) = \sin \frac{\pi}{2} \cos x + \sin x \cos \frac{\pi}{2} = 1 \cdot \cos x + \sin x \cdot 0 = \cos x$ 19. $\sin(180° + \theta)$ $= \sin 180° \cos \theta + \sin \theta \cos 180° = 0 \cdot \cos \theta + \sin \theta \cdot (−1) = -\sin \theta$ 21. $\sin(\pi − \theta) = \sin \pi \cos \theta$

$-\sin\theta\,\cos\pi = 0\cdot\cos\theta - \sin\theta\cdot(-1) = \sin\theta$ 23. $\tan(180°+\theta) = \dfrac{\tan 180° + \tan\theta}{1-\tan 180°\tan\theta} = \dfrac{0+\tan\theta}{1-0\cdot\tan\theta}$

$=\tan\theta$ Th. 3-5 applies. 25. $\tan\left(\dfrac{3\pi}{2}+\theta\right) = \dfrac{\sin\left(\frac{3\pi}{2}+\theta\right)}{\cos\left(\frac{3\pi}{2}+\theta\right)} = \dfrac{\sin\frac{3\pi}{2}\cos\theta + \sin\theta\cos\frac{3\pi}{2}}{\cos\frac{3\pi}{2}\cos\theta - \sin\frac{3\pi}{2}\sin\theta} = -\dfrac{\cos\theta}{\sin\theta} = -\cot\theta$

27. $\tan(\pi-\theta) = \dfrac{\tan\pi - \tan\theta}{1+\tan\pi\tan\theta} = \dfrac{0-\tan\theta}{1+0\cdot\tan\theta} = -\tan\theta$. Theorem 3-6 is applicable. 29. $\tan\dfrac{\pi}{3} =$

$\sqrt{3}$ and $\sqrt{\dfrac{1-\cos\frac{2\pi}{3}}{1+\cos\frac{2\pi}{3}}} = \sqrt{\dfrac{1+\frac{1}{2}}{1-\frac{1}{2}}} = \sqrt{\dfrac{\frac{3}{2}}{\frac{1}{2}}} = \sqrt{3}$ 31. $\tan\dfrac{3\pi}{4} = -1$ and $\dfrac{\sin\frac{3\pi}{2}}{1+\cos\frac{3\pi}{2}} = \dfrac{-1}{1+0} = -1$

33. $\cos\dfrac{2\pi}{3} = -\dfrac{1}{2}$ and $\cos^2\dfrac{\pi}{3} - \sin^2\dfrac{\pi}{3} = \left(\dfrac{1}{2}\right)^2 - \left(\dfrac{\sqrt{3}}{2}\right)^2 = \dfrac{1}{4} - \dfrac{3}{4} = -\dfrac{1}{2}$ 35. $\sin(\alpha+\beta) + \sin(\alpha-\beta) =$

$\sin\alpha\cos\beta + \sin\beta\cos\alpha + \sin\alpha\cos\beta - \sin\beta\cos\alpha = 2\sin\alpha\cos\beta$ 37. $\cot(-\alpha) = \dfrac{\cos(-\alpha)}{\sin(-\alpha)} = \dfrac{\cos\alpha}{-\sin\alpha} = -\cot\alpha$.

True for all $\alpha \ne n\pi, n \in I$ 39. $\sin(\alpha+\beta)\cdot\sin(\alpha-\beta) = (\sin\alpha\cos\beta + \sin\beta\cos\alpha)\cdot(\sin\alpha\cos\beta - \sin\beta$

$\cos\alpha) = \sin^2\alpha\cos^2\beta - \sin^2\beta\cos^2\alpha = \sin^2\alpha(1-\sin^2\beta) - \sin^2\beta(1-\sin^2\alpha) = \sin^2\alpha - \sin^2\alpha\sin^2\beta - \sin^2\beta +$

$\sin^2\beta\sin^2\alpha = \sin^2\alpha - \sin^2\beta$. The statement is true for all real values of α and β. 41. $\sin(\alpha+\beta)\cdot\sin(\alpha-\beta) = (\sin\alpha$

$\cos\beta + \cos\alpha\sin\beta)\cdot(\sin\alpha\cos\beta - \cos\alpha\sin\beta) = \sin^2\alpha\cos^2\beta - \cos^2\alpha\sin^2\beta = (1-\cos^2\alpha)\cos^2\beta - \cos^2\alpha$

$(1-\cos^2\beta) = \cos^2\beta - \cos^2\alpha\cos^2\beta - \cos^2\alpha + \cos^2\alpha\cos^2\beta = \cos^2\beta - \cos^2\alpha$. True for all real α and β.

PAGE 154 CLASSROOM EXERCISES 1. .383 3. .414 5. Quadrant I or II or on the y axis between these quadrants

PAGE 155 WRITTEN EXERCISES

1. $\dfrac{\sqrt{2-\sqrt{3}}}{2}$ 3. $\sqrt{\dfrac{2-\sqrt{3}}{2+\sqrt{3}}}$ 5. $-\dfrac{\sqrt{2-\sqrt{3}}}{2}$ 7. $\dfrac{\sqrt{2+\sqrt{2}}}{2}$ 9. $\sqrt{\dfrac{2+\sqrt{2}}{2-\sqrt{2}}}$ 11. $-\dfrac{\sqrt{2+\sqrt{3}}}{2}$

13. $\dfrac{\sqrt{2-\sqrt{2-\sqrt{3}}}}{2}$ 15. $\dfrac{\sqrt{2-\sqrt{2+\sqrt{2}}}}{\sqrt{2+\sqrt{2+\sqrt{2}}}}$ 17. a. II b. I or II or on the y axis between these quadrants

19. $-\dfrac{12}{13}$ 21. $\dfrac{12}{5}$ 23. $-\dfrac{2}{\sqrt{13}}$

25. $-\dfrac{119}{169}$ 27. $\dfrac{\sqrt{5}}{5}$ 29. $-\dfrac{1}{2}$ 31. $-\dfrac{7}{25}$ 33. $\csc 2\theta = \dfrac{1}{\sin 2\theta} = \dfrac{1}{2\sin\theta\cos\theta} = \dfrac{\csc\theta\,\sec\theta}{2}$

35. $\sec 2\theta = \dfrac{1}{\cos 2\theta} = \dfrac{1}{1-2\sin^2\theta} = \dfrac{1}{\frac{\csc^2\theta - 2}{\csc^2\theta}} = \dfrac{\csc^2\theta}{\csc^2\theta - 2}$ 37. $\cot 2\theta = \dfrac{\cos 2\theta}{\sin 2\theta} = \sqrt{\dfrac{\cos 4\theta + 1}{1-\cos 4\theta}}$

$= \sqrt{\dfrac{1+\cos 4\theta}{1-\cos 4\theta}\cdot\dfrac{1+\cos 4\theta}{1+\cos 4\theta}} = \dfrac{1+\cos 4\theta}{\sin 4\theta}$ 39. $\csc\dfrac{\theta}{2} = \dfrac{1}{\sin\frac{\theta}{2}} = \pm\sqrt{\dfrac{2}{1-\cos\theta}} = \pm\dfrac{\sqrt{2(1-\cos\theta)}}{1-\cos\theta}$

41. $\cos 3\alpha = \cos(\alpha+2\alpha) = \cos\alpha\cos 2\alpha - \sin\alpha\sin 2\alpha = \cos\alpha\cdot(2\cos^2\alpha - 1) - \sin\alpha\cdot 2\sin\alpha\cos\alpha =$

$2\cos^3\alpha - \cos\alpha - 2(1-\cos^2\alpha)\cos\alpha = 2\cos^3\alpha - \cos\alpha - 2\cos\alpha + 2\cos^3\alpha = 4\cos^3\alpha - 3\cos\alpha$

43. $\cos 4\alpha = \cos[2(2\alpha)] = \cos^2 2\alpha - \sin^2 2\alpha = (\cos^2\alpha - \sin^2\alpha)^2 - (2\sin\alpha\cos\alpha)^2 = \cos^4\alpha - 2\cos^2$

$\alpha\sin^2\alpha + \sin^4\alpha - 4\sin^2\alpha\cos^2\alpha = \cos^4\alpha - 2\sin^2\alpha\cos^2\alpha + \sin^4\alpha - 4\sin^2\alpha\cos^2\alpha = \cos^4\alpha - 2$

$(1-\cos^2\alpha)\cos^2\alpha + (1-\cos^2\alpha)(1-\cos^2\alpha) - 4(1-\cos^2\alpha)\cos^2\alpha = \cos^4\alpha - 2\cos^2\alpha + 2\cos^4\alpha + 1 -$

$2\cos^2\alpha + \cos^4\alpha - 4\cos^2\alpha + 4\cos^4\alpha = 8\cos^4\alpha - 8\cos^2\alpha + 1$

1. $\frac{1}{2}\sin\frac{7\pi}{12} + \frac{1}{2}\sin\frac{\pi}{12}$

PAGE 158 WRITTEN EXERCISES
1. $\sin 4x + \sin 2x$ 3. $\cos 7x + \cos 3x$ 5. $-\frac{1}{2}\cos 14x + \frac{1}{2}\cos 6x$ 7. $\frac{1}{2}\sin 12x - \frac{1}{2}\sin 4x$
9. $-2\sin 37° \sin 14°$ 11. $2\cos 87° \sin 44°$ 13. $2\sin\frac{7\pi}{24}\cos\frac{\pi}{24}$ 15. $2\cos\frac{1}{2}\cos\frac{1}{4}$ 17. $\frac{\cos 7t + \cos 5t}{\sin 7t - \sin 5t}$
$= \frac{2\cos 6t \cos t}{2\cos 6t \sin t} = \frac{\cos t}{\sin t} = \frac{\csc t}{\sec t}$ 19. $\frac{\sin 4x + \sin 2x}{\cos 4x + \cos 2x} = \frac{2\sin 3x \cos x}{2\cos 3x \cos x} = \tan 3x = \frac{1}{\cot 3x}$ 21. $\frac{\sin 3x - \sin x}{\cos 3x + \cos x}$
$= \frac{2\cos 2x \sin x}{2\cos 2x \cos x} = \tan x$

PAGES 159-161 CHAPTER OBJECTIVES AND REVIEW
1. a. $\overrightarrow{OA}$ b. O c. $\overrightarrow{OB}$ d. counter-clockwise

3.   5.   7. 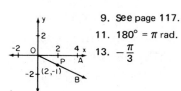 9. See page 117.
11. $180° = \pi$ rad.
13. $-\frac{\pi}{3}$

15. $\frac{77\pi}{36}$ 17. $-330°$ 19. $630°$ 21. $\cos\theta = \frac{x}{r}$ 23. $\cot\theta = \frac{x}{y}$ 25. $\csc\theta\ \frac{r}{y}$

	$\sin\theta$	$\cos\theta$	$\tan\theta$	$\cot\theta$	$\sec\theta$	$\csc\theta$
27.	$\frac{5}{\sqrt{34}}$	$-\frac{3}{\sqrt{34}}$	$-\frac{5}{3}$	$-\frac{3}{5}$	$-\frac{\sqrt{34}}{3}$	$\frac{\sqrt{34}}{5}$
29.	$\frac{1}{\sqrt{5}}$	$\frac{2}{\sqrt{5}}$	$\frac{1}{2}$	$\frac{2}{1}$	$\frac{\sqrt{5}}{2}$	$\frac{\sqrt{5}}{1}$
31.	$\frac{1}{2}$	$-\frac{\sqrt{3}}{2}$	$-\frac{1}{\sqrt{3}}$	$-\frac{\sqrt{3}}{1}$	$-\frac{2}{\sqrt{3}}$	$\frac{2}{1}$

33. 1.7 35. 4.7 37. 2.2 39. $180° - 81° 50'$ 41. $180° + 80° 50'$ 43. 0.5000 45. -0.3420 47. See page
143. 49. $-\frac{\sqrt{2}}{2}$ 51. See page 146. 53. See page 148. 55. $-\frac{\sqrt{2}}{4}(\sqrt{3} - 1)$ 57. $-\frac{\sqrt{3}}{3}$ 59. See page 154.
61. See page 154. 63. $\frac{1}{2}\sqrt{2 - \sqrt{3}}$ 65. $\frac{1}{8}$ 67. $-2\cos\frac{1}{2}\sin\frac{1}{4}$

PAGE 162 CHAPTER TEST
1. a. clockwise b. IV c. See pages 116-117 2. Answers will vary. $-505°, 215°, 575°, -145° \pm n \cdot 360°$
3. a. $\frac{2\pi}{5}$ b. $-\frac{8\pi}{3}$ c. $\frac{\pi}{18}$ 4. a. $50°$ b. $-675°$ c. $114° 35' 29.6''$ 5. a. $\frac{y}{r}$ b. $\frac{x}{r}$ c. $\frac{y}{x}$ d. $\frac{x}{y}$ e. $\frac{r}{x}$ f. $\frac{r}{y}$
6. a. $\sin^2\theta + \cos^2\theta = 1$ b. See page 146. c. See page 147. d. See page 142. e. See page 143. 7. $\sin(\pi - \theta)$
$= \sin\pi\cos\theta - \cos\pi\sin\theta = 0 \cdot \cos\theta - (-1)\sin\theta = \sin\theta$ 8. $\cos 15° = \cos(45° - 30°) = \cos 45° \cos 30°$
$+ \sin 45° \sin 30° = \frac{\sqrt{2}}{2} \cdot \frac{\sqrt{3}}{2} + \frac{\sqrt{2}}{2} \cdot \frac{1}{2} = \frac{\sqrt{2}}{4}(\sqrt{3} + 1)$ 9. $\sin\frac{\pi}{8} = \sin\frac{1}{2}(\frac{\pi}{4})$
$= \sqrt{\frac{1 - \cos\frac{\pi}{4}}{2}} = \sqrt{\frac{1 - \frac{\sqrt{2}}{2}}{2}} = \sqrt{\frac{2 - \sqrt{2}}{4}} = \frac{\sqrt{2 - \sqrt{2}}}{2}$ 10. $\tan 75° = \tan(45° + 30°)$

$$= \frac{\tan 45° + \tan 30°}{1 - \tan 45° \tan 30°} = \frac{1 + \dfrac{1}{\sqrt{3}}}{1 - \dfrac{1}{\sqrt{3}}} = \frac{\sqrt{3} + 1}{\sqrt{3} - 1}$$ 11. $\tan 4° = \dfrac{50}{x}$, $x \approx 715$ meters   12. $\sin 12x - \sin 6x$

13. a. .6561 b. .2309 c. .9336 d. -1.1504 14. $\sin 20° = \dfrac{250}{x}$, $x \approx 731$

CHAPTER 4   APPLYING TRIGONOMETRY

PAGE 166   CLASSROOM EXERCISES

1. $\sin A = \dfrac{50 \sin 110°}{90}$ 3. $b = \dfrac{71 \sin 98°}{\sin 53°}$ 5. The Law of Sines is applicable to all triangles.

PAGES 166-168   WRITTEN EXERCISES

1. $a = 15.41$, $b = 10.90$, $C = 67°$ 3. $A = 9°$, $b \approx 42$, $c \approx 49$ 5. $A = 90°$, $a = 32.5$, $b = 20.7$ 7. $A = 47° 40'$,
$C = 32° 20'$, $c = 10.9$ 9. $\dfrac{a}{\sin A} = \dfrac{b}{\sin B} \rightarrow a \sin B = b \sin A$; therefore $\dfrac{a}{b} = \dfrac{\sin A}{\sin B}$.   11. $AC \approx 52$ $BC = \dfrac{(.3502)(40)}{.7009}$
≈ 20.   13. $AC \approx 241$, height of the tree ≈ 51.   15. a. 1090 meters b. 1060 meters c. 264 meters   17. $\dfrac{a + b}{a - b}$

$$= \frac{\sin A + \sin B}{\sin A - \sin B} = \frac{2 \sin \frac{1}{2}(A + B) \cos \frac{1}{2}(A - B)}{2 \cos \frac{1}{2}(A + B) \sin \frac{1}{2}(A - B)} = \tan \frac{1}{2}(A + B) \cdot \left(\frac{1}{\tan \frac{1}{2}(A - B)} \right) = \frac{\tan \frac{1}{2}(A + B)}{\tan \frac{1}{2}(A - B)}$$

PAGES 171-172   CLASSROOM EXERCISES

1. $A \approx 82° 49'$ $B \approx 41° 25'$ $C \approx 55° 46'$ 3. Three sides or two sides and their included angle   5. a. No b. Yes

PAGES 172-174   WRITTEN EXERCISES

1. $c \approx 5.26$ 3. 24.9   5. 17.6   7. 12.29   9. No solution.   11. One solution.   13. No solution.   15. One solution.
17. No solution.   19. $A = 47° 40'$ 21. $114° 38'$, $84° 44'$ 23. $A \approx 139°$, $B \approx 41°$ 25. $1 = \dfrac{2ab}{2ab}$ and $t =$
$\dfrac{a^2 + b^2 - c^2}{2ab}$; then $1 - t = \dfrac{2ab - (a^2 + b^2 - c^2)}{2ab} = \dfrac{c^2 - a^2 + 2ab - b^2}{2ab} = \dfrac{c^2 - (a - b)^2}{2ab} = \dfrac{(c + a - b)(c - a + b)}{2ab} =$
$\dfrac{(-a + b + c)(a - b + c)}{2ab}$.   27. Since $\cos C = \dfrac{a^2 + b^2 - c^2}{2ab}$, the result follows from Exercise 25.   29. i. $\sin \left(\dfrac{C}{2} \right)$

$$= \sqrt{\frac{1 - \cos C}{2}} = \sqrt{\frac{(-a + b + c)(a - b + c)}{4ab}}; \quad \frac{-a + b + c}{2} = \frac{a + b + c}{2} - a = s - a \text{ and } \frac{a - b + c}{2} = \frac{a + b + c}{2}$$
$- b = s - b$; therefore $\sin \left(\dfrac{C}{2} \right) = \sqrt{\dfrac{(s - a)(s - b)}{ab}}$.   ii. $\cos \left(\dfrac{C}{2} \right) = \sqrt{\dfrac{1 + \cos C}{2}} = \sqrt{\dfrac{(a + b + c)(a + b - c)}{4ab}}$
$= \sqrt{\dfrac{(a + b + c)}{2} \cdot \dfrac{(a + b - c)}{2} \cdot \left(\dfrac{1}{ab} \right)} = \sqrt{\dfrac{s(s - c)}{ab}}$.   iii. $\tan \left(\dfrac{C}{2} \right) = \dfrac{\sin \left(\frac{C}{2} \right)}{\cos \left(\frac{C}{2} \right)} = \sqrt{\dfrac{(s - a)(s - b)}{ab}} \cdot \sqrt{\dfrac{ab}{s(s - c)}}$
$= \sqrt{\dfrac{(s - a)(s - b)}{s(s - c)}}$ iv. $\tan \left(\dfrac{C}{2} \right) = \sqrt{\dfrac{(s - a)(s - b)}{s(s - c)}} = \sqrt{\dfrac{(s - a)(s - b)(s - c)}{s}} \cdot \dfrac{1}{s - c} = \dfrac{P}{s - c}$ 31. $\sin C = 2 \sin \left(\dfrac{C}{2} \right)$
$\cdot \cos \left(\dfrac{C}{2} \right) = 2 \sqrt{\dfrac{(s - a)(s - b)}{ab}} \sqrt{\dfrac{s(s - c)}{ab}} = \dfrac{2}{ab} \sqrt{s(s - a)(s - b)(s - c)}$.

PAGE 177   CLASSROOM EXERCISES

1. Formula 12   3. Formula 5   5. Formula 12   7. $K \approx 26,900$ (square units)   9. $K \approx 4570$ (square units)

1. 19.485 3. No solution. 5. K ≈ 650 7. No solution. 9. .8660 11. No solution. 13. b ≈ 18.7 15. C = 150°

17. K = 96 19. $\dfrac{b^2 \tan \theta}{4}$ 21. r = $\dfrac{K}{s}$ 23. R = OB = $\dfrac{BD}{\sin BOD} = \dfrac{\dfrac{a}{2}}{\sin A} = \dfrac{a}{2 \sin A}$ By the Law of Sines: R =

$\dfrac{a}{2 \sin A} = \dfrac{b}{2 \sin B} = \dfrac{c}{2 \sin C}$ 25. Draw triangle ABC, and drop a perpendicular from C to $\overline{AB}$, to point D.

Consider the case where angles A and B in triangle ABC are acute. Then AD = b cos A, DB = a cos B, so AB =

a cos B + b cos A. Other cases are similar. 27. 2Rr = $\dfrac{2abc}{4K} \cdot \dfrac{K}{s} = \dfrac{abc}{2} \cdot \dfrac{2}{a+b+c} = \dfrac{abc}{a+b+c}$. 29. sin $\left(\dfrac{C}{2}\right)$ =

$\sqrt{\dfrac{(s-a)(s-b)}{ab}}$ and cos $\left(\dfrac{C}{2}\right) = \sqrt{\dfrac{s(s-c)}{ab}}$. Multiplying we get sin $\left(\dfrac{C}{2}\right)$ cos $\left(\dfrac{C}{2}\right) = \sqrt{\dfrac{s(s-a)(s-b)(s-c)}{ab \cdot ab}}$ =

$\dfrac{\sqrt{s(s-a)(s-b)(s-c)}}{ab} = \dfrac{K}{ab}$. Therefore K = ab sin $\left(\dfrac{C}{2}\right)$ cos $\left(\dfrac{C}{2}\right)$.

1. II and IV 3. I and IV 5. II and III

1. $\left\{x : x = \dfrac{3\pi}{4} \pm n\pi, n \in W\right\}$ 3. $\left\{x : x = \pi \pm 2n\pi, n \in W\right\}$ 5. $\left\{x : x = \pm \dfrac{\pi}{3} \pm 2n\pi, n \in W\right\}$

7. $\left\{x : x = \dfrac{\pi}{6} \pm n\pi, n \in W\right\}$ 9. $\left\{x : x = \dfrac{\pi}{3} \pm 2n\pi \text{ or } x = \dfrac{2\pi}{3} \pm 2n\pi, n \in W\right\}$ 11. $\left\{x : x = \dfrac{\pi}{2} \pm 2n\pi, n \in W\right\}$

13. $\left\{x : x = 40° \pm n \cdot 360° \text{ or } x = 140° \pm n \cdot 360°, n \in W\right\}$ 15. $\left\{x : x = \dfrac{3\pi}{4} \pm n\pi \text{ or } x = \dfrac{7\pi}{6} \pm 2n\pi \text{ or } x = \right.$

$\left. -\dfrac{\pi}{6} \pm 2n\pi, n \in W\right\}$ 17. $\dfrac{4}{5}$ 19. $\pm \dfrac{25}{24}$ 21. $\pm \dfrac{7}{24}$ 23. $\pm \dfrac{\sqrt{17}}{4}$ 25. $\pm \dfrac{u}{\sqrt{1-u^2}}$ 27. $\pm \sqrt{1-u^2}$ 29. $\pm \sqrt{1+u^2}$

31. $\pm \dfrac{52}{5\sqrt{313}} \pm \dfrac{36}{5\sqrt{313}}$ 33. $\pm \dfrac{24}{25}$ 35. $\pm \dfrac{336}{527}$ 37. $\pm \dfrac{\sqrt{6}}{2}$

1. π 3. $\dfrac{\pi}{3}$ 5. $\dfrac{\pi}{3}$

1. −45° 3. 31° 5. 60° 7. 30° 9. 22° 11. 4 13. $\dfrac{2}{\sqrt{3}}$ 15. $\dfrac{2}{\sqrt{5}}$ 17. $\dfrac{4}{5}$ 19. $-\dfrac{11}{60}$ 21. $\dfrac{4}{\sqrt{15}}$ 23. This curve has

two branches. For $x \geq 1$, $0 < y \leq \dfrac{\pi}{2}$, and for $x \leq -1$, $-\dfrac{\pi}{2} \leq y < 0$. 25. Let a = Arc sin u. Then cos a =

$\sqrt{1-u^2}$. Thus cos (Arc sin u) = $\sqrt{1-u^2}$. 27. $\dfrac{4}{5}$ 29. $\dfrac{12\sqrt{3}-5}{26}$ 31. $\dfrac{136}{305}$ 33. $-\dfrac{240}{289}$ 35. $\dfrac{336}{527}$ 37. $\dfrac{5}{\sqrt{34}}$

39. tan (Arc tan a + Arc tan 1) = $\dfrac{\tan (\text{Arc tan } a) + \tan (\text{Arc tan } 1)}{1 - \tan (\text{Arc tan } a) \cdot \tan (\text{Arc tan } 1)} = \dfrac{1+a}{1-a}$ 41. tan (Arc cos a + Arc sin b) =

$\dfrac{\tan (\text{Arc cos } a) + \tan (\text{Arc sin } b)}{1 - \tan (\text{Arc cos } a) \cdot \tan (\text{Arc sin } b)} = \dfrac{\sqrt{1-a^2} \cdot \sqrt{1-b^2} + ab}{a\sqrt{1-b^2} - b\sqrt{1-a^2}}$ 43. sin (Arc sin $\dfrac{3}{5}$ + Arc cos $\dfrac{5}{13}$) = sin

(Arc sin $\dfrac{3}{5}$) cos (Arc cos $\dfrac{5}{13}$) + sin (Arc cos $\dfrac{5}{13}$) cos (Arc sin $\dfrac{3}{5}$) = $\dfrac{3}{5} \cdot \dfrac{5}{13} + \dfrac{12}{13} \cdot \dfrac{4}{5} = \dfrac{63}{65}$ 45. tan (2 Arc tan

$\dfrac{1}{3}$ + Arc tan $\dfrac{1}{7}$) = $\dfrac{\tan (2 \text{ Arc tan } \frac{1}{3}) + \tan (\text{Arc tan } \frac{1}{7})}{1 - \tan (2 \text{ Arc tan } \frac{1}{3}) \tan (\text{Arc tan } \frac{1}{7})}$. Now, tan (2 Arc tan $\dfrac{1}{3}$) = $\dfrac{2 \tan (\text{Arc tan } \frac{1}{3})}{1 - \tan^2 (\text{Arc tan } \frac{1}{3})}$, and

tan (Arc tan $\dfrac{1}{7}$) = $\dfrac{1}{7}$; therefore the left side of the equation is equal to

$$\frac{\dfrac{2(\frac{1}{3})}{1-\frac{1}{9}}+\frac{1}{7}}{1-\dfrac{2(\frac{1}{3})}{1-\frac{1}{9}}\cdot\frac{1}{7}}=1; \text{ therefore } 2 \text{ Arc tan } \frac{1}{3}+\text{Arc tan } \frac{1}{7}=\frac{\pi}{4}.$$

PAGE 191   WRITTEN EXERCISES

Note: For Exercise 1-35, $n \in W$.   1. $\left\{x : x = \dfrac{-\pi}{3} \pm 2n\pi \text{ or } x = -\dfrac{2\pi}{3} \pm 2n\pi\right\}$ 3. $\left\{x : x = \pm \dfrac{\pi}{4} \pm 2n\pi\right\}$

5. $\left\{x : x = 150° \pm n \cdot 360° \text{ or } 210° \pm n \cdot 360°\right\}$ 7. $\left\{x : x = \pm 30° \pm n \cdot 360° \text{ or } x = \pm 150° \pm n \cdot 360°\right\}$

9. $\left\{x : x = \pm 30° \pm 360° \cdot n \text{ or } x = \pm 150° \pm n \cdot 360°\right\}$ 11. $\left\{x : x = 26° \; 30' \pm 180° \cdot n \text{ or } x = 116° \; 30' \pm$

$180° \cdot n\right\}$ 13. $\left\{x : x = \pm 180° \cdot n \text{ or } x = 30° \pm 360° \cdot n \text{ or } x = 150° \pm 360° \cdot n\right\}$ 15. $\left\{x : x = 180° \cdot n\right\}$

17. $\left\{x : x = \pm 30° \pm 180° \cdot n\right\}$ 19. θ 21. $\left\{x : x = \pm 360° \cdot n\right\}$ 23. $\left\{x : x = 30° \pm 360° \cdot n \text{ or } x = 150° \pm$

$360° \cdot n\right\}$ 25. $\left\{x : x = -60° \pm 360° \cdot n \text{ or } x = -120° \pm 360° \cdot n\right\}$ 27. $\left\{x : x = \pm 60° \pm 360° \cdot n\right\}$

29. $\left\{x : x = \pm (2n + 1) \cdot 90° \text{ or } x = \pm 45° \pm 180° \cdot n\right\}$.   31. $\left\{x : x = \pm (2n + 1) \cdot 90° \text{ or } x = 54° \pm 360° \cdot\right.$

$\left. n \text{ or } x = 126° \pm 360° \cdot n \text{ or } x = -18° \pm 360° \cdot n \text{ or } n = -162° \pm 360° \cdot n\right\}$.   33. $\left\{x : x = \pm n \cdot 90° \text{ or }\right.$

$\left. x = \pm 120° \pm n \cdot 360°\right\}$ 35. $\left\{x = \pm n \cdot 180° \text{ or } x = \pm 20° \pm n \cdot 120°\right\}$

PAGES 191-192   MID-CHAPTER REVIEW

1. Use $A = 33°$; $B \approx 54° \; 46'$, $C \approx 92° \; 14'$, $c \approx 18$ 2. $A = 78°$, $c = 19.9$, $a = 28.5$ 3. $A \approx 43° \; 30'$, $B \approx 66° \; 30'$

$c \approx 8.2$ 4. $A \approx 22° \; 20'$, $B \approx 27° \; 8'$, $C \approx 130° \; 32'$ 5. $K \approx 223$ 6. $K \approx 10.9$ 7. $\left\{x : x = -\dfrac{\pi}{6} \pm 2n\pi\right\} \cup$

$\left\{x : x = \dfrac{7\pi}{6} \pm 2n\pi\right\}$ 8. $\dfrac{\pm\sqrt{1-u^2}}{u}$ 9. 3.1798   10. $\dfrac{5}{13}$ 11. $\left\{x : x = \dfrac{\pi}{3} \pm n\pi \text{ or } x = \dfrac{2\pi}{3} \pm n\pi\right\}$

12. $\left\{x : x = \pm n\pi \text{ or } x = \dfrac{2\pi}{3} \pm 2n\pi \text{ or } x = \dfrac{4\pi}{3} \pm 2n\pi\right\}$

PAGE 194   WRITTEN EXERCISES

1. $\left\{x : \dfrac{4\pi}{3} \leq x \leq \dfrac{5\pi}{3}\right\}$ 3. $\left\{x : 0 \leq x \leq 1.1 \text{ or } \dfrac{\pi}{2} < x \leq \pi +1.1 \text{ or } \dfrac{3\pi}{2} < x \leq 2\pi\right\}$ 5. $\left\{x : \dfrac{\pi}{4} < x < \dfrac{\pi}{2} \text{ or }\right.$

$\left. \dfrac{5\pi}{4} < x < \dfrac{3\pi}{2}\right\}$ 7. $\left\{x : 0 \leq x \leq \dfrac{\pi}{6} \text{ or } \dfrac{5\pi}{6} \leq x \leq \dfrac{7\pi}{6} \text{ or } \dfrac{11\pi}{6} \leq x \leq 2\pi\right\}$ 9. $\left\{x : \dfrac{\pi}{4} \leq x \leq \dfrac{3\pi}{4} \text{ or }\right.$

$\left. \dfrac{5\pi}{4} \leq x \leq \dfrac{7\pi}{4}\right\}$ 11. $\left\{x : x = 0 \text{ or } \pi \leq x \leq 2\pi\right\}$ 13. $\left\{x : 0 \leq x < \dfrac{\pi}{4} \text{ or } \dfrac{3\pi}{4} < x < \dfrac{5\pi}{4} \text{ or } \dfrac{7\pi}{4} < x \leq 2\pi\right\}$

15. $\left\{x : 0 \leq x \leq \dfrac{2\pi}{3} \text{ or } \dfrac{4\pi}{3} \leq x \leq 2\pi\right\}$ 17. $\left\{x : 0 < x < 2\pi \text{ and } x \neq \pi\right\}$ 19. $\left\{x : \dfrac{\pi}{4} \leq x \leq \dfrac{5\pi}{4}\right\}$
21. $\emptyset$

PAGE 197   CLASSROOM EXERCISES

1. a. $2\sqrt{2} \, (\cos 45° + i \sin 45°)$ b. $3(\cos 270° + i \sin 270°)$ c. $2(\cos (-60°) + i \sin (-60°))$ or $2(\cos 300° +$
$i \sin 300°)$ 3. $x = r \cos \theta$, $y = r \sin \theta$

PAGES 197-198   WRITTEN EXERCISES

1. $4\sqrt{2} \, (\cos 45° + i \sin 45°)$ 3. $1(\cos 300° + i \sin 300°)$ 5. $1(\cos 180° + i \sin 180°)$ 7. $1(\cos 270° + i \sin$

$270°)$ 9. $1(\cos 6° + i \sin 6°)$ 11. $1(\cos 310° + i \sin 310°)$ 13. $\dfrac{1}{4} + \dfrac{\sqrt{3}}{4}i$ 15. $2\sqrt{3} - 2i$ 17. $0 - i$

19. $7.7272 + 2.0704i$ 21. $r(\cos 0° + i \sin 0°)$ or $r(\cos 180° + i \sin 180°)$ 23. If $z_1 = r_1(\cos \theta_1 + i \sin \theta_1)$,

$z_2 = r_2(\cos\theta_2 + i\sin\theta_2) \neq 0 + 0i$ then $\dfrac{z_1}{z_2} = \dfrac{r_1(\cos\theta_1 + i\sin\theta_1)}{r_2(\cos\theta_2 + i\sin\theta_2)} = \dfrac{r_1}{r_2}\dfrac{\cos\theta_1 + i\sin\theta_1}{\cos\theta_2 + i\sin\theta_2}$

$= \dfrac{r_1}{r_2}\dfrac{\cos\theta_1 + i\sin\theta_1}{\cos\theta_2 + i\sin\theta_2} \cdot \dfrac{\cos\theta_2 - i\sin\theta_2}{\cos\theta_2 - i\sin\theta_2}$

$= \dfrac{r_1}{r_2}\dfrac{(\cos\theta_1\cos\theta_2 + \sin\theta_1\sin\theta_2) + i(\sin\theta_1\cos\theta_2 - \sin\theta_2\cos\theta_1)}{\cos^2\theta_2 + \sin^2\theta_2} = \dfrac{r_1}{r_2}[\cos(\theta_1 - \theta_2) + i\sin(\theta_1 - \theta_2)]$

25. $z_1 \cdot z_2 = \dfrac{3}{2}(\cos 120° + i\sin 120°);\ \dfrac{z_1}{z_2} = 6(\cos 40° + i\sin 40°)$ 27. $z_1 \cdot z_2 = \dfrac{4}{3}(\cos 285° + i\sin 285°);$

$\dfrac{z_1}{z_2} = 3(\cos(-15°) + i\sin(-15°))$ 29. $z_1 \cdot z_2 = -1 - i\ \dfrac{z_1}{z_2} = 1 + i$

31. Let $z_1 = r_1(\cos\theta_1 + i\sin\theta_1); z_2 = r_2(\cos\theta_2 + i\sin\theta_2)$

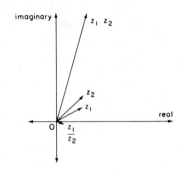

33. $\dfrac{1}{z} = \dfrac{1}{r(\cos\theta + i\sin\theta)} = \dfrac{1}{r} \cdot \dfrac{1}{\cos\theta + i\sin\theta}$

$\cdot \dfrac{\cos\theta - i\sin\theta}{\cos\theta - i\sin\theta} = \dfrac{1}{r} \cdot \dfrac{\cos\theta - i\sin\theta}{\cos^2\theta + \sin^2\theta} = \dfrac{1}{r}$

$\cdot (\cos\theta - i\sin\theta)$ but $\overline{z} = r(\cos\theta - i\sin\theta)$

$\therefore \dfrac{1}{z} = \dfrac{1}{r} \cdot \dfrac{\overline{z}}{r} = \dfrac{1}{r^2} \cdot \overline{z}$

35. $\dfrac{z}{\overline{z}} = \dfrac{r(\cos\theta + i\sin\theta)}{r(\cos\theta - i\sin\theta)} = \dfrac{\cos\theta + i\sin\theta}{\cos\theta - i\sin\theta}$

$\cdot \dfrac{\cos\theta + i\sin\theta}{\cos\theta + i\sin\theta}$

$= \dfrac{(\cos^2\theta - \sin^2\theta) + i(2\sin\theta\cos\theta)}{\cos^2\theta + \sin^2\theta}$

$= \cos 2\theta + i\sin 2\theta$

37. Let $z_1 = r_1(\cos\theta_1 + i\sin\theta_1) \neq 0 + 0i$ and $z_2 = r_2(\cos\theta_2 + i\sin\theta_2) \neq 0 + 0i$. Then $\dfrac{z_1}{z_2} =$

$\dfrac{r_1}{r_2}(\cos(\theta_1 - \theta_2) + i\sin(\theta_1 - \theta_2)) = \dfrac{r_1}{r_2}(\cos 0° + i\sin 0°) = \dfrac{r_1}{r_2}(1 + i \cdot 0) = \dfrac{r_1}{r_2}$, which is real.

PAGE 200 EXERCISES   1. 2420 3. 4420

PAGE 204 CLASSROOM EXERCISES

1. a. $128 + 128\,i$ b. i c. $\dfrac{(-99 + 5\,i)}{19652}$ d. $4(\cos 60° + i\sin 60°)$ 3. $-3, -3\left(-\dfrac{1}{2} + i\dfrac{\sqrt{3}}{2}\right), -3\left(-\dfrac{1}{2} - i\dfrac{\sqrt{3}}{2}\right)$

PAGES 204-205 WRITTEN EXERCISES

1. $2\sqrt{2}(\cos 225° + i\sin 225°); -2 - 2i$ 3. $\cos 0° + i\sin 0°; 1 + 0i$ 5. $\dfrac{1}{32}(\cos 120° + i\sin 120°); -\dfrac{1}{64} + \dfrac{\sqrt{3}}{64}i$ 7. $\cos 90° + i\sin 90°; 0 + i$ 9. $\cos 0° + i\sin 0°, \cos 90° + i\sin 90°, \cos 180° + i\sin 180°, \cos 270° + i\sin 270°$ 11. $\cos 60° + i\sin 60°, \cos 180° + i\sin 180°, \cos 300° + i\sin 300°$ 13. $\sqrt[3]{2}(\cos 40° + i\sin 40°), \sqrt[3]{2}(\cos 160° + i\sin 160°), \sqrt[3]{2}(\cos 280° + i\sin 280°)$ 15. $\cos 45° + i\sin 45°, \cos 225° + i\sin 225°$ 17. Let $(\cos\theta + i\sin\theta) = u + vi, u = \cos\theta, v = \sin\theta$; then $(\cos\theta + i\sin\theta)^4 = \cos 4\theta + i\sin 4\theta$ and $(u + vi)^4 = u^4 + 4u^3(vi) + 6u^2(vi)^2 + 4u(vi)^3 + (vi)^4 = u^4 - 6u^2v^2 + (4u^3v - 4uv^3)i$. Thus $\cos 4\theta + i\sin 4\theta = \cos^4\theta - 6\cos^2\theta\sin^2\theta + \sin^4\theta + (4\cos^3\theta\sin\theta - 4\cos\theta\sin^3\theta)i$. Thus, $\cos 4\theta = \cos^4\theta - 6\cos^2\theta\sin^2\theta + \sin^4\theta, \sin 4\theta =$

$4 \cos^3 \theta \sin \theta - 4 \cos \theta \sin^3 \theta$ 19. $\sqrt[3]{2}(\cos 30° + i \sin 30°)$, $\sqrt[3]{2}(\cos 150° + i \sin 150°)$, $\sqrt[3]{2}(\cos 270° +$

$i \sin 270°)$ 21. $1^3 = 1$, $\omega^3 = (\cos \frac{2\pi}{3} + i \sin \frac{2\pi}{3})^3 = \cos 2\pi + i \sin 2\pi = 1$, $(\omega^2)^3 = (\omega^3)^2 = 1^2 = 1$

23. $r^{-n}[\cos(-n\theta) + i \sin(-n\theta)] = r^{-n}(\cos n\theta - i \sin n\theta)$ 25. $\cos 0 + i \sin 0$, $\cos \frac{2\pi}{3} + i \sin \frac{2\pi}{3}$, $\cos \frac{4\pi}{3} +$

$i \sin \frac{4\pi}{3}$ 27. $\cos 0 + i \sin 0$, $\cos \frac{\pi}{2} + i \sin \frac{\pi}{2}$, $\cos \pi + i \sin \pi$, $\cos \frac{3\pi}{2} + i \sin \frac{3\pi}{2}$ 29. $\cos \frac{3\pi}{8} + i \sin \frac{3\pi}{8}$, $\cos \frac{7\pi}{8} +$

$i \sin \frac{7\pi}{8}$, $\cos \frac{11\pi}{8} + i \sin \frac{11\pi}{8}$, $\cos \frac{15\pi}{8} + i \sin \frac{15\pi}{8}$

PAGE 208 CLASSROOM EXERCISES

1. $(10, -60°)$ and $(-10, 120°)$ 3. See the Solution Key.

PAGE 208 WRITTEN EXERCISES

1. $(\sqrt{2}, 45°)$, $(-\sqrt{2}, 225°)$ 3. $(9, 180°)$, $(-9, 0°)$ 5. $(2, -60°)$, $(-2, 120°)$ 7. $(4\sqrt{5}, 116° 30')$, $(-4\sqrt{5},$

$296° 30')$ 9. $(0, -2)$ 11. $\left(\frac{\sqrt{3}}{2}, \frac{1}{2}\right)$ 13. $\left(-\frac{3}{2}, -\frac{3\sqrt{3}}{2}\right)$ 15. $(0, -5)$ 17. $r \cos \theta = 3$ 19. $2r \cos \theta - r \sin \theta = 3$

21. $r = 4$ 23. $r = -4 \cos \theta$ 25. $r \sin \theta \cdot \tan \theta = 4$ 27. $y = 0$ 29. $x^2 + y^2 = 16$ 31. $y = 6$ 33. $y = 5$ 35. $x_1 =$

$r \cos \theta$, $y_1 = r \sin \theta$ while $x_2 = r \cos (-\theta) = r \cos \theta$, $y_2 = r \sin (-\theta) = r \sin (-\theta) = -r \sin \theta$. Therefore $x_1 =$

x_2 and $y_1 = -y_2$.

PAGE 212 CLASSROOM EXERCISES

1. A circle of radius 2 with center at $(0, 0)$. 3. A straight line through the origin with slope = tan 50°.

PAGES 212-213 WRITTEN EXERCISES

1. A circle of radius 3 with the center at $(0, 0)$. 3. A straight line through origin with slope = tan 75°.

5. A circle of radius $\frac{1}{2}$ with center at $(\frac{1}{2}, 0)$.

7. A circle of radius $\frac{3}{2}$ with the center at $(-\frac{3}{2}, 0)$.

9. A vertical line through $(2, 0)$.

11. Same as the graph of Example 4 on page 211.

13.
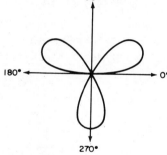

15.
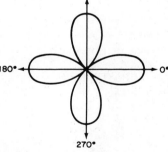

17.
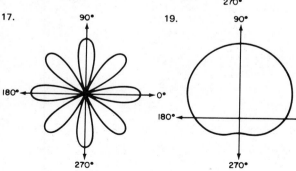

19.

21.
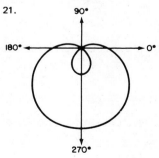

23. Two leaves, each symmetric about the x axis.

25. Case 1 ($\theta > 0$): When $\theta \to 0$, then $r \to \infty$, when $\theta \to \infty$ then $r \to 0$. The graph is as shown. Case 2 ($\theta < 0$: The graph is the reflection of the graph as shown with respect to the 90° line.

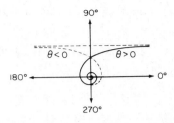

27. Ellipse with center $(\frac{4}{3}, 0)$ and the major axis is the x axis. The equation in Cartesian coordinates is $3x^2 + 4y^2 - 8x - 16 = 0$.

PAGES 215-218   CHAPTER OBJECTIVES AND REVIEW

1. See page 165. 3. 9.30 5. 31° 10′ 7. Answers will vary. 9. 36° 20′ 11. 10.14 13. 20.3 15. An angle whose sine is x. 17. ±150° ±360° · n, n ∈ W 19. $\pm\frac{n\pi}{2}$, n ∈ W 21. ±60° ± 360° · n, n ∈ W 23. $\sin\theta = \frac{1}{3}$
25. $\pm\sqrt{1 - u^2}$ 27. 120°, or $\frac{2\pi}{3}$ 29. 0 31. $\frac{\sqrt{6}}{12}$ 33. $\frac{\sqrt{5}}{2}$ 35. Domain: All real numbers; See page 185 for the graph of y = Arc tan x. 37. $\{x : x = -13° \ 15′ \pm 90° \cdot n, n \in W\}$ 39. $\{x : x = \pm22° \ 30′ + 180° \cdot n, n \in W\}$
41. $\{x : 0 \leq x \leq \frac{\pi}{8}$ or $\frac{3\pi}{8} \leq x \leq \frac{9\pi}{8}$ or $\frac{11}{8}\pi \leq x \leq 2\pi, x \in R\}$ 43. $z = \pm\sqrt{5}(\cos 333° \ 30′ + i \sin 333° \ 30′)$
45. $z = 2(\cos 270° + i \sin 270°)$ 47. $z_1 \cdot z_2 = \frac{3}{2}(\cos \pi + i \sin \pi)$, $\frac{z_1}{z_2} = 6(\cos \frac{\pi}{3} + i \sin \frac{\pi}{3})$ 49. $z = -8i$
51. $\sqrt[4]{2}(\cos \frac{\pi}{12} + i \sin \frac{\pi}{12})$, $\sqrt[4]{2}(\cos \frac{7\pi}{12} + i \sin \frac{7\pi}{12})$, $\sqrt[4]{2}(\cos \frac{13\pi}{12} + i \sin \frac{13\pi}{12})$, and $\sqrt[4]{2}(\cos \frac{19\pi}{12} + i \sin \frac{19\pi}{12})$ 53. (3, 0); (−3, π) 55. (2, $\frac{\pi}{3}$); (−2, $\frac{4\pi}{3}$) 57. $(-\frac{5}{2}, \frac{5\sqrt{3}}{2})$ 59. $(\sqrt{2}, -\sqrt{2})$ 61. The graph of $\theta = -21°$ is a straight line through (0, 0). The line forms an angle of −21° with the positive x axis. 63. See ans. to Ex. 21, page 213 for general shape, except rotated a quarter-turn clockwise. Some points: (0°, .5), (30°, .366), (45°, .2), (60°, 0), (90°, −.5), (120°, −1), (135°, −1.2), (150°, −1.366), (180°, −1.5)

PAGE 218   CHAPTER TEST

1. 42.87 2. 34° 40′ 3. 1856.27 4. 654.5 5. $d^2 = (8,800)^2 + (38,500)^2 - 2(8,800)(38,500)(.2588)$, d = 37,207, 34 sec. 6. $\pm\frac{2}{\sqrt{13}}$ 7. ±2$\sqrt{6}$ 8. $\frac{\sqrt{39}}{8}$ 9. $\frac{\pi}{4}$ 10. $\{x : x = \frac{\pi}{4} \pm n\pi, n \in W\}$ 11. $\{x : x = \frac{\pi}{4} \pm \frac{n\pi}{2}, n \in W\}$
12. $\{x : \frac{\pi}{4} \pm n\pi < x < \frac{3\pi}{4} \pm n\pi\}$ 13. $\sqrt[4]{2}(\cos 30° + i \sin 30°)$, $\sqrt[4]{2}(\cos 120° + i \sin 120°)$, $\sqrt[4]{2}(\cos 210° + i \sin 210°)$, $\sqrt[4]{2}(\cos 300° + i \sin 300°)$ 14. Same graph as that of Exercise 19 on page 213.

PAGES 219-220   CUMULATIVE REVIEW: CHAPTERS 1-4

1. c 3. c 5. a 7. c 9. a 11. b 13. b 15. c 17. b 19. a 21. b

CHAPTER 5   SEQUENCES, SERIES, AND LIMITS

PAGE 225   CLASSROOM EXERCISES

1. 3, 6, 9 3. 3, 9, 27 5. 2, $\frac{4}{3}, \frac{8}{9}, \frac{16}{27}$ 7. −1, $\frac{5}{2}, \frac{17}{4}, \frac{41}{8}$ 9. 1, $\frac{-1}{2}, \frac{+1}{4}, \frac{-1}{8}$ 11. The domain is the positive integers or a subset thereof.

PAGES 225-227   WRITTEN EXERCISES

1. 5, 3, 1, −1, −3, −5 3. 3, 6, 12, 24, 48, 96 5. 4, −4, −4, 4, 4, −4 7. 1, 1, 2, 16, $(32)^3$ = 32,768.

$(65,536)^4$ 9. $5, 5, \frac{5}{2}, \frac{5}{6}, \frac{5}{24}, \frac{1}{24}$ 11. $4, 2, \frac{4}{3}, 1, \frac{4}{5}$ 13. $3, 12, 27, 48, 75$ 15. $1, 3, 5, 7, 9$ 17. $1, 1, 3, 5, 7$

19. $\frac{3}{5}, \frac{4}{7}, \frac{5}{9}, \frac{6}{11}, \frac{7}{13}$ 21. $0, 1, 0, 1, 0$ 23. a. $a_n = n$ b. $a_1 = 1, a_{n+1} = a_n + 1$ 25. a. $a_n = \frac{3}{n!}$ b. $a_1 = 3$,

$a_{n+1} = \frac{a_n}{n+1}$ 27. a. $a_n = (-1)^{n+1}$ b. $a_1 = 1, a_{n+1} = -a_n$ 29. $5, 8, 11, 14$ 31. -14 33. $a_1 = a_1, a_{n+1}$

$= a_n + d$ 35. $\frac{5}{3}, \frac{5}{9}, \frac{5}{27}, \frac{5}{81}$ 37. $\frac{1}{48}$ 39. $a_1 = b_1 = c_1 = 1, a_2 = b_2 = c_2 = \frac{1}{2}, a_3 = b_3 = c_3 = \frac{1}{3}, a_4 = \frac{1}{4}$,

$b_4 = \frac{1}{10}, c_4 = -\frac{1}{4}$ 41. a. $a_n = \frac{n}{n+1}$ b. $a_n = \frac{n}{(n+1) + (n-1)(n-2)(n-3)}$

c. $a_n = \dfrac{n}{(n+) + \frac{1}{2}(n-1)(n-2)(n-3)}$

PAGE 230 CLASSROOM EXERCISES

1. $\langle 0, \frac{3}{4} \rangle$ 3. $\langle -1.1, 1.05 \rangle$ 5. $\langle 1, \infty \rangle$ 7. $\langle -1, 5 \rangle$ neighborhood of 2 with radius 3. 9. $\langle -3, 7 \rangle$, radius = 5

11. $\langle -8, -3 \rangle$ neighborhood of $-5\frac{1}{2}$ with radius $2\frac{1}{2}$. 13. Graphs of sequences are usually on a number line rather than the coordinate plane.

PAGES 230-231 WRITTEN EXERCISES

1. $a_1 = -3, a_2 = -1, a_3 = 1, a_4 = 3, a_5 = 5, a_6 = 7, a_7 = 9$, for n $>$ 7$a_n \in \langle 10, \infty \rangle$ 3. $a_1 = 1, a_2 = \frac{1}{3}, a_3 = \frac{1}{5}$,

$a_4 = \frac{1}{7}, a_5 = \frac{1}{9}$; for n $>$ 5$a_n \in \langle 0, \frac{1}{9} \rangle$ 5. $b_1 = b_3 = b_5 = 1; b_2 = b_4 = -1$; for n $>$ 5$b_n \in \langle -1.1, 1.1 \rangle$

7. $c_1 = \frac{3}{2}, c_2 = \frac{9}{4}, c_3 = \frac{27}{8}, c_4 = \frac{81}{16}, c_5 = \frac{243}{32}$; for n $>$ 5$c_n \in \langle 8, \infty \rangle$ 9. $c_1 = 0, c_2 = -2\frac{1}{4}, c_3 = -2\frac{2}{3}$,

$c_4 = -2\frac{13}{16}, c_5 = -2\frac{22}{25}$; for n $>$ 5$c_n \in \langle -3, -2\frac{22}{25} \rangle$ 11. $\langle 2, 8 \rangle = \{ x : x | x - 5 | < 3, x \in R \}$ 13. $\langle -\frac{5}{2}, \frac{5}{2} \rangle$

$= \{ x : |x| < \frac{5}{2}, x \in R \}$ 15. $\langle -2\frac{1}{4}, \frac{3}{4} \rangle = \{ x : |x + \frac{3}{4}| < \frac{3}{2}, x \in R \}$ 17. $\langle \frac{8}{9}, \frac{10}{9} \rangle$ 19. There is no such

neighborhood, since any neighborhood containing all the terms of $\{ (-1)^n \}$ for n $\geq$ 10 also contains the preceding terms.

PAGE 233 CLASSROOM EXERCISES

1. M = 300 3. M = 1 5. M = 10

PAGES 233-234 WRITTEN EXERCISES

1. a. $a_n > a_{n+1}$ iff $\frac{1}{n} > \frac{1}{n+1}$ iff n + 1 $>$ n (since n and n + 1 $>$ 0) iff 1 $>$ 0. Thus $a_n > a_{n+1}$ for all n $\in$ N

b. M = 200 3. a. $c_n > c_{n+1}$ iff $\frac{1}{2_n} > \frac{1}{2^{n+1}}$ iff 1 $> \frac{1}{2}$. Thus $c_n > c_{n+1}$ for all n $\in$ N b. M = 10, M = 20

5. a. $a_n < a_{n+1}$ iff $-\frac{1}{n} < -\frac{1}{n+1}$ iff $-(n+1) < -n$ iff n + 1 $>$ n iff 1 $>$ 0. Thus $a_n < a_{n+1}$ for all n $\in$ N

b. M = 100 7. a. $c_n < c_{n+1}$ iff $\frac{n}{3n+1} < \frac{n+1}{3(n+1)+1}$ iff $\frac{n}{3n+1}$ iff n(3n + 4) $<$ (3n + 1)(n + 1) iff $3n^2 +$

$4n < 3n^2 + 4n + 1$ iff 0 $<$ 1. Thus, $c_n < c_{n+1}$. b. M = 6

PAGE 238 WRITTEN EXERCISES

1. $\{ a_n : n \geq 2 \}$ 3. $\{ b_n : 5 \leq n \leq 8 \}$ 5. $\{ c_n : 1 \leq n \leq 4 \}$ 7. $\{ d_1, d_2 \}$ 9. $\{ e_n : 6 \leq n \leq 14 \}$

11. a. Both sides of the inequality are multiplied by 10. Th. 1-6, part i. b. Both sides are multiplied by 2n.

Th. 1-6, part i. c. $-10n$ is added to each side of the inequality. Th. 1-5. d. Both sides of the inequality are

multiplied by $-\frac{1}{2}$. Theorem 1-6, part ii. e. Both sides of the inequality are multiplied by $\frac{1}{4}$. Theorem 1-6,

part i. The argument proves that n = 1 is the only positive integer for which $\frac{n-1}{2n} < \frac{1}{10}$. 13. a_2, a_1 lies

outside the neighborhood. 15. a_{501}, 500 terms $(a_1, a_2, \cdots, a_{500})$ lie outside the neighborhood.

17. The first term within the neighborhood is $\left\{a_n : \dfrac{1+R}{2R} < n \le \dfrac{1+R}{2R} + 1\right\}$. All the terms preceding the first term within the neighborhood lie outside the neighborhood.

PAGE 244 WRITTEN EXERCISES

1. The general neighborhood $\langle 3 - \epsilon, 3 + \epsilon \rangle$ was used because the limit of the sequence $\left\{\dfrac{3n+1}{n}\right\}$ is 3 and

therefore the proof must use the general neighborhood of 3 rather than 0. **3.** $\langle -1 - \epsilon, -1 + \epsilon \rangle$

5. $\langle -\dfrac{2}{3} - \epsilon, -\dfrac{2}{3} + \epsilon \rangle$ **7.** $\langle 100 - \epsilon, 100 + \epsilon \rangle$ **9.** $\langle p - \epsilon, p + \epsilon \rangle$ **11.** 2 **13.** $\dfrac{1}{3}$ **15.** 0 **17.** $\left\{\dfrac{\frac{1}{2}n + 1}{n}\right\} \to \dfrac{1}{2}$

iff we can find M such that for $n \ge M$, $a_n \in \langle \dfrac{1}{2} - \epsilon, \dfrac{1}{2} + \epsilon \rangle$ for an arbitrary $\epsilon > 0$. $\dfrac{1}{2} - \epsilon$

$< \dfrac{\frac{1}{2}n + 1}{n} < \dfrac{1}{2} + \epsilon$ iff $1 - 2\epsilon < \dfrac{n+2}{n} < 1 + 2\epsilon$ iff $-2\epsilon < \dfrac{2}{n} < 2\epsilon$ iff $-\epsilon < \dfrac{1}{n} < \epsilon$. Thus $M > \dfrac{1}{\epsilon}$. The

proof for Exercise 19 is similar. For Exercise 19, $M > \dfrac{4}{25\epsilon} - \dfrac{2}{5}$. **21.** Answers will vary. a_n is outside of

$\langle 1 - \dfrac{1}{10}, 1 + \dfrac{1}{10} \rangle$ for all $n > 0$. (The inequality $1 - \dfrac{1}{10} < a_n < 1 + \dfrac{1}{10}$ gives negative values for n.)

PAGES 244-245 MID-CHAPTER REVIEW

1. $1, \dfrac{4}{5}, \dfrac{3}{5}, \dfrac{8}{17}, \dfrac{5}{13}$ **2.** $-\dfrac{1}{2}, -\dfrac{4}{5}, -1 - \dfrac{8}{7}, -\dfrac{10}{8}$ **3.** 4, 5, 7, 11, 19 **4.** $\dfrac{2}{3}, 4\dfrac{1}{3}, \dfrac{2}{3}, 4\dfrac{1}{3}, \dfrac{2}{3}$ **5.** $a_1 = \dfrac{1}{2}, a_2 = \dfrac{2}{3}, a_3 = \dfrac{3}{4}$,

$a_4 = \dfrac{4}{5}, a_5 = \dfrac{5}{6}, a_6 = \dfrac{6}{7}, a_7 = \dfrac{7}{8}, a_8 = \dfrac{8}{9}, a_9 = \dfrac{9}{10}, a_{10} = \dfrac{10}{11}; a_n \in \langle \dfrac{1}{4}, 1 \rangle$ **6.** $b_1 = -2, b_2 = 1, b_3 = -\dfrac{2}{3}, b_4 = \dfrac{1}{2}$,

$b_5 = -\dfrac{2}{5}, b_6 = \dfrac{1}{3}, b_7 = -\dfrac{2}{7}, b_8 = \dfrac{1}{4}, b_9 = -\dfrac{2}{9}, b_{10} = \dfrac{1}{5}; b_n \in \langle -2.1, 1.1 \rangle$ **7.** $d_1 = \dfrac{5}{4}, d_2 = \dfrac{25}{16}, d_3 = \dfrac{125}{64}$,

$d_4 = \dfrac{625}{256}, d_5 = \dfrac{3125}{1024}, d_6 = \dfrac{15,625}{4096}, d_7 = \dfrac{78,125}{16,384}, d_8 = \dfrac{390,625}{65,536}, d_9 = \dfrac{1,953,125}{262,144}, d_{10} = \dfrac{9,765,625}{1,048,576}$;

$d_n \in \langle 1, \infty \rangle$ **8. a.** $b_n = \dfrac{n}{n^2 + 1}$ $b_{n+1} = \dfrac{n+1}{(n+1)^2 + 1} = \dfrac{n+1}{n^2 + 2n + 2}$ $b_n > b_{n+1}$ iff $\dfrac{n}{n^2 + 1} > \dfrac{n+1}{n^2 + 2n + 2}$

iff $n(n^2 + 2n + 2) > (n^2 + 1)(n + 1)$ iff $n^3 + 2n^2 + 2n > n^3 + n^2 + n + 1$ iff $n^2 + n - 1 > 0$. Thus, for all

$n \in N, b_n > b_{n+1}$. **b.** M = 100 **9.** For all $n > 100$, $a_n \in \langle .99, 1.01 \rangle$. **10.** $\dfrac{3}{2}$ **11.** 5 **12.** $\dfrac{5}{3}$

PAGE 248 CLASSROOM EXERCISES

1. Choose $M > \sqrt{\dfrac{1}{2\epsilon}}$

PAGES 248-249 WRITTEN EXERCISES

The proofs for Exercises 1-11 are similar to the proof in Exercise 17, page 232. **1.** $M > \dfrac{1}{\sqrt{3\epsilon}}$

3. $M > \dfrac{\log \epsilon}{\log 3 - \log 4}$ **5.** $M > \dfrac{9}{\epsilon^2} - 2$ **7.** $-\epsilon < \dfrac{\sqrt{n+2}}{n} < \epsilon$ Iff $\dfrac{\sqrt{n+2}}{n} < \epsilon$ (since $\dfrac{\sqrt{n+2}}{n} > -\epsilon$ for

all n) iff $\dfrac{n+2}{n^2} < \epsilon^2$ iff $\dfrac{1}{\epsilon^2} < \dfrac{n^2}{n+2}$. Since $\dfrac{n^2}{n+2} \ge \dfrac{n}{3}$ for all n it is sufficient to solve $\dfrac{1}{\epsilon^2} < \dfrac{n}{3}$ iff $\dfrac{3}{\epsilon^2} < n$.

Thus, $M > \dfrac{3}{\epsilon^2}$ **9.** $M > \sqrt[3]{\dfrac{2}{\epsilon} - 5}$ **11.** $M > \dfrac{\sqrt{1 - \epsilon^2}}{\epsilon}$ **13.** $M > \dfrac{1}{\epsilon}$

PAGE 250 EXERCISES

1. $0.1431 F_{n-2}$ **3.** 0.0269 **5.** $T_n = 0.9(M_{n-1} + F_{n-1}) - cM_{n-1} - kF_{n-1} + 0.27 F_{n-2}$

PAGE 254 CLASSROOM EXERCISES

1. a. 8 **b.** 5 **c.** No **d.** Yes **3.** l.u.b. $c = \sqrt{2}$ **5.** No. If a sequence is not bounded above and is non-decreasing, then its values continue to get larger. Thus, it has no limit.

1. When it is constant, i.e. when $a_1 = a_2 \cdots = a_n$. 3. Yes; a_1 5. Yes. 7. Yes. 9. No. 11. No. 13. (5.) All terms = 0. Therefore bounded above and below by 0. (6.) All terms in $\{-1, 1\}$. Therefore bounded by -1 and 1. (7.) Is bounded by 0 and 1. (8.) Is bounded below by 1. (9) Not bounded. (10.) Is bounded by 3 and 4. (11.) Is bounded by -1 and 1. (12.) Is bounded below by 1. 15. Answers will vary. $\{a_n\} = \{(-1)^n\}$ or $\{b_n\} = \{1 \text{ if } n \text{ is a multiple of } 3, 2 \text{ for all other } n\}$ 17. Let $B = \{-x : x \in A\}$ A, B $\in$ R. A is bounded below, therefore B is bounded above. By the least upper bound axiom B has a l.u.b. in R, b = l.u.b.B and then $-b = g.l.b.A$ 19. Answers will vary. $\{n\}$, $\{(n+1)^2\}$, $\left\{\dfrac{1}{\sin\frac{1}{n}}\right\}$ 21. If a_n is nondecreasing, then $a_1 \leq a_2 \leq a_3 \leq \cdots \leq a_n \leq \cdots$. If a_n is not bounded above there is no real number r such that all $a_n \leq r$. Therefore for any real number p some a_n must be $\geq$ p, and as $a_1 \leq a_2 \leq a_3 \leq \cdots \leq a_n \leq \cdots$ there is an M $\in$ N such that $a_n \geq$ p for all n $\geq$ M.

PAGE 260 CLASSROOM EXERCISES

1. $\sum\limits_{i=3}^{6} |x_i|$ 3. $\sum\limits_{i=1}^{4} (-1)^i x_i$ 5. $\sum\limits_{i=1}^{4} x_i^2$ 7. A sequence is a function whose domain is the set of positive integers. A series is an indicated sum of the terms of a sequence. 9. The sum of the infinite series is defined to be the limit of the sequence of partial sums $\{S_n\}$. If $\{S_n\}$ has a limit, the series is a <u>convergent series</u>. If $\{S_n\}$ has no limit, the series is a <u>divergent series</u>.

PAGES 260-261 WRITTEN EXERCISES

1. Arithmetic. 3. Arithmetic. 5. For n = 1, $\dfrac{1}{2} = \dfrac{2^1 - 1}{2^1} = \dfrac{2-1}{2} = \dfrac{1}{2}$. Assuming $S_k = \dfrac{2^k - 1}{2^k}$, $S_{k+1} = \dfrac{2^k - 1}{2^k}$ $+ \dfrac{1}{2^{k+1}} = \dfrac{2^{k+1} - 2^1 + 1}{2^{k+1}} = \dfrac{2^{k+1} - 1}{2^{k+1}}$ 7. For n = 1, $\dfrac{2}{3} = 2\left[1 - (\tfrac{2}{3})^1\right] = 2\left[\tfrac{1}{3}\right] = \dfrac{2}{3}$.

Assuming $S_k = 2\left[1 - (\tfrac{2}{3})^k\right]$, $S_{k+1} = 2\left[1 - (\tfrac{2}{3})^k\right] + \dfrac{2}{3}(\tfrac{2}{3})^{(k+1)-1} = 2 - 2(\tfrac{2}{3})^k + (\tfrac{2}{3})^{k+1} = 2 - \dfrac{2^{k+1}}{3^k} + \dfrac{2^{k+1}}{3^{k+1}}$ $= 2 - \dfrac{3 \cdot 2^{k+1} - 2^{k+1}}{3^{k+1}} = 2 - 2(\tfrac{2}{3})^{k+1} = 2\left[1 - (\tfrac{2}{3})^{k+1}\right]$ 9. For n = 1, $a = a\dfrac{(1 - r^1)}{(1 - r)}$. Assuming $S_k = a\dfrac{(1 - r^k)}{(1 - r)}$, $S_{k+1} = a\dfrac{(1 - r^k)}{(1 - r)} + ar^{(k+1)-1} = a\left[\dfrac{(1 - r^k)}{(1 - r)} + r^k\right] = a\left[\dfrac{1 - r^k + r^k - r^{k+1}}{(1 - r)}\right] = a\dfrac{(1 - r^{k+1})}{(1 - r)}$ 11. $|2 - 1|$ $+ |2 - 2| + |2 - 3| + |2 - 4| + |2 - 5|$ 13. $(-1)^1(1^2 - 1) + (-1)^2(2^2 - 2) + (-1)^3(3^2 - 3)$ 15. $\dfrac{1}{0 + 1}$ $+ \dfrac{1}{1 + 1} + \dfrac{1}{2 + 1} + \dfrac{1}{3 + 1} + \dfrac{1}{4 + 1}$ 17. $\sum\limits_{i=1}^{4} (5i - 2)$ 19. $\sum\limits_{i=1}^{4} a_i^2$ 21. Yes. 23. No. 25. S = $\dfrac{15}{4}$,

27. For n = 1, $\sum\limits_{i=1}^{1} ca_i = ca_1 = c \sum\limits_{i=1}^{1} a_i$. Assume for n = k, $\sum\limits_{i=1}^{k} ca_i = c \sum\limits_{i=1}^{k} a_i$. Then for n = k + 1, $\sum\limits_{i=1}^{k+1} ca_i = \sum\limits_{i=1}^{k} ca_i + ca_{k+1} = c \sum\limits_{i=1}^{k} a_i + ca_{k+1} = c\left[\sum\limits_{i=1}^{k} a_i + a_{k+1}\right] = c \sum\limits_{i=1}^{k+1} a_i$ 29. For n = 1, $\sum\limits_{i=1}^{1} (a_i + b_i) = a_1 + b_1 = \sum\limits_{i=1}^{1} a_i + \sum\limits_{i=1}^{1} b_i$. Assume for n = k; $\sum\limits_{i=1}^{k} (a_i + b_i) = \sum\limits_{i=1}^{k} a_i + \sum\limits_{i=1}^{k} b_i$. Then for n = k + 1, $\sum\limits_{i=1}^{k+1} (a_i + b_i) = \sum\limits_{i=1}^{k} (a_i + b_i) + a_{k+1} + b_{k+1} = \sum\limits_{i=1}^{k} a_i + \sum\limits_{i=1}^{k} b_i + a_{k+1} + b_{k+1} = \sum\limits_{i=1}^{k} a_i + a_{k+1} + \sum\limits_{i=1}^{k} b_i + b_{k+1}$ $= \sum\limits_{i=1}^{k+1} a_i + \sum\limits_{i=1}^{k+1} b_i$ 31. $\sum\limits_{i=1}^{n} (a_i + c) = \sum\limits_{i=1}^{n} a_i + \sum\limits_{i=1}^{n} c$ by Exercise 29 $= \sum\limits_{i=1}^{n} a_i + cn$ by Exercise 28.

1. a. $|a_n - 0| < 3$ b. $|a_n - 2.8| < 0.7$ c. $|a_n - \frac{1}{2}| < 1$ d. $|a_n - \frac{17}{10}| < \frac{9}{10}$

PAGE 266 WRITTEN EXERCISES

1. $|a_n| < 2$ 3. $|a_n - 2| < .5$ 5. $|a_n - 1| < .01$ 7. $|a_n - 1| < \epsilon$ 9. $\langle -.5, .5 \rangle$ 11. $\langle -1.1, -.9 \rangle$ 13. $\langle -\epsilon, \epsilon \rangle$
15. $\langle .9 - \epsilon, .9 + \epsilon \rangle$ 17. $M \geq 5$ 19. $M \geq 1$ 21. $(\frac{10}{9})^n = (1 + \frac{1}{9})^n \geq 1 + \frac{n}{9} > \frac{n}{9}$. Therefore $(\frac{9}{10})^n < \frac{9}{n}$ and
$(\frac{9}{10})^n < \frac{1}{10}$ if $\frac{9}{n} < \frac{1}{10}$ iff $n > 90$. Thus $M \geq 91$. 23. 0, Theorem 5-4 25. -5, Th. 5-5 27. 0, Theorem 5-4
29. $|\frac{n}{n+1} - 1| = |\frac{n - (n+1)}{n+1}| = |\frac{-1}{n+1}| = \frac{1}{n+1} < \epsilon$ iff $1 < \epsilon \, n + \epsilon$ iff $1 - \epsilon < \epsilon \, n$ iff $\frac{1 - \epsilon}{\epsilon} < n$. Thus
$M > \frac{1 - \epsilon}{\epsilon}$.

PAGE 270 CLASSROOM EXERCISES

1. $\{a_n + b_n\} = \{\frac{8n^2 + 8n + 15}{4n^2 - 25}\}$ 3. $\{a_n \cdot b_n\} = \{\frac{3n^2 - 5n - 2}{4n^2 - 25}\}$

PAGE 271 WRITTEN EXERCISES

1. Converges to $\frac{5}{21}$. 3. Converges to $-\frac{1}{2}$. 5. Converges to $\frac{7}{5}$. 7. Converges to 10. 9. Converges to 16.

11. Converges to $\frac{1}{2}$. 13. Converges to $\frac{1}{3}$. 15. Converges to 5. 17. a. Never. b. Sometimes, convergent

examples $a_n = \frac{1}{n}$ and $b_n = n$, divergent examples $a_n = 1$ and $b_n = n$. c. Sometimes, convergent examples

$a_n = 2$ and $b_n = n^2$, divergent examples $a_n = 3$ and $b_n = (-1)^n$.

PAGES 274-277 CHAPTER OBJECTIVES AND REVIEW

1. $a_1 = 0$; $a_2 = 1$; $a_n = n^2 - 1$; $n \in \{3, 4, 5, \cdots\}$ 3. $\frac{5}{3}, \frac{8}{3}, \frac{11}{3}, \frac{14}{3}, \frac{17}{3}, a_{15} = \frac{47}{3}$ 5. b, $\frac{b}{10}, \frac{b}{10^2}, \frac{b}{10^3}, \frac{b}{10^4}$,
$a_{10} = \frac{b}{10^9}$ 7. $-2, 2, -2, 2, -2, c_{20} = 2$ 9. $a_1 = -1, a_2 = 1, a_3 = 3, a_4 = 5, a_5 = 7, \langle 7, \infty \rangle$ 11. $c_1 = 1, c_2 = .9$,
$c_3 = .81, c_4 = .729, c_5 = .6561, \langle 0, .6561 \rangle$ 13. a. $a_n > a_{n+1}$ iff $\frac{1}{3n} > \frac{1}{3(n+1)}$ iff $\frac{1}{n} > \frac{1}{n+1}$ iff $n + 1 >$
n iff $1 > 0$. This sequence in reverse order proves that $a_n > a_{n+1}, n \in N$. b. $n > 33\frac{1}{3}$ 15. $n \in \{14, 15, \cdots\,$
$23, 24\}$ 17. $n > 5$ 19. $n \in \{18, 19, \cdots, \infty\}$ 21. $a_\infty = 2$ 23. $a_\infty = \frac{1}{2}$ 25. choose $M > \frac{73}{\epsilon}$ 27. An M must

be found such that $\frac{1}{2} - \epsilon < a_n < \frac{1}{2} + \epsilon$ when $n \geq M$, that is, such that $\frac{1}{2} - \epsilon < \frac{n^2 + 1}{2n^2} < \frac{1}{2} + \epsilon$ when $n \geq M$.

This compound inequality is true when $2n^2(\frac{1}{2} - \epsilon) < n^2 + 1$ and $n^2 + 1 < 2(\frac{1}{2} + \epsilon)$, i.e., when $-2n^2 \epsilon < 1$

and $2n^2 \epsilon > 1$. The first part of this compound inequality is true for all $n \in N$ and the second part is true

when $n > \sqrt{\frac{1}{2\epsilon}}$. Thus, choose $M > \sqrt{\frac{1}{2\epsilon}}$. 29. a. Answers will vary. b. All sets in R that are bounded above

have least upper bounds in R. 31. $\sum_{i=1}^{5} a_i^3$ 33. 6, 8, 10, 12, 14 35. $3\frac{1}{2}, 3, 2\frac{1}{2}, 2, 1\frac{1}{2}$ 37. Answers will vary.

39. $\frac{8}{7}$ 41. 0; Theorem 5-4 43. No limit. 45. 0

PAGE 278 CHAPTER TEST

1. $-\frac{1}{2}, \frac{1}{4}, -\frac{1}{6}, \frac{1}{8}, -\frac{1}{10}, \frac{1}{12}, -\frac{1}{14}, b_{100} = \frac{1}{200}, b_{101} = -\frac{1}{202}$ 2. 3, 5, 9, 17, 33, 65, 129 3. 3, 5, 9, 17, 33,
65, 129 Exercise 2 is the recursive definition of the sequence defined in Exercise 3 with the general term.

4. The apparent limit is 0. 5. There does not appear to be a limit. 6. $M = 501$, $M = \frac{1}{2\epsilon} + 1$ 7. 2, $M > \frac{5}{\epsilon} + 2$

8. $\left|\dfrac{3}{n^2}\right| < \epsilon$ iff $\dfrac{3}{n^2} < \epsilon$ iff $\dfrac{n^2}{3} > \dfrac{1}{\epsilon}$ iff $n^2 > \dfrac{3}{\epsilon}$ iff $n > \sqrt{\dfrac{3}{\epsilon}}$. Therefore for an arbitrarily small $\epsilon > 0$ there

exists an $M \in N$ such that for all $n \geq M$, $\dfrac{3}{n^2}$ is within ϵ of 0. 9. Answers will vary. Bounded, $\left\{\dfrac{1}{2^n}\right\}$. Un-

bounded, $\{n\}$. By Theorem 5-3, the first sequence has a limit. 10. 0 11. $\dfrac{2}{3}$ 12. 0 13. $-\dfrac{1}{3}, \dfrac{1}{6}, -\dfrac{1}{9}, \dfrac{1}{12},$

$-\dfrac{1}{15}$ 14. $-1, 1, 3, 5, 7$ 15. $S_n = \dfrac{1 - (\frac{4}{5})^n}{1 - \frac{4}{5}} = 5(1 - (\frac{4}{5})^n)$, $\displaystyle\lim_{n \to \infty} S_n = 5$

CHAPTER 6 FUNCTIONS AND LIMITS

PAGE 284 CLASSROOM EXERCISES   1.1 3. No

PAGES 284-285 WRITTEN EXERCISES

1. 1 3. 2 5. 3 7. 1, 0, 2, −1, 3 9. 20 11. 1 13. Answers will vary. 15. $x_0 = -\dfrac{1}{\epsilon}$ 17. $x_0 = \dfrac{3}{25\epsilon} - \dfrac{1}{5}$

19. $x_0 = \dfrac{1}{\epsilon}$ 21. Any x_0 will suffice. $x_0 \neq \pm 1$ 23. $|x_0| = \dfrac{4}{5\epsilon}$ 25. $|x_0| = \dfrac{1}{\sqrt{\epsilon}}$

PAGES 289-290 WRITTEN EXERCISES

1. $\langle 1.9, 2.1 \rangle$ 3. $\langle \dfrac{599}{300}, \dfrac{601}{300} \rangle$ 5. Impossible. 7. Impossible. 9. $|x^2 - 1| < \dfrac{1}{100}$ iff $|(x - 1)(x + 1)|$

$< \dfrac{1}{100}$ iff $|x - 1||x + 1| < \dfrac{1}{100}$. If $\delta < 1$, then $|x + 1| < 3$. Then the neighborhood of a is $\langle \dfrac{299}{300}, \dfrac{301}{300} \rangle$.

11. $\displaystyle\lim_{x \to 0} f(x) = 0$, $\displaystyle\lim_{x \to 0^+} f(x) = 0$, $\displaystyle\lim_{x \to 0^-} f(x) = 0$. 13. $\displaystyle\lim_{x \to 2} f(x)$ does not exist; $\displaystyle\lim_{x \to 2^+} f(x) = -2$;

$\displaystyle\lim_{x \to 2^-} f(x) = 0$ 15. Answers will vary.

PAGE 294 CLASSROOM EXERCISES   1.11 3. 2 5. 3

PAGES 294-295 WRITTEN EXERCISES

1. 4 3. −3 5. $\dfrac{7}{13}$ 7. Does not exist. 9. 3 11. 28 13. $\dfrac{3}{7}$ 15. Condition iii is not satisfied. 17. Condition iii

is not satisfied. 19. $\displaystyle\lim_{x \to 2} 3x = 6$. Let $\epsilon > 0$ be given. Then you must find $\delta > 0$ such that $|3x - 6| < \epsilon$

whenever $|x - 2| < \delta$ (and $x \neq 2$). Now $|3x - 6| < \epsilon$ iff $3|x - 2| < \epsilon$ iff $|x - 2| < \dfrac{\epsilon}{3}$. You can choose

$\delta = \dfrac{\epsilon}{3}$. 21. $\displaystyle\lim_{x \to 1} x^2 + 2 = 3$ Find δ such that $0 < |x - 1| < \delta$ implies $|x^2 + 2 - 3| = |x - 1| \, |x + 1| < \epsilon$.

Require $\delta \leq 1$; thus $|x - 1| < \delta \leq 1$. Thus, $|x - 1| < 1$ iff $-1 < x - 1$ iff $1 < x + 1 < 3$ and

$|x + 1| < 3$. Hence, $|x^2 + 2 - 3| < \epsilon$ if $|x + 1| < 3$ and $|x - 1| < \dfrac{\epsilon}{3}$. Choose $\delta = \dfrac{\epsilon}{3}$ for $\epsilon \leq 3$ and choose

$\delta = 1$ otherwise. 23. $|k - k| = 0 < \epsilon$ for any $\epsilon > 0$. Thus δ can be any positive number. 25. $P(x)$ is a

polynomial, $\displaystyle\lim_{x \to a} P(x) = \displaystyle\lim_{x \to a} (a_0 x^n + a_1 a^{n-1} + a_2 a^{n-2} + \cdots + a_{n-1} a) = P(a)$.

PAGE 298 CLASSROOM EXERCISES

1. $x = -2$; removable 3. $x = \pm 2$; nonremovable

PAGES 298-300 WRITTEN EXERCISES

1. $\frac{3}{11}$ 3. 1 5. $-1, 2$ 7. 0 9. 1 11. 2 13. None. 15. 2 17. $\frac{5}{3}$ 19. 0 21. $-\frac{1}{8}$ 23. $\lim_{x \to 3^+} \frac{x+3}{(x-3)^2}$

$= +\infty$; $\lim_{x \to 3^-} \frac{x+3}{(x-3)^2} = +\infty$ 25. $\lim_{x \to 2^+} \frac{2}{x^2 - 2x} = +\infty$; $\lim_{x \to 2^-} \frac{2}{x^2 - 2x} = -\infty$ 27. $y = 2$ 29. $y = 3$

31. (27.) $x = 0$ (28.) $x = 2, x = -2$ (29.) $x = 0$ (30.) $x = -\frac{1}{2}$ 33. Yes, $x = 0, x = 2$ 35. $\frac{1}{3}$ 37. $+\infty$

39. $-\infty$ 41. 0 43. 1 45. 0 47. -1 For Exercises 49-51, answers will vary. 49. $R(x) = \frac{1000(x-1)}{(x-1)}$,

$a = 1$ 51. $R(x) = \frac{x}{-x^3}, a = 0$ 53. 0 55. $+\infty$ 57. $\frac{2}{5}$

PAGE 301 MID-CHAPTER REVIEW

1. 1 2. 0 3. $\langle 1.9, 2.1 \rangle$ 4. $\langle 2.995, 3.005 \rangle$ 5. -1 6. $-\frac{1}{3}$ 7. -2 8. ± 2 9. $\lim_{x \to -2^+} f(x) = -\infty$,

$\lim_{x \to -2^-} f(x) = +\infty$ 10. $\lim_{x \to -2^-} f(x) = 0$, $\lim_{x \to -2^+} f(x) = 0$, $\lim_{x \to 2^-} f(x) = -\infty$, $\lim_{x \to 2^+} = +\infty$

PAGE 304 CLASSROOM EXERCISES 1. $6x + 3h$ 3. 3 5. $\frac{-5}{x^2 + xh}$ 7. $6x$ 9. 3 11. $\frac{-5}{x^2}$

PAGES 304-305 WRITTEN EXERCISES

1. $f'(3) = \lim_{h \to 0} \frac{[2(3+h) + 5 - (2 \cdot 3 + 5)]}{h} = \lim_{h \to 0} \frac{2h}{h} = 2$ 3. 0 5. $-\frac{1}{4}$ 7. -5 9. 5 11. $6x_0$ 13. $2x_0 - 3$

15. $3x_0^2$ 17. $2x_0 - 1$ 19. $\frac{1}{2\sqrt{x_0}}$ 21. 2, 1 23. 3, 2 25. Answers will vary. Let $F(x) = \frac{f(x+h) - f(x)}{h}$. Then

$f'(x) = \lim_{h \to 0} F(x) = L$. But $\lim_{h \to 0} F(x) = L$ is equivalent to $\lim_{h \to 0^-} F(x) = L$ and $\lim_{h \to 0^+} F(x) = L$ (see Exercise 15,

page 290). Thus, a function has a derived function at a point if and only if the right and left derived functions are equal at the point.

PAGE 307 EXERCISES 1. The gain will be 9.988, a drop of 0.012. 3. Let $A = 20$ and $B = \frac{19}{300}$.

PAGE 309 CLASSROOM EXERCISES 1. 1 3. -1.7 5. -2 7. 1

PAGE 310 WRITTEN EXERCISES

1. $\frac{2}{3}$ 3. -8 5. 7 7. 3 9. 6 11. 0 13. a. $\frac{y_2 - y_1}{x_2 - x_1}$ b. $\frac{y_2 - y_1}{h}$ c. $\frac{f(x+h) - f(x)}{h}$ d. $\frac{f(x+h) - f(x)}{h}$

15. $f'(-\frac{0}{2 \cdot 1}) = 0$ 17. $f'(-\frac{1}{2 \cdot 2}) = 0$ 19. $f'(-\frac{b}{2a}) = 0$ 21. $f'(x) = -\frac{1}{x^2}$. For x close to 0, $f'(x)$ goes to $-\infty$

and the tangent lines to the graph of $y = f(x)$ to either side of $x = 0$ have negative slopes of increasing steepness.

PAGE 314 CLASSROOM EXERCISES 1. $2x$ 3. $69x^{\frac{1}{2}}$

PAGE 314 WRITTEN EXERCISES

1. $7x^6$ 3. 0 5. $\frac{-100}{x^{101}}$ or $-\frac{100}{x^{101}}$ 7. $50x^9 + 5x^4 - 4x$ 9. $-36x^{-4}$ 11. 448 13. 6 15. $f'(x) = x + 2$, $m =$

$f'(3) = 5, y_1 = f(3) = \frac{21}{2}, y - \frac{21}{2} = 5(x - 3)$ 17. $y = 2x + 3$ 19. $y - \frac{1}{9} = \frac{2}{27}(x - 3)$ 21. $f'(x) = \frac{4}{3}x^{\frac{1}{3}}$,

$m = f'(8) = \frac{8}{3}$, $y_1 = f(8) = 16$, $y - 16 = \frac{8}{3}(x-8)$ 23. $\lim\limits_{h \to 0} \frac{f(x+h)-f(x)}{h} = \lim\limits_{h \to 0} \frac{k-k}{h} = \lim\limits_{h \to 0} 0 = 0$

25. $\lim\limits_{h \to 0} \frac{p(x+h)-p(x)}{h} = \lim\limits_{h \to 0} \frac{f(x+h) \cdot g(x+h) - f(x+h) \cdot g(x) + f(x+h) \cdot g(x) - f(x) \cdot g(x)}{h} = $

$\lim\limits_{h \to 0} f(x+h) \frac{g(x+h)-g(x)}{h} + \lim\limits_{h \to 0} g(x) \frac{f(x+h)-f(x)}{h} = f(x) \, g'(x) + g(x) \, f'(x)$ 27. $-\frac{2}{x^3}$

PAGES 317-319   CHAPTER OBJECTIVES AND REVIEW

1. 1   3. 3   5. $\langle \frac{29}{10}, \frac{31}{10} \rangle$ 7. $x \in (\frac{899}{300}, \frac{901}{300})$ 9. c   11. $M \pm N$ 13. $\frac{M}{N}$, $N \neq 0$ 15. and 17. See the Solution

Key.   19. 8   21. 6

23. 1   25. -6 27. 0   29. $30x^4$ 31. $4x$ 33. $\frac{12-3x}{x^5}$ 35. $\frac{4}{3}x^{\frac{1}{3}}$

PAGE 320   CHAPTER TEST

1. $\lim\limits_{x \to 2} f(x) = 2$ 2. $\lim\limits_{x \to 2^+} f(x) = 2$, $\lim\limits_{x \to 2^-} f(x) = 2$ 3. Yes, since f(2) is defined, $\lim\limits_{x \to 2} f(x)$ exists, and f(2) =

$\lim\limits_{x \to 2} f(x)$ 4. The curve passing through (2, 2) is a smooth continuous line.   5. 0   6. $-\frac{1}{3}$ 7. 1   8. 0   9. $+\infty$

10. $-\infty$ 11. $\lim\limits_{h \to 0} \frac{3(x+h)^2 - (x+h) + 1 - (3x^2 - x + 1)}{h} = \lim\limits_{h \to 0} \frac{3x^2 + 6xh + 3h^2 - x - h + 1 - 3x^2 + x - 1}{h} = $

$\lim\limits_{h \to 0} 6x + 3h - 1 = 6x - 1$ 12. f'(a) is the slope of the line tangent to y = f(x) at point (a, f(a)). See the

diagram on page 308.   13. $16x^2 + 6x - 2$ 14. 0   15. 4   16. $-5x^{-6}$ 17. $\frac{32}{3}x^{\frac{1}{3}}$

CHAPTER 7   ALGEBRAIC FUNCTIONS

PAGE 327   CLASSROOM EXERCISES   1. rational expression, real number coefficients   3. algebraic
expression, integer coefficients   5. rational expression, rational number coefficients

PAGE 327   WRITTEN EXERCISES

1. 4, 3   3. 2, 4   5. 9, -1 7. -3, $-\frac{3}{2}$, -2 9. 0, 0, 2   11. -4, ± 2, 6; y axis; Turning point is (0, -4); Upward.
13. 0, 0, -6; Axis of symmetry is x = 0; Downward.   15. 0, 0 and 2, -8; Axis of symmetry is x = 1; Turning
point is (1, 2); Downward.   17. 0   19. a. -12 b. $-3x_0^2$ 21. Let $p(x) = a_m x^m + a_m x^{m-1} + \cdots + a_0$ and
$q(x) = b_n x^n + b_{n-1} x^{n-1} + \cdots + b_0$ be polynomials over A, with a_m and b_n as leading coefficients. We may
assume without loss of generality that $m > n$. Then $p(x) + q(x) = a_m x^m + \cdots + (a_n + b_n)x^n + \cdots + (a_0 + b_0)$
which after setting $c_i = a_i + b_i$ (i = 0, 1, 2, $\cdots$, n) is certainly a polynomial of degree m over A. (The cases
where $n < m$ and m = n are done in a similar way.) Also true for product of two polynomials.

PAGE 330   CLASSROOM EXERCISES   1. -5, -1, 1

PAGE 330   WRITTEN EXERCISES

1. 51, 6, 56   3. 1, 85, -2, -20, -174 5. $\frac{343}{81}$, $\frac{893}{256}$, 23   7. k = -14 9. k = 10   11. c = 1 and k = 2   13. f(-4) =
-60, f(-3.5) = -47.13, f(-3) = -38, f(-2.5) = -31.88, f(-2) = -28, f(-1.5) = -25.63, f(-1) = -24,
f($-.5$) = -22.38, f(0) = -20, f(.5) = -16.13, f(1) = -10, f(1.5) = $-.88$, f(2) = 12, f(2.5) = 29.38, f(3) = 52,
f(3.5) = 80.63, f(4) = 116

PAGES 334-335 WRITTEN EXERCISES

1. $3x^2 + 10x + 10$, $f(2) = 5$ 3. $-2x^3 + x^2 + x + 7$, -3 5. $9x^2 + 6x + 3$, 3 7. $2x^2 + x + 4$, 0 9. $3x^2 - 6$, 5

11. The degree of $Q(x)$ is $n - m$ and the degree of $r(x)$ is less than m and greater than or equal to zero.

13. $f(-6) = 0$, $f(-2) = 100$, $f(-\frac{1}{3}) = 0$, $f(\frac{1}{2}) = 0$, $f(3) = 450$ The factors are $x + 6$, $x + \frac{1}{3}$, and $x - \frac{1}{2}$. 15. $k = -2$

17. Use synthetic substitution.

$$\begin{array}{cccc} 1 & p & q & \underline{|a} \\ & a & a^2 + ap & \\ \hline 1 & a+p & a^2 + ap + q & \end{array} \qquad \begin{array}{cccc} 1 & p & q & \underline{|b} \\ & b & b^2 + bp & \\ \hline 1 & p+b & b^2 + bp + q & \end{array}$$

Since in each case the remainder is 0, $a^2 + ap + q = 0$ and $b^2 + bp + q = 0$. Now solve for p and q: $q = -a^2 - ap$, $b^2 + bp + (-a^2 - ap) = 0$, or $p(b - a) = a^2 - b^2 = (a + b)(a - b)$. Then $p = \frac{-(b - a)(a + b)}{b - a}$ or $p = -a - b$.

Then $q = -b^2 - b(-a - b) = ab$. 19. $f(-a) = (-a)^n + a^n$. If n is odd, $(-a)^n = -a^n$ and $f(-a) = 0$. Therefore $x + a$ is a factor of $x^n + a^n$. $Q(x) = x^{n-1} - ax^{n-2} + a^2 x^{n-3} - \cdots + \cdots + a^{n-1}$. 21. Let $f(x) = a_3 x^3 + a_2 x^2 + a_1 x + a_0$ and c be a number. To divide $f(x)$ by $x - c$ use synthetic division. $Q(x) = a_3 x^2 + (a_2 + a_c c)x + a_3 c^2 + a_2 c + a_1$ and $r = a_3 c^3 + a_2 c^2 + a_1 c + a_0 = f(c)$. 23. Zeros: $-\frac{1 \pm \sqrt{5}}{2}$; $\left(x - \frac{(1 - \sqrt{5})}{2}\right)\left(x - \frac{(1 + \sqrt{5})}{2}\right)$

25. Zeros: $\pm 2i$; $(x - 2i)(x + 2i)$

PAGE 339 CLASSROOM EXERCISES   1. 1 and -4 3. 2 and -3 5. 1 and -1

PAGE 339 WRITTEN EXERCISES

1. -1 and 0, 1 and 2, 2 and 3 3. -1 and 0, 2 and 3 5. -3 and -2, 1 and 2 7. -2 and -1, 0 and $\frac{1}{2}$, $\frac{1}{2}$ and 1

9. .5 and .6 11. -2.1 and -2.0 13. a. $0 < k < 3$ b. $3 < k < 8$

PAGES 342-343 WRITTEN EXERCISES

1. 2, 3, -4 3. -1, 4 5. $\frac{1}{2}$, $\frac{3}{4}$, 2 7. $\frac{1}{3}$, $\pm\sqrt{2}$ 9. 2, 3, -4 11. -3 13. -3, -1, 3, 5 15. No rational zeros. There is one real zero between 1 and 1.1. 17. $x^3 + 2x^2 - 5x - 6$ 19. -2, which is equal to the opposite of the coefficient of x^2. 21. 6, which is equal to the opposite of the constant term. 23. $-\frac{11}{4}$ 25. $x^3 - x^2 - \frac{11}{4}x + \frac{3}{2} = 0$ 27. $\frac{a_2}{a_3} = -(r_1 + r_2 + r_3)$, $\frac{a_1}{a_3} = r_1 r_2 + r_1 r_3 + r_2 r_3$, $\frac{a_0}{a_3} = -r_1 r_2 r_3$ 29. $\frac{a_3}{a_4} = -(r_1 + r_2 + r_3 + r_4)$, $\frac{a_2}{a_4} = r_1 r_2 + r_1 r_3 + r_1 r_4 + r_2 r_3 + r_2 r_4 + r_3 r_4$, $\frac{a_1}{a_4} = -(r_1 r_2 r_3 + r_1 r_2 r_4 + r_1 r_3 r_4 + r_2 r_3 r_4)$, $\frac{a_0}{a_4} = r_1 r_2 r_3 r_4$

PAGE 345 CLASSROOM EXERCISES

1. 2 has multiplicity 2, -2 has multiplicity 2 3. $+\sqrt{3}i$, $-\sqrt{3}i$, $+i$, $-i$; each has multiplicity 1

PAGES 346-347 WRITTEN EXERCISES

1. -1 has multiplicity 2 and 2 is a simple zero. 3. -2 is a simple zero and -1 has multiplicity 3. 5. 1, $\frac{-1 + i\sqrt{3}}{2}$, and $\frac{-1 - i\sqrt{3}}{2}$ are all simple zeros. 7. i, $-i$, 2i, $-2i$ are all simple zeros. 9. 1, $\frac{-1 + i\sqrt{3}}{2}$, $\frac{-1 - i\sqrt{3}}{2}$ are roots of multiplicity 2. 11. -1, i, and $-i$ are each roots of multiplicity 2. 13. $x^3 - 2x^2 -$

$x + 2$ 15. $x^3 - 4x^2 + 2x + 4$ 17. $x^4 - 4x^3 + 6x^2 - 4x$ 19. $x^4 - 4x^3 + 14x^2 - 20x + 25$ 21. $x^6 + 3x^4 +$ $3x^2 + 1$ 23. $-3i, -\dfrac{1}{2}, 5$ 25. You know by Theorem 7-7 that f(x) has at least one zero, $x = r_1$. This means that by the Factor Theorem $f(x) = (x - r_1)Q_1(x)$, where $Q_1(x)$ has degree $n - 1$. If $n - 1 = 0$ you are done. Otherwise since $Q_1(x)$ is also a polynomial, $Q_1(x)$ has a zero, $x = r_2$. By the Factor Theorem $f(x) = (x - r_1)$ $(x - r_2)Q_2(x)$, where $Q_2(x)$ is of degree $n - 2$. Continue the process and $f(x) = (x - r_1)(x - r_2) \cdots (x - r_n)$ $Q_n(x)$, where $Q_n(x)$ is of degree $n - n = 0$ and therefore f(x) has at most n complex zeros. The reason for "at most" is that some r_i may equal some r_j.

PAGE 350   CLASSROOM EXERCISES

1. $3x^2 + 6x + 3 = 3(x + 1)^2$; $(-1, -1)$ 3. $3x^2 - 3 = 3(x^2 - 1)$; $(-1, -4)$ and $(1, -8)$ 5. $20x^4 + 6x^2$ $= 2x^2(10x^2 + 3)$; $(0, 8)$ 7. $42x^6 - 48x^5 = 6x^5(7x - 8)$; $(0, -5)$, $(\dfrac{8}{7}, \dfrac{-6214867}{823543})$

PAGES 350-351   WRITTEN EXERCISES

1. $(-1, 7)$ is a relative maximum and $(2, -20)$ is a relative minimum. 3. $(0, 0)$ is a relative maximum and $(2, -4)$ is a relative minimum. 5. $(\dfrac{7}{2}, \dfrac{25}{4})$ is a relative maximum. 7. None. 9. $(0,5)$ is a relative maximum and $(\dfrac{4}{3}, \dfrac{103}{27})$ is a relative minimum. 11. $(-1, 10)$ is a relative minimum and $(0, 11)$ is a relative maximum. 13. $(-\dfrac{3}{a}, -\dfrac{9}{a} + c)$ is a relative minimum if $a > 0$ and a relative maximum if $a < 0$. 15. a. 80 feet. b. 128 feet. c. Zero feet. 17. 144 feet. 19. The heights are the same because the graph of the function representing the height is a parabola which has an axis of symmetry t = 5. The points t = 3 and t = 7 on the parabola are symmetric about the line t = 5. 21. b = 18 meters and h = 18 meters.

PAGE 351   MID-CHAPTER REVIEW

1. degree 4, leading coefficient -3 2. slope: -8; y intercept: 5; zero: $x = \dfrac{5}{8}$ 3. $(\dfrac{-7}{2}, \dfrac{-81}{4})$; $x = \dfrac{-7}{2}$; $x = 1$, -8 4. 9 5. 1; -1; 71 6. $Q(x) = x^4 + 5x^3 + 25x^2 + 123x + 615$ 7. $3x^4 + 6x^3 + 12x^2 + 22x + 45$, 89 8. -3 and -2, 0 and 1, 1 and 2 9. $\dfrac{1}{2}, \dfrac{5}{4}, \dfrac{-8}{3}$ 10. $24x^3 - 34x^2 - 19x + 15$ 11. 2 has multiplicity 2; $-1 + \sqrt{3}i$ has multiplicity 2; $-1 - \sqrt{3}i$ has multiplicity 2 12. $(\dfrac{1}{3}, -6\dfrac{23}{27})$ is a relative maximum; $(1, -7)$ is a relative minimum

PAGES 356-357   WRITTEN EXERCISES

1. $(-2, 21)$ is a relative maximum and $(1, -6)$ is a relative minimum. 3. $(0,5)$ is an inflection point and $(\dfrac{3}{2}, \dfrac{53}{16})$ is a relative minimum. 5. $(0, \dfrac{3}{4})$ is a relative maximum and $(-\sqrt{3}, -\dfrac{3}{8})$ and $(\sqrt{3}, -\dfrac{3}{8})$ are relative minima. 7. $(\pm 2, 16)$ are relative maxima and $(0, 0)$ is a relative minimum. 9. $(0, 0)$ is a relative minimum. 11. $(0, -31)$ is a point of inflection. 13. $(0, -1)$ and $(1, 1)$ are points of inflection. 15. $(a, 0)$ is a point of inflection. 17. Point of inflection. 19. None of these. 21. a. 5 and 5 b. 5 and 5 23. 25 and 25

PAGE 360   WRITTEN EXERCISES

1. Functional values: $(-3, 75)$, $(-2, 48)$, $(-1, 27)$, $(0, 12)$, $(1, 3)$, $(2, 0)$, $(3, 3)$; y intercept = 12; Relative minimum = $(2, 0)$; $\lim\limits_{x \to -\infty} f = \lim\limits_{x \to +\infty} f = +\infty$. 3. Functional values: $(-3, -50)$, $(-2, -16)$, $(-1, 0)$, $(0, 4)$, $(1, 2)$, $(2, 0)$, $(3, 4)$; -1 is a single zero and 2 is a zero of multiplicity 2; $(0, 4)$ is a relative maximum and $(2, 0)$ is a relative minimum; $\lim\limits_{x \to -\infty} f = -\infty$ and $\lim\limits_{x \to +\infty} f = +\infty$. 5. Functional values: $(-3, 7)$, $(-2, 18)$, $(-1, 11)$, $(0, -2)$, $(1, -9)$, $(2, 2)$, $(3, 43)$; The zeros of f are between 0 and -1, 1 and 2, and -3 and -4; $(1, -9)$ is a relative minimum and $(-2, 18)$ is a relative maximum; $\lim\limits_{x \to -\infty} f = -\infty$ and $\lim\limits_{x \to +\infty} f = +\infty$. 7. Functional

values: $(-3, 243)$, $(-2, 72)$, $(-1, 11)$, $(0, 0)$, $(1, 3)$, $(2, 8)$, $(3, 27)$; The zeros of f are 0 and $2 \pm \sqrt{2}i$; $(0, 0)$ is a

relative minimum; $\lim\limits_{x \to -\infty} f = \lim\limits_{x \to +\infty} f = +\infty$.   9. Functional values: $(-3, 8)$, $(-2, 0)$, $(-1, 0)$, $(0, 2)$, $(1, 24)$,

$(2, 108)$, $(3, 320)$; The zeros of f are -1 and -2; $(-1\frac{3}{4}, -\frac{27}{256})$ is a relative minimum; $\lim\limits_{x \to +\infty} f = \lim\limits_{x \to -\infty} f = +\infty$;

$(-1, 0)$ and $(-\frac{3}{2}, -\frac{1}{16})$ are points of inflection.   11. Functional values: $(-3, 81)$, $(-2, 16)$, $(-1, 1)$, $(0, 0)$,

$(1, 1)$, $(2, 16)$, $(3, 81)$; $(0, 0)$ is a relative minimum; No points of inflection; $\lim\limits_{x \to +\infty} f = \lim\limits_{x \to -\infty} f = +\infty$.

13. Functional values: $(-3, -343)$, $(-2, -216)$, $(-1, -125)$, $(0, -64)$, $(1, -27)$, $(2, -8)$, $(3, -1)$; $(4, 0)$ is a

point of inflection; $\lim\limits_{x \to -\infty} f = -\infty$ and $\lim\limits_{x \to +\infty} f = +\infty$.   15. Functional values: $(-3, -5887)$, $(-2, -1025)$,

$(-1, -63)$, $(0, -1)$, $(1, 1)$, $(2, 63)$, $(3, 1025)$; $(0, -1)$ and $(1, 1)$ are points of inflection; zero between 0

and 1; $\lim\limits_{x \to -\infty} f = -\infty$ and $\lim\limits_{x \to +\infty} f = +\infty$.   17. Functional values: $(-3, -442)$, $(-2, -101)$, $(-1, -6)$,

$(0, -1)$, $(1, -2)$, $(2, 3)$, $(3, -46)$; zeros between $-.1$ and $-.2$, $-.7$ and $-.6$, 1.2 and 1.3, 2 and 3; relative

minimum between 0 and 1 and relative maxima between -1 and 0 and between 1 and 2; $\lim\limits_{x \to -\infty} f = \lim\limits_{x \to +\infty} f =$

$-\infty$.   19. Functional values: $(-3, -10)$, $(-2, 3)$, $(-1, 6)$, $(0, 5)$, $(1, 6)$, $(2, 15)$, $(3, 38)$; $(\frac{1}{3}, \frac{130}{27})$ is a relative

minimum and $(-1, 6)$ is a relative maximum; $(-\frac{1}{3}, \frac{146}{27})$ is a point of inflection; $\lim\limits_{x \to -\infty} f = -\infty$ and $\lim\limits_{x \to +\infty} f =$

$+\infty$.   21. Functional values: $(-3, 400)$, $(-2, 25)$, $(-1, 0)$, $(0, 1)$, $(1, 16)$, $(2, 225)$, $(3, 1600)$; $(-1, 0)$ is a

relative minimum; $\lim\limits_{x \to -\infty} f = \lim\limits_{x \to +\infty} f = +\infty$.   23. Functional values: $(-3, -640)$, $(-2, -135)$, $(-1, -16)$,

$(0, -1)$, $(1, 0)$, $(2, 5)$, $(3, 80)$; $(1, 0)$ is a point of inflection; $\lim\limits_{x \to -\infty} f = -\infty$ and $\lim\limits_{x \to +\infty} f = +\infty$.   25. Functional

values: $(-3, 100)$, $(-2, 81)$, $(-1, 64)$, $(0, 49)$, $(1, 36)$, $(2, 25)$, $(3, 16)$; $(7, 0)$, is a relative minimum;

$\lim\limits_{x \to +\infty} f = \lim\limits_{x \to -\infty} f = +\infty$.   27. Functional values: $(-3, 625)$, $(-2, 144)$, $(-1, 9)$, $(0, 4)$, $(1, 9)$, $(2, 0)$, $(3, 49)$

Zeros: $-\frac{1}{2}$, 2; $(2, 0)$ is a relative minimum; $(-\frac{1}{2}, 0)$ is a relative minimum; $(\frac{3}{4}, \frac{625}{64})$ is a relative maximum;

$\lim\limits_{x \to -\infty} f = \lim\limits_{x \to +\infty} f = +\infty$.   29. Functional values: $(-3, -648)$, $(-2, -112)$, $(-1, -6)$, $(0, 0)$, $(1, -4)$, $(2, -48)$,

$(3, -162)$; Zeros: 0, 5; $(0, 0)$ is a relative maximum and $(4, -256)$ is a relative minimum; $(3, -162)$ is a point

of inflection; $\lim\limits_{x \to -\infty} f = -\infty$ and $\lim\limits_{x \to +\infty} f = +\infty$.   31. Functional values: $(-3, 64)$, $(-2, 0)$, $(-1, 8)$, $(0, 4)$,

$(1, 0)$, $(2, -16)$, $(3, -200)$; $(-2, 0)$ is a relative minimum and $(-.8, 8.4)$ is a relative maximum; $(1, 0)$ is a

point of inflection; $\lim\limits_{x \to -\infty} f = +\infty$ and $\lim\limits_{x \to +\infty} f = -\infty$.

PAGE 365   CLASSROOM EXERCISES
1. $12x^2 + 12x - 2$ 3. $20x^3 - 24x$

PAGES 365-366   WRITTEN EXERCISES
1. f(x) is concave upward on the interval $\langle -\infty, +\infty \rangle$.   3. f(x) is concave upward on $\langle -\frac{1}{2}, +\infty \rangle$; $(-\frac{1}{2}, \frac{9}{2})$ is an

inflection point.   5. f(x) is concave upward on $\langle -\frac{1}{2}, +\infty \rangle$ and concave downward on $\langle -\infty, -\frac{1}{2} \rangle$; $(-\frac{1}{2}, -\frac{1}{2})$ is

an inflection point.   7. y intercept = 0; Zeros: 0, 2; Relative max: $(\frac{4}{3}, \frac{32}{27})$; Relative min: $(0, 0)$; Point of

inflection = $(\frac{2}{3}, \frac{16}{27})$; Concave upward on $\langle -\infty, \frac{2}{3} \rangle$; Concave downward on $\langle \frac{2}{3}, +\infty \rangle$; $\lim\limits_{x \to +\infty} f(x) = -\infty$ and

$\lim\limits_{x \to -\infty} f(x) = +\infty$.   9. y intercept = 0; Zero: 0; Relative min: $(0, 0)$; Concave upward on $\langle -\infty, +\infty \rangle$; $\lim\limits_{x \to -\infty} f$

$= \lim\limits_{x \to +\infty} f = +\infty$.   11. y intercept = 1; Zeros between -1 and 0; Relative max: $(1, 5)$; Relative min: $(3, 1)$;

Point of inflection = $(2, 3)$; Concave downward on $\langle -\infty, 2 \rangle$; Concave upward on $\langle 2, \infty \rangle$; $\lim\limits_{x \to -\infty} f = -\infty$ and

$\lim_{x \to +\infty} f = +\infty$. **13.** y intercept = 5; Zeros: $1, \dfrac{5 \pm \sqrt{105}}{8}$; Rel. max: $(0, 5)$; Rel. min: $\left(\dfrac{3}{2}, -\dfrac{7}{4}\right)$; Inflection point = $\left(\dfrac{3}{4}, 1\dfrac{5}{8}\right)$; Concave upward on $\left\langle \dfrac{3}{4}, +\infty \right\rangle$; Concave downward on $\left\langle -\infty, \dfrac{3}{4} \right\rangle$; $\lim_{x \to -\infty} f = -\infty$ and $\lim_{x \to +\infty} f = +\infty$. **15.** y intercept = 1; Zeros: ± 1; Rel. max: $(0, 1)$; Rel. min: $(\pm 1, 0)$; Inflection points

$= \left(\pm \dfrac{1}{\sqrt{3}}, \dfrac{4}{9}\right)$; Concave downward on $\left\langle -\dfrac{1}{\sqrt{3}}, \dfrac{1}{\sqrt{3}} \right\rangle$; Concave upward everywhere else; $\lim_{x \to -\infty} f$

$= \lim_{x \to +\infty} f = +\infty$. **17.** y inter. = 25; Zeros between: -4 and -3, 0 and 1, 4 and 5; Rel. max. = $(-2, 69)$; Rel. min. $= (3, -56)$; Infl. pt. $= \left(\dfrac{1}{2}, \dfrac{13}{2}\right)$; Concave down on $\left\langle -\infty, \dfrac{1}{2} \right\rangle$; Concave upward on $\left\langle \dfrac{1}{2}, +\infty \right\rangle$; $\lim_{x \to -\infty} f = -\infty$ and $\lim_{x \to +\infty} f = +\infty$. **19.** y intercept = 0; Zeros: $0, \pm 2$; Rel. max: $(-2, 0)$, $\left(\dfrac{2}{\sqrt{5}}, \dfrac{512}{25\sqrt{5}}\right)$; Relative minima:

$(2, 0)$, $\left(-\dfrac{2}{\sqrt{5}}, -\dfrac{512}{25\sqrt{5}}\right)$; Points of inflection $= \left(\sqrt{\dfrac{12}{5}}, \dfrac{128\sqrt{15}}{125}\right)$, $\left(-\sqrt{\dfrac{12}{5}}, -\dfrac{128\sqrt{15}}{125}\right)$,

$(0, 0)$; $\lim_{x \to -\infty} f = -\infty$ and $\lim_{x \to +\infty} f = +\infty$. **21. a.** The slope of the line passing through $(a, f(a))$, $(b, f(b))$. **b.** The slope of the tangent line to the graph of $y = f(x)$ at the point $(x_0, f(x_0))$. **c.** There is a point $(x_0, f(x_0))$, $a < x_0 < b$, such that the secant line connecting $(a, f(a))$ and $(b, f(b))$ is parallel to the line tangent to $f(x)$ at x_0.

PAGE 369 WRITTEN EXERCISES

1. Functional values: $\left(-2, -\dfrac{1}{3}\right)$, $\left(-1, -\dfrac{1}{2}\right)$, $(0, -1)$, $(2, 1)$, $\left(3, \dfrac{1}{2}\right)$, $\left(4, \dfrac{1}{3}\right)$; no zeros; $x = 1$ is an excluded point; $x = 1$ is a vertical asymptote; $y = 0$ is a horizontal asymptote. **3.** Functional values: $\left(-1, \dfrac{1}{2}\right)$, $\left(0, \dfrac{2}{3}\right)$, $(4, -2)$, $(5, -1)$; no zeros; $x = 3$ is an excluded point; $x = 3$ is a vertical asymptote; $y = 0$ is a horizontal asymptote. **5.** Functional values: $(-6, 12)$, $(-4, -8)$, $(-3, -3)$; one zero at $x = 0$; $x = -5$ is an excluded value and a vertical asymptote; $y = 2$ is a horizontal asymptote. **7.** Functional values: $\left(-6, \dfrac{15}{2}\right)$, $\left(-2, -\dfrac{7}{2}\right)$, $0, -\dfrac{3}{4}$, $\left(\dfrac{3}{2}, 0\right)$; $\dfrac{3}{2}$ is a zero; $x = -4$ is an excluded point and a vertical asymptote; $y = 2$ is a horizontal asymptote. **9.** Functional values: $\left(-3, 4\dfrac{1}{2}\right)$, $\left(-\dfrac{3}{2}, -18\right)$, $(0, 0)$, $\left(1, -\dfrac{1}{2}\right)$, $\left(2, -\dfrac{1}{2}\right)$; 0 is a zero; $x = -1$ and $x = -2$ are excluded points and vertical asymptotes; $y = 0$ is a horizontal asymptote. **11.** Functional values: $(-2, -1)$, $(0, 1)$, $\left(1, \dfrac{1}{2}\right)$, $\left(3, \dfrac{1}{4}\right)$, $\left(4, \dfrac{1}{5}\right)$, $\left(6, \dfrac{1}{7}\right)$; No zeros; $x = -1$ and $x = 5$ are excluded points; $x = -1$ is a vertical asumptote; $y = 0$ is a horizontal asymptote. **13.** Functional values: $\left(-3, \dfrac{24}{23}\right)$, $\left(1, -\dfrac{4}{9}\right)$, $(5, 0)$; 0 and 5 are zeros; $x = -2$ and $x = \dfrac{1}{4}$ are excluded points and vertical asymptotes; $y = \dfrac{1}{4}$ is a horizontal asymptote. **15.** Functional values: $(-4, 21)$, $(-1, 6)$, $(0, 1)$, $\left(1, \dfrac{1}{6}\right)$, $(2, 0)$, $(3, 0)$; 2 and 3 are zeros; $x = -2$ and $x = -3$ are excluded points and vertical asymptotes; $y = 1$ is a horizontal asymptote. **17.** Functional values: $\left(-\dfrac{1}{2}, -\dfrac{4}{3}\right)$, $\left(1, \dfrac{2}{3}\right)$; 0 is a zero; No excluded points or vertical asymptotes; $y = 0$ is a horiz. asymptote. **19.** Same as Ex. 1 except no $g(-2)$ exists. **21.** They are identical except for the zeros of $t(x)$, at which $R_1(x)$ is not defined. **23.** Functional values: $\left(-2, \dfrac{1}{2}\right)$, $\left(-1, \dfrac{1}{3}\right)$, $(1, -1)$, $(3, 3)$, $(4, 2)$; There is a hole at $(0, 0)$; $x = 2$ is an excluded point and a vertical asymptote; $y = 1$ is a horizontal asymptote. **25.** Functional values: $\left(-3, \dfrac{3}{4}\right)$, $\left(-2, \dfrac{2}{3}\right)$, $\left(-1, \dfrac{1}{2}\right)$, $(0, 0)$, $(2, 2)$, $\left(3, \dfrac{3}{2}\right)$, $\left(\dfrac{1}{2}, -1\right)$, $\left(\dfrac{3}{4}, -3\right)$; $x = 1$ is a vertical asymptote and there are no holes.

1. $\langle -\infty, -\sqrt{5}] \cup [\sqrt{5}, +\infty\rangle$ 3. The set of real numbers.

PAGES 373-374 WRITTEN EXERCISES

1. $\langle -\infty, -2] \cup [2, +\infty\rangle$ 3. $\langle -\infty, -2] \cup [2, +\infty\rangle$ 5. $\langle -\infty, 1\rangle$ 7. $\langle -\infty, 1] \cup [2, +\infty\rangle$
9. $[-2, 0] \cup [2, +\infty\rangle$ 11. The set of real numbers. 13. Domain = set of all real numbers; Real zeros are 2,
-2; No vertical or horizontal asymptotes; Functional values: $(-2, 0)$, $(0, -1.587)$, $(1, -1.44)$, $(2, 0)$.
15. Domain = $\langle -\infty, -2] \cup [3, +\infty\rangle$; -2 and 3 are zeros; Functional values: $(-4, \sqrt{14})$, $(-2, 0)$, $(4, \sqrt{6})$,
$(5, \sqrt{14})$. 17. Domain = $\langle 0, +\infty\rangle$, $y = -1$ is a horizontal asymptote, $x = 0$ is a vertical asymptote;
Functional values: $(\frac{1}{2}, -\sqrt{3})$, $(1, -\sqrt{2})$, $(2, -\sqrt{\frac{3}{2}})$. 19. Domain = all real numbers, range $y \geq 0$;
Functional values: $(-2, \sqrt[3]{4})$, $(-1, 1)$, $(1, 1)$, $(2, \sqrt[3]{4})$, $(3, \sqrt[3]{9})$. 21. $y = 1 + \sqrt{1 + x^2}$ has domain = all
real numbers, range = $y \geq 2$; Functional values: $(-3, 4.16)$, $(-1, 2.4)$, $(0, 2)$, $(1, 2.414)$, $(3, 4.16)$. $y = 1$
$- \sqrt{1 + x^2}$ is a mirror image of $y = 1 + \sqrt{1 + x^2}$ about the line $y = 1$. 23. Let $P_0(x) = 1$, $P_1(x) = -2$, and
$P_2(x) = x^2$. 25. $y^4 - 2xy^2 + x^2 - x = 0$, so let $P_0(x) = 1$, $P_1(x) = 0$, $P_2(x) = -2x$, $P_3(x) = 0$, $P_4(x) = x^2 -$
x. 27. $(x^2 + 1)y^3 + (-x) = P_0(x)y^3 + P_3(x) = 0$

PAGE 376 WRITTEN EXERCISES

1. $f(x) = \frac{17}{24}x^3 + \frac{7}{24}x + 1$ 3. $f(x) = x^3 - 12x^2 + 12x$ 5. $f(x) = x^3 - 6x^2 + 11x - 6$ 7. $-\frac{7}{4}x^3 + \frac{45}{4}x^2$
$-\frac{31}{2}x + 3$ 9. $f(2.5) = 33$. At 2:30 the temperature was $33°$. 11. 38

PAGES 379-380 WRITTEN EXERCISES

1. $x = 12\frac{1}{2}$; $y = 25$; $A = 312\frac{1}{2}$ square meters 3. The largest rectangle with a perimeter of 20 meters is a square
with side = 5. 5. $2\sqrt{6}$ by 12 7. First number = $-\frac{1}{4}$, second number = $\frac{1}{4}$, third number = $-\frac{1}{2}$. 9. 35 cents
11. $r = 4$ and $h = 3$ 13. $\frac{2r}{3}, \frac{P}{3}$ 15. $6\sqrt[3]{N^2}$; $3\sqrt[3]{3}$ by $3\sqrt[3]{3}$ by $3\sqrt[3]{3}$

PAGE 381 EXERCISES

1.

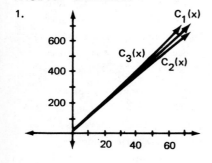

3. a. loss
   b. profit
   c. loss
   d. About 10 or 490

PAGES 383-385 CHAPTER OBJECTIVES AND REVIEW

1. Polynomial; Degree: 3; Leading coefficient: 2 3. Not a polynomial 5. y intercept: 7; Zero: $-\frac{7}{3}$; Slope at
$x = 3$: 3; No axis of Symmetry; No turning point. 7. y intercept: 1; Zero: 1; Slope at $x = 3$: 4; Axis of
symmetry: $x = 1$; Turning point: $(1, 0)$; Upward 9. 2, 110, -2, -2 11. 14, 7, 0, -37

13. $Q(x) = 2x^2 + 7x + 18$, $r = 49$.   15. $x + 1$ 17. $(x + 2)$ and $(x - 2)$ 19. -1 is a real zero and there are real

zeros in the interval $1 \leq x \leq 2$.   21. Possible rational zeros: $0, \pm 1, \pm 3, \pm 5, \pm 15, \pm \frac{1}{2}, \pm \frac{3}{2}, \pm \frac{5}{2}, \pm \frac{15}{2}$; Actual

zeros: $0, -1, -\frac{3}{2}$, and -5 23. Possible rational zeros: $\pm 1, \pm 2, \pm \frac{1}{3}, \pm \frac{2}{3}, \pm \frac{1}{9}, \pm \frac{2}{9}$; Actual zeros: $-1, -\frac{1}{3}$, and $\frac{2}{3}$

25. 0 (multiplicity 2), 2 (multiplicity 2), and $\pm 2i$ 27. $(\sqrt{3}, -10.39)$ is a relative minimum; $(-\sqrt{3}, 10.39)$ is

a relative maximum. $(0, 0)$ is a point of inflection.   29. $(0, 60)$ and $(3, 87)$ are relative minima, and $(2, 92)$ is a

relative maximum. Points of inflection occur at $x \approx 0.78$ and $x \approx 2.55$.   31. y intercept $= -1$; Functional

values: $(-3, -28)$, $(-2, -9)$, $(-1, -2)$, $(0, -1)$, $(1, 0)$, $(2, 7)$, $(3, 26)$; One real zero: 1; $(0, -1)$ is a point of

inflection; As $x \rightarrow +\infty$, $f(x) \rightarrow +\infty$; As $x \rightarrow -\infty$, $f(x) \rightarrow -\infty$.   33. y intercept $= -36$; Functional values:

$(-3, 585)$, $(-2, 306)$, $(-1, 81)$, $(0, -36)$, $(1, 9)$, $(2, 270)$; Zeros: $-0.5, 0.9$, and -9.5; $(-6.27, 1212.07)$ is a

relative maximum and $(0.27, -42.07)$ is a relative minimum. As $x \rightarrow +\infty$, $f(x) \rightarrow +\infty$; As $x \rightarrow -\infty$, $f(x) \rightarrow -\infty$.

35. a. $0, 4$; b. $x = 2$ or $x = -2$; c. $x = 2$ and $x = -2$; d. $y = 1$; e. Functional values: $(-3, 4.2)$, $(-1, -\frac{5}{3})$,

$(0, 0)$, $(1, 1)$, $(3, -\frac{3}{5})$.   37.

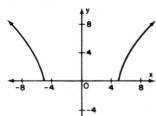

39. $f = -\frac{1}{3}x^2 + \frac{2}{3}x + 3$

41. 150 ft by 120 ft

PAGE 386   CHAPTER TEST

1. $-35, -\frac{340}{27}, 4, 5$ 2. $0, -8, 0, -40, 0$ 3. None; $\pm\sqrt{\frac{5}{3}}, \pm i$ 4. $\pm 3, 0, \frac{2}{3}$ 5. Answers will vary.   6. 6,

because complex zeros must occur in conjugate pairs.   7. Between 0.5 and 0.6   8. Relative maximum at $(0, 0)$;

Relative minima at $(\pm\sqrt{2}, -4)$; Inflection points at $(\pm\sqrt{\frac{2}{3}}, -\frac{20}{9})$.   9. $(1, 0)$ is an inflection point.

10. There is a relative minimum between 1 and 2. There are points of inflection at $x \approx -.47$ and $x \approx -3.53$.

11. See Exercise 8 for maximum and minimum points. y intercept $= 0$; Zeros are 0 and ± 2.   12. Functional

values: $(-3, -54)$, $(-2, -20)$, $(-1, -4)$, $(0, 0)$, $(1, -2)$, $(2, -4)$, $(3, 0)$, $(4, 16)$; y intercept $= 0$; Zeros are 0 and

3, $(0, 0)$ is a relative maximum and $(2, -4)$ is a relative minimum; $(1, -2)$ is a point of inflection.   13. No

maxima or minima; 2 is a zero; $(2, 0)$ is an inflection point and -8 is the y intercept.   14. (11.) Concave

downward on $\langle -\sqrt{\frac{2}{3}}, \sqrt{\frac{2}{3}} \rangle$ and concave upward everywhere else. (12.) Concave upward on $\langle 1, +\infty \rangle$ and

concave downward on $\langle -\infty, 1 \rangle$. (13.) Concave downward on $\langle -\infty, 2 \rangle$ and concave upward on $\langle 2, +\infty \rangle$.

15. Domain $= [-5, 5]$; Maximum $= (0, 6)$; Concave downward everywhere.   16. Functional values: $(-3, 9)$,

$(-1, 1)$, $(0, 0)$, $(1, 1)$, $(3, 9)$; Minimum at $(0, 0)$; Concave upward everywhere and holes at $x = \pm 2$.   17. This

curve has three branches. The first is asymptotic to $x = -1$ and $y = 0$ and $y > 0$ for all x. The second branch is

concave downward, $y < 0$ for all x and it is asymptotic to $x = -1$ and $x = 3$. It has a maximum at $(1, -\frac{1}{4})$. The

third branch is asymptotic to $x = 3$ and $y = 0$ and $y > 0$ for all x.   18. $-\frac{2}{3}x^3 + \frac{3}{2}x^2 + \frac{7}{6}x$ 19. $4, 8$

CHAPTER 8 EXPONENTIAL AND LOGARITHMIC FUNCTIONS

PAGE 391 CLASSROOM EXERCISES 1. $\frac{1}{64}$ 3. 1.8 5. $6y^{-5}$ 7. The qth root of a^p

PAGES 391-392 WRITTEN EXERCISES
1. $\frac{1}{8}$ 3. 343 5. $\frac{1}{8}$ 7. $2xy$ 9. a^5 11. 1 13. 200 15. 27 17. They are equal, at least in some instances. 19. 3
21. 3 23. 256 25. 64 27. 4 29. Let $r_1 = \frac{q_1}{p_1}$ and $r_2 = \frac{q_2}{p_2}$ where p_1 and p_2 are natural numbers and q_1 and

q_2 are integers. a. Proof: $a^{r_1+r_2} = a^{\frac{q_1}{p_1}+\frac{q_2}{p_2}} = a^{\frac{q_1p_2+q_2p_1}{p_1p_2}} = \left(a^{\frac{1}{p_1p_2}}\right)^{q_1p_2+q_2p_1}$ (by 9, page 389)

$= \left(a^{\frac{1}{p_1p_2}}\right)^{q_1p_2} \cdot \left(a^{\frac{1}{p_1p_2}}\right)^{q_2p_1}$ (by 5, page 388) $= a^{\frac{q_1p_2}{p_1p_2}} \cdot a^{\frac{q_2p_1}{p_1p_2}}$ (by 9, page 389) $= a^{r_1} \cdot a^{r_2}$

b. Proof: $a^{r_1-r_2} = a^{\frac{q_1}{p_1}-\frac{q_2}{p_2}} = a^{\frac{q_1p_2-q_2p_1}{p_1p_2}} = \left(a^{\frac{1}{p_1p_2}}\right)^{q_1p_2-q_2p_1}$ (by 9, page 389) $= \frac{\left(a^{\frac{1}{p_1p_2}}\right)^{q_1p_2}}{\left(a^{\frac{1}{p_1p_2}}\right)^{q_2p_1}}$

(by 6, page 388) $= \frac{a^{\frac{q_1p_2}{p_1p_2}}}{a^{\frac{q_2p_1}{p_1p_2}}}$ (by 9, page 389) $= \frac{a^{r_1}}{a^{r_2}}$ c. Proof: $\left(a^p\right)^{\frac{1}{q}}$ is the unique positive number y having

$a^{\frac{1}{p}}$ as its qth power; i.e. $\left(a^p\right)^{\frac{1}{q}} = y$ iff $y^q = a^p$. Now $y^q = a^p$ iff $(y^q)^p = a$ or $y^{pq} = a$. Since $y^{pq} = a$ iff $a^{\frac{1}{pq}}$

$= y$, $a^{\frac{1}{pq}} = y$ and therefore $\left(a^p\right)^{\frac{1}{q}} = a^{\frac{1}{pq}}$.

PAGE 396 CLASSROOM EXERCISES
1. $2^3 \cdot 2^{0.8}$ 3. $5 \cdot 5^{0.632}$ 5. $2^{-2} \cdot 2^{0.49}$ 7. Answers will vary.

PAGES 396-398 WRITTEN EXERCISES

1. 1.2 3. 1.7 5. 0.7 7. 6.1 9. 0.75 11. 11.4 13. 1.3 15. 0.6 17. 14.0 19. 2.3 21. 0.7 23. −1.9
25. $2^{3.31}$ 27. $2^{4.2}$ 29. $2^{4.6}$ 31. $2^{-0.4}$ 33.

35.

PAGE 400 CLASSROOM EXERCISES 1. 7.389 3. 4.482

PAGES 400-401 WRITTEN EXERCISES

1. 2.718, seven terms. 3. 1.0101, three terms. 5. $\frac{1}{2!} - \frac{1}{3!} + \cdots + \frac{(-1)^n}{n!} + \cdots$ 7. 1.44 9. $1 + \frac{1}{13}$
$+ \frac{1}{13^2} + \cdots = \frac{1}{1 - \frac{1}{13}} = \frac{13}{12}$. Therefore, $\frac{1}{13!}(1 + \frac{1}{13} + \frac{1}{13^2} + \cdots) = \frac{1}{13!} \cdot \frac{13}{12} = \frac{1}{12}(\frac{1}{12!})$

$< .000000005$. 11. In Exercise 2, ten terms were needed. $\frac{1}{10!} + \frac{1}{11!} + \frac{1}{12!} + \cdots < \frac{1}{10!}\left(\frac{1}{1 - \frac{1}{10}}\right)$

$= \frac{1}{10!}(\frac{10}{9}) = \frac{1}{9(9!)} < 0.0000005$. Thus, the estimate is accurate to six decimal places.

PAGE 405 CLASSROOM EXERCISES

1. 4.5 3. 2.5353 5. 4.9530 7. 11.0232 9. 3.7434

PAGES 405-406 WRITTEN EXERCISES

1. 0.97 3. 1.1 5. −0.69 7. 0.37 9. 4.48 11. 0.37, 1.35, 4.48, 0.22 respectively. The results should be the same as in Exercises 7-10.

13. a, b.

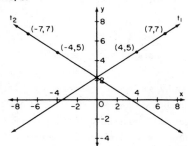

c. (−4, 5)

d. $-\dfrac{2}{3}$

e. (−r, s), −m

15.

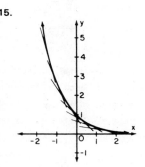

17. The result immediately follows from the observation in Exercise 13. e. that (x, y) is on a graph if and only if (−x, y) is on the mirror image of the graph with respect to the y axis.

PAGE 408 CLASSROOM EXERCISES

1. $6.14 3. $98.36

PAGE 408 WRITTEN EXERCISES

1. $1349.90 3. $1061.70 5. 17.325 years. 7. $\dfrac{69.3}{n}$ years. 9. 23.1%

PAGES 412-413 WRITTEN EXERCISES

1. $N = 2^t N_0$, where N_0 is the number of bacteria at time $t = 0$. 3. 47 days. 5. 303,750 7. $t = 1$
9. $N = (\dfrac{9}{8})^t N_0$ 11. 4.2 years.

PAGE 415 WRITTEN EXERCISES

1. $\dfrac{N(7.7)}{N(0)} = \dfrac{N_0 2^{\frac{-7.7}{385}}}{N_0} = 2^{-0.02} \approx e^{-.0139} \approx 0.986.$ $\dfrac{N(23.1)}{N(0)} \approx 0.96$ 3. a. 0.71 b. 0.13
c. 0.016 5. $x \approx 2000$ years.

PAGES 415-416 MID-CHAPTER REVIEW

1. $\dfrac{1}{16}$ 2. $\dfrac{1}{\sqrt{5}}$, or $\dfrac{\sqrt{5}}{5}$ 3. 1 4. $|\dfrac{x^3}{y}|$ 5. 1.52 6. 0.66 7. 1.32 8. 9.2 9. 19.41 10. 1.768 11. ≈ 0.9
12. $425.76 13. About 5.8 years 14. $\approx$ 11,920 15. 0.354

PAGES 419-420 WRITTEN EXERCISES

1. $f^{-1} : x \to \dfrac{x+2}{3}$ 3. $f^{-1} : x \to \dfrac{2}{x-1}$ 5. $x = \dfrac{y+2}{3}$ 7. $x = \dfrac{2}{y-1}$

9.

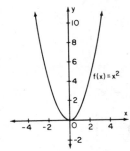

$f(x) = x^2$

a. Since $(-1, 1)$, $(1, 1)$ are elements of f, two x's correspond to $y = 1$. Therefore, there is no inverse for f. b. See the graph at the left. When $x \geq 0$ the graph to the right of the y axis, including the origin, is the graph of $f_1(x) = x^2$; $f_1^{-1}(x) : x \to \sqrt{x}$. When $x < 0$ the graph to the left of the y axis, excluding the origin, is the graph of $f_2(x) = x^2$; $f_2^{-1}(x) : x \to -\sqrt{x}$. c. domain (f) = domain (f_1) $\cup$ domain (f_2)

11. f is strictly decreasing iff for an two elements x_1 and x_2 in the domain of f, $x_1 < x_2$ implies $f(x_1) > f(x_2)$. 13. Proof: Since the slope of $\overline{PQ}$ is $\frac{t-u}{u-t} = -1$ and the slope of $y = x$ is 1, $\overline{PQ}$ is perpendicular to $y = x$. The equation of $\overline{PQ}$ is $y - u = -1(x - t)$. Solve this equation and $y = x$ simultaneously for x and y: $x = \frac{u+t}{2}$ and $y = \frac{u+t}{2}$. Since the midpoint of $\overline{PQ} = (\frac{t+u}{2}, \frac{t+u}{2})$, the line $y = x$ bisects $\overline{PQ}$. 15. The graph of f is a straight line through the point $(0, -4)$ with slope $\frac{2}{3}$. The graph of f^{-1} is a straight line through the point $(-4, 0)$ with slope $\frac{3}{2}$. 17. The slope of the inverse of a linear function is the reciprocal of the slope of the linear function. 19. $f^{-1}(x) = \sqrt{x}$. The slope of the tangent to f^{-1} at $x = 16$ is $\frac{1}{8}$. 21. Since f is a strictly increasing function, it has an inverse, f^{-1}, by Theorem 8-5, and for any x_1 and x_2 in the domain of f, $x_1 < x_2$ implies $f(x_1) < f(x_2)$. But $f^{-1}(f(x_1)) = x_1$ and $f^{-1}(f(x_2)) = x_2$. Thus, $f(x_1) < f(x_2)$ implies $f^{-1}(f(x_1)) < f^{-1}(f(x_2))$, and f^{-1} is a strictly increasing function.

PAGE 425   CLASSROOM EXERCISES

1. a. $x = 2^y$ or $y = \log_2 x$ b. $x = \log_2 y$ 3. $2^3 = 8$ 5. $(16)^{\frac{1}{4}} = 2$

PAGES 425-426   WRITTEN EXERCISES

1. 2.079 3. 2.890 5. 0.406 7. 1.609 9. −1.386 11. 0.511 13. −0.406 15. −1.386 17. 0.511 19. −0.406 21. Answers will vary. 23. $10^5 = x$ 25. $3^y = 25$ 27. $3^y = 25$ 29. Proof: $\log_a \frac{y_1}{y_2}$ $= \log_a (y_1 \cdot (y_2^{-1})) = \log_a (y_1) + \log_a (y_2^{-1}) = \log_a y_1 + (-1) \log_a y_2 = \log_a y_1 - \log_a y_2$ 31. $f : x \to a^x$, so $f(x) = a^x$ and $f(1) = a$. Then $f^{-1}(a) = 1$ or $\log_a a = 1$ 33. $\log_{125} 5 = \frac{1}{3}$ 35. $\log_{36} \frac{1}{6} = -\frac{1}{2}$

37. $\log_{16} 2 = \frac{1}{4}$ 39. −0.6990 41. 0.4080 43. Proof: Let $b = a^{\log_a b}$, $c = a^{\log_a c}$, $bc = a^{\log_a bc}$. Then, $a^{\log_a bc} = a^{\log_a b} \cdot a^{\log_a c}$ or $a^{\log_a bc} = a^{\log_a b + \log_a c}$. So, $\log_a bc = \log_a b + \log_a c$.

PAGES 430-431   WRITTEN EXERCISES

1. 1.0791 3. 0.7781 5. −0.8239 7. 1.6811 9. 2.1070 11. $\frac{3}{2}$ 13. −3 15. −3 17. $\frac{1}{3}$ 19. $\frac{5}{3}$ 21. $\frac{3}{2}$

23. 11 25. 1 27. e 29. $\frac{1}{e^2}$ 31. $\frac{e^2 + 1}{2e^2}$ 33. 1, 100 35. Proof: $\log_a b = x$ is equivalent to $a^x = b$, $\log_b a = y$ is equivalent to $b^y = a$, and $a^{xy} = (a^x)^y = b^y = a = a^1$. Therefore, $xy = 1$. Thus, $x = \frac{1}{y}$ or $\log_a b = \frac{1}{\log_b a}$. 37. Let $\log_a b = A$. Then $a^A = b$. Let $\log_b c = B$. Then $b^B = c$. Let $\log_c d = C$. Then $d = c^C$ $= (b^B)^C = ((a^A)^B)^C = a^{ABC}$. Therefore $\log_a d = ABC = (\log_a b)(\log_b c)(\log_c d)$. 39. −4 41. 2

824   *Answers to Selected Exercises*

1. $f'(x) = e^x$; $f'(\frac{1}{2}) = e^{\frac{1}{2}}$ 3. $f'(x) = \frac{1}{x\ln 2}$; $f'(4) = \frac{1}{4\ln 2}$ 5. $f'(x) = -\frac{1}{x\ln 2}$; $f'(2) = -\frac{1}{2\ln 2}$ 7. $f'(x) = \frac{1}{x\ln b}$;

$f'(\frac{1}{b}) = \frac{b}{\ln b}$ 9. $f'(x) = e^x + \frac{1}{x}$; $f'(x) = e + 1$ 11. (1.) $y - \sqrt{e} = \sqrt{e}\ (x - \frac{1}{2})$ (2.) $y = x - 1$ (3.) $y - 2$

$= \frac{1}{4\ln 2}\ (x - 4)$ (4.) $y - \log_{10} 2 = \frac{1}{2\ln 10}\ (x - 2)$ (5.) $y + 1 = -\frac{1}{2\ln 2}\ (x - 2)$ 13. $f'(x) = \frac{1}{x}\log_{\frac{1}{b}} e$

$= \frac{1}{x}(-1)\log_b e = \frac{-\log_b e}{x}$ 15. $f'(x) = \lim_{h \to 0} (\frac{\ln(a(x+h)) - \ln ax}{h}) = \lim_{h \to 0} (\frac{\ln a + \ln(x+h) - \ln a - \ln x}{h})$

$= \lim_{h \to 0} (\frac{\ln(x+h) - \ln x}{h}) = \frac{1}{x}$ (see p. 433.) 17. let $f(x) = \log_a x$ and $g(y) = a^y$ since $f'(x) = \frac{\log_a e}{x}$, $g'(y) =$

$\frac{x}{\log_a e} = \frac{a^y}{\log_a e} = \frac{a^y}{\frac{\ln e}{\ln a}} = (\ln a)a^y$

1. 19,058 3. 5099 5. 1649 7. No, because of the change in workers and machinary. 9. 171,056 hr; 193,293 by formula. The approximation is better for larger numbers.

1. $x^{\frac{1}{12}}$ 3. $y^{\frac{1}{3}}x^{\frac{1}{2}}$ 5. -32 7. $\frac{3}{5}$ 9. $\frac{5}{6}$ 11. $\frac{2}{3}$ 13. 1.2 15. -1 17. 2.7183 19. Domain: R; Range: $\langle 0, \infty \rangle$; Zeros:

none; y intercept: $e^0 = 1$; Concavity: upward; Asymptote: $y = 0$; See page 403 for a sketch of $y = e^x$.

21. 9.98 23. 0.7 25. 16,971 27. 0.84 29. $f^{-1} : x \to \pm\sqrt{2 - x}$; It is not a function. 31. $\log_3 27 = 3$

33. $\log_8 4 = \frac{2}{3}$ 35. 1.2552 37. $\frac{1}{3}$

1. $\frac{1}{32}$ 2. $x^{-\frac{2}{5}}$ 3. 6 4. 1.35 5. 1.22 6. e 7. $\log_8 4 = \frac{2}{3}$ 8. $2^{-2} = \frac{1}{4}$ 9. $\frac{1}{\log_{10} 5}$ 10. $\log_{10} 5 = \frac{\ln 5}{\ln 10}$

$\approx \frac{\ln 5}{2.303}$ 11. \$182.21 12. Answers will vary. 13. $f(x) = a^x$ and $g(x) = \log_a x$ are inverses since

$a^{(\log_a x)} = \log_a(a^x) = x$. See page 421 for sketch. 14. a. $\frac{1}{x}$ b. e^x 15. As $x \to +\infty$, the slope goes to 0. As $x \to 0$

the slope goes to $+\infty$.

1. c 3. a 5. c 7. d 9. a 11. a 13. d 15. a 17. c 19. c

CHAPTER 9 VECTORS, LINES, AND PLANES

1. First connect the foot of vector A and point C; then construct a parallelogram on it. The side parallel to vector A is the required vector. 3. Approximately $33°$. 5. Construct a parallelogram. The foot of vectors A and B is the foot of $\vec{A} + \vec{B}$ and the fourth vertex is the tip of $\vec{A} + \vec{B}$. The tip of vector B is the foot of $\vec{A} - \vec{B}$, and the tip of vector A is the tip of $\vec{A} - \vec{B}$. 7. Draw a vector equal to vector A that has its foot at the foot of vector B. Call it vector A also. Then construct a parallelogram. The foot of vector A is the foot of $\vec{A} + \vec{B}$ and the tip of vector B is the tip of $\vec{A} + \vec{B}$. The fourth vertex is the foot of $\vec{A} - \vec{B}$; the tip of vector A is the tip of

$\vec{A} - \vec{B}$. **9.** $\vec{A} + \vec{B} = 2\vec{A}$, $\vec{A} - \vec{B} = \vec{0}$. **11.-17.** Answers will vary. **19.** The zero vector is the limiting case of the diagonal of the parallelogram whose adjacent sides are vectors $\vec{A}$ and $-\vec{A}$.

21.

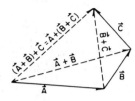

23.

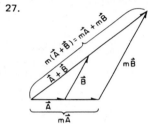

25. The length of $(n\vec{A})$ is $|n||\vec{A}|$ and the length of $m(n\vec{A})$ is $|m|(|n||\vec{A}|) = (|m||n|)(|\vec{A}|) = |(m \cdot n)\vec{A}|$. Therefore, $|m(n\vec{A})| = |(m \cdot n)\vec{A}|$. The direction of $m(n\vec{A})$ is the same as vector A when m and n have the same sign and opposite to that of vector A when m and n are opposite in sign. The same is true for $(m \cdot n)\vec{A}$. **27.** (See figure below) **a.** In the triangles $|\vec{A}|$ and $|\vec{B}|$ are proportional to $|m\vec{A}|$ and $|m\vec{B}|$. The included angles are congruent because a scalar multiple of a vector is parallel to the original vector. Thus, the triangles are similar. It follows that corresponding angles are congruent and $m\vec{A} + m\vec{B}$ has the same direction as $\vec{A} + \vec{B}$ and as $m(\vec{A} + \vec{B})$. **b.** Since corresponding sides are proportional $|m\vec{A} + m\vec{B}| = m|\vec{A} + \vec{B}|$.

27.

PAGE 454 CLASSROOM EXERCISES

1. See page 451. **3.** A linear combination of vectors is the vector sum of 2 or more nonzero vectors with no two parallel to each other. i.e. $\vec{D} = \ell\vec{A} + m\vec{B} + n\vec{C}$

PAGES 454-455 WRITTEN EXERCISES

1. $m \approx \frac{1}{2}$, $n \approx 2$ **3.** $m \approx -\frac{1}{2}$, $n \approx 2$ **5.-11.** Drawings are omitted. **13.** Complete the parallelogram having $m\vec{A}$, $n\vec{B}$ as two adjacent sides and vector $\vec{C}$ as the diagonal. $|\vec{C}| = 1$, $|m\vec{A}| = 1$, $|n\vec{B}| = \sqrt{2}$. $|\vec{A}| = 2$, $|\vec{B}| = 2$

Thus, $m = \frac{1}{2}$, $n = \frac{\sqrt{2}}{2}$. **15.** Complete a parallelogram as in Exercise 13. $\dfrac{\sin 45°}{\sin 60°} = \dfrac{|n||\vec{B}|}{|\vec{C}|}$ Thus, $|n| =$

$\dfrac{|\vec{C}| \sin 45°}{|\vec{B}| \sin 60°} = \dfrac{4 \cdot \frac{\sqrt{2}}{2}}{3 \cdot \frac{\sqrt{3}}{2}} = \dfrac{4\sqrt{2}}{3\sqrt{3}}$. Thus, $n = -\dfrac{4\sqrt{2}}{3\sqrt{3}}$ because $n\vec{B}$ is in the direction opposite to $\vec{B}$.

$\dfrac{\sin 75°}{\sin 60°} = \dfrac{|m||\vec{A}|}{|\vec{C}|} \Rightarrow |m| = \dfrac{\sin 75°}{\sin 60°} \cdot \dfrac{|\vec{C}|}{|\vec{A}|} = \dfrac{0.9659}{\frac{\sqrt{3}}{2}} \cdot \dfrac{4}{2} = \dfrac{3.8636}{\sqrt{3}}$ Therefore, $m = -\dfrac{3.8636}{\sqrt{3}}$.

PAGE 460 CLASSROOM EXERCISES

1. $\gamma = 90°$ **3.** $\cos \alpha = \dfrac{\ell}{k}$, $\cos \beta = \dfrac{m}{k}$, $\cos \gamma = \dfrac{n}{k}$ where $k^2 = \ell^2 + m^2 + n^2$

826   *Answers to Selected Exercises*

PAGE 461 WRITTEN EXERCISES

1. $|\vec{r}| = \sqrt{13}, \theta \approx 56° 20'$ 3. $|\vec{r}| = \sqrt{13}, \theta \approx 236° 20'$ 5. $|\vec{r}| = \sqrt{7}, \theta \approx 319° 10'$ 7. $r = 2, \theta = 150°$
9. $r = 1, \theta = 180°$ 11. $r = 5, \theta = 270°$ 13. No sketches given. 15. $|\vec{PQ}| = \sqrt{m^2 + n^2} = $
$\sqrt{(x_2 - x_1)^2 + (y_2 - y_1)^2}$ 17. 13 19. $2\sqrt{2}$ 21. 6 23. $5\sqrt{2}a$ 25. $\cos^2\alpha + \cos^2\beta + \cos^2\gamma = 1, \frac{3}{4} + \frac{1}{4} + $
$\cos^2\gamma = 0, \gamma = 90°$ 27. $|\vec{A}| = 13$ Thus, $\frac{1}{13}\vec{A} = \frac{12}{13}i - \frac{4}{13}j + \frac{3}{13}k$ is a unit vector in same direction.

PAGE 463 EXERCISES

1.

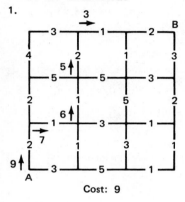

Cost: 9

3.

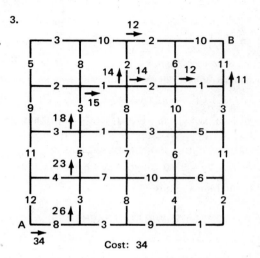

Cost: 34

PAGE 466 CLASSROOM EXERCISES

1. 0 3. $(-1, -\frac{1}{2}, 2)$ 5. $(-\frac{5}{2}, -\frac{3}{2}, -\frac{1}{2})$ 7. $(\frac{a+c}{2}, \frac{b}{2})$

PAGE 467 WRITTEN EXERCISES

1. If $P = (x_1, y_1)$ and $Q = (x_2, y_2)$ then the midpoint of $\vec{PQ}$ is $M = \left(\frac{x_1 + x_2}{2}, \frac{y_1 + y_2}{2}\right)$. Proof: $P = (x_1, y_1, 0)$
and $Q = (x_2, y_2, 0)$. By Theorem 9-4 the midpoint of $\vec{PQ}$ is $\left(\frac{x_1 + x_2}{2}, \frac{y_1 + y_2}{2}, \frac{0 + 0}{2}\right) = \left(\frac{x_1 + x_2}{2}, \frac{y_1 + y_2}{2}\right)$
in the xy plane. 3. $(2, 2, 2)$ 5. $(\frac{3}{2}, \frac{1}{2}, 0)$ 7. $\left(-\frac{1}{2}, -\frac{7}{2}, -\frac{1}{2}\right)$ 9. $(\frac{2a + 1}{2}, b + 1, \frac{2c + 3}{2})$ 11. $(0, 0, 0)$

13. No. The same point would result. 15. $M = \left(\frac{x_2 + 2x_1}{3}, \frac{y_2 + 2y_1}{3}, \frac{z_2 + 2z_1}{3}\right) = (\frac{10}{3}, \frac{7}{3}, \frac{20}{3})$

17. $M = \left(\frac{5x_2 + x_1}{6}, \frac{5y_2 + y_1}{6}, \frac{5z_2 + z_1}{6}\right) = (\frac{7}{3}, -\frac{5}{3}, \frac{14}{3})$ 19. $M = \left(\frac{x_2 + 5x_1}{6}, \frac{y_2 + 5y_1}{6}, \frac{z_2 + 5z_1}{6}\right)$

$= (\frac{11}{3}, \frac{11}{3}, \frac{22}{3})$ 21. $M = (-4, -27, -8)$ 23. $M = (5, 9, 10)$ 25. $x = \frac{px_2 + (q - p)x_1}{q}, y = \frac{py_2 + (q - p)y_1}{q},$
$z = \frac{pz_2 + (q - p)z_1}{q}$

PAGES 471-472 CLASSROOM EXERCISES

1. $x = 1 - 2t, y = 2 - 6t, z = -3 + 10t$ 3. $x = 2 - 5t, y = -1 + 2t, z = 4 + t$ 5. $x = t, y = 2 + t, z = 5 - t$
7. $\ell = -3, m = 7, n = -1$ 9. $\ell = +2, m = +6, n = 10$

1. It is most convenient to use $\vec{r} = \vec{r_0} + t\overrightarrow{AB}$. $xi + yj + zk = -2i + j + 3k + t(3i - 1j - 6k)$ Thus, $x = -2 + 3t$, $y = 1 - t$, $z = 3 - 6t$ and $\frac{x+2}{3} = \frac{y-1}{-1} = \frac{z-3}{-6}$. 3. $xi + yj + zk = 0i + 0j + 0k + t(i + 2j + 3k)$ Thus, $x = 0 + t$, $y = 0 + 2t$, $z = 0 + 3t$ and $\frac{x-0}{1} = \frac{y-0}{2} = \frac{z-0}{3}$. 5. $xi + yj + zk = i + 2j + 5k + t(i - j + 0k)$ Thus, $x = 1 + t$, $y = 2 - t$, $z = 5$ and $\frac{x-1}{1} = \frac{y-2}{-1}$, $z = 5$. 7. $xi + yj + zk = 1i + 2j + 0k + t(2i + j + 0k)$ Thus, $x = 1 + 2t$, $y = 2 + t$, $z = 0$ and $\frac{x-1}{2} = \frac{y-2}{1}$, $z = 0$. 9. $xi + yj = 2i - 3j + t(-6i + 8j)$ Thus, $x = 2 - 6t$, $y = -3 + 8t$ and $\frac{x-2}{-6} = \frac{y+3}{8}$. 11. $xi + yj = 5i - 3j + t(0i + j)$ Thus, $x = 5$, $y = -3 + t$ 13. 0 15. 0 17. $x = 0$, $y = b + tm$, $z = c + tn$ 19. $x = \frac{1}{2} + \frac{1}{2}t$, $y = -2 + \frac{1}{4}t$, $z = \frac{5}{3} + \frac{1}{3}t$ 21. a. $xi + yj + zk = 2i + j + 5k + t(1i + 3j + 2k)$ Thus, $x = 2 + t$, $y = 1 + 3t$, $z = 5 + 2t$. b. $x = 1 + t$, $y = -2 + 3t$, $z = 3 + 2t$ c. $x = 1 - t$, $y = -2 - 3t$, $z = 3 - 2t$ 23. Infinite number. In fact, for each fixed point there are uncountably many parametric equations. 25. $xi + yj = 0i + cj + t(\frac{a}{2}i + (\frac{b}{2} - c)j)$ Thus, $x = 0 + \frac{a}{2}t$, $y = c + (\frac{b}{2} - c)t$; $xi + yj = ai + 0j + t(-ai + \frac{b+c}{2}j)$, $x = a - at$, $y = 0 + (\frac{b+c}{2})t$; $xi + yj = 0i + bj + t(\frac{a}{2}i + (\frac{c}{2} - b)j)$ Thus, $x = 0 + \frac{a}{2}t$, $y = b + (\frac{c}{2} - b)t$

1. $3x - 2y - 8 = 0$ 3. $-4x + 5y + 8 = 0$ 5. x intercept is 2; y intercept is $\frac{8}{3}$. 7. $\lambda = 3$; x intercept is $\frac{3}{2}$, y intercept is $\frac{-9}{2}$; $\vec{A} = i + 3j$

1. $y + 3 = \frac{1}{5}(x - 2)$ 3. $x = -2$ 5. $y = -3$ 7. $y - 1 = -\frac{2}{3}(x - 1)$ 9. $y - 1 = \frac{5}{8}(x - 7)$ 11. $y - 1 = -3(x + 5)$ 13. $y = \frac{2}{7}x$ 15. $\vec{A} = i + 3j$ 17. $\vec{A} = i + j$ 19. $\vec{A} = i - 2j$ 21. $\vec{A} = i + \frac{4}{3}j$ 23. $\vec{A} = 5i + 3j$ 25. No sketches given. 27. $\overrightarrow{P_1P_2} \parallel \overrightarrow{P_3P_4}$ iff $\overrightarrow{P_1P_2} = t\overrightarrow{P_3P_4}$ iff $(x_2 - x_1)i + (y_2 - y_1)j = t[(x_4 - x_3)i + (y_4 - y_3)j]$ iff $(x_2 - x_1) = t(x_4 - x_3)$ and $(y_2 - y_1) = t(y_4 - y_3)$. 29. The hint is sufficient. 31. $\lambda = \frac{-2}{2}$ Thus, $y - 84 = -1(x - 17)$. 33. $\lambda = \frac{-1}{-4}$ Thus, $y + 2 = \frac{1}{4}(x - 3)$. 35. a. $Ax + By + C = 0 \Rightarrow \frac{A}{-C}x + \frac{B}{-C}y = 1 \Rightarrow \frac{x}{\frac{-C}{A}} + \frac{y}{\frac{-C}{B}} = 1$; A, B, C $\neq$ 0

b. a is the x intercept: (a, 0); b is the y intercept: (0, b). 37. a. $\lambda = -\frac{A}{B}$ b. $\vec{A} = i - \frac{A}{B}j$ c. $\vec{D} = Bi - Aj$ and multiples (many other answers also). d. $(y - 3) = \frac{-A}{B}(x - 2)$ or $Ax + By - 3B - 2A = 0$. e. Parallel when $-3B - 2A \neq 5$; Same line when $-3B - 2A = 5$ f. The coefficients of x and y are identical. g. Equations of parallel lines in the plane either have the same pair of coefficients or one pair of coefficients is a nonzero multiple of the other pair.

1.   2.   3.   4.

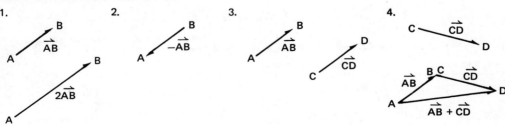

5. $m = \frac{5}{2}$ 6. $n = -\frac{3}{5}$ 7. $m = -\frac{1}{2}$ 8. $n = -\frac{1}{10}$ 9. $\vec{C} = \frac{5\sqrt{2}}{2}\vec{A} + \frac{2.588\sqrt{2}}{3}\vec{B}$ 10. $r = \sqrt{13}$, $\theta \approx 146° \ 20'$
11. $r = \sqrt{13}$, $\theta \approx -33° \ 40'$ 12. $r = \sqrt{13}$, $\theta \approx 213° \ 40'$ 13. $\sqrt{29}$ 14. 7 15. $(\frac{7}{3}, \frac{11}{3})$, $(\frac{11}{3}, \frac{16}{3})$ 16. $x = 1 + 2t$,
$y = 2 + 3t$, $z = 1 + t$; $\frac{x-1}{2} = \frac{y-2}{3} = z - 1$
17. $x = -1 + 4t$, $y = 2t$, $z = 4 - 3t$; $\frac{x+1}{4} = \frac{y}{2} = \frac{z-4}{-3}$ 18. $x = 3 + t$, $y = 6 + t$; $x - 3 = y - 6$ 19. $x = 6 - 7t$,
$y = 2 + t$; $\frac{x-6}{-7} = \frac{y-2}{1}$ 20. $(y + 3) = -\frac{3}{2}(x - 2)$ 21. $\vec{A} = i + 2j$ 22. $\vec{A} = i - 3j$ 23. $\vec{A} = i + j$ 24. $\vec{A} = i - 4j$
25. $\vec{A} = i - 2j$ 26. $\vec{A} = i + \frac{4}{5}j$

PAGES 485-487   WRITTEN EXERCISES

1. $\cos \theta = \frac{1}{\sqrt{2}}$ 3. $\cos \theta = \frac{\sqrt{6}}{3}$ 5. $\cos \theta = 0$ 7. $\cos \theta = \frac{29}{\sqrt{62} \cdot \sqrt{34}}$ 9. $\cos \theta = \frac{-19}{5\sqrt{2} \cdot \sqrt{13}}$

11. $\cos \theta = \frac{-1}{\sqrt{6} \cdot \sqrt{13}}$ 13. $\vec{r} = 2i + 0j + 6k$, $\vec{v} = 4i - 2j - 2k$, $\cos \theta = -\frac{1}{2\sqrt{15}}$

15. $\left.\begin{array}{l}\vec{C} = -3i + 2j \\ \vec{D} = 5i + 3k\end{array}\right\}$ Ex. 7 $\left.\begin{array}{l}\vec{C} = 3j + 2k \\ \vec{D} = 2i - k\end{array}\right\}$ Ex. 8 $\left.\begin{array}{l}\vec{C} = -i + 7j \\ \vec{D} = 2i + 3j\end{array}\right\}$ Ex. 9. There are many other correct answers.

17. $\theta \approx 50°$ 19. $\theta \approx 82°$ 21. $\theta \approx 35°$ 23. (17.) $\frac{-5}{\sqrt{29}}i + \frac{2}{\sqrt{29}}j$, $\frac{i}{\sqrt{10}} - \frac{3}{\sqrt{10}}j$ (18.) $\frac{i}{\sqrt{2}}$

$- \frac{k}{\sqrt{2}}$ and $\frac{i}{\sqrt{10}} - \frac{3}{\sqrt{10}}k$ (19.) $\frac{3}{\sqrt{10}}i + \frac{j}{\sqrt{10}}$ and $\frac{-i}{\sqrt{5}} + \frac{2j}{\sqrt{5}}$ (20.) $\frac{3}{\sqrt{10}}i - \frac{j}{\sqrt{10}}$ and $\frac{2i}{\sqrt{5}}$

$- \frac{j}{\sqrt{5}}$ (21.) $\frac{i}{\sqrt{5}} - \frac{2}{\sqrt{5}}j$ and $\frac{i}{\sqrt{26}} + \frac{5}{\sqrt{26}}j$ (22.) $i - 0j$ and $\frac{2}{\sqrt{5}}i - \frac{j}{\sqrt{5}}$

25. a. $\frac{1 + \lambda_1 \cdot \lambda_2}{\sqrt{1 + \lambda_1{}^2} \cdot \sqrt{1 + \lambda_2{}^2}} = 0 \Rightarrow \lambda_1 \cdot \lambda_2 = -1$ or $\lambda_1 = \frac{-1}{\lambda_2}$ b. If $\lambda_1 \cdot \lambda_2 = -1$ then the lines $\frac{x-a}{1}$

$= \frac{y-b}{\lambda_1}$ and $\frac{x-c}{1} = \frac{y-d}{\lambda_2}$ are perpendicular. Proof: The direction vectors are $\vec{A} = i + \lambda_1 j$ and $\vec{B} = i + \lambda_2 j$.

The lines are perpendicular iff the direction vectors are. But $\vec{A} \cdot \vec{B} = \frac{1 + \lambda_1 \lambda_2}{\sqrt{1 + \lambda_1^2} \cdot \sqrt{1 + \lambda_2^2}} = \frac{1 - 1}{|\vec{A}| \cdot |\vec{B}|} = 0$

Thus the lines are perpendicular. 27. The direction vector for the given line is $\vec{A} = 2i + j + 5k$. Thus a normal
vector is $\vec{N} = 2i + j - k$. A line perpendicular to the given line contains $(1, -3, 1)$ and has direction numbers
$(2, 1, -1)$. The standard equations are: $\frac{x-1}{2} = \frac{y+3}{1} = \frac{z-1}{-1}$

PAGES 490-491   CLASSROOM EXERCISES

1. Perpendicular 3. Perpendicular 5. $\frac{30}{13}$ 7. $5\sqrt{2}$ 9. 0 11. When $m_1 m_2 = -1$ the two lines are perpendicular
where m_1 and m_2 are the nonzero slopes of the two lines

PAGES 491-492   WRITTEN EXERCISES

1. $2x - 3y - 5 = 0$, $3x + 2y - 14 = 0$ 3. $2x - y - 5 = 0$, $x + 2y = 0$ 5. $x - y = 0$, $x + y = 0$ 7. $3x + 3y - 18$
$= 0$, $3x - 3y - 18 = 0$ 9. $y = 9$, $x = 7$ 11. $9y + x - 63 = 0$, $y - 9x - 7 = 0$ 13. (1.) $d = \frac{10}{\sqrt{13}}$;

(2.) $d = \dfrac{6}{\sqrt{5}}$; (3.) $d = \dfrac{5}{\sqrt{5}}$ (4.) $d. = \dfrac{45}{\sqrt{74}}$; (5.) $d = \dfrac{3}{\sqrt{2}}$; (6.) $d = \dfrac{19}{\sqrt{65}}$; (7.) $d = \dfrac{17}{3\sqrt{2}}$;

(8.) $d = 2$; (9.) $d = 12$; (10.) $d = 0$; (11.) $d = \dfrac{66}{\sqrt{82}}$; (12.) $d = \dfrac{19}{\sqrt{13}}$ 15. $\dfrac{7}{\sqrt{13}}$ 17. 4 19. 0

21. $\dfrac{|b|}{\sqrt{m^2 + 1}}$ 23. Median from C: $y - 1 = -\dfrac{5}{2}(x - 5)$. Median from A: $y - 4 = \dfrac{4}{5}(x - 6)$. Median from B:

$y - 3 = -\dfrac{1}{7}(x - 2)$. 25. Bisector of $\overline{AB}$: $(y - 1) = -4(x - 5)$. Bisector of $\overline{AC}$: $(y - 3) = -\dfrac{1}{3}(x - 2)$. Bisector

of $\overline{BC}$: $(y - 4) = \dfrac{3}{2}(x - 6)$. 27. Points $(\dfrac{13}{3}, \dfrac{8}{3})$, $(\dfrac{39}{11}, \dfrac{42}{11})$, and $(\dfrac{52}{11}, \dfrac{23}{11})$ are collinear if a line determined by

two of the points contains the third point. Slope is: $\dfrac{\frac{19}{11}}{\frac{-13}{11}} = \dfrac{-19}{13}$ $(y - \dfrac{42}{11}) = \dfrac{-19}{13}(x - \dfrac{39}{11})$. Try $(\dfrac{13}{3}, \dfrac{8}{3})$ in the

equation: $\dfrac{88}{33} - \dfrac{126}{33} \overset{?}{=} - \dfrac{19}{13}(\dfrac{143}{33} - \dfrac{117}{33})$, $-\dfrac{38}{33} \overset{?}{=} -\dfrac{19}{13}(\dfrac{26}{33}) = -\dfrac{38}{33}$. Thus the 3 points are collinear. (The

line containing these points is the Euler Line.) 29. a. $3i + 2j = \vec{N}$ b. The coefficients are the same as those of

x and y. c. $3(2) + (2)(-5) + 4 = 6 - 10 + 4 = 0$. d. $\vec{PQ} = (x - 2)i + (y + 5)j$. e. Zero. f. $\vec{N} \cdot \vec{PQ} = 3(x - 2) +$

$2(y + 5) = 0$, $3x - 6 + 2y + 10 = 0$, $3x + 2y + 4 = 0$. 31. $\vec{N} \cdot \vec{PQ}$ is the equation of the line with normal $\vec{N}$

and direction vector $\vec{PQ}$.

PAGES 496-497 WRITTEN EXERCISES

1. $\vec{A} \times \vec{B} = -5i - 6j - 7k$ 3. $\vec{A} \times \vec{B} = 2i + 0j - 2k$ 5. $\vec{A} \times \vec{B} = 3i - 18j - 13k$ 7. $\vec{A} \times \vec{B} = 3i + 0j + k$ 9. $\vec{A} \times \vec{B} =$

$-2i + 3j + 0k$ 11. $i \times i = 0$ 13. $i \times k = -j$ 15. $j \times j = 0$ 17. $k \times i = j$ 19. $k \times k = 0$ 21. $\vec{A} \times \vec{B} = -8i + j - 4k$.

Thus, the area of the parallelogram $= |\vec{A} \times \vec{B}| = 9$. 23. (21.) $\sin \theta \approx .7475$, $\theta \approx 48°$ (22.) $\sin \theta \approx 0.8442$,

$\theta \approx 58°$ 25. $\vec{A} = a_1 i + a_2 j + a_3 k$, $\vec{B} = b_1 i + b_2 j + b_3 k$, $\vec{C} = c_1 i + c_2 j + c_3 k$, $\vec{B} + \vec{C}$

$= (b_1 + c_1)i + (b_2 + c_2)j + (b_3 + c_3)k$, $\vec{A} \times (\vec{B} + \vec{C}) = \begin{vmatrix} a_2 & a_3 \\ b_2 + c_2 & b_3 + c_3 \end{vmatrix} i + \begin{vmatrix} a_3 & a_1 \\ b_3 + c_3 & b_1 + c_1 \end{vmatrix} j$

$+ \begin{vmatrix} a_1 & a_2 \\ b_1 + c_1 & b_2 + c_2 \end{vmatrix} k = [a_2(b_3 + c_3) - a_3(b_2 + c_2)]i + [a_3(b_1 + c_1) - a_1(b_3 + c_3)]j$

$+ [a_1(b_2 + c_2) - a_2(b_1 + c_1)]k = [(a_2 b_3 - a_3 b_2) + (a_2 c_3 - a_3 c_2)]i + [(a_3 b_1 - a_1 b_3) + (a_3 c_1 - a_1 c_3)]j$

$+ [(a_1 b_2 - a_2 b_1) + (a_1 c_2 - a_2 c_1)]k = [(a_2 b_3 - a_3 b_2)i + (a_3 b_1 - a_1 b_3)j + (a_1 b_2 - a_2 b_1)k]$

$+ [(a_2 c_3 - a_3 c_2)i + (a_3 c_1 - a_1 c_3)j + (a_1 c_2 - a_2 c_1)k]$

$= \begin{vmatrix} a_2 & a_3 \\ b_2 & b_3 \end{vmatrix} i + \begin{vmatrix} a_3 & a_1 \\ b_3 & b_1 \end{vmatrix} j + \begin{vmatrix} a_1 & a_2 \\ b_1 & b_2 \end{vmatrix} k + \begin{vmatrix} a_2 & a_3 \\ c_2 & c_3 \end{vmatrix} i + \begin{vmatrix} a_3 & a_1 \\ c_3 & c_1 \end{vmatrix} j + \begin{vmatrix} a_1 & a_2 \\ c_1 & c_2 \end{vmatrix} k = \vec{A} \times \vec{B} + \vec{A} \times \vec{C}$

27. $\vec{A} \times \vec{B}$ is perpendicular to $\vec{A}$ and to $\vec{B}$. Therefore $\vec{A} \cdot (\vec{A} \times \vec{B})$ is the dot product of two perpendicular

vectors and $= 0$. 29. Expand $(\vec{A} \times \vec{B}) \times \vec{C}$ and $(\vec{A} \cdot \vec{C})\vec{B} - (\vec{B} \cdot \vec{C})\vec{A}$ and show them to be equal. 31. Area of

triangle $= \dfrac{1}{2}$ Area of Parallelogram. Therefore, area of triangle $= \dfrac{1}{2}|\vec{A} \times \vec{B}| = \dfrac{\sqrt{1667}}{2}$ 33. Do b. first.

b. $\vec{A} \times (\vec{B} \times \vec{C}) = -(\vec{B} \times \vec{C}) \times \vec{A}$ (Theorem 9-12) $= -[(\vec{B} \cdot \vec{A})\vec{C} - (\vec{C} \cdot \vec{A})\vec{B}]$ (By Exercise 29.) $= (\vec{C} \cdot \vec{A})\vec{B} -$

$(\vec{B} \cdot \vec{A})\vec{C}$ a. $(\vec{A} \times \vec{B}) \times \vec{C} = (\vec{A} \cdot \vec{C})\vec{B} - (\vec{B} \cdot \vec{C})\vec{A}$ and $\vec{A} \times (\vec{B} \times \vec{C}) = (\vec{C} \cdot \vec{A})\vec{B} - (\vec{B} \cdot \vec{A})\vec{C}$. Thus,

they are not equal. 35. From p. 493 and Ex. 34b, $\vec{A} \times \vec{B} = i\begin{vmatrix} a_2 & a_3 \\ b_2 & b_3 \end{vmatrix} - j\begin{vmatrix} a_1 & a_3 \\ b_1 & b_3 \end{vmatrix} + k\begin{vmatrix} a_1 & a_2 \\ b_1 & b_2 \end{vmatrix}$ The result follows.

PAGE 501 CLASSROOM EXERCISES

1. $\vec{N} = 3i + 2j - 3k$ 3. $-x + \frac{2}{3}y - z - 3 = 0$

PAGE 501 WRITTEN EXERCISES

1. $3x + 2y - 5z + D = 0$ so $(3 \cdot 1) + (2 \cdot 1) - 5(2) + D = 0$ and $5 - 10 + d = 0 \Rightarrow D = 5$ Thus, $3x + 2y - 5z + 5$

$= 0$ is the equation of the plane. 3. $4x - y - z + 5 = 0$ 5. $\frac{1}{2}x - \frac{2}{3}y + \frac{3}{4}z + 2 = 0$ 7. $-2x + 3y - 4z + 3 = 0$

9. $\vec{A} \times \vec{B} = (i - 3j + 2k) \times (i + j - 4k) = \begin{vmatrix} -3 & 2 \\ 1 & -4 \end{vmatrix} i + \begin{vmatrix} 2 & 1 \\ -4 & 1 \end{vmatrix} j + \begin{vmatrix} 1 & -3 \\ 1 & 1 \end{vmatrix} k = 10i + 6j + 4k$ Thus, $10x + 6y$

$+ 4z + D = 0$. But $(1, 4, 3)$ is in plane; so $10 + 24 + 12 + D = 0 \Rightarrow D = -46$. Therefore, $10x + 6y + 4z - 46 = 0$.

11. $-2x + 12y + 8z - 28 = 0$ 13. The normal to the plane with equation $5x - 2y + 7z + 1 = 0$ is also the normal

of the given plane. Thus, $\vec{N} = 2i + 5j + 0k$ is the normal to one of the countless planes satisfying the conditions.

Its equation is $2x + 5y - 5 = 0$. 15. $2x + y + z = 0$ is one such plane. 17. $\vec{N} = -6i + 6j + 0k$, M$(-2, 4, 2)$,

$-6x + 6y - 36 = 0$ 19. $z = 0, y = 0, x = 0$ 21. $\cos \theta = \dfrac{-2 + 6 + 5}{\sqrt{14} \cdot \sqrt{30}} \approx 0.4392; \theta \approx 64°$

PAGES 507-508 WRITTEN EXERCISES

1. $\vec{N}_1 \times \vec{N}_2 = -i + 6j + 5k$. For $z = 0 \begin{array}{c} 2x - 3y + 1 = 0 \\ 2x + 2y - 4 = 0 \\ -5y + 5 = 0 \end{array}$. So $y = 1$ and $x = 1$. Therefore, $x - 1 = -t, y - 1 = 6t$,

$z - 0 = 5t$. 3. $x - 1 = -9t, y - 0 = 3t, z - 1 = -12t$ 5. $x - 0 = 3t, y - 3 = -9t, z - 2 = -6t$ 7. $\vec{N}_1 \times \vec{N}_2$

$= 0i + 0j + 0k$. No line; the planes are the same. 9. $x - 0 = -3t, y - 1 = -4t, z - 1 = 0$ 11. $\dfrac{|2 - 1 + 6 + 3|}{\sqrt{4 + 1 + 4}}$

$= \dfrac{10}{3}$ 13. $d = \dfrac{9}{2\sqrt{6}}$ 15. $d = \dfrac{10}{\sqrt{11}}$ 17. $d = \dfrac{|D|}{\sqrt{A^2 + B^2 + C^2}}$ 19. a. By def. of $\sin \theta$, $\sin \theta = \dfrac{d}{|\vec{RP}|}$

Thus, $d = |\vec{RP}| \sin \theta$. b. $|\vec{RP} \times \vec{K}| = |\vec{RP}| \cdot |\vec{K}| \cdot \sin \theta$ c. $d = |\vec{RP}| \cdot \sin \theta$ But $\sin \theta = \dfrac{|\vec{RP} \times \vec{K}|}{|\vec{RP}| \cdot |\vec{K}|}$.

Thus, $d = |\vec{RP}| \cdot \dfrac{|\vec{RP} \times \vec{K}|}{|\vec{RP}| \cdot |\vec{K}|} = \dfrac{|\vec{RP} \times \vec{K}|}{|\vec{K}|}$.

PAGES 509-513 CHAPTER OBJECTIVES AND REVIEW

1. A vector has length (or magnitude) and direction. 3. Equal 5. Not equal, the vectors have different directions.

7. All vectors are shown in reduced size.

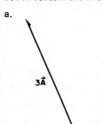

a. $3\vec{A}$

b. $-2\vec{B}$

c. $\vec{B}$ $\vec{A}$ $\vec{A} + \vec{B}$

d. $2\vec{B} + \vec{A}$ $2\vec{B}$ $\vec{A}$

e.

f.

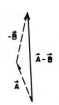

g.

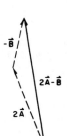

h.

i.

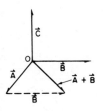

j.

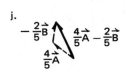

9. See top of page 448 and substitute $\vec{A} + (-\vec{B})$ for $\vec{V}_1 + (-\vec{V}_2)$. 11. Complete the parallelogram with vector C as diagonal. Then m = 2, n = $\frac{4}{5}$.

The vectors in Exercises 13, 15, and 17 are shown in reduced size.

13.

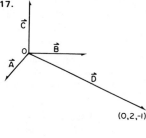

15.

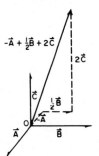

17.

(0, 2, -1)

19. $\sqrt{2}, -45°$ 21. $\sqrt{13}, -33° \, 40'$ 23. 2, 60° 25. $\vec{PQ} = 3i - 2j - k$, $|\vec{PQ}| = \sqrt{14}$ 27. (3, −4) 29. (1, 3)
31. Parametric equations: x = 2 − 2t, y = 3 + t, z = 1; Standard equation: $\frac{2 - x}{-2} = y - 3, z = 1$. 33. Parametric
equations: x = 4 − t, y = 4 − 5t, z = 4 − 2t; Standard equations: $\frac{x - 4}{-1} = \frac{y - 4}{-5} = \frac{z - 4}{-2}$ 35. Parametric
equations: x = 3 + t, y = −2 − $\frac{1}{2}$t; Standard equation: y + 2 = −$\frac{1}{2}$(x − 3) 37. $\vec{A} \cdot \vec{B} = a_1a_2 + b_1b_2 + c_1c_2$
39. $\frac{\sqrt{2}}{2}$ 41. $\frac{+\sqrt{2}}{3}$ 43. Answers will vary. 45. Parallel line: 2x − 3y − 1 = 0; Perpendicular line: 3x + 2y −
8 = 0 47. $\frac{6\sqrt{13}}{13}$ 49. 3i − 2j + 5k 51. 11i − 7j + k 53. $\sqrt{\frac{19}{21}}$ 55. 7x − 2y + 3z − 8 = 0 57. $\vec{N}$ = Ai + Bj + Ck
59. x − $\frac{4}{5}$ = 2t, y − $\frac{11}{5}$ = −7t, z = 5t 61. $\frac{7\sqrt{6}}{6}$

PAGES 513-514 CHAPTER TEST

1. Vectors D and E. Do they form opposite sides of a parallelogram? 2. Vectors D and E and vectors B and C.
3. Same as Exercise 2. 4. Draw vector A. Let the tip of vector A be the foot of vector B; draw vector B. The
vector having foot at the foot of vector A, tip at the tip of vector B is vector A + B. Draw vector E. Let the foot

of vector E be the foot of vector B; draw vector B. Then the vector having foot at the tip of vector E and tip at the tip of vector B is vector B − E. 5. 125° 6. Add vector D to itself twice. The result is $3\vec{D}$. 7. Draw vector A. Then place the foot of $n\vec{D}$ on the foot of vector A and the tip of $m\vec{C}$ on the tip of vector A. The intersecting point of $n\vec{D}$ and $m\vec{C}$ is the foot of $m\vec{C}$ and the tip of $n\vec{D}$. Measure the length of $n\vec{D}$ and $m\vec{C}$. $m \approx \frac{1}{3}$, $n \approx 2\frac{1}{2}$. 8. In a two-space, we have x axis and y axis. Draw a vector having foot on the origin, tip on (1, 0), named i. Draw other vector having foot on origin, tip on (0, 1), named j. i and j are perpendicular and have unit length. In a three-space, we have the x axis, y axis and z axis. Draw i, j and k having the origin as the foot and (1, 0, 0), (0, 1, 0), (0, 0, 1) respectively as the tips. i, j, and k are mutually perpendicular and each has unit length. 9. a. $\vec{PQ} = -3i + 8j$ b. $\vec{PQ} = -i - 8j + 3k$ 10. $|\vec{A}| = \sqrt{4 + 4 + 1} = 3$ 11. a. $xi + yj = 2i + j$ $+ t(-5i + 6j)$, x = 2 − 5t, y = 1 + 6t, $\frac{x-2}{-5} = \frac{y-1}{6}$ b. $xi + yj + zk = i - 3j + 5k + t(i + 8j - 8k)$, x = 1, + t, y = −3 + 8t, z = 5 − 8t, $\frac{x-1}{1} = \frac{y+3}{8} = \frac{z-5}{-8}$ 12. $\vec{A} \cdot \vec{B} = (2)(-3) + (-6)(-1) + (1)(5) = 5$ 13. $\cos\theta$ $= \dfrac{5}{\sqrt{41} \cdot \sqrt{35}}$, $\theta = $ Arc cos $\dfrac{5}{\sqrt{1435}} \approx 82°$ 14. a. $\vec{N} = -29i - 13j - 20k$ b. $\vec{N} = \vec{A} \times \vec{B}$ 15. 5x + 7y − z + 12 16. x + 2z + 5 = 0 17. x = −t, y = −5t, z = −6t

CHAPTER 10 MATRICES, VECTORS, AND LINEAR TRANSFORMATIONS

PAGE 519 CLASSROOM EXERCISES

1. $a_{ij} + b_{ij}$ 3. $(a_{ij} + b_{ij}) + c_{ij}$

PAGES 519-521 WRITTEN EXERCISES

1. $\begin{bmatrix} -10 & -1 & 7 \\ 11 & -1 & -11 \end{bmatrix}$ 3. $\begin{bmatrix} -6 & 2 & 3 \\ 4 & -1 & -2 \end{bmatrix}$ 5. $\begin{bmatrix} 26 & -13 & -11 \\ -13 & 5 & 1 \end{bmatrix}$ 7. $\begin{bmatrix} 0 & 0 & 0 \\ 0 & 0 & 0 \end{bmatrix}$ 9. A − B = X is a matrix such that X + B = A 11. Let A be a matrix in M_2. Then by definition there exists −A such that A + (−A) = (−A) + A = 0. Suppose there is also a B such that A + B = B + A = 0. Then B = B + 0 = B + (A + (−A)) = (B + A) + (−A) (because of associativity) = 0 + −A = −A. Thus, −A is unique. (This is an example of a general theorem: If any system has an associative operation and an inverse for each element, then the inverse is unique. The proof is identical.) To show (−1) A = −A all you need do is show that (−1) A + A = A + (−1) A = 0. This is true because the elements in each sum, (−1) $a_{ij} + a_{ij} = a_{ij} + (-1)$ a_{ij} have zero as their sum. Thus, (−1) A = −A because −A is unique. 13. $p(qA) = p\begin{bmatrix} qa_{11} & qa_{12} \\ qa_{21} & qa_{22} \end{bmatrix} = \begin{bmatrix} pqa_{11} & pqa_{12} \\ pqa_{21} & pqa_{22} \end{bmatrix} = pq\begin{bmatrix} a_{11} & a_{12} \\ a_{21} & a_{22} \end{bmatrix} = pqA$

15. $p(A + B) = p\begin{bmatrix} a_{11} + b_{11} & a_{12} + b_{12} \\ a_{21} + b_{21} & a_{22} + b_{22} \end{bmatrix} = \begin{bmatrix} pa_{11} + pb_{11} & pa_{12} + pb_{12} \\ pa_{21} + pb_{21} & pa_{22} + pb_{22} \end{bmatrix} = \begin{bmatrix} pa_{11} & pa_{12} \\ pa_{21} & pa_{22} \end{bmatrix} + \begin{bmatrix} pb_{11} & pb_{12} \\ pb_{21} & pb_{22} \end{bmatrix} =$ pA + pB 17. $\begin{bmatrix} -6 & 3 \\ 8 & 0 \end{bmatrix}$ 19. $\begin{bmatrix} 0 & -6 \\ 24 & -12 \end{bmatrix}$ 21. $\begin{bmatrix} 6 & -24 \\ 12 & -6 \end{bmatrix}$ 23. $\begin{bmatrix} 30 & -34 \\ -28 & -2 \end{bmatrix}$ 25. $\begin{bmatrix} \frac{5}{3} & 0 \\ -2 & -\frac{1}{3} \end{bmatrix}$

27. Vector A could be represented by a matrix in one row: [2 3 −2] or by a matrix with one column: $\begin{bmatrix} 2 \\ 3 \\ -2 \end{bmatrix}$.

The latter method is used later in this book. 29. a, b, c, d 31. a, b, c 33. a. For any element of D, the associative property holds since D is a subset of C. b. For any element of D, the commutative property holds since D is a subset of C. c. 1 is the identity element. d. Each element of D has an inverse element belonging to D: $i^{-1} = -i$, $(-i)^{-1} = i$, $1^{-1} = 1$, and $-1^{-1} = -1$ 35. Clearly if A = $\begin{bmatrix} a_{11} & a_{12} \\ a_{21} & a_{22} \end{bmatrix}$ is any matrix in M_2, then

$A + 0 = \begin{bmatrix} a_{11} & a_{12} \\ a_{21} & a_{22} \end{bmatrix} + \begin{bmatrix} 0 & 0 \\ 0 & 0 \end{bmatrix}$ = A. Similarly 0 + A = A. Thus 0 is an identity and is unique by Ex. 34.

PAGE 523   CLASSROOM EXERCISES

1. $\begin{bmatrix} 2 & 14 \\ 8 & 1 \end{bmatrix}$ 3. $\begin{bmatrix} 5 & -2 \\ 1 & -3 \end{bmatrix}$

PAGES 523-525   WRITTEN EXERCISES

1. AB = $\begin{bmatrix} 1 & -1 \\ 2 & 2 \end{bmatrix}$, BA = $\begin{bmatrix} 2 & -1 \\ 1 & 1 \end{bmatrix}$, A(2B) = $\begin{bmatrix} 2 & -2 \\ 2 & 4 \end{bmatrix}$, (2A)(3B) = $\begin{bmatrix} 6 & -6 \\ 6 & 12 \end{bmatrix}$ 3. AB = $\begin{bmatrix} 1 & 1 \\ 0 & 0 \end{bmatrix}$, BA = $\begin{bmatrix} -1 & -2 \\ 1 & 2 \end{bmatrix}$,

A(2B) = $\begin{bmatrix} 2 & 2 \\ 0 & 0 \end{bmatrix}$, (2A)(3B) = $\begin{bmatrix} 6 & 6 \\ 0 & 0 \end{bmatrix}$ 5. a. $\begin{bmatrix} 5 & 5 \\ 5 & 10 \end{bmatrix}$ b. $\begin{bmatrix} 1 & 6 \\ 0 & 1 \end{bmatrix}$ 7. $A^2 = \begin{bmatrix} 1 & 0 \\ 0 & 1 \end{bmatrix}$, $A^3 = \begin{bmatrix} 1 & 0 \\ 0 & -1 \end{bmatrix}$, $A^4 = \begin{bmatrix} 1 & 0 \\ 0 & 1 \end{bmatrix}$,

$A^5 = \begin{bmatrix} 1 & 0 \\ 0 & -1 \end{bmatrix}$. Only two elements occur in the set, namely A and I and they alternate. 9. a. (A − B)(A + B) =

A^2 − BA + AB − B^2 b. (A − B)(A + B) $\neq A^2 - B^2$ because BA is not necessarily equal to AB. 11. A^2 =

$\begin{bmatrix} 7 & 4 \\ 6 & 7 \end{bmatrix}$, $-2A = \begin{bmatrix} -2 & -4 \\ -6 & -2 \end{bmatrix}$, $-5I = \begin{bmatrix} -5 & 0 \\ 0 & -5 \end{bmatrix}$, $A^2 - 2A - 5I = \begin{bmatrix} 0 & 0 \\ 0 & 0 \end{bmatrix} = 0$ 13. $A(kB) = \begin{bmatrix} a_{11} & a_{12} \\ a_{21} & a_{22} \end{bmatrix}$

$\begin{bmatrix} kb_{11} & kb_{12} \\ kb_{21} & kb_{22} \end{bmatrix} = \begin{bmatrix} a_{11} kb_{11} + a_{12} kb_{21} & a_{11} kb_{12} + a_{12} kb_{22} \\ a_{21} kb_{11} + a_{22} kb_{21} & a_{21} kb_{12} + a_{22} kb_{22} \end{bmatrix} = k(AB) \,; (kA)B = \begin{bmatrix} ka_{11} & ka_{12} \\ ka_{21} & ka_{22} \end{bmatrix} \begin{bmatrix} b_{11} & b_{12} \\ b_{21} & b_{22} \end{bmatrix} =$

$\begin{bmatrix} ka_{11} b_{11} + ka_{12} b_{21} & ka_{11} b_{12} + ka_{12} b_{22} \\ ka_{21} b_{11} + ka_{22} b_{21} & ka_{21} b_{12} + ka_{22} b_{22} \end{bmatrix} = k(AB)$ Therefore, A(kB) = (kA)B = k(AB) 15. Expand

$(A - \ell_1 I)(A - \ell_2 I)$. The result is $A^2 - \ell_1 IA - A\ell_2 I + \ell_1 \ell_2 I = A^2 - \ell_1 A - A\ell_2 + \ell_1 \ell_2 I = A^2 - (\ell_1 + \ell_2)A +$

$\ell_1 \ell_2 I$. 17. $\begin{bmatrix} -16 & 2 \\ 40 & 33 \\ 10 & 19 \end{bmatrix}$ 19. $\begin{bmatrix} 4 & -3 & -2 & 1 \\ 8 & -6 & -4 & 2 \\ 12 & -9 & -6 & 3 \\ 16 & -12 & -8 & 4 \end{bmatrix}$ 21. $\begin{bmatrix} 2 & -3 \\ 1 & 2 \\ 3 & 0 \end{bmatrix}$ 23. $\begin{bmatrix} 1 & -3 & 0 \\ -1 & 3 & 2 \\ 2 & -1 & -3 \\ -2 & 1 & 1 \end{bmatrix}$

PAGES 528-530   WRITTEN EXERCISES

1. $\begin{bmatrix} 1 \\ 3 \end{bmatrix}$ 3. $\begin{bmatrix} 5 \\ -6 \end{bmatrix}$ 5. $\begin{bmatrix} 6 \\ -3 \end{bmatrix}$ 7. $\begin{bmatrix} -3 \\ 2 \end{bmatrix}$ 9-23. Sketches omitted. 9. $\begin{bmatrix} -2 \\ 6 \end{bmatrix}$ 11. $\begin{bmatrix} -2 \\ 2 \end{bmatrix}$ 13. $\begin{bmatrix} 6 \\ -7 \end{bmatrix}$ 15. $\begin{bmatrix} -4 \\ 12 \end{bmatrix}$ 17. $\begin{bmatrix} 2 \\ 4 \end{bmatrix}$

19. $\begin{bmatrix} 10 \\ -16 \end{bmatrix}$ 21. $\begin{bmatrix} 8 \\ 18 \end{bmatrix}$ 23. $\begin{bmatrix} -8 \\ 14 \end{bmatrix}$ 25. a. Same vector. b. Same vector. c. Same vector. 27. $\begin{bmatrix} -\frac{2}{3} \\ -1 \end{bmatrix}$ 29. $\begin{bmatrix} 4 \\ 5 \end{bmatrix}$

31. Any point on the line x − 2y = 2. 33. $\begin{bmatrix} 8 \\ -30 \end{bmatrix}$ 35. $\begin{bmatrix} 2 & 7 \\ 6 & 19 \end{bmatrix}$

37. $\begin{bmatrix} 6 & 6 & 8 \\ 6 & 8 & 6 \\ 8 & 6 & 6 \end{bmatrix}$ 39. $A(B\vec{r}) = \begin{bmatrix} a_{11} & a_{12} \\ a_{21} & a_{22} \end{bmatrix} \left(\begin{bmatrix} b_{11} & b_{12} \\ b_{21} & b_{22} \end{bmatrix} \begin{bmatrix} x \\ y \end{bmatrix} \right) = \begin{bmatrix} a_{11} & a_{12} \\ a_{21} & a_{22} \end{bmatrix} \begin{bmatrix} b_{11}x + b_{12}y \\ b_{21}x + b_{22}y \end{bmatrix}$

$= \begin{bmatrix} a_{11}(b_{11}x + b_{12}y) + a_{12}(b_{21}x + b_{22}y) \\ a_{21}(b_{11}x + b_{12}y) + a_{22}(b_{21}x + b_{22}y) \end{bmatrix} = \begin{bmatrix} (a_{11}b_{11} + a_{12}b_{21})x + (a_{11}b_{12} + a_{12}b_{22})y \\ (a_{21}b_{11} + a_{22}b_{21})x + (a_{21}b_{12} + a_{22}b_{22})y \end{bmatrix}$

$= \begin{bmatrix} a_{11}b_{11} + a_{12}b_{21} & a_{11}b_{12} + a_{12}b_{22} \\ a_{21}b_{11} + a_{22}b_{21} & a_{21}b_{12} + a_{22}b_{22} \end{bmatrix} \begin{bmatrix} x \\ y \end{bmatrix} = \left(\begin{bmatrix} a_{11} & a_{12} \\ a_{21} & a_{22} \end{bmatrix} \begin{bmatrix} b_{11} & b_{12} \\ b_{21} & b_{22} \end{bmatrix} \right) \begin{bmatrix} x \\ y \end{bmatrix} = (AB)\vec{r}$

41. Proved in a manner similar to the proof in Exercise 39. 43. a. 5 b. −1 c. Does not exist; the matrix is

not n x n.

PAGE 535 WRITTEN EXERCISES

1. -2 3. 1 5. -2 7. 0 9. 0 11. 3 13. (1.) $-\dfrac{1}{2}\begin{bmatrix} 2 & 1 \\ -6 & -4 \end{bmatrix}$ (2.) $\begin{bmatrix} 0 & 1 \\ -1 & 0 \end{bmatrix}$ (3.) $\begin{bmatrix} -1 & 0 \\ 0 & -1 \end{bmatrix}$ (4.) $(-1)\begin{bmatrix} -1 & 0 \\ 0 & 1 \end{bmatrix}$

(5.) $-\dfrac{1}{2}\begin{bmatrix} 5 & -7 \\ -1 & 1 \end{bmatrix}$ (6.) No inverse. (7.) No inverse. (8.) $(-1)\begin{bmatrix} 5 & -8 \\ -2 & 3 \end{bmatrix}$ (9.) No inverse. (10.) $\dfrac{1}{2}\begin{bmatrix} 1 & -3 \\ -5 & 17 \end{bmatrix}$

(11.) $\dfrac{1}{3}\begin{bmatrix} 2 & -55 \\ -3 & 84 \end{bmatrix}$ 15. $\begin{bmatrix} 1 \\ -2 \end{bmatrix}$ 17. No solution. 19. $\begin{bmatrix} -1 \\ 2 \end{bmatrix}$ 21. $\begin{bmatrix} -3 \\ 2 \end{bmatrix}$ 23. $\dfrac{1}{ab}\begin{bmatrix} b & 0 \\ 0 & a \end{bmatrix}$ 25. $\begin{bmatrix} 1 & -k \\ 0 & 1 \end{bmatrix}$

27. $\dfrac{1}{1-a^2}\begin{bmatrix} 1 & -a \\ -a & 1 \end{bmatrix}$

PAGE 537 EXERCISES

1.

Incidence Matrix

	1	2	3	4	5	6	7	8
A	1	0	0	1	1	0	0	0
B	1	1	0	0	0	0	1	0
C	0	1	1	0	0	1	0	0
D	0	0	1	1	0	0	0	1
E	0	0	0	0	1	1	1	1

Route Matrix

	A	B	C	D	E
A	0	1	0	1	1
B	1	0	1	0	1
C	0	1	0	1	1
D	1	0	1	0	1
E	1	1	1	1	0

3.

	A	B	C	D
A	0	1	1	3
B	0	0	1	2
C	0	1	0	1
D	0	0	0	0

This matrix gives the routes without respect to direction.

5. Answers will vary.

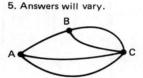

PAGE 540 CLASSROOM EXERCISES

1. $(x, y, z) = (1, 2, 1)$

PAGE 541 WRITTEN EXERCISES

1. $\begin{bmatrix} -3 & 1 & : & -1 \\ 1 & 1 & : & 2 \end{bmatrix} \rightarrow \begin{bmatrix} 1 & 1 & : & 2 \\ -3 & 2 & : & -1 \end{bmatrix} \rightarrow \begin{bmatrix} 1 & 1 & : & 2 \\ 0 & 5 & : & 5 \end{bmatrix} \rightarrow \begin{bmatrix} 1 & 0 & : & 2 \\ 0 & 1 & : & 1 \end{bmatrix} \rightarrow \begin{bmatrix} 1 & 0 & : & 1 \\ 0 & 1 & : & 1 \end{bmatrix}$ $(x, y) = (1, 1)$ 3. $(-1, 2)$

5. $\begin{bmatrix} 1 & -3 & : & 5 \\ -2 & 6 & : & 5 \end{bmatrix} \rightarrow \begin{bmatrix} 1 & -3 & : & 5 \\ 0 & 0 & : & 15 \end{bmatrix}$ Since the last row is all zeros except for the last entry, there is no solution to

the system. 7. $(1, 2, 3)$ 9. $\left(\dfrac{1}{2}, 2, \dfrac{3}{2}\right)$ 11. $(0, 0, 0)$ 13. $(-x_5, 3 + x_5, -1 + x_5, 1 - 2x_5, x_5)$, $x_5 \in R$

15. (10.) $\begin{bmatrix} 1 & 1 & 2 \\ 2 & -1 & 3 \\ 1 & -1 & -1 \end{bmatrix}\begin{bmatrix} x \\ y \\ z \end{bmatrix} = \begin{bmatrix} 2 \\ 5 \\ -2 \end{bmatrix}$ (11.) $\begin{bmatrix} 1 & 5 & -3 \\ 1 & 1 & 1 \\ 2 & -3 & 1 \end{bmatrix}\begin{bmatrix} x \\ y \\ z \end{bmatrix} = \begin{bmatrix} 0 \\ 0 \\ 0 \end{bmatrix}$ (12.) $\begin{bmatrix} 1 & -1 & 1 & -1 \\ 1 & 1 & 1 & 1 \\ 2 & -1 & 1 & -1 \\ -4 & 1 & -2 & 4 \end{bmatrix}\begin{bmatrix} w \\ x \\ y \\ z \end{bmatrix} = \begin{bmatrix} 0 \\ 6 \\ 1 \\ 1 \end{bmatrix}$

(13.) $\begin{bmatrix} 1 & 1 & 1 & 1 & 1 \\ 1 & 0 & 0 & 0 & 1 \\ 2 & 1 & 1 & 0 & 0 \\ 0 & 1 & 1 & 1 & 0 \\ 0 & 0 & 1 & 1 & 1 \end{bmatrix}\begin{bmatrix} x_1 \\ x_2 \\ x_3 \\ x_4 \\ x_5 \end{bmatrix} = \begin{bmatrix} 3 \\ 0 \\ 2 \\ 3 \\ 0 \end{bmatrix}$ (14.) $\begin{bmatrix} 2 & 1 & 3 \\ 1 & 0 & 2 \end{bmatrix}\begin{bmatrix} x_1 \\ x_2 \\ x_3 \end{bmatrix} = \begin{bmatrix} 1 \\ 1 \end{bmatrix}$

17. $\begin{bmatrix} \dfrac{1}{4} & -\dfrac{1}{4} & -\dfrac{1}{4} \\[2mm] \dfrac{7}{24} & \dfrac{1}{24} & -\dfrac{5}{24} \\[2mm] \dfrac{11}{24} & \dfrac{5}{24} & -\dfrac{1}{24} \end{bmatrix}$

PAGE 544 CLASSROOM EXERCISES

1. $\begin{bmatrix} x_1 \\ x_2 \\ x_3 \end{bmatrix} = \begin{bmatrix} -x_3 \\ 2x_3 \\ x_3 \end{bmatrix} = x_3 \begin{bmatrix} -1 \\ 2 \\ 1 \end{bmatrix}$

PAGES 544-545 WRITTEN EXERCISES

1. $\begin{bmatrix} 3 & 2 & -1 & : & 0 \\ 2 & -1 & 2 & : & 0 \end{bmatrix} \to \begin{bmatrix} 1 & \dfrac{2}{3} & -\dfrac{1}{3} & : & 0 \\[2mm] 0 & -\dfrac{7}{3} & \dfrac{8}{3} & : & 0 \end{bmatrix} \to \begin{bmatrix} 1 & 0 & \dfrac{3}{7} & : & 0 \\[2mm] 0 & 1 & -\dfrac{8}{7} & : & 0 \end{bmatrix}$ Thus $\begin{bmatrix} x_1 \\ x_2 \\ x_3 \end{bmatrix} = x_3 \begin{bmatrix} -\dfrac{3}{7} \\[2mm] \dfrac{8}{7} \\[2mm] 1 \end{bmatrix}$ **3.** $\begin{bmatrix} x_1 \\ x_2 \end{bmatrix} = \begin{bmatrix} 0 \\ 0 \end{bmatrix}$

5. $\begin{bmatrix} x_1 \\ x_2 \\ x_3 \end{bmatrix} = x_3 \begin{bmatrix} 0 \\ \dfrac{7}{2} \\ 1 \end{bmatrix}$ **7.** $\begin{bmatrix} x_1 \\ x_2 \\ x_3 \end{bmatrix} = \begin{bmatrix} 0 \\ 0 \\ 0 \end{bmatrix}$ **9.** $\begin{bmatrix} x_1 \\ x_2 \\ x_3 \end{bmatrix} = \begin{bmatrix} \dfrac{2}{3}x_2 - \dfrac{1}{3}x_3 \\ x_2 \\ x_3 \end{bmatrix} = x_2 \begin{bmatrix} \dfrac{2}{3} \\ 1 \\ 0 \end{bmatrix} + x_3 \begin{bmatrix} -\dfrac{1}{3} \\ 0 \\ 1 \end{bmatrix}$

11. $\begin{bmatrix} x_1 \\ x_2 \\ x_3 \\ x_4 \\ x_5 \\ x_6 \end{bmatrix} = x_4 \begin{bmatrix} \dfrac{9}{5} \\ -\dfrac{6}{5} \\ -\dfrac{4}{5} \\ 1 \\ 0 \\ 0 \end{bmatrix} + x_6 \begin{bmatrix} -\dfrac{1}{2} \\ 0 \\ \dfrac{1}{2} \\ 0 \\ -\dfrac{1}{2} \\ 1 \end{bmatrix}$ **13.** $\begin{bmatrix} x_1 \\ x_2 \\ x_3 \end{bmatrix} = x_3 \begin{bmatrix} \dfrac{1}{3}i \\ \dfrac{5}{6}(i-1) \\ 1 \end{bmatrix}$

15. Let x be, successively, 1, 0, −1, 2. $\begin{cases} c_3 + c_2 + c_1 + c_0 = 0 \\ c_0 = 0 \\ -c_3 + c_2 - c_1 + c_0 = 0 \\ 8c_3 + 4c_2 + 2c_1 + c_0 = 0 \end{cases}$ It follows that $c_0 = 0$. Solve the remaining

three equations. $\begin{bmatrix} 1 & 1 & 1 & : & 0 \\ -1 & 1 & -1 & : & 0 \\ 8 & 4 & 2 & : & 0 \end{bmatrix} \to \begin{bmatrix} 1 & 1 & 1 & : & 0 \\ 0 & 2 & 0 & : & 0 \\ 0 & -4 & -6 & : & 0 \end{bmatrix} \to \begin{bmatrix} 1 & 0 & 1 & : & 0 \\ 0 & 1 & 0 & : & 0 \\ 0 & 0 & 1 & : & 0 \end{bmatrix} \to \begin{bmatrix} 1 & 0 & 0 & : & 0 \\ 0 & 1 & 0 & : & 0 \\ 0 & 0 & 1 & : & 0 \end{bmatrix}$ Thus the unique

solution is $(0, 0, 0)$ amd $c_3 = c_2 = c_1 = c_0 = 0$. **17.** $\begin{bmatrix} 1 & 3 & : & 0 \\ 3 & k^2 & : & 0 \end{bmatrix} \to \begin{bmatrix} 1 & 3 & : & 0 \\ 0 & k^2 - 9 & : & 0 \end{bmatrix}$ Thus any $k \in R$ and

$k \neq \pm 3$ will produce only the trivial solution. $k = \pm 3$ will produce an infinite number of solutions.

PAGE 549 CLASSROOM EXERCISES

1. No solution

1. Solution. 3. Solution. 5. Solution. 7. Not a solution. 9. Not a solution. 11. Solution. 13. Only solution

is $(\frac{11}{5}, \frac{2}{5})$ 15. $\begin{bmatrix} 1 & 1 & 2 & : & 2 \\ 2 & 1 & 4 & : & 3 \\ 3 & 1 & 6 & : & 6 \end{bmatrix} \rightarrow \begin{bmatrix} 1 & 1 & 2 & : & 2 \\ 0 & -1 & 0 & : & -1 \\ 0 & -2 & 0 & : & 0 \end{bmatrix} \rightarrow \begin{bmatrix} 1 & 1 & 2 & : & 2 \\ 0 & 1 & 0 & : & 1 \\ 0 & 0 & 0 & : & 2 \end{bmatrix}$ No solution.

17. No solution. 19. $(1, 2, -2, 0, 1, 3)$ 21. $\begin{bmatrix} x_1 \\ x_2 \\ x_3 \\ x_4 \\ x_5 \end{bmatrix} = \begin{bmatrix} 0 \\ -3 \\ 2 \\ 0 \\ 0 \end{bmatrix} + x_4 \begin{bmatrix} \frac{-3}{2} \\ -4 \\ 2 \\ 1 \\ 0 \end{bmatrix} + x_5 \begin{bmatrix} -\frac{1}{2} \\ -2 \\ 1 \\ 0 \\ 1 \end{bmatrix} \begin{bmatrix} 1 \\ -1 \\ 1 \\ -1 \\ 1 \end{bmatrix} \begin{bmatrix} -\frac{1}{2} \\ -5 \\ 3 \\ 0 \\ 1 \end{bmatrix} \begin{bmatrix} 0 \\ -3 \\ 2 \\ 0 \\ 0 \end{bmatrix}$

23. $k = \pm\sqrt{3}$; No solution. $k \neq \pm\sqrt{3}$; One solution. 25. $k = 3$; No solution. $k = -3$; Infinite number of solutions. $k \neq \pm 3$; One solution. 27. Let x_1 = number of units of product B, x_3 = number of units of product C a. Then $5x_1 + 10x_2 + 2x_3 = 100$; $5x_1 + 10x_2 + 4x_3 = 150$; $2x_3 = 50$; $x_3 = 25$. Thus, $(10 - 2x_2)$ units of product A, x_2 units of product B, and 25 units of product C should be produced each day. b. No, there is no unique answer. c. Possible solutions with this restriction are: $x_1 = 0$ and $x_2 = 5$ or $x_1 = 2$ and $x_2 = 4$.

PAGES 552-553 MID-CHAPTER REVIEW

1. $\begin{bmatrix} -1 & 3 \\ -2 & 5 \end{bmatrix}$ 2. $\begin{bmatrix} 3 & -4 \\ -1 & -9 \end{bmatrix}$ 3. $\begin{bmatrix} -10 & 5 \\ 15 & 20 \end{bmatrix}$ 4. $\begin{bmatrix} -5 & 10 \\ -3 & 19 \end{bmatrix}$ 5. $\begin{bmatrix} -11 & -11 \\ -19 & -18 \end{bmatrix}$ 6. $\begin{bmatrix} 0 & 1 \\ 11 & -29 \end{bmatrix}$ 7. $\begin{bmatrix} 0 & 3 \\ 33 & -87 \end{bmatrix}$

8. $\begin{bmatrix} \frac{11}{2} & \frac{11}{2} \\ \frac{19}{2} & 9 \end{bmatrix}$ 9. $\begin{bmatrix} 3 \\ 2 \end{bmatrix}$ 10. $\begin{bmatrix} \frac{11}{5} \\ -\frac{2}{5} \end{bmatrix}$ 11. $\begin{bmatrix} \frac{5}{13} & \frac{3}{13} \\ -\frac{1}{13} & \frac{2}{13} \end{bmatrix}$ 12. 13 13. $(1, -\frac{2}{3}, \frac{5}{3})$ 14. $\begin{bmatrix} x_1 \\ x_2 \\ x_3 \\ x_4 \\ x_5 \end{bmatrix} = x_2 \begin{bmatrix} -2 \\ 1 \\ 0 \\ 0 \\ 0 \end{bmatrix} + x_5 \begin{bmatrix} -3 \\ 0 \\ -4 \\ -2 \\ 1 \end{bmatrix}$

$x_2, x_5 \in R$ Particular solutions: Let $x_2 = 1, x_5 = 1$ $\begin{bmatrix} -5 \\ 1 \\ -4 \\ -2 \\ 1 \end{bmatrix}$ Let $x_2 = -1, x_5 = 0$ $\begin{bmatrix} 2 \\ -1 \\ 0 \\ 0 \\ 0 \end{bmatrix}$

15. $\begin{bmatrix} x_1 \\ x_2 \\ x_3 \\ x_4 \end{bmatrix} = \begin{bmatrix} 1 \\ 0 \\ 0 \\ 0 \end{bmatrix} + x_2 \begin{bmatrix} 1 \\ 1 \\ -1 \\ 0 \end{bmatrix} + x_4 \begin{bmatrix} -1 \\ 0 \\ 0 \\ 1 \end{bmatrix}$ $x_2 = 1, x_4 = 0$ $\begin{bmatrix} 2 \\ 1 \\ -1 \\ 0 \end{bmatrix}$ $x_2 = 0, x_4 = 1$ $\begin{bmatrix} 0 \\ 0 \\ 0 \\ 1 \end{bmatrix}$ $x_2 = 1, x_4 = 1$ $\begin{bmatrix} 1 \\ 1 \\ -1 \\ 1 \end{bmatrix}$

PAGE 556 CLASSROOM EXERCISES

1. $\begin{bmatrix} 1 & 2 \\ 4 & 3 \end{bmatrix} \begin{bmatrix} 3 \\ 1 \end{bmatrix} = \begin{bmatrix} 5 \\ 15 \end{bmatrix}$ 3. $\begin{bmatrix} 1 \\ -3 \end{bmatrix}$

PAGES 556-558 WRITTEN EXERCISES

1.-9. No sketches are given. 1. $\begin{bmatrix} 3 \\ 2 \end{bmatrix}, \begin{bmatrix} 1 \\ -4 \end{bmatrix}, \begin{bmatrix} -4 \\ 3 \end{bmatrix}$ 3. $\begin{bmatrix} 3 \\ 0 \end{bmatrix}, \begin{bmatrix} 8 \\ 0 \end{bmatrix}, \begin{bmatrix} 5 \\ 0 \end{bmatrix}$ 5. $\begin{bmatrix} -1 \\ 2 \end{bmatrix}, \begin{bmatrix} -2 \\ 4 \end{bmatrix}, \begin{bmatrix} 3 \\ -6 \end{bmatrix}$

7. $\begin{bmatrix} 0 \\ 0 \end{bmatrix}, \begin{bmatrix} 0 \\ 0 \end{bmatrix}, \begin{bmatrix} 0 \\ 0 \end{bmatrix}$ 9. $\begin{bmatrix} 2 \\ -1 \end{bmatrix}, \begin{bmatrix} 14 \\ -7 \end{bmatrix}, \begin{bmatrix} 2 \\ -1 \end{bmatrix}$ 11. Every linear transformation of the plane corresponds to a

matrix in M_2. Thus every linear transformation can be represented by a matrix $A = \begin{bmatrix} a_{11} & a_{12} \\ a_{21} & a_{22} \end{bmatrix}$, $a_{ij} \in R$.

But $A \begin{bmatrix} 0 \\ 0 \end{bmatrix} = \begin{bmatrix} 0 \\ 0 \end{bmatrix}$ for all A. Thus $\begin{bmatrix} 0 \\ 0 \end{bmatrix}$ is its own image under every linear transformation of the plane.

13. Let $\begin{bmatrix} x \\ y \end{bmatrix}$ be a vector. Its image is $\begin{bmatrix} 0 & 0 \\ a & b \end{bmatrix}\begin{bmatrix} x \\ y \end{bmatrix} = \begin{bmatrix} 0 \\ ax + by \end{bmatrix}$, which is a vector on the y axis.

15. $\begin{bmatrix} 2 & 3 \\ 1 & 1 \end{bmatrix}\begin{bmatrix} 2 - 3t \\ 1 + 2t \end{bmatrix} = \begin{bmatrix} 4 - 6t + 3 + 6t \\ 2 - 3t + 1 + 2t \end{bmatrix} = \begin{bmatrix} 7 - 0t \\ 3 - t \end{bmatrix}$ The line is x = 7, y = 3 − t. 17. x = 3t, y = −7t

19. a. $\begin{bmatrix} 2 \\ -4 \end{bmatrix}, \begin{bmatrix} 2 \\ -1 \end{bmatrix}, \begin{bmatrix} -1 \\ -1 \end{bmatrix}$ b. $\begin{bmatrix} -2 \\ 4 \end{bmatrix}, \begin{bmatrix} -2 \\ 1 \end{bmatrix}, \begin{bmatrix} 1 \\ 1 \end{bmatrix}$ c. $\begin{bmatrix} 16 \\ -2 \end{bmatrix}, \begin{bmatrix} 10 \\ -5 \end{bmatrix}, \begin{bmatrix} -2 \\ 4 \end{bmatrix}$ d. $\begin{bmatrix} 22 \\ 4 \end{bmatrix}, \begin{bmatrix} 7 \\ 1 \end{bmatrix}, \begin{bmatrix} 4 \\ 1 \end{bmatrix}$

21. Let $A = \begin{bmatrix} a_{11} & a_{12} \\ a_{21} & a_{22} \end{bmatrix}$. Then the image of each point on the line is $\begin{bmatrix} a_{11} & a_{12} \\ a_{21} & a_{22} \end{bmatrix}\begin{bmatrix} a + \ell t \\ b + mt \end{bmatrix} =$

$\begin{bmatrix} a_{11}(a + \ell t) + a_{12}(b + mt) \\ a_{21}(a + \ell t) + a_{22}(b + mt) \end{bmatrix} = \begin{bmatrix} a_{11}a + a_{12}b + (a_{11}\ell + a_{12}m)t \\ a_{21}a + a_{22}b + (a_{21}\ell + a_{22}m)t \end{bmatrix}$ Thus $x \to a_{11}a + a_{12}b + pt$ where $p = a_{11}\ell +$

$a_{12}m$ and $y \to a_{21}a + a_{22}b + qt$ where $q = a_{21}\ell + a_{22}m$. This is a parametric equation of a line.

PAGE 563 CLASSROOM EXERCISES

1. $\begin{bmatrix} 2 \\ 3 \end{bmatrix}, \begin{bmatrix} -2 \\ -3 \end{bmatrix}, \begin{bmatrix} -3 \\ 2 \end{bmatrix}, \begin{bmatrix} 3 \\ -2 \end{bmatrix}$ 3. $\begin{bmatrix} 0 \\ -5 \end{bmatrix}, \begin{bmatrix} 0 \\ 5 \end{bmatrix}, \begin{bmatrix} 5 \\ 0 \end{bmatrix}, \begin{bmatrix} -5 \\ 0 \end{bmatrix}$ 5. $\begin{bmatrix} 2 \\ 2 \end{bmatrix}, \begin{bmatrix} -2 \\ -2 \end{bmatrix}, \begin{bmatrix} -2 \\ 2 \end{bmatrix}, \begin{bmatrix} 2 \\ -2 \end{bmatrix}$

PAGES 563-565 WRITTEN EXERCISES

1. a 3. e 5. a 7. f 9.-15. No graph given. 17. Inverses: $r_{x \text{ axis}}$, $r_{x \text{ axis}}$; $r_{y \text{ axis}}$, $r_{y \text{ axis}}$; $r_{x=y}$, $r_{x=y}$; $r_{y=-x}$,

$r_{y=-x}$ Each transformation is its own image. 19. y = x 21. y = −x 23. y axis 25. x axis 27. x axis and

y axis 29. x axis and y axis 31. y axis 33. none 35. We do only one proof. Let $\begin{bmatrix} x \\ y \end{bmatrix}$ and $\begin{bmatrix} u \\ v \end{bmatrix}$ be two points.

The distance between these points is $\sqrt{(x - u)^2 + (y - v)^2}$. The images under $r_{x \text{ axis}}$ are $\begin{bmatrix} x \\ -y \end{bmatrix}$ and $\begin{bmatrix} u \\ -v \end{bmatrix}$.

The distance between the images is $\sqrt{(x - u)^2 + (-y + v)^2} = \sqrt{(x - u)^2 + (y - v)^2}$. 37. a. $\begin{cases} x = 2 + t \\ y = 1 - 3t \end{cases}$;

$(1\frac{3}{4}, 1\frac{3}{4})$ b. $\begin{cases} x = 1 - 3t \\ y = -2 - t \end{cases}$; (7, 0) c. $\begin{cases} x = -1 + 3t \\ y = 2 + t \end{cases}$; $(0, 2\frac{1}{3})$ d. $\begin{cases} x = -2 - t \\ y = -1 + 3t \end{cases}$; $(-3\frac{1}{2}, 3\frac{1}{2})$

PAGE 568 CLASSROOM EXERCISES

1. $\begin{bmatrix} -\frac{3}{2} + \sqrt{3} \\ \frac{3\sqrt{3}}{2} + 1 \end{bmatrix}$ 3. $\begin{bmatrix} -2 \\ -3 \end{bmatrix}$ 5. $\begin{bmatrix} -3 \\ 2 \end{bmatrix}$

PAGES 568-569 WRITTEN EXERCISES

1. $\begin{bmatrix} 1 & 0 \\ 0 & 1 \end{bmatrix}$ 3. $\begin{bmatrix} 0 & -1 \\ 1 & 0 \end{bmatrix}$ 5. $\begin{bmatrix} 0 & 1 \\ -1 & 0 \end{bmatrix}$ 7. $\frac{1}{2}\begin{bmatrix} 1 & -\sqrt{3} \\ \sqrt{3} & 1 \end{bmatrix}$ 9. Calculate each matrix. 11. a. $\begin{bmatrix} 3 \\ 2 \end{bmatrix}$ b. $\begin{bmatrix} -2 \\ 3 \end{bmatrix}$ c. $\begin{bmatrix} -3 \\ -2 \end{bmatrix}$

d. $\frac{\sqrt{2}}{2}\begin{bmatrix} 5 \\ -1 \end{bmatrix}$ 13. a. $\begin{bmatrix} 4 \\ -3 \end{bmatrix}$ b. $\begin{bmatrix} 3 \\ 4 \end{bmatrix}$ c. $\begin{bmatrix} -4 \\ 3 \end{bmatrix}$ d. $\frac{\sqrt{2}}{2}\begin{bmatrix} 1 \\ -7 \end{bmatrix}$ 15. a. $\begin{bmatrix} -4 \\ 0 \end{bmatrix}$ b. $\begin{bmatrix} 0 \\ -4 \end{bmatrix}$ c. $\begin{bmatrix} 4 \\ 0 \end{bmatrix}$

d. $\frac{\sqrt{2}}{2}\begin{bmatrix} -4 \\ 4 \end{bmatrix}$ 17. a. $\begin{bmatrix} -1 \\ 4 \end{bmatrix}$ b. $\begin{bmatrix} -4 \\ -1 \end{bmatrix}$ c. $\begin{bmatrix} 1 \\ -4 \end{bmatrix}$ d. $\frac{\sqrt{2}}{2}\begin{bmatrix} 3 \\ 5 \end{bmatrix}$ 19. $(-7, 2), (-1, 4), (-3, 6)$ 21. $(-2, -7), (-4, -1),$

$(-6, -3)$ No graph given. 23. $(\sqrt{3} - \frac{7}{2}, 1 + \frac{7\sqrt{3}}{2})$, $(2\sqrt{3} - \frac{1}{2}, 2 + \frac{\sqrt{3}}{2})$, $(3\sqrt{3} - \frac{3}{2}, 3 + \frac{3\sqrt{3}}{2})$ No

graph given. 25. $\begin{cases} x = -2 - 3t \\ y = 1 - 3t \end{cases}$; $\begin{cases} x = \frac{\sqrt{2}}{2}(-1 - 6t) \\[4pt] y = \frac{\sqrt{2}}{2}(3) \end{cases}$; $\begin{cases} x = -1 + 3t \\ y = -2 - 3t \end{cases}$ $\begin{cases} x = 2 + 3t \\ y = -1 + 3t \end{cases}$;

$\begin{cases} x = \frac{\sqrt{3}}{2} - 1 - (\frac{3\sqrt{3}}{2} + \frac{3}{2})t \\[4pt] y = \frac{1}{2} + \sqrt{3} - (\frac{3}{2} - \frac{3\sqrt{3}}{2})t \end{cases}$ 27. $\begin{cases} x = 2 - 5t \\ y = -3 - 2t \end{cases}$; $\begin{cases} x = \frac{\sqrt{2}}{2}(-1 - 7t) \\[4pt] y = \frac{\sqrt{2}}{2}(-5 + 3t) \end{cases}$; $\begin{cases} x = 3 + 2t \\ y = 2 - 5t \end{cases}$; $\begin{cases} x = -2 + 5t \\ y = 3 + 2t \end{cases}$;

$\begin{cases} x = -\frac{3\sqrt{3}}{2} + 1 - (\sqrt{3} + \frac{5}{2})t \\[4pt] y = -\frac{3}{2} - \sqrt{3} + (\frac{5\sqrt{3}}{2} - 1)t \end{cases}$ 29. $\cos\alpha = \dfrac{ac + bd}{\sqrt{a^2+b^2}\cdot\sqrt{c^2+d^2}}$ where α is the acute angle between

$\begin{bmatrix} a \\ b \end{bmatrix}$ and $\begin{bmatrix} c \\ d \end{bmatrix}$. $\cos\phi = \dfrac{(a\cos\theta - b\sin\theta)(c\cos\theta - d\sin\theta) + (a\sin\theta + b\cos\theta)(c\sin\theta + d\cos\theta)}{\sqrt{a^2+b^2}\cdot\sqrt{c^2+d^2}}$

$= \dfrac{ac\cos^2\theta - bc\sin\theta\cos\theta - ad\cos\theta\sin\theta + bd\sin^2\theta + ac\sin^2\theta + bc\sin\theta\cos\theta + ad\sin\theta\cos\theta + bd\cos^2\theta}{\sqrt{a^2+b^2}\cdot\sqrt{c^2+d^2}}$

$= \dfrac{ac(\cos^2\theta + \sin^2\theta) + bd(\sin^2\theta + \cos^2\theta)}{\sqrt{a^2+b^2}\,\sqrt{c^2+d^2}} = \dfrac{ac + bd}{\sqrt{a^2+b^2}\,\sqrt{c^2+d^2}}$ 31. a. If $\begin{bmatrix} t \\ t^3 \end{bmatrix}$ is in V, then $\begin{bmatrix} -t \\ -t^3 \end{bmatrix}$

$= R_{180°}\cdot\begin{bmatrix} t \\ t^3 \end{bmatrix}$ is in V because $\begin{bmatrix} -t \\ -t^3 \end{bmatrix} = \begin{bmatrix} -t \\ (-t)^3 \end{bmatrix}$ b. $R_{180°}\cdot\begin{bmatrix} t \\ \frac{1}{t} \end{bmatrix} = \begin{bmatrix} -t \\ -\frac{1}{t} \end{bmatrix} \in V.$

c. $R_{180°}\cdot\begin{bmatrix} t \\ \pm\sqrt{4-t^2} \end{bmatrix} = \begin{bmatrix} t \\ \pm\sqrt{4-t^2} \end{bmatrix} = \begin{bmatrix} -t \\ \pm\sqrt{4-(-t)^2} \end{bmatrix} \in V.$

PAGE 574 CLASSROOM EXERCISES

1. $\begin{bmatrix} -1 & 4 \\ 7 & 5 \end{bmatrix}$

PAGES 575-576 WRITTEN EXERCISES

1. $BA = \begin{bmatrix} 2 & 1 \\ -3 & -1 \end{bmatrix}\begin{bmatrix} 1 & 2 \\ 1 & 4 \end{bmatrix} = \begin{bmatrix} 3 & 8 \\ -4 & -10 \end{bmatrix}$ 3. $BA = \begin{bmatrix} -17 & 10 \\ -11 & 0 \end{bmatrix}$ 5. (1.) a. $\begin{bmatrix} 21 \\ -26 \end{bmatrix}$ b. $\begin{bmatrix} 16 \\ -20 \end{bmatrix}$ c. $\begin{bmatrix} 4 \\ -6 \end{bmatrix}$ d. $\begin{bmatrix} -9 \\ 12 \end{bmatrix}$

e. $\begin{bmatrix} -14 \\ 18 \end{bmatrix}$ (2.) a. $\begin{bmatrix} 9 \\ 23 \end{bmatrix}$ b. $\begin{bmatrix} 8 \\ 18 \end{bmatrix}$ c. $\begin{bmatrix} 8 \\ 7 \end{bmatrix}$ d. $\begin{bmatrix} -9 \\ -12 \end{bmatrix}$ e. $\begin{bmatrix} -10 \\ -17 \end{bmatrix}$ (3.) a. $\begin{bmatrix} 47 \\ 11 \end{bmatrix}$ b. $\begin{bmatrix} 20 \\ 0 \end{bmatrix}$ c. $\begin{bmatrix} -78 \\ -44 \end{bmatrix}$ d. $\begin{bmatrix} 51 \\ 33 \end{bmatrix}$

e. $\begin{bmatrix} 24 \\ 22 \end{bmatrix}$ (4.) a. $\begin{bmatrix} -1 \\ 3 \end{bmatrix}$ b. $\begin{bmatrix} 0 \\ 2 \end{bmatrix}$ c. $\begin{bmatrix} 4 \\ -1 \end{bmatrix}$ d. $\begin{bmatrix} -3 \\ 0 \end{bmatrix}$ e. $\begin{bmatrix} -2 \\ -1 \end{bmatrix}$ 7. $R_{165°} = R_{120°}\cdot R_{45°} = \frac{1}{2}\begin{bmatrix} -1 & -\sqrt{3} \\ \sqrt{3} & -1 \end{bmatrix}\cdot$

$\frac{\sqrt{2}}{2}\begin{bmatrix} 1 & -1 \\ 1 & 1 \end{bmatrix} = \frac{\sqrt{2}}{4}\begin{bmatrix} -1 & -\sqrt{3} \\ \sqrt{3} & -1 \end{bmatrix}\begin{bmatrix} 1 & -\sqrt{3} \\ -\sqrt{3} & -1 \end{bmatrix}$

9. $R_{195°} = R_{135°} \cdot R_{60°}$. Details are omitted. 11. $AB = \begin{bmatrix} 1 & 0 \\ -2 & 1 \end{bmatrix}\begin{bmatrix} 1 & 3 \\ 0 & 1 \end{bmatrix} = \begin{bmatrix} 1 & 3 \\ -2 & -5 \end{bmatrix}$. Thus, $(1, 2) \rightarrow (7, -12)$;

$(2, 1) \rightarrow (5, -9)$; $(4, 5) \rightarrow (19, -33)$ No. 13. $\begin{cases} x = -5 + 4t \\ y = -2 + t \end{cases}$ 15. Let $A = \begin{bmatrix} a_{11} & a_{12} \\ a_{21} & a_{22} \end{bmatrix}$ and

$B = \begin{bmatrix} b_{11} & b_{12} \\ b_{21} & b_{22} \end{bmatrix}$. Then $\det A = a_{11}a_{22} - a_{12}a_{21}$, $\det B = b_{11}b_{22} - b_{12}b_{21}$.

$AB = \begin{bmatrix} a_{11}b_{11} + a_{12}b_{21} & a_{11}b_{12} + a_{12}b_{22} \\ a_{21}b_{11} + a_{22}b_{21} & a_{21}b_{12} + a_{22}b_{22} \end{bmatrix}$; $\det (AB) = (a_{11}b_{11} + a_{12}b_{21})(a_{21}b_{12} + a_{22}b_{22})$

$- (a_{11}b_{12} + a_{12}b_{22})(a_{21}b_{11} + a_{22}b_{21}) = a_{11}b_{11}a_{21}b_{12} + a_{11}b_{11}a_{22}b_{22} + a_{12}b_{21}a_{21}b_{12} + a_{12}b_{21}a_{22}b_{22}$

$- a_{11}b_{12}a_{21}b_{11} - a_{11}b_{12}a_{22}b_{21} - a_{12}b_{22}a_{21}b_{11} - a_{12}b_{22}a_{22}b_{21} = a_{11}a_{22}(b_{11}b_{22} - b_{12}b_{21})$

$+ a_{12}a_{21}(b_{21}b_{12} - b_{22}b_{11}) = a_{11}a_{22}(b_{11}b_{22} - b_{12}b_{21}) - a_{12}a_{21}(b_{11}b_{22} - b_{12}b_{21})$

$= (a_{11}a_{22} - a_{12}a_{21})(b_{11}b_{22} - b_{12}b_{21}) = \det A \cdot \det B$. 17. a. $A^{-1}A = I$. Thus the vector is its own image.

b. Same as a. 19. $(ai + bj + 0k) \times (ci + 0j + 0k) = \begin{vmatrix} b & 0 \\ 0 & 0 \end{vmatrix}i + \begin{vmatrix} 0 & a \\ 0 & c \end{vmatrix}j + \begin{vmatrix} a & b \\ c & 0 \end{vmatrix}k = 0i + 0j - bck$. Therefore,

the area of the triangle $\frac{1}{2}\sqrt{(bc)^2} = \frac{1}{2}|bc|$. 21. It leaves the area unchanged because $\det R_\theta = 1$.

23. a. $\theta = 0°$ Thus, $r_{y=mx} = \begin{bmatrix} \cos 0° & \sin 0° \\ \sin 0° & -\cos 0° \end{bmatrix} = \begin{bmatrix} 1 & 0 \\ 0 & -1 \end{bmatrix} = r_{x \text{ axis}}$. b. $\theta = 90°$ Thus, $r_{y=mx}$

$= \begin{bmatrix} \cos 180° & \sin 180° \\ \sin 180° & -\cos 180° \end{bmatrix} = \begin{bmatrix} -1 & 0 \\ 0 & 1 \end{bmatrix} = r_{y \text{ axis}}$. c. $\theta = 45°$ Thus, $r_{y=mx} = \begin{bmatrix} \cos 90° & \sin 90° \\ \sin 90° & -\cos 90° \end{bmatrix}$

$= \begin{bmatrix} 0 & 1 \\ 1 & 0 \end{bmatrix} = r_{y=x}$. d. $\theta = 135°$ Thus, $r_{y=mx} = \begin{bmatrix} \cos 270° & \sin 270° \\ \sin 270° & -\cos 270° \end{bmatrix} = \begin{bmatrix} 0 & -1 \\ -1 & 0 \end{bmatrix} = r_{y=-x}$.

PAGE 580 CLASSROOM EXERCISES

1. Translation equations: $x = x' + 0$, $y = y' + 3$. Equation at the line: $3x' + 2y' = 0$

PAGE 580 WRITTEN EXERCISES

1. $(-3, 5)$ 3. $(0, 10)$ 5. $(-7, 12)$ 7. $(5, 5)$ 9. $(4, 1)$ 11. y intercept is $(0, -1)$, translating vector is $\begin{bmatrix} 0 \\ 1 \end{bmatrix}$.

$x = x' - 0$, $y = y' - 1$ Thus, $y' - 1 = 2x' - 1$; so $y = 2x$ is the equation. 13. $2y + 4x = 0$ 15. $y + 5x = 0$

17. The equations are identical to those in Exercises 11-16. 19. The distance d between (x, y) and (u, v) is

$d = \sqrt{(x - u)^2 + (y - v)^2}$. Under a translation with vector $\begin{bmatrix} h \\ k \end{bmatrix}$, $(x, y) \rightarrow (x + h, y + k)$ and $(u, v) \rightarrow (u + h,$

$v + k)$. The distance d' here is $d' = \sqrt{(x + h - u - h)^2 + (y + k - v - k)^2} = \sqrt{(x - u)^2 + (y - v)^2} = d$.

21. $(1, 3) \rightarrow (-6, 7)$, $(4, 5) \rightarrow (-3, 9)$, $(6, 1) \rightarrow (-1, 5)$ 23. $x' + 2 + y' - 1 + 2 = 0$ or $x' + y' + 3 = 0$ 25. $\frac{1}{2}x' - $

$2y' + 3z' = 13$ 27. Answers will vary.

PAGES 581-585 CHAPTER OBJECTIVES AND REVIEW

1. The dimensions of a matrix are the number of rows and columns. 3. Two matrices are equal if and only if

they have the same dimensions and the corresponding entries are equal.

840   *Answers to Selected Exercises*

5. $\begin{bmatrix} 2 & -2 \\ 3 & 5 \end{bmatrix}$ 7. $\begin{bmatrix} 4 & -6 \\ 8 & 10 \end{bmatrix}$ 9. $\begin{bmatrix} 9 & 1 & 1 \\ 4 & 2 & -6 \end{bmatrix}$ 11. $\begin{bmatrix} 70 & 0 & 5 \\ 40 & 15 & -45 \end{bmatrix}$ 13. $\begin{bmatrix} 2 & 2 \\ -1 & -4 \end{bmatrix}$ 15. $\begin{bmatrix} 8 & .2 \\ -3 & 8 \end{bmatrix}$ 17. $\begin{bmatrix} 11 & -13 \\ -5 & 11 \end{bmatrix}$

19. $\begin{bmatrix} 12 & -12 \\ 20 & -6 \end{bmatrix}$ 21. $\begin{bmatrix} -1 \\ 4 \end{bmatrix}$ 23. 25. $\begin{bmatrix} \frac{3}{2} & -\frac{1}{2} \\ 2 & -1 \end{bmatrix}$ 27. $\begin{bmatrix} 1 & -5 \\ 0 & 1 \end{bmatrix}$ 29. x = 7, y = -1 31. $\begin{bmatrix} x_1 \\ x_2 \\ x_3 \end{bmatrix} =$

$\begin{bmatrix} \frac{1}{2} \\ \frac{3}{2} \\ 0 \end{bmatrix} - x_3 \begin{bmatrix} \frac{1}{2} \\ \frac{1}{2} \\ -1 \end{bmatrix}$, $x_3 \in R$ 33. $\begin{bmatrix} x_1 \\ x_2 \\ x_3 \end{bmatrix} = \begin{bmatrix} \frac{1}{2} \\ \frac{3}{2} \\ 0 \end{bmatrix} + x_3 \begin{bmatrix} -\frac{1}{2} \\ -\frac{1}{2} \\ 1 \end{bmatrix}$, $x_3 \in R$ 35. $T(\vec{V_1}) = \begin{bmatrix} 2 \\ -2 \end{bmatrix}$

$T(\vec{V_2}) = \begin{bmatrix} -5 \\ 3 \end{bmatrix}$ $T(\vec{V_3}) = \begin{bmatrix} 5 \\ -6 \end{bmatrix}$ 37. and 39.

(Ex. 37) (Ex. 39)

41. $\frac{1}{\sqrt{2}}\begin{bmatrix} -1 \\ 1 \end{bmatrix}$ 43. $\begin{bmatrix} -2 \\ 0 \end{bmatrix}$ 45. $\begin{bmatrix} 0 & -t \\ 2 & -t \end{bmatrix}$ 47. $\begin{bmatrix} 2 & 3 \\ 9 & 31 \end{bmatrix}$ 49. $\begin{bmatrix} -2 \\ 4 \end{bmatrix}$ 51. $\begin{bmatrix} -4 \\ 9 \end{bmatrix}$ 53. y' = 2x' + 4

PAGES 585-586 CHAPTER TEST

1. No. $a_{22} \neq b_{22}$ 2. a. 3 x 4 b. 3, 7, 0 3. $\begin{bmatrix} 2 & -1 & 0 \\ 1 & -7 & -3 \end{bmatrix}$ 4. $\begin{bmatrix} -4 & -15 & 17 \\ 0 & -1 & 3 \end{bmatrix}$ 5. The matrices are square.

6. a. Yes. b. Yes. c. Yes. d. No 7. det A = ux − vw 8. det A $\neq$ 0 9. $-\frac{1}{7}\begin{bmatrix} -5 & 3 \\ -1 & 2 \end{bmatrix}$ 10. $\begin{bmatrix} 0 & -1 \\ -1 & -k \end{bmatrix}$

11. $\begin{bmatrix} x_1 \\ x_2 \end{bmatrix} = \frac{1}{11}\begin{bmatrix} 20 \\ 19 \end{bmatrix}$ 12. $\begin{bmatrix} x_1 \\ x_2 \end{bmatrix} = \begin{bmatrix} 1 \\ 0 \end{bmatrix} + x_2 \begin{bmatrix} -3 \\ 1 \end{bmatrix}$ 13. $\begin{bmatrix} x_1 \\ x_2 \\ x_3 \end{bmatrix} = x_3 \begin{bmatrix} \frac{7}{3} \\ \frac{1}{3} \\ 1 \end{bmatrix}$ 14. $\begin{bmatrix} x_1 \\ x_2 \\ x_3 \end{bmatrix} = \begin{bmatrix} -1 \\ 1 \\ 1 \end{bmatrix}$ 15. a $\begin{bmatrix} 2 \\ 2 \end{bmatrix}, \begin{bmatrix} 2 \\ 3 \end{bmatrix}, \begin{bmatrix} 2 \\ 4 \end{bmatrix}$

b. Yes, because A is a linear transformation that maps collinear points (lines) onto collinear points.

16. a. $\begin{bmatrix} 1 & -1 \\ 0 & -1 \end{bmatrix}$ b. $\begin{bmatrix} 1 & 0 \\ -3 & -1 \end{bmatrix}$ 17. $\begin{bmatrix} 1 & 0 \\ 0 & 1 \end{bmatrix}$ 18. $\begin{bmatrix} 0 & 1 \\ -1 & 0 \end{bmatrix}$ 19. $\begin{cases} x = 7t + 3 \\ y = 10t + 4 \end{cases}$ 20. $\begin{cases} x = t - 1 \\ y = -t + 4 \end{cases}$ or y = −x + 3

PAGES 587-588 CUMULATIVE REVIEW: CHAPTERS 9-10
1. d 3. b 5. c 7. c 9. c 11. d 13. b 15. b 17. c

CHAPTER 11 THE CONIC SECTIONS

PAGE 591 CLASSROOM EXERCISES 1. circle, parabola, ellipse and hyperbola

PAGE 591 WRITTEN EXERCISES 1. Answers will vary.

PAGE 595 CLASSROOM EXERCISES

1. 6, 5, (±6, 0) 3. 9, 8 (0, ±9) 5. $\frac{x^2}{2} + \frac{y^2}{4} = 1$ 7. $\frac{x^2}{25} + \frac{y^2}{9} = 1$ or $9x^2 + 25y^2 = 225$

PAGES 596-597 WRITTEN EXERCISES

1. Semimajor: 4; semiminor: 2; $(\pm 2\sqrt{3}, 0)$. 3. Semimajor: 6; semiminor: 2; $(0, \pm 4\sqrt{2})$. 5. Semimajor: 6; semiminor: 4; $(\pm 2\sqrt{5}, 0)$. 7. Semimajor: 4; semiminor: $2\sqrt{2}$; $(0, \pm 2\sqrt{2})$. 9. $c = 3$ and $a = 5$. Thus, $b = 4$; $\frac{x^2}{25} + \frac{y^2}{16} = 1$ 11. $c = 2$ and $b = \frac{3}{2}$. Thus, $a = \frac{5}{2}$; $\frac{4x^2}{25} + \frac{4y^2}{9} = 1$ 13. $c = 3$ and $a = 6$. Thus, $b = 3\sqrt{3}$; $\frac{x^2}{27} + \frac{y^2}{36} = 1$ 15. $c = 2$ and $a = 4$. Thus, $b = 2\sqrt{3}$; $\frac{x^2}{12} + \frac{y^2}{16} = 1$ 17. $4x^2 + 9y^2 = 25$ 19. Slope of $\overleftrightarrow{AC} = \frac{y - 0}{x - 2}$; slope of $\overleftrightarrow{BC} =$ $\frac{y - 0}{x + y}$; $\frac{y}{x - 2} \cdot \frac{y}{x + 2} = -4 \Rightarrow y^2 = -4(x^2 - 4) \Rightarrow y^2 + 4x^2 = 16 \Rightarrow \frac{x^2}{4} + \frac{y^2}{16} = 1$. 21. $y^2 = a(x^2 - x_1{}^2) \Rightarrow$ $y^2 - ax^2 = -ax_1{}^2 \Rightarrow \frac{x^2}{x_1{}^2} + \frac{y^2}{-ax_1{}^2} = 1$; $a = $ product of the slopes; slopes $= \frac{y}{x - x_1}, \frac{y}{x + x_1}$; No 23. By Equation 3, $a\sqrt{(x - c)^2 + y^2} = a^2 - cx$ or $\sqrt{(x - c)^2 + y^2} = a - \frac{e}{a}x$. Since $F(c, 0)$ and $p(x, y)$, $\sqrt{(x - c)^2 + y^2} = FP$. Thus, $FP = a - \frac{cx}{a}$.

PAGE 599 CLASSROOM EXERCISES

1. $e = \frac{\sqrt{3}}{2}$, length = 4 3. $e = \frac{\sqrt{3}}{2}$, length = 4 5. $x = \pm \frac{36}{3\sqrt{3}}$ or $x = \pm 4\sqrt{3}$ 7. $x = \pm \frac{50}{\sqrt{30}}$ or $x = \pm \frac{5}{3}\sqrt{30}$

9. Theorem 11-1. An ellipse is the set of all points whose distance from a fixed point F (the focus) is equal to a constant $e(0 < e < 1)$ times the distance to a fixed line d (the directrix). 11. The latus rectum is the focal chord which is perpendicular to the transverse axis.

PAGES 599-600 WRITTEN EXERCISES

1. $a = 4$ and $b = 2$. Thus, $c = 2\sqrt{3}$; $e = \frac{\sqrt{3}}{2}$; Length of latus rectum: 2; Directrices: $x = \pm \frac{8\sqrt{3}}{3}$ 3. $a = 6$ and $b = 2$. Thus, $c = 4\sqrt{2}$; $e = \frac{2\sqrt{2}}{3}$; $\frac{4}{3}$; $y = \pm \frac{9\sqrt{2}}{2}$ 5. $a = 6$ and $b = 4$. Thus, $c = 2\sqrt{5}$; $e = \frac{1}{3}\sqrt{5}$; $\frac{16}{3}$; $x = \pm \frac{18\sqrt{5}}{5}$ 7. $a = 4$ and $b = 2\sqrt{2}$. Thus, $c = 2\sqrt{2}$; $e = \frac{\sqrt{2}}{2}$; 4; $y = \pm 4\sqrt{2}$ 9. $a = 9.45 \times 10^7$, $c = 0.15 \times 10^7$. Thus, $e =$ $\frac{0.15 \times 10^7}{9.45 \times 10^7} = \frac{15}{945} = \frac{1}{63}$. 11. The set of ellipses are such that as e approaches 0, the ellipse approaches a circle. As e approaches 1, the ellipse approaches a straight line. 13. The equation of $\overleftrightarrow{BP}$ is $y - b = \frac{s - b}{r} x$, and its x intercept (M) is $-b \cdot \frac{r}{s - b}$; The equation of $\overleftrightarrow{B'P}$ is $y + b = \frac{s + b}{r} x$, and its x intercept (N) is $b \cdot \frac{r}{s + b}$; $OM \cdot ON = \frac{-br}{s - b} \cdot \frac{br}{s + b} = \frac{-b^2r^2}{s^2 - b^2}$. But $b^2r^2 + a^2s^2 = a^2b^2$, because $P(r, s)$ is on the ellipse. Thus, $b^2r^2 =$ $a^2b^2 - a^2s^2$. $OM \cdot ON = \frac{a^2s^2 - a^2b^2}{s^2 - b^2} = \frac{a^2(s^2 - b^2)}{s^2 - b^2} = a^2$ when $s \neq \pm b$. 15. Let A have coordinates $(a, 0)$, $a < r$. Let P have coordinates (x, y). $AP = \sqrt{(x - a)^2 + y^2}$; $PT = r - PO = r - \sqrt{x^2 + y^2}$; Thus, $\sqrt{(x - a)^2 + y^2} = r - \sqrt{x^2 + y^2}$; $(x - a)^2 + y^2 = r^2 - 2r\sqrt{x^2 + y^2} + x^2 + y^2$; $-2ax + a^2 = r^2 - 2r\sqrt{x^2 + y^2}$; $r^2 - a^2 + 2ax = 2r\sqrt{x^2 + y^2}$; $4a^2r^2x - 4a^3x + 4a^2x^2 + a^4 - 2a^2r^2 + r^4 = 4r^2x^2 + 4r^2y^2$; $-4x^2(r^2 - a^2) + 4a(r^2 - a^2)x + (r^2 - a^2)^2 = 4r^2y^2$; $-4x^2 + 4ax + r^2 - a^2 = \frac{4r^2}{r^2 - a^2}y^2$; $-4(x - \frac{a}{2})^2 + r^2 =$ $\frac{4r^2}{r^2 - a^2}y^2$; $4(x - \frac{a}{2})^2 + \frac{4r^2}{r^2 - a^2}y^2 = r^2$. This is an ellipse.

842   *Answers to Selected Exercises*

PAGE 604 CLASSROOM EXERCISES

1. 5, 3, $\times$ 3. 2, 3, $\times$. 5.

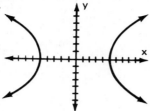

PAGE 604 WRITTEN EXERCISES

1. $a = 4$ and $b = 3$. Thus, $c = 5$; Hyperbola; Vertices: $(4, 0)$, $(-4, 0)$; Foci: $F(\pm 5, 0)$; Endpoints of latera recta: $(5, \pm\frac{9}{4})$, $(-5, \pm\frac{9}{4})$; $e = \frac{5}{4}$ 3. $a = 3$ and $b = 2$. Thus, $c = \sqrt{13}$; Hyperbola; Vertices: $(0, \pm 3)$; Foci: $(0, \pm\sqrt{13})$; Endpoints of latera recta: $(\pm\frac{4}{3}, \sqrt{13})$, $(\pm\frac{4}{3}, -\sqrt{13})$; $e = \frac{\sqrt{13}}{3}$ 5. $a = 1$ and $b = \frac{1}{2}$. Thus, $c = \frac{\sqrt{5}}{2}$; Hyperbola; Vertices: $(0, \pm 1)$; Foci: $(0, \pm\frac{\sqrt{5}}{2})$; Endpoints of latera recta: $(\pm\frac{1}{4}, \frac{\sqrt{5}}{2})$, $(\pm\frac{1}{4}, -\frac{\sqrt{5}}{2})$; $e = \frac{\sqrt{5}}{2}$ 7. $a = 6$ and $b = 6$. Thus, $c = 6\sqrt{2}$; Hyperbola; Vertices: $(0, \pm 6)$; Foci: $(0, \pm 6\sqrt{2})$; Endpoints of latera recta: $(\pm 6, 6\sqrt{2})$, $(\pm 6, -6\sqrt{2})$; $e = \sqrt{2}$ 9. $a = 2$ and $b = \sqrt{21}$. Thus, $c = 5$; Hyperbola; Vertices: $(\pm 2, 0)$; Foci: $(\pm 5, 0)$; Endpoints of latera recta: $(5, \pm\frac{21}{2})$, $(-5, \pm\frac{21}{2})$; $e = \frac{5}{2}$ 11. $a = 2$ and $b = 3$. Thus, $c = \sqrt{13}$; Hyperbola; Vertices: $(0, \pm 2)$; Foci: $(0, \pm\sqrt{13})$; Endpoints of latera recta: $(\pm\frac{9}{2}, \sqrt{13})$, $(\pm\frac{9}{2}, -\sqrt{13})$; $e = \frac{\sqrt{13}}{2}$ 13. $a = 4$ and $b = 3$. Thus, $c = 5$; $\frac{x^2}{16} - \frac{y^2}{9} = 1$ 15. $a = 2$ and $b = \sqrt{5}$. Thus, $c = 3$, $\frac{x^2}{4} - \frac{y^2}{5} = 1$ 17. $a = 3$ and $b = 4$. Thus, $c = 5$; $\frac{x^2}{9} - \frac{y^2}{16} = 1$ 19. $a = 4$ and $b = 3$. Thus, $c = 5$; $\frac{y^2}{16} - \frac{x^2}{9} = 1$ 21. For $\frac{x^2}{25} + \frac{y^2}{9} = 1$, $c = 4$; For $\frac{x^2}{4} - \frac{y^2}{12} = 1$, $c = 4$.

PAGES 607-608 CLASSROOM EXERCISES

1. $y = \pm\frac{6}{5}x$ 3. No asymptotes. (Ellipses do not have asymptotes.) 5. $\frac{y^2}{36} - \frac{x^2}{25} = 1$ 7. $\frac{y^2}{6} - \frac{x^2}{6} = 1$ 9. The asymptotes are perpendicular, i.e. $a = b$.

PAGES 608-609 WRITTEN EXERCISES

1. $\frac{x}{4} \pm \frac{y}{3} = 0$ 3. $\frac{y}{3} \pm \frac{x}{2} = 0$ 5. $2x \pm y = 0$ 7. $y \pm x = 0$ 9. $\sqrt{21}x + 2y = 0$ 11. $3y \pm 2x = 0$ 13. The equations of the asymptotes of $\frac{x^2}{a^2} - \frac{y^2}{b^2} = 1$ are $bx - ay = 0$ and $bx + ay = 0$ or $y = \frac{b}{a}x$ and $y = -\frac{b}{a}x$. Thus, the product of the slopes is $-\frac{b^2}{a^2}$, which is -1 if and only if $b^2 = a^2$. But since $a > 0$ and $b > 0$, $a^2 = b^2$ is equivalent to $a = b$. 15. Yes. 17. $a = 6$, $b = 12$; $\frac{x^2}{36} - \frac{y^2}{144} = 1$ 19. $\frac{10x^2}{16} - \frac{10y^2}{144} = 1$ 21. Let $P(x, y)$ be a point on $x^2 - 4y^2 = 4$. The equations of the asymptotes are $x + 2y = 0$ and $x - 2y = 0$. The distance from P to $x + 2y = 0$ is $\frac{|x + 2y|}{\sqrt{5}}$. The distance from P to $x - 2y = 0$ is $\frac{|x - 2y|}{\sqrt{5}}$. The product is $\frac{|x^2 - 4y^2|}{5} = \frac{4}{5}$, a constant. 23. Foci of ellipse are $(\pm 8, 0)$; $\frac{x^2}{100} + \frac{y^2}{36} = 1$. Foci of hyperbola are $(\pm 8, 0)$; $\frac{x^2}{36} - \frac{y^2}{28} = 1$.

25. $81x^2 - 144y^2 + 2940y = 13{,}600$ 27. Calculate the slope of $\overleftrightarrow{FN}$ and $\overleftrightarrow{FM}$. Show that their product is -1.

29. Slope of $\overleftrightarrow{A'D} = \frac{r}{p + a}$. Slope of $\overleftrightarrow{DA} = \frac{r}{p - a}$. Thus, the slope of $\overleftrightarrow{AX} = -\frac{p - a}{r}$. Equation of $\overleftrightarrow{A'D}$ is $y =$

$\frac{r}{p+a}(x+a)$ (1.) Equation of $\overleftrightarrow{AX}$ is $y = -\frac{p-a}{r}(x-a)$ (2.) Eliminate r between equations (1.) and (2.).

(1.) $r = \frac{y(p+a)}{x+a}$ (2.) $r = \frac{-(p-a)(x-a)}{y}$ Thus, $\frac{y(p+a)}{x+a} = \frac{-(p-a)(x-a)}{y} \Rightarrow y^2 = \frac{-(p-a)}{p+a}(x^2-a^2) \Rightarrow y^2 +$

$\frac{p-a}{p+a}x^2 = \frac{(p-a)a^2}{p+a}$. This is a hyperbola, since $|p| < |a|$.

PAGE 611 EXERCISES   1. $(x, y) = (8, 15)$; 31 panels 3. $(r, d) = (4, 32)$

PAGE 614 CLASSROOM EXERCISES

1. $p = -4$, x axis, to the left 3. $p = -9$, y axis, downward 5. $p = \frac{9}{2}$, x axis, to the right 7. $p = -\frac{13}{2}$, y axis,

downward 9. 16 11. 24 13. A parabola is the set of all points P equidistant from a fixed point and a fixed

line. 15. In the equation for a parabola, there is only one quadratic term.

PAGES 614-615 WRITTEN EXERCISES

1. $p = 1$; Focus: $(1, 0)$; $x = -1$; Endpoints of latus rectum: $(1, \pm 2)$. 3. $p = -\frac{11}{4}$; Focus: $(-\frac{11}{4}, 0)$; $x = \frac{11}{4}$; Endpoints of

latus rectum: $(-\frac{11}{4}, \pm\frac{11}{2})$. 5. $p = -\frac{3}{2}$; Focus: $(-\frac{3}{2}, 0)$; $x = \frac{3}{2}$; Latus rectum: $(-\frac{3}{2}, \pm 3)$. 7. $p = \frac{3}{4}$; Focus:

$(\frac{3}{4}, 0)$; $x = -\frac{3}{4}$; Endpoints of latus rectum: $(\frac{3}{4}, \pm\frac{3}{2})$. 9. $p = \frac{9}{16}$; Focus: $(0, \frac{9}{16})$; $y = -\frac{9}{16}$; Endpoints of

latus rectum: $(\pm\frac{9}{8}, \frac{9}{16})$. 11. $y^2 = -6x$ 13. $y^2 = -16x$ 15. $x^2 = -\frac{7}{2}y$ 17. $x^2 = -12y$ 19. $x^2 = \frac{9}{2}y$

21. $x^2 = -12y$ 23. Vertex is $(0, 0)$. The slopes of the lines are $\frac{2}{1}$ and $-\frac{1}{2}$. Thus, the angle is a right angle.

25. $y^2 = 12(x-1)$ 27. $x^2 = -16(y+2)$ 29. Let d = distance from $P(x, y)$ to the circle. Then $d = OP - r =$

$\sqrt{x^2 + y^2} - r$. Let $\overleftrightarrow{AB}$ be the x axis. Then the distance from P to $\overleftrightarrow{AB}$ is y. Under the given conditions $y = d =$

$\sqrt{x^2 + y^2} - r$. Thus, $y + r = \sqrt{x^2 + y^2}$ and $(y+r)^2 = x^2 + y^2$ or $2yr + r^2 = x^2$ or $x^2 = 2r(y + \frac{r}{2})$. This is a

parabola.

PAGE 616 MID-CHAPTER REVIEW

For Exercises 1-4, and 9-16, the graphs are given in the Solution Key.

1. 12, 8, $(\pm 2\sqrt{5}, 0)$ 2. 12, 8 $(0, \pm 2\sqrt{5})$ 3. 12, 8, $(\pm 2\sqrt{13}, 0)$ 4. 12, 8, $(0, \pm 2\sqrt{13})$ 5. $e = \frac{\sqrt{15}}{5}$; $\ell.r. =$

$\frac{4\sqrt{10}}{5}$; $x = \pm\frac{5\sqrt{6}}{3}$ 6. $e = \frac{\sqrt{35}}{5}$; $\ell.r. = \frac{4\sqrt{10}}{5}$; 7. $e = \frac{\sqrt{3}}{2}$; $\ell.r. = 2$; $x = \pm\frac{8\sqrt{3}}{3}$ 8. $e = \frac{\sqrt{29}}{2}$;

$\ell.r. = 25$; 9. $y = \pm\frac{x}{2}$ 10. $y = \pm\frac{x}{5}$ 11. $y = \pm\frac{4x}{5}$ 12. $y = \pm\frac{3x}{5}$ 13. $F(-3, 0)$, $V(0, 0)$ 14. $F(0, 2)$,

$V(0, 0)$ 15. $F(0, 9)$, $V(0, 0)$ 16. $F(4.5, 0)$, $V(0, 0)$

PAGE 620 CLASSROOM EXERCISES

1. $(3, 2)$, $(6, 2)$, $y = 2$ 3. $(2, 4)$, $(2 - \sqrt{13}, 4)$ and $(2 + \sqrt{13}, 4)$, $\frac{y-4}{2} \pm \frac{(x-2)}{3} = 0$ 5. $(x-1)^2 = -12(y-3)$

7. $\frac{(x-2)^2}{64} + \frac{(y-2)^2}{55} = 1$ 9. $\frac{(x-2)^2}{9} - \frac{(y-1)^2}{7} = 1$

PAGE 621 WRITTEN EXERCISES

1. $a = 3$, $b = 2$, $c = \sqrt{13}$; $\frac{(x-1)^2}{9} - \frac{(y-3)^2}{4} = 1$ 3. $a = \sqrt{7}$, $b = 3$, $c = 4$; $\frac{(x-3)^2}{7} - \frac{(y-2)^2}{9} = 1$

5. $a = 6$, $b = 8$, $c = 10$; $\frac{(x-6)^2}{36} - \frac{y^2}{64} = 1$ 7. $a = 6$, $b = 2\sqrt{5}$, $c = 4$; $\frac{x^2}{36} + \frac{(y-3)^2}{20} = 1$ 9. $a = 3$, $b = 2$,

$c = \sqrt{5}$; $\frac{(x-2)^2}{9} + \frac{(y-3)^2}{4} = 1$ 11. $p = 4$, $(y-3)^2 = 16(x-2)$ 13. $p = 3$, $(x-3)^2 = 12(y+2)$

15. $p = -2$, $(y + 1)^2 = -8(x - 4)$ 17. Consider in each case the y coordinates of the intersection of line

$x = h \pm c$ where c is $\sqrt{a^2 + b^2}$ for the hyperbola and $\sqrt{a^2 - b^2}$ for the ellipse. For the hyperbola the details

are, $b^2(c)^2 - a^2(y - k)^2 = a^2 b^2 \Rightarrow -a^2(y - k)^2 = a^2 b^2 - b^2 c^2 \Rightarrow (y - k)^2 = \dfrac{b^2 c^2 - a^2 b^2}{a^2}$,

$y = k \pm \dfrac{b}{a}\sqrt{c^2 - a^2} = k \pm \dfrac{b^2}{a}$. Thus, the latus rectum has length $\dfrac{2b^2}{a}$. The derivation for the ellipse is similar.

19. $x = h \pm \dfrac{a^2}{c}$

PAGE 625 CLASSROOM EXERCISES   1. $h = -3$, $k = 6$, ellipse 3. $h = \dfrac{-3}{2}$, $k = -1$, hyperbola

PAGE 626 WRITTEN EXERCISES

1. $(x' - h)^2 + (y' - k)^2 - 2(x' - h) - 4(y' - k) - 20 = 0 \Rightarrow (x')^2 - 2x'h + h^2 + (y')^2 - 2y'k + k^2 - 2x' +$

$2h - 4y' + 4k - 20 = 0 \Rightarrow (x')^2 + (y')^2 + (-2h - 2)x' + (-2k - 4)y' + h^2 + k^2 + 2h + 4k - 20 = 0$. Let $h =$

-1, $k = -2$. $x^2 + y^2 + 1 + 4 - 2 - 8 - 20 = 0 \Rightarrow x^2 + y^2 = 25$. 3. $x^2 - 4y^2 = 0$ 5. $y^2 = 6x$ 7. $9x^2 + y^2 = 9$

9. $16x^2 - 4y^2 = 64$ 11. $y^2 + x^2 = 25$ 13. $9x^2 + 4y^2 = 36$

PAGE 631 CLASSROOM EXERCISES

1. $\cos \theta = \dfrac{3}{\sqrt{13}}$, $\sin \theta = \dfrac{2}{\sqrt{13}}$

PAGE 631 WRITTEN EXERCISES

Sketches are not given. Only the standard form of the equation is shown. 1. $\dfrac{y^2}{1} + \dfrac{x^2}{6} = 1$ 3. $\dfrac{x^2}{16} - \dfrac{y^2}{\frac{4}{3}} = 1$

5. $\dfrac{x^2}{12} + \dfrac{y^2}{2} = 1$ 7. $\dfrac{y^2}{\frac{9}{10}} - \dfrac{x^2}{3} = 1$ 9. $\dfrac{x^2}{\frac{12}{25}} - \dfrac{y^2}{\frac{12}{25}} = 1$ 11. $x = \dfrac{1}{\sqrt{2}}(x' + y')$, $y = \dfrac{1}{\sqrt{2}}(-x' + y')$; Thus, $(y' + \dfrac{5\sqrt{2}}{16}) =$

$\dfrac{2\sqrt{2}}{5}(x' - \dfrac{5}{4\sqrt{2}})^2$ Translating, $x'^2 = \dfrac{5\sqrt{2}}{4}y'$. 13. $x'^2 + y'^2 = \dfrac{9}{c^2}$. For $c = \dfrac{1}{2}$, $x'^2 + y'^2 = 36$; for $c = 2$, $x'^2 +$

$y'^2 = \dfrac{9}{4}$; for $c = 3$, $x'^2 + y'^2 = 1$. 15. $x'^2 - y'^2 = \dfrac{1}{c^2}$ For $c = \dfrac{1}{2}$, $\dfrac{1}{c^2} = 4$; $c = 2$, $\dfrac{1}{c^2} = \dfrac{1}{4}$; $c = 3$, $\dfrac{1}{c^2} = \dfrac{1}{9}$

PAGES 634-637 CHAPTER OBJECTIVES AND REVIEW

1. Circle 3. Circle, ellipse, or parabola 5. Major axis $= 4\sqrt{2}$, minor axis $= 4$, Foci: $(2, 0)$, $(-2, 0)$ 7. $\dfrac{x^2}{4^2} +$

$\dfrac{y^2}{5^2} = 1$ 9. Graph is omitted. Endpoints of major axis are $(0, \pm 4)$. Endpoints of minor axis are $(\pm 2, 0)$.

11. $e = \dfrac{\sqrt{3}}{2}$; Length of latera recta $= 2$; Directrices: $y = \dfrac{8\sqrt{3}}{3}$ and $y = -\dfrac{8\sqrt{3}}{3}$ 13. Vertices: $(3, 0)$ and

$(-3, 0)$; Foci: $(5, 0)$, $(-5, 0)$; Endpoints of latera recta: $(-5, \dfrac{16}{3})$ and $(-5, -\dfrac{16}{3})$; $(5, \dfrac{16}{3})$ and $(5, -\dfrac{16}{3})$;

$e = \dfrac{5}{3}$. 15. $\dfrac{y^2}{16} - \dfrac{x^2}{9} = 1$ 17. Graph is omitted. The two wings of the hyperbola open to the left and to the

right and are asymptotic to the lines $y = \pm \dfrac{4}{3}x$. 19. $y = \dfrac{4}{3}x$ and $y = -\dfrac{4}{3}x$. 21. Focus: $(-1, 0)$; Directrix:

$x = 1$; Endpoints of latus rectum: $(-1, -2)$, $(-1, 2)$ 23. $x^2 = -24y$ 25. $x^2 = 10y$ 27. Graph is omitted.

The parabola opens upward. It passes through the origin and is symmetrical about the y axis. 29. $(x - 3)^2 =$

$8(y - 1)$ 31. $3x' + 3(y')^2 = 25\dfrac{2}{3}$ 33. $(x')^2 + 2(y')^2 - 13\dfrac{1}{8} = 0$. 35. Hyperbola 37. Hyperbola

39. Parabola 41. Ellipse 43. Ellipse 45. $(y')^2 - 4(x')^2 = 4$; Translating vector: $\begin{bmatrix} 2 \\ -1 \end{bmatrix}$ 47. $9(y')^2 - 16(x')^2 =$ 225; Translating vector: $\begin{bmatrix} 1 \\ -2 \end{bmatrix}$

PAGES 637-638 CHAPTER TEST

1. $(y - \frac{3}{2})^2 = -3(x - \frac{49}{12})$ 2. a. $\frac{y^2}{9} + \frac{x^2}{8} = 1$ b. $\frac{x^2}{25} + \frac{y^2}{16} = 1$ c. $\frac{(y+3)^2}{36} + \frac{(x-2)^2}{20} = 1$ 3. a. $\frac{y^2}{25} - \frac{x^2}{24} = 1$ b. $\frac{(x-2)^2}{9} - \frac{(y+2)^2}{7} = 1$ c. $\frac{x^2}{64} - \frac{y^2}{36} = 1$ 4. $2\sqrt{6}y \pm 5x = 0$ 5. $\frac{8}{3}$ 6. $x = \frac{19}{2}$ is the equation

of the directrix. 7. $6, 2\sqrt{5}$ 8. Center: $(2, 3)$; Vertices: $(2, 9)$, $(2, -3)$; Foci: $(2, 7)$ $(2, -1)$

9. $4AC - B^2 = 4 \cdot 4 \cdot 3 - 0 > 0$; Ellipse. 10. $4AC - B^2 = 4 \cdot 5 \cdot -4 - 0 < 0$; Hyperbola. 11. $4AC - B^2$ $= 4 \cdot 0 \cdot 3 - 0 = 0$; Parabola. 12. $(h, k) = (1, -2)$; $5x^2 - 4y^2 - 113 = 0$ 13. $\cot 2\theta = \frac{5}{12}$, $\cos 2\theta = \frac{5}{13}$, $\sin \theta = \frac{2}{\sqrt{13}}$, $\cos \theta = \frac{3}{\sqrt{13}}$; $13x^2 - 4 = 0$ 14. $\cot 2\theta = -\frac{7}{24}$, $\cos 2\theta = -\frac{7}{25}$, $\sin \theta = \frac{4}{5}$, $\cos \theta = \frac{3}{5}$; $14x^2 + 64y^2 - \frac{33}{5}x + \frac{56}{5}y - 7 = 0$; $h = -\frac{33}{140}$, $k = \frac{7}{80}$; $14x^2 + 64y^2 - \frac{463}{56} = 0$

CHAPTER 12 GRAPHS IN THREE-SPACE

PAGE 643 CLASSROOM EXERCISES

1. Elliptic cylinder, z axis 3. Hyperbolic cylinder, x axis

5. $\frac{y^2}{a^2} - \frac{z^2}{b^2} = 1$ 7. $Ax + Cz + D = 0$ 9. The graph in three-space of an equation in two variables is a cylinder with its elements parallel to the axis of the unnamed variable.

PAGE 643 WRITTEN EXERCISES

1. Circular cylinder; Center at $(2, 0, 0)$; Elements parallel to z axis. 3. Circular cylinder; Center at $(0, 2, 0)$; Elements parallel to x axis. 5. Sphere with center $(0, 0, 0)$; Radius 2. 7. Parabolic cylinder; Elements parallel to x axis. 9. Elliptic cylinder; Elements parallel to y axis. 11. Elliptic cylinder; Center $(2, 4, 0)$; Elements parallel to z axis. 13. Cylindric surface with directrix as the sine curve; Elements parallel to z axis. 15. a. $x^2 + 4y^2 = 16$ is an elliptical cylinder; Elements parallel to the z axis. b. $x^2 + 4y^2 = 16$ and $z = 2$ is an ellipse in the plane $z = 2$. It can be obtained from (a.) by passing a plane parallel to xy plane through the point $(0, 0, 2)$. 17. Circle in the plane $z = 3$. Cut the sphere with center $(0, 0, 0)$ and radius 4 in Exercise 16 with the plane $z = 3$. 19. Parabola cut from the parabolic cylinder in Exercise 18 with the plane $x = -2$. 21. An ellipse, cut by the plane $y = 1$ from the elliptical cylinder with center $(2, 0, 0)$ in Exercise 20. 23. $d_1 = \sqrt{(x-1)^2 + (y-2)^2 + (z-7)^2}$, $d_2 = \sqrt{(x-1)^2 + (y-5)^2 + (z-7)^2}$ Thus, $(x-1)^2 + (y-2)^2 + (z-7)^2 = (x-1)^2 + (y-5)^2 + (z-7)^2$ or $y^2 - 4y + 4 = y^2 - 10y + 25$ or $6y = 21 \Rightarrow 2y = 7 \Rightarrow y = \frac{7}{2}$. The graph is the plane $y = \frac{7}{2}$.

PAGE 647 CLASSROOM EXERCISES

1. $3x^2 + 3y^2 = 1$, $3y^2 + 3z^2 = 1$, $3x^2 + 3z^2 = 1$, x, y, z axes 3. $4y^2 + 4z^2 = 25$, $x^2 - 4z^2 = 25$, $x^2 - 4y^2 = -25$, x axis

PAGE 647 WRITTEN EXERCISES

1. $\frac{1}{4}(x^2 + z^2) = 0$, $\frac{1}{4}x^2 = y$, $\frac{1}{4}z^2 = y$. This is a surface of revolution about y axis since $\frac{1}{4}(x^2 + z^2) = k$ is the

empty set for $k < 0$, one point for $k = 0$, and a circle for $k > 0$. 3. $9z^2 + 16y^2 = 144$, $9z^2 + 16x^2 = 144$, $16(x^2 + y^2) = 144$. The z axis is the axis of rotation. $16(x^2 + y^2) = 144 - 9k^2 = 9(16 - k^2)$ or $x^2 + y^2 = \frac{9}{16}(16 - k^2)$. For $-4 < k < 4$ the intersection is a circle, for $-4 = k$ or $k = 4$ the intersection is one point, for $k < -4$ or $k > 4$ the intersection is empty. 5. $x^2 + 4y^2 = 36$, $x^2 + 9z^2 = 36$, $4y^2 + 9z^2 = 36$. No axis of rotation. 7. $x^2 + z^2 = 0$, $x^2 + y^2 - 6y = 0$, $z^2 + y^2 - 6y = 0$. The y axis is an axis of rotation. Note that there are two other axes of rotation: the line through $(0, 3, 0)$ parallel to the x axis and the line through $(0, 3, 0)$ parallel to the z axis. 9. $x^2 - 16y^2 = 0$, $x^2 + z^2 = 0$, $-16y^2 + z^2 = 0$. y axis is the axis of rotation. 11. Whenever a pair of the coefficients A, B, and C are identical.

PAGE 652 CLASSROOM EXERCISES

1. yz plane 3. xy plane 5. Sphere 7. Hyperboloid, two sheets 9. Two points P and Q are symmetric with respect to a plane π if an only if π is the perpendicular bisector of the line segment PQ.

PAGES 653-654 WRITTEN EXERCISES

1. Symmetric with respect to yz and xz planes. Traces: $\frac{x^2}{a^2} + \frac{y^2}{b^2} = 0$, $\frac{x^2}{a^2} = cz$, $\frac{y^2}{b^2} = cz$. $z = k$: $\frac{x^2}{a^2} + \frac{y^2}{b^2} = ck$;

ellipse for $k > 0$, a point for $k = 0$, null set for $k < 0$. $y = k$: $\frac{x^2}{a^2} = cz - \frac{k^2}{b^2} = c(z - \frac{k^2}{b^2c})$; parabola for all

$k \in R$. $x = k$: $\frac{y^2}{b^2} = cz - \frac{k^2}{a^2}$, parabola for all $k \in R$. 3. Symmetry with respect to the xy, yz, and xz planes.

Traces: $\frac{x^2}{a^2} + \frac{y^2}{b^2} = 0$, $\frac{x^2}{a^2} - \frac{z^2}{c^2} = 0$, $\frac{y^2}{b^2} - \frac{z^2}{c^2} = 0$. $z = k$: $\frac{x^2}{a^2} + \frac{y^2}{b^2} = \frac{k^2}{c^2}$; ellipse for $k \neq 0$, single point for

$k = 0$. $y = k$: $\frac{x^2}{a^2} - \frac{z^2}{c^2} = -\frac{k^2}{b^2}$; hyperbola for $k \neq 0$, two lines for $k = 0$. $x = k$: $\frac{y^2}{b^2} - \frac{z^2}{c^2} = -\frac{k^2}{a^2}$; hyperbola

for $k \neq 0$, two lines for $k = 0$. 5. Symmetry with respect to xy, xz, and yz planes. Traces: $\frac{x^2}{a^2} - \frac{y^2}{b^2} = 1$,

$\frac{x^2}{a^2} - \frac{z^2}{c^2} = 1$, $\frac{y^2}{b^2} + \frac{z^2}{c^2} = -1$. $z = k$: $\frac{x^2}{a^2} - \frac{y^2}{b^2} = 1 + \frac{k^2}{c^2}$; hyperbola for all k. $y = k$: $\frac{x^2}{a^2} - \frac{z^2}{c^2} = 1 + \frac{k^2}{b^2}$;

hyperbola for all k. $x = k$: $\frac{y^2}{b^2} + \frac{z^2}{c^2} = -1 + \frac{k^2}{a^2}$, ellipse for $k < -a$, $k > a$, for $k = \pm a$ a single point, for

$-a < k < a$, null set. 7. Ellipsoid. 9. Hyperboloid, one sheet. 11. Hyperboloid, two sheets. 13. Elliptic Cone. 15. Elliptic Paraboloid. 17. Hyperbolic Paraboloid. 19. Sphere. 21. Circular cylinder. 23. Elliptic Cone. 25. Circular cylinder. 27. z axis. 29. Sphere. 31. Hyperboloid of one sheet. 33. Circular Paraboloid. 35. Elliptical cylinder. 37. Hyperbolic cylinder. 39. Hyperboloid of one sheet.

PAGE 658 CLASSROOM EXERCISES

1. $(2, 2\sqrt{3}, 2)$ 3. $(0, 1, 9)$ 5. $(2, 0, 0)$ 7. $(\frac{5}{4}, \frac{5}{4}\sqrt{3}, \frac{5\sqrt{3}}{2})$ 9. They are the same except that cylindrical coordinates have a z component.

PAGES 658-659 WRITTEN EXERCISES

1. $(3, 0, 2)$; Thus, $x = 3 \cos 0 = 3$, $y = 3 \sin 0 = 0$, $z = 2$. 3. $(0, 7, 4)$ 5. $(-1, -\sqrt{3}, 3)$ 7. $x = 7 \cos (\frac{\pi}{4}) \cdot$
$\sin 0 = 0$, $y = 7 \sin (\frac{\pi}{4}) \cdot \sin 0 = 0$, $z = 7 \cdot \cos 0 = 7$. 9. $x = 7 \cos (\pi) \cdot \sin \frac{\pi}{2} = -7$, $y = 7 \sin \pi \cdot \sin \frac{\pi}{2} = 0$,
$z = 7 \cos \frac{\pi}{2} = 0$. 11. $x = 8 \cos \frac{\pi}{13} \cdot \sin \pi = 0$, $y = 8 \sin \frac{\pi}{13} \cdot \sin \pi = 0$, $z = 8 \cos \pi = -8$. 13. $\rho^2 = z^2 + r^2 =$
$z^2 + x^2 + y^2$, $\rho = \sqrt{z^2 + x^2 + y^2}$. 15. $\tan \theta = \frac{y}{x}$ 17. $r = \sqrt{x^2 + y^2}$ 19. $x^2 + y^2 + z^2 = 9$, c: $r^2 + z^2 = 9$;

s: $\rho^2 = 9$ or $\rho = 3$ 21. $z^2 = r^2 \Rightarrow z^2 = x^2 + y^2$ or $x^2 + y^2 - z^2 = 0$ in rectangular. s: $\phi = \dfrac{\pi}{4}$ or $\phi = \dfrac{3\pi}{4}$.

23. $\rho = 8 \cos \phi \Rightarrow \dfrac{\rho}{8} = \cos \phi \Rightarrow \dfrac{\rho}{8} = \dfrac{z}{\rho} \Rightarrow \rho^2 = 8z$. r: $\Rightarrow x^2 + y^2 + z^2 = 8z$, c: $\Rightarrow r^2 + z^2 = 8z$.   25. r: $(x^2 + y^2)$

$(x^2 + y^2 + z^2) = 16y^2$, s: $r^2 + z^2 = 16 \sin^2 \theta$

PAGE 661   WRITTEN EXERCISES

1. The curve is a helix. In the first octant some points it passes through are: $(0, 6, 0)$, $(3, 3\sqrt{3}, \dfrac{5\pi}{6})$,

$(3\sqrt{2}, 3\sqrt{2}, \dfrac{5\pi}{4})$, $(3\sqrt{3}, 3, \dfrac{5\pi}{3})$, $(6, 0, \dfrac{5\pi}{2})$ 3. This is an elliptic cone. Some points in the first octant are:

$(0, 0, 0)$, $(\dfrac{\pi\sqrt{3}}{4}, \dfrac{\pi}{4}, \dfrac{2\pi}{3})$, $(\dfrac{3\sqrt{2}\pi}{8}, \dfrac{3\sqrt{2}\pi}{8}, \pi)$, $(\dfrac{\pi}{2}, \dfrac{\sqrt{3}\pi}{2}, \dfrac{4\pi}{3})$, $(0, \dfrac{3\pi}{2}, 2\pi)$.   5. Some points in the first octant

are: $(0, 0, 0)$, $\left(\dfrac{\pi}{6}, \dfrac{\pi}{6}, \dfrac{2}{3}(\dfrac{\pi}{6})^{\frac{2}{3}}\right)$, $\left(\dfrac{\pi}{4}, \dfrac{\pi}{4}, \dfrac{2}{3}(\dfrac{\pi}{4})^{\frac{2}{3}}\right)$, $\left(\dfrac{\pi}{3}, \dfrac{\pi}{3}, \dfrac{2}{3}(\dfrac{\pi}{3})^{\frac{2}{3}}\right)$. All points on the curve in the first octant are

equidistant from the xz and yz planes. 7. Plane curve. Draw the circular cylinder with directrix $x^2 + y^2 = 25$
in the xy plane. Cut the cylinder with the plane $x - z = 0$. Some points the curve passes through in the first

octant are: $(0, 5, 0)$, $(1, \sqrt{24}, 1)$, $(2, \sqrt{21}, 2)$, $(3, 4, 3)$, $(4, 3, 4)$, $(5, 0, 5)$.   9. Plane curve. Draw the circular
cylinder with directrix $x^2 + y^2 - 4y = 0$ in the xy plane. (Circle with center $(0, 2, 0)$ and radius 2.) Cut the
cylinder with the plane $y = 2x$. The curve is an element of the cylinder.   11. In the first octant some points

the curve passes through are: $(0, 0, 0)$, $(1, \dfrac{\sqrt{2}}{2}, \dfrac{1}{3})$, $(2, 2\sqrt{2}, \dfrac{8}{3})$, $(3, \dfrac{9\sqrt{2}}{2}, 9)$, $(4, 8\sqrt{2}, \dfrac{64}{3})$.

PAGES 665-666   CHAPTER OBJECTIVES AND REVIEW

1. See page 640. 3. Parabolic cylinder. 5. Hyperbolic cylinder. 7. Hyperbolic cylinder. 9. Traces: $9x^2 +$
$4y^2 = 36$, $9x^2 + 9z^2 = 36$, $4y^2 + 9z^2 = 36$. y axis is axis of revolution. 11. Traces: $x^2 + 4y^2 = 4$, $x^2 + z^2 = 4$,
$4y^2 + z^2 = 4$. y axis is axis of revolution. 13. Traces: $x^2 - 16y^2 = 0$, $x^2 + z^2 = 0$, $-16y^2 + z^2 = 0$. y axis is
axis of revolution. 15. Elliptic Paraboloid. 17. Sphere. 19. Hyperboloid of 2 sheets. 21. $(r \cos \theta, r \sin \theta, z)$
23. $(\rho \cos \theta \sin \phi, \rho \sin \theta \sin \phi, \rho \cos \phi)$ 25. $(\dfrac{3}{2}, \dfrac{3\sqrt{3}}{2}, -1)$ 27. $(0, 0, 4)$ 29. The graph is not given. Some
points the curve passes through in the first octant are: $(0, 3, 0)$, $(\dfrac{3}{2}, \dfrac{3\sqrt{3}}{2}, \dfrac{\pi}{12})$, $(\dfrac{3\sqrt{2}}{2}, \dfrac{3\sqrt{2}}{2}, \dfrac{\pi}{6})$, $(3, 0, \dfrac{\pi}{4})$

PAGE 666   CHAPTER TEST

1. Parabolic cylinder. 2. $y^2 + z^2 = 25$ 3. $4x^2 + y^2 = 4$, $4x^2 - 4z^2 = 4$, $y^2 - 4z^2 = 4$. No. No circular sections
when cut by planes perpendicular to the axes. 4. $16x^2 - y^2 = 9$, $16x^2 + 16z^2 = 9$, $-y^2 + 16z^2 = 9$. y axis.
5. Hyperboloid of one sheet. 6. $x = 1 \cdot \cos \dfrac{2\pi}{3} \sin \dfrac{3\pi}{4} = 1 \cdot -\dfrac{1}{2} \cdot \dfrac{\sqrt{2}}{2} = -\dfrac{\sqrt{2}}{4}$, $y = 1 \cdot \sin \dfrac{2\pi}{3} \sin \dfrac{3\pi}{4} = 1 \cdot$

$\dfrac{\sqrt{3}}{2} \cdot \dfrac{\sqrt{2}}{2} = \dfrac{\sqrt{6}}{4}$, $z = 1 \cdot \cos \dfrac{3\pi}{4} = -\dfrac{\sqrt{2}}{2}$.   7. $x = 2 \cos \dfrac{\pi}{6} = 2\dfrac{\sqrt{3}}{2} = \sqrt{3}$, $y = 2 \sin \dfrac{\pi}{6} = 2 \cdot \dfrac{1}{2} = 1$, $z = 5$.

CHAPTER 13   INTRODUCTION TO CALCULUS

PAGE 670   CLASSROOM EXERCISES   1. $3x^2 + 4x - 1$ 3. $x^2 e^x + 2xe^x$

PAGE 670   WRITTEN EXERCISES   1. $-4x + 3$ 3. 0 5. $\dfrac{-21}{x^8}$ 7. $\dfrac{1}{x} + e^x - 12x^2$ 9. $3x^2 - 4x - 3$

11. $x^2 e^x + xe^x + 4x - e^x - 2$ 13. $e^x \cdot (\dfrac{1}{x} - x^2 - \dfrac{1}{x^2} - 2x)$ 15. $f'(x) = e^x e^x + e^x e^x = 2e^{2x}$ 17. $4e^{4x}$ 19. ne^{nx}

848   Answers to Selected Exercises

21. Note: To avoid confusion, let $r(x) = h(x)$. $f'(x) = \lim_{h\to 0} \dfrac{\dfrac{r(x+h)}{g(x+h)} - \dfrac{r(x)}{g(x)}}{h} = \lim_{h\to 0} \dfrac{\dfrac{g(x)r(x+h) - r(x)g(x+h)}{g(x+h)g(x)}}{h}$

$= \lim_{h\to 0} \dfrac{g(x)r(x+h) - g(x)r(x) + g(x)r(x) - r(x)g(x+h)}{g(x+h)g(x)h} = \lim_{h\to 0} \dfrac{g(x)[r(x+h) - r(x)]}{g(x+h)g(x)h}$

$-\lim_{h\to 0} \dfrac{r(x)[g(x+h) - g(x)]}{g(x+h)g(x)h} = \lim_{h\to 0} \dfrac{g(x)}{g(x+h)g(x)} \lim_{h\to 0} \dfrac{r(x+h) - r(x)}{h} - \lim_{h\to 0} \dfrac{r(x)}{g(x+h)g(x)} \lim_{h\to 0} \dfrac{g(x+h) - g(x)}{h}$

$= \dfrac{g(x)}{g^2(x)} r'(x) - \dfrac{r(x)g'(x)}{g^2(x)} = \dfrac{g(x)r'(x) - r(x)g'(x)}{g^2(x)}$

PAGE 672 CLASSROOM EXERCISES

1. $r(x) = x^2 + x$, $s(x) = x - 1$, $r'(x) = 2x + 1$, $s'(x) = 1$, $f'(x) = \dfrac{(x-1)(2x+1) - (x^2+x)(1)}{(x-1)^2} = \dfrac{x^2 - 2x - 1}{(x-1)^2}$

3. $r(x) = 4x^2$, $s(x) = 2 - x$, $r'(x) = 8x$, $s'(x) = -1$, $f'(x) = \dfrac{(2-x)(8x) - (4x^2)(-1)}{(2-x)^2} = \dfrac{4x(4-x)}{(2-x)^2}$

PAGE 672 WRITTEN EXERCISES

1. $\dfrac{6x^2(x+3)}{(x+2)^2}$ 3. $\dfrac{2x^2-1}{x^2}$ 5. $\dfrac{1-\ln x}{x^2}$ 7. $\dfrac{b}{a}$ 9. $\dfrac{e^x(x^2+x+1)}{(x+1)^2}$ 11. $\dfrac{2x^2 \ln x - 2x \ln x + 2x^2 - x}{(2x-1)^2} =$

$\dfrac{x(2x \ln x - 2\ln x + 2x - 1)}{(2x-1)^2}$ 13. $\dfrac{2(x+1)}{e^2}$ 15. $f'(x) = -\dfrac{1}{(x-2)^2}$, $f'(4) = -\dfrac{1}{4}$ 17. $f'(x) = \dfrac{4}{(4-x)^2}$,

$f'(0) = \dfrac{1}{4}$ 19. $f'(x) = \dfrac{2x}{(1+x^2)^2} = 0 \Rightarrow x = 0$ 21. $f'(x) = \dfrac{x^2-1}{x^2} = 0 \Rightarrow x = \pm 1$

PAGE 674 CLASSROOM EXERCISES

1. $u(x) = x^2 + 3x$, $u'(x) = 2x + 3$, $f(u) = u^3$, $f'(u) = 3u^2$, $f'(x) = 3(x^2+3x)^2(2x+3)$ 3. $u(x) = x^3 - x$,

$u'(x) = 3x^2 - 1$, $f(u) = u^{\frac{1}{2}}$, $f'(u) = \dfrac{1}{2u^{\frac{1}{2}}}$, $f'(x) = \dfrac{(3x^2-1)}{2(x^3-x)^{\frac{1}{2}}}$

PAGE 674 WRITTEN EXERCISES

1. $5(x+1)^4$ 3. $-10x(x^2+1)^{-6}$ 5. $\dfrac{1}{2}(x^3-x)^{-\frac{1}{2}}(3x^2-1)$ 7. $\dfrac{-4}{x^5}$ 9. $\dfrac{12(2x)^2}{(x+2)^4} = \dfrac{48x^2}{(x+2)^4}$ 11. $2(e^{2x} - e^{-2x})$

13. $\dfrac{-e^{\frac{1}{x}}}{x^2}$ 15. $(x^2+1)(x^3-x)^2(13x^4 + 2x^2 - 3)$ 17. $2x^3e^{x^2}(x^2+2)$ 19. $\dfrac{2x[1 + e^{2x} - 2xe^{2x}]}{(1+e^{2x})^3}$ 21. $2\cos 2x$

23. $4\cot 2x \ln(\sin 2x)$ 25. $f(x) = e^{(a+b)x} \Rightarrow f'(x) = (a+b)e^{(a+b)x}$, $g(x) = e^{ax} \cdot e^{bx} \Rightarrow g'(x) = ae^{ax}e^{bx} +$

$e^{ax}be^{bx} = (a+b)e^{(a+b)x}$, $f'(x) = g'(x)$ 27. $f(x) = \sin(a+b)x$, $f'(x) = (a+b)\cos(a+b)x$, $g(x) =$

$\sin ax \cos bx + \cos ax \sin bx$, $g'(x) = a \cos ax \cos bx - b \sin ax \sin bx - a \sin ax \sin bx + b \cos ax \cos bx =$

$(a+b)\cos ax \cos bx - (a+b)\sin ax \sin bx = (a+b)(\cos ax \cos bx - \sin ax \sin bx) = (a+b)\cos(a+b)x$.

Thus, $f'(x) = g'(x)$'

1. Since $S(3) = 9 - 25 = -16$ and $S(5) = 25 - 25 = 0$, the average velocity is $\dfrac{0 - (-16)}{5 - 3} = \dfrac{16}{2} = 8$ 3. 6.1

5. $\dfrac{S(3 + h) - S(3)}{h} = \dfrac{(3 + h)^2 - 25 - (-16)}{h} = \dfrac{9 + 6h + h^2 - 25 + 16}{h} = 6 + h$ 7. -12 9. -15.96 11. 4, 1,

$-1.7, -1.97, 3h - 2$ 13. $a(t) = 6$, $a(0) = 6$ 15. $v(t) = 4$, $a(t) = 0$, $v(t) = 4$ for all t, $a(t) = 0$ for all t. 17. $v(t) =$

$8t + 12$, $a(t) = 8$, $v(0) = 12$, $v(1) = 20$, $v(2) = 28$, $v(3) = 36$, $v(4) = 44$, $a(t) = 8$ for all t. 19. $v(t) = 64 - 32t$,

$a(t) = -32$, $v(0) = 64$, $v(1) = 32$, $v(2) = 0$, $v(3) = -32$, $v(4) = -64$, $a(t) = -32$ for all t. 21. $v(t) = 6t^2 - 18t$,

$a(t) = 12t - 18$, $v(0) = 0$, $v(1) = -12$, $v(2) = -12$, $v(3) = 0$, $v(4) = 24$, $a(0) = -18$, $a(1) = -6$, $a(2) = 6$,

$a(3) = 18$, $a(4) = 30$ 23. $v(2) = 64$, $v(4) = 0$, $v(6) = -64$ 25. $v(t) = 0$ when $t = 4$, $S(4) = 256$. Yes. 27. Since

$v(t) = 32 - 32t$ and $v(t) = 0$, when $t = 1$, the ball reaches maximum height at 1. 29. $S(t) = 0$ when $t = 2$

PAGE 679 MID-CHAPTER REVIEW

1. $20x^3$ 2. $(4x^3 + x^4)e^x$ 3. $-3x^{-4} + 6x^{-3}$ 4. $(x^2 - 2)e^x$ 5. $3x^2 - 1$ 6. $2e^{2x} + 2e^{-2x}$ 7. $\dfrac{1 - 2x - x^2}{(x^2 + 1)^2}$

8. $\dfrac{x^2 - 6x + 1}{(x - 3)^2}$ 9. $3(x^2 + 6x - 1)^2 (2x + 6)$ 10. $\dfrac{-12x}{(3x^2 - 7)^3}$ 11. $(3x^2 - 2)e^{(x^3 - 2x)}$ 12. $12x^3 - 40x$

13. $f'(x) = 4(2x^2 - 3)^3(4x) = 0$; $x = 0, \pm \dfrac{\sqrt{6}}{2}$ 14. a. $v(t) = 9t^2 - 18$, $a(t) = 18t$ b. $v(0) = -18$, $a(0) = 0$;

$v(1) = -9$, $a(1) = 18$; $v(\sqrt{2}) = 0$, $a(\sqrt{2}) = 18\sqrt{2}$; $v(3) = 63$, $a(3) = 54$ c. $t = 2$

PAGE 681 EXERCISES

1. a. $R'(x) = 8$, none b. $R'(x) = 200 - 10x$, $x = 20$ c. $R'(x) = 540 - \dfrac{x}{9}$, $x = 4860$ 3. a. $P(x) = x - 9$,

$P'(x) = 1$, none b. $P(x) = -5x^2 + 195x - \dfrac{1}{x} - 2000$, $P'(x) = -10x + 195 + \dfrac{1}{x^2}$, $x \approx 19.5$ c. $P(x) = -\dfrac{x^2}{18} +$

$528x - \dfrac{200}{x} - 200$, $P'(x) = -\dfrac{x}{9} + 528 + \dfrac{200}{x^2}$; $x \approx 4752$ 5. a. $D'(x) = -1$, $R'(x) = 8 - 2x$, $x = 4$; b. $D'(x) =$

$\dfrac{-24}{(x + 2)^2}$, $R'(x) = \dfrac{48}{(x + 2)^2}$ No zeros c. $D'(x) = \dfrac{-200}{(x + 10)^2}$, $R'(x) = \dfrac{2000}{(x + 10)^2}$, No zeros

PAGE 685 CLASSROOM EXERCISES 1. $\dfrac{9}{2}$ 3. $\dfrac{15}{4}$

PAGES 685-686 WRITTEN EXERCISES

1. $\Delta x = \dfrac{2 - 0}{2} = 1$, $y_i = \dfrac{3}{2}i$ $\Delta x = \dfrac{3}{2}i$; Therefore, $A_2 = \sum\limits_{i=1}^{2} y_i \Delta x = \sum\limits_{i=1}^{2} \dfrac{3}{2}i = \dfrac{3}{2}(3) = \dfrac{9}{2}$ 3. $A_{16} = \dfrac{51}{16}$ 5. $A_2 = 8$,

$A_4 = 7$, $a_{16} = 6\dfrac{1}{4}$, $A = 6$ 7. $A_2 = 4$, $A_4 = 5$, $a_{16} = 5\dfrac{3}{4}$, $A = 6$ 9. $A_8 = \dfrac{51}{16}$ 11. $A_{16} = \dfrac{1}{8}\sum\limits_{i=1}^{16} \sqrt{i} \approx \dfrac{44.47}{8}$

13. $A_4 = \dfrac{25}{4}$ 15. If $n = 4$, $\Delta x = \dfrac{4 - 2}{4} = \dfrac{1}{2}$

PAGE 688 CLASSROOM EXERCISES 1. 1 3. 42

PAGES 688-689 WRITTEN EXERCISES

1. $\Delta x = \dfrac{1}{2}$, $x_0 = 0$, $y_0 = 0$, $x_1 = \dfrac{1}{2}$, $y_1 = \dfrac{1}{2}$, $x_2 = 1$, $y_2 = \dfrac{2}{2}$, $x_3 = \dfrac{3}{2}$, $y_3 = \dfrac{3}{2}$, $x_4 = 2$, $y_4 = 2$, $T = \dfrac{1}{2}(\dfrac{1}{2} + \dfrac{2}{2} + \dfrac{3}{2} + \dfrac{2}{2})$

$= \dfrac{1}{2}(4) = 2$ 3. $\Delta x = \dfrac{1}{4}$, $x_0 = 1$, $y_0 = 1$, $x_1 = 1 + \dfrac{1}{4} = \dfrac{5}{4}$, $y_1 = (\dfrac{5}{4})^3 = \dfrac{125}{64}$, $x_2 = 1 + \dfrac{2}{4} = \dfrac{6}{4}$, $y_2 = (\dfrac{6}{4})^3 = \dfrac{216}{64}$,

$x_3 = 1 + \frac{3}{4} = \frac{7}{4}$, $y_3 = (\frac{7}{4})^3 = \frac{343}{64}$, $x_4 = 2$, $y_4 = (\frac{8}{4})^3 = \frac{512}{64}$, $\frac{1}{2}y_0 = \frac{1}{2} = \frac{32}{64}$, $\frac{1}{2}y_4 = \frac{256}{64}$,

$T = \frac{1}{4}(\frac{32}{64} + \frac{125}{64} + \frac{216}{64} + \frac{343}{64} + \frac{256}{64}) = \frac{1}{4}(\frac{972}{64}) = \frac{243}{64} \approx 3.80$ 5. 3.45 7. 3.84 9. 732.00 11. 32.78

13. $\Delta x = \frac{b-a}{4}$, $x_0 = a$, $y_0 = ma$, $x_1 = a + \frac{b-a}{4}$, $y_1 = m(a + \frac{b-a}{4})$, $x_2 = a + \frac{2(b-a)}{4}$, $y_2 = m(a + \frac{2(b-a)}{4})$,

$x_3 = a + \frac{3(b-a)}{4}$, $y_3 = m(a + \frac{3(b-a)}{4})$, $x_4 = a + \frac{4(b-a)}{4} = b$, $y_4 = mb$, $\frac{1}{2}y_0 = \frac{ma}{2}$, $\frac{1}{2}y_4 = \frac{mb}{2}$,

$T_4 = \frac{b-a}{4}\left[\frac{ma}{2} + m(a + \frac{b-a}{4}) + m(a + \frac{2(b-a)}{4}) + m(a + \frac{3(b-a)}{4}) + \frac{mb}{2}\right] = \frac{m(b-a)}{4}(\frac{a}{2} + a + \frac{b-a}{4} + a$

$+ \frac{2(b-a)}{4} + a + \frac{3(b-a)}{4} + \frac{b}{2}) = \frac{m(b-a)(b+a)}{2} = \frac{m(b^2 - a^2)}{2}$, $T_8 = \frac{(b-a)}{8}\left[\frac{ma}{2} + m(a + \frac{b-a}{8})\right.$

$+ m(a + \frac{2(b-a)}{8}) + m(a + \frac{3(b-a)}{8}) + m(a + \frac{4(b-a)}{8}) + m(a + \frac{5(b-a)}{8}) + m(a + \frac{6(b-a)}{8}) + m(a + \frac{7(b-a)}{8})$

$\left. + \frac{mb}{2}\right] = \frac{m(b-a)(b+a)}{2} = \frac{m(b^2 - a^2)}{2}$ $T_4 = T_8$ since the region is a trapezoid and therefore $T_4 = T_8$ = area.

PAGE 693 CLASSROOM EXERCISES   1. 6 3. 21

PAGE 693 WRITTEN EXERCISES
1. $A_2^5(2x) = \frac{2}{2}(5^2 - 2^2) = 25 - 4 = 21$ 3. $\frac{63}{2}$ 5. 18.75 7. $A_0^3(x^2) = \frac{3^3 - 0^3}{3} = 9$ 9. $\frac{91}{3}$ 11. 24

13. Since $m < 0$, $A_2^4(-x) = -\frac{(-1)}{2}(4^2 - 2^2) = 6$ 15. $A_{-2}^0(x) = \frac{1}{2}(0^2 - (-2)^2) = -2$. This is true since

$f(x) < 0$ for all $x \in [-2, 0)$. Therefore, $A_{-2}^0 = |-2| = 2$. 17. $\Delta x = \frac{b-a}{n}$, $y_i = p(a + \frac{i(b-a)}{n})^2$, A_n

$= \sum_{i=1}^{n} p(a + \frac{i(b-a)}{n})^2 \frac{2(b-a)}{n} = \frac{p(b-a)}{n} \cdot \sum_{i=1}^{n}(a + \frac{i(b-a)}{n})^2 = \frac{p(b-a)}{n} \cdot \sum_{i=1}^{n}\left[a^2 + \frac{2ai(b-a)}{n}\right.$

$\left. + \frac{i^2(b-a)^2}{n^2}\right] = \frac{p(b-a)}{n}\left[na^2 + \frac{2a(b-a)(n+1)n}{2n} + \frac{(b-a)^2(n(n+1)(2n+1))}{6n^2}\right]$

$= \frac{p(b-a)}{n}\left[na^2 + (ab - a^2)(n+1) + \frac{(b-a)^2(2n^3 + 3n^2 + n)}{6n^2}\right]$

$A_a^b(px^2) = \lim_{n\to\infty}\left[p(b-a)a^2 + p(b-a)(ab - a^2) + \frac{p(b-a)(ab - a^2)}{n} + \frac{p(b-a)(b-a)^2(2n^2 + 3n + 1)}{6n^2}\right]$

$= pa^2b - pa^3 + pab^2 - pa^2b - pa^2b + pa^3 + \lim_{n\to\infty} \frac{p(b-a)(b-a)^2(1 + \frac{3}{2n} + \frac{1}{2n^2})}{3}$

$= pab^2 - pa^2b + \left[\frac{pb^3 - 2pab^2 + pa^2b - pab^2 + 2pa^2b - pa^3}{3}\right]$

$= \frac{3pab^2 - 3pa^2b + pb^3 - 2pab^2 + pa^2b - pab^2 + 2pa^2b - pa^3}{3} = \frac{p(b^3 - a^3)}{3}$ 19. $\frac{1}{4}(b^4 - a^4)$

21. $y_i = \left(a + \frac{i(b-a)}{n}\right)^2 + 1$, $A_n = \sum_{i=1}^{n}\left[\left(a + \frac{i(b-a)}{n}\right)^2 + 1\right]\frac{b-a}{n}$

$= \frac{b-a}{n}\left[\sum_{i=1}^{n}\left(a^2 + \frac{2ai(b-a)}{n} + \frac{i^2(b-a)^2}{n^2}\right) + \sum_{i=1}^{n}1\right]$

$$= \frac{b-a}{n}\left[na^2 + \frac{(2ab-2a^2)n(n+1)}{2n} + \frac{(b-a)^2}{n^2}\left(\frac{n(n+1)(2n+1)}{6}\right) + n\right] = a^2b - a^3 + (ab^2 - 2a^2b + a^3)$$

$$(1 + \tfrac{1}{n}) + \frac{b^3 - 2ab^2 + a^2b - ab^2 + 2a^2b - a^3}{6}(1 + \tfrac{1}{n}).\ (2 + \tfrac{1}{n}) + b - a,\ A_a^b(x^2 + 1) = \lim_{n \to \infty} A_n = a^2b - a^3 + ab^2$$

$$- 2a^2b + a^3 + \frac{b^3 - 2ab^2 + a^2b - ab^2 + 2a^2b - a^3}{3} + b - a = \frac{b^3 - a^3}{3} + b - a \quad 23.\ \frac{b^4 - a^4}{4} + 3(b - a)$$

PAGE 697 CLASSROOM EXERCISES   1. $\frac{8}{3}$ 3. $-\frac{1}{102}$ 5. 2 7. $A_a^b f(x) = \int_a^b f(x)dx$

PAGES 697-698 WRITTEN EXERCISES

1. $\int_0^3 3x^2 dx = 3\int_0^3 x^2 dx = 3\frac{3^3 - 0^3}{3} = 27$ 3. $-\frac{7}{6}$ 5. $\frac{40}{3}$ 7. $\frac{8}{3}$ 9. 25 11. $\frac{-4}{21}$ 13. $\int_1^2 xdx = \frac{2^2 - 1^2}{2}$

$= \frac{3}{2}$ and $\int_2^1 xdx = \frac{1^2 - 2^2}{2} = \frac{-3}{2}$ hence $\int_2^1 xdx = -\int_1^2 xdx$ 15. $\int_{-1}^3 x^4 dx = \frac{244}{5}$ and $\int_3^{-1} x^4 dx = -\frac{244}{5}$

hence $\int_3^{-1} x^4 dx = -\int_{-1}^3 x^4 dx$ 17. $\int_{-2}^0 x^3 dx = -4$ and $\int_0^{-2} x^3 dx = 4$ hence $\int_0^{-2} x^3 dx = -\int_{-2}^0 x^3 dx$ 19. In each

case, $\int_b^a f(x)dx = -\int_a^b f(x)dx$. That is, the integral from x = b to x = a of f(x) is equal to the negative of the

integral from x = a to x = b of f(x). 21. $\int_1^2 2x^2 dx + \int_2^5 2x^2 dx = \frac{248}{3}$, $\int_1^5 2x^2 dx = \frac{248}{3}$ hence $\int_1^2 2x^2 dx$

$+ \int_2^5 2x^2 dx = \int_1^5 2x^2 dx$ 23. $\int_a^c 3x^2 dx + \int_c^b 3x^2 dx = b^3 - a^3$, $\int_a^b 3x^2 dx = b^3 - a^3$ hence $\int_a^c 3x^2 dx$

$+ \int_c^b 3x^2 dx = \int_a^b 3x^2 dx$ 25. $G'(x) = 6x^2 - 1$ 27. $G(b) - G(a) = 2b^3 - b + 2 - (2a^3 - a + 2) = 2(b^3 - a^3)$

$- (b - a)$ 29. $G'(x) = 1$, $\int_a^b G'(x)dx = \int_a^b 1dx = b - a = G(b) - G(a)$ 31. $\int_a^b G'(x)dx = \int_a^b 3x^2 dx = b^3 - a^3$

$= G(b) - G(a)$ 33. $\int_a^b G'(x)dx = \int_a^b 2xdx = b^2 - a^2 = (b^2 - 1) - (a^2 - 1) = G(b) - G(a)$

PAGE 703 CLASSROOM EXERCISES   1. $\frac{64}{3}$ 3. 64

PAGE 703 WRITTEN EXERCISES

1. The curve of $y = 2x - x^2$ intersects x axis at 0 and 2. Thus, $\int_0^2 (2x - x^2)dx = \frac{2(2)^2}{2} - \frac{2^3}{3} - 0 = 4 - \frac{8}{3} = \frac{4}{3}$

3. The curve of $y = x^2 - 9$ intersects x axis at 3. Thus, $\int_1^4 (x^2 - 9)dx = \left|\int_1^3 (x^2 - 9)dx\right| + \int_3^4 (x^2 - 9)dx$

$= \left|9 - 27 - \frac{1}{3} + 9\right| + \frac{64}{3} - 36 - 9 + 27 = \frac{38}{3}$ 5. The curve of $y = 2x - x^2$ intersects $y = -3$ at $x = -1$

and x = 3. Thus, $\int_{-1}^3 [2x - x^2 - (-3)]dx = \frac{32}{3}$. 7. Two curves intersect at $(-2, 8)$, $(2, 8)$ and $(0, 0)$. $\int_{-2}^2 2x^2 dx$

$- \int_{-2}^2 (x^4 - 2x^2)dx = \int_{-2}^2 [2x^2 - (x^4 - 2x^2)]dx = \frac{128}{15}$ 9. The curve $y = x^3 - x^2 - 2x$ intersects x axis at -1,

0, and 2. Thus, $\int_{-1}^0 (x^3 - x^2 - 2x)dx + \left|\int_0^2 (x^3 - x^2 - 2x)dx\right| = \frac{37}{12}$ 11. Two curves intersect at $(-2, -6)$,

$(0, 0)$, and $(2, 6)$. Thus, $\int_{-2}^0 (x^3 - x - 3x)dx + \int_0^2 [3x - (x^3 - x)]dx = 8$ 13. $\int_0^1 x^n dx$ ($n \in W$) is the area

of the region bounded by $y = x^n$, x = 0, x = 1, and the x axis. 15. Decreases. 17. $\int_0^2 (x^2 + x - x)dx = \frac{8}{3}$ 19. No.

PAGE 709   CLASSROOM EXERCISES   1. $\frac{64}{3}\pi$ 3. $\frac{9}{2}\pi$

PAGES 709-710   WRITTEN EXERCISES

1. $\int_0^3 \pi(2x+1)^2 dx = \pi\int_0^3 (4x^2+4x+1)dx = \pi(4\frac{(3)^3}{3} + 4 \cdot \frac{3^2}{2} + 3) = 57\pi$ 3. $\int_0^2 \pi(x^2+1)^2 dx = \frac{206}{15}\pi$

5. $\int_0^2 \pi(x-x^2)^2 dx = \frac{\pi}{30}$ 7. $\int_0^4 \pi[(5x-x^2)^2 - x^2] dx = \frac{384}{5}\pi$ 9. $\int_0^2 \pi[8^2 - (x^3)^2] dx = \frac{768}{7}\pi$

11. $x^2 = y, h = \Delta y, \int_0^2 \pi y\,dy = 2\pi$ 13. $\int_0^1 \pi(y-y^2)dy = \frac{1}{6}\pi$ 15. $\int_0^4 \pi y\,dy = 8\pi$ 17. Since the axis is

the line $y = 4$, the interval is $[0, 2]$. Use the translation equation $y = y' + 4$, or $y' = x^2 - 4$; then $\int_0^2 \pi(x^2-4)^2 dx$

$= \frac{256}{15}\pi$ 19. $\int_0^4 \pi[(-4)^2 - (\sqrt{y}-4)^2] dy = \frac{104}{3}\pi$ 21. $2\int_0^a \pi(\frac{b}{a}\sqrt{a^2-x^2})^2 dx = \frac{4}{3}\pi b^2 a$

PAGES 711-713   CHAPTER OBJECTIVES AND REVIEW

1. $3x^2$ 3. $\frac{2}{x}$ 5. $7e^x x^{-6}(x-5)$ 7. $\frac{x(x-6)}{(x-3)^2}$ 9. $\frac{e^x}{x^2}(x-1)$ 11. $8x(x^2+1)^3$ 13. $3x(x^2-2)^{\frac{1}{2}}$ 15. Average

velocity $= \frac{R(t_2) - R(t_1)}{t_2 - t_1}$, $v(4) = R'(4)$ 17. a. $v(t) = S'(t) = 24t - 6$ b. $a(t) = v'(t) = 24$ c. $v(3) = 24 \cdot 3 -$

$6 = 66$ d. $a(3) = 24$ e. $v(0) = 24 \cdot 0 - 6 = -6$ f. $a(0) = 24$ 19. 4.5 21. ≈ 3.19 23. 66 25. 70 27. $\frac{75}{4}$

29. 172,565,650.3 31. 0 33. -12 35. 702 37. $2\frac{1}{2}$ 39. $\frac{8\sqrt{2}}{3}$ 41. 8π

PAGE 714   CHAPTER TEST

1. $2x - 3 + e^x$ 2. $e^x + xe^x$ 3. $\frac{e^x}{x} + e^x \ln x$ 4. $4(2x-3)(x^2-3x+4)^3$ 5. $\frac{2x^4 + 7x^2 = 1}{(x^2+1)^2}$ 6. $v(t) = 48t - 18t^2$

7. $a(t) = 48 - 36t$ 8. $v(t) = 0$ when $t = 0$ or $t = \frac{48}{18}$ 9. $a(t) > 0$ when $0 < t < \frac{4}{3}$ 10. 18, 48, 54, 0

11. $\frac{54 - 18}{3 - 1} = \frac{36}{2} = 18$ 12. Rectangles: $\frac{17^2}{8^2} = 4\frac{33}{64}$; Trapezoids: $\frac{15^2}{8^2} + \frac{1}{2} = 4\frac{1}{64}$ 13. $\int_0^2 x^3 dx = \frac{1}{4}(2^4 -$

$0^4) = 4$ 14. $\int_{-1}^2 x^3 dx = 3\frac{3}{4}$ 15. $\int_0^5 (3x^2 + 5x^4)dx = 3250$ 16. $\int_1^2 (x+1)(2x-3)dx = \frac{1}{6}$ 17. $\int_0^5 (mx+b)dx =$

$\frac{25m}{2} + 5b$ 18. $\int_0^3 \pi y^2 dx = 36\frac{3}{5}\pi$

PAGES 715-716   CUMULATIVE REVIEW: CHAPTERS 11-13
1. b 3. c 5. d 7. b 9. d 11. b 13. d 15. b 17. c 19. b 21. c 23. b

CHAPTER 14   INTRODUCTION TO PROBABILITY

PAGE 719   CLASSROOM EXERCISES   1. $3 \times 2 = 6$ ways 3. 5^8 or 390,625 ways

PAGES 720-721   WRITTEN EXERCISES
1. The tree diagram is not shown. First draw the three branches corresponding to the chocolate, vanilla, and strawberry ice cream. To each of these, attach five branches corresponding to toppings of marshmallow, chocolate, hot fudge, butterscotch, and crushed nuts. 3. Six 5. 48 7. 105 9. 22 ways; 25 ways 11. 4200
13. 360 15. 1,048,576 17. 1023 19. 2520 21. 90 23. 1440 25. 576

PAGES 724-725 WRITTEN EXERCISES

1. 840 3. 120 5. 120 7. 362,880 9. 729 11. 3360 13. 34,650 15. 10 17. 56 19. 120 21. 362,880 23. 72

25. 2520 27. 10,080 29. 3456 31. $_nP_r = n(n-1)(n-2) \cdots (n-r+1) = n(n-1)(n-2) \cdots (n-r+1) \cdot$

$\dfrac{(n-r+1-1)(n-r+1-2) \cdots 1}{(n-r+1-1)(n-r+1-2) \cdots 1} = \dfrac{n!}{(n-r)!}$

PAGE 729 CLASSROOM EXERCISES   1. $_{52}C_4 = \dfrac{52!}{48!\,4!} = 270,725$ 3. $_5C_2 = \dfrac{5!}{3!\,2!} = 10$

PAGE 729 WRITTEN EXERCISES

1. 35 3. 56 5. 120 7. 220 9. 1287 11. 10 13. 252 15. $\dfrac{52!}{39!\,13!}$ 17. 120 19. 455 21. 1365

23. $_nC_r = \dfrac{n!}{(n-r)!\,r!} = \dfrac{n!}{r!\,(n-r)!} = \dfrac{n!}{[n-(n-r)]!\,(n-r)!} = {_nC_{n-r}}$

PAGES 732-734 WRITTEN EXERCISES

1. 200 3. 66 5. 44 7. 3500 9. 3025 11. 405 13. 32 15. 196 17. 29 19. 469 21. 64 23. 1260

25. 103,776 27. 58,656 29. 1,281,072

31.

Poker Hand	Calculating Formula	Value
Royal Flush	$_4C_1$	4
Straight Flush	$_4C_1 \cdot 9$	36
Four of a Kind	$_{13}C_1 \cdot {_4C_4} \cdot {_{12}C_1} \cdot {_4C_1}$	624
Full House	$_{13}C_1 \cdot {_4C_3} \cdot {_{12}C_1} \cdot {_4C_2}$	3,744
Flush	$_4C_1 \cdot {_{13}C_5} - 40$	5,108
Straight	$10(_4C_1)^5 - 40$	10,200
Three of a Kind	$_{13}C_1 \cdot {_4C_3} \cdot {_{12}C_2} \cdot (_4C_1)^2$	54,912
Two Pairs	$_{13}C_2 \cdot (_4C_2)^2 \cdot {_{11}C_1} \cdot {_4C_1}$	123,552
One Pair	Example 4	1,098,240
Nothing	None	1,302,540

All Possible Five-Card Hands: 2,598,960

PAGE 734 MID-CHAPTER REVIEW

1. 60 2. 12 3. 720 4. 20 5. 120 6. 10 7. 495 8. 8 9. 16

PAGE 739 CLASSROOM EXERCISES

1. $\dfrac{_5C_2 \cdot {_6C_2}}{_{11}C_4} = \dfrac{150}{330} = \dfrac{5}{11}$ 3. $\dfrac{_6C_3 \cdot {_5C_1}}{_{11}C_4} + \dfrac{_6C_4}{_{11}C_4} = \dfrac{100}{330} + \dfrac{15}{330} = \dfrac{23}{66}$ 5. $\dfrac{15}{52}$ 7. $\dfrac{12}{13}$

PAGES 739-741 WRITTEN EXERCISES

1. $\dfrac{3}{13}$ 3. $\dfrac{10}{13}$ 5. $\dfrac{1}{3}$ 7. $\dfrac{1}{2}$ 9. $\dfrac{1}{26}$ 11. $\dfrac{11}{13}$ 13. $\dfrac{5}{13}$ 15. $\dfrac{3}{8}$ 17. $\dfrac{7}{8}$ 19. $\dfrac{1}{2}$ 21. $\dfrac{7}{50}$ 23. $\dfrac{3}{7}$ 25. $\dfrac{3}{7}$ 27. $\dfrac{1}{4}$ 29. $\dfrac{14}{29}$

31. $\dfrac{2}{9}$ 33. $\dfrac{5}{9}$ 35. $\dfrac{4}{7}$ 37. $\dfrac{1}{7}$ 39. $\dfrac{15}{64}$ 41. $\dfrac{1}{64}$ 43. $\dfrac{1}{25}$ 45. $\dfrac{5}{324}$

47.

Poker Hand	(Fractional Form)	(Decimal Form)
Royal Flush	$\dfrac{4}{2{,}598{,}960}$	0.0000015
Straight Flush	$\dfrac{36}{2{,}598{,}960}$	0.000014
Four of a Kind	$\dfrac{624}{2{,}598{,}960}$	0.00024
Full House	$\dfrac{3744}{2{,}598{,}960}$	0.0014
Flush	$\dfrac{5108}{2{,}598{,}960}$	0.0020
Straight	$\dfrac{10{,}200}{2{,}598{,}960}$	0.0039
Three of a Kind	$\dfrac{54{,}912}{2{,}598{,}960}$	0.0211
Two Pairs	$\dfrac{123{,}552}{2{,}598{,}960}$	0.0476
One Pair	$\dfrac{1{,}098{,}240}{2{,}598{,}960}$	0.4226
Nothing	$\dfrac{1{,}302{,}540}{2{,}598{,}960}$	0.5012
Total	1	1.0

PAGE 743   EXERCISES

1. $q = 3.825$ See the Solution Key for the graph.

PAGE 746   CLASSROOM EXERCISES

1. $\dfrac{12}{52}$ or $\dfrac{3}{13}$ 3. $\dfrac{1}{2} \cdot \dfrac{3}{13} = \dfrac{3}{26}$ 5. $\dfrac{12}{52}$ or $\dfrac{3}{13}$

PAGES 746-747   WRITTEN EXERCISES

1. 0.70 3. 0.85 5. 0.30 7. 0.15 9. 0.33 11. 0.11 13. 0.78 15. $\dfrac{1}{2}$ 17. $\dfrac{2}{3}$ 19. $\dfrac{11}{15}$ 21. $\dfrac{14}{15}$ 23. 0.294 25. $\dfrac{1}{5}$
27. $\dfrac{2}{5}$ 29. $\dfrac{7}{10}$ 31. The Venn diagram shows that $p(A)$ will be greater than $p(A \cap B)$ unless A is a subset of B. In this case, $p(A) = p(A \cap B)$. 33. The Venn diagrams show that $p(A \cup B)$ will be greater than $P(B)$ or $p(A)$. The equality holds when either A or B is the null set. 35. 0.33 37. 0.25

PAGE 750   CLASSROOM EXERCISES

1. $\dfrac{10}{36}$ or $\dfrac{5}{18}$ 3. $\dfrac{4}{6}$ or $\dfrac{2}{3}$

PAGE 750   WRITTEN EXERCISES

1. $\dfrac{1}{5}$ 3. $\dfrac{2}{3}$ 5. $\dfrac{1}{4}$ 7. $\dfrac{1}{221}$ 9. $\dfrac{1}{30}$

PAGE 753   CLASSROOM EXERCISES

1. Independent 3. Independent 5. $\dfrac{4}{9} \cdot \dfrac{5}{8} = \dfrac{5}{18}$

PAGES 753-754   WRITTEN EXERCISES

1. $\dfrac{1}{169}$ 3. $\dfrac{1}{36}$ 5. $\dfrac{1}{4}$ 7. $\dfrac{3}{29}$ 9. $\dfrac{51}{145}$ 11. $\dfrac{32}{135}$ 13. $\dfrac{8}{27}$ 15. $\dfrac{1}{221}$ 17. $\dfrac{3}{8}$ 19. $\dfrac{1}{3}$ 21. $\dfrac{25}{64}$ 23. $\dfrac{125}{512}$ 25. $\dfrac{11}{221}$

1. $_5C_2(\frac{1}{4})^2(\frac{3}{4})^3 = \frac{135}{512}$ 3. $_5C_3(\frac{1}{4})^3(\frac{3}{4})^2 = \frac{45}{512}$ 5. $_5C_2(\frac{1}{4})^2(\frac{3}{4})^3 + _5C_1(\frac{1}{4})(\frac{3}{4})^4 + (\frac{3}{4})^5 = \frac{3^3}{4^5}(10 + 15 + 9) =$

$\frac{27(34)}{1024} = \frac{459}{512} \approx .896$

1. $\frac{1}{16}$ 3. 0.161   5. 0.965   7. 0.965   9. 0.004   11. 0.047   13. n = 8   15. 3 and 4   17. In n binomial

trials, the probability of k successes for a specific permutation is $p^k q^{n-k}$. This follows from the definition of

independent events in Section 14-8, generalized to a finite number of events. Since the order of successes and

failures is not important, there are $_nC_k$ combinations of exactly k successes in n trials. Using Probability

Postulate iii, Section 14-5, for mutually exclusive events, we see that the probability of exactly k successes in n

binomial trials is $_nC_k \cdot p^k q^{n-k}$.

1. $\frac{1}{500} \cdot (400) + \frac{499}{500} \cdot 0 = 0.8$

1. 0.2   3. 0.40   5. 12,000   7. You should pay the person two-fifths of the face value, if it is greater than

three.   9. It is worthwhile to pay eight cents.   11. −0.096; No; E is negative.   13. Yes; E is two dollars.

15. 430   17. Suppose that k is the number of successes in n binomial trials. Then the following table can

be constructed.

k	0	1	2	3	...	n
p(k successes)	q^n	npq^{n-1}	$\frac{n(n-1)}{1 \cdot 2}p^2 q^{n-2}$	$\frac{n(n-1)(n-2)}{1 \cdot 2 \cdot 3}p^3 q^{n-3}$	...	p^n

Then, $E(k) = 0 \cdot q^n + 1 \cdot npq^{n-1} + 2 \cdot \frac{n(n-1)}{1 \cdot 2}p^2 q^{n-2} + 3 \cdot \frac{n(n-1)(n-2)}{1 \cdot 2 \cdot 3}p^3 q^{n-3} + \cdots + np^n$

$= np(q^{n-1} + (n-1)pq^{n-2} + \frac{(n-1)(n-2)}{2}p^2 q^{n-3} + \cdots + p^{n-1}) = np(q + p)^{n-1} = np \cdot 1^{n-1} = np.$

1. 15   3. 1024   5. 1   7. $\frac{n!}{r!}$ 9. 1260   11. 12   13. 10   15. 1365   17. 960   19. 9   21. 1170   23. 0.033   25. 360; $\frac{2}{15}$

27. $\frac{25}{52}$ 29. $p(B \mid A) = \frac{p(A \cap B)}{p(A)}$ 31. $\frac{1}{2}$ 33. Dependent   35. 0.513   37. 0.995   39. 50 cents

1. 10   2. 1680   3. $\frac{1}{n}$ 4. $n \cdot (n - 1) \cdot (n - 2) \cdots 1$ 5. 0,1   6. 1   7. $P(E_1), P(E_2)$ 8. $P(E_1 \cap E_2)$

9. $\{(H, H, H), (H, H, T), (H, T, H), (H, T, T), (T, T, T), (T, T, H), (T, H, T), (T, H, H)\}$; $p = \frac{1}{8}$ 10. 35

11. 120   12. 56   13. 0.273   14. $\frac{9}{25}$ 15. 0.343   16. $\frac{1}{6}$ 17. $\frac{1}{6}$ 18. $\frac{5}{6}$ 19. $\frac{5}{18}$ 20. 5

B 4
C 5
D 6
E 7
F 8
G 9
H 0
I 1
J 2